America

The Essential Learning Edition

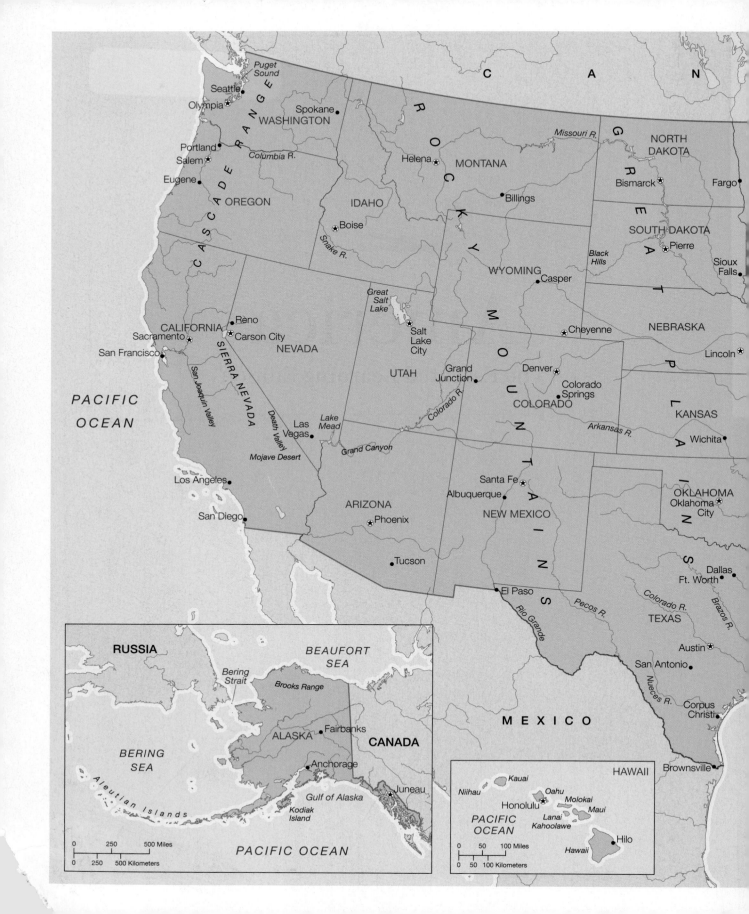

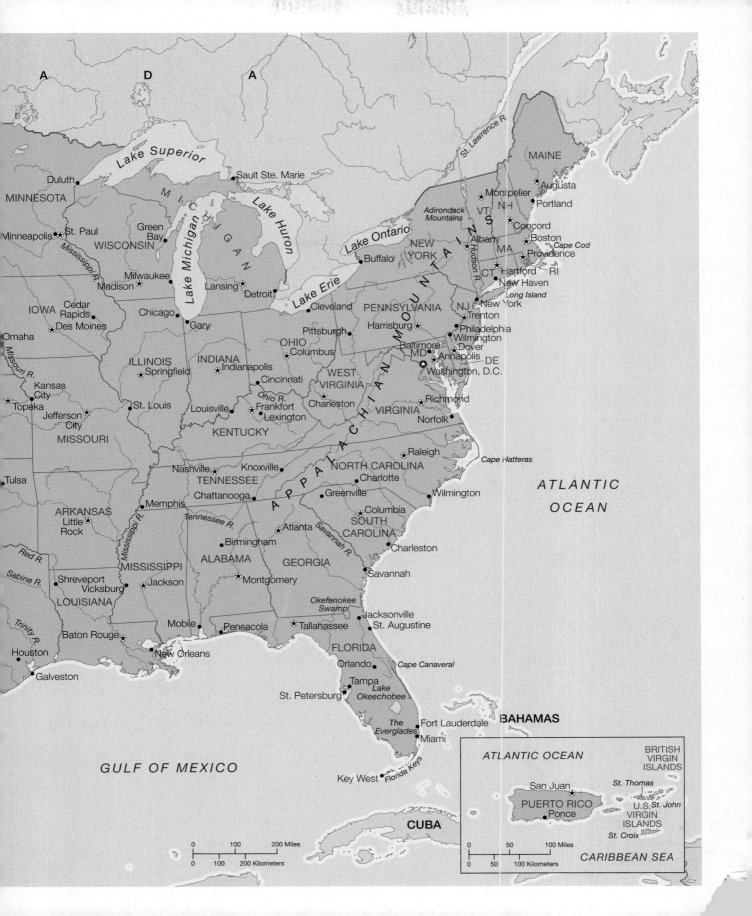

America

The Essential Learning Edition

DAVID EMORY SHI

GEORGE BROWN TINDALL

W. W. Norton & Company, Inc.

New York • London

W. W. Norton & Company has been independent since its founding in 1923, when William Warder Norton and Mary D. Herter Norton first published lectures delivered at the People's Institute, the adult education division of New York City's Cooper Union. The firm soon expanded its program beyond the Institute, publishing books by celebrated academics from America and abroad. By mid-century, the two major pillars of Norton's publishing program—trade books and college texts— were firmly established. In the 1950s, the Norton family transferred control of the company to its employees, and today—with a staff of four hundred and a comparable number of trade, college, and professional titles published each year—W. W. Norton & Company stands as the largest and oldest publishing house owned wholly by its employees.

Editor: Jon Durbin
Developmental Editors: Lisa Moore and John Elliott
Associate Editor: Justin Cahill
Project Editor: Melissa Atkin
Editorial Assistant: Penelope Lin
Marketing Manager, History: Sarah England
Manuscript Editor: Mike Fleming
Managing Editor, College: Marian Johnson
Managing Editor, College Digital Media: Kim Yi
Production Manager: Andy Ensor
Media Editor: Lisa Moore
Media Project Editor: Penelope Lin
Media Editorial Assistant: Chris Hillyer
Design Director: Hope Miller Goodell
Photo Editor: Nelson Colón
Permissions Manager: Megan Jackson
Composition: Graphic World, Inc.
Manufacturing: Courier, Kendallville

The Library of Congress has cataloged the full edition as follows:

Tindall, George Brown.
    America : a narrative history / George Brown Tindall,
David Emory Shi.—9th ed.
      p.   cm.
    Includes bibliographical references and index.
    ISBN 978-0-393-91262-3 (hardcover)
    1. United States—History—Textbooks.   I. Shi, David E.   II. Title.
E178.1.T55 2013   2012034504
973—dc23
    This edition:
    ISBN 978-0-393-93587-5 (pbk.)

W. W. Norton & Company, Inc., 500 Fifth Avenue, New York, NY 10110-0017
wwnorton.com
W. W. Norton & Company Ltd., Castle House, 75/76 Wells Street, London W1T 3QT

1 2 3 4 5 6 7 8 9 0

For Jon Durbin, editor and friend

About the Authors

DAVID SHI is a professor of history and the president emeritus of Furman University. He is the author of several books on American cultural history, including the award-winning *The Simple Life: Plain Living and High Thinking in American Culture* and *Facing Facts: Realism in American Thought and Culture, 1850–1920.*

GEORGE TINDALL recently of the University of North Carolina, Chapel Hill, was an award-winning historian of the South with a number of major books to his credit, including *The Emergence of the New South, 1913–1945* and *The Disruption of the Solid South.*

Lead authors for media and pedagogy

JON LEE (San Antonio College, Texas) served on the American Historical Association/Lumina Tuning Project and educational commissions in the state of Texas to establish discipline-wide historical learning outcomes. He received the "Most Inspirational Professor" award from Phi Theta Kappa Beta Nu. He is the coordinator of the Honors Academy at San Antonio College.

ERIK ANDERSON (San Antonio College, Texas) teaches American history and is involved with the Honors Academy. He also serves as the academic liaison with the Travis Early College High School program at San Antonio College. Anderson earned his doctorate at Brown University.

Contents in Brief

Contents

PART FOUR | A House Divided and Rebuilt   415

PART FIVE | Growing Pains   547

PART SEVEN | The American Age   923

Maps

What's It All About?

Thinking Like A Historian

Preface

The Essential Learning Edition builds upon *America*'s long-established emphasis on history as a storytelling art. It features colorful characters and anecdotes informed by balanced analysis and social texture, all guided by the unfolding of key events. But this Essential Learning Edition, a new addition to the *America* family, includes innovative pedagogical features and tools to help students better understand the most important aspects of American history, to learn how historians study, interpret, and debate the past, and to assess their own progress.

To guide my efforts in crafting the Essential Learning Edition, I asked students and professors at a variety of colleges what they most needed in an introductory survey textbook. Their answers varied, but overall there was a strong consensus on several key points: students want a manageable, inexpensive textbook that focuses on the essentials of American history while telling the dramatic story of the nation's past in vivid but simple language. They stressed that many textbooks overwhelm them, either by flooding them with too much information or by taking too much for granted in terms of the knowledge that students bring to the introductory course. Students also asked for a textbook that would help them more easily identify the most important developments or issues to focus on (and remember) as they read.

To address these student concerns, I have streamlined and compressed the Brief Ninth Edition of *America* to build the Essential Learning Edition. It has 30 chapters as compared to 34 in the Brief Ninth Edition, which means that it nicely fits the chapter per week model for most courses. Moreover, I have trimmed the narrative text of the Brief Ninth Edition by about fifteen percent to focus on the most essential elements of America's past. Finally, because I assumed little or no background knowledge on the part of the student reader, I sought to ensure that the major topics in each chapter are easily grasped and all key terms are clearly identified.

When asked about their needs in a survey text, instructors said much the same as their students, but they also asked for a textbook that introduced students to the nature of historical research, analysis, and debate. Many professors also mentioned the growing importance to them and their institutions of assessing the success of their classes in meeting the learning goals established by their department. Accordingly, I have aligned the Essential Learning Edition with specific learning outcomes for the introductory American history survey course approved by various state and national organizations, including the American Historical Association. To help me make those changes, my innovative editor, Jon Durbin, recruited a talented multi-disciplinary group of professors, pedagogical specialists, developmental editors, instructional designers, reviewers, and copy editors. In particular, Erik Anderson and Jon Lee of San Antonio College in Texas served as the pedagogical specialists and lead media authors for this project. They are both widely recognized as superb teachers and innovative leaders in assessment and community-college instruction. The new pedagogical features in the Essential Learning Edition were a direct outgrowth of their efforts teaching the survey course and working closely with students in a dynamic, collaborative, community-based learning environment in the Honors College at San Antonio College. Moreover, the new pedagogical features of this book and its accompanying media components—including the new Norton InQuizitive program, an adaptive online tool designed to guide student learning—make it much easier for professors to assess their students' performance on a variety of learning levels.

These and other suggestions from students and professors have shaped this Essential Learning Edition. Each of the 30 chapters begins with a list of five or six Core Objectives, carefully designed to help students understand—and remember—the major developments in each period. To make it easier for students to grasp the major developments, I have reorganized every chapter to ensure that the narrative aligns sequentially with the objectives. Each Core Objective appears at the beginning of each major section in the chapter for which it is relevant. Core Objective Flags, unique to this edition, appear in the page margins to highlight topics in the narrative that are essential to understanding the broader Core Objective. Key terms, chosen to reinforce the major concepts, are bolded in the text and defined in the margin, helping students appreciate and remember their significance. At the end of each chapter, new review features are designed to reinforce the Core Objectives, including clear chapter summaries, lists of key terms, and chapter chronologies.

This book breaks new ground by incorporating several new instructional features designed to improve student learning. Maps, for example, are essential to history textbooks, but in this version I have taken the additional step of listing questions underneath each map to help students analyze the implications embedded in maps in a way that promotes active learning.

Interactive maps are but just one example of the innovative elements in this book designed to deepen student learning. Each chapter in the Essential Learning Edition also includes a **What It's All About** feature, which visually summarizes in a graphical format major issues such as:

- Chapter 3: Comparative examination of how different regions of the English colonies were settled and developed.
- Chapter 9: Analyzes sectional conflicts and the role the economic policies of Henry Clay and Andrew Jackson played in those conflicts.
- Chapter 12: Abolitionist versus pro-slavery arguments on slavery.
- Chapter 15: Tracing the legal and legislative road from slavery to freedom for African Americans in the former Confederate States.
- Chapter 23: The First New Deal compared to the Second New Deal.

Another unique new feature, called **Thinking Like a Historian**, helps students better understand—and apply—the research techniques and interpretive skills used by historians. Through carefully selected examples the

Thinking Like a Historian feature highlights the essential role of primary and secondary sources as the building blocks of history and illustrates the ways in which historians have differed in their interpretations of the past. There is one Thinking Like a Historian feature for each major period of American history; each feature takes on a major interpretive issue in that era. In Part I of the activity, students first read excerpts from two original secondary sources that offer competing interpretive views framing that period. In Part II, students then read some of the original primary sources that those same historians used to develop their arguments. Finally, students are asked to answer a series of questions that guide their reading and analysis of the sources.

As always, this new edition also includes new content. As I created the Essential Learning Edition, I have complemented the political narrative by incorporating more social and cultural history into the text. Key new discussions include:

- Chapter 3, Colonial Ways of Life, 1607–1750, includes a new portrait of Antonio, an enslaved African brutalized by his Dutch owner in Maryland in the mid-seventeenth century. There is also new material on the competition among American colonists for British luxury goods in the 1760s and 1770s.
- Chapter 4, From Colonies to States, 1607–1776, has enriched material on the non-importation efforts (boycotts of British goods) led by grassroots Americans prior to the Revolutionary War. It also includes new material about the conversion of American farmers into soldiers after the clash of arms at Lexington and Concord.
- Chapter 5, The American Revolution, 1776–1783, includes more material about slaves who took advantage of the war to escape or join the British forces, and about the ways in which women, Native Americans, and slaves became engaged in the war effort.
- Chapter 6, Creating a "More Perfect Union," 1783–1800, elaborates on Shays's Rebellion and other expressions of agrarian discontent across the nation after the Revolution, and there is also more discussion about how women, Native Americans, and slaves figured into the thinking of the Founding Fathers during the Constitutional Convention in 1787.
- Chapter 7, The Early Republic, 1800–1815, has new material on the way in which the War of 1812 affected slavery/blacks.
- Chapter 8, The Emergence of a Market Economy, 1815–1850, offers new discussions of the emergence of the cotton culture in the South and the plight of the Irish fleeing the famine at home and heading to America.
- Chapter 9, Nationalism and Sectionalism, 1815–1828, more fully discusses the role of labor advocates and unions in forging what would become the Jacksonian movement.
- Chapter 10, The Jacksonian Era, 1828–1840, describes the effect of the Panic of 1837 and the ensuing depression on the working poor.
- Chapter 11, The South and Slavery, 1800–1860, boasts substantial new material related to slavery and African American culture. There is also

a new discussion of a New Orleans slave revolt led by Charles Deslondes in 1811, the largest slave revolt in American history.

- Chapter 12, Religion, Romanticism, and Reform, 1800–1860, includes enriched treatment of the revivalism of the Second Great Awakening, and a completely rewritten discussion of Mormonism.

- Chapter 14, The War of the Union, 1861–1865, adds new material about the social history of the Civil War, including more material on common soldiers, rioting in opposition to the military draft, and backwoods violence rarely included in discussions of the war, such as the summary of the execution of thirteen Unionists in Madison County, North Carolina.

- Chapter 15, Reconstruction, 1865–1877, highlights the circumstances of former slaves—from their perspective. It also includes new examples of the ways in which the Freedmen's Bureau helped negotiate labor contracts between white planters and freedmen.

- Chapter 16, Big Business and Organized Labor, 1860–1900, discusses the emergence of a new middle class during the Gilded Age, and includes substantially revised material on women's and labor history.

- Chapter 17, The South and the West Transformed, 1865–1900, offers a newly rewritten section on the emergence of new racial segregation in the South, and also new material about the everyday realities of Western expansion.

- Chapter 20, The Progressive Era, 1890–1920, provides new sections the attitudes of Theodore Roosevelt and Woodrow Wilson's attitudes and policies concerning race.

- Chapter 21, America and the Great War, 1914–1920, now highlights the war's social effects in the United States, with special attention to women, blacks, and Mexican Americans.

- Chapter 22, A Clash of Cultures, 1920–1929, incorporates new material on the consumer culture, women's history, and revised material on the Harlem Renaissance with a new profile of Zora Neale Hurston.

- Chapter 24, The Second World War, 1933–1945, includes new material about the wartime experience of Mexican Americans.

- Chapter 25, The Cold War and the Fair Deal, 1945–1952, benefits from new coverage of women industrial workers, and also the efforts of Latinos to gain equal rights in the aftermath of World War II.

- Chapter 27, New Frontiers, 1960–1968, showcases a new portrait of Fannie Lou Hamer, a black Mississippi activist, in the section on the early civil rights movements.

- Chapter 28, Rebellion and Reaction, the 1960s and 1970's, includes new material on the women's movement, Mexican Americans, and Native Americans.

In sum, this new *Essential Learning Edition* includes the most dramatic changes ever made in a resilient book that is celebrating its thirtieth year in print.

Media Tools for Students and Instructors

New lead authors for media and pedagogy Jon Lee and Erik Anderson have ensured that the Essential Learning Edition of *America* is supported by an array of digital media with tools faculty need to meet course goals—in the classroom and online—and activities for students to develop core skills in reading comprehension, writing, and analysis.

The Essential Learning Edition Team

I have already introduced you to Erik Anderson and Jon Lee, but our talented team of innovative support authors also includes Brandon Franke (Blinn College), Cathy Parzynski (Montgomery County Community College), Melissa Weinbrenner (Northeast Texas Community College), Brian Cervantez (Tarrant County College), and Laura Farkas (Ivy Tech College–West Lafayette), who have contributed to all of the enriching learning materials we can offer students and instructors for support:

🐰 INQUIZITIVE
Quizzing to Learn

InQuizitive, Norton's new adaptive quizzing platform, uses interactive questions and guided feedback to motivate students to read and understand the text. Varied question types—featuring images, maps, and sources—prompt critical and analytical thinking on each of the chapter's Core Objectives. Robust grading functionality helps instructors track their students' progress on learning outcomes.

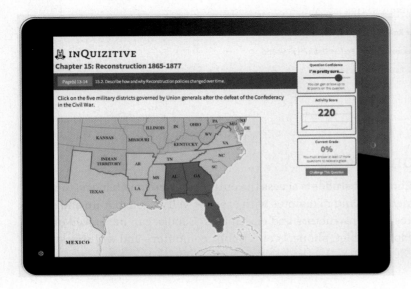

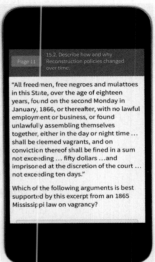

Student Site

This free site offers students access to additional primary source documents and images, Office Hour videos with author David Shi, and iMaps. It is ideal for instructors interested in granting students access to additional material without creating or administering online assignments.

Norton Ebooks

Norton Ebooks let students access the entire book and much more: they can search, highlight, and take notes with ease, as well as collaborate and share their notes with instructors and classmates. Ebooks can be viewed on any device—laptop, tablet, phone, even a public computer—and will stay synced between devices.

Norton Coursepacks

Free Norton Coursepacks (downloadable in Blackboard, WebCT, D2L, and Moodle; additional formats can be provided upon request), include:

- **NEW Gradable Assignments** allow you to assign quizzes based on questions from the text including Assessing the Core Objectives, What's It All About?, and Thinking Like a Historian.
- **NEW Primary Source Exercises** include several primary sources from across cultures with a brief multiple choice exam and a short answer question.
- **Guided Reading Exercises**, keyed to each chapter's Core Objectives, instill the three-step Note-Summarize-Assess pedagogy. Each chapter has one exercise built around passages from the text.
- **Review Quizzes** include targeted feedback that highlights Core Objective, page reference, and difficulty. *Chrono-Quizzes* end each chapter quiz with a matching question.
- **Online Reader** provides over 100 primary-source documents and images.
- **Map Resources** include *iMaps*, where students can peel back each layer to highlight the information they want to see, and *American History Tours*, powered by Google Earth that are dynamic, interactive primary sources that trace geographical developments over time. *Map Worksheets* provide each map without labels for offline relabeling and quizzing.
- **Forum Prompts** for online and hybrid courses are a set of topics that can be used to launch discussions.
- **Key Term Flash Cards** allow students to self-study historical vocabulary.
- Links to **InQuizitive** for each chapter.

Classroom Presentation Tools

- **Lecture PowerPoints** and **Art PowerPoints** feature photographs and maps from the book, retouched for in-class presentation.
- The **Norton American History Digital Archive** includes over 1,700 images, audio and video files that are arranged chronologically and by theme, available online or on DVD.

Instructor's Manual (Melissa Weinbrenner, Northeast Texas Community College)

The Instructor's Manual for The Essential Learning Edition has everything instructors need to prepare lectures and classroom activities: chapter summaries, suggestions for teaching Core Objectives, as well as lecture ideas, classroom activities, and lists of recommended books, films, and websites.

Test Bank (Brandon Franke, Blinn College; Cathy Parzynski, Montgomery County Community College; and Melissa Weinbrenner, Northeast Texas Community College)

The Test Bank features multiple-choice, true/false, and essay questions aligned with the chapter's Core Objectives and classified according to level of difficulty, Bloom's Taxonomy, and the American Historical Association's guidelines for student learning outcomes, offering multiple avenues for content and skill assessment. All Norton test banks are available with Exam-View Test Generator software, allowing instructors to easily create, administer, and manage assessments.

Acknowledgments

The quality and range of reviews on this project were truly exceptional. The book and its accompanying media components benefited from the insights of numerous instructors.

Erik Anderson, San Antonio College
Milan Andrejevich, Ivy Tech College–South Bend
Evan Bennett, Florida Atlantic University
Laura Bergstrom, Ivy Tech College–Sellersburg
Keith Berry, Hillsborough Community College
Albert Broussard, Texas A&M, College Station
Blanche Brick, Blinn College
Cory Burger, Ivy Tech College–Terre Haute
Brian Cervantez, Tarrant County College–Northwest Campus
Michael L. Collins, Midwestern State University
Lee Cowan, Tarrant County College
Thomas A. DeBlack, Arkansas Tech University
Scott Derr, Ivy Tech College–Bloomington
S. Matthew DeSpain, Rose State College
Michael Downs, Tarrant County College–Northeast Campus
Shannon Duffy, Southwest Texas State University
Karen Dunn-Haley, University of California, Davis
Stephen D. Engle, Florida Atlantic University
Laura Farkas, Ivy Tech College–West Lafayette
David Haney, Austin Community College
Andrew Hollinger, Tarrant County College–Southeast Campus
Frances Jacobson, Tidewater Community College
Jon Lee, San Antonio College
Robert MacDonald, Ivy Tech College–Lafayette
Richard McCaslin, University of North Texas–Denton

Suzanne McFadden, Austin Community College

Joel McMahon, Kennesaw State University

Greg Miller, Hillsborough Community College

Catherine Parzynski, Montgomery Community College

R. Lynn Rainard, Tidewater Community College

Hazel Ramos, Glendale Community College

Nicole Ribianszky, Georgia Gwinnett College

Allen Smith, Ivy Tech College–Indianapolis

Bruce Solheim, Citrus College

Mark Stanley, University of North Texas–Denton

Melissa Weinbrenner, Northeast Texas Community College

Once again, I thank my friends and colleagues at W. W. Norton for their consummate professionalism and good cheer, especially Jon Durbin, Justin Cahill, Penelope Lin, Lisa Moore, Chris Hillyer, Melissa Atkin, John Elliott, Mike Fleming, Nelson Colón, Hope Miller Goodell, Debra Morton-Hoyt, Andy Ensor, and Sarah England. In addition, my talented friends Charles Cornwell and Jim Stewart read drafts of numerous chapters, helping me to clarify my descriptions and prune my prose.

Finally, I have dedicated this new version of *America* to Jon Durbin, my tireless editor at W. W. Norton, who is a marketing genius and so much more.

An Old "New" World

History is filled with ironies. The unexpected and unplanned—luck and accidents—often shape events more than intentions. Long before Christopher Columbus happened upon the Caribbean Sea in his effort to find a westward passage to the Indies (a term then used to refer to east Asia), the native peoples he mislabeled *Indians* had occupied and transformed the lands of the Western Hemisphere (also called the Americas—North, Central, and South). The first residents in what Europeans came to call the "New World" had migrated from northeastern Asia nearly 20,000 years ago. By 1492, when Columbus began his famous voyage west from Spain, there were millions of Native Americans living in the Western Hemisphere. Over the centuries, they had developed diverse and often highly sophisticated societies, some rooted in agriculture, and others focused on trade or conquest. The New World was "new" only to the Europeans who began exploring, conquering, and exploiting the region at the end of the fifteenth century.

The Native American peoples were profoundly affected by the arrival of Europeans and Africans. Very different societies collided, each having its own distinct heritage and world view. Indian peoples were exploited, infected, enslaved, displaced, and exterminated. Yet the conventional story of tragic conquest oversimplifies the complex process by which Indians, Europeans, and Africans interacted in the Western Hemisphere. The Native Americans were more than passive victims of European power; they were also trading partners

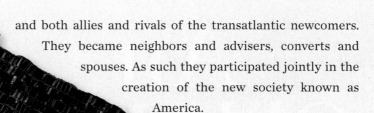

and both allies and rivals of the transatlantic newcomers. They became neighbors and advisers, converts and spouses. As such they participated jointly in the creation of the new society known as America.

The Europeans who risked their lives to settle in the Western Hemisphere were a diverse lot. Young and old, men and women, they came from Spain, Portugal, France, the British Isles, the Netherlands (Holland), Scandinavia, Italy, and the German states (Germany would not become a united nation until the mid–nineteenth century). A variety of motives inspired them to undertake the dangerous transatlantic voyage. Some were adventurers and fortune seekers eager to gain glory and find gold and silver. Others were passionate Christians eager to create kingdoms of God in the New World. Still others were prisoners, debtors, servants, landless peasants, and political or religious exiles. Many were simply seeking a piece of land, higher wages, and greater economic opportunity. A settler in Pennsylvania noted that "poor people (both men and women) of all kinds can here get three times the wages for their labor than they can in England."

Yet such wages did not attract enough workers to keep up with the rapidly expanding colonial economies, so the Europeans early in the seventeenth century turned to Africa for their labor needs. European nations—especially Portugal and Spain—had long been transporting captive Africans to the Western Hemisphere, from Chile to Canada. In 1619 a Dutch warship brought twenty captured Africans to Jamestown, near the coast of Virginia. The Dutch captain exchanged the slaves for food and supplies. This first of many transactions involving enslaved people in British America would transform American society in ways that no one at the time envisioned. Few Europeans during the colonial era saw the contradiction between the promise of freedom in America for themselves and the expanding institution of race-based slavery.

The intermingling of people, cultures, and ecosystems from the continents of Africa, Europe, and the Western Hemisphere gave colonial

American society its distinctive vitality and variety. In turn, the diversity of the environment and the varying climate spawned quite different economies and patterns of living in the various regions of North America. As the original settlements grew into prosperous and populous colonies, the transplanted Europeans had to create new communities and political systems to manage dynamic growth and control rising tensions.

At the same time, bitter rivalries among the Spanish, French, English, and Dutch triggered costly wars fought in Europe and around the world. The monarchs of Europe struggled to manage often-unruly colonies, which, they discovered, played crucial roles in their frequent European wars. Many of the colonists had brought with them to America a feisty independence, which led them to resent government interference in their affairs. A British official in North Carolina reported that the settlers were "without any Law or Order. Impudence is so very high, as to be past bearing." The colonists and their British rulers maintained an uneasy partnership throughout the seventeenth century. But as the royal authorities tightened their control during the mid–eighteenth century, they met resistance from colonists, which exploded into revolution.

DE SOTO AND THE INCAS This 1596 color engraving shows Spanish conquistador Hernando de Soto's first encounter with King Atahualpa of the Inca Empire. Although artist Theodor de Bry never set foot in North America, his engravings reflect travelogues of explorers and Spanish perceptions of Native Americans in the sixteenth century.

The Collision of Cultures

in the 16th Century

Debate continues about when and how the first humans arrived in North America. Until recently, archaeologists had assumed that ancient peoples from northeast Asia, some 12,000 to 15,000 years ago, were the first arrivals in the Western Hemisphere. Those Asian wanderers ("nomads") who hunted the massive woolly mammoths and other big game animals had journeyed 600 miles across the Bering Strait on what was then a treeless land bridge connecting northeastern Siberia with Alaska, when the oceans were much lower than today.

Archaeologists call these first peoples Paleo-Indians ("Old Indians"). Over hundreds of years, as the climate warmed and the glaciers melted, a steady stream of small groups fanned out southward across the entire Western Hemisphere, from the Arctic Circle to the tip of South America. They were skilled "hunter-gatherers" (as well as tool-makers and warriors) whose food consisted of large mammals and edible wild plants, berries, and seeds gathered as they searched for game. As the isolated bands of hunters trekked across the prairies and the plains, they encountered animals unlike those found there today: mastodons, giant sloths, camels, bison, lions, saber-toothed tigers, cheetahs, and massive wolves, beavers, and bears. Recent archaeological discoveries in Pennsylvania, Virginia, and Chile suggest that prehistoric humans may have arrived much earlier than assumed (perhaps 18,000 to

CORE OBJECTIVES INQUIZITIVE

1. Explain why there were so many diverse human societies in the Americas before Europeans arrived.

2. Summarize the major developments in Europe that enabled the Age of Exploration.

3. Describe how the Spanish were able to conquer and colonize the Americas.

4. Assess the impact of the Columbian Exchange between the "Old" and "New" Worlds.

5. Analyze the legacy of the Spanish form of colonization on North American history.

THE FIRST MIGRATION

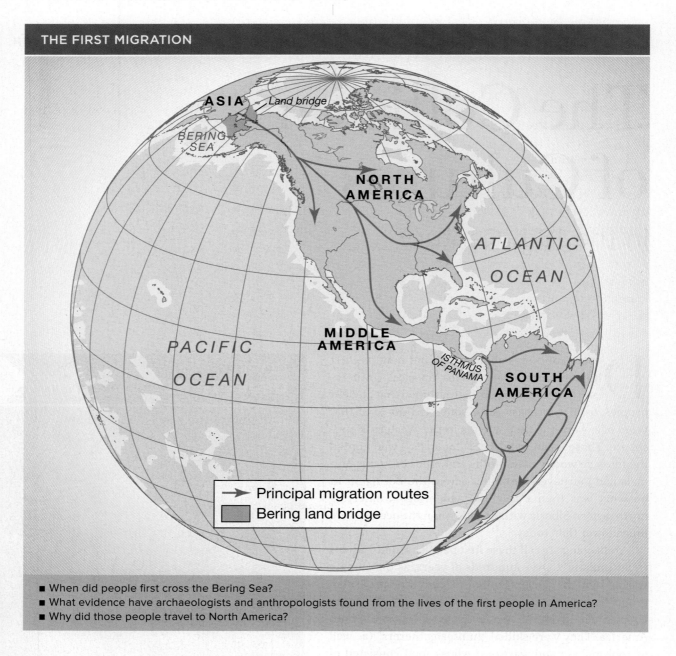

- When did people first cross the Bering Sea?
- What evidence have archaeologists and anthropologists found from the lives of the first people in America?
- Why did those people travel to North America?

40,000 years ago) from various parts of Asia—and some may even have crossed the Atlantic Ocean from southwestern Europe.

Regardless of when ancient humans first set foot on the North American continent, the region eventually became a crossroads for various peoples from around the globe: Europeans, Africans, Asians, and others—all of whom brought with them distinctive backgrounds, cultures, technologies, and motivations that, taken together, helped form the American mosaic.

Early Cultures in the Americas

For at least 15,000 years before the arrival of Europeans, Native Americans had occupied the vastness of North America undisturbed by outside invaders. By the time Christopher Columbus happened upon the Western Hemisphere, the hundreds of Indian societies living in North America may have numbered over 10 million people. They had developed a diverse array of communities in which more than 300 languages were spoken.

Archaeologists have labeled the earliest arrivals in North America the Clovis peoples, named after a site in New Mexico where ancient hunters around 9500 B.C.E. killed tusked woolly mammoths (fourteen feet tall) using distinctive "Clovis" spear points. Clovis people lived in small bands of five to ten families. Over many centuries, as the post–Ice Age climate warmed, sea levels rose, growing seasons lengthened, and snowfall and rainfall lessened, leading many lakes to dry up into deserts. The largest mammals—mammoths, mastodons, giant bison, single-hump camels, huge beavers, sabre-toothed tigers—eventually died out. Hunters shifted from stalking mammoths and mastodons to smaller, yet more abundant mammals: deer, antelope, elk, moose, and caribou.

Global warming diminished grasslands and stimulated forest growth, which provided plants and small animals for human consumption. The ancient Indians adapted to the diverse new environments—coastal forests, grassy plains, southwestern deserts, eastern woodlands—by developing new ways to survive and flourish. Some continued to hunt large animals; others fished and trapped small animals; some gathered wild plants and herbs and collected acorns and seeds; others would farm. Many did some of each. Contrary to the romantic myth of early Indian civilizations living in perfect harmony with nature and one another, indigenous peoples often engaged in warfare and exploited the environment by burning large wooded areas in order to plant fields. They also developed their own nature-centered religions, mastered the use of fire, and improved technology such as spear points, basketry, and pottery.

By about 5000 B.C.E., Native Americans in Mexico had adapted to the warmer climate by transforming themselves into farming societies. They became expert at growing the plant foods that would become the primary crops of the hemisphere: chiefly **maize (corn)** to be ground into flour, beans, and squash, but also chili peppers, avocados, and pumpkins. The annual cultivation of such crops enabled Indian societies to grow larger and more complex, with their own distinctive social, economic, and political institutions.

The Mayas, Incas, and Mexica

Around 1500 B.C.E., farming towns first appeared in Mexico, enabling people to live in one place rather than move with the seasons. The more settled life in turn provided time for the cultivation of religion, art and crafts,

CORE **OBJECTIVE**

1. Explain why there were so many diverse human societies in the Americas before Europeans arrived.

Global warming, and climatic and environmental diversity

Agricultural revolution

maize (corn) The primary grain crop in Mesoamerica yielding small kernels often ground into cornmeal. Easy to grow in a broad range of conditions, it enabled a global population explosion after being brought to Europe, Africa, and Asia.

Mayan society A fresco depicting the social divisions of Mayan society. A Mayan lord, at the center, receives offerings.

science, governmental administration—and frequent warfare. Agriculture supported the development of densely populated cities complete with gigantic pyramids, temples, and palaces in Middle America (Mesoamerica, what is now Mexico and Central America). The Mayas, who dominated Central America for more than 600 years, also developed an elaborate written language and used sophisticated mathematics and astronomy to create a yearly calendar more accurate than the one the Europeans were using at the time of Columbus.

Farther south, as many as 12 million people speaking at least twenty different languages made up the Inca Empire. By the fifteenth century, the Incas' vast realm stretched some 2,500 miles along the Andes Mountains in the western part of South America, transforming their mountainous empire into a flowering civilization with fertile farms fed by irrigation systems, enduring stone buildings, and interconnected networks of paved roads.

During the late thirteenth century, the **Mexica** (Me-SHEE-ka)—whom Europeans later called Aztecs ("People from Aztlán," the place they claimed as their homeland)—began drifting southward from northwest Mexico. They eventually took control of the sweeping valley of central Mexico, where they built the city of Tenochtitlán in 1325 on an island in Lake Tetzcoco, the site of present-day Mexico City. Tenochtitlán would become the largest city in the Western Hemisphere by the end of the fifteenth century.

Warfare was a sacred ritual for the Mexica. Gradually, they expanded their control over neighboring societies in central Mexico, forcing them to pay tribute in goods and services each year and developing a thriving

Vast empires and monumental cities

Tribute and trade

Mexica Otherwise known as "Aztecs," a Mesoamerican people of northern Mexico who founded the vast Aztec Empire in the fourteenth century, later conquered by the Spanish under Hernán Cortés in 1521.

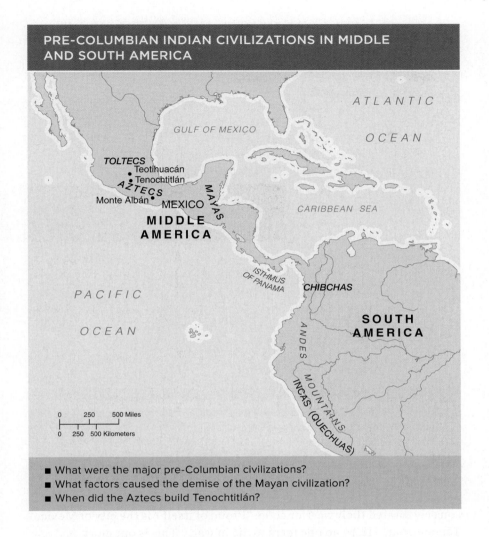

PRE-COLUMBIAN INDIAN CIVILIZATIONS IN MIDDLE AND SOUTH AMERICA

- What were the major pre-Columbian civilizations?
- What factors caused the demise of the Mayan civilization?
- When did the Aztecs build Tenochtitlán?

trade in gold, silver, copper, and pearls as well as agricultural products. Towering stone temples, broad paved avenues, thriving markets, and some 70,000 adobe huts dominated the dazzling capital city of Tenochtitlán. When the Spanish invaded Mexico in 1519, they found a sprawling **Aztec Empire** connected by a network of roads, connecting 371 city-states organized into 38 provinces.

Like most agricultural peoples, the Mexica were intensely spiritual. Their religious beliefs focused on the interconnection between nature and human life and the sacredness of natural elements—the sun, moon, stars, rain, mountains, rivers, and animals. To please the gods and bring good harvests and victory in battle, the Mexica, like most Mesoamericans, regularly offered live human sacrifices—captives, slaves, women, and children. In elaborate weekly rituals, priests used stone knives to cut out the beating hearts of the victims. The need for more sacrificial victims fed the Mexica's relentless warfare against other indigenous groups. A Mexica

Religion, war, tribute, and trade

Aztec Empire A network of more than 300 city-states and upwards of 30 provinces, established in the fourteenth century under the imperialistic Mexica, or Aztecs, in the valley of Mexico.

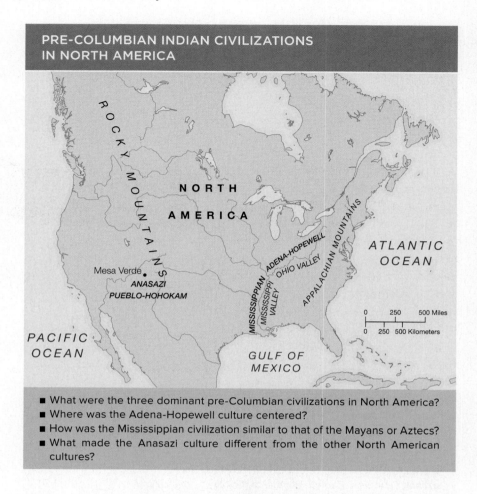

PRE-COLUMBIAN INDIAN CIVILIZATIONS IN NORTH AMERICA

■ What were the three dominant pre-Columbian civilizations in North America?
■ Where was the Adena-Hopewell culture centered?
■ How was the Mississippian civilization similar to that of the Mayans or Aztecs?
■ What made the Anasazi culture different from the other North American cultures?

song celebrated their warrior code: "Proud of itself / is the city of Mexico-Tenochtitlán / Here no one fears to die in war. / This is our glory. . . ."

North American Civilizations before 1500

> **Diverse regional societies**

North of Mexico, numerous indigenous civilizations existed in the present-day United States. They shared several fundamental spiritual myths and social beliefs, especially the sacredness of nature, the necessity of communal living and collective effort, and respect for elders, but they developed in different ways at different times and in different places. In North America alone, there were probably 240 different societies of native peoples speaking many different languages when the Europeans arrived.

> **Southwest pueblo cultures**

The dry Southwest (what is now Arizona, New Mexico, Nevada, and Utah) hosted corn-growing societies, elements of which exist today and heirs to which (the Hopis, Zunis, and others) still live in the multi-story adobe cliffside villages (called *pueblos* by the Spanish) erected by their ancestors. About 500 C.E., the native Hohokam people from present-day

Mexico migrated to southern and central Arizona, where they constructed hundreds of miles of irrigation canals to water their crops. They also crafted decorative pottery and turquoise jewelry, and they constructed temple mounds (earthen pyramids used for sacred ceremonies) similar to those in Mexico. Perhaps because of prolonged drought, the Hohokam society disappeared during the fifteenth century.

The most widespread and best known of the Southwest pueblo cultures were the Anasazi (Ancient Ones). In ancient times they developed extensive settlements in the "Four Corners" region where the modern-day states of Arizona, New Mexico, Colorado, and Utah meet. Anasazi society was remarkable for *not* having a rigid class structure. The religious leaders and warriors worked much as the rest of the people did. And the Anasazi engaged in warfare only as a means of self-defense. (*Hopi* means "Peaceful People.") Environmental factors shaped Anasazi culture and eventually caused its decline. Toward the end of the thirteenth century, a lengthy drought and the pressure of Indian peoples migrating from the north led to the disappearance of Anasazi society.

Cliff Dwellings Ruins of Anasazi cliff dwellings in Mesa Verde National Park, Colorado.

Along the heavily forested northwest Pacific coast, where shellfish, salmon, seals, whales, deer, and edible wild plants were abundant, there was little need for farming. In fact, many of the Pacific Northwest peoples needed to work only two days to provide enough food for a week. Because of plentiful food, the Native American population along the Pacific coast was larger and more concentrated than in other areas. Such social density enabled the Pacific peoples to develop intricate religious rituals and sophisticated woodworking arts, such as those displayed on totem poles. For shelter, they built large, earthen-floored, cedar-plank houses twenty-five to a hundred feet long, where whole bands of families lived together. They also built sturdy, oceangoing canoes carved out of red cedar tree trunks; some were large enough to carry fifty people. Socially, the Indian bands along the Northwest Pacific coast were hierarchical, divided into slaves, commoners, and chiefs. Seashells were used as money. An abundance of food, a mild climate, and a prosperous trading network made the Pacific coast the most densely populated of all the regions in North America.

Pacific Northwest forest and fishing cultures

The peoples living on the Great Plains (Plains Indians), a vast, flat land of cold winters and hot summers west of the Mississippi River, and in the

Plains bison-hunting cultures

Great Basin (present-day Utah and Nevada) include the Arapaho, Blackfeet, Cheyenne, Comanche, Crow, Apache, and Sioux. They were nomadic hunter-gatherers, following on foot enormous herds of bison across a sea of grassland, collecting seeds, nuts, roots, and berries as they roamed. At the center of most hunter-gatherer religions is the idea that the hunted animal is a willing sacrifice provided by the gods ("spirits"). To ensure a successful hunt, these peoples performed sacred rites of gratitude beforehand. Once a buffalo herd was spotted, the hunters would set fires to drive the stampeding animals over cliffs.

East of the Great Plains, in the vast woodlands from the Mississippi River to the Atlantic Ocean, several "mound-building" cultures flourished as predominantly agricultural societies. First the Adena and later the Hopewell peoples (both names derive from the archaeological sites) developed communities along rivers in the Ohio Valley between 800 B.C.E. and 400 C.E. The Adena-Hopewell cultures focused on agriculture, including tobacco. They left behind enormous earthworks and 200 elaborate **burial mounds** shaped like great snakes, birds, and other animals, several of which were nearly a quarter mile long. Evidence from the mounds reveals a complex social structure featuring a specialized division of labor, whereby different groups performed different tasks for the benefit of the society as a whole. Some were fisher folk; others were farmers, hunters, artists, cooks, and mothers.

Like the Adena, the Hopewell also developed an extensive trade network from the Gulf of Mexico to Canada, exchanging exquisite carvings, metalwork, pearls, seashells, copper ornaments, and jewelry. By the sixth century, however, the Hopewell culture disappeared, giving way to a new phase of

Eastern "mound builders"

burial mounds A funereal tradition, practiced in the Mississippi and Ohio Valleys by the Adena-Hopewell cultures, of erecting massive mounds of earth over graves, often shaped in the designs of serpents and other animals.

Great Serpent Mound At over 1,300 feet in length and three feet high, this snake-shaped burial mound in Adams County, Ohio, is the largest of its kind in the world.

Native American development east of the Mississippi River, the Mississippian culture, which flourished from 800 to 1500 C.E. The Mississippians, centered in the southern Mississippi Valley, were also mound-building and corn-growing peoples led by chieftains. They cleared vast tracts of land in order to grow maize, beans, squash, and sunflowers, and they built substantial towns around central plazas and temples. The Mississippi peoples developed a far-flung trading network extending all the way to the Rocky Mountains. Their ability to grow large amounts of corn each year in the fertile flood plains of rivers spurred rapid population growth.

The largest of these advanced regional centers, called "chiefdoms," was **Cahokia** (950–1250 C.E.), in southwest Illinois, just a few miles across the Mississippi River from what is now St. Louis, Missouri. There the Mississippians constructed a huge, intricately planned farming settlement with pole-and-thatch houses, temples (where humans were sacrificed to the gods), monumental public buildings, spacious ceremonial plazas, and over a hundred flat-topped earthen pyramids with thatch-roofed temples on top. At the height of its influence, prosperous Cahokia hosted 15,000 people on some 3,200 acres, making it the largest city north of Mexico. Outlying towns and farming settlements ranged up to fifty miles in all directions.

Cahokia mysteriously vanished after 1400. What caused its collapse remains a mystery, but the most likely reason was environmental. The overcutting of trees may have set in motion ecological changes that doomed the community when a massive earthquake struck around 1200 C.E. The loss of trees led to widespread flooding and the erosion of topsoil that finally forced people to look for better lands for corn growing elsewhere. As Cahokia disappeared, however, its former residents carried with them its cultural traditions, thereby spreading its advanced ways of life to other areas across the Midwest and into the South.

Eastern Woodlands Peoples and European Contact

After the collapse of Cahokia, the **Eastern Woodlands peoples** rose to dominance along the Atlantic seaboard from Maine to Florida and along the Gulf coast to Louisiana. They included three regional groups distinguished by their different languages: the Algonquian, the Iroquoian, and the Muskogean. These are the societies the Europeans would first encounter when they arrived in North America in the sixteenth and seventeenth centuries.

The hundreds of Algonquian-speaking peoples stretched from the New England seaboard to lands along the Great Lakes and into the Upper Midwest and south to New Jersey, Virginia, and the Carolinas. The Algonquians along the coast were skilled at fishing; the inland Algonquians excelled at hunting. All of them practiced agriculture to some extent, regularly burning dense forests to improve soil fertility and provide browsing room for deer. They used canoes made of hollowed-out tree trunks ("dugouts") or made

Cahokia The largest chiefdom and city of the Mississippian Indian culture located in present-day Illinois, and the site of a sophisticated farming settlement that supported up to 15,000 inhabitants.

Eastern Woodlands peoples Various Native American peoples, particularly the Algonquian, Iroquoian, and Muskogean regional groups, who once dominated the Atlantic seaboard from Maine to Louisiana.

Algonquian chief in warpaint
From the notebook of English settler John White, this sketch depicts Native American chief.

Warfare and rivalries

from birch bark to travel down rivers and across lakes. Most Algonquians lived in small, round shelters called *wigwams*. Their villages typically ranged in size from 500 to 2,000 inhabitants, but they often moved their villages with the seasons.

West and south of the Algonquians were the Iroquoian-speaking peoples (including the Seneca, Onondaga, Mohawk, Oneida, and Cayuga nations, as well as the Cherokee and Tuscarora to the south), whose lands spread from upstate New York southward through Pennsylvania and into the upland regions of the Carolinas and Georgia. The Iroquois built no great mounds or templed pyramids. They were farmers who lived together in extended family groups ("clans"), sharing bark-covered "long houses" in towns of 3,000 or more people. The most important crops were corn and squash, both of which figure prominently in Iroquois mythology.

Unlike the patriarchal Algonquian culture, in which men were dominant, in the Iroquoian culture women held the key leadership roles (hence such cultures are called "matriarchal"). As an Iroquois elder explained, "In our society, women are the center of all things. Nature, we believe, has given women the ability to create; therefore it is only natural that women be in positions of power to protect this function." Men and women were not treated as equals. Rather, the two genders operated in two separate social domains. No woman could be a chief; no man could head a clan. Women selected the chiefs, controlled the distribution of property, and planted as well as harvested the crops. After marriage, the man moved in with the wife's family. In part, the Iroquoian matriarchy reflected the frequent absence of Iroquois men, who as skilled hunters and traders traveled extensively for long periods, requiring women to take charge of domestic life in their absence.

War between rival groups of Native Americans, especially the Algonquians and Iroquois, was commonplace, usually as a means of settling feuds or gaining slaves. Success in fighting was a warrior's highest honor. As a Cherokee explained in the eighteenth century, "We cannot live without war. Should we make peace with the Tuscororas, we must immediately look out for some other nation with whom we can engage in our beloved occupation."

The third major Native American group in the Eastern Woodlands included the southern peoples along the Gulf coast who spoke the Muskogean language: the Creeks, Chickasaws, and Choctaws. Like the Iroquois, they were often matrilineal societies, meaning that ancestry was traced only through the mother's line, but they had a more rigid class structure. The Muskogeans lived in towns arranged around a central plaza. In the Lower South, many of their thatch-roofed houses had no walls because of the heat.

Over thousands of years, the native North Americans had displayed remarkable resilience, adapting to the uncertainties of frequent warfare, changing climate, and varying environments. They would display similar resilience in the face of the challenges created by the arrival of Europeans. In the process of adapting their heritage and ways of life to unwanted new realities, the Native Americans played a significant role in shaping America.

The Expansion of Europe

The European exploration of the Western Hemisphere resulted from several key developments during the fifteenth century that transformed Europe by 1492. Dramatic intellectual changes and scientific discoveries affected religion, warfare, family life, and the economy. In addition, the resurgence of the old vices—greed, conquest, exploitation, oppression, racism, and slavery—would help fuel European expansion abroad.

A severe population decline caused by warfare, famine, and plagues (the "Black Death") meant that once-great noble estates no longer had enough agricultural workers to maintain them. By the end of the fifteenth century, medieval feudalism's static agrarian social system, whereby serfs worked for local nobles in order to live on and farm the land, had largely died out. People were no longer forced to remain in the same locality and keep the same social status in which they were born. A new "middle class" of profit-hungry bankers, merchants, and investors emerged, men who were committed to a more dynamic commercial economy driven by innovations in banking, currency, accounting, and insurance.

The growing trade-based economy in Europe freed monarchs from their dependence on feudal nobles, enabling them to unify the scattered cities ruled by princes ("principalities") into large kingdoms with stronger, more centralized governments. The rise of towns, cities, and merchants provided kings and queens with new tax revenues, and lesser agrarian-based nobles were displaced by the emergence of powerful new commercial *nations* governed by these centralized bureaucracies with the power to collect taxes.

At the same time, the rediscovery of ancient Greek and Roman texts spurred an intellectual revolution known as the *Renaissance* (rebirth). Educated people throughout Europe began to challenge prevailing beliefs as well as the absolute authority of rulers and priests. They discussed controversial new ideas about politics, religion, and science, engaged in scientific research, and unleashed their artistic creativity.

This "rebirth" of learning also involved the practical application of new ideas that enabled the Age of Exploration. New knowledge and new technologies made possible the construction of stronger, larger sailing ships armed with cannons and capable of oceanic voyages. The development of more-accurate magnetic compasses, maps, and navigational instruments such as *astrolabes* and *quadrants* enabled sailors to determine their location by reference to the sun or stars. The fifteenth and sixteenth centuries also witnessed the invention of gunpowder, cannons, and firearms—and the printing press.

> **CORE OBJECTIVE**
> **2.** Summarize the major developments in Europe that enabled the Age of Exploration.

> The rise of a middle class

> Powerful new nations

> Innovations in shipbuilding, navigation, and weaponry lead to global revolution in maritime trade

By the end of the fifteenth century, trade between western European nations and across the seas became more important than ever. The Portuguese, blessed with expert sailors and fast new three-masted ships called *caravels*, took the lead in the Age of Exploration during the fifteenth century. Portuguese sailors roamed down the west coast of Africa in search of grains, gold, ivory, spices, and slaves. Eventually, they continued all the way around Africa in search of the fabled Indies (India and Southeast Asia), as well as China and Japan, rich with spices, silk cloth, and other exotic trade goods.

By the end of the fifteenth century, four powerful nations had emerged in western Europe: England, France, Portugal, and Spain. The marriage of King Ferdinand of Aragon and Queen Isabella of Castile in 1469 unified Spain into a single nation. Both monarchs were Christian expansionists. By 1492, they had forcibly expelled all Muslims and Jews from Spain and were making plans for exploring west across the Atlantic Ocean.

The Voyages of Columbus

These were the circumstances that led Christopher Columbus to pursue his own dream of finding an Atlantic route to the Indies. Born in Genoa, Italy, in 1451, the son of a weaver, Columbus took to the sea at an early age, teaching himself geography, navigation, and Latin. By the 1480s he was eager to spread Christianity across the globe. Columbus also wanted to win glory and riches by discovering what he hoped would be a shorter way to the "Indies" by sailing west across the Atlantic Ocean. The tall, red-haired Columbus eventually persuaded Ferdinand and Isabella to finance his voyage in exchange for awarding him a tenth share of any riches he gathered. The legend that the queen had to sell the crown jewels to finance the voyage is as false as the fable that Columbus set out to prove the earth was round rather than flat. Most educated Europeans knew that the earth was round.

On August 3, 1492, Columbus and ninety men and boys, mostly from Spain but from seven other countries as well, set sail on three ships, the *Santa María*, the *Pinta*, and the *Niña*, respectively about sixty, fifty-five, and fifty feet long. From Spain, this little squadron of tiny ships sailed first to Lisbon, Portugal, and then headed west. For weeks they journeyed across the open sea, hoping to sight land at any moment, only to be disappointed. By early October, the worried sailors grew rebellious at the "madness" of sailing blindly and threatened to take over the ships and turn back. Columbus had little choice but to promise that if they did not find land within three days, they would turn back.

Then, at dawn on October 12, a sailor stationed at the masthead yelled, "Tierra! Tierra!" ("Land! Land!"). He had sighted an island in the Bahamas east of Florida that Columbus named San Salvador (Blessed Savior). Columbus mistakenly concluded that they must be near the Indies, so he called the island people *Indios*. At every encounter with these native people, known as Tainos or Arawaks, his first question was whether they had any gold. If they

Christopher Columbus A portrait by Sebastiano del Piombo, ca. 1519.

Lust for gold

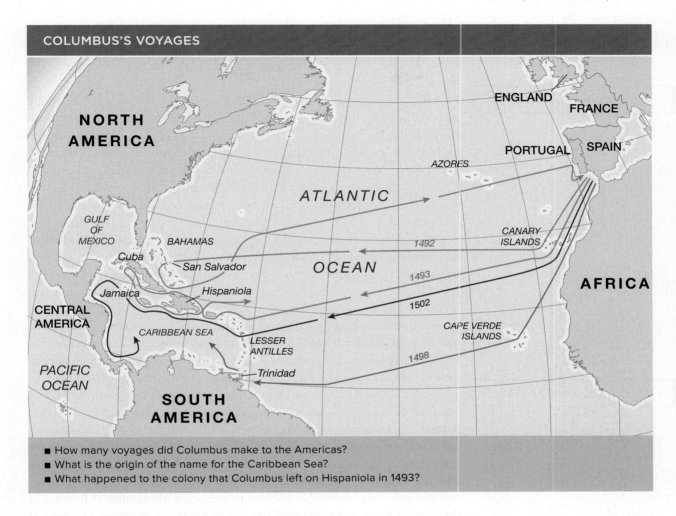

COLUMBUS'S VOYAGES

ENGLAND
FRANCE
PORTUGAL
SPAIN

NORTH AMERICA

AZORES

ATLANTIC

GULF OF MEXICO

BAHAMAS

CANARY ISLANDS

Cuba

San Salvador

OCEAN

1492

Jamaica

Hispaniola

1493

AFRICA

CENTRAL AMERICA

CARIBBEAN SEA

1502

LESSER ANTILLES

CAPE VERDE ISLANDS

PACIFIC OCEAN

Trinidad

1498

SOUTH AMERICA

- How many voyages did Columbus make to the Americas?
- What is the origin of the name for the Caribbean Sea?
- What happened to the colony that Columbus left on Hispaniola in 1493?

had gold, the Spaniards seized it; if they did not, the Europeans forced them to search for it.

After leaving San Salvador, Columbus continued to search for a passage to the Indies through the Bahamas and westward to Cuba. There, Columbus went ashore, sword in one hand, cross in the other, exclaiming that this was the "most beautiful land human eyes have ever beheld." Columbus then sailed eastward to the island he named Hispaniola (now Haiti and the Dominican Republic). There he found indigenous people who wore gold jewelry and introduced him to smoking tobacco.

At the end of 1492, Columbus, still convinced he had reached an outer island of Japan, sailed back across the Atlantic after leaving about forty men on Hispaniola and capturing a dozen Arawaks to present as gifts to the Spanish king and queen. Upon reaching Spain, Columbus received a hero's welcome, which he encouraged through his inflated claims of what he had discovered. Thanks to the newly invented printing press, news of his westward voyage spread rapidly across Europe. The Spanish monarchs,

Ferdinand and Isabella, told Columbus to prepare for a second voyage, instructing him to "treat the Indians very well and lovingly and abstain from doing them any injury." Columbus and his men would repeatedly defy this order.

Treaty of Tordesillas (1494)

The Spanish monarchs also wanted to strengthen their legal claim to the New World in case Portugal decided to send ships across the Atlantic. With the help of the pope (a Spaniard), rivals Spain and Portugal signed the Treaty of Tordesillas (1494), dividing the non-Christian world, with most of the New World given to Spain, and Africa and what would become Brazil granted to Portugal. In practice, this meant that while Spain developed its American empire in the sixteenth century, Portugal provided it with enslaved African laborers.

Flush with the fame resulting from his first voyage, Columbus returned across the Atlantic in 1493 with seventeen ships and 1,400 men. Also on board were Catholic priests eager to convert the native peoples to Christianity. Columbus discovered that the men he had left behind on Hispaniola had lost their senses, raping women, robbing villages, and, as Columbus's son later added, "committing a thousand excesses for which they were mortally hated by the Indians." The Europeans also carried with them a range of infectious diseases—smallpox, measles, typhus—that would prove disastrous for the indigenous peoples, for they had no natural immunities to them.

Vespucci's New World continent

Before he died, Columbus would make two more voyages to the Caribbean. To the end of his life, he insisted that he had discovered the outlying parts of Asia, not a new continent. By one of history's greatest ironies, this led Europeans to name the New World not for Columbus but for another Italian sailor-explorer, Amerigo Vespucci, a talented astronomer. In 1499, with the support of Portugal's monarchy, Vespucci sailed across the Atlantic, navigating by his knowledge of the sun and stars. He landed at Brazil and then sailed along 3,000 miles of the South American coastline in hopes of finding Asia. In the end, Vespucci reported that South America was so large that it must be a *new* continent rather than Asia, as Columbus still believed. In 1507, a German mapmaker paid tribute to Vespucci's navigational skills by labeling the New World using a variant of his first name: America.

Religious Conflict in Europe

At the same time that the voyages of Vespucci and Columbus were prompting other explorers to cross the Atlantic, powerful religious conflicts were tearing Europe apart in ways that would greatly influence settlement in the New World.

When Columbus sailed west in 1492, all of Europe acknowledged the thousand-year-old supremacy of the Roman Catholic Church and its pope in Rome. The brutal efforts of the Spanish to convert native peoples to **Roman Catholicism** illustrated the murderous intensity with which Europeans embraced religious life in the sixteenth century. Spiritual concerns inspired, comforted, and united people. People believed in heaven and hell, devils and

Roman Catholicism The Christian faith and religious practices of the Roman Catholic Church, which exerted great political, economic, and social influence on much of Western Europe and, through the Spanish and Portuguese Empires, on the Americas.

witches, demons and angels, magic and miracles. And Christians were willing to kill and die for their beliefs.

The enforced unity of Catholic Europe began to crack in 1517, however, when Martin Luther (1483–1546), a German priest who taught at the University of Wittenburg, rebelled against the Catholic Church and in the process launched the **Protestant Reformation**. Luther undermined the authority of the Catholic Church by showing that many of its officials were corrupt. He called the pope "the greatest thief and robber that has appeared or can appear on earth." Luther especially criticized the sale of *indulgences* (whereby priests would forgive sins in exchange for money or goods). God alone, through Christ, he insisted, offered people salvation; people could not earn it or buy it. Salvation, in other words, resulted from *belief*. As Luther exclaimed, "By faith alone are you saved!"

> Protestant Reformation

Luther tried to democratize Christianity by urging believers to read the Bible themselves rather than blindly follow the dictates of Catholic priests and the pope. The people themselves represented a "priesthood of all believers," perhaps his most revolutionary idea. To enable people to be their own "priests," Luther produced the first Bible in a German translation.

Catholic officials lashed out at Luther's "dangerous doctrines," calling him a "wild boar" and "a leper with a brain of brass and a nose of iron." Luther fought back with equal fury, declaring that he was "born to war." When the pope expelled Luther from the Catholic Church in 1521 and sentenced him to death, civil war erupted throughout the German principalities (the various German states did not become a united nation until 1871). A powerful German prince protected Luther from the Church's wrath. What had begun as a religious movement now became a political reformation, too. Luther was no longer simply an outspoken priest; he was a spiritual revolutionary, a folk hero, and a political prophet, encouraging German princes and dukes to separate themselves from the Italian papacy. A settlement between warring Lutherans and Catholics did not come until 1555, when each prince was allowed by the Treaty of Augsburg to determine the religion of his subjects.

> Wars and upheavals

Soon after Martin Luther began his revolt against the shortcomings of Catholicism, Swiss Protestants also challenged papal authority. In Geneva, the movement looked to John Calvin (1509-1564), a brilliant French scholar who had fled to that city and brought it under the sway of his powerful beliefs. In his great theological work, *The Institutes of the Christian Religion* (1536), Calvin set forth a stern doctrine. All people, he taught, were damned by Adam's original sin, but the sacrifice of Christ made possible the redemption of those whom God had "elected" and thus had predestined to salvation from the beginning of time.

Intoxicated by godliness, Calvin insisted upon strict morality and hard work, values that especially suited the rising middle class. Moreover, he taught that God valued every form of work, however menial it might be. Calvin also permitted lay members a share in the governance of the church

Protestant Reformation
Sixteenth-century religious movement initiated by Martin Luther, a German monk whose public criticism of corruption in the Roman Catholic Church, and whose teaching that Christians can communicate directly with God, gained a wide following.

through a body of elders and ministers called the presbytery. Calvin's doctrines formed the basis for the German Reformed Church, the Dutch Reformed Church, the Presbyterians in Scotland, some of the Puritans in England (and eventually America), and the Huguenots in France. Through these and other groups, John Calvin exerted a greater effect upon religious belief and practice in the English colonies than did any other leader of the Reformation. His insistence on the freedom of individual believers, as well as his recognition that monarchs and political officials were sinful like everyone else, helped contribute to the evolving ideas in Europe of representative democracy and the importance of separating church power from state (governmental) power.

Catholic Counter-Reformation

Even though the Catholic Church launched a "Counter-Reformation" that reaffirmed basic Catholic beliefs while addressing some of the concerns about priestly abuses raised by Luther, Calvin, and others, the Protestant Reformation spread rapidly across Europe during the sixteenth century. Most of northern Germany, along with Scandinavia, became Lutheran, often calling themselves the "Protesting Estates," from which derived the label "Protestants." The Reformation thus became in part a theological dispute, in part a political movement, and in part a *catalyst* for social change, civil strife, and imperial warfare. Throughout the sixteenth and seventeenth centuries, Catholics and Protestants persecuted, imprisoned, tortured, and killed each other in large numbers in Europe—and in the Americas. Every major international conflict became, to some extent, a religious holy war between Catholic and Protestant nations. Equally important, the Protestant world view, with its emphasis on the freedom of the individual conscience and personal Bible-reading, would play a major role in the colonization of America and the development of the American character.

CORE **OBJECTIVE**

3. Describe how the Spanish were able to conquer and colonize the Americas.

The Spanish Empire

During the sixteenth century, Catholic Spain created the world's most powerful empire. At its height, it encompassed much of Europe, most of the Americas, parts of Africa, and various trading outposts in Asia. But it was the gold and silver looted from the Americas that fueled the engine of Spain's "Golden Empire." By plundering, conquering, and colonizing the Americas and enslaving the native peoples, the Spanish planted Christianity in the Western Hemisphere and gained the resources to rule the world.

Spanish foothold in the Caribbean

The Caribbean Sea served as the funnel through which Spanish power entered the Americas. After establishing colonies on Hispaniola, including Santo Domingo, which became the capital of the West Indies, the Spanish proceeded eastward to Puerto Rico (1508) and westward to Cuba (1511–1514). Their motives, as one soldier explained, were "to serve God and the king, and also to get rich."

Many of the Europeans in the first wave of settlement in the New World died of malnutrition or disease. But the Native Americans suffered far more casualties, for they were ill equipped to resist the European invaders. Disunity everywhere—civil disorder, rebellion, and tribal warfare—left them vulnerable to division and foreign conquest. Attacks by well-armed soldiers and deadly germs from Europe overwhelmed entire native societies.

A Clash of Cultures

The often-violent encounter between Spaniards and Native Americans involved more than a clash between different peoples. It also involved contrasting forms of technological development. The Indians of Mexico used wooden canoes for water transportation, while the Europeans crossed the seas in much larger, heavily armed sailing vessels. The Spanish ships not only carried human cargo, but also steel swords, firearms, explosives, and armor. The wood-tipped arrows and tomahawks used by Native Americans were no match for guns, cannons, smallpox, and warhorses. "The most essential thing in new lands is horses," reported one Spanish soldier. "They instill the greatest fear in the enemy and make the Indians respect the leaders of the army."

> Lethal weapons and warhorses

Cortés's Conquest

The most dramatic European conquest of a major Indian civilization on the North American mainland occurred in Mexico. On February 18, 1519, Hernán Cortés, driven by dreams of gold and glory, set sail for Mexico from Cuba. His fleet of eleven ships carried nearly 600 soldiers and sailors. Also on board were 200 indigenous Cubans, sixteen horses, and cannons. After the Spanish landed on the coast of the Gulf of Mexico, Cortés convinced the local Totomacs to join his assault against the Mexica, their hated rivals. To prevent any of his soldiers, called **conquistadores** (conquerors), from deserting, Cortés had the ships burned, sparing one vessel to carry the expected gold back to Spain. With his small army, cannons, and Indian allies, Cortés brashly set out to conquer the sprawling Mexica (Aztec) Empire, which extended from central Mexico to what is today Guatemala. The nearly 200-mile march of Cortés's army through the mountains to the magnificent Mexica capital of Tenochtitlán took nearly three months.

> Rivals collaborate against the Mexica

Spanish Invaders

As Cortés and his army marched across Mexico, they heard fabulous accounts of Tenochtitlán. With some 200,000 inhabitants, it was the largest city in the Americas and much larger than most European cities. Graced by wide canals, stunning gardens, and formidable stone pyramids, the lake-encircled capital seemed unconquerable. But Cortés made the most of his assets. Through a combination of threats and deceptions, Cortés and his Indian allies entered Tenochtitlán peacefully and captured the emperor,

conquistadores Spanish term for "conquerors," applied to Spanish and Portuguese soldiers who conquered lands held by indigenous peoples in central and southern America as well as the current states of Texas, New Mexico, Arizona, and California.

Cortés in Mexico Page from the *Lienzo de Tlaxcala*, a historical narrative from the sixteenth century. The scene, in which Cortés is shown seated on a throne, depicts the arrival of the Spanish in Tlaxcala.

Montezuma II. Cortés explained to the captive Montezuma why the invasion was necessary: "We Spaniards have a disease of the heart that only gold can cure."

After taking the Mexicas' gold and silver, the Spanish forced them to mine more of the precious metals. Then, in the spring of 1520, disgruntled Mexica decided that Montezuma was a traitor. They rebelled, stoned him to death, and, armed with stone-bladed wooden swords and wicker shields, attacked the Spaniards. Forced to retreat to the mainland, the Spaniards lost about a third of their men. Their 20,000 Indian allies remained loyal, however, and Cortés regrouped his forces. For months, sporadic fighting continued. In 1521, having been reinforced with horse-borne troops (cavalry) from Cuba and thousands more Native Americans eager to defeat the despised Mexica, he surrounded the imperial city for eighty-five days, cutting off its access to water and food and allowing a smallpox epidemic to devastate the inhabitants. For three months, the Mexica bravely defended their capital. Then the siege came to a bloody end. The ravages of smallpox and starvation, as well as the support of 75,000 anti-Mexica Indian allies, help explain how such a small force of determined Spaniards was able to vanquish a proud nation of nearly 1 million people. After 15,000 Mexica were slaughtered, the others surrendered. A merciless Cortés ordered the leaders hanged and the priests devoured by fighting dogs. In two years, Cortés and his disciplined army had conquered a fabled empire that had taken centuries to develop. Cortés became the first governor of New Spain and began a systematic process of replacing the Mexica leaders with Spanish bureaucrats and church officials.

Cortés's conquest of Mexico established the model for waves of plundering conquistadores to follow. Within twenty years, Spain had established a vast empire in Mexico and the Caribbean, which Cortés called "New Spain," based on a pattern of ruthless violence and enslavement of the native

Cortés conquers the Mexica, and Pizarro invades the Inca

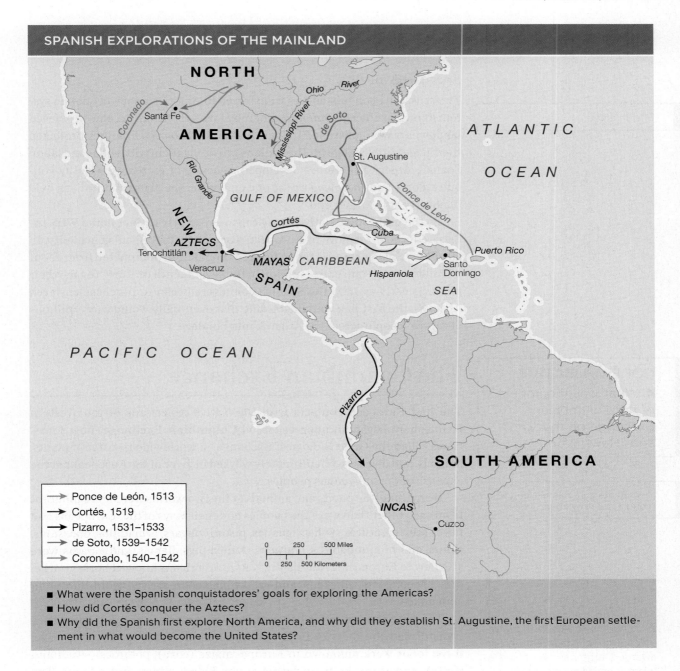

SPANISH EXPLORATIONS OF THE MAINLAND

NORTH AMERICA

Coronado
Santa Fe
Ohio River
Mississippi River
de Soto
St. Augustine

ATLANTIC OCEAN

Rio Grande

GULF OF MEXICO

Ponce de León

Cortés

Cuba

NEW

AZTECS
Tenochtitlán
Veracruz

MAYAS CARIBBEAN
SPAIN

Puerto Rico
Santo Domingo
Hispaniola

SEA

PACIFIC OCEAN

Pizarro

SOUTH AMERICA

INCAS

Cuzco

→ Ponce de León, 1513
→ Cortés, 1519
→ Pizarro, 1531–1533
→ de Soto, 1539–1542
→ Coronado, 1540–1542

0   250   500 Miles
0   250   500 Kilometers

■ What were the Spanish conquistadores' goals for exploring the Americas?
■ How did Cortés conquer the Aztecs?
■ Why did the Spanish first explore North America, and why did they establish St. Augustine, the first European settlement in what would become the United States?

peoples followed by oppressive rule over them—just as the Mexica had done in forming their own empire.

In 1531 another Spaniard, Francisco Pizarro, led a band of soldiers down the Pacific coast from Panama toward Peru, where they brutally subdued the Inca Empire. The Spanish invaders seized the Inca palaces and looted the empire of its gold and silver. From Peru, Spain extended its control southward through Chile by about 1553 and north, to present-day Colombia, by 1538.

Spanish America

Encomienda

The crusading conquistadores transferred to America a socioeconomic system known as the **encomienda**, whereby favored officers became privileged landowners who controlled Indian villages. As *encomenderos*, they protected the villages in exchange for the Indians providing them with goods and labor. Spanish America therefore developed a society of extremes: wealthy conquistadores and *encomenderos* at one end of the spectrum and Indians held in poverty at the other end.

By the mid-1500s, Native Americans were nearly extinct in the West Indies, reduced even more by European diseases than by Spanish brutality. In all of New Spain's empire, the indigenous population plummeted from about 50 million at the outset to 4 million in the seventeenth century. To take their place, as early as 1503 the Spanish colonizers began to purchase enslaved Africans, the first in a wretched traffic that eventually would carry millions of captive people across the Atlantic into bondage.

CORE **OBJECTIVE**

4. What was the impact of the Columbian Exchange on the "Old" and "New" Worlds?

The Columbian Exchange

New plants and animals lead to a global food revolution

The first European contacts with the Native Americans of the Western Hemisphere began an unprecedented **Columbian Exchange**, now sometimes called the Great Biological Exchange—a worldwide transfer of plants, animals, and diseases that ultimately worked in favor of the Europeans at the expense of the indigenous peoples.

If anything, the plants and animals of the two worlds were more different from each other than were the peoples and their ways of life. Europeans had never seen creatures such as iguanas, bison, cougars, armadillos, opossums, sloths, and hummingbirds. Turkeys, guinea pigs, llamas, and alpacas were also new to Europeans. Nor did the Native Americans know of horses, cattle, pigs, sheep, goats, chickens, and rats, which soon arrived from Europe in abundance.

The exchange of plant life between the Americas and Europe/Africa transformed the diets of both hemispheres. Before Columbus's voyage, three foods were unknown in Europe: maize (corn), potatoes (sweet and white), and many kinds of beans (snap, kidney, lima, and others). The white potato, although commonly called Irish, is actually native to South America. Explorers brought it back to Europe, where it thrived. The "Irish potato" was eventually transported to North America by Scots-Irish immigrants during the early eighteenth century. Other Western Hemisphere food plants included peanuts, squash, peppers, tomatoes, pumpkins, pineapples, sassafras, papayas, guavas, avocados, cacao (the source of chocolate), and chicle (for chewing gum). Europeans in turn introduced rice,

encomienda A land-grant system under which Spanish army officers (conquistadores) were awarded large parcels of land taken from Native Americans.

Columbian Exchange The transfer of biological and social elements, such as plants, animals, people, diseases, and cultural practices, among Europe, the Americas, and Africa in the wake of Christopher Columbus's voyages to the New World.

wheat, barley, oats, wine grapes, melons, coffee, olives, bananas, "Kentucky" bluegrass, daisies, and dandelions to the Americas.

Population growth in Europe

The beauty of the biological exchange was that the food plants were more complementary than competitive. Corn, it turned out, could flourish almost anywhere in the world. The nutritious food crops exported from the Americas, especially the potato, thus helped nourish a worldwide population explosion probably greater than any since the invention of agriculture. The new food crops helped spur a dramatic increase in the European population that in turn provided the restless, adventurous young people who would colonize the New World.

By far, however, the most significant aspect of the biological exchange was the transmission of **infectious diseases**. During the three centuries after Columbus's first voyage, Europeans and Africans brought with them deadly diseases that Native Americans had never experienced: smallpox, typhus, malaria, and measles. The results were catastrophic. Far more native people—tens of millions—died from smallpox than from combat. By 1568, just 75 years after Columbus's first voyage, 90 percent of the Indian population had been killed—the greatest loss of human life in history. Unable to explain or cure the diseases, Native American chieftains and religious leaders often lost their stature—and their lives, as they were usually the first to meet the Spanish and thus were the first infected. As a consequence of losing their leaders, the indigenous peoples were less capable of resisting the European invaders.

Spanish Exploration in North America

CORE **OBJECTIVE**
5. Analyze the legacy of Spanish colonization on North American history.

Three centuries of Spanish domination and Hispanic influence

Throughout the sixteenth century, no European power other than Spain held more than a brief foothold in the New World. Spain had the advantage not only of having arrived first but also of having stumbled onto those regions that would produce the quickest profits. While France and England were preoccupied with political disputes and religious conflict, Spain had forged an intense national unity that enabled it to dominate Europe as well as the New World. The treasures seized from Mexico and Peru added to Spain's military and economic power, but the single-minded focus on gold and silver also tempted the Spanish government to live beyond its means. Between 1557 and 1662, the kings of Spain were forced to declare bankruptcy ten times.

For most of the colonial period, much of what is now the United States belonged to Spain, and Spanish culture etched a lasting imprint upon American ways of life. Spain's colonial presence lasted more than three centuries, much longer than either England's or France's. New Spain was centered in Mexico, but its frontier outposts extended from Florida to

infectious diseases Also called contagious diseases, illnesses that can pass from one person to another by way of invasive biological organisms able to reproduce in the bodily tissues of their hosts. Europeans unwittingly brought many such diseases to the Americas, devastating the Native American peoples.

Alaska. Hispanic place-names—San Francisco, Santa Barbara, Los Angeles, San Diego, Santa Fe, San Antonio, Pensacola, and St. Augustine—survive to this day, as do Hispanic influences in art, architecture, literature, music, law, and cuisine.

Juan Ponce de León, then governor of Puerto Rico, made the earliest known exploration of Florida in 1513. Meanwhile, Spanish explorers skirted the Gulf of Mexico coast from Florida to Veracruz, scouted the Atlantic coast all the way to Canada, and established a short-lived colony on the Carolina coast.

In 1539, Hernando de Soto and 600 conquistadores landed on Florida's west coast, traveled north as far as western North Carolina, and then moved westward beyond the Mississippi River and up the Arkansas River, looting and destroying Indian villages along the way. In the spring of 1542, de Soto died near Natchez, Mississippi; the next year, the survivors among his party floated down the Mississippi River, and 311 of the original adventurers found their way to Spanish Mexico. In 1540, Francisco Vásquez de Coronado, inspired by rumors of gold, traveled northward from Mexico into New Mexico and northeast across Texas and Oklahoma as far as Kansas.

The Spanish established provinces in North America not so much as commercial enterprises but as defensive buffers protecting their more lucrative empires in Mexico and South America. In 1565 a Spanish outpost on the Florida coast, St. Augustine, became the first European town in the present-day United States. It included a fort, church, hospital, fish market, and over one hundred shops and houses—all built decades before the first English settlements at Jamestown and Plymouth. While other early American outposts failed, St. Augustine survived as a defensive base perched on the southern edge of a continent.

The Spanish Southwest

The Spanish eventually established other permanent settlements in what are now New Mexico, Texas, and California. Missionaries established Catholic missions, where they imposed Christianity on the Indians and treated them like slaves. After about ten years, a mission would be secularized: its lands would be divided among the converted Indians, the mission chapel would become a parish church, and the inhabitants would be given full Spanish citizenship—including the privilege of paying taxes. The soldiers who were sent to protect the missions were housed in *presidios*, or forts; their families and the merchants accompanying them lived in adjacent villages.

New Mexico A region in the American Southwest, originally established by the Spanish, who settled there in the sixteenth century, founded Catholic missions, and exploited the region's indigenous peoples.

The land that would later be called **New Mexico** was a center of Catholic missionary activity in the American Southwest. In 1598, Juan de Oñate, the rich son of a Spanish mining family in Mexico, received a land grant for the territory north of Mexico above the Rio Grande. He then recruited soldiers and hundreds of Mexican Indians and *mestizos* (the offspring of Spanish fathers and Indian mothers), including women, children, and priests. The caravan of colonists, including animals and carts carrying supplies, began moving north from the mountains above Mexico City. After walking over 800 miles in seven months, they established the colony of "New Mexico" near present-day Santa Fe ("Holy Faith" in Spanish), and sent out expeditions to search for gold and silver. Oñate told the local Indians, called Pueblos, that they now belonged to Spain, but he promised that the Spaniards would bring them peace, justice, prosperity, and protection. If they embraced Christianity, Oñate added, the Indians would receive "an eternal life of great bliss" instead of "cruel and everlasting torment."

Some Indian peoples welcomed the Spanish missionaries as "powerful witches" capable of easing their burdens. Others tried to use the European invaders as allies against rival Indian groups. Still others saw no alternative but to submit. The Indians living in Spanish New Mexico were required to pay tribute to their *encomenderos* and perform personal tasks for them, including sexual favors. Soldiers and priests flogged disobedient Indians.

Before the end of New Mexico's first year as a colony, in December 1598, the Pueblos revolted, killing several soldiers. During three days of relentless fighting, vengeful Spanish soldiers killed 500 Pueblo men and 300 women and children. Survivors were enslaved. Pueblo men over the age of twenty-five had one foot cut off to frighten the others and keep them from escaping or resisting. Children were taken from their parents into a Catholic mission, where, Oñate pledged, they would "attain the knowledge of God and the salvation of their souls."

Spanish New Mexico expanded very slowly. The hoped-for deposits of gold and silver were never found, and a lack of rain for farming blunted the interest of potential colonists. In 1608 the government decided to turn New Mexico into a royal province. The following year it dispatched a royal governor, and in 1610, as the first English settlers were struggling to survive at Jamestown, in Virginia, the Spanish moved the province's capital to Santa Fe, the first permanent seat of government in the present-day United States. By 1630 there were fifty Catholic churches and monasteries in New Mexico, as well as some 3,000 Spaniards.

Roman Catholic missionaries in New Mexico claimed that 86,000 Pueblos had been converted to Christianity during the seventeenth century. In fact, however, resentment among the Indians increased with time. In 1680 a powerful Indian leader named Popé organized a massive rebellion against the Spanish. The Native Americans burned Catholic churches;

Cultural conflict This Peruvian illustration, from a 1612–1615 manuscript by Felipe Guaman Poma de Ayala, shows a Dominican Catholic friar forcing a native woman to weave.

Catholicism in New Spain and the Pueblo Revolt (1680)

tortured, mutilated, and executed priests; and destroyed all relics of Christianity. Popé then established Santa Fe as the capital of his confederacy. The Pueblo Revolt of 1680 was the greatest defeat that Indians ever inflicted on European efforts to conquer the New World. It took fourteen years and four military campaigns for the Spanish to reestablish control over New Mexico.

Horses and the Great Plains

Another major consequence of the Pueblo Revolt was the opportunity it gave Indian rebels to get hundreds of Spanish horses (Spanish authorities had made it illegal for Indians to own horses). The Pueblos in turn established a thriving horse trade with Navajos, Apaches, and others. By 1690, horses were in Texas, and they soon spread across the Great Plains, the vast rolling grasslands extending from the Missouri Valley in the east to the base of the Rocky Mountains in the west.

Horses and bison >

Prior to the arrival of horses, Indians hunted on foot and used dogs as their beasts of burden. But dogs are carnivores, and it was always difficult to find enough meat to feed them. The introduction of the **horse** changed everything, though, providing the Plains Indians with a new source of mobility and power. Horses are grazing animals, and the vast grasslands of the Great Plains offered plenty of forage. Horses could also haul up to seven times as much weight as dogs, and their speed and endurance made the indigenous people much more effective hunters and warriors.

In the short run, the horse brought prosperity and mobility to the Plains Indians. Yet the Indians on horseback eventually killed more bison than the herds could replace. Further, horses competed with the bison for food, often depleting the prairie grass. And as Indians on horses traveled greater distances and encountered more people, infectious diseases spread more widely.

French and Dutch Exploration of America

Spanish rivals for New World wealth >

The success of Spain in conquering much of the Western Hemisphere spurred Portugal, France, England, and the Netherlands (Holland) to begin their own exploration and exploitation of the New World. The French were the first to pose a serious threat. Spanish treasure ships sailing home from Mexico, Peru, and the Caribbean islands offered tempting targets for French privateers (privately owned warships) and pirates. The French also began looking for a passage to Asia through the Americas. In 1524, the French king sent the Italian Giovanni da Verrazano westward across the Atlantic. Upon sighting land (probably at Cape Fear, North Carolina), Verrazano ranged along the coast as far north as Maine. On a second voyage, in 1528, he was killed in the West Indies by Carib Indians.

Unlike the Verrazano voyages, those of Jacques Cartier, beginning in the next decade, led to the first French effort at colonization in North America. During three voyages, Cartier explored the Gulf of St. Lawrence

horse The Spanish introduced horses to the Americas, eventually transforming many Native American cultures.

The Columbian Exchange and the Spanish Empire in North America

The following chart lists examples of organisms and foods exchanged between the Old and New Worlds during the Columbian Exchange that ensued as the Spanish created a vast empire in the Americas. As you review the chart, consider the role that these exchanges played in the Spanish conquest and colonization of North America.

	Old World ⟶ New World	New World ⟶ Old World
Animals	horses, cattle, pigs, sheep, goats, chickens	llamas, turkeys, alpacas, guinea pigs
Food	rice, wheat, barley, oats, wine grapes, melons, coffee, olives, bananas, Kentucky bluegrass, daisies, dandelions	maize, potatoes, snap beans, kidney beans, lima beans, peanuts, squash, peppers, tomatoes, pumpkins, pineapples, sassafras, papayas, guavas, avocadoes, cacao, chicle
Diseases	smallpox, typhus, diphtheria, bubonic plague, malaria, yellow fever, cholera	syphilis

Impact on the Old and New Worlds

1. New foods revolutionized diets in both worlds.
2. The spread of corn in particular led to an explosion of the worldwide population.
3. Infectious diseases, especially smallpox, decimated Native American populations and ways of life, enabled the Spanish to take control over many societies in the Americas, and also led to the beginning of slave importation from Africa.

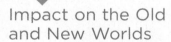

QUESTIONS FOR ANALYSIS

1. How did the biological organisms (plants, animals, and microbes) brought by the Spaniards complement the technological advantages they possessed over Native Americans?

2. How did this biological exchange allow the Spanish to establish political and economic control over many societies in North America?

3. How were food diets revolutionized?

and ventured up the St. Lawrence River, now the boundary between Canada and New York. Twice he got as far as present-day Montreal, and twice he wintered at or near the site of Quebec, near which a short-lived French colony appeared in 1541–1542. From that time forward, however, French kings lost interest in Canada for over half a century.

Greater threats to Spanish power arose from the Dutch and the English. The United Provinces of the Netherlands, which had passed by inheritance

ENGLISH, FRENCH, AND DUTCH EXPLORATIONS

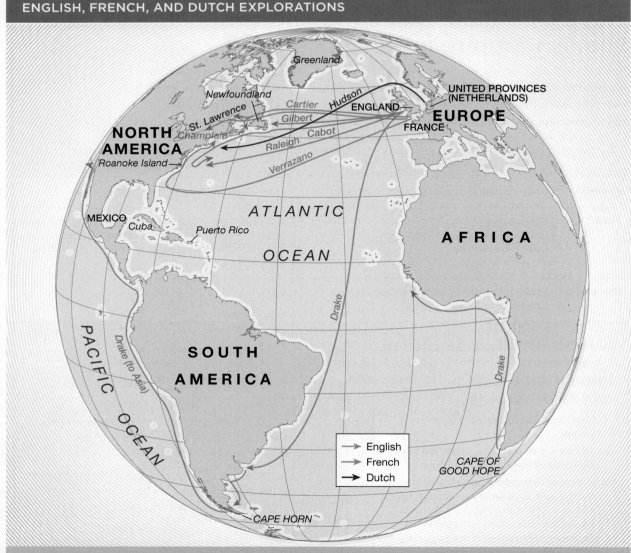

■ Who were the first European explorers to rival Spanish dominance in the New World, and why did they cross the Atlantic?

■ Why was the defeat of the Spanish Armada important to the history of English exploration? What was the significance of the voyages of Gilbert and Raleigh?

to the Spanish king but had become largely Protestant, rebelled against Spanish Catholic rule in 1567. A long, bloody struggle for independence ensued in which Protestant England aided the Dutch. Spain refused to recognize the independence of the Dutch republic for a hundred years, in 1648.

Almost from the beginning of the Protestant Dutch revolt against Catholic Spain, the Dutch plundered Spanish treasure ships in the Atlantic and carried on illegal trade with Spain's colonies. While England's Queen

Elizabeth, a Protestant, steered a tortuous course to avoid open war with Spain, she secretly encouraged both Dutch and English privateers ("sea dogs") to attack Spanish ships and their colonies in the Americas.

The Defeat of the Armada

The English raids on Spanish shipping continued for twenty years before open war erupted between the two nations. Determined to conquer England, Philip II, the king of Catholic Spain who was Queen Elizabeth's brother-in-law and fiercest opponent, assembled in 1588 the massive **Spanish Armada**: 132 warships, 8,000 sailors, and 18,000 soldiers—the greatest invasion fleet in history. On May 28, 1588, the Armada sailed north, determined to conquer the English and restore them to Catholicism. English warships, smaller but faster than those of the Spanish fleet, were waiting for them. As the battle unfolded, the larger Spanish warships could not compete with the speed and agility of the smaller English ships. The English chased the Armada through the English Channel before a terrible storm swept the Spanish fleet into the North Sea, destroying dozens of the world's finest warships. The stunning defeat of Catholic Spain's fearsome Armada greatly strengthened the Protestant cause across Europe.

The great naval victory was the climactic event of Queen Elizabeth's long reign. England at the end of the sixteenth century was surging with new power and optimism, filled with a youthful zest for exploring new worlds. The defeat of the Spanish Armada marked the beginning of England's global naval supremacy and cleared the way for English colonization of America. English colonists could now make their way to North America without fear of Spanish interference.

> The English defeat the Spanish Armada (1588)

English Exploration of America

English efforts to colonize America began a few years before the great battle with the Spanish Armada. In 1578, Queen Elizabeth had given Sir Humphrey Gilbert permission to establish a colony in the "remote heathen and barbarous lands" of America. Gilbert's group set out in 1583, intending to settle near Narragansett Bay (in present-day Rhode Island). He instead landed in fogbound Newfoundland (Canada). With winter approaching and his largest vessels lost, Gilbert and the colonists headed home. On the way back, Gilbert's ship vanished, and he was never seen again.

The next year, Queen Elizabeth asked Sir Walter Raleigh, Gilbert's half-brother and a favorite of the queen, to organize a colonizing mission. Raleigh's expedition discovered the Outer Banks of North Carolina and landed at Roanoke Island. Raleigh named the area Virginia, in honor of childless Queen Elizabeth, the presumably "Virgin Queen," who herself chose the name. After several false starts, Raleigh in 1587 sponsored another expedition of about one hundred colonists, including twenty-six women and children, led by Governor John White. White spent a month on Roanoke Island and then returned to England for supplies, leaving behind his

> The lost Roanoke colony

Spanish Armada A massive Spanish fleet of 130 warships that was defeated at Plymouth in 1588 by the English navy during the reign of Queen Elizabeth I.

The English in Virginia The arrival of English explorers on the Outer Banks, with Roanoke Island at left.

daughter Eleanor and his granddaughter Virginia Dare, the first English child born in the New World. White's journey back to Virginia was delayed because of the naval war with Spain. When he finally returned to America in 1590, he discovered that the Roanoke outpost had been abandoned and looted.

No trace of the "lost colonists" was ever found. Indians may have killed them, or hostile Spaniards—who had certainly planned to attack—may have done the job. The most recent evidence indicates that the "Lost Colony" suffered from a horrible drought that prevented them from growing enough food to survive. While some of the colonists may have gone south, the main group of them appears to have gone north, to the southern shores of Chesapeake Bay, where they lived for some years until they were killed by local Indians.

There was not a single English colonist in North America when the great Queen Elizabeth died in 1603. The Spanish controlled the only colonial outposts on the continent. But that was about to change. Inspired by the success of the Spanish in exploiting the New World, and emboldened by their defeat of the Spanish Armada in 1588, the English—as well as the French and the Dutch—would soon develop American colonial empires of their own, quite different from that of the Spanish.

New Spain at its Height

During the two and a half centuries after 1492, the Spanish developed the most extensive empire the world had ever known. It would span southern Europe and the Netherlands, much of the Western Hemisphere, and parts of

Asia. Yet the Spanish Empire grew so vast that its sprawling size and complexity eventually led to its disintegration.

During the sixteenth century, Spanish America (called New Spain) gradually developed into a settled society. From the outset, the Spanish in the Americas behaved more like occupying rulers than permanent settlers, carefully regulating every detail of colonial administration and life. They were less interested in creating self-sustaining colonial communities than they were devoted to taking gold and silver, and to enslaving the indigenous peoples and converting them to Christianity. Between 1545 and 1660, the Spanish forced Native Americans and Africans to mine 7 million pounds of silver in the New World, twice as much silver as existed in all of Europe in 1492.

The legacy of New Spain is, therefore, decidedly mixed. While connecting the cultures of Europe and the Americas, the Spanish explorers, conquistadores, and priests imposed on the native peoples Catholicism as well as a cruel system of economic exploitation and dependence. That system created terrible disparities in wealth, education, and opportunity that would trigger repeated revolts and political instability. Bartolomé de Las Casas, a courageous Spanish priest in Mexico who tirelessly called for humane treatment of the native peoples, concluded, "The Spaniards have shown not the slightest consideration for these people, treating them (and I speak from firsthand experience, having been there from the outset) . . . as piles of dung in the middle of the road. They have had as little concern for their souls as for their bodies."

New Spain's legacy

■ **Native American Societies** Asian hunter-gatherers came across the Bering Strait by foot and settled the length and breadth of the Americas, forming groups with diverse cultures, languages, and customs. Global warming enabled an agricultural revolution, particularly the growing of *maize*, that allowed former hunter-gatherer peoples to settle and build empires, such as that of the *Mexica*, whose *Aztec Empire* included many subjugated peoples and a vast system of trade and tribute. Some North American peoples developed an elaborate continental trading network and impressive cities like *Cahokia*; their *burial mounds* reveal a complex social organization. The *Eastern Woodlands peoples* that the Europeans would first encounter included both patriarchal and matriarchal societies as well as extensive language-based alliances. The Algonquian, Iroquoian, and Muskogean were among the major Indian nations. Warfare was an important cultural component, leading to shifting rivalries and alliances among indigenous communities and with European settlers.

■ **Age of Exploration** By the 1490s, Europeans were experiencing a renewed curiosity about the world. Warfare, plagues, and famine undermined the old agricultural feudal system in Europe, and in its place arose a middle class that monarchs could tax. Powerful new nations replaced the land estates and cities ruled by princes. A revival of interest in antiquity led to the development of modern science and the creation of better maps and navigation techniques, as well as new weapons and ships. Navies became the critical component of global trade and world power. When the Spanish began to colonize the New World, the conversion of Indians to *Roman Catholicism* was important, but the search for gold and silver was primary.

The national rivalries sparked by the *Protestant Reformation* in Europe shaped the course of conquest in the Americas.

■ **Conquering and Colonizing the Americas** Spanish *conquistadores* such as Hernán Cortés used their advantages in military technology, including steel, gunpowder, and domesticated animals such as *horses*, in order to conquer the powerful Aztec and Inca Empires. European diseases, first introduced by Columbus's voyages, did even more to ensure Spanish victories. The Spanish *encomienda* system demanded goods and labor from the indigenous peoples. As the Indian population declined, the Spanish began to import enslaved Africans.

■ **Columbian Exchange** Contact between the Old World and the New resulted in a great biological exchange, sometimes called the *Columbian Exchange*. Crops such as *maize*, beans, and potatoes became staples in the Old World. Native peoples incorporated into their culture such Eurasian animals as the *horse* and pig. But the invaders also carried *infectious diseases* that set off pandemics of smallpox, plague, and other illnesses to which Indians had no immunity. The Americas were depopulated and cultures destroyed.

■ **Spanish Legacy** Spain left a lasting legacy in the borderlands from California to Florida. Catholic missionaries contributed to the destruction of the old ways of life by exterminating "heathen" beliefs in the Southwest, a practice that led to open rebellion in *New Mexico* in 1598 and 1680. Spain's rival European nation-states began competing for gold and glory in the New World. England's defeat of the *Spanish Armada* cleared the path for English dominance in North America.

KEY TERMS

CHRONOLOGY

by 12,000 B.C.E.	Humans have migrated to the Americas
5000 B.C.E.	Agricultural revolution begins in Mexico
1050–1250 C.E.	The city of Cahokia flourishes in North America
1325	Mexica (Aztec) Empire founded in Central Mexico
1492	Columbus makes his first voyage of discovery in the Americas
1503	Spaniards bring first enslaved Africans to the Americas
1517	Martin Luther launches the Protestant Reformation
1519	Cortés begins the Spanish conquest of Mexico
1531	Pizarro subdues the Inca Empire in South America for Spain
1541	Spaniards build fort at St. Augustine, the first permanent European outpost in the present-day United States
1584–1587	Raleigh's Roanoke Island venture
1588	The English navy defeats the Spanish Armada
1680	Pueblo Revolt

INQUIZITIVE

Go to InQuizitive to see what you've learned—and learn what you've missed—with personalized feedback along the way.

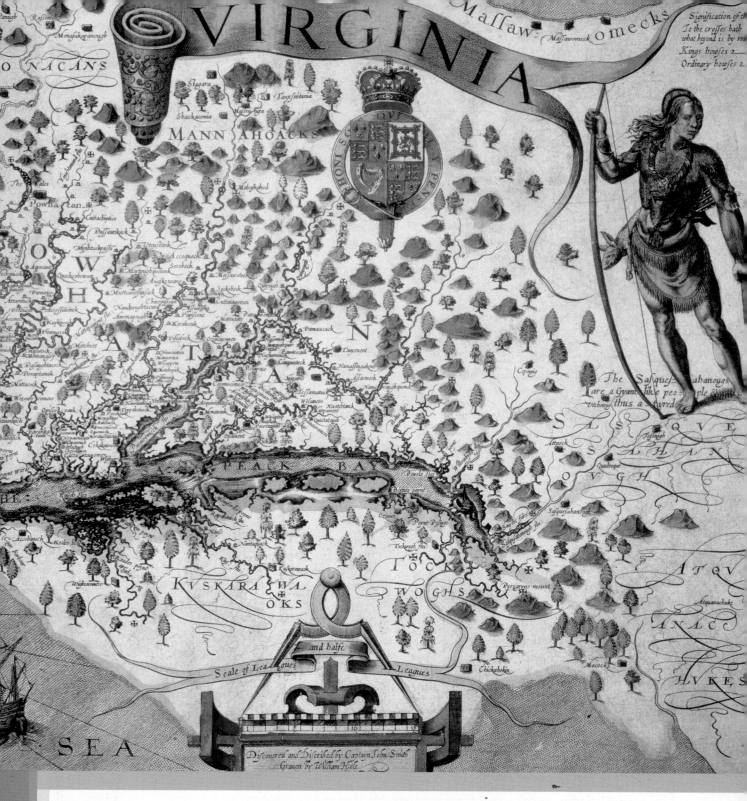

OLD VIRGINIA As one of the earliest explorers and settlers of the Jamestown colony, John Smith put his intimate knowledge of the region to use by creating this seventeenth-century map of Virginia. In the upper right hand corner is a warrior of the Susquehannock, whom Smith called a "G[i]ant-like people."

England and Its American Colonies

1607–1732

The England that Queen Elizabeth governed at the beginning of the seventeenth century was a unique blend of elements. The Church of England mixed Protestant theology with Catholic rituals to produce the Anglican form of Christianity. England was also distinctive in that English rulers shared considerable power with Parliament, the legislature, unlike the absolute monarchs of France and Spain. Even English monarchs took pride in the civil liberties that were born from this evolution of royal power.

The English settlers who poured into coastal America and the Caribbean during the seventeenth century found not a "virgin land" of uninhabited wilderness but a developed region populated by tens of thousands of Indians. As was true in New Spain and New France, European diseases overwhelmed the Native Americans. Smallpox epidemics left the coastal areas "a widowed land." Governor William Bradford, the leader of the Plymouth colony in Massachusetts, reported that the Indians "fell sick of the smallpox, and died most miserably . . . like rotten sheep."

Native Americans dealt with Europeans in different ways. Many resisted, others retreated, and still others developed thriving trade relationships with the newcomers. In some areas, land-hungry colonists quickly displaced or decimated the Indians. In others, Indians found ways to live in cooperation with English settlers—if they were willing to adopt the English way of life. In Massachusetts, a young John Adams, who would one day become the second president of the United States, occasionally visited a neighboring Indian family, "where I never failed to be treated with whortleberries, blackberries, strawberries or apples, plums, peaches, etc."

After creating the Virginia and Maryland colonies in the Chesapeake Bay region and the New England colonies during the first half of the seventeenth century, the English would go on to conquer Dutch-controlled New Netherland, settle Carolina, and eventually fill out the rest of the thirteen original American mainland colonies. In the middle Atlantic region between New England and Maryland, four new colonies taken from the Dutch emerged: New York, New Jersey, Pennsylvania, and Delaware. The diverse American colonies had one thing in common: to one extent or another, they all took part in the enslavement of other peoples, either Native Americans or Africans or both. Slavery, a dreadful practice throughout the world in the seventeenth and eighteenth centuries, enriched a few, corrupted many, and compromised the American dream of equal opportunity for all.

The English Background

People and Profits

Like other European countries, England envied the riches taken from the New World by Spain, especially the enormous amounts of gold and silver. However, the English colonies in America were different from the Spanish colonies. Spanish settlements were royal expeditions; most of the wealth they found became the property of the monarchs who funded the conquistadores. In contrast, English colonization in the Americas was led by two different groups that sometimes overlapped: those seeking freedom from religious persecution in England, both Protestants and Catholics, and those seeking land and profits.

English colonies were thus private business ventures rather than government enterprises. And they were expensive. Few individuals were wealthy enough to finance a colony over a long period. Those interested in colonization thus decided to band together and share the financial risks of starting colonies in the "American wilderness." Investors purchased shares of stock to form "**joint-stock companies**." That way, large amounts of money could be raised and, if a colony failed, no single investor would suffer the whole loss. If a colony succeeded, the profits would be shared among the investors in the joint-stock companies. While Queen Elizabeth and her successors did not fund the colonial expeditions, they did grant the royal charters needed to launch them. The joint-stock companies represented the most important organizational innovation of the

CORE OBJECTIVE

1. Identify the economic, religious, and political motivations for the establishment of England's diverse American colonies.

Joint-stock companies

joint-stock companies
Businesses owned by investors, who purchase shares of stock and share all the profits and losses.

Age of Exploration, and they provided the first instruments of English colonization in America.

The English settlements in America differed in other respects from Spain's far-flung colonies throughout the Western Hemisphere and France's far-reaching trade outposts across Canada and down the Mississippi Valley. The mainland English colonies were more compact, adjoining one another in concentrated geographical areas. England's American empire, therefore, did not focus on conquering sprawling Native American empires as Spain had done in Mexico and Peru. The native peoples along the Atlantic coast of America were less numerous, more scattered, and less wealthy than the Mexica and the Incas.

Unlike the male-dominated French and Spanish colonies, where fur traders and Spanish conquistadores often lived among the Indians and intermarried, most English settlers viewed the Indians as an impediment to be removed as they created family-based agricultural and trading communities. By 1750, English colonists (male and female) outnumbered the French in North America (mostly male) nearly twenty to one—1.3 million to 70,000—while in what became Texas, New Mexico, Arizona, Florida, and California, there were only 20,000 Spaniards.

The English had two primary goals for their American colonies: 1) to provide the mother country with valuable raw materials such as timber for shipmaking, tobacco for smoking, and fur pelts for hats and coats; and, 2) to develop a thriving consumer market in America for English manufactured goods and luxury items. To populate their new colonies, the English encouraged social rebels (including convicts), religious dissenters, and the homeless and landless to migrate to America, thereby reducing social and economic tensions at home.

> Provide raw materials and develop consumer markets

By far, the best way to entice people to become settlers in America was to offer them land and the promise of a better way of life: what came to be called the American dream. Land, plentiful and cheap, was English America's miraculous treasure—once it was taken from the Native Americans.

> Massive immigration

Political Traditions

English colonists brought to America their own political institutions and social folkways. Over the centuries, the island nation of England had developed political practices and principles quite different from those on the continent of Europe. The English rulers shared power with the nobility and a lesser aristocracy called the *gentry*. Their representatives formed the legislature known as the **Parliament**, made up of the hereditary and appointed House of Lords and the elected House of Commons. The most important power allocated to Parliament was the authority to impose taxes. By controlling government tax revenue, the legislature exercised great leverage over the monarchy.

> Parliament, civil rights, and liberties

Parliament Legislature of Great Britain, composed of the House of Commons, whose members are elected, and the House of Lords, whose members are either hereditary or appointed.

England's parliamentary monarchy was unique in sixteenth-century Europe. It began with the Magna Carta (Great Charter) of 1215, a statement of

Puritan New England – Wanted to simplify religion. King James I did not. He banished them from England. Named themselves "Seperatists" and headed for America

...d liberties that nobles had forced the king to approve. The ...stablished the basic principle that everyone was equal before ...person—not even a king or a queen—was above the law.

...nflict and War

...lizabeth, who never married, died in 1603 without a child of ...erit the throne, James VI of Scotland, a distant cousin of Eliza-...King James I of England. While Elizabeth had ruled through ...authority, James claimed to govern by "divine right," by which ...vered only to God.

...s I confronted a divided Church of England, with the reform-...ns in one camp, and the Anglican establishment, headed by ...and bishops, in the other. In seventeenth-century England, ...icized or abandoned the official Anglican Church were called ...Puritans were conservative dissenters who believed that the ...gland needed further "purifying." They demanded that all "papist" (Roman Catholic) rituals be eliminated. No use of holy water. No organ music. No elegant robes (vestments). No jeweled gold crosses. No worship of saints. No kneeling for communion. No tyrannical bishops and archbishops. The Puritans wanted to simplify religion to its basics: people worshipping God in plain, self-governing congregations without all the formal trappings of Catholic and Anglican ceremonies and wealth. They had hoped the new king would support their efforts to "purify" the Church of England. But James I instead sought to banish the Puritans from England.

Some of the Puritans eventually decided that the Church of England should not be fixed but abandoned, so they created their own congregations separate from the Anglican churches, thus earning the name *Separatists*. Such rebelliousness infuriated the leaders of the Church of England, who required people by law to attend Anglican church services. During the late sixteenth century, the Separatists (also called *Nonconformists*) were "hunted & persecuted on every side." English authorities imprisoned Separatist leaders, three of whom were hanged. In 1604, King James I vowed to "make them conform or I will hurry them out of the land or do worse." Many Separatists left England to escape persecution, and some, who would eventually be known as Pilgrims, decided to sail for America.

James's son, Charles I, succeeded his father as king in 1625, and proved to be an even more stubborn defender of absolute royal power. He took the shocking step of disbanding Parliament from 1629 to 1640; he raised taxes without consulting Parliament; and, he persecuted the Puritans. Some fled to Europe; others went to islands in the West Indies. Most of them, however, went to America.

But the monarchy went too far when it tried to impose Anglican forms of worship on Presbyterian Scots. In 1638, Scotland rose in revolt against English tyranny, and in 1640 King Charles, desperate for money to fund his army and save his skin, revived Parliament, ordering its members to raise taxes for

Religious persecution

Puritans English religious dissenters who sought to "purify" the Church of England of its Catholic practices.

the defense of his kingdom against the Scots. The Parliament refused, going so far as to condemn to death the king's chief minister. Militant Puritans took the lead in Parliament, insisting that all bishops in the Church of England be eliminated. In 1642, when the king tried to arrest five members of Parliament, a bloody civil war erupted between Royalists and Parliamentarians. In 1646 parliamentary forces captured King Charles and convicted him of high treason, labeling him a "tyrant, traitor, murderer, and public enemy." He was beheaded in 1649.

Oliver Cromwell, the skilled Puritan commander of the parliamentary army, operated like a military dictator. He extended religious toleration to all Britons except Roman Catholics and Anglicans, but his dictatorship fed growing resentment. After Cromwell's death in 1658, the army allowed new elections for Parliament and in 1660 supported the Restoration of the monarchy under young Charles II, son of the executed king.

Unlike his father, King Charles II agreed to rule jointly with Parliament. His younger brother, the Duke of York (who became James II upon succeeding to the throne in 1685), was less flexible. He openly embraced Catholicism, had political opponents murdered or imprisoned, defied Parliament, and appointed Roman Catholics to key positions.

Execution of Charles I Flemish artist John Weesop witnessed the execution and painted this gruesome scene from memory. He was so disgusted by "a country where they cut off their king's head" that he refused to visit England again.

transfer of power

The English people could bear James II's rule only so long as they expected one of his Protestant daughters, Mary or Anne, to succeed him. In 1688, however, the birth of a royal son who would be reared in the Roman Catholic tradition brought matters to a crisis. Determined to avoid a Catholic monarch, political, religious, and military leaders invited the king's Protestant daughter, Mary Stuart, and her Protestant husband, the ruling Dutch prince William III of Orange, to displace King James II and assume the English throne as joint monarchs. When William landed in England with a Dutch army, his father-in-law, King James II, not wanting to lose his head, fled to France. Amid this dramatic transfer of power, which soon became known as the "Glorious Revolution," Parliament reasserted its right to counterbalance the authority of the monarchy. Kings and queens could no longer suspend Parliament, create armies, or impose taxes without Parliament's consent. The monarchy would henceforth derive its power not from God but from the people.

CORE **OBJECTIVE**

2. Describe the political, economic, social, and religious characteristics of English colonies in the Chesapeake region, the Carolinas, the Middle Colonies, and New England prior to 1700.

Settling the American Colonies

During these tumultuous years in English political and social history, all of England's North American colonies except Georgia were founded. The first waves of colonists were energetic, courageous, and often ruthless, even violent, people willing to risk their lives in hopes of improving them. Many of those who were jobless and landless in England would find their way to America, already in the early seventeenth century viewed as a land of opportunity. Yet what many of them found instead was disease, drought, starvation, warfare, and death.

The Chesapeake Region

In 1606, King James I chartered a joint-stock enterprise called the Virginia Company, owned by merchant investors (including the wealthiest merchant in London) seeking to profit from the gold and silver they hoped would be found. He also gave the Virginia Company a religious mission by ordering the settlers to bring the "Christian religion" to the Indians, who "live in darkness and miserable ignorance of the true knowledge and worship of God." But as was true of many colonial ventures, such missionary activities were quickly dropped in favor of making money. No one foresaw what the first permanent English colony in America would actually become: a place to grow tobacco.

Jamestown

A fragile Jamestown

In 1607, the Virginia Company sent to America three tiny ships carrying about a hundred men and boys, many of them from prominent English families. In May they reached Chesapeake Bay after five storm-tossed months at sea. They chose a river with a northwest bend—in the hope of finding a passage to Asia—and settled about forty miles inland, to avoid Spanish raiders. They called the river the James, in honor of the king, and named their first settlement James Fort, later renamed Jamestown.

On a marshy peninsula fed by salty water and swarming with mosquitoes, the sea-weary colonists built a fort with thatched huts and a church. They struggled to find enough to eat, for most of the colonists were either townsmen unfamiliar with farming or "gentleman" adventurers who despised manual labor. Starvation led them to desperate measures. One hungry man killed, salted, and ate his pregnant wife. His fellow colonists then tortured and executed him. Of the original settlers, only thirty-eight survived the first nine months.

John Smith saves Jamestown

Fortunately for the Virginia colonists, they found an effective leader in Captain John Smith, a twenty-seven-year-old mercenary (a soldier for hire). With the colonists on the verge of starvation, Smith imposed strict military discipline and forced all to work if they wanted to eat. When no gold or silver

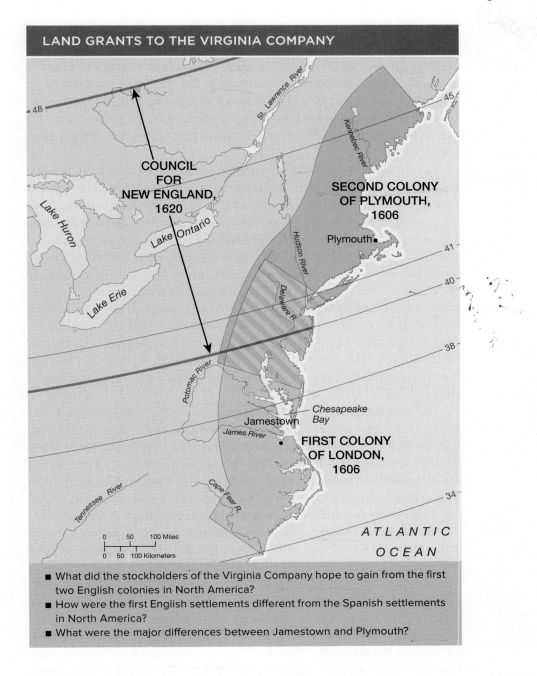

LAND GRANTS TO THE VIRGINIA COMPANY

COUNCIL FOR NEW ENGLAND, 1620

SECOND COLONY OF PLYMOUTH, 1606

Plymouth

FIRST COLONY OF LONDON, 1606

Jamestown

Chesapeake Bay

James River

Cape Fear R.

Tennessee River

Potomac River

Delaware R.

Hudson River

Kennebec River

St. Lawrence River

Lake Huron

Lake Ontario

Lake Erie

ATLANTIC OCEAN

0   50   100 Miles
0   50   100 Kilometers

■ What did the stockholders of the Virginia Company hope to gain from the first two English colonies in North America?

■ How were the first English settlements different from the Spanish settlements in North America?

■ What were the major differences between Jamestown and Plymouth?

was discovered, the Virginia Company shifted its focus to the sale of land, which would rise in value as the colony grew in population. The company recruited more settlers by promising that Virginia would "make them rich." Hundreds of new settlers nearly overwhelmed the infant colony. A new charter also appointed an all-powerful governor. The company then lured new

Grow Tobacco

investors and attracted new settlers by promising to give them land after seven years.

Over the next several years, the Jamestown colony limped along until it gradually found a profitable crop: **tobacco**. The plant had been grown on Caribbean islands for years, and smoking had become a popular habit in Europe. In 1612 Englishman John Rolfe began growing Virginia tobacco for export to England. Virginia's tobacco production soared during the seventeenth century.

Land and liberty

In 1618 Sir Edwin Sandys, a prominent member of Parliament, became head of the Virginia Company and launched a new "**headright**" (land grant) policy: any Englishman who bought a share in the company and could pay for passage to Virginia could have fifty acres upon arrival, and fifty more for any servants he brought along. The following year, the company promised that the settlers would have all the "rights of Englishmen," including a legislature elected by the people, arguing that "every man will more willingly obey laws to which he has yielded his consent." This was a crucial development, for the English had long enjoyed the broadest civil liberties and the least intrusive government in Europe. Now the colonists in Virginia were to enjoy the same rights. On July 30, 1619, the first General Assembly of Virginia met in the Jamestown church, "sweating & stewing, and battling flies and mosquitoes," as it assumed responsibility for governing on behalf of the residents.

The first enslaved Africans

The year 1619 was eventful in other respects. The settlement had outgrown James Fort and was formally renamed Jamestown. Also in that year, a ship with ninety young women aboard arrived in Jamestown. Men rushed to claim them as wives by providing 125 pounds of tobacco for the cost of their transatlantic passage. A third significant development occurred in 1619 when a Dutch ship called the *White Lion* stopped at Jamestown and unloaded "20 Negars," the first Africans known to have reached English America.

By 1624, some 14,000 English men, women, and children had migrated to Jamestown since 1607, but most of them had died; the population in 1624 was still only 1,132. In 1624 an English court dissolved the struggling Virginia Company, and "weak and miserable" Virginia became a royal colony. No longer would the settlers be mere laborers toiling for a distant joint-stock company; they were now free to own private property and start business enterprises. But their governors would thereafter be appointed by the king. Sir William Berkeley, who arrived as Virginia's royal governor in 1642, presided over the colony's rapid growth for most of the next thirty-five years. Tobacco prices surged, and the wealthiest planters began to dominate the social and political life in the colony.

tobacco A "cash crop" grown in the Caribbean as well as the Virginia and Maryland colonies, made increasingly profitable by the rapidly growing popularity of smoking in Europe after the voyages of Columbus.

headright A land-grant policy that promised fifty acres to any colonist who could afford passage to Virginia, as well as fifty more for any accompanying servants. The headright policy was eventually expanded to include any colonists—and was also adopted in other colonies too.

Maryland

In 1634, ten years after Virginia became a royal colony, a neighboring settlement appeared on the northern shore of Chesapeake Bay. Named Maryland in honor of English queen Henrietta Maria, it was granted to Sir George

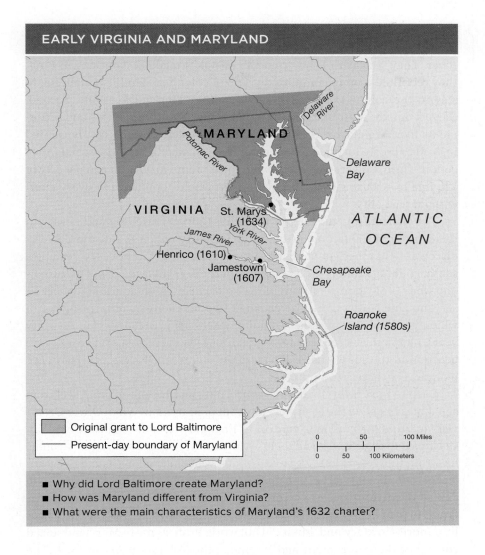

EARLY VIRGINIA AND MARYLAND

Original grant to Lord Baltimore

Present-day boundary of Maryland

■ Why did Lord Baltimore create Maryland?
■ How was Maryland different from Virginia?
■ What were the main characteristics of Maryland's 1632 charter?

Calvert, Lord Baltimore, by King Charles I and became the first *proprietary* colony—that is, it was owned by an individual, not by a joint-stock company. Calvert had created a stir in 1625 when he converted from Anglicanism to Catholicism, which meant he had to resign from his government position as the king's secretary of state. To compensate him for his losses, Calvert asked the king to grant him a charter for an American colony to the north of Virginia. However, Calvert died before the king could act on his request, so the charter was awarded to his son, Cecilius Calvert, the second Lord Baltimore, who actually founded the colony. He wanted Maryland to be a refuge for English Catholics, a persecuted minority in Anglican England. But he also wanted his new colony to be profitable and to avoid antagonizing Protestants, so he instructed his brother, Leonard, the colony's first governor, to ensure that the Catholic colonists worship in private and remain "silent upon all occasions of discourse concerning matters of religion."

Maryland: The first proprietary colony and a refuge for English Catholics

In 1634, Cecilius Calvert and his brother, Leonard, planted the first settlement in coastal Maryland at St. Marys, near the mouth of the Potomac River. They sought to learn from the mistakes made at Jamestown. First, they recruited a more committed group of colonists—families intending to stay in the colony rather than single men seeking quick profits. Second, Calvert did not want Maryland to be a colony of scattered farms and settlements like Virginia, or to become dependent solely on tobacco. He wanted instead to create fortified towns, carefully designed to promote social interaction. Third, Calvert wanted to avoid the extremes of wealth and poverty in Virginia by ensuring that the government would "do justice to every man" without partiality.

The charter from the king gave Cecilius Calvert power to make laws with the consent of the freemen (that is, all property holders). But the Calverts discovered that they could not attract enough Roman Catholics to develop a self-sustaining economy. The majority of the servants who came to the colony were Protestants, both Anglicans and Puritans. In addition, to recruit servants and settlers, the Calverts had to offer them small farms, most of which grew tobacco. Unlike Virginia, which struggled for its first twenty years, Maryland succeeded more quickly because of its focus on growing tobacco from the start. And its long coastline along the Chesapeake Bay gave planters easy access to shipping.

Toleration Act (1649)

Despite the Calverts' caution "concerning matters of religion," sectarian squabbles impeded the early development of Maryland. When Oliver Cromwell and the Puritans took control in England after the English Civil War, Cecilius Calvert feared he might lose the colony. To avoid such a catastrophe, he wrote the Toleration Act (1649) which welcomed all Christians, regardless of their denomination or beliefs (it also promised to execute anyone who denied the divinity of Jesus). Lord Baltimore convinced the Maryland legislature to pass the Toleration Act in the hope that it would protect the Catholic minority in Maryland. But it did not work. Protestants in Maryland seized control of the government and rescinded the Toleration Act in 1654. The once-persecuted Puritans had become persecutors themselves, at one point driving Lord Baltimore out of his own colony. Were it not for the colony's success in growing tobacco, Maryland may well have disintegrated. In 1692, following the Glorious Revolution in England, Catholicism was banned in Maryland. Only after the American Revolution would Marylanders again be guaranteed religious freedom.

New England

Very different English settlements were emerging far to the north of the Chesapeake Bay colonies. Unlike the Jamestown settlers, the New England colonists were often middle-class families that could pay their own way across the Atlantic. There were relatively few servants, and no elite plantation owners. Most male settlers were small farmers, merchants, seamen, or fishermen. New England also attracted more women than did the southern colonies.

Although its soil was not as fertile as that of the Chesapeake region and its growing season was much shorter, New England was a much healthier place to live. Because of its colder climate, settlers avoided the infectious diseases like malaria that ravaged the southern colonies and killed so many during the first waves of settlement. During the seventeenth century, only 21,000 colonists arrived in New England, compared with the 120,000 who went to the Chesapeake Bay colonies. But by 1700, New England's thriving white population exceeded that of Maryland and Virginia. Over several generations, New Englanders had larger families and relatively fewer diseases than their southern counterparts.

Plymouth

The first permanent English settlement in New England was established by a group of ungodly adventurers and pious farm families who were forced to leave England because of their refusal to worship in Anglican churches. (Accordingly, in their own time they were known as Separatists; only much later would this particular group of Separatists be remembered as "the Pilgrims.") They first moved to Holland, only to worry that their children were becoming Dutch. So in September 1620, about a hundred women, men, and children crammed aboard the tiny *Mayflower*, a vessel only 100 feet long, and headed across the Atlantic bound for the Virginia colony, where they had obtained permission to settle. It was hurricane season, and storms blew the ship off course to Cape Cod, just south of what became Boston, Massachusetts. Since they were outside the jurisdiction of any organized government, the forty-one Separatists on board the *Mayflower* signed the **Mayflower Compact**, a formal agreement to abide by the laws made by leaders of their own choosing.

The colonists, both "strangers and pilgrims," as William Bradford wrote in his journal, settled in a deserted Indian village and named their colony Plymouth, after the English port from which they had embarked. Unlike the Jamestown colonists, the Separatists at Plymouth were motivated primarily by religious ideals. The Pilgrims wanted to create a model Christian society living strictly according to God's commandments. This meant "purifying" their church of all Catholic and Anglican rituals and enacting a code of laws and a government structure based upon biblical principles. Such a holy settlement, they hoped, would provide a living example of righteousness for a wicked England to imitate.

Throughout its existence, until it was absorbed into Massachusetts Bay Colony in 1691, the Plymouth colony governed itself on the basis of the Mayflower Compact, which was a covenant (that is, a group contract) to form a church. Thus the civil government grew out of the church government, and the members of each were identical. The signers of the Mayflower Compact at first met as the General Court, which chose the governor

> The Pilgrims at Plymouth and the Mayflower Compact (1620)

Mayflower Compact (1620)
A formal agreement signed by the Separatist colonists aboard the *Mayflower* to abide by laws made by leaders of their own choosing.

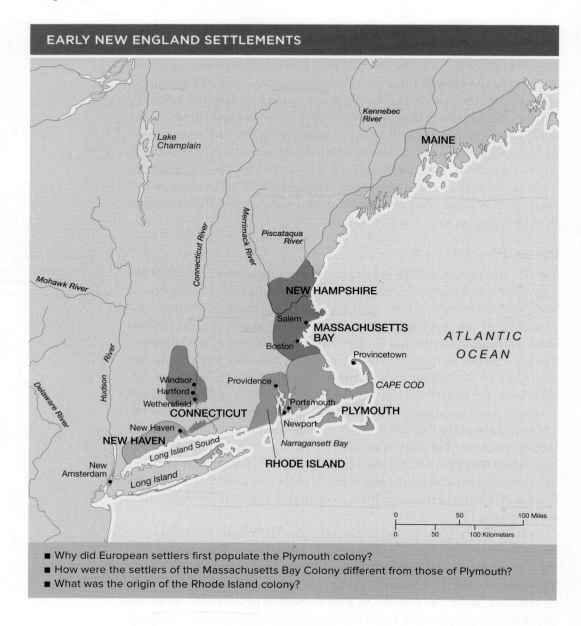

EARLY NEW ENGLAND SETTLEMENTS

■ Why did European settlers first populate the Plymouth colony?
■ How were the settlers of the Massachusetts Bay Colony different from those of Plymouth?
■ What was the origin of the Rhode Island colony?

and his assistants (or council). Others were later admitted as members, or "freemen," but only church members were eligible. Eventually, as the colony grew, the General Court became a legislative body of elected representatives from the various towns.

Massachusetts Bay

Massachusetts Bay Colony
English colony founded by Puritans in 1630 as a haven for persecuted Congregationalists.

The Plymouth colony's population never rose above 7,000, and after ten years it was overshadowed by its much larger neighbor, the **Massachusetts Bay Colony**. That colony, too, was intended to be a holy commonwealth. The

Massachusetts Bay Puritans, however, were different from the Pilgrims. They were non-separating Congregationalists who wanted to purify the Church of England from within. They were called *Congregationalists* because their churches were governed by their congregations rather than by an Anglican bishop in distant England. Their self-governing churches limited membership to "visible saints"—those who could demonstrate receipt of the gift of God's grace.

In 1629, the same year that King Charles I shut down Parliament, the monarchy gave a royal charter to a joint-stock company called the Massachusetts Bay Company. It consisted of a group of Puritans led by John Winthrop, a prosperous lawyer with intense religious convictions. Winthrop wanted the colony to be a haven for persecuted Puritans and a model Christian community—"a city on the hill," as Winthrop declared. To that end, he shrewdly took advantage of an oversight in the company charter: it did not require that the joint-stock company maintain its home office in England. Winthrop's group took its royal charter with them, thereby transferring government authority from London to Massachusetts, where they hoped to govern themselves.

It is hard to exaggerate the crucial role Winthrop played in establishing the Massachusetts Bay Colony, centered on Boston. He was a strong leader who prized stability and order and hated the idea of democracy—the people ruling themselves. Like many Puritan leaders, Winthrop believed that the role of government should be to enforce religious beliefs and ensure social stability. Ironically, the same Puritans who had fled persecution in England did not hesitate to persecute people of other religious views in New England. Catholics, Anglicans, Quakers, and Baptists had no rights in Puritan New England; they were punished, imprisoned, banished, or even executed.

The transfer of the Massachusetts Bay Colony's royal charter, whereby an English trading company evolved into a provincial government, was a unique venture in colonization. Unlike "Old" England, New England had no powerful lords or bishops, kings or queens. The Massachusetts General Court, wherein power rested under the royal charter, consisted of all the shareholders, called freemen. At first, the freemen had no power except to choose "assistants," who in turn chose the governor and deputy governor. In 1634, however, the freemen turned themselves into the General Court, with two or three deputies to represent each town. A final stage in the democratization of the government came in 1644, when the General Court organized itself like the Parliament with a House of Assistants, corresponding roughly to the House of Lords, and a House of Deputies, corresponding to the House of Commons. All decisions had to be ratified by a majority in each house.

Thus, over a period of fourteen years, the joint-stock Massachusetts Bay Company evolved into the governing body of a holy commonwealth in which freemen were given increasing power. Puritans had fled not only religious persecution but also political repression, and they ensured that their

John Winthrop The first governor of the Massachusetts Bay Colony, in whose vision the colony would be as "a city upon a hill."

Puritan New England

Rights and representation in New England

liberties in New England were spelled out and protected. Over time, membership in a Puritan church replaced the purchase of stock as the means of becoming a freeman, or voter, in Massachusetts Bay.

Rhode Island

Rhode Island challenges Puritan control

More by accident than design, the Massachusetts Bay Colony became the staging area for other New England colonies created by people dissatisfied with Puritan control. Young Roger Williams (1603–1683), who had arrived from England in 1631, was among the first to cause problems, precisely because he was the purest of Puritans—a Separatist. He criticized Puritans for not completely cutting their ties to the "whorish" Church of England. Where John Winthrop cherished strict governmental and clerical authority, Williams stubbornly championed individual liberty and criticized the way the Indians were being shoved aside. The combative Williams posed a radical question: If one's salvation depends solely upon God's grace, why bother to have churches at all? Why not give individuals the right to worship God in their own way?

Separation of church and state

In Williams's view, true *puritanism* required complete separation of church and state and freedom from all coercion in matters of faith. "Forced worship," he declared, "stinks in God's nostrils." According to Williams, governments should be impartial regarding religions. Such radical views led the General Court to banish Williams to England. Williams, however, slipped away during a raging blizzard and found shelter among the Narragansett Indians. In 1636 he bought land from the Indians and established the town of Providence at the head of Narragansett Bay, the first permanent settlement in Rhode Island and the first in America to allow complete freedom of religion.

From the beginning, Rhode Island was the most democratic of the colonies, governed by the heads of households rather than by church members. Newcomers could be admitted to full citizenship by a majority vote, and the colony welcomed all who fled religious persecution in Massachusetts Bay. For their part, Puritans came to view Rhode Island as a refuge for rogues. A Dutch visitor reported that Rhode Island was "the sewer of New England. All the cranks of New England retire there." Thus the colony of Rhode Island and Providence Plantations, the smallest in America, began as a sanctuary for those who insisted that governments had no right to impose religious beliefs.

The role of women

Williams was only one of several prominent Puritans who clashed with Governor John Winthrop's stern, unyielding governance of the Bay Colony. Another, Anne Hutchinson, quarreled with Puritan leaders for different reasons. The strong-willed, intelligent wife of a prominent merchant, Hutchinson raised thirteen children and hosted meetings in her Boston home to discuss sermons. Soon, however, the discussions turned into large gatherings (of both men and women) at which Hutchinson shared her strong feelings about religious matters. According to one participant, she "preaches better Gospel than any of your black coats [male ministers]." Blessed with vast biblical knowledge and a quick wit, Hutchinson claimed to know which of her neighbors had truly been saved and which were damned, including ministers.

A pregnant Hutchinson was hauled before the all-male General Court in 1637 for trying to "undermine the Kingdom of Christ," and for two days she sparred on equal terms with the Puritan leaders. Her ability to cite chapter-and-verse biblical defenses of her actions led an exasperated Governor Winthrop to explode: "We are your judges, and not you ours. . . . We do not mean to discourse [debate] with those of your sex." He told Hutchinson that she had "stepped out of your place" as a woman in a man's world. As the trial continued, an overwrought Hutchinson was eventually lured into convicting herself by claiming direct revelations from God—blasphemy in the eyes of Puritans.

In 1638 the General Court banished Hutchinson as a "leper" not fit for "our society." She initially settled with her family and about sixty followers on an island in Narragansett Bay south of Providence. But the hard journey took its toll. Hutchinson grew sick, and her baby was stillborn, leading her critics in Massachusetts Bay to claim that the "monstrous birth" was God's way of punishing her. Hutchinson's spirits never recovered. After her husband's death, in 1642, she moved just north of New Amsterdam (New York City), then under Dutch control. The following year, she and six of her children were massacred by Indians. Her fate, wrote a spiteful John Winthrop, was "a special manifestation of divine justice."

The Trial of Anne Hutchinson In this nineteenth-century wood engraving, Anne Hutchinson stands her ground against charges of heresy from the all-male leaders of Puritan Boston.

Connecticut, New Hampshire, and Maine

New England expands

Connecticut had a more conventional beginning than Rhode Island. In 1636, the Reverend Thomas Hooker led three church congregations from Massachusetts Bay to the Connecticut Valley, where they organized the self-governing colony of Connecticut. In 1639, the Connecticut General Court adopted the Fundamental Orders, a series of laws that provided for a "Christian Commonwealth" like that of Massachusetts, except that voting was not limited to church members. The Connecticut constitution specified that the Congregational churches would be the colony's official religion. The governor was commanded to rule according to "the word of God."

To the north of Massachusetts, most of what are now the states of New Hampshire and Maine was granted in 1622 to Sir Ferdinando Gorges and Captain John Mason. In 1629, Mason and Gorges divided their territory, with Mason taking the southern part, which he named the Province of New Hampshire, and Gorges taking the northern part, which became the Province of Maine. During the early 1640s, Massachusetts took over New Hampshire and in the 1650s extended its authority to the scattered settlements in Maine. This led to lawsuits, and in 1678 English judges decided against Massachusetts in both cases. In 1679, New Hampshire became a royal colony, but Massachusetts continued to control Maine. A new Massachusetts charter in 1691 finally incorporated Maine into Massachusetts.

The Carolinas

From the start, the Carolina colony consisted of two widely separated areas of settlement, which eventually became two different **Carolina colonies**. The northernmost part, long called Albemarle, had been settled in the 1650s by colonists who had drifted southward from Virginia. For half a century, Albemarle remained a remote scattering of farmers along the shores of Albemarle Sound. The eight nobles, called lords proprietor, to whom the king had given Carolina neglected Albemarle and instead focused on more promising sites to the south. They recruited experienced English planters from the Caribbean island of Barbados to bring to southern Carolina the profitable West Indian sugar-plantation system based on the hard labor of enslaved Africans. In a reference to Barbados and the other English colonies in the Caribbean, an English colonist pointed out in 1666 that "these Settlements have been made and upheld by Negroes and without constant supplies of them cannot subsist."

Slavery in the Carolinas

The first English colonists arrived in southern Carolina in 1669 at Charles Town (later named Charleston). Over the next twenty years, half the southern Carolina colonists came from Barbados and other English island colonies in the Caribbean such as Nevis, St. Kitts, and Jamaica. Most of them brought African slaves with them, putting them to work clearing land, cutting wood, planting gardens, and herding cattle. In 1712, the Carolina colony was formally divided in two: North and South.

Religious tolerance

The government of Carolina rested upon one of the most curious documents of colonial history, the Fundamental Constitutions of Carolina, drawn up by one of the eight proprietors, Lord Anthony Ashley Cooper, with the help of his secretary, the renowned philosopher John Locke. Its provisions for a formal titled nobility had little effect in the colony except to encourage a practice of awarding large land grants to prominent Englishmen. From the beginning, however, smaller "headrights" (land grants) were given to every immigrant who could pay for passage across the Atlantic. The Fundamental Constitutions granted religious toleration as a means of encouraging immigration, which gave Carolina a greater degree of religious freedom (extending to Jews and "heathens") than England or any other colony except Rhode Island.

Carolina colonies English proprietary colonies comprised of North and South Carolina, whose semitropical climate made them profitable centers of rice, timber, and tar production.

After rebelling against the lords proprietors, South Carolina became a royal colony in 1719. North Carolina remained under the proprietors' rule for ten more years, until it too became a royal colony. Rice became as much the dominant commercial crop in coastal South Carolina as tobacco was in Virginia and Maryland. Planters discovered that the translucent grain was

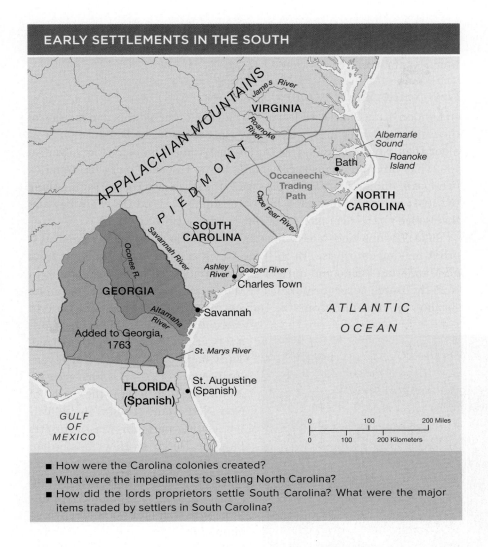

EARLY SETTLEMENTS IN THE SOUTH

APPALACHIAN MOUNTAINS

James River

VIRGINIA

Roanoke River

PIEDMONT

Albemarle Sound

Bath

Roanoke Island

Occaneechi Trading Path

NORTH CAROLINA

Cape Fear River

SOUTH CAROLINA

Savannah River

Oconee R.

Ashley River   Cooper River

Charles Town

GEORGIA

Altamaha River

Savannah

ATLANTIC OCEAN

Added to Georgia, 1763

St. Marys River

St. Augustine (Spanish)

FLORIDA (Spanish)

GULF OF MEXICO

0   100   200 Miles

0   100   200 Kilometers

■ How were the Carolina colonies created?
■ What were the impediments to settling North Carolina?
■ How did the lords proprietors settle South Carolina? What were the major items traded by settlers in South Carolina?

perfectly suited to the growing conditions in the semitropical coastal areas known as the low country. Because rice, like sugarcane and tobacco, was labor-intensive, planters used enslaved Africans to work their rice plantations in the Carolinas. Both Carolinas also had huge forests of yellow pine trees that provided lumber and other key materials for shipbuilding. The resin from trees could be boiled to make tar, which was needed to waterproof the seams of wooden ships (which is why North Carolinians came to be called Tar Heels).

The Middle Colonies and Georgia

The area between New England and the Chesapeake—Maryland and Virginia—included colonies in New York, New Jersey, Delaware, and Pennsylvania. By 1670, the mostly Protestant Dutch had the largest merchant fleet in the world and the highest standard of living. They controlled northern

European commerce and had become one of the most diverse and tolerant societies in Europe—and England's most ferocious competitor in international commerce.

New Netherland Becomes New York

The Dutch in North America

In London, King Charles II decided to pluck out that old thorn in the side of the English colonies in America: **New Netherland**. The Dutch colony was older than New England. The Dutch East India Company (organized in 1602) had hired an English sea captain, Henry Hudson, to explore America in hopes of finding a northwest passage to the spice-rich Indies. Sailing along the coast of North America in 1609, Hudson discovered Delaware Bay and then sailed up the river named for him in what is now New York.

Profits and pluralism

Like Virginia and Massachusetts, New Netherland was created as a profit-making enterprise. In 1610 the Dutch established fur-trading posts on Manhattan Island and upriver at Fort Orange (later called Albany). In 1626 the Dutch governor purchased Manhattan (an Indian word meaning "island of many hills") from the Indians for 60 gilders, or about $1,000 in current values. The Dutch then built a fort at the lower end of the island. The village of New Amsterdam (eventually New York City), which grew up around the fort, became the capital of New Netherland. Unlike their Puritan counterparts in Massachusetts Bay, the Dutch in New Amsterdam were preoccupied more with profits and freedoms than with religion and restrictions. They promoted free enterprise as well as ethnic and religious pluralism.

Castello Plan of New Amsterdam A map of New Amsterdam in 1660, shortly before the English took the colony from the Dutch and christened it New York City.

Dutch settlements gradually emerged wherever fur pelts might be found. In 1638, a Swedish trading company established Fort Christina at the site of present-day Wilmington, Delaware, and scattered settlements up and down the Delaware River. The Dutch in 1655 took control of New Sweden. The chief contribution of the short-lived New Sweden to American culture was the idea of the log cabin, which the Swedes and a few Finnish settlers had brought from the woods of Scandinavia to Delaware.

New Netherland Dutch colony conquered by the English in 1667, out of which four new colonies were created—New York, New Jersey, Pennsylvania, and Delaware.

The New Netherland governors were mostly stubborn autocrats, either corrupt or inept, and especially clumsy at Indian relations. They depended upon a small army for defense, and the colonists, many of whom were not

Dutch, were hardly devoted to the government. New Amsterdam was one of the most ethnically diverse colonial cities—as is New York City today. Its residents included not only the Dutch but also Swedes, Norwegians, Spaniards, Jews, free and enslaved blacks, English, Germans, and Finns. In 1664, the diverse colonists showed almost total indifference when Governor Peter Stuyvesant called them to arms against a threatening English fleet. Stuyvesant blustered and stomped about on his wooden leg but finally surrendered the colony to the English without firing a shot.

The English conquest of New Netherland had been hatched by the Duke of York, who would become King James II. Upon the capture of New Amsterdam, his brother, King Charles II, granted the entire Dutch region to him, and the English promptly renamed both New Netherland and the city of New Amsterdam as New York, in honor of James, and they renamed Fort Orange, farther up the Hudson River, as Albany.

In September 1654, ten years before the English took control of New Netherland, a French ship arrived in New Amsterdam harbor. On board were twenty-three Sephardim, Jews of Spanish-Portuguese descent. Penniless and weary, they had come seeking refuge from Portuguese-controlled Brazil. They were the first Jewish settlers to arrive in North America.

The first Jewish settlers

The Dutch officials embraced the homeless Jews, explaining that they wanted to "allow everyone to have his own belief, as long as he behaves quietly and legally, gives no offense to his neighbor, and does not oppose the government." But it would not be until the late seventeenth century that Jews could worship in public. Such restrictions help explain why the American Jewish community grew so slowly. In 1773, over 100 years after the first Jewish refugees arrived in New Amsterdam, Jews represented only one tenth of 1 percent of the entire colonial population. Not until the nineteenth century would the American Jewish community experience dramatic growth.

New Jersey

Shortly after the conquest of New Netherland, James Stuart, the Duke of York, granted the lands between the Hudson and Delaware Rivers to Sir George Carteret and Lord John Berkeley (brother of Virginia's governor) and named the territory for Carteret's native Jersey, an island in the English Channel. In 1676, by mutual agreement, New Jersey was divided into East and West Jersey, with Carteret taking the east, Berkeley the west. But neither Jersey colony prospered, so in 1702, East and West Jersey were united as the single royal colony of New Jersey.

Pennsylvania

The Quaker sect, as the Religious Society of Friends was called in ridicule (because they were supposed to "tremble at the word of the Lord"), became the most influential of many radical religious groups that emerged from the

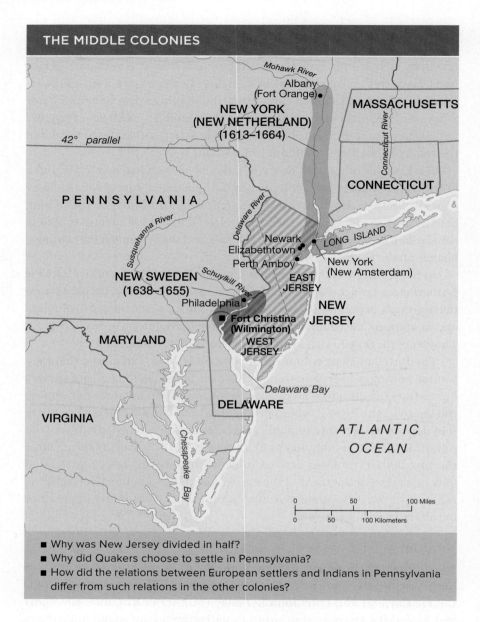

THE MIDDLE COLONIES

- Why was New Jersey divided in half?
- Why did Quakers choose to settle in Pennsylvania?
- How did the relations between European settlers and Indians in Pennsylvania differ from such relations in the other colonies?

turbulence of the English Civil War. Founded in England in 1647 by George Fox, a saintly roving preacher, the Quakers, like the Puritans, rejected the formalism of the Anglican Church. But they did more. The Quakers rebelled against *all* forms of political and religious authority, including salaried ministers, military service, and paying taxes. Quakers insisted that everyone, not just a select few, could experience a personal revelation from God, what they called the "Inner Light." Quakers discarded all formal religious rituals and even a formal ministry, and embraced a fierce pacifism. Some Quakers went barefoot, others wore rags, and a few went naked to demonstrate their "primitive" commitment to Christ. Quakers demanded complete religious freedom for everyone and promoted equality of the sexes, including the full participation of women in religious affairs.

Quakers suffered intense persecution. New England Puritans banned them, tortured them, and executed them. Often, the Quakers seemed to invite such abuse. In 1663, for example, Lydia Wardell, a Quaker in Newbury, Massachusetts, grew so upset with the law requiring everyone to attend Puritan religious services that she arrived at the church naked to dramatize her protest. Puritan authorities ordered her "to be severely whipped," after which she and her husband moved to West Jersey.

The settling of English Quakers in West Jersey encouraged other Friends to migrate, especially to the Delaware River side of the colony, where William Penn's Quaker commonwealth, the colony of Pennsylvania, soon arose. Penn, the son of Admiral Sir William Penn, had become a Quaker as a student at Oxford University. Upon his father's death, he inherited a substantial estate, including a huge tract of land in America. The land was named, at the king's insistence, for Penn's father—Pennsylvania (literally, "Penn's Woods"). Unlike John Winthrop in Massachusetts, Penn encouraged people of different religions to settle in his new colony. By the end of 1681, a town was emerging at the junction of the Schuylkill and Delaware Rivers. Penn called it Philadelphia ("City of Brotherly Love").

> A Quaker-controlled Pennsylvania

The colony's government, which rested on three Frames of Government drafted by Penn, resembled that of other proprietary colonies except that the freemen (taxpayers and property owners) elected the council members as well as the assembly. The governor had no veto, although Penn, as proprietor, did. Penn hoped to show that a government could operate in accordance with Quaker principles, that it could maintain peace and order, and that religion could flourish without government support and with absolute freedom of conscience.

Delaware

In 1682, the Duke of York also granted Penn the area of Delaware, another part of the former Dutch territory (which had been New Sweden before being acquired by the Dutch in 1655). At first, Delaware—taking its name from the Delaware River, which had been named to honor Thomas West, Baron De La Warr (1577–1618), Virginia's first colonial governor—became part of Pennsylvania, but after 1704 it was granted the right to choose its own legislative assembly. From then until the American Revolution, Delaware had a separate assembly but shared Pennsylvania's governor.

Georgia

Georgia was the last of the English colonies to be established—half a century after Pennsylvania. During the seventeenth century, settlers pushed southward into the borderlands between Carolina and Spanish Florida. They brought with them enslaved Africans and a desire to win the Indian trade from the Spanish. Each side used guns, gifts, and rum to court the Indians, and the Indians in turn played off the English against the Spanish.

Georgia established for the "worthy poor"

In 1732, King George II gave the land between the Savannah and Altamaha Rivers to twenty-one trustees appointed to govern the Province of Georgia, named in honor of the king. In two respects, Georgia was unique among the colonies: it was to provide a military buffer against Spanish Florida and also to serve as a social experiment bringing together settlers from different countries and religions, many of them refugees, debtors, or members of the "worthy poor." General James E. Oglethorpe, a prominent member of Parliament, was appointed to head the colony.

In 1733, a band of about 120 colonists founded Savannah on the Atlantic coast near the mouth of the Savannah River. Carefully laid out by Oglethorpe, the old town, with its geometric pattern of crisscrossing roads graced by numerous parks, remains a wonderful example of city planning. Protestant refugees from Austria began to arrive in 1734, followed by Germans and German-speaking Moravians and Swiss, who for a time made the colony more German than English. The addition of Welsh, Highland Scots, Sephardic Jews, and others gave the early colony a diverse character like that of Charleston, South Carolina.

As a buffer against Spanish Florida, the Georgia colony succeeded, but as a social experiment creating a "common man's utopia," it failed. Initially, landholdings were limited to 500 acres in order to promote economic equality. Rum was banned, and the importation of slaves was forbidden. But the idealistic rules soon collapsed as the colony struggled to

Savannah, Georgia The earliest known view of Savannah, Georgia (1734). The town's layout was carefully planned.

become self-sufficient. The regulations against rum and slavery were widely disregarded and finally abandoned. By 1759, all restrictions on land-holding had been removed.

In 1754, Georgia became a royal colony. It developed slowly over the next decade but grew rapidly in population and wealth after 1763. Georgians exported rice, lumber, beef, and pork, and they carried on a lively trade with the islands in the West Indies. Almost unintentionally, the colony had become an economic success and a slave-centered society.

Native Peoples and English Settlers

CORE **OBJECTIVE**

3. Analyze the ways by which English colonists and Native Americans adapted to each other's presence.

The process of creating English colonies in America did not occur in a vacuum: the Native Americans played a crucial role in their development. Most English colonists adopted a strategy for dealing with the Indians quite different from that of the French and the Dutch. Merchants from France and the Netherlands focused on exploiting the profitable fur trade. The thriving commerce in animal skins—especially beaver, otter, and deer—helped spur exploration of the vast American continent. It also enriched and devastated the lives of Indians. To get fur pelts from the Indians, the French and Dutch built trading outposts in upper New York and along the Great Lakes, where they established friendly relations with the Hurons, Algonquins, and other Indians in the region, who greatly outnumbered them. The Hurons and Algonquins also sought French support in their ongoing wars with the mighty Iroquois Nations. In contrast to the French experience in Canada, the English colonists were more interested in pursuing their "God-given" right to hunt and farm on Indian lands and fish in Indian waters.

Food and Land

The English settled along the Atlantic seaboard, where Indian populations were much smaller than those in Mexico or the islands in the Caribbean. Moreover, the various native peoples of North America were fragmented, often fighting among themselves over disputed land. There was no powerful Aztec or Inca Empire to conquer and exploit. In most cases, the English colonists established their own separate communities near Indian villages.

The Jamestown settlers, for example, had come to America expecting to find gold, friendly Indians, and easy living. Most did not know how to exploit the area's abundant game and fish. When some of the starving Jamestown residents tried to steal food from nearby Indian villages, the Indians ambushed and killed them. John Ratcliffe, the initial leader, was captured and skinned alive by women using oyster shells, then burned. Only the effective leadership of John Smith and timely trade with the Indians, who taught the

Agricultural exchanges

EUROPEAN SETTLEMENTS AND INDIAN TRIBES IN EARLY AMERICA

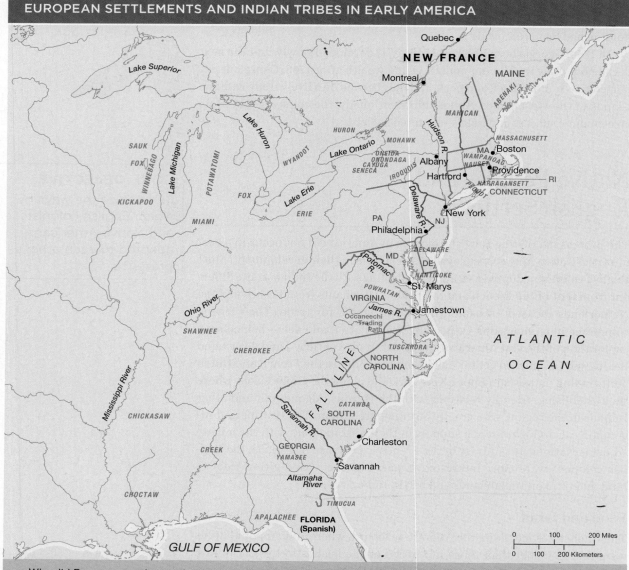

- Why did European settlement lead to the expansion of hostilities among the Indians?
- What were the consequences of the trade and commerce between the English settlers and the southern indigenous peoples?
- How were the relationships between the settlers and the members of the Iroquois League different from those between settlers and tribes in other regions?

ill-prepared colonists to grow corn, enabled a remnant of the original colonists to survive. The short, stocky Smith, a seasoned soldier-for-hire, had himself been wounded in another battle and narrowly escaped execution when the young Indian princess known as Pocahontas convinced the warriors to exchange the Englishman for muskets, hatchets, beads, and trinkets.

Thereafter, the Native Americans around Jamestown fluctuated between exchanging goods with the English and trying to kill them.

By 1616, the discovery that tobacco flourished in Virginia intensified the settlers' lust for more land. English tobacco planters especially coveted the fields already cultivated by Indians because they had already been cleared and were ready to be planted. In 1622, the Indians tried to repel the land-grabbing English. As reported by Captain Smith, the "wild, naked natives" attacked twenty-eight farms and plantations along the James River, "not sparing either age or sex, man, woman, or childe," and killing a fourth of the settlers. Houses were burned, crops destroyed, equipment wrecked, and animals killed or scattered. The English retaliated by decimating the Indian peoples of Virginia. Smith said they were determined to "force the Savages to leave their Country or bring them in . . . fear and subjection."

The Indian peoples of the Chesapeake region were dominated by the **Powhatan Confederacy**. Powhatan was the name for the supreme chief of several hundred villages (of about a hundred people each) organized into thirty chiefdoms in eastern Virginia. At the time, the Powhatan Confederacy may have been the most powerful group of native peoples along the entire Atlantic coast. Largely agricultural people focused on raising corn, they lived in oval-shaped houses framed with bent saplings and covered with bark or mats. Chief Powhatan (his proper name was Wahunsenacawh) forced the rival peoples he had conquered to give him most of their corn. He also traded with the English colonists, exchanging corn and hides for hatchets, swords, and muskets. But he realized too late that the newcomers wanted more than corn; they planned to seize his lands and enslave his people.

Bacon's Rebellion

The relentless stream of new settlers into Virginia exerted constant pressure on Indian lands and produced growing tensions. The largest planters bought up the most fertile land along the coast and rivers, forcing freed servants to become farm workers or try to claim less-fertile land inland. In either case, these landless farmers found themselves at a disadvantage. By 1676, a fourth of the free white men in Virginia were landless. They were forced to roam the countryside, squatting on private property, working at odd jobs, poaching game, or committing other petty crimes to survive.

In the mid-1670s, simmering tensions caused by falling tobacco prices, rising taxes, and crowds of freed servants greedily eyeing Indian lands contributed to the tangled events that came to be called **Bacon's Rebellion**. The royal governor, William Berkeley, noted that "poor, indebted, discontented, and armed" Virginia colonists were ripe for rebellion. The discontent erupted when a squabble between a white planter and native people on the Potomac River led to the murder of the planter's herdsman and, in turn, to retaliation by frontier vigilantes, who killed some two dozen Indians. Frontiersmen then murdered five native chieftains who had sought to negotiate. Enraged Indians took revenge on frontier settlements. Scattered attacks continued

Battles over Indian lands

Intensified conflict with Indians

Powhatan Confederacy
An alliance of several powerful Algonquian tribes under the leadership of Chief Powhatan, organized into thirty chiefdoms along much of the Atlantic coast in the late sixteenth and early seventeenth centuries.

Bacon's Rebellion (1676)
Unsuccessful revolt led by planter Nathaniel Bacon against Virginia governor William Berkeley's administration, which, Bacon charged, had failed to protect settlers from Indian raids.

STRANGE NEWS

FROM

VIRGINIA;

Being a full and true

ACCOUNT

OF THE

LIFE and DEATH

OF

Nathanael Bacon Efquire,

Who was the only Caufe and Original of all the late
Troubles in that COUNTRY.

With a full Relation of all the Accidents which have
happened in the late War there between the
Chriftians and Indians.

LONDON,
Printed for *William Harris*, next door to the Turn-
Stile without *Moor-gate*. 1677.

News of the Rebellion A pamphlet printed in
London provided details about Bacon's
Rebellion.

Religious conversion and land
confiscation

southward to the James River, where Nathaniel Bacon's farm manager was killed. In 1676, when Berkeley refused to take action against the Indian raiders, Bacon defied the governor's authority by assuming command of a group determined to terrorize the "protected and darling Indians." Bacon said he would kill all the Indians in Virginia.

The twenty-nine-year-old Bacon, a graduate of Cambridge University, had been in Virginia only two years. The rebellion he led quickly became a battle of landless servants, small farmers, and even slaves against Virginia's wealthiest planters and political leaders. But Bacon was also the spoiled son of a rich family with a talent for trouble. His ruthless assaults against peaceful Indians and his greed for power and land rather than any commitment to democratic principles sparked his conflict with the governing authorities and the planter elite.

For his part, Governor Berkeley opposed Bacon's plan to destroy the Indians not because he liked Native Americans but because he didn't want to disrupt the profitable deerskin trade with the Indians. Bacon, whose ragtag "army" now numbered in the hundreds, issued a "Declaration of the People of Virginia" accusing Berkeley of corruption and attempted to take the governor into custody. Berkeley's forces resisted—feebly—and Bacon's men burned Jamestown in frustration. Bacon, however, could not celebrate the victory long; he fell ill and died a month later. With Bacon dead, his rebellion gradually disintegrated. Governor Berkeley had twenty-three of the rebels hanged. For such severity, the king denounced Berkeley as a "fool" and recalled him to England, where he died within a year.

Native Americans and Christianity

In the spring of 1621 the Pilgrims in Plymouth were struggling with hunger and disease, just as the Jamestown settlers had before them. And as was true in Virginia, Indian peoples were crucial to their survival. Nevertheless, once they were established the New England Puritans aggressively tried to convert Native Americans to Christianity and "civilized" living. They insisted that Indian converts abandon their religions and languages, their clothes, long hair, names, and villages, forcing them to move to what were called "praying towns" to separate them from their "heathen" brethren.

One reason that Roger Williams of Rhode Island was considered so radical by the Puritan leaders was his insistence that all faiths—including those of the Indians—should be treated equally. He labeled efforts by governments to impose Puritanism on everyone "soul rape."

The relations between the Indians and the Quakers in Pennsylvania were friendly from the beginning, in part because of William Penn's careful policy of purchasing land titles from the Native Americans rather than simply seizing their lands. Penn, like Roger Williams, also took the trouble to learn the

Algonquian ceremony celebrating harvest As with most Native Americans, the Algonquians' dependence on nature for survival shaped their religious beliefs.

local Indian language, something few colonists ever attempted. For some fifty years, the Pennsylvania settlers and the neighboring Indian peoples lived in peace.

The Pequot War

Generally, Indians in the English colonies who fought to keep their lands were forced out. In 1636, settlers in Massachusetts accused a Pequot of murdering a colonist; they took revenge by setting fire to a Pequot village. As the Indians fled the flames, the Puritans killed them—men, women, and children. The militia commander declared that God had guided his actions "to smite our Enemies . . . and give us their land for an Inheritance." Sassacus, the Pequot chief, organized the survivors and counterattacked. During the ensuing Pequot War of 1637, the colonists and their Narragansett allies killed hundreds of Pequots in their village near West Mystic, in the Connecticut Valley. Under the terms of the Treaty of Hartford (1638), the Pequot Nation was dissolved. Only a few colonists regretted the massacre. Roger Williams warned that the lust for land would become "as great a God with us English as Gold was a God with the Spanish." ~funny

> The Pequot Nation destroyed

King Philip's War

After the Pequot War, relations between colonists and Indians improved somewhat, but the continuing influx of English settlers and the decline of the beaver population eventually reduced the Native Americans to poverty. By 1675, the Indians and English settlers had come to fear each other deeply.

> Bloody war between Puritans and Wampanoags

King Philip's War A 1772 engraving by Paul Revere depicts Metacomet (King Philip), leader of the Wampanoags.

The era of peaceful coexistence came to a bloody end during the last quarter of the seventeenth century. Native American leaders, especially the chief of the Wampanoags, Metacomet (known to the colonists as King Philip), resented the English efforts to convert Indians to Christianity. In the fall of 1674, John Sassamon, a Christian Indian who had graduated from Harvard College, warned the English that the Wampanoags were preparing for war. A few months later, Sassamon was found dead in a frozen pond. Colonial authorities convicted three Wampanoags of murder and hanged them. Enraged Wampanoag warriors then burned Puritan farms on June 20, 1675. Three days later, an Englishman shot a Wampanoag, and the Wampanoags retaliated by ambushing and beheading a group of Puritans.

The gruesome violence soon spun out of control. Both sides suffered severe losses in what came to be called **King Philip's War**, or Metacomet's War. The brutal fighting killed more people and caused more destruction in New England in proportion to the population than any American conflict since. Vengeful bands of warriors destroyed fifty towns while killing and mutilating hundreds of men, women, and children. Atrocities occurred on both sides. And Indians fought on both sides.

Within a year, the Narragansetts, after suffering a surprise attack by colonists that killed 300 warriors and 400 women and children, retaliated by destroying Providence, Rhode Island, and were threatening Boston itself, prompting a prominent minister to call this "the saddest time with New England that was ever known." The situation grew so desperate that the colonies passed America's first conscription laws, drafting into the militia all males between the ages of sixteen and sixty.

In the end, staggering casualties as well as shortages of food and ammunition wore down the Indians. Some surrendered, many succumbed to disease, and others fled to the west. Those who remained were forced to move to villages supervised by English officials. Metacomet initially escaped, only to be hunted down and killed. The victorious colonists marched his severed head to Plymouth, where it was displayed atop a pole for twenty years, a gruesome reminder of the English determination to ensure their dominance over Native Americans, once and for all.

Enslaving Indians in Carolina

The quickest way to raise money in the early years of Carolina's development was through trade with Indians, not unlike what the French were doing in Canada. In the late seventeenth century, English merchants began traveling southward from Virginia into the Piedmont region of Carolina, where they developed a prosperous trade with the Catawba Indians. By 1690, traders from Charles Town had made their way up the Savannah River to arrange deals with the Cherokees, Creeks, and Chickasaws. Between 1699 and 1715, Carolina exported to England an average of 54,000 deerskins per year. Europeans, in turn, transformed the valuable hides into leather gloves, belts, hats, work aprons, and book bindings. The growing trade in deerskins entwined

King Philip's War (1675–1678) A war in New England resulting from the escalation of tensions between Native Americans and English settlers; the defeat of the Native Americans led to broadened freedoms for the settlers and their dispossessing the region's Native Americans of most of their land.

Indians in a dependent relationship with Europeans that would prove disastrous to their traditional way of life. Beyond capturing and enslaving Indians, English traders began providing them with goods, firearms, and rum as payment for their capturing rivals to be sold as slaves.

The eight English proprietors of Carolina, meanwhile, wanted the colony to focus on producing the most profitable crops. Such production took time to develop, however. Land had to be cleared and then crops planted, harvested, transported, and sold. These activities required laborers. Some Carolina planters had brought enslaved Africans and white servants with them from the English-controlled islands in the West Indies, but slaves and servants were expensive to purchase and support.

> Native American slave traders

The profitability of captive Indian workers, on the other hand, prompted a frenzy of slaving activity among English settlers. As many as 50,000 Indians, most of them women and children, were sold as slaves in Charles Town between 1670 and 1715. More enslaved Indians were exported during that period than Africans were imported, and thousands more captured Indians were sold to "slavers" who took them to islands in the West Indies through New England ports. The growing trade in enslaved Indians triggered bitter struggles between rival nations, ignited unprecedented colonial warfare, and generated massive internal migrations across the southern colonies.

The Iroquois League

One of the most significant effects of European settlement in North America during the seventeenth century was the intensification of warfare among Indians. The same combination of forces that wiped out the Indian populations of New England and the Carolinas affected the native peoples around New York City and the lower Hudson Valley. The inability of various Indian groups to unite against the Europeans, as well as their vulnerability to infectious diseases, doomed them to conquest and exploitation.

> Iroquois relations with French and English

In the interior of New York, however, a different situation arose. There, sometime before 1600, the Iroquois Nations had forged an alliance so strong that the outnumbered Dutch and, later, English traders were forced to work with them in order to acquire beaver pelts. By the early seventeenth century, some fifty sachems (chiefs) governed the 12,000 members of the **Iroquois League**, known to its members as the *Haudenosaunee*. Its capital was Onondaga, a bustling town a few miles south of what later became Syracuse, New York.

The League was governed by a remarkable constitution, called the Great Law of Peace, which had three main principles: peace, equity, and justice. Each person was to be a shareholder in the wealth or poverty of the nation. The constitution established a Great Council of fifty male *royaneh* (religious-political leaders), each representing one of the female-led clans of the Iroquois Nations. The Great Law of Peace gave essential power to the people. It insisted that every time the *royaneh* dealt with "an especially important matter or a great emergency," they had to "submit the matter to the decision of their people," both men and women, for their consent.

Iroquois League An alliance of the Iroquois Nations, originally formed sometime between 1450 and 1600, that used their combined strength to pressure Europeans to work with them in the fur trade and to wage war across what is today eastern North America.

Wampum belt Woven to certify treaties or record transactions, the white squares likely denote nations and alliances, while the purple often conveys apprehension.

The search for furs and captives led Iroquois war parties to range widely across what is today eastern North America. They gained control over a huge area from the St. Lawrence River south to Tennessee and from Maine west to Michigan. For more than twenty years, warfare raged across the Great Lakes region between the Iroquois (supported by Dutch and English fur traders) and the Algonquians and Hurons (and their French allies). In the 1690s, the French and their Indian allies destroyed Iroquois crops and villages, infected them with smallpox, and reduced the male population by more than a third.

Facing extermination, the Iroquois made peace with the French in 1701. During the first half of the eighteenth century, they stayed out of the struggle between the two rival European powers, which enabled them to play the English off against the French while creating a thriving fur trade for themselves.

CORE **OBJECTIVE**

4. Analyze the role of indentured servants and the development of slavery in colonial America.

Slavery and Servitude in the Colonies

Indentured Servitude

During the seventeenth century, the English colonies, especially Virginia and Maryland along the Chesapeake Bay, grew so fast that they needed more workers than there were settlers. As early as 1619, the connection between growing tobacco and the need for laborers was clear. If "all our riches for the present do consist in Tobacco," explained a Jamestown planter, then it followed that "our principal wealth . . . consisteth in servants." The colonies needed what another planter called "lusty laboring men . . . capable of hard labor, and that can bear and undergo heat and cold."

Indentured servitude solves labor shortage

To solve the labor shortage, the planters at first recruited **indentured servants** from England, Ireland, Scotland, and continental Europe. The term derived from the *indenture*, or contract, which enabled a person to pay for passage to America by promising to work for a fixed number of years (usually between three and seven). As tobacco production soared during the seventeenth century, indentured servants did most of the work. Of the 500,000 English immigrants to America from 1610 to 1775, 350,000 came as indentured servants, most of them Protestants. Not all the servants went voluntarily. Many homeless children in London were "kidnapped" into servitude in America. In addition, Parliament in 1717 declared that convicts could avoid the hangman by relocating to the colonies.

indentured servant Settler who signed on for a temporary period of servitude to a master in exchange for passage to the New World.

Once in the colonies, servants were provided food and a bed by their employer, but their rights were limited. As a Pennsylvania judge explained in 1793, indentured servants occupied "a middle rank between slaves and free men." They could own property but could not engage in trade. Marriage required the master's permission. Masters could whip servants and extend their length of service for bad behavior. Once the indenture ended, usually after four to seven years, the servant could claim the "freedom dues" set by custom and law: money, tools, clothing, food, and occasionally small tracts of land. Indeed, some former servants did very well for themselves. In 1629, seven members of the Virginia legislature were former indentured servants. Such opportunities for servants to assume leading roles in society were much less common in England or Europe, giving people even more reasons to opt for America.

Slavery in North America

In 1700 there were enslaved Africans in every one of the American colonies, and they made up 11 percent of the total population (slaves would comprise more than 20 percent by 1770). But slavery in English North America differed greatly from region to region. Africans were a tiny minority in New England (about 2 percent). Because there were no large plantations in New England and fewer slaves were owned, "family slavery" prevailed, with masters and slaves usually living under the same roof.

Slavery was much more prevalent in the Chesapeake colonies and the Carolinas, where the economy was increasingly dominated by large plantations. By 1730, the black slave population in Virginia and Maryland had become the first in the Western Hemisphere to achieve a self-sustaining rate of population growth. By 1750 about 80 percent of the slaves in the Chesapeake region, for example, had been born there.

African Roots

The transport of African captives, mostly young, across the Atlantic to the Americas was the largest forced migration in world history. Over ten million people eventually made the terrifying journey, the vast majority of whom were taken to Brazil or the Caribbean sugar islands.

Enslaved Africans came from very different places in Africa, spoke as many as fifty different languages, and worshipped many different gods. Some had lived in large kingdoms and others in dispersed villages. Africans had preyed upon other Africans for centuries. Warfare was constant, as rival tribes conquered, kidnapped, enslaved, and sold one another. Slavery in Africa, however, was less brutal than the culture of race-based slavery that developed in the Americas. In Africa, slaves lived with their captors, and their

Indentured servants An advertisement from the *Virginia Gazette*, October 4, 1779, for indentured servants.

> Growth of slavery in the colonies

Different Beginnings, Common Trends: The English Colonies in North America, 1600–1700

The English government oversaw the development of numerous colonies on the Atlantic seaboard of North America in the seventeenth century. By 1700, most of the English colonies were attracting a diverse European population, had eliminated Native American threats to their domain (often through violence), were growing an export trade to other regions in the Atlantic World, and had developed self-governing traditions including elected legislative assemblies. The English colonies were the most prosperous, powerful, and populous region of the continent. Yet, they were a diverse lot.

THE FIRST COLONIES

	Chesapeake Colonies: Virginia and Maryland	New England Colonies: Plymouth, Massachusetts Bay, Rhode Island, Connecticut, New Hampshire	Carolina Colonies and Georgia: North and South Carolina	Middle Colonies: New York, Pennsylvania, New Jersey, Delaware, Georgia
Foundation and Government	Virginia was originally a joint-stock company with an elected assembly; it later became a royal colony. Maryland was the first proprietary colony.	Plymouth Puritans at first were independent, but later absorbed into Massachusetts Bay, a joint-stock company, royally chartered as a self-governing entity with legislative bodies elected by church members.	Proprietorships that later became royal colonies	Proprietorships
Religion	Virginia was officially Anglican. Catholic Maryland also welcomed Protestants.	Puritan New England did not tolerate dissent, but Rhode Island challenged Puritan control as the first colony to establish freedom of religion.	Carolina colonies tolerated many religious communities.	New York inherited a diverse religious community from the previous New Netherland colony. Quaker Pennsylvania also welcomed other religious groups.

	Chesapeake Colonies	New England Colonies	Carolina Colonies and Georgia	Middle Colonies
Economy and Trade	The region primarily cultivated tobacco, using indentured servants and, increasingly, African slaves, who were also exported to England.	New England colonists thrived as small farmers, merchants, seamen, and fishermen.	Colonists brought slaves from the West Indies and created rice plantations. Early on, Carolinians profited from lumber, deerskin trade, and Native American slave trade. Georgia exported rice, lumber, beef, and pork, traded with the West Indies, and became a slave-centered society.	Middle colonists exported furs secured through trade with Native Americans. Many small farmers emerged as well.
Relations with Indians	English colonists traded with the Indians for furs, but also fought several bloody wars with Indians to gain more land for English settlers.	Colonists tried to convert Indians to Christianity without assimilating them into their society. When Indians showed resistance, colonists used force to gain control of Indian lands and to remove them from the region.	The Indian slave trade decimated much of the Indian population, led to devastating wars among various societies, and generated massive internal migrations.	The Pennsylvania government sought peaceful relations with Indians through legally purchased land titles. The Iroquois League maintained its independence from English and French domination in northern New York.

QUESTIONS FOR ANALYSIS

1. Which colonies were founded by joint-stock companies? Which were founded by proprietors? How were the others founded? How did this contribute to self-rule in the colonies?

2. What were the religious distinctions among the colonies? Which colonies were more religiously tolerant than others?

3. Which colonies were more involved with slavery and why? What were the main exports of the different slave-centered regions? What characterized the economies of the other colonies?

4. Which colonies had better relations with Indians?

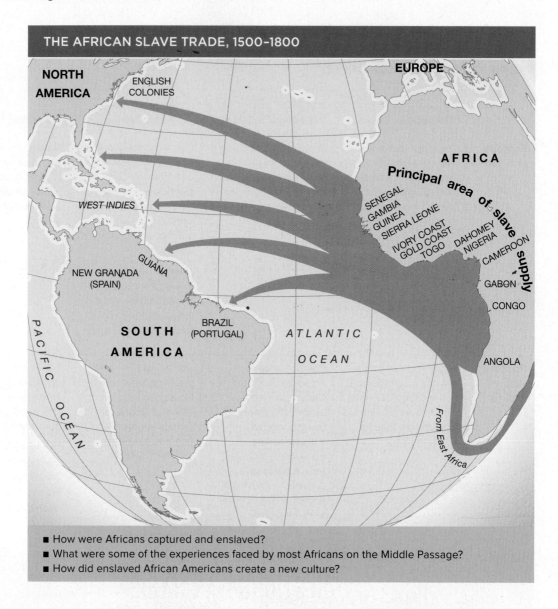

THE AFRICAN SLAVE TRADE, 1500–1800

- How were Africans captured and enslaved?
- What were some of the experiences faced by most Africans on the Middle Passage?
- How did enslaved African Americans create a new culture?

Middle Passage The hellish and often deadly middle leg of the transatlantic "triangular trade" in which European ships carried manufactured goods to Africa, then transported enslaved Africans to the Americas and the Caribbean, and finally conveyed American agricultural products back to Europe.

children were not automatically enslaved. The involvement of Europeans in transatlantic slavery, whereby captives were sold and shipped to other nations, was much worse.

During the seventeenth and eighteenth centuries, African slave traders brought captives to dozens of "slave forts" along the West African coast, where they were sold to European slave traders. Once purchased, the millions of people destined for slavery in the Americas were branded on the back or buttocks with a company mark, chained, and loaded onto horrific slave ships, most of them British-owned, where they were packed as tightly as livestock in the constant darkness below deck. They then were subjected to a four-week to six-month transatlantic voyage, known as the **Middle Passage** (because it was the middle leg of the so-called "triangular trade" that carried European manufactures to Africa, African slaves to America, and American produce and lumber to Europe). One in six captives died along the way. Almost one in every ten of these floating prisons experienced a revolt during the crossing. Some captives committed suicide by jumping off the ships. Yet many of the whites engaged in slave trafficking considered their work highly respectable. "What a glorious and advantageous trade this is," wrote James Houston, who worked for a slave-trading firm. "It is the hinge on which all the trade of this globe moves."

The rapid growth of slavery in the Western Hemisphere was driven by high profits and justified by a widespread racism that viewed Africans as beasts of burden rather than human beings. Once in America, Africans were treated as property ("chattel"), herded in chains to public slave auctions, and sold to the highest bidder. Once purchased, their most common roles were to cook and clean, care for the owner's babies and children, dig ditches, drain swamps, clear, plant, and tend fields, and feed livestock. On large southern plantations that grew tobacco, sugar cane, or rice, groups of slaves were organized into work "gangs" supervised by black "drivers" and white overseers. The slaves were often quartered in barracks, fed like livestock, and issued ill-fitting work clothes and shoes so uncomfortable that many slaves preferred to go barefoot. Colonial laws allowed whites to use brutal means to discipline slaves. They were whipped, branded, shackled, castrated, or sold away, often to the Caribbean islands, where few survived the brutal working conditions of harvesting sugar cane.

> High profits and widespread racism

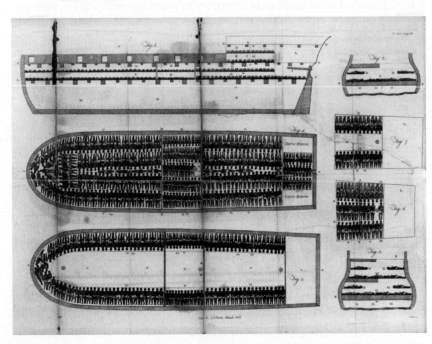

Slave ship One in six Africans died while crossing the Atlantic in ships like this one, from an American diagram ca. 1808.

African cultural heritage in the South The survival of African culture among enslaved Americans is evident in this late-eighteenth-century painting of a South Carolina plantation. The musical instruments and pottery are of African (probably Yoruban) origin.

Slave resistance

Enslaved Africans, however, found ingenious ways to resist being "mastered." Some rebelled against their captors by resisting work orders, sabotaging crops and stealing tools, faking illness or injury, or running away. If caught, runaways faced certain punishment—whipping, branding, and even the severing of an Achilles tendon. Runaways also faced uncertain freedom. Where would black runaways run *to* in a society ruled by whites and governed by racism?

Slave Culture

African and American cultural exchange

Africans who were transported to America brought with them powerful kinship ties. Even though most colonies outlawed slave marriages, many whites believed that slaves would work harder and be more stable if they were allowed to form families. Though families were often broken up when members were sold to different owners, slave culture retained its powerful sense of domestic ties. It also developed gender roles distinct from those of white society. Most enslaved women were field workers as well as wives and mothers responsible for child-rearing and household affairs.

In the process of being forced into lives of bondage in a new world, Africans from diverse homelands forged a new identity as African Americans. At the same time, they wove into American culture many strands of their African heritage, including new words that entered the language, such as *tabby*, *tote*, *goober*, *yam*, and *banana*, as well as the names of the Coosaw, Pee

Dee, and Wando Rivers in South Carolina. More significant are African influences upon American music, folklore, and religious practices. Slaves often used songs, stories, and religious preachings to circulate coded messages expressing their distaste for masters or overseers. The fundamental theme of slave religion, adapted from the Christianity that was forced upon them, was deliverance: God would eventually free African Americans and open the gates to heaven's promised land.

Thriving Colonies

By the early eighteenth century, the English colonies in the New World had outstripped those of both the French and the Spanish as tensions among the three major European powers grew. English America, both the mainland colonies and those in the Caribbean, had become the most populous, prosperous, and powerful of the European empires. American colonists were better fed, clothed, and housed than their counterparts in Europe, where a majority of the people lived in landless poverty. But the English colonization of North America included failures as well as successes. Many settlers found hard labor, desperation, and an early death in the New World. Others flourished only because they were able to exploit Indians, indentured servants, or Africans.

The English created self-governing and profitable American colonies because of crucial advantages they had over their European rivals. The tightly controlled colonial empires created by the monarchs of Spain and France stifled innovation. By contrast, the English organized colonies as profit-making enterprises with a minimum of royal control. Where New Spain was dominated by wealthy men who controlled vast estates and often intended to return to Spain, many English colonists ventured to America because, for them, life in England was intolerable. The leaders of the Dutch and non-Puritan English colonies, unlike their rivals the Spanish and French, welcomed people from a variety of nationalities and religions who came in search of a new life. Perhaps most important, the English colonies enjoyed a greater degree of self-government, which made them more dynamic and creative than their French and Spanish counterparts.

Throughout the seventeenth century, geography reinforced England's emphasis on the concentrated settlements of its colonies. No one great river offered a highway to the interior. The farthest western expansion of English settlement stopped at the eastern slopes of the Appalachian Mountains. To the east lay the wide expanse of ocean, which served not only as a highway for the transport of people, ideas, commerce, and ways of life from Europe to America, but also as a barrier that separated old ideas from new, allowing the English colonies to evolve in a "new world"—while developing new ideas about economic freedom and political liberties that would flower later in the eighteenth century.

CORE **OBJECTIVE**
5. Explain how the English colonies became the most populous, prosperous, and powerful region in North America by 1700.

Organized for profit and self-governing, with widespread land ownership

- **English Background** England's colonization of North America differed from that of its European rivals and reflected its unique traditions and developments in the seventeenth century. While chartered by the Crown, English colonization was funded by *joint-stock companies* or groups of proprietors eager for profits derived from the productive activity of English settlers. Their colonial organization and governments reflected the governmental model of a two-house *Parliament* and long-held English views on civil liberties and representative institutions. The colonization of the eastern seaboard of North America occurred at a time of religious and political turmoil in England, strongly affecting colonial culture and development.

- **English Settlers and Colonization** The early years of Jamestown and Plymouth were grim. The Virginia Company used the *headright* system of granting fifty acres to any Englishmen who bought passage, and in time *tobacco* flourished but this success also laid down roots for a slave-based economy in the South. Sugar, and later rice, plantations developed in the proprietary *Carolina colonies*, which operated with minimal royal intrusion. Family farms and a mixed economy characterized the middle and New England colonies. Religion was the primary motivation for the founding of several colonies. *Puritans* drafted the *Mayflower Compact* and founded *Massachusetts Bay Colony* as a Christian commonwealth outside the structure of the English government and the Anglican Church. Rhode Island was established by Roger Williams, a religious dissenter from Massachusetts. Maryland was founded as a refuge for English Catholics. William Penn, a Quaker, founded Pennsylvania and invited Europe's persecuted religious sects to his colony. The Dutch, with their policy of toleration, allowed members of all faiths to settle in *New Netherland*, but commercial rivalry between the Dutch and the English led to war, during which the Dutch colony of *New Netherland* surrendered to the English in 1664.

- **Indian Relations** Settler–Indian relations were complex. Trade with the *Powhatan Confederacy* in Virginia enabled Jamestown to survive its early years, but brutal armed conflicts such as *Bacon's Rebellion* occurred as settlers invaded Indian lands. Puritans retaliated harshly against Indian resistance in the Pequot War of 1637 and in *King Philip's War* from 1675 to 1676. Among the chief colonial leaders, only Roger Williams and William Penn treated Indians as equals. The powerful *Iroquois League* played the European powers against each other to control territories from Tennessee into Canada.

- **Indentured Servants and Slaves** The colonies increasingly relied on *indentured servants* for their labor supply. European immigrants looking for a better life could pay for passage to America by signing contracts (indentures) that required them to work for several years upon arriving in America. By the end of the seventeenth century, enslaved Africans had replaced indentured servants as the primary form of labor to produce tobacco in the Chesapeake. The demand for slaves in the sugar plantations of the West Indies drove European slave traders to organize the transport of Africans via the dreaded *Middle Passage* across the Atlantic. With the supply of slaves seemingly inexhaustible, the Carolinas soon adopted African slavery to cultivate rice. African cultures fused with others in the Americas to create a native-born African American culture.

- **Thriving English Colonies** By 1700, England had become a great trading empire. English America was the most populous and prosperous region of North America. Minimal royal interference in the proprietary for-profit colonies and widespread landownership encouraged settlers to put down roots for a sustainable future. Religious diversity attracted a variety of investors. By relying increasingly on slave labor, the southern colonies provided England with tobacco and other plantation crops.

KEY TERMS

CHRONOLOGY

1603	James I takes the throne of England
1607	The Virginia Company establishes Jamestown, the first permanent English colony
1612	John Rolfe begins growing tobacco for export in Virginia
1614	The Dutch charter the New Netherland Company
1619	First Africans arrive in English America
1620	The Plymouth colony is founded by Pilgrims; Pilgrims agree to the Mayflower Compact
1622	War between Indians and colonists begins in Virginia
1630	Massachusetts Bay Colony is founded by Puritans
1634	Settlement of Maryland begins
1637	The Pequot War in New England
1642–1651	The English Civil War (Puritans vs. Royalists)
1649	The Toleration Act in Maryland
1660	Restoration of English monarchy
1669	Charles Town is founded in the Carolina Colony
1675–1676	King Philip's War in New England
1676	Bacon's Rebellion erupts in Virginia
1681	Pennsylvania is established
1733	Georgia is founded

InQUIZITIVE

Go to InQuizitive to see what you've learned—and learn what you've missed—with personalized feedback along the way.

THE ARTISANS OF BOSTON (1766) While fishing, shipbuilding, and maritime trade dominated New England economies, many young men entered apprenticeships under master craftsmen in the hopes of becoming blacksmiths, carpenters, gunsmiths, printers, candlemakers, leather tanners, and more.

Colonial Ways of Life

1607–1750

The process of carving a new civilization out of an abundant "New World" involved sometimes-violent encounters among European, African, and Indian cultures. Warfare, duplicity, displacement, and enslavement were often the tragic results. Yet on another level the process of transforming the American continent was not simply a story of conflict but also one of blending and accommodation, a story of diverse peoples and resilient cultures engaged in the everyday tasks of building homes, planting crops, trading goods, raising families, enforcing laws, and worshipping gods. Those who colonized America during the seventeenth and eighteenth centuries were part of a massive social migration occurring throughout Europe and Africa. Everywhere, it seemed, people were in motion—moving from farms to villages, from villages to cities, and from homelands to colonies.

People moved for various reasons. Most English and European settlers were responding to rapid population growth and the rise of commercial agriculture, which squeezed poor farm workers off the land. Many of the landless and jobless rural poor drifted into cities like London, Edinburgh, Dublin, and Paris, where they struggled to survive in growing urban ghettos. That most Europeans in the seventeenth and eighteenth centuries were desperately poor helps explain why so many were willing to risk their lives by migrating to the American colonies. Others journeyed to America in search of political security or

CORE
OBJECTIVES INQUIZITIVE

1. Explain the major factors that contributed to the demographic changes that took place in the English colonies during the eighteenth century.

2. Describe women's various roles in the English colonies.

3. Compare the societies and economies of the southern, middle, and New England colonies.

4. Describe the creation of race-based slavery during the seventeenth century and its impact on the social and economic development of colonial America.

5. Analyze the impact of the Enlightenment and Great Awakening on American thought.

religious freedom. A tragic exception was the Africans, who were captured and transported to new lands against their will.

Those who initially settled in colonial America were mostly young (more than half were under twenty-five years old), male, and poor. Almost half were servants or slaves, and during the eighteenth century, England would transport more than 50,000 convicts to the North American colonies as a way to relieve overcrowded jails and provide needed workers in the colonies. Only about a third of the settlers came with their families. Once in America, many of the newcomers kept moving within and across colonies in search of better lands or new business opportunities, such as trading with the native peoples who controlled the profitable fur trade. This extraordinary migration of adventurous people created many of America's enduring institutions and values, as well as its distinctive spirit and restless energy.

CORE **OBJECTIVE**

1. Explain the major factors that contributed to the demographic changes that took place in the English colonies during the eighteenth century.

The Shape of Early America

Population Growth

The early months and years of England's colonies in America exacted a fearsome toll: many in the first wave of settlement died of disease, starvation, or warfare with Native Americans. But once colonial life became more settled and secure, the colonies grew rapidly. On average, the American population doubled every twenty-five years during the colonial period. By 1750, the number of colonists had passed 1 million; by 1775, it approached 2.5 million. By comparison, the combined population of England, Scotland, and Ireland in 1750 was 6.5 million.

Plentiful land, scarce labor, and better living conditions

The extraordinary increase of the colonial population, explained Philadelphia's Benjamin Franklin, a keen observer of many things, resulted from two facts: land in America was plentiful and cheap, and laborers were scarce and expensive. The opposite conditions prevailed in Europe. There, the "enclosure movement" had led nobles—who had traditionally opened their estates to all farmers for common purposes, such as grazing animals—to fence their lands and focus on large-scale commercial ("cash") crops and herds, such as sheep. Many surrounding landless farmers were thus displaced, creating widespread unemployment, homelessness, and starvation. As a result, America's plentiful lands lured migrants eager to have their own farms. Once in the colonies, the settlers tended to have large families, in part because farm children could lend a hand in the fields; once grown, they could find new land for themselves, if need be.

Birth and Death Rates

Rapid population growth

Colonists tended to marry and start families at an earlier age than in Europe. In England, the average age at marriage for women was twenty-six; in America, it dropped to twenty. Men in the colonies also married at a younger age. The **birth rate** rose accordingly, since women who married younger had time for about two additional pregnancies during their childbearing years.

Equally responsible for the fast-growing colonial population was a much lower **death rate** than that in Europe. By the middle of the seventeenth century, infants had a better chance of reaching maturity in New England than in England, and adults lived longer in the colonies. Lower mortality rates in the colonies resulted from several factors. Since fertile land was plentiful, famine seldom occurred after the early years of colonization, and, although the winters were more severe than in England, firewood was abundant. Being younger—the average age in 1790 was sixteen—Americans on the whole were less susceptible to disease than were Europeans. That they were more scattered than in Europe also meant they were less exposed to infectious diseases. That began to change as colonial cities grew larger and more dense. By the mid–eighteenth century, the colonies experienced levels of disease much like those in the cities of Europe.

Colonial farm This plan of a newly cleared American farm shows how trees were cut down with axes and the stumps left to rot.

"Women's Work" in the Colonies

In contrast to the colonies of New Spain and New France, English America had far more women, which largely explains the difference in population growth rates among the European empires competing in the Americas. But higher numbers of women did not mean greater equality. Most European colonists brought to America deeply rooted convictions about the inferiority of women. As one New England minister stressed, "the woman is a weak creature not endowed with [the] strength and constancy of mind [of men]." Women, as had been true for centuries, were expected to obey and serve their husbands, nurture their children, and do the hard daily work required to maintain their households ("domestic" life). Women in most colonies could not vote, hold office, attend schools or colleges, bring lawsuits, sign contracts, or become ministers.

In the eighteenth century, "**women's work**" typically involved activities in the house, garden, and fields. Yet the scarcity of workers in the colonies created new opportunities for women. In the towns, women commonly served as tavern hostesses and shopkeepers and occasionally also worked as doctors, printers, upholsterers, painters, and silversmiths. Often, these

> CORE **OBJECTIVE**
> **2.** Describe women's various roles in the English colonies.

birth rate Proportion of births per 1,000 of the total population.

death rate Proportion of deaths per 1,000 of the total population; also called *mortality rate*.

women's work Traditional term referring to routine tasks in the house, garden, and fields performed by women; eventually expanded in the colonies to include medicine, shopkeeping, upholstering, and the operation of inns and taverns.

The First, Second, and Last Scene of Mortality **(ca. 1776)** Prudence Punderston's needlework shows the domestic path, from cradle to coffin, followed by most colonial women.

women were widows carrying on their dead husbands' trade or business. Such working widows became accustomed to some measure of social authority in the "man's world" of eighteenth-century economic life.

One woman who exercised leadership outside the home was South Carolinian Elizabeth Lucas Pinckney (1722–1793). After her father, a British army officer, was called back to the Caribbean island of Antigua (where the family had come from), fifteen-year-old Eliza cared for her ailing mother and younger sister in Charleston, South Carolina, while managing three plantations worked by enslaved Africans. She decided to grow a West Indian plant called *indigo*, which provided a much-coveted blue dye for coloring fabric. Indigo made her family a fortune, as it did for many other plantation owners on the Carolina coast.

The shortage of women in the first years of colonial settlement at times made them more highly valued than they were in Europe. In addition, the Puritan emphasis on a well-ordered family life led to laws protecting wives from physical abuse and allowing for divorce. In addition, colonial laws gave wives greater control over the property they contributed to a marriage or that was left after a husband's death. But such exceptions did not change the basic status of women: the age-old notions of women being subordinate to men remained firmly entrenched in colonial America. As a boy in Massachusetts claimed in 1662, the superior aspect of life was "masculine and eternal; the feminine inferior and mortal."

> Overall inferior status but new opportunities and greater property rights for women under the law

Society and Economy in the Colonies

In the early eighteenth century, England and Scotland merged. The Act of Union in 1707 announced a new name for the joint monarchies: Great Britain. Its colonies—now referred to as the British American colonies—were part of a complex North Atlantic commercial network, trading sugar, wheat, tobacco, rum, rice, and many other commodities, as well as African and Indian slaves, with Great Britain and its highly profitable island colonies in the West Indies such as Bermuda, Barbados, and Jamaica. In addition, American merchants also traded ("smuggled") with Spain, France, Portugal, Holland, and their colonies, which were often at war with Britain and therefore officially off limits to Americans. Out of necessity, the colonists were dependent on Britain and Europe for manufactured goods and luxury items such as wine, glass, and jewelry.

The colonies were blessed with abundant natural resources, but they struggled to find enough laborers for their rapidly expanding economy. The primary solution to the shortage of workers in the colonies was indentured servitude. This practice, whereby servants agreed to work for four to seven years in exchange for their "master" paying for their travel to America, accounted for probably half the white settlers (mostly from England, Ireland, Scotland, or Germany) in all the colonies outside New England. These unfree workers brought their own cultures to the regions where they lived, creating a diverse ethnic mix, especially in the southern and middle colonies. During the late seventeenth and eighteenth centuries, however, the southern colonies turned from using indentured servants to purchasing life-long Indian or African slaves to satisfy the growing demand for agricultural workers on vast tobacco and rice plantations.

The Southern Colonies

As the southern colonies matured, inequalities of wealth became more visible and social life grew more divided by marked differences in status. The use of enslaved Indians and Africans to grow tobacco, sugar cane, rice, and indigo created enormous wealth for a few large landowners and their families. Socially, the planters and merchants increasingly became a class apart. They dominated the colonial legislatures, bought luxury goods from London and Paris, and built brick mansions with formal gardens like those in England—all the while looking down upon their social "inferiors," both white and black.

Warm weather and plentiful rainfall enabled the southern colonies to grow the **staple crops** (most profitable) valued by the mother country: tobacco, rice, sugar cane, and indigo. In the Chesapeake region of the Upper South, Virginia, as King Charles I put it, was "founded upon smoke." Tobacco

> **CORE OBJECTIVE**
> **3.** Compare the societies and economies of the southern, middle, and New England colonies.

> A rapidly expanding economy

> Rising inequality and a slave-based economy in the South

staple crop A profitable market crop, such as cotton, tobacco, or rice, that predominates in a given region.

Virginia plantation wharf Southern colonial plantations were often constructed along rivers, with easy access to oceangoing vessels, as shown on this 1730 tobacco label.

production soared during the seventeenth century. "In Virginia and Maryland," wrote a royal official in 1629, "tobacco . . . is our All, and indeed leaves no room for anything else." The same was true for rice cultivation along the South Carolina coast. Over time, the rice planters became the wealthiest group in the British colonies, forcing their slaves to "work for hours in mud and water." Using only hand tools, slaves transformed the landscape of coastal South Carolina and, eventually, Georgia, removing trees from swamps and wetlands infested with snakes, alligators, and mosquitos. They then created a system of floodgates to allow workers to drain or flood the rice fields as needed.

As plantations grew in size, the demand for enslaved laborers, first male Indians and later Africans, rose dramatically. Almost 90 percent of the Africans transported to the American mainland went to the southern colonies. South Carolina had a black majority throughout the eighteenth century. As one visitor observed, "Carolina looks more like a negro country than like a country settled by white people."

New England

New England townships

There was remarkable diversity among the American colonies during the seventeenth century and after. Few New England colonists, for example, owned huge tracts of land, as was common in Carolina, Virginia, Maryland, and Dutch New Netherland. In New England, settlers, often already gathered into a church congregation, would ask the general court for a township and then divide its acreage in roughly equal parcels: those who invested more or had larger families or greater status might receive more land. Over time, as the population grew, the land was divided into separate farms more distant from the original village.

Religion

Church and state

Whenever towns were founded, the first public structure built was usually a church. The New England Puritans believed that God had created a *covenant*, or contract, in which people formed a congregation for common worship. This led to the idea of people joining together to form governing bodies too, but "democracy" was not part of Puritan political thought.

Housing in colonial New England This frame house, built in the 1670s, belonged to Rebecca Nurse, one of the women hanged as a witch in Salem Village in 1692.

Puritan leaders sought to do the will of God, not to follow the will of the people, and the ultimate source of authority in Puritan New England was not majority rule but the Bible as interpreted by ministers and magistrates (political leaders). By law, every town had to collect taxes to support a church. And every resident—whether a church member or not—was required to attend midweek and Sunday religious services. The average New Englander heard 7,000 sermons in a lifetime.

Over time, Puritan New England experienced a gradual erosion of religious commitment. More and more children and grandchildren of the original "visible saints" could not give the required testimony of spiritual conversion. In 1662, a group of Boston ministers created the "Half-Way Covenant," whereby baptized children of church members could be admitted to a "halfway" membership, but they could neither vote in church nor take communion. A further blow to Puritan ideals came with the Massachusetts royal charter of 1691, which required toleration of religious dissenters (such as Quakers) and based the right to vote in public elections on property ownership rather than church membership.

The strains accompanying Massachusetts's transition from Puritan utopia to royal colony reached a tragic climax in the witchcraft hysteria at Salem Village (now the town of Danvers) in 1692. Belief in witchcraft was widespread throughout Europe and the colonies in the seventeenth century. Prior to the dramatic episode in Salem, almost 300 New Englanders (mostly middle-aged women) had been accused of practicing witchcraft, and more than 30 had been hanged.

The Salem episode was unique in its scope and intensity, however. During the winter of 1691–1692, several adolescent girls became fascinated with the fortune telling and voodoo practiced by Tituba, a West Indian slave. The

Salem witch trials

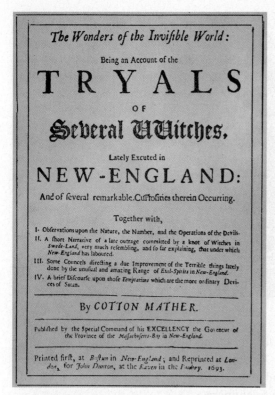

The Wonders of the Invisible World Title page of the 1693 London edition of Cotton Mather's account of the Salem witchcraft cases. Mather, a prominent Boston minister, warned his congregation that the devil's legions were assaulting New England.

entranced girls began to behave oddly—shouting, barking, crawling, and twitching for no apparent reason. When asked who was tormenting them, the girls claimed that three women—Tituba, Sarah Good, and Sarah Osborne—were Satan's servants. Authorities then arrested the three accused women. They were tried and two were hanged. Within a few months, the village jail was filled with townspeople—men, women, and children—all accused of practicing witchcraft. As the accusations multiplied, leaders of the Massachusetts Bay Colony began to worry that the witch hunts were out of control. The governor finally intervened when his own wife was accused of serving the devil. He disbanded the special court in Salem and ordered the remaining suspects released. Nineteen people had been hanged—all justified by the Biblical verse that tells believers not to "suffer a witch to live." More than 100 others had been jailed. A year after it had begun, the witchcraft frenzy was finally over.

What explains Salem's hysteria? It may have represented nothing more than theatrical adolescents trying to enliven the dreary routine of everyday life. Some historians have stressed that most of the accused witches were women, many of whom had in some way defied the traditional roles assigned to females. Still another interpretation suggests that the witchcraft accusations may have reflected the hysteria caused by frequent Indian attacks occurring just north of Salem, along New England's northern frontier. Whatever its actual causes, the witchcraft controversy reflected the peculiar social tensions of Salem Village. Nothing quite like it occurred anywhere else in the colonies.

Economy

Early New England farmers and their families led hard lives. Simply clearing the many rocks from the glacier-scoured soil might require sixty days of hard work per acre. The growing season was short, and, unlike in the southern colonies, no staple crops like tobacco or rice grew in the colder climate. The crops and livestock were those familiar to rural England: wheat, barley, and oats; cattle, pigs, and sheep.

Fishing and farming

Not all New England towns were founded as religious communities. In coastal towns, residents were often more devoted to catching fish and engaging in trade or operating taverns than worship. After a Puritan minister delivered his first sermon to a congregation in the port of Marblehead, a crusty fisherman scolded him for being so spiritual: "You think you are preaching to the people of the Bay. Our main end is to catch fish." Cod, a tasty fish that can weigh hundreds of pounds, had been a regular element of the European diet for centuries, and the waters off the New England coast had the heaviest concentrations of cod in the world. Whales, too, were numerous in New England waters and supplied oil for lighting and lubrication. The waters off New England, unlike the farms, supplied plenty of cod for export to Europe, with lesser grades of fish going to the West Indies as food for slaves. The fishing and whaling activities spurred shipbuilding, which in turn facilitated a profitable trade with Europe and other colonies.

The system of trade in New England and the middle colonies differed from that in the South in two respects: the lack of staple crops—tobacco, rice, and indigo—to exchange for English goods was a relative disadvantage, but New England's shipbuilding, fishing, and maritime trading were very profitable enterprises. After 1660, in order to protect England's own agricultural and fishing economies, the government in London placed high duties (taxes) on certain colonial exports—fish, flour, wheat, and meat—while leaving the door open to timber, furs, whale oil, tobacco, and indigo, products in great demand in the home country.

Profitable fisheries Fishing for, curing, and drying cod in Newfoundland in the early 1700s. The rich fishing grounds of the North Atlantic provided New Englanders with a prosperous industry for centuries.

The New England colonies eventually specialized in shipping goods to foreign markets through what came to be called the "**triangular trade**," in which New Englanders shipped rum to the west coast of Africa, where they exchanged it for slaves; ships then took the enslaved Africans to sell in the West Indies; they then returned home with various Caribbean commodities, including molasses, from which they manufactured more rum. In another version of the trading triangle, they shipped products such as meat and fish to the West Indies, where they acquired sugar and molasses, which they then transported to England, and returned to America with manufactured goods and luxury items from Britain and Europe.

The Middle Colonies

Both geographically and culturally, the middle colonies (New York, Pennsylvania, New Jersey, Delaware, and Maryland) stood between New England and the South, including aspects of both regions. As such, they more completely reflected the diversity of colonial life and more fully foreshadowed the pluralism of America.

The primary crops in the middle colonies were those of New England but more plentiful, owing to more fertile soil and a longer growing season. The middle colonies harvested crop surpluses for export to the slave-based plantations of the South and the West Indies: wheat, barley, oats,

"Triangular" trade networks

triangular trade A network of trade in which exports from one region were sold to a second region; the second sent its exports to a third region that exported its own goods back to the first country or colony.

ATLANTIC TRADE ROUTES

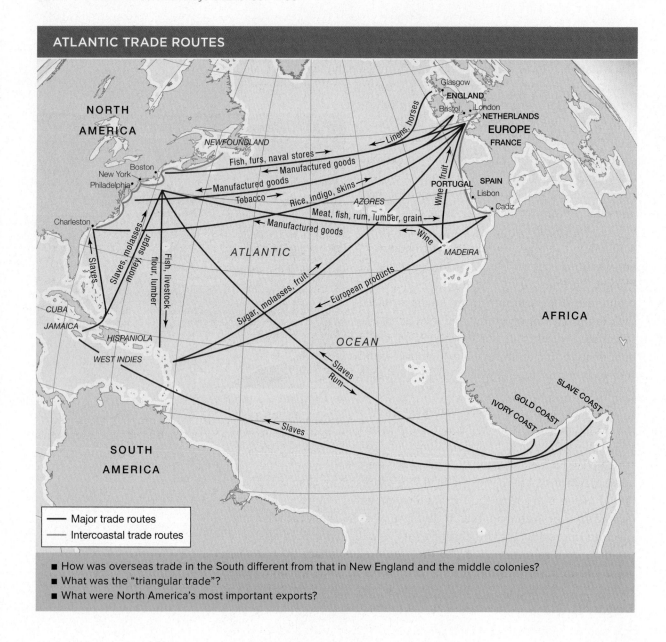

— Major trade routes
— Intercoastal trade routes

- How was overseas trade in the South different from that in New England and the middle colonies?
- What was the "triangular trade"?
- What were North America's most important exports?

as well as livestock. Three great rivers—the Hudson, the Delaware, and the Susquehanna—and their tributaries gave the middle colonies access to the backcountry of Pennsylvania and New York, which opened up a rich fur trade with Native Americans. As a consequence, the region's bustling trade, centered in New York City, Philadelphia, and Baltimore, rivaled that of New England.

Dutch *patroonship*

Land policies in the middle colonies followed the *headright* system in distributing fifty acres to any settler who had paid his own passage and fifty more if the settler brought servants. In New York, the early royal governors continued the Dutch practice of the *patroonship*, whereby influential men (called *patroons*) were granted vast estates on Long Island and throughout the Hudson and Mohawk River valleys north of New York City. The *patroons* controlled self-contained estates farmed by tenants (renters) who paid fees to use the landlord's mills, warehouses, and docks.

In the makeup of their population, the middle colonies differed from both New England's Puritan settlements and the biracial plantation colonies to the south. In New York and New Jersey, for instance, Dutch culture and language lingered. Along the Delaware River near Philadelphia, the first settlers—a small number of Swedes and Finns—were overwhelmed by an influx of English and Welsh Quakers, followed in turn by other European ethnic groups of Germans, Irish, and Scots-Irish. By the mid-eighteenth century, the middle colonies were the fastest growing region in North America.

Ethnic diversity in the middle colonies

The Germans came to America (primarily Pennsylvania) mainly from the Rhineland region of Europe that suffered from brutal religious wars that pitted Protestants against Catholics. William Penn's recruiting brochures in German translation circulated throughout central Europe, and his promise of religious freedom in Pennsylvania appealed to many persecuted sects, especially the Mennonites, German Baptists whose beliefs resembled those of the Quakers.

In 1683, a group of Mennonites founded Germantown, near Philadelphia. They were the first among a surge of German migration in the eighteenth century, a large proportion of whom paid their way to America as indentured servants, or "redemptioners," as they were commonly called. The waves of German immigrants during the eighteenth century alarmed many British colonists. Benjamin Franklin worried that the Germans "will soon . . . outnumber us."

Throughout the eighteenth century, the feisty Scots-Irish moved still farther out into the Pennsylvania backcountry. ("Scotch-Irish" is the more common but inaccurate name for the Scots-Irish, a mostly Presbyterian population transplanted from Scotland to northern Ireland by the English government a century earlier in order to give Catholic Ireland a more Protestant tone.) There were so many Scots-Irish streaming into Pennsylvania during the eighteenth century that the colony could not contain them all, so they kept moving southwest into the fertile valleys in central Virginia and western Carolina.

Land was the great magnet attracting the Scots-Irish. They were, said a recruiting agent, "full of expectation to have land for nothing" and were "unwilling to be disappointed." In most cases, the lands they "squatted on" were claimed by Native Americans. In 1741 a group of Delaware Indians protested to Pennsylvania authorities that the Scots-Irish intruders were taking "our land" without giving "us anything for it." If the colonial government did not stop the flow of whites, the Delawares threatened, then they would "drive them off."

The Scots-Irish and the Germans became the largest non-English ethnic groups in the colonies. Other ethnic minorities also enriched the population

A tradition of social tolerance

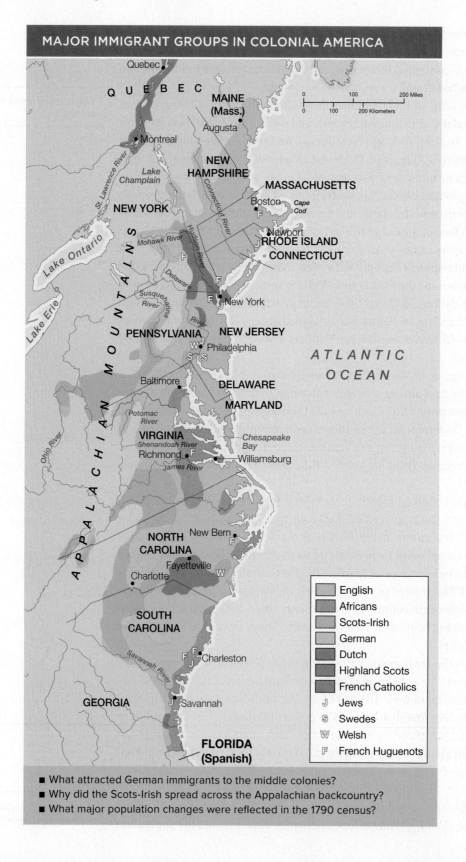

MAJOR IMMIGRANT GROUPS IN COLONIAL AMERICA

Legend:
- English
- Africans
- Scots-Irish
- German
- Dutch
- Highland Scots
- French Catholics
- J Jews
- S Swedes
- W Welsh
- F French Huguenots

- What attracted German immigrants to the middle colonies?
- Why did the Scots-Irish spread across the Appalachian backcountry?
- What major population changes were reflected in the 1790 census?

in the middle colonies: Huguenots (French Protestants whose religious freedom had been revoked in 1685, forcing many to leave France), Irish, Welsh, Swiss, and Jews. New York had inherited from the Dutch a tradition of ethnic and religious tolerance, which had given the colony a diverse population before the English conquest: French-speaking Walloons (a Celtic people from southern Belgium), French, Germans, Danes, Portuguese, Spaniards, Italians, Bohemians, Poles, and others, including some New England Puritans. The Sephardic Jews who landed in New Amsterdam in 1654 quickly founded a synagogue there.

The eighteenth century saw soaring population growth in British North America, during which the colonies grew even more diverse. In 1790, the white population was 61 percent English; 14 percent Scottish and Scots-Irish; 9 percent German; 5 percent Dutch, French, and Swedish; 4 percent Irish; and 7 percent "unidentifiable," a category that included people of mixed origins as well as "free blacks." If one adds to the 3,172,444 whites in the 1790 census the 756,770 nonwhites, without even considering the almost 100,000 Native Americans that went uncounted, only about half the nation's inhabitants, and perhaps fewer, could trace their origins to England.

Race-Based Slavery in the Colonies

By the eighteenth century, the economy in the southern colonies had become utterly dependent on enslaved workers, either Indians or Africans. The profound economic, political, and cultural effects of African slavery in the Americas would be felt far into the future. Most Europeans during the colonial period viewed **race-based slavery** as a normal aspect of everyday life in an imperfect world; few considered it a moral issue. They instead believed that God determined one's "station in life." Slavery was thus considered a "personal misfortune" dictated by God rather than a social evil. It was not until the late eighteenth century that large numbers of white Europeans and Americans began to raise ethical questions about slavery.

Initially, during the early seventeenth century, many of the first Africans in America were treated like indentured servants, with a limited term of service. Those who finished their term of indenture gained their freedom, and some of them, as "free blacks," themselves acquired black slaves and white servants. Gradually, however, life-long slavery for African Americans became the custom—and the law—of the land. Slaves cost more than did indentured servants, but they served for life, so they were an increasingly shrewd investment. By the 1660s, colonial legislatures had begun to legalize the institution of race-based slavery, with strict slave codes regulating their lives. During the colonial era, slavery was legal in all the colonies but was most prevalent in the South.

> CORE **OBJECTIVE**
> **4.** Describe the creation of race-based slavery during the seventeenth century and its impact on the social and economic development of colonial America.

> Legalization of lifelong slavery

race-based slavery Institution that uses racial characteristics and myths to justify enslaving a people by force.

Racial Prejudice

As slavery in the American colonies grew more widespread, the role of race grew more prominent. Did a deep-rooted color prejudice lead to race-based slavery, or did the practice of slavery over time produce the racial prejudice? More than a century before the English arrived in America, the Portuguese and Spanish had established a global trade in enslaved Africans—the word "negro" is Spanish for "black." English settlers often enslaved Indian captives, as had the Spanish and Portuguese before them. However, the Europeans did not enslave other Europeans who were captured in warfare. Color was the crucial difference, or at least the crucial rationalization used to justify the institution of slavery and its brutalities.

Deep-rooted color prejudice

The English in the seventeenth century associated the color black with darkness and evil; they considered the different appearance, behavior, and customs of Africans, as well as the indigenous peoples of America, as representing "savagery" and "heathenism." The colonial Virginians justified slavery by convincing themselves that blacks (and Indians) were naturally lazy, treacherous, and stupid, among other shortcomings. Throughout history, dominant peoples have repeatedly assigned ugly traits to those they enslaved. And in the seventeenth and eighteenth centuries, American colonists readily justified enslaving Africans because they were deemed both "heathens" and "aliens."

African Slavery in North America

African slave trading networks

The continent of Africa during the sixteenth and seventeenth centuries experienced almost constant civil wars among competing groups and kingdoms. Africans kidnapped and sold each other into slavery in large numbers. Slave-trading networks crisscrossed the African continent. Eventually, over 10 million Africans made the forced journey into slavery across the Atlantic, most of them destined for the Spanish and Portuguese colonies. Their great ethnic diversity is often overlooked. Some came from lands as remote from each other as Angola and Senegal, thousands of miles distant, and they spoke many different languages. Many of the Africans taken to North America came in ships built in New England and owned by merchants in Boston and Newport. Most of the enslaved were young—twice as many men as women—between the ages of fifteen and thirty.

Virginia and Maryland plantation owners favored slaves from West Africa, where the cultivation of yams (sweet potatoes) was similar to the cultivation of tobacco. Fulani from West and Central Africa were prized as cattle herdsmen. South Carolina rice planters preferred slaves from Africa's "Rice Coast," especially Gambia, where rice cultivation was commonplace. Owners of slaves from the lowlands of Africa used their talents as boatmen in the coastal waterways. In a new colonial society, many slaves became skilled workers: blacksmiths, carpenters, coopers (barrel makers), bricklayers, and the like. Many enslaved women worked as household servants and midwives, helping to deliver babies.

Colonial Race Relations

Enslaved workers were eventually used in virtually every activity within the expanding colonial economy. To be sure, the vast majority were agricultural workers, often performing strenuous labor from dawn to dusk in oppressive heat and humidity. Jedidiah Morse, a prominent minister in Charleston, South Carolina, admitted in the late eighteenth century that "no white man, to speak generally, ever thinks of settling a farm, and improving it for himself, without negroes." In 1750, the vast majority of slaves in the American colonies were in Virginia and Maryland, numbering about 150,000, compared with 60,000 in South Carolina and Georgia, and only 33,000 in all the northern colonies.

Most slaves in the northern colonies lived in towns or cities, which gave them more opportunities to circulate within the larger society than

Slavery in New Amsterdam (1642) African slaves had become a mainstay of the economy so early on in American history that they appear hefting tobacco in this early and rare engraving of the Dutch colony New Amsterdam, later known as New York.

their southern counterparts living on large plantations distant from town. By 1740, New York City was second only to Charleston in the percentage of slaves in colonial cities. Most of the enslaved blacks in New York City came from the Caribbean sugar islands rather than directly from Africa. As the number of slaves increased in the congested city, racial tensions mounted and occasionally exploded. In 1712, several dozen slaves revolted; they started fires and then used swords, axes, and guns to kill whites who rushed to fight the fires. Called out to restore order, the militia captured twenty-seven slaves. Six committed suicide, and the rest were executed; some were burned alive.

New York officials thereafter passed a series of ordinances—a "black code"—strictly regulating slaves. Any slave caught with a weapon, for example, would be whipped, and owners could punish their slaves as they saw fit, as long as they did not kill them. New York and other states modeled their **slave codes** after those in South Carolina—which had been written in 1691 and allowed whites to abuse blacks verbally and physically. In 1680 the Virginia legislature had ordered thirty lashes with a whip "if any negro or other slave shall presume to lift up a hand in opposition against any Christian." Even the enlightened Thomas Jefferson, who owned almost three hundred slaves, ordered that runaways be "severely flogged."

At its most basic level, slavery is a system in which the powerless are brutalized by the powerful. Slaves who ran away in colonial America faced

Slave codes

slave codes Ordinances passed by a colony or state to regulate the behavior of slaves, often including severe punishments for infractions.

ghastly punishments when caught; many were hanged or burned at the stake. Antonio, a west African man shipped as a slave to New Amsterdam and then to Maryland during the first half of the seventeenth century, worked in the tobacco fields alongside indentured servants and enslaved Native Americans. Antonio tried to escape several times. After his last attempt, in 1656, his owner, a young Dutch planter named Syman Overzee, recaptured Antonio (a "dangerous Rogue"), whipped his "bare back" with branches from a pear tree, poured hot grease into his wounds, then tied him to a ladder where he slowly died. Overzee was charged with murder—and acquitted.

> Stono Rebellion

In a few cases, as had happened in New York City, slaves organized armed rebellions, stealing weapons, burning and looting plantations, and occasionally killing their masters. In 1739, some twenty slaves attacked a store in Stono, South Carolina, south of Charleston. They killed the owner, seized weapons, and headed toward freedom in Spanish-controlled Florida, gathering more recruits along the way. Within a few days, the slaves participating in the **Stono Rebellion** had killed twenty-five whites, whereupon the militia caught up with them. Most of the rebels were killed, and in the weeks that followed, some sixty more were captured by enraged planters who "cut off their heads and set them up at every Mile Post."

Slavery in the Western Hemisphere was a rapidly growing phenomenon by the time of the American Revolution. It was driven by high profits and justified by a pervasive racism. Although race-based slavery entailed the dehumanization of an entire class of human beings, white Europeans believed they were justified in doing so because of the supposed "backwardness" of Africans and Indians. Not even the American Revolution's ideals of freedom and equality (for whites) would change that attitude.

CORE **OBJECTIVE**
5. Analyze the impact of the Enlightenment and the Great Awakening on the colonies.

First Stirrings of a Common Colonial Culture

By the middle of the eighteenth century, the thirteen colonies were rapidly growing and maturing. Schools and colleges were springing up, and the standard of living was rising as well. More and more colonists were able to read about the latest ideas circulating in London and Paris while purchasing the latest consumer goods from Europe.

During the eighteenth century, prosperous Americans became addicted to buying the latest "baubles" from Britain. The rage for British luxury goods, especially fine clothing and beaver hats, heightened social inequality, especially in the cities. Many ministers and laymen complained that wealthy Americans were so preoccupied with buying luxury goods from London that they were ignoring their religious commitment to Christian ideals. In 1714, a Bostonian regretted the "great extravagance that people are fallen into, far

Stono Rebellion (1739) A slave uprising in South Carolina that was brutally quashed, leading to executions as well as a severe tightening of the slave codes.

beyond their circumstances, in their purchases, buildings, families, expenses, apparel—generally in their whole way of living."

English merchants required Americans to buy their goods only with *specie* (gold or silver coins). This left little "hard money" in the colonies themselves. American merchants tried various ways to get around the shortage of specie. Some engaged in *barter*, using commodities such as tobacco or rice as currency in exchange for manufactured goods and luxury items from England. The issue of money—what kind and how much—would become one of the major subjects of dispute between the colonies and Britain leading to the Revolution.

> Commerce and culture

Colonial Cities

The American colonies were mostly populated by farmers or farm workers. Colonial cities hugged the coastline or, like Philadelphia, sprang up on rivers large enough to handle oceangoing vessels. Never comprising more than 10 percent of the colonial population, the large coastal cities had a disproportionate influence on commerce, politics, society, and culture. By the end of the colonial period, Philadelphia, with some 30,000 people, was the largest city in the colonies. New York City, with about 25,000, ranked second; Boston numbered 16,000; Charleston, 12,000; and Newport, Rhode Island, 11,000.

The urban social elite was dominated by wealthy merchants and property owners served by a middle class of shop owners, innkeepers, and skilled craftsmen. Almost two thirds of the urban male workers were artisans, people who made their living at handicrafts. They included carpenters and coopers (barrel makers), shoemakers and tailors, silversmiths and blacksmiths, sailmakers, stonemasons, weavers, and potters. At the bottom of the social order were sailors, manual laborers, servants, and slaves.

> An urban elite and city problems

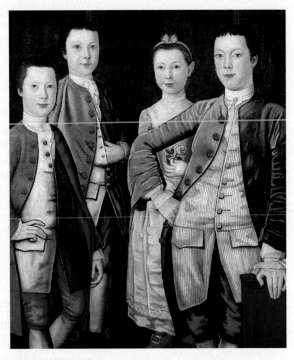

Colonial cities were busy, crowded, and dangerous. The use of open fireplaces for heating led to frequent fires that in turn led to the development of fire companies. Rising crime and violence required increased policing of neighborhoods by sheriffs and local militias. Colonists also were concerned about the poor and homeless. The number of Boston's poor receiving assistance from colonial authorities rose from 500 in 1700 to 4,000 in 1736; in New York City, the number rose from 250 in 1698 to 5,000 in the 1770s. In colonial America, those designated "helpless" among the destitute poor, especially the disabled, elderly, widows, and orphans, were often provided money, food, clothing, and firewood by the county, town, or city. In some towns, "poorhouses" were built to house the homeless poor and provide them with jobs.

***The Rapalje Children* (1768)** John Durand painted the children of a wealthy Brooklyn merchant wearing clothing typical of upper-crust urban society.

Comparing the Three English Colonial Regions

The following charts highlight some important social, cultural, and economic characteristics of the three regions of colonial America: the southern, middle, and New England colonies.

The Southern Colonies	
Colonies (and Cities)	Virginia, Maryland, North Carolina, South Carolina, Georgia (Charleston, Baltimore)
Economy and Climate	Warm and wet, best suited for staple crops: tobacco, rice
Religious Character	Anglicanism in Virginia, the Carolinas, and Georgia; Catholicism in Maryland with religious toleration
Immigrant Groups	Mostly biracial: English and Africans
Equality/Inequality	High rates of inequality: many slaves, indentured servants, landless whites at one extreme and wealthy gentry at the other

The Middle Colonies	
Colonies (and Cities)	New York, Pennsylvania, Delaware, New Jersey (Philadelphia, New York)
Economy and Climate	Commercial crossroads with mixed economy: foodstuffs for export and trade, fur trade with Native Americans; temperate climate with longer growing season
Religious Character	Pluralistic: Anglican, Protestant, and Jewish, with freedom of religion in Pennsylvania
Immigrant Groups	Diverse: Dutch, Swedes, Scots-Irish, Finns, English, Germans, Swiss, French, Welsh, Africans
Equality/Inequality	Moderate inequality: more small-farm ownership and extensive trade with Native Americans

Travel and taverns: The circulation of new ideas

The Urban Web

The first American roads were Indian trails that were widened with frequent travel, then made into roads. Overland travel was initially by horse or by foot. The first public stagecoach line opened in 1732. Taverns and inns were important in the colonial era, since travel at night was treacherous. (During this period it was said that when the Spanish settled an area, they would first

The New England Colonies	
Colonies (and Cities)	Massachusetts, Rhode Island, Connecticut, New Hampshire (Boston, Newport)
Economy and Climate	Mixed economy: fishing, shipbuilding, shipping and trade, small farms; triangular trade of slaves and rum; cold and harsh climate with short growing season
Religious Character	Largely Puritan Congregationalists with limited religious toleration, except Rhode Island
Immigrant Groups	Mostly English
Equality/Inequality	Greatest level of equality in the colonies: Congregational faith–based towns with few slaves

QUESTIONS FOR ANALYSIS

1. Which region had the largest cities, and why?

2. How did geography and climate contribute to the different economies of each region?

3. Which region was the most religiously diverse, and why? Which was the least diverse, and why?

4. Which region appeared to be the most ethnically diverse, and why? Which was the least diverse, and why?

5. What factors help explain the different level of social inequality in the various colonies?

build a church; the Dutch, in their settlements, would first erect a fort; and the English, in theirs, would first construct a tavern.) By the end of the seventeenth century, there were more taverns in America than any other business. Colonial taverns and inns were places to eat, drink, relax, read a newspaper, play cards, gossip about people or politics, learn news from travelers, or conduct business.

Tavern culture A tobacconist's business card from 1770 captures men talking in a Philadelphia tavern while they drink ale and smoke pipes.

A postal system

Taverns served as a forum for conversation and social interaction, but long-distance communication was more complicated. Postal service in the seventeenth century was almost nonexistent—people gave letters to travelers or sea captains in hopes they would be delivered. Under a parliamentary law of 1710, the postmaster of London named a deputy in charge of the colonies, and a postal system eventually encompassed most of the Atlantic seaboard. Benjamin Franklin, who served as deputy postmaster for the colonies from 1753 to 1774, sped up the service with shorter routes and night-traveling mail riders.

Freedom of the press

More reliable mail delivery gave rise to newspapers in the eighteenth century. Before 1745, twenty-two newspapers had been started: seven in New England, ten in the middle colonies, and five in the South. An important landmark in the progress of freedom of the press was John Peter Zenger's trial for publishing criticisms of New York's royal governor in his newspaper, the *New-York Weekly Journal*. Zenger was imprisoned for ten months and brought to trial in 1735. English common law held that one might be punished for "libel," or criticism that fostered "an ill opinion of the government." Zenger's lawyer startled the court with his claim that the editor had published the truth—which the judge ruled an unacceptable defense. The jury, however, held the editor not guilty. The libel law remained standing as before, but editors thereafter were emboldened to criticize officials more freely.

The Enlightenment in America

Enlightenment A revolution in thought begun in Europe in the seventeenth century that emphasized reason and science over the authority and myths of traditional religion.

The most significant of the new European ideas circulating in eighteenth-century America grew out of a burst of innovative intellectual activity known as the **Enlightenment**. The Enlightenment celebrated rational inquiry, scientific research, and individual freedom. Enlightened people were those who sought the truth, wherever it might lead, rather than remain content with believing dogmas passed down through the ages or taken from the Bible. Curious, well-educated, and well-read people were no longer willing simply to accept biblical explanations of the universe as sufficient and complete. Immanuel Kant, the eighteenth-century German philosopher, summed up the Enlightenment point of view by saying: "Dare to know! Have the courage to use your own understanding." He and others used the power of reason to analyze the workings of nature. To do so, they employed new tools like microscopes and telescopes to engage in close observation, scientific experimentation, and precise mathematical calculation.

The Enlightenment, often called the Age of Reason, was triggered by a scientific revolution in which the ancient view that the earth was at the center of the universe was overthrown in the early sixteenth century by the controversial heliocentric (sun-centered) solar system described by Nicolaus Copernicus, a Polish astronomer who was also a Catholic priest. His theory in 1533 that the earth orbits the sun was scorned by Catholic officials before it was later confirmed by other scientists.

> The scientific revolution

The climax to the scientific revolution came in 1687 when Englishman Isaac Newton (1642–1727) announced his controversial theory of the earth's gravitational pull. Newton challenged biblical notions of the world's workings by depicting a mechanistic universe moving in accordance with natural laws that could be grasped by human reason and explained by mathematics. He implied that natural laws rather than God's actions govern all things, from the orbits of the planets to the science of human relations: politics, economics, and society.

Some enlightened people believed in **Deism**, which carried Newton's scientific outlook to its logical conclusion, claiming that God created the world and designed its "natural laws," and these laws, not God directly, govern the operation of the universe. In other words, Deists insisted that God planned the universe and set it in motion, but no longer interacted directly with the earth and its people. So the rational God of the Deists was nothing like the intervening God of the Christian tradition, to whom believers prayed for daily guidance and direct support. Evil in the world, according to the Deists, resulted not from humanity's inherent *sinfulness* as outlined in the Bible but from human *ignorance* of the rational laws of nature. Therefore the best way to improve both society and human nature, according to Deists such as Thomas Jefferson and Benjamin Franklin, was by cultivating Reason, which was the highest Virtue (Enlightenment thinkers often capitalized both words). By doing so, by using education, reason, and scientific analysis, societies were bound to improve their knowledge as well as their quality of life. Faith in human progress was thus one of the most important beliefs of the Enlightenment.

> Deism

Equally important was the enlightened notion of political freedom. Both Jefferson and Franklin were intrigued by the English political philosopher John Locke (1632–1704), who maintained that "natural law"

Deism Enlightenment thought applied to religion, emphasizing reason, morality, and natural law rather than scriptural authority or an ever-present God intervening in the daily life of humans.

called for a government resting on the consent of the governed and respecting the "natural rights" of all. It was not far from such an idea to finding justification for revolution against tyrannical monarchies, like those governing Great Britain and France.

The Age of Reason in America

Benjamin Franklin epitomized the Enlightenment in the eyes of both Americans and Europeans. Born in Boston in 1706, a descendant of Puritans, Franklin left home at the age of seventeen, bound for Philadelphia. There, before he was twenty-four, he bought a print shop where he edited the *Pennsylvania Gazette*, one of the leading newspapers in the colonies. When he was twenty-six, he published *Poor Richard's Almanack*, a collection of seasonal weather forecasts, puzzles, household tips, and witty sayings about success and happiness. Before he retired from business at the age of forty-two, Franklin had founded a public library, started a fire company, helped create the academy that became the University of Pennsylvania, and organized a debating club that grew into the American Philosophical Society.

Benjamin Franklin A champion of reason, Franklin was an inventor, philosopher, entrepreneur, and statesman.

Benjamin Franklin was devoted to scientific investigation. Skeptical and curious, pragmatic and irreverent, he was an inventive genius. His wide-ranging scientific experiments ranged across the fields of medicine, meteorology, geology, astronomy, and physics, among others. He developed the Franklin stove, the lightning rod, bifocal spectacles, and a glass harmonica.

Franklin's love of science and reason clashed with prevailing Christian beliefs. Although raised as a Presbyterian, he became a Deist who prized science and reason over orthodox religion. He questioned the divinity of Jesus and the assumption that the Bible was truly the word of God. Like the European Deists, Franklin came to believe in a God that had created a universe directed by natural laws, laws that curious people could discover through the use of reason and the scientific method. For Franklin and others in the eighteenth century, to be "enlightened" meant developing the confidence and capacity to think for oneself, to think critically rather than simply accepting what tradition dictated as truth.

The Great Awakening

The growing popularity of Enlightenment rationalism posed a direct threat to traditional religious life in Europe and America. But religious faith has always shown remarkable resilience in the face of challenging new ideas. This was certainly true in the early eighteenth century, when the American colonies experienced a widespread revival of spiritual zeal designed to restore the primacy of emotion in the religious realm.

Religious response to the Enlightenment

Between 1700 and 1750, when the controversial ideas of the Enlightenment were circulating among the best educated colonists, hundreds of new Christian congregations were founded. Most Americans (85 percent) lived in colonies with an "established" church, meaning that the colonial government officially endorsed—and collected taxes to support—a single official denomination. The Church of England, also known as Anglicanism, was the "established" church in Virginia, Maryland, Delaware, and the Carolinas. Puritan Congregationalism was the official faith in New England. In New York, Anglicanism vied with the Dutch Reformed Church for control. Pennsylvania had no single state-supported church, but Quakers dominated the legislative assembly. New Jersey and Rhode Island had no official denomination and hosted numerous Christian splinter groups.

Most colonies organized religious life on the basis of well-regulated local parishes, which defined their theological boundaries and defended them against people who did not hold to the same faith. In colonies with official religions, people of other faiths could not preach without the permission of the local parish. Then, in the 1730s and 1740s, the parish system was thrown into turmoil by the arrival of outspoken traveling evangelists, called *itinerants*, who claimed that most of the local parish ministers were incompetent. In their emotionally charged sermons, the itinerants, several of whom were white women and African Americans, insisted that Christians must be "reborn" in their convictions and behavior.

During the early 1730s, a widespread sense of religious decline and the need for "rebirth" helped spark a series of emotional revivals known as the **Great Awakening**. The revivals began in the southern colonies and quickly spread up the Atlantic coast to New England. Whole towns were swept up in the ecstasy of renewed spiritual passion. Unlike the Enlightenment, which affected primarily the intellectual elite, the evangelical energies unleashed by the Great Awakening appealed mostly to the masses. As a skeptical Benjamin Franklin observed of the Awakening, "Never did the people show so great a willingness to attend sermons. Religion is become the subject of most conversation." The Awakening was the first popular movement before the American Revolution that affected all thirteen colonies, and as such it helped create ties across the colonies that would later help coordinate revolutionary activities against the British government.

> Traveling evangelists and intense revivals

In 1734–1735, a remarkable spiritual transformation occurred in the congregation of Jonathan Edwards, a prominent Congregationalist minister in the western Massachusetts town of Northampton. One of America's most brilliant philosophers and theologians, Edwards had entered Yale College in 1716, at age thirteen, and graduated at the top of his class four years later. In 1727, Edwards was named minister of the Congregational church in Northampton. He was shocked at the town's lack of religious conviction. Edwards claimed that the young people of Northampton were preoccupied with sinful pleasures; they indulged in "lewd practices" that "corrupted others." Christians had also become obsessed with making and spending money. He also warned that the rebellious new ideas associated with the Enlightenment were eroding the importance of religious life. Edwards attacked Deists

Great Awakening Emotional religious revival movement that swept the thirteen colonies from the 1720s through the 1740s.

Jonathan Edwards One of the foremost preachers of the Great Awakening.

for believing that "God has given mankind no other light to walk by but their own reason."

To counteract the secularizing forces of the Enlightenment, Edwards resolved to restore the emotional side of religion. "Our people," he said, "do not so much need to have their heads stored [with new scientific knowledge] as to have their hearts touched [with spiritual intensity]." His own vivid descriptions of the sufferings of hell and the delights of heaven helped rekindle spiritual intensity among his congregants. By 1735, Edwards could report that "the town seemed to be full of the presence of God; it never was so full of love, nor of joy." To judge the power of the religious awakening, he thought, one need only observe that "it was no longer the Tavern" that drew local crowds, "but the Minister's House."

While Jonathan Edwards was promoting a revival of religious emotion in Puritan New England, William Tennent, an Irish-born Presbyterian revivalist, was stirring souls in Pennsylvania. He and his sons charged that many of the local ministers were "cold and sapless," afraid to "thrust the nail of terror into sleeping souls." Tennent's oldest son, Gilbert, defended their aggressive (and often illegal) tactics by explaining that he and other traveling evangelists invaded parishes only when the local minister showed no interest in the "Getting of Grace and Growing in it." The Tennents caused great anxiety because they preached to those at the bottom of the social scale—farmers, laborers, sailors, and servants. By promoting a passionate piety, urging people to renounce their ministers, and attacking the luxurious excesses of the wealthiest and most powerful colonists, the radical evangelists threatened to disrupt the social order in the colonies. Competition was emerging in colonial religious life. Worried members of the colonial elite charged that the radical revivalists were spreading "anarchy, levelling, and dissolution."

The most celebrated promoter of the Great Awakening was a young English minister, George Whitefield, whose reputation as a spellbinding evangelist preceded him to the colonies. Congregations were lifeless, he claimed, "because dead men preach to them." Too many ministers were "slothful shepherds and dumb dogs." Whitefield set out to restore the fires of religious intensity in American congregations. In the autumn of 1739, the twenty-five-year-old evangelist began preaching to huge crowds across the colonies. A disgusted Bostonian described a revival meeting's theatrics: "The meeting was carried on with . . . some screaming out in Distress and Anguish . . . some again jumping up and down . . . some lying along on the floor. . . . The whole with a very great Noise, to be heard at a Mile's Distance, and continued almost the whole night." Benjamin Franklin, who went to see Whitefield preach in Philadelphia, got so carried away by the fiery sermon that he emptied his pockets into the collection plate.

Jonathan Edwards took advantage of the energies stirred up by Whitefield to spread his own revival gospel throughout New England. The Great

Jonathan Edwards: "Sinners in the Hands of an Angry God"

Awakening reached its peak in 1741 when Edwards delivered his most famous sermon, "Sinners in the Hands of an Angry God." It was designed in part to frighten people into seeking salvation. Edwards reminded the congregation that hell is real and that God "holds you over the pit of hell, much as one holds a spider, or some loathsome insect, over the fire, abhors you, and is dreadfully provoked. . . . He looks upon you as worthy of nothing else, but to be cast into the fire." When Edwards finished, he had to wait several minutes for the agitated congregants to quiet down before he led them in a closing hymn.

The Great Awakening made religion intensely personal by creating both a deep sense of spiritual guilt and a yearning for redemption. Yet while the Great Awakening saved souls, it also undermined many of the established churches by emphasizing that individuals, regardless of wealth or social status, could receive God's grace without the guidance of their local ministers. It also gave people more religious choices. During the Great Awakening, the major denominations fractured: Presbyterians divided into "Old Side" critics of revivalism and "New Side" supporters; Congregationalists into "Old Light" and "New Light" factions. Jonathan Edwards regretted the emergence of warring factions. We are "like two armies," he said, "separated and drawn up in battle array, ready to fight one another." New England religious life would never be the same.

> Challenges to established churches

Individualism and Colonial Culture

The energies of the Great Awakening subsided by 1750, but like its very different counterpart movement, the Enlightenment, it set in motion powerful currents that still flow through American life. Ministers could no longer control the direction of religious life as more and more people took charge of their own spirituality and new denominations sprouted like mushrooms. The Great Awakening implanted in American culture the evangelical impulse and the emotional appeal of revivalism. By encouraging the creation of new denominations, the Awakening heightened the need for the toleration of many religious persuasions rather than just one's own.

In some respects, however, the conflict between the emotional forces unleashed by the Awakening and the rational analyses of the Enlightenment led by different roads to similar ends. Both movements cut across all of the colonies and thereby helped bind them together. Both movements emphasized that individuals should have the freedom to take responsibility for their own lives and salvation. By urging believers to exercise their own spiritual judgment, the revivals weakened the authority of the established churches and their ministers, just as colonial resentment of British economic regulations would later weaken the colonists' loyalty to the king. As such, the Great Awakening and the Enlightenment helped nurture an American commitment to individual freedom and resistance to authority that would play a key role in the rebellion against British tyranny in 1776.

> Emerging individualism

Reviewing the
CORE OBJECTIVES | INQUIZITIVE

■ **Colonial Demographics** Cheap land lured most poor immigrants to America, and the initial shortage of women eventually gave way to a more equal gender ratio and a tendency to earlier marriage than in Europe, leading to higher *birth rates* and larger families. People also lived longer on average in the colonies than in Europe. The lower *death rates* led to rapid population growth in the colonies.

■ **Women in the Colonies** English colonists brought their traditional beliefs and prejudices with them to America, including convictions about the inferiority of women. Colonial women remained largely confined to *women's work* in the house, yard, and field. Over time, though, necessity created new opportunities for women outside their traditional roles.

■ **Colonial Differences** A thriving colonial trading economy sent raw materials such as fish, timber, and furs to England in return for manufactured goods. The expanding economy created new wealth and a rise in the consumption of European goods, and it fostered the expansion of slavery. Agriculture diversified: tobacco was the *staple crop* in Virginia, rice in the Carolinas. Plantation agriculture based on slavery became entrenched in the South. New England's prosperous shipping industry created a profitable *triangular trade* among Africa, America, and England. By 1790, German, Scots-Irish, Welsh, and Irish immigrants and other European ethnic groups had settled in the middle colonies, along with members of religious groups such as Quakers, Jews, Huguenots, and Mennonites.

■ **Race-Based Slavery** Deep-rooted color prejudice led to *race-based slavery*. Africans were considered "heathens" whose supposed inferiority entitled white Americans to use them for slaves. Diverse Africans brought skills from Africa to build America's economy. The use of African slaves was concentrated in the South, where landowners used them to produce lucrative *staple crops*, such as tobacco, rice, and indigo, but slaves lived in cities, too, especially New York. As the population of slaves increased, race relations grew more tense, and *slave codes* were created to regulate the movement and activities of enslaved people. Sporadic slave uprisings, such as the *Stono Rebellion*, occurred in both the North and South.

■ **The Enlightenment and the Great Awakening** Printing presses, higher education, and city life created a flow of new ideas that circulated via long-distance travel, tavern life, the postal service, books, and newspapers. The attitudes of the *Enlightenment* were transported along international trade routes. Sir Isaac Newton's scientific discoveries culminated in the belief that reason could improve society. Benjamin Franklin, who believed that people could shape their own destinies, became the face of the Enlightenment in America. *Deism* expressed the religious views of the Age of Reason. By contrast, during the 1730s, a revival of faith, the *Great Awakening*, swept through the colonies. New congregations formed as evangelists insisted that Christians be "reborn." Individualism, not orthodoxy, was stressed in this first popular religious movement in America's history.

KEY TERMS

birth rate *p. 81*
death rate *p. 81*
women's work *p. 81*
staple crops *p. 83*

triangular trade *p. 87*
race-based slavery *p. 91*
slave codes *p. 93*
Stono Rebellion (1739) *p. 94*

Enlightenment *p. 98*
Deism *p.99*
Great Awakening *p. 101*

CHRONOLOGY

1660s	Colonial assemblies legalize lifelong slavery
1683	German Mennonites arrive in Pennsylvania
1687	Sir Isaac Newton publishes his theory of universal gravitation
1691	South Carolina passes first slave codes; other states follow
1692	Salem witch trials
1712	Slave revolt in New York City; New York passes stricter laws governing slaves
1730	Chesapeake region's slave population achieves self-sustaining rate of population growth
1730s–1740s	The Great Awakening
1739	Stono Rebellion
1750	Colonial population passes 1 million
1775	Colonial population passes 2.5 million

INQUIZITIVE

Go to InQuizitive to see what you've learned—and learn what you've missed—with personalized feedback along the way.

BOSTON TEA PARTY Disguised as Native Americans, a swarm of Patriots seized three British ships and dumped more than three hundred chests of East India Company tea into the Boston harbor.

From Colonies to States

1607–1776

Four great naval European powers—Spain, France, Britain, and the Netherlands (Holland)—created colonies in North America during the sixteenth and seventeenth centuries as part of their larger fight for global supremacy. Throughout the eighteenth century, wars raged across Europe, mostly pitting the Catholic nations of France and Spain against Protestant Great Britain and the Netherlands, but at times the battle lines were complicated by other considerations of economics, alliances, and political opportunism. The tensions and fighting increasingly spread across the high seas to the Americas. By the middle of the eighteenth century, North America had become a primary battleground, involving both colonists and the Native Americans who were allied with different European powers.

Spain's sparsely populated settlements in the borderlands north of Mexico were small and weak compared to those in the British colonies. The Spanish in what is now the American Southwest as well as Texas and California failed to create settlements with self-sustaining economies. Instead, Spain emphasized the conversion of native peoples to Catholicism, prohibited manufacturing within its colonies, strictly limited trade with Native Americans, and searched—in vain—for gold.

The French and the British, however, developed a thriving trade with Native Americans (trade that included supplying Indians with firearms), but the fierce rivalry between the British and the French gradually shifted the

CORE
OBJECTIVES INQUIZITIVE

1. Compare how the British and French empires administered their colonies before 1763.

2. Analyze the effects of the French and Indian War and how the war changed relations among the European powers in North America.

3. Describe how, after the French and Indian War in the 1760s, the British tried to strengthen their control over the colonies and then summarize the colonial responses.

4. Explain the underlying factors amid the events in the 1770s that led the colonies to declare their independence from Britain.

balance of power in Europe. By the end of the eighteenth century, Spain would be in decline, leaving France and Great Britain to fight for supremacy. The nearly constant warfare around the globe led Great Britain to tighten its control over the American colonies in order to raise the funds needed to combat France and Spain and to fill the ranks of its military forces. Tensions over the British effort to preserve its empire at the expense of American freedoms would lead first to rebellion and eventually to revolution.

Troubled Neighbors

CORE **OBJECTIVE**

1. Compare how the British and French empires administered their colonies before 1763.

New France

The actual settlement of New France began in 1605, when the enterprising soldier-explorer Samuel de Champlain, the "Father of New France," founded Port-Royal in Acadia, along the Canadian coast. Then, three years later, Champlain established Quebec, to the west, along the St. Lawrence River (Quebec is an Algonquian word meaning "where the river narrows"). Champlain was the first European to explore and map the Great Lakes.

French fur trading companies, religious restrictions, and limited immigration

Until his death in 1635, Champlain governed New France on behalf of trading companies exploiting the fur trade with the Indians. The merchant-investors in the trading companies sponsored Champlain's voyages in hopes of creating a prosperous commercial colony. But in 1627 the French government ordered that only Catholics could live in New France. This restriction stunted its growth—as did the harsh winter climate. As a consequence, the number of French who colonized Canada was *much* smaller than the number of British, Dutch, and Spanish colonists in other North American colonies, and they were almost all men.

Coureurs des bois

Champlain knew that the greatly outnumbered French could survive only by befriending the native peoples. To that end, he dispatched young French trappers and traders to live with the indigenous peoples, learn their languages and customs, marry native women, and serve as ambassadors of New France. These hardy woodsmen, called *coureurs des bois* (runners of the woods) pushed into the forested regions around the Great Lakes and developed a thriving fur trade with the native peoples.

Royal control

In 1663, French king Louis XIV changed struggling New France into a royal colony led by a governor-general who managed an administrative structure modeled after that of the monarchy in France. New France was fully subject to the French king. The colonists had no political rights or representative government, and public meetings could not be held without official permission. Louis dispatched soldiers and new settlers, including shiploads of young women, known as the King's Daughters, to provide wives for the mostly male colonists. The king also awarded large grants of land, called *seigneuries*, as a lure to aristocratic settlers. The poorest farmers usually rented land from the *seigneur*.

THE FRENCH IN NORTH AMERICA

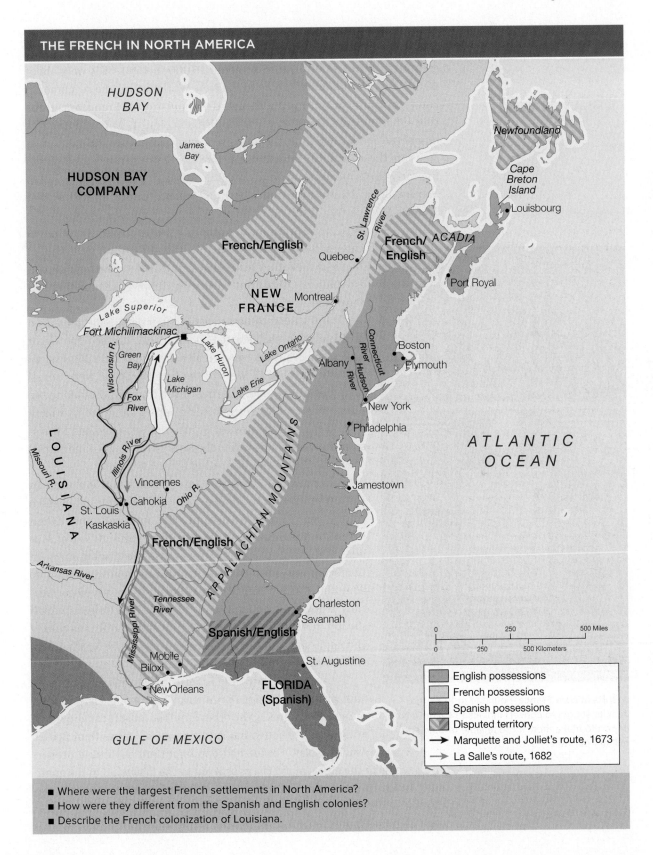

- Where were the largest French settlements in North America?
- How were they different from the Spanish and English colonies?
- Describe the French colonization of Louisiana.

But none of these efforts worked to transform New France from being essentially a fur trading outpost. The tiny French population of New France grew from about 4,000 in 1665 to about 15,000 in 1690. Still, only about 40,000 French immigrants came to the New World during the seventeenth and eighteenth centuries, even though the population of France was three times that of Spain. By 1750, when the British colonists in North America numbered about 1.5 million, the total French population was 70,000.

From their Canadian outposts along the Great Lakes, French explorers in the early 1670s moved southward down the Mississippi River to the Gulf of Mexico. Louis Jolliet, a fur trader born in Quebec, teamed up with Father Jacques Marquette, a Jesuit priest fluent in Indian languages, to explore the Wisconsin River south to the Mississippi River. Traveling in canoes, they paddled south to within 400 miles of the Gulf of Mexico, where they turned back for fear of encountering Spanish soldiers. Other French explorers followed their pathbreaking expedition.

In 1682, René-Robert Cavelier, sieur de La Salle, organized an expedition that started in Montreal, crossed the Great Lakes, and eventually made it all the way down the Mississippi River to the Gulf of Mexico, the first European to do so. La Salle hoped to create a string of fur trading posts along the entire length of the river. While stopping along the riverbank in Arkansas, he claimed for France the vast Ohio and Mississippi Valleys—all the way to the Rocky Mountains—and named the region Louisiana, after King Louis XIV.

Settlement of the Louisiana territory finally began in 1699, when Pierre Le Moyne, sieur d'Iberville, established a colony near Biloxi, Mississippi. The main settlement then moved to Mobile Bay and, in 1710, to the present site of Mobile, Alabama. For nearly fifty years, the driving force in Louisiana was Jean-Baptiste Le Moyne, sieur de Bienville. Sometimes called the Father of Louisiana, he served periodically as governor, and in 1718 he founded New Orleans, which shortly thereafter became the capital of the Louisiana colony encompassing much of the interior of the entire North American continent.

Jesuits in New France Founded in 1539, the Jesuits sought to convert Indians to Catholicism, in part to make them more reliable trading and military partners.

Two centuries later, the American historian Francis Parkman wrote that "France in America had two heads, one amid the snows of Canada, the other amid the [sugar] canebrakes of Louisiana." Although having far fewer colonists than British America, New France had one important advantage over its rival: access to the great inland rivers that led to the heartland of the continent. In the Illinois region, scattered French settlers began farming the fertile soil, while Jesuits established missions to convert the Indians at places such as Terre Haute ("High Land," in what is now Indiana) and Des Moines

("Of the Monks," in present-day Iowa—the name probably shortened from Rivière des Moines, or "River of the Monks"). Because of geography as well as deliberate policy, however, New France remained during the eighteenth century a vast wilderness traversed by a mobile population of traders, trappers, missionaries, and mainly Indians. By building closer bonds and encroaching far less upon Native American lands, the French won Native American allies against the more numerous British Americans. For well over a century, in fact, Native Americans would determine the military balance of power within North America.

> Native American allies

The British System

The British colonies in North America were quite different from those of New France. Within the more diverse British colonies, governments typically included a governor and a legislative assembly. As chief executives, the governors of each colony were appointed by the king. Few of the royal governors were especially gifted administrators, but they could appoint and remove officials, command the militia, and grant pardons to people convicted of crimes.

However, the American colonists enjoyed some rights and powers absent in Britain—as well as in New France. The British colonies in America, unlike the Spanish, French, or Dutch colonies, had *elected* legislative assemblies. Whether called the House of Burgesses (Virginia), the House of Delegates (Maryland), or the House of Representatives (Massachusetts) or simply the Assembly, the "lower" houses in each colony were chosen by popular vote. Not all colonists could vote, however. Only adult males owning a specified amount of property could vote. Women, Native Americans, and African Americans were excluded from the political process. But because property holding was widespread in America, a greater proportion of the male population could vote in the colonies than anywhere else in the world.

> Elected legislative assemblies

The most important political trend in eighteenth-century America was the growing power of the colonial legislatures. Like Parliament, the colonial assemblies controlled the budget, and they could pass laws and regulations. Most of the colonial assemblies also influenced the royal governors by controlling their salaries. Throughout the eighteenth century, the assemblies expanded their power and influence relative to the royal governors. Unlike the situation in New France, where the governor-general exercised almost absolute power and there were no legislative assemblies and an absence of ethnic and religious diversity, self-government in British America became first a habit, then a cherished "right."

Mercantilism

Throughout much of the seventeenth and eighteenth centuries, British officials exercised what one politician called a **salutary neglect** by not strictly enforcing the laws regulating the American colonies, especially those

salutary neglect Informal British policy during the first half of the eighteenth century that allowed the American colonies freedom to pursue their economic and political interests in exchange for colonial obedience.

involving trade restrictions. Smuggling was commonplace, a way to escape paying taxes on goods imported from other countries. The perpetual struggle between Parliament and the British kings made it difficult to develop either consistent colonial policies around the world or to create effective means of enforcing such policies. The English Civil War (1642–1646) sharply reduced the flow of money and people from Britain to America and created great confusion regarding Britain's colonial policies.

> From salutary neglect to mercantilism

The 1651 victory of Oliver Cromwell's Puritan army over Royalist forces in the English Civil War had direct effects in the colonies. As Britain's new ruler, Cromwell ended the tradition of "salutary neglect" in favor of **mercantilism**, a political and economic policy adopted by most of the European monarchs during the seventeenth century. In a mercantile system, the government would take control of all economic activities. Key industries were regulated, taxed, or "subsidized" (supported by payments from the government). People with specialized skills or knowledge of new industrial technologies, such as textile machinery, were not allowed to leave the country.

Mercantilism also supported the creation of global empires. Colonies, it was assumed, enriched their founding nation in several ways: (1) by providing silver and gold as well as the raw materials (furs, fish, grains, timber, sugar, tobacco, indigo, tar, etc.) needed to supply food and produce goods; (2) by creating a captive market of colonial consumers who would be forced to buy goods created in the home country; (3) by relieving social tensions and political unrest in the home country, because colonies could provide a new home for the growing numbers of poor, unemployed, and imprisoned; and (4) by prohibiting its colonies from producing goods that would compete with manufacturers in the "mother country."

Navigation Acts

Such mercantilist assumptions prompted Oliver Cromwell to adopt the first in a series of **Navigation Acts** intended to increase Britain's colonial revenues. The Navigation Act of 1651 required that all goods imported to or exported from Britain be carried *only* in ships built in Britain and owned by Britons. The law was intended to hurt the rival Dutch—but because the Dutch controlled New Netherland (New York, West and East Jersey, and Delaware) and because the law applied not only to Britain but also to Britain's American colonies, the Navigation Act of 1651 thus had tremendous effect in North America. American merchants resented such a regulation because the Dutch shippers charged much less to transport American goods than the British. By 1652, Britain and the Netherlands were at war, the first of three naval conflicts that erupted between 1652 and 1674 as a result of the intense economic competition between the two Protestant European rivals.

After the British monarchy was restored in 1660, the new royalist Parliament passed the Navigation Act of 1660, which specified that certain colonial products such as tobacco were to be shipped *only* to Britain or to other

mercantilism Policy of Great Britain and other imperial powers of regulating colonial economies to benefit the mother country.

Navigation Acts (1650–1775) Restrictions passed by the British Parliament to control colonial trade and bolster the mercantile system.

British colonies, not European nations. The Navigation Act of 1663, also known as the Staples Act, required that *all* shipments of goods from Europe to America stop first in Britain, be offloaded, and be taxed before their reshipment to the colonies.

In 1664, a British fleet of warships conquered New Netherland, removing the Dutch rival from North America. Over time, the Navigation Acts worked as planned: by 1700, the British had surpassed the Dutch as the world's leading maritime power. Virtually all of the products sent to and from America from Europe and Africa were carried in British ships. What the British government did not predict or fully understand was that the mercantile system would arouse growing resentment in the colonies.

Navigation Acts target Dutch

Resentment in the British Colonies

Colonial merchants and shippers loudly complained about the Navigation Acts. New England, which shipped 90 percent of all American exports, was particularly hard hit. In 1678, a defiant Massachusetts legislature declared that the Navigation Acts had no legal standing in the colony. Six years later, in 1684, King Charles II tried to teach the rebellious colonists a lesson by revoking the royal charter for Massachusetts.

The following year, in 1685, King Charles II died and was succeeded by his brother, the Duke of York, now crowned King James II. The new king reorganized all of the New England colonies into a single royal colony called the Dominion of New England. In 1686, the newly appointed royal governor, Sir Edmund Andros, arrived in Boston to take control. Andros imposed new taxes as well as the Anglican religion, ignored the authority of town governments, strictly enforced the Navigation Acts, and punished American smugglers who tried to avoid regulation altogether.

Dominion of New England

The Glorious Revolution

In 1688, the Dominion of New England added the former Dutch provinces of New York, East Jersey, and West Jersey to its control, just a few months before the **Glorious Revolution** erupted in Britain in December. When news reached Boston that the Catholic King James II had been forced to flee to France and that he would be replaced by his Protestant daughter Mary and her Protestant husband William III (the ruling Dutch Prince) as the new king and queen of Great Britain, Boston staged its own revolution. A group of merchants, ministers, and militiamen (citizen-soldiers) arrested Governor Andros and his aides and removed Massachusetts Bay Colony from the new Dominion. Within a few weeks, the other colonies that had been absorbed into the Dominion also restored their independence.

William and Mary, the new British monarchs, allowed all of the colonies to regain their former status except Massachusetts Bay and Plymouth, which after some delay were united under a new charter in 1691 as the royal colony of Massachusetts Bay. But William and Mary were also determined to crack

Glorious Revolution (1688) Successful coup, instigated by a group of English aristocrats, that overthrew King James II and instated William of Orange and Mary, his English wife, to the British throne.

down on American smuggling and rebelliousness. They appointed new royal governors in Massachusetts, New York, and Maryland. In Massachusetts, the new governor was given authority to veto acts of the colonial assembly, and he removed the Puritans' religious qualification for voting.

> Natural rights vs. royal absolutism

The Glorious Revolution in Britain had significant long-term effects on American history in that the removal of King James II revealed that a hated monarch could be deposed. (The revolution was called "Glorious" because it took place with very little bloodshed, unlike the English Civil War a generation earlier; indeed, the long-standing geographical designation "Great Britain" for the island shared by England, Scotland, and Wales would soon be revived as the official name of the nation.) A powerful justification for revolution appeared in 1690 when the English philosopher John Locke published his *Two Treatises on Government*, which had an enormous impact on political thought in the colonies. Locke rejected the "divine" right of monarchs to govern with absolute power. He also insisted that people are endowed with **natural rights** to life, liberty, and property. After all, as Locke noted, it was the need to protect those "natural" rights that led people to establish governments in the first place. When rulers failed to protect the property and lives of their subjects, Locke argued, the people had the right—in extreme cases—to overthrow the monarch and change the government.

Warfare in the Colonies

> CORE **OBJECTIVE**
>
> **2.** Analyze the effects of the French and Indian War and how the war changed relations among the European powers in North America.

The Glorious Revolution of 1688 transformed relations among the great powers of Europe. The Protestant William and Mary, the new British King and Queen, were passionate foes of Catholic France's Louis XIV. The new king William organized an alliance of European nations against the French in a transatlantic war known in the American colonies as King William's War (1689–1697). It was the first of four major wars fought in Europe and the colonies over the next seventy-four years. In each case, Britain and its European allies fought against Catholic France or Spain and their allies. By the end of the eighteenth century, the struggle between the British and the French would shift the balance of power in Europe.

The French and Indian War

natural rights An individual's basic rights (life, liberty, and happiness) that should not be violated by any government or community.

By far, the most significant conflict between Britain and France in North America was the French and Indian War (1754–1763). Unlike the three previous wars between Britain and France and their allies, it ended with a decisive victory. Sparked by competing claims over the Indian lands in the vast Ohio Valley, the "most fertile country of America," the stakes were high. Both the British and the French governments believed that whoever controlled the "Ohio Country" would come to control the entire continent.

MAJOR CAMPAIGNS OF THE FRENCH AND INDIAN WAR

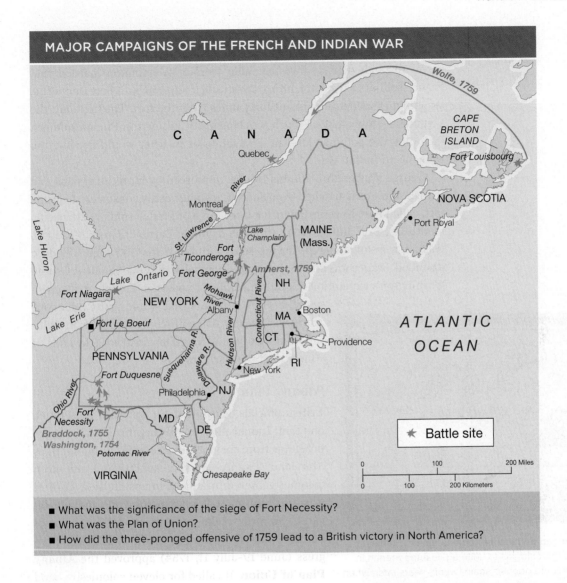

- What was the significance of the siege of Fort Necessity?
- What was the Plan of Union?
- How did the three-pronged offensive of 1759 lead to a British victory in North America?

To defend their interests in the Ohio Valley, the French pushed south from Canada and built forts in upstate New York and western Pennsylvania. When the Virginia governor learned of the French forts, he sent a twenty-one-year-old Virginia militia officer, Major George Washington, to warn the French to leave the area. With an experienced guide and a few others, Washington made his way on foot and by horseback, canoe, and raft over 450 miles to Fort Le Boeuf (just south of Lake Erie, in northwest Pennsylvania) in late 1753. He demanded that the French withdraw from the Ohio Country; the French captain refused. A frustrated George Washington returned to Virginia through the deepening snow. A few months later, in the spring of 1754, George Washington went back to the Ohio Country. This time he led 150 inexperienced volunteer soldiers and Indian allies to build a fort where the Allegheny, Monongahela, and Ohio Rivers converged (where the city of Pittsburgh later developed). After two months of difficult travel through densely-forested, hilly terrain, Washington learned that French soldiers had beaten him to the strategic site and built Fort Duquesne. Washington made camp about forty miles from the fort. The next day, the Virginians ambushed a French scouting party, killing ten French soldiers, including the commander—the first fatalities in what would become the French and Indian War.

George Washington and his troops, reinforced by more Virginians and British soldiers dispatched from South Carolina, hastily constructed a crude fort, called Fort Necessity, which a large force of French soldiers attacked a month later, on July 3, 1754. After the day-long Battle of Great Meadows, Washington surrendered, having seen a third of his 300 men killed or wounded. France was now in undisputed control of the Ohio Country. George Washington's expedition not only had failed to oust the French; it also triggered a series of events that would ignite a massive world war. As a British politician exclaimed, "the volley fired by a young Virginian in the backwoods of America set the world on fire."

Albany Plan

British officials, worried about war with the French and their Indian allies, hastily organized a meeting of delegates from the northern colonies as far south as Maryland. Twenty-one representatives from seven colonies gathered in Albany, in upstate New York. It was the first time that a large group of colonial delegates had met to take joint action. At the urging of Pennsylvania's Benjamin Franklin, the Albany Con-

The first American political cartoon Benjamin Franklin's exhortation to the colonies to unite against the French in 1754 would become popular again twenty years later, when the colonies faced a different threat.

Albany Plan of Union (1754)
A failed proposal by the seven northern colonies in anticipation of the French and Indian War, urging the unification of the colonies under one Crown-appointed president.

gress (June 19–July 11, 1754) ... the **Albany** ... s to band ... the king.

Each colonial as ... and council," which woul ... risdiction over Indian affa ...

But the Alba ... e colonial legislatures, eag ... o wanted simply a milita ... Benjamin Franklin later m ... adopted, may have postp ... e colonial revolution.

With the fai ... ecided to force a showdo ... erica. In June 1755, a Br ... Acadia, a colony of New ... tish then

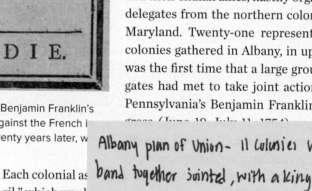

[Handwritten note:] Albany plan of Union— 11 Colonies Would band together jointed, with a king appointed by the king. Would create legislature regarding native american affairs.

— Was too radical, British officials resented it, colonial powers wanted to maintain their own legislative powers.

expelled 11,500 of the Catholic French residents, called Acadians. They were put on ships and scattered throughout the British colonies, from Maine to Georgia. Hundreds uprooted by the "Great Expulsion" eventually found their way to French Louisiana, where they became known as Cajuns (the name derived from *Acadians*).

Braddock's Defeat

In 1755, the British government also sent a thousand soldiers to Virginia to force the French out of the Ohio Country. The British commander, General Edward Braddock, was a stubborn, overconfident officer who had no experience fighting in the American wilderness. Braddock viewed Native Americans with contempt, and his ignorance of Indian warfare would prove fatal. With the addition of some American militiamen, including George Washington as a volunteer officer, Braddock's force hacked a 125-mile-long road west through the rugged Allegheny Mountains toward Fort Duquesne. The British were on the verge of success when, on July 9, 1755, six miles from Fort Duquesne, they were ambushed by French soldiers and Indians. Attacked on three sides, the British troops suffered horrific losses. General Braddock died from his wounds. Twenty-three-year-old George Washington, his coat riddled by four bullets, helped other officers lead a hasty retreat.

The French and Indians had killed 63 of 86 British officers, 914 out of 1,373 soldiers, and captured the British cannons, supplies, and secret papers. It was one of the worst British defeats in history. Twelve of the wounded British soldiers left behind on the battlefield were stripped and burned alive by Indians. A devastated George Washington wrote his brother that the British army had "been scandalously beaten by a trifling body of men." The vaunted redcoats "broke & run as sheep before hounds," but the Virginians "behaved like Men and died like Soldiers."

From La Roque's *Encyclopédie des Voyages* An Iroquois warrior in an eighteenth-century French engraving.

A World War

Braddock's stunning defeat sent shock waves through the colonies. Inspired by the news, Indians allied with the French attacked American families living on isolated farms throughout western Pennsylvania, Maryland, and Virginia. It was not until May 1756, however, that Britain and France formally declared war; the **French and Indian War** in America would become known as the Seven Years' War in Europe. A worldwide war between the Protestant and Catholic nations, it would eventually be fought on four continents and three oceans around the globe. In the end, it would redraw the map of the world.

In 1759, the French and Indian War reached its climax with a series of British triumphs on land and at sea around the world. The most decisive British victory was at Quebec, the gateway to French Canada. Thereafter, the war in North America dragged on until 1763. In the South, fighting flared up between the Carolina settlers and the Cherokee Nation. A force of British regulars and colonial militia broke Cherokee resistance in 1761.

The French and Indian War becomes the Seven Years' War

French and Indian War (Seven Years' War) (1756–1763) The last and most important of four colonial wars between England and France for control of North America east of the Mississippi River.

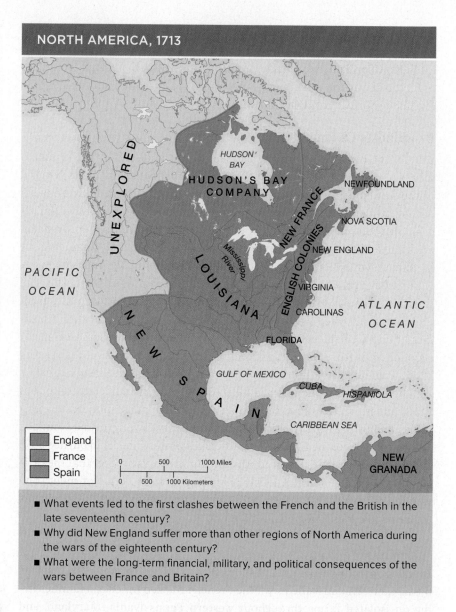

NORTH AMERICA, 1713

UNEXPLORED

HUDSON BAY

HUDSON'S BAY COMPANY

NEWFOUNDLAND

NEW FRANCE

NOVA SCOTIA

NEW ENGLAND

ENGLISH COLONIES

Mississippi River

LOUISIANA

VIRGINIA

PACIFIC OCEAN

CAROLINAS

ATLANTIC OCEAN

NEW SPAIN

FLORIDA

GULF OF MEXICO

CUBA

HISPANIOLA

CARIBBEAN SEA

NEW GRANADA

England
France
Spain

0   500   1000 Miles
0 500 1000 Kilometers

- What events led to the first clashes between the French and the British in the late seventeenth century?
- Why did New England suffer more than other regions of North America during the wars of the eighteenth century?
- What were the long-term financial, military, and political consequences of the wars between France and Britain?

George III The young king of a victorious empire.

Meanwhile, the much larger Seven Years' War played out around the globe, with skirmishes in South America, Africa, India, and the Philippines in addition to British gains in North America. Most of the fighting, though, was in Europe, where Great Britain's allies, especially Prussia, and the nations allied with France and Spain, primarily Austria, Sweden, and Russia, ravaged each other. Hundreds of towns and cities were plundered and destroyed and over a million people killed.

On October 25, 1760, King George II arose at 6 A.M., as was his habit, then drank his morning chocolate milk, and suddenly, unexpectedly, died on his toilet. His death shocked the nation, in part because the new twenty-two-year-old king, George III, was inexperienced and despised by his grandfather, George II. The boyish king turned into a strong-willed leader. He

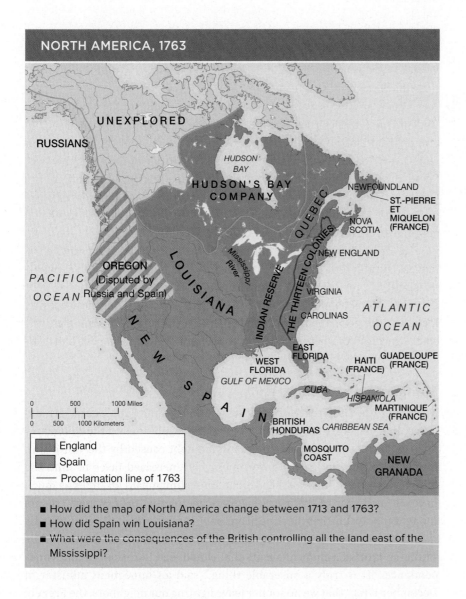

NORTH AMERICA, 1763

UNEXPLORED

RUSSIANS

HUDSON BAY

HUDSON'S BAY COMPANY

NEWFOUNDLAND

ST.-PIERRE ET MIQUELON (FRANCE)

QUEBEC

NOVA SCOTIA

NEW ENGLAND

Mississippi River

OREGON (Disputed by Russia and Spain)

PACIFIC OCEAN

LOUISIANA

INDIAN RESERVE

THE THIRTEEN COLONIES

VIRGINIA

ATLANTIC OCEAN

CAROLINAS

N E W   S P A I N

EAST FLORIDA

WEST FLORIDA

GULF OF MEXICO

HAITI (FRANCE)

GUADELOUPE (FRANCE)

CUBA

HISPANIOLA

MARTINIQUE (FRANCE)

BRITISH HONDURAS

CARIBBEAN SEA

MOSQUITO COAST

NEW GRANADA

| 0 | 500 | 1000 Miles |
| 0 | 500 | 1000 Kilometers |

■ England
■ Spain
— Proclamation line of 1763

■ How did the map of North America change between 1713 and 1763?
■ How did Spain win Louisiana?
■ What were the consequences of the British controlling all the land east of the Mississippi?

oversaw the military defeat of France and Spain, which made Great Britain the ruler of an enormous world empire and a united kingdom brimming with confidence and pride. Within three years of George III's ascension to the throne, Britain became the largest, richest, and most powerful empire in the world. And the American colonists celebrated the great British victories with as much excitement and pride as did the British themselves.

The Treaty of Paris (1763)

More territory was transferred from the vanquished to the victors as a result of the French and Indian War than any other war before or since. In the **Treaty of Paris**, signed in February 1763, victorious Britain took several profitable French "sugar island" colonies in the West Indies, most of the French colonies in India, and all of France's North American possessions east of the Mississippi River: all of Canada and all of what was then called

Treaty of Paris (1763) Settlement between Great Britain and France that ended the French and Indian War.

Spanish Florida (including much of present-day Alabama and Mississippi). The hugely profitable fur trade that the French had developed with the Indians was now transferred to the British, as were the rich fishing grounds off the Atlantic coast of Canada.

> The British gain most of North America; the Spanish gain the Louisiana Territory

British Americans were delighted with the outcome of the war. As a New England minister declared, Great Britain had reached the "summit of earthly grandeur and glory." The British now controlled most of the continent of North America. In compensation for its loss of Florida in the Treaty of Paris, Spain received from France the vast Louisiana Territory (including New Orleans and all French land west of the Mississippi River). The loss of Louisiana left France with no territory on the continent. British power reigned supreme over North America east of the Mississippi River.

But Britain's spectacular military success also created massive challenges. Humiliated France thirsted for revenge; a new war was a constant possibility. The British victory was also costly; Britain's national debt doubled during the war. The cost of maintaining the North American empire, including the permanent stationing of British soldiers in the colonies, was staggering. And the victory meant that Britain now had to manage half a *billion* acres of new colonial territory in North America.

Managing a New Empire

> Colonists taxed to pay staggering British debts

No sooner was the Treaty of Paris signed than young King George III and his cabinet began strictly enforcing economic regulations on the colonies as a means of reducing the crushing national debt caused by the world war. During the war, the British government had increased taxes to fund the military expenses. In 1763, the average Englishman paid 26 times as much in taxes each year as the average American colonist paid. British leaders thought it only fair that the Americans should pay more of the expenses for maintaining and defending the colonies. Many Americans disagreed, thus setting in motion a chain of events that would lead to revolution and independence. "It is truly a miserable thing," said a Connecticut minister in December 1763, "that we no sooner leave fighting our neighbors, the French, but we must fall to quarreling among ourselves."

Pontiac's Rebellion (1763)
A series of Native American attacks on British forts and settlements after France ceded to the British its territory east of the Mississippi River, as part of the Treaty of Paris without consulting France's Native American allies.

Royal Proclamation of 1763
Proclamation drawing a boundary along the Appalachian Mountains from Canada to Georgia in order to minimize occurrences of settler–Native American violence; colonists were forbidden to go west of the line.

Pontiac's Rebellion

From the beginning, the colonists in America had always pushed westward, and the lust for new lands only increased after 1763. Tens of thousands of European immigrants arrived each year, lured by promises of free land, low taxes, and religious freedom. No sooner had the war with France ended than colonists began squabbling over Indian-owned land west of the Appalachian Mountains that the French had ceded to the victorious British in the Treaty of Paris. Native American leaders, none of whom attended the meetings leading to the Treaty of Paris in 1763, were shocked to learn that the French had "given" their lands to the British. They demanded to know "by what right the French could pretend" to transfer Native American lands to the British.

In a desperate effort to recover their lands, Indians fought back in the spring of 1763, capturing most of the British forts around the Great Lakes and in the Ohio Valley. They also raided colonial settlements in Pennsylvania, Maryland, and Virginia, destroying hundreds of farm cabins and killing several thousand people.

The widespread Indian attacks in the spring and summer of 1763 came to be called **Pontiac's Rebellion** because of the prominent role played by the inspiring Ottawa chief. The British government eventually negotiated an agreement with the Indians that allowed British troops to reoccupy the frontier forts in exchange for a renewal of the fur trade. Still, as Chief Pontiac stressed, the Indians denied British claims to their territory under the terms of the Treaty of Paris. He told a British official that the "French never conquered us, neither did they purchase a foot of our Country, nor have they a right to give it to you."

To help keep peace with the Indians, King George III issued the **Royal Proclamation of 1763**, which drew an imaginary "proclamation line" along the crest of the Appalachian Mountains from Canada in the north to Georgia in the south. White settlers ("our loving subjects") were forbidden to go west of the line in order to ensure that the Indians would not be "molested or disturbed" on their ancestral lands. For the first time, American territorial expansion was to be curtailed by royal officials. The British government sent 10,000 soldiers to enforce the new boundary line separating Indians and whites and to ensure that the former French colonists in Canada did not cause trouble. Yet in practice the Proclamation Line was impossible to enforce. Land-hungry settlers defied its boundaries and continued to push across the Appalachian ridges into Indian country. By 1767, an Indian chief was complaining that whites were "making more encroachments on their Country than ever they had before."

Tightening Control over the Colonies

CORE **OBJECTIVE**

3. Describe how, after the French and Indian War in the 1760s, the British tried to strengthen their control over the colonies and then summarize the colonial responses.

The Royal Proclamation of 1763 was the first of several efforts by the British government after the French and Indian War to increase control over the colonies. Little did the king and his ministers know that their efforts would spark a revolution.

Grenville's Colonial Policy

New taxes and regulations

Just as the Proclamation of 1763 was being drafted, a new British government led by George Grenville began to grapple with the huge debts the government had accumulated during the war—and the added expenses of maintaining large numbers of British troops in America. George Grenville's colonial policy declared that the Americans, whom he called the "least taxed

The Road to the American Revolution

The French and Indian War (1754–1763) redrew the map of the world. It was sparked by competing claims over the Native American lands in the vast Ohio Valley. The military defeat of France and Spain made Great Britain the ruler of an enormous world empire. American colonists celebrated the British victories with as much excitement and pride as did the British themselves. The British victory gave them control of most of the North American continent, although Native Americans still claimed most of it as their own. The following timeline highlights important features in the British government's attempts to manage its empire in North America after the French and Indian War, leading up to the American Revolution.

1763 Treaty of Paris; Royal Proclamation Line

- In the Treaty of Paris, Britain acquires all of France's North American possessions east of the Mississippi River, as well as Spanish Florida (Florida, Alabama, and Mississippi), but Native Americans refuse to recognize the Treaty and fight for their lands.

- King George III ends fighting with Native Americans and issues the Royal Proclamation of 1763 to prevent American colonists from settling west of the Appalachian Mountains; colonists ignore the Proclamation.

1764 American Revenue Act (Sugar Act); Currency Act

- Sugar Act cuts the import tax on molasses in an attempt to deter colonial distillers from smuggling molasses from the French, but also imposes new import duties on textiles, wine, coffee, indigo, and sugar in order to raise new revenue from the colonists.

- Currency Act prohibits colonies from printing more paper money in order to ensure the payment of colonial debt to British merchants in gold and silver coins.

1765 Stamp Act; Quartering Act

- Stamp Act orders colonists to pay a tax on all printed materials.

- Quartering Act requires colonies to feed and house British troops.

1766 Boycotts, Protests; Stamp Act Repealed; Declaratory Act

- A humiliated Parliament repeals the Stamp Act after widespread colonial protests and boycotts of British goods but issues the Declaratory Act announcing that it has authority to pass any law regulating the colonies.

1767 Townshend Acts; Revenue Act

- Townshend Acts shut down the New York colonial assembly in retaliation for its defiance of the Quartering Act (the assembly quickly yields).

- A new Revenue Act imposes taxes on the colonies' glass, lead, paint, paper, and tea imports.

British warships target American smugglers

people in the world," must pay for the British troops defending them. Grenville also resented the large number of American smugglers who avoided paying taxes on imported goods. Americans after the war went on a buying binge, eager to purchase the latest fashionable items from Britain and France, and they preferred buying from smugglers—it was cheaper. So Grenville ordered colonial officials to tighten the enforcement of the Navigation Acts, and he sent warships to capture American smugglers.

Revenue Act repealed; Boston Massacre

- Parliament repeals all taxes imposed by the Revenue Act except for that on tea.
- Tensions with British troops spark the Boston Massacre.

Tea Act

- Parliament, in an effort to bail out the British East India Company, passes the Tea Act, which allows the company to sell its tea to the colonists without paying any taxes.

Boston Tea Party; Coercive Acts

- Bostonians defy the Tea Act by destroying the British East India Company's tea at the Boston Tea Party.
- Parliament passes the Coercive Acts, which close the port of Boston, direct local authorities to house and feed British troops, repeal the right of Massachusetts colonists to elect many civic officials, and ban all town meetings held without the Royal Governor's permission.

Continental Congress; Conciliatory Proposition; Continental Army; Olive Branch Petition

- The First Continental Congress meets to oppose the Coercive Acts and to assert the colonies' autonomy from Parliament.
- In response, British prime minister sends to each colony a Conciliatory Proposition to eliminate all of Parliament's revenue-generating schemes in any colony that volunteers to pay its share for the defense and governance of the colony.

- British soldiers clash with Massachusetts Minutemen at Lexington and Concord in Massachusetts.
- The Second Continental Congress appoints George Washington to lead a new Continental army.
- While suffering terrible losses, British forces defeat Americans at the Battle of Bunker Hill outside of Boston.
- King George III rejects the Continental Congress's Olive Branch Petition urging reconciliation.

Declaration of Independence

- The Continental Congress authorizes all thirteen colonies to form independent state governments.
- The Continental Congress adopts the Declaration of Independence.

QUESTIONS FOR ANALYSIS

1. How did British citizens in Britain and in the American colonies respond differently to the British Empire's acquisition of Native American lands after the Treaty of Paris?

2. What were the overall goals of Britain's colonial policy after the French and Indian War?

3. How did British policy change in response to the colonists' opposition?

4. Judging from this timeline, were there opportunities for a compromise between the British and American colonists before the colonists' declaration of independence?

The Sugar Act

Grenville realized that his new effort to enforce the often-violated Molasses Act of 1733 posed a serious threat to New England's prosperity. Making rum in New England out of molasses, a sweet syrup made from sugarcane was quite profitable, especially if the molasses could be smuggled in from Caribbean islands controlled by the French. The tax on molasses, therefore, was not mainly intended to raise revenue for the British government but to force New England rum producers to buy molasses from the British islands in the Caribbean rather than from the French. To ease the burden of the tax on imported molasses, Grenville put through the American Revenue Act of 1764, commonly known as the Sugar Act, which cut the tax on molasses in half. Doing so, he believed, would reduce the temptation to smuggle molasses or to bribe royal customs officers. But the Sugar Act contained a catch: it also added new duties (taxes) on other goods (sugar, wines, coffee, spices) imported into America. The new revenues generated by the Sugar Act, Grenville estimated, would help pay for "the necessary expenses of defending, protecting, and securing, the said colonies and plantations."

The Sugar Act raised the stakes over British regulations in the colonies. For the first time, Parliament had adopted so-called external duties (taxes) designed to raise *revenues* from the colonies and not merely intended to *regulate* trade with other nations. As such, it was viewed as violating a basic British principle by taxing the colonists without their consent, since the colonies had no representatives in Parliament.

The Currency Act

Another of Grenville's new regulatory measures, the Currency Act of 1764, was equally hated in the colonies. It prohibited the colonies from printing more paper money, and stipulated that all payments for British goods must be in gold or silver coins or a commodity like tobacco. This caused the value of existing paper money to plummet and dried up much of American commerce. As a Philadelphia newspaper noted, "The Times are Dreadful, Dismal, Doleful, Dolorous, and DOLLAR-LESS."

The Quartering Act

Then, in 1765, Grenville persuaded Parliament to pass the Quartering Act as part of his new system of colonial regulations. The Quartering Act required the colonies to feed and house British troops. Such a step seemed perfectly appropriate to Grenville, since he and many others in Britain believed that the Americans should contribute to the expense of defending the colonies. In the view of many Americans, however, the Quartering Act was yet another form of tax as well as another form of repression. Many Americans saw no need for so many British soldiers in colonial cities. If the British were there to defend against Indians, why weren't they positioned closer to the Indians? Some colonists decided that the Quartering Act was actually an effort to use British soldiers to bully the Americans.

The Stamp Act

Britain's prime minister, George Grenville, excelled at doing the wrong thing—repeatedly. The Sugar Act, for example, did not produce more revenue for Great Britain; the cost of enforcing it, in fact, was four times greater than the additional revenue it generated. Yet Grenville worsened the situation by pushing through an even more controversial measure to raise money in America: a stamp tax. On February 13, 1765, Parliament passed the **Stamp Act**, which created special paper with tax stamps embossed on it. The colonists would have to purchase stamped paper for virtually every possible use: newspapers, pamphlets, bonds, leases, deeds, licenses, insurance policies, college diplomas, even playing cards. The requirement was to go into effect November 1, nine months later. The Stamp Act was especially important because it affected all the colonists, not just New England merchants and shippers, and it was the first effort by Parliament to place a direct—or "internal"—tax specifically on American goods and services rather than an "external" tax on imports and exports.

The Whig Point of View

Grenville's colonial policies outraged many Americans. Unwittingly, the prime minister had stirred up a storm of protest and set in motion a violent debate about the proper relationship between Great Britain and her American colonies. Slowly, more and more colonists began developing what could be called an American rather than a British point of view. It was not based on a common ancestry, a shared religion, or even a common culture. Rather, the American perspective involved taking for granted certain essential principles and practices: self-government, equality of economic opportunity, religious freedom, and territorial expansion. Now, all of those deeply embedded values seemed threatened by Parliament's determined efforts to tighten control over its colonies after 1763. In the late eighteenth century, the Americans who opposed British policies began to call themselves Whigs, a name earlier applied to British critics of royal power, and to label the king and his "corrupt" government ministers and Parliamentary supporters as "Tories," a word meaning friends of the king.

In 1764 and 1765, American Whigs decided that Grenville was violating their rights in several ways. A professional army was usually a weapon used by tyrants, and now, with the French defeated and Canada solidly under British control, thousands of British soldiers remained in the colonies. Were the troops there to protect the colonists or to scare them into obedience?

Other factors heightened colonial fears. British citizens had the right to be taxed only by their elected representatives in Parliament, but Americans had no such representatives. British leaders countered that the colonists were "virtually" represented in Parliament, whose members were sworn to represent not simply their own districts but Britons everywhere. After all, Grenville and other British authorities argued, Americans were like many individuals and groups in Britain that had no voice in elections to Parliament because of high property qualifications for voting. They were instead

> Virtual representation

Stamp Act (1765) Act of Parliament requiring that all printed materials in the American colonies use paper with an official tax stamp in order to pay for British military protection of the colonies.

provided with **virtual representation** by all of the members of Parliament acting in the national interest.

William Pitt, a staunch supporter of American rights in Parliament, dismissed Grenville's concept of "virtual representation" as "the most contemptible idea that ever entered into the head of a man." Many others, in both Britain and America, agreed. Sir Francis Bernard, the royal governor of Massachusetts, correctly predicted that the new stamp tax "would cause a great Alarm & meet much Opposition" in the colonies.

Protests in the Colonies

George Grenville had assumed that, because a stamp tax had been in place in Britain for years, it would not create much resistance in the American colonies. He was wrong. The Stamp Act aroused fierce resentment among the colonists. A New Yorker wrote that "this single stroke has lost Great Britain the affection of all her colonies." In a flood of pamphlets, speeches, and resolutions, critics repeated a slogan familiar to all Americans: "No taxation without representation [in Parliament]."

Stamp Act Resolutions

Through the spring and summer of 1765, this simmering resentment boiled over at meetings, parades, bonfires, and other demonstrations. The protesters, calling themselves **Sons of Liberty**, emerged in every colony, often meeting beneath "liberty trees"—in Boston a great elm, in Charleston, South Carolina, a live oak. In New York City, the Sons of Liberty erected "liberty poles" as symbols of their resistance (British soldiers would tear them down almost as soon as they were put up). In Virginia, Patrick Henry convinced the assembly to pass the "Stamp Act Resolutions," which asserted yet again that the colonists could not be taxed without being consulted by the British government or represented in the British Parliament.

In mid-August 1765, nearly three months before the Stamp Act was to take effect, a mob of angry Bostonians plundered the homes of the royal lieutenant governor and the royal official in charge of enforcing the stamp tax. Thoroughly shaken, the Boston stamp agent resigned, and stamp agents throughout the colonies were hounded out of office. By November 1, its effective starting date, the Stamp Act was dead.

The Nonimportation Movement

Americans opposed to the Stamp Act knew that the most powerful form of leverage they had against the British was economic. To demonstrate their resolve and to put pressure on the British government, colonists by the thousands signed nonimportation agreements, promising not to buy any British goods. These boycotts of imported British products were an especially effective tactic because American consumers had become a major boon to the British economy during the eighteenth century. Now this was at risk, and many London merchants sided with the Americans against the

virtual representation The idea that the American colonies, although they had no actual representative in Parliament, were "virtually" represented by all members of Parliament.

Sons of Liberty First organized by Samuel Adams in the 1770s, groups of colonists dedicated to militant resistance against British control of the colonies.

proposed Stamp Act, fearful of losing their profitable business with their overseas customers.

The nonimportation movement of the 1760s and 1770s enabled women to play a significant public role in the resistance against Britain's colonial policies. Calling themselves **Daughters of Liberty**, many colonial women quit buying imported British clothes and made their own. The Daughters of Liberty also participated in public "spinning bees," whereby groups of women would gather in the town square to weave and spin yarn and wool into fabric, known as "homespun."

Americans saw the effort to boycott British products not only as a means of exerting political pressure on Parliament but also as a way to restore their own virtue. A Rhode Islander declared that a primary cause of America's problems was the "luxury and extravagance" brought on by their freewheeling purchases of British goods. The nonimportation movement would help Americans restore "our frugality, industry, and simplicity of manners." Plain living soon became a sign of American patriotism. A Boston minister claimed that those who could not do without British luxury goods and be satisfied with "plainness and simplicity" did not deserve to be American citizens.

Boycotts

Colonial Unity

The surprisingly effective boycotts of British imported goods strengthened colonial unity as Americans discovered that they had more in common with each other than with their fellow British subjects in Great Britain. The Virginia assembly struck the first official blow against the Stamp Act with the Virginia Resolves, a series of resolutions inspired by the fiery young Patrick Henry. Virginians, Henry declared, were entitled to all the rights of Englishmen, and Englishmen could be taxed only by their own

Virginia Resolves

Daughters of Liberty Colonial women who protested the British government's tax policies by boycotting British products, such as clothing, and who wove their own fabric, or "homespun."

elected representatives. Newspapers spread the Virginia Resolves throughout the colonies, and other colonial assemblies hastened to follow Virginia's example.

The Stamp Act Congress, and the Declaration of Rights and Grievances

In 1765, the Massachusetts House of Representatives invited the other colonial assemblies to send delegates to meet in New York to discuss their opposition to the Stamp Act. Nine responded, and from October 7 to 25, 1765, the so-called Stamp Act Congress formulated a Declaration of the Rights and Grievances of the Colonies. The delegates insisted that they would accept no taxes being "imposed on them" without "their own consent, given personally, or by their representatives." Parliament, in other words, had no right to tax people who were unrepresented in that body. Grenville responded to the American slogan "No taxation without representation!" by denouncing his colonial critics as "ungrateful" for all of the benefits provided them by the British government.

Repeal of the Stamp Act

The storm had scarcely broken before Grenville was out of office in London and the Stamp Act was repealed. Grenville had lost the confidence of the king, who replaced him with Lord Rockingham in July 1765. Pressure from British merchants hurt by the colonial boycott convinced the Rockingham-led government that the Stamp Act was a mistake. In February 1766, a humiliated Parliament repealed the Stamp Act. To save face, it also passed the Declaratory Act, which asserted the power of Parliament to govern the colonies "in all cases whatsoever." The repeal of the Stamp Act set off excited demonstrations throughout the colonies. Perhaps the worst was over, they hoped.

The Townshend Acts Fan the Flames

In July 1766, King George III replaced Lord Rockingham with William Pitt, the former prime minister who had exercised heroic leadership during the French and Indian War. For a time in 1767, the guiding force in the Pitt ministry was the witty but reckless Charles Townshend, the treasury chief whose "abilities were superior to those of all men," said a colleague, "and his judgment [common sense] below that of any man."

More taxes under Townshend

In 1767, Townshend, determined like his predecessors to extract more revenue from the colonies in order to pay for the costs of governing and defending them, pushed his ill-fated plan through Parliament; a few months later he died at age forty-two, leaving behind a bitter legacy: the **Townshend Acts**. Among Townshend's new policies, the Revenue Act of 1767, which taxed colonial imports of glass, lead, paint, paper, and tea, was the most hated. The Revenue Act of 1767 posed an even more severe threat to colonial assemblies than Grenville's taxes had done, for Townshend planned to use the new tax revenues to pay the royal governors in the colonies and thereby release them from financial dependence upon the colonial assemblies.

Townshend Acts (1767) Parliamentary measures to extract more revenue from the colonies; the Revenue Act of 1767, which taxed tea, paper, and other colonial imports, was one of the most notorious of these policies.

The Crisis Grows

American Patriots

The Townshend Acts surprised and angered the colonists. As American rage bubbled over, loyalty to Britain waned. Firebrand Samuel Adams of Boston emerged as the most radical of American rebels. Early in 1768, he and the Boston attorney James Otis convinced the Massachusetts assembly to circulate a letter they had written to the other colonies. The letter's tone was polite and logical: it restated the illegality of taxation without colonial representation in Parliament and invited the support of other colonies. British officials ordered the Massachusetts assembly to withdraw the Adams-Otis letter. The assembly refused, and the king ordered the assembly dissolved.

In response to an appeal by the royal governor of Massachusetts, 4,000 British troops were sent to Boston in October 1768 to maintain social order. **Loyalists**, as the American Tories who supported the king and Parliament were often called, welcomed the soldiers; **Patriots**, the name for those rebelling against British authority, viewed the British troops as an occupation force intended to crush dissent. Meanwhile, in London the king appointed a new chief minister, Frederick, Lord North, in January 1770.

The Boston Massacre

By 1770, the American nonimportation agreements were strangling British trade with the colonies and causing unemployment in Britain. The impact of the colonial boycott of British products persuaded Lord North to modify the Townshend Acts—just in time to prevent tensions from getting out of hand. In Boston, the British soldiers (called "lobsterbacks" or "redcoats" because of their red uniforms) had become a constant source of irritation to Patriots. Crowds heckled the soldiers, many of whom earned the abuse by harassing and intimidating Americans.

On March 5, 1770, a group of rowdies began taunting and throwing icicles at a British guard. Soldiers rushed to his aid. Then someone rang the town fire bell, drawing a larger crowd to the scene. At their head, or so the story goes, was Crispus Attucks, a runaway African American slave. Attucks and others continued to bait the British troops. Finally, a soldier was knocked down; he rose to his feet and fired into the crowd, as did others. When the smoke cleared, five people lay dead or dying, and eight more were wounded.

The so-called **Boston Massacre** sent shock waves throughout the colonies and all the way to London. Late in April 1770, Parliament repealed all the Townshend duties except for the tea tax. Colonial discontent diminished for two years thereafter. The redcoats left Boston, but they remained stationed nearby in Canada, and the British navy still patrolled the New England coast chasing smugglers.

CORE OBJECTIVE

4. Explain the underlying factors amid the events in the 1770s that led the colonies to declare their independence from Britain.

Samuel Adams Adams was the fiery organizer of the Sons of Liberty.

British troops and the Boston Massacre

Loyalists Colonists who remained loyal to Britain before and during the Revolutionary War.

Patriots Colonists who rebelled against British authority before and during the Revolutionary War.

Boston Massacre (1770) Violent confrontation between British soldiers and a Boston mob on March 5, 1770, in which five colonists were killed.

The Bloody Massacre Paul Revere's engraving of the Boston Massacre.

The *Gaspée* Incident

The *Gaspée* incident

Then in 1772, a naval incident further eroded the colonies' fragile relationship with the mother country. Near Warwick, Rhode Island, the HMS *Gaspée*, a British warship, ran aground while chasing suspected smugglers, and its hungry crew went ashore and seized local sheep, hogs, and chickens. An angry crowd from the town then boarded the ship, shot the captain, removed the crew, and set fire to the vessel.

The *Gaspée* incident symbolized the anti-British anger felt by growing numbers of Americans. When the British tried to take the suspects to London for trial, Americans organized in protest. Thomas Jefferson remembered that it was the threat of transporting Americans for trials in Britain that reignited anti-British activities in Virginia. Likewise, in response to the fallout from the *Gaspée* incident, Samuel Adams in Boston organized the **Committee of Correspondence**, which issued a statement of American rights and grievances and invited other towns to do the same. Similar committees sprang up across Massachusetts and in other colonies, forming a network of rebellion. A Massachusetts Loyalist called the committees "the foulest, subtlest, and most venomous serpent ever issued from the egg of sedition." The crisis was escalating. "The flame is kindled and like lightning it catches from soul to soul," reported Abigail Adams, the high-spirited and politically astute wife of future president John Adams.

Committee of Correspondence Group organized by Samuel Adams in retaliation for the *Gaspée* incident to address American grievances, assert American rights, and form a network of rebellion.

The Boston Tea Party

The new British prime minister, Lord North, soon provided the colonists with the spark to ignite colonial resentment. In 1773, he tried to bail out the struggling East India Company, which had in its British warehouses some 17 million pounds of tea that it desperately needed to sell before the tea rotted. Under the Tea Act of 1773, the government would allow the grossly mismanaged company to send its tea directly to America without paying any taxes. British tea merchants could thereby undercut the prices charged by their American competitors, most of whom were smugglers who bought tea from the Dutch. At the same time, King George III told Lord North that his job was to "compel obedience" in the colonies; North ordered British authorities in New England to clamp down harder on American smuggling.

The Committees of Correspondence, backed by Boston merchants, alerted colonists to the new danger. The British government, they said, was trying to purchase colonial submission with cheap tea. They saw the reduction in the price of tea as a clever trick to make them accept taxation without consent. Before the end of the year, large shipments of tea left Britain for the major colonial ports. In Boston, enraged colonists decided that their passion for liberty outweighed their love for tea. On December 16, 1773, scores of Patriots disguised as Indians boarded three British ships in Boston harbor and dumped 342 chests of East India Company tea overboard—cheered on by a crowd lining the shore.

The **Boston Tea Party** pushed British officials to the breaking point. They had tolerated criticism, evasion, and occasional violence, but the destruction of so much valuable tea convinced the king and his advisers that a forceful response was required. "The colonists must either submit or triumph," George III wrote to Lord North, who decided to make an example of Boston to the rest of the colonies. "We are now to establish our authority [over the colonies]," North said, "or give it up entirely." In the end, his reassertion of royal control helped make a revolution that would cost Britain far more than three shiploads of tea.

> Boston Tea Party

The Coercive Acts

In 1774, Parliament enacted a cluster of harsh laws, called the **Coercive Acts** (referred to by Americans as the "Intolerable" Acts), to punish rebellious Boston. The Boston Port Act closed the harbor from June 1, 1774, until the city paid for the lost tea. A new Quartering Act ordered local authorities to provide lodging for British soldiers. Finally, the Massachusetts Government Act made all of the colony's officials appointive rather than elective and ordered that no town meeting could be held without the royal governor's consent. In May, Lieutenant-General Thomas Gage, commander in chief of British forces in North America, was named governor of Massachusetts and assumed command of the British soldiers in Boston.

Boston Tea Party (1773) Demonstration against the Tea Act of 1773 in which the Sons of Liberty, dressed as Indians, dumped hundreds of chests of British-owned tea into Boston Harbor.

Coercive Acts (1774) Four parliamentary measures that required the colonies to pay for the Boston Tea Party's damages: imposed a military government, disallowed colonial trials of British soldiers, and forced the quartering of troops in private homes.

Elsewhere, colonists rallied to help Boston, raising money, sending supplies, and boycotting, as well as burning, British tea. In Williamsburg, when the Virginia assembly met in May, a young member of the Committee of Correspondence, Thomas Jefferson, suggested that June 1, the effective date of the Boston Port Act, become an official day of fasting and prayer in Virginia. The royal governor responded by dissolving the assembly, whose members then retired to the Raleigh Tavern where they decided to form a Continental Congress to represent all the colonies.

The First Continental Congress

The First Continental Congress

On September 5, 1774, the fifty-five delegates making up the First Continental Congress assembled in Philadelphia. During seven weeks of meetings, the Congress endorsed the Suffolk Resolves, which urged Massachusetts to resist British tyranny with force. The Congress then adopted a Declaration of American Rights, which proclaimed once again the rights of Americans as British citizens and denied Parliament's authority to regulate internal colonial affairs.

Finally, the First Continental Congress adopted the Continental Association of 1774, which recommended that every colony organize committees to enforce a complete boycott of all imported British goods. These elected committees became the organizational network for the resistance movement. Seven thousand men across the colonies served on the committees of the Continental Association, and many more thousands of women put the boycotts into practice. The committees required colonists to sign an oath refusing to purchase British goods. Those who refused to sign were punished; some were tarred and feathered.

Such efforts to gain economic self-sufficiency helped unify the diverse colonies. Thousands of ordinary men and women participated in the boycott of British goods, and their sacrifices on behalf of colonial liberties provided the momentum leading to revolution. For all of the attention given to colonial leaders such as Samuel Adams and Thomas Jefferson, it was common people who enforced the boycott, volunteered in Patriot militia units, attended town meetings, and exerted pressure on royal officials in the colonies. As the people of Pittsfield, Massachusetts, declared in a petition, "We have always believed that the people are the fountain of power."

Last Minute Compromise

In London, King George fumed. He wrote Lord North that "blows must decide" whether the Americans "are to be subject to this country or independent." In early 1775, Parliament declared that Massachusetts was officially "in rebellion" and prohibited the New England colonies from trading with any nation outside the British Empire. On February 27, 1775, Lord North issued the Conciliatory Propositions, which offered to resolve the festering dispute by eliminating all taxes on any colony that voluntarily paid both its share for military defense and the salaries of the royal governors. In other words, North was asking the colonies to tax themselves. By the time the Conciliatory Propositions arrived in America, shooting had already started.

Bold Talk of War

While most of the Patriots believed that Britain would back down in the face of united colonial resistance, in Virginia Patrick Henry dramatically declared that war was unavoidable. He urged Americans to prepare for combat. The twenty-nine-year-old Henry, a farmer and storekeeper turned lawyer, claimed that the colonies "have done everything that could be done to avert the storm which is now coming on," but their efforts had been met only by "violence and insult." Freedom, the defiant Henry shouted, could be bought only with blood. If forced to choose, he supposedly shouted, "give me liberty"—then paused dramatically, clenched his fist as if it held a dagger, and plunged it into his chest—"or give me death." Loyalists shouted "Treason!" But even more of those present stood and applauded.

As Patrick Henry had predicted, events during 1775 quickly moved toward armed conflict. By mid-1775, the king and Parliament had effectively lost control of their colonies; they could neither persuade nor force the Patriots to accept new regulations and revenue measures. In Boston, General Gage warned his British superiors that armed conflict with the Americans would unleash the "horrors of civil war." Lord Sandwich, the head of the British navy, was not worried by the idea of warfare. He dismissed the rebels as "raw, undisciplined, cowardly men." Major John Pitcairn, a British army officer, agreed, writing home from Boston in 1775 that "one active campaign, a smart action, and burning two or three of their towns, will set everything to rights."

Patrick Henry of Virginia Henry famously declared "Give me liberty, or give me death!"

Lexington and Concord

Major Pitcairn soon had his chance to quash the rebel resistance. On April 14, 1775, the British army in Boston received secret orders to stop the "open rebellion" in Massachusetts. General Gage had decided to arrest rebel leaders such as Samuel Adams and seize the American militia's gunpowder stored at Concord, sixteen miles northwest of Boston. After dark on April 18, some 700 redcoats secretly boarded boats in Boston and crossed the Charles River after midnight, then set out westward on foot to Lexington. When Patriots got wind of the plan, Paul Revere and William Dawes mounted their horses for their famous "midnight ride" to warn the rebel leaders that the British were coming.

In the gray dawn light of April 19, the British advance guard of 238 redcoats found Captain John Parker, a veteran of the French and Indian War, and about seventy "Minutemen" (Patriot militia who could assemble at a "minute's" notice), lined up on the Lexington town square, while about a hundred villagers watched. Parker and his men intended only a silent

Shots fired at Lexington and Concord

protest, but Major Pitcairn of the Royal Marines rode onto the Lexington Green, swinging his sword and yelling, "Disperse, you damned rebels! You dogs, run!" The outnumbered militiamen had already begun backing away when someone, perhaps an onlooker, fired a shot, whereupon the British soldiers began wildly shooting at the Minutemen, then charged them with bayonets, leaving eight dead and ten wounded. Jonathan Harrington, a militiaman who was shot in the back, managed to crawl across the Green, only to die on his doorstep.

The British officers quickly brought their men under control and led them to Concord, announcing their arrival with fifes and drums. In Concord, they searched buildings for hidden military supplies, destroying what they found. While marching out of the town, they encountered American riflemen at the North Bridge. Shots were fired, and a dozen or so British soldiers were killed or wounded. More important, the short skirmish and ringing church bells alerted hundreds, then thousands, of rebel farmers, ministers, craftsmen, and merchants from nearby communities to grab their muskets.

By noon, the British began a ragged retreat back to Lexington. Less than a mile out of Concord, they suffered the first of many ambushes. The narrow road back to Boston turned into a gauntlet of death as hundreds of rebel marksmen fired on the British troops from behind stone walls, trees, barns, and houses. "It was a day full of horror," one of the soldiers recalled. "The Patriots seemed maddened." By nightfall, the redcoat survivors were safely back in Boston, having suffered three times as many dead and wounded as the Americans. A British general reported to London that the feisty Americans had earned his respect: "Whoever looks upon them as an irregular mob will find himself much mistaken."

LEXINGTON AND CONCORD, APRIL 19, 1775

★ Battle site

- Describe the outbreak of shooting on Lexington Green.
- Why did the Americans' tactics along the road between Concord and Lexington succeed?
- Why did the British march on Concord in the first place?

Outright Rebellion

The colonial resistance movement had grown into an outright rebellion, but few Patriots in 1775 were yet calling for American independence. They still considered themselves British subjects whose rights had been repeatedly violated by an arrogant king and a misguided Parliament. When the Second Continental Congress convened at Philadelphia on May 10, 1775, the delegates gathered under a British flag. Most Americans in 1775 still wanted

The Battle of Lexington (1775) Amos Doolittle's impression of the Battle of Lexington as combat begins between the Royal Marines and the Minutemen.

Parliament to restore their rights so that they could go back to being loyal British colonists.

Meanwhile, the British army in Boston was encircled and under siege by American militia units and small groups of musket-toting men who had raced from all across New England to join in the rebellion. They were still farmers, not trained soldiers, and the uprising was not yet an army; it lacked an organized command structure and effective support system. The Patriots also lacked training, discipline, cannons, muskets, bullets, gunpowder, and blankets. They did not even have a name for their ragtag army. But they did have a growing sense of confidence and resolve. As a Massachusetts Patriot warned in urging Americans to join the revolt, "Our all is at stake. Death and devastation are the instant consequences of delay. Every moment is infinitely precious."

With each passing day in the spring of 1775, war fever infected more and more colonists. "Oh that I were a soldier!" John Adams wrote to his wife Abigail from Philadelphia. "I will be. I am reading military books. Everybody must, and will, and shall be a soldier." On the very day that Congress met, the British Fort Ticonderoga, on Lake Champlain in upstate New York near the Canadian border, fell to a Patriot force of "Green Mountain Boys" led by Ethan Allen of Vermont and Massachusetts volunteers under Benedict Arnold. Two days later, the Patriots captured a smaller British fort at Crown Point, north of Ticonderoga.

The Spreading Conflict

On June 15, 1775, the Second Continental Congress unanimously selected forty-three-year-old George Washington to lead a new national professional army. Washington's service in the French and Indian War had made him one of the few experienced American officers. And he *looked* like a leader. Tall and strong, he was a superb horseman and fearless fighter. Washington humbly accepted the new responsibility but refused to be paid.

The Battle of Bunker Hill

On Saturday, June 17, the very day that George Washington was named commander in chief, Patriot militiamen engaged British forces in their first major clash, the Battle of Bunker Hill (adjoining Breed's Hill was the battle's actual location).

> The First Battle: Bunker Hill

Twenty-four hundred British troops advanced up the hill in tight formation through waist-high grass and across pasture fences as Americans watched from behind their earthworks. The militiamen, mostly farmers, waited until the redcoats had come within thirty paces, then loosed a volley that shattered the front British ranks. The British re-formed their lines and attacked again, but the Patriot riflemen forced them to retreat a second time. During the third British assault, the colonials ran out of gunpowder and retreated in panic and confusion. "I jumped over the walls," Peter Brown remembered, "and ran for about half a mile while [musket] balls flew like hailstones and cannons roared like thunder."

The British took the high ground but were too tired to pursue the rebels. Victory came at a high price. The British suffered 1,054 casualties, over twice the American losses. "A dearly bought victory," reported British general Henry Clinton; "another such would have ruined us." The two armies, American and British, settled in for a nine-month stalemate around Boston, each hoping for a negotiated end to the crisis.

"Open and Avowed Enemies"

> Olive Branch Petition rejected

Three weeks after the Battle of Bunker Hill, on July 6 and 8, 1775, the Continental Congress sent the king the Olive Branch Petition, urging him to negotiate with his angry colonies. When the Olive Branch Petition reached London, however, King George refused even to look at it. On August 22, he declared the American rebels "open and avowed enemies."

Independence

***Common Sense* (1776)** Popular pamphlet written by Thomas Paine attacking British principles of hereditary rule and monarchical government, and advocating a declaration of American independence.

The Revolutionary War was well underway in January 1776 when Thomas Paine, a recent English emigrant to America, provided the Patriot cause with a stirring pamphlet titled ***Common Sense***. Until it appeared, colonial grievances had been mainly directed at the British Parliament; only a few colonists then considered independence an option. Paine, however, directly attacked the British monarchy. The "common sense" of the matter, he

The coming revolution The Continental Congress votes for independence, July 2, 1776.

stressed, was that King George III had caused the rebellion. Americans, Paine urged, should abandon the British monarchy and declare their independence: "The blood of the slain, the weeping voice of nature cries, 'tis time to part." Only by declaring independence, Paine predicted, could the colonists gain the crucial support of France and Spain: "The cause of America is in great measure the cause of all mankind." Paine added that the "sun had never shone on a cause of greater worth."

Within three months, more than 150,000 copies of Paine's stirring pamphlet were circulating throughout the colonies, an enormous number for the time. "*Common Sense* is working a powerful change in the minds of men," George Washington reported. Paine's *Common Sense* inspired the colonial population from Massachusetts to Georgia, helping to convince British subjects still loyal to the king to embrace the radical notion of independence. The momentum for independence was building. In Congress, the Pennsylvanian John Dickinson, perhaps the most underrated of the "Founding Fathers," urged delay. On June 1, he warned that independence was a dangerous step since America had no national government or European allies. But his was a lone voice of caution.

In June 1776, one by one, the colonies authorized their delegates in the Continental Congress to take the final step. On June 7, Richard Henry Lee of Virginia moved "that these United Colonies are, and of right ought to be, free

Declaration of Independence

Declaration of Independence The Declaration in its most frequently reproduced form, an 1823 engraving by William J. Stone.

Declaration of Independence (1776) Formal statement, principally drafted by Thomas Jefferson and adopted by the Second Continental Congress on July 4, 1776, that officially announced the thirteen colonies' break with Great Britain.

and independent states." Lee's resolution passed on July 2, a date that "will be the most memorable epoch in the history of America," John Adams wrote to his wife, Abigail. The more memorable date, however, became July 4, 1776, when the Congress formally adopted the **Declaration of Independence**.

Jefferson's Declaration

In June 1776, thirty-three-year-old Thomas Jefferson wrote a first draft of a statement of independence that was submitted to the Congress. Others then edited and polished Jefferson's document. The resulting Declaration of Independence was crucially important not simply because it marked the creation of a new nation but because of the ideals it expressed. It insisted that "all men are created equal" in having the right to maintain governments of their own choosing. Governments, in Jefferson's words, derive "their just Powers from the consent of the people," who are entitled to "alter or abolish" those governments when they deny citizens their "unalienable rights" to "life, Liberty, and the pursuit of Happiness." Because King George was trying to impose "an absolute Tyranny over these States," the "Representatives of the United States of America" therefore declared the thirteen "United Colonies" to be "Free and Independent States."

News of the Declaration of Independence so excited New Yorkers that they toppled a statue of King George and had it melted down to make 42,000 bullets for the war. General George Washington ordered the Declaration read to every unit in the Continental army. Benjamin Franklin acknowledged how high the stakes were: "Well, Gentlemen," he told the Congress, "we must now hang together, or we shall most assuredly hang separately."

The Contradictions of Slavery

George Washington had declared that Boston's fight against British tyranny "now is and ever will be considered as the cause of America (not that we approve their conduct in destroying the Tea)." The alternative, Washington warned, was to become "tame and abject slaves, as the blacks we rule over with such arbitrary sway [absolute power]." Washington and other American slaveholders, such as Thomas Jefferson, were in part so resistant to "British tyranny" because they witnessed every day what actual slavery was like—for the blacks under their control. Jefferson acknowledged their moral hypocrisy. "Southerners," he wrote to a French friend, are "jealous of their own liberties but trampling on those of others." The contradiction between American slaveholders demanding liberty from British oppression was not lost on other observers at the time, either. Phillis Wheatley, the first African American writer to see her poetry published in America, highlighted the "absurdity" of white colonists claiming their freedom while continuing to exercise "oppressive power" over enslaved Africans.

"We Always Had Governed Ourselves"

In explaining the causes of the Revolution, historians have highlighted many factors: the clumsy British efforts to tighten their regulation of colonial trade, the restrictions on colonists eager to acquire western lands, the growing tax burden, the mounting debts to British merchants, the lack of American representation in Parliament, and the role of revolutionary agitators such as Samuel Adams and Patrick Henry in stirring up anti-British feelings.

Phillis Wheatley An autographed portrait of America's first African American poet.

Each of those factors (and others) helped ignite the Revolutionary War. Yet colonists sought liberty from British tyranny for many reasons, not all of which were selfless or noble. The Boston merchant John Hancock embraced the Patriot cause in part because he was the region's foremost smuggler. Paying more British taxes would have cost him a fortune. Likewise, South Carolina's Henry Laurens and Virginia's Landon Carter, wealthy planters, worried that the British might abolish slavery in the future.

The difficult decision to declare independence from Great Britain was not simply about "taxation without representation." A larger issue had emerged by 1776. Many Americans had become determined to develop their own society in the ways they wished. Yes, most American "Patriots" still spoke the same language and worshipped the same God as the British, but they no longer thought the same way about things that mattered. Rebellious Americans wanted to trade freely with the world and to expand what Jefferson called their "empire of liberty" westward, across the Appalachians.

Perhaps the last word on the complex causes of the Revolution should belong to Levi Preston, a Minuteman from Danvers, Massachusetts. Asked late in life about the British efforts to impose new taxes and regulations on the colonists, Preston responded by asking his young interviewer, "What were they? Oppressions? I didn't feel them." He was then asked, "What, were you not oppressed by the Stamp Act?" Preston replied that he "never saw one of those stamps . . . I am certain I never paid a penny for one of them." What about the tax on tea? "Tea-tax! I never drank a drop of the stuff; the boys threw it all overboard." His interviewer finally asked why he decided to fight for independence. "Young man," Preston explained, "what we meant in going for those Redcoats was this: we always had governed ourselves, and we always meant to. They didn't mean we should."

■ **British and French Colonies** New France followed the model of absolute power in governing its far-flung trading outposts. Few French colonists settled in the vast geography of Canada and the Louisiana territory, but friendships with Native Americans and a profitable fur trade kept the balance of power in North America. On the other hand, the British policy of *salutary neglect* allowed the British colonies a large degree of self-government, until the British government's decision to rigidly enforce its policy of *mercantilism*, as seen in such measures as the *Navigation Acts*, became a means for Britain to enrich its global empire. The *Glorious Revolution* in Great Britain inspired new political philosophies that challenged the divine right of kings with the *natural rights* of free men.

■ **The French and Indian War** Four European wars affected America between 1689 and 1763 as the British and French, joined by their allies, fought each other throughout the world. Worried colonies joined together to create the *Albany Plan of Union*, which was ultimately rejected but formed an early blueprint for an independent American government. The *Seven Years' War* (1754–1763), known as the *French and Indian War* in the American colonies, was the first world war, eventually won by the British. In the *Treaty of Paris* in 1763, France lost all its North American possessions, Britain gained Canada and Florida, and Spain acquired the vast Louisiana territory. With the war's end, Native Americans were no longer regarded as essential allies and so had no recourse when settlers squatted on their lands. They fought to regain control in *Pontiac's Rebellion*, and Great Britain, weary of war, negotiated peace in the *Royal Proclamation of 1763*. But land-hungry settlers ignored the Proclamation Line intended to protect Indian lands. The 1763 Treaty of Paris also set the stage for conflict between the mother country and the American colonies as Britain tried to make the colonies pay for their own defense.

■ **British Colonial Policy** After the French and Indian War, the British government was saddled with an enormous national debt. To reduce that burden, George Grenville's colonial policy tried to implement various taxes to compel colonists to pay for their own defense. Colonists resisted, claiming that they could not be taxed by Parliament because they were not represented in Parliament. Colonial reaction to the *Stamp Act* of 1765 was the first sign of real trouble for British authorities. Conflicts between Whigs and Tories intensified when the *Townshend Acts* imposed additional taxes. The *Sons of Liberty* and the *Daughters of Liberty* mobilized resistance, particularly through nonimportation agreements. The boycotts of British goods were successful, helping convince Parliament to repeal the Stamp Act.

■ **Road to the American Revolution** But the crisis worsened. Spontaneous resistance led to the *Boston Massacre*; organized protesters later staged the *Boston Tea Party*. The British response, called the *Coercive Acts*, sparked further violence between *Patriots* and *Loyalists*. The First Continental Congress formed *Committees of Correspondence* to organize and spread resistance. Thomas Paine's pamphlet *Common Sense* helped kindle revolutionary fervor as well as plant the seed of independence, and conflicts over trade regulations, taxes, and expansion now erupted into war. In the heat of battle, compromise became less likely, and finally impossible, and the Continental Congress delivered its *Declaration of Independence*.

KEY TERMS

CHRONOLOGY

1651	First Navigation Act passed by Parliament
1688–1689	Glorious Revolution
1756–1763	Seven Years' War (French and Indian War)
1754	Albany Plan of Union
1763	Pontiac's Rebellion begins
1763	Treaty of Paris ends Seven Years' War
1763	Royal Proclamation Act
1764–1765	Sugar Act and Stamp Act
1765	Stamp Act Congress
1766	Repeal of the Stamp Act
1767	Townshend Acts
1770	Boston Massacre
1773	Tea Act and Boston Tea Party
1774	Coercive Acts
1774	First meeting of Continental Congress
1775	Military conflict at Lexington and Concord
1775	Continental Congress creates an army
1776	Thomas Paine publishes *Common Sense*
1776	Continental Congress declares independence

INQUIZITIVE

Go to InQuizitive to see what you've learned—and learn what you've missed—with personalized feedback along the way.

DEBATING the Origins of the American Revolution

History is more than just the memorization of *what* happened. It also involves interpreting *why* the past unfolded as it did. In seeking to understand *why*, historians often find themselves disagreeing. This happens for many reasons. Historians themselves are influenced by their own outlook and the society they live in. Historians can revise their thinking in light of fresh information from newly discovered *primary sources*. They can also interpret previously examined sources in new ways by applying new methodologies and theories. The study of how interpretations of history have changed is called *historiography*. It is the history of the field of history! For Part 1, *A Not-So-"New" World*, the case study of the origins of the American Revolution demonstrates how historians can disagree because they use different types of sources. Thus it is an excellent topic for sharpening your historiographical skills.

For this exercise you have two tasks:

PART 1: Compare the two secondary sources on the American Revolution.
PART 2: Using primary sources, evaluate the arguments of the two secondary sources.

PART I Comparing and Contrasting Secondary Sources

Below are excerpts from two prominent historians of the American Revolution who are at odds over its origins. The first piece comes from Bernard Bailyn of Harvard University, who has explored how the American Revolution was shaped by *ideology*—the system of ideas, ideals, and beliefs that undergird political and economic theory and practice. Bailyn focuses on the way that ideas from the English Whigs, who argued that the English constitution limited the power of the king (see page 125), influenced American Revolutionaries. The author of the second excerpt, Gary Nash of the University of California, Los Angeles, has studied the role that common people, as well as the economic forces that affected their lives, played in the American Revolution. Nash seeks to uncover not just the Whig ideology that is the focus of Bailyn's work, but also the ideas and forces that motivated the masses to participate in this great struggle. While Bailyn and Nash agree on much, their work illustrates how different methodologies lead to different historical interpretations. On the one hand, Bailyn looks at the ideas and writings of the Revolutionary elite—their ideas and arguments—to explain what people actually did. On the other hand, Nash examines the actions and economic circumstances of Revolutionaries who produced no written records in order to understand their motivations. So while Bailyn seeks to understand the causes of the Revolution through the writing of the colonial elite, Nash looks at the actions of common people to understand why they participated in this struggle.

Compare the views of these two historians by answering the following questions. Be sure to find specific examples in the text to support your answers.

■ What is the topic of each excerpt?

■ Are there any similarities between these two excerpts?

■ According to each author, what role did ideology play in the origins of the American Revolution?

■ According to each author, what role did economics and material conditions play in the origins of the Revolution?

■ What type of primary sources does each author mention?

■ What might account for the differences (if any) in interpretation between the authors?

Secondary Source 1

Bernard Bailyn, *The Ideological Origins of the American Revolution* (1992)

Study of the pamphlets [thin booklets] confirmed my rather old-fashioned view that the American Revolution was above all else an ideological, constitutional, political struggle and not primarily a controversy between social groups undertaken to force changes in the organization of the society or the economy. It confirmed too my belief that intellectual developments in the decade before Independence led to a radical idealization and conceptualization of the previous century and a half of American experience, and that it was this intimate relationship between Revolutionary thought and the circumstances of life in eighteenth-century America that endowed the Revolution with its peculiar force and made it so profoundly a transforming event. But if the pamphlets confirmed this belief, they filled it with unexpected details and gave it new meaning.

. . . I began to see a new meaning in phrases that I, like most historians, had readily dismissed as mere rhetoric and propaganda: "slavery," "corruption," "conspiracy." These inflammatory words were used so forcefully by writers of so great a variety of social statuses, political positions, and religious persuasions; they fitted so logically into the pattern of radical and opposition thought; and they reflected so clearly the realities of life in an age in which monarchical autocracy flourished, in which the stability and freedom of England's "mixed" constitution was a recent and remarkable achievement, and in which the fear of conspiracy against constituted authority was built into the very structure of politics, that I began to suspect that they meant something very real to both the writers and their readers: that there were real fears, real anxieties, a sense of real danger behind these phrases, and not merely the desire to influence by rhetoric and propaganda the inert minds of an otherwise passive populace. The more I read, the less useful, it seemed to me, was the whole idea of propaganda in its modern meaning when applied to the writings of the American Revolution. . . . In the end I was convinced that the fear of a comprehensive conspiracy against liberty throughout the English speaking world—a conspiracy believed to have been nourished in corruption, and of which, it was felt, oppression in America was only the most immediately visible part—lay at the heart of the Revolutionary movement.

Source: Bailyn, Bernard. *The Ideological Origins of the American Revolution*. Cambridge, Mass.: Belknap Press of Harvard University Press, 1992. xx–xxiii.

Secondary Source 2

Gary Nash, "Social Change and the Growth of Prerevolutionary Urban Radicalism" (1976)

One of the purposes of this essay is to challenge these widely accepted notions that the "predicament of poverty" was unknown in colonial America, that the conditions of everyday life among "the inarticulate" had not changed in ways that led toward a revolutionary predisposition, and that "social discontent," "economic disturbances," and "social strains" can generally be ignored in searching for the roots of the Revolution. I do not suggest that we replace an ideological construction with a mechanistic economic interpretation, but argue that a popular ideology, affected by rapidly changing economic conditions in American cities, dynamically interacted with the more abstract Whig ideology borrowed from England. These two ideologies had their primary appeal within different parts of the social structure, were derived from different sensibilities concerning social equity, and thus had somewhat different goals. The Whig ideology, about which we know a great deal through recent studies, was drawn from English sources, had its main appeal within upper levels of colonial society, was limited to a defense of constitutional rights and political liberties, and had little to say about changing social and economic conditions in America or the need for change in the future. The popular ideology, about which we know very little, also had deep roots in English culture, but it resonated most strongly within the middle and lower strata of society and went far beyond constitutional rights to a discussion of the proper distribution of wealth and power in the social system. It was this popular ideology that undergirded the politicization of the artisan and laboring classes in the cities and justified the dynamic role they assumed in the urban political process in the closing decades of the colonial period.

To understand how this popular ideology swelled into revolutionary commitment within the middle and lower ranks of colonial society, we must first comprehend how the material conditions of life were changing for city dwellers during the colonial period and how people at different levels of society were affected by these alterations. We cannot fathom this process by consulting the writings of merchants, lawyers, and upper-class politicians, because their business and political correspondence and the tracts they wrote tell us almost nothing about those below them in the social hierarchy. But buried in more obscure documents are glimpses of the lives of both ordinary and important people—shoemakers and tailors as well as lawyers and merchants. The story of changing conditions and how life in New York, Philadelphia, and Boston was experienced can be discerned, not with perfect clarity but in general form, from tax, poor relief, and probate records.

The crescendo of urban protest and extralegal activity in the prerevolutionary decades cannot be separated from the condition of people's lives. . . . The willingness of broad segments of urban society to participate in attacks on narrowly concentrated wealth and power—both at the polls where the poor and propertyless were excluded, and in the streets where everyone, including women, apprentices, indentured servants, and slaves, could engage in action—should remind us that a rising tide of class antagonism and political

consciousness, paralleling important economic changes, was a distinguishing feature of the cities at the end of the colonial period. It is this organic link between the circumstances of people's lives and their political thought and action that has been overlooked by historians who concentrate on Whig ideology, which had its strongest appeal among the educated and well-to-do.

Source: Nash, Gary. "Social Change and the Growth of Prerevolutionary Urban Radicalism." *The American Revolution: Explorations in the History of American Radicalism*. Ed. Alfred F. Young. Dekalb, Ill.: Northern Illinois University Press, 1976. 6–7.

PART II Using Primary Sources to Evaluate Secondary Sources

When historians are faced with competing interpretations of the past, they often look at *primary* source material as part of the process of evaluating the different arguments. Below are a selection of primary source materials relating to the origins of the American Revolution.

The first document is an excerpt from a series of letters by Pennsylvania Quaker John Dickinson that he published anonymously under the pen name "A Farmer." Dickinson wrote the first letter in 1767, following the British Parliament's suspension of the New York Assembly for failure to comply with the Quartering Act of 1765, which required the colonies to provide British troops with food and shelter.

The second document is an excerpt from a letter sent by Massachusetts Bay Governor Francis Bernard to British officials in London following the Stamp Act Riots in Boston during August of 1765. The riots begun on August 13 with an attack upon the house of Andrew Oliver, who was responsible for the collection of the tax. This act of destruction was widely celebrated by Samuel Adams and other Sons of Liberty. A few days later a mob ransacked and looted the house of the lieutenant-governor, Thomas Hutchinson. This mob acted without the support of Adams or other elite leaders.

Carefully read each of the following primary sources and answer the following questions. Decide which of the primary source documents support or refute Bailyn's and Nash's arguments about this period. You may find that some documents do both, but for different parts of each historians' interpretation. Be sure to identify which specific components of each historian's argument the documents support or refute.

■ Which of the two historians' *arguments* is best supported by the *primary source* documents? Or if you find

that both arguments are well supported by the evidence, why do you think the two historians had such different interpretations about the period?

■ Based on your comparison of the two historians' arguments and your analysis of the primary sources, what have you learned about historiography and the ways historians interpret the past?

Primary Source 1

John Dickinson, "Letter from a Farmer in Pennsylvania" (1767)

My dear COUNTRYMEN,

I am a FARMER settled after a variety of fortunes, near the banks of the river *Delaware* in the province of *Pennsylvania*. . . . Being master of my time, I spend a good deal of it in a library. . . . I believe I have acquired a greater share of knowledge in history, and the laws and constitution of my country, than is generally attained by men of my class. . . . From my infancy I was taught to love humanity and liberty. Inquiry and experience have since confirmed my reverence for the lessons then given me, by convincing me more fully of their truth and excellence. . . . With a good deal of surprise I have observed, that little notice has been taken of an act of Parliament, as injurious in its principle to the liberties of these colonies, as the STAMP ACT was: I mean the act for suspending the legislation of New-York. . . . It [the Act] is a parliamentary assertion of the *supreme authority* of *the British legislature* over these colonies in *the part of taxation*; and is intended to COMPEL *New-York* into a submission to that authority. It seems therefore to me as much a violation of the liberty of the people of that province, and consequently of all these colonies, as if the parliament had sent a number of regiments to be quartered upon them till they should comply. For it is evident, that the suspension is meant as a compulsion; and the *method* of compelling is totally indifferent. It is indeed probable that the sight of red coats, and the beating of drums would have been most alarming, because people are generally more influenced by their eyes and ears than by their reason: But whoever seriously considers the matter, must perceive, that a dreadful stroke is aimed at the liberty of these colonies: For the cause of *one* is the cause of *all*. If the parliament may lawfully deprive *New-York* of any of its rights, it may deprive any, or all the other colonies of their rights; and nothing can possibly so much encourage such attempts, as a mutual inattention to the interests of each other. *To divide, and thus to destroy*, is the first political maxim in attacking those who are powerful by their union. He certainly is not a wise man, who folds his arms and reposes himself at home, viewing with unconcern the flames that have invaded his neighbour's house, without any endeavors to extinguish them.

Source: Dickinson, John. "Letters from a Farmer." *Letters from a Farmer in Pennsylvania, to the Inhabitants of the British Colonies.* Ed. R. T. H. Halsey. New York: The Outlook Company, 1903. 6–12.

Primary Source 2

Governor Francis Bernard, "Letter to the Lords of Trade" (1765)

The disorders of the town having been carried to much greater lengths than what I have informed your lordships of. After the demolition of Mr. Oliver's house was found so practicable and easy, and that the government was obliged to look on, without being able to take any one step to prevent it, and the principal people of the town publicly avowed and justified the act; the mob, both great and small, became highly elated, and all kinds of ill-humours were set on foot; everything that, for years past, had been the cause of any unpopular discontent, was revived; and private resentments against persons in office worked

themselves in, and endeavored to exert themselves under the mask of the public cause. . . . Towards evening, some boys began to light a bonfire before the town-house, which is an usual signal for a mob. Before it was quite dark, a great company of people gathered together, crying 'Liberty and Property;' which is their usual notice of their intention to plunder and pull down a house.

. . .

The lieutenant-governor [Thomas Hutchinson] . . . was at supper with his family when he received advice that the mob was coming to him. . . . As soon as the mob had got into the house, with a most irresistible fury, they immediately looked about for him, to murder him, and even made diligent enquiry whither he was gone. They went to work with a rage scarce to be exemplified by the most savage people. Every thing moveable was destroyed in the most minute manner, except such things of value as were worth carrying off. . . . It was now becoming a war of plunder, of general leveling, and taking away the distinction of rich and poor: so that those gentlemen, who had promoted and approved the cruel treatment of Mr. Oliver, became now as fearful for themselves as the most loyal person in the town could be. When first the town took this new turn, I was in hopes that they would have disavowed all the riotous proceedings; that of the first night, as well as the last. But it is no such thing; great pains are taken to separate the two riots: what was done against Mr. Oliver is still approved of, as a necessary declaration of their resolution not to submit to the Stamp Act.

Source: Bernard, Francis. "Extract from a Letter to the Lords of Trade, dated August 31, 1765." *The Parliamentary History of England, from the Earliest Period to the Year 1803. From which Last-Mentioned Epoch It is Continued Downwards in the Work Entitled, "The Parliamentary Debates."* Vol. XVI. A. D. 1765–1771. London: Printed by T. C. Hansard, Peterborough-Court, Fleet-Street: for Longman, Hurst, Rees, Orme, & Brown; J. Richardson; Black, Parry, & Co.; J. Hatchard; J. Ridgway; E. Jeffery; J. Booker; J. Rodwell; Cardock & Joy; R. H. Evans; E. Budd; J. Booth; and T. C. Hansard, 1813. 129–131.

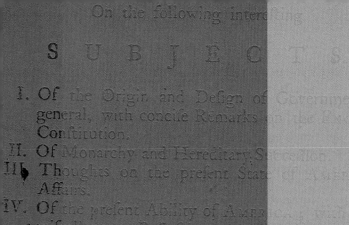

URNING of the FRIGATE PHILADELPHIA in the HARBOUR of TRIPOLI, 16ᵗʰ Feb. 1804.

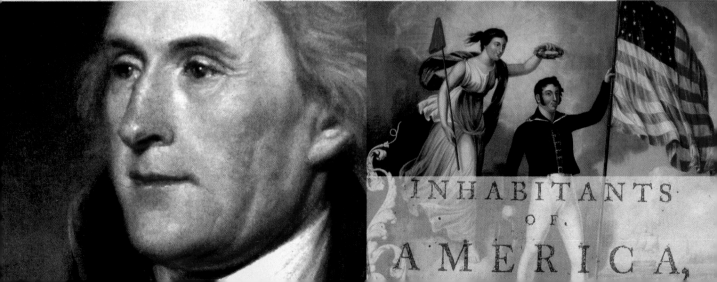

INHABITANTS OF AMERICA,

Building a Nation

The signing of the Declaration of Independence in early July 1776 thrilled the rebellious colonists and forced other Americans to make a life-or-death choice: to remain loyal subjects of King George III and thus traitors to the new United States of America, or to embrace the rebellion and become traitors to Great Britain. It was one thing for Patriot leaders to declare American independence and quite another to win it on the battlefield. The odds greatly favored the British; fewer than half of the colonists were Patriots who *actively* supported the Revolution, and many others—the Loyalists—fought against it. The political stability of the new nation was uncertain, and General George Washington found himself facing the world's greatest military power with a poorly supplied, often unpaid, and inexperienced army.

Yet the Revolutionaries would persevere and prevail. Washington and his lieutenants were skilled in taking advantage of geography. They knew the American landscape much better than the British. Even more important was the decision by the French to join the war against Britain. The Franco-American military alliance, negotiated in 1778, was the decisive event in the war. In 1783, after eight years of sporadic fighting and heavy human and financial losses, the British gave up the fight and their American colonies.

While fighting the British, the Patriots also had to create new governments for themselves. Colonies suddenly became co-equal states. The deeply ingrained resentment of British imperial rule led the Americans to give more power to the individual states than to the new national government. As Thomas Jefferson declared, "Virginia is my country." Such powerful local ties help explain why the Articles of Confederation, the original American constitution organizing the thirteen states into a nation, provided only minimal national authority when it was ratified in 1781. Final power to make and execute laws remained with the states. After the Revolutionary War, the flimsy political bonds authorized by the Articles of Confederation could not meet the needs of the new nation. This realization led to the calling of the Constitutional Convention in 1787. The process of drafting and approving the new constitution prompted a heated debate about the respective powers granted to the states and the national government, a debate that became the central theme of American political thought ever since.

The Revolution also unleashed social forces that would help reshape American culture. What would be the role of women, African Americans, and Native Americans in the new nation? How would the different economies of the various regions of the new United States be developed? Who would control access to the vast Native American lands to the west of the original thirteen states? How would the United States of America relate to the other nations of the world?

These questions gave birth to the first national political parties in the United States. During the 1790s, the Federalist party, led by George Washington and Alexander Hamilton, and the first Republican party, led by Thomas Jefferson and James Madison, furiously debated the political and economic future of the new nation. With Jefferson's election as president in 1800, the Republicans gained the upper hand in national politics and would remain dominant for the next quarter century. In the process, they presided over a maturing republic that aggressively expanded westward at the expense of the Native Americans, embraced industrial development, engaged in a second war with Great Britain, and witnessed growing tensions between North and South over slavery.

THE DEATH OF GENERAL MERCER AT THE BATTLE OF PRINCETON (CA. 1789–1831) Hot on the heels of the American victory in Trenton, New Jersey, was another unexpected win for George Washington (center, on horseback) and his men in the Battle of Princeton. One of the casualties, however, was Washington's close friend General Hugh Mercer (bottom), who became a rallying symbol for the revolution.

The American Revolution

1776–1783

Few foreign observers thought the upstart American revolutionaries could win a war against the world's richest and most powerful empire—and, indeed, the Americans did end up losing most of the battles in the Revolutionary War. But they outlasted the British, eventually forcing them to grant independence to the United States of America. This stunning result reflected the tenacity of the Patriots as well as the difficulties the British faced in fighting a transatlantic war thousands of miles from home.

What began as a war for independence became both a civil war between Americans (Patriots versus Loyalists), joined by their Indian allies, and a world war involving numerous "allied" European nations. The crucial development during the war was the ability of the United States to forge military alliances with France, Spain, and the Netherlands, all of which were eager to humble Great Britain and seize its colonies around the world. Those nations provided the American revolutionaries desperately needed money, supplies, soldiers, and warships. Ninety percent of the gunpowder used by American soldiers came from Europe.

Wars, of course, affect civilians as well as combatants. America's War of Independence unleashed unexpected social and political changes, as the effort to win the war required "common people" to take a more active role in governments at all levels, local, state, and national.

CORE OBJECTIVES INQUIZITIVE

1. Explain the challenges faced by both British and American military leaders in fighting the Revolutionary War.

2. Identify key turning points in the Revolutionary War, and explain how they changed the direction of the war.

3. Describe the ways in which the American Revolution was also a civil war.

4. Examine how the Revolutionary War was an "engine" for political and social change.

5. Compare the impact of the Revolutionary War on African Americans, women, and Native Americans.

After all, as the Declaration of Independence asserted, governments derive "their just powers from the consent of the governed." And the "common people" readily took advantage of the new opportunities provided by republicanism. In Virginia, voters in 1776 elected a new state legislature that, as an observer noted, "was composed of men not quite so well dressed, nor so politely educated, nor so highly born" as had been the case in the past.

> **CORE OBJECTIVE**
>
> **1.** Explain the challenges faced by both British and American military leaders in fighting the Revolutionary War.

Mobilizing for War

British Military Power

The British Empire sent some 35,000 soldiers and half of its huge navy across the Atlantic to put down the American rebellion. To aid their war effort, the British also hired foreign soldiers (mercenaries). Almost 30,000 Germans served in the British armies in America. Most of them were from the German state of Hesse-Cassel—thus they became known to Americans as *Hessians*. The British also recruited American Loyalists, Native Americans, and African Americans to fight on their behalf, but there were never as many as British leaders had hoped. Further, it was a formidable challenge for the British to keep their large army in America supplied. They initially assumed that there would be enough food for their troops and forage for their horses in America. But they quickly realized that most of the supplies would have to come from Britain. It took two to three months for ships to make the Atlantic crossing, depending upon the weather, and the war in America soon became terribly expensive.

> American challenges: Massive British forces

The British government under Lord North led Great Britain into a far-away war without a clear strategy for waging it. Initially, the British focused on blockading New England's seaports in order to strangle American trade and eventually force the Americans to give up. When that failed, the British military leaders sought to destroy George Washington's Continental army in New York. Despite their initial success in driving the Americans out of the city, the British generals failed to pursue the retreating Continental army. The British next tried to drive a wedge between New England and New York, splitting the colonies in two. That too would fail, leading to the final British strategy: moving their main army into the southern colonies in hopes of rallying Loyalists in that region to beat back the Revolutionaries. Although victorious in most conventional battles against the Americans, the British never fastened upon an overall strategy to defeat the Patriot cause. Ultimately, the Americans—fighting in their homeland for their independence and generously aided by the French—were able to outlast the British in a war of endurance.

The Continental Army

> American challenges: Finance and supply for the military, citizen-soldiers

While the Patriots had the advantage of fighting on their home ground—the American commanders knew the terrain and the people—but they also had to create an army and navy from scratch, and with little money.

Recruiting, supplying, equipping, training, and paying soldiers and sailors were monumental challenges for the new nation. At the start of the fighting, there were no uniforms, and American weapons were "as various as their costumes."

The Patriot army that encircled the British in Boston in 1775 was little more than a poorly trained militia made up of lightly armed volunteers who had enlisted for six months. Unlike the professional soldiers in the British army, these part-time **citizen-soldiers** were mostly poor American farmers or recent immigrants who had been indentured servants. They often came and went as they pleased, gambled frequently, and drank liquor freely. The states rarely provided their share of the war's expenses, and the Continental Congress reluctantly had to allow the Patriot armies to take supplies directly from farmers in return for promises of future payment.

Before the war for independence, American militiamen (citizen-soldiers) were primarily a home guard—civilians called out from their farms and shops on short notice to defend their local communities. To repel an attack, the militiamen somehow mustered themselves; once the danger was past, they disappeared, for there were chores to do at home. Many of the local militiamen were unreliable and ungovernable. They "come in, you cannot tell how," General Washington said in exasperation, "go, you cannot tell when, and act you cannot tell where, consume your provisions, exhaust your stores [supplies], and leave you at last at a critical moment." Once the war started, American leaders knew that they could not win against veteran British and German soldiers using only militiamen. They needed a professional army of their own, with full-time soldiers enlisted from all thirteen colonies. As he recruited such an army, General Washington was pleased to see that the men from different colonies were developing a national (or "continental") viewpoint, in which they thought of themselves as fighting for a new *nation*, not just protecting their particular communities like militiamen. Washington thus decided to call it the *Continental army*. What the Continental army needed most were capable officers, intensive training, strict discipline, and multi-year enlistment contracts. He soon began whipping his new army into shape. Recruits who violated army rules were jailed, flogged, or sent packing. Some deserters were hanged.

George Washington at Princeton Commissioned for Independence Hall in Philadelphia, this 1779 painting by Charles Willson Peale portrays Washington as the hero of the Battle of Princeton.

Native Americans and the Revolution

Both the British and Americans recruited Indian allies to "take up the hatchet" and fight with them, but the British were far more successful, because they promised to protect Indian lands. The peoples making up the Iroquois League split their allegiances, with most Mohawks, Onondagas, Cayugas, and Senecas, led by Mohawk Joseph Brant and Seneca Old Smoke, joining the British, and most Oneidas and Tuscaroras supporting the Patriots. The Cherokees also joined the British in hopes of driving out American settlers who had taken their lands. Most Indians in New England tried to remain neutral or sided with the Patriots. The Stockbridge Indians in Massachusetts, mostly Mahicans, formed a company of Minutemen who fought alongside Patriot

American and British challenges: Recruiting Native Americans

citizen-soldiers Part-time non-professional soldiers, mostly poor farmers or recent immigrants who had been indentured servants, who played an important role in the Revolutionary War.

units. They pledged that "wherever your armies go, there we will go; you shall always find us by your side; and if providence calls us to sacrifice our lives in the field of battle, we will fall where you fall, and lay our bones by yours. Nor shall peace ever be made between our nation and the Red-Coats until our brothers—the white people—lead the way." But however much the British or Americans claimed Native Americans as allies, most Indians engaged in the war as a means of protecting themselves and their own interests.

Disaster in Canada

In July 1775, the Continental Congress authorized an ill-fated attack against Quebec, in the vain hope of rallying support for the American rebellion among the French inhabitants in Canada. One Patriot detachment, under General Richard Montgomery, headed toward Quebec by way of Lake Champlain along the New York–Canadian border; another, under General Benedict Arnold, struggled westward through the dense Maine woods. The American units arrived outside Quebec in September, exhausted and hungry. A silent killer then ambushed them: smallpox. As the deadly virus raced through the American camp, General Montgomery faced a brutal dilemma. Most of his soldiers had signed up for short tours of duty, and many of them were scheduled for discharge at the end of the year. He could not afford to wait until spring for the smallpox to subside. Seeing little choice but to fight, Montgomery ordered a desperate attack on the British forces at Quebec during a blizzard, on December 31, 1775.

The assault on New Year's Eve was a disaster. Montgomery was killed early in the battle and Benedict Arnold was wounded. Over 400 Americans were taken prisoner. The rest of the Patriot force retreated to its camp outside the walled city and appealed to the Continental Congress for reinforcements. The smallpox virus spread throughout the American army. As fresh troops arrived, they too fell victim to the deadly virus. General Benedict Arnold warned George Washington in February 1776 that the runaway disease would soon lead to "the entire ruin of the Army." The British, sensing the weakness of the American force, attacked and sent the ragtag Patriots on a frantic retreat up the St. Lawrence River to the American-held city of Montreal and eventually back to New York and New England.

Quebec was the first military setback for the Revolutionaries. It would not be the last. By the summer of 1776, Americans knew that their quest for independence would be neither short nor easy, for King George and the British government were determined to crush the revolt and restore their Empire. To do so, they were willing to gather the most powerful fighting force in the world.

Washington's Narrow Escape

On July 2, 1776, the day the Continental Congress voted for independence, British redcoats landed on undefended Staten Island, across New York City's harbor from Manhattan. They were the first wave in a determined effort to smash the American Revolution. During the summer of 1776, a massive British fleet of 427 warships carrying 32,000 British and German troops, 1,200 cannons, and 10,000 sailors began landing on Long Island near New York City. It was the largest seaborne military expedition in history. "I could not believe my eyes," recalled a Pennsylvania militiaman. "I declare that I thought all London was afloat."

Meanwhile, Washington could gather only about 19,000 poorly trained militiamen and recruits in the new Continental army. It was too small a force to defend New York, but the Continental Congress wanted to keep the city in Patriot hands. Although a veteran of frontier fighting, Washington had never commanded a large force or supervised artillery (cannon) units. As he confessed to the Continental Congress, he had no "experience to move [armies] on a large scale" and had only "limited . . . knowledge . . . in military matters." In 1776 he was still learning the art of generalship, and the British invasion of New York taught him some costly and painful lessons.

Short of weapons and greatly outnumbered, the American army suffered a humiliating defeat at the Battle of Long Island. Had the British moved more quickly, they could have trapped Washington's entire army as it fled across lower Manhattan. But the British rested as the main American force made a miraculous escape northward, crossed the Hudson River, and retreated into New Jersey and over the Delaware River into eastern Pennsylvania.

By December 1776, the American Revolution was near collapse as winter arrived. A British officer reported that many of the "rebels" were "without shoes or stockings, and several were observed to have only linen drawers . . . without any proper shirt. They must suffer extremely." Washington had only 3,000 men left under his command, as thousands of militiamen had simply gone home to sit out the winter or tend to their farms. Unless a new army could be raised quickly, Washington warned, "I think the game is pretty near up."

But help emerged from an unexpected source: Englishman Thomas Paine. Having opened the eventful year of 1776 with his inspiring pamphlet *Common Sense*, Paine now composed *The American Crisis*, in which he wrote these stirring lines:

> These are the times that try men's souls: The summer soldier and the sunshine patriot will, in this crisis, shrink from the service of his country; but he that stands it NOW deserves the love and thanks of man and woman. Tyranny, like Hell, is not easily conquered. Yet we have this consolation with us, that the harder the conflict, the more glorious the triumph.

Paine's rousing pamphlet boosted Patriot morale. Soon the Continental Congress's decision to offer army recruits cash, land, clothing, and blankets would provide further support for what Paine's pamphlet inspired.

Thomas Paine's *Common Sense*
Thomas Paine's inspiring pamphlet was originally published anonymously because the British viewed its content as evidence of treason.

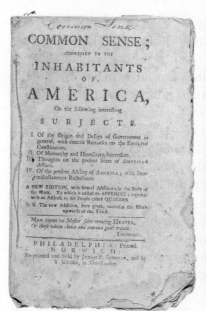

In December 1776, General William Howe, commander in chief of the British forces, settled down with his married Loyalist mistress (twenty-five-year-old Elizabeth Loring) to wait out the winter in New York City. (Eighteenth-century armies rarely fought during the winter months.) By not pursuing the Americans as they retreated from Long Island and later Manhattan, Howe had lost a great opportunity to end the Revolution. In coming months, he would continue to miss chances to destroy the struggling Continental army, leading one American general to conclude that Howe "shut his eyes, fought his battles, drank his bottle and had his little whore."

A Desperate Gamble

George Washington, however, was not ready to hibernate for the winter. He decided that the morale of his men and the hopes of the nation required "some stroke" of good news after the devastating defeats they had suffered around New York City. So he launched a desperate gamble to achieve a much-needed victory before more of his soldiers decided to return home. On Christmas night 1776, Washington led some 2,400 men, packed into forty-foot-long boats, from Pennsylvania across the icy, swollen Delaware River into New Jersey. Near dawn at Trenton, the Americans surprised 1,500 sleeping Hessians. It was a total rout, from which only 500 Hessians escaped. Just two of Washington's men were killed and four wounded, one of whom was James Monroe, the future president. A week later, the Americans again crossed the Delaware River and won another battle at Princeton before taking shelter in winter quarters at Morristown, in the hills of northern New Jersey. A British officer grumbled that the Americans had "become a formidable enemy." The American victories at Princeton and Trenton saved the cause of independence. A wave of Americans signed up to serve in Washington's army.

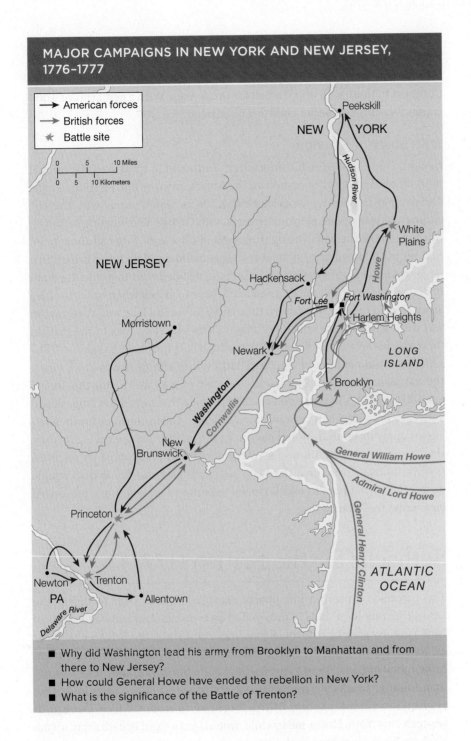

MAJOR CAMPAIGNS IN NEW YORK AND NEW JERSEY, 1776–1777

→ American forces
→ British forces
✳ Battle site

- Why did Washington lead his army from Brooklyn to Manhattan and from there to New Jersey?
- How could General Howe have ended the rebellion in New York?
- What is the significance of the Battle of Trenton?

Winter in Morristown

During the winter at Morristown in early 1777, George Washington's army nearly disintegrated as six-month enlistment contracts expired and deserters fled the brutal weather, inadequate food, and widespread disease. One soldier recalled that "we were absolutely, literally starved.... I saw several of the men roast their old shoes and eat them."

American challenges: Demoralized troops

Only about a thousand Continental soldiers and a few militiamen stuck out the Morristown winter. With the spring thaw, however, recruits began arriving to claim the $20 and 100 acres of land offered by the Continental Congress to those who would enlist for three years. With a new army of 9,000 troops, Washington began planning his strategy for 1777.

A Strategy of Evasion

British challenges: American evasion and selective confrontation, and high supply costs

General Howe, the British commander, continued to think in conventional military terms, hoping to maneuver the American army into fighting a single decisive battle that the superior British forces would surely win, thereby ending the war in one glorious engagement. George Washington, however, refused to take the bait. The fighting around New York City had shown him that his outmanned army almost certainly could not defeat the British in a large battle. The only way to beat them, he decided, was to evade the main British army, carefully select when and where to attack when opportunities arose, and, in the end, wear down the enemy forces in a long war. Washington was willing to concede control of major cities like New York to the British, for it was his army, "not defenseless towns, [that] they have to subdue." The Americans did not have to win large battles; they simply had to avoid losing the war. Britain, on the other hand, could win only by destroying the American will to resist. Victory would come to the side that fought the longest, and with each passing year it became more difficult—and expensive—for the British to supply its large army and navy in America. During the next eight years, the Americans would follow a strategy of evasion punctuated by selective confrontations. Over time, the British government and the British people would tire of the human and financial expense of conducting a prolonged war across the Atlantic.

CORE **OBJECTIVE**
2. Identify key turning points in the Revolutionary War, and explain how they changed the direction of the war.

Setbacks for the British (1777)

The carefully conceived but poorly executed British plan to defeat the "American rebellion" in 1777 involved a three-pronged assault on the state of New York. By gaining control of that important state, the British would cut off New England from the rest of the colonies. The plan called for a British army, based in Canada and led by General John Burgoyne, known as "Gentleman Johnny," to advance southward from Quebec via Lake Champlain to the Hudson River, while another British force moved eastward from Oswego, in western New York. Howe, meanwhile, would lead a third British army up the Hudson River from New York City. As often happens with ambitious, complicated war plans, however, the British failed in their execution—and in their communications with one another. At the last minute, Howe changed his mind and decided to move his army south to attack the Patriot capital, Philadelphia. General Washington withdrew most of his men from New Jersey to meet the British threat in Pennsylvania. On September 11, 1777, at

Brandywine Creek, southwest of Philadelphia, the British overpowered the Americans and then occupied Philadelphia, the largest and wealthiest American city. The members of the Continental Congress were forced to flee the city. Washington and his army had to withdraw to winter quarters twenty miles away at Valley Forge, while Howe and his men remained in the relative comfort of Philadelphia.

The Campaign of 1777

Meanwhile, an overconfident General Burgoyne (nicknamed "General Swagger") led his mistress and army (including 225 women and 500 children) southward from Canada through dense forests and across rivers and creeks toward New York's Lake Champlain in June 1777. The heavily laden army struggled to cross the wooded, marshy terrain in upstate New York.

The American army commander in New York facing Burgoyne's redcoats was General Horatio Gates. In 1745, Gates and Burgoyne had joined the same British regiment. Now they were commanding opposing armies. As Patriot militiamen converged from across central New York, Burgoyne pulled his dispirited forces back to the village of Saratoga, where the reinforced American army surrounded the outnumbered and now-stranded British army, which was desperate for food.

In the ensuing, three-week-long **Battles of Saratoga**, Gates's army surrounded the outnumbered British forces, cutting off their supply lines. Desperate to retreat back to Canada, the British twice tried—and failed—to break through the encircling Americans. On October 17, 1777, Burgoyne surrendered his outnumbered and nearly starving army, turning over 5,800 troops, 7,000 muskets, and forty-two brass cannons to Gates. Burgoyne's shocking surrender prompted former British prime minister William Pitt to tell Parliament, "*You cannot conquer America.*" King George was devastated by the news, falling "into agonies on hearing the account" of Burgoyne's defeat.

Alliance with France

The surprising American victory at Saratoga was a strategic turning point because it convinced the French, who had lost four wars to the British in the previous eighty years, to sign two crucial treaties in early 1778 that created an American **alliance with France**. Under the Treaty of Amity and Commerce, France officially recognized the new United States and offered trade concessions, including important privileges to American shipping. Next, under the Treaty of Alliance, both parties agreed, first, that if France entered the war, both countries would fight until American independence was won; second, that neither would conclude a "truce or peace" without "the formal consent of the other"; and third, that each would guarantee the other's possessions in America "from the present time and forever against all other powers." France further bound itself to seek neither Canada nor other British possessions on the mainland of North America. In the end, it

General John Burgoyne Commander of Britain's northern forces. Burgoyne and most of his troops surrendered to the Americans at Saratoga on October 17, 1777.

Battles of Saratoga (1777)

Battles of Saratoga (1777) Decisive defeat of 5,000 British troops under General John Burgoyne in several battles near Saratoga, New York, in October 1777; the American victory helped convince France to enter the war on the side of the Patriots.

alliance with France Critical diplomatic, military, and economic alliance between France and the newly independent United States, codified by the Treaty of Amity and Commerce and the Treaty of Alliance (1778).

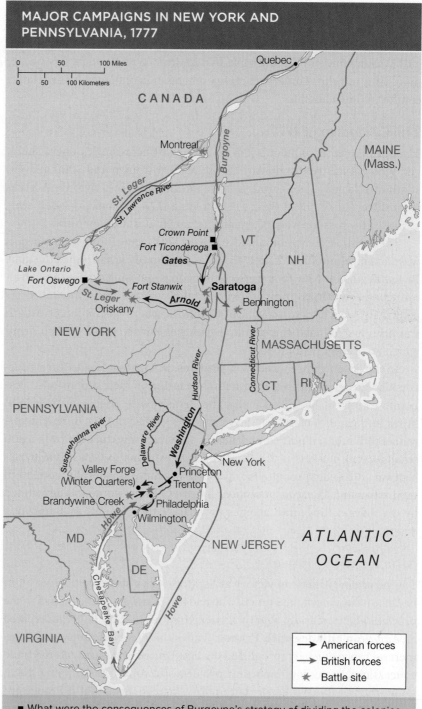

MAJOR CAMPAIGNS IN NEW YORK AND PENNSYLVANIA, 1777

- What were the consequences of Burgoyne's strategy of dividing the colonies with two British forces?
- How did life in Washington's winter camp at Valley Forge transform the American army?
- Why was Saratoga a turning point in the American Revolution?

was the intervention of the French army and navy on behalf of the struggling Americans that determined the outcome of the war. By June 1778, British vessels had fired on French ships and the two nations were at war once again. The Americans would also form alliances with the Spanish (1779) and the Dutch (1781), but neither of those allies provided as much support as the French.

After the British defeat at Saratoga and the news of the French alliance with the United States, the British Parliament tried to end the war by granting all the demands that the American rebels had made before they declared independence. But the Continental Congress would not negotiate until Britain recognized American independence and withdrew its forces. King George refused.

Valley Forge and Stalemate

For George Washington's army at **Valley Forge**, near Philadelphia, the winter of 1777–1778 was a time of intense suffering. The American forces endured unrelenting cold, hunger, and disease. Some soldiers lacked shoes and blankets, and their makeshift log-and-mud huts offered little protection from the howling winds and bitter cold. By February, 7,000 troops were too ill for duty. More than 2,500 soldiers died at Valley Forge; another 1,000 deserted. Fifty officers resigned on one December day. Several hundred more left before winter's end.

Desperate for relief, Washington sent troops across New Jersey, Delaware, and the Eastern Shore of Maryland to confiscate horses, cattle, and hogs in exchange for "receipts" promising future payment. By March 1778 the once-gaunt troops at Valley Forge saw their strength restored. Their improved health enabled Washington to begin a rigorous training program, designed to bring unity to his ragtag array of soldiers. Because few of the regimental commanders had any formal military training, their troops lacked leadership, discipline, and skills. To remedy this defect, Washington turned to an energetic Prussian soldier of fortune, Friedrich Wilhelm, baron von Steuben, who used an interpreter and frequent profanity to instruct the troops in the fundamentals of close-order drill: how to march in formation and how to handle their weapons properly.

Steuben was one of a number of foreign volunteers who joined the American army at Valley Forge. Another European was a twenty-year-old red-haired Frenchman named Gilbert du Motier, Marquis de Lafayette. A wealthy idealist excited by the American cause, Lafayette offered to serve for no pay in exchange for being named a general. General Washington was initially skeptical of the young French aristocrat, but Lafayette soon became the commander in chief's most trusted aide. The French general also proved to be a courageous soldier and able diplomat.

The Continental army's morale rose when the Continental Congress promised extra pay and bonuses after the war. The good news from France

Winter of 1777-1778 at Valley Forge

Valley Forge (1777–1778) American military encampment near Philadelphia, where more than 3,500 soldiers deserted or died from cold and hunger in the winter.

about the formal military alliance also helped raise the Patriots' spirits. In the spring of 1778, British forces withdrew from Pennsylvania to New York City, with the American army in hot pursuit. Once the British were back in Manhattan, Washington's army encamped at nearby White Plains. From that time on, the major campaigns and battles in the North settled into a long stalemate.

War in the West

Terror tactics in Indian country

The one significant American military success of 1778 occurred in the west. The Revolution had created two wars. In addition to the main conflict between British and American armies in the east, a frontier guerrilla war of terror and vengeance pitted Indians and Loyalists against isolated Patriot settlers along the northern and western frontiers. In the Ohio Valley as well as western New York and Pennsylvania, the British urged frontier Loyalists and their Indian allies to raid farm settlements and offered to pay bounties for American scalps.

To end the English-led attacks, early in 1778 young George Rogers Clark took 175 Patriot frontiersmen on flatboats down the Ohio River. On the evening of July 4, the Americans captured English-controlled Kaskaskia (in present-day Illinois). Then, without bloodshed, Clark took Cahokia (in present-day Illinois across the Mississippi River from St. Louis) and Vincennes (in present-day Indiana). After the British retook Vincennes, Clark marched his men (almost half of them French volunteers) through icy rivers and flooded prairies, sometimes in water neck deep, and prepared to attack the astonished British garrison. Clark's men, all hardened woodsmen, captured five Indians carrying American scalps. Clark ordered his men to kill the Indians in sight of the fort. After watching the terrible executions, the British surrendered.

While Clark's Rangers were in the Indiana territory, a much larger American military expedition moved through western Pennsylvania to attack Iroquois strongholds in western New York, where Loyalists ("Tories") and their Indian allies had been terrorizing frontier settlements throughout the summer of 1778. Led by Mohawk chief Joseph Brant, the Iroquois had killed hundreds of militiamen along the Pennsylvania frontier. In response, George Washington sent 4,000 men under General John Sullivan to crush "the hostile tribes" and "the most mischievous of the Tories." At Newton, New York, on August 29, 1779, Sullivan's soldiers burned about forty Seneca and Cayuga villages, together with their orchards and food supplies, leaving many of the Indians homeless and without enough food to survive. The campaign broke the power of the Iroquois Confederacy for all time, but sporadic fighting continued until the end of the war.

In the Kentucky territory, Daniel Boone and his small band of settlers repeatedly clashed with the Shawnees and their British and Loyalist allies. In 1778, Boone and some thirty men, aided by their wives and children,

Joseph Brant This 1786 portrait of Thayendanegea (Joseph Brant) by Gilbert Stuart features the Mohawk leader who fought against the Americans in the Revolution.

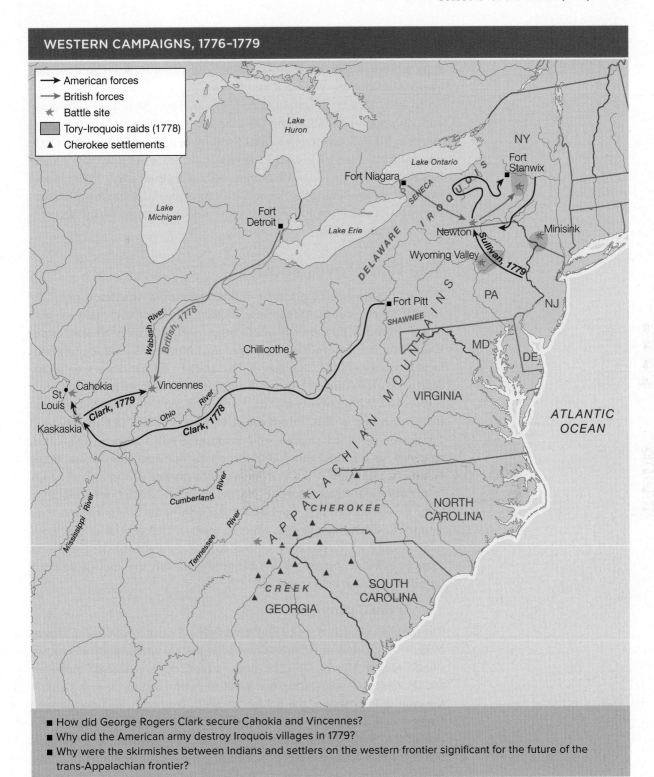

WESTERN CAMPAIGNS, 1776–1779

Legend:
- → American forces
- → British forces
- ✳ Battle site
- ▨ Tory-Iroquois raids (1778)
- ▲ Cherokee settlements

Lake Huron

Lake Michigan

Lake Ontario

Lake Erie

NY

Fort Niagara

Fort Stanwix

SENECA

IROQUOIS

Minisink

Newton

Wyoming Valley

Sullivan, 1779

Fort Detroit

DELAWARE

Wabash River

British, 1778

Fort Pitt

SHAWNEE

PA

NJ

Chillicothe

MD

DE

St. Louis

Cahokia

Vincennes

Clark, 1779

Ohio River

Clark, 1778

VIRGINIA

ATLANTIC OCEAN

Kaskaskia

Mississippi River

Cumberland River

Tennessee River

APPALACHIAN MOUNTAINS

CHEROKEE

NORTH CAROLINA

SOUTH CAROLINA

CREEK

GEORGIA

- How did George Rogers Clark secure Cahokia and Vincennes?
- Why did the American army destroy Iroquois villages in 1779?
- Why were the skirmishes between Indians and settlers on the western frontier significant for the future of the trans-Appalachian frontier?

held off an assault by more than 400 Indians at Boonesborough. Later, Boone himself was twice shot and twice captured. Indians killed two of his sons, a brother, and two brothers-in-law. His daughter was captured, and another brother was wounded four times.

In early 1776, a delegation of northern Indians—Shawnees, Delawares, and Mohawks—had talked the Cherokees into striking at frontier settlements in Virginia and the Carolinas. Swift retaliation had followed as Carolina militiamen led by Andrew Pickens burned dozens of Cherokee villages just east of the Blue Ridge Mountains, destroying their corn, orchards, and livestock. By weakening the major Native American nations along the frontier, the American Revolution cleared the way for white settlers to seize Indian lands after the war.

The War Moves South

In late 1778, the new commander of British forces in America, General Sir Henry Clinton, sent 3,000 redcoats, Hessians, and Loyalists to take the port city of Savannah, on the southeast Georgia coast, and roll northeast toward Charleston, South Carolina gathering momentum by enlisting support from local Loyalists and the Cherokee, led by Chief Dragging Canoe, who promised to leave the ground "dark and bloody." Initially, Clinton's southern strategy worked. Within twenty months, the British and their allies had defeated three American armies, seized the strategic port cities of Savannah and Charleston occupied Georgia and much of South Carolina, and killed, wounded, or captured some 7,000 American soldiers. The success of the "southern campaign" led a British official to predict a "speedy and happy termination of the American war." But his optimistic prediction fell victim to three developments: first, the Loyalist strength in the South was less than estimated; second, the British effort to unleash Indian attacks convinced many undecided backcountry settlers to join the Patriot side; and, third, some British and Loyalist soldiers behaved so harshly that they drove other Loyalists to switch to the rebel side.

War in the Carolinas

The Carolina campaign took a major turn when British forces, led brilliantly by generals Clinton and Charles Cornwallis, bottled up an American army in Charleston. On May 12, 1780, the American general surrendered Charleston and its 5,500 defenders, the single greatest Patriot loss of the war. General Cornwallis, in charge of the British troops in the South, defeated a much larger American force at Camden, South Carolina. Cornwallis had Georgia and most of South Carolina under British control by 1780. Much of the fighting in the Carolinas was a civil war pitting Americans against Americans, Patriots fighting Loyalists, and both sides looted farms and plantations and tortured, scalped, and executed prisoners.

The Battle of King's Mountain

Cornwallis's two most ruthless cavalry officers, Sir Banastre Tarleton and Major Patrick Ferguson, who were in charge of training Loyalist militiamen, eventually overreached themselves. In a war without mercy, the British officers often let their men burn Patriot farms, liberate slaves, and destroy livestock. Major Ferguson sealed his doom when he threatened to march over the Blue Ridge Mountains, hang the mostly Scots-Irish Presbyterian frontier Patriot leaders ("backwater barbarians"), and destroy their farms. Instead, the feisty "overmountain men" from southwestern Virginia and western North and South Carolina (including "Tennesseans") went hunting for Ferguson and his army of Carolina Loyalists.

On October 7, 1780, the two sides clashed near King's Mountain, a heavily wooded ridge along the North Carolina border with South Carolina. There, in a ferocious hour-long battle, Patriot sharpshooters devastated the Loyalist troops. Major Ferguson, the only British soldier in the battle, had boasted beforehand that "all the rebels in hell could not push him off" King's Mountain. His body was riddled with seven bullet holes. Seven hundred Loyalists were captured, twenty-five of whom were later hanged. "The division among the people is much greater than I imagined," an American officer wrote to one of General Washington's aides. The Patriots and Loyalists, he said, "persecute each other with . . . savage fury."

| The Battle of King's Mountain (1780) |

As with so many confrontations during the war in the South, the Battle of King's Mountain was like an extended family feud. Seventy-four sets of brothers fought on both sides, and twenty-nine sets of fathers and sons. After the battle, Patriot captain James Withrow refused to help his Loyalist brother-in-law, who had been badly wounded. "Look to your friends for help," he said, leaving him to die on the battlefield. When Withrow's wife learned how her husband had treated her brother, she asked for a separation. Five brothers in the Goforth family from Rutherford County, North Carolina, fought at King's Mountain; three were Loyalists, two were Patriots. Only one of them survived. Two of the brothers, Preston and John Preston, both excellent riflemen fighting on opposite sides, recognized each other during the battle, took deadly aim as if in a duel, and fired simultaneously, killing each other.

The Battle of King's Mountain was a crucial American victory, for it undermined the British strategy in the South. Thomas Jefferson later said that the Battle of King's Mountain was "the turn of the tide of success." After King's Mountain, the British forces under Cornwallis retreated back into South Carolina and found it virtually impossible to recruit more Loyalists. By proving that the British and their Loyalist supporters could be beaten, the Battle of King's Mountain inspired farmers to join Patriot units under colorful leaders such as Francis Marion, "the Swamp Fox," and Thomas Sumter, "the Carolina Gamecock."

The Tide Turns in the South

In late 1780, the Continental Congress chose a new commander for the American army in the South: General Nathanael Greene, "the fighting Quaker" of Rhode Island. A former blacksmith blessed with unflagging patience, he was George Washington's ablest general—and well suited to the drawn-out war against the British forces. From Charlotte, North Carolina, where Greene arrived in December 1780, he moved his army eastward while sending General Daniel Morgan, one of the heroes of the Battle of Saratoga, with about 700 men on a sweep to the west of Cornwallis's headquarters at Winnsboro, South Carolina.

American victory at Cowpens

On January 17, 1781, Morgan's force took up positions near Cowpens, an area of cattle pastures in northern South Carolina, and lured Tarleton's army into an elaborate trap. Tarleton, long celebrated for his bravery but hated for his brutality, rushed his men forward, only to be ambushed by Morgan's cavalry. Tarleton himself escaped, but 110 British soldiers were killed and more than 700 were taken prisoner. Cowpens was the most complete tactical victory for the American side in the Revolution (Morgan called it a "devil of a whipping") and was one of the few times that Americans won a battle in which the two sides were evenly matched. When British general Cornwallis learned of the American victory, he snapped his sword in two, saying that the news "broke my heart."

After the victory at Cowpens, Morgan's army moved into North Carolina and linked up with Greene's troops. Greene lured Cornwallis's starving army north, then attacked the redcoats at Guilford Courthouse (near what became Greensboro, North Carolina) on March 15, 1781. The Americans lost the battle but inflicted such heavy losses that Cornwallis left behind his wounded and marched his men off toward Wilmington, on the North Carolina coast, to rest and take on supplies from British ships. The British commander reported that the Americans had "fought like demons." Greene then resolved to go back into South Carolina in the hope of drawing Cornwallis after him, or forcing the British to give up the state. Greene joined forces with local guerrilla bands led by Francis Marion and Thomas Sumter. Together they worked to win the war by using hit-and-run tactics that prolonged the fighting.

A War of Endurance

The Revolutionary War had become a contest of endurance, and the Americans held the advantage in time, men, and supplies. They knew they could outlast the British as long as they avoided a catastrophic defeat in any single battle. "We fight, get beat, rise, and fight again," General Greene said. By September 1781, the Americans had narrowed British control in the South to Charleston and Savannah, although local Patriots and Loyalists would continue to battle each other for more than a year in the backcountry, where there was "nothing but murder and devastation in every quarter," Greene said.

Meanwhile, General Cornwallis had pushed his British army northward from Wilmington, reasoning that before the Carolinas could be subdued, Virginia must be eliminated as a source of American reinforcements and supplies. In May 1781, the British marched into southeastern Virginia. There, the former American general Benedict Arnold, who had switched sides in the war, was eager to strike at the American forces. Arnold had earlier plotted to sell out his former American command of West Point, a critically important fortress on the Hudson River north of New York City. Only the lucky capture of a British spy, Major John André, had exposed Arnold's plot. Warned that his plan had been discovered, Arnold had joined the British in New York City, while the Americans hanged André as a spy.

Yorktown

When Cornwallis and his army joined up with Arnold's at Petersburg, Virginia, their combined British forces totaled 7,200 men. As the Americans approached, Cornwallis picked York-

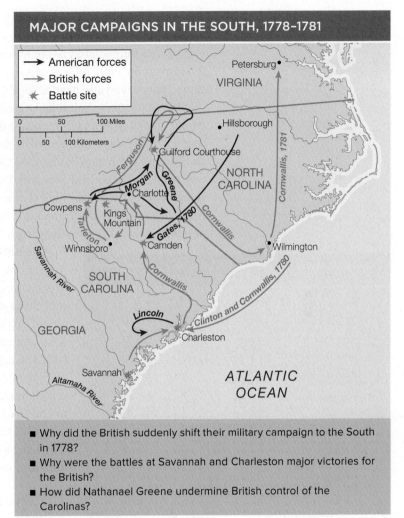

MAJOR CAMPAIGNS IN THE SOUTH, 1778-1781

→ American forces
→ British forces
✷ Battle site

- Why did the British suddenly shift their military campaign to the South in 1778?
- Why were the battles at Savannah and Charleston major victories for the British?
- How did Nathanael Greene undermine British control of the Carolinas?

town, Virginia, a small tobacco port between the York and James Rivers on the Chesapeake Bay, as his base of operations. He was not worried about an American attack, since General Washington's main force seemed preoccupied with attacking New York, and the British navy controlled American waters. In July 1780, the French had finally managed to land 6,000 soldiers at Newport, Rhode Island, which the British had given up in order to concentrate on the South, but the French army had been bottled up there for a year, blockaded by the British fleet. As long as the British navy maintained supremacy along the coast, the Americans could not hope to win the war.

In May 1781, however, the elements for a combined Franco-American action suddenly fell into place. Indeed, it is impossible to imagine an American victory in the Revolution without the assistance of the French. As Cornwallis's army moved into Virginia, Washington persuaded the commander of the French army in Rhode Island to join in an attack on the British army in New York. The two armies linked up in July, but before they could strike, word came from the West Indies that Admiral François-Joseph-Paul de Grasse

> Yorktown: French forces tip the balance and British surrender

was headed for the Chesapeake Bay with his large French fleet and some 3,000 soldiers. The unexpected news led General Washington to change his strategy. He immediately began moving his army south toward Yorktown. At the same time, French ships slipped out of the British blockade at Newport, Rhode Island, and also headed south.

On August 30, Admiral de Grasse's fleet reached Yorktown, and French troops landed to join the Americans confronting Cornwallis's army. On September 6, the day after a British fleet appeared, de Grasse attacked and forced the British navy to abandon Cornwallis's army, leaving them with no way to get fresh food and supplies. De Grasse then sent ships up the Chesapeake to ferry down the soldiers who were marching south from New York, bringing the total American and French armies to 16,000 men—more than double the size of Cornwallis's army.

YORKTOWN, 1781

The **Battle of Yorktown** commenced on September 28, 1781. The combined American and French troops soon closed off Cornwallis's last route of escape and began bombarding the besieged British troops with artillery. On October 17, 1781, a glum Cornwallis surrendered. Two days later, the British force of more than 7,000 marched out and laid down their weapons. Cornwallis himself claimed to be too ill to participate. His report to the British commander in chief was brief: "I have the mortification to inform your Excellency that I have been forced to surrender the troops under my command."

The Treaty of Paris (1783)

Any lingering British hopes of victory vanished at Yorktown. In London, Lord North reacted to the news of the surrender as if he had "taken a ball [bullet] in the breast." The prime minister exclaimed: "Oh God, it is all over." In December 1781, King George decided to send no more troops to America. On February 27, 1782, Parliament voted to end the war, and on March 20, Lord North resigned. In part, the British leaders chose peace in America so that they could concentrate on their continuing global war with France and Spain.

Upon learning of the British decision to negotiate, the Continental Congress named a group of prominent Americans to go to Paris to discuss terms with the British. The commissioners included John Adams, who was then representing the United States in the Netherlands; John Jay, minister (ambassador) to Spain; and Benjamin Franklin, already in France. The cranky John Adams was an odd choice since, as Thomas Jefferson said, "He hates [Benjamin] Franklin, he hates John Jay, he hates the French, he hates the

Battle of Yorktown (1781) Last major battle of the Revolutionary War; General Cornwallis, along with over 7,000 British troops, surrendered to George Washington at Yorktown, Virginia, on October 17, 1781.

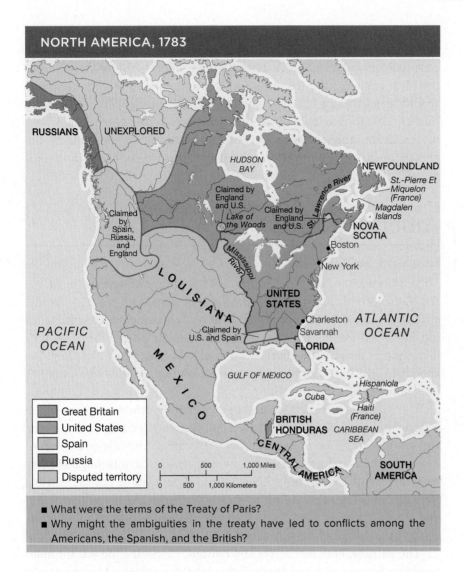

NORTH AMERICA, 1783

RUSSIANS UNEXPLORED

HUDSON BAY

NEWFOUNDLAND

St.-Pierre Et Miquelon (France)

Magdalen Islands

Claimed by England and U.S.

Lake of the Woods

Claimed by England and U.S.

St. Lawrence River

NOVA SCOTIA

Boston

Claimed by Spain, Russia, and England

Mississippi River

New York

LOUISIANA

UNITED STATES

PACIFIC OCEAN

Charleston ATLANTIC OCEAN

Claimed by U.S. and Spain

Savannah

MEXICO

FLORIDA

GULF OF MEXICO

Hispaniola

Cuba

Haiti (France)

BRITISH HONDURAS CARIBBEAN SEA

CENTRAL AMERICA

SOUTH AMERICA

Legend:
- Great Britain
- United States
- Spain
- Russia
- Disputed territory

0   500   1,000 Miles
0   500   1,000 Kilometers

■ What were the terms of the Treaty of Paris?
■ Why might the ambiguities in the treaty have led to conflicts among the Americans, the Spanish, and the British?

English." In the end, Franklin and Jay did most of the work leading to the peace treaty.

The negotiations with the British dragged on for months until, on September 3, 1783, the Treaty of Paris was signed. Its provisions were quite favorable to the United States—Franklin, Jay, and Adams had done very well. Great Britain recognized the independence of the thirteen former colonies and—surprisingly—agreed that the Mississippi River was America's western boundary, thereby more than doubling the territory of the new nation. The boundaries of the United States created by the treaty covered some 900,000 square miles, most of which were *west* of the Proclamation Line of 1763, a vast region long inhabited by Indians and often referred to as *Transappalachia*. Native American leaders were given no role in the negotiations, and Indians were by far the biggest losers in the final treaty.

The treaty's unclear references to America's northern and southern borders would be a source of dispute for years. Florida, as it turned out, passed back to Spain from Britain. As for the prewar debts owed by Americans to British merchants, the U.S. negotiators promised that British merchants should "meet with no legal impediment" in seeking to collect money owed them. And on the tender point of the thousands of Loyalist Americans whose homes, lands, and possessions had been seized by state governments, the negotiators agreed that the Continental Congress would "earnestly recommend" to the states that the confiscated property be restored.

CORE **OBJECTIVE**

3. Describe the ways in which the American Revolution was also a civil war.

American Society at War

Choosing Sides

The Revolution was as much a brutal civil war among Americans (including the Native American peoples allied with both sides) as it was a prolonged struggle against Great Britain. The necessity of choosing sides divided families and friends, towns and cities. Benjamin Franklin's illegitimate son, William, for example, was the royal governor of New Jersey. An ardent Loyalist, he sided with Great Britain during the Revolution, and his Patriot father later removed him from his will.

Colonists divided

The colonists were divided into three groups: Patriots, who formed the Continental army and fought in state militias; Loyalists, or Tories, as the Patriots mockingly called them; and a less committed middle group swayed mostly by the better organized and more energetic Patriots. Loyalists may have represented 20 percent of the American population, but the Patriots were probably the largest of the three groups. Some Americans (like Benedict Arnold) switched sides during the war, and there were numerous deserters, spies, and traitors on both sides.

The Patriots, both moderates and radicals, supported the war for independence because they had finally decided that the only way to protect their liberty was to separate themselves from British control and also from the British monarchy and aristocracy. Patriots also wanted to establish an American republic, a unique form of government in the late eighteenth century that would convert them from being *subjects* of a king to being *citizens* with the power to elect their own government and pursue their own economic interests. "We have it in our power," wrote Thomas Paine, "to begin the world over again. . . . The birthday of a new world is at hand."

Loyalists oppose independence

The Loyalists, also called Tories, Royalists, or "King's Men," had no desire to "dissolve the political bands" with Britain, as the Declaration of Independence demanded. Instead, as some 700 of them in New York City said in a petition to British officials, they "steadily and uniformly opposed" this "most unnatural, unprovoked Rebellion." Where the Patriots rejected the monarchy, the Loyalists staunchly upheld royal authority and appreciated being defended by British soldiers. The British Empire, they felt, had

***Four Soldiers* (ca. 1781)** This illustration by a French lieutenant captures the varied appearances of Patriot forces in the war (left to right): a black soldier (freed for joining the 1st Rhode Island Regiment), a New England militiaman, a frontiersman, and a French soldier.

long championed Protestantism, commerce, and liberty. Loyalists believed that the British constitution was more likely to protect their rights and liberties than the American aristocrats parading as revolutionaries. They viewed the Revolution as an act of treason and were horrified by the idea of independence.

Loyalists were most numerous in the seaport cities, especially New York City and Philadelphia, as well as the Carolinas, but they came from all walks of life. Governors, judges, and other royal officials were almost all Loyalists; most Anglican ministers also preferred the mother country, as did many Anglican worshippers. In the backcountry of New York and across the Carolinas, many small farmers who had largely been unaffected by the controversies over British efforts to tighten colonial regulations rallied to the British side. More New York men joined Loyalist regiments than the Continental army. Many Loyalists calculated that the Revolution would fail or feared that it would result in mob rule. In few places, however, were there enough Loyalists to assume control without the support of British troops.

The Loyalists Flee

The Loyalists suffered greatly for their stubborn support of King George and for their refusal to pledge allegiance to the new United States. During and after the Revolution, their homes, farms, and lands were confiscated, and many were assaulted and executed by Patriots (and vice versa). After the American victory at Yorktown, tens of thousands of panicked Loyalists headed to seaports to board British ships to flee the new United States. Thousands of African Americans, mostly runaway slaves, also flocked to New York City, Charleston, and Savannah, with many of their angry owners in hot pursuit.

The Fate of the Loyalists **(1783)** After the Revolution, many Loyalists fled to British colonies in the Caribbean and Canada. This British cartoon shows Patriots, depicted as "savages let[ting] loose," mercilessly hanging and scalping the Loyalists.

> Loyalist, African American, and Native American refugees

Some 80,000 desperate refugees—white Loyalists, free blacks, freed slaves, and Indians who had allied with the British—scattered throughout the British Empire, transforming it in the process. The largest number of Loyalist exiles landed in Canada, including 3,500 former slaves who had been given their freedom in exchange for joining the British army.

The departure of so many Loyalists from America was one of the most important social consequences of the Revolution. Their confiscated homes, vast tracts of land, and vacated jobs created new social, economic, and political opportunities for Patriots.

> CORE **OBJECTIVE**
>
> **4.** Examine how the Revolutionary War was an "engine" for political and social change.

War as an Engine of Change

Like all major wars, the Revolution had unexpected effects on political, economic, and social life. It not only secured American independence and created a unique system of self-governance, but it also began a process of societal change that has remained a defining element in the American experiment in representative democracy. The turmoil of eight years of war upset traditional social relationships and affected the lives of people who had long been discriminated against—African Americans, women, and Native Americans. In important ways, then, the Revolution was much more than simply a war for independence. It was an engine for political experimentation and social change.

A Political Revolution

> Debating the forms of government

The Americans had won their War of Independence. Had they experienced a political revolution as well? Years later, former President John Adams insisted that the Revolution had begun long before the shooting started: "The Revolution was in the minds and hearts of the people.... This radical change in the principles, opinions, sentiments, and affections of the people, was the real American Revolution." Yet Adams's observation notwithstanding, the war itself ignited a prolonged debate about what new forms of government would best serve the new American republic.

Republican Ideology

American revolutionaries embraced a **Republican ideology** instead of the monarchical outlook that had long dominated Europe. The new American republic was not a democracy in the purest sense of the word. In ancient Greece, the Athenians practiced *direct democracy*, which meant that the citizens voted on all major decisions affecting their society, not unlike the town meetings in New England villages today. The new United States, rather, was technically a *representative democracy*, in which property-holding white men governed themselves through the concept of republicanism, whereby they elected representatives, or legislators, to make key decisions on their behalf. As Thomas Paine observed, representative democracy had many advantages over monarchies, one of which was greater transparency: "Whatever are its excellencies and defects, they are visible to all."

To preserve the delicate balance between liberty and power in the new American republic, the Revolutionary leaders believed that their new governments must protect the rights of individuals and states from being violated by the national government. The war for independence thus sparked a wave of new **state constitutions** that remains unique in history. Not only was a new nation coming into being, but also new state-level governments were also being created, all of which were designed to reflect the principles of the "republican ideology" limiting the powers of government so as to protect the people's rights.

State Governments

Most of the political experimentation between 1776 and 1787 occurred at the state level in the form of written constitutions in which the people granted limited authority to their governments. The first state constitutions created governments much like the colonial governments, but with *elected* governors and senates instead of royally *appointed* governors and councils. Most of the constitutions also included a bill of rights that protected the time-honored rights of freedom of speech, trial by jury, freedom from self-incrimination, and the like. Most of them limited the powers of governors and strengthened the powers of the legislatures.

The Articles of Confederation

Once the American colonies had declared their independence in 1776, the Patriots needed to form a *national* government as well as thirteen *state* governments in the midst of the war. Before March 1781, the Continental Congress had exercised emergency powers without any legal or official authority. Plans for a permanent form of government emerged quickly,

> Representative democracy and individuals' rights

Republican ideology Political belief in representative democracy in which citizens govern themselves by electing representatives, or legislators, to make key decisions on the citizens' behalf.

state constitutions Charters that define the relationship between the state government and local governments and individuals, also protecting their rights from violation by the national government.

however. As early as July 1776, a committee appointed by the Continental Congress had produced a draft constitution called the *Articles of Confederation and Perpetual Union*. When the **Articles of Confederation** finally were ratified (approved by the states) five years later, in March 1781, they essentially legalized the way things had been operating since independence had been declared. The Confederation government reflected the long-standing American fears of monarchy by not even allowing for a president or chief executive. The Confederation Congress was given full power over foreign affairs and over disputes between the states. But the Confederation Congress had no courts and no power to enforce its resolutions and ordinances. It also had no power to levy taxes and had to rely for its own budgetary needs on requisitions from the states, which state legislatures often ignored.

> Limited government and states' rights

The states were in no mood to create a strong central government. The Confederation Congress, in fact, had less power than the colonists had once accepted in Parliament, since it could not regulate interstate and foreign commerce. For certain important acts, moreover, a "special majority" was required. Nine states had to approve measures dealing with war, treaties, coinage, finances, and the army and navy. Unanimous approval from the states was needed to levy tariffs (often called "duties," or taxes) on imports. Amendments to the Articles also required unanimous ratification by the states. The Confederation had neither an executive nor a judicial branch; there was no administrative head of government (only the president of the Confederation Congress, chosen annually) and no federal courts.

For all its weaknesses, however, the Confederation government represented the most practical structure for the new nation. After all, the Revolution on the battlefields had yet to be won, and an America besieged by British armies and warships could not risk divisive debates over the distribution of power that other forms of government might have entailed. The new state governments were not willing in 1776 to create a strong national government that might threaten their liberties.

Expansion of Political Participation

Participation in the Revolutionary army or militia excited men who previously had taken little interest in politics. The new political opportunities afforded by the creation of state governments led more ordinary citizens to participate than ever before. The property qualifications for voting, which already admitted an overwhelming majority of white men, were lowered after 1776. As a group of farmers explained, "no man can be free and independent" unless he possesses "a voice . . . in the most important officers in the legislature." In Pennsylvania, Delaware, North Carolina, and Georgia, any male taxpayer could vote. In addition, farmers, tradesmen, and shopkeepers were soon elected to state legislatures. In general, a higher percentage of American males could vote in the late eighteenth and early nineteenth century than their counterparts in Great Britain.

Articles of Confederation The first form of government for the United States, ratified by the original thirteen states in 1781; weak in central authority, it was replaced by the U.S. Constitution drafted in 1787.

A Social Revolution

The Revolutionary War helped excite a sense of common nationality. American nationalism embodied a stirring idea. This new nation, unlike the Old World nations of Europe, was not rooted in antiquity. Its people, except for the Native Americans, had not inhabited it over many centuries, nor did they all share the same ethnic background. "The American national consciousness," one observer wrote, "is not a voice crying out of the depth of the dark past, but is proudly a product of the enlightened present, setting its face resolutely toward the future."

A social revolution

Political revolutions often spark social revolutions. What did the Revolution mean to those workers, servants, farmers, and freed slaves who participated? Many hoped that the Revolution would remove, not reinforce, the elite's traditional political and social advantages. Many wealthy Patriots, on the other hand, would have been content to replace royal officials with the rich, the wellborn, and the able—and let it go at that. The poor did not overthrow the rich during the American Revolution, but the new republic's social fabric was visibly different after the war. The energy created by the concepts of liberty, equality, and democracy changed the dynamics of American social and political life in ways that people could not have imagined in 1776. The Philadelphia doctor and scientist Benjamin Rush recognized that unexpected changes were on the way: "The American war is over: but this is far from being the case with the American Revolution. On the contrary, but the first act of the great drama is closed."

Freedom of Religion

The Revolution also tested traditional religious loyalties and set in motion important changes in the relationship between church and government. Before the Revolution, Americans *tolerated* religious dissent; after the Revolution, Americans insisted on complete *freedom* of religion as embodied in the principle of separation of church and state. The Anglican Church, established as the official religion in five colonies and parts of two others, was especially vulnerable to changes prompted by the

Religious development The Congregational Church developed a national presence in the early nineteenth century. Lemuel Haynes, depicted here, was its first African American preacher.

war. Anglicans tended to be pro-British, and non-Anglicans, notably Baptists and Methodists, outnumbered Anglicans in all states except Virginia. All but Virginia eliminated tax support for the church before the fighting was over, and Virginia did so soon afterward. Although Anglicanism survived in the form of the new Episcopal Church, it never regained its pre-Revolutionary stature.

Religious freedom

In 1776, the Virginia Declaration of Rights guaranteed the free exercise of religion, and in 1786 the **Virginia Statute of Religious Freedom** (written by Thomas Jefferson) declared that "no man shall be compelled to frequent or support any religious worship, place or ministry whatsoever" and "that all men shall be free to profess, and by argument to maintain, their opinions in matters of religion." These statutes, and the Revolutionary ideology that justified them, helped shape the course that religious life would take in the new United States: diverse and voluntary rather than monolithic and enforced by the government. Even religious life was revolutionized.

CORE **OBJECTIVE**

5. Compare the impact of the Revolutionary War on African Americans, women, and Native Americans.

Equality and Its Limits

The Paradox of Slavery

The sharpest irony of the American Revolution is that Britain offered enslaved blacks more opportunities for freedom than did the new United States. In November 1775, the British promised freedom to slaves, as well as indentured servants, who would fight for the Loyalist cause. Thousands of slaves took advantage of the offer. Harry Washington, for example, was born in Africa, became one of George Washington's slaves in 1763, escaped to join the British army, and served in the Revolutionary War as a corporal in one of the black regiments organized by the British army. The British recruitment of slaves outraged George Washington, Thomas Jefferson, and other white plantation owners in Virginia, where 40 percent of the population was black. Twenty-three slaves escaped from Jefferson's Monticello plantation. The man who drafted the Declaration of Independence eventually reclaimed six of them, only to sell them for their "disloyalty" in seeking liberty for themselves.

In the end, however, the British policy of recruiting slaves into the military backfired. The "terrifying" prospect of British troops arming slaves persuaded many southerners to join the Patriot cause, and for many whites, especially in Virginia, the Revolution became primarily a war to defend slavery. Edward Rutledge of South Carolina said that the British decision to arm slaves did more to create "an eternal separation between Great Britain and the colonies than any other expedient." Slaves accused of disloyalty faced terrible punishment. In 1775, Thomas Jeremiah, a free black, was convicted and executed in Charleston, South Carolina, for telling slaves that British troops were coming "to help the poor Negroes."

In response to the British recruitment of enslaved African Americans, at the end of 1775 General Washington authorized the enlistment of free blacks—but not slaves—into the American army. Southerners, however, convinced the Continental Congress to instruct Washington in February 1776 to enlist no more African Americans, free or enslaved. But as the American war effort struggled, some states ignored southern wishes. Massachusetts organized two all-black army units, and Rhode Island organized one, which also included Indians. However, two states, South Carolina and Georgia, refused

Virginia Statute of Religious Freedom (1786) A Virginia law, drafted by Thomas Jefferson in 1777 and enacted in 1786, that guarantees freedom of, and from, religion.

to allow any blacks to serve in the Patriot forces. About 5,000 African Americans fought on the Patriot side, and most of them were free blacks from northern states.

The white Belknap family of Framingham, Massachusetts, freed their African American slave Peter Salem so that he might enlist in the Massachusetts militia. Salem was with the Minutemen at Concord in 1775 and also fought alongside other blacks at the Battles of Bunker Hill and Saratoga. Another former slave who fought at Bunker Hill, Salem Poor, was commended after the battle for being a "Brave & gallant Soldier" who "behaved like an experienced officer, as well as an excellent soldier."

In the end, the British army, which liberated 20,000 enslaved blacks during the war, was a far greater instrument of emancipation than the American forces. Most of the newly freed blacks found their way to Canada or to British colonies on Caribbean islands.

While thousands of free blacks and runaway slaves fought in the war, the vast majority of African Americans did not choose sides so much as they chose freedom. Several hundred thousand enslaved blacks, mostly in the southern states, took advantage of the disruptions caused by the war to seize their freedom. In the North, which had far fewer slaves than the South, the ideas of liberty and freedom that inspired the Patriots led most states to end slavery, either during the war or shortly afterward. In other words, the ideals of the Revolution provided the impulse to end slavery in the North, while at the same time, many southerners were prompted to join the Revolution to keep the British from freeing their slaves. These paradoxical attitudes would continue to shape the political disputes of the young nation.

British recruit and free slaves, while slavery abolished in the North

The Status of Women

The idea of liberty spawned by the Revolution applied to the status of women as much as to that of African Americans. The legal status of women in the colonies was governed by British common law, which essentially treated them like children, limiting their roles to child-rearing and maintaining the household. Women could not vote or hold office. Nor could they preach. Few had access to formal education. Boys were taught to read and write; girls were taught to read and sew. Most New England women in the eighteenth century could not write their own names. Until married, women were subject to their fathers. Once a woman married, she essentially became the property of her husband, and her goods became his. A married woman had no right to buy, sell, or manage property. Technically, any wages a wife earned belonged to the husband. Women could not sign contracts or sue others or testify in court. A husband could beat and even rape his wife without fearing legal action. Divorces were extremely difficult to obtain; wives were required to obey their husbands.

Yet the Revolution offered women new opportunities to broaden their social roles. Women supported the armies in various ways. They handled supplies, served as messengers or spies, and worked as camp followers, cooking, cleaning, and nursing the soldiers. Wives often followed their

Abigail Adams Abigail Adams, wife of John Adams, in a 1766 portrait. Though an ardent Patriot, Adams and other women like her saw few changes in women's rights emerging in the new United States.

soldier-husbands to camp and on occasion took their place in battle. In 1777, some 400 armed women mobilized to defend Pittsfield, Vermont. The men of the town had gone off to fight when a band of Loyalists and Indians approached the village. In a day-long battle, the women held off the attackers until help arrived. A few women disguised themselves and fought as ordinary soldiers. An exceptional case was Deborah Sampson, who joined a Massachusetts regiment as "Robert Shurtleff" and served from 1781 to 1783 by the "artful concealment" of her gender. Ann Bailey did the same. In 1777 she cut her hair, dressed like a man, and used a husky voice to enlist in the Patriot army in New York as "Samuel Gay." Bailey performed so well that she was promoted to corporal, only to eventually be discovered and dismissed.

Early in the Revolutionary struggle, Abigail Adams, one of the most learned, spirited, and independent women of the time, wrote to her husband, John: "In the new Code of Laws which I suppose it will be necessary for you to make, I desire you would remember the Ladies. . . . Do not put such unlimited power into the hands of the Husbands." Since men were "Naturally Tyrannical," she wrote, "why then, not put it out of the power of the vicious and the Lawless to use us with cruelty and indignity with impunity." Otherwise, "if particular care and attention is not paid to the Ladies we are determined to foment a Rebellion, and will not hold ourselves bound by any Laws in which we have no voice, or Representation." Husband John responded that he could not help but "laugh" at her proposals. While surprised that women might be dissatisfied, he insisted on retaining the traditional privileges enjoyed by males: "Depend upon it, we know better than to repeal our Masculine systems." If women were to be granted equality, he warned, then "children and apprentices" and "Indians and Negroes" would also demand equal rights and freedoms.

Thomas Jefferson shared Adams's stance. In his view, there was no place in the new American republic for female political participation. When asked about women's voting rights, he replied that "the tender breasts of ladies were not formed for political convulsion." Improvements in the status of women would have to wait. New Yorker Margaret Livingston admitted as much in 1776 when she wrote her daughter that "our Sex are *doomed* to be obedient [to men] at every stage of life so that we shan't be great gainers by this contest [the Revolutionary War]."

Little progress for women

Native Americans and the Revolution

The war for American independence had lasting effects on the Indians in the southern backcountry and in the Old Northwest territory west of New York and Pennsylvania. Most Native Americans sought to remain neutral in the war, but both British and American agents urged the chiefs to fight on their side. The result was the disintegration of the alliance among the six nations making up the Iroquois League. Most Mohawks, for example, accepted British promises to protect them from encroachments by American settlers on their lands. The Oneidas, on the other hand, fought with the Patriots. Indians on both sides attacked villages, burned crops, and killed civilians.

From Subjects to Citizens

The concepts of liberty, equality, and democracy changed the dynamics of American social and political life. As Americans won their War of Independence, they began to re-define their relationships with one another and develop new systems of government that reflected their view of themselves as independent citizens, not the subjects of any king.

Ideology	Americans embraced republicanism where political power was exercised by officials elected by citizens. They rejected all forms of monarchism or aristocracy. White men who owned certain amounts of property could vote in elections and enjoyed full rights as citizens.
Religion	Many state governments moved from the principle of religious tolerance to complete religious freedom for all citizens.
African Americans	During and after the Revolution, northern states began implementing policies to end slavery, concluding that the institution was incompatible with liberty. Southern states did not follow suit. Many slaveholders there had joined the Revolutionary side because they feared a British victory would result in freedom for their slaves.
Gender	Although women made significant contributions to the war for independence, men maintained control of politics, dismissing many women's appeals for political participation and voting rights.
Native Americans	While some Native Americans sided with the American Revolutionary cause, most did not. After independence, Americans continued to view them as a threat to future expansion and opportunity in the West.

QUESTIONS FOR ANALYSIS

1. Did Americans experience a *political* revolution after they won independence from Britain?

2. What was at the heart of the experiment in self-rule for the states?

3. How did the Revolution lead to broader political rights and expand civil liberties?

4. What were the ironies of the Revolution for African Americans, women, and Native Americans? Were there victories?

The new American government assured its Indian allies that it would respect their lands and their rights. But the American people adopted a very different goal: they used the disruptions of war to destroy and displace many Native Americans. Once the war ended and independence was secured, there was no peace for the Indians. The new U.S. government turned its back on most of the pledges made to Native Americans. By the end of the eighteenth century, land-hungry whites were again pushing into Indian territories on the western frontier. Independence for Americans would bring growing ex-ploitation of Native Americans.

Displacement and destruction of Native Americans

■ **Military Challenges** In 1776 the British had the mightiest army and navy in the world. The Americans had to create an army—the Continental army—and sustain it. To defeat the British, George Washington realized that the Americans had to turn unreliable *citizen-soldiers* into a disciplined fighting force. He decided to wage a long, costly war, wagering that the British army was fighting thousands of miles from its home base and would eventually give up in order to cut its losses.

■ **Turning Points** The French were likely allies for the colonies from the beginning of the conflict because they resented their losses to Britain in the Seven Years' War. After the British defeat at the *Battles of Saratoga* the first major turning point, France agreed to fight with the colonies until independence was won. Washington's ability to hold his ragged forces together despite daily desertions and two especially difficult winters in Morristown and *Valley Forge,* the second and third major turning points. The British lost support on the frontier and in their southern colonies when terrorist tactics backfired. The Battle of King's Mountain drove the British into retreat, and the *alliance with France* meant that French supplies and the French fleet would tip the balance and ensure the American victory at the *Battle of Yorktown*, which were the final turning points.

■ **Civil War** The American Revolution was also a civil war, dividing families and communities. There were at least 100,000 Loyalists in the colonies. They included royal officials, Anglican ministers, wealthy southern planters, and the elite in large seaport cities; they also included many humble people, especially recent immigrants. After the hostilities ended, many Loyalists, including slaves who had fled their plantations to support the British cause, left for Canada, the West Indies, or Great Britain.

■ **A Political and Social Revolution** The American Revolution disrupted and transformed traditional class and social relationships. American revolutionaries embraced a *Republican ideology* in contrast to a monarchy, and more white men gained the right to vote as property requirements were removed. But fears of a monarchy being re-established led colonists to vest power in the states rather than a powerful national government under the *Articles of Confederation*. The states wrote new *state constitutions* that instituted more elected positions. Most included bills of rights that protected individual liberties. The *Virginia Statute of Religious Freedom* led the way in guaranteeing the separation of church and state, and religious toleration was transformed into religious freedom for all, including Roman Catholics and Jews.

■ **African Americans, Women, and Native Americans** Northern states began to free slaves after the Revolutionary War, but southern states refused to do so. Although many women had undertaken nontraditional roles during the war, afterward they remained largely confined to the domestic sphere, with no changes to their legal or political status. The Revolution had catastrophic effects on Native Americans, regardless of which side they had embraced during the war. During and after the Revolution, American settlers seized Native American land, often in violation of existing treaties.

KEY TERMS

citizen-soldiers *p. 153*
Battles of Saratoga (1777) *p. 159*
alliance with France *p. 159*
Valley Forge (1777–1778) *p. 161*

Battle of Yorktown (1781) *p. 168*
Republican ideology *p. 173*
state constitutions *p. 173*

Articles of Confederation *p. 174*
Virginia Statute of Religious
    Freedom (1786) *p. 176*

CHRONOLOGY

1776 British forces seize New York City

General Washington's troops defeat British forces at the Battle of Trenton

States begin writing new constitutions

1777 American forces defeat British in a series of battles at Saratoga, New York

1778 Americans and French form a crucial military alliance

George Rogers Clark's militia defeats British troops in the Mississippi Valley

American forces defeat the Iroquois Confedercy at Newtown, New York

British seize Savannah and Charleston

1780 Patriots defeat Loyalists at the Battle of King's Mountain

1781 British invasion of southern colonies turned back at the Battles of Cowpens and Guilford Courthouse

American and French forces defeat British at Yorktown, Virginia

1781 Articles of Confederation are ratified

Continental Congress becomes Confederation Congress

1783 Treaty of Paris is signed, formally ending Revolutionary War

1786 Virginia adopts the Statute of Religious Freedom

INQUIZITIVE

Go to InQuizitive to see what you've learned—and learn what you've missed—with personalized feedback along the way.

WASHINGTON AS A STATESMAN AT THE CONSTITUTIONAL CONVENTION (1856) This painting by Junius Brutus Stearns is one of the earliest depictions of the drafting of the Constitution, capturing the moment after the convention members, including George Washington (right), decided to present the Constitution to the public.

Creating a "More Perfect Union"

1783–1800

The unlikely American victory in the Revolutionary War stunned the world, but the Patriots had little time to celebrate, for they faced the overwhelming task of creating the world's first large republic. The transition from war to peace was neither simple nor easy. Forging a new nation out of thirteen rebellious colonies posed huge challenges during and after the war. The period from the drafting of the Declaration of Independence in 1776, through the creation of the new Constitution in 1787, and ending with the election of Thomas Jefferson as president in 1800 was an especially turbulent time during which the new nation experienced growing political divisions, foreign troubles, and courageous statesmanship.

During the so-called Critical Period between 1783 and 1787, Americans developed sharp differences of opinion about national economic policies, international relations, and the proper relationship of the states to the national government. In the end, differences over those key issues created powerful tensions that gave birth to the nation's first political parties and, to this day, continue to complicate the American experiment in federalism (the sharing of power among national, state, and local governments).

CORE OBJECTIVES INQUIZITIVE

1. Identify the strengths and weaknesses of the Articles of Confederation and explain how they contributed to the creation of a new U.S. Constitution in 1787.

2. Describe the political innovations that the 1787 Constitutional Convention developed for the new nation.

3. Summarize the major debates surrounding the ratification of the Constitution and how they were resolved.

4. Compare the Federalists' vision for the United States with that of their Republican opponents during the 1790s.

5. Explain how attitudes toward Great Britain and France shaped American politics in the late eighteenth century.

The Confederation Government

During the 1780s, the widespread American distrust of centralized government power, originally directed at the British monarchy, was redirected toward the new American government under the Articles of Confederation. The union of states created in 1776 was a wartime alliance of necessity that, politically and economically, often functioned poorly. Riots and rebellions protesting government policies erupted with growing frequency after the Revolutionary War ended in 1783. The weaknesses of the Confederation government in dealing with such turmoil led political leaders to design a new national constitution and federal government in 1787, both of which proved to be more effective—and lasting—than the Confederation government.

A Loose Alliance of States

By design, the Articles of Confederation, drafted in 1776 and 1777 and approved by the states in 1781, had created not so much a united nation as a loose alliance ("confederation") of thirteen independent states. America's first national government under the Articles of Confederation had only one component, a one-house (unicameral) congress. There was no president, no executive branch, no separate national judiciary (court system). State legislatures appointed the members of the Confederation Congress; each state, regardless of size or population, had one vote. This meant that Rhode Island, with 68,000 people, had the same power in Congress as Virginia, with over 747,000 inhabitants. Altering the Articles of Confederation required a *unanimous* vote of both the Congress and the thirteen state legislatures; given this difficulty, they were never amended.

The Confederation Congress was weak by design, in order to ensure that it did not violate the rights of the thirteen states. It had little authority or resources, leading George Washington to call it "a half-starved, limping government, always moving upon crutches and tottering at every step." The Confederation Congress could neither regulate trade between the states or with other nations, nor pay off the country's large war debts; it could approve treaties with other nations but had no power to enforce their terms; it could call for the raising of an army but could not force men to fill the ranks. The Congress had no power to enforce its own laws and ran up a budget deficit every year of its existence. Because most of the states did not provide sufficient contributions to pay for the national government, the Confederation Congress resorted to printing paper money called Continentals, whose value plummeted as more were printed, leading to the joking phrase, "Not worth a Continental."

An Important Foundation

Yet in spite of its limitations, the weak Confederation Congress somehow managed to survive the war years and to lay important foundations for the new national government. The Articles of Confederation were crucially important in supporting the political concept of "republicanism," which meant that the American Republic would be governed not by kings or queens or nobles but "by the authority of the people."

The Confederation government also concluded the strategically important Treaty of Paris with Great Britain in 1783, ending the Revolutionary War. Perhaps most important, the Confederation established the basic principles of land distribution and territorial government that would guide America's westward expansion for decades to come.

Successes: Support of "republicanism" and negotiation of Treaty of Paris (1783)

Land Policy

In ending the Revolutionary War and transferring Britain's North American colonies to America's Confederation government, the Treaty of Paris doubled the size of the United States. Between 1784 and 1787, the Confederation Congress issued three major policies, called *ordinances*, providing for the orderly development of the vast territories west of the thirteen original states in an effort to generate revenue for the national government. These documents—among the most important in American history—created the procedures that the United States would follow in its eventual expansion all the way to the Pacific.

In 1784 Thomas Jefferson drafted the first federal land ordinance, which urged states to drop their competing claims to Indian-held territory west of the Appalachian Mountains, north of the Ohio River, and east of the Mississippi River. That way, the vast, unmapped area could be divided into as many as seventeen *new* states. When a western territory's population equaled that of the smallest existing state (Rhode Island), the territory would be eligible for statehood. The Confederation Congress, after rejecting Jefferson's proposal that slavery be banned from the new territories, passed the Land Ordinance of 1784.

The next year, the Confederation Congress created the Land Ordinance of 1785, which outlined a plan of land surveys and sales that would stamp a rectangular pattern on what was called the Northwest Territory (the sprawling area that would become the states of Ohio, Michigan, Indiana, Illinois, and Wisconsin). Wherever Indian lands were purchased—or taken—they were divided into six-mile-square townships laid out along a grid of lines running east-west and north-south. Each township was in turn divided into thirty-six sections one mile square (640 acres), with each section divided into four farms. The 640-acre sections of "public lands" were to be sold at auctions, the proceeds of which went into the national treasury.

Success: Creation of land ordinances

The Northwest Ordinance

The third major land policy created by the Confederation Congress was the **Northwest Ordinance** of 1787. It outlined two key principles: that the new western territories could become states that would be treated as equals rather than as colonies, and that slavery was banned from the western region (but slaves already there would remain slaves). The Northwest Ordinance

Northwest Ordinance (1787) Land policy for new western territories in the Ohio Valley that established the terms and conditions for self-government and statehood while also banning slavery from the region.

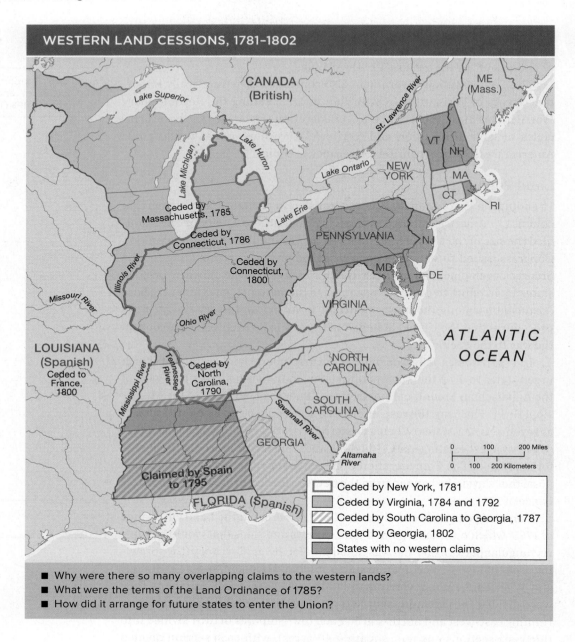

WESTERN LAND CESSIONS, 1781–1802

CANADA (British)

Lake Superior

Lake Michigan

Lake Huron

Lake Ontario

Lake Erie

St. Lawrence River

ME (Mass.)

VT

NH

NEW YORK

MA

CT

RI

Ceded by Massachusetts, 1785

Ceded by Connecticut, 1786

Ceded by Connecticut, 1800

PENNSYLVANIA

NJ

MD

DE

Illinois River

Missouri River

Ohio River

VIRGINIA

LOUISIANA (Spanish)

Ceded to France, 1800

Mississippi River

Tennessee River

Ceded by North Carolina, 1790

NORTH CAROLINA

SOUTH CAROLINA

Savannah River

GEORGIA

Altamaha River

ATLANTIC OCEAN

Claimed by Spain to 1795

FLORIDA (Spanish)

0   100   200 Miles

0   100   200 Kilometers

☐	Ceded by New York, 1781
▨	Ceded by Virginia, 1784 and 1792
▨	Ceded by South Carolina to Georgia, 1787
▨	Ceded by Georgia, 1802
▨	States with no western claims

■ Why were there so many overlapping claims to the western lands?
■ What were the terms of the Land Ordinance of 1785?
■ How did it arrange for future states to enter the Union?

also included a promise (which would be repeatedly broken) that Indian lands "shall never be taken from them without their consent."

The Northwest Ordinance specified that a new territory would become a state through a three-stage process. First, Congress would appoint a territorial governor and other officials to create a legal code, keep the peace, and administer justice. Second, when the territorial population of adult males reached 5,000, a legislature would be elected. Third, when a territory's population reached 60,000 "free inhabitants," it could create a state constitution and apply to Congress for statehood. In 1803, Ohio was the first territory to be granted statehood in this way.

Foreign Tensions

After the Revolutionary War, the Confederation government confronted issues with Great Britain and Spain that it was powerless to resolve. Both European nations kept trading posts and forts on American soil, in violation of the Treaty of Paris (1783). Another major irritant in U.S.-British relations was the seizure of Loyalist property (homes, farms, plantations, slaves, businesses, etc.) by Patriots during and after the war. The British government demanded that the United States pay the Loyalists for their losses. With Spain, the chief issues were the disputed southern boundary of the United States along the Gulf of Mexico and the right of Americans to send boats or barges filled with their crops and products down the Mississippi River to the valuable Spanish-controlled port of New Orleans. In 1784 the Spanish governor in New Orleans closed the lower Mississippi River to American boats and barges, thus cutting off settlers in Tennessee and Kentucky from world commerce.

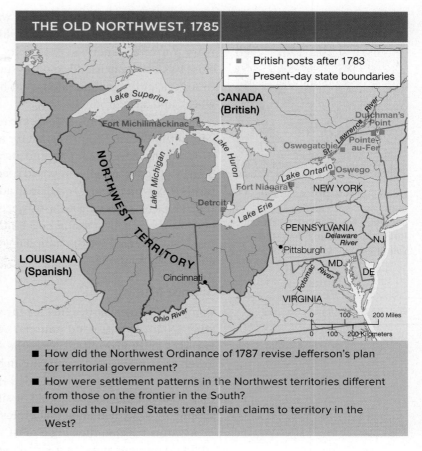

THE OLD NORTHWEST, 1785

- British posts after 1783
- Present-day state boundaries

- How did the Northwest Ordinance of 1787 revise Jefferson's plan for territorial government?
- How were settlement patterns in the Northwest territories different from those on the frontier in the South?
- How did the United States treat Indian claims to territory in the West?

The Spanish governor of Florida also provided firearms to Creeks who resisted American encroachment on their lands in south Georgia. Led by the powerful chief Alexander McGillivray, the son of a Scottish planter and trader and a half-French, half-Creek mother, the Creeks forced whites off their tribal lands. The Spanish argued that all of the land west of the Appalachian Mountains "belongs to the free and independent nations of Indians, and you [Americans] have no right to it." American frontiersmen disagreed violently with the Spanish position, but the Confederation Congress was powerless to help them.

Trade and the Economy

The Confederation government also struggled to manage complex economic issues. Seven years of warfare against Great Britain had nearly bankrupted the new nation. The plantation economies of the southern states were hard hit by the escape of tens of thousands of enslaved workers during and after

> Failure: Regulation of interstate commerce and foreign relations

Domestic industry American craftsmen, such as this cabinetmaker, favored tariffs on foreign goods that competed with their own products.

Failure: No national currency

the war. And the national economy was devastated by the loss of its trading network with the British Empire, which before the Revolution was the primary source of American prosperity. The British decision after the war to close its Caribbean island colonies such as Bermuda, Jamaica, and Barbados to American trade eliminated what had been a thriving market for timber, wheat, and farm products.

Merchants and shippers eager to revive the profitable trade relationships within the British Empire called for an economic war against Great Britain to force the government to end its restrictions on American commerce. Some state governments imposed special taxes on British vessels and special tariffs (taxes on imports) on British goods. The British responded by sending their ships to states whose tariffs were lower. In essence, the American states ended up competing against each other for foreign trade. By 1787, a clear need had emerged for the national government to regulate interstate trade and foreign relations.

Scarce Money

Complex financial issues further threatened the stability of the new nation after 1783. There was no national currency and only a handful of banks. Farmers who had profited during the war now found themselves squeezed by lower crop prices and mounting debts and taxes. Creditors (people who loaned money to others) demanded that debtors (mostly farmers) pay back their loans or mortgages in gold or silver coins, which were always in short supply. By 1785, demands that states print new paper currency to supplement coins became the single most divisive issue in politics. Farmers saw adding paper currency as a simple way to raise prices for their crops and livestock and thereby help them pay their debts and taxes. In 1785–1786, seven states began issuing their own paper money to help farmers and to pay the cash bonuses promised to war veterans. The Rhode Island legislature issued so much paper money that creditors fled the state to avoid being paid in paper currency of such unstable value.

Shays's Rebellion

In neighboring Massachusetts, however, the legislature took a different stance. Hard-pressed farmers in the western part of the state, many of them military veterans who had not received their promised pay during the war, urged the state to issue new paper money and demanded more time to pay the taxes owed on their lands. When the Massachusetts legislature adjourned in 1786 without providing paper money or any other relief from taxes and debts, three rural counties erupted in revolt.

Led by thirty-nine-year-old Daniel Shays, who had served as a captain in the Revolutionary War, armed gangs of angry farmers forced judges to stop farm foreclosures. Shays urged them on, yelling "Close down the courts!" Shays and his followers wanted to use corn and wheat as money in paying their debts and taxes. The state government responded by sending 4,400 militiamen armed with cannons to suppress the rebellion. They scattered Shays's debtor army with a single volley that left four farmers dead. The farmers ran for the hills; Shays fled to Vermont.

The rebels nevertheless won a victory of sorts, as the state legislature decided to eliminate some of the taxes and fees on farmers. But the most important consequence of **Shays's Rebellion** was to spread panic among wealthy Americans. In Massachusetts, Abigail Adams dismissed Shays and his followers as "ignorant, restless desperadoes, without conscience or principles." In Virginia, George Washington was equally disturbed. "Good God!" he exclaimed. America needed a "government by which our lives, liberty, and properties will be secured."

Shays's Rebellion Shays and his followers demanded a more flexible monetary policy and the right to postpone paying taxes until the postwar agricultural depression lifted.

The events in Massachusetts, he feared, might tempt other angry debtor groups around the country to violate the law and disturb the peace.

Creating the Constitution

In the wake of Shays's Rebellion, many public officials agreed with Virginian James Madison that the "crisis is arrived." It was time to empower the national government to bring order and stability to the new nation.

The Constitutional Convention

In 1787, the Confederation Congress called for a special convention to gather in Philadelphia's Old State House (now Independence Hall) for the "purpose of revising the Articles of Confederation." Twelve of the thirteen states eventually participated; tiny Rhode Island refused. Twenty-nine delegates began meeting on May 25, 1787 (altogether, fifty-five men served as delegates at one time or another). After four months of deliberations carried out in stifling heat behind closed windows and locked doors, thirty-nine delegates signed the new federal constitution on September 17. Only three refused to sign what has become the longest functioning written constitution in the world.

The durability of the ideas and institutions contained in the Constitution is a lasting testimony to the men who made it. The convention delegates were surprisingly young; their average age was forty-two, and the youngest was twenty-six. Most of the framers of the Constitution, later dubbed the "Founding Fathers," were members of the nation's political and economic elite (Thomas Jefferson and John Adams did not participate because they

> CORE **OBJECTIVE**
>
> **2.** Describe the political innovations that the 1787 Constitutional Convention developed for the new nation.

Shays's Rebellion (1786–1787) Storming of the Massachusetts federal arsenal in 1787 by Daniel Shays and 1,200 armed farmers seeking debt relief from the state legislature through issuance of paper currency and lower taxes.

were serving as diplomats in Europe). Twenty-six delegates were college graduates; two were college presidents. Thirty-four were lawyers. Nearly all were considered "gentlemen" or "natural aristocrats."

Yet they were also practical men of experience, tested in the fires of the Revolutionary War. Twenty-two had served in the military during the conflict (five were captured and imprisoned by the British), seven had been state governors, and eight had helped write their state constitutions. Most had been members of the Continental Congress, and eight had signed the Declaration of Independence. In the summer of 1787, they gathered in Philadelphia "to form a more perfect union," as the preamble to the new Constitution asserted.

Drafting the Constitution

George Washington served as presiding officer of the Constitutional Convention but participated little in the debates. The governor of Pennsylvania, eighty-one-year-old Benjamin Franklin, the oldest delegate, was in such poor health that he had to be carried to the meetings each day in a special chair, borne aloft by inmates from the Philadelphia jail. Like Washington, Franklin said little from the floor but provided a wealth of experience, wit, and common sense behind the scenes.

Most active in the debates was James Madison. He was the ablest political theorist in the group and the central figure at the convention. The thirty-six-year-old Madison, a Virginia attorney, had arrived in Philadelphia with trunks full of books about political theory and a head full of ideas about how to strengthen the Confederation. Barely five feet tall and weighing only one hundred thirty pounds (a colleague said he was "no bigger than half a piece of soap"), he was too frail to serve in the Revolutionary army. Although painfully shy and soft-spoken, Madison had an agile mind, a huge appetite for learning, and a lifelong commitment to public service. He was determined to create a new constitution that would ensure the "supremacy of national authority." The logic of his arguments—and his willingness to support repeated compromises—proved decisive in shaping the new constitution. "Every person seems to acknowledge his greatness," one delegate said of Madison.

Most delegates agreed with Madison that their young nation needed a stronger national government and less powerful state governments. A New Hampshire delegate explained that he "saw no more reason to be afraid of the central [national] government than of the state governments."

The two basic and interrelated assumptions of the Constitutional Convention were that the national government must have direct authority over the citizenry rather than governing the people only through the state governments, and that the national government must derive its "sovereignty" (powers) directly from the people rather than from the state governments. The insistence on the authority of "the people" was the most important political innovation since the Declaration of Independence, for by declaring

James Madison This 1783 miniature shows Madison at thirty-two years old, just four years before he would assume a major role in drafting the Constitution.

Innovation: All authority derived from "the people"

the Constitution to be the voice of "the people," the founders authorized the federal government to limit the powers of the individual states.

Experience with the Articles of Confederation had persuaded the delegates that an effective national government needed new authority to collect taxes, borrow and issue money, regulate commerce and international relations, fund an army and navy, and make laws binding upon individual citizens. Experience also suggested to them that the states must be stripped of certain powers: to print paper money, make treaties with other nations, wage war, and levy taxes (tariffs) on imported goods. This concept of dividing governmental authority between the national government and the states came to be called **federalism**, another major contribution of the new American republic to the rest of the world.

> Innovation: Federalism

The Virginia and New Jersey Plans

James Madison drafted the framework for the initial discussions at the Constitutional Convention. His proposals, called the Virginia Plan, started with a revolutionary suggestion: that the delegates scrap their original instructions to *revise* the Articles of Confederation and instead create an entirely *new* federal constitution. The Virginia Plan called for a new Congress divided into two houses: a lower House of Representatives and an upper house, to be called the Senate. States with larger populations, such as Virginia and Pennsylvania, would have more representatives in Congress than the smaller states.

Critics of the Virginia Plan submitted an alternative written by William Paterson of New Jersey. The New Jersey Plan sought to keep the existing structure of equal representation of the states in a unicameral (one-house) Congress but gave Congress the power to levy taxes and regulate commerce, and the authority to name a chief executive as well as a supreme court.

After intense debate over the two plans, the dispute was resolved by the Great Compromise (sometimes called the Connecticut Compromise), which used elements of both plans in creating a new legislative structure for the national government. The more populous states won apportionment (the number of delegates representing each state) by population in the proposed House of Representatives, while the delegates who sought to protect states' power won equality of representation in the Senate, where each state would have two members.

> Innovation: The Great Compromise

The Structure of the Federal Government

The delegates at the 1787 Constitutional Convention were preoccupied with *power*: who should have it and how it would be used and controlled. The new constitution created a "federal" structure in which each citizen is governed by both a state government and the national government. To prevent power from being abused, each branch of the new national government—executive, legislative, and judicial—was given a separate sphere of authority as well as

> Innovation: Separation of powers

federalism Concept of dividing governmental authority between the national government and the states.

the responsibility to counterbalance the other branches, called the **separation of powers**, to keep any one of the three branches of the government from growing too powerful.

Legislature (Congress)

As a result of the Great Compromise, the delegates at the Constitutional Convention embedded the concept of a separation of powers in the new Congress. It would have two "houses," each intended to counterbalance the other, with one (the House of Representatives) representing the voters at large and the other, the Senate, representing the state legislatures. The "lower house" of Congress, the House of Representatives, was designed to be closer to the voters, who elected its members every two years. Under the Articles of Confederation, none of the members of Congress had been chosen by popular vote; all of them had been elected by state legislatures. James Madison argued that allowing individual citizens to elect at least one part of the new legislature was "essential to every plan of free government." The upper house, or Senate, was intended to be a more elite group, elected for six-year terms, not by voters directly, but by state legislatures. The Senate was intended to be a conservative force, using its power, when necessary, to overrule either the House of Representatives or the president. The more prestigious Senate, explained Madison, would help "protect the minority of the opulent against the majority."

Executive (President)

The delegates at the Constitutional Convention struggled mightily over the design of a new executive branch of government. Most of them expected the Congress to be the dominant branch of the new national government. Some delegates urged that a board of three men, modeled after the *triumvirate* of ancient Rome, collectively serve as the nation's chief executive. But a majority of delegates soon opted for a single president. Alexander Hamilton, a delegate from New York who was a celebrated attorney and the former chief of staff for General George Washington during the Revolution, wanted the president to serve for life, but the delegates eventually decided that the president should be held accountable to the people by standing for election every four years. The president could veto acts of Congress, subject to being overridden by a two-thirds vote in each house. The president was named the nation's chief diplomat as well as the commander in chief of the armed forces, and was responsible for the execution of the laws.

But the powers of the new president were also to be limited in key areas. The chief executive could neither declare war nor make peace; those powers were reserved for Congress. Unlike the British monarch, moreover, the president could be removed from office. The House of Representatives could impeach the chief executive and other civil officers on charges of treason, bribery, or "other high crimes and misdemeanors." An impeached president could be removed from office if two-thirds of the Senate voted for conviction.

separation of powers Strict division of the powers of government among three separate branches (executive, legislative, and judicial) which, in turn, check and balance each other.

To preserve the separation of the three branches, the president would be elected not by the Congress, but by "electors" chosen by "the people" in local elections. The number of "electors" in each state would vary depending upon the combined number of congressional representatives and U.S. senators. This "Electoral College" was a compromise between those wanting the president elected by a vote in Congress and those preferring election by a popular vote of qualified citizens.

Judiciary (Court System)

The third proposed branch of government, the judiciary, sparked surprisingly little debate. The Constitution called for a national supreme court headed by a chief justice. The role of the national judiciary was not to make laws (which was reserved to Congress) or execute or enforce the laws (which was reserved to the presidency) but to interpret the law as applied to specific cases and to ensure that every citizen received equal justice under the law. The U.S. Supreme Court was given final authority in interpreting the U.S. Constitution as well as in adjudicating disputes arising from the various state constitutions. Furthermore, Article VI of the Constitution declared that the federal Constitution, federal laws, and treaties are "the supreme Law of the Land." That is, when federal laws and state laws conflicted, the federal law would triumph.

"We the People"

The men who drafted the new constitution claimed to be representing all of the American people. The Constitution begins with the words: "We the people." In fact, however, there were important groups of Americans left out of the Constitution's protections. Native Americans, for example, were not considered federal or state citizens unless they paid taxes, which very few did. The Constitution declared that Native American "tribes" were not part of the United States but instead were separate "nations." Only the U.S. Congress, not the states or individuals, could negotiate treaties with the Indian nations. Not until 1924 would Native Americans qualify for American citizenship.

Dealing with Slavery

Of all the issues that emerged during the Constitutional Convention, none was more explosive than the question of slavery. Many of the framers viewed slavery as an embarrassing contradiction to the principles of liberty and equality expressed in the Declaration of Independence and the new Constitution. A New Jersey delegate declared that slavery was "utterly inconsistent with the principles of Christianity and humanity."

By contrast, delegates from the southern states strenuously defended slavery. During the eighteenth century, the agricultural economies of Maryland, Virginia, the Carolinas, and Georgia had become dependent upon huge numbers of enslaved laborers, and delegates from those states were determined to protect the future of slavery. Caught in the middle were Virginia slaveholders like George Washington, Thomas Jefferson, and James Madison, who hated slavery but saw no way to eliminate it without civil war. Madison told the Convention that the "distinction of color" had created "the most oppressive dominion ever exercised by man over man."

Because the southern delegates would have walked out of the convention, the framers did not even consider abolishing slavery, nor did some of them view slaves as human beings whose rights should be protected. Such moral blindness to basic human dignities reflected the prevailing attitudes among most white Americans at the time.

But if the slaves were not to be freed or their rights to be acknowledged, how were they to be counted? Since the size of state delegations in the proposed House of Representatives was based on population, southern delegates argued that slaves should be counted along with whites. Northerners said it made no sense to count slaves for purposes of political representation when slaves were not treated as people but as property. The delegates finally agreed to a compromise proposed by James Wilson of Pennsylvania, whereby three-fifths of "all other persons" (that is, the enslaved) would be included in a state's population count as a basis for apportioning a state's congressional delegation.

Limitation: Failure to deal with slavery

By design, the original Constitution never specifically mentions the word *slavery*. Instead it speaks of "free persons" and "all other persons," and of persons "held to service of labor." The word *slavery* would not appear in the Constitution until the Thirteenth Amendment (1865) abolished slavery at the end of the Civil War. Under the 1787 Constitution, the national government had no authority to deal with slavery in the states. The success of southern delegates in getting slaves counted for purposes of calculating a state's representation in the House of Representatives and the Electoral College would give the southern states disproportionate power in the Congress by increasing the number of southern votes in the House of Representatives. This, in turn, increased southern influence in the Electoral College, since the number of each state's electors was to be the total of its senators and representatives. It was thus no accident that in the nation's first sixteen presidential elections, between 1788 and 1848, all but four chose a southern slaveholder. The pro-slavery nature of the Constitution prompted the fiery abolitionist William Lloyd Garrison to declare in the 1830s that the framers of the document had forged a "covenant with death and an agreement with hell."

***Charles Calvert and His Slave* (1761)**
In military regalia, the five-year-old descendant of Lord Baltimore towers over his slave, dressed as a drummer boy.

The Absence of Women in the Constitution

While the delegates found the debates over slavery contentious, they considered irrelevant any discussion of political rights for women. Yet not all women were willing to maintain their traditional subordinate role. During and after the Revolutionary War, there were many declarations of independence, many forms of resistance to old ways of doing things, indeed many personal "revolutions"—some successful, some not. Just as the experiences of the Revolutionary War led many African Americans to seize their freedom, some brave women demanded political equality for themselves.

Eliza Yonge Wilkinson, born in 1757 to a wealthy plantation family living on an island south of Charleston, South Carolina, lost her husband early in the war. In June 1780, after Wilkinson was assaulted and robbed by "inhuman" British soldiers during their forty-day siege of Charleston, she became a fiery Patriot who "hated Tyranny in every shape." Wilkinson's "saucy" personality led her to be openly critical of the British during their eighteen-month occupation of the city. She assured a friend that "We may be *led*, but we never will be *driven*!" And she showed great courage and resilience in helping American prisoners of war while managing her family's plantations during the war. Such unconventional experiences led Wilkinson to expect greater freedom for women after the war. "The men say we have no business [with politics]," she wrote to a friend. "It is not our sphere! I won't have it thought that because we are the weaker sex as to bodily strength, my dear, we are capable of nothing more than minding the dairy, visiting the poultry-house, and all such domestic concerns." Wilkinson demanded more. "They won't even allow us the liberty of thought, and that is all I want."

> Limitation: No political rights for women

With more and more women like Wilkinson calling themselves "perfect statesmen" and "great Politician[s]," Judith Sargent Murray, an essayist, playwright, and poet in Gloucester, Massachusetts, predicted the dawn of "a new era of female history" after the Revolution. She argued that the rights and liberties fought for by Patriots belonged not just to men but to women, too. In her essay "On the Equality of the Sexes," written in 1779 but not published until 1790, she, like Eliza Wilkinson, challenged the prevailing view that men had greater intellectual capacities than women. She insisted instead that whatever differences existed between the knowledge displayed by men and women resulted from prejudice and discrimination that prevented women from having access to formal education and worldly experience.

Like many other of the most radical voices of the Revolutionary era, Murray's support for gender equality was met largely by shock and disapproval among both men and women. At the Constitutional Convention in Philadelphia, there was never any formal discussion of women's rights, nor does the Constitution even include the word *women*. The "Founding Fathers" still defined politics and government as realms for men only. Writing from Paris, Thomas Jefferson expressed the hope that American "ladies" would be "contented to soothe and calm the minds of their husbands returning ruffled from political debate" rather than getting involved themselves. Neither Jefferson nor most Americans, he added, were "prepared" to support women holding elected office.

CORE **OBJECTIVE**
3. Summarize the major debates surrounding the ratification of the Constitution and how they were resolved.

The Fight for Ratification

The final draft of the Constitution was submitted to the states for approval (ratification) on September 28, 1787. Thus began the greatest public debate in world history up to that point. For the first time, the diverse peoples making up a large nation were able to discuss, debate, and decide by a peaceful vote how they would be governed. In the fierce ten-month-long debate, those supporting the new Constitution were called Federalists; their opponents became **anti-Federalists**. The two factions formed the seeds for America's enduring two-party political system.

A Fiery Debate

States' rights vs. expanding federal authority

Among the supreme legacies of the dramatic debate over the Constitution is *The Federalist Papers*, a collection of 85 essays published in 1787 and 1788. Written in support of the new Constitution by James Madison of Virginia and Alexander Hamilton and John Jay of New York, the essays defended the principle of a strong national government.

In perhaps the most famous Federalist essay, Number Ten, James Madison argued that the size and diversity of the expanding nation would make it impossible for any single faction to form a dangerous majority that could dominate the federal government. This contradicted the conventional wisdom of the time, which insisted that republics could survive only in small nations like Switzerland. Large republics, it was thought, would self-destruct as a result of warring factions. Not so, Madison insisted. Given a balanced federal government, a large republic could work better than a small one. "Extend the [geographic] sphere," he wrote, "and you take in a greater variety of parties and interests; you make it less probable that a majority of the whole will have a common motive to invade the rights of other citizens."

anti-Federalists Opponents of the Constitution as an infringement on individual and states' rights, whose criticism led to the addition of a Bill of Rights to the document. Many anti-Federalists later joined Thomas Jefferson's Democratic-Republican party.

The Federalist Papers Collection of eighty-five essays, published widely in newspapers in 1787 and 1788, written by Alexander Hamilton, James Madison, and John Jay in support of adopting the proposed U.S. Constitution.

Anti-Federalists v. Federalists

The anti-Federalists opposed the new Constitution by highlighting the dangers of placing more power in the hands of the central government. They predicted that the new federal government would eventually grow corrupt and tyrannical. Mercy Otis Warren of Massachusetts, the most prominent woman in the new nation to write regular political commentary, warned that the proposed constitution would put "shackles on our own necks." She and other anti-Federalists emphasized the absence of a bill of rights to protect individuals and states from the growing power of the national government.

The Federalists, also called nationalists, had several advantages in the prolonged national debate over the Constitution. First, they had a concrete proposal; their opponents had nothing to offer instead of the Constitution but criticism. Second, the Federalist leaders were on average 10–12 years younger than the anti-Federalists, and many of them had been members of the Constitutional Convention who were familiar with the disputed issues in the document. Third, the Federalists were more unified, better organized, and better able to manage the national debate.

By contrast, the anti-Federalist leaders—Virginians Patrick Henry, George Mason, Richard Henry Lee, and future president James Monroe; George Clinton of New York; Samuel Adams, Elbridge Gerry, and Mercy Otis Warren of Massachusetts; and Luther Martin and Samuel Chase of Maryland—were mostly older figures whose careers and reputations had been established well before the Revolution.

Regardless of the voices on each side, the tension between preserving states' rights and expanding federal authority at the center of the debate over ratification would not end in 1787; it became a defining drama of American politics thereafter.

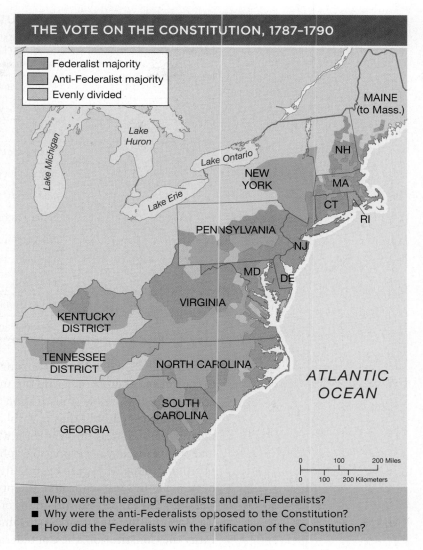

THE VOTE ON THE CONSTITUTION, 1787–1790

Federalist majority
Anti-Federalist majority
Evenly divided

MAINE (to Mass.)
Lake Michigan
Lake Huron
Lake Ontario
Lake Erie
NH
NEW YORK
MA
CT
RI
PENNSYLVANIA
NJ
MD
DE
VIRGINIA
KENTUCKY DISTRICT
TENNESSEE DISTRICT
NORTH CAROLINA
ATLANTIC OCEAN
SOUTH CAROLINA
GEORGIA

0   100   200 Miles
0   100   200 Kilometers

■ Who were the leading Federalists and anti-Federalists?
■ Why were the anti-Federalists opposed to the Constitution?
■ How did the Federalists win the ratification of the Constitution?

The States Decide

The heated debate over ratification of the Constitution at times boiled over into violence. Riots erupted in several cities. Newspapers took sides, leading one New Englander to remark that the papers were being "read more than the Bible."

Amid the intense debate, ratification of the new Constitution gained momentum at the end of 1787. The state legislatures in Delaware, New Jersey, and Georgia voted unanimously in favor of ratification. Massachusetts, still sharply divided in the aftermath of Shays's Rebellion, was the first state legislature in which the outcome was close, approving the Constitution by a vote of 187 to 168.

RATIFICATION OF THE CONSTITUTION

Order of Ratification	State	Date of Ratification
1	Delaware	December 7, 1787
2	Pennsylvania	December 12, 1787
3	New Jersey	December 18, 1787
4	Georgia	January 2, 1788
5	Connecticut	January 9, 1788
6	Massachusetts	February 6, 1788
7	Maryland	April 28, 1788
8	South Carolina	May 23, 1788
9	New Hampshire	June 21, 1788
10	Virginia	June 25, 1788
11	New York	July 26, 1788
12	North Carolina	November 21, 1789
13	Rhode Island	May 29, 1790

On June 21, 1788, New Hampshire became the ninth state to ratify the Constitution, thereby meeting the minimum number of states needed for approval. But the new Constitution and the government it created could hardly succeed without the approval of Virginia, the largest, wealthiest, and most populous state, or New York, which had the third highest population and occupied a key position geographically. Both states included strong opposition groups who were eventually won over by the same pledge as had been made in Massachusetts—the promise of adding a bill of rights to the Constitution to specify protections of individual rights.

Upon notification that New Hampshire had become the ninth state to ratify the Constitution, the Confederation Congress selected New York City as the temporary national capital and fixed the date for the first national elections in 1788–1789.

The Bill of Rights

Protecting individual rights vs. the power of the state

The Constitution was adopted, but because of the spirited resistance it faced, in May 1789, James Madison proposed to the new Congress the cluster of constitutional amendments designed to protect individual rights from the power of the state. As Thomas Jefferson explained, a "bill of rights is what the people are entitled to against every government on earth, general or particular, and what no just government should refuse." After considerable discussion and debate, Congress approved twelve amendments in September 1789. By the end of 1791, the necessary three-fourths of the states had approved *ten* of the twelve proposed amendments, now known as the **Bill of Rights**.

Bill of Rights (1791) First ten amendments to the U.S. Constitution, adopted in 1791 to guarantee individual rights and to help secure ratification of the Constitution by the states.

The First Amendment declared that "Congress shall make no law respecting an establishment of religion or prohibiting the free exercise thereof." This statement has since become one of the most controversial principles of American government. The men who drafted and amended the Constitution made no direct mention of God, for they were determined to protect freedom of religion from government interference and coercion.

In the late eighteenth century, the United States was virtually alone among nations in not declaring a single "established" religion funded by the government. France and Spain, for example, were officially Roman Catholic nations; Great Britain was Anglican. In addition, when the Bill of Rights was ratified, most states still used tax revenues to support a single established religion. Dissenters, the members of other churches, were tolerated but forced to pay taxes for the state-supported religion, and they were often prohibited from voting or holding political office.

The First Amendment changed that at the national level. It prohibited the federal government from endorsing or supporting any religion or interfering with the religious choices that people make. As Thomas Jefferson later explained, the First Amendment erected a "wall of separation between Church and State."

The other original amendments to the Constitution provided safeguards for individual rights of speech, assembly, and the press; the right to own firearms; the right to refuse to house soldiers; protection from unreasonable searches and seizures; the right to refuse to testify against oneself; the right to a speedy public trial, with an attorney present, before an impartial jury; and protection against "cruel and unusual" punishment. The Tenth Amendment addressed the widespread demand that "powers not delegated to the United States by the Constitution, nor prohibited by it to the States, are reserved to the States respectively, or to the people."

The ten amendments constituting the Bill of Rights were written in broad language that seemed to exclude no one, but in fact, the first ten amendments technically applied only to property-owning white males. Whole groups of Americans were officially left out of its protections. Native Americans were entirely outside the constitutional system, defined as an "alien people" in their own land. Like the Constitution itself, the Bill of Rights gave no protections to enslaved Americans. Instead of constitutional rights, they were governed by state "slave codes" that regulated every aspect of their lives. They had no access to the legal system: they could not go to court, make contracts, or own property. Similar restrictions applied to women, who could not vote in most state and national elections.

A Flexible Framework

"Our constitution is in actual operation," Benjamin Franklin wrote to a friend in 1789; "everything appears to promise that it will last; but in this world nothing is certain but death and taxes." George Washington was even more uncertain about the nation's future under the new plan of government. He predicted that the Constitution would not "last for more than twenty years."

The Constitution has lasted much longer, of course, and in the process it has provided a model of resilient republican government whose features have been repeatedly borrowed by other nations. The Constitution, in other words, was not *completed* in 1787 but instead is a living experiment, just as the United States is a living experiment in republicanism. It was, however, flawed from the beginning, just as the nation was flawed, for by evading the issue of slavery, the framers of the Constitution unwittingly allowed growing tensions over the expansion of slavery to reach the point in 1861 where there could be no political solution—only civil war.

CORE **OBJECTIVE**

4. Compare the Federalists' vision for the United States with that of their Republican opponents during the 1790s.

The Federalist Era

It was one thing to ratify a new U.S. Constitution and quite another to make the new federal government run smoothly. During the 1790s, the debates between Federalists and anti-Federalists over the new government gave birth to the nation's first political parties: Federalists and Republicans (also called the Democratic Republicans or **Jeffersonian Republicans**).

The two political parties came to represent two very different visions of America's future development. In 1790, the United States was predominantly a rural society, and 80 percent of households were involved in agricultural production. Only a few cities—Philadelphia, New York City, and Boston—had more than 5,000 residents. The Republicans were mostly southerners like Thomas Jefferson and James Madison who wanted America to remain a nation of small farmers and few cities. The Federalists sharply disagreed. Led by Alexander Hamilton, they embraced urban and commercial growth. Hamilton became the champion of northern efforts to promote trade, banking, finance, and manufacturing as the most essential elements of America's future economy.

The Constitution provided a framework for nationhood but not a blueprint; it left unanswered many questions about the actual structure and conduct of the new government. As James Madison acknowledged, "We are in a wilderness without a single footstep to guide us." On the whole, the Jeffersonian Republicans promoted a strict interpretation of the Constitution, while Federalists believed that the language of the Constitution should be interpreted broadly to enable the new federal government to take decisive action when necessary. One of George Washington's greatest challenges as the nation's first president was to bridge the growing divides between Federalists and Republicans, northerners and southerners, merchants and planters.

Jeffersonian Republicans
Political party founded by Thomas Jefferson in opposition to the Federalist Party led by Alexander Hamilton and John Adams; also known as the Democratic-Republican Party.

A New Government

On March 4, 1789, the new Congress convened its first meeting in New York City. In April, the presiding officer of the Senate certified that George Washington, with 69 votes, was the unanimous choice of the Electoral College to be president. John Adams, with 34 votes, became vice president. George Washington was a reluctant first president, but he agreed to serve because he had been "summoned by my country." A self-made man who had lost his father at age eleven and had little formal education, he had never visited Europe. Vice President John Adams groused that Washington was "too illiterate, unlearned, unread for his station and reputation."

But George Washington had virtues that John Adams lacked. As a French diplomat commented after watching the inaugural ceremony, Washington "has the soul, look, and figure of a hero in action." He was a military hero who had married a wealthy young widow and become a prosperous planter. Washington brought to his new office a remarkable capacity for leadership that helped keep the young republic from disintegrating. Although capable of angry outbursts, Washington was remarkably self-disciplined; he possessed extraordinary stamina and patience, integrity and resolve, courage and resilience. Few doubted that he was the best person to lead the new nation.

Shaping a Federal Union

America's first president took charge of a tiny national government that faced massive challenges. George Washington had a larger staff at his plantation in northern Virginia than he did as president. During the summer of 1789, Congress created executive departments corresponding to those formed under the Confederation. To lead the Department of State, Washington named Thomas Jefferson, recently back from his diplomatic duties in France. To head the Department of the Treasury, Washington picked his brilliant thirty-four-year-old wartime aide, Alexander Hamilton, now a celebrated New York lawyer.

The Rise of American Capitalism

In 1776, the same year that Americans were declaring their independence from the British monarchy, Adam Smith, a Scottish philosopher, published a pathbreaking book titled *An Inquiry into the Nature and Causes of the Wealth of Nations*. It provided the first full description of a modern *capitalist* economy and its social benefits. Like the American Revolution, *The Wealth of Nations* was a declaration of independence from Great Britain's mercantilist system. Under mercantilism, national governments exercised tight controls over economic life in the contest for world power. In *The Wealth of Nations*, Smith argued for just the opposite. Instead of controlling economic activity, governments should allow energetic individuals and efficient businesses to compete freely for profits in the marketplace. Doing so would provide the

Alexander Hamilton Secretary of the Treasury from 1789 to 1795.

Alexander Hamilton's economic reforms

best path to individual success and national prosperity. Smith also explained that modern capitalism involved diverse national economies in which all of the major sectors were flourishing: agriculture, trade, banking, finance, and manufacturing.

Alexander Hamilton greatly admired *The Wealth of Nations* and embraced the idea of a diverse capitalist economy in which the engine of competition drove prosperity. America's first secretary of the Treasury was determined to use the energies of capitalism to transform a weak cluster of states into a global economic power comparable to Great Britain. He also recognized, however, that the fragile American republic's economy required temporary government assistance to enable it to compete with the much more advanced economies of Europe. In addition, the federal treasury was virtually empty. Something had to be done quickly to generate enough cash for the new federal government to operate. To that end, Hamilton submitted to Congress a series of brilliant reports between January 1790 and December 1791. **Alexander Hamilton's economic reforms** outlined his bold vision for the new nation's economic development.

Paying Debts

The United States was born in debt. And it fell to Alexander Hamilton to figure out how the debts should be repaid. In the first of two "Reports on Public Credit" sent to Congress, Hamilton outlined how the new federal government should absorb the massive debt that the states and the Confederation had incurred during the War of Independence. Some argued that the debts should not be repaid. Hamilton countered that not paying war debts was unjust and dishonorable. Only by paying its debts in full could the new nation gain credibility among the leading nations of the world. He also explained that the state debts from the Revolution were a *national* responsibility because all Americans had benefited from the war for independence. A federal debt, he claimed, would be a "national blessing," provide a "mechanism for national unity," and promote long-term prosperity.

James Madison led the opposition to Hamilton's "debt-funding" plan in Congress. Madison did not question whether the war-related debt should be paid; he was troubled, however, that far more debt was owed to northerners than to southerners. The gridlock over the debt issue ended in the summer of 1790 with a secret deal. In return for northern votes in favor of locating the permanent national capital on the Potomac River between Maryland and Virginia, Madison pledged to seek enough southern votes in Congress to pass Hamilton's debt-assumption plan. The Compromise of 1790 worked as planned. The national capital would be moved from New York City to Philadelphia for ten years, after which it would be settled at a new federal city (soon to be called Washington) on the Potomac River in the new federal District of Columbia. Once implemented, Hamilton's debt-financing plan was an immediate success. By making the United States

Alexander Hamilton's economic reforms Various measures designed to strengthen the nation's capitalist economy and generate federal revenue through the promotion of new industries, the adoption of new tax policies, the payment of war debts, and the establishment of a national bank.

financially solvent, he set in motion the greatest economic success story in history.

Raising Federal Revenue

Governments have three basic ways to raise money to pay their bills: they can impose taxes or fees on individuals, businesses, and specific products; they can borrow money by selling interest-paying government bonds to investors; and, they can print currency. To raise urgently needed funds, Congress in 1789, with the approval of Washington and Hamilton, imposed a 5 percent tariff tax on a wide variety of imported items.

The creation of federal tariffs marked but the beginning of Hamilton's ambitious effort to put the new capitalist republic on sound financial footing. His next effort, in 1791, was to convince Congress to impose federal taxes, called "excises," on specific items: carriages, sugar, salt, and alcoholic beverages. The new tax on whiskey outraged many frontier farmers because it taxed their most profitable commodity. During the eighteenth and early nineteenth centuries, nearly all Americans drank alcoholic beverages: beer, hard cider, ale, wine, rum, brandy, or whiskey. In the areas west of the Appalachian Mountains, the primary cash commodity was liquor distilled from grains (mostly corn and rye) or fruit (peaches and apples). It was far easier for western farmers to convert their crops to liquor and then take it across the mountains or down the Mississippi River than it was to transport the bulky grains or fruits. Unlike grain and fruit crops, distilled spirits could be easily stored, shipped, or sold—and at higher profits. A bushel of corn worth 25¢ could yield two and a half gallons of liquor, worth ten times as much.

> Hamilton's revenue plan: The first federal taxes

A National Bank

After securing congressional approval for federal tariffs, Hamilton called for the establishment of a national bank modeled after the powerful Bank of England. Once again, Madison and Jefferson led the opposition, arguing that the Constitution said nothing about a national bank and therefore the government could not create one. Hamilton and his supporters countered that creating a bank was an "implied power" within the Constitution. Congress ended up agreeing with Hamilton, with virtually all northern Congressmen voting for the new bank while most southerners opposed it. But the fundamental debate between Jefferson and Hamilton over how to interpret the Constitution has continued to this day: should government officials be allowed to stretch the original language of the Constitution to adjust to new realities?

> Hamilton's National Bank

The **Bank of the United States** (B.U.S.) would have three primary responsibilities: (1) to hold government funds and make transfers of monies to other nations; (2) to provide loans to the federal government and to other banks to promote economic development; and (3) to manage the nation's money supply by regulating the power of state-chartered banks to issue paper currency (called banknotes). The B.U.S. could issue banknotes as needed to address the chronic shortage of gold and silver coins.

Bank of the United States (1791) National bank responsible for holding and transferring federal government funds, making business loans, and issuing a national currency.

The Bank of the United States
Proposed by Alexander Hamilton, the bank opened in Philadelphia in 1791.

Encouraging Manufactures

In the "Report on Manufactures," the last of his major proposals to Congress, Hamilton called for the federal government to help launch new industries that would reduce America's dependence on manufactured goods imported from Europe, especially Great Britain. Industrialization, Hamilton believed, would accomplish several goals: diversify an American economy overly dependent on agriculture; improve productivity through greater use of machinery; encourage immigration to entice skilled workers from abroad; and create more opportunities for economic expansion.

To encourage industrial development, Hamilton recommended that the federal government provide financial incentives to help people start new industries and spur inventors to create new technologies. He claimed that such government support was needed to enable new American companies to compete "on equal terms" with companies in the more advanced economies of Europe. Finally, Hamilton asked Congress to fund an improved transportation system across the young nation, including the development of roads, canals, and rivers for commercial traffic.

Hamilton's "Report on Manufactures"

Few of Hamilton's pro-industry proposals were enacted in the 1790s because of strong opposition among southerners. But his ideas were not forgotten. They provided an arsenal of arguments for the advocates of manufacturing and transportation improvements in years to come.

Hamilton's Achievement

Largely owing to the skillful Hamilton, the Treasury Department during the early 1790s accumulated a surplus that enabled it to begin paying off the Revolutionary War debts, and foreign capitalists began to invest heavily in the growing American economy. A Boston merchant reported in late 1790 that the United States had never "had a brighter sunshine of prosperity. . . .

Our agricultural interest smiles, our commerce is blessed, our manufactures flourish." Yet however beneficial Hamilton's policies were to the nation's long-term economic development, they continued to arouse fierce opposition among Republicans.

The Republican Alternative

By supporting industry and commerce as well as the expansion of federal authority at the expense of the states, Hamilton infuriated a growing number of people, especially in the agricultural South and western frontier. Because the southern states had virtually no manufacturing enterprises and much less varied commercial activity than New York and New England, Thomas Jefferson, James Madison, and other Republicans viewed Hamilton's economic policies as discriminating against them. The tax on whiskey infuriated frontier farmers in western Pennsylvania.

> Regional economic differences

The increasingly bitter disputes between Secretary of the Treasury Hamilton and Secretary of State Jefferson soon fractured President Washington's cabinet. Hamilton was an intense American nationalist, but he very much admired the powerful British economy and its political system (a limited monarchy and a parliament governed by a constitution). The British government was, he observed, "the best model the world ever produced," and he wanted Great Britain to remain America's largest trading partner. He also remained devoted to a strong central government and a powerful national bank. By contrast, Jefferson was anti-British and pro-French; he loved French culture, cuisine, and wine. Unlike Hamilton, the Virginian hated banks and big cities. His dream for America was to preserve a decentralized agrarian republic made up primarily of small farmers. "Those who labor in the earth," he wrote, "are the chosen people of God, if ever he had a chosen people, whose breasts He has made His peculiar deposit for genuine and substantial virtue." Jefferson feared that Hamilton's campaign for American industries would produce a growing class of landless factory workers who were dependent upon others for their livelihood and therefore subject to political manipulation and economic exploitation.

> Hamilton and Jefferson's conflicting visions

By mid-1792, Hamilton and Jefferson could no longer hide their hatred for each other. The two strongest members of the cabinet became mortal enemies—as well as the leaders of two emerging parties. Part of the opposition to Hamilton's financial proposals grew out of opposition to Hamilton himself. The brashly confident Hamilton acted as if he were President Washington's prime minister. As a Congressman said in 1791, Hamilton "is all powerful and fails in nothing which he attempts." Jefferson, twelve years older than Hamilton, told a friend that he and his rival "daily pitted [fought] in the cabinet like two cocks [roosters]." President Washington begged his chief officers to put an end to the "wounding suspicions and irritating charges." They did not. In September 1792, Jefferson told President Washington that "I was duped ... by the Secretary of the Treasury, and made a fool for forwarding his [economic] schemes, not then sufficiently understood by

Thomas Jefferson A 1791 portrait by Charles Willson Peale.

me; and of all the errors of my political life, this has occasioned the deepest regret."

CORE **OBJECTIVE**

5. Explain how attitudes toward Great Britain and France shaped American politics in the late eighteenth century.

Foreign and Domestic Crises

In 1789, the same year that George Washington became president, frenzied violence erupted in France, as masses of enraged people, inspired in part by the example of the American Revolution, revolted against the monarchy and sent shock waves throughout Europe. By 1792, when Washington was unanimously reelected to serve a second term as president, the **French Revolution** was careening out of control. The radicals executed the king and queen as well as hundreds of aristocrats. On February 1, 1793, the revolutionary government declared war on archenemy Great Britain, as well as the Netherlands and Spain. Thereafter, the most violent of the French revolutionaries—called *Jacobins*—used guillotines to execute thousands of political prisoners and Catholic priests.

Neutrality proclamation

Secretary of State Thomas Jefferson, the former U.S. ambassador to France, called for the United States to aid revolutionary France in its war against the European monarchies. "To back away from France," he claimed, "would be to undermine the cause of republicanism in America." But President Washington (and Alexander Hamilton) wanted no part of the European conflict. On April 22, 1793, Washington announced that the United States would not take sides in the war; it would be "friendly and impartial toward the belligerent powers." Instead of settling matters, however, Washington's neutrality proclamation brought to a boil the ugly feud between Hamilton and Jefferson. In 1793, Jefferson urged his friend James Madison to "take up your pen" and cut Hamilton "to pieces" in the newspapers.

Citizen Genet

While not wanting the United States to get involved in the European war, President Washington did accept Jefferson's argument that the United States should recognize the new French revolutionary government (becoming the first nation to do so). The French government then sent its first ambassador to the United States—the impulsive thirty-year-old Edmond-Charles-Édouard Genet.

Citizen Genet, as he quickly became known (a nod to newly egalitarian France), landed at Charleston, South Carolina, to a hero's welcome. He then openly violated America's neutrality by recruiting four American privateers (privately owned warships) to capture English and Spanish merchant vessels. He also conspired with frontiersmen and land speculators to organize an attack on Spanish Florida and Louisiana.

As Genet made his way to Philadelphia, then America's capital, he was greeted along the way by large crowds cheering the French Revolution. Once in Philadelphia, Genet continued his reckless efforts to draw America into

French Revolution Revolutionary movement beginning in 1789 that overthrew the monarchy and transformed France into an unstable republic before Napoleon Bonaparte assumed power in 1799.

Daniel Boone Escorting Settlers through the Cumberland Gap by George Caleb Bingham.

passage that more than 300,000 settlers would use over the next twenty-five years.

Washington's Farewell

By 1796, George Washington had decided that two terms as president were enough. He was eager to retire to Mount Vernon, his beloved home in northern Virginia. He would leave behind a formidable record of achievement: the organization of a national government, a prosperous economy, the recovery of territory from Britain and Spain, a stable northwestern frontier, and the admission of three new states: Vermont (1791), Kentucky (1792), and Tennessee (1796).

On September 17, 1796, Washington delivered a farewell address to the nation in which he stressed that the United States should avoid getting involved in Europe's quarrels and wars. It was, he said, "our true policy to steer clear of permanent alliances with any portion of the foreign world." The key word here is *permanent*. Washington agreed that "temporary alliances for extraordinary emergencies" might be needed. His warning against permanent foreign entanglements would serve as a fundamental principle in U.S. foreign policy until the early twentieth century.

The Election of 1796

With George Washington out of the race, the United States had its first contested election for president in 1796. The logical choice of the Federalists would have been Alexander Hamilton. But since he had not been born in the United States, Hamilton could not be president. And his illegitimate birth, as well as his bold leadership within the cabinet, had created enemies, even among the Federalists. Vice President John Adams dismissed Hamilton as "a Creole bastard" who was "the incarnation of evil." So the Federalist "caucus," a group of leading congressmen, chose Adams as their presidential candidate. Thomas Pinckney of South Carolina, fresh from his diplomatic triumph in Spain, also ran as a Federalist candidate (at this time there were no candidates for the vice presidency; whoever came in second, regardless of party affiliation, became the vice president). As expected, the Republicans chose Thomas Jefferson. Aaron Burr, a brilliant young attorney and senator from New York, also ran as a Republican.

The campaign of 1796 was nasty. Republicans labeled Adams a closet monarchist because of his alleged elitism (Adams wanted people to refer to the President of the United States as "His Highness"). The Federalists countered that Jefferson was a French-loving atheist eager for another war with Great Britain. They also charged that the philosophical Jefferson was not decisive enough to be president. The increasing strength of the Republicans, fueled by the smoldering resentment of Jay's Treaty as far too lenient with the British, nearly swept Jefferson into office. Instead, Adams became president and Jefferson became his opponent's vice president by winning 68 electoral votes to Adams's 71.

The Adams Administration

Vain and prickly, opinionated and stubborn, John Adams had crafted a distinguished career as a Massachusetts lawyer, as a leader in the Revolutionary movement, as the hardest-working member of the Continental Congress, as a talented diplomat in France, Holland, and Great Britain, and as George Washington's vice president.

Adams lusted for the presidency, but he refused to compromise his principles to ensure his election. He was an independent thinker with a combative spirit and fiery temper who fought as often with his fellow Federalists as he did with his Republican opponents. Benjamin Franklin said Adams was "always an honest man, often a wise one, but sometimes . . . absolutely out of his senses."

Adams had many virtues, however. He was fiercely patriotic, intelligent, experienced, and conscientious. No one had served the new nation with as much dedication and energy. He had helped persuade the Continental

John Adams Political philosopher and politician, Adams was the first president to take up residence in the White House, in early 1801.

Congress to declare independence and assisted Jefferson in drafting the Declaration of Independence. Adams had also helped negotiate the Treaty of Paris, which ended the Revolutionary War in 1783.

The Quasi-War with France

As America's second president, Adams inherited a naval "quasi-war" with France, a by-product of revolutionary France's angry reaction to Jay's Treaty between the United States and Great Britain. When John Jay accepted the British insistence that food and military supplies being shipped from the United States to nations at war with Britain would be seized, the French announced that they would retaliate by confiscating American cargo headed for British ports. By the time of Adams's inauguration, in 1797, French naval vessels had plundered some 300 American ships and severed diplomatic relations with the United States.

President Adams immediately tried to restore good relations with France. In 1797, he sent three U.S. diplomats to Paris to negotiate a settlement of the dispute. But when the Americans arrived in Paris, they were accosted by three French officials (labeled "X," "Y," and "Z" by Adams in his report to Congress), who announced that negotiations could begin only if the United States paid a bribe of $250,000.

Such bribes were common eighteenth-century diplomatic practice, but the answer from the humiliated American side was "no, no, not a sixpence." When the so-called XYZ Affair was reported to Congress, American hostility toward France soared. Many Republicans—with the notable exception of Vice President Jefferson—joined the chorus crying for revenge. President

Quasi-war with France

Conflict with France A cartoon indicating the anti-French sentiment generated by the XYZ affair. The three American negotiators (at left) reject the Paris Monster's demand for money.

Federalists vs. Republicans

With the ratification of the Constitution, the new federal government set out to address the challenges confronting the young nation and set a course for the future. Within President Washington's cabinet and the Congress, divisions quickly emerged as to what the federal government should do regarding financial and other economic matters, western expansion, and how to deal with the fallout from the French Revolution.

Competing Visions	Federalists	Republicans
The Federal Government	Federalists favored a strong national government that would rule the citizenry directly rather than through the states.	Republicans feared a strong national government would return the country to monarchy and trample on individual liberty.
The Constitution	Federalists favored an interpretation of the Constitution that included "implied powers" to give the national government the authority to address issues as they arose.	Jefferson and other Republicans feared excessive government power and favored a strict interpretation of the Constitution that limited the national government and protected individual and states' rights. They demanded a Bill of Rights.
The Economy	As secretary of the Treasury, Hamilton wanted to transform the United States into a global economic power comparable to Great Britain by promoting the growth of cities and commerce. Federalists did not engage issues of slavery and women's rights.	Jefferson and his Republican allies envisioned an egalitarian, agrarian nation. They championed farmers over bankers and feared that inequalities and corruption would arise from the growth of manufacturing and cities. Republicans also did not engage issues of slavery and women's rights.
Western Expansion	Hamilton and Federalists favored building up the population of the East Coast rather than encouraging rapid western expansion.	Republicans favored policies that promoted westward expansion and land ownership and farming rather than urban-industrial development.

The Convention of 1800

Adams asked Congress to authorize the construction of more warships and the expansion of the army. By the end of 1798, an undeclared naval war (a quasi-war) with France had begun in the West Indies. The success of the American navy in capturing nearly 100 French ships, combined with other French defeats around the world, now led the French government to ask for negotiations. In a treaty called the Convention of 1800, the Americans won the best terms they could from the French, including the end of the military alliance with the United States dating back to the Revolutionary War. The American government was eager to end the alliance to avoid being drawn into future European wars involving France. The Senate quickly ratified the agreement, which became effective on December 21, 1801.

Competing Visions	Federalists	Republicans
Debt and Revenue	Hamilton believed that it was the responsibility of the federal government to pay off all Revolutionary War debts, including those of the states, and promoted an ongoing national debt funded by taxes that would be used to continually invest in the economy.	Republicans agreed to the need for paying Revolutionary debts, but opposed an ongoing national debt and federal taxes.
The Bank of the United States	Hamilton favored the creation of a publicly chartered Bank of the United States to secure a sound currency, issue government bonds, and manage the federal government's revenue.	Republicans argued that the Constitution did not give the national government the authority to create a national bank and so opposed the creation of the Bank of the United States.
The French Revolution	Hamilton and Federalists were suspicious of the French Revolution, which they viewed as excessive, and were opposed to continuing the military alliance with France.	Republicans, while acknowledging the excesses of the French Revolution, welcomed its elimination of the monarchy and wanted the United States to support the new French Republic.

QUESTIONS FOR ANALYSIS

1. What were the major disputes between the Federalists and the Republicans?

2. How did their political competition influence the future direction of the United States?

3. What were the results of the Federalist and Republican battles in the 1790s?

The War at Home

The naval war with France sparked an intense debate between Federalists eager for war and the Republicans most sympathetic to France. Pro-French Thomas Jefferson told a French official that President Adams was "a vain, irritable, stubborn" man. In 1797, Vice President Jefferson secretly sponsored a vicious pamphlet that described Adams as a deranged monarchist intent upon naming himself king of the United States. Adams, who learned of his vice president's efforts to undermine his presidency, regretted losing Jefferson as a friend but "felt obliged to look upon him as a man whose mind is warped by prejudice."

Jefferson and other Republicans were convinced that the real purpose of the French crisis was to provide Federalists with an excuse to quiet their American critics. The infamous **Alien and Sedition Acts of 1798** seemed to confirm the Republicans' suspicions. These vengeful acts, passed amid the surge of patriotic war fever, limited freedom of speech and the press as well as the liberty of "aliens" (immigrants who had not yet gained citizenship). John Adams's support for the Alien and Sedition Acts would prove to be the greatest mistake of his presidency.

Three of the four Alien and Sedition acts reflected hostility to French immigrants, many of whom had become militant Republicans in the United States. The Naturalization Act lengthened from five to fourteen years the residency requirement for U.S. citizenship. The Alien Act empowered the president to deport "dangerous" aliens, and the Alien Enemies Act authorized the president in wartime to expel or imprison enemy aliens at will. Finally, the Sedition Act outlawed writing, publishing, or speaking anything of "a false, scandalous and malicious" nature against the government or any of its officers.

In response, Thomas Jefferson and James Madison drafted the Kentucky and Virginia Resolutions, passed by the legislatures of both states in 1798. The resolutions denounced the Alien and Sedition Acts as "alarming infractions" of constitutional rights and argued that the states should "nullify" (reject and ignore) acts of Congress that violated the First Amendment's guarantee of free speech. In attacking the Alien and Sedition Acts, Jefferson was suggesting something more dangerous: disunion. George Washington told Patrick Henry in Virginia that Jefferson was threatening to "dissolve the union or produce coercion."

Republican Victory in 1800

The furor over the Alien and Sedition Acts influenced the pivotal presidential election of 1800. The Federalists nominated John Adams for a second term and added Charles Cotesworth Pinckney to the ballot. But many leading Federalists continued to snipe at Adams and his policies, especially his refusal to declare war against France. New York's Alexander Hamilton, for example, publicly questioned Adams's fitness to be president, citing his "disgusting egotism."

Thomas Jefferson and Aaron Burr, the Republican candidates, represented the alliance of the two most powerful states, Virginia and New York, where Burr was a prominent political figure. The Federalists again attacked Jefferson for supporting the radical French Jacobin revolutionaries. His election, they claimed, would bring civil war and anarchy to America. Jefferson's supporters portrayed him as a passionate idealist and optimist who was the friend of farmers and the courageous champion of states' rights, limited government, and personal liberty.

In the **election of 1800**, Jefferson and Burr tied for the lead with 73 electoral votes each. Adams received only 65. The tie vote in the Elec-

Alien and Sedition Acts of 1798 Four measures passed during the undeclared war with France that limited the freedoms of speech and press and restricted the liberty of immigrants.

election of 1800 Presidential election involving Thomas Jefferson and John Adams; resulted in the first Democratic-Republican victory after the Federalist administrations of George Washington and John Adams.

THE ELECTION OF 1800

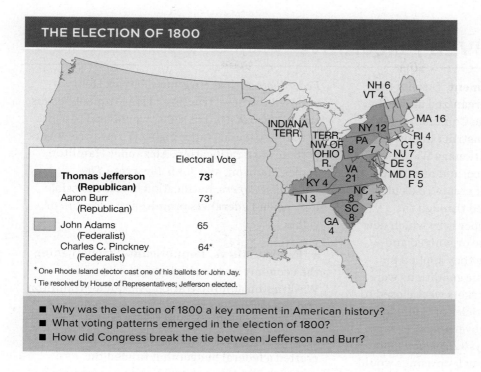

	Electoral Vote
Thomas Jefferson (Republican)	73†
Aaron Burr (Republican)	73†
John Adams (Federalist)	65
Charles C. Pinckney (Federalist)	64*

* One Rhode Island elector cast one of his ballots for John Jay.
† Tie resolved by House of Representatives; Jefferson elected.

■ Why was the election of 1800 a key moment in American history?
■ What voting patterns emerged in the election of 1800?
■ How did Congress break the tie between Jefferson and Burr?

toral College for Jefferson and Burr sent the choice of the president to the House of Representatives (a constitutional defect corrected in 1804 by the Twelfth Amendment). It took thirty-six ballots for the House of Representatives to choose Thomas Jefferson as the new president, making Burr the vice president.

Before the Federalists turned over power to the Jeffersonian Republicans on March 4, 1801, Congress passed the Judiciary Act of 1801. It was intended to ensure Federalist control of the judicial system by creating sixteen federal circuit courts with a new judge for each. Before he left office, Adams appointed Federalists to all the new positions. The defeated Federalists, in the words of Jefferson, "had retired into the judiciary as a stronghold." They would never again exercise political power.

A bitter John Adams refused to attend Thomas Jefferson's inauguration in the new federal capital in Washington, D.C. Instead, unnoticed and unappreciated, the ex-president boarded a stagecoach for the 500-mile trip to his home in Massachusetts. He and Jefferson would not communicate for the next twelve years. As Adams returned to his Massachusetts farm with his wife, Abigail, he told his eldest son, John Quincy, who would later become the nation's sixth president, that anyone governing the new United States faced "a hard, laborious, and unhappy life."

■ **Confederation Government** Despite the weak form of government organized under the *Articles of Confederation*, the Confederation government managed to construct important alliances during the Revolutionary War, help win the War of Independence, and negotiate the Treaty of Paris (1783). It created executive departments and established through the *Northwest Ordinance* the process by which new western territories would be organized and governments formed before they applied for statehood. Postwar economic conditions were difficult because British markets were closed to American trade and the Articles of Confederation did not allow the national government to raise taxes to fund its debts. *Shays's Rebellion* made many Americans fear that such uprisings would eventually destroy the new republic unless the United States formed a stronger national government.

■ **Constitutional Convention** Delegates gathered at the convention in Philadelphia in 1787 to revise the existing government, but almost immediately they decided to scrap the Articles of Confederation and start over. An entirely new document emerged, which created a system called *federalism* in which a strong national government with clear *separation of powers* between executive, legislative, and judicial branches functioned alongside state governments with clearly designated responsibilities. Arguments about how best to ensure that the rights of individual states were protected and also that "the people" were represented in the new Congress were resolved by establishing a Senate, with equal representation for each state, and a House of Representatives, the number of whose delegates was determined by population counts.

■ **Ratification of the Constitution** Ratification of the Constitution was hotly contested, *Anti-Federalists* such as Virginia's Patrick Henry opposed the new structure of government because the absence of a bill of rights would lead to a loss of individual and states' rights. To sway New York State toward ratification, Alexander Hamilton, James Madison, and John Jay wrote *The Federalist Papers*. Ratification became possible only when Federalists promised to add a bill of rights.

■ **Federalists vs. Republicans** Strengthening the economy was the highest priority of the Washington administration. Alexander Hamilton and the *Federalists*, wanted to create a diverse economy in which agriculture was balanced by trade, finance, and manufacturing. Hamilton crafted a federal budget that funded the national debt through tariff and tax revenues, and he created a national bank, the first *Bank of the United States*. Thomas Jefferson and others, known as the *Republicans* worried that Hamilton's plans violated the Constitution and made the federal government too powerful. They envisioned a nation dominated by farmers and planters where the rights of states would be protected against federal power.

■ **Trouble Abroad** With the outbreak of war throughout much of Europe during the *French Revolution*, George Washington's policy of neutrality violated the terms of the 1778 treaty with France. At the same time, Americans sharply criticized *Jay's Treaty* with the British for giving too much away. French warships began seizing British and American ships and an undeclared war was underway. Federalists supported Washington's approach, whereas Republicans were more supportive of France. During the presidency of John Adams, the United States fought an undeclared naval war with the French, which led to the controversial *Alien and Sedition Acts* of 1798.

KEY TERMS

CHRONOLOGY

1781	Articles of Confederation take effect
1783	Treaty of Paris ends the war for independence
1784–1785	Land Ordinances
1786–1787	Shays's Rebellion
1787	Northwest Ordinance
	The Constitutional Convention is held in Philadelphia
1787–1788	*The Federalist Papers* are published
1789	President George Washington is inaugurated
1791	Bill of Rights is ratified
	Bank of the United States is created
1793	Washington issues a proclamation of neutrality
1794	Jay's Treaty is negotiated with England
	Whiskey Rebellion in Pennsylvania
	U.S. Army defeats Indians in the Battle of Fallen Timbers
1795	Treaty of Greenville
	Pinckney's Treaty is negotiated with Spain
1796	John Adams is elected president
1798–1800	Quasi-War with France
1798	Alien and Sedition Acts are passed
1800	Thomas Jefferson is elected president

INQUIZITIVE

Go to InQuizitive to see what you've learned—and learn what you've missed—with personalized feedback along the way.

WE OWE ALLEGIANCE TO NO CROWN (CA. 1814) The War of 1812 generated a renewed spirit of
nationalism, inspiring Philadelphia sign-painter John Archibald Woodside to create this patriotic
and iconic painting.

The Early Republic

1800–1815

When President Thomas Jefferson took office in early 1801, the United States and its western territories reached from the Atlantic Ocean to the Mississippi River. Nine of ten Americans lived on the land, with most of them growing enough food and raising enough livestock to maintain their households but rarely producing surpluses for sale outside the community. Nevertheless, Americans were rapidly developing a commercial economy, buying and selling goods with people around the world as well as with one another. The American desire to increase its trade and grow its economy was, according to Congressman Henry Clay, "a passion as unconquerable as any with which nature has endowed us. You may attempt to regulate [it]—[but] you cannot destroy it." Everywhere people were on the make and on the move, leading one newspaper to claim that what made America different from other nations was "the almost universal ambition to get forward."

1. Summarize the major domestic political developments that took place during Thomas Jefferson's administration.

2. Describe how foreign events impacted the United States during the Jefferson and Madison administrations.

3. Explain the primary causes of the American decision to declare war on Great Britain in 1812.

4. Analyze the most significant outcomes of the War of 1812 on the United States.

The new president claimed that the United States was the "world's best hope" for social progress because it had the "strongest government on earth." The future was bright, Jefferson believed, for Americans could achieve anything they attempted. "Whatever they can, they will," he predicted. Everywhere he looked, Jefferson saw energetic Americans at work. Westward expansion, surging economic development, rapid population growth, and intense political activity preoccupied Americans at the start of the new century. As retiring president John Adams observed, "There is no people on earth so ambitious as the people of America . . . because the lowest can aspire as freely as the highest."

In 1800 the United States, with 5.3 million people, was predominantly a rural society. Almost a million Americans were enslaved. The rapidly growing nation was also becoming younger. Two-thirds of American males in 1800 were under age twenty-five. Their prospects seemed unlimited, their optimism unrestrained.

The spirit of opportunistic independence affected free African Americans as well as whites. Free blacks represented the fastest-growing segment of the population during the early nineteenth century. Many had gained their freedom during the Revolutionary War by escaping, joining the British army, or serving in the American army. Every state except South Carolina and Georgia had promised freedom to slaves who fought the British. Afterward, anti-slavery organizations exerted increasing pressure on the South to end the degrading practice, as state after state in the North outlawed slavery. Massachusetts, for example, freed its slaves in 1780, during the Revolutionary War, citing Thomas Jefferson's phrase from the Declaration of Independence declaring that "all men are created equal."

Thomas Jefferson described the United States in the early years of the nineteenth century as an "empire of liberty" spreading westward across the continent. (He ignored the process by which Americans violated the liberty of Native Americans and Hispanics—people of Mexican or Spanish descent—in the process of moving west.) Native Americans fiercely resisted the invasion of their ancestral lands but ultimately succumbed to a federal government and a federal army determined to relocate them. Most whites, however, were less concerned about Indians than they were about seizing their own opportunities. A British visitor remarked that the Americans were a "restless people, always on the lookout for something better or more profitable." During the early years of the nineteenth century, the new nation set about forging its identity and earning its place among the great powers of the world. But it was not easy. It would take another war with Great Britain—the War of 1812—to ensure the independence of the rowdy American republic.

CORE **OBJECTIVE**

1. Summarize the major domestic political developments that took place during Thomas Jefferson's administration.

Jeffersonian Republicanism

The "People's President"

The 1800 presidential campaign between Federalists and Jeffersonian Republicans had been so fiercely contested that some had predicted civil war as the House of Representatives prepared to decide the outcome of the disputed election. But on March 4, 1801, the fifty-seven-year-old Thomas Jefferson was inaugurated without incident, leading some people to call his election "the peaceful revolution," for it was one of the first public elections in modern history that saw the peaceful transfer of power from one party to another.

Jefferson was the first president to be inaugurated in the new national capital named Washington, District of Columbia. The new city, still raw and unfinished, was crisscrossed with muddy avenues connecting a scattering of buildings clustered around two centers, Capitol Hill and the "President's Palace." Cows grazed along the Mall.

At his intentionally informal inauguration ceremony, Jefferson emphasized his sympathies for the plain style of the "common" people. Instead of wearing a ceremonial sword and riding in an elegant horse-drawn carriage, as George Washington and John Adams had done, the third president left his boarding house and rode his horse alone down stump-strewn Pennsylvania Avenue to the unfinished Capitol building. (Jefferson sold the presidential carriage.) He entered the Senate chamber, took the presidential oath, and then read his inaugural address in a barely audible voice. Jefferson's deliberate display of **Republican simplicity** set the tone for his administration. He wanted Americans to notice the difference between the monarchical trappings of the Federalists and the down-to-earth simplicity and frugality of the Republicans. He did not wear fancy clothes or host elegant parties. Jefferson often answered the door of the president's house himself, wearing a robe and slippers.

In his inaugural address, the tall, thin Virginian, his red hair now streaked with grey, imagined "a rising nation, spread over a wide and fruitful land, traversing all the seas with the productions of their industry, engaged in commerce with nations" across the globe. Although determined to overturn many Federalist policies and programs, he urged Americans to temper their political partisanship and work together. "We are all Republicans— we are all Federalists," Jefferson stressed, noting that "every difference of opinion is not a difference of principle." He asked Americans to "unite with one heart and one mind." It was a brilliant speech, but Jefferson's appeal for a united nation proved illusory, in part because he himself retained his own anti-Federalist prejudices. In a letter to a British friend, Jefferson described the Federalists as "insane" men: "Their leaders are a hospital of incurables."

Jefferson in Office

The inauguration of Thomas Jefferson ushered in a new, more democratic era in American life. An increasing proportion of white males gained the right to vote as state after state reduced or eliminated requirements that voters own property. In many northern states, the percentage of eligible voters went from 20 percent to 80 percent by eliminating or reducing the property requirements. Men of humble origins, some of whom were uneducated and illiterate, began to displace the social and political elite in the state legislatures. And over half of the members of the Republican-controlled Congress

Expanded political participation

Republican simplicity
Deliberate attitude of humility and frugality, as opposed to monarchical pomp and ceremony, adopted by Thomas Jefferson in his presidency.

were newly elected. Unlike John Adams, George Washington, and the Federalists, Thomas Jefferson and the Republicans urged states to expand the electorate so that more men of simple means could vote and hold office. Diehard Federalists were horrified by the "democratization" of politics. "We are sliding down into the mire of a democracy," moaned Fisher Ames of Massachusetts.

Thomas Jefferson was a bundle of contradictions. On one hand, he was a wealthy, slave-owning planter with expensive tastes in food, wine, and furnishings. Charming and brilliant, he was an inventive genius of wide learning and many abilities. He designed the state capitol in Richmond, Virginia, as well as his thirty-three-room mountaintop mansion near Charlottesville called *Monticello* (Little Mountain). Yet while he lived the luxurious life of a slaveholding planter, Jefferson consistently championed the "honest heart" of the common people. His faith in expanding the number of eligible voters and his determination to reduce the power of the national government opened a more democratic era in American life in which the founding generation of aristocratic "gentlemen" such as John Adams and George Washington were gradually displaced in positions of power by men from more common backgrounds.

For all of his natural shyness and admitted weakness as a public speaker, Jefferson was the first president to pursue the role of party leader and political wheeler-dealer, openly cultivating congressional support at frequent dinner parties and elsewhere. In the new president's cabinet, the leading figures were Jefferson's best friend, neighbor, and political ally, Secretary of State James Madison, and Secretary of the Treasury Albert Gallatin, a Swiss-born Pennsylvania Republican whose financial skills had won him the

The Capitol building This 1806 watercolor was painted by its architect Benjamin Henry Latrobe and inscribed to Jefferson. The iconic dome would be added later, after the building was damaged in the War of 1812.

respect of the Federalists. To cultivate Federalist-controlled New England, Jefferson chose men from that region for the positions of attorney general, secretary of war, and postmaster general. In lesser offices, however, Jefferson often succumbed to pressure from the Republicans to remove Federalists. In one area—the judiciary—he removed the offices altogether.

Marbury v. Madison

In 1802, at Jefferson's urging, the Republican-controlled Congress repealed the Judiciary Act of 1801, which the Federalists had passed just before the transfer of power to the Jeffersonian Republicans on March 4, 1801. The Judiciary Act of 1801 was intended to ensure Federalist control of the judicial system by creating sixteen federal circuit courts and appointing—for life—a new Federalist judge for each. The controversy over rescinding the judgeships sparked the precedent-setting case of **Marbury v. Madison** (1803), the first in which the U.S. Supreme Court declared a federal law unconstitutional.

The case involved the appointment of Maryland Federalist William Marbury as justice of the peace in the District of Columbia. Marbury's "midnight" letter of appointment, or commission, signed by President Adams just two days before he left office, was still undelivered when Madison took office as secretary of state, and President Jefferson directed Madison to withhold it. Marbury then filed suit to force Madison to deliver his commission.

The Supreme Court's unanimous opinion, written by Chief Justice John Marshall, a brilliant Virginia Federalist and fierce critic of Jefferson, his cousin, held that Marbury deserved his commission but denied that the Court had jurisdiction in the case. The Federal Judiciary Act of 1789, which gave the Court authority in such proceedings, was unconstitutional, the Marshall court ruled, because the Constitution specified that the Court should have original jurisdiction only in cases involving foreign ambassadors or nations. The Court, therefore, could issue no order in the case. With one bold stroke, Marshall had reprimanded the Jeffersonian Republicans while avoiding an awkward confrontation with an administration that might have defied his order. More important, with the *Marbury* ruling the Court declared a federal law invalid on the grounds that it violated provisions of the Constitution.

Marshall stressed that the Supreme Court was empowered "to say what the law is." In other words, the Marbury decision granted to the Supreme Court a power not mentioned in the Constitution: the right of *judicial review*, or deciding whether acts of Congress were constitutional. So even though William Marbury never gained his judgeship, Marshall established that the Supreme Court decided constitutional interpretations. This was such an astonishing decision that the Court did not declare another federal law unconstitutional for fifty-four years. Since then, however, the Court has struck down over 150 acts of Congress and over 1,100 acts of state legislatures.

Marbury v. Madison (1803)

Marbury v. Madison **(1803)** First Supreme Court decision to declare a federal law—the Judiciary Act of 1789—unconstitutional.

Jefferson's Economic Policies

Athough John Marshall got the better of Thomas Jefferson in court, the president's first term included a series of triumphs in domestic affairs. Jefferson did not set out to dismantle all of Alexander Hamilton's Federalist economic program, despite his harsh criticism of it. Instead, following the advice of Treasury secretary Gallatin, Jefferson, who like many other southern planters never understood the function of banks and hated them, learned to accept the national bank as essential to economic growth. He did, however, reject Hamilton's insistence that a federal debt was a national "blessing" because it gave bankers and investors who lent money to the government a direct financial stake in the success of the new republic. Jefferson believed that a large federal debt would bring high taxes and government corruption, so he set about paying down the debt by slashing the federal budget. If it were not eliminated, Jefferson told Gallatin, "we shall be committed to the English career of debt, corruption, and rottenness, closing with revolution. The discharge of the debt, therefore, is vital to the destinies of the government."

Shrinking the government

In his first message to Congress in 1801, Jefferson promised to reduce the size, expense, and power of the federal government ("too complicated, too expensive"), shrink the government bureaucracy, and restore the authority of the sovereign states. He fired all federal tax collectors and cut the military budget in half, saying that the state militias provided the nation with adequate protection. Jefferson's was the first government in history that intentionally reduced its scope and power.

Jefferson once admitted that he had a peculiar affection for the "men from the Western side of the mountains." To address the grievances of grain farmers and backwoods distillers, Jefferson repealed the federal whiskey tax that Alexander Hamilton had instituted in 1791. Fortunately for Jefferson, the prosperous economy enabled the federal budget to absorb the loss of the whiskey taxes. Revenues from federal tariffs on imports rose, and the sale of government-owned western lands soared. Continuing conflicts in Europe increased American shipping traffic to the nations at war and further padded the federal Treasury.

Western Expansion

Where Alexander Hamilton always faced east, looking to Great Britain for his model of national greatness, Thomas Jefferson looked to the west for his inspiration, across the mountains and even across the Mississippi River. Only by expanding westward, he believed, could America avoid the social turmoil and misery common in the crowded cities of Europe. Only by "enlarging the empire of liberty" could America remain a nation primarily of farmers.

To ensure westward settlement, Jefferson and the Republicans strove to reduce the cost of federal lands, and appreciative settlers flocked to buy property in the western territories. Ohio's admission to the Union in 1803 increased the number of states to seventeen. Land sales west of the Appalachian Mountains skyrocketed in the early nineteenth century as settlers shoved Indians aside and established homesteads.

The Louisiana Purchase

The **Louisiana Purchase** of 1803 was a brilliant diplomatic achievement that more than doubled the territory of the United States. The purchase included 875,000 square miles of land extending far beyond the boundaries of present-day Louisiana. It comprised the entire Mississippi Valley west of the river to the Rocky Mountains. Six states in their entirety, and most or part of nine more, would eventually be carved out of the Louisiana Purchase.

The Louisiana Purchase (1803)

In 1801, soon after Jefferson learned that Spain had transferred the Louisiana Territory to Napoleonic France, he sent Robert R. Livingston to Paris to acquire the area. Spain in control of the Mississippi River outlet was bad enough, but the power-hungry Napoléon in control could only mean serious trouble for the United States. "The day that France takes possession of New Orleans," Jefferson wrote Livingston, "we must marry ourselves to the British fleet and nation"—an unhappy prospect for the French-loving Jefferson.

Early in 1803, Jefferson sent James Monroe, his trusted Virginia friend, to assist Livingston. Their initial goal was simply to acquire the city of New Orleans, strategically situated along the banks of the Mississippi River near its outlet at the Gulf of Mexico. Over the years, New Orleans under Spanish and French rule had become a dynamic crossroads community where people of all races and classes intermingled, reinventing themselves as Americans, while taking advantage of the city's control of the commerce floating down the mighty Mississippi. For years, Americans living in Tennessee and Kentucky had threatened to secede if the federal government did not ensure that they could send their crops and goods down the river to New Orleans.

No sooner had Monroe arrived in Paris than the French surprised him and Livingston by asking if the United States would buy not just New Orleans but *all* of France's immense Louisiana Territory. Livingston quickly snapped up the offer. Napoléon was willing to sell the Louisiana Territory because his army in Saint-Domingue (Haiti) had been decimated by a massive slave revolt and an epidemic of yellow fever. After losing 57,000 French soldiers to disease and warfare, Napoléon decided to cut French losses in the Americas by selling the Louisiana Territory—and thereby helping to finance his ongoing war with Great Britain. The transfer of the vast region, Napoléon said, "strengthens forever the power of the United States, and I have just given to England a maritime rival [the United States] that will sooner or later humble her pride."

By the Treaty of Cession, dated April 30, 1803, the United States obtained the Louisiana Territory for about $15 million. This surprising turn of events presented Jefferson with a "noble bargain"—as well as a constitutional dilemma. Nowhere did the Constitution mention the purchase of territory. Was such an action legal? Jefferson admitted that the purchase was not

Louisiana Purchase (1803) President Thomas Jefferson's purchase of the Louisiana Territory from France for $15 million, doubling the size of U.S. territory.

authorized by the Constitution, but he allowed his desire to expand the American republic to trump his legal concerns. He hoped "that the good sense of our country will correct the evil of loose construction [of the Constitution] when it shall produce ill effects."

Jefferson and other Republicans supported the Louisiana Purchase for several reasons. Acquiring the territory, the president explained, would serve "the immediate interests of our Western citizens" and promote "the peace and security of the nation in general" by removing French control and creating a protective buffer separating the United States from the rest of the world. Besides, Jefferson and his supporters argued, if the nation waited to pass a constitutional amendment to enable the acquisition, Napoléon might change his mind.

New England Federalists, however, were not convinced. They worried that the growing numbers of Americans moving west were driving up wages on the Atlantic coast by reducing the workforce and lowering the value of real estate in their region. They also cringed at the prospect that new western states would likely be settled by southern slaveholders who were Jeffersonian Republicans. In a reversal that anticipated many more reversals on constitutional issues, Federalists found themselves arguing for strict construction of the Constitution in opposing the Louisiana Purchase. Jefferson and the Republicans brushed aside Federalist reservations; the opportunity to almost double the size of the United States outweighed any legal reservations.

Jefferson called a special session of Congress on October 17, 1803, whereupon the Senate ratified the treaty by an overwhelming vote of 26–6. On December 20, 1803, U.S. officials took formal possession of the sprawling Louisiana Territory. At first the Spanish kept West Florida, but in 1810 American settlers revolted against Spanish rule and proclaimed the Republic of West Florida, which was quickly annexed and occupied by the United States as far east as the Pearl River. In 1813, with Spain itself a battlefield for French and British forces, Americans took over the rest of West Florida, out of which the states of Mississippi and Alabama would emerge. Legally, as the U.S. government has claimed ever since, all these areas were included in the Louisiana Purchase, the most significant event of Jefferson's presidency. From Tennessee, Andrew Jackson wrote Jefferson to congratulate him on acquiring the Louisiana Territory. "Every face wears a smile, and every heart leaps with joy."

Lewis and Clark

In the American imagination, beginning with the first colonists, the West, first meaning the Appalachian Mountains, then the Ohio and Mississippi Valleys, then the part of the continent closer to the Pacific Ocean, was always a magical place where dreams could be fulfilled. Thomas Jefferson had long been fascinated by the mysterious region west of the Mississippi River. To

One of Lewis and Clark's maps
In their journals, Lewis and Clark sketched detailed maps of unexplored regions.

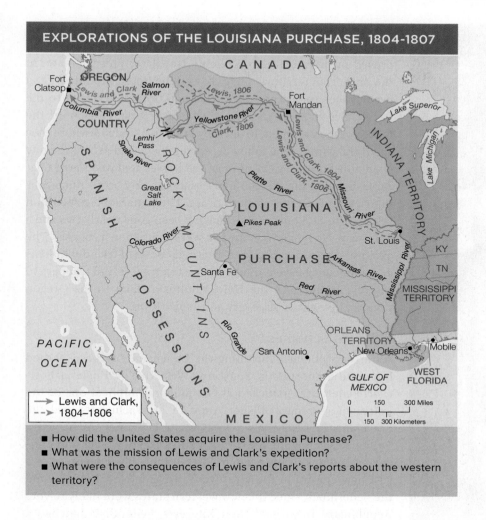

EXPLORATIONS OF THE LOUISIANA PURCHASE, 1804-1807

Lewis and Clark, 1804–1806

- How did the United States acquire the Louisiana Purchase?
- What was the mission of Lewis and Clark's expedition?
- What were the consequences of Lewis and Clark's reports about the western territory?

learn more about its geography, its flora and fauna, and its prospects for trade and agriculture, he asked Congress in 1803 to fund a scientific expedition to the territory. Congress approved, and Jefferson appointed former army officers Meriwether Lewis and William Clark, both Virginians, to lead what we now refer to as the **Lewis and Clark expedition**. Lewis was then serving as Jefferson's private secretary. Clark, it was said, was "a youth of solid and promising parts, and as brave as Caesar."

In 1804 the "Corps of Discovery," numbering nearly fifty men, set out from a small village near St. Louis to follow the muddy Missouri River northward through some of the most rugged wilderness in North America, in part to determine whether the river made its way to the Pacific Ocean. Six months later, near the Mandan Sioux villages in what would become North Dakota, they built Fort Mandan and wintered in relative comfort, sending downriver a barge loaded with maps, soil samples, and live specimens of creatures such as the prairie dog and the magpie, previously unknown in America.

Lewis and Clark expedition

Lewis and Clark expedition (1804) Led by Meriwether Lewis and William Clark, a mission to the Pacific coast commissioned for the purposes of scientific and geographical exploration.

Sacagawea Of the many memorials devoted to Sacagawea, this statue by artist Alice Cooper was unveiled at the 1905 Lewis and Clark Centennial Exposition before another pioneering woman: feminist Susan B. Anthony.

In the spring, Lewis and Clark added to their main party a remarkable young Shoshone woman named Sacagawea, who proved an enormous help as a guide, translator, and negotiator in the uncharted territory. They crossed the Rocky Mountains and used canoes to descend the Snake and Columbia Rivers to the Pacific Ocean. Near the future site of Astoria, Oregon, at the mouth of the Columbia River, they built Fort Clatsop, where they spent the winter. The following spring they headed back, having overcome hunger by eating dogs and horses, and weathered blizzards, broiling sun, fierce rapids, raging grizzly bears, numerous injuries, and swarms of mosquitoes. The remarkable expedition returned to St. Louis in 1806, having been gone nearly two and a half years. No longer was the Far West an unknown country. The explorers' accurate maps and exciting reports of friendly Indians and abundant beavers quickly attracted traders and trappers to the region and gave the United States a claim to the Oregon Country by right of discovery and exploration.

Political Schemes

Jefferson's policies, including the Louisiana Purchase, earned him solid support in the South and West. In New England, however, Federalists panicked at the political implications of the Louisiana Purchase. Fisher Ames of Massachusetts said the Louisiana Territory was a great waste of money, for it was a "wilderness unpeopled with any beings except wolves and wandering Indians." Ames also predicted that the acquisition of a vast new empire in the West would weaken New England and the Federalists, since the new western states were likely to vote Republican. To protect their interests, Federalists hatched a scheme to link New York politically to New England by trying to elect Vice President Aaron Burr, a Republican rival of Jefferson, as governor of New York. Burr chose to drop his Republican affiliation and run for governor as an independent candidate. Several prominent Federalists opposed the scheme. Alexander Hamilton, for example, urged Federalists not to vote for Burr, calling him "a dangerous man, and one who ought not to be trusted with the reins of government." To his surprise, Burr ended up losing the election to the Republican candidate, who had been endorsed by Jefferson.

Hamilton was among those Burr blamed for his defeat. An angry Burr demanded that Hamilton make a public retraction of his critical remarks, and, when Hamilton refused to do so, Burr challenged him to a duel. At dawn on July 11, 1804, the two proud men met near Weehawken, New Jersey, across the Hudson River from New York City. Both men fired, but only Hamilton, whose son had been killed in an earlier duel at the same location, was hit. Mortally wounded, he died the next day. Upon learning that he had been charged with murder by New Jersey authorities, Burr, who was still the vice president, fled to South Carolina, where his daughter lived.

In the meantime, the presidential campaign of 1804 began when a congressional caucus of Republicans renominated Jefferson and chose George Clinton of New York as the vice presidential candidate. By then, to avoid the problems associated with parties running multiple candidates for the presidency, Congress had passed, and the states would soon ratify, the Twelfth Amendment, stipulating that the national electors use separate ballots to vote for the president and vice president. The Federalist candidates, Charles C. Pinckney and Rufus King, never had a chance. Jefferson and Clinton won 162 of the 176 electoral votes. It was the first landslide election in American history.

Divisions in the Republican Party

Freed from strong opposition—Federalists made up only a quarter of the new Congress—the dominant Republican majority began to fragment into warring factions. Fiery Virginian John Randolph (described by a colleague as "an object of admiration and terror") was initially a loyal Jeffersonian, but over time he emerged as the most colorful of the anti-Jefferson "Old Republicans"—mostly southerners who were more consistent than Jefferson in defending states' rights and strict construction of the Constitution. As the imperious Randolph admitted, "The *old* Republican party is already ruined, past redemption," but he tried to save it nonetheless. "I am an aristocrat," he declared. "I love liberty. I hate equality." He and other Old Republicans opposed any compromise with the Federalists, any expansion of federal authority at the expense of states' rights, any new taxes or tariffs, and any change in the nation's agrarian way of life. The Jeffersonian Republicans, on the other hand, were more moderate, pragmatic, and nationalistic in their orientation. As Jefferson demonstrated, they were willing to compromise their states' rights principles to maintain tariffs on imports and a national bank, and to stretch the "implied powers" of the Constitution to accommodate the Louisiana Purchase.

The Burr Conspiracy

Meanwhile, New Yorker Aaron Burr continued to plot and scheme. Sheer brilliance and opportunism had carried him to the vice presidency in 1800. He might easily have become the next president, but a taste for backroom deal-making was his tragic flaw. After the controversy over his duel with Alexander Hamilton subsided, Burr focused on a cockeyed scheme to carve out his own personal empire in the West. What came to be known as the Burr Conspiracy was hatched when Burr and General James Wilkinson plotted to get the Louisiana Territory to secede from the Union and declare itself an independent republic. Earlier, Burr had secretly sought British support for his scheme to separate "the western part of the United States in its whole extent."

Aaron Burr Burr graduated from what is now Princeton University, where he changed his course of study from theology to law.

In late 1806, Burr floated down the Mississippi River with 100 volunteers, only to be arrested and transported to Richmond, Virginia, to face trial for treason before Chief Justice John Marshall. President Jefferson became personally involved, urging the court to convict Burr. In the end, however, Burr was acquitted. With further charges pending, he skipped bail and took refuge in France. He returned in 1812 and resumed practicing law in New York.

Slave Trade Legislation

President Jefferson had little time to fret over the escapades of Aaron Burr; other pressing issues demanded his attention. On December 2, 1806, in his annual message to Congress, Jefferson deplored the "violations of human rights" caused by the continuing trafficking in enslaved Africans. He reminded the Congress that the Constitution stipulated that the international slave trade could be outlawed on January 1, 1808. Congress agreed, and in 1807 the president signed a landmark bill that stopped the importation of enslaved Africans into the United States. At the time, South Carolina was the only state that still permitted the foreign slave trade. The new law ending the importation of slaves did nothing to stop the buying and selling of slaves within the United States, however. In fact, the banning of slaves imported from Africa made the enslaved in America even more valuable, and the number of slave auctions actually increased.

CORE **OBJECTIVE**

2. Describe how foreign events impacted the United States during the Jefferson and Madison administrations.

War in the Mediterranean and Europe

The Barbary Pirates

Issues of foreign relations emerged early in Jefferson's first term, when events in the distant Mediterranean Sea gave him second thoughts about the need for American warships. On the Barbary Coast of North Africa, the Islamic rulers of Morocco, Algiers, Tunis, and Tripoli had for years specialized in piracy, preying upon European and American ships. After the Revolution, **Barbary pirates** continued to capture American vessels and enslave the crews. The U.S. government made ransom payments, first to Morocco in 1786, then to the others in the 1790s. In 1801, however, the pasha (ruler) of Tripoli upped his demands and declared war on the United States. Jefferson sent warships to blockade Tripoli. A naval war dragged on until 1805, punctuated in 1804 by the notable exploit of Lieutenant Stephen Decatur, who slipped into Tripoli Harbor by night and set fire to the frigate *Philadelphia*, which had been captured (along with its crew) after it ran aground. The pasha finally settled for a $60,000 ransom and released the *Philadelphia*'s crew, whom he had held hostage for more than a year. It was still ransom (called "tribute" in the nineteenth century), but far less than

Barbary pirates North Africans who waged war (1801–1805) on the United States after Jefferson refused to pay tribute (a bribe) to protect American ships.

Burning of the Frigate Philadelphia Lieutenant Stephen Decatur set fire to the captured *Philadelphia* during the United States' standoff with Tripoli over the enslavement of American sailors.

the $300,000 the pasha had demanded at first and much less than the cost of war.

Naval Harassment by Britain and France

In his first term, Jefferson had been able to avoid most foreign entanglements, particularly the new war in Europe pitting Napoleonic France against Great Britain. But during his second term, the expanding European war (1803–1815) forced him to take action to protect America's economic interests. In May 1806, Britain's desperate war with France led it to declare a naval blockade of the entire European coast to prevent merchant ships from making port in France. Because the United States was officially "neutral" in the war, its ships technically were allowed by international law to carry cargo from the islands in the French and Spanish West Indies through the British blockade to French ports. But the British quickly decided to end such commerce.

The tense situation posed a dilemma for American merchants. If they agreed to British demands to stop all trading with the French, they would be subject to seizure by the French navy, and vice versa. French and British efforts to control trade across the Atlantic soon brought Americans into the war. Hundreds of American ships were intercepted and their cargoes seized.

For American seamen, the danger was heightened by the British practice of *impressment*, whereby British naval personnel forcibly boarded American ships and captured sailors they claimed were British citizens who had deserted the British navy. American merchant ships paid seamen more than twice as much as did the Royal Navy, so thousands of British sailors had

"Impressment"

deserted the navy to work on American ships. Needing 12,000 new sailors each year to man its growing fleet of warships, the British wanted their deserters back, but they often did not bother to determine the citizenship of those they took off American vessels and "impressed" into service for the British navy. The British often "impressed" American citizens who had been born in Britain, claiming "once a British citizen, always a British citizen," even if the United States had granted citizenship.

To Americans, the British practice of impressment assaulted the honor and dignity of the newly independent nation. As Senator John Quincy Adams, the son of former president John Adams, groused, impressment was "kidnapping on the ocean." Between 1803 and 1811, some 6,200 American sailors were "impressed" into the British navy.

In early 1807, Napoléon responded to the British blockade of Europe by sending French warships to blockade the ports of Great Britain. The British then announced that they would no longer allow any foreign ships to trade with the French islands in the Caribbean.

> The *Chesapeake* Incident (1807)

The United States was again caught in the crossfire between the two warring European powers. On June 22, 1807, the British warship HMS *Leopard* stopped a U.S. vessel, the *Chesapeake*, about eight miles off the Virginia coast. After the *Chesapeake*'s captain refused to allow the British to search his ship for British deserters, the *Leopard* opened fire, killing three Americans and wounding eighteen. The *Chesapeake* was forced to surrender. A British search party seized four men, one of whom was later hanged for desertion from the British navy.

Preparation for War to Defend Commerce Shipbuilders, like those pictured here constructing the *Philadelphia*, played an important role in the war efforts against America's many rivals.

The British attack on the *Chesapeake* was both an act of war and a national insult. The *Washington Federalist* editorialized: "We have never, on any occasion, witnessed . . . such a thirst for revenge." Public anger was so great that President Jefferson could have declared war on the spot. He later wrote that the *Chesapeake* incident "put war into my hand, I had only to open it and let havoc loose." In early July, Jefferson called his cabinet members to meet in Washington, D.C. He then issued a proclamation banning all British warships from American waters and called on state governors to mobilize their militia units. But like John Adams before him, Jefferson resisted war fever, in part because the United States was not prepared for war. Jefferson's caution outraged his critics. A politician eager for war called Jefferson a "dish of skim milk curdling at the head of our nation."

The Embargo

Not ready for war, President Jefferson convinced Congress to cut off all American trade with Europe. As Jefferson said, his choices were "war, embargo, or nothing." The unprecedented **Embargo Act** (December 1807) stopped all American ships from leaving for foreign ports. All trade with foreign nations was banned. Jefferson and his secretary of state, James Madison, assumed that the loss of trade with America would quickly force the warring nations of Europe to quit violating American rights—but Jefferson and Madison were sorely wrong, as neither Britain nor France yielded.

With each passing month, the embargo devastated the American economy, especially in New England, where merchants howled because the embargo cut off their primary industry: oceangoing commerce. The value of American exports plummeted from $48 million in 1807 to $9 million a year later. Shipbuilding declined by two-thirds, and prices for farm crops were cut in half. New England's once-thriving port cities—Boston, Salem, and Providence—were like ghost towns. Thirty thousand unemployed American sailors wandered the streets, drinking and cursing Jefferson's unpopular embargo. Meanwhile, smuggling grew rampant, especially along the border with Canada. While American merchant ships sat idle, the British gained a near monopoly on trade with Canada and the islands in the West Indies. Americans in every region but especially New England grew furious at "Jefferson's embargo." A Bostonian wrote the president to report that he was "in a starving condition" and accused Jefferson of being "one of the greatest tyrants in the whole world." Another told the president that he had paid $400 to four friends "to shoot you if you don't take off the embargo."

The embargo turned American politics upside down. Jefferson, the nation's leading spokesman for reducing the power of the federal government, now found himself expanding federal power into every aspect of the nation's economic life. The tiny U.S. Navy was deployed to enforce the embargo. In effect, the United States blockaded its own shipping, cutting off the profitable

Embargo Act (1807)

Embargo Act (1807) A law promoted by President Thomas Jefferson prohibiting American ships from leaving for foreign ports, in order to safeguard them from British and French attacks. This ban on American exports proved disastrous to the U.S. economy.

Anti-Jefferson sentiment
This 1807 Federalist cartoon compares Washington (left, flanked by a British lion and American eagle) and Jefferson (right, with a snake and a lizard). Below Jefferson are volumes of French philosophy while Washington's volumes simply read: *Law*, *Order*, and *Religion*.

trade with foreign nations in an effort to avoid war by exerting "peaceable coercion" against Britain and France. New England Federalists, eager to renew trade with Europe, now used the argument that their states' rights were being violated by the national government.

The outrage over "Jefferson's embargo" demoralized the president and other Republicans and helped revive the Federalist party in New England, which charged that the president was trying to help the French by shutting off American trade with London. At the same time, farmers and planters in the South and West also suffered; they needed to sell their surplus grain, cotton, and tobacco. A gloomy Jefferson finally accepted failure and repealed the ill-conceived embargo in 1809, shortly before he ended the "splendid misery" of his presidency and retired "to my family, my books, and my farms" in Virginia. No one, he said, could be more relieved "on shaking off the shackles of power."

President Jefferson learned a hard lesson that many of his successors would also confront: a second term is rarely as successful as the first. As Jefferson admitted, "No man will ever carry out of that office [the presidency] the reputation which carried him into it." In the election of 1808, the presidency passed to another prominent Virginian, Jefferson's close friend and fellow Republican, Secretary of State James Madison. The Federalists, backing Charles C. Pinckney of South Carolina and Rufus King of New York, won only 47 electoral votes to Madison's 122.

James Madison and the Drift to War

In his inaugural address, President Madison observed that he inherited a situation "full of difficulties." He soon made them worse. Although he may have been a talented legislator and the "Father of the Constitution," he proved to be a poor chief executive. When members of Congress questioned several of his cabinet appointments, the president backed down and ended up naming second-rate men to key positions. In fact, Madison's sparkling wife, Dolley, was the only truly excellent member of his inner circle. Seventeen years younger than the president and twice his size, she was a superb First Lady who excelled at using the White House to entertain political leaders and foreign dignitaries. Journalists called her the "Queen of Washington City."

From the beginning, Madison's presidency was entangled in foreign affairs and crippled by his lack of executive experience. Madison and his advisers repeatedly overestimated the young republic's diplomatic leverage and military strength in shaping foreign policy. The result was humiliation.

Like Jefferson, Madison insisted on upholding the principle of freedom of the seas for the United States and other neutral nations, but he was unwilling to create a navy strong enough to enforce it. He continued the policy of "peaceable coercion," which was just as ineffective for Madison as it had been for Jefferson. In place of the ill-conceived embargo, Madison convinced Congress to pass the Non-Intercourse Act (1809), which reopened trade with all countries *except* France and Great Britain and their colonies. It also authorized the president to reopen trade with France or Great Britain if either stopped violating American rights.

Non-Intercourse Act (1809)

Madison's restrictions on American trade sparked an economic recession and brought no change in the British navy's misbehavior on the high seas. By 1811, the United States was again on the verge of war, with Americans seriously divided again about whether Britain or France was more responsible for violating American shipping rights. When the British refused to give in, Madison reluctantly asked Congress to declare war on June 1, 1812. If the United States did not defend its rights as a neutral nation, the president explained, then Americans were "not independent people, but colonists and vassals."

On June 5, the House of Representatives voted for war 79–49. Two weeks later, the Senate concurred by a narrower vote, 19–13. Every Federalist in Congress resisted what they called "Mr. Madison's War"; 80 percent of Republicans supported it. The southern and western states wanted war; the northeastern states, fearful of losing their essential maritime trade, opposed it. By declaring war, Republicans hoped to unite the nation, discredit the Federalists, and put an end to British-led Indian attacks along the Great Lakes and in the Ohio Valley. To generate popular support, Jefferson advised Madison that he needed, above all, "to stop Indian barbarities. The conquest of Canada will do this." Jefferson and others lusting for war presumed that the French Canadians were eager to rise up against their British rulers. With their help, the Republicans assumed, American invaders would easily conquer Britain's northern colony. It did not work out that way.

America declares war on Great Britain (1812)

CORE **OBJECTIVE**

3. Explain the primary causes of the American decision to declare war on Great Britain in 1812.

The War of 1812

In the **War of 1812** the United States found itself in yet another conflict with Great Britain, barely thirty years after the Revolutionary War had ended. It was the first time in American history that Congress formally used its war-making powers detailed in the Constitution. Great Britain did not want the war; it was preoccupied with defeating Napoléon in Europe. In fact, on June 16, 1812, the British government sought to avert war by deciding to quit interfering with American shipping. But President Madison and the Republicans were not satisfied; they said the war would proceed in order to put an end to the British practice of impressment as well as British-inspired Indian attacks. Why the United States chose to declare the war remains a puzzle still debated among historians.

American Shipping Rights and Honor

British impressment of U.S. sailors and invasion of shipping rights

The main cause of the war—the repeated British violations of American shipping rights and the practice of "impressing" sailors off American ships dominated President Madison's war message. Most of the votes for war came from congressmen representing rural regions from Pennsylvania southward and westward, where farmers and planters grew surpluses for export to Europe. They had real economic interests that were being hurt by the raids on American merchant ships. However, the representatives from the New England states, which bore the brunt of British attacks on U.S. shipping, voted *against* the declaration of war, 20–12. As a New England minister roared, let the "southern *Heroes* fight their own battles."

One explanation for this seeming inconsistency is that many Americans in the South and West, especially Tennessee and Kentucky, voted for war because they believed America's national honor was at stake. A proud Tennessean, Andrew Jackson, declared that he was eager to fight "for the re-establishment of our national character." When asked what the United States would "lose by maintaining the peace," Kentucky Congressman Henry Clay, the new Speaker of the House, answered forcefully: "Commerce, character, a nation's best treasure, honor!" In the popular phrase of the time, the war was needed to protect "Free Trade and Sailors' Rights!"

Native American Conflicts

War of 1812 (1812–1815)
Conflict fought in North America and at sea between Great Britain and the United States over American shipping rights and British-inspired Indian attacks on American settlements. Canadians and Native Americans also fought in the war on each side.

Another factor leading to war was the growing number of British-allied Indian attacks in the Ohio Valley. During the early nineteenth century, land-hungry settlers and speculators kept moving into Indian lands. The constant pressure on Native Americans to sell land repeatedly forced or persuaded Indians to sign treaties they did not always understand. It was an old story, dating from the Jamestown settlement, but one that took a new turn with the rise of two brilliant Shawnee leaders, Tecumseh and his brother, Tenskwatawa.

Tecumseh (Shooting Star) knew that the fate of the native peoples in America depended on their being unified. His hope was to create a single Indian nation powerful enough, with British assistance, to fend off further American expansion. His half brother Tenskwatawa (the "Open Door"), a one-eyed recovering alcoholic with a fierce temper who was known as "the Prophet" and claimed to have been visited by the Great Spirit, gained a large following among Native Americans for his repeated prediction that the white Americans ("children of the devil") were on the verge of collapse. He demanded that the indigenous peoples abandon all things European: clothing, customs, Christianity, and especially liquor. If they did so, the Great Spirit would reward them by turning the whites' gunpowder to sand.

From his large village called Prophetstown on the Tippecanoe River in northern Indiana, Tecumseh, inspired by his brother's spiritual message, traveled in 1811 from Canada to the Gulf of Mexico to form alliances with other Native American nations (Shawnee and Creek; Cherokee and Mohegan; Miami, Delaware, and Kickapoo; Choctaw and Chickasaw; Chippewa and Ottawa) to defend their hunting grounds. "The whites have driven us from the sea to the lakes," he declared. "We can go no further." Tecumseh disavowed the many treaties whereby indigenous peoples had "sold" ancient Indian lands. "No tribe," he declared, "has the right to sell [land], even to each other, much less to strangers. . . . Sell a country!? Why not sell the air, the great sea, as well as the earth? Didn't the Great Spirit make them all for the use of his children?" No land transfer to whites was valid without the consent of all the Indian peoples, he insisted, since they held the land in common.

William Henry Harrison, governor of the Indiana Territory, learned of Tecumseh's bold plans, met with him twice, and described him as "one of those uncommon geniuses who spring up occasionally to produce revolutions and overturn the established order of things." Yet Harrison vowed to eliminate Tecumseh and his dream of a unified Indian nation. In the fall of 1811, he gathered 1,000 troops and advanced on Tecumseh's capital, Prophetstown, while the Indian leader was away. His brother Tenskwatawa was lured into making a foolish attack on Harrison's encampment. The **Battle of Tippecanoe** was a disastrous defeat for the Native Americans. Harrison's troops burned the village and destroyed its supplies. **Tecumseh's Indian Confederacy** went up in smoke, and he fled to Canada.

The Lust for Canada and Florida

Some Americans wanted war with Great Britain because they wanted to acquire Canada, not only as a means of expanding American territory and eliminating the British presence there, but also as a way to gain a monopoly over the lucrative fur trade with the indigenous peoples ("First Nations") in Canada. That there were nearly 8 million Americans in 1812 and only 300,000 Canadians led many pro-war Americans to believe that the

Tecumseh Shawnee leader who tried to unite Indian tribes in defense of their lands, later killed in 1813 at the Battle of the Thames.

The British-allied Indian attacks in Ohio Valley

Battle of Tippecanoe (1811) Battle in northern Indiana between U.S. troops and Native American warriors led by prophet Tenskwatawa, the brother of Tecumseh.

Tecumseh's Indian Confederacy A group of Native American nations under leadership of Shawnee leader Tecumseh and Tenskwatawa; its mission of fighting off American expansion was thwarted in the Battle of Tippecanoe (1811), when the confederacy fell apart.

conquest of sparsely populated Canada would be quick and easy. Jefferson had told Madison that the American "acquisition of Canada" was simply a "matter of marching" north with a military force.

U.S. desire to acquire Canada and Florida

The British were also vulnerable far to the south. East Florida, which the British had returned to Spain in 1783, posed a threat to the Americans because Spain was too weak (or simply unwilling) to prevent Indian attacks across the border with Georgia. In the absence of effective Spanish control of the border, British agents and traders remained in East Florida, smuggling goods and conspiring with Indians along the coast of the Gulf of Mexico. Spanish Florida had also long been a haven for runaway slaves from Georgia and South Carolina. Many Americans living along the Florida-Georgia border hoped that the war against Great Britain would enable them to oust the British and Spain from Florida and make it an American territory.

War Fever

Defending America's "national honor"

Such concerns helped generate excited support for a war against Great Britain. In the Congress that assembled in late 1811, young new representatives from southern and western districts shouted for war in defense of "national honor" and to rid the Northwest of the "Indian problem." Among the "war hawks" were Henry Clay of Kentucky and John C. Calhoun of South Carolina. After they entered the House, John Randolph of Virginia said, "We have heard but one word . . . one eternal monotonous tone—Canada! Canada! Canada!" Clay, the new Speaker of the House, was a tall, rawboned man who yearned for war. He was all "for resistance by the *sword*," and boasted that the Kentucky militia alone could conquer British Canada.

Clay's bravado inspired others. "I don't like Henry Clay," Calhoun said. "He is a bad man, an imposter, a creator of wicked schemes. I wouldn't speak to him, but, by God, I love him" for wanting war. When Calhoun heard about Madison's decision for war, he threw his arms around Clay's neck and led his war-hawk colleagues in an Indian war dance. Virginian James Monroe was also delighted by the onset of a "manly war."

In New England and much of New York, however, there was little enthusiasm for the war. Another conflict with Great Britain threatened to cripple the region's dominant industry, shipping, since Great Britain remained the region's largest trading partner. Federalists not only criticized President Madison for declaring war; a few of them, both men and women, were charged with being British spies ("the blackest treason"—but technically not yet a crime for civilians to do so) while others were caught smuggling goods to the British. Other Americans who opposed the war discouraged men from enlisting in the military and making loans to the government. In 1814 the Massachusetts governor secretly asked the British what they would do if New England seceded from the United States. Republicans dismissed the anti-war Federalists as traitors. Former president Jefferson claimed that the "Republicans are the nation," implying that the Federalists were British loyalists.

War Preparations

As it turned out, the war hawks would get neither Canada nor Florida because the United States was unprepared for war, both financially and militarily. The emphasis of Republican presidents Jefferson and Madison on small federal budgets and military cutbacks proved to be an ineffective way to win a war, and Madison, a small, soft-spoken man, lacked the military qualities needed to inspire national confidence and resolve. He was no George Washington.

Moreover, the national economy was weak. In 1811, despite pleas from the Treasury secretary, Congress had let the charter of the Bank of the United States expire. In addition, once war began, the mighty British navy blockaded American ports and cut off imports, a major source of national revenue. By March 1813, Albert Gallatin warned Madison that the U.S. Treasury had "hardly enough money to last till the end of the month." Furthermore, the demise of the Bank of the United States brought confusion to the nation's financial system. Loans were needed to cover the war's costs, and northeastern opponents of the war were reluctant to lend money to the federal government.

The military situation was almost as bad. When the War of 1812 began, the U.S. Army numbered only 3,287 ill-trained and poorly equipped men, led by mostly incompetent officers with little combat experience. In January 1812, Congress authorized an army of 35,000 men, but a year later, just 18,500 had been recruited, many of them poor Irish immigrants who hated the English—and then only by enticing them with promises of land and cash bounties. President Madison refused to allow free blacks or slaves to serve in the army, so he was forced to plead with the state governors to provide militiamen, only to see the Federalist governors in anti-war New England refuse. The British, on the other hand, had thousands of soldiers stationed in Canada and the West Indies. And, as was true during the Revolutionary War, the British, offering food, guns, and ammunition, recruited more Native American allies than did the Americans in 1812. In all, more than two dozen Indian nations participated in the war.

The U.S. Navy was in better shape than the army, with able officers and well-trained seamen, but there were only sixteen warships, compared to Britain's 600. In the first year of the war, the navy produced the only U.S.

U.S. Naval victories John Bull (the personification of England) "stung to agony" by *Wasp* and *Hornet*, two American ships that clinched early victories in the War of 1812.

victories, in isolated duels with British vessels. But courageous American seamen could not stop the British from blockading the U.S. coast, except for New England, where the British hoped to strengthen anti-war sentiment. The lopsided military strength of the British led President Madison to mutter that the United States was in "an embarrassing situation."

A Continental War

The War of 1812 was really three wars fought on three separate fronts. One theatre of conflict was the Chesapeake Bay along the coast of Maryland and Virginia, including Washington, D.C. The second was in the South, in Alabama, Mississippi, and West and East Florida, culminating in the Battle of New Orleans in 1815. In that region, American forces led by General Andrew Jackson invaded lands owned by the Creeks and the Spanish. The third war might be more accurately called the Canadian-American War. It began in what is now northern Indiana and Ohio, southeastern Michigan, and regions around Lakes Huron and Michigan. There the fighting raged back and forth along the ill-defined border between the United States and British Canada.

The War in the North

The only place where the United States could attack the British on land was Canada. There the war would essentially become a civil war, very much like the American Revolution. One side—Canadians, many of whom were former American Loyalists who had fled north in 1783—remained loyal to the British Empire, while the Americans and a few French Canadians sought to push Britain out of North America. Indians armed with British-supplied weapons dominated the heavily wooded area around the Great Lakes. Michigan's governor recognized that the British and their Indian allies were dependent on each other: "The British cannot hold Upper Canada without the assistance of the Indians," but the "Indians cannot conduct a war without the assistance of a civilized nation [Great Britain]."

For the American assault on British Canada, President James Madison approved a three-pronged plan. It called for one U.S. army to move north through upstate New York, along Lake Champlain, to take Montreal, while another was to advance into Upper Canada by crossing the Niagara River between Lakes Ontario and Erie. The third attack would come from the west, with an American force moving east into Upper Canada from Detroit, Michigan. The plan was to have all three attacks begin at the same time in order to force the British troops in Canada to split up. Like so many complex war plans, this one was a disaster, in large part because the Americans could barely field one army, not three, and communications among the various commanders was spotty at best.

In July 1812, General William Hull, a Revolutionary War veteran and governor of the Michigan Territory, marched his disorganized and poorly supplied army across the Detroit River into Canada, announcing to the Canadians, most of them French, that he was there to free them from "tyranny and oppression." But the Americans were soon pushed back to Detroit by a smaller number of British troops and their Indian allies. Sickly and distracted by too much whiskey, the timid Hull was tricked by the opposing British commander's threats to unleash thousands of Indian warriors led by Tecumseh. Fearing a massacre by "savages," Hull suddenly surrendered his entire force to the British bluff. His capitulation, giving up 2,500 troops and loads of weapons and munitions that the Americans could not afford to lose, shocked the nation and opened the Old Northwest region to raids by British troops and their Indian allies. Madison and the Republicans felt humiliated; the American soldiers appeared to be cowards. In Kentucky, a Republican said General Hull must be a "traitor" or "nearly an idiot" or "part of both." Hull was eventually put on trial and sentenced to death, only to be pardoned by President Madison and dismissed from the army.

The second prong of the American invasion plan, the assault on Montreal, never got off the ground. The third American attack began at dawn on October 13, 1812. U.S. troops led by General Stephen Van Rensselaer, New York's wealthiest landowner, rowed across the Niagara River from Lewiston, New York, to invade at the Canadian village of Queenston, but suffered a

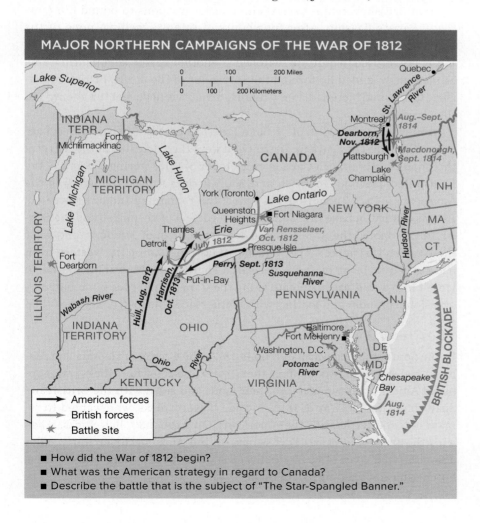

MAJOR NORTHERN CAMPAIGNS OF THE WAR OF 1812

- How did the War of 1812 begin?
- What was the American strategy in regard to Canada?
- Describe the battle that is the subject of "The Star-Spangled Banner."

crushing defeat in the Battle of Queenston Heights. Some 925 American soldiers surrendered, and Van Rensselaer resigned his command in shame. Many Americans lost hope that they could win the war. In early 1813, a Kentuckian warned that any more military disasters would result in "disunion," and the "cause of Republicanism will be lost."

Thereafter, in the northern borderland between the United States and Canada, a powerful alliance of British troops, Canadian militiamen, and Indians repeatedly repelled U.S. invasion attempts. The bruised Americans then sought to gain naval control of the Great Lakes and other inland waterways along the Canadian border. If the Americans could break the British naval supply line and secure Lake Erie, they could divide the British and their Indian allies. In 1813 at Presque Isle, Pennsylvania, (near Erie), twenty-eight-year-old Oliver Hazard Perry supervised the construction of warships from timber cut in nearby forests. By the end of the summer, Commodore Perry set out in search of the British, finally finding them at Lake Erie's Put-in-Bay on September 10. After completing preparations for battle, Perry told his aide, "This is the most important day of my life."

Two British warships used their superior weapons to pound the *Lawrence*, Perry's flagship. After four hours of intense shelling, none of the *Lawrence*'s guns were working, and most of the crew were dead or wounded. But Perry refused to quit. He switched to another vessel, kept fighting, and, miraculously, ended up forcing the surrender of the entire British squadron. Hatless and bloodied, Perry reported that "we have met the enemy and they are ours."

American naval control of Lake Erie forced the British to evacuate Upper Canada. They gave up Detroit and were then defeated at the Battle of the Thames in southern Canada on October 5, 1813. During the battle, the British fled, leaving Tecumseh and 500 warriors to face the wrath of the Americans. When Tecumseh was killed, the remaining Indians retreated. Perry's victory on Lake Erie and the army's defeat of Tecumseh and the British force enabled the Americans to recover control of Michigan and seize the Western District of Upper Canada. At last, the war on the western front had turned in favor of the Americans. Thereafter, the war in the north lapsed into a military stalemate along the Canadian border punctuated by occasional plunder and looting, with neither side able to dislodge the other.

The Creek War

In the South, too, the war flared up in 1813. The Creeks in Georgia and Alabama had split into two factions: the Upper Creeks (or Red Sticks), who opposed American expansion into their lands and sided with the British and Spanish during the War of 1812, and the Lower Creeks, who wanted to remain on good terms with the Americans. On August 30, Red Sticks, allied with the British, attacked Fort Mims, on the Alabama River thirty miles above the Gulf coast town of Mobile, killing 553 men, women, and children, butchering and scalping half of them.

The massacre outraged Americans, especially those eager to remove the Native Americans from the Mississippi Territory (which then included Alabama). Thirsting for revenge, Andrew Jackson, commanding general of the Army of West Tennessee, recruited about 2,500 volunteers and headed south. Jackson was a natural warrior and a gifted commander. From a young age, he had embraced violence, gloried in it, and prospered by it. He had a volcanic temper and a ferocious will that inspired obedience and loyalty. He told all "brave Tennesseans" that their "frontier [was] threatened with invasion by the savage foe" and that the Indians were advancing "with scalping knives unsheathed, to butcher your wives, your children, and your helpless babes. Time is not to be lost."

Jackson's volunteers crushed the Red Sticks in Alabama. The decisive battle occurred on March 27, 1814, at Horseshoe Bend on the Tallapoosa River. Jackson's soldiers and their Cherokee and Creek allies surrounded a Red Stick fort, set fire to it, and shot the Indians as they tried to escape. Nine hundred of them were killed, in-

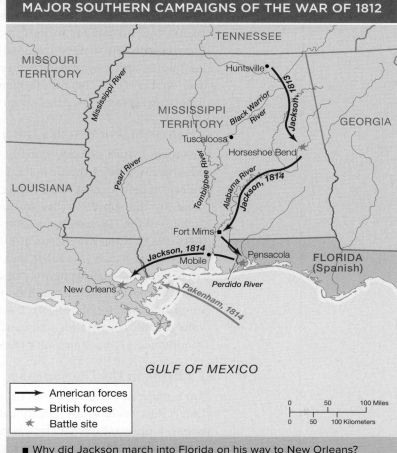

MAJOR SOUTHERN CAMPAIGNS OF THE WAR OF 1812

American forces
British forces
Battle site

■ Why did Jackson march into Florida on his way to New Orleans?
■ Why did he have the advantage in the Battle of New Orleans?
■ Why was the Battle of New Orleans important to the Treaty of Ghent?

cluding 300 who drowned in a desperate effort to cross the river. Jackson reported to his wife that the *"carnage was dreadful."* His men had "regained all the scalps taken from Fort Mims." Fewer than fifty of Jackson's soldiers were killed.

The Battle of Horseshoe Bend was the worst defeat ever inflicted upon Native Americans. With the Treaty of Fort Jackson, signed in August 1814, the devastated Red Stick Creeks were forced at gunpoint to give up two-thirds of their land—some 23 million acres—including southwest Georgia and much of Alabama. Red Eagle, chief of the Red Sticks, told Jackson: "I am in your power. . . . My people are all gone. I can do no more but weep over the misfortunes of my nation." For his part, Jackson declared that "the power of the Creeks is I think forever broken." President Madison rewarded Jackson by naming him a major general in the regular army of the United States.

Soon after the Battle of Horseshoe Bend, events in Europe took a dramatic turn when the British, Spanish, and Portuguese armies repelled

French emperor Napoléon's effort to conquer Spain and Portugal. Now free to deal with the United States, the British in the summer of 1814 sent 16,000 veteran soldiers from Europe to try again to invade America from Canada. The British navy extended their blockade to include the New England ports, and they bombarded coastal towns from Delaware to Florida. The final piece of the British plan was to seize New Orleans and sever American access to the Mississippi River, lifeline of the western states.

Thomas Macdonough's Naval Victory

The main British military effort in the War of 1812 focused on launching a massive invasion of the United States from Canada. But the outnumbered American defenders at Plattsburgh, New York, along Lake Champlain, were saved by the superb ability of Commodore Thomas Macdonough, commander of the U.S. naval squadron. On September 11, 1814, the British soldiers attacked the Americans at Plattsburgh while their warships engaged Macdonough's navy in a battle that surprisingly ended with the entire British fleet either destroyed or captured. The Battle of Lake Champlain (also called the Battle of Plattsburgh) forced the British to abandon the northern campaign. The British forces retreated back into Canada. When the British officers came aboard the American flagship to surrender, Macdonough said, "Gentlemen, return your swords to your scabbards; you are worthy of them."

Fighting in the Chesapeake

The American naval victory at Lake Champlain could not have been more timely. Just weeks before, U.S. forces had suffered the most humiliating experience of the war as British troops captured and burned Washington, D.C. In August 1814, 4,000 British soldiers landed at Benedict, Maryland, and headed briskly for the American capital, thirty-five miles away. Thousands of frightened Americans fled the city. President Madison frantically called out the poorly led and untrained militia, then courageously left the White House (Madison was the first president to call it that) to encourage the soldiers confronting the British army. But their feeble defense disintegrated in the face of the British attack.

On August 24 the British marched unopposed into the American capital. British officers ate a meal in the White House that had been prepared for Madison and his wife, Dolley, who had fled the grounds just in time, after first saving a copy of the Declaration of Independence and George Washington's portrait. The vengeful British, aware that American troops had earlier burned the Canadian capital at York (Toronto), then torched the White House, the Capitol, the Library of Congress, and most other government buildings. A tornado the next day compounded the damage, but a violent thunderstorm dampened both the fires and the enthusiasm of the British forces, who headed north to assault Baltimore.

The destruction of Washington, D.C., infuriated Americans. A Baltimore newspaper reported that the "spirit of the nation is roused." That spirit of determination showed itself when fifty British warships sailed into Baltimore Harbor on September 13 while the British army assaulted the city on land. About a thousand Americans held Fort McHenry on an island in the harbor. The British fleet unleashed a nightlong bombardment of the fort. Yet the Americans refused to surrender. Francis Scott Key, a Washington, D.C., lawyer and occasional poet, watched the siege from a British ship, having been sent to negotiate the release of a captured American. The sight of the American flag still flying over Fort McHenry at dawn meant that the city had survived the British onslaught. The scene inspired Key to scribble the verses of what came to be called "The Star-Spangled Banner," which began, "Oh, say can you see by the dawn's early light?" Later revised and set to the tune of an English drinking song, it eventually became America's national anthem. The inability of the British to conquer Fort McHenry led them to abandon the attack on Baltimore.

The Burning of the Capitol This 1817 etching of the burnt Capitol shows shackled slaves (bottom right) and angels overhead. It appeared in a book arguing that the destruction of "the temple of freedom" was a sign that God disapproved of slavery.

The war in the Chesapeake, despite the destruction of Washington, D.C., was ultimately a British failure, since the invading army was forced to withdraw to its ships and leave the region. Still, the British raids into Maryland and Virginia were terribly unsettling to Americans, especially slaveholders, because the presence of British troops encouraged thousands of slaves to run away and join the invaders. As had happened during the Revolutionary War, the British promised freedom to slaves who aided or fought with them, and almost 3,000 ran away to join British units before eventually being taken to Canada. One of them, Jeremiah West, wrote his former owner in Virginia in 1818: "Thank God I can enjoy all comforts under the flag of England and here I shall remain." Another liberated slave from Virginia declared that "we have as much right to fight for our liberty as any men."

The Aftermath of the War

CORE **OBJECTIVE**
4. Analyze the most significant outcomes of the War of 1812 on the United States.

While the fighting raged in the United States, American diplomats had begun meetings in Ghent, near Brussels in present-day Belgium, to discuss ending the war. The negotiations were at a standstill when news arrived of the American victory at the Battle of Lake Champlain and the failure of the British invasion of Baltimore. The British grew more flexible, but negotiations dragged on throughout the fall. Finally, on Christmas Eve, 1814, the diplomats reached an agreement to stop the fighting.

The Treaty of Ghent (1814)

The Treaty of Ghent

The war-weary British decided to end the war in part because of military setbacks but also because London merchants were eager to renew the profitable trade with America. The British government had also concluded that the war was not worth the cost (the prime minister said he had come to recognize the "inconvenience of the continuation of the war"). By the **Treaty of Ghent**, signed on December 24, 1814, the two sides agreed to end the war, return the prisoners, and restore the previous boundaries. The British also pledged to stop spurring Indian attacks along the Great Lakes. What had begun as an American effort to protect its honor, end impressment, and invade and conquer Canada had turned into a second war of independence against the world's greatest empire. Although the Americans lost the war for Canada and saw their national capital captured and burned, they won the southern war to defeat the Indians and take their lands. More important, the treaty saved the fragile and splintered republic from possible civil war and financial ruin.

The Battle of New Orleans

Because it took six weeks for news of the Treaty of Ghent to reach the United States, fighting continued in America. Along the Gulf coast during December 1814, forty-seven-year-old General Andrew Jackson had, without authorization, invaded the Panhandle region of Spanish Florida and taken Pensacola, putting an end to British efforts to organize Indian attacks on American settlements. In mid-December he was back in Louisiana, where he supervised efforts to defend New Orleans. A British fleet, with some 8,000 seasoned soldiers fresh from victory over Napoléon Bonaparte in Europe, took up positions just south of New Orleans, the second busiest port in the United States (after New York City). The British hoped to capture New Orleans and thereby control the entire Mississippi Valley. New England Federalists, fed up with "Mr. Madison's War," predicted that New Orleans would be lost; some called for Madison's impeachment.

British general Sir Edward Pakenham's painfully careful approach—he waited weeks until he had cannons in place to support his soldiers—gave Jackson time to organize hundreds of slaves "loaned" by planters to erect American defenses around New Orleans. The Americans built up an almost invulnerable position, but Pakenham rashly ordered a frontal assault at dawn on January 8, 1815. His brave but blundering redcoats, including all-black units from the Caribbean islands, ran into a murderous hail of artillery shells and rifle fire. Before the British withdrew, nearly 2,000 had been wounded or killed, including Pakenham and two other generals. American casualties were minimal. A British naval officer wrote that there "never was a more complete failure." When the British finally boarded their ships to leave America, several hundred runaway slaves joined them.

Treaty of Ghent (1814) Agreement between Great Britain and the United States that ended the War of 1812.

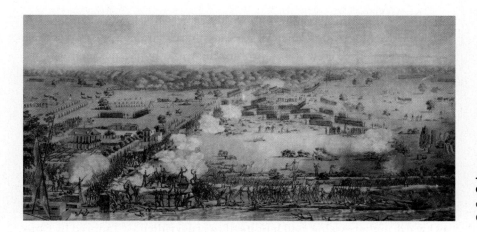

Jackson's army defends New Orleans Andrew Jackson's defeat of the British at New Orleans, January 1815.

Battle of New Orleans (1815)

Although the **Battle of New Orleans** occurred after the Treaty of Ghent had already been signed in Europe, it was still a vitally important psychological victory, as the treaty had yet to be officially ratified by either the United States or Great Britain. Had the British won at New Orleans, they might have tried to revise the treaty in their favor. Jackson's lopsided victory ensured that both governments would act quickly to officially approve the treaty. The unexpected American triumph at New Orleans also generated a wave of patriotic nationalism that would later help transform Jackson into a dynamic president eager to move the nation into an era in which the "common man" would be celebrated. The rough-hewn Jackson, wrote a southerner in April 1815, "is everywhere hailed as the savior of the country. . . . He has been feasted, caressed, & I may say idolised."

The Hartford Convention

Weeks before the Battle of New Orleans, many New Englanders, fed up with the war and the loss of revenue caused by the stoppage of trade, tried to take matters into their own hands at a meeting in Hartford, Connecticut. The **Hartford Convention** was the climax of New England's disgust with "Mr. Madison's War." The region, dominated by Federalists, had managed to remain detached from the war politically while still profiting from smuggling. Both Massachusetts and Connecticut had refused to contribute soldiers to the war effort, and merchants had continued to sell supplies to British troops in Canada. In 1814, however, the British navy extended its blockade to New England, occupied Maine, and raided several coastal towns. Even Boston seemed threatened. Instead of rallying to the American flag, however, Federalists in the Massachusetts legislature voted in October 1814 to hold a convention of New England states to protest the war.

On December 15, 1814, the Hartford Convention assembled with delegates from Massachusetts, Rhode Island, Connecticut, Vermont, and New Hampshire. The convention proposed seven constitutional amendments designed to limit Republican (and southern) influence: abolishing the

Battle of New Orleans (1815)
Final major battle in the War of 1812, in which the Americans under General Andrew Jackson unexpectedly and decisively countered the British attempt to seize the port of New Orleans, Louisiana.

Hartford Convention (1815)
A series of secret meetings in December 1814 and January 1815 at which New England Federalists protested American involvement in the War of 1812 and discussed several constitutional amendments, including limiting each president to one term, designed to weaken the dominant Republican party.

counting of slaves in determining a state's representation in Congress, requiring a two-thirds supermajority rather than a simple majority vote to declare war or admit new states, prohibiting trade embargoes lasting more than sixty days, excluding foreign-born people from holding federal office, limiting the president to one term, and barring successive presidents from the same state (a provision clearly directed at Virginia).

Their call for a later convention in Boston carried the unmistakable threat of secession—the possibility of New England leaving the United States—if these demands were dismissed. Yet the threat quickly evaporated. In February 1815, when messengers from Hartford reached Washington, D.C., they found the battered capital celebrating the good news from New Orleans. "Their position," according to a French diplomat, was "awkward, embarrassing, and lent itself to cruel ridicule." Ignored by Congress and the president, the Hartford delegates swiftly withdrew their recommendations. The incident proved fatal to the Federalist party, which never recovered from the shame of disloyalty stamped on it by the Hartford Convention. News of the victory at New Orleans and the arrival of the peace treaty from Europe transformed the national mood. Almost overnight, President Madison had gone from being denounced to being hailed a national hero.

The War's Legacies

There was no clear victor in the War of 1812, nor much clarification about the issues that ignited the war. The Treaty of Ghent ended the fighting but failed to address the reasons why President Madison had declared war in the first place: the disputes about maritime rights and the British practice of impressment.

"Second war of independence"

But that did not mean that the war was without consequences. For all the clumsiness with which it was fought, the war generated an intense patriotism across much of the nation and reaffirmed American independence. The young republic was at last secure from British or European threats. "By the war," said Secretary of State James Monroe, "we have acquired a character and a rank among the other nations, which we did not enjoy before." The nation grew more confident and more powerful by surviving a "second war of independence" against the greatest power on earth. America emerged from the fighting with new symbols of nationhood and a new gallery of heroes. The people, observed Treasury secretary Albert Gallatin, "are more American; they feel and act more as a nation; and I hope that the permanency of the Union is thereby better secured."

Economic independence

The war also propelled the United States toward economic independence, as the wartime interruption of trade with Europe encouraged the growth of American manufactures. The British blockade of the American coast during the war created a shortage of cotton cloth in the United States, leading to the creation of the nation's first cotton-manufacturing industry, in Waltham, Massachusetts. By the end of the war, there were over a hundred cotton mills in New England and sixty-four more in Pennsylvania. "Our people have 'cotton mill fever,' as it is called," said Moses Brown of Rhode Island. "Every place [is] almost occupied with cotton mills." Even Thomas Jefferson admitted in 1815 that his beloved agricultural republic had been transformed: "We must now place the manufacturer by the agriculturalist." After nearly forty years of independence, the new American republic was emerging as an agricultural, commercial, and industrial world power. "Never did a country occupy more lofty ground," said U.S. Supreme Court Justice Joseph Story in 1815. "We have stood the contest, single-handed, against the conqueror of Europe; and we are at peace, with all our blushing victories thick crowding on us."

Emergence as a world power

One of the strangest results of the War of 1812 and its aftermath was a reversal of attitudes toward government policy by the Republicans and the Federalists. The wartime experience taught James Madison and the Republicans some lessons in nationalism. First, the British invasion of Washington, D.C., impressed upon Madison the necessity of a strong army and navy. Second, the lack of a national bank had greatly complicated the financing of the war; state banks were so unstable and in such turmoil that it was difficult for states and the federal government to raise the funds needed to support the war effort. In 1816, Madison, who had been formerly opposed to a national bank, changed his mind and created the Second Bank of the United States. Third, the rise of new industries during the war prompted business owners to call for increased tariffs on imports to protect the new American companies from unfair foreign competition. Madison went along, despite his criticism of tariffs in the 1790s.

While Madison reversed himself by embracing nationalism and a broader interpretation of the Constitution, the Federalists similarly reversed themselves and took up Madison's and Jefferson's original emphasis on states' rights and strict construction of the Constitution as they tried to defend the special interests of their regional stronghold, New England. It was the first great reversal of partisan political roles in constitutional interpretation. It would not be the last.

Reversal of political roles for Republicans and Federalists

While no borders changed because of the War of 1812, the end of the fighting proved devastating to all of the eastern Indian nations, most of which had fought with the British. By agreeing to the Treaty of Ghent, the British essentially abandoned their Indian allies. None of their former lands were returned to them, and the British vacated their frontier forts that had long served as supply centers for the Indians. The Lakota chief Little Crow expressed the betrayal felt by all of the British-allied Native Americans when he rejected the consolation gifts from the British commander: "After we have fought for you, endured many hardships, lost some of our people, and awakened the vengeance of our powerful neighbors, you make peace for yourselves. . . . You no longer need our service; you offer us these goods to pay us for [your] having deserted us. But no, we will not take them; we hold them and yourselves in equal contempt." In the years after the war, the United

Managing Foreign Policy in the Early Republic

In his farewell address as president, George Washington warned Americans to avoid entanglements with Europe. During the administrations of Jefferson and Madison, however, avoiding such entanglements became increasingly difficult. Below are four events in which America became involved beyond its borders.

Event	Causes	Reactions	Outcomes
War with the Barbary pirates (1801–1804)	Barbary pirates demand increased payments in exchange for ceasing attacks on U.S. ships in Mediterranean Sea.	Jefferson sends U.S. Navy to blockade Tripoli, on the north African coast.	After demanding $300,000, the pasha of Tripoli settles for $60,000 as "tribute" to free captured Americans.
Louisiana Purchase (1803)	After the devastation of the French army in Haiti, Napoléon seeks funds to finance France's war against Great Britain. Americans desire free navigation of the Mississippi River and access to New Orleans.	Napoléon sells the French Louisiana Territory to the United States for about $15 million.	Louisiana Purchase nearly doubles U.S. territory. The Lewis and Clark expedition (1804) maps the West and establishes U.S. claims on Oregon Country.
Embargo Act (1807)	As part of their war against each other, British and French navies interfere with U.S. shipping. British navy increases impressment of American sailors. United States wishes to avoid foreign entanglements and trade freely with all European nations.	Congress and Jefferson pass the Embargo Act (1807), forbidding American ships from traveling to foreign ports.	U.S. exports plummet, devastating the U.S. economy. Jefferson declines to seek a third term as president. President Madison reopens U.S. trade with all nations, except Britain and France.

States negotiated over 200 treaties with native peoples that transferred Indian lands to America and created reservations west of the Mississippi River where the Indians were relocated.

> Westward expansion

As the Indians were pushed out, tens of thousands of Americans moved west into the Great Lakes region and southwest into Georgia, Alabama, and Mississippi after the war, occupying more territory in a single generation than had been settled in the 150 years of colonial history. With nearly an

(CONTINUED)

Event	Causes	Reactions	Outcomes
War of 1812 (1812–1815)	British navy continues to interfere with U.S. shipping in Great Britain's war with France. Americans are land-hungry for British Canada and seek end to British influence over Native Americans.	United States declares war on Great Britain. United States fails to capture Canada. British troops burn Washington, D.C. United States forces defeat British forces and their Native American allies in the Battles of Lake Champlain (1814) and New Orleans (1815), and the West.	United States and Great Britain end the war with the Treaty of Ghent. United States experiences surge in patriotism and economic independence. The Hartford Convention weakens the Federalist Party. The Republican Party seeks to increase federal government's economic and military power.

QUESTIONS FOR ANALYSIS

1. What interests shaped American foreign affairs?

2. What were the common causes of U.S. foreign involvement?

3. How did foreign events affect U.S. domestic affairs and politics?

entire continent to explore and exploit, Americans streamed westward. Between 1800 and 1820, the trans-Appalachian population rose from 300,000 to 2 million. By 1840, more than 40 percent of Americans lived west of the Appalachians in eight new states. At the same time, the growing significance of slavery and its controversial extension into new western territories set in motion an explosive national debate that would test again the grand American experiment in republican government.

Reviewing the
CORE OBJECTIVES | INQUIZITIVE

- **Jefferson's Administration** The Jeffersonian Republicans did not dismantle much of Hamilton's Federalist economic program, but they did repeal the whiskey tax, cut back on government expenditures, and promoted what was called *republican simplicity* whereby they championed the virtues of smaller government and plain living. While Republicans idealized the agricultural world that had existed prior to 1800, the first decades of the 1800s were a period of explosive economic and population growth in the United States, transforming the nation. Large-scale commercial agriculture and exports to Europe flourished; Americans moved west in huge numbers. The *Louisiana Purchase,* which resulted from negotiations with French emperor Napoléon Bonaparte following French setbacks in Haiti, their colony in the Caribbean, dramatically expanded the boundaries of the United States. Jefferson's *Lewis and Clark Expedition* explored the new region and published reports that excited interest in the Far West. In *Marbury v. Madison* (1803), the Federalist chief justice of the Supreme Court, John Marshall, declared a federal act unconstitutional for the first time. With that decision, the Court assumed the right of judicial review over acts of Congress and established the constitutional supremacy of the federal government over state governments.

- **War in Europe** Thomas Jefferson sent warships to subdue the *Barbary pirates* and negotiated with the Spanish and French to ensure that the Mississippi River remained open to American commerce. Renewal of war between Britain and France in 1803 complicated matters for American commerce with Europe. Neither country wanted its enemy to purchase U.S. goods, so both declared blockades of each other's ports. In retaliation, Jefferson convinced Congress at the end of 1807 to pass the *Embargo Act,* which prohibited all foreign trade.

- **War of 1812** Renewal of the European war in 1803 created conflicts with Britain and France. Neither country wanted its enemy to purchase U.S. goods, so both declared blockades. In retaliation, Jefferson had Congress pass the Embargo Act, which prohibited all foreign trade. James Madison ultimately declared war over the issue of neutral shipping rights and the fear that the British were inciting Native Americans to attack frontier settlements.

- **Aftermath of the War of 1812** The *Treaty of Ghent* (1814) ended the war by essentially declaring it a draw. A smashing American victory in January of 1815 at the *Battle of New Orleans* occurred before news of the peace treaty had reached the continent, but the lopsided American triumph helped to ensure that the treaty would be ratified and enforced. One effect of the conflict over neutral shipping rights was to establish the economic independence of the United States, as goods previously purchased from Great Britain were now manufactured at home. During and after the war, Federalists and Republicans seemed to exchange roles: delegates from the waning Federalist party met at the *Hartford Convention* (1815) to defend states' rights and threaten secession, while Republicans now promoted nationalism and a broad interpretation of the Constitution.

KEY TERMS

CHRONOLOGY

1800	U.S. population reaches over 5,000,000
1801	Thomas Jefferson inaugurated as president in Washington, D.C.
	Barbary pirates harass U.S. shipping and capture American sailors; the pasha of Tripoli declares war on the United States
1803	Supreme Court issues *Marbury v. Madison* decision
	Louisiana Purchase
1804–1806	Lewis and Clark expedition
1804	Jefferson overwhelmingly reelected
1807	British interference with U.S. shipping increases
1808	International slave trade ended in the United States
1811	Defeat of Tecumseh's Indian Confederacy at the Battle of Tippecanoe
1812	Congress declares war on Britain
	U.S. invasion of Canada
1813–1814	Creek War
1814	British capture and burn Washington, D.C.
	Hartford Convention
1815	Battle of New Orleans
	News of the Treaty of Ghent reaches the United States

INQUIZITIVE

Go to InQuizitive to see what you've learned—and learn what you've missed—with personalized feedback along the way.

DEBATING Thomas Jefferson and Slavery

One of the more difficult tasks that historians face is assessing the beliefs and actions of historical figures within an ethical framework. Should individuals be assessed by the standards of their time or by those of today? Should we hold celebrated historical figures to a higher ethical standard? For Part II, *Building a Nation*, the complex relationship of Thomas Jefferson to slavery demonstrates how historians can disagree when they evaluate historic individuals from an ethical perspective.

This exercise involves two tasks:

PART 1: Compare the two secondary sources on Thomas Jefferson and slavery.

PART 2: Using primary sources, evaluate the arguments of the two secondary sources.

PART I Comparing and Contrasting Secondary Sources

Below are secondary sources from two scholars who have written on the question of Jefferson and his relationship with slavery. The first is from Douglas L. Wilson, Professor Emeritus of English and Co-Director of the Lincoln Studies Center at Knox College; the second is written by Paul Finkelman, Professor of Law and Public Policy at the Albany Law School. In these selections, Wilson and Finkelman explore one of the great contradictions in early American history: that Thomas Jefferson, an outspoken critic of slavery and writer of perhaps the most famous phrase in American history, "All men are created equal," was himself a slave owner. Further complicating the matter was Jefferson's relationship with Sally Heming, a slave with whom he likely had several children. Both passages grapple with the issue of *presentism*, the application of present day ideas and beliefs onto the past.

Compare the views of these two scholars by answering the following questions. Be sure to find specific examples in the selections to support your answers.

■ How does each author address the issue of presentism?

■ What ethical standards do each of the authors use to evaluate Jefferson?

■ What type of evidence do they offer when evaluating Jefferson?

■ How does each author think Jefferson meets or fails to meet the ethical standard the author established?

■ What ethical standard would you use?

Secondary Source 1

Douglas L. Wilson, "Thomas Jefferson and the Character Issue" (1992)

How could the man who wrote that "All men are created equal" own slaves? This, in essence, is the question most persistently asked of those who write about Thomas Jefferson, and by all indications it is the thing that contemporary Americans find most vexing about him . . . The question carries a silent assumption that because he practiced slave holding, Jefferson must have somehow believed in it, and must therefore have been a hypocrite. My belief is that this way of asking the question . . . reflects the pervasive presentism of our time. Consider, for example, how different the question appears when inverted and framed in more historical terms: How did a man who was born into a slave holding society, whose family and admired friends owned slaves, who inherited a fortune that was dependent on slaves and slave labor, decide at an early age that slavery was morally wrong and forcefully declare that it ought to be abolished?

But when the question is explained in this way, another invariably follows: If Jefferson came to believe that holding slaves was wrong, why did he continue to hold them? . . . Obstacles to emancipation in Jefferson's Virginia were formidable, and the risk was demonstrably great that emancipated slaves would enjoy little, if any, real freedom and would, unless they could pass as white, be more likely to come to grief in a hostile environment. In short, the master whose concern extended beyond his own morality to the well-being of his slaves was caught on the horns of a dilemma. Thus the question of why Jefferson didn't free his slaves only serves to illustrate how presentism involves us in mistaken assumptions about historical conditions — in this case that an eighteenth-century slave holder wanting to get out from under the moral stigma of slavery and improve the lot of his slaves had only to set them free.

Although we may find Jefferson guilty of failing to make adequate allowance for the conditions in which blacks were forced to live, Jefferson did not take the next step of concluding that blacks were fit only for slavery. This rationalization of slavery was indeed the common coin of slave holders and other whites who condoned or tolerated the "peculiar" institution, but it formed no part of Jefferson's thinking. In fact, he took the opposite position: that having imposed the depredations of slavery on blacks, white Americans should not only emancipate them but also educate and train them to be self-sufficient, provide them with necessary materials, and establish a colony in which they could live as free and independent people.

Source: Wilson, Douglas L. "Thomas Jefferson and the Character Issue." *The Atlantic Monthly* 270, no. 5 (November 1992), pp. 57–74.

Secondary Source 2

Paul Finkelman, "Jefferson and Slavery" (1993)

An understanding of Jefferson's relationship to slavery requires analysis of his statements on and beliefs about the institution and an account of his actions as a public leader and a private individual. Scrutinizing the contradictions between Jefferson's professions and his actions does not impose twentieth-century values on an eighteenth-century man. Because he was the author of the Declaration of Independence and a leader of the American Enlightenment, the test of Jefferson's position on slavery is not whether he was better than the worst of his generation, but whether he was the leader of the best; not whether he responded as a southerner and a planter, but whether he was able to transcend his economic interests and his sectional background to implement the ideals he articulated. Jefferson fails the test. When Jefferson wrote the Declaration, he owned over 175 slaves. While many of his contemporaries freed their slaves during and after the Revolution, Jefferson did not.

In the fifty years from 1776 until his death in 1826, a period of extraordinary public service, he did little to end slavery or to dissociate himself from his role as the master of Monticello. To the contrary, as he accumulated more slaves he worked assiduously to increase the productivity and the property values of his labor force. Nor did he encourage his countrymen to liberate their slaves, even when they sought his blessing. Even at his death Jefferson failed to fulfill the promise of his rhetoric. In his will he emancipated only five bondsmen, condemning nearly two hundred others to the auction block . . .

. . . He knew slavery was wrong. It could not have been otherwise for an eighteenth-century natural law theorist. Many of his closest European and American friends and colleagues were leaders of the new abolition societies. Jefferson was part of a cosmopolitan "republic of letters" that was overwhelmingly hostile to slavery. But, for the most part, he suppressed his doubts, while doing virtually nothing to challenge the institution. On this issue Jefferson's genius failed him. As David Brion Davis observes, "Jefferson had only a theoretical interest in promoting the cause of abolition."

Jefferson could not live without slaves. They built his house, cooked his meals, and tilled his fields. In contrast to George Washington, Jefferson failed to carefully manage his lands and finances and lived beyond his means. Washington refused to traffic in slaves. Chronically in debt, Jefferson overcame his professed "scruples about selling negroes but for delinquency or on their own request," selling scores of slaves in order to make ends meet. Jefferson could not maintain his extravagant life style without his slaves and, to judge from his lifelong behavior, his grand style was far more important than the natural rights of his slaves. . . . Throughout his life, as he condemned slavery, Jefferson almost always implied that, however bad it was for slaves, the institution was somehow worse for whites. His concerns about the institution had more to do with its effect on whites and white society than on its true victims. . . . Jefferson's concerns were solely with the "morals and manners" of the master class. He was concerned that slavery leads to despotism by the masters; but he never expressed regret for the mistreatment of the slave. Similarly, throughout his life Jefferson expressed his fears of miscegenation and a weakening of white society through contact with blacks. He favored some form of colonization that would put blacks "beyond the reach of mixture."

Source: Finkelman, Paul. "Jefferson and Slavery: 'Treason Against the Hopes of the World.'" In *Jeffersonian Legacies,* ed. Peter S. Onuf. Charlottesville, Va.: The University Press of Virginia, 1993, pp. 181–221.

Using Primary Sources to Evaluate Secondary Sources

When historians are faced with competing interpretations of the past, they often look at primary source material as part of the process of evaluating the different arguments. Below are a selection of primary source materials relating to Thomas Jefferson's relationship with slavery. The first document is an excerpt from a draft of the Declaration of Independence largely written by Thomas Jefferson. This excerpt was removed from the final version of the declaration. The second document is a selection from Jefferson's 1785 book on the state of Virginia, relating to slaves and slavery. The third document is a letter Jefferson wrote while serving in Paris as the U.S. minister (ambassador) to France in 1788, while the fourth is a letter from April 1820 expressing his feelings regarding the Missouri compromise which admitted Missouri as a slave state and created a northern boundary for slavery in the western territories.

Carefully read each of the following primary sources and answer the following questions. Decide which of the primary source documents support or refute Wilson's and Finkelman's arguments about Jefferson. You may find that some documents do both, but for different parts of each historian's interpretation. Be sure to identify which specific components of each historian's argument the documents support or refute.

■ Which of the two historians' *arguments* is best supported by the *primary source* documents? Or, if you find that both arguments are well supported by the evidence, why do you think the two historians had such different interpretations about Jefferson?

■ Based on the ethical standard you choose in part I and these documents, how would *you* assess Jefferson's relationship with slavery? You may consider how Jefferson's views change over time.

■ What has using primary sources to evaluate the Wilson and Finkelman arguments taught you about making ethical assessments of historical figures?

Primary Source 1

Thomas Jefferson, a draft section omitted from the Declaration of Independence (1776)

He [King George III] has waged cruel war against human nature itself, violating its most sacred rights of life & liberty in the persons of a distant people [Africans] who never offended him, captivating & carrying them into slavery in another hemisphere, or to incur miserable death in their transportation thither. This piratical warfare, the opprobrium of infidel powers, is the warfare of the Christian king of Great Britain. Determined to keep open a market where men should be bought & sold, he has prostituted his negative for suppressing every legislative attempt to prohibit or to restrain this execrable (disgusting) commerce: and that this assemblage of horrors might want no fact of distinguished die, he is now exciting those very people to rise in arms among us, and to purchase that liberty of which he has deprived them, & murdering the people upon whom he also obtruded them; thus paying off former crimes committed against the liberties of one people, with crimes which he urges them to commit against the lives of another.

Source: Jefferson, Thomas. "Thomas Jefferson, June 1776, Rough Draft of the Declaration of Independence," 1776. *The Thomas Jefferson Papers Series 1. General Correspondence. 1651–1827.* American Memory, Library of Congress, Washington, D. C.

Primary Source 2

Thomas Jefferson, *Notes on the State of Virginia* (1787)

It will probably be asked, Why not retain and incorporate the Blacks into the State [after emancipation], and thus save the expense of supplying, by importation of white settlers, the vacancies they will leave? Deep-rooted prejudices entertained by the Whites; ten thousand recollections by the Blacks, of the injuries they have sustained; new provocations; the real distinctions which nature has made; and many other circumstances, will divide us into parties, and produce convulsions, which will probably never end but in the extermination of the one or the other race. To these objections, which are political, may be added others, which are physical and moral. . . . Comparing them by their faculties of memory, reason, and imagination, it appears to me, that in memory they are equal to the Whites; in reason much inferior, . . . and that in imagination they are dull, tasteless and anomalous . . . .

To our reproach it must be said, that though for a century and a half we have had under our eyes the races of Black and of Red men, they have never yet been viewed by us as subjects of natural history. I advance it therefore as a suspicion only, that the Blacks, whether originally a distinct race, or made distinct by time and circumstances, are inferior to the Whites in the endowments both of body and mind. It is not against experience to suppose, that different species of the same genus, or varieties of the same species, may possess different qualifications. Will not a lover of natural history then, one who views the gradations in all the races of animals with the eye of philosophy, excuse an effort to keep those in the department of man as distinct as nature has formed them? This unfortunate difference of colour, and perhaps of faculty, is a powerful obstacle to the emancipation of these people. Many of their advocates, while they wish to vindicate the liberty of human nature, are anxious also to preserve its dignity and beauty. Some of these, embarrassed by the question 'What further is to be done with them?' join themselves in opposition with those who are actuated by sordid avarice (greed) only. Among the Romans emancipation required but one effort. The slave, when made free, might mix with, without staining the blood of his master. But with us a second is necessary, unknown to history. When freed, he is to be removed beyond the reach of mixture . . . . There must, doubtless, be an unhappy influence on the manners of our people, produced by the existence of slavery among us. The whole commerce between master and slave is a perpetual exercise of the most boisterous passions, the most unremitting despotism on the one part, and degrading . . . . For if a slave can have a country in this world, it must be any other in preference to that in which he is born to live and labor for another.

Source: Jefferson, Thomas. "Laws, Query XIV." In *Notes on the State of Virginia*. London: Printed for John Stockdale, Opposite Burlington-House, Piccadilly, 1787, pp. 229–271.

Primary Source 3

Thomas Jefferson, Letter to M. Warville (February 11, 1788)

Sir,

I am very sensible of the honor you propose to me, of becoming a member of the society for the abolition of the slave-trade. You know that nobody wishes more ardently, to see an abolition, not only of the trade, but of the condition of slavery: and certainly nobody will be more willing to encounter every sacrifice for that object. But the influence and information of the friends to this proposition in France will be far above the need of my association. I am here as a public servant, and those whom I serve, having never yet been able to give their voice against the practice, it is decent for me to avoid too public a demonstration of my wishes to see it abolished. Without serving the cause here, it might render me less able to serve it beyond the water. I trust you will be sensible of the prudence of those motives, therefore, which govern my conduct on this occasion, and be assured of my wishes for the success of your undertaking, and the sentiments of esteem and respect, with which I have the honor to be, Sir, your most obedient, humble servant,

Th: Jefferson.

Source: Jefferson, Thomas. "Jean Plumard Brissot de Warville to Thomas Jefferson, February 11, 1788," 1788. *The Thomas Jefferson Papers Series 1. General Correspondence. 1651–1827.* American Memory, Library of Congress, Washington, D. C.

Primary Source 4

Thomas Jefferson, Letter to John Holmes (April 22, 1820)

I thank you, dear Sir, for the copy you have been so kind as to send me of the letter to your constituents on the Missouri question [the admission of Missouri as slave state] . . . The cession of that kind of property[slaves] (for so it is misnamed) . . . would not cost me a second thought, if, in that way, a general emancipation and expatriation could be effected: and, gradually, and with due sacrifices, I think it might be. But as it is, we have the wolf by the ears, and we can neither hold him, nor safely let him go. Justice is in one scale, and self-preservation in the other. Of one thing I am certain, that as the passage of slaves from one State to another, would not make a slave of a single human being who would not be so without it, so their diffusion over a greater surface would make them individually happier, and proportionally facilitate the accomplishment of their emancipation . . . .

Th: Jefferson.

Source: Jefferson, Thomas. "Thomas Jefferson to John Holmes, April 22, 1820," 1820. *The Thomas Jefferson Papers Series 1. General Correspondence. 1651–1827.* American Memory, Library of Congress, Washington, D. C.

A CARD.

BLOUNT & DAWSON,
NERAL BROKERS

the Purchase and Sale of NEGROES and OTHER
PROPERTY.

AVANNAH,   GEORGIA.

en the Office and New Jail completed by Wm Wright. Esq.. we are
rd secure and good accommodations for all negroes left with us for Sale
eping. would respectfully solicit a share of public patronage.

Two Doors East of J, Bryan & Co., opposite
the State Bank.

LOUNT.   W. C. DAWSON.

leased the above gentlemen my office and jail. would take pleasure in
ding them to my patrons and the public generally.

WM. WRIGHT.

An Expanding Nation

During the nineteenth century, the United States experienced a wrenching change from being a predominantly agrarian society to having a more diverse economy, with factories and cities emerging alongside farms and towns. The pace of life quickened, and American ambitions mushroomed. Between 1790 and 1820, the nation grew rapidly; its boundaries expanded and its population—both white and black—soared while the number of Native Americans continued its long decline. By the early 1820s, the total number of enslaved Americans was more than two and a half times greater than in 1790, and the number of free blacks doubled. The white population of the United States grew just as rapidly.

Accompanying the industrialization of the economy was the relentless expansion of the United States westward. Until the nineteenth century, most of the population was clustered near the seacoast and along rivers flowing into the Atlantic Ocean. The great theme of early-nineteenth-century American history was the migration of millions of people westward across the Allegheny and Appalachian Mountains into the Middle West. Waves of adventurous Americans then crossed the Mississippi River and spread out across the Great Plains. By the 1840s, Americans had reached the Pacific Ocean, transported there by horses, wagons, canals, flatboats, steamboats, and eventually railroads and steamships.

While the feverish expansion into the West brought more conflict with Native Americans, Mexicans, the British, and the Spanish, most Americans believed it was their God-given destiny to spread across the continent—at whatever cost and at whomever's expense. These developments—the emergence of a market economy and the growth of the nation—made the second quarter of the nineteenth century a time of restless optimism. Americans were nothing if not brash and self-assured. In 1845, an editorial in the *United States Journal* claimed that "we, the American people, are the most independent, intelligent, moral, and happy people on the face of the earth." The republic governed by highly educated "natural aristocrats" such as Thomas Jefferson, James Madison, James Monroe, and John Quincy Adams gave way to the frontier democracy promoted by Andrew Jackson. Americans began to demand government of, by, and for the people.

During the first half of the nineteenth century, two very different societies—North and South—developed in the United States. The North was the more dynamic and faster-growing region. It embraced the Industrial Revolution, large cities, foreign immigrants, and the ideal of "free labor." By contrast, the South remained rural, agricultural, and increasingly committed to enslaved labor as the backbone of its economy. Two great underlying fears worried southerners: the daily threat of slave uprisings and the growing possibility that a northern-controlled Congress might abolish slavery. The planter elite's aggressive efforts to preserve and expand slavery stifled reform impulses in the South and ignited a prolonged political controversy with the North that would eventually lead to civil war.

The so-called Jacksonian Era during the first half of the nineteenth century celebrated individual freedom and self-expression. Religious life, for example, experienced another wave of energetic revival centered on the

power of individuals to embrace Christ and attain salvation on their own. Such an emphasis on individualism and freedom of expression shaped cultural life in general.

The Romantic movement, originating in Europe and then spreading to America, applied democratic ideals to philosophy, religion, literature, and the fine arts. In New England, Ralph Waldo Emerson and Henry David Thoreau joined other "transcendentalists" in promoting a radical individualism. At the same time, activists of all types fanned out to reform and even "perfect" American society by creating public schools accessible to all children, working to abolish slavery, combating the consumption of alcohol, and striving to improve living conditions for the disabled, the insane, the poor, and the imprisoned.

LACKAWANNA VALLEY (1855) Often hailed the father of American landscape painting, George Inness was commissioned by a railroad company to capture its trains coursing through the lush Lackawanna River Valley in northeastern Pennsylvania. New inventions and great technological growth would continue to change the American landscape.

The Emergence of a Market Economy

1815–1850

A mid the postwar celebrations in 1815, Americans set about transforming their victorious young nation. Within a year or so after war's end, prosperity returned as British and European markets again welcomed American ships and commerce. During the war, the cutting off of trade with Britain and Europe had forced the United States to develop more factories and mills of its own, spurring the development of the more diverse economy that Alexander Hamilton had championed in the 1790s. Between 1815 and 1850, the United States became a transcontinental power, expanding all the way to the Pacific coast. Hundreds of thousands of land-hungry people streamed westward toward the Mississippi River and beyond. In just six years following the end of the war in 1815, six new states were added to the Union (Alabama, Illinois, Indiana, Mississippi, Missouri, and Maine).

The lure of cheap land and plentiful jobs, as well as the promise of political and religious freedom, attracted millions of European immigrants in the first half of the nineteenth century. They were not always welcomed. Ethnic prejudices, religious persecution, and language barriers made it difficult for many new immigrants, mostly from Ireland and Germany, to adapt to American culture.

In the Midwest and West, large-scale commercial agriculture emerged as big farms grew corn, wheat, pigs, and cattle to be sold in distant markets. In the South, cotton became so profitable and widespread that it increasingly dominated the region's economy, luring farmers and planters (wealthy farmers with hundreds or even thousands of acres worked by large numbers of slaves) into the new states of Alabama, Mississippi, Louisiana, and Arkansas. Cotton cloth was the first great consumer product of the Industrial Age. As the cotton culture expanded into new southern territories and states, it required growing numbers of enslaved workers, many of whom were sold and relocated from Virginia and the Carolinas. Meanwhile, the Northeast experienced an industrial revolution that reshaped the region's economy as mills and factories began to dot the landscape and transform the nature of work; most of the early mill workers were young farm women. In the North and Midwest, an urban middle class emerged as Americans left farms and moved to towns and cities, drawn primarily by jobs in new mills, factories, and banks.

By 1850, the United States had become one of the world's major commercial and manufacturing nations—and the fastest growing. The dynamic economy also generated changes in most other areas, from politics to the legal system, from the family to social values. These social and economic developments in turn helped expand prosperity and freedom for whites and free blacks. These changes also prompted vigorous political debates over economic policies, transportation improvements, and the extension of slavery into the new territories. The economy was being transformed into a national marketplace enabled by dramatic improvements in communication and transportation. In the process, the nation began to divide into three powerful regional political blocs—North, South, and West—whose shifting alliances would shape political life until the Civil War.

CORE **OBJECTIVE**

1. Describe how changes in transportation and communications altered the economic landscape during the first half of the nineteenth century.

market economy Large-scale manufacturing and commercial agriculture that emerged in America during the first half of the nineteenth century, displacing much of the pre-market subsistence and barter-based economy and producing boom-and-bust cycles while raising the American standard of living.

The Market Revolution

During the first half of the nineteenth century, a market revolution transformed the young American economy. In the eighteenth century, most Americans were part of what was called a local "household economy." That is, they produced enough food, livestock, and clothing for their own family's needs and perhaps a little more to barter (exchange) with their neighbors. During the nineteenth century, however, more and more farmers began producing surplus crops and livestock to sell, for cash, in more distant regional markets reached by rivers, canals, and roads. Such large-scale commercial agriculture, often called a **market economy**, produced boom-and-bust cycles, but overall the standard of living rose and Americans experienced unprecedented opportunities for economic gain and geographic mobility. The transition from a traditional household economy to a modern market economy was neither easy nor simple; it involved massive changes in the way people lived, worked, traveled, and voted.

Transportation

Speed is the defining aspect of modern life. The most important break-throughs in creating the national market economy were dramatic improvements in transportation. Until the nineteenth century, travel in America had been slow, tedious, and expensive. It took a stagecoach four days to travel from New York City to Boston. Because of long travel times, many farm products could only be sold locally before they spoiled. That changed during the first half of the nineteenth century. An array of innovations in transportation—larger horse-drawn wagons, called *Conestogas*; new roads; canals; steamboats; and railroads—knit together the expanding national market for goods and services and greatly accelerated the pace of life. During the first quarter of the nineteenth century, stagecoaches increased their speed as the quality of roads improved. In addition, stagecoach lines began using continual relays, or "stages," of fresh horses made available every 40 miles or so. This made travel faster, less expensive, and more accessible to more people.

> A revolution in transportation

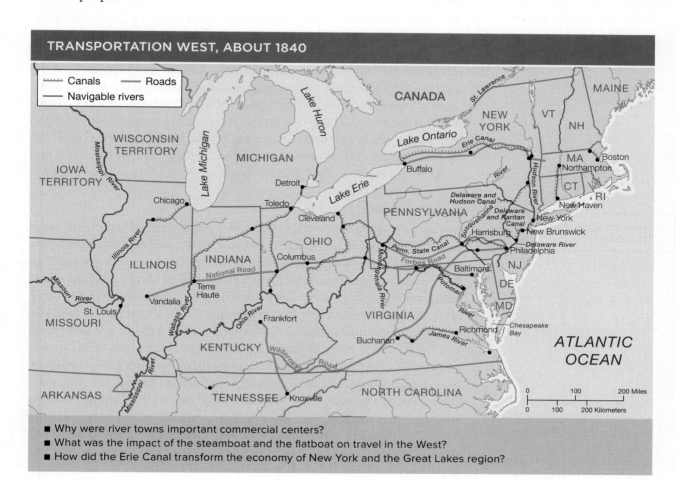

TRANSPORTATION WEST, ABOUT 1840

- Why were river towns important commercial centers?
- What was the impact of the steamboat and the flatboat on travel in the West?
- How did the Erie Canal transform the economy of New York and the Great Lakes region?

Traveling the western waters Steamboats at the levee at St. Paul, Minnesota, in 1859.

New Roads

Road transportation: Building turnpikes

As settlers moved west, people demanded better roads. In 1795 the Wilderness Road, along the trail first blazed by Daniel Boone twenty years earlier, was opened to wagon and stagecoach traffic, thereby easing the over-the-mountains route from North Carolina into Kentucky and Tennessee. To the northeast, a movement for graded and paved roads (using packed-down crushed stones) gathered momentum after the Philadelphia-Lancaster Turnpike was completed in 1794 (the term *turnpike* derives from a pole, or pike, at the tollgate, which was turned to admit the traffic in exchange for a small fee). By 1821, some 4,000 miles of turnpikes had been built, and stagecoach and freight companies emerged to move more people and cargo at lower rates.

Water Transportation

Water transportation: Steamboats

By the early 1820s, the turnpike boom was giving way to dramatic advances in water transportation. River steamboats, flatboats, and canal barges carried people and goods far more cheaply than did horse-drawn wagons. The first steamboat appeared when Robert Fulton and Robert R. Livingston sent the *Clermont* north up the Hudson River from New York City in 1807. Thereafter, the use of wood-fired **steamboats** spread rapidly to other eastern rivers and to the sprawling Ohio and Mississippi river systems, opening nearly half the continent to water traffic. By bringing two-way traffic to the Mississippi Valley (the third-largest drainage system in the world, surpassed only by the Amazon and the Congo), steamboats created a transcontinental market and an agricultural empire that produced much of the nation's timber, wheat, corn, cattle, and hogs. By 1836, there were 750 steamboats operating on American rivers, more than twice the number in Europe. Steamboats transformed St. Louis, Missouri, from a sleepy frontier village into a booming river port. New Orleans developed even faster. By 1840, it was the wealthiest and third largest American city, having developed a thriving trade with

steamboats Ships and boats powered by wood-fired steam engines that made two-way traffic possible in eastern river systems, creating a transcontinental market and an agricultural empire.

the Caribbean islands and the new Latin American republics that had overthrown Spanish rule.

Canals also sped the market revolution. The historic **Erie Canal** in New York spurred the creation of a national economy. After it opened in 1825, having taken eight years to build, the new canal drew eastward much of the midwestern trade that earlier had been forced to make the long journey down the Ohio and Mississippi Rivers to the Gulf of Mexico. The Erie Canal had enormous economic and political consequences, tying together the regional economies of the Midwest and the East while further isolating the Deep South.

The remarkable Erie Canal, forty feet wide and four feet deep, extended 364 miles across New York from Albany to Buffalo. Additional branches soon put most of the state within its reach. The canal, built by tens of thousands of manual laborers, mostly Irish immigrants, brought a "river of gold" to New York City in the form of an unending stream of goods going to and from the Midwest. The Erie Canal reduced travel time from New York City to Buffalo from twenty days to six, and the cost of moving a ton of freight plummeted from $100 to $5. Such dramatic improvements enabled New York City to rush past Boston, New Orleans, and Baltimore and become the nation's busiest port. The success of the New York canal system inspired the construction of more canals in other states. By 1837, there were 3,000 miles of canal waterways across the nation.

> Water transportation: Canal systems

Railroads

But the canal era was short-lived. During the second quarter of the nineteenth century, a more versatile and powerful form of transportation emerged: the railroad. In 1825, the year the Erie Canal was completed, the world's first steam-powered railway began operating in England. Soon thereafter, a railroad-building craze struck the United States. In 1830 the nation had only 23 miles of railroad track. Over the next twenty years, railroad coverage grew to 30,626 miles.

> Railroads connect the continent

The railroad surpassed other forms of transportation because of its speed, carrying capacity, and reliability. **Railroads** could carry more people and freight faster, farther, and cheaper. The early trains averaged ten miles per hour, more than twice the speed of stagecoaches and four times that of boats and barges. The ability of railroads to operate year-round also gave them a huge advantage over canals that froze over in winter and dirt roads that became rivers of mud during rainstorms.

In addition, railroads provided indirect benefits by encouraging new western settlement and the expansion of commercial agriculture. Building railroads stimulated the national economy not only by improving transportation but by creating a huge demand for iron, wooden crossties, bridges, locomotives, freight cars, and equipment of various kinds needed to operate railroads. Perhaps most important, railroads enabled towns and cities not served by canals or turnpikes to compete economically. In other words, the

Erie Canal (1817) Most important and profitable of the many barge canals built in the early nineteenth century, connecting the Great Lakes to the Hudson River, and conveying so much cargo that it made New York City the nation's largest port.

railroads Steam-powered vehicles that improved passenger transportation, quickened western settlement, and enabled commercial agriculture in the nineteenth century.

THE GROWTH OF RAILROADS, 1850 AND 1860

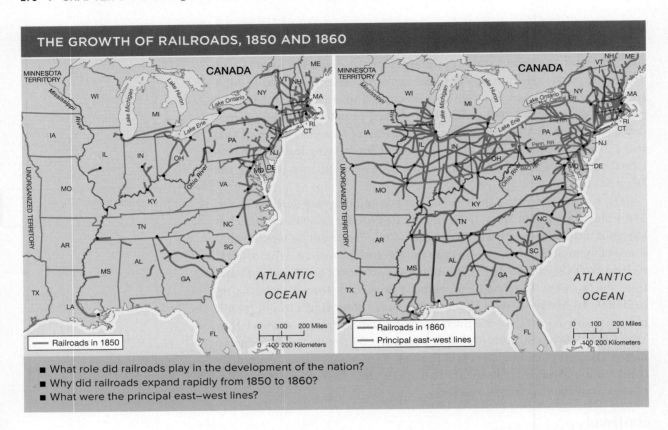

- What role did railroads play in the development of the nation?
- Why did railroads expand rapidly from 1850 to 1860?
- What were the principal east–west lines?

railroads eventually changed what in the eighteenth century had been a cluster of mostly local markets into an interconnected national market-place for goods and services. Railroads thereby expanded the geography of American capitalism, making possible larger industrial and commercial enterprises.

Ocean Transportation

Ocean transportation: Clipper ships enable high-speed ocean travel

The year 1845 brought a great innovation in ocean transport with the launching of the first clipper ship, the *Rainbow*. Built for speed, the sleek **clipper ships** were the nineteenth-century equivalent of the supersonic jetliner. They were twice as fast as the older merchant ships. Long and lean, with taller masts and more sails, they cut dashing figures during their brief but colorful career, which lasted less than two decades. It was the American thirst for Chinese tea that prompted the clipper boom. Asian tea leaves had to reach the market quickly after harvest, and the fast clipper ships made this possible. Even more important, the discovery of gold in California in 1848 lured thousands of prospectors and entrepreneurs from the Atlantic seaboard. The massive wave of would-be miners generated an urgent demand for goods on the West Coast, and the clippers met it. In 1854 the *Flying Cloud* took eighty-nine days and eight hours to travel from

clipper ships Tall, slender ships favored over older merchant ships for their speed; ultimately gave way to steamships because clipper ships lacked cargo space.

Building a clipper ship This 1833 oil painting captures the Messrs. Smith & Co. Ship Yard in Manhattan, where shipbuilders are busy shaping timbers to construct a clipper ship.

New York to San Francisco, less than half as long as the trip would have taken in a conventional ship. But clippers, while fast, lacked ample space for cargo or passengers. After the Civil War, the clipper ship would give way to the steamship.

Communications

Innovations in transportation also helped spark amazing improvements in communications, which knit the nation closer together. At the beginning of the nineteenth century, traveling any distance was slow and difficult. It took days—often weeks—for news to travel along the Atlantic seaboard. For example, after George Washington died in 1798 in Virginia, the news of his death did not appear in New York City newspapers until a week later. By 1829, it was possible to deliver President Andrew Jackson's inaugural address from Washington, D.C., to New York City by relay horse riders in less than twenty hours. Mail deliveries also improved. The number of U.S. post offices soared from 75 in 1790 to 28,498 in 1860. In addition, the mass production of newspapers enabled by new steam-powered printing presses reduced their cost from six cents to a penny each, enabling virtually everyone to benefit from the news contained in the "penny press."

But the century's most important advance in communications occurred with the development of a national electromagnetic **telegraph system**,

telegraph system System of electronic communication invented by Samuel F. B. Morse that could transmit messages instantaneously across great distances.

invented by Samuel F. B. Morse, a portrait painter turned inventor. In May 1844, Morse sent the first intercity telegraph message from Washington, D.C. to Baltimore, Maryland. It read: "What Hath God Wrought?" By the end of the decade, most major cities were connected by telegraph lines. By enabling people to communicate faster and more easily across long distances, the electrical telegraph system triggered many changes, not the least of which was helping railroad operators to schedule trains more precisely and thus avoid collisions. A New Orleans newspaper claimed that with the invention of the telegraph "scarcely anything now will appear to be impossible."

The Role of Government

Taken together, the communications and transportation improvements of the first half of the nineteenth century reshaped the contours of economic, social, and political life. Steamboats, canals, and railroads helped connect the western areas of the country with the East, boost trade, open up the Far West for settlement, and spark dramatic growth in cities such as Buffalo, Cleveland, and Chicago. Between 1800 and 1860, an undeveloped nation of scattered farms, primitive roads, and modest local markets was transformed into an engine of capitalist expansion, urban energy, and global reach.

Government financing for internal improvements

The dramatic transportation improvements were financed by both state governments and private investors. Unlike in Europe, virtually all of the railroads in the United States were built by private companies and investors rather than by the national government. But the federal government helped, too, despite intense political debates over whether it was constitutional to use federal funds or assets like government-owned land to finance such "internal improvements." The national government bought stock in turnpike and canal companies and, after the success of the Erie Canal, awarded land grants to several western states in order to support canal and railroad projects. By 1860, Congress had given railroad companies more than 20 million acres of federal lands. The national government also sent federal cavalry troops to "pacify" the Indians along the route of the railroads.

The Industrial Revolution

CORE OBJECTIVE
2. Explain the impact of the Industrial Revolution on the way people worked and lived.

The concentration of population in cities, coupled with the transportation and communication revolutions, greatly increased the number of potential customers for a given product. This in turn gave rise to *mass production*, whereby companies used new technologies (machine tools) to produce much greater quantities of products which could be sold at lower prices while generating higher profits. The application of water-powered mills and coal-powered steam engines, as well as the application of new technologies to make manufacturing more efficient, sparked an industrial revolution in Europe and America from the mid-eighteenth century to the late nineteenth century. The **Industrial Revolution**, centered on the invention of the steam engine, was the most important development in human history since the advent of agriculture. Prior to 1800, most products were made by hand by skilled artisans. That changed quickly with the development, first, of textile machinery, soon followed by a dazzling array of machinery invented to manufacture almost everything. Factories, mills, and industrial plants emerged during the first half of the nineteenth century to replace many artisans and craftsmen making clothing, shoes, clocks and watches, furniture, firearms, and an array of other items.

American Technology

During the nineteenth century, Americans became known around the world for their "practical" inventiveness. Between 1790 and 1811, the U.S. Patent Office approved an annual average of seventy-seven new patents certifying new inventions; by the 1850s, the Patent Office was approving more than 28,000 new inventions each year. Many of those new inventions generated dramatic changes. In 1844, for example, Charles Goodyear patented a process for "vulcanizing" rubber, which made the product stronger, more elastic, waterproof, and winter-proof. Vulcanized rubber was soon being used for a variety of products, from shoes and boots to seals, gaskets, and hoses and, eventually, tires. In 1846 Elias Howe patented his design of the sewing machine, soon improved upon by Isaac Merritt Singer, who founded the Singer Sewing Machine Company, which first produced only industrial sewing machines for use in textile mills but eventually offered machines for home use. The availability of sewing machines helped revolutionize "women's work." Sewing machines dramatically reduced the time for making clothes at home, thus freeing up more leisure time for many women.

> American inventiveness: The sewing machine (1846)

Technological advances helped improve living conditions; houses could be larger, better heated, and better illuminated. The first sewer systems helped clean up cities by ridding their streets of human and animal waste. Mechanization of factories meant that more goods could be produced faster with less labor, and machines also enabled industries to produce "standardized parts" that could be assembled by unskilled workers. Machine-made clothes using standardized forms fit better and were cheaper than those sewn by hand; machine-made newspapers and magazines were more abundant and affordable, as were clocks, watches, guns, and plows.

Another such invention would launch an economic revolution. In 1792 Eli Whitney, a recent Yale graduate from New England, visited Mulberry Grove plantation in coastal Georgia, where he "heard much said of the difficulty of ginning cotton"—that is, separating the fibers from the seeds. The person who invented a "machine" to gin cotton, it was said, would become wealthy overnight. A few days later, Whitney devised a simple mechanism (he called it "an absurdly simple contrivance"), using nails attached to a roller, to remove the seeds from cotton bolls. Whitney's **cotton gin** (short for *engine*) proved to be fifty times more productive than a hand laborer.

Industrial Revolution Major shift in the nineteenth century from hand-made manufacturing to mass production in mills and factories using water-, coal-, and steam-powered machinery.

cotton gin Hand-operated machine invented by Eli Whitney that quickly removed seeds from cotton bolls, enabling mass production of cotton in nineteenth-century America.

Almost overnight, the cotton gin made cotton America's most profitable cash crop, and in the process transformed southern agriculture and northern industry.

Cotton

During the first half of the nineteenth century, southern-grown **cotton** became the dominant force driving the national economy and the controversial efforts to expand slavery into the western territories. Cotton became so profitable that it was called "white gold"; it brought enormous wealth to southern planters and merchants as well as New England textile mill owners and New York shipowners. Until the nineteenth century, most clothing had been made of wool, linen, or silk. Cotton was a more comfortable fabric, but until the cotton "gin" was invented, it was much more expensive to produce. By 1812, because of the widespread use of cotton gins, the cost of producing cotton yarn had plunged by 90 percent. The spread of textile mills in Britain and Europe during the late eighteenth century created a rapidly growing global market for cotton. By the mid-nineteenth century, people worldwide were wearing more-comfortable and easier-to-clean cotton clothing. When British textile manufacturers chose the less brittle American cotton over the varieties grown in the Caribbean, Brazil, and India, the demand for southern cotton skyrocketed, as did its price. During the first half of the nineteenth century, cotton became America's largest export. By 1860, British textile mills were processing a billion pounds of cotton a year, 92 percent of which came from the American South. The commercial growing of cotton for world markets spread plantation slavery across the South, spurred the development of textile mills in New England, and expanded the shipping fleets of New York City.

Cotton first engulfed the Piedmont region of the Carolinas and Georgia, between the coast and the mountains. After the War of 1812, it migrated into the contested Indian lands to the west—Tennessee, Alabama, Florida, Mississippi, Louisiana, Arkansas, and Texas. New Orleans became a bustling port—and active slave market—because of the cotton being grown throughout the region and shipped down the Mississippi River. From the mid-1830s to 1860, cotton accounted for more than half of American exports. The South harvested raw cotton, and northern buyers and shipowners carried it to New England, Great Britain, and France, where textile mills spun the fiber into thread and fabric.

The Expansion of Slavery

Cotton is a labor-intensive crop, requiring 70 percent more labor than corn. While a person could pick as much as fifty pounds of cotton in a day, that same person working all day could separate barely one pound of fiber from seeds. With the invention of the cotton gin, the demand for cotton increased and southerners solved the labor problem by using lots of slaves to plant the fields and pick the cotton. As a result, the price of slaves soared with the price of cotton. As farmland in Maryland and Virginia lost its fertility after

cotton White fibers harvested from plants that made comfortable, easy-to-clean products, especially clothing; the most valuable cash crop driving the economy in nineteenth-century United States and Great Britain.

years of relentless tobacco planting, which strips soil of its nutrients, many whites shifted to growing corn and wheat (the climate in Maryland and Virginia was too cold for cotton). Many Virginia and Maryland planters sold their surplus slaves to work in the new cotton-growing areas in Alabama and Mississippi. Between 1790 and 1860, some 835,000 slaves were "sold south." In 1790, planters in Virginia and Maryland had owned 56 percent of all the slaves in the United States; by 1860, they owned only 15 percent. A new cotton farmer in Mississippi urged a friend in Kentucky to sell his farm and join him: "If you could reconcile it to yourself to bring your negroes to the Mississippi Territory, they would certainly make you a handsome fortune in ten years by the cultivation of Cotton." Slaves became so valuable that stealing slaves became a common problem in the southern states, especially Alabama and Mississippi.

Cotton production expands slavery

Farming the West

The westward flow of planters and slaves to Alabama and Mississippi mirrored another migration through the Ohio Valley and the Great Lakes region, where Native Americans had been forcibly pushed westward. By 1860, more than half the nation's population lived west of the Appalachian Mountains. The fertile farmlands in the Midwest—Ohio, Michigan, Indiana, Illinois, and Iowa—drew farmers from the rocky hillsides of New England and the exhausted soils of Virginia. A new national land law of 1820 reduced the price of federal land. Even that was not enough for westerners, however. They demanded "preemption," the right of squatters (people who simply built a cabin and started farming without actually purchasing government land) to purchase land at the minimum price, and "graduation," the progressive reduction of the price of land that did not sell immediately.

Congress eventually responded to the land mania with two bills. Under the Preemption Act of 1830, squatters could get 160 acres at the minimum price of $1.25 per acre. Under the Graduation Act of 1854, prices of unsold lands were to be lowered in stages over thirty years.

Technology also enabled greater agricultural productivity. The development of effective iron plows (rather than wooden plows) greatly eased the backbreaking job of tilling the soil. In 1819, Jethro Wood of New York introduced an iron plow with separate parts that could be easily replaced when worn out or broken. Further improvements would follow, including Vermonter John Deere's steel plow (1837), whose sharp edges could cut through the tough prairie grass in the Midwest and the Great Plains. By 1845, Massachusetts alone had seventy-three plants making more than 60,000 plows per year. Most were sold to western farmers, illustrating the emergence of a national marketplace for goods and services made possible by the transportation revolution.

Growth of commercial agriculture: Steel plows (1837) and mechanical reapers (1831)

Other technological improvements quickened the growth of commercial agriculture, whereby huge farms produced surplus for national and world markets. By the 1840s, new mechanical seeders had replaced the process of

McCormick's Reaping Machine This illustration appeared in the catalog of the Great Exhibition, held at the Crystal Palace in London in 1851. The plow eased the transformation of rough plains into fertile farmland, and the reaping machine accelerated farm production.

sowing seed by hand. Even more important, in 1831 twenty-two-year-old Virginian Cyrus Hall McCormick (1809–1884) invented a mechanical reaper pulled by horses to harvest wheat, a development as significant to the agricultural economy of the Midwest, Old Northwest, and Great Plains as the cotton gin was to the South. McCormick tinkered with his reaping machine for almost a decade. In 1847 the **McCormick reaper** began selling so fast that he moved to Chicago and built a manufacturing plant. Within a few years he had sold thousands of the giant farm machines, transforming the scale of commercial agriculture. Using a handheld sickle, a farmer could harvest a half acre of wheat a day; with a McCormick reaper, two people could work twelve acres a day. By reducing the number of workers needed, such new agricultural machines helped send displaced laborers to work on railroads and in textile mills, iron foundries, shoe factories, coal mines, oil fields, and other new industries in towns and cities.

Early Textile Manufacturers

Rise of the factory system: Steam-powered mills

While technological breakthroughs such as the cotton gin, mechanical harvester, and railroads had quickened agricultural development and created a national economy, other technology altered the economic landscape even more profoundly by giving rise to the factory system. Mills and factories were initially powered by water wheels and then by coal-fired steam engines that dramatically increased productivity. The shift from water power to steam as a source of energy is what enabled the growth of the textile industry (and industries of all types), initiating an industrial revolution destined to end Britain's domination of the world economy.

McCormick reaper Mechanical reaper invented by Cyrus Hall McCormick in 1831 that dramatically increased the production of wheat.

In 1800, the output of America's factories amounted to only one-sixth of Great Britain's production. The growth of American textile production was slow and faltering until Thomas Jefferson's embargo in 1807 stimulated the production of cloth made in America. By 1815, hundreds of textile mills in New England, New York, and Pennsylvania were producing thread, cloth, and clothing. By 1860, the output of America's factories would be a third and by 1880 two-thirds that of the British industrial economy.

After the War of 1812, British textile companies flooded American markets with cheap cotton cloth. Such "dumping" nearly killed the infant American textile industry by lowering the prices of thread and cloth. A delegation of New England mill owners traveled to Washington, D.C., to demand a federal tariff (tax) on imported cloth to deter the British from selling their cloth in the United States for less than the prices charged by American manufacturers. The efforts of the American mill owners to gain political assistance created a culture of industrial lobbying for Congressional tariff protection that continues to this day.

What the mill owners neglected to admit was that import tariffs hurt American consumers by forcing them to pay higher prices. Over time, as the Scotsman Adam Smith explained in his book on capitalism, *The Wealth of Nations* (1776), consumers not only pay higher prices for foreign goods as a result of tariffs, but they also pay higher prices for domestic goods, since businesses invariably take advantage of opportunities to raise the prices charged for their products. Tariffs helped "protect" American industries from foreign competition, but competition is the engine of innovation and efficiency in a capitalist economy. New England shipping companies opposed higher tariffs because they would reduce the amount of goods being sent across the Atlantic from Britain and Europe. Many southerners also opposed tariffs because of fears that Britain and France would retaliate with tariffs on American cotton and tobacco shipped to their ports. In the end, the New England mill owners won the political debate. Congress passed the Tariff of 1816, which placed a tax on imported cloth. Such tariffs were a major factor in the industrialization of America during the nineteenth century. By impeding foreign competition, they enabled American manufacturers to dominate the national marketplace.

Import tariffs

The Lowell System

The factory system sprang full-blown upon the American scene at Waltham, Massachusetts, in 1813, when a group known as the Boston Associates constructed the first textile mill in which the processes of spinning yarn and weaving cloth by machinery (copied from English mills) were brought together under one roof. In 1822, the Boston Associates, led by Francis Cabot Lowell, developed another cotton mill at a village along the Merrimack River twenty-eight miles north of Boston, which they renamed Lowell. It soon became the model for mill towns throughout New England, often referred to as the **Lowell system**.

Lowell system Model New England factory communities that provided employees, mostly young women, with meals, a boardinghouse, moral discipline, and educational opportunities.

Technological Innovation and a National Marketplace

In the first half of the nineteenth century, technological innovations or improvements dramatically changed the economic landscape. They transformed the way Americans traveled, transported goods, farmed, and manufactured products. Indeed, by the 1830s what had once been a series of local markets loosely connected to each other had become a national market economy: farmers, manufacturers, financiers, publishers, and others could envision a single extensive, nationwide market through which to sell their products and increase their profits. But the rise of a national market economy did not create economic or social uniformity across the nation. Regional differences among the North, West, and South, already present, continued to grow. To examine this development, review the two charts below.

TECHNOLOGICAL INNOVATIONS AND IMPROVEMENTS

Transportation	Agriculture	Manufacturing
More extensive graded and paved roads (the Wilderness Road)	Mass production of cotton gins that mechanically separate seed from fiber	New and improved machinery to mass-produce standardized parts
More extensive canals (Erie Canal)	Mass production of steel plows that open up more land to cultivation	Use of coal-burning steam engines to power factories
Steamboats (powered by steam engines)	Mass production of mechanical reapers to harvest wheat	Vulcanization, a process that made rubber more durable
Railroads (powered by steam engines)		
Clipper ships that shorten the time of transoceanic travel and transportation		

REGIONAL ECONOMIC DEVELOPMENTS

North	West	South
Northeastern states underwent an industrial revolution. Factories, using new and improved machinery and steam engines, began mass producing textiles, shoes, iron, clocks, and guns for national consumption.	Western states' agriculture greatly expanded due to improvements in transportation. Steel plows opened up more land for production, and mechanical reapers vastly increased the productivity of individual farmers.	Southern states saw a vast expansion of the cotton plantation economy. The use of slaves to cultivate cotton, and the cotton gin to process the cotton, vastly increased the amount available for export.

QUESTIONS FOR ANALYSIS

1. How did technological innovations bring Americans together?

2. How did technological innovations create different regional patterns of economic development?

3. How did the emergence of a national market reinforce these different regional patterns?

Lowell system

The founders of the Lowell system had a much larger vision than just improved industrial efficiency; they also sought to develop model industrial communities. To avoid the crowded, wretched life of the English textile-mill villages, they located their four- and five-story brick-built mills along rivers in the countryside. Factory workers at Waltham and Lowell were mostly young women aged 15 to 30 from farm families. Mill owners preferred to hire women because of their skill in operating machines and their willingness to stomach the mind-numbing boredom of operating spinning machines and looms for wages lower than those paid to men (even though their wages, $2–5 per week, were the highest in the world for women). Moreover, by the 1820s there was a surplus of women in New England because so many men had migrated westward in search of cheap land and new economic opportunities. In the early 1820s, a steady stream of single women began flocking toward Lowell to work in the mills. To reassure worried parents, the mill owners promised to provide the "Lowell girls" with tolerable work, prepared meals, comfortable boardinghouses (four girls to a room), moral discipline, and educational and cultural opportunities.

Initially the "Lowell idea" worked pretty much according to plan. The "Lowell girls" lived in dormitories staffed by housemothers who enforced church attendance and evening curfews. Despite thirteen-hour work days and five-and-a-half day workweeks (longer hours than those imposed upon prison inmates), some of the women found the time and energy to form study groups, publish a literary magazine, and attend lectures. The mill managers required bedtime curfews, church attendance, and only limited contact with men.

Mill girls Massachusetts mill workers of the mid-nineteenth century, photographed holding shuttles.

But Lowell soon lost its innocence as it grew—and as the owners accumulated "unbelievable profits." Greed led mill owners to produce too much cloth, which depressed prices. Wages were cut, and the pace of work was quickened. By 1834, the Lowell women began going on strike to protest the deteriorating working and living conditions. The mill owners were not pleased. They labeled the 1,500 striking women "ungrateful" and "unfeminine"—and tried to get rid of the strike's leaders. One mill manager reported that "we have paid off several of these Amazons & presume that they will leave town on Monday."

The economic success of the New England textile mills raises an obvious question: why didn't the South build its own mills close to the cotton fields to keep its profits in the region? A few mills did appear, but they struggled to find workers because white farmers resisted factory work, and planters refused to allow slaves to leave the fields. African Americans, it was assumed, could not work efficiently indoors, and cotton planters considered textile mills an inefficient use of their labor resources. Agricultural slavery had made them rich. Why should they change?

Industrialization, Cities, and the Environment

Rapid growth of cities

The rapid growth of commerce and industry spurred the growth of cities. Lowell's population in 1820 was 200. By 1830, it was 6,500 and ten years later had soared to 21,000. By 1840, there were thirty-two mills and factories in operation, and the once rural town of Lowell had become an industrial city—busy, grimy, and bleak. Other similar factory centers sprouted up across New England, displacing forests, farms, and villages while filling the air with smoke, noise, and stench. In addition, the profusion of dams—built to harness water to turn the mill wheels—flooded pastures and decimated fish populations, spawned urban growth that in turn polluted the rivers, and aroused intense local resentment. In 1859, farmers far upstream of the big Massachusetts textile factories tried to destroy a massive dam in Lake Village, New Hampshire, but their axes and crowbars caused little damage. By then, the Industrial Revolution could not be stopped. The textile system was not only transforming lives and property—it was reshaping nature as well.

Between 1820 and 1840, the number of Americans engaged in manufacturing increased 800 percent, and the number of city dwellers more than doubled. As Thomas Jefferson and other agrarians feared, the United States was rapidly becoming a global industrial power, second only to Great Britain, producing its own clothing and shoes, iron and engines. Between 1790 and 1860, the proportion of urban to rural populations grew from 3 percent to 16 percent. Because of their strategic locations along rivers flowing into the ocean, the Atlantic seaports of New York City, Philadelphia, Baltimore, and Boston remained the largest cities. New Orleans became the nation's fifth-largest city

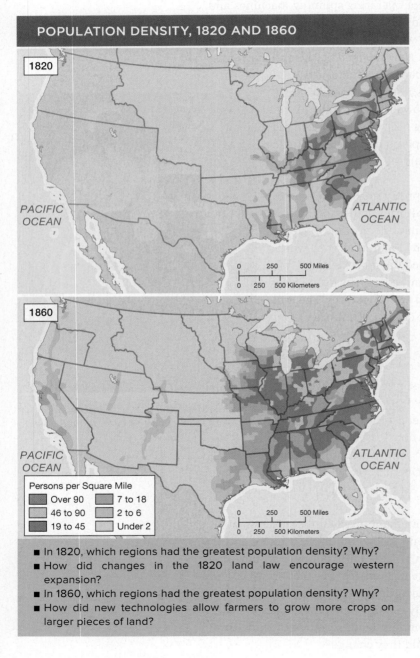

POPULATION DENSITY, 1820 AND 1860

1820

PACIFIC OCEAN

ATLANTIC OCEAN

0   250   500 Miles
0   250   500 Kilometers

1860

PACIFIC OCEAN

ATLANTIC OCEAN

Persons per Square Mile
- Over 90
- 46 to 90
- 19 to 45
- 7 to 18
- 2 to 6
- Under 2

0   250   500 Miles
0   250   500 Kilometers

- In 1820, which regions had the greatest population density? Why?
- How did changes in the 1820 land law encourage western expansion?
- In 1860, which regions had the greatest population density? Why?
- How did new technologies allow farmers to grow more crops on larger pieces of land?

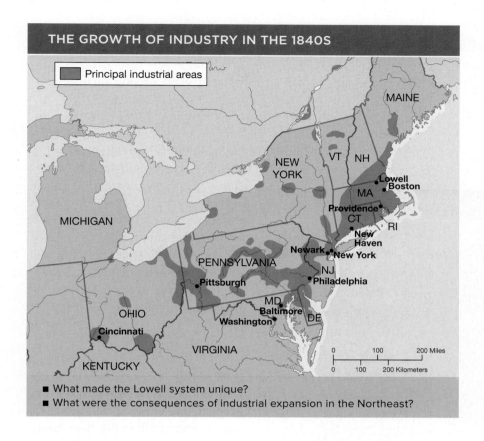

THE GROWTH OF INDUSTRY IN THE 1840S

Principal industrial areas

- What made the Lowell system unique?
- What were the consequences of industrial expansion in the Northeast?

because of its role in shipping goods that were floated down the Mississippi River to the East Coast and to Europe. New York outpaced all its competitors in growth. By 1860, it was the first city to reach a population of more than 1 million, largely because of its superior harbor and its access to the commerce floating down the Hudson River from the Erie Canal.

Immigration

During the forty years from the outbreak of the Revolution to the end of the War of 1812, immigration had slowed to a trickle. The French Revolution and the Napoleonic Wars restricted travel to and from Europe until 1815. Thereafter, however, the number of immigrants to America rose steadily, and throughout the nineteenth century the United States remained a magnet for immigrants. People on ships packed with humanity arrived from all over the world, eager to experience the American Dream—the shimmering, seductive promise that in the United States everyone had a chance to become something else, something better. After 1837, a worldwide financial panic and economic slump accelerated the tempo of immigration to the

CORE **OBJECTIVE**

3. Analyze how immigration altered the nation's population and shaped its politics.

United States. American employers began aggressively recruiting foreigners, in large part because they were often willing to work for lower wages than Americans.

Massive increase in immigration

The years from 1845 to 1854 saw the greatest proportional influx of immigrants in U.S. history, 2.4 million, or about 14.5 percent of the total population in 1845. In 1860, America's population was 31 million, with more than one of every eight residents foreign born. British immigrants continued to arrive in the United States in large numbers during the first half of the nineteenth century. By the 1850s, the rapid development of California was also attracting the Chinese, and Scandinavians and Norwegians began immigrating and settling mostly in Wisconsin and Minnesota, where the climate and woodlands reminded them of home. But by far, the largest number of immigrants between 1840 and 1860 came from Ireland and Germany.

The Irish

A prolonged agricultural crisis that brought immense social hardships caused many Irish to flee their homeland in the mid-nineteenth century for North America. Irish farmers primarily grew potatoes; in fact, fully a third of the people were dependent on the potato harvest for survival. In 1845, an epidemic of potato fungus triggered what came to be called the Irish potato famine. The average adult male in Ireland ate five pounds of potatoes a day. So when the fungus destroyed the potato crop, more than a million people died, and almost two million more left Ireland, whose total population was eight million. Most of them traveled to Canada and the United States. As one group of exiles explained, "All we want to do is get out of Ireland; we must be better anywhere but here." America, they knew, had plenty of paying jobs and "plenty to eat."

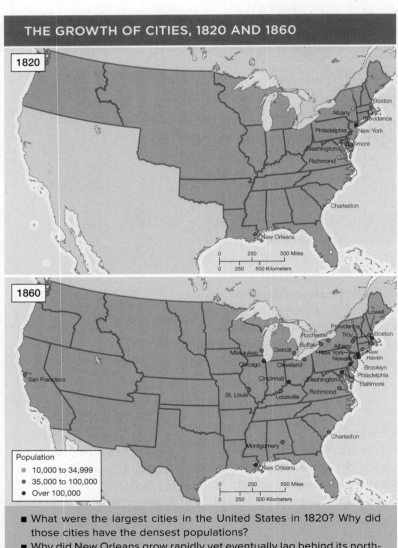

THE GROWTH OF CITIES, 1820 AND 1860

1820

Boston
Albany
Providence
Philadelphia   New York
Washington   Baltimore
Richmond

Charleston

New Orleans

0   250   500 Miles
0   250   500 Kilometers

1860

Lowell
Providence
Rochester   Troy   Boston
Buffalo   Albany
Detroit   New York   New Haven
Milwaukee   Newark
Chicago   Cleveland   Brooklyn
Cincinnati   Philadelphia
San Francisco   Washington   Baltimore
St. Louis   Louisville   Richmond

Montgomery   Charleston

New Orleans

Population
○ 10,000 to 34,999
● 35,000 to 100,000
● Over 100,000

0   250   500 Miles
0   250   500 Kilometers

■ What were the largest cities in the United States in 1820? Why did those cities have the densest populations?
■ Why did New Orleans grow rapidly yet eventually lag behind its northeastern counterparts?
■ Why did Chicago, Pittsburgh, Cincinnati, and St. Louis become major urban centers in the mid-nineteenth century?

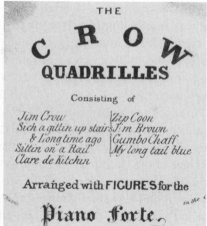

The Crow Quadrilles This sheet-music cover, printed in 1837, shows eight vignettes caricaturing African Americans. Minstrel shows enjoyed nationwide popularity while reinforcing racial stereotypes.

By the 1850s, the Irish made up more than half the population of Boston and New York City and were almost as dominant in Philadelphia. Most of them were crowded into filthy, poorly ventilated tenements (low-income urban apartment buildings) that were plagued by high crime rates, deadly diseases, prostitution, and alcoholism. The archbishop of New York described the Irish as "the poorest and most wretched population that can be found in the world." One Irishman lamented that he worked like "a slave for the Americans."

Irish immigrants confronted humiliating stereotypes and intense anti-Catholic prejudice. Many employers posted signs reading "No Irish Need Apply." Irish Americans, however, could be equally mean-spirited toward other groups, such as free African Americans, who competed with them for low-wage jobs. In 1850, the *New York Tribune* expressed concern that the Irish, having escaped from "a galling, degrading bondage" in their homeland, voted against proposals for equal rights for blacks and frequently arrived at the polls shouting, "Down with the Nagurs! Let them go back to Africa, where they belong." For their part, many African Americans viewed the Irish with equal contempt. In 1850, a slave expressed a common sentiment: "My Master is a great tyrant, he treats me badly as if I were a common Irishman."

But many enterprising Irish immigrants forged remarkable careers. Twenty years after arriving in New York, Alexander T. Stewart became the owner of the nation's largest department store and thereafter accumulated vast real estate holdings in Manhattan. Michael Cudahy, who began working at age fourteen in a Milwaukee meatpacking business, became head of the Cudahy Packing Company and developed a process for the curing of meats under refrigeration. Dublin-born Victor Herbert emerged as one of America's most revered composers, and Irish dancers and playwrights came to dominate the stage. Irishmen were equally successful in the boxing arena and on the baseball diamond. And it was Irish manual laborers who built much of nineteenth-century America, including the Erie Canal, much of the national railway network, and most of the relentless construction in the nation's rapidly expanding cities.

Irish immigration: Unskilled labor and the growth of Roman Catholicism

Perhaps the greatest collective achievement of the Irish immigrants was stimulating the growth of the Roman Catholic Church in the United States. Years of persecution had instilled in Irish Catholics a fierce loyalty to the doctrines of the church as "the supreme authority over all the affairs of the world." Such passion for Catholicism generated both unity among Irish Americans and fear among American Protestants. By 1860, Roman Catholicism had become the largest denomination in the United States.

The Germans

German immigration: Skilled and diverse workers

A new wave of German immigration peaked in 1854, just a few years after the crest of Irish arrivals, when 215,000 Germans arrived in U.S. ports. These immigrants included a large number of learned, cultured, professional people—doctors, lawyers, teachers, engineers—some of whom were refugees from the failed German revolution of 1848. In addition to an array of political opinions, the Germans brought with them a variety of religious preferences. Most of them were Protestants (usually Lutherans), a third were Roman Catholics, and a significant number were Jews. Among the German immigrants who prospered in the New World were Heinrich Steinweg, a piano maker who in America changed his name to Steinway and became famous for the quality of his instruments, and Levi Strauss, a Jewish tailor who followed the gold rush to California and began making work pants, later dubbed "Levi's."

Unlike the Irish, Germans settled more often in rural areas than in cities. Many were independent farmers, skilled workers, and shopkeepers who were able to establish themselves immediately. More so than the Irish, they migrated in families and groups. This clannish quality helped them better sustain elements of their language and culture in the New World. More of them also tended to return to their native country. About 14 percent of the Germans eventually went back to their homeland, compared with just 9 percent of the Irish.

Nativism

Nativism: Anti-Catholic violence

Not all Americans welcomed the flood of immigrants. Many "nativists," people born in the United States, resented the newcomers, with their strange languages and customs, and sought to restrict or stop immigration altogether. The flood of Irish and German Catholics aroused Protestant hostility. There were also fears that German immigrants were bringing to America dangerous political ideas such as socialism and communism, and that the Irish were voting solely for the Democratic party. In 1844, armed clashes between Protestants and Catholics in Philadelphia caused widespread injuries and deaths.

Nativists pursued organized efforts to stop the tide of immigrants. The Order of the Star-Spangled Banner, founded in New York City in 1849, grew into a powerful new political organization known officially as the American party. Members pledged never to vote for any foreign-born or Catholic candidates. When asked about the secretive organization, they were told to say, "I know nothing," a phrase which gave rise to the informal name for the American party: the **Know-Nothing party**. For a while, the Know-Nothings appeared to be on the brink of major-party status. In the state and local campaigns of 1854, they carried one election after another. They swept the Massachusetts legislature, winning all but two seats in the lower house, and that fall they elected more than forty congressmen.

The Know-Nothings demanded that immigrants and Roman Catholics be excluded from public office and that the waiting period for naturalization (earning citizenship) be extended from five to twenty-one years, but the party never developed enough strength to enact such legislation. Nor did Congress restrict immigration in any way during that period. For a while, the Know-Nothings threatened to control New England, New York, and Maryland and showed strength elsewhere, but the anti-Catholic movement subsided when slavery became the focal issue of the 1850s.

Nativism: The Know-Nothings

Organized Labor and New Professions

CORE **OBJECTIVE**
4. Evaluate the impact of the expanding "market economy" on workers, professionals, and women.

While most Americans continued to work as farmers during the nineteenth century, a growing number found employment in new or expanding enterprises: textile mills, shoe factories, banks, railroads, publishing, retail stores, teaching, preaching, medicine, law, construction, and engineering. Technological innovations (steam power, power tools, and new modes of transportation) and their social applications (mass communication, turnpikes, the postal service, banks, and corporations) fostered an array of new industries and businesses that transformed the nature of work for many Americans, both men and women.

Early Unions

Proud apprentices, journeymen, and master craftsmen, who controlled their labor and invested their work with an emphasis on quality rather than quantity, resented the spread of mills and factories populated by masses of "half-trained" workers, often young women as in the Lowell textile mills, dependent upon an hourly wage and subject to the sharp fluctuations of the larger economy. Skilled workers in American cities before and after the Revolution were called artisans, craftsmen, or mechanics. They made or

Nativists Native-born Americans who viewed immigrants as a threat to their job opportunities and way of life.

Know-Nothing party Nativist, anti-Catholic third party organized in 1854 in reaction to large-scale German and Irish immigration.

The shoe factory When Philadelphia shoemakers went on strike in 1806, a court found them guilty of a "conspiracy to raise wages." Here, shoemakers work in the bottoming room at a Massachusetts shoe factory.

Creation of National Trades' Union (1834)

repaired shoes, hats, saddles, silverware, jewelry, glass, ropes, furniture, and a broad array of other products. During the 1820s and 1830s, artisans who emphasized quality and craftsmanship found it hard to compete with the low prices made possible by the new factories and mass-production workshops.

In the early nineteenth century, a growing fear that they were losing status led artisans in the major cities to become involved in politics and unions. At first, these workers organized themselves into interest groups representing their individual skills or trades. Such "trade associations" were the first type of labor unions. They pressured politicians for tariffs to protect their industries from foreign imports, provided insurance benefits, and drafted regulations to improve working conditions. In addition, they sought to control the number of tradesmen in their profession so as to maintain wage levels.

Early labor unions faced major legal obstacles—in fact, they were prosecuted as unlawful conspiracies. In 1806, for instance, Philadelphia shoemakers were found guilty of conspiring "to raise their wages." The court's decision broke the union. In 1842, though, the Massachusetts Supreme Court issued a landmark ruling in *Commonwealth v. Hunt* declaring that forming a trade union was not in itself illegal, nor was a demand that employers hire only members of the union. The court also said that union workers could strike if an employer hired laborers who refused to join the union.

Until the 1820s, labor organizations took the form of local trade unions, each confined to one city and one craft or skill. From 1827 to 1837, however, organization on a larger scale began to take hold. In 1834 the **National Trades' Union** was formed to organize all of the citywide trade unions into a stronger national association. At the same time, shoemakers, printers, carpenters, and weavers established national craft unions. But all the national groups and most of the local ones vanished during the terrible economic depression in the late 1830s.

The Rise of the Professions

The dramatic social changes of the first half of the nineteenth century opened up an array of new **professions**. Bustling new towns required new services—retail stores, printing shops, post offices, newspapers, schools, banks, law firms, medical practices, and others—that created more high-status professions than had existed before. By definition, professional workers are those who have specialized knowledge and training. In 1849, Henry Day delivered a lecture on "The Professions" at the Western Reserve School of Medicine. He declared that the most important social functions in modern life were the professional skills. In fact, Day claimed, American society had become utterly dependent upon "professional services."

Teaching

Teaching was one of the fastest-growing vocations in the first half of the nineteenth century. Horace Mann of Massachusetts was instrumental in promoting the idea of free public education for all children as the best way to transform youths into disciplined, judicious republican citizens. Many states, especially in the North, agreed, and the number of schools exploded during the second quarter of the nineteenth century. New schools required teachers, and Horace Mann helped create "normal schools" around the nation to train young people to be teachers. Public schools initially preferred men as teachers, usually hiring them at age seventeen or eighteen. The pay was so low that few stayed in the profession their entire career, but for many educated, restless young adults, teaching offered independence and social status, as well as an alternative to the rural isolation of farming. Church groups and civic leaders started private academies, or seminaries, for girls.

Law, Medicine, and Engineering

Teaching was a common stepping-stone for men who became lawyers. In the decades after the Revolution, growing numbers of young men would teach for a year or two before joining an experienced attorney as an apprentice (what today would be called an *intern*). They would learn the practice of law in exchange for their labors. (There were no law schools in the first half of the nineteenth century.) The absence of formal standards for legal training helps explain why there were so many attorneys in the pre–Civil War period.

National Trades' Union Formed in 1834 to organize all local trade unions into a stronger national association; dissolved amid the economic depression in the late 1830s.

professions Occupations requiring specialized knowledge of a particular field; the Industrial Revolution and its new organization of labor created an array of professions in the nineteenth century.

Like attorneys, physicians in the early nineteenth century often had little formal academic training. Healers of every stripe assumed the title of *doctor* and established medical practices without regulation. Most were self-taught or had learned their profession by assisting a physician for several years, occasionally supplementing their internships with a few classes at the handful of medical schools. By 1860, there were 60,000 self-styled physicians, many of whom were "quacks" or frauds. As a result, the medical profession lost the public's confidence.

The industrial expansion of the United States also spurred the profession of engineering, a field that would eventually become the nation's largest professional occupation for men. Specialized expertise was required for the design and construction of canals and railroads, the development of machine tools and steam engines, and the building of roads, bridges, and factories. By the outbreak of the Civil War, engineering had become one of the largest professions in the nation.

> **New professions for men:**
> Lawyers, doctors, engineers

"Women's Work"

> **New professions for women:**
> Teachers and nurses

During the first half of the nineteenth century, despite the influx of young women into New England textile mills, most women still worked primarily in the home or on a farm. The only professions readily available to them were nursing (often midwifery, the delivery of babies) and school teaching. Many middle-class women spent their time outside the home doing religious and social-service work. Then as now, women were the backbone of most churches.

A few women, however, courageously pursued careers in male-dominated professions. Elizabeth Blackwell of Ohio managed to gain admission to Geneva Medical College (now Hobart and William Smith College) in western New York despite the disapproval of the faculty. When she arrived at her first class, a hush fell upon the students "as if each member had been struck with paralysis." Blackwell had the last laugh when she finished first in her class in 1849, but thereafter the medical school refused to admit any more women. The first American woman to earn a medical degree, Blackwell went on to start the New York Infirmary for Women and Children and later had a long career as a professor of gynecology at the London School of Medicine for Women.

Equal Opportunities

The dynamic market economy that emerged during the first half of the nineteenth century helped spread the idea that individuals should have an equal opportunity to better themselves in the workplace through their abilities and hard work. Equality of opportunity, however, did not assume equal outcomes. Americans wanted an equal chance to earn unequal amounts of wealth. In America, observed a journalist in 1844, "one has as good a chance as another according to his talents, prudence, and personal exertions." The same ideals that prompted so many white immigrants to risk everything to come to the United States, however, were equally appealing to those groups that still did not enjoy equal opportunities to pursue their American dream: African Americans and women. By the 1830s, they, too, began to demand their right to "life, liberty, and the pursuit of happiness." Such desires of "common people" to pursue economic opportunities would quickly spill over into the political arena. The great theme of political life in the first half of the nineteenth century would be the continuing democratization of opportunities for white men, regardless of income or background, to vote and hold office.

■ **Transportation and Communication Revolutions** Canals and other improvements in transportation such as the *steamboat* that could be used on the nation's rivers and lakes allowed goods to reach markets more quickly and cheaply, helping to create a national *market economy* in which people bought and sold goods at larger distances. *Clipper ships* shortened the amount of time to transport goods across the oceans. The *railroads* (which expanded rapidly during the 1850s) and the *telegraph system* diminished the isolation of the West and united the country economically and socially. The *Erie Canal (1817)* contributed to New York City's emerging status as the nation's economic center even as it spurred the growth of Chicago and other midwestern cities. Improvements in transportation and communication linked rural communities to a worldwide marketplace.

■ **The Industrial Revolution** Inventions in machine tools and technology spurred an *Industrial Revolution* during the nineteenth century. The *cotton gin* dramatically increased cotton production, and a rapidly spreading *cotton* culture boomed in the South, with a resultant increase in slavery. Other inventions, such as John Deere's steel plow and the mechanized *McCormick reaper*, helped Americans, especially westerners, farm their land more efficiently and more profitably. In the North, mills and factories, at first water powered and eventually powered by coal-fired steam engines, spread rapidly. They initially produced textiles for clothing and bedding from southern cotton, as well as iron, shoes, and other products. The federal government's tariff policy encouraged the growth of domestic manufacturing, especially cotton textiles, by reducing imports of British cloth. Between 1820 and 1840, the number of Americans engaged in manufacturing increased 800 percent. Many mill workers, such as the women employed in the *Lowell system* of New England textile factory communities, worked long hours for low wages in unhealthy conditions. Industrialization, along with increased commerce, helped spur the growth of cities. By 1860, 16 percent of the population lived in urban areas.

■ **Immigration** The promise of cheap land and good wages drew millions of immigrants to America. By 1844, 14.5 percent of the population was foreign born. Many of those who arrived in the 1840s came not just from the Protestant regions of Northern Europe that had supplied most of America's previous immigrants. The devastating potato famine led to an influx of poor Irish Catholic families. By the 1850s, they represented a significant portion of the urban population in the United States, constituting a majority in New York and Boston. German migrants, many of them Catholics and Jews, migrated to the country at the same time. Not all native-born Americans welcomed the immigrants. *Nativists* became a powerful political force in the 1850s, with the *Know-Nothing party* nearly achieving major-party status with its message of excluding immigrants and Catholics from the nation's political community.

■ **Workers, Professionals, and Women** Skilled workers (artisans) in American cities had long formed trade associations to protect their members and to lobby for their interests. As the *Industrial Revolution* spread, some workers expanded these organizations nationally, forming the *National Trades' Union*. The growth of the *market economy* also expanded opportunities for those with formal education to serve in new or expanding *professions*. The number of physicians, teachers, engineers, and lawyers grew rapidly. By the mid-nineteenth century, women, African Americans, and immigrants began to agitate for equal social, economic, and political opportunities.

KEY TERMS

CHRONOLOGY

1793	Eli Whitney invents the cotton gin
1794	Philadelphia-Lancaster Turnpike is completed
1795	Wilderness Road opens
1807	Robert Fulton and Robert Livingston launch steamship transportation on the Hudson River in New York
1825	Erie Canal opens in upstate New York
1831	Cyrus McCormick invents a mechanical reaper
1834	National Trades' Union is organized
1837	John Deere invents the steel plow
1842	Massachusetts Supreme Judicial Court issues *Commonwealth v. Hunt* decision
1845	The *Rainbow*, the first clipper ship, is launched
1845	Irish Potato Famine
1846	Elias Howe invents the sewing machine
1848	California gold rush begins
1855	Know-Nothing party (American party) formed

INQUIZITIVE

Go to InQuizitive to see what you've learned—and learn what you've missed—with personalized feedback along the way.

PARADE OF THE VICTUALLERS (1821) On a beautiful day in March 1821, Philadelphia butcher William White organized a parade celebrating America's own high-quality meats. Many townspeople watched from their windows and balconies, while the spectators below could also enjoy the foods of various street vendors, such as the African American oyster peddler (bottom left). This watercolor by John Lewis Krimmel captures the new, vibrant nationalism that emerged in America after the War of 1812.

Nationalism and Sectionalism

1815–1828

After the War of 1812, the British navy stopped interfering with American shipping, and Americans were freed from British restrictions on their economic activities. The United States could now grow new industries and exploit new markets around the globe. It was not simply Alexander Hamilton's financial initiatives and the capitalistic energies of wealthy investors and speculators that sparked America's dramatic economic growth in the early nineteenth century. It was also the strenuous efforts of ordinary men and women who were willing to take risks, uproot families, use unstable paper money issued by unregulated local banks, purchase factory-made goods, and tinker with new machines and tools. In short, by 1828 the agrarian republic nestled along the Atlantic seaboard was poised to become a sprawling commercial nation connected by networks of roads and canals as well as regional economic relationships—all energized by a restless spirit of enterprise, experimentation, and expansion.

But for all of the energy and optimism exhibited by Americans after the war, the fundamental tension between *nationalism* and *sectionalism* remained: how to balance the particular issues and purely sectional concerns of the nation's three regions—North, South, and West—with the national interest? Each region (that is, each section) had different economic interests and political goals. Complicating the tensions between nationalists and sectionalists, some of whom changed their perspective over time, with sectionalists becoming nationalists and vice versa,

CORE OBJECTIVES INQUIZITIVE

1. Analyze how the new spirit of nationalism that emerged after the War of 1812 affected economic policies and judicial decisions.

2. Summarize the issues and ideas that promoted sectional conflict during this era.

3. Explain the emergence of the "Era of Good Feelings" and the factors that led to its demise.

4. Identify the federal government's diplomatic accomplishments during this era, and analyze their impact.

5. Evaluate the influence of Andrew Jackson on national politics in the 1820s and the developments that enabled him to become president.

was the ongoing debate over the meaning of the U.S. Constitution and whether its language should be interpreted loosely or strictly. Some sectionalists were single-mindedly focused on promoting their region's priorities: shipping and commerce in the Northeast, slave-based agriculture in the South, low land prices and transportation improvements in the West. Nationalists, on the other hand, tried to find policies and offer proposals that would serve the interests of the nation as a whole. This required each region to compromise, to recognize that no single section could get all it wanted without threatening the survival of the nation. Of all the issues dividing the young American republic, the passions aroused by slavery proved to be the most difficult to resolve.

CORE **OBJECTIVE**

1. Analyze how the new spirit of nationalism that emerged after the War of 1812 affected economic policies and judicial decisions.

A New Nationalism

Postwar Nationalism and Economic Policy

After the War of 1812, Americans experienced a wave of patriotic excitement. They had won their independence from Britain for a second time. A surge of prosperity fed a widespread sense of optimism about the young nation's future. In his first message to Congress in late 1815, President James Madison revealed how much the challenges of the war, especially the weaknesses of the armed forces and the national economy, had changed his attitudes toward the role of the federal government. Now, he and other leading Republicans such as South Carolina's John C. Calhoun reversed themselves and acted like nationalists rather than states' rights sectionalists. They abandoned many of Thomas Jefferson's presidential policies (reducing the armed forces and opposing a national bank, for example) in favor of *economic* nationalism developed earlier by Federalists Alexander Hamilton and George Washington as a means of preserving political unity. Many Republicans such as Jefferson and Madison, once they were in charge of actually running the government, discovered that many of the Federalist policies, such as a strong national bank, were in fact wise. Madison, for example, now supported a larger army and navy, a national bank, and tariffs to protect American manufacturers from foreign competitors. "The Republicans have out-Federalized Federalism," one New Englander remarked after Madison's speech.

The Bank of the United States

After President Madison and congressional Republicans allowed the charter for the First Bank of the United States to expire, in 1811, the nation's finances fell into a muddle. States began chartering new local banks with little or no regulation, and their banknotes (paper money) flooded the economy with different currencies of uncertain value. Imagine trying to do business on a national basis when each state-chartered bank had its own currency, which often was not accepted by other banks or in other states.

In response to the growing financial turmoil and the financial problems that emerged during the war, Madison and most of the younger generation of Republicans swallowed their longstanding reservations about a powerful national bank. In 1816, Madison urged Congress to establish a **Second Bank of the United States** (B.U.S.). The B.U.S., which could establish branches throughout the states, was intended primarily to create a stable national currency that would promote economic growth. With the help of Clay and Calhoun, Congress created the new B.U.S., which, like its predecessor, was based in Philadelphia and was designated to hold and disburse all federal government funds.

> Economic nationalism: New national bank and currency

A Protective Tariff

The long controversy with Great Britain over shipping rights convinced most Americans of the need to develop their own manufacturing sector in order to end their dependence on British goods. Efforts to develop American iron and textile industries, begun in New York and New England during the Embargo of 1807, which ended American trade with other nations, had accelerated during the War of 1812, since the war cut off American access to European goods. After the war ended, however, the British flooded American markets with their less-expensive products. Northern business leaders urged Congress to create federal tariffs to protect their infant industries from what they called "unfair" British competition. Congress responded by passing the **Tariff of 1816**, which placed a 20–25 percent tax on a long list of imported goods. Like so many government policies, tariffs benefited some regions (the Northeast) more than others (the South), thus worsening sectional tensions and grievances.

> Economic nationalism: Tariff of 1816 and federal financing for "internal improvements"

Internal Improvements

The third major element of economic nationalism in the first half of the nineteenth century involved federal financing of **internal improvements**, which meant the construction of roads, canals, and harbors intended to benefit the flow of goods and people. During the War of 1812, American military leaders had also grown frustrated by the difficulty of moving troops through the western region. In 1803, when Ohio became a state, Congress had ordered that 5 percent of the money from land sales in the state would go toward building a National Road from the Atlantic coast into Ohio and westward. Construction finally began in 1811. The road was cleared eighty feet wide with a twenty-foot-wide, stone-paved strip down the middle. Originally called the Cumberland Road, it was the first interstate roadway financed by the federal government. By 1818 the road was open from Cumberland, Maryland, westward to Wheeling, Virginia (now West Virginia), where it crossed the Ohio River. By 1838 the road extended 600 miles farther westward to Vandalia, Illinois. By reducing transportation costs and opening up new markets, the National Road helped accelerate

Second Bank of the United States Established in 1816 after the first national bank's charter expired; it stabilized the economy by creating a sound national currency, by making loans to farmers, small manufacturers, and entrepreneurs, and by regulating the ability of state banks to issue their own paper currency.

Tariff of 1816 Taxes on various imported items, to protect America's emerging iron and textile industries from British competition.

internal improvements Construction of infrastructural projects intended to facilitate the flow of goods and people.

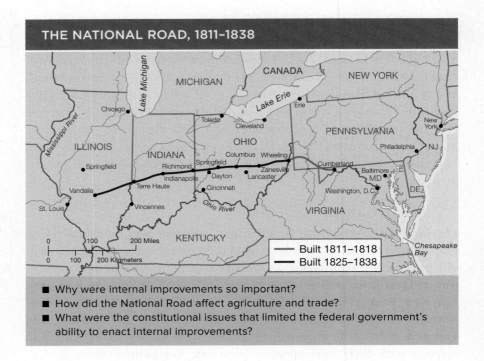

THE NATIONAL ROAD, 1811–1838

Built 1811–1818
Built 1825–1838

■ Why were internal improvements so important?
■ How did the National Road affect agriculture and trade?
■ What were the constitutional issues that limited the federal government's ability to enact internal improvements?

John Marshall A pillar of judicial nationalism, Marshall was appointed chief justice of the U.S. Supreme Court at the young age of forty-six, ruling on *Marbury v. Madison* just two years later.

the settlement of the West and the emergence of a truly national market economy, with the commercialization of agriculture, whereby farmers increasingly sold their produce and livestock to distant rather than merely local markets. But using federal money to finance such "internal improvements" remained controversial. Critics concerned about the expansion of federal power argued that the U.S. Constitution did not allow for such activities; only the local and state governments, or private investors, should fund road, canal, and harbor projects.

Postwar Nationalism and the Supreme Court

The postwar emphasis on nationalism also flourished in the Supreme Court, where Chief Justice John Marshall strengthened the constitutional powers of the federal government at the expense of states' rights. Marshall was a consistent nationalist. He viewed his cousin Thomas Jefferson and his Republican followers as a dangerous threat to the nation because they preferred states' rights over federal authority. During Marshall's early years on the Court (he served thirty-four years altogether), his judicial nationalism affirmed that the Supreme Court had the authority (and responsibility) to judge the constitutionality of state and federal legislative actions (oversight called *judicial review*). In *Marbury v. Madison* (1803) the Court had, for the first time, struck down a federal law as unconstitutional. In the cases of *Martin v. Hunter's Lessee* (1816) and *Cohens v. Virginia* (1821), the Court ruled

Sectional Conflict and Economic Policies

After the War of 1812, Congress created many policies that would arouse fierce debate over several decades. Policies regarding the monetary system, tariffs, and internal improvements ignited sectional conflict as people viewed specific policies as damaging to their varied regional interests.

Federal Initiative	Northeast Region Economy (manufacturing, shipping, investment, some commercial farming)	Southern Region Economy (plantation-based agriculture, esp. cotton cultivation)	Western Region Economy (commercial farming)	Congressional Action
Protective Tariff	Opposed by shippers Supported by manufacturers	Opposed	Supported	Tariff of 1816 passed
National Bank	Generally supported	Generally opposed	Intensely opposed, due to Western shortage of hard currency	Second Bank of the United States created
Internal Improvements	Opposed	Opposed	Supported	National Road is built

QUESTIONS FOR ANALYSIS

1. How were the regions diverging economically?

2. How did the different economies in each section shape their support or opposition to the tariff, the Bank of the United States, and federally financed internal improvements?

3. How did sectional conflict affect politics at the national level?

4. Which policies did Congress enact and sustain? Which proved more difficult to pursue?

that the U.S. Constitution, as well as the laws and treaties of the United States, could remain the supreme law of the land only if the Court could review the decisions of state courts.

Protecting Contract Rights

Judicial nationalism: *Dartmouth College v. Woodward* (1819)

In the fateful year of 1819, the Supreme Court made two more major decisions that limited the powers of states and strengthened the power of the federal government. One of them, ***Dartmouth College v. Woodward***, involved an attempt by the New Hampshire legislature to alter a provision in Dartmouth College's charter under which the college's trustees elected their own successors. In 1816 the state's Republican legislature, offended by the Federalist majority on the college's board, placed Dartmouth under a new board of trustees named by the governor. The college's original group of trustees sued to block the move. They lost in the state courts but won on appeal to the Supreme Court. The college's original charter, wrote John Marshall in drafting the Court's opinion, was a valid contract that the state legislature had violated, an act forbidden by the Constitution. This decision implied a new and enlarged definition of *contract* that seemed to put corporations beyond the reach of the states that had chartered them. Thereafter, states commonly wrote into the charters incorporating businesses and other organizations provisions making them subject to state oversight. Such provisions were then part of the "contract."

Protecting A National Currency

Judicial nationalism: *McCulloch v. Maryland* (1819)

The second major Supreme Court case of 1819 was Marshall's single most important interpretation of the constitutional system: ***McCulloch v. Maryland***. James McCulloch, a clerk in the Baltimore branch of the federal Bank of the United States, had refused to apply state taxes to B.U.S. currency, as required by a Maryland law. Indicted by the state, McCulloch, acting for the bank, appealed to the Supreme Court, which handed down a unanimous judgment upholding the power of Congress to charter the B.U.S. and denying the state's right to tax it. In a lengthy opinion, Chief Justice Marshall said that Maryland's effort to tax the national bank conflicted with the supreme law of the land. One great principle that "entirely pervades the Constitution," Marshall wrote, is "that the Constitution and the laws made in pursuance thereof are supreme: . . . They control the Constitution and laws of the respective states, and cannot be controlled by them." The effort by a state to tax a federal bank therefore was unconstitutional, for the "power to tax involves the power to destroy"—which was precisely what the legislatures of Maryland and several other states had in mind with respect to the national bank. The Marshall court ruled that Congress had the right (that is, one of its "implied powers") to take any action not forbidden by the Constitution as long as the purpose of such laws was within the "scope of the Constitution."

Dartmouth College v. Woodward (1819) Supreme Court ruling that enlarged the definition of *contract* to put corporations beyond the reach of the states that chartered them.

McCulloch v. Maryland (1819) Supreme Court ruling that declared it unconstitutional for states to tax the Bank of the United States.

Gibbons v. Ogden (1824) Supreme Court case that gave the federal government the power to regulate interstate commerce.

***Steamboat Travel on the Hudson River* (1811)** This watercolor of an early steamboat was painted by a Russian diplomat, Pavel Petrovich Svinin, who was fascinated by early techological innovations and the unique culture of America.

Regulating Interstate Commerce

John Marshall's last great judicial decision, ***Gibbons v. Ogden*** (1824), established the federal government's supremacy in regulating interstate commerce. In 1808, the New York legislature granted Robert Fulton and Robert R. Livingston the exclusive right to operate steamboats on the state's rivers and lakes. Fulton and Livingston then gave Aaron Ogden the exclusive right to ferry people and goods up the Hudson River between New York and New Jersey. Thomas Gibbons, however, operated ships under a federal license that competed with Ogden. On behalf of a unanimous Court, Marshall ruled that the monopoly granted by the state to Ogden conflicted with the federal license issued to Gibbons.

Thomas Jefferson detested John Marshall's judicial nationalism. The Court's ruling in the *Gibbons* case, said the eighty-two-year-old former president, revealed how "the Federal branch of our Government is advancing towards the usurpation of all the rights reserved to the States, and the consolidation in itself of all powers, foreign and domestic."

> Judicial nationalism: *Gibbons v. Ogden* (1824)

Debates over the American System

> CORE **OBJECTIVE**
> **2.** Summarize the issues and ideas that promoted sectional conflict during this era.

The major economic initiatives debated by Congress after the War of 1812—the national bank, federal tariffs, and federally-financed roads and canals—were interrelated pieces of a comprehensive economic plan to strengthen and unify the nation called the **American System**. The term was coined by Republican Henry Clay, the powerful Congressional leader from Kentucky who would serve three terms as Speaker of the House before becoming a U.S. senator Clay was a leading *nationalist*. He insisted that "I know of no South, no North, no East, no West to which I owe my allegiance. The Union is my country." Clay saw in the American System a way for the United States to become independent of the British economically while tying together the diverse regions of the nation politically.

In promoting the American System, Clay sought to give each region or section of the country its top economic priority. He argued that high tariffs on imports were needed to block the sale of British products in the United States in order to protect fragile new American industries from unfair foreign competition. To convince the skeptical western states to support the tariffs wanted by New England manufacturers, Clay called for the federal government to use tariff revenues to build much-needed infrastructure in the frontier West: roads, canals, and other "internal improvements" were desperately needed to enable speedier travel and the shipment of goods. Second, Clay's American System would raise prices for the purchase of federal lands and "distribute" the additional revenue to the states to help finance more roads, bridges, and canals. Third, Clay endorsed a strong national bank to create a single national currency and to regulate the often unstable state and local banks.

Clay was the era's supreme political deal-maker and economic nationalist. In many respects, he assumed responsibility for sustaining Alexander Hamilton's vision of a strong federal government nurturing a diversified national economy that combined agriculture, industry, and commerce. The debates over the merits of the American System would continue throughout the first half of the nineteenth century. The success of Clay's program depended on each section's willingness to compromise in order to maintain national unity. For a while, it worked.

> Regional differences over the American System

The much-discussed American System aroused both widespread support and intense opposition. Critics argued that higher prices for federal lands would discourage western migration and that tariffs benefited the northern manufacturing sector at the expense of southern and western farmers and the "common" people, who had to pay higher prices for the goods produced by tariff-protected industries. Many westerners and southerners also feared that the Philadelphia-based Second Bank of the United States would become so powerful that it could dictate the nation's economic future at the expense of states' rights and the needs of particular sections of the nation. Missouri senator Thomas Hart Benton predicted that cash-strapped western towns would now be at the mercy of a powerful national bank in Philadelphia. The West, he feared, would be "devoured" by the East and its national banking system. Westerners, Benton worried, "are in the jaws of the monster! A lump of butter in the mouth of a dog! One gulp, one swallow, and all is gone!"

American System Economic plan championed by Henry Clay of Kentucky that called for federal tariffs on imports, a strong national bank, and federally-financed internal improvements—roads, bridges, canals—all intended to strengthen the national economy and end American dependence on Great Britain.

The bitter debate over the B.U.S. helped set the pattern of deepening sectional disputes among the North, South, and West on the economic issues associated with Henry Clay's American System. Support for federal spending on internal improvements came largely from the West, which badly needed good roads, bridges, canals, and port facilities to connect its economy to the other regions. Many New Englanders and southerners opposed the use of federal money to finance transportation projects in the West, arguing that such projects should be paid for by the states. On his last day in office, in 1817, President Madison vetoed a bill that would have funded more internal improvements because he could not find a provision in the Constitution authorizing such federal expenditures. Nor was he willing to claim that such funding was an "implied power" within the Constitution. As a result, internal improvements remained, with few exceptions, the responsibility of the states for another hundred years. The federal government did not enter the field again on a large scale until passage of the Federal Highways Act of 1916.

In championing his American System, Henry Clay was forced to resolve explosive sectional conflicts over slavery in the western territories and states. Many of the Americans pouring across the Appalachian Mountains took with them a commitment to cotton production and the slave system that supported it. The possibility of new western states becoming "slave states" created the greatest political controversy of the nineteenth century. Former president Thomas Jefferson admitted that the issue scared him "like a firebell in the night." It "awakened and filled me with terror. I considered it at once as the knell of the Union." Jefferson realized that the United States, which he and others had worked so hard to create and nurture, was increasingly at risk of disintegrating over the future of slavery, the explosive issue that no longer could be avoided. And like Thomas Jefferson, Henry Clay lived with the daily contradiction of being a slave owner opposed to the expansion of slavery.

> Conflict over extending slavery into the western states

"Era of Good Feelings"

James Monroe

As James Madison approached the end of his presidency, he, as Thomas Jefferson had done before him, turned to a fellow Virginian, another secretary of state, to be his successor. For Madison that man was James Monroe, who went on to win the Republican nomination. In the 1816 election, Monroe overwhelmed his Federalist opponent, Rufus King of New York, with 183 to 34 votes in the Electoral College. The "Virginia dynasty" of presidents continued.

Like George Washington, Thomas Jefferson, and James Madison, Monroe was a slaveholding Virginia planter. At the outbreak of the Revolutionary War, he was beginning his studies at the College of William and Mary. He

> CORE **OBJECTIVE**
> **3.** Explain the emergence of the "Era of Good Feelings" and the factors that led to its demise.

James Monroe Portrayed as he began his presidency in 1817.

joined the army at the age of sixteen, served under George Washington during the Revolution, and later studied law with Jefferson. Washington called him a "brave, active, and sensible army officer."

Tall, blue-eyed James Monroe was eminently qualified to be president. He had served as a representative in the Virginia assembly, as governor of the state, as a representative in the Confederation Congress, as a U.S. senator, and as U.S. minister (ambassador) to Paris, London, and Madrid. Under President Madison, he served as secretary of state and doubled as secretary of war. South Carolina's John C. Calhoun, who would serve as Monroe's secretary of war, said that the new president was "among the wisest and most cautious men I have ever known." Thomas Jefferson was even more lavish with his praise. He noted that Monroe was "a man whose soul might be turned wrong side outwards without discovering a blemish to the world."

Monroe's administration began with the nation at peace and its economy flourishing. A Boston newspaper said the new president's arrival in office coincided with an "Era of Good Feelings" and the label became a popular catchphrase for the strong economy and political good will during Monroe's administration. In 1820 Monroe would be re-elected without opposition; by then, the Federalists were so weak that they did not even put up a candidate. The Republican party was dominant.

The nationalist priorities during the so-called Era of Good Feelings did not last long, however, for sectional loyalties continued to battle with national perspectives. Two crucial events signaled the end of the Era of Good Feelings and warned of stormy times ahead: the financial Panic of 1819 and the political conflict over statehood for Missouri.

The Panic of 1819

> End of Era of Good Feelings: Collapse of cotton prices

The financial **Panic of 1819** was caused by the sudden collapse of cotton prices after British textile mills quit buying high-priced American cotton—the nation's leading export—in favor of cheaper cotton from other parts of the world, especially Egypt and India. The collapse of cotton prices was especially devastating for southern planters, but it also reduced the world demand for other American goods. New American factory owners struggled to find markets for their goods and to fend off more-experienced foreign competitors. The financial panic thus renewed sectional tensions between northern and southern economic interests.

Other factors caused the financial panic to become a prolonged economic recession. Business owners, farmers, and land speculators had recklessly borrowed money to fuel their business ventures. In many cases, land speculators had purchased large tracts of government land, paying only a fourth of the full cost, and then sold the parcels to settlers with the understanding that they would pay the remaining installments. With the collapse of crop prices and the decline of land values during and after 1819, both speculators and settlers saw their income plummet.

Panic of 1819 A financial panic that began a three-year economic crisis triggered by reduced demand in Europe for American cotton, declining land values, and reckless practices by local and state banks.

The equally reckless lending practices of the numerous new state banks compounded the economic confusion. To generate more loans, the banks issued more paper money. Even the Second Bank of the United States, which was supposed to bring financial stability to the nation, was caught up in the easy-credit mania. In 1819 newspapers revealed a case of extensive fraud and embezzlement in the Baltimore branch of the Bank of the United States. The disclosure prompted the appointment of Langdon Cheves, a former congressman from South Carolina, as the new president of the B.U.S. Cheves rescued the bank from near ruin, but only by putting pressure on state banks to keep more gold coins in their vaults to back up the loans they were making. State banks in turn put pressure on their debtors, who found it harder to renew old loans or to get new ones. The economic depression lasted about three years, and many people blamed the B.U.S. After the panic passed, resentment of the national bank lingered, especially in the South and the West.

> End of the Era of Good Feelings: Financial Panic of 1819

The Missouri Compromise

As the financial panic deepened into a depression, another cloud appeared on the horizon: the onset of a fierce sectional controversy between North and South over expanding slavery into the new western territories. By 1819 the United States had an equal number of slave and free states—eleven of each. The Northwest Ordinance (1787) had banned slavery north of the Ohio River, and the Southwest Ordinance (1790) had authorized slavery south of the Ohio. In the vast region west of the Mississippi River, however, no move had been made to extend the dividing line across the vast Louisiana Territory, where slavery had existed since the days when France and Spain first colonized the area. At the time, the Missouri Territory encompassed all of the Louisiana Purchase except the state of Louisiana and the Arkansas Territory. The old French town of St. Louis became the funnel through which settlers, largely southerners who brought their slaves with them, rushed westward beyond the Mississippi River.

In 1819, residents in the Missouri Territory asked the House of Representatives, where members from free states outnumbered those from slave states, to approve legislation enabling them to draft a constitution and apply for statehood, its population having passed the minimum of 60,000 white settlers. At that point, Representative James Tallmadge Jr., a New York Republican, stunned Congress by proposing a resolution banning the transport of any more slaves into Missouri. Tallmadge's resolution enraged southern slave owners, many of whom had developed a profitable trade selling slaves to be taken out west. Any effort to restrict slavery in the western territories, southern congressmen threatened, could lead to "disunion" and civil war. In addition, southerners worried that the addition of Missouri as a free state would tip the balance in the Senate against the slave states. After fiery debates, the House, with its northern majority, passed

> End of the Era of Good Feelings: Tallmadge Amendment

THE MISSOURI COMPROMISE, 1820

Legend:
- Free states
- Slave states
- States and territories covered by the compromise

- What caused the sectional controversy over slavery in 1819?
- What were the terms of the Missouri Compromise?
- What was Henry Clay's solution to the Missouri constitution's ban on free blacks in that state?

End of the Era of Good Feelings: Missouri Compromise

the Tallmadge Amendment on an almost strictly sectional vote. The Senate, however, rejected it—similarly along sectional lines.

At about the same time, Maine, which had been part of Massachusetts, applied for statehood. The Senate decided to link Maine's request for statehood with Missouri's, voting to admit Maine as a free state and Missouri as a slave state, thus maintaining the key political balance between free and slave states. Illinois senator Jesse Thomas further extended the so-called **Missouri Compromise** by introducing an amendment to exclude slavery in the rest of the Louisiana Purchase north of latitude 36°30′, Missouri's southern border. Slavery thus would continue in the Arkansas Territory and in the new state of Missouri but would be excluded from the remainder of the sprawling area west of the Mississippi River. By a close vote, the Thomas Amendment passed the House on March 2, 1820.

Then another problem arose. The pro-slavery faction that dominated Missouri's constitutional convention inserted in the proposed state constitution a ban on free blacks and mulattoes (mixed-race people) from residing in the state. This clearly violated the U.S. Constitution. Free blacks were already citizens of many states, including the slave states of North Carolina and Tennessee.

Missouri Compromise (1820) Legislative decision to admit Missouri as a slave state while prohibiting slavery in the area west of the Mississippi River and north of the parallel 36°30′.

The renewed controversy threatened to unravel the deal to admit Missouri as a state until Speaker of the House Henry Clay formulated a "second" Missouri Compromise whereby Missouri's admission as a state would depend upon assurances from its legislature that it would never deny free blacks their constitutional rights. The Missouri legislature approved Clay's suggestion but denied that it had any power to bind the people of the state to the pledge. On August 10, 1821, Missouri became the twenty-fourth state, and the twelfth where slavery was allowed.

Nationalists praised the Missouri Compromise for resolving difficult issues that threatened the stability of the Union. But the ferocity of the debate over the extension of slavery revealed that the compromise had settled little. Sectionalism erupted even within the president's cabinet. President Monroe, a Virginian, insisted that any effort to restrict the spread of slavery violated the spirit if not the language of the Constitution. His secretary of state, the future president John Quincy Adams of Massachusetts, disliked the Missouri Compromise for the opposite reason: because it sustained the Constitution's immoral "bargain between freedom and slavery." A great divide was widening between the nation's two sections: the North dominated by shipping, commerce, manufacturing, and small farms, the South becoming more and more dependent on cotton and slavery.

Henry Clay of Kentucky Clay entered the Senate at twenty-eight, despite the requirement that senators be at least thirty years old. Here, Clay is pictured on a fifty-dollar bill issued in the 1860s.

Nationalist Diplomacy

The efforts of Henry Clay to promote economic nationalism and John Marshall to affirm *judicial* nationalism were reinforced by efforts to practice *diplomatic* nationalism. John Quincy Adams, the secretary of state in the Monroe administration and the son of former president John Adams, aggressively exercised America's growing power abroad so as to clarify and expand the nation's boundaries. He also wanted to establish the nation's dominance in the Western Hemisphere. He thus supported the efforts of Spain's remaining colonies to declare their independence and form their own republics modeled after the American example.

Relations with Britain

The Treaty of Ghent had ended the War of 1812, but it left unsettled several remaining disputes between the United States and Great Britain. American statesmen were eager to resolve those disputes in ways that would reinforce economic nationalism. During James Monroe's presidency, John Quincy Adams oversaw the negotiations of two important treaties, the Rush-Bagot Agreement of 1817 (named after the diplomats who arranged it) and the Convention of 1818, both of which eased tensions with Great Britain. In the Rush-Bagot Agreement, the two nations agreed to limit the number of warships on the Great Lakes between Canada and the United States. The Convention of

> CORE **OBJECTIVE**
> **4.** Identify the federal government's diplomatic accomplishments during this era, and analyze their impact.

> The Rush-Bagot Agreement of 1817 and the Convention of 1818

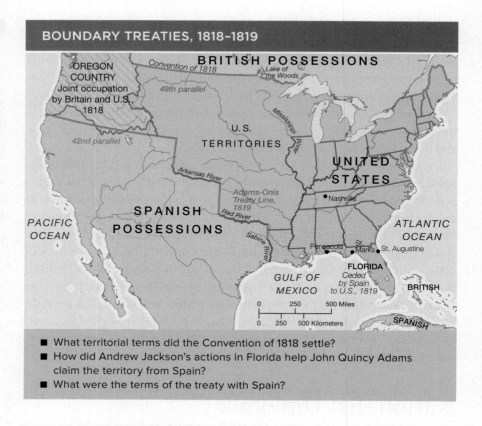

BOUNDARY TREATIES, 1818-1819

- What territorial terms did the Convention of 1818 settle?
- How did Andrew Jackson's actions in Florida help John Quincy Adams claim the territory from Spain?
- What were the terms of the treaty with Spain?

1818 finally settled the disputed northern limit of the Louisiana Purchase by extending America's northern boundary along the 49th parallel westward from what would become Minnesota to the crest of the Rocky Mountains. West of that point, the Oregon Country would be jointly occupied by the British and the Americans, though the boundary remained unsettled.

The Extension of Boundaries

The heightened sense of American nationalism after the War of 1812 revealed itself in continuing efforts to expand the nation's boundaries. Spanish control over Florida during the early nineteenth century was more a technicality than an actuality. Spain, once dominant in the Americas and the world, was now a declining power, unable to enforce its obligations under Pinckney's Treaty of 1795 to keep Indians in the region from raids into American territory. In 1816, U.S. soldiers clashed with a group of escaped slaves who had taken over a British fort (renamed Negro Fort) on the Apalachicola River in West Florida, in the present-day Florida Panhandle. At the same time, Seminole Indians were fighting white settlers in the area. In 1817, Americans burned a Seminole village on the border, killed five Indians, and dispersed the rest.

At that point, Secretary of War John C. Calhoun ordered federal troops to crush the Seminoles. To do so, he summoned General Andrew Jackson from

***Massacre of the Whites by Indians and Blacks in Florida* (1836)** Published in a southerner's account of the Seminole War, this is one of the earliest known depictions of African Americans and Native Americans fighting as allies.

Nashville, Tennessee, to lead an army into Florida. Jackson's orders allowed him to pursue Indians into Spanish territory but not to attack any Spanish forts. A frustrated Jackson pledged to President Monroe that if the United States wanted Spanish Florida, he could conquer it in sixty days.

When it came to Spaniards or Indians, few white Tennesseans—and certainly not Jackson, the hero of the Battle of New Orleans—bothered with legal technicalities. In early 1818, without presidential approval, General Jackson ordered his force of 2,000 federal soldiers, volunteer Tennessee militiamen, and Indian allies among the Creeks to cross into Spanish Florida from their encampment in south Georgia. In April, the Americans assaulted a Spanish fort at St. Marks and destroyed several Seminole villages along the Suwannee River. They also captured and court-martialed British traders accused of provoking Indian attacks. When told that a military trial of the British citizens was illegal, Jackson gruffly replied that the laws of war did not "apply to conflicts with savages." Jackson ordered the immediate execution of the British traders, an illegal action that angered the British government and alarmed Monroe's cabinet. But the Tennessee general kept moving. In May, he captured Pensacola, the Spanish capital of West Florida, and established a provisional American government.

While Jackson's military exploits in what came to be called the Seminole War excited American expansionists, they aroused resentment in Spain and concern in Washington, D.C. Spain demanded that its territory be returned and that Jackson be punished. Monroe's cabinet was at first prepared to disavow Jackson's illegal acts, especially his direct attack on Spanish posts. Privately, Secretary of War Calhoun criticized Jackson for disobeying orders—a stand that would later cause bad blood between these two proud men. But Jackson was highly popular with the public. He also had an important friend, Secretary of State John Quincy Adams. Adams realized that Jackson's conquest of Florida had strengthened his own hand

Andrew Jackson
The controversial general was painted by Anna Claypoole Peale in 1819, the year of his military exploits in Florida. The niece of famed portraitist Charles Willson Peale, she captures the confident demeanor that made Jackson so popular with the public.

Transcontinental Treaty (1819)
Treaty between Spain and the United States that clarified the boundaries of the Louisiana Purchase and arranged for the transfer of Florida to the United States in exchange for cash.

in negotiating with the Spanish minister to purchase the territory. American forces withdrew from Florida, but negotiations resumed with the knowledge that the U.S. Army could retake Florida at any time.

With the fate of Florida a foregone conclusion, Adams turned his eye to a larger goal: a precise definition of the western boundary of the Louisiana Purchase and—his boldest stroke—extension of its boundary all the way to the Pacific coast. In lengthy negotiations with Spain, Adams gradually gave ground on American claims to Texas, then a province of New Spain. But in the final version of the deal, he stuck to his demand that the boundary of the Louisiana Purchase extend all the way to the Pacific Ocean. In 1819, Adams convinced the Spanish to sign the **Transcontinental Treaty** (also called the Adams-Onís Treaty), which gave all of Florida to the United States in return for the U.S. government paying $5 million to settle claims of American citizens against the Spanish government. Florida thus became a U.S. territory. In 1845, it would become a state. The treaty also clarified the western boundary separating the Louisiana Territory from New Spain, explaining that it would run from the Gulf of Mexico north along the Sabine River separating Louisiana from Texas and then in stair-step fashion up to the Red River, along the Red, and up to the Arkansas River. From the source of the Arkansas it would go north to the forty-second parallel and then west to the Pacific coast.

The Monroe Doctrine

Perhaps the most important diplomatic policy crafted by President James Monroe and Secretary of State John Quincy Adams was a determined effort to end all European colonialism in the Western Hemisphere. The Spanish, British, French, Portuguese, Dutch, and Russians still controlled one or more colonies. One consequence of the Napoleonic Wars raging across Europe and the French occupation of Spain and Portugal was a series of independence movements among the Spanish colonies. Within little more than a decade after the flag of rebellion was first raised in 1809 in Ecuador, Spain had lost almost its entire empire in the Americas: La Plata (later Argentina), Bolivia, Chile, Ecuador, Peru, Colombia, Mexico, Paraguay, Uruguay, and Venezuela had all proclaimed their independence, as had Portuguese Brazil, and the United States was the first nation in the world to recognize them as new nations. The only areas still under Spanish control were the islands of Cuba and Puerto Rico and the colony of Santo Domingo on the island of Hispaniola.

In 1823, rumors circulated that the monarchs of Europe were planning to help Spain recover its Latin American colonies by military force. The British foreign minister, George Canning, told the United States that the two countries should jointly oppose any new incursions by Spain, France, and Russia in the Western Hemisphere. Monroe initially agreed with the British proposal—if the London government would agree to recognize the independence of the new nations of Latin America. Adams, however, urged the president to go it alone in prohibiting European involvement in the hemisphere. Adams knew that, as a practical matter, the British navy would stop any aggressive action by European powers in Latin America. The British, moreover, wanted the United States to agree not to acquire any more Spanish territory, including Cuba. Adams preferred to avoid any such commitment.

Monroe incorporated the substance of Adams's views into his annual message to Congress in December 1823. The **Monroe Doctrine**, as it was named a generation later, contained four major points: (1) that "the American continents . . . are henceforth not to be considered as subjects for future colonization by any European powers"; (2) that the political system of the European monarchies was different from that of the United States, which would "consider any attempt on their part to extend their system to any portion of this hemisphere as dangerous to our peace and safety"; (3) that the United States would not interfere with existing European-controlled colonies; and (4) that the United States would keep out of the internal affairs of European nations and their wars.

> Monroe Doctrine (1823)

Although the Monroe Doctrine was a dramatic assertion of American nationalism and became one of the cherished principles of American foreign policy, it had no standing in international law; it was merely a bold statement sent by an American president to Congress. Certainly, none of the European nations recognized the legitimacy of the Monroe Doctrine. The Russian ruler, czar Alexander I, viewed it with "profound contempt." The Russians then controlled Alaska and claimed to own the Oregon Territory as well. Symbolically, however, the Monroe Doctrine was an important statement of American intentions to prevent European involvement in the Western Hemisphere and an example of the young nation's determination to take its place among the world's great powers.

The Rise of Andrew Jackson

CORE **OBJECTIVE**
5. Evaluate the influence of Andrew Jackson on national politics in the 1820s and the developments that enabled him to become president.

America had become a one-party political system after the War of 1812. The refusal of the Federalists to support the war effort against Great Britain had virtually killed the party. In 1820 Monroe was reelected without opposition; the Federalists were so weak they did not even nominate a candidate. While the Republican party was dominant for the moment, however, it was about to follow the Federalists into oblivion. If Monroe's first term was the Era of Good Feelings, his second term became the Era of Bad Feelings, as sectional controversies among the North, South, and West erupted into disputes so violent that they gave birth to a new political party: the Democrats.

One-Party Politics

Almost from the start of James Monroe's second term, in 1821, leading Republicans began positioning themselves to be the next president. Three members of the president's cabinet became active candidates: Secretary of

Monroe Doctrine (1823) U.S. foreign policy that barred further colonization in the Western Hemisphere by European powers and pledged that there would be no American interference with any existing European colonies.

War John C. Calhoun, Secretary of the Treasury William H. Crawford, and Secretary of State John Quincy Adams. Speaker of the House Henry Clay also hungered for the presidency. And a new force appeared in former general Andrew Jackson, a celebrated military hero and the hated enemy of the British, Spanish, Red Stick Creeks, and Seminoles. Jackson had only recently entered the national political scene, having been elected to the U.S. Senate from Tennessee in 1823. The emergence of four strong Republican candidates revealed how fractured the party had become.

Presidential Nominations

In 1822, the Tennessee legislature named Jackson as its choice to succeed President Monroe. Two years later, a mass meeting of Pennsylvanians also endorsed Jackson for president and John C. Calhoun for vice president. Meanwhile, the Kentucky legislature had nominated its favorite son, Henry Clay, in 1822. The Massachusetts legislature nominated John Quincy Adams in 1824. That same year, a group of Republican congressmen nominated William Crawford of Georgia.

Crawford's friends emphasized his devotion to states' rights and strict construction (interpretation) of the Constitution. For his part, Henry Clay continued to champion the economic nationalism of his "American System." Adams shared Clay's belief that the national government should finance internal improvements to stimulate economic development, but he was less strongly committed to tariffs. And meanwhile, Jackson tried to capitalize on his own popularity as a military hero. Thomas Jefferson remained skeptical, believing that Jackson lacked the education and polish to be president: "He is one of the most unfit men I know."

As a self-made military hero, Jackson was an attractive candidate, especially to voters of Irish and Scots-Irish backgrounds. In Jackson, the Irish immigrants found a hero. The son of poor Scots-Irish colonists, he was beloved for having defeated the hated English in the Battle of New Orleans. In addition, the Irish immigrants' distaste for aristocracy, which they associated with centuries of English rule, attracted them to a politician who claimed to represent "the common man."

The "Corrupt Bargain"

The results of the 1824 election were inconclusive. In the Electoral College, Jackson had 99 votes, Adams 84, Crawford 41, and Clay 37. But Jackson did not have the necessary majority of the total votes. In such a circumstance, as in the 1800 election, the Constitution specified that the House of Representatives would make the final decision from among the top three candidates. By the time the House could convene, however, Crawford had suffered a stroke and was ruled out. Whatever else might have been said about the outcome between Jackson and Adams, one thing seemed apparent—the election revealed how deeply divided the nation had become. Sectionalism had defeated nationalism as the Republicans split into warring regional factions. The election was a particularly humiliating defeat for Henry Clay and his American System; voters in New England and New York opposed his call for federal funding of internal improvements, and the South rejected his promotion of the protective tariff.

Now that the deadlocked election had been thrown into the House of Representatives, however, Clay's influence, as Speaker, would be decisive. He scorned the other candidates, but he had little trouble choosing from among them, since he regarded Jackson, his western rival, as a "military chieftain" unfit for the office. Clay disliked Adams, and vice versa, but Adams supported most of what Clay wanted, particularly high tariffs, internal transportation improvements, and a strong national bank. Clay also expected Adams to name him secretary of state, the office that usually led to the White House. A deal between Clay and Adams broke the election deadlock. Clay endorsed Adams, and the House of Representatives elected Adams with 13 state delegation votes to Jackson's 7 and Crawford's 4.

The victory proved costly for Adams, however, as it united his foes and crippled his administration before it even began. Jackson dismissed Clay as a "scoundrel," the "Judas of the West," who had entered into a **"corrupt bargain"** with Adams. Clay would never live down Jackson's claim that he had sold his vote to make Adams president. Almost immediately after the 1824 decision, Jackson's supporters launched a campaign to elect him president in 1828. Crawford's supporters soon moved into the Jackson camp. So, too, did the new vice president, John C. Calhoun of South Carolina, who had run on the ticket with both Adams and Jackson but favored Jackson. (Until the political parties created presidential nominating conventions in 1832, state legislatures could nominate candidates, thus at times creating several nominees from each party).

Corrupt bargain (1824)

John Quincy Adams

John Quincy Adams was one of the ablest men, hardest workers, and finest intellects ever to enter the White House. Yet he also was one of the most ineffective presidents, undercut from the start of his administration by the controversy surrounding his deal with Henry Clay to make him president. In his inaugural address, Adams admitted to voters that he was "less possessed of your confidence . . . than any of my predecessors." Like his father, the stiff and formal Adams lacked the common touch and the politician's gift for compromise. A stubborn, snobbish man, Adams saw two brothers and two sons die from alcoholism. Adams himself suffered from chronic bouts of depression that reinforced his grim self-righteousness and tendency toward self-pity, qualities that did not endear him to fellow politicians or the public. He acknowledged the "defects" in his character, but confessed that he could not change his ways.

Adams's first message to Congress included a grand blueprint for national development, set forth in such a blunt way that it became a disaster for

"corrupt bargain" Scandal in which presidential candidate and Speaker of the House, Henry Clay, secured John Quincy Adams's victory over Andrew Jackson in the 1824 election, supposedly in exchange for naming Clay secretary of state.

him politically. In the boldness and magnitude of its conception, his vision of an expanded federal government outdid the plans of Alexander Hamilton, James Monroe, and Henry Clay. The federal government, Adams stressed, should finance internal improvements (roads, canals, harbors, and bridges), create a national university, support scientific explorations, build astronomical observatories, and establish a department of the interior to manage the vast federal lands. To refrain from using broad federal powers, Adams insisted, "would be treachery to the most sacred of trusts."

Adams's explicit support for increasing the powers of the federal government was so controversial that it led to the death of the Republican party and sparked the emergence of a new party system. Those who agreed with the economic nationalism of Adams and Clay began calling themselves National Republicans. The opposition—the growing party of those supporting Andrew Jackson and states' rights—began calling themselves Democratic Republicans; they would eventually drop the name Republican and become simply Democrats.

President Adams's outspoken efforts to expand the scope of the federal government and his refusal to play backroom politics with Congress condemned his administration to utter frustration from the start. Congress largely ignored his ambitious domestic proposals, and in foreign affairs the triumphs he had scored as secretary of state had no sequels during his presidency.

John Quincy Adams A brilliant man but an ineffective leader, he appears here in his study in 1843. He was the first U.S. president to be photographed.

The Election of Andrew Jackson

Thus the stage was set for the savage **election of 1828**. Both sides engaged in vicious partisan attacks, including false claims that Jackson was the son of a prostitute whose husband was a slave. Adams's supporters denounced Jackson as a hot-tempered, ignorant barbarian, a gambler and slave trader who had participated in numerous duels and frontier brawls, a man whose fame rested upon his reputation as a killer. In addition, his enemies dredged up the story that Jackson had lived in adultery with his wife, Rachel, before they were legally married. (In fact, they had lived together for two years in the mistaken belief that her divorce from her first husband had been approved. As soon as the divorce was official, Andrew and Rachel had remarried.) A furious Jackson blamed Henry Clay for the slurs against his wife. He called Clay "the basest, meanest scoundrel that ever disgraced the image of his god."

election of 1828 Bitter presidential contest between Democrat Andrew Jackson and National-Republican John Quincy Adams (running for re-election), resulting in Jackson's victory.

The Jacksonians, for their part, were equally vicious, condemning Adams as an aristocrat and monarchist, a professional politician who had never had a real job, had been corrupted by foreigners in the courts of Europe, and had allegedly delivered up an American girl to serve the lust of Czar Alexander I while serving as ambassador to Russia. They stressed that Adams despised the common people and that he had gained the presidency in 1824 by a "corrupt bargain" with Clay.

In the 1828 campaign, Jackson held most of the advantages. As a military hero and a fabled Indian fighter, he was beloved in the western and southern states, and as a plantation owner, lawyer, and slaveholder, he had the trust of the southern elite. Debtors and small bankers who hated the national bank also embraced Jackson, and he benefited from a growing spirit of democracy in which many voters viewed Adams as an elitist. When Adams's supporters began referring to Jackson as a "jackass," Jackson embraced the name, using the animal as a symbol for his "tough" campaign. The jackass eventually became the enduring symbol of the Democratic party.

The Rise of the "Common Man" in Politics

Jackson's campaign explicitly appealed to the "common" voters, many of whom were able to vote in a presidential election for the first time. After the Revolution, and especially after 1800, more and more white men had gained the right to vote. In 1776 Pennsylvania had given voting rights to all adult males (black or white) who paid taxes. Vermont, immediately upon its admission to statehood in 1791, became the first state to allow all men to vote, whether they owned property or not. Kentucky, admitted to the Union in 1792, became the second. Tennessee, admitted as a state in 1796, had only a modest property-owning qualification for voting. New Jersey in 1807 and Maryland and South Carolina in 1810 abolished property and taxpaying requirements for voting, and after 1815 the new western states entered the Union with either suffrage for all white men or a low taxpaying requirement. Connecticut in 1818, Massachusetts in 1821, and New York in 1821 abolished property requirements for voting.

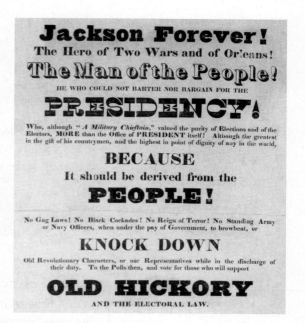

Jackson Forever Proclaiming Jackson a "man of the people," this 1828 poster identifies him with the democratic impulse of the time.

The "democratization" of politics, in which more and more men were allowed to vote, also affected many free black males in northern states, half of which allowed blacks to vote alongside whites. Rufus King, a member of the New York delegation to the Constitutional Convention in 1787, declared that in New York, "a citizen of color was entitled to all the privileges of a citizen . . . [and] entitled to vote."

The extension of voting rights to people with little or no wealth led to the election of politicians sprung from the people rather than the social elite. Jackson, a frontiersman of humble origin who had scrambled up the political ladder by will and tenacity, fit this more democratic ideal. "Adams can write," went one of the campaign slogans, "but Jackson can fight." The former general could write, too, though he once said that he had no respect for a man who could think of only one way to spell a word.

> Democratization of voting

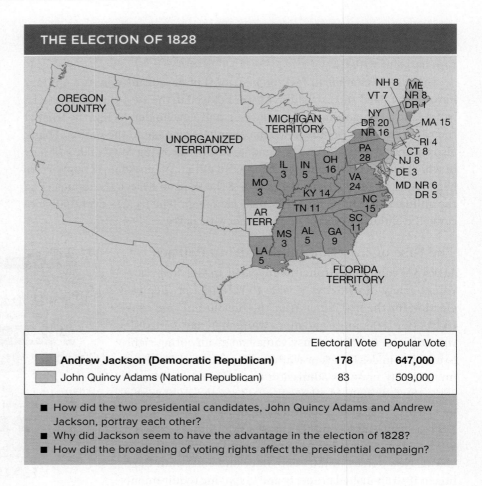

THE ELECTION OF 1828

		Electoral Vote	Popular Vote
	Andrew Jackson (Democratic Republican)	**178**	**647,000**
	John Quincy Adams (National Republican)	83	509,000

- How did the two presidential candidates, John Quincy Adams and Andrew Jackson, portray each other?
- Why did Jackson seem to have the advantage in the election of 1828?
- How did the broadening of voting rights affect the presidential campaign?

Labor Politics

Political participation by labor unions and reformers

With the widespread removal of property qualifications for voting, the working class became an important political force in the form of the Workingmen's parties, first formed in Philadelphia in 1828, and followed soon thereafter by parties in New York City and Boston. The Workingmen's parties were reformist groups in the nation's largest cities devoted to promoting the interests of laborers, including shorter working hours, public schools, allowing all males to vote regardless of the amount of property owned. The Workingmen's parties faded quickly, however. The inexperience of labor politicians left these reformist groups prey to manipulation by political professionals. In addition, major national parties, especially the Democrats, co-opted some of their issues. Labor parties also proved vulnerable to charges of social radicalism, and the courts typically sided with business owners, not workers. Yet while the working-class parties elected few candidates, they did succeed in drawing notice to their demands, many of which attracted the support of middle-class reformers. Above all, they promoted free public education for all children and sought to end the practice of imprisoning people for not paying their debts, causes that won widespread popular support. The labor parties and unions also called for a ten-hour workday to prevent employers from abusing workers. In large part because of his background as a "common man," union members loved Andrew Jackson.

President Jackson

When the 1828 election returns came in, Jackson had won by a comfortable margin. The electoral vote was 178 to 83, and the popular vote was about 647,000 to 509,000 (the figures vary). Adams had won New Jersey, Delaware, all of New England (except 1 of Maine's 9 electoral votes), 16 of the 36 electoral votes from New York, and 6 of the 11 from Maryland. The rest belonged to Jackson. The new president, the first to come from a western state, entered office still seething with resentment at the way his opponents had smeared the reputation of his wife, who had died a few days after learning of the political attacks on her and her "tarnished" marriage. President-elect Jackson wept at her funeral while reading the inscription on her gravestone: "A being so gentle, so virtuous, slander might wound but could not dishonor." Now, he relished the chance to take revenge on those whose attacks had caused Rachel's heart attack and death. More important, Jackson wanted to launch a new "democratic" era in American political development that would silence his critics, restore government to "the people," and take power away from the Eastern "elite."

■ **Nationalism** After the War of 1812, the federal government pursued many policies to strengthen the national economy. The *Tariff of 1816* protected American manufacturing from foreign competition, and the *Second Bank of the United States* provided a stronger currency. Madison, Monroe, and Adams all promoted an active economic role for the federal government, including a national bank, a protective tariff, and federally-funded *internal improvements,* such as roads and canals. Led by John Marshall, the Supreme Court limited the powers of states and strengthened the power of the federal government in *Dartmouth College v. Woodward (1819)* and *McCulloch v. Maryland (1819).* The Marshall court interpreted the Constitution as giving Congress the right to take any action not forbidden by the Constitution as long as the purpose of such laws was within the "scope of the Constitution." In *Gibbons v. Ogden (1824),* the Marshall court protected contract rights against state action and established the federal government's supremacy over interstate commerce, thereby promoting growth of the national economy.

■ **Sectionalism** Henry Clay's American System supported economic nationalism by endorsing a national bank, a protective tariff, and federally-funded internal improvements, such as roads and canals. Many Americans, however, remained more tied to the needs of their particular sections of the country. People in the different regions—North, South, and West—disagreed about which economic policies best served their interests. As settlers streamed west, the extension of slavery into the new territories became the predominant political concern, eventually requiring both sides to compromise repeatedly to avoid civil war.

■ **Era of Good Feelings** James Monroe's term in office was initially labeled the Era of Good Feelings because it began with peace and prosperity. Two major events spelled the end of the Era of Good Feelings: the financial *Panic of 1819* and the controversial *Missouri Compromise (1820).* The explosive growth of the cotton culture transformed life in the South, in part by encouraging the expansion of slavery, which moved west with southern planters. But in 1819 the sudden collapse of world cotton prices devastated the southern economy and soon affected the national economy as well. The Missouri Compromise, a short-term solution to the issue of allowing slavery in the western territories, exposed the emotions and turmoil that the tragic system generated.

■ **National Diplomacy** The main diplomatic achievements of the period between the end of the War of 1812 and the coming civil war concerned the extension of America's contested boundaries and the resumption of trade with its old enemy, Great Britain. To the north, U.S. diplomatic achievements established northern borders with Great Britain. To the south, the *Transcontinental Treaty (1819)* with Spain extended the boundaries of the United States. The *Monroe Doctrine (1823)* declared that the Americas were no longer open to colonization and proclaimed American neutrality in European affairs.

■ **The Election of 1828** The demise of the Federalists ended the first party system in America, leaving the Republicans as the only political party in the nation. The seeming unity of the Republicans was shattered by the election of 1824, which Andrew Jackson lost as a result of what he believed was a *"corrupt bargain"* between John Quincy Adams and Henry Clay. Andrew Jackson won the presidency in the *election of 1828* by rallying southern and western voters with his appeal to the common man. His election opened a new era in national politics that reflected the democratization of voting in most states (at least for white men) and the development of political organizations that rallied voters to particular personalities and issues.

KEY TERMS

CHRONOLOGY

1811	Construction of the National Road begins
1816	Second Bank of the United States is established
	First "protective" tariff goes into effect
1817	Rush-Bagot Agreement between the United States and Great Britain creates an unfortified border between the United States and Canada
1818	The Convention of 1818 establishes the northern border of the Louisiana Purchase at the 49th parallel and the joint occupation of Oregon by the United States and Great Britain
1819	Supreme Court issues *McCulloch v. Maryland* decision
	United States and Spain agree to the Transcontinental Treaty
	Tallmadge Amendment
1820	Congress accepts the Missouri Compromise
1821	Florida, Maine, and Missouri become states
1823	President Monroe enunciates the principles of the Monroe Doctrine
1824	Supreme Court issues *Gibbons v. Ogden* decision
	John Quincy Adams wins the presidential election by what some critics claim is a "corrupt bargain" with Henry Clay
1828	Andrew Jackson wins presidential contest

INQUIZITIVE

Go to InQuizitive to see what you've learned—and learn what you've missed—with personalized feedback along the way.

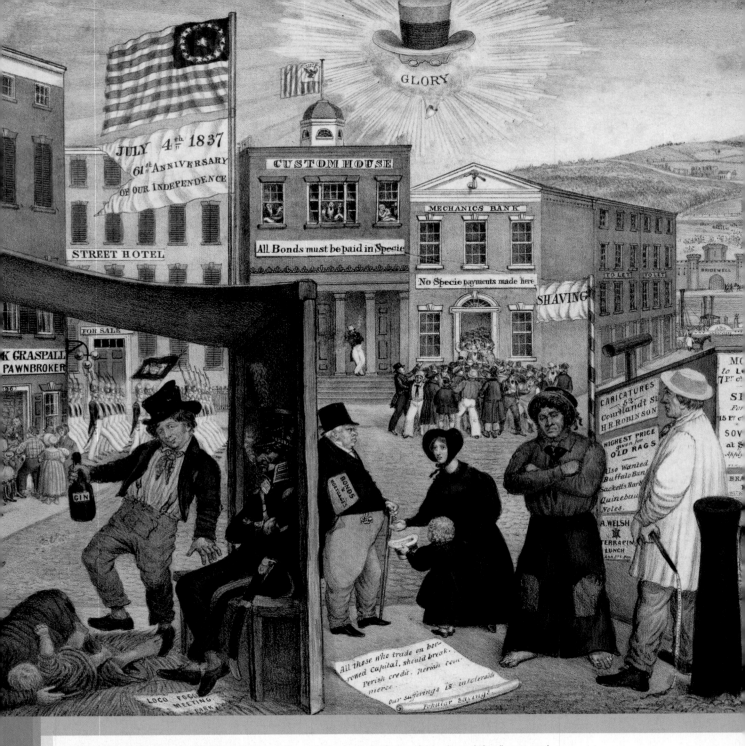

HARD TIMES IN THE JACKSONIAN ERA Although Andrew Jackson championed the "poor and humble," his economic policies contributed to the Panic of 1837, a financial crisis that hit the working class the hardest. This cartoon illustrates New York City during the seven-year depression: a frantic mob storms a bank, while in the foreground, a widow begs on the street with her child, surrounded by a banker or landlord and a barefoot sailor. At left, there is a drunken member of the Bowery Toughs gang and a down-on-his-luck militiaman. The cartoonist places the blame on Jackson, whose hat, glasses, and pipe overlook the scene. The white flag at left wryly states: "July 4, 1827, 61st Anniversary of Our Independence."

The Jacksonian Era

1828–1840

Andrew Jackson was the first president from a western state (Tennessee), the first to have been born in a log cabin, the first not to have come from a prominent colonial family, and the last to have participated in the Revolutionary War. Born in 1767 along the border between the two Carolinas, he grew up in a struggling single-parent household. Jackson's father was killed in a farm accident three weeks before Andrew was born, forcing his widowed mother Elizabeth to scratch out a living as a housekeeper.

During the Revolution, the Jackson boys joined in the fighting against the British, and one of Andrew's brothers died in battle. In 1781, fourteen-year-old Andrew was captured and imprisoned. When he refused to shine a British officer's boots, the officer slashed him with a sword, leaving ugly scars on his head and arm. Soon after her son was released, Elizabeth Jackson, who had helped nurse injured American soldiers, died of cholera. The orphaned Andrew Jackson thereafter despised the British, blaming them for the deaths of his brother and mother.

Andrew Jackson loved a good fight. During one duel in 1806 with a man who had insulted his wife, Jackson let his opponent fire first. For his gallantry, the future president received a bullet that wedged itself next to his heart and nearly killed him. He nevertheless straightened himself, patiently took aim, and killed his foe. "I should have hit him," Jackson claimed, "if he had shot me through the brain."

CORE
OBJECTIVES INQUIZITIVE

1. Describe Andrew Jackson's major beliefs regarding the common man, the presidency, and the proper role of government in the nation's economy.

2. Evaluate Jackson's response to the nullification crisis.

3. Analyze Andrew Jackson's legacy regarding the status of Indians in American society.

4. Explain the causes of the economic depression of the late 1830s and the emergence of the Whig party.

5. Assess the strengths and weaknesses of Jackson's transformational presidency.

After the Revolution, the self-taught Jackson became a frontier attorney in backwoods Tennessee, where he dealt mostly with disputes over land claims. He moved to Nashville in 1788, where he fell in love with Rachel Donelson Robards, a woman he lived with before she was legally divorced from her first husband. The Jacksons developed a happy marriage, but gossip about the origins of their relationship dogged them until Rachel's heart attack and death in December 1828.

In 1796, when Tennessee became a state, voters elected Jackson to the U.S. House and then to the Senate, where he served only a year before returning to Tennessee and becoming a judge. The ambitious Jackson made a lot of money, first as an attorney, then as a buyer and seller of horses, land, and slaves. Jackson eventually owned a hundred slaves on his large cotton plantation, called the Hermitage, near Nashville. Like most of his neighbors, he had no moral reservations about slavery and at times could be a cruel master. After one of his slaves escaped, Jackson offered a large reward for his recapture, and promised "ten dollars extra for every hundred lashes a person will give [him] to the amount of three hundred." When not farming or raising racehorses, Jackson served as the iron-willed commander of the Tennessee militia.

Many American political leaders cringed at the thought of the rough-hewn, short-tempered Jackson, who had run roughshod over international law in his war against the British and Seminoles in Florida, presiding over the nation. "His passions are terrible," said elderly Thomas Jefferson. John Quincy Adams scorned Jackson "as a barbarian and savage who could scarcely spell his name." Jackson dismissed such criticism as an example of the "Eastern elite" trying to control American politics.

Concerns about Jackson's fitness for the presidency were heightened by the riotous scene at the White House after his inauguration ceremony in March 1829. In a symbolic effort to reach out to the "common" people, Jackson opened the party to anyone. To his surprise, the huge crowd of jubilant Democrats quickly turned into a drunken mob. Dishes and glasses were smashed and furniture broken. Revelers in the presidential mansion stood in muddy boots on chairs, ripped down drapery, and trampled on rugs. Supreme Court Justice Joseph Story said he had never seen such "a mixture" of people in the White House. "The reign of KING MOB seemed triumphant," he wrote. The partying crowd was finally lured out of the White House when the liquor barrels were carried out onto the lawn.

Jackson was a quite different kind of president from George Washington, Thomas Jefferson, and James Madison. He smoked a corncob pipe and chewed tobacco. Tall and lean—over six feet tall but only 140 pounds—with penetrating eyes, a long nose, jutting chin, and iron-gray hair that intensified his steely personality, *Old Hickory* (a nickname given to Jackson by his soldiers because he was as tough as the hard wood of a hickory tree) loved the rough-and-tumble combat of political life. "I was born for a storm," he once boasted. "A calm [life] does not suit me."

In his extraordinary novel *Moby-Dick* (1851), Herman Melville observed that it was the "great democratic God" who picked "up Andrew Jackson from the pebbles; who didst hurl him upon a warhorse; who didst thunder him higher than a throne!" General Jackson did indeed take the nation by storm. No political figure was so widely loved or more deeply hated. As a self-made soldier, politician, and planter, Jackson craved wealth and fame, and he won both. He symbolized the emergence of the "market revolution" in the economy and the "common man" in politics (he meant white men only) and stamped his name and, more important, his ideas, personality, and values on an entire era of American history.

Jacksonian Democracy

During the 1820s and 1830s, American political life was transformed as more and more working men were allowed to vote and hold office. Most of the new western states admitted to the Union reduced property-owning requirements for voting and allowed virtually any white male to run for elected office. "The principle of universal suffrage," announced the *U.S. Magazine and Democratic Review*, "meant that white males of age constituted the political nation." Jacksonian Democrats expanded economic opportunity and political participation for the "common man" (white factory workers, craftsmen and mechanics, small farmers, and land-hungry frontiersmen). Andrew Jackson promised to protect "the poor and humble" from the "tyranny of wealth and power." His goal was to elevate the "laboring classes" of white men who "love liberty and desire nothing but equal rights and equal laws." Jackson's concept of greater democracy, however, did not include women, African Americans, or Native Americans.

Jackson was the first president to view himself as a representative of "the people." As such, he expected to exercise expanded executive powers at the expense of the legislative and judicial branches. The ruling political and economic elite must be removed, he said, for "the people" are "the government, the sovereign power" in the United States, and they had elected him president. In general, Jackson and the Democrats believed that "the world is governed too much." The nation's seventh president wanted to reduce federal spending, pay off the federal debt (a "national curse"), destroy the Second Bank of the United States, and remove the "ill-fated race" of Indians from the East so that they could retain their way of life while white Americans exploited their ancestral lands. In pursuing these ambitious goals, he exercised presidential authority more boldly than any of his predecessors.

Jackson's heroic stature and combative personality attracted enthusiastic supporters among westerners as well as workingmen in the East. Jackson was also an openly partisan president. He actively lobbied Congress and benefited from a national Democratic party "machine" run by his trusted

CORE **OBJECTIVE**

1. Describe Andrew Jackson's major beliefs regarding the common man, the presidency, and the proper role of government in the nation's economy.

Promoting the "common man"

Expanded presidential authority

All Creation Going to the White House In this depiction of Jackson's inauguration party, satirist Robert Cruikshank draws a visual parallel to Noah's Ark, suggesting that people of all walks of life were now welcome to the White House.

secretary of state (later his vice-president) Martin Van Buren, a New York lawyer with a shrewd political sense whose investments had made him rich.

The Spoils System and Presidential Conventions

The spoils system

To dislodge the eastern political elite, Jackson replaced many federal officials with his own supporters. Government jobs, he argued, belonged to the people, not to career bureaucrats. During his two presidential terms, Jackson replaced about a fifth of the federal officeholders with his own friends and supporters, not all of whom were qualified for their new positions. Such partisan behavior came to be called "the spoils system," since, as a prominent Democrat declared, "to the victor goes the spoils."

Birth of presidential nominating conventions

Jackson also sought to "democratize" the way that presidential candidates were selected. Since the presidency of George Washington, most nominees had been chosen by party "caucuses" of prominent congressmen and senators. Jackson hated the idea of legislators nominating presidents. Their doing so had led to the "corrupt bargain" between Henry Clay and John Quincy Adams that had denied him the presidency and instead elected Adams to succeed James Monroe in 1824. In 1832, he would convince the Democrats to stage their first presidential nominating convention as a means of involving more people in the process of selecting a candidate. The innovation of presidential nominating conventions reinforced Jackson's image as a man of the people fighting against entrenched special interests.

The Eaton Affair

From the outset, Andrew Jackson's administration was divided between supporters of Secretary of State Martin Van Buren and those of Vice President John C. Calhoun of South Carolina, both of whom wanted to succeed Jackson as president. Jackson turned mostly to Van Buren for advice. But

Calhoun, a Yale graduate of towering intellect and fiery determination, could not be taken lightly. Although earlier a nationalist, he now was determined to defend southern interests, especially the preservation of the slave-based cotton economy that had made him a rich planter.

In his rivalry with Calhoun, Van Buren had luck on his side in the form of a social scandal known as the Peggy Eaton affair. John Eaton, a former Tennessee senator, was a close friend of Jackson who had managed his 1824 presidential campaign. Three months before Eaton became Jackson's secretary of war, he had married his mistress, Peggy O'Neale Timberlake, whose husband, a naval officer, had reportedly committed suicide upon learning of her affair with Eaton. Eaton's enemies criticized the "unseemly haste" of the marriage, and Peggy Eaton, the lively, flirtatious daughter of an Irish tavern owner, was not a virtuous woman in the eyes of the proper ladies of Washington. Floride Calhoun, the vice president's wife, especially objected to Mrs. Eaton's lowly origins and unsavory past. She pointedly snubbed her, and the other cabinet wives followed suit.

> The politics of social scandal

Mrs. Eaton's plight reminded Jackson of the mean-spirited gossip that had plagued his own wife, Rachel. He strenuously defended Mrs. Eaton, insisting that she was as pure "as a virgin." His cabinet members, however, were unable to cure their wives of what the unmarried Van Buren dubbed "the Eaton Malaria." Mrs. Eaton finally withdrew from the social scene in Washington, and her husband resigned from the cabinet. The outraged Jackson linked the social abuse heaped on Peggy Eaton to his arch-enemy, John C. Calhoun. Secretary of War Eaton was the only cabinet member who did not support Calhoun's plan to be the next president. In a vengeful rage, Jackson concluded that Vice President Calhoun was one of the "most dangerous men living—a man devoid of principle" who "would sacrifice his friend, his country, and forsake his god, for selfish personal ambition."

Jackson decided that the only way to restore harmony in his warring cabinet was to disband it and start over. On April 4, 1829, the president accepted John Eaton's resignation. Four days later, Martin Van Buren resigned. The rest of the cabinet members left in following weeks, enabling Jackson to appoint a new group of senior officers. "A revolution has taken place in the Capitol of the United States," announced the newspaper headlines. Thereafter, Jackson relied more upon the advice of his so-called "kitchen cabinet," an informal group of close friends and supporters. Critics claimed that Jackson did not have the skill to lead the nation. One newspaper announced that the ship of state "is sinking and the rats are flying! The hull is too leaky to mend, and the hero of two wars and a half has not the skill to keep it afloat."

> Jackson's "kitchen cabinet"

Internal Improvements

Concerns that Jackson was not in control of things quickly disappeared, however, for he decisively used his executive authority to limit the role of the federal government—while at the same time delivering additional blows to John C. Calhoun and to Henry Clay, the man Jackson blamed for

> Jackson vetoes the Maysville Road Bill

King Andrew the First
Opponents considered Jackson's veto of the Maysville Road Bill an abuse of power. This cartoon shows "King Andrew" trampling on the Constitution, internal improvements, and the Bank of the United States.

Second Bank of the United States National bank established in 1816 when the charter for the First Bank of the United States expired.

The Bank War Political struggle in the early 1830s between President Jackson and financier Nicholas Biddle over the renewing of the Second Bank's charter.

having "stolen" the 1824 election from him. In 1830, Congress passed a bill supported by Calhoun and Clay that authorized the use of federal monies to build a sixty-mile-long road from Maysville, Kentucky, to Lexington, Kentucky, Clay's hometown. President Jackson, urged on by Martin Van Buren, vetoed the bill on the grounds that the proposed road was a "purely local matter," being solely in the state of Kentucky, and thus outside the domain of Congress; funding such local projects would require a constitutional amendment. Clay was stunned. "We are all shocked and mortified by the rejection of the Maysville road," he wrote a friend. But he had no luck convincing Congress to override the presidential veto.

The Bank War

Jackson showed the same principled stubbornness in dealing with the national bank as he did in vetoing the Maysville Road Bill. The charter for the First Bank of the United States (B.U.S.) had expired in 1811 and had been renewed in 1816 as the **Second Bank of the United States**, which soon became the largest corporation in the nation and the only truly national business enterprise. The second B.U.S. held all federal funds (mostly from land sales) and also issued paper money (backed by gold and silver) as the national currency. With twenty-nine branches around the nation, the B.U.S. had helped accelerate business expansion. It had also supplied a stable currency by forcing the 464 state banks to keep enough gold coins in their vaults to back their own paper currency, which they loaned to people and businesses. With federal revenues soaring from land sales during the early 1830s, the B.U.S., led by the brilliant but arrogant Nicholas Biddle, had accumulated massive amounts of money—and economic power.

Even though the national bank was beneficial to the infant American economy, it had been controversial from the start. Local banks and state governments, especially in the South and West, feared the growing power of the "monopolistic" national bank. Southerners and westerners claimed that the small group of B.U.S. directors, most of whom lived in the Northeast, were preventing the state banks from lending as much as they wanted and impeding businesses from borrowing as much as they wanted.

Throughout his life Andrew Jackson had hated banks and bankers, whom he called "vipers and thieves." He admitted that he had "always been afraid of banks"—especially the national bank—because they exercised too much power over the economy and the people. Jackson spoke for many Americans who felt that banks favored the "rich and powerful" men in the East. Jackson also distrusted paper money because banks printed too much of it, causing prices to rise (inflation). He wanted only coins to be used for economic transactions. "I think it right to be perfectly frank with you," Jackson told Nicholas Biddle in 1829. "I do not dislike your Bank any more than [I dislike] all banks."

Early on, the president resolved to destroy the B.U.S., pledging "to put his foot upon the head of the monster and crush him to the dust." The national bank may have become too powerful, but **The Bank War** between Jackson and Biddle revealed that the president never truly understood the bank's

Rechartering the Bank
Jackson's effort to defeat the recharter of the B.U.S. is likened to fighting a hydra, a many-headed serpent from Greek mythology. Just as the hydra would sprout two heads when one was severed, for every one B.U.S. supporter that Jackson subdued, even more B.U.S. supporters would emerge to take his place.

role or policies. The national bank had provided a stable currency for the expanding economy, as well as a mechanism for controlling the pace of economic growth by regulating the ability of branch banks and state banks to issue paper currency.

The Recharter Effort

Although the second B.U.S. charter would run through 1836, Nicholas Biddle could not afford to wait until then for its renewal. Leaders of the National Republican party, especially Henry Clay and Daniel Webster (who was legal counsel to the B.U.S. as well as a senator), told Biddle that he needed to get the charter renewed before the 1836 presidential election. They assured Biddle that the Congress would renew the charter. And Biddle himself grew overconfident about his bank's future. "This worthy President thinks because he has scalped Indians . . . he is to have his way with the Bank." Biddle thought otherwise. "I have been for years in the daily exercise of more personal authority than any President habitually enjoys." But Biddle and his political allies failed to grasp both Jackson's tenacity and the depth of public resentment toward the national bank. Jackson's disgust for the B.U.S. reflected the concerns of many voters. In the end, Biddle, Clay, and the National Republicans unintentionally handed Jackson a popular issue on the eve of the election.

Early in the summer of 1832, both houses of Congress passed the Bank Recharter Bill. On July 10, 1832, however, Jackson vetoed the bill, sending it back to Congress with a blistering criticism of the bank's monopoly powers. Jackson claimed that the B.U.S. was both unconstitutional (although the

Jackson vetoes renewal of B.U.S. charter

Supreme Court disagreed) and "dangerous to our liberties." The B.U.S. made "the rich richer and the potent more powerful" while discriminating against "the humble members of society—the farmers, mechanics, and laborers" who were justified in their complaints about the "injustice" of the national bank. Daniel Webster accused Jackson of using the bank issue "to stir up the poor against the rich." But Webster could not convince the Senate to override the veto, thus setting the stage for a nationwide financial crisis and a dramatic presidential campaign. The overriding issue in the 1832 election was the future of the Bank of the United States.

CORE OBJECTIVE

2. Evaluate Jackson's response to the nullification crisis.

Nullification

The vetoes of the Maysville Road bill and the B.U.S. recharter illustrated Jackson's forceful personality. He eventually would veto twelve congressional bills, more than all of the previous presidents combined. Critics claimed that his behavior was "monarchical" in its frequent defiance of the will of Congress. Jackson, however, remained determined to strengthen the executive branch in order to strengthen the Union. His commitment to nationalism over sectionalism was nowhere more evident than in his handling of the nullification crisis in South Carolina.

Calhoun and the Tariff

Vice President John C. Calhoun became Andrew Jackson's fiercest critic. In part because of his personal feud with the president, the brilliant but brittle South Carolinian had abandoned his earlier stance as an economic nationalist and had become the leading states' rights advocate for the South. Conditions in his home state led him to change his political position. The financial panic of 1819 had sparked a nationwide depression, and throughout the 1820s, South Carolina had suffered from a collapse in cotton prices. The state lost almost 70,000 residents who moved west during the 1820s; it would lose nearly twice that number in the 1830s, with many moving to Texas.

Most South Carolinians blamed their economic woes on the Tariff of 1828, which aroused such hatred it was referred to as the **"Tariff of Abominations."** By taxing British textiles coming into U.S. markets, the 1828 tariff on imported cloth hurt southern cotton growers by reducing British demand for raw cotton from America. It also hurt southerners by raising the prices they had to pay for imports.

The tariff debate revealed how the North and South had developed into quite different regions, with different economic interests and different ways of protecting those interests. Massachusetts was prospering while South Carolina was struggling. But the tariff was not the only factor explaining South Carolina's problems. Thousands of acres of farmland across the state were exhausted from constant overplanting. In addition, South Carolina

"Tariff of Abominations" (1828) Tax on imported goods, including British cloth and clothing, that strengthened New England textile companies but hurt southern consumers, who experienced a decrease in British demand for raw cotton grown in the South.

cotton planters now faced competition from the new cotton-growing states in the Old Southwest: Alabama, Mississippi, Louisiana, and Arkansas.

In a lengthy pamphlet called the *South Carolina Exposition and Protest* (1828), written in secret by John C. Calhoun, the South Carolinian claimed that the Tariff of 1828 favored the interests of New England textile manufacturing over southern agriculture. Under such circumstances, he argued, a state could "nullify," or veto, a federal law it deemed unconstitutional. **Nullification** was the ultimate weapon for those determined to protect states' rights against federal authority. As President Jackson and others pointed out, however, allowing states to pick and choose which federal laws they would follow would have created national confusion.

> Calhoun's theory of nullification

The Webster-Hayne Debate

The controversy over the Tariff of 1828 simmered until 1830, when the great Webster-Hayne debate in Congress sharpened the lines between the respective proponents of states' rights and national authority. In a fiery speech, Senator Robert Y. Hayne of South Carolina, a rising star among southern defenders of states' rights, argued that the Union was created by the states, and the states therefore had the right to nullify federal laws.

> Webster-Hayne debate: States' rights vs. national unity

Senator Daniel Webster of Massachusetts then rose to defend the North—and the Union. Blessed with a thunderous voice and a theatrical

nullification Right claimed by some states to veto a federal law deemed unconstitutional.

***Webster Replying to Senator Hayne* (1848)** The eloquent Massachusetts senator challenges the argument for nullification in the Webster-Hayne debate.

flair, Webster presented a nationalistic view of the Constitution, arguing that if a single state could nullify a federal law, then the Union would be a "rope of sand." How could there ever be a "nation" in which the individual states could pick and choose which federal laws to follow? For America to remain a nation, Webster said, a state could neither nullify a federal law nor secede from the Union. South Carolina's defiance of federal authority, he charged, "is nothing more than resistance by *force*—it is disunion by *force*—it is secession by *force*—it is Civil War."

Webster's closing statement was printed in virtually every newspaper in the nation: "Liberty and Union, now and forever, one and inseparable." Abraham Lincoln later called it "the very best speech ever delivered." In the end, Webster had the better argument. The Union and majority rule meant more to westerners, including President Jackson, than the abstractions of states' rights and nullification. And most political leaders agreed with Webster that the states could not act separately from the national government. As Jackson said, the Constitution and its laws were "supreme."

The Split with Calhoun

Jackson: The preservation of the Union

Like Calhoun, Jackson was a cotton-planting southern slaveholder, so many southerners expected him to support their resistance to the federal tariff. Jackson was sympathetic—until Calhoun and South Carolina threatened to "nullify" federal laws they did not like. He then turned on Calhoun and South Carolina with the same angry force he had directed toward the advancing British army at New Orleans in 1815. On April 13, 1830, the Democratic party hosted the first annual Jefferson Day dinner to honor the birthday of the former president. When it was Jackson's turn to propose a toast to Jefferson's memory, he raised his glass, glared at Calhoun, and announced: "Our Union—It must be preserved!" Calhoun then stood and countered with a toast to "the Union, next to our liberty most dear! May we all remember that it can only be preserved by respecting the rights of the States and distributing equally the benefit and the burden of the Union!" Jackson's toast had set off a bombshell that exploded the plans of Calhoun and the nullifiers. The rift between the two proud men prompted Jackson to take a dramatic step: he removed all of Calhoun's supporters from his cabinet. Five of eight cabinet members were forced to resign.

The South Carolina Nullification Ordinance

In the fall of 1831, Jackson announced his willingness to serve a second term as president. He also tried to defuse the confrontation with South Carolina by calling on Congress to reduce the tariff. Congress responded with the Tariff of 1832, which lowered duties on many imported items, although tariffs on cloth and iron remained high.

The new tariff, however, was not enough to satisfy Calhoun and others in his home state. South Carolina seethed with resentment toward Jackson and the federal government. One hotheaded South Carolina congressman called the Union a "foul monster." He and other white South Carolinians, living in the only state where enslaved Africans were a majority of the population, feared that if the northern representatives in Congress were powerful enough to create such discriminatory tariffs, they might eventually vote to end slavery. Calhoun declared that the "peculiar domestic institutions of the southern states" (by which he meant slavery) were at stake in the debate over tariff policy.

In November 1832, a South Carolina state convention overwhelmingly adopted a Nullification Ordinance that repudiated the "unconstitutional" federal tariff acts of 1828 and 1832 (declaring them "null, void, and no law"). If federal authorities tried to use force to collect the tariffs, South Carolina would secede from the Union, they vowed. The reassembled state legislature then chose Senator Robert Hayne as governor and elected Calhoun to succeed him as senator. Calhoun resigned as vice president so that he could defend the nullification policy in the Senate.

> South Carolina Nullification Ordinance

Jackson's Firm Response

In the nullification crisis, South Carolina, "feisty as a gamecock," found itself standing alone. Other southern states expressed sympathy, but none endorsed nullification. President Jackson's public response was moderate. He promised to use "firmness and forbearance" with South Carolina but stressed that nullification "means insurrection and war; and the other states have a right to put it down."

In private, however, Jackson was furious. He threatened to hang Calhoun, Hayne, and other "nullifiers" if there was any bloodshed. "Surely the president is exaggerating," Governor Hayne of South Carolina remarked to Senator Thomas Hart Benton of Missouri. Benton, who years before had been in a fistfight with Jackson, replied: "I have known General Jackson a great many years, and when he speaks of hanging it is time to look for a rope."

In his annual message to the nation, delivered December 4, 1832, Jackson appealed to the people of South Carolina not to follow false leaders such as Calhoun: "The laws of the United States must be executed. . . . Those who told you that you might peaceably prevent their execution, deceived you. . . . Their object is disunion. . . . Disunion by armed force is treason."

Clay's Compromise

President Jackson then sent federal soldiers and a warship to Charleston to uphold national authority. Governor Hayne responded by mobilizing the state militia, and the two sides verged on civil war. In early 1833, the president requested from Congress the **"Force Bill"** authorizing him to use the U.S. Army to "force" compliance with federal law in South Carolina. At that point, the nullifiers backed down; the South Carolina legislature postponed the actual enforcement of the nullification ordinances in hopes that a

The "Force Bill" (1833) Legislation, sparked by the nullification crisis in South Carolina, that authorized the president's use of the army to compel states to comply with federal law.

compromise might be reached. Passage of the compromise bill in Congress depended upon the support of Senator Henry Clay, himself a slaveholding planter, who finally yielded to those urging him to save the day for the Union. A fellow senator told Clay that these "South Carolinians are good fellows, and it would be a pity to see Jackson hang them." Clay agreed. On February 12, 1833, he circulated a plan to reduce the federal tariff gradually. It was less than South Carolina preferred, but it got the nullifiers out of the dilemma they had created. Calhoun supported the compromise: "He who loves the Union must desire to see this agitating question [the tariff] brought to a termination."

On March 1, 1833, Congress passed the compromise tariff and the Force Bill, and the next day Jackson signed both. Calhoun rushed home to convince the rebels in his state to back down. The South Carolina convention then met and rescinded its nullification of the tariff acts. In a face-saving gesture, the delegates nullified the Force Bill, which Jackson no longer needed. Both sides were able to claim victory. Jackson had upheld the supremacy of the Union, and South Carolina had secured a reduction of the federal tariff. But there was still the fundamental issue of southern slaveholders feeling increasingly threatened by growing anti-slavery sentiment in the North. "The struggle, so far from being over," a defiant Calhoun wrote, "is not more than fairly commenced."

CORE **OBJECTIVE**

3. Analyze Andrew Jackson's legacy regarding the status of Indians in American society.

Jackson's Indian Policy

If President Jackson's firm stance against nullification constituted his finest hour, his forcible removal of Indians from their ancestral lands was one of his lowest moments. Like most white frontiersmen, Jackson viewed Indians as barbarians without rights, who should be treated as "subjects," not "nations." After his election in 1828, he recommended that the Eastern Indians be moved to the Great American Desert west of the Mississippi River, in what became Oklahoma. State laws in Alabama, Georgia, and Mississippi had already abolished tribal units and stripped them of their powers, rejected ancestral Indian land claims, and denied Indians the right to vote or testify in court. Jackson claimed that relocating the Eastern Indians was a pragmatic act of mercy, a "wise and humane policy" that would save the Indians from "utter annihilation" if they tried to hold on to their lands.

Indian Removal

Indian Removal Act (1830) Law permitting the forced relocation of Indians to federal lands west of the Mississippi River in exchange for the land they occupied in the East and South.

In response to a request from Jackson, Congress in 1830 debated the **Indian Removal Act**, which authorized the president to disavow earlier treaty commitments and force the 74,000 Indians remaining in the East and South to move to federal lands west of the Mississippi River. Relocating the Native Americans was President Jackson's top priority. But it provoked opposition, not only among the Indian peoples but also among

American reformers, who deluged Congress with petitions that criticized the removal policy and warned that the policy would bring "enduring shame" on the nation. Even David "Davy" Crockett of Tennessee, a frontiersman like President Jackson, opposed the forced removal of the Indian nations. But to no avail. In late May 1830, Congress narrowly passed and Jackson eagerly signed the Indian Removal Act.

By 1835, some 46,000 Indians had been relocated across the Mississippi River at government expense. The policy was enacted with remarkable speed, but not fast enough to satisfy whites in the South and Southwest. Unlike in the Ohio Valley and the Great Lakes region, where the flow of white settlers had constantly *pushed* the Indians westward, settlers in the Old Southwest moved across Kentucky, Tennessee, and Georgia into Florida, Alabama, and Mississippi, *surrounding* the so-called Five Civilized Tribes: the Cherokee, Choctaw, Chickasaw, Creek, and Seminoles—the Indian peoples who had taken on many features of white society, abandoning traditional hunting practices to develop farms, build roads, schools, and churches, and create trading posts and newspapers. Many Cherokees, Creeks, and Choctaws had married whites, adopted their clothing and food, and converted to Christianity.

Most of the northern Indians were too weak to resist being relocated. But in Illinois and the Wisconsin Territory, the Black Hawk War erupted in 1832. The Illinois militia mobilized to expel the Sauk and Fox peoples, chased them into the Wisconsin Territory, ignored the Indians' effort to surrender under a white flag, and massacred women and children as they tried to escape across the Mississippi River. Six weeks later, their leader, Black Hawk, was captured and imprisoned. After eight months, President Jackson ordered that he be brought to Washington, D.C. by carriage, steamboat, and railroad, to impress upon the Indian leader the greatness and power of the United States before releasing him.

| Resistance: Black Hawk War (1832) |

In the South, the Seminoles, led by Osceola (called by U.S. soldiers "the still unconquered red man") resisted the federal removal policy from 1835 to 1842 by fighting a guerrilla war in the swamps of the Florida Everglades—the longest, most expensive, and deadliest war ever fought by Native Americans. But the Seminoles' heroic resistance waned after 1837, when Osceola, the most famous Native American of the time, was captured, imprisoned, and left to die at Fort Moultrie near Charleston, South Carolina. After 1842, only a few hundred Seminoles remained, hiding out in the swamps. It was not until 1934 that the few surviving Seminoles in Florida became the last Native American tribe to end their war with the United States.

| Resistance: Seminole guerrilla war |

The Trail of Tears

The Cherokee Nation occupied northwest Georgia and the mountainous areas of Alabama, Tennessee, and North Carolina. In 1827, the Cherokees, relying upon their established treaty rights, adopted a constitution as an

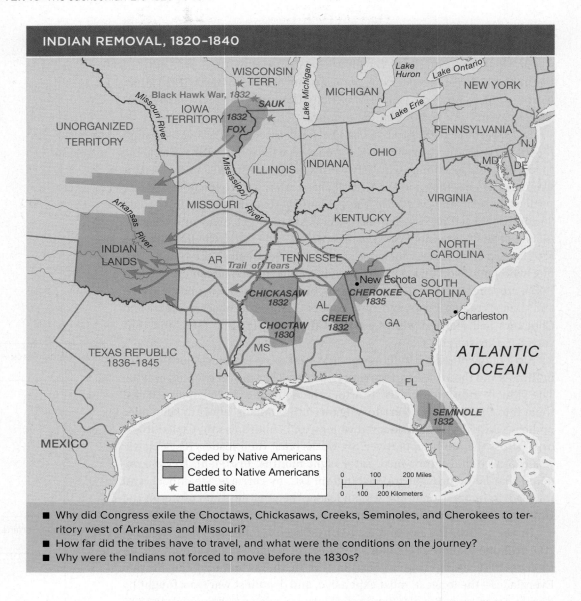

INDIAN REMOVAL, 1820–1840

- Why did Congress exile the Choctaws, Chickasaws, Creeks, Seminoles, and Cherokees to territory west of Arkansas and Missouri?
- How far did the tribes have to travel, and what were the conditions on the journey?
- Why were the Indians not forced to move before the 1830s?

independent nation in which they declared that they were not subject to the laws or control of any state or the federal government. In 1828, shortly after Jackson's election, Georgia announced that after June 1, 1830, the authority of state law would extend to the Cherokees living within the boundaries of the state. According to the Georgia state government, the Cherokees would no longer be a "nation within a nation."

Cherokee Nation v. Georgia (1831) and *Worcester v. Georgia* (1832)

Of all the so-called Civilized Tribes, the Cherokees had come closest to adopting the customs of white America. But the discovery of gold in north Georgia in 1829 fed whites' appetite for Cherokee land and attracted trespassing prospectors. The Cherokees sought relief in the Supreme Court. In

Cherokee Nation v. Georgia (1831), Chief Justice John Marshall ruled that the Cherokees were a "domestic dependent nation" rather than a foreign state. He added, however, that the Cherokees had "an unquestionable right" to their lands "until title should be extinguished by voluntary cession to the United States." The following year, the Supreme Court ruled in *Worcester v. Georgia* (1832) that the Cherokee Nation was "a distinct political community" within which Georgia law had no force. Both of these Supreme Court decisions had the effect of favoring the Cherokee argument that their ancestral lands could not be taken from them.

President Jackson, however, refused to enforce the Court's "wicked" decisions, claiming that he had no constitutional authority to intervene in Georgia. Jackson's rejection of the Court's ruling reflected his many contradictions. When dealing with Indians in Georgia, he refused to interfere with the state's refusal to abide by U.S. Supreme Court rulings. By contrast, in the nullification crisis with South Carolina, he used military force to deny the right of a state to defy the federal government.

Meanwhile, the Indians were forced out. There was nothing for the Cherokees (who had fought with Jackson as allies against the Creeks) to do but sign a treaty, which they did in 1835. They gave up their land in the Southeast (about 100 million acres) in exchange for 32 million acres in the "Indian Territory" to the west of Arkansas—part of present-day Oklahoma. By 1838, 17,000 Cherokees had been evicted and moved west on the **Trail of Tears**, an eight-hundred-mile forced journey mostly on foot. Four thousand of the refugees died along the way. A few held out in the mountains and acquired title to federal land in North Carolina; they became known as the "Eastern Band" of Cherokees.

Cherokees divided While many Cherokee elite fought against Jackson's policies, Elias Boudinot, editor of the first Native American newspaper, *Cherokee Phoenix*, signed the Indian Removal Treaty in 1835. He was subsequently murdered.

Trail of Tears (1838–1839) The Cherokees' eight-hundred-mile journey from the southern Appalachians to Indian Territory.

Trail of Tears Thousands of Cherokees died on a nightmarish forced march from Georgia to Oklahoma after being forced from their native lands.

CORE **OBJECTIVE**

4. Explain the causes of the economic depression of the late 1830s and the emergence of the Whig party.

Political Battles

Jackson's controversial policies regarding the Indians, nullification, and the B.U.S. aroused so much opposition that new political parties were formed to oppose him. Some congressional opponents talked of impeaching him. Jackson received so many death threats that he decided his political opponents were trying to kill him. In January 1835, the threat became real. After attending the funeral service for a member of Congress, Jackson was leaving the Capitol when an unemployed English-born housepainter named Richard Lawrence emerged from the shadows and pointed a pistol at the president's heart—only a few feet away. When he pulled the trigger, however, the gun misfired. Jackson lifted his walking stick and charged at Lawrence, who pulled out another pistol, but it, too, miraculously misfired, and he was arrested. Jackson charged that his political foes, including John C. Calhoun, had planned the attack. A jury, however, decided that Lawrence, the first person to try to kill a U.S. president, was insane and ordered him confined in an asylum.

A Third Party

In 1832, for the first time in a presidential election, a third party entered the field. The Anti-Masonic party grew out of popular hostility toward the Masonic fraternal order, a large, all-male social organization that originated in Great Britain early in the eighteenth century. By 1830, there were some 2,000 Masonic "lodges" scattered across the United States with about 100,000 members, including Andrew Jackson and Henry Clay.

The Anti-Masonic party

Suspicions of the Masonic order as a secret elite organization intent on undermining democracy gave rise to the grassroots movement known as the Anti-Masonic party. More than 100 Anti-Masonic newspapers emerged across the nation. Their common purpose was to stamp out an organization that was contaminating the "heart of the republic." Former president John Quincy Adams said that disbanding the "Masonic institution" was the most important issue facing "us and our posterity."

Opposition to a fraternal organization was hardly the foundation upon which to build a lasting political party, but the Anti-Masonic party had three important firsts to its credit: in addition to being the first third party, it was the first party to hold a national convention to nominate a presidential candidate and the first to announce a platform of specific policy goals.

The 1832 Election

The Democrats and the National Republicans followed the example of the Anti-Masonic party by holding presidential nominating conventions of their own. In December 1831, the National Republicans assembled in Baltimore to nominate Henry Clay. Eager to demonstrate popular support for his own party's candidates, Jackson endorsed the idea of a nominating convention for the Democratic party as well.

The Democratic convention, also meeting in Baltimore, first adopted the two-thirds rule for nomination (which prevailed until 1936, when the requirement became a simple majority), then named Martin Van Buren as Jackson's running mate. The Democrats, unlike the other two parties, adopted no formal platform and relied to a substantial degree upon the popularity of the president to carry their cause.

The outcome was an overwhelming endorsement of Jackson in the Electoral College, with 219 votes to 49 for Clay, and a solid victory in the popular vote, 688,000 to 530,000. William Wirt carried only Vermont, winning seven electoral votes. Wayward South Carolina, unable to stomach either Jackson or Clay, delivered its 11 votes to Governor John Floyd of Virginia.

The Removal of Government Deposits

Jackson interpreted his lopsided reelection as a "decision of the people against the bank." Jackson ordered the Treasury Department to transfer federal monies from the national bank to twenty-three state banks—called "pet banks" because many were in the western states and were run by friends and allies of Jackson. Transferring the government's deposits from the B.U.S. to the pet banks was probably illegal, and the Senate, led by Henry Clay, voted on March 28, 1834, to censure Jackson for it, the only time an American president has been reprimanded in this way as opposed to actual impeachment. Jackson was so angry about being censured that he wanted to challenge Clay to a duel to "bring the rascal to a dear account."

Meanwhile, Nicholas Biddle refused to surrender. He ordered the B.U.S. to quit making loans and demanded that state banks exchange their paper currency for gold or silver coins as quickly as possible. Through such deflationary policies that reduced the amount of money circulating in the economy, the desperate Biddle was trying to create a depression, and thus reveal the importance of maintaining the national bank. An infuriated Jackson said the B.U.S. under Biddle was "trying to kill me, but I will kill it!"

Jackson prevailed. The B.U.S. would shut down by 1841. With the restraining effects of Biddle's national bank removed, hundreds of new state banks sprouted like mushrooms, each printing its own paper currency to lend to land speculators and new businesses. Sales of federal- or state-owned lands rose from 4 million acres in 1834 to 20 million in 1836. At the same time, the states plunged themselves heavily into debt to finance the building of roads and canals. By 1837, total state indebtedness had soared. The irony of Jackson's war on the national bank was that it sparked the dangerous misbehavior among small state banks that he most feared. As Senator Thomas Hart Benton, one of Jackson's most loyal supporters, said in 1837, he had not helped kill the B.U.S. to create a "wilderness of local banks. I did not join in putting down the paper currency of a national bank to put up a national paper currency of a thousand local banks."

> Jackson's war on the B.U.S.

The Money Question

The Distribution Act (1836) >

The surge of unstable paper money being issued by state banks peaked in 1836, when events combined suddenly to destroy the value of the bank notes. Two key developments, the **Distribution Act** and the Specie Circular, would combine to devastate the nation's financial system and throw the surging economy into a sudden tailspin. During the 1830s, the federal government was acquiring huge amounts of cash from the sale of government-owned lands. For a time, the annual surpluses from land sales were used to pay off the federal debt. The debt, reduced to $7 million by 1832, was completely paid off by 1835, the first time that any nation had done so.

And the federal surplus continued to mount. In June 1836, Congress decided that the money from land sales should be "distributed" to the states in proportion to each state's representation in Congress. The distribution of the surplus resulted in the withdrawal of federal funds from the state banks. In turn, the state banks had to require many borrowers to repay their loans immediately so that the banks could replace the lost federal funds. This situation caused even greater disarray in the already unstable banking sector.

Specie Circular (1836) >

A month after the Distribution Act was signed into law, Andrew Jackson signed the Specie Circular, which announced that the federal government would accept only gold or silver coins in payment for land. The requirement that only "specie" (coins) be accepted for federal land purchases put an added strain on the nation's already-tight supplies of gold and silver. Eastern banks had to transfer much of their gold and silver reserves to western banks, where most federal lands were being sold. As banks reduced their reserves of gold and silver, they had to reduce their lending. Soon, the once-bustling economy began to slow into a recession.

The Whig Coalition

Whigs vs. "King Andrew I" >

Jackson had removed the Indians from the eastern United States and had slain the dual monsters of nullification in South Carolina and the national bank in Philadelphia, and many loved him for it. But in 1834, a new anti-Jackson coalition emerged, united chiefly by their hostility to the president's authoritarian style. Jackson's domineering manner had given rise to the nickname "King Andrew I." His Democratic followers were deemed Tories, supporters of the "tyrannical" king, and his opponents became known as the **Whig party**, a name that linked them to the Patriots of the American Revolution (as well as the parliamentary opponents of the Tories in Britain).

The Whigs grew out of the National Republican party of John Quincy Adams, Henry Clay, and Daniel Webster. They also attracted members of the Anti-Masonic and Democratic parties, who for one reason or another were irritated by Jackson's stand on the national bank, states' rights, and his disregard of the Supreme Court, among other grievances. Of the forty-one Democrats in Congress who had voted against Jackson on rechartering the national bank, twenty-eight had joined the Whigs by 1836, including David

Distribution Act (1836) Law requiring distribution of the federal budget surplus to the states, creating chaos among unregulated state banks dependent on such federal funds.

Whig party Political party founded in 1834 in opposition to the Jacksonian Democrats; supported federal funding for internal improvements, a national bank, and high tariffs on imports.

Crockett, the famous frontiersman and storyteller now representing Tennessee in the House of Representatives. For the next twenty years, the Whigs and the Democrats would be the two major political parties, and so for a second time a **two-party system** emerged.

Most Whigs supported Clay and his "American System" of economic nationalism. They favored federal support for internal improvements—roads, bridges, canals—to foster economic growth. They also supported a national bank and high tariffs. In the South, the Whigs tended to be bankers and merchants. In the West, the Whigs were farmers who valued government-funded internal improvements. Unlike the Democrats, who attracted Catholic voters from Germany and Ireland, Whigs tended to be native-born Protestants—Congregationalists, Presbyterians, Methodists, and Baptists—who promoted social reforms such as the abolition of slavery and legislation to prohibit the sale of alcoholic beverages.

> Whigs support Clay's "American System"

The Election of 1836

In 1835, eighteen months before the presidential election, the Democrats nominated Jackson's handpicked successor, Vice President Martin Van Buren. The Whig coalition, united chiefly in its opposition to Jackson, adopted a strategy of multiple candidacies, hoping to throw the election into the House of Representatives. The Whigs put up three favorite sons: Daniel Webster, nominated by the Massachusetts legislature; Hugh Lawson White, chosen by anti-Jackson Democrats in the Tennessee legislature; and William Henry Harrison of Indiana, nominated by a predominantly Anti-Masonic convention in Harrisburg, Pennsylvania. In the South, the Whigs made heavy inroads by arguing that only a southerner—that is, Hugh White—could be trusted as president. But their complicated multi-candidate strategy failed. In the popular vote of 1836, though, Van Buren outdistanced the entire Whig field, with 765,000 votes to 740,000 for the three Whigs. Van Buren won 170 electoral votes; Harrison, 73; White, 26; and Webster, 14.

Martin Van Buren Van Buren earned the nickname the "Little Magician," for not only his short stature but also his "magical" ability to exploit his political and social connections.

The Eighth President

Martin Van Buren was the first president of Dutch ancestry. Although trained as an attorney, he had spent most of his adult life as a skillful politician whose ability to organize and manipulate the New York political "machine" earned him the nickname the "Little Magician." Elected governor of New York in 1828, he had resigned to join Andrew Jackson's cabinet and became vice president in 1833. He had been Jackson's closest adviser and ally.

The Panic of 1837

Fortunately for Jackson, the financial **Panic of 1837** did not erupt until he was out of the White House. His successor got the blame. The financial panic President Van Buren inherited mushroomed into an economic depression lasting seven years. During the mid-1830s, the already-precarious economy was tipped over by a depression in Great Britain, America's largest trading

two-party system Domination of national politics by two major political parties, such as the Whigs and Democrats during the 1830s and 1840s.

Panic of 1837 A financial calamity in the United States brought on by a dramatic slowdown in the British economy and falling cotton prices, failed crops, high inflation, and reckless state banks.

partner, which resulted in a sharp drop in demand for American cotton and caused English capitalists to cut back on their investments in the U.S. economy. On top of everything else, in 1836 there had been a failure of the wheat crop, the export of which in good years had helped offset the drain of gold payments abroad. In April 1837, some 250 businesses failed in New York City alone.

As a newspaper editorial complained in December 1836, the nation's economy "has been put into confusion and dismay by a well-meant, but *extremely mistaken*" pair of decisions by Congress and President Jackson: the destruction of the B.U.S. and the Distribution Act. Adding to the stresses on the economy was the Specie Circular. Its requirement that all federal land purchases be transacted in gold or silver caused government land sales to plummet, thus pinching the federal budget. American banks were forced to borrow gold from European banks, but they could not get enough to prevent a financial panic and a deepening depression.

In April 1836, *Niles' Weekly Register*, the nation's leading business journal, reported that the economy was "approaching a momentous crisis." The government was lucky to sell land for $3 an acre that had been going for $10 an acre. States had to cancel plans to build roads, bridges, railroads, canals, and ports. Forty percent of the state banks shut their doors. Even the federal government itself, having put most of its gold and silver in state banks, was verging on bankruptcy. The *National Intelligencer* newspaper reported in May that the federal treasury "has not a dollar of gold or silver in the world!"

The poor, as always, were particularly hard hit during the economic slump. By the fall of 1837, a third of the nation's workers were jobless, and those still fortunate enough to have jobs had their wages slashed. At the same time, prices for food and clothing soared. As the winter of 1837 approached, a New York City journalist reported that 200,000 people were "in utter and hopeless distress with no means of surviving the winter but those provided by charity." The nation had a "poverty-struck feeling." Every part of the country was "a scene of suffering, of anguish, and distress."

The unprecedented economic calamity sent shock waves through the political system. Critics called the president "Martin Van Ruin" because he did not believe that he or the government had any responsibility to rescue hard-pressed farmers, bankers, or businessmen, or to provide relief for the jobless and homeless. He did call a special session of Congress in 1837, which canceled the distribution of the federal surplus to the states because there was no longer any surplus to distribute.

An Independent Treasury

Independent Treasury Act (1840) System created by Van Buren that moved federal funds from favored state banks to the U.S. Treasury, whose financial transactions could only be in gold or silver.

Van Buren believed that the federal government should stop risking its deposits in shaky state banks. Instead, he wanted to establish an independent treasury system whereby the government would keep its funds in its own bank vaults and do business entirely in gold or silver, not paper currency. At his urging, Congress passed the **Independent Treasury Act** on July 4, 1840.

Although it lasted little more than a year (the Whigs repealed it in 1841), it would be restored in 1846.

The "Log Cabin and Hard Cider" Campaign

By 1840, an election year, the Van Buren administration had become the target of growing discontent. The president won re-nomination easily enough but could not get the Democratic convention to agree on his vice-presidential choice, which was left up to the Democratic electors.

Because of the economic depression, the Whigs were confident they would win the 1840 presidential election. At their nominating convention, they passed over Henry Clay, the Kentucky legislator who had been Jackson's consistent foe, in favor of William Henry Harrison, whose credentials were impressive: victor at the Battle of Tippecanoe against Tecumseh's Shawnees in 1811, former governor of the Indiana Territory, and former congressman and senator from Ohio. To rally their states'-rights wing, the Whigs chose for vice president John Tyler of Virginia.

The Whigs had no platform, since they believed that the economic depression was enough to ensure their victory. But they hit upon a catchy campaign slogan: "Tippecanoe and Tyler Too." And they soon had a rousing campaign theme, which the *Baltimore Republican*, a Democratic newspaper, unwittingly supplied when it declared that General Harrison, at 67 the oldest candidate yet to seek the presidency, was the kind of man who would spend his retirement "in a log cabin [sipping apple cider] on the banks of the Ohio [River]." The Whigs seized upon the cider and log cabin symbols to depict Harrison as a simple man sprung from the people, in contrast to President

Uncle Sam's Pet Pups!
A woodcut showing William Henry Harrison luring "Mother Bank," Andrew Jackson, and Martin Van Buren into a barrel of hard (alcoholic) cider. While Jackson and Van Buren sought to destroy the Bank of the United States, Harrison promised to reestablish it, hence his providing "Mother Bank" a refuge in this scene.

Creating a Two-Party System: Democrats vs. Whigs

While controversial, Andrew Jackson had a broad appeal to the voters in his time and left an enduring mark on the presidency of the United States. A man of strong convictions, Jackson championed the common man against the wealthy and privileged, but his economic policies led the nation into financial depression. His often contradictory policies and positions brought about intense opposition that eventually coalesced into the Whig party, a rival to his Democratic political organization. By 1840, there were two nationally competitive political parties in the United States. Each party competed at the national level, and each party had to create coalitions of voters, many of whom had differing views on major issues. However, no politician would prove as popular as Andrew Jackson or would win two successive terms to the presidency until Abraham Lincoln did so nearly thirty years after him.

Jackson's Positions and Policies	Democrats on Jackson's Policies	Whigs on Jackson's Policies	Regions on Jackson's Policies
Equality of Opportunity Jackson believed that all white men should rise and fall according to their own talents. He hated elitism and social deference.	Support	Support	**Strong support** in Northeast (especially factory workers) and West (especially frontiersmen)
Internal Improvements Jackson opposed government spending on internal improvements, which he felt favored certain regions.	**Opposition** to federally funded internal improvements	**Support** for federally funded internal improvements	**Strong support** in West (farmers needed internal improvements to help transport agricultural products to national markets)
Second Bank of the United States Jackson distrusted bankers and viewed the national bank as a government-sanctioned monopoly favoring the rich and privileged, as well as the Northeast, where the first B.U.S. was located.	**Opposition** to rechartering the Second Bank of the United States	**Support** for rechartering the Second Bank of the United States	**Support** in Northeast **Strong opposition** in West

Van Buren's wealthy, aristocratic lifestyle. (Harrison was actually from one of Virginia's wealthiest families).

As expected, Van Buren lost by the thumping margin of 234 votes to 60 in the Electoral College. The Whigs had promised a return to prosperity

Jackson's Positions and Policies	Democrats on Jackson's Policies	Whigs on Jackson's Policies	Regions on Jackson's Policies
Tariffs Jackson believed in lowering taxes but had no strong position on tariffs, until Southern opposition to tariffs convinced him to support lowering them.	**Support** for lowering tariffs	**Opposition** to lowering tariffs	**Support** in Northeast **Strong opposition** in South
Nullification A strong supporter of the Union, Jackson stood down South Carolina when it declared the Tariffs of 1828 and 1832 unconstitutional and not applicable in its borders.	**Opposition** to nullification	N/A (did not yet exist as a party)	**Support** in South (especially South Carolina) **Opposition** in West and North
Indian Policy Jackson did not believe that Native Americans should be part of America's economic, political, and social fabric. Congress approved his forcible removal of Native Americans to the West.	**Support** for forced removal of Native Americans	**Opposition** to forced removal of Native Americans	**Support** in South and Southwest by whites (especially settlers moving into areas surrounding the Cherokee, Choctaw, Chickasaw, Creek, and Seminoles)

QUESTIONS FOR ANALYSIS

1. Who could vote during the 1830s, and how did Jackson's views appeal to voters?

2. How did Jackson's policies lead to a second two-party system, this time made up of Democrats and Whigs? In what particular regions was Jackson's message most popular? In what regions were the Whigs the most popular?

3. Why did Jackson generate support across the country among voters from a variety of occupations and a variety of incomes?

without explaining how such prosperity was to be generated. It was simply time for a change. What was most remarkable about the election of 1840 was the turnout. Over 80 percent of white American men voted, many for the first time—the highest turnout before or since.

CORE **OBJECTIVE**

5. Assess the strengths and weaknesses of Jackson's transformational presidency.

Assessing the Jacksonian Era

The nation Andrew Jackson governed as president was vastly different from that led by George Washington and Thomas Jefferson. In 1828 the United States boasted twenty-four states and nearly 13 million people, many of them recent arrivals from Germany and Ireland. The national population was growing at a phenomenal rate, doubling every twenty-three years. During the Jacksonian Era, the nation witnessed booming industrialization, rapidly growing cities, rising tensions between the North and South over slavery, accelerating westward expansion, and the emergence of the second two-party system, featuring Democrats and Whigs. A surge in foreign demand for southern cotton and other American goods, along with substantial British investment in an array of new American enterprises, helped generate an economic boom and a transportation revolution. That President-elect Jackson rode to his inauguration in a horse-drawn carriage and left Washington, D.C., eight years later on a train symbolized the dramatic changes occurring in American life.

A New Political Landscape

The Whigs may have captured the presidency in 1840, but the Jacksonian Democrats had permanently altered American politics. A transformational figure in a transformational era, Andrew Jackson initiated a new era in American politics. He enabled the "common man" to play a greater role in the political arena at the same time that working men were forming labor unions to increase their economic power. He helped establish the modern Democratic party and attracted to it the working poor from eastern cities as well as farmers from the South and East. He saved the Union by suppressing the nullification crisis through a nimble combination of force and compromise. And, in 1835, he paid off the national debt.

In Jackson's 1837 farewell address, he looked back over eight controversial years in the White House and stressed that he had worked on behalf of "the farmer, the mechanic, and the laboring classes of society—the bone and sinew of the country—men who love liberty and desire nothing but equal rights and equal laws." But his concept of "the people" was limited to a "white men's democracy," as it had been for all earlier presidents, and the phenomenon of Andrew Jackson, the heroic symbol of the times, continues to spark historical debate.

White men's democracy

A Controversial Presidency

President Jackson's repeated charges that the "rich and powerful" too often controlled the government for their own "selfish purposes" obscured the fact that in practice Andrew Jackson, along with his advisers and supporters, proved to be as opportunistic and manipulative as the Eastern political and economic elite they displaced. The Jacksonians were largely men "on the make" who promoted greater democracy for the nation while pursuing greater wealth for themselves. Accordingly, Jackson's opponents challenged the sincerity of his commitment to "the people." As Henry Clay charged in 1833, Jackson often seemed to be seeking "the concentration of all power in the hands of one man." But in Jackson's view, the president was the only government official chosen by *all* the people, unlike senators and representatives, and this gave the chief executive the responsibility—and expanded powers—to serve the good of all the people.

Jackson's forceful use of that presidential power was not always wise, however. His controversial decision to eliminate the national bank led to a prolonged depression. One of Jackson's opponents once wrote a letter to the president brutally outlining his faults: "Your besetting sins are ambition and the love of money. . . . You are naturally and constitutionally irritable, overbearing and tyrannical. . . . When you become the enemy of any man you will put him down if you can, no matter by what means, fair or foul. . . . You are miserably deficient in principle, and have seldom or never had power without abusing it."

| A controversial presidency |

Limited Equality

While a typical white American was better off than the average European in 1840, the supreme irony of the so-called age of the common man—that is, of Jacksonian democracy—is that it was actually an era of growing economic and social *in*equality. Jacksonian Democrats championed political equality for white males, giving everyone, regardless of wealth, the right to vote and hold office. They also promoted equality of opportunity, not equality of outcomes, and certainly not equality of wealth. "Distinctions in society will always exist under every just government," Jackson observed. "Equality of talents, or education, or of wealth cannot be produced by human institutions." Jacksonian Democrats wanted every white man to have an equal chance to compete in the political arena and to grow rich, but they never promoted equality of results.

| Jacksonian equality of opportunity |

During the years before the Civil War, the notion of young men rising from rags to riches was a popular myth. Speaking to the Senate in 1832, Henry Clay claimed that almost all the successful factory owners he knew were "enterprising, self-made men, who have whatever wealth they possess by patient and diligent labor." In fact, however, those who started out poor and uneducated seldom made it to the top. In 1828, the top 1 percent of New York's families (those worth $34,000 or more) held 40 percent of the wealth, and the top 4 percent held 76 percent of the wealth. Similar circumstances prevailed in Philadelphia, Boston, and other cities. But Jackson and others who celebrated the "common man" and talked frequently of "equality" never expected people to be equal in wealth. "True republicanism," one commentator explained, "requires that every man shall have an equal chance—that every man shall be free to become as *unequal* as he can." That is what Jackson believed as well.

| Jacksonian economic and social inequality |

■ **Jackson's Views and Policies** The Jacksonians sought to democratize the political process and expand economic opportunity for the "common man" (that is, "poor and humble" white men). As the representative of "the people," he expanded the role of the president in economic matters, reducing federal government spending and eliminating the powerful *Second Bank of the United States*. His *Bank War* painted the national bank as full of "vipers and thieves" and was hugely popular, but Jackson did not understand its long-term economic consequences. In addition, his views on limited government were not always reflected in his policies. He left the high taxes on imports from the *"Tariff of Abominations" (1828)* in place until opposition in the South created a national crisis.

■ **Nullification Controversy** The concept of *nullification*, developed by South Carolina's John C. Calhoun, enabled a state to disavow a federal law. When a South Carolina convention nullified the Tariffs of 1828 and 1832, Jackson requested that Congress pass a *"Force Bill" (1833)* authorizing the U.S. Army to compel compliance with the tariffs. After South Carolina, under the threat of federal military force, accepted a compromise tariff put forth by Henry Clay, the state convention nullified the force bill. The crisis was over, with both sides claiming victory.

■ **Indian Removal Act of 1830** The *Indian Removal Act of 1830* authorized the relocation of eastern Indians to federal lands west of the Mississippi River. The Cherokees used the federal court system in *Cherokee Nation v. Georgia* and *Worcester v. Georgia* to try to block this relocation. Despite the Supreme Court's decisions in their favor, President Jackson forced them to move; the event and the route they took came to be known as the *Trail of Tears (1838–1839)*. By 1840 only a few Seminoles and Cherokees remained in remote areas of the Southeast.

■ **Democrats and Whigs** Jackson's arrogant behavior, especially his use of the veto, led many to regard him as "King Andrew I." Groups who opposed him organized a new party, known as the *Whig party*, thus producing the country's *two-party system*. Two acts—the *Distribution Act (1836)* and the Specie Circular—ultimately destabilized the nation's economy. Andrew Jackson's ally and vice president, Martin Van Buren, succeeded him as president, but Jacksonian bank policies led to the financial *Panic of 1837* and an economic depression. Van Buren responded by establishing the *Independent Treasury Act (1840)* to safeguard the nation's economy but offered no help for individuals in distress. The economic calamity ensured a Whig victory in the election of 1840.

■ **The Jackson Years** Andrew Jackson's America was very different from the America of 1776. Most white men had gained the vote when states removed property qualifications for voting, but political equality did not mean economic equality. Democrats wanted every American to have an equal chance to compete in the marketplace and in the political arena, but they never promoted equality of results. Inequality between rich and poor widened during the Jackson Era.

KEY TERMS

CHRONOLOGY

1828	Andrew Jackson wins presidential election
	"Tariff of Abominations" goes into effect
1830	Congress passes the Indian Removal Act
	Andrew Jackson vetoes the Maysville Road Bill
	The Eaton affair divides Andrew Jackson's warring cabinet
1831	Supreme Court issues *Cherokee Nation v. Georgia* decision
1832	Supreme Court issues *Worcester v. Georgia* decision
	South Carolina passes Nullification Ordinance
	Andrew Jackson vetoes the Bank Recharter Bill
1833	Congress passes the Force Bill, authorizing military force in South Carolina
	Congress passes Henry Clay's compromise tariff with Jackson's support
1836	Democratic candidate Martin Van Buren is elected president
1837	Financial panic deflates the economy
1838–1839	Eastern Indians are forced west on the Trail of Tears
1840	Independent Treasury Act established
1840	Whig candidate William Henry Harrison is elected president

INQUIZITIVE

Go to InQuizitive to see what you've learned—and learn what you've missed—with personalized feedback along the way.

THE OLD SOUTH One of the enduring myths of the South is captured in this late nineteenth-century painting of a plantation on the Mississippi River: strong slaves tending the lush cotton fields, a paddle steamer easing down the wide river, and the planter's family retiring in the cool of their white-columned mansion. Novels and films like *Gone with the Wind* (1939) would perpetuate the notion of the Old South as a stable, paternalistic agrarian society led by white planters who were the "natural" aristocracy of virtue and talent within their communities.

The South and Slavery

1800–1860

O f all the regions of the United States during the first half of the nineteenth century, the Old South (that is, the pre–Civil War South) was the most distinctive. The southern states remained rural and agricultural long after the rest of the nation had embraced urban-industrial development. By the 1840s, the North and South had developed different economies and political goals. The North wanted high tariffs on imported manufactured goods to "protect" its new mills and factories from foreign competition. Southerners, on the other hand, favored "free trade"—no tariffs—because they wanted to buy British goods in exchange for the raw cotton they sold to British textile mills.

The rapid settlement of the western territories during the first half of the nineteenth century set in motion a ferocious competition between North and South for political influence in the West. Would the new western territories and states be "slave" or "free"? Much was riding on that issue, since congressional representatives and senators from the newly admitted western states would tip the delicate political balance in Washington, D.C., one way or the other, slave or free.

The efforts of southerners to expand slavery in the face of growing criticism from the North ignited

CORE
OBJECTIVES INQUIZITIVE

1. Explain the various factors that made the South distinct from the rest of the United States during the early nineteenth century.

2. Discuss the role that cotton production and slavery played in the South's economic and social development.

3. Distinguish among the major groups within southern white society and explain why each group was committed to the continuation and expansion of slavery.

4. Describe the impact of slavery on African Americans, both free and enslaved, throughout the South.

5. Analyze how enslaved peoples responded to the inhumanity of their situation.

a prolonged political controversy that would end in civil war. Many southerners, then and since, despised being told what to do by others—especially outsiders. And white southerners especially resented northern demands for the abolition of slavery. A prickly defensiveness came to define southern attitudes and actions. The nineteenth-century white South became famous for its defiant pride, its violence-prone sense of honor, and its spirited independence, all rooted in the region's commitment to cotton and race-based slavery.

CORE **OBJECTIVE**

1. Explain the various factors that made the South distinct from the rest of the United States during the early nineteenth century.

The Distinctiveness of the Old South

Climate, geography, and the plantation system

Explanations of what set the Old South apart from the rest of the nation generally focus on the impact of the region's climate and geography in shaping its culture and economy, and on the effects of human decisions and actions over many years. The South's warm, humid climate was ideal for the cultivation of profitable commercial crops such as tobacco, cotton, rice, indigo, and sugar cane. Those cash crops led to the plantation system of large commercial agriculture and its dependence upon enslaved labor. Unlike the North, the South had few large cities, few banks, few railroads, and few factories. Most of the commerce in the South was related to the storage, distribution, and sale of agricultural products, especially cotton. With the cotton economy booming, there was little reason to create robust financial and industrial sectors.

A Triracial Culture

While geography and climate were key factors in shaping the South's economy and culture, what made the region most distinctive was the diminishing presence of Native Americans and the expanding institution of race-based slavery. During the early decades of the nineteenth century, all three groups—blacks, whites, and Indians—regularly intermingled and adopted aspects of each other's cultures. By 1840, however, few Native Americans remained in the South; most had been forced onto lands in the West.

The South's "peculiar institution"

As the number of Native Americans declined in the South, the number of enslaved African Americans increased. Most southern whites did not own slaves (also called bondpeople), but they supported what was often called the South's **"peculiar institution"** because slavery was so central to the society's way of life. The phrase enabled southerners to avoid using the charged word *slavery*, while the adjective *peculiar* implied that slavery was *unique* to the South. What virtually all white southerners shared during the first half of the nineteenth century was an often brutal racial prejudice against both Native Americans and African Americans.

"peculiar institution" Phrase used by whites in the antebellum South to refer to slavery without using the word slavery.

Assumptions of White Superiority

The profitability and convenience of owning slaves—as well as the psychological appeal of racial superiority among those who did not own slaves—created a sense of racial unity that bridged class differences among whites. Poor whites who owned no slaves could still claim racial superiority to enslaved blacks. Because of race-based slavery, explained Georgia attorney Thomas R. Cobb, every white "feels that he belongs to an elevated class. It matters not that he is no slaveholder; he is not of the inferior race; he is a free-born citizen." In reality, only a very few southerners owned great plantations, but many southern whites dreamed of acquiring large land-holdings and becoming members of a "natural" aristocracy within their communities.

> Belief in racial superiority

The Old South differed from other sections of the country, too, in its high proportion of native-born Americans, both whites and blacks. The South attracted few overseas immigrants after the Revolution. One reason for the lack of foreign migrants was that the main shipping lines connected Europe to northern ports such as Boston, New York City, and Philadelphia. Most immigrants were penniless; they could not afford to travel to the South. Moreover, European immigrants, most of whom were manual laborers, could not compete with slave labor and the poor whites already living in the South.

Conflicting Myths

Southerners, a North Carolina editor wrote, are "a mythological people, created half out of dream and half out of slander, who live in a still-legendary land." He was referring to the conflicting visions of the South that emerged before the Civil War and have since defined the region. A powerful belief among white southerners—that the South was both different *and* better than the North—was central to the self-image of white southerners, then and since. The white South's increasing defensiveness about slavery reflected the economic and political elite's proud sense of its region's distinctiveness and superiority. The dominance of farming remained a vital regional characteristic, whether pictured as the Jeffersonian small farmer living by his manual labor or the lordly planter overseeing his slaves. "We want no manufactures; we desire no trading, no mechanical or manufacturing classes," an Alabama politician told an English visitor. The agrarian ideal and the penchant in the South for fighting, guns, horsemanship, and the military painted a picture of the Old South as full of honest small farmers and aristocratic gentlemen, young belles and beautiful ladies, who led leisurely lives of well-mannered graciousness, honor, and courage, all the while sipping mint juleps in a world of white-columned mansions.

> Myth of the Old South: Agrarian "aristocracy"

In defending the South and slavery from northern abolitionists, southerners claimed that their region was morally superior to the North. Kind planters supposedly provided happy slaves with food, clothing, shelter, and security—in contrast to a North populated with greedy bankers and heartless factory owners who treated their wage laborers worse than slaves. John C. Calhoun insisted that in the northern states where slavery had been banned, "the condition of the African, instead of being improved, has become worse," while in the South, the Africans "have improved greatly in every respect."

In this mythic version of the Old South, slavery is a positive good benefiting both slaves and owners rather than a necessary evil that must one day disappear, as Thomas Jefferson and George Washington had insisted at the end of the eighteenth century. In *Aunt Phillis's Cabin; or, Southern Life As It Is* (1852), novelist Mary Henderson Eastman stresses "the necessity of the existence of slavery at present in our Southern States, and that, as a general thing, the slaves are comfortable and contented, and their owners humane and kind."

The contrasting myth of the Old South was a much darker one developed by northern abolitionists who pictured the region as being caught in the grip of an outdated economic system that led whites to exploit blacks and Native Americans. In this version, the theme of violence runs deep. The white planters were rarely "natural aristocrats" like Thomas Jefferson. More often, they were ambitious self-made men, humble in origins, who had seized opportunities to become rich by planting and selling cotton—and trading in slaves. Many of these farmers-turned-planters were portrayed by abolitionists such as Harriet Beecher Stowe as crude capitalists who raped enslaved women, brutalized slaves, and lorded over their local communities with arrogant disdain. They treated slaves like cattle, broke up slave families, and sold slaves "down the river" to toil in the Louisiana sugar mills and rice plantations.

Like all myths, both of these warring images of the Old South contained elements of truth and distortion. Yet myths often shape human perceptions and actions more than reality. Certainly that has been true in the American South, which itself is a fabric made of many different threads. The mythic image of slavery as a beneficial system for blacks, however, fails the test of credibility. As a bondwoman who escaped to freedom in Canada recalled, "I look upon slavery as the worst evil that ever was. My life has been taken from me in a measure by it. If any are disposed to apologize for slavery, it would be well for them to try it awhile."

A Variety of Souths

For all the common threads tying the Old South together, it in fact included three distinct subregions with different economic interests and diverging degrees of commitment to slavery. Throughout the first half of the nineteenth century, the seven states of the Lower South (South Carolina, Georgia, Florida, Alabama, Mississippi, Louisiana, and parts of Texas) grew increasingly dependent upon labor-intensive cotton production—and the large-scale cultivation of cotton was utterly dependent on slave labor. A traveler in Mississippi observed in 1835 that all of the ambitious whites wanted "to sell cotton in order to buy negroes—to make more cotton to buy negroes"—forever. By 1860, slaves represented nearly half the population of the Lower South.

The states of the Upper South (Virginia, North Carolina, Tennessee, and Arkansas) had more diversified agricultural economies—a mixture of large commercial plantations and small family farms, or "yeoman" farms, where crops were grown mostly for local or personal use rather than for sale in national or international markets. Many southern states also had large areas without slavery, especially in the mountains of Virginia, the western Carolinas, eastern Tennessee, and northern Georgia.

In the Border South (Delaware, Maryland, Kentucky, and Missouri), slavery was disappearing both because cotton could not thrive in those states and because of widespread—and growing—abolitionist sentiment. By 1860, 90 percent of Delaware's black population and half of Maryland's were already free.

> Distinctive southern economies in Upper, Border, and Lower states

What the three subregions shared was opposition to the immediate abolition of slavery. White slave owners in the Border South, who held far fewer slaves than their counterparts in the Lower South, often adopted an attitude of paternalism toward slaves by incorporating them into their households and, to a degree, treating them as if they were family members. A few prominent slave owners actually worked to end slavery by stopping the African slave trade, which officially ended in 1807. Others supported "colonization" efforts to ship slaves and freed blacks to Africa or encouraged owners upon their deaths to free their slaves, as did George Washington.

Slave owners in the Lower South, however, had a disproportionately large investment in slavery. They increasingly believed that only constant supervision, intimidation, and punishment would keep the fast-growing population of bondpeople under control, in part because the working and living conditions for the enslaved were so brutal. "I'd rather be dead," said a white overseer in Louisiana, "than a nigger in one of those big [sugar cane] plantations."

The greatest fear of whites in the Lower South was an organized slave revolt as had occurred in 1791 in French-controlled Saint-Domingue—a decade later to become the independent Republic of Haiti—where plantations and factories were burned, and whites, who were outnumbered by the slaves ten to one, were slaughtered. "For our declaration of independence," one of the rebel leaders announced, "we should have the skin of a white man for parchment, his skull for an inkwell, his blood for ink, and a bayonet for a pen!" At the same time, as the dollar value of slaves soared, thanks to the dramatically increasing demand for cotton, white planters from the Lower South led efforts to transplant slavery into the new western territories.

CORE **OBJECTIVE**

2. Discuss the role that cotton production and slavery played in the South's economic and social development.

The Cotton Kingdom

Tobacco, Rice, Sugar, and Livestock

During the first half of the nineteenth century, cotton became the most profitable cash crop in the South. But other crops were grown as well. Tobacco, the region's first main cash crop, had been the economic mainstay of Virginia and Maryland during the colonial era and was also common in North Carolina. After the Revolution, as the tobacco fields in the Chesapeake lost their fertility, the tobacco economy spread into Kentucky and as far west as Missouri. Since rice was the most expensive crop to produce, requiring floodgates, irrigation ditches, and machinery, it was limited to large plantations in the coastal areas ("low country") of the Carolinas and Georgia, where fields could easily be flooded and drained by tidal rivers flowing into the ocean. Sugar cane, like rice, was also an expensive crop to produce, and it required expensive machinery to grind the cane to release the sugar syrup. In addition to such staple crops, the South led the nation in the production of livestock: hogs, horses, mules, and cattle.

The Lower South

Massive migration to Lower South / Old Southwest

Cotton, however, eventually outpaced all the other crops, thanks largely to the invention of the cotton gin that so dramatically increased productivity. In 1805, a visiting Frenchman reported that "the great profits derived from cotton" were enticing an "immense number" of people to the Lower South. At the end of the War of 1812, annual cotton production in the United States was less than 150,000 bales (a bale is a bundle of cotton weighing between 400 and 500 pounds). In 1860, production was 4 *million* bales. As the oldest southern states—Virginia and the Carolinas—experienced soil

Atop the cotton kingdom This photograph offers a glimpse of the staggering rates of cotton production. These cotton bales are so densely packed and plentiful that men are walking upon them at this Galveston, Texas port.

exhaustion from the overplanting of tobacco and cotton, farmers and planters moved to inexpensive cotton lands in the region called **The Old Southwest**—western Georgia, Alabama, Mississippi, Louisiana, Arkansas, and, eventually, Texas.

The Old Southwest region's low land prices and fertile soil served as a powerful magnet, luring hundreds of thousands of settlers when the seaboard economy faltered during the 1820s and 1830s. Where an acre of land in South Carolina produced only 300 pounds of cotton, an acre in Alabama could generate 800 pounds. A planter who moved to the Mississippi Territory urged a friend back in Kentucky to join him: "If you could . . . bring your negroes to the Miss. Terr., they would certainly make you a handsome fortune in ten years by the cultivation of Cotton." An Alabaman wrote to his father than he had "never seen such a Migration in my life" as huge numbers of Americans picked up and moved to the Old Southwest. A North Carolinian reported that the "*Alabama Fever* . . . has *carried off* vast numbers of our citizens." Between 1810 and 1840, the combined population of Georgia, Alabama, and Mississippi increased from about 300,000 (252,000 of whom were in Georgia) to 1,657,799. More than 40 percent of the new residents were enslaved blacks, many of whom had been moved in chained gangs (called "coffles") from plantations and slave markets in the Carolinas, Virginia, and New Orleans, a "city of bustle and business."

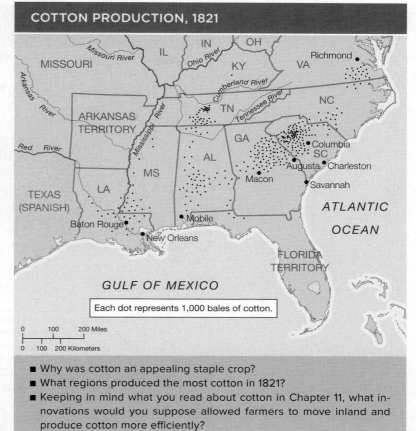

COTTON PRODUCTION, 1821

Each dot represents 1,000 bales of cotton.

0   100   200 Miles
0   100   200 Kilometers

■ Why was cotton an appealing staple crop?
■ What regions produced the most cotton in 1821?
■ Keeping in mind what you read about cotton in Chapter 11, what innovations would you suppose allowed farmers to move inland and produce cotton more efficiently?

The Spreading Cotton Kingdom

By 1860, the center of the "**cotton kingdom**" stretched from eastern North Carolina, South Carolina, and Georgia through the fertile Alabama-Mississippi "black belt" (so called for the color of the fertile soil), through Louisiana, on to Texas, and up the Mississippi Valley as far as southern Illinois. As cotton prices soared, farmers began shifting away from growing other crops, in part because cotton could be grown on small farms, unlike sugar cane and rice. Many tobacco farmers in Virginia and Maryland pulled up stakes and moved west and south into the "cotton belt." In addition, the emergence of steamboats enabled the Mississippi River to become the cotton

The Old Southwest Region covering western Georgia, Alabama, Mississippi, Louisiana, Arkansas, and Texas, where low land prices and fertile soil attracted droves of settlers after the American Revolution.

cotton kingdom Cotton-producing region, relying predominantly on slave labor, that spanned from North Carolina west to Louisiana and reached as far north as southern Illinois.

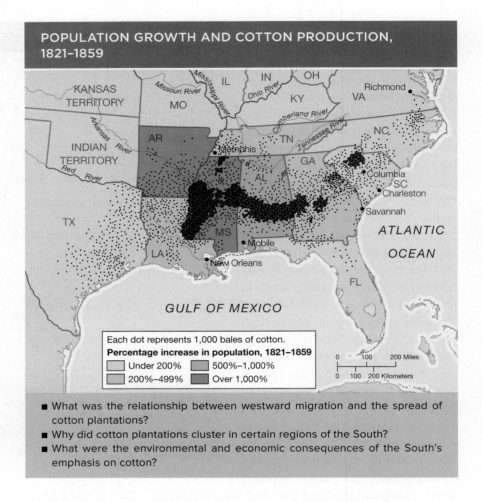

POPULATION GROWTH AND COTTON PRODUCTION, 1821–1859

Each dot represents 1,000 bales of cotton.
Percentage increase in population, 1821–1859
- Under 200%
- 500%–1,000%
- 200%–499%
- Over 1,000%

- What was the relationship between westward migration and the spread of cotton plantations?
- Why did cotton plantations cluster in certain regions of the South?
- What were the environmental and economic consequences of the South's emphasis on cotton?

highway. Millions of bales were sent downriver to New Orleans, where merchant ships took the cotton to New York, New England, Great Britain, and France.

| Cotton boom expands slavery |

By 1860, Alabama, Mississippi, and Louisiana were the three top-producing cotton states in the nation. At the same time, more millionaires per capita lived in Natchez, Mississippi, along the great river, than anywhere else in the world. The rapid expansion of the cotton belt throughout the South ensured that the region became more, rather than less, dependent on enslaved black workers. More than half of the slaves in the South worked in cotton production.

Slavery became such a powerful engine of economic development in the South that it resisted any criticism and helps explain why southerners became so defiantly defensive about preserving slavery. By 1860, the dollar value of enslaved blacks outstripped the value of *all* American banks, railroads, and factories combined. The South led the nation in exports because of King Cotton. The result was staggering wealth for a few; the twelve richest counties in the United States in 1860 were all in the South. A land surveyor described the economic boom drawing hordes of people to Louisiana: "Money, Negroes, Sugar, Cotton, and Land seem to engross all their time and attention."

The soaring profitability of cotton made some southerners brashly over-confident. In a speech to the U.S. Senate in 1858, South Carolina's former governor, James Henry Hammond, a Democrat who owned a huge cotton plantation worked by slaves, warned the North: "You dare not make war on cotton. No power on earth dares make war upon it. Cotton is King."

What Hammond failed to acknowledge was that the southern economy had grown dangerously dependent on European (largely British and French) demand for raw cotton. By 1860, Britain was importing more than 80 percent of its cotton from the South. Hammond and other southern leaders failed to anticipate what they could least afford: a sudden collapse in world demand for southern cotton that began in 1860. The expansion of the British textile industry peaked in 1860, but by then the Lower South was locked into large-scale cotton production for generations to come.

> Increased southern dependence on Britain

White Social Groups in the South

CORE **OBJECTIVE**
3. Distinguish among the major groups within southern white society and explain why each group was committed to the continuation and expansion of slavery.

White Planters

Although there were only a few giant plantations in each southern state, their owners exercised disproportionate influence in economic, political, and social life. As a western Virginian observed in the mid-1830s, "the old slaveholding families exerted a great deal of control . . . and they affected the manner and prejudices of the slaveholding part of the state." The large planters in each state behaved like an aristocracy, controlling political, economic, and social life. "The planters here are essentially what the nobility are in other countries," claimed a self-serving James Henry Hammond. "They stand at the head of society and politics. . . . Slavery does indeed create an aristocracy—an aristocracy of talents, of virtue, or generosity, and courage." The largest planters were determined to retain their control over southern society. To do so, they frequently defended their right to rule their neighbors. "Inequality is the fundamental law of the universe," declared one planter.

What distinguished a plantation from a farm, in addition to its size, was the use of a large number of slaves supervised by overseers. A clear-cut distinction between management and labor set the planter apart from the small slaveholder, who often worked side by side with slaves. If, as historians have agreed, one had to own at least twenty slaves to be called a **planter**, only one out of every thirty whites in the South in 1860 was a planter. The 1860 U.S. Census listed eleven planters with 500 slaves and one with as many as 1,000. The planters, making up less than 4 percent of the white men in the South, held more than half the slaves, and the number of slaveholders was only

planters Owners of large farms in the South that were worked by twenty or more slaves and supervised by overseers.

Cotton and the Transformation of the South

Between 1800 and 1860, the production of cotton transformed the southern region of the United States. The following chart explores the growth of cotton production and slavery, as well as where slavery and cotton production was concentrated in the region by 1860.

FACT 1
Increased Cotton Production
In 1815, the South produced 150,000 bales of cotton. By 1860, it produced 4 million bales. Cotton was the nation's leading export.

FACT 2
Increased Number of Slaves
In 1790, there were 700,000 slaves in the United States. In 1830, there were 2 million. By 1860, there were 4 million.

FACT 3
Concentration of Slaves
By 1860, more than half of all slaves worked on cotton plantations.

FACT 4
Concentration of Cotton Production
Cotton production was concentrated in the fertile "black belt" regions of The Old Southwest, eventually stretching westward from the Carolinas and Georgia all the way to Texas. In 1860, Louisiana, Mississippi, and Alabama were the top-producing cotton states.

FACT 5
Concentration of Slave Ownership
In 1860, whites who owned twenty or more slaves were considered planters. They constituted only 4 percent of the white population. Only roughly 25 percent of white families owned slaves, most owning fewer than twenty.

FACT 6
Value of Slaves
By 1860, the dollar value of slaves outstripped the value of all American banks, railroads, and factories combined.

FACT 7
Value of Cotton
Southern cotton fueled the growth of the modern textile industry, particularly in Europe. By 1860, Great Britain imported 80 percent of its raw cotton from the American South. Southern planters, dependent on slavery, grew overconfident that their economic and social system was indestructible.

QUESTIONS FOR ANALYSIS

1. Why did southerners invest so much in cotton production?
2. Where was cotton production concentrated?
3. How did increased cotton production affect slavery?
4. How did increased cotton production affect the distribution of wealth in the South?

383,637 out of a total white population of 8 million. But assuming that each family numbered five people, then almost two million people, or roughly a fourth of the South's white population, had a direct interest in slavery.

Few planters were wealthy enough not to work. Most of them were full-time commercial farmers who spent their days, including weekends, carefully managing their agricultural business. Most planters had begun their careers as land traders, investors, cotton merchants (called "factors"), and farmers. Over time, they made enough money to acquire a plantation worked by slaves. Frederick Stanton, a cotton broker near Natchez, Mississippi, became a planter with 444 slaves working 15,000 acres of cotton.

Success as a cotton planter required careful monitoring of the world markets for cotton, land, and slaves as well as careful management of the workers and production. When not working, planters enjoyed hunting, horse racing, and cards. As a plantation slave recalled, his master on Sundays liked to "gamble, run horses, or fight game-cocks, discuss politics, and drink whisky, and brandy and water all day long."

> The planter elite

From colonial times, most southern white men, but especially the planter and political elite, embraced a social code centered on an easily offended sense of personal honor in which a man was expected to defend his reputation—with words, fists, or guns. Duels to the death were the ultimate expression of personal honor and manly courage. Although not confined to the South, dueling was much more common there than in the rest of the nation, a fact that gave rise to the observation that southerners would be polite until they were angry enough to kill you. Many of the most prominent southern leaders—congressmen, senators, governors, editors, and planters—engaged in duels, although dueling was technically illegal in many states. The roster of participants included President Andrew Jackson of Tennessee and Senator Henry Clay of Kentucky.

> Honor and violence: Dueling

The Plantation Mistress

The **plantation mistress**, like the master, seldom led a life of idle leisure, nor was she a frail, helpless creature focused solely on planning parties and balls. Although the mistress of the plantation had slaves to wait on her and attend to her needs, she also supervised the domestic household in the same way as the planter took care of the cotton business, overseeing the supply and preparation of food and linens, the housecleaning and care of the sick, and many other details, including the birthing of babies. A plantation slave reported that her mistress "was with all the slave women every time a baby was born. Or, when a plague of misery hit the folks, she knew what to do and what kind of medicine to chase off the aches and pains." The son of a Tennessee slaveholder remembered that his mother and grandmother were "the busiest women I ever saw." Mary Boykin Chesnut, a plantation mistress in South Carolina, complained that "there is no slave, after all, like a wife." She admitted that she herself had few rights in the household, since her husband was the "master of the house." Planters ruled their wives and children as well

Mary Boykin Chesnut Her diary describing the Civil War was republished in 1981 and won the Pulitzer Prize.

plantation mistress Matriarch of a planter's household, responsible for supervising the domestic aspects of the estate.

as their slaves, and southern white women were even more confined to the "domestic arena" than their counterparts in the North. Virginian George Fitzhugh, a celebrated Virginia attorney and writer, spoke for most southern men when he explained that a "man loves his children because they are weak, helpless, and dependent. He loves his wife for similar reasons."

White women living in a slaveholding culture confronted a double standard in terms of moral and sexual behavior. They were expected to be examples of Christian morality and sexual purity, and to "obey" their fathers and husbands, even as their husbands, brothers, and sons often followed an unwritten rule of self-indulgent hedonism. "God forgive us," Mary Chesnut wrote in her diary, "but ours is a monstrous system. Like the patriarchs of old, our men live all in one house with their wives and their [enslaved] concubines [lovers]; and the mulattoes [people of mixed races] one sees in every family partly resemble the white children. Any lady is ready to tell you who is the father of all the mulatto children in everybody's household but her own. Those, she seems to think, drop from the clouds." Such a double standard reinforced the arrogant authoritarianism displayed by many white planters. Yet for all their private complaints and daily burdens, few plantation mistresses spoke out against the male-dominated social order and racist climate.

Overseers and Drivers

White overseers

The whites who worked on the large plantations were usually *overseers* who managed the slaves to ensure that they worked hard and efficiently. They generally came from the middle class of white farmers or skilled workers, or were younger sons of planters. Most hoped to become slaveholders themselves. They moved often, seeking better wages and cheaper land. A Mississippi planter described white overseers as "a worthless set of vagabonds." Usually, the highest managerial position a slave could hope for on a plantation was that of *driver*, a man whose job was to oversee a small group ("gang") of slaves. There were, however, a few black overseers. Francis Frederic, a slave in Kentucky, remembered that his grandmother's white master was a "hard one." He appointed her son, a slave, as the plantation's overseer. After the planter discovered that Frederic's grandmother had committed the crime of attending a prayer meeting, he ordered her son to give her "forty lashes with a thong of a raw cow's-hide, her master standing over her the whole time blaspheming and threatening what he would do if her son did not lay it on."

"Plain White Folk"

"plain white folk" Yeoman farmers who lived and worked on their own small farms, growing food and cash crops to trade for necessities.

The most numerous white southerners were the small farmers—the **"plain white folk"** who were usually uneducated and often illiterate, eking out hardscrabble lives of bare self-sufficiency separate from the market revolution. These small farmers ("yeomen") lived with their families in simple two-room cabins, raised a few hogs and chickens, grew some corn and cotton, and traded with neighbors more than they bought from stores. Women on these farms worked in the fields during harvest time but spent most of their days doing household chores. Some of these "middling" farmers owned a handful of slaves with whom they worked alongside, but most had none. In the backcountry and mountainous regions of the South, small farmers dominated the social structure; there were few plantations in western North Carolina and Virginia, upcountry South Carolina, eastern Tennessee, northern Georgia, and northern Alabama.

Southern farmers tended to be fiercely independent and suspicious of government authority, and they overwhelmingly identified with the Democratic party of Andrew Jackson and the spiritual energies of the evangelical Protestant denominations such as Baptists and Methodists. Although only a minority of the small farm owners held slaves, most supported the slave system for both economic and racial reasons. They feared that the slaves, if freed, would compete with them for land and jobs, and they enjoyed the privileged status that race-based slavery afforded them. As a white farmer told a northern traveler, "Now suppose they [slaves] was free. You see they'd all think themselves as good as we." James Henry Hammond and other wealthy white planters frequently reminded their poorer white neighbors who owned no slaves that "in a slave country, every freeman is an aristocrat" because blacks are beneath them in the social order. Such racist sentiments pervaded the Lower South—and much of the rest of the nation—throughout the nineteenth century.

"Poor Whites"

Visitors to the Old South often had trouble telling small farmers apart from the "poor whites," a category of desperately poor people relegated to the least desirable land, living on the fringes of polite society, often in the upland areas or in the Appalachian Mountains. The "poor whites," often derided as "crackers," or "hillbillies," were often day laborers or squatters who owned neither land nor slaves. Some 40 percent of white southerners worked as "tenants," renting land from others, or as farm laborers, toiling for others. And what land they owned was often the least desirable for farming. They were often forced to take refuge in the pine barrens, the mountain hollows, and the swamps after having been pushed aside by the more enterprising and the more successful. They usually lived in log cabins or shacks and often made their own clothing, barely managing each year to keep their families clothed, warm, dry, and fed. The "poor whites" were regularly satirized and caricatured. In 1860, D. R. Hundley wrote in *Social Relations in Our Southern States* that the poor white southerner was descended from criminals deported to America from Great Britain. "He is bony and lank, with a sallow complexion, awkward manners, and a natural stupidity or dullness of intellect that almost surpasses belief."

Slave codes

Black Society in the South

However immoral and degrading, slavery was one of the fastest-growing elements of national life during the first half of the nineteenth century. Owning, working, and selling slaves was the quickest way to wealth and social status in the nineteenth-century South. In 1790, the United States had fewer than 700,000 black slaves. By 1830 it had more than 2 million, and by 1860 almost 4 million. As the enslaved population grew, slave owners felt the need to develop a complex system of rules, regulations, and restrictions to govern the slaves' daily lives. Throughout the seventeenth and well into the eighteenth century, slavery had largely been an uncodified system of forced labor. Slaves were initially treated like indentured servants, who worked for a designated number of years and then, at some point after they had fulfilled their service, would be freed.

After the American Revolution, however, slavery became a highly regulated institution centered on lifelong service. Slaves were treated like property rather than people; babies became slaves at birth; slaves could be moved, sold, rented, whipped, or raped, as their master saw fit. Formal **slave codes** in each state governed the treatment of slaves in order to deter runaways or rebellions. Some state codes, for example, prohibited slaves from gathering in groups of more than three. Slaves could not leave their owner's land or household without permission or stay out after dark (curfew) without an identification pass. "No slave dare leave the plantation to which he belongs," said Charles Ball, a bondman who lived in several states, explained, not for a "single mile" or a "single hour, by night . . . practice to leave their owners' property without a pass from the overseer, or master."

Some codes made it a crime for slaves to learn how to read and write, for fear that they might use notes to plan a revolt. A former Kentucky slave, John W. Fields, remembered that the white slaveholders "were very harsh if we were caught trying to learn or write. . . . Our ignorance was the greatest hold the South had on us." If a white was caught teaching a slave to read, they were subject to a fine and imprisonment. Fields also explained that the slaves in his rural community were never allowed to go to town for fear that they might hatch an escape. Slaves in most states could not testify in court, legally marry, own firearms, or hit a white man, even in self-defense. Yet despite such restrictions and brutalities, the enslaved managed to create their own community and culture within the confines of the slave system.

"Free Persons of Color"

In the South, free persons of color tended to live in cities. In fact they were anything but free; they occupied an uncertain social status between slavery and freedom. In South Carolina, for example, free blacks had to pay

slave codes Codes governing the treatment of slaves in each state in order to deter runaways and rebellions.

an annual tax and were not allowed to leave the state. After 1823, they were required to have a white "guardian." Blacks became "free" in a number of ways. Over the years, some slaves were able to purchase their freedom, and others were freed ("manumitted") by their owners. By 1860, there were approximately 250,000 free blacks in the slave states, most of whom lived in coastal cities such as Baltimore, Charleston, Mobile, and New Orleans. Some were tailors or shoemakers or carpenters; others worked as painters, bricklayers, butchers, blacksmiths, or barbers. Still others worked on the docks or on steamships. Free black women usually worked as seamstresses, laundresses, or house servants. Free blacks had more rights than slaves. They could enter into contracts, marry, own property (including slaves of their own), and pass on their property to their children.

Among the free black population were a large number of **mulattoes**, people of mixed racial ancestry. The census of 1860 reported 412,000 mulattoes in the United States, or about 10 percent of the black population—probably a drastic undercount. In cities such as Charleston, South Carolina, and especially New Orleans, Louisiana, "colored" society occupied a status somewhere between that of blacks and that of whites. Some mulattoes built substantial fortunes and even became slaveholders themselves. In Louisiana, a mulatto, Cyprien Ricard, paid $250,000 for an estate that had ninety-one slaves. In Natchez, Mississippi, William Johnson, son of a white father and a mulatto mother, operated three barbershops, owned 1,500 acres of land, and held several slaves. Black slaveholders were few in number, however. The 1830 census reported that 3,775 free blacks, about 2 percent of the total free black population, owned 12,760 slaves. Most often, black slaveholders were free blacks who bought their own family members with the express purpose of freeing them.

The Trade in Slaves

The rapid increase in the slave population mainly occurred naturally, through slave births, especially after Congress and President Thomas Jefferson outlawed American involvement with the African slave trade in 1808. But banning the importation of slaves from Africa also had the effect of increasing the cash value of slaves in the United States. This in turn convinced some owners to treat their slaves better. As one planter remarked in 1849, "The time has been that the farmer would kill up and wear out one Negro to buy another, but it is not so now."

The dramatic rise in the dollar value of enslaved workers prompted better treatment for many. "Massa was purty good," one ex-slave recalled. "He treated us jus' 'bout like you would a good mule." Another said his master "fed us reg'lar on good, 'stantial food, jus' like you'd tend to you hoss [horse], if you had a real good one." A slave born in 1850 had a life expectancy of 36 years; the life expectancy of whites was 40 years. Some slaveholders hired white wage laborers, often Irish immigrants, for dangerous work rather than risk the lives of the more valuable slaves.

Yarrow Mamout As an enslaved African Muslim, Mamout purchased his freedom, acquired property, and settled in present-day Washington, D.C. Charles Willson Peale executed this portrait in 1819 when Mamout was over 100 years old.

mulattoes Mixed-race people who constituted most of the South's free black population.

Once the African slave trade was outlawed, the slave-trading network *within* the United States became even more important. Selling slaves for profit became big business, and slave markets and auction houses sprang up in every southern city. Most often, slaves along the Atlantic coast were sold and moved from the worn-out lands of Virginia and the Carolinas into the booming Old Southwest. Perhaps the worst aspect of the domestic slave trade was the separation of children from parents and husbands from wives. "Them days was hell," a former slave woman named Delia Garlic remembered. "Babies were snatched from their mother's breast and sold to speculators. Chilrens was separated from sisters and brothers and never saw each other again. Course they cried. You think they not cry when they was sold like cattle?" Only Louisiana and Alabama (from 1852) prohibited separating a child younger than ten from his or her mother, and no state prevented the separation of a slave husband from his wife.

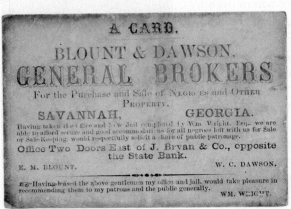

The business of slavery This advertisement for the Blount & Dawson guarantees its clients "secure and good accommodations for all negroes left with us for Sale or Safe-Keeping" in its newly acquired jail, opposite the state bank.

Almost a million captive blacks were "sold South" and taken to the Old Southwest during the first half of the nineteenth century. A third of the transplanted slaves were transported with their owners. The other two-thirds were sold at auctions where slaves were stripped to show their physique and often told to jump and dance to display their agility. White owners—as well as Indians who purchased enslaved blacks—worked the slaves especially hard in the "howling wilderness" of the Old Southwest, cutting down vast forests, operating sawmills, draining swamps, clearing land, building roads, and planting cotton. A white Virginian noted in 1807 that "there is a great aversion amongst our Negroes to be carried to distant parts, and particularly to our new countries [in the Old Southwest]."

Rural and Urban Slavery

The vast majority of slaves across the South were **field hands**, both men and women, including children, organized into work gangs, usually supervised by a black "driver" or white overseer. Plantation slaves were usually housed in one- or two-room wooden shacks or log cabins with dirt floors. The wealthiest planters built slave cabins out of brick. A set of clothes was distributed twice a year, but shoes were generally provided only in winter; slaves went barefoot most of the year. About half of all slave babies died in their first year, a rate more than twice that of whites. The food provided slaves was cheap and monotonous: cornmeal, pork, molasses, and chicken.

Solomon Northup, a free-born African American from New York with a wife and three children, was kidnapped in 1845 by slave traders, taken first to Washington, D.C., and then to New Orleans, and eventually sold to a

field hands Slaves who toiled in the cotton or cane fields in organized work gangs.

THE SLAVE POPULATION, 1820 AND 1860

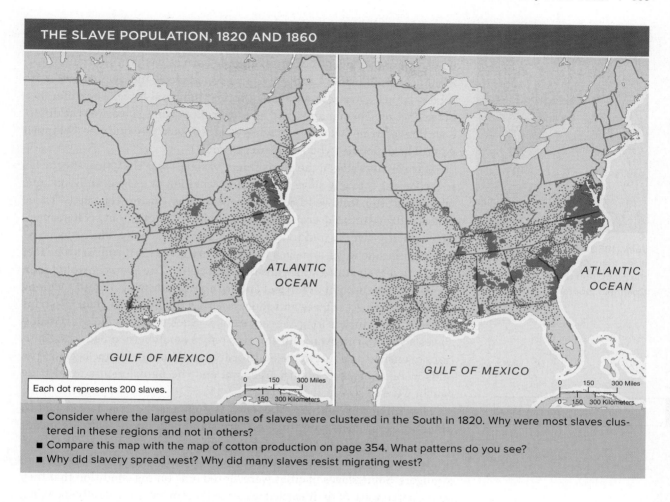

ATLANTIC OCEAN

GULF OF MEXICO

Each dot represents 200 slaves.

0   150   300 Miles
0   150   300 Kilometers

ATLANTIC OCEAN

GULF OF MEXICO

0   150   300 Miles
0   150   300 Kilometers

- Consider where the largest populations of slaves were clustered in the South in 1820. Why were most slaves clustered in these regions and not in others?
- Compare this map with the map of cotton production on page 354. What patterns do you see?
- Why did slavery spread west? Why did many slaves resist migrating west?

"repulsive and coarse" Louisiana cotton planter. More than a decade later, he was able to gain his freedom. In *Twelve Years a Slave* (1853), he wrote about his living and working conditions as a slave. His bed "was a plank twelve inches wide and ten feet long. My pillow was a stick of wood. The bedding was a coarse blanket." The log cabin where he and others slept had a dirt floor and no windows. Each day, "an hour before daylight, the horn is blown. Then the slaves arouse, prepare their breakfast . . . and hurry to the field." If found in their "quarters after daybreak," or if they failed to harvest enough cotton, he added, slaves were flogged. "It was rarely that a day passed by without one or more whippings. . . . The crack of the lash, and the shrieking of the slaves, can be heard from dark till bed time, on Epps' plantation, any day almost during the entire period of the cotton-picking season."

Field hands worked from sunrise to sunset, six days a week. Amanda McDaniel, enslaved in Georgia, remembered that her parents "had to get

Brutal force and rural slaves

***Jack* (1850)** Daguerreotype of a slave identified only as Jack, on the plantation of B. F. Taylor in Columbia, South Carolina.

up at four o'clock every morning and feed the stock [cattle, pigs, horses, and mules] first. By the time it was light enough to see they had to be in the fields where they hoed the cotton and the corn as well as the other crops." Although some owners and slaves developed close and even affectionate relationships, slavery was a system rooted in brutal force. The difference between a good owner and a bad one, according to one slave, was the difference between one "who did not whip you too much" and one who "whipped you till he'd bloodied you and blistered you."

Slave owners staged the punishment of slaves into theatrical spectacles to strike fear into any slave considering rebellion or escape. In Louisiana, whippings often followed a horrific procedure, as a visitor reported: "Three stakes is drove into the ground in a triangular manner, about six feet apart. The culprit [slave] is told to lie down . . . flat on his belly. The arms is extended out, side ways, and each hand tied to a stake hard and fast. The feet is both tied to the third stake, all stretched tight." The overseer would then step back "seven, eight or ten feet and with a rawhide whip about 7 feet long . . . lays on with great force and address across the Buttocks," cutting strips of flesh "7 or 8 inches long at every stroke." Such cruelties led over 50,000 slaves a year to run away. But this was only a small percentage of the millions of enslaved people in the South. Most chose not to escape because the odds were so stacked against freedom, and the punishments for getting caught were so severe.

Slaves living in southern cities such as Richmond or Atlanta had a much different experience from those on farms and plantations. City life meant that slaves interacted not only with their white owners but also with the extended interracial community—shopkeepers and police, neighbors and strangers. Some slaves in cities were "hired out" on the condition that they paid a percentage of their earned wages to their owners. Generally speaking, slaves in cities enjoyed greater mobility and freedom than their counterparts in rural areas living on isolated farms or plantations.

| Greater mobility for city slaves |

Slave Women

Although enslaved men and women often performed similar chores, they did not experience slavery in the same way. "Slavery is terrible for men," the former North Carolina slave Harriet Jacobs stressed in her autobiography, *Incidents in the Life of a Slave Girl*, "but it is far more terrible for women. Superadded to the burden common to all, they have wrongs, and sufferings, and mortifications peculiarly their own."

| Female slaves and reproduction |

Once slaveholders realized how profitable a fertile female slave could be over time by giving birth to babies that could later be sold, they "encouraged" female slaves to have as many children as possible. A South Carolina planter named William Johnson explained in 1815 that the "interest of the owner is to obtain from his slaves labor *and increase* [in their numbers]." Some owners rewarded pregnant slaves by giving them less work and more food, and rewarded new mothers with dresses and silver dollars.

But if motherhood provided enslaved women with greater stature and benefits, it also was exhausting. Within days after childbirth, the mothers were put to work spinning, weaving, or sewing. A few weeks thereafter, they were sent back to the fields; breast-feeding mothers were often forced to take their babies with them, strapped to their backs. Enslaved women were expected to do "man's work": cut trees, haul logs, spread fertilizer, plow fields, dig ditches, slaughter animals, hoe corn, and pick cotton. As an escaped slave reported, "Women who do outdoor work are used as bad as men."

Once women passed their childbearing years, around the age of forty, their workload increased. Slaveholders put middle-aged women to work full-time in the fields or performing other outdoor labor. On large plantations, elderly women, called *grannies*, kept the children during the day while their mothers worked outside. Slave women worked as cooks and seamstresses, midwives and nurses, healers and folk doctors.

Enslaved girls, women, and some men were often sexually abused by their owners, both men and women. James Henry Hammond, the prominent South Carolina planter and political leader who confessed that he only succeeded "when everything is under my control," had a long affair with one of his female slaves, Sally Johnson, who bore several of his children, and then began another affair with one of her daughters, twelve-year-old Louisa. (A lusty man with voracious sexual appetites, Hammond also had scandalous affairs with four teen-aged nieces and two daughters of his sister-in-law). Sometimes a white master or overseer would rape a woman in the fields or cabins. Sometimes a woman would be locked in a cabin with a male slave whose task was to impregnate her. Enslaved women responded to sexual assaults in different ways. Some seduced their owner away from his wife. Others fiercely resisted the sexual advances—and were usually whipped or even killed for their disobedience. Some women aborted or killed their babies rather than see them grow up in slavery.

> Female slaves and sexual abuse

Slave family in a Georgia cotton field The invention of the cotton gin sent cotton production soaring, deepening the South's dependence on slavery.

Celia

A single historical example helps illustrate the exploitation, deprivation, and vulnerability of enslaved people. The tragic story of a teenager named Celia reveals the complexity of slavery and the limited options available to the enslaved. As Celia discovered, slaves often could improve their circumstances only by making horrible choices that offered no guarantee of success.

In 1850, fourteen-year-old Celia was purchased by Robert Newsom, a Missouri farmer who told his daughters that he had bought the girl to be their servant. In fact, however, the recently widowed Newsom wanted a sexual slave. After purchasing Celia, he raped her, and for the next five years, he treated her as his mistress, even building her a brick cabin fifty yards from his house. During that time, she gave birth to two children, presumably his offspring.

On June 23, 1855, the sixty-five-year-old Newsom entered Celia's cabin, ignored her frantic appeals, and kept assaulting her until she struck and killed him with a large stick. Celia was not allowed to testify at her murder trial because she was a slave. The judge and jury, all white men, pronounced her guilty, and on December 21, 1855, she was hanged. The grim story of Celia's abusive owner and brief life illustrates the lopsided power structure in southern society at the time. Celia bore a double burden, that of a slave and of a woman living in a male-dominated society rife with racism and sexism.

CORE **OBJECTIVE**

5. Analyze how enslaved peoples responded to the inhumanity of their situation.

Forging a Slave Community

To generalize about slavery is to miss the diversity of its experiences. Enslaved African Americans were victims of terrible injustice and abuse, but such an obvious truth neglects important evidence of their endurance, resilience, and achievement. The Africans who were brought to America represented a variety of ethnic, linguistic, and tribal origins. Wherever they could, they forged their own sense of community, asserted their individuality, and devised ingenious ways of resisting their confinement. African American folklore invented stories of resistance such as "Brer [Brother] Rabbit," where the smart little rabbit eludes the animals stalking it by hiding in a patch of prickly briars. Many **spirituals**, sacred folk songs, expressed a longing to be free. Although most slaves were prohibited from marrying, the law did not prevent them from choosing partners and forging a family life within the rigid constraints of the slave system.

The Slave Family

Slave marriages had no legal status, but many slaveholders accepted unofficial marriages as a stabilizing influence on the plantation. Sometimes they performed the marriages themselves or had a minister officiate. Whatever the formalities, the norm for the slave community, as for the white, was the nuclear family, with the father regarded as the head of the household. Most slave children were socialized by means of the nuclear family, which afforded

spirituals Songs with religious messages sung by slaves to help ease the strain of field labor and to voice their suffering at the hands of their masters and overseers.

some degree of independence from white influence. Childhood was short for slaves. At five or six years of age, children were put to work; they collected trash and firewood, picked cotton, scared away crows from planted fields, weeded gardens and fields, and ran errands. By age ten they were full-time field hands. The frequent buying and selling of slaves meant that children were often separated from their parents and sold to new masters. In Missouri, one enslaved woman saw six of her seven children, aged one to eleven, sold to six different owners. Given the fragility of the family, enslaved African Americans often extended the fellowship of family to those who worked together, with older slave women being addressed as "granny," or co-workers as "sis" or "brother." Such efforts to create a sense of extended family resembled similar kinship practices in Africa. One white teacher visiting a slave community observed that they "all belonged to one immense family."

African American Religion

Among the most important elements of African American culture was its dynamic religion, a unique mixture of African, Caribbean, and Christian elements often practiced in secret because many slaveholders feared enslaved workers might use group religious services as a means of organizing rebellions. Slaves found in religion both relief for the soul and release for their emotions. Most Africans brought with them to the Americas belief in a Creator, or Supreme God, whom they could recognize in the Christian God, and whom they might identify with Christ, the Holy Ghost, and the saints. But they also maintained beliefs in spirits, magic, and conjuring. Most slave owners tried to erase African religion and spirituality from the slave experience.

Plantation Burial (1860) The slaves of Mississippi governor Tilghman Tucker gather together in the woods to bury and mourn for one of their own. The painter of this scene, Englishman John Antrobus, would serve in the Confederate Army during the Civil War.

By 1860, about 20 percent of adult slaves had joined Christian denominations. Many others displayed aspects of the Christian faith in their forms of worship but were not considered Christians. As a white minister observed, "Their notions of the Supreme Being; of the character and offices of Christ and of the Holy Ghost; of a future state; and of what constitutes the holiness of life are indefinite and confused." Some slaves had "heard of Jesus Christ, but who he is and what he has done for a ruined world, they cannot tell."

African American religion and spirituals

Slaves found the Bible inspiring in its support for the poor and oppressed, and they embraced its promise of salvation through the sacrifice of Jesus. Likewise, the lyrics of religious spirituals helped slaves endure the strain of field labor. The abolitionist Frederick Douglass, himself a former slave, stressed that "slaves sing most when they are most unhappy." Spirituals offered them deliverance from their worldly woes. One popular spiritual, "Go Down, Moses," derived from the plight of the ancient Israelites held captive in Egypt, says: "We need not always weep and moan, / Let my people go. / And wear these slavery chains forlorn, / Let my people go."

Slave Rebellions

Southern whites feared slave uprisings more than anything. As a prominent Virginian explained, a slave revolt would "deluge the southern country with blood." Any sign of resistance or rebellion therefore risked a brutal response. In 1811, for example, two of Thomas Jefferson's nephews, Lilburn and Isham Lewis, tied a seventeen-year-old slave named George to the floor of their Kentucky cabin and killed him with an axe in front of seven other slaves, all because George had run away several times. They then handed the axe to one of the slaves and forced him to dismember the body and put the pieces in the fireplace. The Lewises, who had been drinking heavily, wanted "to set an example for any other uppity slaves."

Slave rebellions

The overwhelming authority and firepower of southern whites made organized resistance by slaves very risky. The nineteenth-century South witnessed only four major slave insurrections. In 1800, a slave named Gabriel Prosser, who worked as a blacksmith on a plantation near Richmond, Virginia, hatched a revolt involving perhaps a thousand other slaves. They planned to seize key points in the city, capture the governor, James Monroe, and overthrow the white elite. Gabriel expected the "poor white people" to join their effort. But someone alerted whites to the scheme. Gabriel and twenty-six of his fellow "soldiers" were captured, tried, and hanged. Before his execution, Gabriel explained that he was only imitating George Washington: "I have ventured my life in endeavoring to obtain the liberty of my countrymen." A white Virginian who observed the hangings noted that the rebels on the gallows displayed a "sense of their [natural] rights, [and] a contempt for danger."

In early 1811, the largest slave revolt in American history occurred just north of New Orleans in the Louisiana Territory, where wealthy sugarcane planters had acquired one of the largest populations of slaves in North America, five times as many as the whites who owned them. Many of those slaves were ripe for revolt. Sugarcane was known as a "killer crop" because the working conditions were so harsh that many slaves died from exhaustion in the heat and humidity of Louisiana.

Late on January 8, a group of slaves broke into their owner's plantation house along the east bank of the Mississippi River. The planter was able to escape, but his son was hacked to death. The leader of the assault was Charles Deslondes, a trusted slave overseer. Deslondes and his fellow rebels seized weapons, horses, and militia uniforms from the plantation. Reinforced by more slaves and emboldened by liquor, the rebels headed toward New Orleans, burning houses and killing whites along the way. Over the next two days, the ranks of the rebels swelled to over 200. But their success was short-lived. Angry whites—as well as several free blacks who were later praised for their "tireless zeal and dauntless courage"—suppressed the insurrection. U.S. Army units and militia joined the effort. Dozens of slaves were killed or wounded; most who fled were captured over the next week. "We made considerable slaughter," reported one white planter. Deslondes had his hands severed and thighs broken before he was shot and his body burned. As many as 100 slaves were tortured, killed, and beheaded. Their severed heads were placed on poles along the Mississippi River in order to strike fear into enslaved workers. A month after the rebellion was put down, a white resident noted that "all the negro difficulties have subsided and gentle peace prevails."

Denmark Vesey Revolt

The Denmark Vesey plot in Charleston, South Carolina, discovered in 1822, involved a similar effort to assault the white population. Vesey, born in 1767 on the Caribbean island of St. Thomas, was purchased by a slave trader based in Charleston. In 1799 he purchased a lottery ticket and won $1,500, which he used to buy his freedom, joining 3,600 other free blacks in Charleston. He thereafter opened a carpentry shop and organized a Bible study class in the African Methodist Episcopal (AME) Church.

In 1822, Vesey and several slaves developed a plan for a massive slave revolt. They would first capture the city's arsenal and distribute its hundreds of rifles to free and enslaved blacks. All whites in the city would then be killed, along with any blacks who refused to join the rebellion. Vesey then planned to burn the city, seize ships in the harbor, and head for the black republic of Haiti, where slaves in the former French sugar colony, then called Saint-Domingue, had staged a successful revolt in 1791.

The Vesey plot never got off the ground, however. As Vesey and others secretly tried to recruit slaves, one of them told his master what was going on. Soon Vesey and a hundred other supposed slave rebels were captured and tried. The court found Vesey guilty of plotting a slave uprising intended to "trample on all laws, human and divine; to riot in blood, outrage, rapine . . . and conflagration, and to introduce anarchy and confusion in their most horrid forms." Vesey and thirty-four others were executed; three dozen more were transported to Spanish Cuba and sold. The AME church in Charleston where Vesey hatched his plan was closed and demolished. When told that he would be hanged, Vesey replied that "the work of insurrection will go on."

Denmark Vesey's planned rebellion led officials in South Carolina to place even more restrictions on the mobility of free blacks and black religious gatherings. It also influenced John C. Calhoun to abandon the nationalism of his early political career and become the South's most forceful spokesman for states' rights.

Nat Turner Rebellion

The Nat Turner insurrection of August 1831, in a rural area of Virginia where enslaved blacks greatly outnumbered free whites, again panicked whites throughout the South. Turner, a trusted black overseer, was also a preacher who believed God had instructed him to lead a slave rebellion. The revolt began when a small group of slaves joined Turner in methodically killing his owner's family. They then repeated the process at other farmhouses, where other slaves joined in. Before the revolt ended, fifty-seven whites had been killed, most of them women and children. Turner later explained that he had also killed the "man who was to me a kind master." Federal troops, Virginia militiamen, and volunteers, driven by anger and fear, indiscriminately killed hundreds of slaves in the process of putting down the rebels. A Virginia newspaper said the behavior of the white vigilantes was comparable in "barbarity to the atrocities of the insurgents." Seventeen slaves were hanged; several were decapitated, with their severed heads placed on poles along the highway. Turner, called the "blood-stained monster," avoided capture for six weeks. He then was tried, found guilty, and hanged. His dead body was dismembered, with body parts given to the victims' families.

More than any other slave uprising, **Nat Turner's Rebellion** terrified white southerners by making real the lurking fear that enslaved blacks might revolt. The Virginia legislature responded by restricting the ability of slaves to learn to read and write and gather for religious meetings. "We were no more than dogs," an enslaved woman recalled. "If they caught us with a piece of paper in our pockets, they'd whip us. They was afraid we'd learn to read and write, but I never got the chance." Throughout the South after Nat Turner's Rebellion, states created vigilante groups of whites, slave owners as well as non-owners, who would patrol their communities looking for runaways. A former slave highlighted the "thousand obstacles thrown in the way of the flying slave. Every white man's hand is raised against him—the patrollers are watching for him—the hounds are ready to follow on his track, and the nature of the country is such as renders it impossible to pass through it with any safety."

Nat Turner's Rebellion (1831)
Insurrection in rural Virginia led by black overseer Nat Turner, who murdered slave owners and their families; in turn, federal troops indiscriminately killed hundreds of slaves in the process of putting down Turner and his rebels.

The Lure of Freedom

But slaves kept running away—a powerful example of the enduring lure of freedom and the extraordinary courage of those who yearn for it. Frederick Douglass decided that risking death was better than staying in bondage: "I had as well be killed running as die standing." As Douglass implied, the odds were stacked against escape, in part because most slaves could not read, had no maps, and could not use public transportation such as stage-coaches, steamboats, and railroads. Blacks, whether free or enslaved, had to have an identity pass or official emancipation papers to go anywhere on their own. Most runaways were tracked down by bloodhounds or bounty hunters. Even in the 1850s—the height of efforts by many northerners to help runaways through the "underground railroad," a secret network of safe houses and abolitionists—only about 1,000 slaves each year made it to safety.

Runaways: The "underground railroad"

But slaves who did not escape resisted in other ways. They often faked illness, engaged in sabotage, stole or broke tools, or destroyed crops or live-stock. Yet there were constraints on such behavior, for laborers would likely eat better on a prosperous plantation than on a struggling one. And the shrewdest slaveholders knew that offering rewards was more profitable than inflicting pain.

Everyday forms of resistance

The South—a Region Apart

The recurring theme of southern politics and culture from the 1830s to the outbreak of civil war in 1861 was the region's determination to remain a society dominated by whites who lorded over people of color. Slavery increasingly became the paramount issue controlling all else in the South. A South Carolinian asserted that "slavery with us is no abstraction—but a great and vital fact. Without it, our every comfort would be taken from us."

Protecting the right of southerners to own, transport, and sell slaves in the new western territories became the overriding focus of southern political leaders during the 1830s and after. As a Mississippi governor insisted in 1850, slavery "is entwined with our political system and cannot be separated from it." It was race-based slavery that provided the South's prosperity as well as its growing sense of separateness from the rest of the nation.

Throughout the 1830s, southern state legislatures were "one and indivisible" in their efforts to preserve race-based slavery. They shouted defiance against northern abolitionists who called for an end to the immorality of slavery. Virginia's General Assembly, for example, declared that only the southern states had the right to control slavery and that such control must be "maintained at all hazards." The Georgia legislature agreed, announcing that "upon this point there can be no discussion—no compromise—no doubt." The increasingly militant efforts of northerners to restrict or abolish slavery helped reinforce the sense of southern unity while provoking an emotional defensiveness that would result in secession and war—and the unexpected end of slavery.

■ **The Southern Distinctiveness** The South remained rural and agricultural in the first half of the nineteenth century as the rest of the nation embraced urban industrial development. The region's climate favored the growth of cash crops such as tobacco, rice, indigo, and, increasingly, cotton. These crops led to the spread of the plantation system of large commercial agriculture dependent on enslaved labor. The Southern planter elite sought not only to preserve slavery in the nineteenth century but also to expand it, despite growing criticism of this *"peculiar institution"* outside the region.

■ **A Cotton Economy** Throughout the pre–Civil War era the South became increasingly committed to a cotton economy. Despite efforts to diversify the economy, the wealth and status associated with cotton, as well as soil exhaustion and falling prices from Virginia to Georgia, prompted the westward expansion of the plantation culture to *The Old Southwest.* Moreover, sons of southern planters wanted to take advantage of cheap land on the frontier in order to make their own fortunes. Slaves were worked harshly as they prepared the terrain for cotton cultivation and experienced the breakup of their families. By 1860, the *cotton kingdom* stretched from the Carolinas and Georgia through eastern Texas and up the Mississippi River to Illinois. More than half of all slaves worked on cotton plantations.

■ **Southern White Culture** White society was divided between the planter elite, or those who owned at least twenty slaves or more, and all the rest. *Planters* made up around 4 percent of the white population and exercised a disproportionately powerful political and social influence. Other whites owned a few slaves, but most owned none. A majority of whites were *"plain white folk"*— simple farmers who raised corn, cotton, hogs, and chickens. Southern white women spent most of their time on household chores. The *plantation mistress* supervised her home and household slaves. Most whites were fiercely loyal to the institution of slavery. Even those who owned no slaves feared the competition they believed they would face if slaves were freed, and they enjoyed the privileged status that race-based slavery gave them.

■ **Southern Black Culture** As slavery spread and the southern economy became more dependent on slave labor, the enslaved faced more regulations and restrictions on their behavior. The vast majority of Southern blacks were slaves who served as *field hands.* They had few rights and could be bought and sold and moved at any time. Their movements were severely limited and they had no ability to defend themselves. Any violation of these restrictions could result in severe punishments. Most Southern blacks were slaves, but a small percentage were free. Many of the free blacks were *mulattoes*, having mixed-race parentage. Free blacks often worked for wages in towns and cities.

■ **African American Resistance and Resilience** Originally, slaves were treated more as indentured servants, eligible for freedom after a specified number of years, but during the eighteenth century *slave codes* codified practices of treating slaves as property rather than people. The enslaved responded to their oppression in a variety of ways. Although many slaves attempted to run away, only a few openly rebelled because the consequences were so harsh. Organized revolts such as *Nat Turner's Rebellion (1831)* in Virginia were rare. Most slaves survived their hardships by relying on their own communities, family ties, and Christian faith, and by developing their own culture, such as the singing of *spirituals* to express frustration, sorrow, and hope for their eventual deliverance.

KEY TERMS

CHRONOLOGY

1790	Enslaved population of the United States nearly reaches 700,000
1791	Slave revolt in Saint-Domingue (Haiti)
1800	Gabriel conspiracy in Richmond, Virginia
1808	U.S. participation in the international slave trade is outlawed
1811	Charles Deslondes revolt in Louisiana
1814	Annual cotton production in the United States is 150,000 bales
1822	Denmark Vesey conspiracy is discovered in Charleston, South Carolina
1830	U.S. slave population exceeds 2 million
1831	Nat Turner leads slave insurrection in Virginia
1840	Population in the Old Southwest tops 1.5 million
1852	Harriet Beecher Stowe's *Uncle Tom's Cabin* is published
1860	Annual cotton production in the United States reaches 4 million bales
	Slave population in the United States reaches 4 million

INQUIZITIVE

Go to InQuizitive to see what you've learned—and learn what you've missed—with personalized feedback along the way.

THE VOYAGE OF LIFE: CHILDHOOD (1839–1840) In his *Voyage of Life* series, Thomas Cole draws upon both the religious revivalism and Romantic ideals of the period to depict the four stages of a man's life: childhood (shown above), youth, manhood, and old age. In this painting, an infant drifts along the River of Life with his guardian angel into the fertile landscape from the dark cave, meant to be "emblematic of our earthly origin, and the mysterious Past."

Religion, Romanticism, and Reform

1800–1860

During the first half of the nineteenth century, the world's largest—and youngest—republic was a nation of contrasts. Europeans traveling in America marveled at its restless energy and expansive optimism, its commitment to democratic ideals, and its remarkable capitalist spirit. However, visitors also noticed that the dynamic young republic was experiencing growing pains as the market revolution continued to excite a lust for profits and to widen economic inequality. At the same time, sectional tensions over economic policies, and increasingly heated debates over the morality and future of slavery, made for a combative political environment whose conflicts were mirrored in social and cultural life.

Unlike nations of the Old World, which had long been steeped in history and romance, the United States in the early nineteenth century was a young nation whose founding leaders had embraced the rational ideas of the Enlightenment. Those "reasonable" ideas about government and the pursuit of happiness, most vividly set forth in Thomas Jefferson's Declaration of Independence, influenced religion, literature, and the arts, as well as various social reform movements. Politics was not the only contested battleground during the first half of the nineteenth century; religious and cultural life also experienced intense conflicts and radical new outlooks.

CORE OBJECTIVES INQUIZITIVE

1. Describe the major changes in the practice of religion in America in the early nineteenth century, and analyze their impact.

2. Examine the emergence of transcendentalism in American culture in the early nineteenth century.

3. Explain the origins of the major social reform movements in the early nineteenth century, and analyze their influence on American society and politics.

4. Analyze the impact on American society and politics of the emergence of the anti-slavery movement.

After the Revolution, many Americans were as interested in religious salvation as political engagement. Christian evangelists democratized the path to salvation at the same time that Jacksonian Democrats democratized the political process. So-called free-will ministers assured people that they could *choose* to be saved by embracing Jesus's promise of salvation just as more men who owned no property were allowed to *choose* their elected officials.

Christian activists assumed that the United States had a God-mandated mission to provide a shining example of representative government, much as Puritan New England had once stood as an example of an ideal Christian community. The concept of America having a special *mission* to create an ideal society still carried strong spiritual overtones. This ideal also contained an element of perfectionism—and an element of impatience when reality fell short of expectations. The combination of widespread religious energy and intense social activism brought major reforms and advances in human rights during the first half of the nineteenth century. It also brought disappointments that at times triggered cynicism and disillusionment.

CORE **OBJECTIVE**

1. Describe the major changes in the practice of religion in America in the early nineteenth century, and analyze their impact.

Religion

The contrasting currents of the rational Enlightenment and the spiritual Great Awakening, now mingling, now parting, flowed from the colonial period on into the nineteenth century. In different ways they eroded the old Calvinist view that people were innately sinful and that God had chosen only a select few for heavenly salvation ("predestination"). As time passed, many believers embraced a more optimistic religious outlook. Just as Enlightenment rationalism stressed humanity's natural goodness rather than its sinfulness and encouraged a belief in progress through social reforms and individual improvement, Protestant churches in the early nineteenth century stressed that people were capable of perfection through the guiding light of Christ.

Rational Religion

Deistical societies

Enlightenment ideas during the eighteenth century, including the religious concept of *Deism*, inspired prominent leaders such as Thomas Jefferson and Benjamin Franklin. Deists believed in a rational God—creator of the rational universe—and that all people were created as equals. They prized science and reason over traditional religion and blind faith. Interest in Deism increased after the American Revolution. In every major city, Deist societies emerged, and college students in particular took delight in criticizing conventional religion. Through the use of reason and scientific research, Deists believed, people might grasp the natural laws governing the universe. Deists rejected the belief that every statement in the Bible was literally true. They were skeptical of miracles and questioned the divinity of Jesus. Deists also defended free speech and opposed religious coercion.

Unitarianism and Universalism

Most Christians could hardly distinguish Deism from atheism, but the same ideals of Enlightenment rationalism that excited Deists soon began to make deep inroads into American Protestantism as well. The old Puritan churches in and around Boston proved especially vulnerable to the appeal of religious liberalism. Boston's progress—or, some would say, its degeneration—from Puritanism to prosperity had persuaded many wealthy families that they were anything but sinners at the mercy of an angry God. By the end of the eighteenth century, many well-educated New Englanders were embracing Unitarianism, a belief system that emphasizes the oneness ("unity") and compassion of a loving God, the natural goodness of humankind, and the superiority of calm reason over emotional forms of worship. **Unitarians** believe that Jesus was a saintly man but was not divine. People are not inherently sinful, Unitarians stress; people are capable of doing tremendous good by following the teachings of Jesus, and *all* people are eligible for the gift of salvation from a God of boundless love. Boston became the center of the Unitarian movement, which flourished chiefly within Congregational churches. During the early nineteenth century, "liberal" churches adopted the name *Unitarian*. Although Unitarianism never attracted large numbers of followers, many of its believers were among the best-educated and wealthiest New Englanders.

A parallel religious movement, Universalism, attracted a different—and much larger—social group: the working poor. In 1779, John Murray, a British clergyman and former Methodist, founded the first Universalist church, in Gloucester, Massachusetts. **Universalists** stressed that salvation was available to everyone; it was "universal," not for just a predestined few. God, it teaches, is too merciful to condemn anyone to eternal punishment. "Thus, the Unitarians and Universalists were in fundamental agreement," wrote one historian, "the Universalists holding that God was too good to damn man; the Unitarians insisting that man was too good to be damned." Although both sects remained relatively small, they exercised a powerful influence over intellectual life, especially in New England.

The Second Great Awakening

During the first Great Awakening in the early 1700s, traveling evangelists had stirred up religious life by challenging the established denominations, particularly Anglicanism, and promoting a more intense and personal relationship with God. In addition, Anglicanism suffered from being aligned historically with the Church of England and lost its status as the official religion in most states after the American Revolution. To help erase their pro-British image, Virginia Anglicans renamed themselves *Episcopalians*. But even the new name did not prevent the denomination from losing its leadership position in the South. Newer denominations, especially Baptists and Methodists, 20 percent of whom were African Americans, emerged and

Unitarians

Universalists

Unitarians Members of the liberal New England Congregationalist offshoot, who profess the oneness of God and the goodness of rational man, often well-educated and wealthy.

Universalists Members of a New England religious movement, who believed in a merciful God and universal salvation, often from the working class.

attracted masses of followers. These new Christian sects were organized in accord with more democratic principles, allowing individual congregations to exercise more power on their own than did the elaborate governance structures of the Anglican Church.

Second Great Awakening

Around 1800, the United States experienced a much larger wave of religious revivals called the **Second Great Awakening**, the first having swept across the American colonies in the first half of the eighteenth century. On and off over the next forty years, the flames of revivalism raced across the country in response to the dramatic economic growth and social changes transforming American life. The nation's rampant materialism furnished evangelical ministers with plenty of ammunition, as did soaring crime rates. Without religion, revivalists warned, the American republic would give way to "unbridled appetites and lust."

Statistics reveal the impact of the evangelical revivals. In 1780, there were only fifty Methodist churches in America; by 1860, there were 20,000, far more than any other denomination. The percentage of Americans who joined Protestant churches increased sixfold between 1800 and 1860. Thus, one of the major effects of the Second Great Awakening was that more Americans than ever were joining and supporting churches.

The Second Great Awakening involved two different centers of activity. One developed among the elite New England colleges that were founded as religious centers of learning, then spread westward like a wildfire across New York into Pennsylvania and Ohio, Indiana, and Illinois. The other emerged in the backwoods of Tennessee and Kentucky and spread across rural America. Both the urban and rural phases of Protestant revivalism shared a simple message: salvation is available not just to a select few, as the Calvinists had claimed, but to *anyone* who repents and embraces Christ.

Frontier Revivals

Traveling evangelists

In its frontier phase, the Second Great Awakening, like the first, generated tremendous excitement and dramatic behavior. It gave birth, moreover, to two religious phenomena—the traveling backwoods evangelist and the camp meeting—that helped keep the fires of revivalism and spiritual intensity burning. People found the supernatural inside as well as outside of churches; they readily believed in magic, dreams, visions, miraculous healing, and speaking in tongues. Evangelists and "exhorters" with colorful nicknames such as Jumpin' Jesus or Crazy Dow or Mad Isaac found ready audiences among lonely frontier folk hungry for spiritual intensity and a sense of community. Revivals in the backwoods were family-oriented, community-building events; they truly represented social democracy, bridging social, economic, political, and even racial divisions. Women, especially, flocked to the rural revivals, readily gave their souls to Jesus, and served as the backbone of religious life on the frontier.

At the end of the eighteenth century, ministers visiting the new western territories reported that there were few frontier churches and few people

Second Great Awakening
Religious revival movement that arose in reaction to the growth of secularism and rationalist religion; spurred the growth of the Baptist and Methodist churches.

attending them. To remedy the situation, evangelists began to stoke the fires of religious fervor. The first camp meeting occurred in 1801 on a Kentucky hillside called Cane Ridge. Some 10,000 people came from miles around, camping in tents under the stars. White and black ministers from many denominations preached day and night, often chanting their sermons in ways that prompted listeners to cry: "Amen!" "Hallelujah!" "Lord, have mercy!"

Like the revivals of the earlier Great Awakening, the **frontier revivals** generated intense emotions. One participant observed that "some of the people were singing, others praying, some crying for mercy." He added that "shrieks and shouts" punctuated every sermon. Soon, camp meeting revivals were occurring in every state. But not all were swept up in the religious emotionalism. Frances Trollope, a distinguished British woman writer who toured the United States in 1827, attended a frontier revival and thought the participants behaved like raving lunatics. She fled the roiling scene in panic.

Religious revivalism Frontier revivals and prayer meetings ignited religious fervor within both minister and participant. In this 1830s camp meeting, the women are so intensely moved by the sermon that they shed their bonnets and fall to their knees.

Baptists and Methodists

The frontier revivals included many Presbyterians but were dominated by Baptists and Methodists. The Baptist theology was grounded in biblical fundamentalism—a certainty that every word and story in the Bible are literally true. Unlike the earlier Puritans, however, the Baptists believed that everyone could gain salvation in heaven by choosing (via "free will") to receive God's grace and by being baptized as adults. The Baptists also stressed the social equality of all before God, regardless of wealth, status, or education.

The Methodists, who shared with Baptists the belief that everyone could gain salvation by an act of "free will," developed the most effective evangelical method of all: the "circuit rider," a traveling evangelist on horseback, who sought out converts in remote frontier settlements. The system began with Francis Asbury, a tireless British-born revivalist who scoured the Ohio Valley for lost souls, traveling across fifteen states and preaching thousands of sermons. Asbury established a mobile evangelism perfectly suited to the frontier environment and the new democratic age.

After Asbury, Peter Cartwright emerged as the most successful circuit rider and became famous for his highly charged sermons. Cartwright had

> Growth of Baptist and Methodist denominations

frontier revivals Religious revival movement within the Second Great Awakening, that took place in frontier churches in western territories and states in the early nineteenth century.

grown up in one of the most violent and lawless regions of frontier Kentucky. His brother was hanged as a murderer and his sister was said to be a prostitute. At age sixteen, he converted to Methodism, and the following year became an "exhorter," preaching the faith even though he was not yet an ordained minister. By age eighteen, Cartwright began roaming across Kentucky, Tennessee, Ohio, and Indiana, and for more than twenty years preached a sermon a day. His message was simple: salvation is free for all to embrace.

Revivalism and African Americans

Equal participation for African Americans

African Americans were especially attracted to the emotional energies of the Methodist and Baptist churches. Richard Allen, who would later help found the African Methodist Episcopal (AME) Church, said in 1787 that "there was no religious sect or denomination that would suit the capacity of the colored people as well as the Methodist." He decided that the "plain and simple gospel suits best for any people; for the unlearned can understand [it]." Even more important, the Methodists actively recruited blacks. They were "the first people," Allen noted, "that brought glad tidings to the colored people." The Baptists did as well. As African Americans joined white Baptist or Methodist churches, they infused the congregations with exuberant energy and the emotional songs called *spirituals*.

During the early nineteenth century, the energies of the Great Revival, as the Second Great Awakening was called, spread through the western states and into more settled regions back East, and Americans were building a thousand new churches each year. The fastest growth was along the frontier, where the camp meetings were an expression of the frontier's democratic spirit; they welcomed "all sorts and conditions" of people. Revivals were typically held in late summer or fall, when farm work eased. People came from far and wide, camping in wagons, tents, or crude shacks. African Americans, whether enslaved or free, were encouraged to attend.

Black Methodists Holding a Prayer Meeting (1811) This caricature of an African American Methodist meeting in Philadelphia shows a preacher in the church doorway, while his congregation engages in exuberant prayer.

Camp Meetings and Women

The largest meetings tended to be ecumenical affairs, with Baptist, Methodist, and Presbyterian ministers working as a team. Crowds often numbered in the thousands, and the unrestrained atmosphere at times got out of hand.

Mass excitement swept up even the most skeptical onlookers, and infusions of the spirit sparked strange behavior. Some went into trances; others contracted the "jerks," laughed "the holy laugh," babbled in unknown tongues, or got down on all fours and barked like dogs to "tree the devil," as a hound might tree a raccoon.

But dwelling on the bizarre aspects of the camp meetings gives a distorted view of an activity that offered a welcome social outlet to isolated rural folk. This was especially true for women, for whom the camp meetings provided a communal alternative to the rigors and loneliness of farm life. Women, in fact, played the predominant role at camp meetings, as they had in earlier revivals. Evangelical ministers repeatedly applauded the spiritual energies of women and affirmed their right to give public witness to their faith.

Camp meetings provided opportunities for women to participate as social equals to men, both as preachers and parishioners. Jarena Lee, a free black who lived in the Philadelphia area, was the first African American woman to be allowed to preach in the African Methodist Episcopal Church (AME). As she wrote, "If the man may preach, because the Saviour died for him, why not the woman? Seeing [as] he died for her also. Is he not a whole Saviour, instead of a half one, as those who hold it wrong for a woman to preach, would seem to make it appear?" Lee became a tireless revivalist during the 1830s, walking as many as twelve miles a day. According to her own records, she "traveled 2,325 miles and preached 178 sermons."

> Religious leadership for women

The organizational needs of large revivals offered ample opportunities for women to exercise leadership roles outside the home, including service as traveling evangelists themselves. Phoebe Worrall Palmer, for example, hosted prayer meetings in her New York City home that included men as well as women, a controversial innovation for the time. She then traveled across the United States as a camp meeting "exhorter," assuring listeners that they could gain a life without sin, what then was called "perfectionism" or "holiness."

Women like Phoebe Palmer found public roles within evangelical religion because of its emphasis on individual religious experiences rather than conventional male-dominated church structures. Palmer claimed a woman's right to preach by citing the biblical emphasis on obeying God rather than man. "It is always right to obey the Holy Spirit's command," she stressed, "and if that is laid upon a woman to preach the Gospel, then it is right for her to do so; it is a duty she cannot neglect without falling into condemnation."

Such opportunities to assume traditional male religious roles reinforced women's self-confidence and expanded their horizons. Their religious enthusiasm often inspired them to pursue social reforms, including expanded educational opportunities for women and the right to vote. So in many ways and on many levels, the energies of the revivals helped spread a more democratic faith among people living on the frontier.

Religion and Reform

Regions swept up by revival fever were compared to forests devastated by fire. Western New York, in fact, experienced such intense levels of evangelical activity that it was labeled the *burned-over district* because it was so often fired by the flames of the Holy Spirit. One reason the area was such a hotbed of evangelical activity was that it was being transformed by the Erie Canal, which opened in 1825. Both the construction of and traffic on the canal turned many "canal towns" into rollicking scenes of lawlessness: gambling, prostitution, public drunkenness, and crime. Such widespread sinfulness made the region ripe for revivalism.

The most successful evangelist in the burned-over district was a Presbyterian minister named Charles Grandison Finney. In the winter of 1830–1831, he preached with "a clear, shrill voice" for six months in Rochester, then a canal boomtown in upstate New York. In the process, he generated some 100,000 conversions and became the most celebrated minister in the country. Finney claimed that he was enabling "the greatest revival of religion . . . since the world began." While rural camp meeting revivals attracted farm families and other working-class groups, Finney's audiences in the Northeast attracted more prosperous seekers. "The Lord," Finney declared, "was aiming at the conversion of the highest classes of society." In 1836, he built a huge church in New York City to accommodate his rapidly growing congregation.

Finney focused on the question that had preoccupied Protestantism for centuries: what role can the individual play in earning salvation? The Puritans and other Calvinists had argued that people could neither earn nor choose salvation. They believed in "predestination": that salvation was a gift of God to a select few. In contrast, Finney and other "free will" evangelists wanted to democratize the opportunity for salvation by insisting that everyone, rich or poor, black or white, could *choose* to be "saved" simply by embracing the promise of Jesus.

Finney's democratic gospel combined faith and good works: revival led to efforts at social reform. "The great business of the church," Finney insisted, is "to reform the world." By embracing Christ, a convert could thereafter be free of sin, but Christians also had an obligation to improve society. Christians should "aim to be holy and not rest satisfied until they are as perfect as God." Finney helped found an array of groups designed to reform various social ills: alcoholism, prostitution, war, and slavery. The revivals thus provided much of the energy behind the sweeping reform impulse that characterized the age.

The Mormons

The spiritual stirrings of the Second Great Awakening also helped produce new religious groups. The burned-over district in western New York gave rise to several religious movements, the most important of which was Mormonism. Its extraordinary founder, Joseph Smith Jr., the child of

Finney and the "burned-over" district

Joseph Smith and *The Book of Mormon*

intensely religious Vermont farm folk who settled in the village of Palmyra in western New York, was born and raised amid the excitement of the Second Great Awakening. In 1823, the eighteen-year-old Smith reported that an angel named Moroni had led him to a hillside near his father's farm, where he had unearthed golden tablets on which was etched a lost "gospel" of the Bible that describes a group of ancient Israelites ("Nephites") who crossed the Atlantic on barges and settled America 2,000 years before Columbus. Smith, who could barely read, set about translating and dictating to others the "reformed Egyptian" inscriptions on the plates (which no one else ever saw before he returned them to Moroni). Smith convinced a friend to mortgage his farm to pay for the publication of the first 5,000 copies of the 500-page text he called *The Book of Mormon: An Account Written by the Hand of Mormon upon Plates Taken from the Plates of Nephi*.

With this remarkable book as his gospel, young Smith began telling the story of his "marvilous [sic] experience" and gathering converts ("saints") who shared his desire to live together in accordance with the teachings of Jesus. Eventually, convinced that his religious authority came directly from God, Smith formed what he called the Church of Jesus Christ of Latter-day Saints, more popularly known as **Mormons**. God "is a man like one of you," Smith told his followers. His was a democratic faith run by plain people and intended for all people.

In his self-appointed role as Prophet, Smith criticized the sins of the rich, preached universal salvation, dismissed all Christian denominations (Protestant and Catholic) as frauds, denied that there was a hell, urged his followers to avoid liquor, tobacco, and hot drinks, and promised that the Second Coming of Christ was looming. Within a few years, the charismatic Smith, whom the Mormons simply called Joseph, had gathered thousands of converts, most of them poor New England farmers who, like Smith's family, had migrated to western New York. "The people fairly adored him," said a Mormon woman.

From the outset, the Mormon "saints" upset both their neighbors and the civil authorities. Mormons stood out with their secret rituals, their refusal to abide by local laws and conventions, and their clannishness: they worshipped together, voted together, and traveled together. Smith denied the legitimacy of civil governments and the U.S. Constitution. As a result, no community wanted to host him and his "peculiar people." In their search for a refuge from persecution and for the "promised land," the ever-growing contingent of Mormons moved from western New York to Ohio, then to Missouri, and finally, in 1839, to the half-built town of Commerce, Illinois, on swampy land along the west bank of the Mississippi River. They renamed the town Nauvoo (a crude transliteration of a Hebrew word meaning "beautiful land").

Within a few years, thanks to Smith's organizing genius and absolute authority, Nauvoo had become a bustling, well-planned community of 12,000, with an impressive, neo-classical temple overlooking the river. The community was run according to strict Mormon principles. There were no saloons or brothels. A New York newspaper reported that the Mormons at

Mormons Members of the Church of Jesus Christ of Latter-day Saints, which dismissed other Christian denominations, emphasizing universal salvation and a modest lifestyle; often persecuted for their secrecy and clannishness.

Nauvoo were "organizing a religious empire in the far west that will aston-ish the world." Joseph Smith, "the Prophet," became the community's reli-gious dictator: he was Nauvoo's leading planner, businessman, and political czar. He owned the hotel and general store, published the newspaper and sold real estate, served as mayor, chief justice, and commander of the city's 2,000-strong army (the Nauvoo Legion), and was the trustee of the church. Smith's lust for power grew as well. He began excommunicating dissidents, and in 1844 he announced his intention to become America's president. He proclaimed that the United States should peacefully acquire not only Texas and Oregon but all of Mexico and Canada, and that slavery should be ended.

Smith also caused controversy by practicing "plural marriage" (polyg-amy); he accumulated over two dozen wives and encouraged other Mormon leaders to do the same. In 1844, a crisis arose when Mormon dissenters, in-cluding Smith's first wife, Emma, denounced his polygamy. The result was not only a split in the church but also an attack on Nauvoo by non-Mormons from neighboring counties. When Smith ordered Mormons to destroy an op-position newspaper, he and his brother Hyrum were arrested and charged with treason. On June 27, 1844, a mob stormed the jail in the nearby town of Carthage and killed the Smith brothers. Joseph Smith, the thirty-eight-year-old prophet, had become a martyr. A New York newspaper predicted that his death would kill Mormonism: "They cannot get another Joe Smith. The holy city must tumble into ruins."

But in Brigham Young, the Mormons found a new and, in many ways, bet-ter leader. Strong-minded, intelligent, authoritarian, and a compelling speaker (as well as husband eventually to dozens of wives, who bore fifty-six children), Young was a Vermont-born carpenter who in 1813 moved with his family to western New York, where he became an early convert to Mormon-ism. In 1844, he was elected to succeed Smith.

Nauvoo continued to arouse the suspicions of non-Mormons, leading Young to look for another home for his flock. Their new destination was 1,300 miles away in the isolated, barren valley near the Great Salt Lake in Utah, a vast, sparsely populated area that was part of Mexico. In early 1846, in wagons and on foot, 12,000 Mormons started their grueling exodus across Nebraska and Wyoming to their new Zion, the "promised land" of Utah. On a good day they traveled only about ten miles. The first to arrive at the Great Salt Lake in July 1847 found "a broad and barren plain hemmed in by the mountains . . . the paradise of the lizard, the cricket and the rattlesnake." But Brigham Young declared that "this is the place" for the Mormons to settle. It was "a good place to make saints."

By the end of 1848, the Mormons had developed an efficient irrigation system for their farms, and over the next decade they brought about a spec-tacular greening of the desert. At first they organized their own state, named Deseret (meaning "Land of the Honeybee"), and elected Young gov-ernor. But their independence was short-lived. In 1848, Mexico signed the Treaty of Guadalupe Hidalgo, transferring to the United States what is now

Brigham Young Young was the president of the Mormons for thirty years.

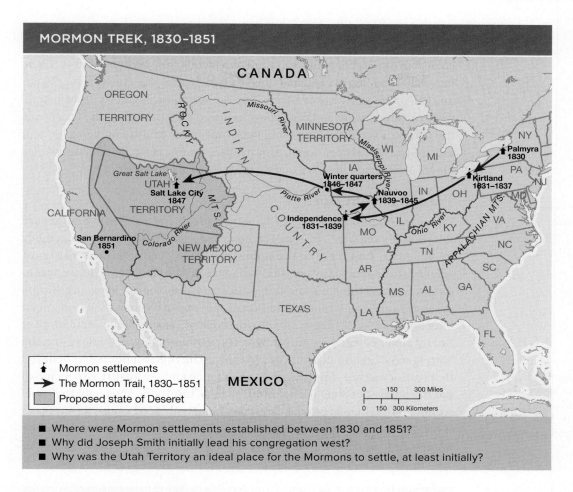

MORMON TREK, 1830–1851

Mormon settlements

The Mormon Trail, 1830–1851

Proposed state of Deseret

■ Where were Mormon settlements established between 1830 and 1851?
■ Why did Joseph Smith initially lead his congregation west?
■ Why was the Utah Territory an ideal place for the Mormons to settle, at least initially?

California, Nevada, Utah, Texas, and parts of Arizona, New Mexico, Colorado, and Wyoming. Two years later, Congress incorporated the Utah Territory, including the Mormons' Salt Lake settlement, into the United States. Nevertheless, when Brigham Young was named the territorial governor, the new arrangement gave the Mormons virtual independence. For more than twenty years, Young ruled the territory with an iron hand, allowing no dissent and defying federal authority. Not until 1896, after the Mormons disavowed the practice of polygamy, was Utah admitted as a state.

Romanticism in America

The revival of religious life during the early 1800s was one of many efforts throughout the United States and Europe to unleash the stirrings of the spirit. Another great cultural shift from the scientific rationalism of the Enlightenment was the Romantic movement in thought, literature, and the arts. It began in Europe, as young people rebelled against the well-ordered

CORE **OBJECTIVE**
2. Examine the emergence of transcendentalism in American culture in the early nineteenth century.

rational world promoted by the eighteenth-century Enlightenment. Were there not, after all, more things in the world than reason, science, and logic could box up and explain: spontaneous moods, impressions, and feelings; mysterious, unknown, and half-seen things? In areas in which science could neither prove nor disprove concepts, the Romantics believed that people were justified in having faith. They preferred the stirrings of the heart over the calculations of the head, nonconformity over traditional behavior, and the mystical over the rational. Americans also embraced the Romantics' emphasis on individualism, idealizing the virtues of common people.

Transcendentalism

The most intense advocates of Romantic ideals in the United States were the transcendentalists of New England, America's first group of rebellious intellectuals committed to reshaping the nation's cultural life. What **transcendentalism** actually entailed is hard to define. The name derived from its emphasis on thoughts and things that *transcend* (or rise above) the limits of reason and logic. Transcendentalism, said one of its champions, meant an interest in areas "a little beyond" the scope of reason. Transcendentalism thus at times seemed irrational, rejecting both religious orthodoxy and the "corpse-cold" rationalism of Unitarianism. The transcendentalists believed that reality was not simply what you can touch and see; reality also included the unexplored realms of the mind, such as intuition. Above all, the transcendentalists believed in "self-reliance" and embraced a pure form of personal spirituality uncorrupted by organized religion. Transcendentalists wanted individuals to look *within* themselves, not follow the guidance of

transcendentalism Philosophy of New England writers and thinkers who advocated personal spirituality, self-reliance, social reform, and harmony with nature.

***The Indian's Vespers* (1847)**
Asher B. Durand's painting of a Native American saluting the sun captures the Romantic ideals of personal spirituality and the uncorrupted natural world that swept America in the wake of the Enlightenment.

ministers, for spiritual insights. They also wanted to unleash a romantic spirituality in harmony with nature. All people, they believed, had the capacity for self-realization, enabling them to tap the divine potential ("spark") present in all of God's creatures and creations. By the 1830s, New England transcendentalism had become the most influential force in American culture.

In 1836, an informal discussion group known as the Transcendental Club began to meet in Boston and nearby Concord to discuss philosophy, literature, and religion. They teasingly called themselves the "club of the like-minded," quipped a Boston preacher, "because no two . . . thought alike." The club included liberal clergymen, militant reformers, writers such as Theodore Parker, George Ripley, Henry David Thoreau, Nathaniel Hawthorne, and brilliant women such as Elizabeth Peabody, her sister Sophia (who married Hawthorne in 1842), and Margaret Fuller. Fluent in six languages, Fuller organized a transcendentalist discussion group and edited its magazine, the *Dial* (1840–1844), for two years before the duty fell to Ralph Waldo Emerson, the high priest of transcendentalism.

Ralph Waldo Emerson

More than anyone else, Ralph Waldo Emerson embodied the transcendentalist gospel promoting individual freedom and "self-culture." Tall and slender, with bright blue eyes, he became the most popular speaker in the United States during the second quarter of the nineteenth century, in part because Emerson led the crusade to end America's dependence on European literary and artistic traditions. Emerson strove to help "extract the tapeworm of Europe from America's body," to "cast out the passion for Europe," and replace it with "the passion for America," exhorting the young republic to shed its cultural inferiority complex and create its own distinctive literature and art.

> Emerson and cultural nationalism

Descended from a line of New England Calvinist ministers and the son of a Unitarian preacher, Emerson graduated from Harvard College in 1821 and became a Unitarian parson in 1829, but he quit the "cold and cheerless" denomination three years later and turned away from all organized religions because they stifled free thinking. "In the Bible," he explained, "you are not directed to be a Unitarian or a Calvinist or an Episcopalian." Such group identities disgusted him. After traveling in Europe, where he met England's greatest Romantic writers, Emerson settled in Concord to take up the life of an essayist, poet, and lecturer ("preacher to the world") promoting radical individualism. He now found God in nature and came to believe in human perfectibility. Emerson celebrated the virtues of optimism, self-reliance, and the individual's unlimited potential. In 1836 he published the pathbreaking book *Nature*, which helped launch the Transcendental movement. In it, he stressed that sensitive people could "transcend" the material world and discover the "spirit" animating the universe. Individuals, in other words, could exercise godlike powers.

The spirit of self-reliant individualism in Emerson's lectures and writings provided the energetic core of the transcendentalist outlook. "The

American Scholar," a speech he delivered at Harvard in 1837, urged young Americans to put aside their reverence for European culture and explore the beauties and freedoms of their own new world. The speech was "our intellectual Declaration of Independence," said one observer.

"Self-Reliance" (1841)

Emerson's essay "Self-Reliance" (1841) is crammed with crisply formulated assertions that express the distinctive transcendentalist outlook:

> Whoso would be a man, must be a nonconformist.... Nothing is at last sacred but the integrity of your own mind.... It is easy in the world to live after the world's opinion; it is easy in solitude to live after our own; but the great man is he who in the midst of a crowd keeps with perfect sweetness the independence of solitude.... A foolish consistency is the hobgoblin of little minds, adored by little statesmen and philosophers and divines.... Speak what you think now in hard words and tomorrow speak what tomorrow thinks in hard words again, though it contradict everything you said today.... To be great is to be misunderstood.

Emerson's democratic belief that every man and woman possessed godlike virtues inspired generations. He was a down-to-earth transcendentalist who championed a self-reliant individualism that reinforced the democratic energies inspiring Jacksonian America.

Henry David Thoreau

Emerson's philosophical young friend and neighbor, Henry David Thoreau, practiced the thoughtful self-reliance that Emerson preached. "I like people who can do things," Emerson stressed, and Thoreau, fourteen years his junior, could do many things: carpentry, masonry, painting, surveying, sailing, gardening. The son of a man who was a pencil maker and a woman who was a domineering reformer, Thoreau displayed a powerful sense of uncompromising integrity and prickly individuality. "If a man does not keep pace with his companions," Thoreau wrote, "perhaps it is because he hears a different drummer."

Thoreau marched to a different drummer all his life. He once described himself as "a mystic, a transcendentalist, and a natural philosopher." Born in 1817, he attended Harvard, where he exhausted the library's resources before graduating. After a brief stint as a teacher, during which he got in trouble for refusing to cane his students, Thoreau worked with his father making pencils. But like Emerson, he made frequent escapes to admire the beauties of nature. Thoreau viewed "the indescribable innocence" of nature as a living bible; the earth to him was a form of poetry, full of hidden meanings and life-giving energies. Walks in the woods inspired him more than attending church. He also showed no interest in the scramble for wealth, for it too often corrupted the pursuit of happiness. "The mass of men," he wrote, "lead lives of quiet desperation" because they were preoccupied with making money rather than pursuing happiness. Thoreau became famous for his

Henry David Thoreau Thoreau was a lifelong abolitionist.

strong opinions and frankness. Most of what his neighbors deemed good, he believed "in his soul to be bad."

A born rebel, Thoreau yearned to experience the "extremities" of life and not be bound by stuffy traditions, unjust laws, "good behavior," or the opinions of his elders. "I have lived thirty years on this planet," he wrote, "and I have yet to hear the first syllable of valuable advice from my seniors. They have told me nothing, and probably cannot tell me anything." He committed himself to leading what Emerson called a simple life centered on "plain living and high thinking." He loved to be alone, wrapped in his own thoughts and free to think for himself.

Thoreau rented a room at the Emersons' home for a time, tending the family garden and taking long walks with his host. "I delight much in my young friend," Emerson wrote, "who seems to have as free and erect a mind as any I have ever met." In 1844, when Emerson bought fourteen acres along Walden Pond, Thoreau decided to embark upon an unusual experiment in self-reliance. On July 4, 1845, at age twenty-seven, he took to the woods to live in a tiny, one-room cabin he had built for $28 on Emerson's land at Walden Pond, just a few miles outside of Concord. Having decided that a "man is rich in proportion to the number of things he can do without," Thoreau wanted to free himself from the constraints of conventional life and devote his time to gardening, studying nature, swimming in the pond, and recording his thoughts and observations in his journal. "I went to the woods because I wished to live deliberately," he wrote in *Walden, or Life in the Woods* (1854), ". . . and not, when I came to die, discover that I had not lived."

Thoreau's *Walden* (1854)

During Thoreau's two years at Walden Pond, the United States declared war against Mexico, largely in order to acquire Texas, then part of Mexico. He felt it was an unjust war pushed by southern cotton planters eager to add more slave territory. His disgust for the war led him to refuse to pay taxes, for which he was put in jail (for only one night; an aunt paid the tax). This incident inspired him to write his now-classic essay, "Civil Disobedience" (1849), which would later influence Martin Luther King Jr. in shaping the civil rights movement in the 1950s and '60s. "If the law is of such a nature that it requires you to be an agent of injustice to another," Thoreau wrote, "then, I say, break the law." Until his death in 1862, Thoreau continued to attack slavery and applaud those who worked to undermine it. "The law will never make men free," he insisted. "It is men who have got to make the law free." The continuing influence of Thoreau's creed of taking individual action against injustice shows the impact that a thoughtful person can have on the world of action.

"Civil Disobedience" (1849)

An American Literature

Thoreau and Emerson portrayed the transcendentalist movement as an expression of moral idealism; critics dismissed it as outrageous self-centeredness. Though the transcendentalists attracted only a small following in their own time, they inspired a generation of writers that produced the first great age of American literature. The half decade of 1850 to 1855 witnessed an outpouring of extraordinary writing in the United States, a nation that had long suffered an inferiority complex about the quality of its arts. Those five years saw the writing of *Representative Men* by Emerson, *Walden* by Thoreau, *The Scarlet Letter* and *The House of the Seven Gables* by Nathaniel Hawthorne, *Moby-Dick* by Herman Melville, *Leaves of Grass* by Walt Whitman, and hundreds of unpublished poems by Emily Dickinson.

Literary Giants

Emily Dickinson, the most strikingly original of the New England poets, spent much of her life in her second-story bedroom in Amherst, Massachusetts, writing poetry that few people saw during her lifetime. Only a handful of her almost 1,800 poems were published (anonymously) before her death, in 1886. As she once prophetically wrote, "Success is counted sweetest / By those who ne'er succeed." Neither she nor her sister married, and they lived out their lives in their parents' home. Perhaps it was Dickinson's severe eye trouble during the 1860s that caused her solitary withdrawal from the larger society; perhaps it was the aching despair generated by her love for a married minister. Whatever the reason, her intense isolation and lifelong religious doubts led her to probe her own shifting psychological state. Her often-abstract themes were elemental: life, death, fear, loneliness, nature, and above all, God, a "Force illegible," "a distant, stately lover."

Emily Dickinson Dickinson offered the world of New England literature a fresh female voice.

The most provocative writer during the nineteenth century was New Yorker Walt Whitman. The swaggering Whitman was a startling figure, with his frank sexuality and homoerotic overtones. There was something elemental in Whitman's overflowing character, something bountiful and generous and compelling—even his faults and inconsistencies were ample. Born on a Long Island farm, he moved with his family to Brooklyn, where he worked as a teacher, journalist, a Democratic party activist, and an editor of the *Brooklyn Eagle*. Whitman frequently took the ferry across the East River to bustling Manhattan. The city's restless energies fascinated him, and he gorged himself on the urban spectacle: the vibrant vistas of shipyards, crowds, factories, and shop windows.

When Whitman first met Ralph Waldo Emerson, he had been "simmering, simmering," but Emerson "brought him to a boil" with his emphasis on defying tradition and celebrating the commonplaces of life, all of which found their way into his controversial first book of poems, *Leaves of Grass* (1855), which often dispensed with stanzas and rhymes. Whitman introduced his new book by declaring that "I celebrate myself, and sing myself." He wanted to leave the past behind. He was a pioneer on behalf of "a new mightier world, a varied world," a "world of labor" and "common people." Although *Leaves of Grass* was banned in Boston, Emerson found it "the most extraordinary piece of wit and wisdom that America has yet contributed," but more-conventional critics shuddered at the shocking frankness of Whitman's sexual references. Thoreau, however, loved the earthy poetry. He described Whitman as "the greatest democrat the world has seen."

Walt Whitman This engraving of a thirty-seven-year-old Walt Whitman appeared in his acclaimed poetry collection, *Leaves of Grass*.

The Reform Impulse

CORE **OBJECTIVE**

3. Explain the origins of the major social reform movements in the early nineteenth century, and analyze their influence on American society and politics.

In 1842, the monthly *Gazette* reported that the "spirit of reform is in every place" across America. The United States in the first half of the nineteenth century was awash in reform movements led by dreamers and activists who saw injustice and fought to correct it. Lyman Beecher, a champion of evangelical Christian revivalism (as well as the father of writer Harriet Beecher Stowe), stressed that the Second Great Awakening was not focused simply on promoting individual conversions; it was also intended to "reform human society." Evangelical societies fanned out across America to organize Sunday schools to spread the gospel and distribute Bibles to the children of the working poor. Other reformers tackled urgent social issues such as dreadful conditions in prisons and workplaces, care of the disabled, reducing the consumption of alcoholic beverages (temperance), women's rights, and the abolition of slavery. Some reformers proposed legislative remedies for social ills; others stressed personal conversion or private philanthropy. Whatever the method or approach, earnest social reformers mobilized in great numbers during the second quarter of the nineteenth century. That they often met resistance, persecution, violence, and even death testified to the sincerity of their convictions and the power of their example.

***Politics in an Oyster House* (1848)** Commissioned by social activist John H. B. Latrobe, this painting captures the public debates that were fueled by newspapers and other print periodicals.

While an impulse to "perfect" people and society helped excite the reform movements, social and economic changes helped spur many reformers themselves, most of whom were women. The rise of an urban middle class offered growing numbers of women more time to devote to societal concerns. Prosperity enabled them to hire cooks and maids, often Irish immigrants, who in turn freed them from household chores. As had been true for two centuries, many women used their free time to join churches and charitable organizations, most of which were led by men.

Temperance

The **temperance** crusade to reduce alcohol consumption was perhaps the most widespread of the reform movements. The census of 1810 reported some 14,000 distilleries producing 25 million gallons of alcoholic spirits each year. William Cobbett, an English reformer who traveled in the United States, noted in 1819 that one could "go into hardly any man's house without being asked to drink wine or spirits, even *in the morning*." In 1826, a group of ministers in Boston organized the American Society for the Promotion of Temperance, which sponsored lectures, press campaigns, and the formation of local and state societies. A favorite device was to ask each person who took the pledge to put by his or her signature a T for "total abstinence." With that a new word entered the language: *teetotaler*.

temperance A widespread reform movement led by militant Christians that focused on reducing the use of alcoholic beverages.

The American Temperance Union

In 1833, the society organized a national convention in Philadelphia, where the American Temperance Union was formed. Like nearly every reform movement of the day, temperance had a wing of absolutists. They would accept no compromise with Demon Rum and carried the day with a resolution that liquor was evil and ought to be prohibited by law. The Temperance Union, at its spring convention in 1836, called for abstinence from all alcoholic beverages—which caused moderates to abstain from the temperance movement instead.

Prisons and Asylums

Prison and asylum reform

The Romantic impulse often included the liberal belief that people are innately good and capable of improvement. Such an optimistic view brought about major changes in the treatment of prisoners, the disabled, and dependent children. Public institutions (often called asylums) arose that were dedicated to the treatment of social ills. If removed from society, the theory went, the needy and the deviant could be made whole again. Unhappily, however, the asylums had a way of becoming breeding grounds for brutality and neglect.

Gradually, the idea of the penitentiary developed as a new approach to reforming criminals. It would be a place where the guilty paid for their crimes but also underwent rehabilitation. An early model of the new system, widely copied, was the Auburn Penitentiary, which opened in New York in 1816. The prisoners at Auburn had separate cells and gathered only for meals and group labor. Discipline was severe. The men were marched out in lockstep and never put face-to-face or allowed to talk. But they were reasonably secure from abuse by their fellow prisoners. The system, its advocates argued, had a beneficial effect on the prisoners and saved money, since the workshops supplied prison needs and produced goods for sale at a profit. By 1840, there were twelve Auburn-type penitentiaries scattered across the nation.

The Romantic reform impulse also found an outlet in the care of the insane. Before 1800, few hospitals provided care for the mentally ill. The insane were usually confined at home with hired keepers, or in jails or almshouses, where homeless debtors were housed. In the years after 1815, however, asylums that separated the disturbed from the criminal began to appear.

Dorothea Dix reforms care for the mentally ill

The most important figure in heightening awareness of the plight of the mentally ill was Dorothea Lynde Dix. A pious Boston schoolteacher, she was asked to instruct a Sunday-school class at the East Cambridge House of Correction in 1841. There she found a roomful of insane people who had been completely neglected. She was so disturbed by the scene that she began a two-year investigation of jails and almshouses in Massachusetts. In a report to the state legislature in 1843, she revealed that insane people were confined "in *cages, closets, cellars, stalls, pens! Chained, naked, beaten with rods,* and *lashed* into obedience." Those managing asylums dismissed her charges as "slanderous lies," but she won the support of leading reformers. From Massachusetts she carried her campaign throughout the country and abroad. By 1860 she had persuaded twenty states to heed her advice, thereby helping to transform social attitudes toward mental illness.

Women's Rights

Dorothea Dix was but one sterling example of the countless middle-class women who devoted themselves to improving the quality of life in America. Others argued that women should first focus on enhancing home life. In 1841, Harriet Beecher Stowe's sister, Catharine Beecher, a leader in the public education movement and founder of women's schools in Connecticut and Ohio, published *A Treatise on Domestic Economy*, which became the leading handbook promoting the **cult of domesticity**, a powerful ideology that called upon women to celebrate their role as manager of the household and the children. While Beecher upheld high standards in women's education, she accepted the prevailing view that the "woman's sphere" was inside the home. She, and many other prominent women, argued that young women should be trained not for the workplace but in the domestic arts—managing a kitchen, running a household, and nurturing the children. Women, explained a Philadelphia doctor, were crucial to the future of the Republic because they instructed their children "in the principles of liberty and government." This *cult of domesticity* was especially strong among Mormons. From its inception, the Mormon Church was patriarchal, ruled by men. Women were limited to running the household and raising the children.

The official status of women during the first half of the nineteenth century remained much as it had been in the colonial era. They were barred from the ministry and most other professions. Higher education was hardly an option. Women could not serve on juries, nor could they vote. A wife often had no control over her property or even her children. She could not make a will, sign a contract, or bring suit in court without her husband's permission. Her subordinate legal status was similar to that of a minor or a free black.

Gradually, however, women began to protest, and men began to listen. The organized movement for women's rights emerged in 1840, when the anti-slavery movement split over the question of women's right to participate. Women decided then that they needed to organize on behalf of their own emancipation.

In 1848, two prominent advocates of women's rights, Lucretia Mott, a Philadelphia Quaker, and Elizabeth Cady Stanton, a graduate of New York's Troy Female Seminary who refused to be merely "a household drudge," called a convention to discuss "the social, civil, and religious condition and rights of women." On July 19, 1848, the **Seneca Falls Convention** issued a clever paraphrase of the Declaration of Independence. Called the **Declaration of Sentiments**, it proclaimed that "all men and women

Cult of domesticity

cult of domesticity Pervasive nineteenth-century ideology urging women to celebrate their role as manager of the household and nurturer of the children.

Seneca Falls Convention (1848) Convention organized by feminists Lucretia Mott and Elizabeth Cady Stanton to promote women's rights and issue the pathbreaking Declaration of Sentiments.

Declaration of Sentiments (1848) Document based on the Declaration of Independence that called for gender equality, written primarily by Elizabeth Cady Stanton and signed by Seneca Falls Convention delegates.

Elizabeth Cady Stanton and Susan B. Anthony Stanton (left, in 1856) was a young mother who called the Seneca Falls Convention, while Anthony (right, in 1848) started as an anti-slavery and temperance activist in her twenties. The two would meet in 1851 and form a lifelong partnership in the fight for women's suffrage.

are created equal." All laws that placed women "in a position inferior to that of men, are contrary to the great precept of nature, and therefore of no force or authority." Such language was too strong, too radical, for most of the 1,000 delegates, and only about a third of them signed the document. Nevertheless, the Seneca Falls gathering represented an important first step in the evolving campaign for women's rights.

From 1850 until the Civil War, leaders of the women's rights movement held annual conventions, delivered lectures, and circulated petitions. The movement struggled in the face of meager funds and widespread anti-feminist sentiment. A mother and housewife criticized the women reformers for "aping mannish manners" and wearing "absurd and barbarous attire." The typical feminist, she claimed, "struts and strides, and thinks that she proves herself superior to the rest of her sex." The movement's eventual success resulted from the work of a few undaunted women who refused to be stopped by the odds against them.

Susan B. Anthony, already active in temperance and anti-slavery groups, joined the crusade in the 1850s. Unlike Stanton and Mott, she was unmarried and therefore able to devote most of her attention to the women's crusade. As one observer put it, Stanton "forged the thunderbolts and Miss Anthony hurled them." Both were young when the movement started, and both lived into the twentieth century, focusing after the Civil War on demands for women's suffrage (the right to vote).

Women's suffrage

The fruits of the women's rights movement ripened slowly. Women did not gain the vote in national elections in the nineteenth century, but they did make legal gains. In 1839, Mississippi became the first state to grant married women control over their property; by the 1860s, eleven more states had done so. Still, the only jobs open to educated women in any number were nursing and teaching. Both professions brought relatively lower status and pay than "man's work," despite the skills, training, and responsibilities involved.

Early Public Schools

Early America, like most rural societies, offered few educational opportunities for the masses. That changed in the first half of the nineteenth century as reformers lobbied for **public schools** serving all children, rich or poor. The working poor wanted free schools to give their children an equal chance to pursue the American dream. In 1830, the Workingmen's party of Philadelphia called for "a system of education that shall embrace equally all the children of the state, of every rank and condition." Education, it was argued, would improve manners and at the same time reduce crime and poverty.

A well-informed citizenry equipped with knowledge not only for gaining employment but also for good citizenship was another of the basic premises of a republic. If political power resided with the people, as the Constitution asserted, then the citizenry needed to be well-educated. Literacy in Jacksonian America was surprisingly widespread. In 1840, according to census data, some 78 percent of the total population and 91 percent of the white population could read and write. Ever since the colonial period, in fact, Americans had had a higher literacy rate than that in Europe. Most children were taught to read at home, in church (Sunday school), or in private schools. By 1830, however, no state had a public school system in the modern sense.

> Highest literacy rates in the world

Horace Mann of Massachusetts, a state legislator and attorney, led the early drive for statewide, tax-supported school systems open to everyone, regardless of class, race, or ethnicity, including immigrant children. He sponsored the creation of a state board of education, and then served as its leader. Mann went on to promote many reforms in Massachusetts, including the first state-supported "normal school" for the training of teachers, a state association of teachers, and a minimum school year of six months. He saw the public school system as a way not only to ensure that everyone had a basic level of knowledge and skills but also to reinforce values such as hard work and clean living. "If we do not prepare children to become good citizens, if we do not enrich their minds with knowledge," Mann warned, "then our republic must go down to destruction." Such a holistic education, Mann argued, would enhance social stability and equal opportunity, as well as give women opportunities for rewarding work outside the home, as teachers. Mann said they could become "mothers away from home" for the children they taught. In 1846, Catharine Beecher organized a Board of National Popular Education, which recruited unmarried women to serve as public school teachers in the Midwest.

> Horace Mann's "normal school"

public schools Elementary and secondary schools funded by the state and free of tuition.

By the 1840s, most states in the North and Midwest, but not the South, had joined the public school movement. The initial conditions for public education, however, were seldom ideal. Funds for buildings, books, and equipment were limited; teachers were poorly paid and often poorly prepared. Most students going beyond the elementary grades attended private academies, often organized by churches. Such schools, begun in colonial days, multiplied until in 1850 there were more than 6,000 of them.

In 1821, the Boston English High School opened as the nation's first free public secondary school, set up mainly for students not going on to college. By a law of 1827, Massachusetts required every town of five hundred or more residents to have a high school; in towns of four thousand or more, the school had to offer Latin, Greek, rhetoric, and other college-preparatory courses. Public high schools became well established only after the Civil War. In 1860 there were barely three hundred in the whole nation.

By 1850, half of the white children between ages 5 and 19 were enrolled in schools, the highest percentage in the world. But very few of those students were southerners. The South had very few public schools until after the Civil War. In most states, enslaved children were prohibited from learning to read and write or attend school. A former slave recalled that his owner "didn't teach 'em nuthin' but work." The South had some 500,000 illiterate whites, more than half the total in the country. In the South, North Carolina led the way in state-supported education, enrolling more than two-thirds of its white school-age population by 1860. But the school year was only four months long because of the rural state's need for children to do farm work. The prolonged disparities between North and South in the number and

The George Barrell Emerson School, Boston (ca. 1850) Although higher education for women initially met with some resistance, seminaries, like this one, started in the 1820s and 1830s, taught women mathematics, physics, and history, as well as music, art, and social graces.

quality of educational opportunities help explain the growing economic and cultural differences between the two regions. Then, as now, undereducated people were more likely to remain economically deprived, less healthy, and less engaged in political life.

Utopian Communities

Amid the pervasive climate of reform during the early nineteenth century, the quest for utopia—communities with innovative social and economic relationships—flourished. Plans for ideal communities had long been an American passion, at least since the Puritans set out to build a wilderness Zion in New England. More than 100 **utopian communities** sprang up between 1800 and 1900. Many of them were *communitarian* experiments in that they emphasized the welfare of the entire community rather than individual freedom. Some experimented with "free love," socialism, and special diets.

Those communities founded by the Shakers (officially the United Society of Believers in Christ's Second Appearing) proved to be long lasting. Ann Lee (known as Mother Ann Lee) arrived in New York from England with eight followers in 1774. Believing religious fervor to be a sign of inspiration from the Holy Ghost, Mother Ann and her followers had strange fits in which they saw visions and issued prophecies (predictions about the future). These manifestations later evolved into a ritual dance—hence the name "Shakers." Shaker doctrine held God to be a dual personality. In Christ, the masculine side was revealed; in Mother Ann, the feminine element. Mother Ann preached celibacy to prepare Shakers for the perfection that was promised them in heaven.

Shakers

Mother Ann died in 1784, but the group found new leaders, and the movement spread from New York into New England, Ohio, and Kentucky. By 1830 about twenty groups were flourishing. In these Shaker communities all property was held in common. Shaker farms were among the nation's leading sources of garden seed and medicinal herbs, and many of their products, including clothing, household items, and especially furniture, were prized for their simple beauty.

John Humphrey Noyes, founder of the Oneida Community, had a very different vision of the ideal community. The son of a Vermont congressman, Noyes attended Dartmouth College and Yale Divinity School. But in 1834 he was expelled from Yale and his license to preach was revoked after he announced that he was "perfect" and free of all sin. In 1836 Noyes gathered a group of "Perfectionists" around his home in Putney, Vermont. Ten years later, he announced a new doctrine, "complex marriage," which meant that every man in the community was married to every woman, and vice versa. "In a holy community," he claimed, "there is no more reason why sexual intercourse should be restrained by law, than why eating and drinking should be." Authorities thought otherwise, and Noyes was charged with adultery for practicing his theology of "free love" (he coined the term). He fled to New York and

The Oneida Community

utopian communities Ideal communities that offered innovative social and economic relationships to those who were interested in achieving salvation.

in 1848 established the Oneida Community, which had more than 200 members by 1851 and became famous for its production of fine silverware.

Brook Farm

Brook Farm in Massachusetts was the most celebrated utopian community because it grew out of the transcendental movement. George Ripley, a Unitarian minister and transcendentalist, conceived of Brook Farm as a kind of early-day think tank, combining high philosophy and plain living. In 1841 he and several dozen like-minded utopians moved to the 175-acre farm nine miles southwest of Boston. Brook Farm became America's first secular utopian community. One of its members, novelist Nathaniel Hawthorne, called it "our beautiful scheme of a noble and unselfish life." Its residents shared the tasks of maintaining the buildings, tending the fields, and preparing the meals. They also organized picnics, dances, lectures, and discussions. The place survived, however, mainly because of an excellent school that drew tuition-paying students from outside. In 1846, Brook Farm's main building burned down, and the community spirit died in the ashes.

Utopian communities, with few exceptions, quickly ran out of steam. The communal social experiments had little impact on the outside world, where reformers wrestled with the sins of the multitudes. Among all the targets of the reformers' zeal, one great evil would take precedence over the others: human bondage. Transcendentalist reformer Theodore Parker declared that slavery was "the blight of this nation, the curse of the North and the curse of the South." The paradox of American freedom being coupled with American slavery, of what novelist Herman Melville called "the world's fairest hope linked with man's foulest crime," would inspire the climactic crusade of the age, abolitionism, one that would ultimately sweep the nation into an epic civil war.

CORE **OBJECTIVE**

4. Analyze the impact on American society and politics of the emergence of the anti-slavery movement.

The Anti-Slavery Movement

The men who drafted the U.S. Constitution in 1787 hoped to keep the new nation from splitting apart over the question of the slavery. They negotiated compromises that avoided dealing with the issue. But most of them knew that there eventually would be a day of reckoning. That day approached as the nineteenth century unfolded.

Early Opposition to Slavery

Efforts to weaken or abolish slavery increased after 1800. The first organized emancipation movement appeared in 1816 with the formation of the **American Colonization Society**, whose mission was to raise funds to "repatriate" free blacks back to Africa. Its supporters included such prominent figures as James Madison, James Monroe, Henry Clay, John Marshall, and Daniel Webster. Some supported the colonization movement because of

American Colonization Society Established in 1816, an organization whose mission was to return freed slaves to Africa.

their opposition to slavery; others saw it as a way to get rid of potentially troublesome free blacks. "We must save the Negro," as one missionary explained, "or the Negro will ruin us." Leaders of the free black community denounced the colonization idea from the start. The United States of America, they stressed, was their native land. Nevertheless, in 1821, agents of the American Colonization Society acquired land in West Africa that became the nucleus of a new nation. In 1822, African Americans were transported to what became the Republic of Liberia. But the African colonization movement received only meager support. In all, only about 15,000 American blacks went to Africa, a tiny figure compared with the number of slave births each year in the United States.

From Gradualism to Abolitionism

In the early 1830s, blacks in Boston and whites in the anti-slavery movement adopted an aggressive new strategy. Its initial efforts to promote a *gradual* end to slavery by prohibiting it in the western territories and encouraging owners to free their slaves gave way to demands for *immediate* **abolition** everywhere. A zealous white Massachusetts activist named William Lloyd Garrison illustrated the change in outlook.

William Lloyd Garrison A vocal abolitionist and an advocate of immediate emancipation.

In 1831, free blacks in Boston helped convince Garrison to launch a new anti-slavery newspaper, *The Liberator*, which became the voice of the first civil rights movement. In the newspaper's first issue, he renounced "the popular but pernicious doctrine of gradual emancipation." He would promote immediate abolition because slavery was a crime against humanity and a sin before God. The crusading Garrison dreamed of true racial equality in all spheres of American life. In pursuing that dream he vowed to be "as harsh as truth, and as uncompromising as justice. . . . I am in earnest—I will not equivocate—I will not excuse—I will *not retreat a* single inch—AND I WILL BE HEARD."

Garrison's fierce courage in denouncing slavery outraged slave owners in the South as well as some whites in the North. In 1835, a mob of angry whites dragged him through the streets of Boston at the end of a rope. The Georgia state legislature promised a $5,000 reward to anyone who kidnapped Garrison and brought him south for trial. A southern slaveholder warned Garrison "to desist your infamous endeavors to instill into the minds of the negroes the idea that 'men must be free.'" Garrison reminded his critics that, however violent his language, he was opposed to the use of force. "We do not preach rebellion," he stressed. The prospect "of a bloody insurrection in the South fills us with dismay," but "if any people were ever justified in throwing off the yoke of their tyrants, the slaves are the people."

During the 1830s, Garrison became the nation's most unyielding foe of slavery. Two prominent New York City evangelical merchants, Arthur and Lewis Tappan, provided financial support for *The Liberator*. In 1833, they

abolitionism Movement that called for an immediate end to slavery throughout the United States.

joined with Garrison and a group of Quaker reformers, free blacks, and evangelicals to organize the American Anti-Slavery Society. That same year, Parliament ended slavery throughout the British Empire by passing the Emancipation Act, whereby slaveholders were paid to give up their "human property." In 1835, the Tappans hired the famous revivalist Charles G. Finney to head the anti-slavery faculty at Oberlin, a new college in northern Ohio that would be the first to admit black students.

The American Anti-Slavery Society, financed by the Tappans, created a national network of newspapers, offices, and chapters, almost all of which were affiliated with a local Christian church. By 1840, some 160,000 people belonged to the American Anti-Slavery Society, which stressed that "slaveholding is a heinous crime in the sight of God, and that the duty, safety, and best interests of all concerned, require its *immediate abandonment*." The society even argued that blacks should have complete social and civil rights. In 1835, the group began flooding the South with anti-slavery pamphlets and newspapers. Infuriated southern slaveholders called for state and federal laws to prevent the distribution of the literature, and post offices began destroying what was called "anti-slavery propaganda."

The most radical figure among the mostly white Garrisonians was David Walker, a free black man who owned a clothing store in Boston. In 1829, he published *Walker's Appeal*, a pamphlet which denounced the hypocrisy of Christians in the South for defending slavery and urged slaves to revolt. "Are we men?" he asked. "I ask you, O my brethren, are we MEN? Did our Creator make us to be slaves to dust and ashes like ourselves?" Walker shocked whites by encouraging rebellious slaves to use the "crushing arm of power" to gain their freedom. "Woe, woe will be to you if we have to obtain our freedom by fighting."

> **The American Anti-Slavery Society (1833)**

> **Walker's Appeal (1829)**

A Split in the Movement

As the abolitionist movement spread, debates over tactics intensified. The Garrisonians felt that slavery had corrupted virtually every aspect of American life: politics, the economy, and social and religious life. Garrison himself came to embrace every important reform movement of the day: abolition, temperance, pacifism, and women's rights. He also championed equal social and legal rights for African Americans. His unconventional religious ideas led him to break with the established Protestant churches, which to his mind were in league with slavery. The federal government was all the more so. The U.S. Constitution, he said, was "a covenant with death and an agreement with hell." Garrison refused to vote and encouraged others to do the same, arguing that the American republic could not continue to proclaim the ideal of liberty while tolerating the reality of slavery. He fiercely believed that the South could simply be shamed into ending slavery.

Other reformers were more practical. They saw American society as fundamentally sound and they concentrated on purging it of slavery. Garrison struck them as an unrealistic fanatic. A showdown came in 1840 on the issue of women's rights. Women had joined the abolition movement from the start, but largely in groups without men. At that time, women were rarely allowed to speak to organizations that included men. Then the activities of the Grimké sisters brought women's rights to center stage.

Women's rights and abolition

Sarah and Angelina Grimké, daughters of a wealthy South Carolina family, were raised in luxury and served by many slaves. In 1821, soon after her father's death, Sarah moved from Charleston to Philadelphia, joined the Society of Friends (Quakers), and renounced slavery as a sin. Angelina soon left home and joined her. In 1835 the two sisters joined the abolitionist movement, speaking to women's groups in what were called "parlor meetings." By 1835 they had joined the circle of female abolitionist leaders. After they appealed to southern Christian women to put an end to slavery, the mayor of Charleston told their mother that her daughters would be jailed if they ever returned home.

The energetic Grimké sisters traveled throughout the northern states, speaking first to audiences of women and eventually to both women and men. Their unconventional behavior in speaking to mixed-gender audiences prompted criticism from male reformers. The chairman of the Connecticut Anti-Slavery Society declared, "No woman shall speak or vote where I am a moderator." Catharine Beecher reminded the Grimké sisters that women occupy "a subordinate relation in society to the other sex" and that they should limit their activities to the "domestic and social circle" rather than public organizations. Angelina Grimké stoutly rejected such arguments. "It is a woman's right," she insisted, "to have a voice in all laws and regulations by which she is to be governed, whether in church or in state." Soon, she and her sister began linking their efforts to free the slaves with their desire to free women. "Men and women are CREATED EQUAL!" Sarah Grimké insisted. "Whatever is right for man to do is right for woman." The Grimké sisters joined others in claiming that women were being kept in "domestic slavery" by male traditionalists.

The debate over the role of women in the anti-slavery movement finally exploded at the Anti-Slavery Society's meeting in 1840, where the Garrisonians convinced a majority of delegates that women should participate equally in the organization. The Tappans and their supporters walked out of the convention and formed the American and Foreign Anti-Slavery Society.

A third faction of the American Anti-Slavery Society also broke with Garrison. Its members had grown skeptical that the nonviolent "moral suasion" promoted by Garrison would ever lead to abolition. In 1840, they formed the Liberty Party in an effort to elect an American president who would abolish slavery. Their nominee, James Gillespie Birney, executive secretary of the American Anti-Slavery Society, was a former slaveholder turned abolitionist. In the 1840 election, he polled only 7,000 votes, but in 1844 he won 60,000. From that time forward an anti-slavery party contested

The Liberty Party (1840)

every national election until the Thirteenth Amendment officially ended slavery in 1865.

Black Anti-Slavery Activity

Although many whites worked courageously to end slavery, most of them, unlike Garrison, adopted the racist attitudes common at the time, insisting that blacks were socially inferior to whites. Freedom for slaves, in other words, did not mean social equality for blacks. Many white abolitionists, for example, expected free blacks to take a backseat in the movement to end slavery. Yet despite such discrimination, many free African Americans such as David Walker, Sarah Parker Redmond, and Sarah Mapps Douglass, among others, were active in white anti-slavery societies. Former slaves such as Henry Bibb and William Wells Brown, both escapees from Kentucky, and Frederick Douglass, who had escaped from Maryland, were the most effective critics of the South's "peculiar institution."

Brown was just twenty years old and illiterate when he escaped from his owner, a steamboat pilot on the Ohio River. An Ohio Quaker named Wells Brown helped him escape, and Brown adopted his name in the process of forging a new identity as a free man. Brown settled in Cleveland, Ohio, married, had three children, and helped numerous runaway slaves escape to Canada. By 1842 he had learned to read and write and began to publish columns in abolitionist newspapers. In 1847 Brown moved to Boston, where the Massachusetts Anti-Slavery Society hired him as a traveling lecturer. That same year, the organization published his autobiography, *Narrative of William W. Brown, A Former Slave, Written by Himself,* which became a best-seller. Brown gave thousands of speeches in America and Europe calling for an end to slavery and equality for both blacks and women. He repeatedly stressed that the African American "is endowed with those intellectual and amiable qualities which adorn and dignify human nature."

Narrative of the Life of Frederick Douglass (1845)

Through his writings and dazzling speeches, Douglass became the best-known black man in America. "I appear before the immense assembly this evening as a thief and a robber," he told a Massachusetts group in 1842. "I stole this head, these limbs, this body from my master, and ran off with them." Fearful of capture after publishing his *Narrative of the Life of Frederick Douglass, An American Slave, Written by Himself* (1845), he left for an extended lecture tour of the British Isles, returning two years later with enough money to purchase his freedom. He then started an abolitionist newspaper for blacks, the *North Star*, in Rochester, New York. He named the newspaper after the star that runaway slaves used to guide them at night toward freedom.

The female counterpart to Frederick Douglass was Sojourner Truth. Born to slaves in the Dutch farming culture of upstate New York in 1797, Sojourner Truth was given the name Isabella "Bell" Hardenbergh but

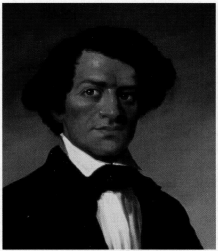

Frederick Douglas and Sojourner Truth Both Douglass and Truth were leading abolitionists and captivating orators.

renamed herself in 1843 after experiencing a conversation with God, who told her "to travel up and down the land" preaching against slavery. Having been a slave until she was freed by a New York law in 1827, Sojourner Truth was able to speak with conviction and knowledge about the evils of the "peculiar institution" and the inequality of women. She traveled throughout the North during the 1840s and 1850s, urging audiences to support women's rights and the immediate abolition of slavery. As she told the Ohio Women's Rights Convention in 1851, "I have plowed, and planted, and gathered into barns, and no man could head me—and ar'n't I a woman? I have borne thirteen children, and seen 'em mos' all sold off into slavery, and when I cried out with a mother's grief, none but Jesus heard—and ar'n't I a woman?"

Through such compelling testimony, Sojourner Truth demonstrated the powerful intersection of abolitionism and feminism. In the process, she tapped the distinctive energies that women brought to reformist causes. "If the first woman God ever made was strong enough to turn the world upside down all alone," she concluded in her address to the Ohio gathering, "these women together ought to be able to turn it back, and get it right side up again!"

> Black abolitionists and women's rights

Underground Railroad

While runaways often made it out of slavery on their own, many were aided by the **Underground Railroad**, a vast national network of secret routes and "safe houses," where free blacks and white abolitionists called "conductors" concealed runaway slaves in basements, attics, barns, and wagons before helping the fleeing "passengers" to the next "station" and eventually to freedom, often over the Canadian border.

Underground Railroad A secret system of routes and safe houses through which runaway slaves were led to freedom in the North.

The Underground Railroad

In many northern cities, blacks and whites organized "vigilance committees" to protect from and thwart the slave catchers. In February 1851, Shadrach Minkins, a "stout, copper-colored man" who worked as a waiter at a Boston coffee house, was seized by U.S. marshals claiming that he was a runaway slave from Virginia. During a court hearing, a group of black and white members of the anti-slavery Boston Vigilance and Safety Committee active in the Underground Railroad startled the judge and observers by rushing in, overcoming armed guards, and snatching "the trembling prey of the slave hunters." Abolitionists hid him for days in Boston before taking him to safety in Canada, where he married an Irish woman and had four children. An outraged President Millard Fillmore issued a proclamation demanding that citizens obey the law and that those responsible for "kidnapping" Minkins be prosecuted. None of the Bostonians charged in the case were convicted.

Between 1810 and 1850, tens of thousands of other southern slaves ran away and fled north. Escaped slaves would make their way, usually at night, from one station to the next. The conductors included free-born blacks, white abolitionists, former slaves, and Native Americans. Many of them were motivated by religious concerns. Quakers, Presbyterians, Methodists, and Baptists participated. A few courageous runaway slaves returned to the South to organize more escapes. Harriet Tubman, the most celebrated runaway, was born a slave in Maryland in 1820 but escaped to Philadelphia in 1849. During the 1850s she risked everything to venture back to the South nineteen times to help some 300 slaves, including her parents, escape over several years. She "never lost a passenger."

Reactions to Abolitionism

Even in the North, abolitionists confronted hostile white crowds who disliked blacks or found anti-slavery agitation bad for business. In 1837, a mob in Illinois killed Elijah P. Lovejoy, editor of an anti-slavery newspaper, giving the movement a martyr to the causes of both abolition and freedom of the press.

Mob violence

Lovejoy had begun his career as a Presbyterian minister in New England. He moved to St. Louis, in slaveholding Missouri, where his newspaper repeatedly denounced alcohol, Catholicism, and slavery. When a pro-slavery mob destroyed his printing office, he moved across the Mississippi River to a warehouse in Alton, Illinois, where he tried to start an anti-slavery society. There mobs twice more destroyed his printing press. When a new press arrived, Lovejoy and several supporters armed themselves and took up defensive positions. On November 7, 1837, thugs began hurling stones and firing shots into the building. One of Lovejoy's allies fired back, killing one of the rioters. The mob then set fire to the warehouse, shouting, "Kill every damned abolitionist as he leaves." A shotgun blast killed Lovejoy. His murder aroused a frenzy of indignation. Former president John Quincy

Adams said that Lovejoy's death sent "a shock as of an earthquake through-out the continent." At one of the hundreds of memorial services across the North, a grizzled John Brown rose, raised his right hand, and declared, "Here, before God, in the presence of these witnesses, from this time, I consecrate my life to the destruction of slavery!" Brown and other militants decided that only violence would dislodge the sin of slavery.

The Defense of Slavery

The growing strength and visibility of the abolitionist movement prompted southerners to launch an equally aggressive defense of slavery. During the 1830s and after, pro-slavery leaders worked out an elaborate rationale for what they considered the benefits of slavery. The Bible was cited; had not the patriarchs of the Hebrew Bible held people in bondage? Had not Saint Paul advised servants to obey their masters and told a runaway servant to return to his master? And had not Jesus remained silent on the subject?

Soon even bolder arguments emerged to defend the South's "peculiar institution." In February 1837, South Carolina's John C. Calhoun, the most prominent southern political leader, told the Senate that slavery was not evil. Instead, it was "good—a great good," rooted in the Bible. He brazenly asserted that the "savage" Africans brought to America "had never existed in so comfortable, so respectable, or so civilized a condition, as that which is now enjoyed in the Southern states." If slavery were abolished, Calhoun warned, the principle of white racial supremacy would be compromised: "the next step would be to raise the negroes to a social and political equality with the whites." What is more, Calhoun and other defenders of slavery claimed, blacks could not be expected to work under conditions of freedom. They were too shiftless, the argument went, and if freed, they would be a danger to themselves and to others. White workers, on the other hand, feared the competition for jobs if slaves were freed. Calhoun's strident defense of slavery as a "positive good" led Henry Clay of Kentucky, himself a slave owner, to describe Calhoun as "a rigid, fanatic, ambitious, selfishly partisan and sectional turncoat with too much genius and too little common sense, who will either die a traitor or a madman."

The increasingly heated debate over slavery drove a wedge deeply between North and South. In 1831, William Lloyd Garrison noted that the "bond of our Union is becoming more and more brittle." He predicted—correctly—that an eventual "separation between the free and slave States" was "unavoidable." By mid-century, a large number of Americans, mostly Whigs, had decided that southern slavery was an abomination that should not be allowed to expand into the new western territories. The militant reformers who were determined to prevent slavery from expanding outside the South came to be called "free soilers," and their crusade to improve American life would reach a fiery climax in the Civil War.

Southern white resistance

Abolitionism

Revolutions in transportation and communication allowed more Americans to share ideas, explore new ways of thinking, and connect with other like-minded individuals. But this often caused rifts in American society as many groups and individuals increasingly challenged social norms and institutions. Nothing divided Americans and generated more debate than abolitionism. Abolitionists not only called for an immediate end to slavery, but also demanded full social and political equality for African Americans. Though appealing to many reformers, particularly Christian evangelicals, it drew an equally passionate yet hostile response from its opponents. Furthermore, abolitionism propelled discussion of the place of all men and women in American society, questions that often divided abolitionists themselves.

Reactions to Abolitionism	North	South	African Americans	Women
General Position	**Pro-Abolition** Inspired by the Second Great Awakening, northern supporters considered slavery a sin.	**Pro-Slavery** Most southerners viewed abolition as a threat to the cotton economy and the social fabric of white supremacy.	**Pro-Abolition** Plantation economy and southern culture split slave families and legalized brutality toward African Americans.	**Pro-Abolition** Many women viewed abolition as part of broader reform movements advocating universal suffrage and gender equality.
Main Goals and Issues	Immediate emancipation, full political and social equality for African Americans Disagreed over tactics and relationship to other reform movements	Slavery improved "the condition of the African" by bringing Christianity and civilization to a "savage," inferior race	Immediate emancipation, full political and social equality, access to education Some called for a violent overthrow of slavery (such as *Walker's Appeal*)	Immediate emancipation, full political and social equality, access to education
Major Figures	■ William Lloyd Garrison ■ Arthur and Lewis Tappan ■ Charles G. Finney ■ James Birney ■ John Brown	■ Senator John C. Calhoun	■ Frederick Douglass ■ Sojourner Truth ■ Harriet Tubman	■ Angelina and Sarah Grimké ■ Sojourner Truth ■ Harriet Tubman ■ Lucretia Mott ■ Elizabeth Cady Stanton ■ Susan B. Anthony

(CONTINUED)

Reactions to Abolitionism	North	South	African Americans	Women
Key Events	■ 1831 – Garrison publishes *The Liberator*, first anti-slavery newspaper ■ 1833 – American Anti-Slavery Society is formed ■ 1837 – Abolitionist editor Elijah Lovejoy murdered by pro-slavery mob ■ 1840 – Liberty Party is formed	■ 1831 – Nat Turner's Rebellion ■ 1830s – Stricter slave codes adopted ■ 1835 – "Anti-slavery propaganda" made illegal in South after abolitionists distribute pro-abolition literature	■ 1816 – First African American church founded in Philadelphia ■ 1845 – *Narrative of the Life of Frederick Douglass* published ■ 1850s – Underground Railroad reaches its height; "vigilance committees" established	■ 1830s – Anti-Slavery Society splits over participation of women ■ 1840 – Emergence of women's rights movement ■ 1851 – Sojourner Truth delivers "Ar'n't I a Woman" speech
Outcomes by 1860	■ Many northerners continued to oppose abolition ■ Many northern politicians refused discussion of slavery issue	■ Slave codes further strengthened ■ Southern Baptist and Methodist denominations dissociated themselves from northern counterparts over slavery issue	■ Underground Railroad brings more than 300,000 to freedom in 1850s–1860s ■ Join forces with women's rights movement ■ National leaders and platforms for abolitionism emerge	■ Association of women's rights and abolitionist movements caused southern women to also oppose women's rights

QUESTIONS FOR ANALYSIS

1. How did residents of northern and other free states respond to abolitionists?

2. How did southerners respond?

3. How did abolitionism affect many African Americans and women?

4. How did abolitionism change American attitudes towards slavery and social reform?

■ **Religious Developments** Starting in the late eighteenth century, *Unitarians* and *Universalists* in New England challenged the notion of predestination and advocated that all humans are capable of good deeds and could receive salvation, not just a select few. Echoing these ideas with their conception of salvation by free will, the preachers of the *Second Great Awakening* generated widespread interest among Protestants in *frontier revivals*. The more democratic sects, such as Baptists and Methodists, gained huge numbers of converts, especially among women and African Americans. Religion went hand in hand with reform in the "burned-over district" in western New York, which was also the birthplace of several religious movements, including the Church of Jesus Christ of Latter-day Saints (the *Mormons*).

■ **Transcendentalists** embraced a moral and spiritual idealism (Romanticism) in reaction to scientific rationalism and Christian orthodoxy. In their writings, they sought to "transcend" reason and the material world and encourage more independent thought and reflection. At the same time, *transcendentalism* influenced the works of novelists, essayists, and poets, who created a uniquely American literature. A cultural nationalism emerged with political ideals for a more moral American society.

■ **Social Reform Movements** The *cult of domesticity* celebrated a "woman's sphere" in the home and argued that young women should be trained not for the workplace but in the domestic arts—managing a kitchen, running a household, and nurturing the children. However, the rise of an urban middle class offered growing numbers of women more time to devote to societal concerns. Social reformers—many of them women—sought to improve society and eradicate social evils. The most widespread movement was for *temperance,* the elimination of excessive drinking. Many were also active in reforming prisons and asylums. At the *Seneca Falls Convention of 1848,* social reformers launched the women's rights movement with the *Declaration of Sentiments (1848)*. In many parts of the country, social reformers called for greater access to education through *public schools* for the nation's young, which would also offer women an occupation outside the home. One educational reformer, Horace Mann, said that teaching was a way for women to become "mothers away from home" for the students. Amid the pervasive climate of reform during the early nineteenth century, more than 100 *utopian communities* were established, including the Shakers, Brook Farm, and the Oneida Community.

■ **Anti-Slavery Movement** Northern opponents of slavery promoted several solutions, including the *American Colonization Society's* call for gradual emancipation and the deportation of African Americans to colonies in Africa. *Abolitionism* emerged in the 1830s, demanding an immediate end of slavery. Some abolitionists went even further, calling for full social and political equality among the races, although they disagreed over tactics. Abolitionist efforts in the North provoked a strong reaction among southern whites, stirring fears for their safety and resentment of interference. Yet many northerners shared the belief in the racial inferiority of Africans and were hostile to the tactics and message of the abolitionists. African Americans in the North joined with abolitionists to create an *Underground Railroad,* a network of safe havens to help slaves escape their bondage in the South.

KEY TERMS

CHRONOLOGY

1779	Universalist Church founded in Massachusetts
1816	Auburn Penitentiary opens in New York
1826	Ministers organize the American Society for the Promotion of Temperance
1830–1831	Charles G. Finney begins preaching in upstate New York
1830	Percentage of American churchgoers has doubled since 1800
	Joseph Smith reveals *The Book of Mormon*
1831	William Lloyd Garrison begins publishing *The Liberator*
1833	American Anti-Slavery Society is founded
1836	Transcendental Club holds its first meeting
1837	Abolitionist editor Elijah P. Lovejoy is murdered
1840	Abolitionists form the Liberty Party
1840s	Methodists have become largest Protestant denomination in America
1845	*Narrative of the Life of Frederick Douglass* is published
1846	Mormons, led by Brigham Young, make the difficult trek to Utah
1848	At the Seneca Falls Convention, feminists issue the Declaration of Sentiments
	John Humphrey Noyes establishes the Oneida Community
1851	Sojourner Truth delivers her famous speech "Ar'n't I a Woman?"
1854	Henry David Thoreau's *Walden, or Life in the Woods* is published

INQUIZITIVE

Go to InQuizitive to see what you've learned—and learn what you've missed—with personalized feedback along the way.

DEBATING Separate Spheres

Politics and present-day events often influence *historiography*, the study of how interpretations of history change over time. In the 1960s, *social* history gained popularity. Drawing on methodologies from the social sciences, historians emphasized the importance of processes and structures in societies and applied them to groups that had been ignored by previous generations of historians. Three concepts of great importance to social historians are *race, class*, and *gender*. For Part 3, *An Expansive Nation*, we will see how historians use these concepts to debate the importance of the "separate spheres" ideology. This ideology emerged during a period where rapid industrialization spurred the growth of the middle class. In the first half of the nineteenth century, before the Civil War, the "separate spheres" ideology promoted separate and distinct roles for women and men. The female sphere was within the home and focused on domesticity, while the male sphere was outside the home and was centered on economic and political competition.

For this exercise you have two tasks:

PART 1: Compare the two secondary sources on women and separate spheres.

PART 2: Using primary sources, evaluate the arguments of the two secondary sources.

PART I Comparing Secondary Sources

Below are secondary sources from two social historians who have written on the separate spheres ideology in American life before the Civil War. The first is from Catherine Clinton of Queens University in Belfast, Ireland; the second from Nancy Hewitt of Rutgers, the State University of New Jersey. Both Clinton and Hewitt use race, class, and gender analysis to look at how separate spheres impacted American women and how women responded to that ideology.

Compare the views of these two scholars by answering the following questions. Be sure to find specific examples in the selections to support your answers.

- What is the subject of each article?

- What classes of women does each author focus on?

- According to each author, how did the ideology of separate spheres impact American women?

- In what ways does each author use race, class, and gender in constructing her argument?

Secondary Source 1

Catherine Clinton, "The Ties that Bind" (1984)

The nineteenth century ushered in a social as well as an economic revolution for American women. The refinement of middle-class ideology profoundly affected females during the antebellum [pre-Civil War] era. . . . The creation of the cult of domesticity, the redefinition of the home as women's domain, was a delicate process designed to channel women's contributions into a proper course. . . .

[I]nstead of liberty and equality, subordination and restriction were drummed into women, a refrain inherited from the colonial era. Women's only reward was lavish exaltation of their vital and unmatchable contributions to the civic state as mothers. This rejuvenated ethic was accompanied by a confinement to the domestic sphere.

Once segregated from men by the confines of a new ideological order, women set about turning their liabilities into assets. Forbidden traditional pathways to success, post-Revolutionary women pursued other means of achieving esteem and influence within their society. These alternatives were pioneered by women who were in search of new influence but who refrained from invading the male domain—not for the sake of modesty, but rather as a strategy. . . .

Woman's domain was, despite confinement, expansive. She was charged with the moral, spiritual, and physical well-being of her entire family. . . . She was supervisor of the education of her children, tender of the heath, and the symbol of the home. These indispensable functions, although primarily carried out within the home, were not restricted to it. Women perceived that they might extend female jurisdiction into the public and hitherto exclusively male realm by using their "domestic" role as a lever—wedging themselves into positions of power, however limited, through exploitation of their domesticity. In the early decades of the century, creative women took their rather circumscribed nooks and crannies, within the culture, and turned them into springboards. Women's talents and contributions were soon apparent within the larger social arena.

Source: Clinton, Catherine. "The Ties that Bind." *The Other Civil War, American Women in the Nineteenth Century.* New York: Hill and Wang, first published in 1984; revised edition, 1999, 40-42.

Secondary Source 2

Nancy A. Hewitt, "Beyond the Search for Sisterhood: American Women's History in the 1980s" (1985)

The bonds that encircled past generations of women were initially perceived as restrictive, arising from female victimization at the hands of patriarchs in such institutions as medicine, education, the church, the state, and the family. Historians soon concluded, however, that oppression was a double-edged sword; the counterpart of subordination in or exclusion from male-dominated domains was inclusion in an all-female enclave. The concept of womanhood, it soon appeared, "bound women together even as it bound them down." The formative works in American women's history have focused on the formation of these separate sexual spheres, particularly among the emerging urban bourgeoisie in the first half of the nineteenth century. Reified in prescriptive literature, realized in daily life, and ritualized in female collectivities, this 'woman's sphere' came to be seen as the foundation of women's culture and community in antebellum [pre-Civil War] America. . . . The community that has become the cornerstone of North American women's history was discovered within the Victorian middle class. . . . Yet evidence from the lives of slaves, mill operatives, miners' wives, immigrants, and southern industrial workers as well as from "true women" indicates that there was no single woman's culture or sphere. There was a culturally dominant definition of sexual spheres promulgated by an economically, politically, and socially dominant group. That definition was firmly grounded in the sexual division of labor appropriate to that class, just as other definitions developed based on the sexual division of labor in other class and racial groups. All of these divisions were characterized by sufficient sex-stereotyping to assure the formation of distinct female circles of labor and distinct rituals and values rooted in that laboring experience. To date historians have focused on the parallels in the establishment of women's spheres across classes, races, and ethnic groups and have asserted certain commonalities among them, assuming their common origin in the modernization of society during the nineteenth century. A closer examination now reveals that no such universal sisterhood existed, and in fact that the development of a sense of community among various classes of women served as a barrier to an all-embracing bond of womanhood. Finally, it is now clear that privileged women were willing to wield their sex-specific influence in ways that, intentionally or unintentionally, exploited other women in the name of "true-womanhood."

Source: Hewitt, Nancy A. "Beyond the Search for Sisterhood: American Women's History in the 1980s." *Social History* 10 (1985), pp. 299-321.

PART II **Using Primary Sources to Evaluate Secondary Sources**

When historians are faced with conflicting interpretations of the past, they often look at primary source material as part of the process of evaluating the different arguments. Below are three excerpts from political statements by three remarkable but very different women. The first is from Lucretia Mott, a middle class and highly educated woman who became a Quaker speaker, leading abolitionist, and co-organizer of the first women's rights conventions, the Seneca Falls Convention. The second excerpt is from Sojourner Truth, a former slave and leading abolitionist. The final excerpt is from Harriett Robinson, who at the age of ten began work in the textile mills of Lowell, Massachusetts. Robinson went on to write her autobiography, and was involved in the women's suffrage movement. While not all of these documents directly engage with the term "separate spheres," each address women's place in American society.

Carefully read each of the following primary sources and answer the following questions. Decide which of the primary source documents support or refute Clinton and Hewitt's arguments about women's separate sphere. You may find that some documents do both but for different parts of each historian's interpretation. Be sure to identify which specific components of each historian's argument the documents support or refute.

■ How did the ideology of separate spheres impact the lives of these three women?

■ What can we learn about separate spheres from those primary sources that do not directly discuss the concept?

■ Which of the primary sources do you think Clinton and Hewitt would find most useful, and how might they use them to support their argument?

■ Which of the secondary sources do you think is best supported by the primary source evidence?

■ What have these primary sources taught you about using race, class, and gender in historical analysis?

Primary Source 1

Lucretia Mott, *Discourse on Women* (1849)

This age is notable for its works of mercy and benevolence—for the efforts that are made to reform the inebriate and the degraded, to relieve the oppressed and the suffering. Women as well as men are interested in these works of justice and mercy. They are efficient co-workers, their talents are called into profitable exercise, their labors are effective in each department of reform. The blessing to the merciful, to the peacemaker is equal to man and to woman. It is greatly to be deplored, now that she is increasingly qualified for usefulness, that any view should be presented, calculated to retard her labors of love.

   Why should not woman seek to be a reformer? . . . [I]f she is to fear to exercise her reason, and her noblest powers, lest she should be thought to "attempt to act the man," and not "acknowledge his supremacy"; if she is to be satisfied with the narrow sphere assigned her by man, nor aspire to a higher, lest she should transcend the bounds of female delicacy; truly it is a mournful prospect for woman. We would admit all the difference, that our great and beneficent Creator has made, in the relation of man and woman, nor would we seek to disturb this relation; but we deny that the present position of woman, is her true sphere of usefulness: nor will she attain to this sphere, until the disabilities and disadvantages, religious, civil, and social, which impede her progress, are removed out of her way. These restrictions have enervated her mind and paralyzed her powers. . . . So far from her "ambition leading her to attempt to act the man," she needs all the encouragement she can receive, by the removal of obstacles from her path, in order that she may become a "true woman." As it is desirable that man should act a manly and generous part, not "mannish," so let woman be urged to exercise a dignified and womanly bearing, not womanish. Let her cultivate all the graces and proper accomplishments of her sex, but let not these degenerate into a kind of effeminacy, in which she is satisfied to be the mere plaything or toy of society, content with her outward adorning's, and with the tone of flattery and fulsome adulation too often addressed to her. True, nature has made a difference in her configuration, her physical strength, her voice, etc.—and we ask no change, we are satisfied with nature. But how has neglect and mismanagement increased this difference! It is our duty to develop these natural powers, by suitable exercise, so that they may be strengthened "by reason of use."

Source: Mott, Lucretia. *Discourse on Women*. Philadelphia, Penn.: T.B. Peterson, 1850.

Primary Source 2

Sojourner Truth, "And Ar'n't I a Woman?" (1851)

And ar'n't I a woman? Look at me! Look at my arm! (*And she bared her right arm to the shoulder, showing her tremendous muscular power*.) I have plowed, and planted, and gathered into barns, and no man could head me—and ar'n't I a woman? I could work as much and eat as much as a man when I could get it and bear de lash as well—and ar'n't I a woman? I have borne thirteen children, and seen 'em mos' all sold off to slavery, and when I cried out with my mother's grief, none but Jesus heard me—and ar'n't I a woman? . . . If my cup won't hold but a pint, and your'n holds a quart, wouldn't ye be mean not to let me have my little half-measure full? . . . He say women can't have as much rights as men, 'cause Christ wan't a woman! Whar did your Christ come from? . . . From God and a woman! Man had nothin' to do with Him.

Source: Truth, Sojourner. "And Ar'n't I a Woman?" (Speech at the Ohio Women's Rights Convention, 1851, Akron, Ohio). *History of Woman Suffrage*, Vol 1.1848-1861. Ed. Elizabeth Cady Stanton, Susan B. Anthony, and Matilda Joslyn Gage. Rochester, New York: Susan B. Anthony, 1887.

Primary Source 3

Harriett H. Robinson, *Loom and Spindle or Life among the Early Mill Girls* **(1898)**

One of the first strikes of cotton-factory operatives that ever took place in this country was that in Lowell, in October, 1836. When it was announced that the wages were to be cut down, great indignation was felt, and it was decided to strike, en masse. This was done. The mills were shut down, and the girls went in procession from their several corporations to the "grove" on Chapel Hill, and listened to "incendiary" speeches from early labor reformers. One of the girls stood on a pump, and gave vent to the feelings of her companions in a neat speech, declaring that it was their duty to resist all attempts at cutting down the wages. This was the first time a woman had spoken in public in Lowell, and the event caused surprise and consternation among her audience. . . . It was estimated that as many as twelve or fifteen hundred girls turned out, and walked in procession through the streets. They had neither flags nor music, but sang songs, a favorite (but rather inappropriate) one being a parody on "I won't be a nun."

"Oh ! isn't it a pity, such a pretty girl as I—

Should be sent to the factory to pine away and die?

Oh ! I cannot be a slave,

I will not be a slave,

For I'm so fond of liberty

That I cannot be a slave."

Source: Robinson, Harriett H. *Loom and Spindle or Life among the Early Mill Girls.* New York and Boston: Thomas Y. Crowell and Company, 1898.

...l unanimously at 1.15 o'clock, P. M., Dece...
20th, 1860.

FOR SALE HERE

AN EDITION FOR THE MILLION, COMPLETE IN 1 Vol., PRICE 37 1-2 CENT...
" " IN GERMAN, IN 1 Vol., PRICE 50 CENTS.
" " IN 2 Vols., CLOTH, 6 PLATES, PRICE $1.50.
SUPERB ILLUSTRATED EDITION, IN 1 Vol., WITH 153 ENGRAVINGS,
PRICES FROM $2.50 TO $5.00.

A House Divided and Rebuilt

During the first half of the nineteenth century, Americans, restless and energetic, were mostly optimistic about the future as their young nation matured into a global power. The United States had already become the world's largest republic. Its population continued to grow rapidly, economic conditions were improving, and tensions with Great Britain had eased. Above all, Americans continued to move westward, where vast expanses of cheap government-owned land lured farmers, ranchers, and miners. By the end of the 1840s, the United States—yet again— had dramatically expanded its territory, from Texas west to California and the Pacific Northwest. In the process of dislodging Native Americans and Mexicans, it assembled a continental empire from the Atlantic to the Pacific.

This extraordinary surge of territorial expansion was not an unmixed blessing, however. How to deal with the new western territories became the nation's flashpoint issue as the differences between America's three distinctive regions—North, South, and West—became more divisive. During the first half of the nineteenth century, a series of political compromises had glossed over the fundamental issue of slavery, but growing numbers of anti-slavery activists opposed efforts to extend slavery into the new western territories. Moreover, the 1850s brought a new generation of national politicians who were less willing to compromise. The continuing debate over allowing slavery into new territories eventually led more and more Americans to decide that the nation could not survive half-slave and half-free. Something had to give.

In a last-ditch effort to preserve the institution of slavery, eleven southern states seceded from the Union and declared themselves a separate Confederate nation. That, in turn, prompted northerners, led by President Abraham Lincoln, to support a civil war to restore the Union. No one realized in 1861 how costly that war would become: more than 700,000 soldiers and sailors would die in four years of fighting. Nor did anyone envision how sweeping the war's effects would be upon the nation's future. The northern victory in 1865 restored the Union and helped accelerate America's transformation into a modern nation-state. A national consciousness began to replace the sectional divisions of the prewar era, and a Republican-led Congress passed a wave of federal legislation to promote industrial and commercial development and western expansion. In the process the United States began to leave behind the Jeffersonian dream of America as a decentralized agrarian republic.

Although the Civil War also ended slavery, the status of the freed African Americans remained uncertain and even life-threatening. Former slaves found themselves legally free, but few had property, homes, education, or training. Although the Fourteenth Amendment (1868) guaranteed the civil rights of African Americans and the Fifteenth Amendment (1870) declared that black men could vote, southern officials often ignored the new laws, and African Americans continued to suffer social abuse and physical harm.

The restoration of the former Confederate states to the Union did not come easily. Bitterness and resistance grew among the defeated southerners. Although former Confederate leaders were initially stripped of the right to vote and hold office, they continued to exercise considerable authority in political and economic matters. In 1877, when the last federal troops were removed from the occupied South, former Confederates declared themselves "redeemed" from the stain of Northern military occupation. By the end of the nineteenth century, most states of the former Confederacy had developed a system of legal discrimination against blacks that re-created many aspects of slavery.

EMIGRANTS CROSSING THE PLAINS, OR THE OREGON TRAIL (1869) German American painter Albert Bierstadt captures the majestic sights of the frontier, though the transcontinental trek was also grueling and bleak for many pioneers.

Western Expansion and Southern Secession

1830–1861

During the 1840s and after, wave after wave of Americans moved west. "If hell lay to the west," one pioneer declared, "Americans would cross heaven to get there." By 1860, some 4.3 million Americans had crossed the mile-wide Mississippi River and spread out across the Great Plains. Westward expansion was especially important to southerners, many of whom wanted new lands to plant cotton using slave labor. In addition, southerners had long enjoyed disproportionate political power because of the provision in the U.S. Constitution that counted slaves as part of the population in determining the number of Congressional seats for each state. Thirteen of the first sixteen presidents were from the South, and most Congressional leadership positions were held by southerners. But southern political influence began to wane as the industrializing Midwest and Northeast grew more rapidly, increasing those regions' representation in Congress. Southerners wanted new western states to boost pro-southern representation in Congress as a means of ensuring that slavery would never be threatened by northern abolitionists. As a Mississippi senator

CORE OBJECTIVES INQUIZITIVE

1. Explain how, why, and where Americans moved west of the Mississippi River during the 1830s and 1840s.

2. Examine the impact of the Mexican-American War on national politics.

3. Describe how the federal government tried to resolve the issue of slavery in the western territories during the 1850s.

4. Analyze what appealed to northern voters about the Republican party and how that led to Abraham Lincoln's victory in the 1860 presidential contest.

5. Explain why seven southern states seceded from the Union shortly after Lincoln's election in 1860.

explained, "I would spread the blessings of slavery . . . to the uttermost ends of the earth." Such motives made the addition of new western territory controversial. Would the territory be slave or free?

Emigrants moved west largely for economic reasons. "To make money was their chief object," said a pioneer woman in Texas, "all things else were subsidiary to it." Trappers and farmers, miners and merchants, hunters, ranchers, teachers, servants, and prostitutes, among others, headed west to seek their fortune. Others—such as the Mormons and Christian missionary organizations—sought religious freedom and the chance to win converts to their faith. The Indians and Hispanics who had long inhabited the region were swept aside by the onslaught of Americans, all enabled by presidents and congressmen eager to complete the nation's expansion to the Pacific coast.

CORE **OBJECTIVE**

1. Explain how, why, and where Americans moved west of the Mississippi River during the 1830s and 1840s.

Moving West

In 1845, a New York newspaper editor and Democratic-party propagandist named John L. O'Sullivan gave a catchy name to America's aggressive spirit of westward expansion. "Our manifest destiny," he wrote, "is to overspread the continent allotted by Providence for the free development of our yearly multiplying millions." The phrase "**manifest destiny**" assumed that the United States had a God-given right to extend its rapidly growing Christian republic and capitalist civilization across the continent from the Atlantic to the Pacific—and beyond. This widely embraced notion of manifest destiny offered a powerful religious justification for territorial expansion, even at the expense of the prior claims of Native Americans and Hispanics, Spaniards and the British, on western lands.

Western migration: Population growth, land, and Overland Trails

The Western Frontier

Most of the western pioneers during the second quarter of the nineteenth century were American-born whites from the Upper South and the Midwest. Only a few free African Americans joined in the migration. What spurred the massive migration westward was the continuing population explosion in the United States and the desire for land.

Although some people traveled by sea to California, most went overland. Between 1841 and 1867, some 350,000 men, women, and children made the difficult trek to California or Oregon, while hundreds of thousands of others settled along the way in areas such as Colorado, Texas, and Arkansas. Most of the pioneers who made their way westward on the **Overland Trails** traveled in family groups. Oregon-bound wagon trains usually left Missouri in late spring and completed the grueling 2,000-mile trek in six months. By 1845, some 5,000 people were making the journey annually. The discovery of gold in California in 1848 brought some 30,000 pioneers along the Oregon Trail in 1849. By 1850, the peak year of travel along the trail, the annual count had risen to 55,000.

manifest destiny The widespread belief that America was "destined" by God to expand westward across the continent into lands claimed by Native Americans as well as European nations.

Overland Trails Trail routes followed by wagon trains bearing settlers and trade goods from Missouri to the Oregon Country, California, and New Mexico, beginning in the 1840s.

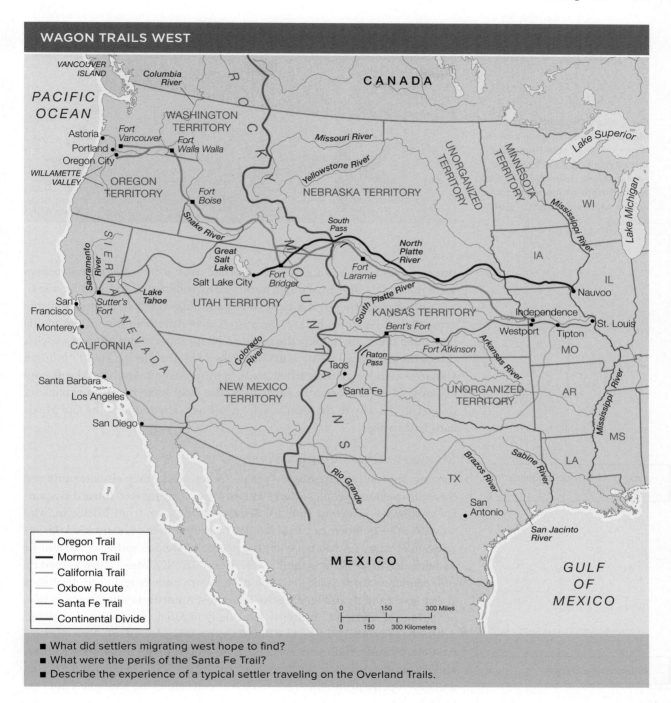

WAGON TRAILS WEST

Legend:
- Oregon Trail
- Mormon Trail
- California Trail
- Oxbow Route
- Santa Fe Trail
- Continental Divide

- What did settlers migrating west hope to find?
- What were the perils of the Santa Fe Trail?
- Describe the experience of a typical settler traveling on the Overland Trails.

Plains Indians

More than 325,000 Indians inhabited the Southwest, the Great Plains, California, and the Pacific Northwest in 1840, when the great migration of American settlers into the region began. The Native Americans were divided into more than 200 nations, each with its own language, religion, cultural

> Conflicts over Indian lands

Fur Traders Descending the Missouri (1845) Originally titled "French-Trader, Half-Breed Son," this oil painting depicts a white settler sailing down the river with his half–Native American son—not an uncommon sight in early America.

practices, and system of governance. Some were primarily farmers; others were nomadic, following buffalo herds; many Indian nations were hostile to each other, resulting in frequent wars and raids—often to control hunting grounds or to acquire horses. Because Native American life on the plains depended upon the buffalo, the influx of white settlers and hunters posed a direct threat to the Indians' survival. When federal officials could not force Indian leaders to sell their tribal lands, fighting ensued. And after the discovery of gold in California in early 1848, the tidal wave of white expansion flowed all the way to the west coast, engulfing Native Americans and Mexicans in its wake.

Mexico and the Spanish West

> Mexico gains independence from Spain (1821)

As American settlers trespassed across Indian lands, they also encountered Spanish-speaking peoples. Many whites were as prejudiced toward Hispanics as they were toward Indians. Senator Lewis Cass from Michigan, who would be the Democratic candidate for president in 1848, expressed the expansionist view: "We do not want the people of Mexico, either as citizens or as subjects. All we want is their . . . territory." In 1821, Mexico had gained its independence from Spain, but the new nation had struggled to develop a stable government and an effective economy. Americans were eager to take advantage of Mexico's instability, especially in Mexico's sparsely populated northern provinces—areas that included present-day Texas, New Mexico, Arizona, Nevada, California, and portions of Colorado, Oklahoma, Kansas,

> American fur traders

and Wyoming. American fur traders streamed into New Mexico and Arizona and developed a profitable trade in beaver pelts along the Santa Fe Trail east to St. Louis.

The Rocky Mountains and Oregon Country

> British-American joint occupation of the Oregon Country

During the early nineteenth century, the Far Northwest consisted of the Nebraska, Washington, and Oregon Territories. The Oregon Country included what became the states of Oregon, Idaho, and Washington, as well as parts of Montana, Wyoming, and the Canadian province of British Columbia. It was an unsettled region claimed by both Great Britain and the United States. By the Convention of 1818, the two nations had agreed to "joint occupation" of the Oregon Country.

Word of Oregon's fertile soil, plentiful rainfall, and magnificent forests gradually spread eastward. By the late 1830s, a trickle of emigrants—farmers, missionaries, fur traders, and shopkeepers—was flowing along the Oregon Trail, a 2,000-mile footpath connecting the Missouri River near St. Louis with Oregon. Soon, however, **Oregon Fever** swept the nation. In 1841 and 1842, the first sizable wagon trains made the trip, and in 1843 the movement became a mass migration. One pioneer remembered that the wagon trains were like mobile communities. "Everybody was supposed to rise at daylight, and while the women were preparing breakfast, the men rounded up the cattle, took down the tents, yoked the oxen to the wagons, and made everything ready to start" once breakfast was over. They found Oregon in a "primitive state" requiring backbreaking work to create self-sustaining homesteads. Women worked as hard as men, day and night. "I am a very old woman," reported twenty-nine-year-old Sarah Everett. "My face is thin, sunken, and wrinkled, my hands bony, withered, and hard." Another Oregon pioneer warned that a "woman that cannot endure almost as much as a horse has no business here." By 1845 there were about 5,000 settlers in Oregon's Willamette Valley.

The Settlement of California

California was also a powerful magnet for new settlers and adventurers. By the nineteenth century, Spanish Catholic missionaries, aided by Spanish soldiers, had control over most of the coastal Indians. The friars (priests) lured the local Indians into "missions" by offering gifts or impressing them with their "magical" religious rituals. Once inside the missions, the Indians were baptized as Catholics, taught Spanish, and stripped of their native heritage. Soldiers living in the missions enforced the will of the friars, and rebellious Indians were whipped or imprisoned. Mission Indians died at an alarming rate; the Native American population along the California coast declined from 72,000 in 1769 to 18,000 by 1821. Saving souls cost many lives.

For all of its rich natural resources, California remained thinly populated well into the nineteenth century. Californians took comfort that Mexico City, the Mexican capital, was too far away to exercise effective control over them. Between 1821, when Mexico gained its independence, and 1841, Californians, including many recent American arrivals, staged ten revolts against Mexican governors.

Yet the shift from Spanish to Mexican rule did produce one dramatic change in California. In 1824, Mexico passed a colonization act that granted hundreds of huge *ranchos* (estates) to prominent Mexicans. Yet the *rancheros* (largest landowners) wanted more, especially the vast estates controlled by the Catholic missions, which were usually on the most fertile and valuable land. In 1833–1834, they persuaded the Mexican government to pass the "secularization act" which allowed the government to take the missions,

> Oregon Fever

Oregon Fever The lure of fertile land and economic opportunities in the Oregon Country that drew thousands of settlers westward, beginning in the late 1830s.

Huge *ranchos* dominate
Mexican-owned California

release the Indians from church control, and transfer the missions' vast farmlands to *rancheros*. Within a few years, some 700 new *rancho* grants of 4,500 to 50,000 acres were issued along the California coast. These sprawling ranches resembled southern plantations—but the death rate among brutalized Indian workers was twice as high as that among enslaved blacks in the Lower South.

California: Sutter's Fort

Among the most ambitious white immigrants in California in the mid-nineteenth century was John A. Sutter, a Swiss settler who had founded a colony of European emigrants. At the junction of the Sacramento and American Rivers (later the site of the city of Sacramento), Sutter built an enormous fort to protect the settlers and their shops. New Helvetia (Americans called it Sutter's Fort), completed in 1843, stood at the end of what became the most traveled western route through the Sierra Nevada mountains, the California Trail, which forked southward off the Oregon Trail and led through the mountains. By the start of 1846, there were perhaps 800 Americans in California, along with approximately 10,000 *Californios* (settlers of Hispanic descent).

American Settlements in Texas

"Texians" settle lands in northern Mexico

The American passion for new western land focused on the closest of all the northern Mexican borderlands, Texas. During the 1820s, the United States had twice offered to buy Texas, but the Mexican government refused to sell. Mexicans were frightened and infuriated by the idea of America acquiring their "sacred soil." But that is what happened anyway. The leading promoter of American settlement in Texas was Stephen Fuller Austin, a visionary land developer (*empresario*) who convinced Mexican leaders that he could recruit energetic American families to settle in Texas and thereby create a "buffer" on the northern frontier between the feared Comanche Indians and the Mexican settlements to the south. Thousands of hardy souls settled in Austin's Anglo-Texas "colony." They were mostly ranchers or farmers drawn to the fertile lands in the river valleys that sold for only a few cents an acre—much less than the price of federal land in the United States. A few of the settlers were wealthy planters who brought large numbers of

American pioneers This 1850 photograph captures only a few of the thousands of pioneers who headed west for brighter futures.

slaves with them at a time when Mexico prohibited the importation of slaves. By 1830, the coastal region of Texas had far more Americans living there than Hispanics—about 20,000 white settlers (Anglo-Texans, or "Texians"), and 1,000 enslaved blacks, brought to grow and harvest cotton.

In 1828, José María Sánchez, a Mexican official, visited Austin's settlement in Texas and warned that the effort to take Texas from Mexico "will start from this colony" because the Mexican government was not taking "vigorous measures to prevent it."

The Texas War for Independence

Mexican officials were so worried about the cultural tensions created by too many non-Catholic and slave-owning Americans living in Texas that in April 1830 they abruptly outlawed immigration from the United States and built forts to enforce the new law. But Americans, who viewed the Mexicans and their army with contempt, kept coming. By 1835, the Texians and their enslaved blacks outnumbered the *Tejanos* (Hispanic Texans) ten to one.

Changing political circumstances in Mexico aggravated the growing tensions. In 1834, General Antonio López de Santa Anna, the Mexican president, suspended the national congress and became a dictator, calling himself the "Napoleon of the West." Texians feared that Santa Anna planned to free "our slaves and to make slaves of us." When Santa Anna imprisoned Stephen Austin in 1834, Texians decided that they must gain their independence from Mexican control. After Austin was released from jail eighteen months later, he called for Texians to revolt: "War is our only resource. There is no other remedy. We must defend our rights, ourselves, and our country by force of arms." He urged that Texas become fully American, promote slavery, and join the United States. In the fall of 1835, wary Texians followed Austin's lead and rebelled against Santa Anna's "despotism." A furious Santa Anna ordered all Americans expelled, all Texians disarmed, and all rebels arrested and executed. As sporadic fighting erupted, hundreds of armed volunteers from southern states rushed to assist the 30,000 Texians in the **Texas Revolution** against a Mexican nation of 7 million people. "The sword is drawn!" Austin proclaimed.

| Texas Revolution (1835–1836) |

The Alamo and Goliad

At San Antonio, in southern Texas, General Santa Anna's army assaulted a small group of fewer than 200 Texians, Tejanos, and American volunteers holed up in an abandoned Catholic mission called the Alamo. The rebels were led by William B. Travis, a hot-tempered, twenty-six-year-old Alabama lawyer and teacher who had recently been named a lieutenant colonel in the newly formed Texian Army. Travis ignored orders to retreat from the Alamo, insisting that "death was preferable to disgrace." Among the other Americans at the Alamo, the most celebrated was David Crockett, the Tennessee frontiersman, bear hunter, and sharpshooter who had fought Indians under Andrew Jackson and served as an anti-Jackson Whig congressman. He told his fellow defenders that he had come "to aid you all that I can in your noble cause."

In February 1836, Santa Anna demanded that the Americans in the Alamo surrender. Travis answered with cannon fire. He then sent urgent

| The Alamo |

Texas Revolution (1835–1836) Conflict between Texas colonists and the Mexican government that resulted in the creation of the separate Republic of Texas in 1836.

The Alamo David Crockett, pictured fighting with his rifle over his head, joined the legendary battle to defend the Alamo against the Mexican army.

appeals for help, while promising that *"I shall never surrender or retreat. . . . VICTORY OR DEATH!"* But help did not come, and Santa Anna launched a series of assaults against the outnumbered defenders. For eleven days, the Mexicans were thrown back and suffered heavy losses. Then, on March 6, the defenders of the Alamo were awakened by the sound of Mexican bugles playing the dreaded "Degüello" ("No Mercy to the Defenders"). Colonel Travis shouted: "The Mexicans are upon us—give 'em Hell!" Wave after wave of Santa Anna's men attacked from every side. They were twice forced back, but on the third try they broke through the battered north wall. Out of bullets, the rebels fought with tomahawks, knives, and rifle butts, but in the end, virtually all were killed or wounded.

A handful of Alamo defenders, perhaps including Crockett, survived and were captured. General Santa Anna ordered them hacked to death with swords. A Mexican officer wrote that the captives "died without complaining and without humiliating themselves before their torturers." The only survivors of the Alamo were a handful of women, children, and slaves. It was a complete victory for the Mexicans, but a costly one, for the Battle of the Alamo claimed more than 600 Mexican lives and provided a rallying cry for angry Texians thereafter. While Santa Anna proclaimed a "glorious victory," his aide wrote ominously in his diary, "One more such 'glorious victory' and we are finished."

The furious fighting at the Alamo turned the rebellion into a war for Texas independence. On March 2, 1836, during the siege of the Alamo, delegates from all fifty-nine Texas towns met at the village of Washington-on-the-Brazos, 150 miles northeast of San Antonio. There they signed a declaration of independence. Over the next seventeen days, the delegates drafted a constitution for the new Republic of Texas and established a government. Two weeks later, at the Battle of Coleto, a Mexican force again defeated a smaller Texian army, many of them recently arrived volunteers from southern states. The Mexicans marched the 465 captured Texians to a fort in the nearby town of Goliad. Despite pleas from his own men to show mercy, Santa Anna ordered the captives killed as "pirates and outlaws." On Palm Sunday, March 27, 1836, 303 Texians were marched out of Goliad and then killed. The massacres at the Alamo and Goliad fueled a burning desire for revenge among the Texians.

The Battle of San Jacinto

The commander in chief of the Texian Army was the remarkable Sam Houston, a hard-drinking frontiersman born in Virginia to Scots-Irish immigrants. At age fourteen, after his father died, Houston had moved with his mother and siblings to eastern Tennessee, where he lived among the Cherokees for a time. Like David Crockett, he had served under General Andrew Jackson during the War of 1812 before becoming an attorney, a U.S. congressman, and governor of Tennessee. He resigned the governorship two years later because his aristocratic young wife had left him, claiming she had discovered that he had sustained a "dreadful injury" in the Creek War that had left him impotent (a falsehood). In 1829, Houston joined the Cherokee migration westward to the Arkansas Territory, where he married a Cherokee woman and was formally "adopted" by the Cherokee Nation. In December 1832, he moved to Texas and immediately joined the rebellion against Mexico.

A giant of a man said to drink "a barrel of whiskey a day," Houston was fearless, a quality sorely needed by the Texians as they struggled against the much larger Mexican army. After learning of the massacre at the Alamo, Houston's outnumbered troops retreated, hoping that Santa Anna's pursuing army would make a mistake. On April 21, 1836, the cocky Mexican general walked into a trap, when Houston's army surprised the Mexicans near the San Jacinto River, about twenty-five miles southeast of the modern city of Houston. The Texians and Tejanos charged, yelling "Remember the Alamo." They overwhelmed the panic-stricken Mexicans, most of whom had been caught napping during the afternoon *siesta*.

The battle lasted only eighteen minutes; Houston's troops then spent the next two hours slaughtering fleeing Mexican soldiers. It was, said a Texian, a "frightful sight to behold." Some 630 Mexicans were killed and 700 captured. The Texians lost only nine men. Santa Anna escaped in his underwear but was captured the next day. He bought his freedom by signing a treaty recognizing the independence of the Republic of Texas, with the Rio Grande as its southern boundary with Mexico. The Texas Revolution had been accomplished in seven weeks.

The Battle of San Jacinto (1836)

The Lone Star Republic

The Republic of Texas (1836)

In 1836, the Lone Star Republic, as Texians nicknamed their new nation, drafted a constitution for Texas that legalized slavery and banned free blacks, elected Sam Houston its first president, and voted overwhelmingly for annexation by the United States. No one expected the huge Republic of Texas, with only 40,000 people, to remain independent for long.

The American president at the time was Houston's friend and former commander, Andrew Jackson, who eagerly wanted Texas to join the Union. But Jackson decided it was better to wait a few years. He knew that adding Texas as a slave state would ignite an explosive sectional quarrel between North and South that would fracture the Democratic party and endanger the election of New Yorker Martin Van Buren, Jackson's handpicked successor. Worse, any effort to add Texas to the Union would likely mean a war with Mexico, which refused to recognize Texan independence. So Jackson delayed official recognition of the Republic of Texas until his last day in office, early in 1837. Van Buren, Jackson's successor, did as predicted: he avoided all talk of Texas annexation during his single term as president.

The Tyler Presidency and Texas

When William Henry Harrison became president in 1841, he was the oldest man (sixty-eight) and the first Whig to win the office. The Whigs had first emerged in opposition to Andrew Jackson and continued to promote strong federal government support for industrial development and economic growth: high tariffs to deter imports and funding for internal improvements. Yet Harrison was elected primarily on the strength of his military record and because he had avoided taking public stances on controversial issues. In the end, it mattered little, for Harrison served the shortest term of any president.

Tyler assumes the presidency after Harrison's death (1841)

On April 4, 1841, exactly one month after his inauguration, he died of pneumonia, and John Tyler of Virginia became president. When the Whigs had chosen Tyler as their vice-presidential nominee in 1840, no one expected him to become president. The powerful anti-Jackson Whig, Senator Henry Clay, had wanted a southerner to balance the Whig ticket but expected that he would dominate the Harrison presidency.

Tyler, however, was not so easily dominated. At fifty-one, the tall, thin, slave-owning Virginian was the youngest president to date, but he had lots of political experience, having served as a state legislator, governor, congressman, and senator. Originally a Democrat, Tyler had broken with the party over President Andrew Jackson's "condemnation" of South Carolina's attempt to nullify federal laws. Tyler believed that South Carolina had a constitutional right to secede from the nation.

Now, as president, Tyler was stubbornly opposed to everything associated with the Whig party's "American System," Clay's celebrated program of economic nationalism that called for the federal government to support industrial development. Like Thomas Jefferson, Tyler also endorsed territorial expansion, and soon after becoming president in 1841, he began working to make Texas the twenty-eighth American state.

When Congress met in a special session in 1841, Henry Clay introduced a series of controversial resolutions. He called for the repeal of the Independent Treasury Act and the creation of another Bank of the United States, proposed to revive the distribution program whereby the money raised from federal land sales was given to the states, and urged that tariffs be raised on imported goods. The "haughty and imperious" Clay then set about pushing his program through Congress. "Tyler dares not resist. I will drive him before me," he said. With more tact Clay might have avoided a series of nasty disputes with Tyler over financial issues. But for once, driven by his inextinguishable quest to be president, Clay, the Great Compromiser, lost his instinct for compromise.

Although Tyler agreed to the repeal of the Independent Treasury Act and signed a higher tariff bill, the president vetoed Clay's pet project: a new national bank. Clay responded by attacking the president in Congress, calling him a traitor to his party. He also convinced Tyler's entire cabinet to resign, with the exception of Secretary of State Daniel Webster. Tyler replaced the defectors with anti-Jackson Democrats who, like him, had become Whigs. The Whigs then expelled Tyler from the party. By 1842, Tyler had become a president without a party, shunned by both Whigs and Democrats, but loved by those promoting territorial expansion.

> Tyler vetos national bank bill

The political turmoil coincided with the continuing economic depression. Bank failures mounted, and unemployment soared. People rioted in the streets of Philadelphia, and an armed rebellion flared up in Rhode Island over the failure of the state to allow non-landowners to vote. The self-assured Tyler, however, refused to let either the sputtering economy or an international crisis with Great Britain deflect him from his determination to annex more territory into the United States.

Tensions with Britain

In late 1841, slaves being transported from Virginia to Louisiana on the American ship *Creole* revolted and took charge of the ship after killing a slave trader. They sailed into Nassau, in the Bahamas, where British authorities set 128 of them free (Great Britain had abolished slavery throughout its empire in 1834). It was the most successful slave revolt in American history. Southerners were furious, and the incident mushroomed into an international crisis with Great Britain. Secretary of State Daniel Webster demanded that the slaves be returned as American property, but the British refused. (The dispute was not settled until 1853, when Britain paid $110,000 to the owners of the freed slaves.)

At this point, the British government decided to send Alexander Baring, Lord Ashburton, to meet with Webster. The meetings concluded with the signing of the Webster-Ashburton Treaty (1842), which provided for joint

> Webster-Ashburton Treaty (1842)

naval patrols off the coast of Africa to police the outlawed slave trade. The treaty also resolved a long-standing dispute over the northeastern U.S. boundary with British Canada.

Efforts to Annex Texas

Texas annexation treaty defeated

In April 1843, South Carolinian John C. Calhoun, then secretary of state, sent to the Senate for ratification a treaty annexing Texas. But there it died by a vote of 35–16. Northern senators, many of whom were abolitionists, refused to add another slave state. Others were concerned that annexing Texas would trigger a war with Mexico.

Texan leaders were frustrated that their new independence had not led to annexation. Houston threatened to expand the Republic of Texas to the Pacific. But with little money in the treasury, a rising government debt, and continuing tensions with Mexico, which insisted that it remained at war with Texas, this was mostly talk. The Lone Star Republic also had no infrastructure—no banks, no schools, no industries. It remained largely a frontier community of scattered log cabins. Houston decided that Texas had only two choices: annexation to the United States or closer economic ties to Great Britain, which extended formal diplomatic recognition to the republic and began buying cotton from Texas planters. Meanwhile, thousands more Americans poured into Texas. The population more than tripled between 1836 and 1845, from 40,000 to 150,000, and the enslaved black population grew even faster than the white population.

The Election of 1844

James K. Polk elected president (1844)

Leaders in both political parties hoped to keep the divisive Texas issue out of the 1844 presidential campaign. Whig Henry Clay (of Kentucky) and Democrat Martin Van Buren (of New York), the leading candidates for each party's nomination, agreed that adding Texas to the Union would be a mistake. Van Buren's southern supporters, including Andrew Jackson, abandoned him because he opposed annexation. At the Democratic Convention, annexationists, including Jackson, nominated James Knox Polk, former Speaker of the House and former governor of Tennessee. Like Tyler, Polk was an aggressive expansionist who wanted to make the United States a transcontinental global power. On the ninth ballot, he became the first "dark horse" (unexpected) candidate to win a major-party nomination. The Democrats' platform called for the annexation of both the Oregon Country and Texas.

The 1844 presidential election proved to be one of the most significant in American history. By promoting southern and western expansionism, the Democrats offered a winning strategy, one so popular that it forced Whig candidate Henry Clay to alter his position on Texas at the last minute; he now claimed that he had "no personal objection to the annexation" if it could be achieved "without dishonor, without war, with the common consent of the Union, and upon just and fair terms."

Clay's change of heart on Texas shifted more anti-slavery votes to the new Liberty party (the anti-slavery party formed in 1840), which increased its count in the presidential election from about 7,000 in 1840 (the year it was founded) to more than 62,000 in 1844. In the western counties of New York, the Liberty party drew enough votes from Clay and the Whigs to give the state to Polk and the Democrats. Had he carried New York, Clay would have won the national election by seven electoral votes. Instead, Polk won a narrow national plurality of 38,000 popular votes (the first president since John Quincy Adams to win without a majority) but a clear majority of the Electoral College, 170–105. Clay had lost his third and last effort to win the presidency. Clay could not understand how he could have lost to Polk, a "third-rate" politician lacking natural leadership abilities.

Polk wins 1844 election

Yet Polk had been surprising people his whole career. Born near Charlotte, North Carolina, he graduated first in his class at the University of North Carolina, then moved to Tennessee, where he became a successful lawyer and planter, entered politics, and served fourteen years in Congress (four as Speaker of the House) and two years as governor. At age forty-nine, often called "Young Hickory" because of his admiration for Andrew Jackson, Polk was America's youngest president up to that time. Yet he worked so hard during his four years in the White House that his health failed, and he died in 1849, at fifty-three, just three months after leaving office.

The State of Texas

Texas, the political hot potato, had been added to the Union just before Polk became president. In his final months in office, President John Tyler had asked Congress to annex Texas by joint resolution, which required only a simple majority in each house rather than the two-thirds Senate vote needed to ratify a *treaty*. The resolution narrowly passed, with most Whigs opposed. On March 1, 1845, in his final presidential action, President Tyler signed the resolution admitting Texas to the Union as the twenty-eighth state, and fifteenth slave state, on December 29, 1845. By 1850, the population—both white and black—had soared by almost 50 percent. (The census then did not include Native Americans.) By 1860, Texas was home to 600,000 people, most of them southerners intent on growing cotton.

Texas becomes a state (1845)

Polk's Goals

Like Andrew Jackson, the slave-owning Polk sought to avoid any public discussion of the merits or future of slavery while focusing on four major objectives, all of which he accomplished: 1) reduce tariffs on imports; 2) re-establish the Independent Treasury ("We need no national banks!"); 3) settle the Oregon boundary dispute with Britain; and 4) acquire California from Mexico. Polk's top priority was territorial expansion. He wanted to add Oregon, California, and New Mexico to the Union. In keeping with longstanding Democratic beliefs, Polk wanted lower tariffs to allow more foreign goods to compete in the American marketplace, and thereby help drive consumer prices down. Congress agreed by approving the Walker Tariff of 1846, named after Robert J. Walker, the secretary of the Treasury.

In the same year, Polk persuaded Congress to restore the Independent Treasury Act that President Martin Van Buren had signed into law in 1840 and the Whig-dominated Congress had repealed the next year. The act established independent treasury deposit offices separate from private or state banks to receive all federal government funds. The system was intended to replace the Second Bank of the United States, which Jackson had "killed," so as to offset the rapid growth of unregulated state banks, whose reckless lending practices had helped cause the depression of the late 1830s. The new Independent Treasury established by Polk entrusted the federal government, rather than favored state banks, with the exclusive management of government funds and required that all disbursements be made in gold or silver, or paper currency backed by gold or silver. Polk also sought to reverse Whig policy on the federal funding of roads and harbors. Twice he vetoed Whig-passed bills for federally funded infrastructure projects. His blows to Whig economic policies satisfied the slaveholding South but angered northerners who wanted higher tariffs to protect their industries from British competition and westerners who wanted federally financed roads and harbors for their bustling new economies.

Tariff of 1846 This political cartoon illustrates the public outcry—represented by a Quaker woman brandishing switches, ready to whip Polk—against the Tariff of 1846, one of the lowest in the nation's history.

Oregon

Meanwhile, the dispute with Great Britain over the Oregon Country boundary heated up as expansionists insisted that Polk take the whole region rather than split it with the British. In his inaugural address, Polk said that the American claim to the enormous Oregon Country was "clear and unquestionable," and he was willing to go to the brink of war to achieve his goals. "If we do have war," Polk said, "it will not be our fault."

Fortunately for the reckless Polk, the British were not willing to risk war over a remote wilderness territory. In 1846, they suggested extending the border between the United States and British Canada westward to the Pacific coast along the 49th parallel. On June 15, James Buchanan, Polk's secretary of state, signed what was called the Buchanan-Pakenham Treaty, which did just that.

Buchanan-Pakenham Treaty (1846): Oregon becomes American territory

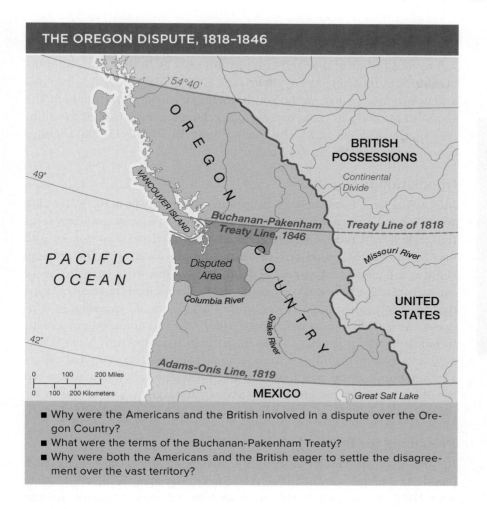

THE OREGON DISPUTE, 1818–1846

- Why were the Americans and the British involved in a dispute over the Oregon Country?
- What were the terms of the Buchanan-Pakenham Treaty?
- Why were both the Americans and the British eager to settle the disagreement over the vast territory?

The Mexican-American War

The Outbreak of War

On March 6, 1845, two days after James K. Polk took office, the Mexican government broke off relations with the United States to protest the annexation of Texas. The president was willing to wage war against Mexico to acquire California, but he did not want Americans to fire the first shot. So Polk ordered several thousand U.S. troops under General Zachary Taylor to advance some 150 miles south of the Texas frontier and take up positions around Corpus Christi, near the Rio Grande. The U.S. troops were knowingly in disputed territory; Mexico recognized neither the American annexation of Texas nor the Rio Grande boundary.

On the evening of May 9, 1845, Polk learned that Mexican troops had attacked U.S. soldiers north of the Rio Grande. Eleven Americans were killed. Polk's scheme to provoke an attack had worked. In his war message to Congress, the president claimed that war was the only response to

CORE **OBJECTIVE**
2. Examine the impact of the Mexican-American War on national politics.

Westward expansionism and war fever

Mexican aggression. Mexico, he reported, "has invaded our territory, and shed American blood upon the American soil." Congress quickly passed the war resolution and authorized the recruitment of 50,000 soldiers. The outbreak of fighting thrilled many Americans. "LET US GO TO WAR," screamed a New York newspaper. In the South, where expansion fever ran high, the war with Mexico was immensely popular. So many men rushed to volunteer that thousands had to be turned back. Eventually, 112,000 whites served in the war (blacks were banned).

Opposition to the War

In New England, however, there was much less enthusiasm for "Mr. Polk's War." Congressman John Quincy Adams, who voted against the war resolution, called it "a most unrighteous war" designed to extend slavery into new territories. Many other New Englanders involved with the growing abolitionist movement denounced the war as the work of pro-slavery southerners. The fiery Boston abolitionist William Lloyd Garrison charged that the war against Mexico was one "of aggression, of invasion, of conquest." A few miles away, in Concord, Henry David Thoreau spent a night in jail rather than pay taxes that might help fund the war. Most Whigs across the North, including a young Illinois congressman named Abraham Lincoln, opposed the war, stressing that President Polk had maneuvered the Mexicans to attack. The United States, they argued, had no reason for placing its army in the disputed border region between Texas and Mexico.

Preparing for Battle

Regardless of the conflict's legitimacy, the United States was again ill prepared for a major war. At the outset, the regular army numbered barely over 7,000, in contrast to the Mexican force of 32,000. Before the war ended, the U.S. military had grown to almost 79,000 troops, many of whom were frontier toughs lacking uniforms, equipment, and discipline. Repeatedly, some of these soldiers engaged in plunder, rape, and murder. Yet the American troops outfought the larger Mexican forces, which had their own problems with training, discipline, morale, supplies, and munitions. The Mexican-American War would last two years, from March 1846 to April 1848, and would be fought on four fronts: southern Texas, central Mexico, New Mexico, and California. Early in the fighting, General Zachary Taylor's army scored two victories over Mexican forces north of the Rio Grande, at Palo Alto (May 8) and Resaca de la Palma (May 9). On May 18, Taylor's army crossed the Rio Grande and occupied Matamoros. These quick victories brought General Taylor, a Whig, instant popularity, and Polk agreed to public demands that Taylor be made overall commander.

The Annexation of California

California becomes an American territory (1846)

Along the Pacific coast, the conquest of Mexican territory was under way before news of the start of the Mexican-American War had arrived. Near the end of 1845, John C. Frémont, an army officer and ardent expansionist

Zachary Taylor Like Andrew Jackson, Taylor was a popular war hero whose public support paved the way to presidency.

known as "the Pathfinder" for having helped map the eastern half of the Oregon Trail, recruited a band of sixty frontiersmen and headed into California's Sacramento Valley, where they encouraged Americans to declare their independence from Mexico. They captured Sonoma on June 14, 1846, proclaimed the Republic of California, and hoisted a flag featuring a grizzly bear and star, a version of which would later become the state flag. But the Bear Flag Republic lasted only a month. In July, the commodore of the U.S. Pacific Fleet, having heard of the outbreak of hostilities, sent troops ashore to raise the American flag and claim California as part of the United States.

Before the end of July, another navy officer, Robert F. Stockton, led the American occupation of Santa Barbara and Los Angeles, on the southern California coast. By mid-August 1846, Mexican resistance had evaporated. On August 17, Stockton declared himself governor, with Frémont as military governor in the north. At the same time, another American military expedition headed for New Mexico. On August 18, General Stephen Kearny and a small army entered Santa Fe. Kearny then led 300 men westward toward southern California, where they joined Stockton's forces at San Diego. They took control of Los Angeles on January 10, 1847, and the remaining Mexican forces surrendered.

U.S. Army takes New Mexico (1846)

War in Northern Mexico

Both California and New Mexico had been taken from Mexican control before General Zachary Taylor fought his first major battle in northern Mexico. In September 1846, Taylor's army assaulted the fortified city of Monterrey, which surrendered after a five-day siege. Then the old dictator General Antonio López de Santa Anna, forced out of power in 1845, got word to Polk from his exile in Cuba that he would end the war if he were allowed to return. Polk assured the Mexican leader that the U.S. government would pay well for any territory taken from Mexico. In August 1846, on Polk's orders, Santa Anna was permitted to return to Mexico. But the crafty Santa Anna had lied. Soon he was again president of Mexico and in command of the Mexican army. As it turned out, however, he was much more talented at raising armies than leading them in battle. In October 1846, Santa Anna prepared to attack. When the Mexican general invited the outnumbered Americans to surrender, Zachary Taylor responded, "Tell him to go to hell." That launched the hard-fought Battle of Buena Vista (February 22–23, 1847), in northern Mexico. Both sides claimed victory, but the Mexicans lost five times as many killed and wounded as the Americans. However, one of the U.S. soldiers killed was Henry Clay Jr., "the pride and hope" of his famous father who had lost to Polk in the 1844 presidential campaign. The elder Clay, devastated by his son's death, condemned Polk's "unnecessary" war of "offensive aggression" and opposed any effort to use the war as a means of acquiring Mexican territory "for the purpose of introducing slavery into it."

The Battle of Buena Vista (1847)

Meanwhile, the long-planned American assault on Mexico City had begun on March 9, 1847, when General Winfield Scott's army landed on the beaches south of Veracruz and began marching toward the Mexican capital. After a series of battles in which they overwhelmed the Mexican defenses, U.S. forces entered Mexico City on September 13. News of the victory thrilled American expansionists. The editor John O'Sullivan, who had coined the phrase "manifest destiny," shouted, "More, More, More! Why not take all of Mexico?"

The Treaty of Guadalupe Hidalgo

Treaty of Guadalupe Hidalgo (1848)

After the fall of Mexico City, Santa Anna resigned and fled the country. Peace talks began on January 2, 1848. By the **Treaty of Guadalupe Hidalgo**, signed on February 2, Mexico gave up all claims to Texas north of the Rio Grande and transferred control of California and New Mexico to the United States. In return for half a million square miles of territory—more than half of Mexico—the United States agreed to pay $15 million. The Senate ratified the treaty on March 10, 1848. By the end of July, the last remaining U.S. soldiers had left Mexico.

The War's Legacies

An expanded United States

The United States lost 1,733 soldiers from combat in the Mexican-American War. Another 4,152 were wounded, and far more—11,550—died of disease. The war remains the deadliest in American history in terms of the percentage of soldiers killed. Out of every 1,000 U.S. soldiers in Mexico, some 110 died. The next highest death rate would be in the Civil War, with 65 dead out of every 1,000 participants. As a result of the conflict, the United States acquired the future states of California, Nevada, and Utah and parts of New Mexico, Arizona, Colorado, and Wyoming. Except for a small addition made by the Gadsden Purchase of 1853, these annexations rounded out the continental United States and nearly doubled its size.

THE GADSDEN PURCHASE, 1853

- Why did the U.S. government purchase from Mexico the land south of the Gila River?
- What was the route of the new Southern Pacific railroad?
- How did the debate over the national railroad open up sectional conflicts?

The victory in Mexico also helped end the long economic depression. As the years passed, however, the Mexican-American War was increasingly seen as a shameful war of conquest and imperialistic plunder directed by a president bent on territorial expansion for the sake of slavery. Ulysses S. Grant, who fought in the war, later called it "one of the most unjust wars ever waged by a stronger against a weaker nation."

Treaty of Guadalupe Hidalgo (1848) Treaty between United States and Mexico that ended the Mexican-American War.

Slavery in the Territories

President Polk acquired more new territory for the United States than any president before or since. Yet he naively assumed that expanding the nation to the Pacific would strengthen "the bonds of Union." He was wrong. No sooner was Texas annexed and gold discovered in California than a violent debate erupted over the extension of slavery into the new territories. That debate, spurred by growing southern fears that a larger, richer, and more powerful North would eventually abolish slavery, culminated in a controversial war that nearly destroyed the Union.

CORE OBJECTIVE
3. Describe how the federal government tried to resolve the issue of slavery in the territories during the 1850s.

The Wilmot Proviso

The Mexican-American War was less than three months old when a new political conflict erupted over slavery. On August 8, 1846, a Democratic congressman from Pennsylvania, David Wilmot, delivered a speech to the House of Representatives in which he endorsed the earlier annexation of Texas as a slave state. But slavery had come to an end in the rest of Mexico, he noted, and if any *new* Mexican territory should be acquired as a result of the war, he declared, "God forbid that we should be the means of planting this institution [slavery] upon it." If any additional land should be acquired from Mexico, Wilmot proposed, slavery would be banned there, in part because he and other northerners were "jealous of the power of the South" and did not want any new states joining the slave-state alliance.

The proposed **Wilmot Proviso** re-ignited the debate over the westward extension of slavery. The issue had been lurking for a generation, ever since the Missouri controversy of 1819–1821. The Missouri Compromise had provided a temporary solution by protecting slavery in states where it already existed but not allowing it in newly acquired territories north of the 36th parallel. Now, with the addition of the territories taken from Mexico, the stage was set for an even more explosive debate.

In 1846, the House of Representatives adopted the Wilmot Proviso, but the Senate balked. When Congress reconvened in December 1846, President Polk dismissed the proviso as "mischievous and foolish." He convinced Wilmot to withhold his amendment from any bill dealing with the annexation of Mexican territory. By then, however, others were ready to take up the cause. In one form or another, Wilmot's idea of restricting the expansion of slavery would continue to crop up in Congress. Abraham Lincoln later recalled that during his one term as a congressman, in 1847–1849, he voted for it "as good as forty times."

Senator John C. Calhoun of South Carolina, meanwhile, countered Wilmot's proviso with his own plan, which he presented to the Senate on February 19, 1847. Calhoun insisted that Wilmot's effort to exclude slaves from territories acquired from Mexico would violate the Fifth Amendment, which forbids Congress to deprive any person of life, liberty, or property

Wilmot Proviso (1846)

Wilmot Proviso (1846)
Proposal by Congressman David Wilmot, a Pennsylvania Democrat, to prohibit slavery in any land acquired in the Mexican-American War.

without due process of law. Slaves, he argued, were *property*. By this clever stroke of logic, Calhoun turned the Bill of Rights into a guarantee of slavery. Senator Thomas Hart Benton of Missouri, himself a slaveholder but also a nationalist eager to calm sectional tensions, found in Calhoun's stance a set of dangerous abstractions "leading to no result." Wilmot and Calhoun between them, he said, had fashioned a pair of scissors. Neither blade alone would cut very well, but joined together they could sever the nation in two.

Popular Sovereignty

The "popular sovereignty" plan

Benton and others tried to deflect the brewing conflict over slavery. President Polk was among the first to suggest simply extending the Missouri Compromise, dividing free and slave territory at the latitude of 36°30′, all the way to the Pacific Ocean. Senator Lewis Cass of Michigan suggested that the citizens of a territory "regulate their own internal concerns in their own way," like the citizens of a state. Such an approach would take the issue of slavery in new territories out of Congress and put it in the hands of those directly affected. "**Popular sovereignty**," as Cass's idea was called, appealed to many Americans.

Polk had promised to serve only one term, and having accomplished his major goals, he refused to run again in 1848. Cass won the Democrats' presidential nomination, but the party refused to endorse his "popular sovereignty" plan. Instead, it simply denied the power of Congress to interfere with slavery in the states and criticized all efforts by anti-slavery activists to bring the question before Congress. The Whigs devised an even more ingenious strategy in the process of selecting a presidential candidate. Once again, as in 1840, they passed over their party leader, Henry Clay, in favor of General Zachary Taylor, whose fame had grown since the Battle of Buena Vista. Taylor, born in Virginia and raised in Kentucky, was a Louisiana resident who owned more than 100 slaves. But he was an unusual slaveholder in that he vigorously opposed the extension of slavery into new western territories.

The Free-Soil Coalition

The Free-Soil party

As it had done in the 1840 election, the Whig party in 1848 adopted no platform in an effort to avoid the divisive issue of slavery. But the anti-slavery crusade was not easily silenced. Americans who worried about slavery but shied away from calling for outright abolition could readily endorse the exclusion of slavery from the western territories. The Northwest Ordinance and the Missouri Compromise supplied honored precedents for doing so. As a result, "free soil" in the new territories became the rallying cry for a new political party: the Free-Soil coalition, which focused on preventing the spread of slavery into the western territories.

The **Free-Soil party** attracted three major groups: northern Democrats opposed to slavery, anti-slavery northern Whigs, and members of the abolitionist Liberty party, created in 1840. In 1848, at a convention in Buffalo,

popular sovereignty Legal concept by which the white male settlers in a new U.S. territory would vote to decide whether to permit slavery.

Free-Soil party A political coalition created in 1848 that opposed the expansion of slavery into the new western territories.

The Wilmot Proviso Taylor would refuse to veto the proviso as president, even though he was a slave owner. This political cartoon, "Old Zack at Home," points out his seeming hypocrisy.

New York, Free-Soilers nominated former Democratic president Martin Van Buren as their candidate. The party's platform stressed that slavery would not be allowed in the western territories. The new anti-slavery party infuriated John C. Calhoun and other southern Democrats. Calhoun called Van Buren a "bold, unscrupulous, and vindictive demagogue." The impact of the Free-Soil party on the election was mixed. The Free-Soilers split the Democratic vote enough to throw New York to the Whig Zachary Taylor, and they split the Whig vote enough to give Ohio to the Democrat Lewis Cass. But Van Buren's 291,000 third-party votes lagged well behind the totals of 1,361,000 for Taylor and 1,222,000 for Cass. Taylor won with 163–127 electoral votes.

The California Gold Rush

Meanwhile, a new issue had emerged to complicate the debate over the western territories. On January 24, 1848, on the property of John A. Sutter along the south fork of the American River (Sutter's Fort), gold was discovered in the Mexican province of California, which nine days later would be transferred to the United States through the treaty ending the Mexican-American War. Word of the gold strike spread quickly. In 1849 nearly 100,000 Americans, mostly men, set off for California, eager to find riches; by 1854, the number would top 300,000. So many men left New England as part of the **California Gold Rush** that it would be years before the region's gender ratio evened out again.

The gold rush was the greatest mass migration in American history—and one of the most significant events in the first half of the nineteenth century. Between 1851 and 1855, California produced almost half of the

California Gold Rush (1849) A massive migration of gold hunters, mostly men, who transformed the economy of California after gold was discovered in northern California.

world's output of gold. The infusion of California gold into the U.S. economy triggered a surge of prosperity that eventually helped finance the Union military effort in the Civil War. The gold rush also transformed the sleepy coastal village of San Francisco into the nation's largest city west of Chicago. In addition, it shifted the nation's center of gravity westward, spurred the construction of railroads and telegraph lines, and excited dreams of an American empire based in the Pacific.

Gold miners Chinese immigrants and white settlers mine for gold in the Auburn Ravine of California in 1856.

California Statehood

New president Zachary Taylor opposed the expansion of slavery into new territories and states. In 1849, he decided to use California's request for statehood to end the stalemate in Congress over slavery. Why not make California and New Mexico free states immediately, he reasoned, and bypass the issue of slavery? But Californians, in desperate need of organized government, were ahead of him. By December 1849, without consulting Congress, they had put a free-state (no-slavery) government into operation. New Mexico responded more slowly, but by 1850 Americans there had also adopted a free-state constitution.

The Compromise of 1850

In his annual message on December 4, 1849, President Taylor endorsed immediate statehood for California and urged Congress to avoid injecting slavery into the issue. The new Congress, however, was in no mood for simple solutions. By 1850, tensions over slavery were boiling over. Irate southerners threatened to leave the Union if Taylor brought California and New Mexico in as free states. "I avow before this House and country, and in the presence of the living God," shouted Robert Toombs, a Georgia congressman, "that if by your legislation you seek to drive us [slaveholders] from the territories of California and New Mexico . . . and to abolish slavery in this District [of Columbia] . . . I am for disunion."

Compromise of 1850

The spotlight fell on the Senate, where an all-star cast—Henry Clay, John C. Calhoun, and Daniel Webster (all of whom would die within two years), with William H. Seward, Stephen A. Douglas, and Jefferson Davis in supporting roles—staged one of the great dramas of American politics: the **Compromise of 1850**, a series of resolutions intended to reduce the tensions between North and South.

Compromise of 1850 A package of five bills presented to the Congress by Henry Clay intended to avoid secession or civil war by reducing tensions between North and South over the status of slavery.

The Great Debate

With southerners threatening secession, Congressional leaders in early 1850 again turned to Clay, now 72, who, as Abraham Lincoln said, was "regarded by all, as *the* man for the crisis." Unless some compromise could be found, Clay warned, a "furious" civil war would fracture the Union. On January 29, 1850, having gained support from Webster, Clay presented to Congress eight resolutions meant to settle the "controversy between the free and slave states, growing out of the subject of slavery." He proposed (1) to admit California as a free state; (2) to organize the territories of New Mexico and Utah without restrictions on slavery, allowing the residents to decide the issue for themselves; (3) to deny Texas its extreme claim to much of New Mexico; (4) to compensate Texas by having the federal government pay the pre-annexation Texas debts; (5) to retain slavery in the District of Columbia, but (6) to abolish the sale of slaves in the nation's capital; (7) to adopt a more effective federal fugitive slave law; and, (8) to deny congressional authority to interfere with the interstate slave trade. His complex cluster of proposals became in substance the Compromise of 1850, but only after seven months of negotiations punctuated by the greatest debates in Congressional history.

On March 4, a grim John C. Calhoun, the uncompromising defender of slavery, left his sickbed to sit in the Senate chamber and listen to a colleague read his defiant speech, in which he blamed the North for inciting civil war by opposing slavery in the territories. Clay's compromise should be rejected, Calhoun urged. The South simply needed Congress to protect the rights of slave owners to take their "property" into the new territories. Otherwise, Calhoun warned, the "cords which bind" the Union would be severed. The southern states would leave the Union (secede) and form their own national government.

Three days later, Calhoun, who would die in just three weeks, returned to the Senate to hear Daniel Webster speak. "I wish to speak today," Webster began, "not as a Massachusetts man, not as a Northern man, but as an American. . . . I speak today for the preservation of the Union." The geographic extent of slavery had already been determined, Webster insisted, by the Northwest Ordinance in 1787 and by the Missouri Compromise in 1820. He criticized extremists on both sides and suggested that some new territories should become slave states and others free states.

Webster's evenhanded speech was savaged by northerners for betraying the region's anti-slavery ideals. On March 11, William Seward, the Whig senator from New York, declared that *any* compromise with slavery was "radically wrong and essentially vicious." There was, he said, "a *higher law* than the Constitution," and it demanded the abolition of slavery.

Compromise Efforts

On July 4, 1850, supporters of the Union staged a grand rally at the base of the unfinished Washington Monument in Washington, D.C. President Zachary Taylor went to hear the speeches and lingered in the heat and humidity. Five days later, he died of a violent stomach disorder, likely caused by tainted food or water.

Taylor's sudden death strengthened the chances of a compromise in Congress. His successor, Vice President Millard Fillmore, supported Clay's

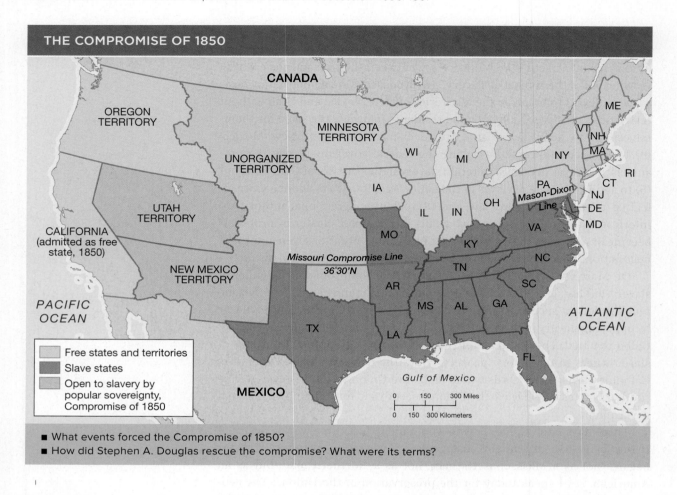

THE COMPROMISE OF 1850

Free states and territories
Slave states
Open to slavery by popular sovereignty, Compromise of 1850

■ What events forced the Compromise of 1850?
■ How did Stephen A. Douglas rescue the compromise? What were its terms?

proposals. It was a strange switch: Taylor, the Louisiana slaveholder, had been ready to make war on his native South; Fillmore, who southerners thought opposed slavery, was ready to make peace.

At this point, young senator Stephen A. Douglas of Illinois, a rising star in the Democratic party who was friendly to the South, rescued Clay's faltering plan. Short and stocky, brash and brilliant, Douglas suggested that the best way to approve Clay's "comprehensive scheme" was to break it up into separate proposals and vote on each of them, one at a time. The plan worked. By September 20, President Fillmore had signed the last of the measures into law, claiming that they represented a "final" solution to sectional tensions over slavery. True, the Compromise of 1850 had defused an explosive situation and settled each of the major points at issue, but it only postponed secession and civil war for ten years.

In its final version, the Compromise of 1850 included the following elements: (1) California entered the Union as a free state, ending forever the old balance of free and slave states; (2) the Texas–New Mexico Act made New Mexico a territory and set the Texas state boundary at its present location. In return for giving up its claims, Texas was paid $10 million, which secured payment of the state's debt; (3) the Utah Act set up the Utah Territory and gave the territorial legislature authority over "all rightful subjects of legislation" (including slavery); (4) a Fugitive Slave Act required the federal government and northern states to help capture and return runaway slaves to the South; and, (5) as a gesture to anti-slavery groups, the public sale of slaves, but not slavery itself, was abolished in the District of Columbia.

The Fugitive Slave Act

The **Fugitive Slave Act** was the most controversial element of the Compromise of 1850. It did more than strengthen the hand of slave catchers; it provided a strong temptation to kidnap free blacks in northern "free" states, claiming that they were runaway slaves. The law denied fugitives a jury trial. In addition, federal marshals could require citizens to help locate and capture runaways: violators could be imprisoned for up to six months and fined $1,000. Abolitionists fumed. "This filthy enactment was made in the nineteenth century, by people who could read and write," Ralph Waldo Emerson marveled in his diary. He advised neighbors to break the new law "on the earliest occasion." The occasion soon arose in Detroit, Michigan, where only military force stopped the rescue of a fugitive slave by an outraged group in October 1850. There were relatively few such incidents, however. In the first six years of the Fugitive Slave Act, only three runaways were forcibly rescued from slave catchers. On the other hand, probably fewer than two hundred were returned to bondage during those years. The Fugitive Slave Act was a powerful emotional and symbolic force deepening the anti-slavery impulses in the North.

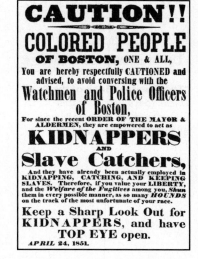

Threats to free blacks This 1851 notice warned free blacks about police and others who could easily, under the new Fugitive Slave Act, kidnap and sell them back into slavery.

Uncle Tom's Cabin

During the 1850s, anti-slavery forces found their most persuasive new weapon not in the Fugitive Slave Act but in the fictional drama of Harriet Beecher Stowe's best-selling novel, *Uncle Tom's Cabin* (1852). Stowe, whose father, husband, and five brothers were Congregationalist ministers, epitomized the powerful religious underpinnings of the abolitionist movement. While living in Cincinnati, Ohio, during the 1830s and 1840s, she helped runaway slaves who had crossed the Ohio River from Kentucky. Stowe was disgusted with the Fugitive Slave Act of 1850. In the spring of 1850, having moved to Maine, she began writing *Uncle Tom's Cabin*, urged on by her anti-slavery family. "The time has come," she wrote, "when even a woman or a child who can speak a word for freedom and humanity is bound to speak."

Uncle Tom's Cabin was a smashing commercial success. The first printing sold out within two days, and by the end of its first year in print, the book had sold 300,000 copies in the United States and over a million in Great Britain. Soon it was translated in thirty-seven different languages. By 1855 *Uncle Tom's Cabin* had become "the most popular novel of our day." The novel revealed how the brutal realities of slavery harmed everyone associated with it. The abolitionist leader Frederick Douglass, a former slave himself, said that *Uncle Tom's Cabin* was like "a flash" that lit "a million

Fugitive Slave Act (1850) Part of the Compromise of 1850, a provision that authorized federal officials to help capture and then return escaped slaves to their owners without trials.

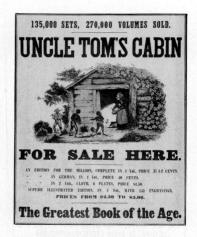

135,000 SETS, 270,000 VOLUMES SOLD.

UNCLE TOM'S CABIN

FOR SALE HERE.

AN EDITION FOR THE MILLION, COMPLETE IN 1 Vol. PRICE 37 1/2 CENTS.
" " IN GERMAN, IN 1 Vol. PRICE 50 CENTS.
" " IN 2 Vols. CLOTH, 6 PLATES, PRICE $1.50.
SUPERB ILLUSTRATED EDITION, IN 1 Vol. WITH 153 ENGRAVINGS,
PRICES FROM $2.50 TO $5.00.

The Greatest Book of the Age.

"The Greatest Book of the Age"
Uncle Tom's Cabin, as this advertisement indicated, was an influential best seller.

camp fires in front of the embattled host of slavery." Slaveholders were incensed by the book, calling Stowe that "wretch in petticoats." One of them mailed her a parcel containing the severed ear of a disobedient slave.

The Election of 1852

In 1852, the Democrats chose boyishly handsome Franklin Pierce of New Hampshire as their presidential candidate; their platform endorsed the Compromise of 1850. For their part, the Whigs repudiated the lackluster Millard Fillmore, who had faithfully supported the Compromise of 1850, and chose General Winfield Scott, a hero of the Mexican-American War and a Virginia native. Scott, however, was an inept politician and carried only Tennessee, Kentucky, Massachusetts, and Vermont. Pierce overwhelmed him in the Electoral College, 254–42, although the popular vote was fairly close: 1.6 million–1.4 million. The third-party Free-Soilers mustered only 156,000 votes for John P. Hale, in contrast to the 291,000 they had tallied for Van Buren in 1848.

The forty-eight-year-old Pierce had fought in the Mexican-American War and was, like James Polk, touted as another Andrew Jackson despite his undistinguished record as a congressman and senator. He eagerly promoted western expansion, even if it meant adding more slave states to the Union, but he also acknowledged that the nation had recently survived a "perilous crisis" that was defused by the Compromise of 1850. He urged both North and South to avoid aggravating the other. But as a Georgia editor noted, the feud between the two regions might be "smothered, but never overcome." Pierce, the youngest president to date, was timid and indecisive, unable to unite the warring factions of his own party. By the end of his first year in office, Democratic leaders had decided he was a failure. By trying to be all things to all people, Pierce was labeled a "doughface": a "Northern man with Southern principles."

The Kansas-Nebraska Crisis

Kansas-Nebraska Act (1854)

During the mid-nineteenth century, Americans discovered the vast markets of Asia. As the amount of trade with China and Japan grew, merchants and manufacturers called for a transcontinental railroad line connecting the eastern seaboard with the Pacific coast to facilitate both the flow of commerce with Asia and the settlement of the western territories. Those promoting the building of a railroad linking the far-flung regions of the new United States did not realize that the issue would renew sectional rivalries and reignite the debate over the westward extension of slavery. In 1852 and 1853, Congress debated several proposals for a transcontinental rail line. Secretary of War Jefferson Davis of Mississippi favored a southern route across the territories acquired from Mexico. Senator Stephen A. Douglas of Illinois insisted that Chicago be the transcontinental railroad's Midwest hub. To promote that idea, he urged Congress in 1854 to pass the **Kansas-Nebraska Act** so that the vast territory west of Missouri and Iowa could be settled.

Kansas-Nebraska Act (1854)
Controversial legislation that created two new territories taken from Native Americans, Kansas and Nebraska, where residents would vote to decide whether slavery would be allowed (popular sovereignty).

New western territories, however, raised again the worrisome question of whether slavery would be allowed in them. To win the support of southern legislators, Douglas championed the principle of "popular sovereignty," whereby voters in each new territory could decide themselves whether to allow slavery. It was a clever way to get around the 1820 Missouri Compromise, which excluded slaves north of the 36th parallel, where Kansas and Nebraska were located. Southerners demanded even more, so Douglas, even though he knew it would "raise a hell of a storm," supported the formal repeal of the Missouri Compromise and the creation of *two* new territorial governments rather than one: Kansas, west of Missouri, and Nebraska, which then included the Dakotas, west of Iowa and Minnesota. In Congress, Douglas masterfully assembled the votes for his Kansas-Nebraska Act. President Pierce helped get several reluctant Democrats to vote for the measure (though about half the northern Democrats refused to yield), and in 1854 it passed by a vote of 37–14 in the Senate and 113–100 in the House. The anti-slavery faction in the Congress, mostly Whigs, had been crushed.

But Douglas's passion for the new rail line backfired. However honest his motives in promoting the Kansas-Nebraska Act, he had blundered politically, damaging his presidential chances and setting the country on the road to civil war by pushing the slavery issue back to the forefront of national concerns. In abandoning the long-standing Missouri Compromise boundary line and allowing territorial voters to decide the issue of slavery, Douglas unwittingly inflamed the tensions between North and South.

The Emergence of the Republican Party

CORE **OBJECTIVE**

4. Analyze the appeal of the Republican party to northern voters and how it led to Abraham Lincoln's victory in the 1860 presidential contest.

The dispute over the Kansas-Nebraska Act destroyed the already weakened Whig party. Northern Whigs now gravitated toward two new parties. One was the American ("Know-Nothing") party, which had emerged in response to the surge of mostly Catholic immigrants from Ireland and Germany. The anti-Catholic "Know-Nothings" embraced nativism (opposition to foreign immigrants) and proposed that citizenship be denied to newcomers. In the early 1850s, Know-Nothings won several local elections in Massachusetts and New York.

Anti-Catholic "Know-Nothings"

The other new party, the Republicans, attracted even more northern Whigs. The party was formed in 1854 when the anti-slavery "conscience Whigs" split from the southern pro-slavery "cotton Whigs" and joined with independent Democrats and Free-Soilers to form a new Republican party whose members initially stood for only one principle: the exclusion of slavery from the western territories. A young Illinois congressman named Abraham Lincoln made the transition from being a Whig to a Republican. He said that the passage of Douglas's Kansas-Nebraska Act angered him "as he had

New Republican party (1854)

never been before" and transformed his views on slavery. Unless the North mobilized to stop the efforts of pro-slavery southerners, Lincoln believed, the future of the Union was endangered. From that moment on, Lincoln focused his career on reversing the Kansas-Nebraska Act and preventing the extension of slavery into any new territories.

"Bleeding Kansas"

After the passage of the Kansas-Nebraska Act in 1854, attention turned to the plains of Kansas, where opposing elements gathered to stage a rehearsal for civil war. While Nebraska would become a free state, Kansas was up for grabs. According to the Kansas-Nebraska Act, the people living in the Kansas Territory were "perfectly free to form and regulate their domestic institutions [including slavery] in their own way, subject only to the Constitution." This is what was meant by "popular sovereignty." But the law said nothing about *when* Kansans would decide about slavery, so each side tried to gain political control of the fifty-million-acre territory.

Rival groups for and against slavery in the North and South recruited emigrants to move to the new territory. "Every slaveholding state," said an observer, "is furnishing men and money to fasten slavery upon this glorious land, by means no matter how foul." When Kansas's first federal governor arrived in 1854, he scheduled an election for a territorial legislature in 1855. On election day, several thousand hard-fisted "border ruffians" from Missouri crossed into Kansas, illegally elected pro-slavery legislators, and vowed to kill every "God-damned abolitionist in the Territory." The governor denounced the fraudulent vote but did nothing to alter the results, for fear of being killed himself. The territorial legislature expelled its few anti-slavery members and declared that the territory would be open to slavery.

"Bleeding Kansas" (1856)

Outraged free-state advocates in Kansas rejected this "bogus" government and elected their own delegates to a constitutional convention which met in Topeka in 1855, drafted a state constitution excluding slavery, and applied for statehood. By 1856, a free-state "governor" and "legislature" were functioning in Topeka; thus there were two illegal governments in the Kansas Territory. And soon there was a civil war in Kansas, which journalists called "**Bleeding Kansas**."

In May 1856, a pro-slavery mob of Missourians and Alabamans decided to invade the free-state town of Lawrence, Kansas. David Atchison, a former U.S. senator from Missouri, urged the southern raiders not "to slacken or stop until every spark of free-state, free-speech, free-niggers, or free in any shape is quenched out of Kansas." As they prepared to teach the "damned abolitionists a southern lesson," Atchison yelled: "Boys, this is the happiest day of my life!" The mob then rampaged through the town, destroying the newspaper, burning the governor's house, and demolishing the Free-State Hotel.

The "Sack of Lawrence" resulted in just one casualty, but the excitement aroused a passionate white abolitionist named John Brown. He believed that slavery was the most wicked of sins and that blacks deserved both

Bleeding Kansas (1856)
A series of violent conflicts in the Kansas Territory between anti-slavery and pro-slavery factions over the status of slavery.

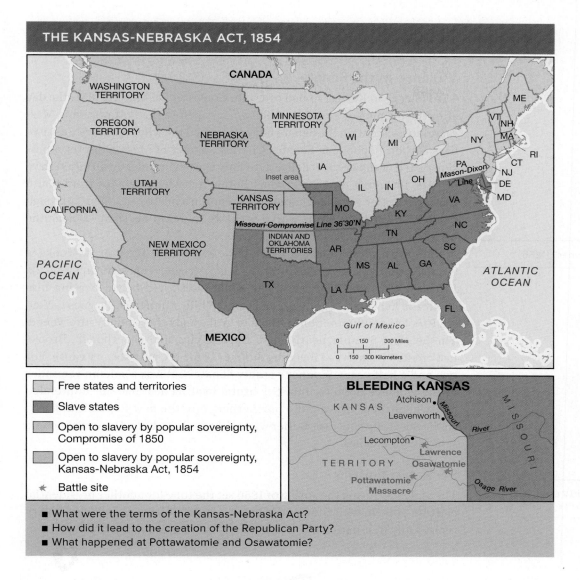

THE KANSAS-NEBRASKA ACT, 1854

CANADA

WASHINGTON TERRITORY

OREGON TERRITORY

NEBRASKA TERRITORY

MINNESOTA TERRITORY

WI

MI

ME

VT
NH
MA

NY

RI
CT

UTAH TERRITORY

CALIFORNIA

Inset area

KANSAS TERRITORY

IA

IL

IN

OH

MO

PA
Mason-Dixon
Line

NJ
DE

MD

VA

KY

Missouri Compromise Line 36°30'N

NEW MEXICO TERRITORY

INDIAN AND OKLAHOMA TERRITORIES

AR

TN

NC

SC

PACIFIC OCEAN

MS

AL

GA

ATLANTIC OCEAN

TX

LA

FL

MEXICO

Gulf of Mexico

0   150   300 Miles

0   150   300 Kilometers

☐ Free states and territories

☐ Slave states

☐ Open to slavery by popular sovereignty, Compromise of 1850

☐ Open to slavery by popular sovereignty, Kansas-Nebraska Act, 1854

✳ Battle site

BLEEDING KANSAS

KANSAS

Atchison

Leavenworth

Missouri River

M I S S O U R I

Lecompton

TERRITORY

Lawrence

Osawatomie

Pottawatomie Massacre

Osage River

■ What were the terms of the Kansas-Nebraska Act?

■ How did it lead to the creation of the Republican Party?

■ What happened at Pottawatomie and Osawatomie?

liberty and full social equality in the United States. A newspaper reporter said that the selfless Brown was a "strange" and "iron-willed" old man with a "fiery nature and a cold temper, and a cool head—a volcano beneath a covering of snow." Two days after the attack on Lawrence, Brown set out with four of his sons for Pottawatomie, Kansas, a pro-slavery settlement near the Missouri border. There they dragged five men from their houses and hacked them to death with swords. One of the murdered men had had his fingers and arms cut off. "God is my judge," Brown told one of his sons upon their return from the raid. "We were justified under the circumstances." Without "the shedding of blood," he added, "there is no remission of sins."

The Pottawatomie Massacre (May 24–25, 1856) set off a guerrilla war in the Kansas Territory. On August 30, Missouri ruffians raided the free-state settlement at Osawatomie, Kansas. They looted and burned the houses and shot Frederick Brown, John's son, through the heart. By the end of 1856, about 200 settlers on both sides had been killed in "Bleeding Kansas."

Violence in the Senate

The violence in Kansas spilled over into Congress. On May 22, 1856, the day after the burning of Lawrence and two days before the Pottawatomie Massacre, an incident on the Senate floor electrified the whole country. Just two days earlier, Republican Senator Charles Sumner of Massachusetts, a passionate foe of slavery, had delivered a fiery speech in which he insulted slave owners, including Andrew Pickens Butler, an elderly senator from South Carolina. Butler, Sumner charged, had "chosen a mistress . . . who . . . though polluted in the sight of the world, is chaste [pure] in his sight—I mean the harlot [prostitute], Slavery."

> "Bleeding Sumner" (1856)

Sumner's speech enraged Butler's young cousin Preston S. Brooks, a South Carolina congressman with a hair-trigger temper. On May 22, Brooks confronted Sumner at his Senate desk and began beating him about the head with a gold-headed cane. While stunned colleagues looked on, Brooks beat Sumner until his cane broke and others finally intervened. The helpless Sumner nearly died. In satisfying his rage, though, Brooks had created a martyr—"Bleeding Sumner"—for the anti-slavery cause. For two and a half years, Sumner's empty Senate seat was a solemn reminder of the violence done to him. His brutal beating also had an unintended political effect: it drove more northerners into the new Republican party. In the South, by contrast, Butler was celebrated as a hero. Dozens of people sent him new canes.

Sectional Politics

> Republican party opposed to expanding slavery

The violence during the spring of 1856 set the tone for another presidential election—one in which the major parties could no longer evade the slavery issue. At its first national convention, the Republican party fastened on an

"Bully" Brooks attacks Charles Sumner This outbreak of violence in Congress worsened the strains on the Union.

eccentric military hero, John C. Frémont, "the Pathfinder," who had led the conquest of Mexican-controlled California. The Republican platform also owed much to the Whigs. It favored federal funding for a transcontinental railroad and, in general, more government-financed internal improvements. It condemned the repeal of the Missouri Compromise, the Democratic party's policy of territorial expansion, and the "barbarism" of slavery. For the first time, a major-party platform had taken a stand against slavery.

In picking a presidential candidate, the Democrats dumped the widely unpopular Franklin Pierce. The president had become the most hated person in the nation by 1856, and he remains the only elected president to be denied re-nomination by his own party. Instead, the Democrats nominated James Buchanan of Pennsylvania, a former senator and secretary of state who had long sought the nomination. The Democratic platform endorsed the Kansas-Nebraska Act, called for vigorous enforcement of the fugitive slave law, and stressed that Congress should not interfere with slavery in states or territories. In the campaign of 1856, the Republicans had very few southern supporters and only a handful in the border slave states of Delaware, Maryland, Kentucky, and Missouri, where fear of disunion held many Whigs in line. Buchanan thus went into the campaign as the candidate of the only remaining national party. Frémont swept the northernmost states with 114 electoral votes, but Buchanan added five free states—Pennsylvania, New Jersey, Illinois, Indiana, and California—to his southern majority for a total of 174.

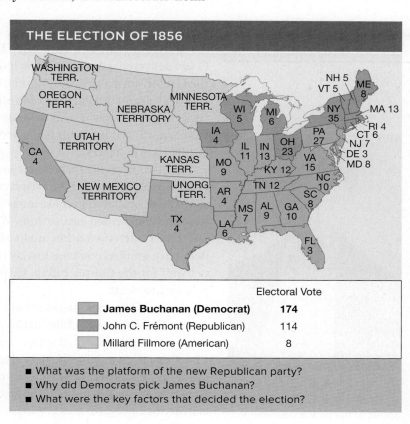

THE ELECTION OF 1856

	Electoral Vote
James Buchanan (Democrat)	**174**
John C. Frémont (Republican)	114
Millard Fillmore (American)	8

- What was the platform of the new Republican party?
- Why did Democrats pick James Buchanan?
- What were the key factors that decided the election?

President Buchanan

The sixty-five-year-old Buchanan, America's first unmarried president, tall and solid, his head topped with a mane of white hair, had built his impressive political career on his commitment to states' rights and his aggressive promotion of territorial expansion. He believed that saving the Union depended upon the nation making concessions to the South. Republicans charged that he lacked the backbone to stand up to the southern slaveholders who dominated the Democratic majorities in Congress. His choice of four slave-state men and only three free-state men for his cabinet seemed another bad sign. It was.

During James Buchanan's first six months in office in 1857, two major events brought about his undoing: (1) the Supreme Court decision in the *Dred Scott* case, and (2) new troubles in strife-torn Kansas. For all of Buchanan's experience as a legislator and diplomat, he failed to handle either of those issues with confidence or strength. The Financial Panic of 1857 only made a bad situation worse for both the new president and the nation as a whole. By 1857, the American economy was growing too fast. Too many railroads and factories were being built even as European demand for American corn and wheat was slackening. The result was a financial panic triggered by the failure of the Ohio Life Insurance and Trust Company on August 24, 1857.

The Dred Scott Case

The *Dred Scott* case (1857)

On March 6, 1857, two days after Buchanan's inauguration, the Supreme Court delivered a decision in the long-pending case of ***Dred Scott v. Sandford***. Scott, born a slave in Virginia, had been taken to St. Louis in 1830 and sold to an army surgeon, who took him to Illinois, then to the Wisconsin Territory (later Minnesota), and finally back to St. Louis in 1842. While in the Wisconsin Territory, Scott had married Harriet Robinson, and they eventually had two daughters.

In 1846, Dred Scott filed suit in the Missouri courts, claiming that his residence in Illinois and the Wisconsin Territory had made him free because slavery was outlawed in those areas. A jury decided in his favor, but the state supreme court ruled against him. When the case rose on appeal to the U.S. Supreme Court, the nation anxiously awaited its opinion on whether freedom once granted could be lost by returning to a slave state. Buchanan did not wait for the Court's ruling. He privately pressured one of the judges to rule against Scott.

Dred Scott Scott's lawsuit over his family's freedom fanned the flames of the nation's debate on slavery.

Seven of the nine justices were Democrats, five of whom were southerners. The vote was 7–2 against Scott. Seventy-nine-year-old Chief Justice Roger B. Taney, a devoted supporter of the South and of slavery, wrote the Court's majority opinion. He ruled that Scott lacked legal standing because, like all former slaves, he was not an American citizen. At the time the Constitution was adopted, Taney claimed, blacks "had for more than a century been regarded as . . . so far inferior, that they had no rights which the white man was bound to respect." On the issue of Scott's residency, Taney argued that the Missouri Compromise of 1820 had deprived citizens of property by prohibiting slavery in selected states, an action "not warranted by the Constitution."

***Dred Scott v. Sandford* (1857)** U.S. Supreme Court ruling that slaves were not U.S. citizens and therefore could not sue for their freedom and that Congress could not prohibit slavery in the western territories.

The upshot was that the Supreme Court had declared an act of Congress unconstitutional for the first time since *Marbury v. Madison* (1803). Congress had repealed the Missouri Compromise in the Kansas-Nebraska Act three years earlier, but the *Dred Scott* decision now challenged the concept of "popular sovereignty." If Congress itself could not exclude slavery from a territory, as Taney argued, then neither could a territorial government created by an act of Congress.

Yet instead of settling the issue of slavery in the territories, Taney's ruling fanned the flames. Pro-slavery advocates greeted the Court's opinion as binding, and President Buchanan approved. Republicans, on the other hand, were outraged by the *Dred Scott* decision because it nullified their anti-slavery program. They threatened to remove the justices and reverse the decision if they secured control of the federal government.

The Lecompton Constitution

Meanwhile, in the Kansas Territory, the struggle over slavery continued with both sides resorting to voting trickery and violence. Just before Buchanan's inauguration, in early 1857, the pro-slavery territorial legislature called for a constitutional convention. The governor vetoed the measure, but the legislature overrode his veto. The governor resigned in protest, and President Buchanan replaced him with Robert J. Walker. With Buchanan's approval, Walker pledged to the free-state Kansans (who made up an overwhelming majority of the residents) that the new constitution would be submitted to a fair vote. But when the pro-slavery constitutional convention, meeting at Lecompton, drafted a constitution under which Kansas would become a slave state, those opposed to slavery boycotted the vote on the new constitution.

> Lecompton Constitution (1858)

At that point, President Buchanan took a fateful step. Influenced by southern advisers and politically dependent upon powerful southern congressmen, he endorsed the pro-slavery Lecompton convention, sparking a new wave of outrage across the northern states. Stephen A. Douglas, the most prominent Midwestern Democrat, broke with the president over the issue, siding with anti-slavery Republicans because the people of Kansas had been denied the right to decide the issue. Douglas told a newspaper reporter that "I made Mr. James Buchanan, and by God, sir, I will unmake him." The rigged election in Kansas went as predicted: 6,226 for the constitution with slavery, 569 for the constitution without slavery.

Meanwhile, a new acting governor had convened the anti-slavery legislature, which called for another election to vote the Lecompton Constitution up or down. Most of the pro-slavery settlers boycotted this election. The result, on January 4, 1858, was overwhelming: 10,226 voted against the Lecompton Constitution, while only 138 voted for it. In April 1858, the U.S. Congress ordered that Kansans vote again on the Lecompton Constitution. On August 2, 1858, voters rejected the Lecompton Constitution, 11,300 to 1,788. With that vote, Kansas cleared the way for its eventual admission as a free state in 1861.

Douglas versus Lincoln

The controversy over slavery in Kansas put severe strains on the Democratic party. To many, Stephen A. Douglas, one of the few remaining Democrats with support in both the North and the South, seemed the best hope for national unity and union. The year 1860 would give him a chance for the presidency, but first he had to secure his home base in Illinois, where in 1858 he faced re-election to the Senate.

To oppose him, Illinois Republicans selected a rustic lawyer from Springfield, Abraham Lincoln, the former Whig legislator. Lincoln had served in the Illinois legislature and in 1846 had won a seat in the U.S. Congress. After a single unremarkable term in Washington, D.C., he returned to Springfield. In 1854, however, the Kansas-Nebraska Act drew Lincoln back into the political arena. Lincoln hated slavery but was no abolitionist. He did not believe that the nation should force the South to end slavery, but he did insist that slavery not be expanded into new western territories. In 1856, Lincoln joined the rapidly growing Republican party, and two years later he emerged as the obvious choice to oppose Douglas for the Senate seat. Because he was the underdog, Lincoln sought to raise his profile by challenging Douglas to a series of debates across the state.

The **Lincoln-Douglas debates** took place from August 21 to October 15, 1858. They attracted tens of thousands of spectators and transformed the contest for an Illinois Senate seat into a battle for the future of the Republic. The two men differed as much physically as they did politically. Douglas was barely five feet tall, stocky with a big head. Lincoln was tall and thin, well over six feet tall. The basic political difference between the two men, Lincoln argued, lay in Douglas's indifference to the immorality of slavery. Douglas, he said, did not care whether slavery in the territories was "voted up, or voted down." Douglas was preoccupied only with process ("popular sovereignty"); Lincoln claimed to be focused on principle. He insisted that the American government could not "endure, permanently half *slave* and half *free*. . . . It will become *all* one thing, or *all* the other." If Lincoln had the better of the argument in the long view, Douglas had the better of a close election, but, while a losing cause, Lincoln's energetic campaign had elevated him to being a national figure.

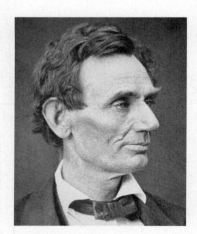

Abraham Lincoln A lanky and rawboned small-town lawyer, Lincoln challenged Douglas to debate him in 1858.

Lincoln-Douglas debates (1858) In the Illinois race between Republican Abraham Lincoln and Democrat Stephen A. Douglas for a seat in the U.S. Senate, a series of seven dramatic debates focusing on the issue of slavery in the territories.

An Outnumbered South

By the late 1850s, national politics was undergoing profound changes. In May 1858, the free state of Minnesota entered the Union; in February 1859, another non-slave territory, Oregon, gained statehood. The slave states of the South were quickly becoming a minority, and their political insecurity deepened into paranoia. At the same time, political tensions over slavery were becoming more violent. In 1858, members of Congress engaged in the largest brawl ever staged on the floor of the House of Representatives, with more than fifty legislators shoving, punching, and wrestling one another.

Like the scuffling congressmen, more and more Americans began to feel that slavery could be ended or defended only with violence. The editor of a pro-slavery Kansas newspaper wanted to kill abolitionists: "If I can't kill a man, I'll kill a woman; and if I can't kill a woman, I'll kill a child." Some southerners were already talking of secession. In 1858, former Alabama congressman William L. Yancey, a member of a group of hot-tempered southern secessionists called "fire-eaters," threatened that it would be easy "to precipitate the Cotton States into a revolution."

John Brown's Raid

Such violent threats to maintain slavery drove John Brown into a desperate act. On the cool, rainy night of October 16, 1859, iron-willed Brown launched his supreme effort to end slavery. From a Maryland farm, he crossed the Potomac River with about twenty men, mostly unmarried and in their twenties, including three of Brown's sons and five African Americans. Under cover of darkness, they approached the federal rifle arsenal in Harpers Ferry, Virginia (now West Virginia), a factory town some sixty miles northwest of Washington, D.C. Brown's mad scheme was to give the arsenal's muskets to thousands of slaves in the area, in the hope of triggering mass uprisings across the South. "I want to free all the negroes in this state," Brown said. "If the citizens interfere with me, I must burn the town and have blood."

Brown and his comrades took the town by surprise, cut the telegraph lines, and occupied the arsenal. He then sent a handful of men to kidnap several prominent slave owners and spread the word for local slaves to rise up and join the rebellion. But only a few slaves heeded the call. By dawn, enraged townsmen had surrounded the raiders. Brown and a dozen of his men, along with eleven white hostages (including George Washington's great-grandnephew, the area's most prominent resident) and two of their slaves, remained holed up for thirty-two hours. Meanwhile, hundreds of armed men poured into Harpers Ferry to capture Brown and his raiders. Lieutenant Colonel Robert E. Lee arrived with a force of U.S. Marines, having been dispatched from Washington, D.C., by President Buchanan. On the morning of October 18, the marines broke down the arsenal's barricaded doors and rushed in. The siege was over. Altogether, Brown's men had killed four townspeople and wounded another dozen. Of their own group, ten were killed (including two of Brown's sons) and five were captured; another five escaped.

Brown and his accomplices were quickly convicted of treason, murder, and "conspiring with Negroes to produce insurrection." At his sentencing, Brown delivered one of America's classic speeches: "Now, if it is deemed necessary that I should forfeit my life for the furtherance of the ends of justice, and mingle my blood further with the blood of my children and with the blood of millions in this slave country whose rights are disregarded by wicked, cruel, and unjust enactments, I say, let it be done." For weeks, as Brown waited in his cell to be executed, he continued to crusade against slavery by mailing a stream of letters, many of which were printed in anti-slavery newspapers.

Brown was hanged on December 2, 1859. (Among the crowd watching the execution was a popular young stage actor named John Wilkes Booth, who would later assassinate Abraham Lincoln.) If Brown had failed to ignite a massive slave rebellion, he had achieved two things: he had become a martyr for the anti-slavery cause, and he had set off a panic throughout the slaveholding South. "John Brown may be a lunatic," said a Boston newspaper, but

> Raid on Harpers Ferry (1859)

John Brown On his way to the gallows, Brown predicted that slavery would end only "after much bloodshed."

if so, "one-fourth of the people of Massachusetts are madmen." The transcendentalist leader Ralph Waldo Emerson called Brown a "saint" who had made "the gallows glorious like a cross." The leading black abolitionist, former slave Frederick Douglass, called Brown "our noblest American hero" whose commitment to ending slavery "was far greater than mine."

Outlawing anti-slavery activity

John Brown's daring but hopeless attack on Harper's Ferry stirred the South's worst nightmare: that armed slaves would revolt. Caught up in a frenzy of fear, southerners equated Brown's violent abolitionism with the Republican party. Throughout the fall and winter of 1859–1860, wild rumors of abolitionist conspiracies and slave insurrections swept through the southern states, leading many to outlaw any anti-slavery activity. Some 300 abolitionists were murdered or forced out of the region. "We regard every man in our midst an enemy to the institutions of the South," said the *Atlanta Confederacy*, "who does not boldly declare that he believes African slavery to be a social, moral, and political blessing."

The Democrats Divide

Amid such emotional hysteria the nation mobilized for another presidential election, destined to be the most fateful in its history. In April 1860 the squabbling Democrats gathered for what would become a disastrous presidential nominating convention in Charleston, South Carolina, a pro-slavery hotbed where Northern delegates in their hotel rooms could hear the sound of drums beating each evening, a warning to free blacks that they must be off the streets after sunset. Stephen A. Douglas's northern supporters tried to straddle the divisive issue of slavery by promising southerners to defend the "peculiar institution" in their region while assuring northerners that slavery would not spread to new states. Southern firebrands, however, demanded federal protection for slavery in the territories as well as the states. When the pro-slavery advocates lost the platform fight, delegates from eight southern states walked out of the convention. "We say, go your way," exclaimed a Mississippi delegate to Douglas's supporters, "and we will go ours."

The Democratic convention then dissolved into factions. Douglas's supporters reassembled in Baltimore on June 18 and nominated him for president. Southern Democrats met first in Richmond and then in Baltimore, where they adopted the pro-slavery platform defeated in Charleston and named John C. Breckinridge, vice president under Buchanan, as their candidate. Thus another cord of union had snapped: the last remaining national party had split into northern and southern factions. The fracturing of the Democratic party made a Republican victory in 1860 almost certain.

Lincoln's Election

The Republican nominating convention was held in May in the fast-growing city of Chicago, where everything suddenly came together for Abraham Lincoln, the uncommon common man who won the presidential nomination over New York senator William H. Seward. The resulting cheer, wrote one journalist, was "like the rush of a great wind." Inside the convention building, the "wildest excitement and enthusiasm" swelled to a "perfect roar." The convention reaffirmed the party's opposition to the extension of slavery and, in an effort to gain broader support, endorsed a series of traditional Whig policies promoting national economic expansion: a higher protective tariff, free farms on federal lands out west, and federally financed internal improvements, including a transcontinental railroad.

The rival Democratic and Republican presidential nominating conventions revealed that opinions about the future of slavery were becoming more radical in the Northeast and the Lower South. Attitude followed latitude. In the border states of Maryland, Delaware, Kentucky, and Missouri, the prevailing sense of moderation aroused former Whigs to make one more try at reconciliation. Meeting in Baltimore a week before the Republicans met in Chicago, they reorganized themselves as the Constitutional Union party and nominated John Bell of Tennessee for president. Their platform centered on a vague statement promoting "the Constitution of the Country, the Union of the States, and the Enforcement of the Laws."

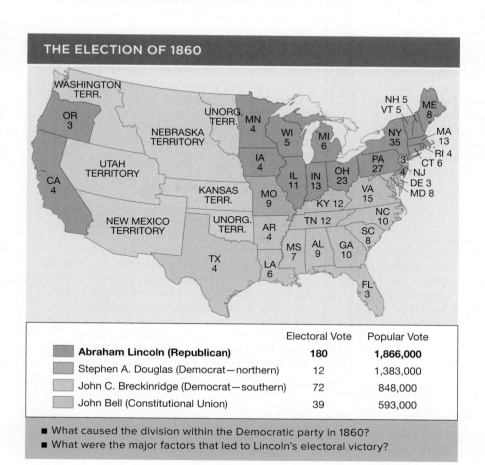

THE ELECTION OF 1860

	Electoral Vote	Popular Vote
Abraham Lincoln (Republican)	**180**	**1,866,000**
Stephen A. Douglas (Democrat—northern)	12	1,383,000
John C. Breckinridge (Democrat—southern)	72	848,000
John Bell (Constitutional Union)	39	593,000

- What caused the division within the Democratic party in 1860?
- What were the major factors that led to Lincoln's electoral victory?

Slavery, Territorial Expansion, and Secession

In 1840, Whigs and Democrats dominated national and state politics. They each drew significant support from voters in free and slave states, North and South, East and West. They each avoided discussing the issue of slavery and instead debated the merits of an active federal government and its involvement in the economy and ordinary people's lives. By 1860, the Whig party had disappeared, the Democrats had split between supporters from free and slave states, and a new party—the Republican party dedicated to stopping the expansion of slavery into American territories—had gained the majority of support among voters in the free states. The election of Abraham Lincoln that year provoked the secession crisis in which eleven slave states eventually revoked their membership in the federal union.

Texts

Texas

In the waning days of the Tyler administration, Congress annexed Texas and in 1845 it was admitted to the Union as a slave state. Settlers from southern states had begun moving into this northern Mexican province in the 1820s, bringing their slaves with them to grow cotton, even though the Mexican government discouraged the use of African slave labor in the province. Ultimately, the "Texian" settlers revolted and in 1836 established an independent Republic of Texas that they hoped the United States would soon annex. However, Presidents Jackson and Van Buren postponed any discussion of annexation in an effort to avoid a national controversy over the expansion of slavery within the United States.

The Oregon Country

Until 1846, the entire Oregon Country—Oregon, Washington, Idaho, and parts of Wyoming, Montana, and British Columbia—was jointly claimed by both the United States and Great Britain. The Buchanan-Pakenham Treaty divided the region between them with the United States controlling the land below the 49th parallel. Oregon's status as a free-soil territory caused little dispute.

California and New Mexico

In the Treaty of Guadalupe Hidalgo (1848), the federal government purchased from Mexico the territories of California and New Mexico (which included the current states of Utah, Nevada, Arizona, New Mexico, and part of Colorado). Even before the war officially ended, many anti-slavery politicians attempted to ban the expansion of slavery into this vast new territory. After the election of the Whig candidate Zachary Taylor, the discovery of gold in California, and the ensuing rapid migration of settlers into that region starting in 1849, Congress had to address the issue head-on when California applied for statehood in 1850 as a free state.

The Compromise of 1850

Congress ultimately agreed to California's status as a free state, but left the issue of slavery up to the settlers themselves, a compromise known as "popular sovereignty," thus leaving the possibility of future slave states joining the Union. Congress also pleased opponents of slavery by ending the slave trade in the District of Columbia, but at the same time, as part of the Compromise, Congress also passed the controversial Fugitive Slave Act, which enhanced the ability of slave owners to recapture slaves who had escaped to free states, demonstrating the federal government's support for the rights of slave owners.

The Kansas-Nebraska Act

In 1854, Senator Stephen Douglas of Illinois persuaded Congress to renounce the Missouri Compromise of 1820 and allow some of the territory from the Louisiana Purchase to be opened up to the expansion of the slave system. The Kansas-Nebraska Act allowed for the organization of a Kansas Territory in which the issue of slavery would be determined through a vote by the settlers, called "popular sovereignty." The new Republican party was founded in opposition to the Kansas-Nebraska Act, attracting politicians from the Democratic, Whig, and Free-Soil parties into a broad coalition that opposed any further efforts to expand slavery into the territories.

Bleeding Kansas

Anti- and pro-slavery settlers rushed to the newly organized Kansas territory in 1855. Disputes, often violent, flared between each side. Eventually each faction created a territorial constitution supporting their position. President James Buchanan, a northern Democrat, sided with the pro-slavery faction. Nevertheless, anti-slavery settlers ultimately prevailed, and by 1858 Kansas was on its way to becoming a free state.

The *Dred Scott* Decision

In its 1857 *Dred Scott* decision, the U.S. Supreme Court weighed in on the issue of the expansion of slavery into the western territories. Enslaved Dred Scott had sued his owner on the basis that he and his owner had lived for a substantial amount of time in territory where slavery was prohibited by the Missouri Compromise. The Court ruled against him, dismissing his standing as a U.S. citizen because of his race and deciding further that the Constitution did not allow Congress to prohibit slavery from any territory. Thus, the *Dred Scott* decision ruled that the 1820 Missouri Compromise was unconstitutional.

The Lower South secedes

In 1860, Abraham Lincoln, the Republican nominee for president, won a small plurality of the vote by carrying every free state (but none of the slave states). Southerners, especially those in the cotton states, feared that the anti-slavery views of Lincoln and the Republicans would incite slave insurrections and the destruction of the cotton economy. Before Lincoln was inaugurated in March 1861, seven southern states passed secession ordinances and formed the Confederate States of America.

QUESTIONS FOR ANALYSIS

1. How did American expansion intensify the national debate over slavery in the territories? What was the political significance of whether territories were "free" or "slave"?

2. How did the slavery controversy make the annexation of new states so controversial and lead to the Compromise of 1850?

3. Why did violence over slavery escalate after the passage of the Kansas-Nebraska Act? What role did Bleeding Kansas and the Kansas-Nebraska Act play in national politics?

4. Why did the *Dred Scott* decision by the Supreme Court make compromise more difficult?

5. What role did territorial expansion play in the secession of the states of the Lower South in 1860?

The bitterly contested presidential campaign in 1860 thus became a choice between Lincoln and Douglas in the North (Lincoln was not even on the ballot in the South), and between Breckinridge and Bell in the South. Douglas, the only candidate to mount a nationwide campaign, promised that he would "make war boldly against" extremists in both regions: "Northern abolitionists and Southern disunionists." But his effort to preserve the Union by preserving slavery did no good.

By midnight on November 6, Lincoln's victory was clear. In the final count he had 39 percent of the total popular vote, the smallest plurality ever, but he won a clear majority (180 votes) in the Electoral College. He carried *all* eighteen free states and *none* of the slave states.

Abraham Lincoln elected president (1860)

The Response in the South

CORE **OBJECTIVE**

5. Explain why seven southern states seceded from the Union soon after Lincoln's election in 1860.

Between November 8, 1860, when Lincoln was elected, and March 4, 1861, when he was inaugurated, the United States of America disintegrated. The election of Lincoln panicked southerners who believed that the Republican party, as a Richmond, Virginia, newspaper asserted, was founded for one reason: "hatred of African slavery."

Southern fears of a Lincoln presidency

South Carolina, which had long been the state most resistant to federal authority, viewed Lincoln's election as the final signal to abandon the Union. After Lincoln's victory, South Carolina's entire delegation of U.S. congressmen and senators resigned. Federal district judge Andrew McGrath in Charleston also resigned, dramatically ripping off his federal robe. The South Carolina legislature then appointed a convention to decide whether the state should secede from the Union. Among the convention delegates were former governors, four former U.S. senators, the presidents of Furman University and Limestone College, and a dozen ministers, all of whom assumed that Lincoln would try to abolish slavery. Nearly all of the delegates owned slaves. Twenty-seven owned a hundred or more slaves, and one delegate, former governor John Manning, owned more than 650 slaves. One of the delegates, Thomas Jefferson Withers, declared that the "true question for us all is how shall we sustain African slavery in South Carolina from a series of annoying attacks."

South Carolina's slaveholding elite pushes secession

South Carolina then was the third wealthiest state in the Union. It had a higher percentage of slaves in its population (60 percent) than any other state, and its political leadership was dominated by slave-owning hotheads. It had been a one-party state (Democratic) for decades, and it was then the only state in the Union that did not allow its citizens to vote in presidential elections; the state legislature, controlled by white planters, did the balloting.

Meeting in Charleston on December 20, 1860, the special convention, most of whose 169 delegates were wealthy slave owners, unanimously approved an Ordinance of Secession, explaining that President-elect Lincoln was a man "whose opinions and purposes are hostile to slavery."

David Jamison Rutledge, the man who presided over the secession convention, announced that "the Ordinance of Secession has been signed and ratified, and I proclaim the State of South Carolina an Independent Commonwealth." (Jamison would have four sons killed in the Civil War and see his house burned to the ground by Union soldiers.) James L. Petigru, one of the few Unionists in Charleston, claimed that those who voted for secession were lunatics. South Carolina, he quipped, "is too small to be a Republic and too large to be an insane asylum." As the news of secession spread through Charleston, church bells rang and shops closed. New flags were unfurled and cadets at The Citadel, the state's military college, fired artillery salutes. "THE UNION IS DISSOLVED!" screamed the headline of the *Charleston Mercury*, a pro-secession newspaper. One Unionist in Charleston kept a copy of the newspaper, scribbling on the bottom of it: "You'll regret the day you ever done this. I preserve this to see how it ends."

Buchanan's Waiting Game

The nation's gravest crisis needed a bold, decisive president, but lame-duck James Buchanan was timid and hesitant. He blamed the crisis on fanatical abolitionists, but then declared that secession was illegal, only to claim that he lacked the constitutional authority to force a state to rejoin the Union. In the face of Buchanan's inaction, all the southerners in his cabinet resigned, and secessionists in the South seized federal forts. Among those federal forts was Fort Sumter, nestled on a tiny island at the mouth of Charleston Harbor, in the very jaws of the Confederacy. When South Carolina secessionists demanded that Major Robert Anderson, a Kentucky Unionist, surrender the undermanned federal fort, he refused, vowing to hold on at all costs. On January 5, 1861, President Buchanan sent an unarmed ship, the *Star of the West*, to resupply Fort Sumter. As the ship approached Charleston Harbor on January 9, Confederate cannons opened fire and drove it away. It was an act of war, but Buchanan chose to ignore the challenge and ride out the remaining weeks of his term, hoping that one of several compromise proposals would succeed in averting war.

"The Union Is Dissolved!" A newspaper headline announcing South Carolina's secession from the Union.

Secession of the Lower South

By February 1, 1861, the seven states of the Lower South—South Carolina, Mississippi, Florida, Alabama, Georgia, Louisiana, and Texas—had seceded. Although the states' secession ordinances mentioned various grievances against the federal government, including tariffs on imports, they made clear that the primary reason for leaving the Union was the preservation of slavery. Texas's ordinance explained that the purpose of secession and the formation of the Confederacy was to *secure the rights of the slave-holding*

> The formation of the Confederacy

States in their domestic institutions." The Texas convention, displaying the paternalistic racism at work in secession, called African Americans "an inferior and dependent race" for whom slavery was actually "beneficial."

On February 4, 1861, representatives of the seceding states, 90 percent of whom were slave owners, met in Montgomery, Alabama, where they adopted a constitution for the Confederate States of America. It mandated that "the institution of negro slavery, as it now exists in the Confederate States, shall be recognized and protected." Mississippi's Jefferson Davis was elected president, with Alexander H. Stephens of Georgia as vice president. The tiny, sickly Stephens left no doubt about why the Confederacy was formed. "Our new government," he declared, "is founded upon . . . the great truth that the negro is not equal to the white man; that slavery, subordination to the superior [white] race, is his natural and normal condition." In mid-February 1861, President Jefferson Davis ominously claimed that "the time for compromise is now passed."

Final Efforts at Compromise

> The Crittenden Compromise fails (1861)

Amid the secession fever, several members of Congress desperately sought a compromise that would avert a civil war. On December 18, 1860, Senator John J. Crittenden of Kentucky proposed a series of resolutions that allowed for slavery in the new western territories *south* of the 1820 Missouri Compromise line (36°30′ parallel) and guaranteed the preservation of slavery where it already existed. President-elect Lincoln, however, opposed any plan that would allow for the extension of slavery westward, and the Senate defeated the Crittenden Compromise, 25–23. Several weeks later, in February 1861, twenty-one states sent delegates to a peace conference in Washington, D.C. Former president John Tyler presided, but the peace convention's proposal, substantially the same as the Crittenden Compromise, failed to win the support of either house of Congress. The only proposal that met with any success was a constitutional amendment guaranteeing slavery where it existed. Many Republicans, including Lincoln, were prepared to go that far to save the Union, but no farther.

As it happened, after passing the House, the slavery amendment, needing a two-thirds majority, passed the Senate without a vote to spare, 24–12, on the dawn of Lincoln's inauguration day, March 4, 1861. It would have become the Thirteenth Amendment, with the first use of the word *slavery* in the Constitution, but the states never ratified it. When a Thirteenth Amendment was eventually ratified, in 1865, it did not guarantee slavery—it abolished it.

Lincoln's Inauguration

In mid-February 1861, Abraham Lincoln boarded a train in Springfield, Illinois, that would carry him to Washington, D.C., for his presidential inauguration. Along the way, he told the New Jersey legislature that he was "devoted to peace" but warned that "it may be necessary to put the foot down." At the end of the weeklong journey, Lincoln reluctantly agreed that threats against his life made it too risky for him to enter the capital in daylight. Accompanied by bodyguards, he passed through Baltimore unnoticed on a night train and slipped into Washington, D.C., before daybreak on February 23, 1861.

In his March 4 inaugural address, the fifty-two-year-old Lincoln repeated his pledge not "to interfere with the institution of slavery in the states where it exists." But the immediate question facing the nation and the new president had shifted from slavery to secession. Lincoln insisted that "the Union of these States is perpetual." No state, he stressed, "can lawfully get out of the Union." He pledged to defend "federal forts in the South," such as Fort Sumter, but beyond that "there will be no invasion, no using of force against or among the people anywhere." Lincoln closed by appealing for regional harmony:

> We are not enemies, but friends. We must not be enemies. Though passion may have strained, it must not break our bonds of affection. The mystic chords of memory, stretching from every battlefield and patriot grave to every living heart and hearthstone all over this broad land, will yet swell the chorus of the Union, when again touched, as surely they will be, by the better angels of our nature.

Southerners were not impressed, however. A North Carolina newspaper warned that Lincoln's inauguration speech made civil war "inevitable." On both sides, people assumed that if fighting erupted, it would be over quickly and that their daily lives would go on as usual. The new president of the United States continued to seek a peaceful solution. But in early 1861, the possibility of compromise waned and civil war grew more likely.

The End of the Waiting Game

On March 5, 1861, his first day in office, President Lincoln learned that time was running out for the federal troops at Fort Sumter. Major Robert Anderson reported that his men had enough food for only a few weeks, and that Confederates were encircling the fort with a "ring of fire." On April 4, 1861, Lincoln ordered that ships be sent to resupply the sixty-nine soldiers at Fort Sumter. His counterpart, Jefferson Davis, president of the Confederate states, was determined to stop any effort to resupply the fort. On April 11, Confederate general Pierre G. T. Beauregard, a Louisiana native who had studied under Robert Anderson at West Point, demanded that his former professor surrender Fort Sumter. Major Anderson refused. At 4:30 on the morning of April 12, the Confederate shelling of Fort Sumter began. After some thirty-four hours, his ammunition exhausted, the outgunned Anderson lowered the "stars and stripes." The Civil War had begun.

Civil War begins (April 12, 1861)

Reviewing the
CORE OBJECTIVES | INQUIZITIVE

■ **Westward Migration** In the 1830s, Americans came to believe in *"manifest destiny"*— that the U.S. expansion to the Pacific coast was divinely ordained. A population explosion and the lure of cheap, fertile land prompted large numbers of Americans to endure the hardships of the *Overland Trails* to Oregon (*"Oregon Fever"*) and California. Many southerners moved to the Mexican province of Texas with their slaves to grow cotton. The Mexican government would not sanction slavery, however, and in 1830 forbade further immigration. Texians rebelled, winning their independence from Mexico in the *Texas Revolution*. But Texas would not become a state for another decade because the U.S. was determined to avoid war with Mexico and the divisive issue of adding another slave state to the Union.

■ **Mexican-American War** When the United States finally annexed Texas, the Mexican government refused to recognize the loss of its northern province. President Polk sought to acquire California, New Mexico, and Texas, but negotiations failed. When Mexican troops crossed the Rio Grande and fired on U.S. soldiers, Polk urged Congress to declare war. U.S. forces prevailed, despite experiencing high casualties. By the terms of the *Treaty of Guadalupe Hidalgo* (1848), Mexico ceded California and New Mexico to the United States and gave up claims to land north of the Rio Grande.

■ **Slavery in the Territories** The *Wilmot Proviso* (1846), never became law but, by declaring that slavery prohibited in the newly acquired Mexican territories, stirred anti-slavery sentiment. The new *Free-Soil party* also demanded that slavery be banned in the new territories. But the *California Gold Rush* of 1849 escalated tensions. Most Californians wanted their territory to be a free state. Southerners feared losing federal protection of their "peculiar institution" if free states outnumbered slave states. Some political leaders urged the voters in each territory to decide with *popular sovereignty*. The much celebrated *Compromise of 1850* allowed California to enter the Union as a free state, established the territories of Texas, New Mexico, and Utah without direct reference to slavery, banned the slave trade in Washington, D.C., and passed a stronger *Fugitive Slave Act*. Tensions turned violent with the passage of the *Kansas-Nebraska Act* (1854), which overturned the Missouri Compromise by allowing slavery in the territories where it had been banned in 1820.

■ **The Republican Party's Appeal** Northerners were outraged by violent pro-slavery mobs as the territory of Kansas prepared to enter the Union. Yet anti-slavery zealots were equally violent, such as John Brown in *Bleeding Kansas*. The Supreme Court's pro-slavery *Dred Scott v. Sandford* (1857) decision further fueled sectional conflict. Northern voters increasingly gravitated toward the anti-slavery Republican party. Republicans also advocated for protective tariffs and the development of national infrastructure, which appealed to northern manufacturers and commercial farmers. In the 1860 presidential election, Lincoln carried every free state and won a clear electoral college victory.

■ **The Secession of the Lower South** South Carolina seceded from the Union a month after Lincoln's presidential victory. Before Lincoln was even inaugurated, six other states had joined South Carolina to form the Confederate States of America, claiming a right to secede in order to ensure the preservation of slavery. South Carolinians fired at Fort Sumter in Charleston Harbor, and so the Civil War began.

KEY TERMS

CHRONOLOGY

1821	Mexico gains independence from Spain
1836	American "Texians" are defeated at the Alamo
1842	United States and Great Britain agree to the Webster-Ashburton Treaty
1845	United States annexes Texas
1846	Mexican-American War begins
1848	Treaty of Guadalupe Hidalgo ends Mexican-American War
1849	California Gold Rush begins
1854	Congress passes the Kansas-Nebraska Act
	The Republican party is founded
1856	Bleeding Kansas and Bloody Sumner
1857	*Dred Scott v. Sandford* and Lecompton Constitution
1858	Lincoln-Douglas debates
1859	John Brown's raid at Harpers Ferry, Virginia
1860–1861	Seven southern states secede from the Union
March 4, 1861	Abraham Lincoln is inaugurated president
April 1861	Fort Sumter falls to Confederate forces

INQUIZITIVE

Go to InQuizitive to see what you've learned—and learn what you've missed—with personalized feedback along the way.

LINCOLN'S DRIVE THROUGH RICHMOND (1866) Shortly after the Confederate capital of Richmond, Virginia, fell to Union forces in April 1865, President Abraham Lincoln visited the war-torn city. His carriage was swarmed by enslaved blacks who were freed by the war, as well as whites whose loyalties were with the Union.

The War of the Union

1861–1865

The fall of Fort Sumter started the war of the Union and triggered a wave of patriotic bluster on both sides. A southern woman prayed that God would "give us strength to conquer them, to exterminate *them*, to lay waste every Northern city, town and village, to destroy them utterly." By contrast, the writer Nathaniel Hawthorne reported from Massachusetts that his transcendentalist friend Ralph Waldo Emerson was "breathing slaughter" as the Union army prepared for its first battle.

Many southerners, then and since, argued that the Civil War was not about slavery but about the South's effort to defend states' rights. Confederate president Jefferson Davis, for example, claimed that the war was fought on behalf of the states' right to secede from the Union and the South's need to defend itself against a "tyrannical majority," by whom he meant those who had elected President Abraham Lincoln, the anti-slavery Republican. "All we ask," he said, "is to be let alone."

For his part, Lincoln stressed repeatedly that the war's goal was simply to restore the Union. In an 1862 letter, he declared that the "paramount object in this struggle *is* to save the Union, and is *not* either to save or to destroy slavery. If I could save the Union without freeing *any* slave I would do it, and if I could save it by freeing *all* the slaves I would do it; and if I could save it by freeing some and leaving others alone I would also do that." If the southern states

CORE OBJECTIVES INQUIZITIVE

1. Identify the respective advantages of the North and South and explain how they affected the military strategies of the Union and the Confederacy.

2. Evaluate Lincoln's decision to issue the Emancipation Proclamation and its impact on the war.

3. Analyze how the war affected social and economic life in the North and South.

4. Describe the military turning points in 1863 and 1864 that ultimately led to the Confederacy's defeat.

5. Explain how the Civil War changed the nation.

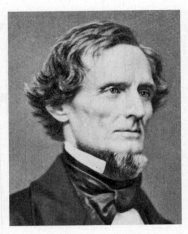

Jefferson Davis President of the Confederacy.

returned to the Union, he promised, they could retain their slaves. None of the Confederate states accepted Lincoln's offer, in large part because most white southerners were convinced that Lincoln was lying. The "Black Republican," as they called the president, was determined to end slavery, no matter what he said.

However much Jefferson Davis and other southerners argued that secession and the war were about states' rights, the states of the Lower South seceded in 1860–1861 to preserve slavery. The South Carolina Declaration on the Immediate Causes of Secession was quite clear on the matter, highlighting the "increasing hostility on the part of the non-slaveholding states to the institution of slavery." Southerners claimed their *right* to secede from the Union, but protecting slavery was the *reason* southern leaders repeatedly used to justify secession and war. In 1860, William Preston of South Carolina declared: "Cotton is not our king—slavery is our king. Slavery is our truth. Slavery is our divine right." As Lincoln noted in his second inaugural address, everyone knew that slavery "was somehow the cause of the war."

CORE **OBJECTIVE**

1. Identify the respective advantages of the North and South and explain how they affected the military strategies of the Union and the Confederacy.

Mobilizing Forces in the North and South

On April 15, three days after the Confederate attack on Fort Sumter, President Lincoln called upon the loyal states to supply 75,000 soldiers to suppress the rebellion. Volunteers on both sides flocked to military recruiting offices. The pro-slavery Senator Stephen Douglas now insisted, "There are only two sides to the question [of civil war]. Every man must be for the United States or against it. There can be no neutrals in this war, only patriots—or traitors." The Civil War would force everyone—men and women, white and black, immigrants and Native Americans, free and enslaved—to choose sides. Thousands of southerners fought for the Union; thousands of northerners fought for the Confederacy. Thousands of European volunteers fought on both sides.

Taking Sides

The first seven states that seceded were all from the Lower South—South Carolina, Mississippi, Florida, Alabama, Georgia, Louisiana, and Texas—where the cotton economy was strongest. All the states in the Upper South, especially Tennessee and Virginia, had areas (mainly in the mountains) where whites were poor, slaves were scarce, and Union support was strong. Nevertheless, the outbreak of actual fighting led four more southern slave states to join the Confederacy: Virginia, Arkansas, Tennessee, and North Carolina.

In east Tennessee, however, the mountain counties would supply more volunteers to the Union army than to the Confederate cause, and people living in western Virginia were so loyal to the Union that they split off and

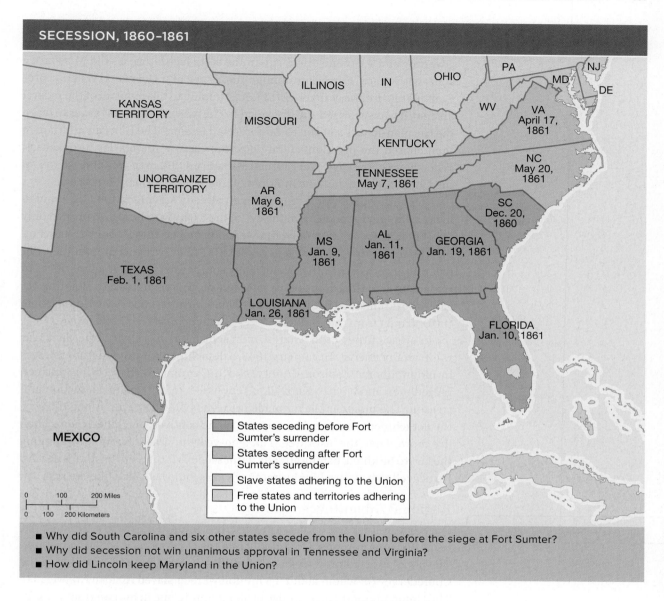

SECESSION, 1860–1861

PA
NJ
OHIO
IN
ILLINOIS
MD
DE
WV
VA
April 17,
1861
KANSAS
TERRITORY
MISSOURI
KENTUCKY
NC
May 20,
1861
TENNESSEE
May 7, 1861
UNORGANIZED
TERRITORY
AR
May 6,
1861
SC
Dec. 20,
1860
MS
Jan. 9,
1861
AL
Jan. 11,
1861
GEORGIA
Jan. 19, 1861
TEXAS
Feb. 1, 1861
LOUISIANA
Jan. 26, 1861
FLORIDA
Jan. 10, 1861
MEXICO

States seceding before Fort Sumter's surrender
States seceding after Fort Sumter's surrender
Slave states adhering to the Union
Free states and territories adhering to the Union

0   100   200 Miles
0   100   200 Kilometers

■ Why did South Carolina and six other states secede from the Union before the siege at Fort Sumter?
■ Why did secession not win unanimous approval in Tennessee and Virginia?
■ How did Lincoln keep Maryland in the Union?

formed the new state of West Virginia. Of the border states, Delaware remained firmly in the Union, but Maryland, Kentucky, and Missouri went through bitter struggles to decide which side to support. "I think to lose Kentucky is nearly the same as to lose the whole game," Lincoln said to a friend, explaining the situation in his home state. "Kentucky gone, we cannot hold Missouri, nor, as I think, Maryland." Kentuckian Mary Todd Lincoln, the president's wife, saw her youngest brother join the Confederate army, as did three of her half-brothers and a brother-in-law.

If Maryland had seceded, Confederates would have surrounded Washington, D.C. To keep Maryland in the Union, Lincoln had pro-Confederate leaders arrested, including Baltimore's mayor and chief of police. The fragile neutrality of Kentucky lasted till September 3, when Confederate and Union armies moved into the divided state. Kentucky voters elected a secessionist governor and a Unionist majority in the state legislature, as did Missouri, a state with many European immigrants, especially Germans. When a pro-Confederate militia gathered in St Louis, hoping to take control of the federal arsenal, it was surprised and disarmed by German immigrants "eager to teach the German-haters a never-to-be-forgotten lesson." The German militiamen then chased the pro-Confederate governor across the border to Arkansas. When news of the Civil War reached Missouri, 4,200 men volunteered to join the Union army; all but one hundred of them were German Americans.

The outbreak of war forced the men already serving in the U.S. Army to make an agonizing choice. On the eve of the Civil War, the U.S. Army had only 16,400 men, about 1,000 of whom were officers. Of these, about 25 percent, like the future Confederate general Robert E. Lee, resigned to join the Confederate army. On the other hand, many southerners made great sacrifices to remain loyal to the Union. Some left their native region once the fighting began; others remained in the South but found ways to support the Union. Some 100,000 men from the southern states fought *against* the Confederacy.

In areas of the South where Union sentiment was strong, the Civil War was brutally uncivil. In January 1863, a detachment of Confederate soldiers in mountainous Madison County, North Carolina, was escorting thirteen ragged men and boys to Knoxville, Tennessee, to be tried for desertion and treason. The prisoners never made it to Knoxville, however. Along the way, the detachment stopped, lined up five of the captives, and killed them. Then five more. Then the last three. Thirteen-year-old David Shelton was among the last to be killed, having already witnessed his father and brother's deaths. He begged to be spared for his mother's sake, but was killed like the rest.

Regional Advantages

| Union advantage: Population |

Once battle lines were finally drawn, the Union held twenty-three states, including four border slave states, while the Confederacy had eleven states. The population count was about 22 million in the Union to 9 million in the Confederacy (of whom about 3.5 million were enslaved African Americans). The Union therefore had an edge of about four to one in human resources. To help balance the odds, the Confederacy mobilized 80 percent of its military-age white men, a third of whom would die during the four-year war.

| Union advantage: Greater industrial development, railroads, and ships |

An even greater advantage for the North was its industrial development. As the southern character Rhett Butler complains in the classic movie *Gone with the Wind* (1939), "Why, all we have [in the South] is cotton and slaves and arrogance." The hated Yankees, he adds, have "the factories, the foundries, the shipyards, the iron and coal mines—all the things we haven't got." The southern states produced just 7 percent of the nation's manufactured goods on the eve of the war. The Union states produced 97 percent of the firearms and 96 percent of the railroad equipment. The North's advantage in transportation, particularly ships, also weighed heavily as the war went on. At the start of the war, the Union had ninety warships while the South at first had no navy at all. Federal gunboats and transports played a direct role in securing the Union's control of the Mississippi River and its larger tributaries, which provided easy invasion routes into the center of the Confederacy. And early on, the Union navy's blockade of the major southern ports sharply reduced the amount of cotton that could be exported to Britain and France as well as the flow of goods (including military weapons) imported from Europe. In addition, the Union had more wagons and horses than the Confederacy, and an even more impressive edge in the number of railroad locomotives.

The Confederacy, however, enjoyed a major geographic advantage: it could fight a defensive war on its own territory. In warfare, it is usually easier to defend than to attack. And in the Civil War, 90 percent of the time, armies that assaulted well-defended positions were beaten. Many Confederate leaders assumed that if their new nation could hold out long enough, perhaps the North would lose the will to continue the war.

> Confederate advantage: Waging a defensive war on its own territory

As the two sides mobilized for the first battles, the Confederate armies had more experienced military leaders and better horsemen. Many Confederates also displayed a brash sense of confidence in facing the more numerous and better equipped Union forces. After all, had not the Revolutionaries of 1776 defeated a much stronger British army? "Britain could not conquer three million [Americans]," a Louisianan declared, and "the world cannot conquer the South."

> Confederate advantage: Experienced military leaders

The War's Early Strategies

After the fall of Fort Sumter, excited civilians on both sides pressured the generals to strike quickly. "Forward to Richmond!" screamed a New York newspaper headline. In the summer of 1861, Jefferson Davis allowed the battle-hungry General Beauregard to hurry the main Confederate army to Manassas Junction, a railroad crossing in northern Virginia, about twenty-five miles southwest of Washington. Lincoln hoped that the Union army (often called *Federals*) would overrun the outnumbered Confederates (often called *Rebels*) and quickly push on to Richmond, only 107 miles to the south. "What a picnic," predicted a New York soldier, "to go down South for three months and clean up the whole business."

> Union strategy: Capture the Confederate capital

First Bull Run

When word reached Washington, D.C. that the two opposing armies were converging for battle, hundreds of congressmen and civilians packed picnic lunches and rode in carriages or on horseback to watch the romantic spectacle. It was a hot, dry day on July 21, 1861, when 37,000 untested Union recruits in colorful uniforms breezily marched to battle, some of them breaking ranks to eat blackberries or drink water from streams along the way. Many of them died with the berries still staining their lips as they engaged the Confederates dug in behind a branch of the Potomac River called Bull Run near

> Confederate advantage: Victory at First Battle of Bull Run (1861)

First Bull Run Moments before battle, a spectator in a top hat chats with Union soldiers (bottom right), while an artist sketches the passing troops heading to war (at left).

the vital Manassas Junction railroad station. The Union troops almost won early in the afternoon. "We fired a volley," wrote a Massachusetts private, "and saw the Rebels running. . . . The boys were saying constantly, in great glee, 'We've whipped them.' 'We'll hang Jeff Davis from a sour apple tree.' 'They're running.' 'The war is over.'" But Confederate reinforcements poured in to tip the balance. Amid the furious fighting, a South Carolina officer, soon to be killed himself, rallied his troops by pointing to the courageous example of Thomas Jackson's men: "Look! There is General Jackson with his Virginians, standing like a stone wall!" Jackson ordered his men to charge the faltering Union ranks, urging them to "yell like furies!" From that day forward, "Stonewall" became Jackson's nickname, and he would be the most celebrated—and feared—Confederate commander.

The Union army's retreat from Bull Run turned into a panicked rout (the "great skedaddle") as fleeing soldiers and terrified civilians clogged the road to Washington, D.C. But the Confederates were themselves so disorganized and exhausted that they failed to give chase. Unionists were devastated. New Yorker George Templeton Strong, a wealthy attorney and civic leader, wrote that "we are utterly and disgracefully routed, beaten, whipped by secessionists."

The First Battle of Bull Run (or First Manassas)[*] was a sobering experience for both sides, each of which had underrated the other's strength and tenacity. Much of the romance—the colorful uniforms, bright flags, and rousing songs—gave way to the agonizing realization that this would be a long, costly struggle. *Harper's Weekly* bluntly warned: "From the fearful day at Bull Run dates war. Not polite war, not incredulous war, but war that breaks hearts and blights homes."

Thomas "Stonewall" Jackson The aggressive commander of a Confederate brigade at Bull Run, Jackson would later die of friendly fire in the Battle of Chancellorsville.

---

[*] The Federals most often named battles for natural features; the Confederates, for nearby towns—thus Bull Run (Manassas), Antietam (Sharpsburg), Stones River (Murfreesboro), and the like.

The Union's "Anaconda" Plan

The Battle of Bull Run demonstrated that the war would not be decided with one sudden stroke. General Winfield Scott, the seasoned seventy-five-year-old commander of the Union war effort, devised a three-pronged strategy that called first for the Army of the Potomac, the main Union army, to defend Washington, D.C., and exert constant pressure on the Confederate capital at Richmond. At the same time, the Federal navy's blockade of southern ports would cut off the Confederacy's access to foreign goods and weapons. The third and final component of the plan called for other Union armies to divide the Confederacy by pushing south along the crucial inland water routes: the Mississippi, Tennessee, and Cumberland Rivers. This so-called **Anaconda Plan** was intended to slowly trap and crush the southern resistance, like an anaconda snake strangling its prey.

> Union strategy: Naval blockade and control of inland rivers

Confederate Strategy

The Confederate war plan was simpler. Jefferson Davis was better prepared than Lincoln at the start of the war to guide military strategy. A graduate of the U.S. Military Academy at West Point, he had served as an officer during the Mexican War and was U.S. secretary of war from 1853 to 1857. If the Union forces could be held off and the war prolonged, as Davis and others hoped, then the British or French, desperate for southern cotton, might be persuaded to join their cause. Or, perhaps a long war would change public sentiment in the North and force Lincoln to seek a negotiated settlement. So while armies were forming in the South, Confederate diplomats were seeking military and financial assistance in London and Paris, and Confederate sympathizers in the North were urging an end to the Union's war effort.

> Confederate strategy: A lengthy war to erode northern morale

The Confederate representatives in Paris won a promise from France to recognize the Confederacy as a new nation *if* Great Britain would do the same. But the British foreign minister refused to work with the Confederates, partly in response to pressure from President Lincoln and partly out of Britain's desire to maintain its trade with the United States. Confederate leaders had assumed that Britain would support the South in order to get its cotton. "The cards are in our hands!" crowed the *Mercury*, a Charleston newspaper. "And we intend to play them out to the bankruptcy of every cotton factory in Great Britain and France for the acknowledgement of our independence." As it turned out, however, the British, although eventually losing 400,000 jobs in their textile mills, were able to import enough cotton from their Asian colony, India, to maintain production of cloth. In the end, Confederate diplomacy in Europe was more successful in getting military supplies than in gaining official recognition of the Confederacy as an independent nation.

> Confederate strategy: Cotton diplomacy in Europe

Forming Armies

Once the fighting began, President Lincoln called for 500,000 more men, a staggering number at the time and one that the Confederacy struggled to match. "War! And volunteers are the only topics of conversation or thought," wrote a student at Ohio's Oberlin College. "I cannot study. I cannot sleep,

Anaconda Plan Union's primary war strategy calling for a naval blockade of major southern seaports and then dividing the Confederacy by gaining control of the Tennessee, Cumberland, and Mississippi Rivers.

and I don't know as I can write." In Illinois, Ulysses S. Grant, a graduate of the U.S. Military Academy at West Point who had fought in the Mexican-American War, rejoined the army in 1861, explaining that there "are but two parties now—traitors and patriots—and I want hereafter to be ranked with the latter." Confederates were equally committed to their cause. Charleston, wrote Mary Chesnut, the literary wife of a prominent planter, was "crowded with soldiers" who feared "the war will be over before they get a sight of the fun." Tennessee's twenty-one-year-old Sam Watkins reported that everyone in his town "was eager for the war."

The basic unit of the nineteenth-century U.S. Army was the regiment, about a thousand soldiers, and during the Civil War most regiments on both sides were made up of friends, neighbors, and relatives from the same local community. Ethnic groups also formed their own regiments. A quarter of the Union troops were foreign-born. The Union army, for example, included a Scandinavian regiment (the 15th Wisconsin Infantry), a French regiment (the 55th New York Infantry), a Polish Legion (the 58th New York Infantry), and a mixed regiment of Poles, Hungarians, Germans, Spaniards, and Italians (the 39th New York Infantry). Many immigrant soldiers spoke no English. They were attracted to serve by many motives: a strong belief in the Union cause, cash bonuses, regular pay, or the need for a steady job. Whatever the reason, the high proportion of immigrants in the Union army gave it an ethnic diversity absent in the Confederate ranks. Many of the first Confederate army units chose flamboyant names: the Frontier Guards, Rough-and-Ready Grays, Game Cocks, Tigers, Cherokee Lincoln Killers, Tallapoosa Thrashers, and Raccoon Roughs.

In the Confederacy, the smaller male population than in the North forced Jefferson Davis to enact a conscription law (a mandatory military draft). On April 16, 1862, all white males aged eighteen to thirty-five were declared members of the army for three years, and those already in uniform were required to serve until the war ended. Many resented being

Union soldiers Smoking their pipes, these soldiers share a moment of rest and a bottle of whiskey.

drafted. "From this time until the end of the war," a Tennessee soldier wrote, "a soldier was simply a machine, a conscript. . . . All our pride and valor had gone, and we were sick of war and cursed the Southern Confederacy." In 1862, the upper age for military service was raised to forty-five; and in 1864, the age range was further extended to fifty. But age often did not matter, since recruiting officers frequently decided for themselves which boys "were old enough."

The Confederate conscription law included controversial loopholes, however. First, a draftee might escape service either by providing an able-bodied "substitute" who was not of draft age or by paying $500 in cash. Second, elected officials and key civilian workers, as well as planters with twenty or more slaves, were exempted from military service. Many among the planter elite argued that if they left to fight in the army, their slaves would escape or riot. Equally galling to many Confederate soldiers was the behavior of wealthy officers who brought their enslaved servants with them to army camps.

The Union took nearly another year to force men into service. In 1863, with the war going badly for the Federal armies, the government began to draft men aged twenty to forty-five. But many younger men served in the war. The Union army had over a thousand soldiers under the age of fifteen, some of whom served as regimental "drummer boys"; one of these was just nine years old. As in the South, there were ways for northerners to avoid military service. Exemptions were granted to selected federal and state officeholders and to others on medical or compassionate grounds. In the North, a draftee might pay $300 to avoid service. The fathers of Theodore and Franklin Roosevelt paid for substitutes, as did two future presidents, Chester A. Arthur and Grover Cleveland. Such exemptions led to bitter complaints on both sides about the conflict being "a rich man's war and a poor man's fight." Widespread public opposition to the draft emerged in both the North and South.

The average Civil War soldier or sailor was twenty-five years old, stood five feet eight inches, and weighed 143 pounds. A third of the southern soldiers could neither read nor write. One in nine would be killed or wounded. Half of the Union soldiers and two-thirds of the Confederates were farmers. Army camps featured their own libraries, theatrical stages, churches, and numerous "mascot" pets—and monotonous routine. A witty Pennsylvania private wrote home that "the first thing in the morning is drill. Then drill, then drill again. Then drill, drill, a little more drill, then drill, lastly drill."

Blacks in the South

As had happened during the Revolutionary War and the War of 1812, enslaved African Americans took advantage of the confusion created by the war to run away, engage in sabotage, join the Union war effort, or pursue their own interests. A plantation owner in Tennessee was disgusted by the war's effect on his slaves, as he confessed in his diary: "My Negroes all at home, but working only as they see fit, doing little." Some of them had

> Union advantage: Slaves run away from southern owners

reported that they had "rather serve the federals than work on the farm." Later, he revealed that when Union armies arrived in the area, his slaves had "stampeded" to join the Yankees: "Many of my servants have run away and most of those left had [just] as well be gone, they being totally demoralized and ungovernable." Some enslaved blacks escaped and served as spies or guides for Union forces; others later in the war escaped to join the Union army or navy.

Fighting in the West

During the Civil War, fighting spilled across the Mississippi River into the Great Plains and all the way to California. In 1862 a small Confederate army tried to conquer the New Mexico territory, which then included Arizona, but was repelled. Amid sporadic fighting, western settlement slowed but did not stop. New discoveries of gold and silver in the Sierra Nevada mountains in eastern California and in Montana and Colorado lured more prospectors and their suppliers. Dakota, Colorado, and Nevada gained territorial status in 1861, Idaho and Arizona in 1863, and Montana in 1864. Silver-rich Nevada gained statehood in 1864.

Kansas and Indian Territory

The most intense fighting west of the Mississippi occurred along the Kansas-Missouri border, where the disputes that had developed between the proslavery and anti-slavery settlers in the 1850s turned into brutal guerrilla warfare. The most prominent pro-Confederate leader in the area was William Quantrill. He and his followers, mostly teenagers, fought under a black flag, meaning that they would kill anyone who surrendered. In destroying Lawrence, Kansas, in 1863, Quantrill ordered his men to "kill every male and burn every house." By the end of the day, 182 boys and men had been massacred. Their opponents, the Jayhawkers, responded in kind. They tortured and hanged pro-Confederate prisoners, burned houses, and destroyed livestock.

Many Indian nations were caught up in the Civil War. Indian regiments fought on both sides, and in Oklahoma they fought against each other. Indians among the "Five Civilized Tribes" held African-American slaves and felt a bond with southern whites. Oklahoma's proximity to Texas influenced the Choctaws and Chickasaws to support the Confederacy. The Cherokees, Creeks, and Seminoles were more divided in their loyalties. For them, the Civil War fractured their unity. The Cherokees, for example, split in two, some supporting the Union and others the Confederacy.

Kentucky and Tennessee

Little happened of military significance east of the Appalachian Mountains before May 1862. On the other hand, important battles occurred in the West (from the Appalachians to the Mississippi River). In western Kentucky,

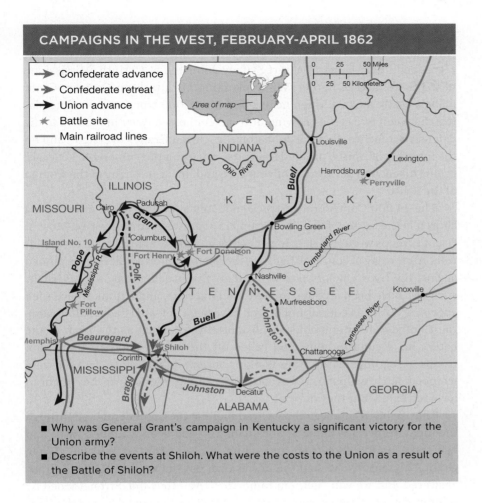

CAMPAIGNS IN THE WEST, FEBRUARY-APRIL 1862

- Confederate advance
- Confederate retreat
- Union advance
- Battle site
- Main railroad lines

Area of map

0   25   50 Miles
0   25   50 Kilometers

INDIANA

ILLINOIS

MISSOURI

Ohio River

Louisville

Lexington

Harrodsburg

Perryville

Buell

K E N T U C K Y

Cairo   Paducah

Grant

Columbus

Island No. 10

Fort Henry   Fort Donelson

Bowling Green

Cumberland River

Mississippi R.

Pope

Polk

Nashville

Fort Pillow

T E N N E S S E E

Murfreesboro

Knoxville

Buell

Johnston

Tennessee River

Memphis

Beauregard

Shiloh

Chattanooga

Corinth

MISSISSIPPI

Bragg

Johnston   Decatur

GEORGIA

ALABAMA

- Why was General Grant's campaign in Kentucky a significant victory for the Union army?
- Describe the events at Shiloh. What were the costs to the Union as a result of the Battle of Shiloh?

Confederate general Albert Sidney Johnston had perhaps 40,000 men stretched over some 150 miles. Early in 1862, General Ulysses S. Grant, a superb horseman but inexperienced commander, made the first Union thrust against the weak center of Johnston's overextended lines. Moving on boats out of Cairo, Illinois, and Paducah, Kentucky, the Union army steamed up the Tennessee River and captured Fort Henry in northern Tennessee on February 6. Grant then moved quickly overland to attack nearby Fort Donelson, where, on February 16, some 12,000 Confederates surrendered.

This first major Union victory touched off wild celebrations throughout the North. President Lincoln's delight, however, was tempered by the death in the White House of his eleven-year-old son Willie, who succumbed to typhoid fever. The tragedy "overwhelmed" the president. It "showed me my weakness as I had never felt it before," Lincoln confessed to a friend. A White House staff member said she had never seen "a man so bowed down in grief."

Shiloh

After defeats in Kentucky and Tennessee, the Confederate forces in the West regrouped under General Albert Sydney Johnston at Corinth, Mississippi, near the Tennessee border. While planning his attack on Corinth, Grant made a costly mistake when he exposed his 42,000 troops on a rolling plateau between two creeks flowing into the Tennessee River and failed to dig defensive trenches. General Johnston recognized Grant's oversight, and on the morning of April 6 ordered a surprise attack on the vulnerable Federals, urging his men to be "worthy of your race and lineage; worthy of the women of the South."

The 44,000 Confederates struck suddenly at Shiloh, a whitewashed log church in the center of the Union camp in southwestern Tennessee. Most of Grant's troops were still sleeping or eating breakfast; many died in their bedrolls. After a day of confused fighting, the fleeing Union soldiers were pinned against the river. One of them wrote that "this is going to be a great battle, such as I have been anxious to see for a long time, and I think I have seen *enough* of it." The Federals might well have been defeated had not Johnston, the Confederate commander, been mortally wounded at the peak of the battle; his second in command called off the attack, allowing the Union troops to regroup. Private Sam Watkins observed that "those Yankees were whipped, fairly whipped, and according to all the rules of war they ought to have retreated. But they didn't."

Union victory: Battle of Shiloh

That night, as Union gunboats fired shells at the Confederates all through the night, General William T. Sherman, who had been wounded twice and had three horses shot from under him, visited Grant as rain fell. "Well, Grant," he said, "we've had the devil's own day, haven't we?" "Yes," Grant answered. But we will "lick 'em tomorrow." And they did. Strengthened by reinforcements, Grant's troops took the offensive the next day, and the Confederates glumly withdrew twenty miles to Corinth. The Union army was too battered to pursue.

Union strategy: "Complete conquest"

Shiloh, a Hebrew word meaning "Place of Peace," was the largest and costliest battle in which Americans had ever engaged up to that point. Some 100,000 men had fought each other, and a quarter of them had been killed or wounded. The 3,477 killed were more than had been killed in all of the War of 1812. Grant remembered that the battlefield was so littered with corpses that he could not walk in any direction without "stepping on dead bodies." He now realized that the only way the cruel war would end would be through "complete conquest." Like so many battles to come, Shiloh was a story of missed opportunities and lucky accidents. Throughout the Civil War, winning armies would fail to pursue their retreating foes, thus allowing the wounded opponent to slip away and fight again.

After Shiloh, Union general Henry Halleck, already jealous of Grant's success, spread a false rumor that Grant had been drinking during the battle. Some urged Lincoln to fire Grant, but the president refused: "I can't spare this man; he fights." Halleck, however, took Grant's place as field commander, and as a result the Union thrust in the Mississippi Valley southward ground to a halt.

New Orleans

Just three weeks after the Battle of Shiloh, the Union won a great naval victory at New Orleans, as sixty-year-old David G. Farragut's warships blasted their way past Confederate forts under cover of darkness to take control of the largest city in the Confederacy. Union general Benjamin F. Butler, a cross-eyed Massachusetts Democrat, thereafter served as the military governor of captured New Orleans. When a Confederate sympathizer ripped down a Union flag, Butler had him hanged. After a Rebel woman leaned out her window and emptied her chamber pot on the head of newly promoted Admiral Farragut, General Butler decreed that any woman who was disrespectful of Union soldiers would be treated as a "woman of the town plying her avocation" (that is, as a prostitute). Residents of the captured towns thereafter referred to General Butler as "the Beast," but they also quit harassing his soldiers. By shutting off the flow of goods, especially cotton, coming down the Mississippi River to the Gulf of Mexico, the loss of New Orleans was a devastating blow to the Confederate economy as the Union army took control of 1,500 cotton plantations and 50,000 slaves in the Mississippi Valley. The slave system was "forever destroyed and worthless" in Louisiana, reported a northern journalist. "New Orleans gone—and with it the Confederacy?" a worried Mary Chesnut wrote in Richmond.

> Union seizes New Orleans

Perryville

In the late summer of 1862, Confederate General Braxton Bragg's Army of Mississippi, 30,000 strong, used railroads to link up with General Edmund Kirby Smith's Army of East Tennessee. Their goal was to invade the North by taking control of the border state of Kentucky. They hoped to recruit volunteers for the Confederacy as well as push the Union army out of the state across the Ohio River. After early success, the Confederates installed a governor in Frankfort, only to cancel the inaugural ball because of the approaching Union Army of Ohio led by General Don Carlos Buell. The two forces met at the village of Perryville in central Kentucky in October 1862. In the ensuing battle, the outnumbered Confederates attacked the Union lines, pushing them back over a mile. But when Bragg learned that Union reinforcements were rushing to the battle, he, against the advice of his officers, ordered the Army of Mississippi to withdraw south toward Tennessee. After the Battle of Perryville, the Union retained control of Kentucky for the rest of the war. Jefferson Davis was so upset by Bragg's timid leadership that he ordered him to Richmond for a tongue lashing.

> Union victory: Battle of Perryville (1862)

Fighting in the East

The fighting in the East remained fairly quiet for nine months after the Battle of Bull Run. In the wake of the Union defeat, Lincoln had appointed General George B. McClellan, Stonewall Jackson's classmate at West

Point and a former railroad president, as head of the Army of the Potomac. The thirty-four-year-old McClellan, who encouraged journalists to call him "Little Napoleon," set about building the Union's most powerful, best-trained army. Yet for all of his self-confidence and organizational ability, McClellan's cautiousness would prove crippling. Months passed while he remained in a state of perpetual preparation, building and training his massive army to meet the superior numbers of Confederates he mistakenly believed were facing him. Worried that the Union was running out of money, Lincoln finally lost his patience and ordered McClellan to attack. "[You] must strike a blow," he told his reluctant commander.

McClellan's Peninsular Campaign

In mid-March 1862, McClellan finally moved his huge army of 122,000 men on 400 ships and barges down the Potomac River and the Chesapeake Bay to the mouth of the James River at the tip of the Yorktown peninsula, southeast

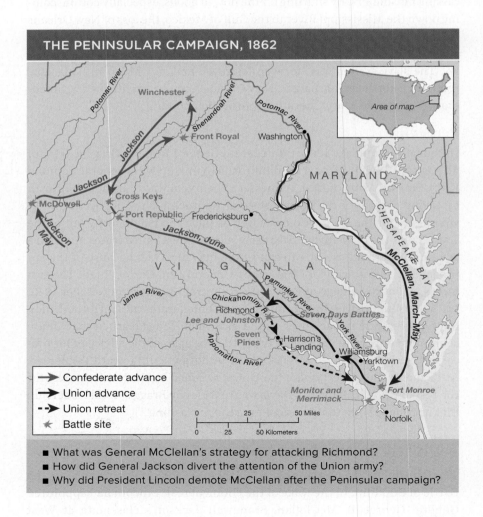

THE PENINSULAR CAMPAIGN, 1862

- → Confederate advance
- → Union advance
- -→ Union retreat
- ⋆ Battle site

■ What was General McClellan's strategy for attacking Richmond?
■ How did General Jackson divert the attention of the Union army?
■ Why did President Lincoln demote McClellan after the Peninsular campaign?

of Richmond, Virginia. McClellan's "Peninsular Campaign" boldly put the Union forces within sixty miles of the Confederate capital. Thousands of residents fled the city in panic, but McClellan waited too long to strike, overestimating the number of Confederate defenders. As a frustrated Lincoln told McClellan, the war could be won only by *engaging* the rebel army, not by endless maneuvers and efforts to occupy Confederate territory. "Once more," Lincoln told his commanding general, "let me tell you, it is indispensable to *you* that you strike a blow."

On May 31, 1862, it was the Confederate general Joseph E. Johnston who struck the first blow at McClellan's army along the Chickahominy River, six miles east of Richmond. In the Battle of Seven Pines (Fair Oaks), only the arrival of Federal reinforcements, who somehow crossed the swollen river, prevented a disastrous Union defeat. Both sides took heavy casualties, and General Johnston was severely wounded. At this point, Robert E. Lee assumed command of the Confederates' main army, the Army of Northern Virginia, a development that changed the course of the war. Dignified yet fiery, the brilliant Lee, fluent in French and Latin, had graduated second in his class at West Point. During the Mexican War, he had impressed General Winfield Scott as the "very best soldier I ever saw in the field." In 1857, Scott predicted that Lee would become America's greatest military leader. Now, as the commander of the Army of Northern Virginia, Lee would prove to be a daring, even reckless, strategist who was as aggressive as McClellan was timid. "He is silent, inscrutable, strong, like a God," said a Confederate officer.

On July 9, when President Lincoln visited McClellan's headquarters on the coast of Virginia, the general complained that the administration had failed to support him and lectured the president at length on military strategy. Such insubordination was ample reason to remove McClellan. After returning to Washington, Lincoln called Henry Halleck from the West to take charge as general in chief. Miffed at his demotion, McClellan angrily dismissed Halleck as an officer "whom I know to be my inferior."

Robert E. Lee Military adviser to President Jefferson Davis and commander of the Army of Northern Virginia.

> Robert E. Lee takes command of Confederate forces

Lincoln's search for a "fighting general" Abraham Lincoln and George B. McClellan confer at Antietam, October 4, 1862.

Second Bull Run

Confederate victory: Second Battle of Bull Run

Lincoln and Halleck ordered McClellan to move his troops back to Washington, D.C., and join forces with General John Pope, commander of the Union Army of Virginia, in a new assault on Richmond. Pope declared that his goal "was attack and not defense." In a letter to his wife, a jealous McClellan predicted—accurately—that "Pope will be thrashed and disposed of" by Lee's army. Lee moved northward to strike Pope's army before McClellan's troops arrived. The Confederate commander knew that his only chance was to drive a wedge between the two larger Union armies so that he could deal with them one at a time. Violating a basic rule of military strategy, Lee riskily divided his forces, sending Stonewall Jackson's "foot cavalry" around Pope's flank to attack his supply lines in the rear. At the Second Battle of Bull Run (or Manassas), fought in exhausting heat on almost the same site as the earlier battle, a confused Pope assumed that he faced only Jackson, but Lee's main army by that time had joined in. On August 30, 1862, a crushing Confederate attack drove the larger Union army from the field, giving the Confederates a sensational victory and leading one disheartened Union officer to confess from his death bed that "General Pope had been outwitted. . . . Our generals have defeated us." In contrast, a Rebel soldier from Georgia wrote home that "General Lee stands now above all generals in modern history. Our men will follow him to the end."

CORE **OBJECTIVE**

2. Evaluate Lincoln's decision to issue the Emancipation Proclamation and its impact on the war.

Emancipation

The Confederate victories in 1862 devastated northern morale and convinced Lincoln that he had to take bolder steps to win the war over an enemy fighting for and aided by enslaved labor. Now the North had to assault slavery itself. Once fighting began in 1861, the Union's need to keep the border slave states (Delaware, Kentucky, Maryland, and Missouri) in the Union had dictated caution on the volatile issue of emancipation. Beyond that, Lincoln had to contend with a deep-seated racial prejudice among most northerners, who were willing to allow slavery to continue in the South. Lincoln himself harbored doubts about his constitutional authority to emancipate slaves.

Slaves in the War

"Contrabands of war"

The expanding war forced the issue. As Federal forces pushed into the Confederacy, runaway slaves began to turn up in Union army camps, and the commanders did not know whether to declare them free. One general designated the fugitive slaves "contrabands of war," and thereafter the slaves who sought protection and freedom with Union forces were known as **contrabands.**" Some Union officers put the contrabands to work digging trenches and building fortifications; others simply set them free.

Lincoln, meanwhile, began to edge toward emancipation. On April 16, 1862, he signed an act that abolished slavery in the District of Columbia; on

contrabands Runaway slaves who sought refuge in Union military camps or who lived in areas of the Confederacy under Union control.

Contrabands Former slaves on a farm in Cumberland Landing, Virginia, 1862.

June 19 another act excluded slavery from the western territories. Still, Lincoln insisted that the war was about restoring the Union, not ending slavery in the South. Like most northerners, he was more determined to end secession than to end slavery.

But the course of the war changed Lincoln's outlook and transformed the conflict into a struggle for human freedom. In the summer of 1862, Lincoln decided that emancipation of slaves in the Confederate states was necessary to win the war. Many of the more than 3 million enslaved laborers in the Confederacy, he knew, were being forced to aid the Rebel war effort. Further, morale in the North needed a boost, and public opinion was swinging toward emancipation. In July 1862, Lincoln confided to his cabinet that "decisive and extreme measures must be adopted." Emancipation, he said, had become "a military necessity, absolutely necessary to the preservation of the Union. We must free the slaves or be ourselves subdued." Secretary of State William H. Seward agreed, but advised Lincoln to delay the announcement until after a Union battlefield victory to avoid being viewed as desperate.

> Emancipation: Military necessity

Antietam

Robert E. Lee made his own momentous decision in the summer of 1862: he would invade Maryland and thereby force the Union army to leave northern Virginia and relieve the pressure on Richmond, the Confederate capital. He also hoped to gain official recognition of the Confederate nation from Great Britain and France, which would bring desperately needed military supplies to the Confederacy. In addition, Lee and Jefferson Davis hoped to capture

Maryland, with its many Confederate supporters, and separate it from the Union. For those reasons and others, in September 1862, Lee and his troops, many of them ragged and barefoot and all of them underfed, pushed north into western Maryland.

Battle of Antietam (1862)

On September 17, 1862, the Union and Confederate armies clashed in the furious **Battle of Antietam** (Sharpsburg). Had not Union soldiers discovered Lee's detailed battle plans, wrapped around three cigars, which one of his officers had carelessly dropped on the ground, the Confederates might have won. Instead, McClellan, if he moved quickly, could attack Lee's outnumbered forces while they were scattered and on the move. But, as always, McClellan moved slowly, enabling Lee to regroup his scattered units at Sharpsburg, along Antietam Creek. There the poorly coordinated Union army launched repeated attacks. The fighting was savage; a Union officer counted "hundreds of dead bodies lying in rows and in piles." The scene after "five hours of continuous slaughter" was "sickening, harrowing, horrible. O what a terrible sight!"

The next day, Lee braced for another Union attack, but it never came. That night, cloaked by fog and drizzling rain, the battered Confederates slipped south back across the Potomac River to the safety of Virginia. "The 'barefoot boys' have done some terrible fighting," a Georgian wrote his parents. "We are a dirty, ragged set [of soldiers], mother, but courage & heroism find many a true disciple among us."

Although the battle was technically a draw, Lee's northern invasion had failed. McClellan, never known for his modesty, claimed that he "had fought the battle splendidly." To him, the Battle of Antietam was "the most terrible battle of the age." Indeed, it was the bloodiest single day in American military history. Some 6,400 soldiers on both sides were killed, twice as many as at Shiloh, and another 17,000 were wounded. The Confederate people, said a soldier, wanted "an active [military] campaign, and General Lee has certainly given it to us."

President Lincoln was pleased that Lee's army had been forced to retreat, but he was disgusted by McClellan's failure to attack the retreating Confederates and win the war. The president sent a sarcastic message to the general: "I have just read your dispatch about sore-tongued and fatigued horses. Will you pardon me for asking what the horses of your army have done . . . that fatigues anything?" Failing to receive a satisfactory answer, Lincoln again relieved McClellan of his command of the Army of the Potomac and assigned him to recruiting duty in New Jersey. Never again would McClellan command troops, but he would challenge Lincoln for the presidency in 1864 as a Democrat.

The Battle of Antietam had several important results. It revived sagging northern morale, dashed the Confederacy's hopes of forging alliances with Great Britain and France, and convinced Abraham Lincoln to free the slaves in the Confederate states as a military necessity.

Battle of Antietam (1862)
Turning-point battle near Sharpsburg, Maryland, leaving over 20,000 soldiers dead or wounded, in which Union forces halted a Confederate invasion of the North.

Emancipation Proclamation

The victory at Antietam convinced President Lincoln to take a momentous step. Using his powers as commander in chief of the armed forces, by the stroke of a pen, he changed the conflict from a war to restore the Union to a struggle to end slavery. On September 22, 1862, five days after the battle, he signed the **Emancipation Proclamation**, which announced that "as a necessary war measure" all slaves in the Rebel states were to be made "forever free" on January 1, 1863. He added that free blacks and escaped slaves would now be welcomed into the Union army and navy. The Emancipation Proclamation did not free the 500,000 enslaved blacks in the four Union border states of Delaware, Kentucky, Maryland, and Missouri, or the 300,000 slaves in Tennessee, western Virginia, coastal Carolina, and parts of Louisiana which were back under Union control. As he signed the Emancipation Proclamation, Lincoln said, "I never, in my life, felt more certain that I was doing the right thing than I do in signing this paper." Simply restoring the Union was no longer the purpose of the war; the transformation of the South was now the goal.

> Emancipation Proclamation: Civil War becomes a struggle to end slavery

Reactions to Emancipation

Although Lincoln's proclamation technically freed only the slaves where Confederates remained in control, many slaves in both the North and the South claimed their freedom anyway. As Lincoln had hoped, word of his landmark proclamation spread rapidly among the slave community in the Confederacy, arousing hopes of freedom, creating general confusion in the cities, and encouraging thousands to escape to approaching Union armies. George Washington Albright, an enslaved teen in Mississippi, recalled that white planters tried to prevent slaves from learning about the Proclamation but word of it slipped through the "grapevine." His father, in fact, was inspired by Lincoln's declaration to escape and join the Union army. The younger Albright served as a "runner" for the 4Ls ("Lincoln's Legal Loyal League"), a secret group created to spread the news about the proclamation to slaves throughout the region.

> Union armies liberate Confederate slaves

Confederate leaders were outraged by Lincoln's action, predicting it would ignite a race war in the South. By contrast, Frederick Douglass, the African American abolitionist leader, was overjoyed at Lincoln's "righteous decree" for he knew that, despite its limitations, it would inspire abolitionists in the North and set in motion the eventual end of slavery throughout the United States.

As Lincoln had hoped, the Emancipation Proclamation did indeed aid the Union war effort, not only by enlisting blacks in the army and navy but also by undermining support for the Confederacy in Europe. The conversion of the Civil War from a conflict simply to restore the Union into a crusade to end slavery gave the federal war effort greater moral legitimacy in

Emancipation Proclamation (1863) Military order issued by President Abraham Lincoln that freed slaves in areas still controlled by the Confederacy.

Union view of the Emancipation Proclamation A thoughtful Lincoln composes the proclamation with the Constitution and the Holy Bible in his lap. The Scale of Justice hangs on the wall behind him.

the eyes of Europeans. At the same time, however, many northern Democrats savagely attacked Lincoln's proclamation, calling it dictatorial, unconstitutional, and catastrophic. "We Won't Fight to Free the Nigger," proclaimed one popular banner. A Massachusetts army officer agreed. "I am a strong Union man," he said, "but I am not willing to shed one drop of blood to fight Slavery."

As the war continued and Union armies advanced into the southern states, they liberated the slaves. At Camp Saxton, a former plantation on the coast of South Carolina near Beaufort, the 1st South Carolina Volunteers, a new Union army regiment made up of former slaves, gathered on January 1, 1863, to celebrate the Emancipation Proclamation. After the proclamation was read aloud, it was "cheered to the skies." As Colonel Thomas W. Higginson, a noted white abolitionist from Massachusetts who was the new unit's commander, unfurled an American flag, the black troops spontaneously began singing "My Country 'Tis of Thee / Sweet land of liberty / Of thee I sing!" Higginson reported his emotional reaction: "I never saw anything so electric; it made all other words cheap; it seemed the choked voice of a race at last unloosed. Just think of it!—the first day they had ever had a country, the first flag they had seen which promised anything to their people."

Fredericksburg

In his search for a new general to lead the Union war effort, Lincoln now made the worst choice of all. In the fall of 1862, he turned to 38-year-old Ambrose E. Burnside, a tall, imposing figure whose distinctive facial hair gave rise to the term "sideburns." Twice before, Burnside had turned down the job because he felt unfit for so large a command. He was right, as it turned out. Burnside was an eager fighter but a poor strategist who, according to

Confederate view of the Emancipation Proclamation
Surrounded by demonic faces hidden in his furnishings, Lincoln pens the proclamation with a foot trampling on the Constitution. The devil holds the inkwell before him.

Fanny Seward, the secretary of state's daughter, had "ten times as much heart as he has head." And the Union army soon paid for his mistakes.

On December 13, 1862, Burnside foolishly sent the 122,000 men in the Army of the Potomac west across the icy Rappahannock River to assault Lee's outnumbered forces, who were well entrenched on a line of ridges and behind stone walls west of Fredericksburg, Virginia, midway between Richmond and Washington, D.C. Confederate cannons and muskets chewed up the advancing federal soldiers as they crossed half a mile of open land. The assault was, a Union general regretted, "a great slaughter-pen," more like murder than warfare. Wave after wave of blue-clad troops surged toward the well-protected Confederates. None of the Union soldiers made it. The awful scene led Lee to remark: "It is well that war is so terrible—we should grow too fond of it." After attempting fourteen assaults and taking 12,600 casualties, compared with fewer than 5,300 for the Confederates, a weeping Burnside told his men to withdraw back across the river as darkness fell. As Burnside rode past his retreating men, his aide called for three cheers for their commander. All he got was sullen silence.

The year 1862 ended with forces in the East deadlocked and the Union advance in the West stalled. Union morale plummeted: northern Democrats were victorious in the fall Congressional elections, sharply reducing the Republican majorities in the House and the Senate. Many Democrats were calling for a negotiated peace. Republicans—even Lincoln's own cabinet members—grew increasingly critical of the president's leadership. "If there is a worse place than hell," Lincoln sighed, "I am in it." Newspapers circulated rumors that Lincoln was going to resign. General Burnside, too, was under fire, with some of his own officers eager to testify publicly to his shortcomings. One of them claimed that the general was "fast losing his mind."

> Lincoln loses support over deadlocked war

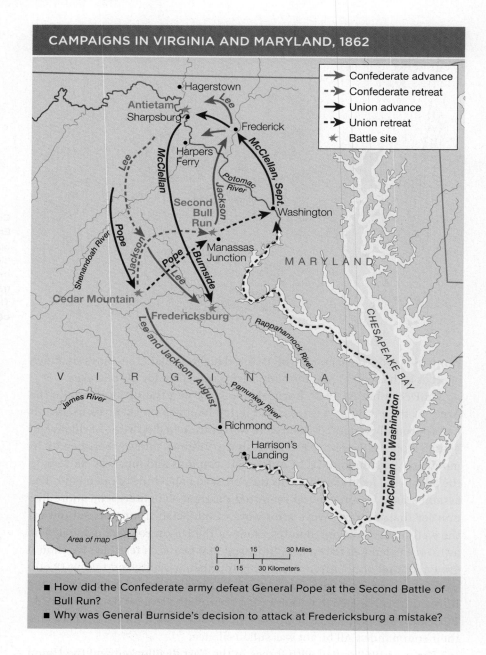

CAMPAIGNS IN VIRGINIA AND MARYLAND, 1862

Legend:
- → Confederate advance
- ⇢ Confederate retreat
- → Union advance
- ⇢ Union retreat
- ✳ Battle site

- Hagerstown
- Antietam
- Sharpsburg
- Harpers Ferry
- Frederick
- Second Bull Run
- Washington
- Manassas Junction
- Cedar Mountain
- Fredericksburg
- Richmond
- Harrison's Landing

MARYLAND
VIRGINIA

Shenandoah River
Potomac River
Rappahannock River
James River
Pamunkey River
CHESAPEAKE BAY

Lee, *McClellan*, *Jackson*, *Pope*, *Burnside*, *McClellan, Sept.*, *Lee*, *Pope*, *Lee and Jackson, August*, *McClellan to Washington*

Area of map

| 0 | 15 | 30 Miles |
| 0 | 15 | 30 Kilometers |

- How did the Confederate army defeat General Pope at the Second Battle of Bull Run?
- Why was General Burnside's decision to attack at Fredericksburg a mistake?

New York City Draft Riots

Northern resistance to the war effort

Lincoln's proclamation freeing slaves in the Confederacy created anxiety and anger among many laborers in the North who feared that freed southern blacks would eventually migrate north and take their jobs. In New York City, such fears erupted into violence. In July 1863, a group of 500 wage workers, led by volunteer firemen, assaulted the army draft office, shattering its windows, then burning it down. When the city police superintendent arrived at the scene, he was beaten unconscious, and the outnumbered policemen were forced to retreat. The rioters, now swollen by thousands of working-class whites, mostly Irishmen and including women and children, ruthlessly took out their frustrations over the unfair military draft on blacks. Mobs rampaged through the streets of Manhattan, randomly assaulting African Americans, beating them, dragging them through the streets, and lynching a disabled black man while chanting "Hurrah for Jeff Davis." Thugs also burned down over fifty buildings, including the mayor's home, police stations, two Protestant churches, and the Colored Orphan Asylum, forcing 233 children to flee. The violence went on for three days, killing 105 people and injuring thousands. Only the arrival of federal soldiers put an end to the rioting. Thousands of terrified blacks thereafter moved out of the city for fear of continuing racial violence. Similar riots occurred in other northern cities, including Boston.

Blacks in the Military

In July 1862, in an effort to strengthen the Union war effort, the U.S. Congress had passed the **Militia Act**, which authorized the army to use freed slaves as laborers or soldiers (they were already eligible to serve in the navy). But Lincoln did not encourage the use of freed slaves as soldiers because he feared the reaction in the border states where slavery remained in place. It was only after issuing the Emancipation Proclamation in September that the Union army aggressively recruited blacks. On May 22, 1863, the U.S. War Department created the Bureau of Colored Troops to recruit free blacks and freed slaves. More than 180,000 blacks enlisted in the new U.S. Colored Troops. Some 80 percent of them were from southern states, and 38,000 of them gave their lives. In the navy, African Americans accounted for about a fourth of all enlistments; of these, more than 2,800 died. Initially, blacks were not allowed in combat, but the need to win the prolonged war changed that. Once in battle, they fought tenaciously. A white Union army private reported in the late spring of 1863 that the black troops "fight like the Devil."

To be sure, a still-powerful racism in the North influenced the status of African Americans in the Union military. Many people who opposed slavery did not support racial equality. Black soldiers and sailors were placed in all-black units led by white officers. They were also paid less than whites ($7 per month for black recruits versus $16 for white recruits) and were ineligible for the enlistment bonus paid to whites. Still, as Frederick Douglass declared, "this is no time for hesitation. . . . This is our chance, and woe betide us if we fail to embrace it." Service in the Union army provided former slaves a unique opportunity to grow in confidence, awareness, and maturity. A northern social worker in the South Carolina Sea Islands was "astonished" at the positive effects of "soldiering" on ex-slaves: "Some who left here a month ago to join [the army were] cringing, dumpish, slow," but now they "are ready to look you in the eye—are wide awake and active." By mid-1863, African American units were fighting in battles. Commenting on Union victories at Port Hudson and Milliken's Bend, Louisiana, Lincoln reported that "some of our commanders . . . believe that . . . the use of colored troops constitutes the heaviest blow yet dealt to the rebels."

Black Union Army Sergeant Wearing his sergeant uniform and sword, he poses with a copy of J. T. Headley's *The Great Rebellion* in his hand.

Militia Act (1862) Congressional measure that permitted freed slaves to serve as laborers or soldiers in the United States Army.

CORE **OBJECTIVE**

3. Analyze how the war affected social and economic life in the North and South.

The War behind the Lines

Feeding, clothing, and supplying the vast armies required tremendous sacrifices on the home fronts, both North and South. Farms and villages were transformed into battlefields, churches became makeshift hospitals, civilian life was disrupted, and families grieved the soldiers who would not be coming home.

Women and the War

While breaking the bonds of slavery, the Civil War also loosened traditional restraints on female activity. "No conflict in history," a journalist wrote at the time, "was such a woman's war as the Civil War." Women on both sides played prominent roles. They worked in mills and factories, sewed uniforms, composed patriotic poems and songs, and raised money and supplies. In Greenville, South Carolina, when T. G. Gower went off to fight, his wife Elizabeth took over the family business, converting their carriage factory to produce military wagons and ambulances. Three thousand northern women worked as nurses with the U.S. Sanitary Commission, a civilian agency that provided medical relief and other services for soldiers. Other women, black and white, supported the freedmen's aid movement to help impoverished freed slaves.

In the North alone, some 20,000 women served as nurses or other health-related volunteers. The most famous nurses were Dorothea Lynde Dix and Clara Barton, both untiring volunteers in service to the wounded and the dying. Barton explained that her place was "anywhere between the bullet and the battlefield." Dix declared that nurses should be "sober, earnest, self-sacrificing, and self-sustained" women between the ages of thirty-five and fifty who could "bear the presence of suffering and exercise entire self-control" and who could be "calm, gentle, quiet, active, and steadfast in duty." Barton, who later founded the American Red Cross, claimed that the war advanced by fifty years the progress of women in gaining social and economic equality.

In many southern towns and counties, the home front became a world of white women and children and African American slaves. A resident of Lexington, Virginia, reported that there were "no men left" in town by mid-1862. Women suddenly found themselves full-time farmers or plantation managers, clerks, and teachers. Hundreds of women disguised themselves as men and fought in the war, and dozens served as spies. Others traveled with the armies, cooking meals, writing letters, and assisting with amputations. New Yorker Mary Edwards Walker, a Union battlefield surgeon, was captured and imprisoned by the Confederates for spying. She was the only woman in the war (and since) to be awarded the Congressional Medal of Honor, the nation's highest military award. In 1864, President Lincoln told a soldier that all the praise of women over the centuries did not do justice "for their conduct during the war."

Clara Barton She oversaw the distribution of medicines to Union troops and would later help found the American Red Cross.

Susie King Taylor Born into slavery, she served as a nurse in Union-occupied Georgia and operated a school for freedmen.

Government during the War

While freeing the slaves was a momentous social and economic revolution, an even broader political revolution began as a result of power in Congress shifting from the South to North after secession. Before the war, southern Democratic congressmen exercised considerable influence, but once the secessionists had abandoned Congress to the Republicans, a dramatic change occurred. Several Republican economic projects that had been stalled by southern opposition were adopted before the end of 1862. Congress passed a higher tariff bill to raise government revenue and "protect" American businesses from foreign competition. For the rest of the nineteenth century, U.S. manufacturers were the most protected in the world in terms of high federal tariffs discouraging foreign imports. The Republican Congress also approved construction of a transcontinental railroad to run westward through Omaha, Nebraska, to Sacramento, California. A **Homestead Act** granted 160 acres of public land to settlers who agreed to work the land for five years. The National Banking Act followed in 1863. It created a new federal banking system that effectively eliminated paper currency issued by state banks and created a system of national banks that could issue paper money. Two other key pieces of legislation were the **Morrill Land Grant Act** (1862), which provided federal aid to state-supported colleges and universities teaching "agriculture and mechanic arts," and the Contract Labor Act (1864), which encouraged the importation of immigrant labor. Congress also created a new cabinet-level agency, the Department of Agriculture. All of these wartime measures had long-term significance for the growth of the national economy—and the expansion of the federal government.

> Expanding a national economy and federal government

Union Finances

In December 1860, as southern states announced their plans to secede, the federal treasury was virtually empty. There was not enough cash on hand to fund a massive war. To meet the war's huge expenses, Congress focused on three options: raising taxes, printing paper money, and selling government bonds to investors. The taxes came chiefly in the form of the Morrill Tariff on imports and taxes on manufactures and nearly every profession. A butcher, for example, had to pay thirty cents for every head of beef he slaughtered, ten cents for every hog, and five cents for every sheep.

> Financing the war: Internal Revenue Service

In 1862, Congress created the Internal Revenue Service to implement the first income tax on citizens and corporations. The first income tax rate was 3 percent on those with annual incomes more than $800. The tax rate went up to 5 percent on incomes over $10,000. Yet very few people paid the taxes. Only 250,000 people out of a population of 39 million had income high enough to pay taxes. The concept of "progressive" taxation, in which tax rates rose with designated income levels, horrified Representative Justin S. Morrill, a Vermont Republican who had authored the Land Grant Act and the Tariff Act of 1862. He argued that the government should not tax "a man

Homestead Act (1862)
Legislation granting "homesteads" of 160 acres of government-owned land to settlers who agreed to work the land for at least five years.

Morrill Land Grant Act (1862)
Federal statute that allowed for the creation of land-grant colleges and universities, which were founded to provide technical education in agriculture, mining, and industry.

Financing the war: Legal Tender Act (1862)

[more] because he is richer than another. The very theory of our institutions is entire equality, that we make no distinction between the rich man and the poor man." Morrill lost the argument.

The new federal tax revenues trickled in so slowly—in the end they would meet only 21 percent of wartime expenditures—that Congress in 1862 resorted to printing paper money. Beginning with the Legal Tender Act of 1862, Congress ultimately authorized $450 million in paper currency, which soon became known as *greenbacks* because of the color of the ink used to print the bills. The decision to print paper money was extremely important for the economy. Unlike previous paper currencies issued by local banks, greenbacks could not be exchanged for gold or silver. Instead, their value relied upon public trust in the government. Many bankers were outraged by the issuance of the greenbacks, but the desperate need to finance the war demanded extreme measures. The federal government also relied upon the sale of bonds to help finance the war effort. A Philadelphia banker named Jay Cooke (sometimes tagged the "Financier of the Civil War") mobilized a nationwide campaign to sell $2 billion in government bonds to private investors.

Confederate Finances

Financing the Confederate war effort: Taxation, currency troubles, soaring inflation, and social unrest

Confederate finances were a disaster by comparison. The Confederate government had to create a treasury and a revenue-collecting system from scratch. Moreover, the South's agrarian economy was land-rich but cash-poor compared to that of the North. While the Confederacy owned 30 percent of America's assets (businesses, land, slaves) in 1861, its currency in circulation was only 12 percent of that in the North. In its first year, the Confederacy created a property tax, which should have yielded a hefty amount of revenue. But the collection of the taxes was left to the states, and the result was chaos. In 1863, the desperate Confederate Congress began taxing nearly everything, but enforcement was poor and evasion easy. Altogether, taxes covered no more than 5 percent of Confederate war costs; bond issues accounted for less than 33 percent; and treasury notes (paper money), for more than 66 percent. Over the course of the war, the Confederacy issued more than $1 billion in paper money, which, along with a shortage of consumer goods, caused prices to soar. By 1864 a turkey sold in the Richmond market for $100, flour brought $425 a barrel, and bacon was $10 a pound.

Such rampant inflation (price increases) caused great distress. Poverty drove some southerners to take desperate measures. Frustrations over the burdens of war increasingly erupted into rioting, looting, military desertions, and mass protests against the Confederate government. A poor farmer in Alabama refused to serve in the Confederate army because the war was being fought to preserve the "infurnal negroes" owned by wealthy planters. David Harris, another farmer, deserted from the army because the cause was lost: "I am now going to work instead of to the war," he wrote home.

Union Politics and Civil Liberties

Within his own Republican party, Lincoln faced a radical wing composed mainly of militant abolitionists. Led by Thaddeus Stevens in the House and Charles Sumner in the Senate, the Radical Republicans wanted Union armies to seize southern plantations and give the land to the former slaves. The majority of Republicans, however, continued to back Lincoln's reluctance to confiscate private property.

The Democratic party in the North suffered the loss of its southern wing and the death of its leader, Stephen A. Douglas, in June 1861. By and large, northern Democrats favored the war only for the purpose of restoring the Union "as it was" before 1860, giving reluctant support to Lincoln's war policies but opposing Republican economic legislation. So-called War Democrats, such as Tennessee senator Andrew Johnson and Secretary of War Edwin M. Stanton, backed Lincoln's policies, while a peace wing of the party preferred an end to the fighting, even if that meant risking the Union.

An extreme fringe of the peace wing flirted with outright disloyalty. The **Copperhead Democrats** (poisonous snakes), as they were called, were strongest in states such as Ohio, Indiana, and Illinois. They openly sympathized with the Confederacy and called for an end to the war.

Such support for the enemy led Lincoln to crack down hard. Like all wartime leaders, he faced the challenge of balancing the urgent needs of winning a war with the protection of civil liberties. Early in the war, Lincoln assumed emergency powers, including the power to suspend the writ of *habeas corpus*, which guarantees arrested citizens a speedy hearing before a judge. The Constitution states that the right of *habeas corpus* may be suspended only in cases of rebellion or invasion, but Supreme Court justice Roger Taney and several congressional leaders argued that Congress alone had the authority to take such action. By the Habeas Corpus Act of 1863, Congress authorized the president to suspend the writ. Thereafter, Union soldiers and local sheriffs arrested many Confederate sympathizers in the northern states. Union general Henry Halleck arrested one Missourian for saying, "[I] wouldn't wipe my ass with the stars and stripes."

> Violation of civil liberties in the North

Confederate Politics and States' Rights

Unlike Lincoln, Jefferson Davis never had to face a presidential contest. He and his vice president, Alexander Stephens, were elected without opposition in 1861 for a six-year term. But discontent grew as the war dragged on. Poor white southerners expressed bitter resentment of the planter elite while food grew scarce and prices skyrocketed. A bread riot in Richmond on April 2, 1863, ended only when President Davis himself threatened to shoot the protesters (mostly women).

Davis's greatest challenge came from the southern politicians who had embraced secession and then criticized the powers of the Confederate government in Richmond. As a general reported, "The state of feeling between the President [Davis] and Congress is bad—could not be worse." Critics

Copperhead Democrats
Democrats in northern states who opposed the Civil War and argued for an immediate peace settlement with the Confederates; Republicans labeled them "Copperheads," likening them to poisonous snakes.

asserted states' rights against the authority of the Confederate government, just as they had against the Union. Georgia's governor Joseph Brown hated Jefferson Davis, explaining that he joined the Confederacy to "sustain the rights of the states and prevent the consolidation of the Government, and I am still a *rebel* . . . no matter who may be in power."

States' rights vs. war effort

Among other fatal flaws, the Confederacy suffered from Davis's difficult personality. Whereas Lincoln was a pragmatist, Davis, blind in one eye and suffering chronic headaches, was a brittle ideologue with a stinging temper. Once he made a decision, nothing could change his mind, and he could never admit a mistake. One southern politician said that Davis was "as stubborn as a mule." Such a personality was ill suited to the chief executive of an infant—and fractious—nation. Cabinet members resigned almost as soon as they were appointed. During the four years of the Confederacy, there were three secretaries of state and six secretaries of war. Vice President Stephens carried on a running battle against President Davis's "military despotism," claiming Davis was so "timid, petulant, peevish, and obstinate" that he eventually left Richmond in 1862 to sulk at his Georgia home.

Chancellorsville

After the Union disaster at Fredericksburg at the end of 1862, Lincoln turned to General Joseph Hooker, a hard-fighting, hard-drinking leader whose fierceness had earned him the nickname "Fighting Joe." With a force of 130,000 men, the largest Union army yet gathered, and a brilliant plan, an overconfident Hooker failed his leadership test at Chancellorsville, not a town but a solitary home, the Chancellor House, surrounded by woods in eastern Virginia, in the first week of May, 1863. "My plans are perfect. . . . May God have mercy on General Lee," Hooker boasted, "for I will have none." He spoke too soon. The always bold Robert E. Lee, with perhaps half as many troops, split his army in thirds and gave Hooker a lesson in the art of elusive mobility when Stonewall Jackson's 28,000 Confederates again surprised the Union army, smashing into its exposed right flank, and forcing it to retreat. "It was pandemonium," recalled a Union soldier. "My God, my God," moaned Lincoln when he heard the news. "What will the country say?" The Confederate victory at Chancellorsville was the peak of Lee's military career, but it would also be his last significant victory.

CORE **OBJECTIVE**

4. Describe the military turning points in 1863 and 1864 that ultimately led to the Confederacy's defeat.

The Faltering Confederacy

The Confederate strategy of fighting largely a defensive war worked well in the early years of the war. As the armies maneuvered for battle in the spring of 1863, Robert E. Lee's superior generalship boosted Confederate spirits—until Lincoln found a commanding general as capable as Lee: Ulysses S. Grant.

Vicksburg

While Lee's army held the Federals at bay in the East, Ulysses S. Grant had been inching his army down the Mississippi River toward the Confederate stronghold of Vicksburg, a busy commercial town situated on high bluffs overlooking a sharp horseshoe bend in the river. Capturing the Rebel stronghold, Grant stressed, "was of the first importance." Vicksburg was the only rail and river junction between Memphis, Tennessee, and New Orleans. President Lincoln said Vicksburg held the "key" to a Union victory in the war. If Union forces could gain control of the Mississippi River, they could split the Confederacy in two and prevent Western food and livestock from reaching the Confederate armies in the East. While the Union navy ran gunboats and transports past the Confederate cannons overlooking the river, Grant moved his army eastward on a campaign through Mississippi that Lincoln later called "one of the most brilliant in the world." Grant captured Jackson, Mississippi, before pinning the 31,000 Confederates inside Vicksburg so tightly that "not a cat could have crept out . . . without being discovered."

In the **Battle of Vicksburg**, Grant decided to wear down the encircled Confederates through constant bombardment and gradual starvation. The Rebel soldiers and the city's residents were hopelessly trapped; they could neither escape nor be reinforced nor resupplied with food and ammunition. As the weeks passed, the besieged Confederates ate their horses and mules, then dogs and cats, and, finally, rats. The Confederate commander at Vicksburg wrote Jefferson Davis that the situation was "hopeless." A group of soldiers pleaded with their commander: "If you can't feed us, you had better surrender us, horrible as that idea is."

Battle of Vicksburg: Gaining control of the Mississippi River

Gettysburg

Vicksburg's plight led Davis to ask Robert E. Lee to send troops to break the siege. Lee, however, had a better idea. He would make another daring strike into the North in hopes of forcing the Union army surrounding Vicksburg to retreat. He also hoped that his northern offensive would persuade peace-seeking northern Copperhead Democrats to end the war on terms favorable to the Confederacy. A Confederate general said the invasion would "either destroy the Yankees or bring them to terms." Or be a disaster for Lee.

In June 1863, the fabled Army of Northern Virginia, which Lee said was made up of "invincible troops" who would "go anywhere and do anything if properly led," again moved northward across western Maryland, taking thousands of animals and wagons as well as throngs of slaves to support the army. The Confederates moved quickly. As a Rebel soldier said, he had enjoyed "breakfast in Virginia, whiskey in Maryland, and supper in Pennsylvania." A Maryland woman reported that the Confederate soldiers were "the dirtiest I ever saw, a most ragged, lean, and hungry set of wolves."

Once the Union commanders realized the Confederates were again moving north, they gave chase, but Lee lost track of the Federals because of the unexplained absence of General J. E. B. Stuart's 5,000 horse soldiers,

Battle of Vicksburg (1863) A protracted battle in northern Mississippi in which Union forces under Ulysses Grant besieged the last major Confederate fortress on the Mississippi River, forcing the inhabitants into starvation and then submission.

"A Harvest of Death" Timothy H. O'Sullivan's grim photograph of the dead at Gettysburg.

Battle of Gettysburg: Confederate counterstrategy— a northern offensive

Battle of Gettysburg (1863)
A monumental three-day battle in southern Pennsylvania, widely considered a turning point in the war, in which Union forces successfully countered a second Confederate invasion of the North.

who were Lee's "eyes and ears." Stuart, it turned out, had decided to create a panic in the Union capital by threatening an attack on Washington, D.C. On June 28, Lee uttered in exasperation: "I cannot think what has become of Stuart. I ought to have heard from him long before now."

Neither side expected Gettysburg, a crossroads farming town of 2,400 people in southeastern Pennsylvania, a land of rocky ridges and green hillsides crisscrossed with fences, to be the site of a monumental battle. Both armies were caught by surprise when Confederate troops entered the town at dawn on June 30 and encountered Union cavalry units that had been tracking their movements. The main forces of both sides—65,000 Confederates and 85,000 Federals—then raced to the scene, and on July 1, the two armies commenced the **Battle of Gettysburg**, the most dramatic contest of the war. As they prepared to fight, a Union cavalryman who sensed the importance of the coming battle, yelled at the soldiers from New York and Pennsylvania: "You stand alone, between the Rebel army and your homes. Fight like hell!"

Initially, the Confederates pushed the Federals out of the town, but the Union troops retreated into stronger positions on high ridges to the south and west. The new Union commander, the cautious and conservative General George Meade, rushed reinforcements to his new lines along the heights overlooking the town. On July 2, wave after wave of screaming Confederates assaulted Meade's army, pushing the Federal lines back across blood-soaked wheat fields and through peach orchards, but never breaking through. A wounded Confederate officer scrawled a note before he died: "Tell my father I died with my face to the enemy." Some 16,000 were killed or wounded on both sides during the inconclusive second day of fighting. But worse was yet to come.

The next day, July 3, against the advice of his senior general, James Longstreet, Robert E. Lee staked everything on one final assault on the well-defended Union lines along Cemetery Ridge. At about two o'clock on the broiling summer afternoon, three Confederate infantry divisions—about 12,500 men in all—emerged from the woods into the brilliant sunlight and prepared for a gallant but doomed attack. General George Pickett, commander of the lead division, told them to "Charge the enemy and remember Old Virginia!"

With drums pounding and bugles blaring, a gray wave began a desperate, mile-long advance up a grassy slope crisscrossed with wooden fences. Awaiting them behind a low stone wall at the top of the ridge were 120 Union cannons and thousands of rifles. It was suicide. As a Union soldier remembered, the Confederates "came on in magnificent order with the step of men who believed themselves invincible." Once the Federals were ordered to fire, the attacking Confederates were "enveloped in a dense cloud of dust. Arms, heads, blankets, guns, and knapsacks were tossed into the clear air." Only a few Rebels made it to the top of the ridge. A general climbed atop the stone wall and shouted: "Come on, boys! Give them the cold steel! Who will follow me?" Two minutes later, he was dead—as was the Confederate assault—when Union soldiers held in reserve rushed to close the gap in their lines.

Pickett's charge

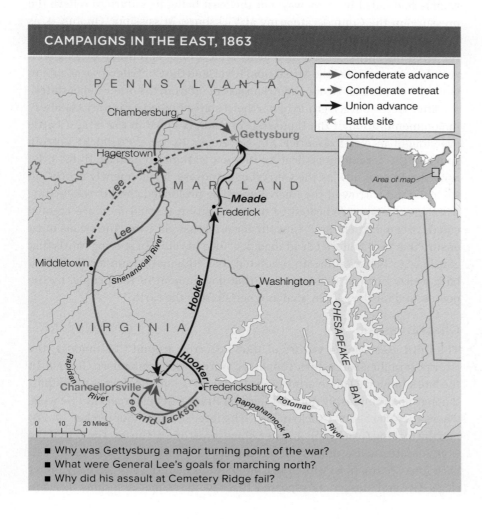

CAMPAIGNS IN THE EAST, 1863

- Why was Gettysburg a major turning point of the war?
- What were General Lee's goals for marching north?
- Why did his assault at Cemetery Ridge fail?

What General Lee had called the "grand charge" was, in the end, a grand failure. As he watched the survivors returning from the bloody field, Lee muttered, "All this has been my fault." He then ordered General Pickett to prepare his battered division for another attack, only to have Pickett tartly reply: "General Lee, I have no division now." Half of his men lay dead or wounded. Some 42,000 on both sides were killed, wounded, or missing over three days at Gettysburg. A Union soldier who witnessed the slaughter on the final day wrote home: "Great God! When will this horrid war stop?"

Again, as after Antietam, Lee's mangled army was forced to retreat back to Virginia in a driving rain—and again, the Federals failed to give chase. Had General Meade pursued Lee's army across Maryland, he might have ended the war, but yet again the winning army failed to capitalize on its victory. President Lincoln was outraged that Meade allowed the Confederates to get away: "We had them within our grasp!" he thundered to his assistant. Lee had escaped to fight again—and the war would grind on for another twenty-one months.

The last Confederate invasion of the North was over. Lee's desperate gamble had failed in every way, not the least being its failure to relieve the pressure on the Confederate army at Vicksburg, Mississippi. On July 4, as Lee's army left Pennsylvania, the Confederate commander at Vicksburg surrendered his entire 30,000-man army after a forty-seven-day siege. Union vessels now controlled the Mississippi River, and the Confederacy was split in two, with Louisiana, Texas, and Arkansas cut off from the other Rebel states.

After Gettysburg, a group of northern states funded a military cemetery in commemoration of the thousands of soldiers killed in the largest battle ever fought in North America. On November 19, 1863, President Lincoln spoke at the ceremony dedicating the new national cemetery. In his brief remarks, known now as the Gettysburg Address, he eloquently expressed the pain and sorrow of the uncivil war. The prolonged conflict was testing whether a nation "dedicated to the proposition that all men are created equal . . . can long endure." Lincoln declared that all living Americans must ensure that the "honored dead" had not "died in vain." In stirring words that continue to inspire, Lincoln predicted that "this nation, under God, shall have a new birth of freedom—and that government of the people, by the people, and for the people, shall not perish from the earth."

Chattanooga

> The Battle of Chattanooga: South loses the war in the West

The third great Union victory of 1863 occurred around Chattanooga, the river port railhead of eastern Tennessee and gateway to northern Georgia. In the late summer, a Union army led by General William Rosecrans took Chattanooga and then rashly pursued General Bragg's Rebel forces into Georgia, where they clashed at Chickamauga. The intense battle (September 19–20) had the makings of a Union disaster, since it was one of the few times that the Confederates had a numerical advantage. The battered Union forces fell back into Chattanooga while the Confederates held the city virtually under siege. General Rosecrans reported that "we have met a serious disaster.

Enemy overwhelmed us, drove our right, pierced our center, and scattered troops there." Lincoln urged him to hang on: "If we can hold Chattanooga, and East Tennessee, I think [the] rebellion must dwindle and die." The Union command rushed in reinforcements, and on November 24 and 25, the Federal troops dislodged the Confederates from Lookout Mountain and Missionary Ridge, thereby gaining effective control of east Tennessee. The South had lost the war in the West.

The North Prevails

The dramatic Union victories at Vicksburg, Gettysburg, and Chattanooga turned the tide against the Confederacy. General Lee offered his resignation to Jefferson Davis, but it was refused. He told Lee he could not find a better commander. During the summer and fall of 1863, however, Lincoln's generals in the East lost the momentum that Gettysburg had provided, thereby allowing the Army of Northern Virginia to nurse its wounds and regroup. By 1864, the tenacious Lee was ready to renew the war: "in fine spirits and anxious for a fight." Still, the tone had changed. Earlier, Confederate leaders assumed they could actually win the war and secure their independence. Now, they began to worry about defeat. A Confederate officer in Richmond, writing in his diary after the defeats at Gettysburg and Vicksburg, noted that just a few months earlier the Confederacy had been on the "pinnacle of success—today absolute ruin seems to be our fortune. The Confederacy totters to its destruction." Mary Chesnut of South Carolina confessed in her diary that the war was not going well for her beloved Confederacy. On January 1, 1864, she wrote: "God help my country!"

A Wartime Election

War or no war, 1864 was still a presidential election year. Radical Republicans, upset with the lengthy Union war effort, tried to prevent Lincoln's nomination for a second term, but he consistently outmaneuvered them. Once Lincoln was assured of the party's nomination, he selected Andrew Johnson, a "war Democrat" from Tennessee, as his running mate on the "National Union" ticket, so named to promote bipartisanship during the war. At their 1864 national convention in Chicago, the Democrats called for an immediate end to the war. They nominated General George B. McClellan, the former Union commander who had sparred with Lincoln, his commander in chief, often calling him a "gorilla" and "an idiot." The Confederates hoped that if they could gain a military advantage it might help lead to Lincoln's defeat in November.

Lincoln doubted that the war-weary voters would give him a second term. To boost his reelection chances in the 1864 election, the president brought his best general, Ulysses S. Grant, to Washington, D.C., in March 1864, gave him overall command of the Union war effort, and promised him all the troops and supplies he needed. A New York newspaper reported that Lincoln's presidency was now "in the hands of General Grant, and the failure of the General will be the overthrow of the president."

> Ulysses S. Grant takes command of Union forces

Ulysses S. Grant At his headquarters in City Point (now Hopewell), Virginia.

Grant's Strategy

The cigar-chewing Grant was a hard-nosed warrior. One soldier said that Grant always looked like he was "determined to drive his head through a brick wall and was about to do it." The Union commander had a simple concept of war: "Find out where your enemy is, get to him as soon as you can, and strike him as hard as you can, and keep moving on"—regardless of the number of dead and wounded.

Grant dramatically changed the Union military strategy. He planned for the three largest Union armies, one in Virginia, one in Tennessee, and one in Louisiana to launch offensives in the spring of 1864 in which the fighting would never cease. No more short battles followed by long pauses. The Union would force the outnumbered Confederates to keep fighting constantly, thereby wearing them out. Grant assigned his trusted friend and fierce fighter, General William Tecumseh Sherman, a rail-thin, red-haired Ohioan, to lead the Union army in Tennessee and apply Grant's strategy of "complete conquest" to invade Georgia and the heart of the Confederacy. Grant and Sherman would now wage total war, confiscating or destroying civilian property that might be of use to the military. It was a ruthless and costly plan, but in the end effective.

Grant's Pursuit of Lee

In May 1864, the Union's massive Army of the Potomac, numbering about 115,000 soldiers to Lee's 65,000, moved south across the Rappahannock and Rapidan Rivers in eastern Virginia. In the nightmarish Battle of the Wilderness (May 5–6), the armies fought blindly through dense woods thick with vines, thorns, and briars. It was a hellish scene; the tangled underbrush caught fire from exploding artillery shells, and many wounded men burned to death. Grant's men suffered heavier casualties than the Confederates, but the Rebels were running out of replacements. Always before, when bloodied by Lee's troops, Union forces had pulled back to rest and recover, but Grant continued to push southward, keeping the pressure on Lee. "Whatever happens," he assured Lincoln, "we will not retreat." Grant "was like a bulldog," Lincoln said. "Let him get his teeth in, and nothing can shake him loose."

In the first days of June 1864, just as Republican party leaders were gathering to renominate Lincoln as their presidential candidate for the fall election, Grant attacked Lee's well-entrenched army at Cold Harbor near the Chickahominy River, ten miles east of Richmond. In twenty minutes, almost 4,000 attacking Federals, caught in a blistering cross-fire, were killed or wounded. A Confederate commander reported that "it was not war; it was murder."

Grant later admitted that the botched attack was his greatest mistake. Critics, including Lincoln's wife Mary, called him "the Butcher" after Cold Harbor. Yet he knew that his massive army could replace its dead and wounded; the Confederates could not. While the Confederates were winning battles, they were losing more and more men who could not be replaced.

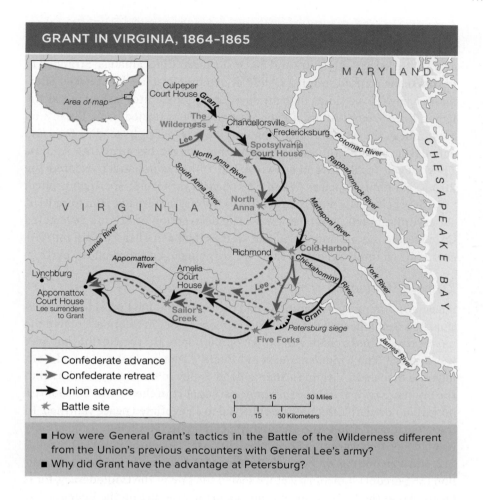

GRANT IN VIRGINIA, 1864–1865

Area of map

MARYLAND

Culpeper Court House • Grant

The Wilderness

Chancellorsville • • Fredericksburg

Potomac River

Lee

North Anna River

Spotsylvania Court House

Rappahannock River

South Anna River

VIRGINIA

North Anna

Mattaponi River

CHESAPEAKE BAY

James River

Appomattox River

Richmond •

Cold Harbor

Chickahominy River

York River

Lynchburg •

Amelia Court House

Lee

Appomattox Court House Lee surrenders to Grant

Sailor's Creek

Grant

Petersburg siege

James River

Five Forks

→ Confederate advance
⇢ Confederate retreat
→ Union advance
★ Battle site

0   15   30 Miles
0   15   30 Kilometers

■ How were General Grant's tactics in the Battle of the Wilderness different from the Union's previous encounters with General Lee's army?
■ Why did Grant have the advantage at Petersburg?

Grant kept the pressure on. He brilliantly maneuvered his battered forces around Lee's army and headed for Petersburg, twenty-five miles south of Richmond, where the major railroads converged. The opposing armies then dug in along long lines of trenches above and below Petersburg. Grant telegraphed Lincoln that he intended "to fight it out on this line if it takes all summer." For nine months, the two armies faced each other down. Grant's troops, twice as numerous as the Confederate army, were generously supplied by Union vessels moving up the James River, while Lee's men, hungry and cold, wasted away. Petersburg had become Lee's prison while disasters piled up for the Confederacy elsewhere.

Sherman Pushes through the South

Meanwhile, General Sherman moved his army south from Chattanooga through the Georgia mountains toward the crucial railroad hub of Atlanta. He sent a warning to the city's residents intended to frighten them: "prepare for my coming." By the middle of July, Sherman's troops had reached the outskirts of Atlanta, trapping the Confederate soldiers there. Their commander, General John Bell Hood of Texas, was a recklessly aggressive

The burning of Atlanta

fighter. A Confederate senator's wife said that "a braver man, a purer patriot, a more gallant soldier never breathed than General Hood." He had had an arm shattered at Gettysburg and had lost a leg at Chickamauga. Strapped to his horse, he refused simply to "defend" Atlanta; instead, he attacked Sherman's army. Three times in eight days, the Confederates lashed out at the Union lines around Atlanta. Each time they were turned back. Finally, on September 1 the outnumbered Confederates, desperately needing food and supplies, evacuated the city. Sherman then moved his army into Atlanta. They stayed until November, when the Union commander ordered the 20,000 residents to leave. When city officials protested, Sherman replied: "War is cruelty." His men then set fire to the city's railroads, iron foundries, shops, mills, hotels, and businesses. The destruction of Atlanta devastated Confederate morale. Mary Chesnut "felt as if all were dead within me, forever." She gloomily predicted that "we are going to be wiped off the earth."

Lincoln Reelected

> Abraham Lincoln reelected (1864)

Sherman's conquest of Atlanta turned the tide of the 1864 presidential election. As a Republican senator said, the Union victory in Georgia "created the most extraordinary change in public opinion here [in the North] that ever was known." The Union conquest of Mobile, Alabama, in August, and Confederate defeats in Virginia's Shenandoah Valley in October contributed to the dramatic revival of Lincoln's political support in the North. The South's hope that northern discontent would lead to a negotiated peace vanished. In the **election of 1864**, the Democratic candidate, McClellan, carried only New Jersey, Delaware, and Kentucky, with just 21 electoral votes to Lincoln's 212, and won only 1.8 million popular votes (45 percent) to Lincoln's 2.2 million (55 percent). Lincoln's victory sealed the fate of the Confederacy, for it ensured that the Union armies would keep the pressure on the Rebels.

While Confederate forces made their last stands, Abraham Lincoln prepared for his second term as president. He was the first president since Andrew Jackson to have been reelected. The weary commander in chief had made many mistakes and weathered constant criticism during his first term, but with the war nearing its end, Lincoln now received well-deserved praise. The *Chicago Tribune* observed that the president "has slowly and steadily risen in the respect, confidence, and admiration of the people."

Sherman's "March to the Sea"

In November 1864, Sherman's army began its fabled **"March to the Sea,"** advancing rapidly through Georgia, where no organized Confederate armies remained. He planned to "whip the rebels, to humble their pride, to follow them into their inmost recesses, and make them fear and dread us." Hood's Confederate army, meanwhile, went in the opposite direction, pushing northward into Tennessee, trying to lure Sherman into chasing them. But the Union commander refused to take the bait. He was determined to push southward through Georgia and into South Carolina, the seedbed of secession.

election of 1864 Abraham Lincoln's successful re-election campaign, capitalizing on Union military successes in Georgia, to defeat his Democratic opponent, former general George B. McClellan, who ran on a peace platform.

Sherman's "March to the Sea" (1864) The Union army's devastating march through Georgia from Atlanta to Savannah led by General William T. Sherman, intended to demoralize civilians and destroy the resources the Confederate army needed to fight.

In the Battle of Franklin (November 30, 1864), near Nashville, General Hood, against the advice of his generals, sent his army across two miles of open ground defended by dug-in Union troops backed by cannons. It was another example of valiant suicide. In a few hours, Hood lost six generals and 1,750 men, more than had been killed in "Pickett's Charge" at Gettysburg. A Confederate captain, scarred by the battle's senseless butchery, wrote that the "wails and cries of the widows and orphans made at Franklin, Tennessee, will heat up the fires of the bottomless pit to burn the soul of General J. B. Hood for murdering their husbands and fathers." Finally, in the Battle of Nashville (December 15–16), the Federals scattered what was left of Hood's army. A few days later, Hood was relieved of his command. One of Hood's soldiers said that he was a "brave, good, noble, and gallant" man, "but as a general he was a failure."

Meanwhile, Sherman's 62,000 soldiers pushed southward across Georgia. His troops lived off the land, destroying plantations, farms, crops, and rail lines. Sherman said he wanted to "make Georgia howl" so as to convince the people to surrender. "We are not only fighting hostile armies," Sherman explained, "but a hostile people" who must "feel the hard hand of war." By the time Sherman's army arrived in Savannah, on the coast, after a month of plundering their way across the Georgia countryside, his troops had freed more than 40,000 slaves, burned scores of plantations, and destroyed railroads. On December 24, 1864, Sherman sent a whimsical telegram to President Lincoln offering him the city of Savannah as a Christmas present. After the war, a Confederate officer acknowledged that Sherman's march through Georgia was well conceived and well managed. "I don't think there was ever

William Tecumseh Sherman
Sherman's campaign developed into a war of maneuver, without the pitched battles of Grant's campaign, but he pushed relentlessly through Georgia.

Destroying southern railroads
Sherman's troops cut a swath of destruction across Georgia in his "March to the Sea." Here, Union troops rip up railroad tracks in Atlanta.

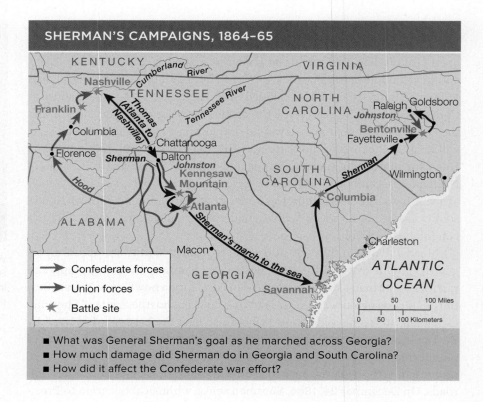

SHERMAN'S CAMPAIGNS, 1864–65

■ What was General Sherman's goal as he marched across Georgia?
■ How much damage did Sherman do in Georgia and South Carolina?
■ How did it affect the Confederate war effort?

an army in the world that would have behaved better, in a similar expedition, in an enemy country. Our army certainly wouldn't have."

After occupying Savannah, Sherman's army crossed the Savannah River into South Carolina, the "hell-hole of secession." Sherman reported that his "whole army is burning with an insatiable desire to wreak vengeance upon South Carolina. I almost tremble at her fate, but feel she deserves all that seems in store for her." The Union army burned more than a dozen South Carolina towns, including the state capital of Columbia, which was captured on February 17, 1865.

During the late winter and early spring of 1865, the shrinking Confederacy found itself besieged on all sides. Defeat was in the air. But Jefferson Davis rejected any talk of surrender. If the Confederate armies should be defeated, he wanted the soldiers to scatter and fight an unending guerrilla war. "The war came and now it must go on," he stubbornly insisted, "till the last man of this generation falls in his tracks, and his children seize his musket and fight our battle."

Appomattox

Confederate surrender at Appomattox Court House

During the spring of 1865, General Grant's army kept pushing, probing, and battering the Rebels defending Petersburg, Virginia, twenty miles south of Richmond. The badly outnumbered Confederates were slowly starving. Something had to give. On April 2, 1865, Lee's army tried to break out of

Petersburg in a desperate flight south. But the Union army was in hot pursuit. On April 7, Grant sent a note to Lee urging him to surrender. With his army virtually surrounded, Lee recognized that "there is nothing left for me to do but go and see General Grant, and I would rather die a thousand deaths."

On April 9 (Palm Sunday) the tall, dignified Lee, in his formal dress uniform, met the short, mud-spattered Grant in the village of **Appomattox Court House**. Grant displayed extraordinary generosity in keeping with Lincoln's desire for a gracious peace. At Lee's request, he let the Confederates keep their pistols, horses, and mules, and he ensured that none of them would be tried for treason, despite the demands of many Radical Republicans in Congress. Lee then confessed that his men were starving, and Grant ordered that they be provided 25,000 rations. After signing the surrender documents, Lee mounted his horse and returned to his army.

The next day, as the gaunt, hungry Confederate troops formed ranks for the last time, Joshua Chamberlain, the Union general in charge of the surrender ceremony, ordered his soldiers to salute their foes as the Rebel soldiers paraded past to give up their weapons. His Confederate counterpart signaled his men to do likewise. Chamberlain remembered that there was not a sound—no trumpets or drums, no cheers or jeers, simply an "awed stillness . . . as if it were the passing of the dead." The remaining Confederate forces surrendered in May. Jefferson Davis fled Richmond by train ahead of the advancing Federal troops, only to be captured in Georgia by Union cavalry on May 10. He was eventually imprisoned in Virginia for two years.

The brutal war was at last over. Upon learning of the Union victory, John Wilkes Booth, a popular young actor in Washington, D.C., wrote in his diary that "something decisive and great must be done" to avenge the Confederate defeat.

A Transforming War

The Civil War was the most traumatic event in American history. "We have shared the incommunicable experience of war," reflected Oliver Wendell Holmes Jr., the twice-wounded Union officer who would one day become the nation's leading jurist. "We have felt, we still feel, the passion of life to its top. . . . In our youth, our hearts were touched by fire." In Virginia, elderly Edmund Ruffin, the arch secessionist planter who had been given the honor of firing the first shots at Fort Sumter, was so distraught by the Confederate surrender that he put his rifle barrel in his mouth and blew off the top of his head.

The long war changed the nation in profound ways. A *New York Times* editorial said that the war left "nothing as it found it. . . . It leaves us a different people in everything." The war's terrible ferocity shattered countless lives and destroyed the South's economy, many of its railroads and factories, much of its livestock, and several of its cities. The former Confederacy was a

> CORE **OBJECTIVE**
> **5.** Explain how the Civil War changed the nation.

Appomattox Court House Virginia village where Confederate general Robert E. Lee surrendered to Union general Ulysses S. Grant on April 9, 1865.

Why Was the North Victorious in the Civil War?

Historians have long debated the reasons for the Union's defeat of the Confederacy in the Civil War and will continue to do so. Clearly, the North had many advantages, particularly in population and economic and financial resources.

	North	South
Population	22 million people	9 million people
Manufacturing	93% of nation's manufactured goods 97% of nation's firearms 96% of nation's railroad equipment	7% of nation's manufactured goods
Finance	**Nation's financial center** Banking reforms during the war allowed the Union to sell $2 billion in bonds to private investors and print $450 million in paper money	**Land-rich but cash-poor** Struggle to raise revenue to support the war; printing over $1 billion in paper currency without backing by revenue collection or bonds resulted in rampant inflation
Geography	Securing Union's border states gave Union troops greater access to rivers on which to launch their invasions	Much of war was fought in the South, giving Confederacy a "home-field advantage" and support from civilian population Challenge for Union to conquer large geographical area of Confederacy

landscape of ruin, wreckage, and bankruptcy. In 1860, the northern and southern economies were essentially equal in size. By 1865, the southern economy's productivity had been cut in half. Many among the southern economic and political leaders had either been killed during the war or had seen their plantations and businesses destroyed.

The Union Preserved

Expansion of federal government and power shift to the North

The war also ended the Confederacy and preserved the Union, shifted the political balance of power from South to North, in Congress the U.S. Supreme Court, and the presidency, and boosted the northern economy. The Homestead Act (1862) made more than a billion acres in the West available to the landless. The war greatly expanded the power and scope of the federal government at the expense of states' rights. In 1860, the annual federal budget was $63 million; by 1865, it was over $1 billion. In winning the war, the federal government had become the nation's largest employer.

	North	South
African Americans and Slavery	**Militia Act (1862)** Authorized African American enlistment into Union Army Some 180,000 served, over 80% in South	More than 30% of population, or 3.5 million, were slaves at the start of Civil War **Emancipation Proclamation (1863)** damaged southern economy, encouraged slaves to run away, enlist with Union, or passively resist in the South; eliminated chance of a European power (such as England or France) becoming Confederate military ally
Leadership	The pragmatic President Lincoln favored tenacious generals such as Ulysses S. Grant and William T. Sherman, over the cautious and weak Grant and Sherman developed the "total war" strategy that defeated Confederate forces in the West and eventually subdued the Confederate rebellion	Rigid and doctrinaire, President Davis was unable to maintain political support or public confidence South started with superior military leaders, but many were killed throughout war Southern governors asserted states' rights and resisted Davis's efforts to centralize power and drive war effort

QUESTIONS FOR ANALYSIS

1. What were the Union's key advantages?

2. How did President Lincoln's decision to make the Civil War a fight to end slavery affect the outcome?

3. Given critical Northern advantages, why was the Confederacy able to hold out for so long?

By the end of the war, the Union was spending $2.5 million per day on the military effort. Samuel Colt of New Haven, Connecticut, manufactured Colt pistols for the army. "Run the armory day and night with double sets of hands," he told his foreman. The war-related expenditures by the Union generated whole new industries to meet the military's needs for weapons, uniforms, food, equipment, and supplies. The massive amount of preserved food required by the Union armies, for example, helped create the canning industry and transformed Chicago into the meatpacking capital of the world. Federal contracts also accelerated the growth of new industries such as iron/steel and petroleum products, thus laying the groundwork for the postwar economic boom led by tycoons such as J. Pierpont Morgan, John D. Rockefeller, Andrew W. Mellon, and Andrew Carnegie. Ohio senator John Sherman, in a letter to his brother, General William T. Sherman, said the war had dramatically expanded the vision "of leading capitalists" who now talk of earning "millions as confidently as formerly of thousands."

The war boosts northern industries

The First "Modern" War

In many respects, the Civil War became the first modern war. Its scope and scale were unprecedented, as it was fought across the entire continent, from Pennsylvania to New Mexico and from Florida to Kansas. One of every twelve men on both sides served in the war, and few families were unaffected. Over 730,000 soldiers and sailors (37,000 of whom were blacks fighting for the Union side) died in the conflict, 50 percent more than the number who would die in the Second World War. Of the surviving combatants, 50,000 returned home with one or more limbs amputated. Disease, however, was the greatest threat to soldiers, killing twice as many as were lost in battle. Some 50,000 civilians were also killed during the war.

Unlike previous conflicts, much of the fighting in the Civil War was "modern" in that it was distant, impersonal, and mechanical. Men were often killed at long distance, without ever knowing who had fired the shots that felled them. The opposing forces used an array of new weapons and instruments of war: cannons with "rifled," or grooved, barrels for greater accuracy; repeating rifles; ironclad ships; railroad artillery; the first military telegraph; observation balloons; and, wire entanglements. The war was also modern in that civilians could follow its activities by reading the popular newspapers that sent reporters to the front lines, or by visiting exhibitions of photographs taken at the battlefields and camps.

Social Changes Wrought by the War

The war also generated significant social changes. Women's roles were transformed. "No conflict in history," a journalist wrote at the time, "was such a woman's war as the Civil War." The requirements of war enabled women to become nurses, farm or business managers, and executives of new organizations. So many ministers left their congregations to become military chaplains that lay people, especially women, assumed even greater responsibility for religious activities in churches and synagogues. The war's awful carnage took a terrible personal toll on women. Hundreds of thousands of women were widowed by the war or saw their lives permanently transformed by the return of husbands with missing limbs or ghastly wounds.

The war also transformed the religious life of African Americans, many of whom saw the war and emancipation as a modern biblical Exodus: God's miraculous intervention on behalf of a chosen people in bondage. In those areas of the South taken over by Union armies, freed slaves were able to create their own churches for the first time.

Thirteenth Amendment

By far, however, the most important result of the war was the liberation of slaves. Lincoln had not intended to end slavery when the war began, but the course of the war changed his mind. The Emancipation Proclamation had freed only those slaves in areas still controlled by the Confederacy. As the war entered its final months, however, freedom for all slaves emerged more fully as a legal reality. Three major steps occurred in January 1865, three months before the war ended: Missouri and then Tennessee abolished slavery by state action, and, at the insistent urging of President Lincoln, the U.S. House of Representatives passed an amendment to the U.S. Constitution that banned slavery everywhere. Upon ratification by three-fourths of the reunited states, the **Thirteenth Amendment** became law eight months after the war ended, on December 18, 1865. It removed any lingering doubts about the legality of emancipation. By then, in fact, slavery remained only in the border states of Kentucky and Delaware.

The Debate Continues

In some respects, the Civil War has not yet been resolved. Historians have provided conflicting assessments of the Union victory. Some have focused on the inherent weaknesses of the Confederacy: its lack of industry and railroads, the tensions between the states and the central government in Richmond, poor political leadership, faulty political-military coordination and communication, the expense of preventing slave rebellions and runaways, and the advantages in population and resources enjoyed by the North. Still others have highlighted the erosion of Confederate morale in the face of terrible food shortages, soaring prices, and unimaginable human losses.

The debate over why the North won and the South lost will probably never end, but as in other modern wars, firepower and manpower were essential factors. Robert E. Lee's own explanation retains an enduring accuracy: "After four years of arduous service marked by unsurpassed courage and fortitude, the Army of Northern Virginia has been compelled to yield to overwhelming numbers and resources." Whatever the reasons, the North's victory resolved a key issue: no state could divorce itself from the Union. The Union, as Lincoln had insisted, was indissoluble, now and forever.

Thirteenth Amendment (1865) Amendment to the U.S. Constitution that freed all slaves in the United States.

■ **Civil War Strategies** Southerners were optimistic when the war began. The Confederates had a geographic advantage in that they were fighting a defensive war on their own territory. Confederate diplomacy also anticipated massive support from Britain and France, support that never materialized. The Union, however, held strong advantages in terms of population and industrial development. The Union quickly launched a campaign to seize the Confederate capital, Richmond, Virginia. Initial hopes for a rapid victory died at the First Battle of Bull Run. The Union then adopted the *Anaconda Plan*, which involved imposing a naval blockade on southern ports and slowly crushing resistance on all fronts.

■ **Emancipation Proclamation** Gradually, Lincoln came to see that winning the war required ending slavery. He justified the *Emancipation Proclamation* (1862) as a military necessity because it would deprive the South of its captive labor force. After the *Battle of Antietam* in September 1862, he announced his plans to free the slaves. He hoped that southern states would return to the Union before his January 1, 1863 deadline, when all slaves living in areas under Confederate control were declared free. Many slaves freed themselves by escaping to Union army camps. In July 1862, with the *Militia Act*, Congress had declared that freed slaves could join the Union army. During 1863, blacks, both free and freed, joined the Union army in large numbers, giving the Union military a further advantage over the Confederacy. Although the Emancipation Proclamation announced the war aim of abolishing slavery, it freed only those in areas still under Confederate control.

■ **Wartime Home Fronts** The Union government proved much more capable with finances than did its Confederate counterparts. Through a series of tariffs, income taxes, bond issues, and banking reforms, the Union was better able to absorb the war's soaring costs. In the absence of the southern Democrats in Congress, the Republican-controlled Congress also created a cabinet-level Department of Agriculture, approved a higher tariff, a transcontinental railroad, a *Homestead Act*, and a Contract Labor Act, all of which accelerated Union settlement of the West and the growth of a national economy. The Confederate finances, on the other hand, were pitiful in the cash-poor South. The Confederate treasury department was forced to print so much money that it created spiraling inflation of consumer prices and civil unrest. Also, most of the warfare took place in the South; thus, although the North had more casualties, the physical impact on the South was much greater.

■ **The Winning Union Strategy** The Union victories at the *Battles of Vicksburg* and *Gettysburg* in July 1863 were a major turning point of the war. With the capture of Vicksburg, Union forces cut the Confederacy in two, depriving armies in the east of western supplies and manpower. General Robert E. Lee and the Army of Northern Virginia lost a third of its troops after the defeat at Gettysburg, forcing the Confederates to adopt a defensive strategy. In 1864, Lincoln placed General Ulysses S. Grant in charge of the Union's war efforts, and he initiated a strategy to make the best use of the Union's advantages in manpower and supplies. For the next year, his forces constantly attacked Lee's in Virginia while, farther south, General William T. Sherman conquered Georgia and South Carolina. *Sherman's "March to the Sea"* across Georgia destroyed plantations, railroads, and morale. Sherman's successes helped propel Lincoln to victory in the *election of 1864*. After that, southern resistance wilted, forcing Lee to surrender his army to General Grant at *Appomattox Court House* in April 1865.

■ **The Significance of the Civil War** The Civil War involved the largest number of casualties of any American war. The Union's victory changed the course of the nation's development. Most important, the Civil War brought about the destruction of slavery. Not only did the power of the federal government increase as a result of the war, but the center of political and economic power shifted away from the South and the planter class. The Republican-controlled Congress enacted many pieces of legislation favored by northern voters that would drive the nation's economic development for the rest of the century.

KEY TERMS

CHRONOLOGY

April 1861	Virginia, North Carolina, Tennessee, and Arkansas join Confederacy; West Virginia splits from Virginia to stay with Union
July 1861	First Battle of Bull Run (Manassas)
March–July 1862	Peninsular Campaign
April–August 1862	Battles of Shiloh, Second Bull Run, and Antietam; New Orleans seized by Union forces
July 1862	Congress passes the Militia Act
September 1862	Lincoln issues Emancipation Proclamation
May–July 1863	Siege of Vicksburg, Battle of Gettysburg
November 1863	Battle of Chattanooga
March 1864	General Grant takes charge of Union military operations
September 1864	General Sherman seizes and burns Atlanta
November 1864	Lincoln is reelected
	Sherman's "March to the Sea"
April 9, 1865	General Lee surrenders at Appomattox Court House
1865	Thirteenth Amendment is ratified

INQUIZITIVE

Go to InQuizitive to see what you've learned—and learn what you've missed—with personalized feedback along the way.

***A VISIT FROM THE OLD MISTRESS* (1876)** This powerful painting by Winslow Homer depicts a plantation mistress visiting her former slaves in the postwar South. Although their living conditions are humble, these freedwomen stand firmly and eye-to-eye with the woman who kept them in bondage.

Reconstruction

1865–1877

In the spring of 1865, the Civil War was finally over. The United States was a "new nation," said an Illinois congressman, because it was now "wholly free." At a frightful cost of over 700,000 lives and the destruction of the southern economy, the Union had won the terrible war, and some 4 million enslaved Americans in the South and border states had seized their freedom. This was the most dramatic social change in the history of the nation. No longer would enslaved workers be whipped by their white owners, nor sold and separated from their families, nor prevented from learning to read and write or attending church. "I felt like a bird out of a cage," said former slave Houston Holloway from Georgia. "Amen. Amen. Amen. I could hardly ask to feel any better than I did that day."

In some places it took longer for freedom to be recognized and enforced. In 1865, Henry Adams left the Louisiana plantation where he had been enslaved "to see whether I am free by going without a pass." A group of whites confronted him on the road, asked the name of his owner, and beat him when he declared that "I now belong to no one." Some slaves rushed to give themselves new names to symbolize their new status. Other slaves left plantations and farms for cities, where, as one of them said, "freedom was free-er."

The ratification of the Thirteenth Amendment to the U.S. Constitution in December 1865 was intended to end all doubt about the status of former slaves by abolishing slavery everywhere. Now the nation faced the huge task of "reconstructing" and reuniting a ravaged South while helping to transform ex-slaves into free workers and equal citizens. It would not be easy. As

CORE
OBJECTIVES INQUIZITIVE

1. Identify the federal government's major challenges in reconstructing the South after the Civil War during the period from 1865 to 1877.

2. Describe how and why Reconstruction policies changed over time.

3. Assess the attitudes of white and black southerners toward Reconstruction.

4. Analyze the political and economic factors that helped lead to the end of Reconstruction in 1877.

5. Explain the significance of Reconstruction for the nation's future.

a South Carolina planter threatened a federal official in the fall of 1865, "The war is not over."

The postwar Reconstruction Era, from 1865 to 1877, was a period during which former slaves became citizens. In addition, political leaders of the Reconstruction Era wrestled with how best to bring the Confederate states back into the Union. Those years witnessed a complex debate about the role of the federal government in ensuring civil rights. Some northerners wanted the former Confederate states returned to the Union with little or no changes in the South's social, political, and economic life. Others wanted the former Confederate political and military leaders imprisoned or executed and the South rebuilt in the image of the rest of the nation. Still others wanted the federal government to spend less time focused on the defeated South and more time promoting northern economic growth and westward expansion. Although the Reconstruction Era lasted only twelve years, it was one of the most significant periods in U.S. history. The decisions that were made and the policies enacted are still shaping American life nearly a hundred and fifty years later.

CORE **OBJECTIVE**

1. Identify the federal government's major challenges in reconstructing the South after the Civil War during the period from 1865 to 1877.

The War's Aftermath in the South

The former Confederacy presented a sharp contrast to the victorious North. Throughout the South, people were emotionally exhausted; many lives had been shattered. In 1866, the state of Mississippi spent a fifth of its annual budget on artificial limbs for Confederate soldiers. Property values had collapsed. In the year after the war ended, eighty-one plantations in Mississippi were sold for less than a tenth of what they had been worth in 1860. Confederate money was worthless; personal savings had vanished. Confederate general Braxton Bragg returned to his "once prosperous" Alabama home to find "all, all was lost, except my debts."

Many of the largest southern cities—Richmond, Atlanta, Columbia—were in ruins; most railroads were damaged or destroyed; many southerners, white and black, were homeless and hungry. Emancipation wiped out $4 billion invested in slavery, which had enabled the explosive growth of the cotton culture. But the expansion in the cotton market was over. Not until 1879 would the cotton crop again equal the record harvest of 1860; tobacco production did not regain its prewar level until 1880; the sugar crop of Louisiana did not recover until 1893; and the old rice industry along the coast of South Carolina and Georgia never regained its prewar levels of production or profit. In 1860, just before the Civil War, the South generated 30 percent of the nation's wealth; in 1870, only ten years later, it produced but 12 percent.

Deciding the status of Confederate states and freed slaves

The process of forming new state governments in the South first required deciding the official status of the seceded states: Were they now conquered

Richmond after the Civil War Before evacuating the capital of the Confederacy, Richmond, Virginia, local mobs set fire to warehouses and factories to prevent their falling into Union hands. Pictured here is one of Richmond's burnt districts in April 1865. Women in mourning attire walk among the shambles.

territories? If so, then the Constitution assigned Congress authority to re-create their state governments. But what if, as Abraham Lincoln had argued, the Confederate states had never officially left the Union because the act of secession was itself illegal? In that circumstance, the president would be responsible for re-forming state governments. Whichever branch of government—Congress or the President—directed the reconstruction of the South, it would have to address the most complicated and controversial issue: What would be the political, social, and economic status of the freed slaves? Were they citizens? If not, what was their status as Americans?

The Battle over Political Reconstruction

CORE **OBJECTIVE**
2. Describe how and why Reconstruction policies changed over time.

The reconstruction of former Confederate states actually began during the war and went through several phases, the first of which was Presidential Reconstruction. With Union forces advancing into the South during the fighting, President Lincoln in 1862 had named army generals to serve as temporary military governors for conquered Confederate areas. By the end of 1863, he had formulated a plan for regular governments in those states liberated from Confederate rule.

Lincoln's Wartime Reconstruction Plan

Presidential Reconstruction: Lincoln's Proclamation of Amnesty and Reconstruction

In late 1863, President Lincoln issued a Proclamation of Amnesty and Reconstruction, under which any former Rebel state could form a Union government whenever a number equal to 10 percent of those who had voted in 1860 took an oath of allegiance to the Constitution and the Union and received a presidential pardon acquitting them from treason charges. Certain groups, however, were excluded from the pardon: Confederate government officials; senior officers of the Confederate army and navy; judges, congressmen, and military officers of the United States who had left their federal posts to aid the rebellion; and those who had abused captured African American soldiers.

But northern politicians disagreed over who had the authority to restore Rebel states to the Union. Many Republicans, especially the so-called Radicals, who were most committed to black civil rights, argued that Congress, not the president, should supervise Reconstruction. By contrast, a few conservative and most moderate Republicans supported Lincoln's program that immediately restored pro-Union southern governments. The **Radical Republicans**, however, favored a drastic transformation of southern society through which freed slaves would be granted full citizenship rights. Many Radical Republican leaders, motivated primarily by strongly felt religious values and moral ideals, believed that all people, regardless of race, were equal in God's eyes. They wanted no compromise with the "sin" of racism.

The Radicals also hoped to reconstruct southern society by replacing the white, Democratic planter elite with a new generation of small farmers, along with wage-earning and middle-class Republicans, both black and white, who would help replace the all-white Democratic party in the South. "The middling classes who own the soil, and work it with their own hands," explained Radical leader Thaddeus Stevens, "are the main support of every free government."

In 1864, with the war still raging, the Radical Republicans tried to take charge of Reconstruction by passing the Wade-Davis Bill, sponsored by Senator Benjamin Franklin Wade of Ohio and Representative Henry Winter Davis of Maryland. In contrast to Lincoln's 10 percent plan, the Wade-Davis Bill required that a *majority* of white male citizens declare their allegiance to the Union before a Confederate state could be re-admitted.

Lincoln vetoes Wade-Davis Bill

But the Wade-Davis Bill never became law: Lincoln vetoed it as being too harsh. In retaliation, Republicans issued the Wade-Davis Manifesto, a public statement that accused Lincoln of exceeding his constitutional authority. Unfazed by the criticism, Lincoln moved ahead with his efforts to restore the Confederate states to the Union. He also rushed to provide assistance to the freed slaves in the South.

The Freedmen's Bureau

Radical Republicans Congressmen who identified with the abolitionist cause and sought swift emancipation of the slaves, punishment of the Rebels, and tight controls over former Confederate states.

In early 1865, Congress approved the Thirteenth Amendment to the Constitution, officially abolishing slavery everywhere in the United States. The amendment, and the war that enabled it, liberated 4 million slaves, but what

ormer slaves, most of whom had no land, no home,
n? Throughout the major northern cities, people
ht of the former slaves had formed Freedmen's Aid
and recruit volunteers to help the African Americans
urches did the same. But the needs far exceeded such

did freedom mean for the f
no food, and no educatio
concerned about the plig
Societies to raise funds
in the South. Many ch
grassroots efforts.
It soon fell

federal government to take charge of coordinating ef-
sperate plight of the former slaves. On March 3, 1865,
eedmen's Bureau (within the War Department) to
men and their wives and children." It was the first
iding assistance directly to people rather than to
Oliver O. Howard, commissioner of the Freed-
eed slaves "must be free to choose their own
labor." He sent Freedmen's Bureau agents to
tracts between blacks and white landown-
ents also provided the former slaves with
d helped set up schools and pay teachers.
rvising over 4,000 new schools in the South
udents, many of whose teachers were initially
the North. The Freedmen's Bureau also helped for-
sh connection with their family members. Marriages
rohibited during slavery were now made legal through the
the Freedmen's Bureau.

Freedmen's Bureau (1865)

Freedmen's Bureau Federal Reconstruction agency established to protect the legal rights of former slaves and to assist with their education, jobs, health care, and land ownership.

Freedmen's school in Virginia Throughout the former Confederate states, the Freedmen's Bureau set up schools for former slaves, such as this one.

Lincoln assassinated
(April 14, 1865)

The Assassination of Lincoln

Abraham Lincoln offered his last view of Reconstr[uction] of his life. On April 11, 1865, he rejected calls by Ra[dicals for] construction. He wanted "no persecution, no bloody [work," no ha]Confederate leaders nor any extreme efforts to restru[cture] and economic life. Three days later, on April 14, 1865, t[he president and his] wife Mary went to see a play at Ford's Theatre in Washi[ngton. Lincoln] was sitting defenseless as John Wilkes Booth slipped in[to the] presidential box. Booth, a famous actor [and con]federate, fired his small pistol point-bla[nk into the presi]dent's head. As Lincoln slumped forward, [Booth pulled] out a knife, stabbed Lincoln's aide, and jump[ed from the] box to the stage, breaking his leg in the proce[ss. Booth] mounted a waiting horse and fled the city. The [president] died nine hours later. Eleven days later, Booth w[as found] hiding in a barn in Virginia, where he was shot and [killed].

Johnson's Plan

Lincoln's murder shocked and saddened the nation a[nd] propelled into the White House Vice President Andre[w] Johnson of Tennessee, a combative man with a quick temper and fierce prejudices (he hated both the white southern elite and the idea of racial equality). Johnson was a pro-Union Democrat who had joined Lincoln's National Union ticket in 1864 as a gesture of wartime bipartisan unity. Like Lincoln, he was a self-made man.

Born in poverty in Raleigh, North Carolina, Johnson never attended school. At age thirteen he relocated to Greeneville, in the mountains of east Tennessee, where he became a tailor and eventually served as the mayor, a state legislator, governor, congressional representative, and U.S. senator.

Paying respect The only photograph of Lincoln in his coffin, displayed here in New York's City Hall rotunda.

Johnson's supporters were primarily the small farmers and working poor across the state. He called himself a Jacksonian Democrat "in the strictest meaning of the term. I am for putting down the [Confederate] rebellion, because it is a war [of wealthy plantation owners] against democracy." He had long disliked the planter elite, whom he dismissed as "a bloated, corrupted, damnable aristocracy." But Johnson shared the racist attitudes of most southern whites, rich and poor. "Damn the negroes," he exclaimed to a friend during the war. "I am fighting those traitorous aristocrats, their masters."

Johnson's plan to restore the Confederate states to the Union closely resembled Lincoln's lenient plan. In May 1865, the president issued a new Proclamation of Amnesty that excluded not only those ex-Confederates whom Lincoln had barred from a presidential pardon but also banned anyone with property worth more than $20,000. Johnson was determined to keep the wealthiest southerners from regaining political power in the former Confederate states. Surprisingly, however, he eventually gave pardons to most of the white "aristocrats" he claimed to despise. What brought about this change of heart? Johnson had apparently decided that he could buy the political support of prominent southerners by pardoning them, improving his own chances of reelection.

Johnson's "Restoration" Plan included the appointment of a Unionist as provisional governor in each southern state, with authority to call a convention of men elected by "loyal" (that is, not Confederate) voters. Each state convention had to ratify the Thirteenth Amendment ending slavery before it could be readmitted to the Union. Johnson also encouraged the state conventions to consider giving a few blacks voting rights, especially those with some education or with military service so as to "disarm" the "radicals who are wild upon" giving *all* African Americans the right to vote. Except for uncompromising Mississippi, each state of the former Confederacy held a convention that met Johnson's requirements but ignored his suggestion about giving voting rights to a few blacks.

> Presidential Reconstruction: Johnson's "Restoration" Plan

Andrew Johnson A pro-Union Democrat from Tennessee.

The Radical Republicans

Johnson's initial assault on the southern planter elite won him the support of the Radical Republicans, but not for long. Many Radicals who wanted "Reconstruction" to provide social and political equality for blacks were frustrated by Johnson's efforts to bring the South back into the Union as quickly as possible. The leading Radical Republicans, such as Thaddeus Stevens of Pennsylvania and Charles Sumner of Massachusetts, wanted to deny former Confederates the right to vote in order to keep them from electing the old planter elite and to enable the Republican party to gain a foothold in the Democratic region. Stevens argued that the Civil War was a *"radical* revolution": the "whole fabric of southern society must be changed" in order to "revolutionize southern institutions, habits, and manners." Stevens and other Radicals wanted the federal government to confiscate the largest southern plantations, divide them into small farms, and give them to former slaves. And the Radicals claimed they had the authority to do so. The iron-willed Stevens, for example, viewed the Confederate states as "conquered provinces," subject to the absolute will of the U.S. Congress, not the president. Andrew Johnson, however, balked at such an expansion of federal authority. At base, he was committed to the states' rights to control their affairs rather than to an intrusive federal government. "White men alone must manage the South," Johnson told a visitor.

Unreconstructed Southerners

After the war most white southerners found their lives in turmoil. And it was only natural that former Confederates nursed bitter grievances against the North and the federal government. Many shared the attitude expressed by a North Carolinian in 1866 who said he felt the "bitterest hatred toward the North." He and others wanted to rebuild the new South as it had been before the war, the fabled "Old South," and they were determined to do so in their own way and under their own leadership. They saw no need for their beloved region to be "reconstructed" by outsiders.

Johnson's "Restoration" Plan Plan to require southern states to ratify the Thirteenth Amendment, disqualify wealthy ex-Confederates from voting, and appoint a Unionist governor.

So when the U.S. Congress met in December 1865, for the first time since the end of the war, the new state governments in the postwar South looked remarkably like the former Confederate governments. Southern voters had refused to extend voting rights to the newly freed slaves. Instead, they had elected as new U.S. senators and congressmen Georgia's Alexander Stephens, former vice president of the Confederacy, and four Confederate generals, eight colonels, and six Confederate cabinet members. The outraged Republicans in Congress denied seats to all such "Rebel" officials.

Then in May and July of 1866, white mobs murdered African Americans in Memphis and New Orleans. The massacres, Radical Republicans argued, resulted from Andrew Johnson's lenient policy toward white supremacists. "Witness Memphis, witness New Orleans," Massachusetts senator Charles Sumner cried. "Who can doubt that the President is the author of these tragedies?" The riots against blacks helped motivate Congress to pass the Fourteenth Amendment that year, extending federal civil rights protections to blacks.

| Black codes |

The violence directed against southern blacks was partly sparked by black protests over restrictive laws being passed by the new all-white southern state legislatures. These "**black codes**," as a white southerner explained, were intended to make sure "the ex-slave was not a free man; he was a free Negro." A northerner visiting the South said the black codes in each state were intended to enforce a widespread insistence that "the blacks at large belong to the whites at large."

The black codes varied from state to state, but some provisions were common in many of them. While black marriages were recognized, blacks could not vote or serve on juries or testify against whites. They could own property, but they could not own farmland in Mississippi or city property in South Carolina. In Mississippi, every black male over the age of eighteen had to be apprenticed to a white, preferably a former slave owner. Any blacks not apprenticed or employed by January 1866 would be jailed as "vagrants." If they could not pay the vagrancy fine—and most of them could not—they were forced to work as convict laborers for whites. In other words, aspects of slavery were simply being restored in new ways. As a reporter observed, southern whites never agreed that "freedom for the negro means the same thing as freedom for them." The black codes infuriated Republicans. "We [Republicans] must see to it," Senator William Stewart of Nevada resolved, "that the man made free by the Constitution of the United States is a freeman indeed." And that is what they set out to do.

Johnson's Battle with Congress

| The Civil Rights Act (1866) |

Largely because of southern whites' resistance to Reconstruction, by the end of 1865, the Radical Republicans had gained a majority in Congress and were warring with Andrew Johnson over the control of Reconstruction. Johnson started the fight when he vetoed a bill renewing funding for the Freedmen's Bureau. On February 22, three days after the veto vote, Johnson criticized the Radical Republicans for promoting black civil rights. Moderate Republi-

black codes Laws passed in southern states to restrict the rights of former slaves.

cans thereafter deserted the president and supported the Radicals. President Johnson had become in their eyes "an alien enemy of a foreign state," Thaddeus Stevens declared. In mid-March 1866, the Radical-led Congress passed the pathbreaking Civil Rights Act, which declared that "all persons born in the United States" (except Indians) were citizens entitled to "full and equal benefit of all laws."

The new legislation enraged President Johnson. Congress, he fumed, had no authority to grant citizenship to blacks, who did not deserve it. The Civil Rights Act discriminated against the "white race." Johnson vetoed the bill, but this time, on April 9, 1866, Congress overrode the presidential veto. It was the first time in history that Congress had overturned a presidential veto of a major bill. From that point on, President Johnson, a stubborn loner unable to accept criticism or compromise, steadily lost both public and political support in the fight over Reconstruction.

"(?) Slavery Is Dead (?)" (1867) Thomas Nast's cartoon argues that blacks were still being treated as slaves despite the passage of the Fourteenth Amendment. This detail illustrates a case in Raleigh, North Carolina: a black man was whipped for a crime despite federal orders specifically prohibiting such forms of punishment.

Congressional Reconstruction

To remove all doubt about the legality of the new Civil Rights Act, Congress passed the **Fourteenth Amendment** to the U.S. Constitution on June 16, 1866. It went far beyond the Civil Rights Act by guaranteeing citizenship to anyone born in the United States, except Native Americans. It also prohibited any efforts to violate the civil rights of "citizens," black or white; to deprive any person "of life, liberty, or property, without due process of law"; or to "deny any person . . . the equal protection of the laws." With the Fourteenth Amendment, the federal government was assuming responsibility for protecting the civil rights of Americans.

> Passage of the Fourteenth Amendment (1866)

As 1866 drew to an end, the fall congressional elections revealed the growing split between President Andrew Johnson and the Radical Republicans. To win votes for his favored candidates, Johnson went on a speaking tour of the Midwest. But his efforts backfired when several of his speeches turned into ugly shouting contests between him and his critics. In Cleveland, Ohio, Johnson described the Radical Republicans as "factious, domineering, tyrannical" men, and he exchanged hot-tempered insults with a heckler. Radical Republicans claimed that Johnson was behaving like a "drunken imbecile."

The 1866 congressional elections were a devastating defeat for Johnson and the Democrats; in each house, Radical Republican candidates won more than a two-thirds majority, the margin required to override presidential vetoes. On March 2, 1867, Congress passed, over President Johnson's

Fourteenth Amendment (1866) Amendment to the U.S. Constitution guaranteeing equal protection under the law to all U.S. citizens, including former slaves.

Congressional Reconstruction:
The Military Reconstruction,
Command of Army, and Tenure
of Office Acts (1867)

vetoes, three crucial laws creating what came to be called **Congressional Reconstruction**: the Military Reconstruction Act, the Command of the Army Act, and the Tenure of Office Act.

The Military Reconstruction Act was the capstone of the Congressional Reconstruction plan. It abolished all of the new governments "in the rebel States" established under President Johnson's lenient reconstruction policies. In their place, Congress established military control over the defeated South. One state, Tennessee, was exempted because it had already ratified the Fourteenth Amendment. The other ten ex-Confederate states were divided into five military districts, each commanded by a general who acted as governor.

The Military Reconstruction Act required each state to create a new constitution that guaranteed the right of African American males to vote. (Women—black or white—did not yet have the vote and were not included in the discussions. The Radical Republicans were not so radical when it came to promoting the equality of women.) Once the new state constitution was ratified by a majority of voters in that state and accepted by Congress, a newly elected state legislature had to ratify the Fourteenth Amendment before regaining its state's representation in Congress.

The Command of the Army Act directed that all army orders from the president go through the army's commanding general, Ulysses S. Grant. The Radical Republicans feared that, to manage Reconstruction in the South, President Johnson would appoint generals who would be too lenient. So they bypassed the president and entrusted General Grant to enforce Congressional Reconstruction in the South.

The Tenure of Office Act required Senate permission for the president to remove any federal official whose appointment the Senate had confirmed. This act was intended to prevent Andrew Johnson from firing Secretary of War Edwin Stanton, the president's most outspoken critic in the cabinet. Stanton had openly criticized Johnson's lenient approach to the South and had allied himself with the Radicals.

Congressional Reconstruction thus sought to ensure that the freed slaves could participate in the creation of new state governments in the former Confederacy. As Thaddeus Stevens explained, the Congressional Reconstruction plan was designed to create a "perfect republic" based on the principle of *equal rights* for all citizens. "This is the promise of America," he insisted. "No More. No Less."

Impeaching the President

The first two years of Congressional Reconstruction saw dramatic changes in the South. One by one, a new set of southern state legislatures rewrote their constitutions and ratified the Fourteenth Amendment. Radical Republicans now seemed fully in control of Reconstruction, but one person still stood in their way—Andrew Johnson. During 1867 and early 1868, more and more Radicals decided that the defiant Democratic president must be removed from office.

Congressional Reconstruction
Phase of Reconstruction directed by Radical Republicans through the passage of three laws: the Military Reconstruction Act, the Command of the Army Act, and the Tenure of Office Act.

Johnson himself opened the door to impeachment (the formal process by which Congress charges the president with "high crimes and misdemeanors") when he tried to fire Secretary of War Edwin Stanton. The sharp-tongued Stanton had exasperated Johnson by refusing to resign from the cabinet despite his harsh criticism of the president's Reconstruction policy. Radical Republicans had passed the Tenure of Office Act in 1866 to make it illegal for Johnson to remove Stanton for championing their cause. Johnson, who considered the Tenure of Office Act an illegal restriction of presidential power, fired Stanton on August 12, 1867, appointing General Ulysses S. Grant in his place. To the Republicans, this was a declaration of war. John F. Farnsworth, an Illinois Congressman, denounced the president as an "ungrateful, despicable, besotted, traitorous man."

The Radical Republicans now saw their chance. By removing Stanton without congressional approval, Johnson had violated the law. On February 24, 1868, the Republican-dominated House passed eleven articles of impeachment (that is, specific charges against the president), most of which dealt with Stanton's firing, and all of which were flimsy. In reality, the essential grievance against the president was that he had opposed the policies of the dominant Radical Republicans. According to Secretary of the Navy Gideon Welles, Radical Republicans were so angry at Johnson that they would have tried to remove him had he been accused of stepping on a dog's tail.

> Johnson's presidency in crisis

The first Senate trial of a sitting president began on March 5, 1868, and continued until May 26, with Chief Justice Salmon P. Chase presiding. It was a dramatic spectacle before a packed gallery of journalists, foreign dignitaries, corporate executives, and political leaders, all eager to watch the first effort to impeach a president. Thaddeus Stevens, the Radical leader, did not need to be convinced that Johnson should be removed. As the trial began, he warned the president: "Unfortunate, unhappy man, behold your doom!"

Trial of Andrew Johnson In this *Harper's Weekly* illustration, Johnson is seated at the center of the foreground among his defense committee. The galleries of the Senate are packed with men and women watching the proceedings.

The five-week impeachment trial ended in May 1868 in stunning fashion, but not as the Radicals had hoped. In the end, the Senate voted 35 to 19 for conviction, only *one* vote short of the two-thirds needed for removal from office. Senator Edmund G. Ross, a young Radical from Kansas, cast the deciding vote in favor of acquittal, knowing that his vote would ruin his political career. "I almost literally looked down into my open grave," Ross explained afterwards. "Friendships, position, fortune, everything that makes life desirable . . . were about to be swept away by the breath of my mouth." Ross was thereafter shunned by the Republicans. He lost his reelection campaign and died in near poverty.

The effort by Radicals to remove Johnson was in the end a grave political mistake, for it ended up weakening public support for Congressional Reconstruction. Nevertheless, the Radical cause did gain something: to avoid being convicted, President Johnson had privately agreed to stop obstructing Congressional Reconstruction.

Republican Rule in the South

Passage of the Fifteenth Amendment (1870)

In June 1868, Congressional Republicans agreed that eight former Confederate states—all but Virginia, Mississippi, and Texas—had met the tough new conditions for readmission to the Union. Virginia, Mississippi, and Texas were readmitted in 1870, with the added requirement that they ratify the **Fifteenth Amendment**, which gave voting rights to African American men. As the prominent black leader Frederick Douglass, himself a former slave, had declared in 1865, "slavery is not abolished until the black man has the ballot."

The Fifteenth Amendment, submitted to the states in 1869 and ratified in 1870, prohibited states from denying any person the vote on grounds of "race, color, or previous condition of servitude." Susan B. Anthony and Elizabeth Cady Stanton, leaders of the movement to secure voting rights for women, demanded that the Fifteenth Amendment be revised to include women as well as black men. As Anthony stressed in a famous speech, the U.S. Constitution says: "we, the people; not we, the white male citizens; nor yet we, the male citizens; but we, the whole people, who formed the Union—women as well as men." But most men remained unreconstructed when it came to female voting rights. Radical Republicans tried to deflect the issue by declaring that it was the "Negro's hour," and women would have to wait—another fifty years, as it turned out.

CORE **OBJECTIVE**

3. Assess the attitudes of white and black southerners toward Reconstruction.

Reconstruction in Practice

When a federal official asked Garrison Frazier, a former slave in Georgia, if he and others wanted to live among whites or among themselves, he said that they preferred "to live by ourselves, for there is a prejudice against us in the South that will take years to get over." In forging new lives in freedom, Frazier and many other former slaves then set about creating their own social institutions.

The Reconstruction of Black Social Life

The northern victory in the Civil War led to a striking transformation of African American religious life in the South. Many former slaves identified their struggle for freedom with the biblical Hebrews, who were led out of

Fifteenth Amendment (1870)
Amendment to the U.S. Constitution forbidding states to deny any male citizen the right to vote on grounds of "race, color or previous condition of servitude."

slavery into the "promised land." Emancipation demonstrated to them that God was on *their* side. Before the war, slaves who were allowed to attend white churches were forced to sit in the back. After the war, with the help of many northern Christian missionaries, both black and white, ex-slaves eagerly established their own African American churches.

The black churches were the first social institution the former slaves could control, and they quickly became the crossroads for African American community life. Black ministers emerged as social and political leaders as well as preachers. One could not be a real minister, one of them claimed, without looking "out for the political interests of his people."

Many African Americans became Baptists or Methodists, in part because these were already the largest denominations in the South and in part because they reached out to the working poor. In 1866 alone, the African Methodist Episcopal (AME) Church gained 50,000 members. By 1890, over 1.3 million African Americans in the South had become Baptists, nearly three times as many as had joined any other denomination.

> African American churches

African American communities in the postwar South also rushed to establish schools. Starting schools, said one former slave, was the "first proof" of freedom. Most plantation owners had denied education to blacks in part because they feared that literate slaves would read abolitionist literature and organize uprisings. After the war, the white elite worried that formal education would encourage poor whites and poor blacks to leave the South in search of better social and economic opportunities. "They didn't want us to learn nothin'," one former slave recalled. "The only thing we had to learn was how to work."

> African American schools

White opposition to education for blacks made education all the more important to African Americans. South Carolina's Mary McLeod Bethune, the fifteenth child of former slaves, rejoiced in the opportunity to gain an education: "The whole world opened to me when I learned to read." She walked five miles to school as a child, then earned a scholarship to college, and went on to become the first black woman to found a school that became a four-year college: what is today known as Bethune-Cookman University, in Daytona Beach, Florida.

African Americans in Southern Politics

Participation in the Union army or navy had given many former slaves their first opportunity to express their loyalty to the American nation. A Virginia freedman explained that the United States was "now *our* country," paid for "by the blood of our brethren" who died while serving in the Union military during the Civil War. Serving in the military enabled many former slaves to learn to read and write. Black veterans would also form the core of the first generation of African American political leaders in the postwar South.

Any African American participation in southern political life was a first. With many ex-Confederates denied voting rights, new African American voters helped elect some six hundred blacks—most of them former slaves—as Republican state legislators under Congressional Reconstruction. In

> African American vote

African American political figures of Reconstruction
Blanche K. Bruce (left) and Hiram Revels (right) served in the U.S. Senate. Frederick Douglass (center) was a major figure in the abolitionist movement.

Louisiana, Pinckney Pinchback, a northern free black and former Union soldier, was elected lieutenant governor. Several other African Americans were elected lieutenant governor, state treasurer, or secretary of state. There were two black senators in Congress, Hiram Revels and Blanche K. Bruce, both Mississippi natives who had been educated in the North, as well as fourteen black members of the U.S. House of Representatives during Reconstruction.

African American elected officials

White southern Democrats were appalled at the election of black Republican politicians. They complained that freed slaves were illiterate and had no civic experience or appreciation of political issues and processes. In this regard, of course, blacks were no different from millions of poor or immigrant white males who had been allowed to vote for years. Some freedmen frankly confessed their disadvantages. Beverly Nash, an African American delegate to the South Carolina convention of 1868, told his colleagues: "I believe, my friends and fellow-citizens, we are not prepared for this suffrage [the vote]. But we can learn. Give a man tools and let him commence to use them, and in time he will learn a trade. So it is with voting."

Land, Labor, and Disappointment

A few northerners argued that what the former slaves needed most was neither the right to vote nor the opportunity to be paid laborers on plantations but their own land, where they could gain economic self-sufficiency. "What is freedom," Ohio Congressman James A. Garfield, a former general and future president, asked in 1865. "Is it the bare privilege of not being chained? If this is all, then freedom is a bitter mockery, a cruel delusion." Freed slaves felt the same way. Freedom, explained a black minister from Georgia, meant

Freedmen Voting in New Orleans The Fifteenth Amendment, ratified in 1870, guaranteed at the federal level the right of citizens to vote regardless of "race, color, or previous condition of servitude." But former slaves had been registering to vote—and voting in large numbers—in some state elections since 1867, as in this scene.

the freedom for blacks to "reap the fruit of our own labor, and take care of ourselves."

In several southern states, former slaves had been "given" land by Union armies after they had taken control of Confederate areas during the war. But such transfers of white-owned property to former slaves were reversed during 1865 by President Andrew Johnson. In South Carolina, the Union general responsible for evicting former slaves urged them to "lay aside their bitter feelings, and become reconciled to their old masters." But the assembled freedmen shouted "No, never!" and "Can't do it!" They knew that ownership of land was the foundation of their freedom. Yes, they had no deeds or titles for the land they now worked, but it had been "earned by the sweat of *our* brows," said a group of Alabama freedmen.

President Johnson, however, was insistent that the federal government had no right to take land from former Confederates. Tens of thousands of former slaves were forced to return their farms to the white owners. In addition, it was virtually impossible for former slaves to get loans to buy farm land because there were so few banks in the postwar South, and few of these were willing to lend to blacks. The sense of betrayal among the former slaves was profound. An ex-slave in Mississippi whose farm was returned to its white owner said the former slaves were left with nothing: "no *land*, no *house*, not so much as a place to lay our head."

Sharecropping replaces slavery

The intensity of racial prejudice in the South often blocked the efforts of federal troops and officials to protect the former slaves. In late June 1865, for example, Thomas Ferguson, a white plantation owner near Charleston, South Carolina, signed a contract with sixty-five of his former slaves. It called for them to "cultivate" his fields in exchange for "half of the crop raised after having deducted the seed of rice, corn, peas & potatoes." This labor system of **sharecropping**—where the landowner provided land, seed, and tools to a poor farmer in exchange for a *share* of the crop—essentially re-enslaved the workers because, as a federal army officer objected, no matter "how much they are abused, they cannot leave without permission of the owner." If they chose to leave, they would forfeit any right to a portion of the crop, and any workers who violated the terms of the contract could be evicted from the plantation, leaving them jobless and homeless—and subject to arrest. Across the former Confederacy, most white plantation owners and small farmers were determined to continue to control the lives of African Americans.

Sharecroppers A family is shown outside their Virginia home in this 1899 photograph, taken by Frances Benjamin Johnston, one of the earliest American female photojournalists.

With little money or technical training, many freed blacks preferred sharecropping over working for wages, since it freed them from day-to-day supervision by white landowners. But over time, most sharecroppers, black and white, found themselves deeper in debt to the landowner, with little choice but to remain tied to the same discouraging system of dependence that, over the years, felt much like slavery. As a former slave acknowledged, he and others had discovered that "freedom could make folks proud but it didn't make 'em rich."

"Carpetbaggers" and "Scalawags"

Most of the top positions in the new Republican southern state governments went to whites, who were dismissed as "carpetbaggers" and "scalawags" by their critics. Carpetbaggers were allegedly opportunistic northerners who rushed South with all their belongings in cheap suitcases made of carpeting ("carpetbags") to grab political power. Some northerners were indeed corrupt opportunists. However, most of the northerners in the postwar South were Union military veterans who had arrived as early as 1865 or 1866, drawn back to the South by the desire to rebuild the region's devastated economy. Others were Union soldiers who never returned home after fighting in the South. New Yorker George Spencer, for example, arrived in

sharecropping A farming system developed after the Civil War by which landless workers farmed land in exchange with the landowner for farm supplies and a share of the crop.

Alabama with the Union army during the war and decided to pursue his "chances of making a fortune" in selling cotton and building railroads. He eventually was elected to the U.S. Senate.

Many other so-called carpetbaggers were teachers, social workers, or ministers motivated by a genuine desire to help free blacks and poor whites improve the quality of their lives. Union general Adelbert Ames stayed in the South after the war because he felt a "sense of Mission with a large M" to help the former slaves develop healthy communities. He served as the military governor of Mississippi before being elected as a Republican U.S. senator in 1870. In 1873 Ames ran for governor of Mississippi in a bitter campaign against another white Republican, a "scalawag" named James Lusk Alcorn, a former Confederate general who owned the largest plantation in the Mississippi Delta and had served as Mississippi's governor from 1870 to 1871. Alcorn wrote his wife that "southerners must make the Negro their friend or the path ahead will be red with blood and damp with tears." Ames won the gubernatorial contest in 1873 and served as governor from 1874 to 1876 before resigning in the face of a resurgent white Democratic party.

Carpetbagger The cartoonist's caption to this critique of carpetbaggers reads: "The bag in front of him, filled with others' faults, he always sees. The one behind him, filled with his own faults, he never sees."

Most so-called scalawags were southerners who had opposed secession but supported the Confederacy once the war started, and then became Republicans after the war was over. Several distinguished figures became scalawags, including the former Confederate general James Longstreet, who decided after the war that the Old South must change its ways. He became a successful cotton broker in New Orleans, joined the Republican party, and supported the Congressional Reconstruction program. Another unlikely scalawag was Joseph E. Brown, the former Confederate governor of Georgia, who urged southerners to support Republicans because they were the only source of economic investment in the devastated region.

Southern Resistance and White "Redemption"

The scalawags, or southern white Republicans, were especially hated by southern Democrats, who often called them traitors. A Nashville, Tennessee, newspaper editor dismissed them as the "merest trash." Most southern whites viewed secession not as a mistake but as a noble "lost cause." At the same time, they viewed federal efforts at reconstruction as a tragedy. And they used all means possible—legal and illegal—to "redeem" their beloved South from northern control, Republican rule, and black assertiveness. An Alabama planter admitted that southern whites simply "can't learn to treat the freedmen like human beings." White southern ministers, for example, assured their congregations that God endorsed white supremacy. In an attempt to reunite the Protestant denominations of the north and south, many northern religionists became "apostles of forgiveness" for their southern

> Reconstruction's final phase: Southern white resistance and "redemption"

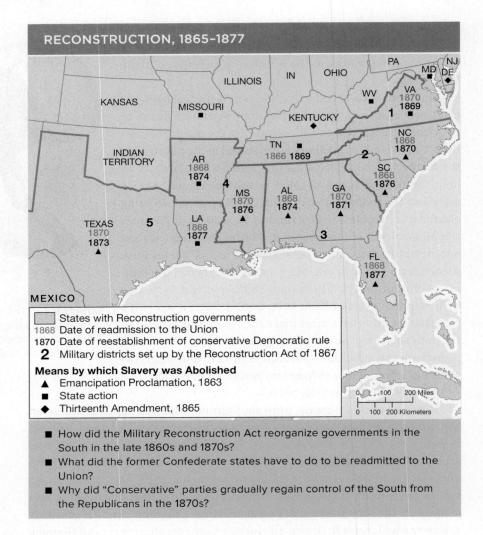

RECONSTRUCTION, 1865–1877

Legend:
- States with Reconstruction governments
- 1868 Date of readmission to the Union
- 1870 Date of reestablishment of conservative Democratic rule
- 2 Military districts set up by the Reconstruction Act of 1867

Means by which Slavery was Abolished
- ▲ Emancipation Proclamation, 1863
- ■ State action
- ◆ Thirteenth Amendment, 1865

■ How did the Military Reconstruction Act reorganize governments in the South in the late 1860s and 1870s?

■ What did the former Confederate states have to do to be readmitted to the Union?

■ Why did "Conservative" parties gradually regain control of the South from the Republicans in the 1870s?

White violence against black political participation

white brethren. Even abolitionists such as the Reverend Henry Ward Beecher, whose sister Harriet Beecher Stowe had written *Uncle Tom's Cabin* (1857), called for southern whites—rather than federal officials or African Americans themselves—to govern the South after the war.

The Civil War had brought freedom to enslaved African Americans, but it did not bring them protection against exploitation or abuse. The "black codes" created by white state governments in 1865 and 1866 were the first of many continuing efforts to deny equality to African Americans. With each passing year, southern whites used terror, intimidation, and violence to prevent blacks from exercising their political rights. Hundreds were killed across the South and many more injured in systematic efforts to "keep blacks in their place." In Texas a white farmer, D. B. Whitesides, told a former slave named Charles Brown that his newfound freedom would do him "damned little good . . . as I intend to shoot you"—and he did, shooting Brown in the chest as he tried to flee. Whitesides then rode his horse beside the wounded

Brown and asked, "I got you, did I Brown?" "Yes," a bleeding Brown replied. "You've got me good." Whitesides yelled that the wound would teach "niggers [like you] to put on airs because you are free."

Such ugly incidents revealed a harsh truth: the death of slavery did not mean the birth of true freedom for many African Americans. For a growing number of southern whites, resistance to Congressional Reconstruction and "Radical rule" became more and more violent. Several secret terrorist groups emerged to harass, intimidate, and even kill scalawags, carpetbaggers, and African Americans. The **Ku Klux Klan** (KKK), for instance, was formed in 1866 in Pulaski, Tennessee. The name *Ku Klux* was derived from the Greek word *kuklos* meaning "circle" or "band" (and *Klan* comes from the English word *clan*, or family). The Klan, and other groups like it, began initially as a social club, with costumes and secret rituals. At first a group of pranksters, its members soon turned to intimidation of blacks and white Republicans throughout the South. Their motives were varied—anger over the Confederate defeat, resentment against federal soldiers occupying the South, complaints about having to pay black workers, and an almost paranoid fear that former slaves might seek violent revenge against whites. Klansmen rode about at night in white sheets and masks spreading horrendous rumors, issuing threats, burning schools and churches. "We are going to kill all the Negroes," a white supremacist declared during one massacre.

"Worse Than Slavery" This Thomas Nast cartoon condemns the Ku Klux Klan for promoting conditions "worse than slavery" for southern blacks after the Civil War.

The Legacy of Republican Rule

Yet for all of the violent opposition directed against the Republican state governments, the new constitutions they created remained in effect for some years after the end of Radical Republican control, and later constitutions incorporated many of their most progressive features. Among the most significant innovations brought about by the Republican state governments were those intended to increase the participation of the common people in the political process: protecting black voting rights, restructuring legislatures to reflect shifting populations, and making more state offices elective to weaken the "good old boy" tradition of rewarding political supporters with state government jobs. In South Carolina, former Confederate leaders opposed the Republican state legislature not simply because of its black members but because poor whites were also enjoying political clout for the first time, thereby threatening the traditional power of wealthy white plantation owners and merchants.

Given the hostile circumstances under which the Republican state governments operated in the South, their achievements were remarkable. They constructed an extensive railroad network and established public, though racially segregated, school systems—schools funded by state governments

Radical Republican achievements

Ku Klux Klan A secret terrorist organization founded in Pulaski, Tennessee, in 1866 targeting former slaves who voted and held political offices, as well as people the KKK labeled as carpetbaggers and scalawags.

and open to all children. Some six hundred thousand black pupils were enrolled in southern schools by 1877. State governments under the Radicals also gave more attention to the poor and to orphanages, asylums, and institutions for the deaf and the blind of both races. Public roads, bridges, and buildings were repaired or rebuilt. African Americans achieved rights and opportunities that would repeatedly be violated in coming decades but never completely taken away, at least in principle: equality before the law and the rights to own property, attend schools, learn to read and write, enter professions, and carry on business.

Yet several of the Republican state governments also engaged in corrupt practices. Bribes and kickbacks, whereby companies were awarded government contracts and then secretly rewarded officials with cash or stock, were commonplace. In Louisiana, the twenty-six-year-old Illinois carpetbagger, Henry Clay Warmoth, a Union war veteran and attorney, somehow turned an annual salary of $8,000 into a million-dollar fortune over four years serving as governor (he was impeached and removed from office). "I don't pretend to be honest," he admitted. "I only pretend to be as honest as anybody in politics." As was true in the North and the Midwest at the time, southern state governments awarded money to corporations, notably railroads, under conditions that invited shady dealings. In fact, some railroads were funded but never built at all. Republican state legislators doubled and even tripled their salaries. Bribery was rampant. Such corruption was not invented by the Radical Republican regimes, nor did it die with them. Governor Warmoth recognized as much: "Corruption is the fashion" in Louisiana, he explained.

CORE **OBJECTIVE**
4. Analyze the political and economic factors that helped lead to the end of Reconstruction in 1877.

The Grant Years and Northern Disillusionment

Democrat Andrew Johnson's crippled presidency created an opportunity for Republicans to elect one of their own in 1868. Both parties wooed Ulysses S. Grant, the "Lion of Vicksburg" credited by most Americans with the Union victory in the Civil War. His falling-out with President Johnson, however, had pushed him toward the Republicans.

The Election of 1868

The Republican party platform of 1868 endorsed Congressional Reconstruction. More important than the party platform, however, were the public expectations driving the election of Ulysses S. Grant, a heroic soldier whose campaign slogan was "Let us have peace."

African American votes help elect President Grant (1868)

The Democrats, not surprisingly, charged the Republican Congress with subjecting the South "to military despotism and Negro supremacy." They nominated Horatio Seymour, the wartime governor of New York and a passionate critic of Congressional Reconstruction. His vice-presidential running mate, Francis P. Blair Jr., a former Union general from Missouri who had served in Congress, appealed directly to white bigotry when he denounced Republicans for promoting equality for "a semi-barbarous race" of black men who sought to "subject the white women to their unbridled lust." A Democrat later said that Blair's egregiously "stupid and indefensible" remarks cost Seymour a close election. Grant swept the Electoral College, 214 to 80, but his popular majority was only 307,000 out of a total of almost 6 million votes. More than 500,000 African American voters accounted for Grant's margin of victory. The efforts of Radical Republicans to ensure that southern blacks had voting rights had paid off. When Grant was inaugurated in March 1869, a sullen Andrew Johnson refused to attend.

Grant had proved himself a great military leader, but as the youngest president ever (forty-six years old at the time of his inauguration), he was not nearly as bold a politician as he had been a general. He passively followed the lead of Congress and was often blind to the political forces and self-serving influence peddlers around him. A failure as a storekeeper before the Civil War, he was awestruck by men of wealth who lavished gifts on him, including houses. He also showed poor judgment in his selection of cabinet members. During Grant's two terms in office, his seven cabinet officers changed a total of twenty-four times. Some of them were out-and-out crooks who betrayed his trust and engaged in criminal behavior. His former comrade-in-arms, General William T. Sherman, said he felt sorry for his former commander because so many supposedly "loyal" Republicans used him for their own selfish gains.

Scandals

President Grant's new administration soon fell into a cesspool of scandal. In the summer of 1869, two unprincipled financial schemers, Jay Gould and James Fisk Jr. (known as "Jubilee Jim"), infamous for their bribing of politicians and judges, plotted with the president's brother-in-law to create a public craze for gold by purchasing massive quantities of the precious yellow metal to drive up its value. The only danger to the scheme lay in the possibility that the federal Treasury would burst the bubble by selling large amounts of its gold supply, which would deflate the value of gold by putting more in circulation. When President Grant was seen in public with Gould and Fisk, people assumed that he supported their gold scheme. As the rumor spread in New York City's financial district that the president endorsed the run-up in gold, its value soared.

On September 24, 1869—soon to be remembered as "Black Friday"—the scheme of Gould and Fisk to drive up the price of gold worked to perfection. Starting at a price of $150 an ounce, the bidding on Wall Street in New York City started rising, first to $160, then $165, leading more and more investors across the nation and around the world to join the stampede. Then, around noon, President Grant and his Treasury secretary realized what was happening and began selling huge amounts of government gold. Within fifteen minutes, the bubble created by Fisk and Gould burst, and the price of gold plummeted to $138. People who had bought gold in large amounts lost fortunes.

> Corruption in the Grant administration

Their agony, said a New Yorker, "made one feel as if the Battle of Gettysburg had been lost and the Rebels were marching down Broadway." Soon, the turmoil spread to the entire stock market, claiming thousands of victims. As Fisk noted, "It was each man drag out his own corpse." For weeks after the gold bubble collapsed, the financial markets were paralyzed and business confidence was rudely shaken. Congressman James Garfield wrote privately to a friend that President Grant had compromised his presidential integrity by his "indiscreet acceptance" of gifts from Fisk and Gould and that any investigation of "Black Friday" would lead "into the parlor of the President."

The plot to corner the gold market was only the first of several scandals that rocked the Grant administration. More disclosures of corruption followed, some involving members of the president's cabinet. The secretary of war, it turned out, had accepted bribes from merchants who traded with Indians at army posts in the West. In St. Louis, whiskey distillers—dubbed the "whiskey ring" in the press—bribed federal agents to avoid taxes, bilking the government out of millions of dollars in revenue. Grant's personal secretary was enmeshed in that scheme, taking large sums of money and other valuables in return for inside information.

There is no evidence that Grant himself was ever involved in any of the frauds, but his poor choice of associates earned him widespread criticism. Democrats scolded Republicans for their "monstrous corruption and extravagance" and launched thirty-six investigations into supposedly corrupt acts during Grant's administration.

The Money Supply

Greenbacks vs. gold coins

Complex financial issues—especially monetary policy—dominated Grant's presidency. Prior to the Civil War, the economy operated on a gold standard. That is, state banks issued paper money which could be exchanged for an equal value of gold coins. So both gold coins and state bank notes circulated as the nation's currency. **Greenbacks** (because of the dye color used on the printed dollars) were issued during the Civil War to help pay for the war.

When a nation's supply of money grows faster than the economy itself, prices for goods and services increase (inflation). This is what happened during the Civil War when the greenbacks were issued. After the Civil War, the U.S. Treasury assumed that the greenbacks issued during the conflict would be recalled from circulation so that consumer prices would decline and the nation could return to a "hard-money" currency—gold, silver, and copper coins—which had always been viewed as more reliable in value than paper currency. The most vocal supporters of a return to "hard money" were eastern creditors (mostly bankers and merchants to whom others owed money) who did not want their debtors to pay them in paper currency. Critics of the gold standard tended to be farmers and other debtors. These so-called soft-money advocates opposed taking greenbacks out of circulation because shrinking the supply of money would bring lower prices (deflation) for their crops and livestock, thereby reducing their income and making it harder for

greenbacks Paper money, issued during the Civil War, that sparked currency debates after the war.

them to pay their long-term debts. In 1868 congressional supporters of such a "soft-money" policy—mostly Democrats—had forced the Treasury to stop the withdrawal of greenbacks from circulation.

President Grant sided with the "hard-money" camp. On March 18, 1869, he signed the Public Credit Act, which said that the investors who purchased government bonds to help finance the war effort must be paid back in gold coins rather than paper currency. It was the first act of Congress that Grant signed, and it soon generated a decline in consumer prices (deflation) that hurt debtors, helped creditors, and in the process ignited a ferocious political debate over the merits of "hard" and "soft" money that would last throughout the nineteenth century—and beyond.

> Public Credit Act (1869)

Financial Panic

Grant's effort to withdraw the greenbacks from circulation unintentionally helped cause a major economic collapse. During 1873, some twenty-five railroads stopped paying their bills, leading Jay Cooke and Company, the nation's leading business lender, to go bankrupt on September 18, 1873. The resulting financial **Panic of 1873** triggered a deep economic depression. Thousands of businesses closed, and three million people lost their jobs. Those with jobs saw their wages slashed. In the major cities, unemployed, homeless Americans roamed the streets and formed long lines at charity soup kitchens.

> Panic of 1873

The terrible contraction of the economy led the U.S. Treasury to reverse course and begin printing more greenbacks. For a time, the supporters of paper money celebrated, but in 1874, President Grant vetoed a bill to issue even more greenbacks. His efforts to remove paper money from circulation pleased his supporters but only prolonged what was then the nation's worst economic depression in its history.

Liberal Republicans

The sudden collapse of the nation's economy in 1873 also contributed to northerners' losing interest in Reconstruction. Liberal Republicans, a new faction in the Republican party, called for ending federal Reconstruction efforts in the South and promoted "civil service reforms" designed to end the "patronage system" whereby new presidents rewarded political supporters with federal government jobs. In 1872 the Liberal Republicans held their own national convention, at which they accused the Grant administration of corruption, incompetence, and "despotism." They nominated an unlikely presidential candidate: Horace Greeley, the prominent editor of the *New York Tribune* and a longtime champion of a variety of causes: abolitionism, socialism, vegetarianism, and spiritualism. His image as an eccentric was complemented by his record of hostility to the Democrats, whose support the Liberal Republicans needed if they were going to win the election. The Democrats nevertheless gave their nomination to Greeley as the only hope of beating Grant.

> Reconstruction loses support

Panic of 1873 Financial collapse triggered by President Grant's efforts to withdraw greenbacks from circulation and transition the economy back to hard currency.

The result was predictable. Greeley, the shared candidate of the Liberal Republicans and Democrats, carried only six southern states and none in the North. Grant won thirty-one states and carried the national election by 3,598,235 votes to Greeley's 2,834,761. An exhausted Greeley confessed that he was "the worst beaten man who ever ran for high office." He died three weeks later.

White Terror

Violence against blacks escalates

President Grant initially fought hard to enforce federal efforts to reconstruct the postwar South. But southern resistance to "Radical rule" increased and turned brutally violent. In Grayson County, Texas, a white man and two friends murdered three former slaves because they wanted to "thin the niggers out and drive them to their holes."

Klansmen focused their terror on prominent Republicans, black and white. In Mississippi they killed a black Republican leader in front of his family. Three white "scalawag" Republicans were murdered in Georgia in 1870. That same year an armed mob of whites assaulted a Republican political rally in Alabama, killing four blacks and wounding fifty-four. In South Carolina white supremacists were especially active—and violent. In 1871, some five hundred masked men laid siege to South Carolina's Union County jail and eventually lynched eight black prisoners. In March 1871, the Klan killed thirty African Americans in Meridian, Mississippi.

Enforcement Acts (1870–1871)

At the urging of President Grant, Republicans in Congress struck back at such racial violence with three Enforcement Acts (1870–1871). The first of these measures imposed penalties on anyone who interfered with any citizen's right to vote. A second measure dispatched federal election supervisors and marshals to monitor elections in southern districts where political terrorism flourished. The third, called the Ku Klux Klan Act, outlawed the main activities of the KKK—forming conspiracies, wearing disguises, resisting officers, and intimidating officials. In 1871, the federal government singled out nine counties in upcountry South Carolina as a center of Klan-instigated violence and jailed several hundred people. In general, however, the Enforcement Acts were not consistently applied. As a result, the efforts of southern whites to use violence to thwart Reconstruction escalated in the 1870s. On Easter Sunday in 1873 in Colfax, Louisiana, a mob of white vigilantes disappointed by local election results attacked a group of black Republicans, slaughtering eighty-one. It was the bloodiest racial incident during the Reconstruction period.

Southern "Redeemers"

The Ku Klux Klan's impact on southern politics varied from state to state. In the Upper South, it played only a modest role in helping Democrats win local elections. But in the Lower South, Klan violence and intimidation had more serious effects. In overwhelmingly black Yazoo County, Mississippi, vengeful whites used terrorism to reverse the political balance of power. In the 1873 elections, for example, the Republicans cast 2,449 votes and the Democrats 638; two years later the Democrats polled 4,049 votes, the Republicans 7. Throughout the South, the activities of the Klan and other white supremacists disheartened black and white Republicans alike. "We are helpless and unable to organize," wrote a Mississippi scalawag. We "dare not attempt to canvass [campaign for candidates], or make public speeches." At the same time, during the 1870s northerners displayed a growing weariness with efforts to use federal troops to reconstruct the South and protect civil rights. "The plain truth is," noted the *New York Herald,* "the North has got tired of the Negro."

The erosion of northern interest in civil rights resulted from more than weariness, however. Western expansion, Indian wars, and political controversy over economic issues distracted attention from southern resistance to Republican rule and black rights. Given the violent intensity of diehard former Confederates' efforts to resist Reconstruction, it would have required far more patience, conviction, and resources for the federal government to protect the civil rights of blacks in the South. Republican political control in the South gradually loosened as all-white "Conservative" parties mobilized the anti-Reconstruction vote. White Democrats—the so-called **redeemers** who supposedly "saved" the South from Republican control and "black rule"—emotionalized the race issue to excite the white electorate and intimidate black voters. Where persuasion failed to work, Democrats were willing to use trickery. As one enthusiastic Democrat boasted, "The white and black Republicans may outvote us, but we can outcount them."

> Resurgence of the southern white elite

Republican political control collapsed in Virginia and Tennessee as early as 1869; in Georgia and North Carolina it ended in 1870, although North Carolina had a Republican governor until 1876. Reconstruction lasted longest in the Deep South states with the largest black population; there, whites abandoned Klan masks for barefaced intimidation in paramilitary groups such as the Mississippi Rifle Club and the South Carolina Red Shirts. By 1876, Radical Republican regimes survived only in Louisiana, South Carolina, and Florida, and those collapsed after the elections of that year.

The return to power of the old white political elite in the South undermined the country's commitment to Congressional Reconstruction. The collapse of the economy and the much-publicized political scandals hurt Republicans in the 1874 congressional elections, in which the Democrats won control of the House of Representatives and gained seats in the Senate.

> Democrats win control of Congress (1874)

The Compromise of 1877

President Grant, despite the controversies swirling around him, wanted to run again in 1876, but many Republicans had lost confidence in his leadership and opposed the idea of his becoming the nation's first three-term president. In the summer of 1875, Grant acknowledged defeat and announced his retirement, admitting that he had entered the White House

redeemers Postwar white Democratic leaders in the South who supposedly saved the region from political, economic, and social domination by northerners and blacks.

with "no political training" and had made "errors in judgment." James Gillespie Blaine of Maine, former Speaker of the House, emerged as the Republican front-runner to succeed Grant, but he, too, bore the taint of scandal when it was revealed that he had promised political favors to railroad executives in exchange for shares of stock in the company.

The scandal led the Republican Convention to pass over Blaine in favor of Ohio's favorite son, Rutherford B. Hayes. Elected governor of Ohio three times, most recently as a "hard money" advocate of gold rather than greenbacks, Hayes had also made a name for himself as a civil service reformer by trying to reduce the number of government jobs subject to political appointment. But his chief virtue was that he offended neither Radicals nor reformers. As a journalist put it, he was "obnoxious to no one."

The Democratic Convention was uncharacteristically harmonious from the start. The nomination went on the second ballot to Samuel J. Tilden, a wealthy corporate lawyer and reform governor of New York.

The 1876 campaign raised no burning issues. Both candidates favored the trend toward relaxing federal authority in the South. As Hayes said privately, he did not approve of "bayonet rule" by federal troops in the South. In the absence of strong ideological differences, Democrats aired the Republicans' dirty linen. In response, Republicans waved "the bloody shirt," whereby they linked the Democratic party to secession, civil war, and the outrages committed against Republicans in the South. As Robert G. Ingersoll, the most celebrated Republican public speaker of the time, insisted: "The man that assassinated Abraham Lincoln was a Democrat. . . . Soldiers, every scar you have on your heroic bodies was given you by a Democrat!"

Disputed election of 1876

Despite the lack of major issues, the 1876 election generated the most votes of any national election in U.S. history up to that point. Early election returns pointed to a victory for the Democrat Tilden. Nationwide, he outpolled Hayes by almost 300,000 votes. By midnight following Election Day, Tilden had won 184 electoral votes—just one vote short of victory. Hayes went to bed that night convinced that he had lost. But overnight, Republican activists realized that the election hinged on nineteen disputed electoral votes from Florida, Louisiana, and South Carolina. The Democrats needed only one of the challenged votes to claim victory; the Republicans needed all nineteen. Republicans in those key states had engaged in election fraud while Democrats had used physical intimidation to keep black voters at home. But each of the three states was then governed by a Republican who appointed the election boards, each of which reported narrow victories for Hayes. The Democrats immediately challenged the results.

In all three of the disputed southern states, rival election boards sent in conflicting counts. The nation watched and wondered as the politicians bickered about the contested election. The Constitution offered no guidance in this unprecedented situation. Days, then weeks, passed with no solution. Finally, on January 29, 1877, the Congress set up a special Electoral Commission to settle the dispute. It met daily for weeks trying to verify the disputed vote counts in the three contested southern states. Finally, on March 1, 1877, the commission voted 8 to 7 along party lines in favor of Hayes. On March 2, 1877, the House of Representatives declared Hayes president by an electoral vote of 185 to 184. Tilden decided not to protest the decision. His campaign manager explained that they preferred "four years of Hayes's administration to four years of civil war."

Hayes's victory hinged on the defection of key southern Democrats, who, it turned out, had made a number of secret deals with the Republicans. On February 26, 1877, prominent Ohio Republicans (including future president James A. Garfield) and powerful southern Democrats struck a private bargain—the **Compromise of 1877**—at Wormley's Hotel in Washington, D.C. The Republicans promised that if Hayes were named president, he would remove the last federal troops from the South, letting the state Republican governments there collapse.

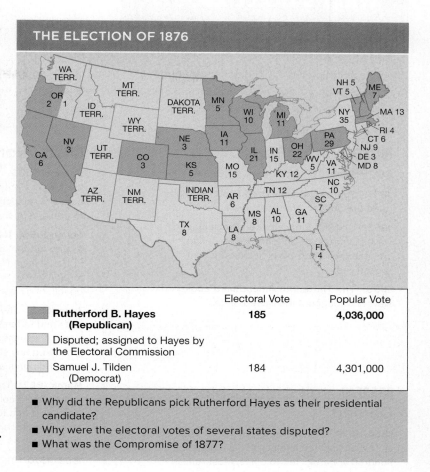

THE ELECTION OF 1876

	Electoral Vote	Popular Vote
Rutherford B. Hayes (Republican)	**185**	**4,036,000**
Disputed; assigned to Hayes by the Electoral Commission		
Samuel J. Tilden (Democrat)	184	4,301,000

- Why did the Republicans pick Rutherford Hayes as their presidential candidate?
- Why were the electoral votes of several states disputed?
- What was the Compromise of 1877?

The End of Reconstruction

In 1877, newly inaugurated President Hayes fulfilled his pledge: he withdrew federal troops from Louisiana and South Carolina, whose Republican governments collapsed soon thereafter. Hayes insisted that it was not his fault. "The practical destruction of the Republican organization in the South was accomplished before my southern policy was announced." Over the next thirty years, the protection of black civil rights in the South crumbled under the pressure of restored white Democratic rule. As Henry Adams, a former Louisiana slave, observed in 1877, "The whole South—every state in the South—has got [back] into the hands of the very men that held us as slaves." New white state governments in the South rewrote their constitutions, rid their administrations of "carpetbaggers, scalawags, and blacks," and cut back spending. "The Yankees helped free us, so they

Compromise of 1877 Secret deal forged by congressional leaders to resolve disputed election of 1876; Republican Rutherford B. Hayes, who had lost the popular vote, was declared the winner in exchange for his pledge to remove federal troops from the South, marking the end of Reconstruction.

From Slave to Citizen

The following timeline highlights important developments in the legal status of African Americans during the Civil War and Reconstruction. The timeline breaks the legal status of African Americans into three phases:

PHASE I From Slaves to Freedmen

1857 Supreme Court's *Dred Scott* decision ruled that African Americans were not citizens.

1863 Lincoln's **Emancipation Proclamation** freed slaves in areas still under rebellion during the Civil War, but their citizenship status remained unresolved.

1865 The **Thirteenth Amendment** abolished slavery throughout the United States.

PHASE II From Freedmen to Citizen

Summer 1865 As the war ended, southern states in the former Confederacy adopted a series of **black codes** to restrict the freedom of African Americans and to preserve many aspects of slavery.

March 1866 Republicans in Congress passed a **Civil Rights Act** that declared all persons born in the United States (except Native Americans) and not subject to any foreign power, were citizens entitled to full and equal benefit of all laws.

June 1866 The **Fourteenth Amendment** reaffirmed the state and federal citizenship of anyone born or naturalized in the United States (except Native Americans) and prohibited any state from allowing any citizen to be denied civil rights and equal protection of the laws.

March 1867 The **Military Reconstruction Act** called for new state constitutions in former Confederate states that had to guarantee the voting rights of African Americans (males) and to ratify the Fourteenth Amendment.

1869–1870 The **Fifteenth Amendment** to the U.S. Constitution prohibited states from denying the vote on the basis of "race, color, or previous condition of servitude."

PHASE III Full Citizenship Denied

1866–1870 African American men in southern states participated in elections at high rates. Six hundred were elected to office. Most African American voters and office holders supported the Republican Party.

1870–1877 White terrorist organizations such as the Ku Klux Klan used violence to suppress African American voting and other forms of political participation. Over time, northern voters lost interest in the process of Reconstruction.

1877 President Hayes withdrew the last federal troops from the South. Over the next several decades, southern states severely curtailed the civil rights of African Americans, including their political participation.

QUESTIONS FOR ANALYSIS

1. What events and movements prompted the federal government to redefine the standing of African Americans in American society between 1857 and 1877?

2. Which of these reforms were widely accepted and which were strongly resisted?

3. How did the Thirteenth, Fourteenth, and Fifteenth Amendments to the U.S. Constitution affect the nation's politics?

4. Why did the federal government abandon its pursuit of racial equality?

say," a former North Carolina slave named Thomas Hall remembered, "but [in 1877] they let us be put back in slavery again."

Reconstruction's Significance

After the Civil War, Congressional Reconstruction gave African Americans an opportunity to experience freedom—but not security or equality. As Thomas Hall noted in acknowledging the end of Reconstruction, African Americans were no longer slaves but they remained dependent "on the southern white man for work, food, and clothing," and most southern whites remained hostile to the notion of civil rights and social equality. The collapse of Congressional Reconstruction in 1877 had tragic consequences, for it allowed the South to renew long-standing patterns of discrimination against African Americans.

Yet for all of the unfulfilled promises of Congressional Reconstruction, it left an enduring legacy—the Thirteenth, Fourteenth, and Fifteenth Amendments—not dead in 1877 but dormant, waiting to be reawakened during the second reconstruction of civil rights in the 1950s and 1960s. If Reconstruction's experiment in interracial democracy did not provide true social equality or substantial economic opportunities for African Americans, it did create the essential constitutional foundation for future advances in the quest for equality and civil rights—not just for African Americans but for women and other minority groups as well. Until the pivotal Reconstruction Era, the states were responsible for protecting citizens' rights. Thereafter, thanks to the Fourteenth and Fifteenth Amendments, blacks had gained equal rights (in theory), and the federal government assumed responsibility for ensuring that states treated blacks equally in terms of their basic civil rights. Congressional Reconstruction was a half-way revolution, sighed the former governor of North Carolina Jonathan Worth, and "nobody can anticipate the action of revolutions." A hundred years later, the cause of civil rights would be embraced again by the federal government—this time permanently.

CORE OBJECTIVE

5. Explain the impact of Reconstruction on the nation's future.

Racial discrimination continues

Thirteenth, Fourteenth, and Fifteenth Amendments lay groundwork for future civil rights movements

■ **Reconstruction Challenges** With the defeat of the Confederacy and the passage of the Thirteenth Amendment, the federal government had to develop policies and procedures to address a number of difficult questions: What was the status of the defeated states and how would they be reintegrated into the nation's political life? What would be the political status of the former slaves and what would the federal government do to integrate them into the nation's social and economic fabric?

■ **Reconstruction over Time** Abraham Lincoln and his successor, southerner Andrew Johnson, wanted a lenient and quick plan for Reconstruction. The *Freedmen's Bureau* attempted to educate and aid freed slaves, negotiate labor contracts, and reunite families. Lincoln's assassination led many northerners to favor the *Radical Republicans*, who wanted a more transformative plan designed to end the grasp of the old plantation elite on the South's society and economy. Southern whites resisted and established *black codes* to restrict the lives of blacks. *Congressional Reconstruction* responded by stipulating that to reenter the Union, former Confederate states had to ratify the *Fourteenth* and *Fifteenth Amendments* to the U.S. Constitution in order to expand and protect the rights of African Americans. Congress also passed the Military Reconstruction Act, which used federal troops to protect the voting rights and civil rights of African Americans.

■ **Views of Reconstruction** Many former slaves found comfort in their families and the independent churches they established, but land ownership reverted to the old white elite, reducing newly freed black farmers to *sharecropping*. African Americans enthusiastically participated in politics, with many serving as elected officials.

Along with white southern Republicans (scalawags) and northern carpetbaggers, they worked to rebuild the southern economy. Many white southerners, however, blamed their poverty on freed slaves and Republicans, and they supported the *Ku Klux Klan*'s violent intimidation of the supporters of these Reconstruction efforts and the goal of "redemption," or white Democratic control of Southern state governments.

■ **Political and Economic Developments and the End of Reconstruction** Scandals during the Grant administration involved an attempt to corner the gold market and the "whiskey ring's" plan to steal millions of dollars in tax revenue. In the face of these troubles and the economic downturn caused by both the *Panic of 1873* over railroad defaults and disagreement over whether to continue the use of *greenbacks* or return to the gold standard, northern support for Reconstruction eroded. Southern white *redeemers* were elected in 1874, successfully reversing the political progress of Republicans and blacks. In the *Compromise of 1877*, Democrats agreed to the election of Republican Rutherford B. Hayes, who put an end to the Radical Republican administrations in the southern states.

■ **The Significance of Reconstruction** Southern state governments quickly renewed long-standing patterns of discrimination against African Americans, but the Fourteenth and Fifteenth Amendments remained enshrined in the Constitution, creating the essential constitutional foundation for future advances in civil rights. These amendments give the federal government responsibility for ensuring equal treatment and political equality within the states, a role it would increasingly assume in the twentieth century.

KEY TERMS

CHRONOLOGY

1865	Congress sets up the Freedmen's Bureau
April 14, 1865	Lincoln assassinated
1865	Johnson issues Proclamation of Amnesty
	All-white southern state legislatures pass "black codes"
1866	Ku Klux Klan organized
	Congress passes the Civil Rights Act
1867	Congress passes the Military Reconstruction Act
	Freedmen begin participating in elections
1868	Fourteenth Amendment is ratified
	The U.S. House of Representatives impeaches President Andrew Johnson; the Senate fails to convict him
1868	Grant elected President
	Six former Confederate states readmitted to the Union
1869	Reestablishment of white conservative rule ("redeemers") in some former Confederate states
1870	Fifteenth Amendment ratified
1870	First Enforcement Acts passed in response to white terror in the South
1872	Grant wins reelection
1873	Panic of 1873 triggers depression
1877	Compromise of 1877 ends Reconstruction

INQUIZITIVE

Go to InQuizitive to see what you've learned—and learn what you've missed—with personalized feedback along the way.

DEBATING Reconstruction

Historians' interpretations of the past change over time. This happens for many reasons. Historians can revise their thinking in light of information from newly discovered *primary sources*. They can also interpret previously examined sources in new ways by applying new methodologies and theories. Finally, historians themselves are influenced by the values of their own society and times. Present-day events or particular personal interests can influence how historians think about the past. The study of how interpretations of history have changed is called *historiography*. It is the history of the field of history. For Part 4, *A House Divided*, the case study of Debating Reconstruction demonstrates how the views of historians have changed dramatically over time.

For this exercise you have two tasks:

PART 1: Compare the two secondary sources on Reconstruction.

PART 2: Using primary sources, evaluate the arguments of the two secondary sources.

PART I **Comparing and Contrasting Secondary Sources**

Two *secondary sources*, the work of prominent historians from different eras, are included below for you to review. The first selection comes from William Dunning's (1857–1922) *Reconstruction, Political and Economic, 1865–1877*, written in 1907. Dunning was born on the eve of the Civil War to a well-to-do New Jersey family and began his studies at Columbia University soon after the end of Reconstruction. He lived during a time when racial segregation and white supremacy were the unchallenged law of the land, and he wrote some of the first academic texts on Reconstruction. Dunning was such a compelling force in the first half of the twentieth century that the many historians trained and influenced by him are referred to as the "Dunning School." He was particularly hostile to political idealists, a group which, in his mind, included abolitionists and Radical Republicans. Like many historians of his day, Dunning never questioned his own objectivity. However, later academics and activists have noted that his writings reflect the political beliefs and prejudices of his generation.

Interpretations of Reconstruction have undergone many changes since Dunning's time. The second excerpt, written 101 years later, is from Eric Foner's *The Story of American Freedom*. Born in 1943, Foner is the son of civil rights activists (one of them a historian) deeply concerned with the plight of African Americans. Foner completed his Ph.D. in 1969 during the height of the civil rights movement. Widely regarded as a leading contemporary historian of Reconstruction, Foner's writing on the period brings together much of the scholarship that has revised "Dunning School" interpretations of Reconstruction, particularly as they described the role of African Americans in American society.

Before you begin reading these excerpts, it may be helpful to review Chapter 15 on the transition from President Andrew Johnson's Restoration Plan to Congressional Reconstruction.

Compare the work of these two historians by answering the following questions. Be sure to support your answers with specific examples drawn from the selections by Dunning and Foner.

■ What is the topic of each excerpt? What period of Reconstruction is the author writing about? What groups are examined in American society?

■ Generally, how does each author portray the Reconstruction process? What in each author's writing leads you to believe that this is how the author feels about Reconstruction? How do those feelings—whether positive or negative—affect each author's point of view?

■ How would you describe the similarities between these two excerpts?

■ What are the major differences in interpretation between the excerpts?

- What is the main argument each historian makes about the topic?

- How do these interpretations compare to that presented in Chapter 15?

- These two excerpts were written 101 years apart. How might this have influenced the development of their arguments?

Secondary Source 1

William Dunning, from *Reconstruction, Political and Economic, 1865–1877*

It was, indeed, no novelty for the people of the South to be subject to government by the United States army. . . . The reasoning by which the policy of Congress was justified in the North was regarded in the South as founded on falsehood and malice. So far as the "black codes" were concerned, it was pointed out that they could not be alleged as evidences of a tendency to restore slavery or introduce peonage [dependence], since the offensive acts had in many of the states been repealed by the legislatures themselves, and in all had been duly superseded by the civil rights act. The much-exploited outrages on freedmen and Unionists were declared to be exaggerated or distorted reports of incidents which any time of social tension must produce among the criminal classes. The rejection of the Fourteenth Amendment was considered as merely a dignified refusal by honorable men to be the instruments of their own humiliation and shame.

Under all these circumstances the southerners felt that the policy of Congress had no real cause save the purpose of radical politicians to prolong and extend their party power by means of negro suffrage [voting rights]. This and this alone was the purpose for which major-generals had been empowered to remodel the state governments at their will, to exercise through general orders the functions of executive, legislature, and courts, and to compel the white people to recognize the blacks as their equals wherever the stern word of military command could reach. It was as inconceivable to the southerners that rational men of the North should seriously approve of negro suffrage per se as it had been in 1860 to the northerners that rational men of the South should approve of secession per se. Hence, in the one case as in the other, a craving for political power was assumed to be the only explanation of an otherwise unintelligible proceeding.

Source: Dunning, William. *Reconstruction, Political and Economic, 1865–1877*. New York: Harper & Bros., 1907. 109–12.

Secondary Source 2

Eric Foner, from *The Story of American Freedom*

Rejecting the idea that emancipation implied civil or political equality or opportunities to acquire property or advance economically, rights northerners deemed essential to a free society, most white southerners insisted that blacks must remain a dependent plantation workforce in a laboring situation not very different from slavery. During Presidential Reconstruction—the period from 1865 to 1867 when Lincoln's successor, Andrew Johnson, gave the white South a free hand in determining the contours of Reconstruction—southern state governments enforced this view of black freedom by enacting the notorious Black Codes, which denied blacks equality before the law and political rights and imposed on them mandatory year-long labor contracts, coercive apprenticeship regulations, and criminal penalties for breach of contract. Through these laws, the South's white leadership sought to ensure that plantation agriculture survived emancipation.

Thus, the death of slavery did not automatically mean the birth of freedom. But the Black Codes so flagrantly violated free labor principles that they invoked the wrath of the Republican North. Southern reluctance to accept the reality of emancipation resulted in a monumental struggle between President Andrew Johnson and the Republican Congress over the legacy of the Civil War. The result was the enactment of laws and constitutional amendments that redrew the boundaries of citizenship and expanded the definition of freedom for all Americans. . . .

Much of the ensuing conflict over Reconstruction revolved around the problem, as Senator Lyman Trumbull of Illinois put it, of defining "what slavery is and what liberty is." . . . By 1866, a consensus had emerged within the Republican Party that civil equality was an essential attribute of freedom. The Civil War had elevated "equality" to a status in the vocabulary of freedom it had not enjoyed since the Revolution. . . . In a remarkable, if temporary, reversal of political traditions, the newly empowered national state now sought to identify and protect the rights of all Americans.

Source: Foner, Eric. *The Story of American Freedom*. New York: W. W. Norton & Company, 1998. 103–105.

PART II Using Primary Sources to Evaluate Secondary Sources

When historians are faced with competing interpretations of the past, they often look at primary source material as part of the process of evaluating the different arguments. In the following selections, you'll find *primary sources* relating to the period of Reconstruction.

Carefully read each of the following primary sources and answer the following questions. Decide how the primary source documents support or refute Dunning's and Foner's arguments about this period. You may find that some documents do both, but for different parts of each historian's interpretation. Be sure to identify which specific components of each historian's argument the documents support or refute.

■ Which of the two historian's arguments is best supported by the primary source documents? Or if you find that both arguments are well supported by the evidence, why do you think the two historians had such different interpretations about the period?

■ Based on your comparison of the two arguments and your analysis of the primary sources, how has the interpretation of Reconstruction by historians shifted over time? What can you conclude about historiography from the work of these two historians?

Primary Source 1
Union Army General Carl Schurz, from *Report on the Condition of the South*

A belief, conviction, or prejudice, or whatever you may call it, so widely spread and apparently so deeply rooted as this, that the negro will not work without physical compulsion, is certainly calculated to have a very serious influence upon the conduct of the people entertaining it. It naturally produced a desire to preserve slavery in its original form as much and as long as possible—and you may, perhaps, remember the admission made by one of the provisional governors, over two months after the close of the war, that the people of his State still indulged in a lingering hope slavery might yet be preserved—or to introduce into the new system that element of physical compulsion which would make the negro work. Efforts were, indeed, made to hold the negro in his old state of subjection, especially in such localities where our military forces had not yet penetrated, or where the country was not garrisoned in detail. Here and there planters

succeeded for a limited period to keep their former slaves in ignorance, or at least doubt, about their new rights; but the main agency employed for that purpose was force and intimidation. In many instances negroes who walked away from the plantations, or were found upon the roads, were shot or otherwise severely punished, which was calculated to produce the impression among those remaining with their masters that an attempt to escape from slavery would result in certain destruction. A large proportion of the many acts of violence committed is undoubtedly attributable to this motive.

Source: Schurz, Carl. *Report on the Condition of the South*, 1865, 39TH CONGRESS, SENATE. Ex. Doc., 1st Session, No. 2, p. 19.

Primary Source 2
Mississippi Vagrant Law, 1865

All freedmen, free negroes and mulattoes in this State, over the age of eighteen years, found on the second Monday in January, 1866, or thereafter, with no lawful employment or business, or found unlawfully assembling themselves together, either in the day or night time, and all white persons so assembling themselves with freedmen, free negroes or mulattoes, or usually associating with freedmen, free negroes or mulattoes, on terms of equality, or living in adultery or fornication with a freed woman, free negro or mulatto, shall be deemed vagrants, and on conviction thereof shall be fined in a sum not exceeding, in the case of a freedman, free negro, or mulatto, fifty dollars, and a white man two hundred dollars, and imprisoned at the discretion of the court, the free negro not exceeding ten days, and the white man not exceeding six months.... All fines and forfeitures collected under the provisions of this act shall be paid into the county treasury for general county purposes, and in case any freedman, free negro or mulatto shall fail for five days after the imposition of any fine or forfeiture upon him or her for violation of any of the provisions of this act to pay the same, that it shall be, and is hereby, made the duty of the sheriff of the proper county to hire out said freedman, free negro or mulatto, to any person who will, for the shortest period of service, pay said fine and forfeiture and all costs....

Source: Mississippi Vagrant Law, *Laws of Mississippi, 1865*, 90 in *Documentary History of Reconstruction: Political, Military, Social, Religious, Educational & Industrial, 1865 to the Present Time*. Ed. Walter Lynwood Fleming. Cleveland, Oh.: The Arthur H. Clark Company, 1906. 283–86.

Primary Source 3

Civil Rights Act of 1866

Be it enacted, . . . That all persons born in the United States and not subject to any foreign power, excluding Indians not taxed, are hereby declared to be citizens of the United States; and such citizens, of every race and color, without regard to any previous condition of slavery or involuntary servitude, except as a punishment for crime whereof the party shall have been duly convicted, shall have the same right, in every State and Territory in the United States, to make and enforce contracts, to sue, be parties, and give evidence, to inherit, purchase, lease, sell, hold, and convey real and personal property, and to full and equal benefit of all laws and proceedings for the security of person and property, as is enjoyed by white citizens, and shall be subject to like punishment, pains and penalties, and to none other, any law, statute, ordinance, regulation, or custom, to the contrary notwithstanding.

Source: Civil Rights Act of 1866, *United States Statutes at Large*, vol. xiv, 27 [April 9, 1866].

Primary Source 4

Radical Republican Thaddeus Stevens, from "The Advantages of Negro Suffrage"

Unless the rebel States, before admission, should be made republican in spirit, and placed under the guardianship of loyal men, all our blood and treasure will have been spent in vain. . . . There is more reason why colored voters should be admitted in the rebel States than in the Territories. In the States they form the great mass of the loyal men. Possibly with their aid loyal governments may be established in most of those States. Without it all are sure to be ruled by traitors; and loyal men, black and white, will be oppressed, exiled, or murdered. . . . Have not loyal blacks quite as good a right to choose rulers and make laws as rebel whites? In the second place, it is a necessity in order to protect the loyal white men in the seceded States. The white Union men are in a great minority in each of those States. With them the blacks would act in a body; and it is believed that in each of said States, except one, the two united would form a majority, control the States, and protect themselves. Now they are the victims of daily murder. They must suffer constant persecution or be exiled. . . . Another good reason is, it would insure the ascendency of the Union party. . . . I believe . . . that on the continued ascendency of that party depends the safety of this great nation. If impartial suffrage is excluded in the rebel States, then every one of them is sure to send a solid rebel representative delegation to Congress, and cast a solid rebel electoral vote. . . . I am for negro suffrage in every rebel State. If it be just, it should not be denied; if it be necessary, it should be adopted; if it be a punishment to traitors, they deserve it.

Source: Stevens, Thaddeus. *Congressional Globe*, January 3, 1867, 252. In *Documentary History of Reconstruction: Political, Military, Social, Religious, Educational & Industrial, 1865 to the Present Time*. Ed. Walter Lynwood Fleming. Cleveland, Oh.: The Arthur H. Clark Company, 1906. 149–50.

Growing Pains

The defeat of the Confederacy in 1865 restored the Union and in the process helped accelerate America's transformation into an agricultural empire and an industrial powerhouse. A stronger sense of nationalism began to replace the regional conflicts of the prewar era. During and after the Civil War, the Republican-led Congress pushed through legislation to promote industrial and commercial development as well as western expansion at the same time that it was "reconstructing" the former Confederate states. In the process of settling the rest of the continent, ruthlessly forcing Indians onto reservations, and exploiting the continent's natural resources, the United States forged a dynamic new industrial economy serving an increasingly national and even international market for American goods.

Fueled by innovations in mass production and mass marketing as well as advances in transportation and communications such as transcontinental railroads and transatlantic telegraph systems, huge corporations began to dominate the economy by the end of the nineteenth century. As the prominent social theorist William Graham Sumner remarked, the relentless process of industrial development "controls us all because we are all in it. It creates the conditions of our own existence, sets the limits of our social activity, and regulates the bonds of our social relations."

Late-nineteenth-century American life drew much of its energy from the mushrooming industrial cities. "This is the age of cities," declared Midwestern writer Hamlin Garland. "We are now predominantly urban." But the transition from an economy made up of mostly small local and regional businesses to one dominated by large-scale national and international corporations affected rural life as well. As early as 1869, novelist Harriet Beecher Stowe reported that the "simple, pastoral" America "is a thing forever gone. The hurry of railroads, and the rush and roar of business" had displaced the Jeffersonian ideal of America remaining a nation of small farms and few cities. For more and more Americans, their work day began with the shriek of a factory whistle rather than a crowing rooster. She exaggerated, of course. Small farms and small towns survived the impact of the Industrial Revolution, but farm folk, as one New Englander stressed, must now "understand farming as a business; if they do not it will go hard with them." The friction between the new forces of the national marketplace and the traditional folkways of small-scale family farming generated social unrest and political revolts (what one writer called "a seismic shock, a cyclonic violence") during the last quarter of the nineteenth century.

The clash between tradition and modernity, sleepy farm villages and bustling cities, peaked during the 1890s, one of the most strife-ridden decades in American history. A deep economic depression, political activism by farmers, and violent conflicts between industrial workers and employers transformed the presidential campaign of 1896 into a clash between rival visions of America's future. The Republican candidate, William McKinley, campaigned on modern urban and industrial values. By contrast, William Jennings Bryan, the nominee of both the Democratic and the Populist parties, was an eloquent defender of America's rural past. McKinley's victory proved to be a turning point in the nation's political and social history. By 1900 the United States had emerged as one of the world's greatest industrial powers, and it would thereafter assume a new leadership role in world affairs—for good and for ill.

CARNEGIE STEEL COMPANY Steelworkers operate the dangerous and magnificent Bessemer converters at Andrew Carnegie's huge steel mill in Pittsburgh, Pennsylvania.

Big Business and Organized Labor

1860–1900

After the Civil War, America witnessed a wild scramble for wealth and an epidemic of political corruption as people rushed to take advantage of boundless economic possibilities. The massive production of supplies for the war effort stimulated a dramatic expansion of the economy that quickened in the years after the war. From 1865 to 1900, the United States experienced the highest rate of economic growth in the world, more than double that of its closest rival, Great Britain. By 1900, American industries and farms dominated global markets in textiles, steel, and oil, wheat and cotton, timber and meat packing.

Such phenomenal economic growth generated profound social changes. Millions of young adults left farms and villages to work in factories, mines, and mills in the fast-growing cities. Women entered the workplace in growing numbers, mostly as clerks, typists, secretaries, teachers, nurses, and seamstresses. And workers in many industries, especially railroads, coal mines, and steel mills, joined unions in an effort to gain better working conditions and higher wages. Strikes—often accompanied by violence—became commonplace during the late nineteenth century as wage laborers sought economic justice.

Rapid industrialization resulted from many factors, not the least of which was the emergence of remarkable and often ruthless business titans who took full advantage of new opportunities, innovative

CORE OBJECTIVES INQUIZITIVE

1. Explain the primary factors that stimulated unprecedented industrial and agricultural growth in the late nineteenth century.

2. Describe the entrepreneurs who pioneered the growth of Big Business, the goals they aimed to achieve, and the strategies they used to dominate their industries.

3. Evaluate the role of the federal government in the nation's economic development during this period.

4. Analyze the ways in which the social class structure and the lives of women changed in the late nineteenth century.

5. Evaluate the efforts of workers to organize unions to promote their interests during this era.

technologies, and political lobbying (including bribery) to grow huge businesses (called *trusts*) that dominated their respective industries. While amassing phenomenal personal wealth and exercising disproportionate political influence, the post–Civil War business leaders also aroused intense criticism. Slowly but insistently, reformers emerged to demand that the government step in to regulate the freewheeling entrepreneurs. By the end of the century, a massive reform movement would force all levels of government—local, state, and federal—to restrain the excesses of the nation's largest businesses to preserve social stability.

CORE **OBJECTIVE**

1. Explain the primary factors that stimulated unprecedented industrial and agricultural growth in the late nineteenth century.

The Causes of Industrial Growth

Several factors converged after the Civil War to accelerate economic growth and industrial development. America's vast natural resources—land, rivers, forests, oil, coal, water, iron ore—created a huge advantage over other nations. At the same time, a flood of immigrants provided an army of new low-wage workers and also expanded the national market of consumers. Between 1865 and 1900, over 15 million newcomers arrived in the United States. In addition, inventors, research laboratories, and business owners developed labor-saving machinery and mass-production techniques that spurred dramatic advances in efficiency and productivity. Farms, canneries, factories, slaughterhouses, mines, mills, refineries, and other businesses turned out more products more cheaply, enabling more people to buy more of them. These technological advances created *economies of scale*, whereby larger business enterprises, including commercial farms, were able to afford expensive new machinery and large workforces that made them more productive than smaller enterprises.

Causes of industrial growth:
1) vast natural resources,
2) flood of immigrants,
3) technological innovations

Innovative business leadership also spurred economic growth. A group of shrewd, determined entrepreneurs created huge new national corporations, some of which became virtual monopolies in industries like oil, steel, sugar, and meatpacking. As one wealthy investor said, a new breed of ruthlessly focused capitalists had emerged after the Civil War, driven by the "same all-pervading, all-engrossing anxiety to grow rich."

The Second Industrial Revolution

Second Industrial Revolution
Beginning in the late nineteenth century, a wave of technological innovations, especially in iron and steel production, steam and electrical power, and telegraphic communications, all of which spurred industrial development and urban growth.

The dramatic increases in economic productivity were spurred by the **Second Industrial Revolution**, which began in the mid–nineteenth century and was centered in the United States and Germany. This revolution resulted from three related developments. The first was the creation of modern transportation and communication systems that gave farmers and factory owners access to national and international markets. The completion of transcontinental railroads and the development of larger, faster steamships helped expand markets worldwide, as did the laying of the telegraph cable under the Atlantic Ocean to connect the United States with Europe.

During the 1880s, a second major breakthrough—the creation of electrical power—accelerated the pace of change in industrial and urban development. Electricity dramatically increased the power, speed, and efficiency of machinery. It also spurred urban growth by making possible trolley and subway systems as well as elevators that enabled the construction of taller buildings.

The third major catalyst for the Second Industrial Revolution was the systematic application of scientific research to industrial processes. In new laboratories staffed by graduates of new research universities and often funded by corporations or wealthy business owners, scientists (mostly chemists) and engineers discovered dramatic new ways to improve industrial processes. Researchers figured out, for example, how to refine kerosene and gasoline from crude oil, and how to make steel more efficiently and in much larger quantities.

Using these improved processes, inventors developed new products—telephones, typewriters, phonographs (record players), adding machines, sewing machines, cameras, zippers, farm machinery—that resulted in lower prices for an array of consumer items. These advances, in turn, expanded the scope and scale of industrial organizations. Capital-intensive industries, those requiring massive investments in specialized equipment, such as steel and oil, as well as processed food and tobacco, began emphasizing mass production and distribution across national and international markets. Serving customers across the nation and around the world required more sophisticated strategies of marketing and advertising, thus expanding those industries. Between 1870 and 1900, expenditures on advertising increased more than tenfold. As early as 1867, a journalist complained that advertisements were invading "every department of life."

> The Second Industrial Revolution: Modern transportation systems and electrical power

> The Second Industrial Revolution: Improvement of industrial processes

Corporate Farming

At the same time that the industrial sector of the economy was experiencing rapid growth and an ever-increasing concentration of ownership and production into huge companies, the agricultural sector was also shifting quickly to a large-scale market model of operation. Corporations developed huge "bonanza" farms (growing mostly wheat and corn) that defied the nation's tradition of small-scale family farming. Bonanza farms appeared first in the Dakotas and Minnesota before spreading across the West. They were run like factories by professional, college-educated managers, who during harvest season would hire hundreds of migrant workers to bring in the crop. Bonanza farms using the latest machinery and scientific techniques became internationally famous for their productivity and efficiency. By 1870, America had become the world's leading agricultural producer, sending massive amounts of grain to foreign markets abroad. In addition, with the start of the

> Large-scale farming: "Bonanza farms"

commercial cattle industry, the processes of slaughtering and packing meat became major industries too. So the farm sector directly stimulated the industrial sector of the economy.

Technological Innovations

Technological innovations spur productivity

After the Civil War, technological innovations spurred phenomenal increases in industrial productivity. The U.S. Patent Office, which had recorded only 276 inventions during the 1790s, registered almost 235,000 new patents a century later, in the 1890s. The list of commercial innovations after the Civil War was lengthy: barbed wire; mechanical harvesters, reapers, and combines; refrigerated rail cars; air brakes for trains; machine tools; steam turbines; typewriters; sewing machines; vacuum cleaners; and countless others. Few, if any, inventions of the time could rival the importance of the telephone, which twenty-nine-year-old Alexander Graham Bell, a Scottish immigrant, patented in 1876. Four years later, Bell perfected the long-distance telephone lines that revolutionized communication. By 1895, there were over 300,000 telephones in use. Before the end of the century, the internal-combustion engine, motion picture, and automobile were stimulating new industries that would flourish in the twentieth century.

New job options for women: Office work and sweatshops

New inventions changed the nature of work. The development of typewriters, for example, brought a flood of women workers into business offices, which had been mostly all male. Because women were presumed to have greater dexterity in their fingers, owners hired them to operate typewriters, in part because they could be paid much less than men. Clerical positions soon became the fastest-growing job category for women. Likewise, the

Office typists Newly entrusted with typewriters, women occupied the secretarial positions at many offices, such as the Remington Typewriter Company, pictured here.

introduction of sewing machines for the mass production of clothing and linens opened new doors to women—if not usually pleasant ones to walk through. So-called sweatshops emerged in the major cities, where large numbers of mostly young women worked long hours stitching textiles in cramped, stifling conditions.

Technological discoveries transformed daily life, none more so than the creations of inventor Thomas Alva Edison. In the laboratory at his "science village" in Menlo Park, New Jersey, Edison promised to produce "a minor invention every ten days and a big thing every six months or so." He invented the phonograph in 1877 and the electric light bulb in 1879. Altogether he created or perfected hundreds of new devices and processes, including the storage battery, dictaphone, mimeograph copier, electric motor, and motion picture camera and projector.

Until the 1880s the United States was lit mostly by flickering kerosene or gas lamps. In 1882 the Edison Electric Illuminating Company, later renamed General Electric, supplied electrical current to eighty-five customers in New York City, launching the electric utility industry. The invention of electric motors enabled factories to locate wherever owners wished; they no longer had to cluster around waterfalls and coal deposits for a ready supply of energy.

> Edison and electricity

Railroads Leading the Way

More than any other industry, the railroads symbolized the impact of innovative technologies on the economic revolution during the second half of the nineteenth century. No other form of transportation played so large a role in the development of the interconnected national marketplace. Railroads moved people and goods faster and farther than anything else could, and they did so in any weather. Towns that had rail stations thrived; those that did not died. A town's connection to a railroad, observed Anthony Trollope, a celebrated British writer touring the United States, was "the first necessity of life, and gives the only hope of wealth."

Although the first great wave of railroad building had occurred in the 1850s, the most spectacular growth took place during the quarter century after the Civil War. Between 1865 and 1873, 35,000 miles of new track were laid across the nation, as much as had been built in the previous thirty years. The national rail network grew to nearly 200,000 miles by 1897, more than all of Europe combined.

> Railroads' contributions to the economic boom

The transcontinental rail lines led the way, helping to populate the Great Plains and the Far West by enabling more people to move west and ship their farm products back east. Railroads were expensive enterprises that required huge capital investments to purchase engines and cars and construct track, trestles, and bridges. The financing of railroads also involved complex transactions. Railroads became the first industry to contract with "investment banks" to raise capital by selling shares of stock to investors

Chinese railroad workers Using horse-drawn carts, picks, shovels, and dynamite, Chinese laborers played a large role in constructing the Transcontinental Railroad's Central Pacific track.

The Union Pacific meets the Central Pacific The celebration of the first transcontinental railroad's completion took place in Promontory, Utah, on May 10, 1869.

around the world. They were also the largest consumers in the economy, stimulating other industries through their vast purchases of iron and steel, coal, timber, leather (for seats), and glass. In addition, railroad companies were the nation's largest employers. By the 1870s, the Pennsylvania Railroad alone had 55,000 employees.

But the railroads also brought problems. Many freewheeling developers cared more about making money than building good railroads. In their race to build new lines, companies overlooked dangerous working conditions that caused thousands of laborers to be killed or injured. Too many unneeded railroads were built; by the 1880s, there were twice as many railroad companies as the economy could support. Some railroads were poorly or even criminally managed and went bankrupt. Railroad lobbyists helped to corrupt state and federal legislators, as the votes of politicians were "bought" with cash or shares of stock in the new railroad companies. As the head of the Union Pacific Railroad admitted, "Our method of doing business is founded upon lying, cheating, and stealing—all bad things."

Building the Transcontinentals

After the Civil War, railroad tracks in the South were gradually rebuilt and expanded. But the most spectacular achievements were the transcontinental lines built west of the Mississippi River across plains and deserts, over roaring rivers and deep canyons, and around and through the nation's tallest mountains, all the way to the Pacific coast. The Pacific Railway Act (1862) authorized the construction of a rail line to be built by the Union Pacific Railroad Company westward from Omaha, Nebraska, and by the Central Pacific Railroad Company eastward from Sacramento, California. Both companies began construction during the war, but most of the work was done after 1865.

By connecting the nation from ocean to ocean, the transcontinental railroads enabled the creation of a truly national market for goods and services, including tourism. In 1872 Congress created Yellowstone, the first national park, and railroads began bringing tourists to the park in northwest Wyoming ten years later. Furthermore, as they pushed into sparsely populated western states and territories, the railroad companies became the region's primary real estate developers. They transported millions of settlers from the East, many of them immigrants who were eager to buy land. The railroads changed the economic and political as well as physical landscape, and enabled the United States to emerge as a world power.

The first transcontinental railroads were extremely expensive to build compared with lines in the East. Because the routes passed through long stretches of unpopulated desert areas, construction materials as well as workers and their food and water had to be hauled long distances. Camps had to be built for housing. Crossing high mountains required extensive use of dynamite and costly tunnels and bridges. Harsh weather caused frequent work disruptions. The high costs made the railroad owners dependent on government financial support, which came in the form of substantial loans and cash subsidies as well as massive grants of "public" land taken from the Indians. The owners also relied on federal troops to crush the Native Americans whose ancestral lands were along the rail route.

The transcontinental railroads were, in the words of General William Tecumseh Sherman, the "work of giants." Their construction required heroic feats by workers and engineers who laid the rails, built the bridges, and

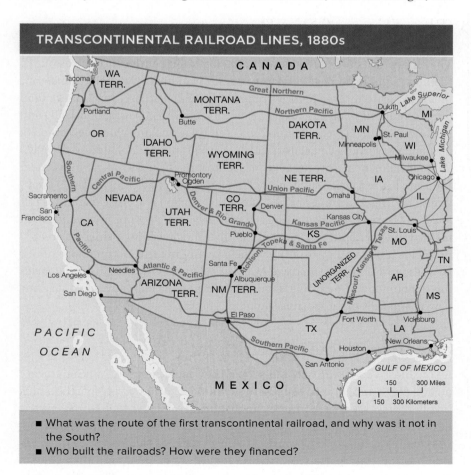

TRANSCONTINENTAL RAILROAD LINES, 1880s

■ What was the route of the first transcontinental railroad, and why was it not in the South?

■ Who built the railroads? How were they financed?

gouged out the tunnels amid dangerous working conditions and severe weather. Some 10,000 men worked on the two railroads as they raced to connect with one another. The Union Pacific crews were composed largely of young, unmarried former Civil War soldiers, both Union and Confederate, along with ex-slaves and Irish and German immigrants. The Central Pacific crews were mainly Chinese workers lured to America either earlier by the California gold rush or more recently by railroad jobs. Most of these "coolie" laborers were single men eager to make money to take back to their homeland, where they could then afford to marry and buy a parcel of land. Their temporary status and dreams of a good life back in China made them more willing than American laborers to endure the low pay and dangerous working conditions.

The Union Pacific had built 1,086 miles of track compared with the Central Pacific's 689 when the race ended at Promontory Summit in the Utah Territory. There, on May 10, 1869, president of the Central Pacific, Leland Stanford, drove a gold spike symbolizing the completion of the first transcontinental railroad. Others soon followed along routes to the north and south.

The Rise of Big Business

CORE **OBJECTIVE**

2. Describe the entrepreneurs who pioneered the growth of Big Business, the goals they aimed to achieve, and the strategies they used to dominate their industries.

The emergence of "Big Business" in the late nineteenth century was one of the most significant developments in American history. Corporations grew much larger than ever before, transacting business across the nation and often around the world. They were also much more powerful politically and socially, forming a web of interconnected relationships with each other to influence governors, legislators, Congress, and presidents. Before the Civil War, most businesses were small, local enterprises run by their owners. After 1865, much of America suddenly got bigger—towns and cities, ships, locomotives, factories, machines, mines, and mills—and business organizations followed the same path in creating the most sweeping economic revolution in history. But the rapid expansion in the size and power of businesses created problems along with prosperity. "The growing wealth and influence of our large corporations," warned the *New York Times*, "is one of the most alarming phenomena of our time. Our public companies already wield gigantic power, and they use it like unscrupulous giants."

The Growth of Corporations

Rise of limited liability corporations and elimination of competition

As businesses grew in size and scope, they took many forms. Some were owned by an individual, usually their founder; others were partnerships involving several owners. Increasingly during the late nineteenth century, however, large companies that served national and international markets were converted into "corporations"—legal entities that separate the *ownership* of an enterprise from the *management* of its operations. Once a corporation is registered ("chartered" or "incorporated") with a state government, it can raise money to operate ("capital") by selling shares of stock—representing partial ownership of the company—to people not otherwise involved with it, although those who found and manage a corporation usually own stock in it as well. Shareholders elect a board of directors who appoint and evaluate the corporation's executives ("management") and can replace them. One of the most important benefits of a corporation is "limited liability": stockholders share in the profits generated by a corporation, but they cannot be held personally liable for its debts if it fails.

Competition is supposed to be the great virtue of capitalism, since it forces businesses to produce better products and lower prices. But as many American businesses grew larger and became giant corporations, some of them came to view competition as a burden. To try to eliminate it, competing companies selling similar products often formed secret "pools" whereby they agreed to keep their prices the same. Pools rarely lasted, however, because one or more of the participants usually violated the agreement by cutting prices. The more effective strategy for the most aggressive companies was to drive out or buy out their weaker competitors.

Strategies like these, as well as the specific methods used to carry them out, aroused considerable controversy. In the process of forming huge companies and eliminating competition, many business leaders cut ethical corners, bribed politicians, exploited workers, and broke laws. When asked how people might react to the shady methods he used to build his network of railroads, William Henry Vanderbilt famously replied: "The public be damned!"

The Barons of Business

Most of the men (few women had such opportunities) who created big businesses and huge fortunes in the late nineteenth century were driven by a compulsive desire to become rich and influential. From the first days of the Jamestown colony in Virginia during the early seventeenth century, the drive to build a fortune has been one of the most powerful forces shaping American life. During and after the Civil War, becoming rich became a dominant ideal for many Americans. "To secure wealth is an honorable ambition," stressed Russell Conwell, a prominent Baptist minister from Philadelphia who crisscrossed the nation preaching the benefits of hard work and its just rewards. "Money is power," he explained, and "every good man and woman ought to strive for power, to do good with it when obtained. I say, get rich! get rich!"

The richly varied industrial and financial giants who emerged after the Civil War personified the values celebrated in Conwell's speech. They were outsized men of grit and genius who found innovative—and occasionally illegal—ways to increase production, create efficiencies, and eliminate competition. Three entrepreneurs, in particular, stand out in this period for their shrewdness, ruthlessness, and remarkable achievements: John D. Rockefeller, Andrew Carnegie, and John Pierpont Morgan.

Rise of industrial and financial giants

John D. Rockefeller Co-founder of Standard Oil Company.

Strategy: Horizontal and vertical integration

Standard Oil Company
Corporation under the leadership of John D. Rockefeller that attempted to dominate the entire oil industry through horizontal and vertical integration.

monopoly Corporation so large that it effectively controls the entire market for its products or services.

John D. Rockefeller

Born in New York in 1839, John D. Rockefeller moved as a youth to Cleveland, Ohio. Soon thereafter, his father abandoned the family. Raised by his mother, a devout Baptist, Rockefeller developed a single-minded passion for systematic organization and self-discipline, and as a young man in the 1860s, he decided to bring order and rationality to the chaotic new boom-and-bust oil industry. Fiercely ambitious and a hard bargainer, he was obsessed with precision, efficiency, tidiness, and money. (A childhood friend recalled that he was "mad about money, though sane about everything else.") He said little, rarely smiled, and hardly ever laughed.

The railroad and shipping connections around Cleveland made it a strategic location for serving the booming oil fields of nearby western Pennsylvania. The first oil well in the United States began producing in 1859 in Titusville, Pennsylvania, and led to the Pennsylvania oil rush of the 1860s. Because oil could be refined into kerosene, then widely used for lighting, heating, and cooking, the economic importance of the oil rush soon outstripped that of the California Gold Rush ten years earlier. Well before the end of the Civil War, oil refineries sprang up in Pittsburgh and Cleveland. Of the two cities, Cleveland had better rail service, so Rockefeller focused his energies there.

In 1870, Rockefeller teamed up with Henry M. Flagler, Samuel Andrews (inventor of an inexpensive means of refining crude oil), and his brother William Rockefeller to establish the **Standard Oil Company** of Ohio. Although the company quickly became the largest oil refiner in the nation, Rockefeller wanted more. His goal was to eliminate his competitors and win control of the entire oil industry, for once he gained a near monopoly, he could raise oil prices as he saw fit. During the 1870s, Rockefeller pursued a strategy of consolidating control called horizontal integration, in which a dominant corporation in a particular industry buys or forces out most of its competitors. In a few cases, Rockefeller hired former competitors as executives, but only "the big ones," he said, "those who have already proved they can do a big business. As for the others, unfortunately they will have to die." By 1879, Standard Oil controlled more than 90 percent of the oil refining in the nation. Still, that was not enough for Rockefeller, who intended "to secure the entire refining business of the world." His goal was a **monopoly**, a business that grows so large that it effectively controls an entire industry.

Rockefeller was ruthlessly efficient in his efforts to dominate the oil industry. He was adept at reducing expenses, incorporating the latest technologies, and eliminating waste while paying "nobody a profit." Because he shipped so much oil by rail, for example, he forced railroads to pay him secret "rebates" on his oil shipments, enabling him to pay less for shipping than his competitors paid. Most important, instead of depending upon the products or services of other firms, known as middlemen, Standard Oil eventually owned everything needed to produce, refine and deliver oil, from wells to the finished product. The company had its own pipelines, built factories to make

The rise of oil Crowding this Pennsylvania farm are wooden derricks that extracted crude oil.

its own wagons and storage barrels, did its own hauling, owned storage tanks and tanker ships, and did whatever else it needed to produce crude oil, refine it into kerosene, gasoline, and lubricants, and then sell it. In economic terms, this business strategy is called vertical integration. A vertically integrated corporation owns all of the different businesses needed to produce and sell its product.

During the 1870s, Standard Oil bought so many of its competitors that, in an effort to limit its economic power, many state legislatures outlawed the practice of one corporation owning stock in competing ones. In 1882, Rockefeller tried to get around such laws by organizing the Standard Oil Trust, a new way of merging businesses. A **trust** is an arrangement that gives a person or corporation (the "trustee") the legal power to manage another person's money or another company. Instead of owning other companies outright, the Standard Oil Trust controlled more than thirty companies spread across several states by having their stockholders transfer their shares "in trust" to Rockefeller and eight other trustees. In return, the stockholders received "trust certificates," which paid them annual dividends from the Trust's earnings. The Standard Oil Trust gave Rockefeller a virtual monopoly over the American oil industry.

> Strategy: Corporate trusts, e.g., the Standard Oil Trust

But the formation of huge corporate trusts, a practice widely copied by the cattle, liquor, sugar, tobacco, salt, and leather industries, among others, generated intense criticism. In 1890, Congress responded by passing the Sherman Anti-Trust Act, which declared that efforts to monopolize industries and thereby "restrain" competition were illegal. Its language was so vague and unclear, however, that it proved to be virtually toothless.

> Sherman Anti-Trust Act

State laws against monopolies were initially more effective than the Sherman Act in controlling trusts. In 1892, Ohio's Supreme Court ordered the Standard Oil Trust dissolved because it was behaving like a monopoly. A furious Rockefeller then found another way of keeping control of his

trust Business arrangement that gives a person or corporation (the "trustee") the legal power to manage another person's money or another company without owning those entities outright.

numerous companies: creating a **holding company**, a huge corporation that controls other companies by "holding" most or all of their stock certificates. A holding company produces nothing itself; it simply owns a majority of the stock in other companies.

Rockefeller was convinced that ending competition among companies by creating a near monopoly was a good thing for the nation. Monopolies, he insisted, were the natural result of capitalism at work. "It is too late," he declared in 1899, "to argue about the advantages of [huge] industrial combinations. They are a necessity. The day of individualism is gone. Never to return." That year, Rockefeller brought his entire industrial empire under the direction of the Standard Oil Company of New Jersey, a gigantic holding company. By 1904, 318 holding companies in the United States controlled more than 5,300 factories.

Andrew Carnegie

Like Rockefeller, Andrew Carnegie, who created the largest steel company in the world during the late nineteenth century, rose from boyhood poverty to fabulous riches in his adult life. Born in Scotland, he migrated with his family in 1848 to Allegheny County, Pennsylvania. At age thirteen, he went to work in a textile mill. In 1853 he became personal secretary to Thomas Scott, then district superintendent of the Pennsylvania Railroad and later its president. When Scott moved up, Carnegie, bright and competitive, shrewd and charming, and driven by a fierce desire to succeed, took his place as superintendent. During the Civil War, when Scott became assistant secretary of war in charge of transportation, Carnegie went with him to Washington, D.C., and helped develop a military telegraph system.

Carnegie kept on moving—from telegraphy to railroading to bridge building and then to steelmaking and investments. In the early 1870s, he decided "to concentrate on the manufacture of iron and steel and be master in that." A tiny man (barely five feet tall) with giant ambitions, Carnegie wanted not simply to excel in the steel industry; he wanted to dominate it, just as John D. Rockefeller was doing with oil. Like Rockefeller, Carnegie accumulated vast wealth for the pure pleasure of the pursuit of it, and he often treated his workers ruthlessly.

Until the mid–nineteenth century, steel, which is stronger and more flexible than iron, could be made only from wrought iron—itself expensive since it had to be imported from Sweden—and only in small quantities. Bars of wrought iron were heated with charcoal over days to add carbon to carbon-free wrought iron. It took three tons of coke, a high-burning fuel derived from coal, to produce one ton of steel. As a result, steel was too costly to make in large quantities.

That changed in the 1850s, when England's Sir Henry Bessemer invented what became known as the Bessemer converter, a process by which high-quality steel could be produced more quickly by blasting air (oxygen) through the molten iron in the furnace. In the early 1870s, Carnegie

Andrew Carnegie Established the Carnegie Steel Company.

Strategy: Continuous innovation, e.g., the Bessemer converter

holding company Corporation established to own and manage other companies' stock rather than to produce goods and services itself.

decided to concentrate his operations on steel because Bessemer's process had made it so inexpensive to produce and the railroad industry needed massive amounts of it. As more steel was produced, its price dropped and its industrial uses soared. In 1860, the United States produced only 13,000 tons of steel. By 1880, production had reached 1.4 million tons annually. Between 1880 and 1900, Carnegie dominated the steel industry, expanding his own business by acquiring competitors or driving them out of business by cutting prices and taking their customers.

Carnegie was never a technical expert on steel. But he was a quick-witted and resilient promoter, salesman, and organizer—and a ferocious competitor. He insisted upon up-to-date machinery and equipment and, like Rockefeller, he expanded quickly and cheaply by purchasing struggling competitors. He also preached a philosophy of continuous innovation to reduce operating costs: "Cut the prices, scoop the market, run the mills full; watch the costs, and profits will take care of themselves."

Like Rockefeller, Carnegie sought to expand his industry by vertical integration, gaining control of every phase of the steel-making business, including the raw materials needed to make steel. He owned coal mines in West Virginia, bought huge deposits of iron ore in Michigan and Wisconsin, and transported the ore in his own ships across the Great Lakes and then by rail to his steel mills in Pittsburgh. The result was phenomenal. By 1900, the **Carnegie Steel Company** produced more steel each year than was produced in all of Great Britain. With 20,000 employees, it was the largest industrial company in the world. And Carnegie worked his people hard. His mills operated nonstop, with two twelve-hour shifts every day and night, the only exception being the Fourth of July.

Carnegie insisted that what he, Rockefeller, and other titans of industry were doing was simply the wave of the future. Rockefeller agreed, saying that the formation of huge trusts was simply "the working out of a law of nature and a law of God."

J. Pierpont Morgan

Unlike Rockefeller and Carnegie, J. Pierpont Morgan was born to wealth. His father was a partner in a large English bank. After attending school in Switzerland and university in Germany, the younger Morgan was sent in 1857 to work in New York City for a new enterprise, **J. Pierpont Morgan and Company**. The firm, under various names, invested European money into American businesses and grew into a financial power by helping competing corporations merge and by purchasing massive amounts of stock in American companies and selling them at a profit.

Morgan took over poorly run companies, appointed new executives, and supervised operations. Like Rockefeller and Carnegie, he believed in capitalism but hated the chaos of competition with other companies. In his view, high profits required order and stability, and stability required consolidating competitors into trusts that he would own and manipulate.

J. Pierpont Morgan Despite his privileged upbringing and financial success, he was self-conscious about his deformed nose, caused by chronic skin diseases.

Carnegie Steel Company Corporation under the leadership of Andrew Carnegie that came to dominate the American steel industry.

J. Pierpont Morgan and Company An investment bank under the leadership of J. Pierpont Morgan that bought or merged unrelated American companies, often using capital acquired from European investors.

Strategy: Mergers to eliminate competition, e.g., United States Steel Corporation

Morgan recognized early on the importance of railroads, and he acquired and reorganized one struggling rail line after another. By the 1890s, he controlled a sixth of the nation's railway system. But his crowning triumph was the consolidation of the steel industry. After a rapid series of mergers, he bought out Carnegie's huge steel and iron holdings in 1901. Morgan added scores of related companies to form the new United States Steel Corporation, the world's first billion-dollar corporation, employing 168,000 people. It was the climactic event in the efforts of the great financial capitalists to reduce industrial competition.

The "Gospel of Wealth"

However harsh the methods employed by the "captains of industry"—a term favored by their supporters—these men were convinced that they benefited the general public by accelerating the Industrial Revolution, creating jobs, and growing the economy. In his essay "The Gospel of Wealth" (1889), Carnegie argued that "not evil, but good, has come to the [Anglo-Saxon] race from the accumulation of wealth by those who have the ability and energy that produces it." But he also felt the need to justify his incredible wealth and denounced the "worship of money." Like other business barons, he and Rockefeller made colossal personal fortunes, but they gave much of their money away, mostly to support education and medicine.

Philanthropy

By 1900, Rockefeller had become the world's leading philanthropist. "I have always regarded it as a religious duty," he said late in life, "to get all I could honorably and to give all I could." He donated more than $500 million during his lifetime, including tens of millions to fund Baptist causes and $35 million to found the University of Chicago. His philanthropic influence continues today through the Rockefeller Foundation. As for Carnegie, after retiring from business at age sixty-five, he declared that the "man who dies rich dies disgraced" and devoted himself to dispensing his $400 million fortune for the public good. Calling himself a "distributor" of wealth (he disliked the term *philanthropy*), he gave huge sums to numerous universities, built 2,500 public libraries around the country, and helped fund churches, hospitals, parks, and halls for meetings and concerts, including New York City's Carnegie Hall.

CORE **OBJECTIVE**
3. Evaluate the role of government in the nation's economic development during this period.

The Alliance of Business and Politics

The building of big businesses by Rockefeller, Carnegie, Morgan, and others depended on more than just their skills as entrepreneurs. Such corporations also developed cozy relationships with local, state, and federal officials, a process of buying influence ("lobbying") that continues to this day. Big Business has legitimate political interests, but, because of its size and resources, it also sometimes exercises a corrupt influence on government. Never was

Celebrating Big Business
A lavish dinner celebrated the merger of the Carnegie and Morgan interests in 1901. The shape of the banquet table is meant to symbolize a rail.

this conflicting role more evident than during the decades after the Civil War. The *New York Times* noted that the largest corporations "control the Legislatures."

Federal and Republican Support for Business

During and after the Civil War, the Republican party and the U.S. government grew increasingly allied with Big Business. A key element of this alliance was tariff policy, one of the most important political issues throughout the nineteenth century. Since 1789, the federal government had imposed tariffs—taxes on imported goods—both to raise revenue and to benefit American manufacturers, by forcing their foreign competitors to raise the prices of their products. In 1861, as the Civil War was starting, the Republican-dominated Congress enacted the Morrill Tariff, which doubled the tax rates on hundreds of imported items as a means of raising money for the war and of rewarding the businesses that supported Abraham Lincoln and the Republican party.

> High tariffs on imported goods

After the war, President Ulysses S. Grant and later Republican presidents and Congresses continued the party's commitment to high tariffs despite complaints that the tariffs increased consumer prices by restricting foreign imports and thereby relieving American manufacturers of the need to keep their prices down to be competitive. Farmers in the South and Midwest resented federal tariffs because they had to sell their crops in an open world market but had to buy manufactured goods whose prices were artificially high because of tariffs. Farmers and other advocates of "free world trade," including most southern Democrats, generally wanted Congress to lower or eliminate tariffs.

Introduction of national paper currency and land grants for homesteads and technical colleges

During the Civil War, the Republican-dominated Congress also passed other key pieces of legislation related to the economy. The Legal Tender Act of 1862 for the first time authorized the federal government to issue paper money to help pay for the war. The new national currency was called "greenbacks" because of its green color. Having a uniform paper currency rather than a hodgepodge of paper money issued by numerous state banks was essential to a modern national economy. To that end, the National Banking Act (1863) created new national banks authorized to issue greenbacks, which discouraged state banks from continuing to issue their own paper money.

At the same time, Congress also took steps to tie the new states and territories of the West into the national economy. The U.S. government owned vast amounts of western land, most of it acquired from the Louisiana Purchase of 1803 and the Oregon Treaty with Britain in 1846. In the Homestead Act of 1862, Congress provided free 160-acre homesteads to settlers on this land. By encouraging widespread western settlement, the Homestead Act promoted economic growth by creating new markets for goods and services and spurring railroad construction to connect frontier communities with major cities. The Morrill Land Grant Act of the same year transferred to each state 30,000 acres of federal land for each member of Congress the state had. The sale of those lands provided funds for states to create colleges of "agriculture and mechanic arts," such as Iowa State University and Kansas State University. The new "land grant" universities were created specifically to support economic growth by providing technical training needed by farmers as well as by rapidly growing industries such as mining, steel, petroleum, transportation, forestry, and construction (engineering). As already noted, Congressional authorization for construction

Homesteaders An African American family poses outside of their log and sod cabin in 1889.

of the first transcontinental railroad and generous federal subsidies, loans, and land grants for the project provided additional boosts to the nation's economic development.

Laissez-Faire Theory and Corrupt Practices

Government's *laissez-faire* approach to business

Equally important in propelling the postwar economic boom was what government did *not* do. It did not regulate the activities of big businesses in any significant way or impose high corporate taxes, nor did it provide any meaningful oversight of business operations or working conditions for wage earners. In general, both Congress and the presidents in this period accepted the economic doctrine of **laissez-faire**, a French phrase meaning "let them do as they will," which opposed government interference in the economy. Business leaders spent time—and money—ensuring that government officials did not regulate their businesses. For their part, members of Congress as well as state legislators were usually eager to help the new titans of industry and finance in exchange for campaign contributions and, often, direct bribes for looking the other way.

A Changed Social Order

CORE **OBJECTIVE**
4. Analyze the ways in which the social class structure and the lives of women changed in the late nineteenth century.

During the late nineteenth century, industrialization transformed not only the economy and the workplace; it also transformed social life. Class divisions became more visible. The growing gap between rich and poor was like "social dynamite," said the Reverend Josiah Strong in 1885. The Massachusetts reformer Lydia Maria Child noticed with alarm the growing class consciousness in America. The rich, she reported, "do not intermarry with the middle classes; the middle classes do not intermarry with the laboring class," nor did different classes "mix socially."

The Ways of the Wealthy

"The Gilded Age"

The financiers and industrialists who dominated social, economic, and political life in post–Civil War America amassed such fabulous wealth and showed it off so publicly that the period is still called "the Gilded Age." The name came from a popular novel by Mark Twain and Charles Dudley Warner, *The Gilded Age: A Tale of Today* (1872), which mocked the crooked dealing and lavish wealth of political leaders and of the business elite, often called "robber barons" by their critics. During the Gilded Age, the share of the nation's wealth owned by the richest 10 percent of families tripled, to more than three-fourths in 1900. In 1861, there were only a few dozen millionaires in the United States. By 1900, there were over 4,000. Most of them were white Protestants who voted Republican, except for the small number of wealthy southern Democrats.

laissez-faire An economic doctrine holding that businesses and individuals should be able to pursue their economic interests without government interference.

Many of the *nouveaux riches* (French for "newly rich") indulged in what came to be called "conspicuous consumption," competing with each other to host the fanciest parties and live in the largest and most extravagantly furnished houses. In 1869, E. L. Godkin, the editor of the *Nation* magazine, wrote that New York City was being flooded by rich "barbarians"—and the following years provided considerable evidence for his accusation. One tycoon gave a lavish dinner honoring his dog and presented it with a $15,000 diamond necklace. At a party at New York's Delmonico's restaurant, the guests smoked cigarettes wrapped in $100 bills. Mrs. Bradley Martin received such a torrent of criticism after spending $368,000 on a banquet that she and her husband fled to England. When the rich were not attending such excessive parties, they were relaxing in monumental mansions overlooking the cliffs at Newport, Rhode Island, atop Nob Hill in San Francisco, along Chicago's Lake Shore Drive and New York City's Fifth Avenue, and down the "Main Line" in suburban Philadelphia.

"Who knows how to be rich in America?" Godkin asked. "Plenty of people know how to get money, but . . . to be rich properly is, indeed, a fine art. It requires culture, imagination, and character."

A Growing Middle Class

Rise of white middle-class professionals

It was left to the fast-growing middle class to display such "character" by practicing its traditional virtues of self-discipline and restraint, simplicity and frugality. The term "middle class" had first appeared in the 1830s and had become commonplace by the 1870s, as more and more Americans came to view themselves as members of a distinct social class between the ragged and the rich. The middle class, explained the Chicago writer George Ade in an 1895 essay, "The Advantage of Being 'Middle Class,'" meant those people who "work either with hand or brain, who are neither poverty-stricken nor offensively rich."

Accompanying the spread of huge corporations after the Civil War was a rising standard of living for many people. While the rich were getting much richer, a lot of other people were also becoming better off. Most middle-class Americans working outside the home were salaried employees of large businesses, people making up a new class of "white-collar" professionals: editors, engineers, accountants, supervisors, managers, marketers, and realtors. Others, with women a growing share of the total, were clerks, secretaries, salespeople, and government employees, including teachers and librarians. At the same time, the number of attorneys, physicians, professors, journalists, nurses, and social workers rose dramatically.

Middle-Class Women

Women admitted to colleges and professional jobs

The growing middle-class female presence in the workforce partly reflected the increasing number of women who were gaining access to higher education. Dozens of women's colleges were founded after the Civil War, and many

College women By the end of the century, women made up more than a third of all college students. Here, an astronomy class at New York's Vassar College is underway in 1880.

formerly all-male colleges began admitting women. By 1900, in fact, a third of college students were women. "After a struggle of many years," a New York woman boasted, "it is now pretty generally admitted that women possess the capacity to swallow intellectual food that was formerly considered the diet of men exclusively." To be sure, college women were often steered into home economics classes and "finishing" courses intended to perfect their house-keeping or social skills. Still, the doors of the professions—law, medicine, science, and the arts—were at least partially opened.

In this context, then, the "woman question" that created so much public discussion and controversy in the second half of the nineteenth century involved far more than the issue of voting rights; it also concerned the liberation of at least some women from the home and from longstanding limits on their social roles and even character traits. In addition to new jobs and professions, middle-class women took advantage of other, often new public venues for female interaction: charitable associations, women's clubs, literary societies, and church work. "If there is one thing that pervades and characterizes what is called the 'woman's movement,'" E. L. Youmans, a prominent science writer, remarked, "it is the spirit of revolt against the home, and the determination to escape from it into the outer spheres of activity."

The "woman question"

Neurasthenia

Yet such determination to escape the "cult of domesticity" often came at a high price. Many women who wanted to play a more active role in the public world contracted a peculiar affliction called neurasthenia, a draining psychological and physical disorder whose symptoms usually included insomnia, hysteria, headaches, depression, and a general state of fatigue. Although neurasthenia plagued both sexes, it most often affected college-educated middle-class women. Some prominent men tried to use this finding to force women back into the "cult of domesticity." George M. Beard, a neurologist who popularized the term *neurasthenia*, concluded—incorrectly—that women were "more nervous, immeasurably, than men," and that female neurasthenics tended to be women who had become "overly active" outside the home. This association of neurasthenia with independence led one doctor to insist that the malady provided the best "argument against higher education of women."

Many prominent women understandably objected to such self-serving male arguments. Charlotte Perkins Gilman, for instance, intended her short story "The Yellow Wallpaper" as a piece of "pure propaganda" to expose the horrors of the "rest cure" she was subjected to at age twenty-seven. A doctor had ordered her to "live as domestic a life as possible; have your child with you all the time; lie down an hour after each meal; have but two hours intellectual life a day; and *never touch pencil, brush, or pen as long as you live.*" This regimen, Gilman explained, took her "as near lunacy as one can, and come back."

Social worker Jane Addams also struggled with neurasthenia. After graduating in 1881 from Rockford College in Illinois, she found few opportunities to use her degree and lapsed into a state of depression during which she developed an intense "desire to live in a really *living* world." Middle-class women, she charged, were "so besotted with our [sentimental] novel reading that we have lost the power of seeing certain aspects of life with any sense of reality because we are continually looking for the possible romance." Addams's intense desire to engage "real life" eventually led her to found Hull House, the famous "settlement house" in Chicago. There, she and other social workers helped immigrants make the transition to American life, and young women like herself "could learn of life from life itself" rather than from books.

The examples of Addams and others helped convince many other middle-class women to enter the "real" world. By 1890, a magazine called *The Arena* could urge progressive-minded people to recognize the traditional view of women as homebodies for what it was: "hollow, false, and unreal." More and more people did just that. Upon returning from England to America in 1904, the illustrious writer Henry James reported that the predominance of "new" women and their struggle for autonomy had become "the sentence written largest in the American sky." Several years later he applauded the shifting emphasis "from the idea of woman's weakness to the idea of her strength."

Jane Addams She believed that social service requires a "scientific" observation of one's community in order to "see the needs" and provide "data for legislation" reform.

The Ladies' Home Journal

Middle-class women and domestic life

Not all middle-class women, however, wanted to venture out into the public world long dominated by men. Many of them identified more with the domestic life that was the focus of numerous mass-circulation magazines for women, the most popular of which was the *Ladies' Home Journal.* By 1892, it had 700,000 subscribers; in 1910 the number reached almost 2 million, the largest circulation of any magazine in the world.

Edward Bok, a Dutch immigrant raised in Brooklyn, New York, became editor of *Ladies' Home Journal* in 1889 at the age of twenty-six. For the next thirty years, he used the magazine as a means of providing a "great clearing house of information" to the large and rapidly growing urban middle class. The *Journal* included departments focused on sewing, cooking, religion, politics, and fiction. Bok was no feminist; "my idea," he stressed, "is to keep women in the home." There, he believed, they would maintain a high moral tone for society, for women were "better, purer, conscientious, and morally stronger than men." In particular, Bok saw the middle-class woman as the crucial "steadying influence" between the "unrest among the lower classes and [the] rottenness among the upper classes."

Bok's view of the ideal life for a woman was a far cry from the extravagant spending of the super-rich. It included "a healthful diet, simple, serviceable clothing, a clean, healthy dwelling-place, open-air exercise, and good reading." Bok preached contentment rather than conspicuous consumption, a message directed not just to his middle-class readers but also to the growing class of working poor. In a Christmas editorial, though, he recognized that "it is a hard thing for those who have little to believe that the greatest happiness of life is with them: that it is not with those who have abundance."

Mennen's Toilet Powder This advertisement appeared in the Independence Day edition of *Ladies' Home Journal* in 1908, suggesting that a homemaker's ability to protect her family from skin discomforts was her own declaration of independence.

The Working Class

The continuing demand for unskilled workers by railroads, factories, mills, mines, slaughterhouses, and sweatshops attracted new groups to the workforce: immigrants above all, but also growing numbers of women and children. In addition, millions of rural folk, especially young people, gave up farming and formed a migratory stream from the agricultural regions of the South and Midwest to the cities.

Although wage levels rose overall during the Gilded Age, there was a great disparity between the pay for skilled and unskilled workers. During the recessions and depressions that occurred about every six years on average, the unskilled workers were the first to be laid off or to have their wages slashed. In addition, working conditions were difficult and often dangerous for those at the bottom of the occupational scale. The average workweek during the late nineteenth century was fifty-nine hours, or nearly six ten-hour days. Most steelworkers put in a twelve-hour day. The death rate in the crowded working-class neighborhoods of major cities was much higher than in the countryside. American industry had the highest rate of workplace accidents and deaths in the world, and there were virtually no safety regulations or government inspections. Few machines had safety devices; few factories or mills had fire escapes. Respiratory diseases were common in mines and unventilated buildings. In the seven years between 1888 and 1894,

16,000 railroad workers were killed and 170,000 maimed in on-the-job accidents. The United States was the only industrial nation with no insurance program to cover medical expenses for on-the-job injuries.

Working Women

Difficult, "unskilled" labor for working-class women

The Second Industrial Revolution transformed the nature of the workplace in ways that meant that mills, mines, factories, and large businesses needed far more unskilled workers than skilled ones. To fill these jobs, employers recruited women and children for many of the unskilled jobs because they were willing to work for lower wages than men. In addition to those laboring over typewriters, sewing machines, or textile looms, millions of women worked as maids, cooks, or other domestic laborers. In the manufacturing sector, women's wages averaged $7 a week, compared to $10 for unskilled men. A social worker sent to investigate working conditions for women reported that it was widely assumed in many factory settings that a married woman would accept lower wages because she "has a man to support her" (which was by no means always true). The number of women working for wages outside the home tripled between 1870 and 1900, when 5 million women (17 percent of all women) held full-time jobs. This development led one male editor to joke that he was being drowned "by the rising tide of femininity" in the workplace.

In a letter to the editor of the *Nation* in 1867, a "working woman" described the changing nature of gender roles in American life. Most middle-class women, she acknowledged, still lived in a "world of love, of a sweet and guarded domesticity, of drawing-rooms and boudoirs, of dainty coquetries, of quiet graces, where they flourish like fair flowers in a south window." But each year "thousands of women" were entering a different world "of mud, carts, ledgers, packing-boxes, counting-houses, paste, oils, leather, iron, boards, committees, big boots, and men who . . . meet women on a cool, business level of dollars and cents."

Child Labor

Child labor

After the Civil War, a growing number of wage laborers were children who worked full time for meager wages under unhealthy conditions. Most young people had always worked in America; farms required everyone to pitch in. After the Civil War, however, millions of children took up work outside the home or off the farm, sorting coal, stitching clothes, shucking oysters, peeling shrimp, canning food, blowing glass, tending looms in textile mills, and operating other kinds of machinery. Parents desperate for income felt forced to put their children to work. By 1880, one of every six children under age fourteen in the nation was working full time; by 1900, the United States had almost 2 million child laborers. In Pennsylvania, West Virginia, and eastern Kentucky, soot-smeared boys worked in the coal mines. In New England and the South, thousands of children worked in dusty textile mills where, during the night shift, they had water thrown in their faces to keep them awake. In the southern mills, a fourth of the employees were below

Children in industry These four young boys performed the dangerous work of mine helpers in West Virginia around 1900.

the age of fifteen, and children as young as eight were laboring alongside adults twelve hours a day, six days a week. As a result, they received little or no education. Factories, mills, mines, and canneries were especially dangerous places for children, who suffered three times as many accidents as adult workers and higher rates of respiratory diseases as well. A child working in a southern textile mill was only half as likely to reach the age of twenty as a child who did not work in a mill.

The "Dreadful Chill of Change"

When the famous writer Henry James returned to the United States in the first decade of the twentieth century after a long stay in England, he was shocked by the "dreadful chill of change" transforming American social life. Urban-industrial development and western expansion had generated unparalleled prosperity, but the United States, he feared, had lost much of its social stability and cohesion. In 1885, one writer said that wage workers, by attempting to organize unions in order to improve their leverage with management, were unleashing "a seismic shock, a cyclonic violence" that threatened to tear society apart.

Organized Labor

During the Gilded Age, thousands of wage workers struggled to organize in an effort to force employers to recognize their needs and concerns. Yet the working poor who tried to form unions to improve their pay and working conditions faced huge obstacles. Most elected officials sided with business owners rather than workers. Another factor impeding the growth of labor

CORE **OBJECTIVE**

5. Assess the efforts of workers to organize unions in order to promote their interests during this era.

unions was that much of the workforce was made up of immigrants who spoke different languages and often distrusted those from other ethnic groups. Nonetheless, with or without unions, workers during the Gilded Age began to stage frequent strikes in response to wage cuts and other grievances. Strikes often led to violence. Perhaps at no time before or since have class tensions—both social and cultural—been as bitter as they were during the last quarter of the nineteenth century.

The Great Railroad Strike of 1877

The Great Railroad Strike of 1877

After the financial panic of 1873, the major rail lines in the East cut the wages of their workers. In 1877, the companies announced another 10 percent wage cut, which led most of the railroad workers at Martinsburg, West Virginia, to walk off the job and block the tracks in order to shut down all traffic. The Great Railroad Strike of 1877 spread quickly to hundreds of other cities and towns, and the resulting violence left more than 100 people dead and millions of dollars in damaged property. In Pittsburgh, thousands of striking workers burned thirty-nine buildings and destroyed more than 1,000 rail cars and locomotives. State militiamen called in from Philadelphia dispersed a crowd at the cost of twenty-six lives, but looting and burning continued until federal troops finally ended it. A reporter described the scene as "the most horrible ever witnessed, except in the carnage of war. There were fifty miles of hot rails, ten tracks side by side, with as many miles of ties turned into glowing coals and tons on tons of iron car skeletons and wheels almost at white heat." Eventually the disgruntled workers, lacking organized bargaining power, had little choice but to drift back to work. The strike failed.

For many Americans, the Great Railroad Strike raised the possibility of what a Pittsburgh newspaper saw as "a great civil war in this country between labor and capital." Equally disturbing to those in positions of corporate and political power was the presence of many women among the protesters. A Baltimore journalist noted that the "singular part of the disturbances is the very active part taken by the women, who are the wives and mothers of the [railroad] firemen."

The Sandlot Incident

The Sandlot Incident

In California the national railroad strike indirectly gave rise to a working-class political movement. In 1877, a meeting held in a sandy San Francisco lot to express sympathy for the railroad strikers ended with attacks on passing Chinese workers. In the aftermath of the so-called Sandlot Incident, white mobs attacked Chinatown, home to 25,000 Chinese, mostly males, who experienced the worst forms of discrimination and segregation. The depression of the 1870s had hit the West Coast especially hard, and the Chinese were handy scapegoats for frustrated white laborers who believed the Asians

"The Chinese Must Go" In this advertisement for the Missouri Steam Washer, the American-made machine drives the stereotype of the Chinese laundryman back to China, playing on the growing anti-Chinese sentiments in the 1880s.

had taken their jobs. Soon an Irish immigrant, Denis Kearney, had organized the Workingmen's Party of California, whose platform called for the United States to stop Chinese immigration. A gifted agitator who had only recently become a naturalized American, Kearney lectured the "sand-lotters" about the "foreign peril" and blasted the rich railroad barons for exploiting the poor. The Workingmen's movement peaked in 1879, when its candidates were elected as state legislators and as mayor of San Francisco. Although Kearney failed to build a lasting movement, his anti-Chinese theme became a national issue. In 1882, Congress voted to prohibit Chinese immigration for ten years.

The Workingmen's Party of California

Toward Permanent Unions

As the size and power of corporations increased during the second half of the nineteenth century, efforts to build a national labor union movement gained momentum. During the Civil War, because of the increased demand for skilled labor, so-called "craft unions" made up of workers skilled in a particular handicraft grew in strength and number. Yet there was no overall connection among such groups until 1866, when the National Labor Union (NLU) convened in Baltimore.

The NLU was more interested in advocating for new state and local laws to improve workplace conditions than in bargaining with employers about wages and hours. It advocated improvements such as the eight-hour workday, workers' cooperatives (in which workers, collectively, would create and own their own large-scale manufacturing and mining operations), "greenbackism" (the printing of paper money to inflate the currency and thereby relieve debtors), and equal voting rights for women and African Americans. Like most such organizations in the nineteenth century, however, the NLU did not allow women as members. As one official explained the attitude of male unionists, "Woman was created to be man's companion," not his competitor in the workplace who would cause his wages to fall.

After William Sylvis, the head of the NLU, died suddenly in 1869 at the age of forty-one, its support fell away, and by 1872 the union had disbanded. The NLU was not a total failure, however. It was influential in persuading Congress to enact an eight-hour workday for federal employees and to repeal the 1864 Contract Labor Act, which was passed during the Civil War to encourage the importation of laborers through an arrangement, similar to the indentured servitude of colonial times, that allowed employers to pay for the passage of foreign workers to America; in exchange, the workers were committed to work for a specified number of years. Employers had taken advantage of the Contract Labor Act to recruit foreign laborers willing to work for lower wages than their American counterparts.

The Knights of Labor

In 1869, another labor group of national standing had emerged: the Noble Order of the **Knights of Labor**. The union grew slowly at first, but even as other unions collapsed during the depression of the 1870s, it spread more rapidly. The Knights of Labor endorsed the reforms advanced by previous workingmen's groups, including the creation of a bureau of labor statistics and mechanics' lien laws (to ensure payment of wages), the elimination of convict-labor competition, the establishment of the eight-hour work day and worker cooperatives, and the use of paper currency. One plank in the platform, far ahead of the times, called for equal pay for equal work by men and women. Throughout its existence, the Knights of Labor condemned violence, class warfare, and socialism; they preferred boycotts to strikes as a

Knights of Labor A national labor organization with a broad reform platform; reached peak membership in the 1880s.

Knights of Labor This national union was the most egalitarian union during the Gilded Age.

way to pressure employers. The Knights allowed as members all who had ever worked for wages, except lawyers, doctors, bankers, and those who sold liquor. Theoretically, it was one big union of all workers, skilled and unskilled, men and women, immigrants and African Americans.

In 1879, Terence V. Powderly, the thirty-year-old mayor of Scranton, Pennsylvania, became head of the Knights of Labor. Born of Irish immigrant parents, Powderly had started working for a railroad at age sixteen. Frail, sensitive to criticism, and indecisive at critical moments, he was in many ways unsuited to his new job. He was temperamentally opposed to strikes, and when they did occur, he did not always support the local groups involved. Yet the Knights owed their greatest growth to strikes that occurred under his leadership. In the early 1880s the Knights increased their membership from about 100,000 to more than 700,000.

> Rise of the Knights of Labor and Terence V. Powderly

Anarchism

One of the many challenges facing the labor union movement was growing hostility from middle-class Americans who came to view unionized workers, especially those involved in clashes with police, as "radicals" or "anarchists." Anarchists believed that government—any government—was a device used by powerful capitalists to oppress and exploit the working poor. They dreamed of the eventual disappearance of government altogether, and some were willing to use bombs and bullets to achieve their revolutionary goal. Many European anarchists immigrated to the United States during the last quarter of the nineteenth century. Although most anarchists disavowed violence, the terrorists among them ensured that the label "anarchist" provoked frightening images in the minds of many Americans.

Labor-related violence increased during the 1880s as the gap between the rich and working poor widened. Between 1880 and 1900, 6.6 million hourly workers participated in more than 23,000 strikes nationwide. Chicago, the fastest-growing city in the nation, was a hotbed of labor unrest and a magnet for immigrants, especially German and Irish laborers, some of whom were socialists or anarchists who endorsed violence as a means of transforming the capitalist system. The Chicago labor movement's foremost demand was for an eight-hour workday, and what came to be called the **Haymarket Riot** grew indirectly out of prolonged agitation for this goal.

The Haymarket Riot

In May 1886, some 40,000 Chicago workers went on strike in support of an eight-hour workday. On May 3, violent clashes between strikers and "scabs" (nonunion workers who defied the strike) erupted outside the McCormick Harvesting Machine plant, where farm equipment was made. The police arrived, shots rang out, and two strikers were killed. The killings infuriated the

Haymarket Riot (1886) Violent uprising in Haymarket Square, Chicago, where police clashed with labor demonstrators in the aftermath of a bombing.

leaders of the tiny anarchist movement in Chicago, which included many women. They printed leaflets demanding "Revenge!" and "Workingmen, to Arms!" Calls went out for a mass protest the following night at Haymarket Square.

On the evening of May 4, after listening to long speeches complaining about low wages and long working hours, the crowd in Haymarket Square was beginning to break up when policemen arrived and ordered the people to disperse. At that point, someone threw a bomb toward the police. The police then fired into the crowd, killing and wounding people, including other policemen. Throughout the night, police arrested scores of people. The next day, all labor meetings were banned in the city, and newspapers across the nation printed sensational headlines about anarchists terrorizing Chicago. One New York paper demanded stern punishment for "the few long-haired, wild-eyed, bad-smelling, atheistic, reckless foreign wretches" who promoted such unrest.

At trials during the summer of 1886, seven anarchist leaders, all but one of them German speakers, were sentenced to death despite the lack of any evidence linking them to the bomb thrower, whose identity was never established. In a statement to the court after being sentenced to be hanged, Louis Lingg declared that he was innocent of the bombing but was proud to be an anarchist who was "in favor of using force" to attack the abuses of the capitalist system. Lawyers for the anarchists appealed the convictions to the Illinois Supreme Court. Meanwhile, petitions from around the world arrived at the Illinois governor's office appealing for clemency. One of the petitioners was Samuel Gompers, the founding president of the American Federation of Labor (AFL), which would soon replace the faltering Knights of Labor as the nation's leading union. "I abhor anarchy," Gompers stressed, "but I also abhor injustice when meted out even to the most despicable being on earth."

On November 10, 1887, Louis Lingg committed suicide in his cell. That same day, the governor commuted the sentences of two of the convicted conspirators to life imprisonment. The next day the four remaining condemned men were hanged. Two hundred thousand people lined the streets of Chicago as their caskets were taken for burial. To labor militants around the world, the executed anarchists were working-class martyrs; to the police and the economic elite in Chicago, they were demonic assassins. In his novel *The Titan*, Theodore Dreiser wrote that the Haymarket Riot "had brought to the fore, once and for all, as by a flash of lightning, the whole problem of mass against class."

Samuel Gompers The head of the American Federation of Labor strikes an assertive pose.

The Decline of the Knights of Labor

After the Haymarket Riot, tensions between workers and management reached a fever pitch. In 1886 alone there were 1,400 strikes across the country involving 700,000 workers. But the violence in Chicago had triggered widespread public hostility to the Knights of Labor and labor groups in general. Despite his best efforts, Terence Powderly could never separate in the public mind the Knights from the anarchists, since one of those convicted of conspiracy in the bombing was a member of the union. Powderly clung to leadership until 1893, but after that the union evaporated. Besides fear of its supposed radicalism and the failure of a railroad strike in 1886, membership in the Knights also declined because its leaders spent more time promoting national reforms than focusing on better wages and working conditions.

The Knights nevertheless attained some lasting achievements, among them an 1880 federal law providing for the arbitration of labor disputes and the creation of the federal Bureau of Labor Statistics in 1884 as well as several state labor bureaus. Another of their successes was the Foran Act of 1885, which, though poorly enforced, penalized employers who imported immigrant workers so that they could pay lower wages. And by their example, the Knights also spread the idea of unionism and initiated a new type of union organization: the industrial union, which included all skilled and unskilled workers within a particular industry, such as railroad workers or miners.

Gompers and the AFL

The craft unions, representing skilled workers, generally opposed efforts to unite with industrial unionism. Leaders of the craft unions feared that joining with unskilled laborers would mean a loss of their craft's identity and a loss of skilled workers' greater bargaining power. Thus, in 1886, delegates from twenty-five craft unions meeting in Columbus, Ohio, organized the **American Federation of Labor** (AFL). Its structure differed from that of the Knights of Labor in that it was a federation of many separate national unions, each of which was largely free to act on its own in dealing with business owners.

Formation of the American Federation of Labor (AFL)

Samuel Gompers served as president of the AFL from its founding until his death, in 1924, with only one year's interruption. Born in England of Dutch Jewish ancestry, Gompers came to the United States as a teenager, joined the Cigarmakers' Union in 1864, and became president of his New York City local union in 1877. Unlike Terence Powderly and the Knights of Labor, Gompers focused on concrete economic gains—higher wages, shorter hours, better working conditions—and avoided utopian ideas or politics.

The AFL at first grew slowly, but by 1890 it had surpassed the Knights of Labor in membership. By the turn of the century, it claimed 500,000 members in affiliated unions; in 1914, on the eve of World War I, it had 2 million; and in 1920 it reached a peak of 4 million. But even then the AFL embraced less than 15 percent of the nation's nonagricultural workers. In fact, all unions, including the railroad brotherhoods unaffiliated with the AFL,

American Federation of Labor Founded in 1886 as a national federation of trade unions made up of skilled workers.

accounted for little more than 18 percent of those workers. Organized labor's strongholds were in transportation and the building trades. Most of the larger manufacturing industries—including steel, textiles, tobacco, and meatpacking—remained almost untouched. Gompers never opposed industrial unions, and several became important affiliates of the AFL: the United Mine Workers, the International Ladies Garment Workers, and the Amalgamated Clothing Workers. But the AFL had its greatest success in organizing skilled workers.

Two incidents in the 1890s stalled the emerging industrial-union movement: the **Homestead Steel Strike** of 1892 and the **Pullman Strike** of 1894. These violent labor conflicts represented the climactic economic events of the Gilded Age. Each pitted workers in a bitter contest against one of the nation's largest and most influential corporations. The two strikes not only represented a test of strength for the organized labor movement but also served to reshape the political landscape.

The Homestead Steel Strike

The Homestead Steel Strike

The Amalgamated Association of Iron and Steel Workers, founded in 1876, was the largest craft union. At the massive iron and steel mill at Homestead, Pennsylvania, near Pittsburgh, the union had enjoyed friendly relations with Andrew Carnegie's company until the stern Henry Clay Frick became company chairman and chief executive in 1889. A showdown was delayed until 1892, however, when the union contract came up for renewal. Carnegie, who had previously expressed sympathy for unions, went on a lengthy hunting trip in his native Scotland, leaving the rigid Frick to handle the difficult negotiations. Yet Carnegie knew what was in the works: a cost-cutting reduction in the number of highly paid skilled workers through the use of labor-saving machinery. It was a deliberate attempt to smash the union. "Am with you to the end," he wrote to Frick after leaving for Scotland.

As negotiations dragged on, the company announced on June 25 that it would stop negotiating with the union on June 29 unless an agreement was reached. A strike—or, more properly, a lockout of unionists, in which management closed down the mill to try to force the union to make concessions—began on that date. Frick told journalists that he was determined to have "absolute control of our plant and business." To that end, he built a twelve-foot-high fence around the plant and equipped it with watchtowers, searchlights, barbed wire, and high-pressure water cannons. He also hired a private army of 316 men from the Pinkerton Detective Agency to protect what was soon dubbed Fort Frick. Before dawn on July 6, 1892, the "Pinkertons" floated up the Monongahela River on two barges pulled by a tugboat.

Thousands of unionists and supporters, many of them armed, were waiting on shore. A fourteen-hour battle broke out in which seven workers and three Pinkertons were killed and dozens wounded. Hundreds of women on

Homestead Steel Strike (1892) Labor conflict at the Homestead steel mill near Pittsburgh, Pennsylvania, culminating in a battle between strikers and private security agents hired by the factory's management.

Pullman Strike (1894) A national strike by the American Railway Union, whose members shut down major railways in sympathy with striking workers in Pullman, Illinois; ended with intervention of federal troops.

shore shouted, "Kill the Pinkertons!" In the end, the Pinkertons surrendered, having agreed to be tried for murder, and were marched away to taunts from crowds lining the streets. A week later, the Pennsylvania governor dispatched 4,000 state militiamen to Homestead, where they surrounded the steel mill and dispersed the picketing workers. Frick then hired strikebreakers to operate the mill. He refused to resume negotiations: "I will never recognize the union, never, never!"

The strike dragged on until November, but by then the union was dead and its leaders had been charged with murder and treason. The union cause was not helped when Alexander Berkman, a Lithuanian anarchist, tried to assassinate Frick on July 23, shooting him twice in the neck and stabbing him three times. Despite his wounds, Frick fought back fiercely and, with the help of staff members, subdued the would-be assassin. Much of the local sympathy for the strikers evaporated. As a union leader explained, Berkman's bullets "went straight through the heart of the Homestead strike." Penniless and demoralized, the defeated workers ended their walkout on November 20 and accepted the company's harsh wage cuts. Only a fifth of the strikers were hired back; the rest were "blacklisted" to prevent other steel mills from hiring them. Carnegie and Frick, with the support of local, state, and national government officials, had eliminated the union.

The Pullman Strike

The Pullman Strike of 1894 was an even more notable confrontation between workers and management, as it paralyzed the economies of the twenty-seven states and territories making up the western half of the nation. It involved a dispute at Pullman, Illinois, a "model" industrial suburb of Chicago owned by the Pullman Palace Car Company, which made passenger train cars (called "Pullmans" or "sleeping cars"). Employees who built rail cars were required to live in the town's 1,400 cottages, which had been built to high standards, with gas heat and indoor plumbing. With 12,000 residents, the town of Pullman also boasted a library, a theater, a school, a church (without a congregation), parks and playgrounds, and a glass-roofed shopping mall owned by the company. There were no saloons, however, nor any social clubs, newspapers, or private property not owned by the company. No political activities, including election of local officials, were allowed.

As a "company town," Pullman was of much higher quality than the many villages in the South owned by textile mills, and the death rate there was less than half of that in neighboring communities. Yet over time, many workers complained that they did not like living under the thumb of the company's owner, George Pullman.

During the terrible depression of 1893, George Pullman laid off 3,000 of his 5,800 employees and cut wages 25 to 40 percent for the rest, but did not lower rents for housing or the price of food in the company store. In the spring of 1894, desperate workers joined the American Railway Union,

The Pullman Strike

The Growth of Big Business and Its Impact on Late-19th-Century America

The growth of Big Business in the late nineteenth century dramatically reshaped the lives of millions of Americans. Large corporations led the way in making the United States into the world's leading nation in manufacturing and the majority of the American labor force into factory workers and miners rather than farmers. The growth of Big Business made manufactured products and industrial resources like electricity widely available to Americans and enriched the nation as a whole. But the concentration of wealth in the hands of a relatively few corporate leaders and wealthy investors provoked profound discontent among millions of Americans frustrated by low wages and harsh working conditions.

Entrepreneurs of Big Business

■ John D. Rockefeller, Standard Oil

■ Andrew Carnegie, Carnegie Steel

■ J. Pierpont Morgan, J. Pierpont Morgan and Company

Goals of Big Business

■ Bring order and stability to various sectors of the economy

■ Increase profits and destroy competitors

Strategies Pursued by Big Business

. . . to become a monopoly:

■ **Horizontal integration:** A dominant corporation within an industry buys or forces out its competition to become a monopoly.

■ **Vertical integration:** A corporation owns all the different businesses needed to produce and sell its products to become a monopoly.

. . . to avoid government regulation:

■ **Limited liability corporations:** Ownership and management are separated, and stockholders share in the corporation's profits but are not liable for its debts.

■ **Trusts:** Granted authority to manage people's investments or companies, for an annual dividend.

■ **Holding companies:** Producing nothing but controlling a majority of stock in other companies.

. . . to maintain a monopoly:

■ Continuous innovation, cost reduction, investment in technology, elimination of waste.

■ At times, exploitation of workers, illegal activity, bribery and/or control of public officials through campaign funding and other contributions.

Consequences of Big Business

... for better:

■ Created jobs, reduced unemployment

■ Increase in supply of affordable products improved quality of life for many

... for worse:

■ Increased economic inequality, with 10% of Americans controlling 75% of the nation's wealth by 1900

■ American economy dominated by Big Business, with 318 holding companies controlling more than 5,300 factories by 1904

■ Increased corruption in all major political parties and levels of government

Reactions to Big Business

General public

■ Appreciated the technological innovations, increased access to new goods and services, employment opportunities, and other benefits

■ Disturbed many who believed competition was great virtue of capitalism

Federal and state governments and courts

■ Attempted to outlaw corrupt Big Business practices, though corporations found ways around legislation, which was often vague and hard to enforce

■ Officials usually supported rights of corporations over its workers, even sending in federal troops to suppress strikes, e.g., the Homestead Strike of 1892 and the Pullman Strike of 1894

Labor unions and workers

■ Combated exploitation, poor working conditions, lowered wages, and layoffs by negotiating with corporation owners, lobbying for pro-worker legislation, and striking

■ Lost public support when violence resulted from their efforts

■ Involvement of socialists and anarchists, in addition to the violence, led many to see labor activism as radical and frightening

QUESTIONS FOR ANALYSIS

1. What were the overall goals of Big Business?

2. What strategies were used to pursue these goals?

3. What were the consequences of the rise of Big Business?

4. How did the government and the public react to the growth of Big Business?

Eugene V. Debs Founder of the American Railway Union, and later the presidential candidate for the Socialist Party of America.

founded the previous year by Eugene V. Debs. The charismatic Debs was a child of working-class immigrants who had quit school at age fourteen to work for an Indiana railroad. By the early 1890s, he had become a tireless spokesman for labor radicalism, and he strove to organize all railway workers—skilled or unskilled—into the American Railway Union, which soon became a powerful labor organization. He quickly turned his attention to the Pullman controversy, urging the workers to obey the laws and avoid violence. After George Pullman fired three members of a workers' grievance committee, the workers went on strike on May 11, 1894.

In June, after Pullman refused Debs's plea for a negotiated settlement, the Railway Union workers stopped handling trains containing Pullman rail cars. By the end of July, they had shut down most of the railroads in the Midwest, cutting off all traffic through Chicago. To keep the trains running, railroad executives hired strikebreakers, and the U.S. attorney general, a former lawyer for railroad companies, swore in 3,400 special deputies to protect them. Angry workers assaulted strikebreakers and destroyed property.

Finally, on July 3, President Grover Cleveland sent 2,000 federal troops into the Chicago area, claiming it was his duty to ensure delivery of the mail. Meanwhile, the attorney general convinced a federal judge to sign an "injunction," an official court decree, prohibiting the labor union from interfering with the delivery of mail and interstate commerce. On July 13, the union called off the strike. A few days later, a judge cited Debs for violating the injunction, and he served six months in jail. The Supreme Court upheld the decree in the case of *In re Debs* (1895) on broad grounds of national sovereignty: "The strong arm of the national government may be put forth to

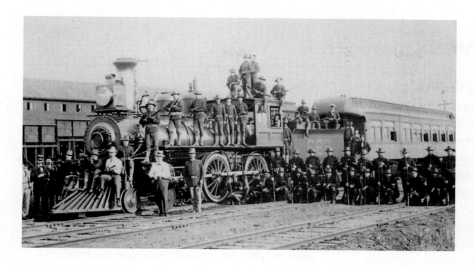

The Pullman Strike Federal troops guarding the railroads, 1894.

brush away all obstructions to the freedom of interstate commerce or the transportation of the mails." Debs emerged from jail as a socialist who would later run for president. In 1897, George Pullman died of a heart attack, and the following year, the city of Chicago annexed the town of Pullman. A reporter for the *Nation* noted that despite the town's attractive features, what the workers wanted most was the chance to own a house of their own. "Mr. Pullman," he explained, "overlooked this peculiar American characteristic."

Economic Success and Excess

For all of the stress and strain caused by the industrialization of the American economy, the nation's productivity soared in the late nineteenth century. By 1900, the United States was producing a third of the world's goods. The corporate empires created by a generation of outsized business leaders created enormous fortunes for a few and real improvements in the quality of life of the many. The majority of American workers for the first time now labored in factories and mines rather than on farms. "One can hardly believe," observed the philosopher John Dewey, "there has been a revolution in history so rapid, so extensive, so complete." The urban-industrial revolution and gigantic new corporations had transformed the size, scope, and power of the American economy, for good and for ill. As the twentieth century dawned, an unregulated capitalist economy had gotten recklessly out of balance—and only government intervention could restore economic fairness and social stability.

■ **The Causes of Industrial Growth** During the late nineteenth century, agricultural and industrial production increased sharply. The national railroad network increased to nearly 200,000 miles, the most of any nation in the world. Farmers and industrialists expanded their production for both national and international markets. The *Second Industrial Revolution* saw the expanded use of electrical power, the application of scientific research to industrial processes, and other commercial innovations that brought new products to market and improved methods for producing and distributing them.

■ **The Rise of Big Business** Many businesses transformed themselves into limited-liability corporations and grew to enormous size and power in this period, often ignoring ethics and the law in doing so. Leading entrepreneurs like John D. Rockefeller, Andrew Carnegie, and J. Pierpont Morgan were extraordinarily skilled at organizing and gaining control of particular industries. Companies such as Rockefeller's *Standard Oil* and *Carnegie Steel* practiced both vertical integration, through which they controlled all the various enterprises needed to produce and distribute their products, and horizontal integration, in which they absorbed or eliminated their competitors. To consolidate their holdings and get around laws prohibiting *monopolies*, they created *trusts* and eventually *holding companies* in an effort to bring "order and stability" to the marketplace.

■ **The Alliance of Business and Politics** The federal government encouraged economic growth after the Civil War by imposing high tariffs on imported products, granting public land to railroad companies and settlers in the West, establishing a stable currency, and encouraging the creation of "land grant" universities to spur technical innovation and research. Equally important, local, state, and federal governments made little effort to regulate the activities of businesses. This *laissez-faire* policy allowed entrepreneurs to experiment with new methods of organization, but also created the conditions for rampant corruption and abuses.

■ **A Changed Social Order** The huge fortunes of the "Gilded Age" flowed to a few prominent families, and social class tensions worsened as productivity increased. While the business and financial elite showed off their new wealth with extravagant homes and parties, the urban and industrial workforce was largely composed of unskilled workers, including recent immigrants, former farmers, and growing numbers of women and children. Business owners and managers showed little concern for workplace safety, and accidents and work-related diseases were common. Industrialization and the rise of Big Business also increased the number of people considering themselves part of the middle class. Middle-class women increasingly went to college, took business and professional jobs, and participated in other public activities despite male resistance.

■ **Organized Labor** It was difficult for unskilled workers to organize effectively into unions, in part because of racial and ethnic tensions among laborers, language barriers, and the efforts of owners and supervisors to undermine unionizing efforts. Business owners often hired "strikebreakers," usually immigrant workers who were willing to take jobs at the prevailing wage because they were so desperate for a job. Business owners often relied on the support of political leaders, who would mobilize state and local militias and federal troops against strikers. Nevertheless, several unions did organize and advocate for workers' rights at a national level, including the National Labor Union and the *Knights of Labor*. After the violence associated with the *Haymarket*

Riot and the *Homestead Steel Strike* and *Pullman Strike*, many Americans grew fearful of unions and viewed them as politically radical. Craft unions made up solely of skilled workers became more successful at organizing, such as the *American Federation of Labor*.

KEY TERMS

laissez-faire p. 567

Second Industrial Revolution p. 552

monopoly p. 560

Standard Oil Company p. 560

trust p. 561

holding company p. 562

Carnegie Steel Company p. 563

J. Pierpont Morgan and Company p. 563

Knights of Labor p. 576

Haymarket Riot (1886) p. 577

American Federation of Labor p. 579

Homestead Steel Strike (1892) p. 580

Pullman Strike (1894) p. 580

CHRONOLOGY

1859	First oil well is struck in Titusville, Pennsylvania
1861	Congress creates the Morrill Tariff
1869	First transcontinental railroad is completed
1876	Alexander Graham Bell patents his telephone
1876	Thomas A. Edison invents incandescent lightbulb
1880s	Widespread use of electrical power begins
1882	John D. Rockefeller organizes the Standard Oil Trust
1886	Haymarket Riot
1886	American Federation of Labor is organized
1892	Homestead Steel Strike
1894	Pullman Strike
1901	J. Pierpont Morgan creates the U.S. Steel Corporation

INQUIZITIVE

Go to InQuizitive to see what you've learned—and learn what you've missed—with personalized feedback along the way.

MINING ON THE COMSTOCK (1877) The Comstock Lode was one of the largest gold and silver mines to be discovered in America, yielding over $300 million over two decades. This illustration shows a cutaway of the Comstock Lode, revealing the complex network of shafts and supports, as well as the various tasks of miners within its tunnels.

The South and the West Transformed

1865–1900

After the Civil War, the devastated South and the untamed West provided two frontiers of enticing opportunities for economic enterprise. The war-devastated South had to be rebuilt; the sparsely settled territories and states west of the Mississippi River were ripe for the development of farms, businesses, railroads, and towns. Banks and financiers in America and Europe took advantage of these conditions to invest heavily in both regions. While both the South and West offered huge forests, valuable minerals, and plentiful opportunities for industrial projects, this was particularly true of the western region between the Mississippi River and California.

Throughout the first half of the nineteenth century, the Great Plains had been viewed as a barren landscape suitable only for Indians and animals. Half the state of Texas, for instance, was still not settled at the end of the Civil War. After 1865, however, the federal government encouraged western settlement and economic development. The construction of transcontinental railroads, the military conquest of the Indians, and the policy of distributing government-owned lands at low cost to settlers, ranchers, miners, and railroads combined to lure millions of pioneers and enterprising capitalists westward. Charles Goodnight, a Texas cattle rancher, recalled that "we were adventurers in a great land . . . fresh and full of the zest of darers." By 1900, a New West and a New South

CORE OBJECTIVES InQuizitive

1. Analyze the ways in which a "New South" emerged economically in the late nineteenth century.

2. Describe the crop-lien system that emerged in the South and explain how it shaped the region after the Civil War.

3. Explain how and why white southerners took away African Americans' right to vote and adopted "Jim Crow" segregation laws at the end of the nineteenth century.

4. Identify the various groups of migrants to the West after the Civil War and the reasons they went there.

5. Describe the experiences of miners, farmers, ranchers, and women in the West in the late nineteenth century.

6. Evaluate the impact on Native Americans of the federal government's policies in the West after the Civil War.

7. Describe how the South and West had changed by 1900.

had emerged, and eleven new states had been created out of the western territories.

The Myth of the New South

After the Civil War, the South fought an inner civil war over the future of the region. Many white southerners embraced the "Lost Cause," a romanticized interpretation of the war that pictured the Confederates as noble, chivalrous defenders of the distinctive southern way of life against a tyrannical federal government headed by Abraham Lincoln. Southerners devastated by defeat were haunted by a lingering nostalgia for the mythic Old South of white-columned plantations, white supremacy, and cotton-generated wealth produced by armies of enslaved blacks. As one southerner said, his native region remained "old-fashioned, medieval, provincial, worshipping the dead."

At the same time, no region has inspired a more tenacious *pride of place*, a localism anchored in family life enlivened by visions of a mythic past. The Mississippi writer Eudora Welty once explained that in the South, "feelings are bound up with place." *Home* and *history* are two of the most revered words in southern life. Nineteenth-century southerners did not simply live in the present and dream of the future. They were forever glancing backward in the process of moving forward. Their romanticized common history provided much of the script for the ongoing drama of their lives. As William Faulkner recognized in his novel *Intruder in the Dust*, "The past isn't dead. It's not even past."

Other prominent southerners, however, looked more to the future, a future much different than the Old South. They called for a New South where the region's predominantly agricultural economy would be diversified by an expanded industrial sector.

The tireless champion of the New South ideal during the 1880s was Henry Woodfin Grady (1850–1889), the powerful managing editor of the *Atlanta Constitution*. In 1886, he told a New York City audience that there had been an Old South "of slavery and secession—that South is dead. There is now a New South of union and freedom—that South, thank God, is living, breathing, and growing every hour." The Old South, he added, "rested everything on slavery and agriculture, unconscious that these could neither give nor maintain healthy growth."

Grady saw the New South becoming "a perfect democracy" of small farms growing varied crops. This healthy agricultural sector would be complemented by new mills, factories, and cities. The postwar South, Grady claimed, held the promise of a real democracy, one no longer run by the planter aristocracy and no longer dependent upon slave labor. He imagined a New South with "a hundred farms for every plantation, fifty homes for every palace—and a diversified industry that meets the complex needs of this complex age."

Many southerners shared Henry Grady's vision of a New South dotted with new industries. The Confederacy, they concluded, had lost the war because it had relied too much upon King Cotton—and slavery. In the future, the New South must follow the North's example ("out-Yankee the Yankees") and develop a strong industrial sector to go along with its agricultural foundation. Promoters of a New South also stressed that more-efficient farming, using the latest machinery and technical expertise, was essential in the still-backward South; that more-widespread vocational training was urgently needed; and that racial harmony built upon the acceptance by blacks of white supremacy would provide a stable social environment for economic growth.

Developing a Textile Industry

The chief accomplishment of the New South was a dramatic expansion of the region's textile industry, which produced thread and cotton-based bedding and clothing. From 1880 to 1900, the number of cotton mills in the South grew from 161 to 400, the number of mill workers (most of whom were white, with women and children outnumbering men) increased fivefold, and the demand for cotton products went up eightfold. Tens of thousands of dirt-poor farm folk—many of them children—rushed to take jobs in the new textile mills that blossomed after the war. Seventy percent of southern textile mill workers were under the age of twenty-one, and many were under the age of fourteen. A dawn-to-dusk job in a mill paying fifty cents a day "was much more interesting than one-horse farming," noted one worker, "because you can meet your bills." Those bills were usually paid to the mill owner, who provided ramshackle housing and basic supplies to the workers in his company village—for a fee. By 1900, the South had surpassed New England as the largest producer of cotton fabric in the nation.

> Cotton fabrics

The Tobacco Industry

Tobacco growing and cigarette production also increased significantly in the New South. Essential to the rise of the tobacco industry was the Duke family of Durham, North Carolina. At the end of the Civil War, the story goes, Washington Duke took a barnload of tobacco, dried it, and, with the help of his two sons, hitched two mules to his wagon, and set out across the state, selling tobacco in small pouches as he went. By 1872 the Dukes had a factory producing 125,000 pounds of tobacco annually, and Washington Duke prepared to settle down and enjoy success.

His son James Buchanan "Buck" Duke wanted even greater success, however. He poured large sums into advertising schemes and perfected the mechanized mass production of cigarettes. Duke also undersold competitors in their own markets and cornered the supply of ingredients needed to make cigarettes. Eventually his primary competitors agreed to join forces

> Tobacco and cigarettes

Southern smokes Allen & Ginter was a major tobacco manufacturer that joined the American Tobacco Company. This advertisement, featuring black laborers in the tobacco fields, plays to the southern nostalgia for the "Old Dominion" before the Civil War.

American Tobacco Company Business founded in 1890 by North Carolina's James Buchanan Duke, who combined the major tobacco manufacturers of the time, controlling 90 percent of the country's booming cigarette production.

Redeemers Post–Civil War Democratic leaders who supposedly saved the South from Yankee domination and preserved the primarily rural economy.

with him, and in 1890 Duke brought most of them into the **American Tobacco Company**, which controlled nine tenths of the nation's cigarette production. A ferociously hard worker, Duke was well on his way to becoming one of the wealthiest and most powerful men in the nation. "I needed no vacation or time off," Duke explained. "There ain't a thrill in the world to compare with building a business and watching it grow before your eyes."

Other New South Industries

Effective use of other abundant natural resources helped revitalize the South along the Appalachian Mountain chain from West Virginia to Alabama. Coal production in the South (including West Virginia) grew from 5 million tons in 1875 to 49 million tons by 1900. At the southern end of the mountains, Birmingham, Alabama, sprang up during the 1870s in the shadow of Red Mountain, so named for its iron ore, and boosters soon tagged the steelmaking city the "Pittsburgh of the South."

Urban and industrial expansion as well as rapid population growth created a need for housing, and after 1870 lumbering became a thriving industry in the South, as housing required wood. Northern investors bought up vast pine forests throughout the region and set about clear-cutting them. By 1900, lumber had surpassed textiles in annual economic value.

The Redeemers

Henry Grady's vision of a New South celebrated the heroic **Redeemers**, the conservative, pro-business politicians in the Democratic Party who had supposedly rescued the white South from the hell of federally imposed Reconstruction and embraced a new vision of industrial progress grounded in white supremacy. The supporters of these white Democratic leaders referred to them as Redeemers because they supposedly saved the South from Yankee domination and "black rule" during the Reconstruction Era.

The Redeemers included a rising class of lawyers, merchants, railroad executives, mill owners, and entrepreneurs who wanted a more diversified economy based upon industrial development and railroad expansion along with cuts in state taxes and expenditures, including those for the public-school systems started after the war. "Schools are not a necessity," claimed a Virginia governor. Louisiana cut back so much on school funding that the percentage of residents unable to read and write actually increased between 1880 and 1900. Black children in particular suffered from such cutbacks. But the Redeemers did not want educated African Americans. "What I want here is Negroes who can make cotton," explained a white planter, "and they don't need education to help them make cotton."

The Failings of the New South

CORE **OBJECTIVE**

2. Describe the crop-lien system that emerged in the South and explain how it shaped the region after the Civil War.

Despite the development of some mills and factories, by the end of the nineteenth century the South had fallen far short of the diversified economy that Henry Grady and others had envisioned in the mid-1880s. The South in 1900 remained the least industrial, least urban, least educated, and least prosperous region in the nation. Per capita income in the South in 1900 was only 60 percent that of the national average. The typical southerner was less likely to be tending a textile loom or a steel furnace than, as the saying went, facing the eastern end of a westbound mule or risking his life in an Appalachian coal mine. The postwar South remained dependent on the North for investment capital and for manufactured goods.

Henry Grady had also called for more diversified agriculture, but cotton remained king after the Civil War, even though it never regained the huge profitability it had generated in the 1850s. By the 1880s, southern farmers were producing as much cotton as they had before the war, but were earning far less money because the world price for cotton declined throughout the decade. "Cotton planting has been a mania," one observer noted. "The neglected corn field with all its consequences is a part of southern history."

Southern Poverty

Grady also hoped that growing numbers of southern farmers would own their own land by the end of the nineteenth century. But the opposite occurred. The majority of southern farmers struggled merely to survive after the Civil War, and many of them actually lost ownership of the land that they worked each year. A prolonged decline in crop prices that affected the entire economy during the last third of the nineteenth century made it more difficult than ever to own farm land. By 1890, falling rates of farm ownership in the Lower South dispelled Grady's dream as the region sank deeper and deeper into poverty. By 1900, 70 percent of farmers did not own the land they worked, and in no southern state were more than half of farmers landowners.

Because most southern communities had no banks after the Civil War, people had to find ways to operate with little or no cash. Many rural areas adopted a barter economy in which a local "crossroads" or "furnishing" merchant would provide food, clothing, seed, fertilizer, and other items to poor farmers "on credit" in exchange for a share (or "lien") of their crops when harvested.

Origins of the crop-lien system

The Crop-Lien System

The southern farmers, white and black, who participated in the **crop-lien system** fell into three distinct categories: small farm owners, sharecroppers, and tenants. The farms owned by most southerners were small and financially fragile; they did not generate much cash income. As a result, even

crop-lien system Credit system used by sharecroppers and share tenants who pledged a portion ("share") of their future crop to local merchants or land owners in exchange for farming supplies, food, and clothing.

"Free slaves" Sharecroppers painstakingly pick cotton while their white overseer observes them from atop his horse.

owners had to pledge a portion of their future crop to the local merchant in return for supplies purchased "on credit."

Tenant farmers and sharecroppers

Sharecroppers, mostly blacks who had nothing to offer but their labor, worked 20–40 acres of an owner's land in return for shelter, seed, fertilizer, mules, supplies, and food—as well as a share of the crop, generally about half. Share tenants, mostly white farmers who were barely better off, might have their own mule or horse, a plow and tools, and a line of credit with the nearby country store, but they still needed to rent land to farm. A few paid their rent in cash, but most, like sharecroppers, pledged a share of the harvested crops to the landowner. Usually, the tenant farmers were able to keep a larger share of the crop (about 60 percent) than the sharecroppers, which meant that landowners often preferred to rent acreage to "croppers" rather than tenants. And many African American sharecroppers worked for the same planter who had earlier owned them as slaves. "The colored folks," said a black Alabama sharecropper, "stayed with the old boss man and farmed and worked on the plantations. They were still slaves, but they were free slaves." Eighty percent of southern blacks lived on farms in the late nineteenth century. African American Ned Cobb, an Alabama sharecropper, recalled that his father "put me to plown' the first time at nine years old, right after my mother died." He plowed "barefoot" on rocky land.

The crop-lien system was terribly inefficient and even corrupting. The overwhelming focus on planting cotton or tobacco year after year stripped the soil of its fertility and stability, causing disastrous erosion as topsoil during storms washed into nearby creeks and rivers whose banks caved in, creating ever-deepening gullies. In addition, landowners required croppers and tenants to grow only a "cash crop," usually cotton or tobacco. This meant that the landless farmers could not grow their own vegetable gardens; they had to get their food from the local merchant in exchange for promised cotton. And because most farmers did not own the land they worked, the cabins they lived in, or the tools they used, they had little incentive to enrich the soil or maintain buildings and equipment owned by the

sharecroppers Poor, mostly black farmers who would work an owner's land in return for shelter, seed, fertilizer, mules, supplies, and food, as well as a substantial share of the crop produced.

landlord. "The tenant," explained a South Carolina–born economist, Matthew B. Hammond, "is interested only in the crop he is raising, and makes no effort to keep up the fertility of the land." The tenant system of farming, he concluded, had been "more wasteful and destructive than slavery was anywhere."

The crop-lien system was in essence a post–Civil War version of economic slavery for poor whites as well as blacks. Georgia's Tom Watson said that the masses of landless farmers were "like victims of some horrid nightmare . . . powerless—oppressed—shackled." The landowner or merchant (often the same person) decided what crop would be planted and how it would be cultivated, harvested, and sold. The landowner could enter a tenant or cropper's cabin whenever he pleased. In good times, croppers and tenants barely broke even; in bad times, they struggled to survive. Sharecroppers and share tenants were among the poorest people in the nation—for three generations. Most of them lived in poor health in rude shacks; they had little or no education, rarely enough healthy food, and little hope for a better future.

> Crop-lien system: Inefficient, corrupt, a form of slavery, and self-defeating

Those who worked the farms of large landowners developed an intense suspicion of them, for landlords often swindled the workers by not giving them their fair share of the crops. Landlords kept the books, handled the sale of the crops, and gave the cropper or tenant his share of the proceeds after deducting for all the items supplied during the year, plus interest that

> Economic stagnation

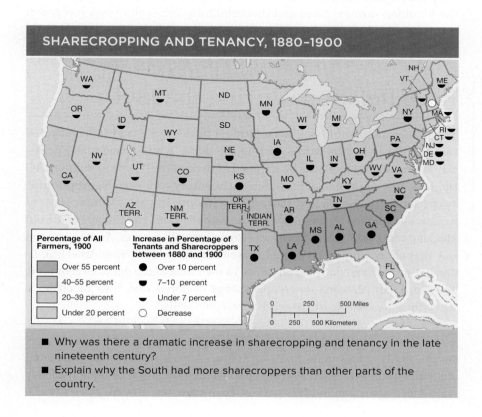

SHARECROPPING AND TENANCY, 1880–1900

Percentage of All Farmers, 1900
- Over 55 percent
- 40–55 percent
- 20–39 percent
- Under 20 percent

Increase in Percentage of Tenants and Sharecroppers between 1880 and 1900
- ● Over 10 percent
- ◗ 7–10 percent
- ◗ Under 7 percent
- ○ Decrease

0   250   500 Miles
0   250   500 Kilometers

- Why was there a dramatic increase in sharecropping and tenancy in the late nineteenth century?
- Explain why the South had more sharecroppers than other parts of the country.

ranged, according to one newspaper, "from 24 percent to grand larceny." Often, the cropper or tenant received nothing at the end of a harvest but a larger debt to be rolled over to next year's crop. Over time, the high interest charged on the credit offered by the local store or landowner, coupled with sagging prices for cotton and other crops, created a hopeless cycle of perennial debt among small farmers, sharecroppers, and share tenants.

Falling Cotton Prices

The one-crop system of southern agriculture was self-defeating. As cotton production soared during the last quarter of the nineteenth century, largely because of dramatic growth in Texas cultivation, the price paid for raw cotton fell steadily. "Have you all felt the effects of the low price of cotton," Mary Parham of Amite, Louisiana, wrote to her father in 1892. "It nearly ruined us. I did not get my house built. The farmers are very blue here. But [they are] getting ready to plant cotton again." As the price declined, desperate farmers planted even more cotton, which only accelerated the decline in price.

In the 1870s, annual production of cotton was about 2.6 billion pounds, which brought an average price of 11.77 cents per pound. In the 1880s, the average annual production was 3 billion pounds at 10.44 cents per pound. By 1896, the average price of cotton was down to 7.72 cents. The average annual income of white southerners in 1900 was about half that of Americans outside the South. Eleven percent of whites in the South were illiterate, twice the national average. The poorest people in the nation's poorest region were the 9 million former slaves and their children. Per capita black income in 1900 was a third of that of southern whites, and the black illiteracy rate in the South was nearly 50 percent, almost five times higher than that of whites.

CORE **OBJECTIVE**

3. Explain how and why white southerners took away African Americans' right to vote and adopted "Jim Crow" segregation laws at the end of the nineteenth century.

Race Relations during the 1890s

The desperate plight of southern farmers in the 1880s and 1890s affected race relations—for the worse. During the 1890s, white farmers and politicians demanded that blacks be stripped of their voting rights and other civil rights as well. At the end of the nineteenth century, a violent "**Negrophobia**" swept across the South and much of the nation. In part, the new wave of racism was spurred by the revival in the United States and Europe of the old idea that the Anglo-Saxon "race" was superior to other races. Another reason was that many whites had come to resent any signs of African American financial success and political influence in the midst of the decade's economic downturn. An Alabama newspaper editor declared that "our blood boils when the educated Negro asserts himself politically."

Disenfranchising African Americans

By the 1890s, a new generation of African Americans born and educated since the end of the Civil War was determined to gain true equality. They were more assertive and less patient than their parents. "We are not the

Negrophobia A violent new wave of racism that spread in the late nineteenth century largely spurred by white resentment for African American financial success and growing political influence.

Negro from whom the chains of slavery fell a quarter century ago, most as-suredly not," a black editor announced. A growing number of young white adults, however, were equally determined to keep "Negroes in their place."

The Mississippi Plan

Mississippi led the way to the near-total loss of voting rights by blacks—and many poor whites as well. The so-called **Mississippi Plan**, a series of state constitutional amendments in 1890, set the pattern of disenfran-chisement that nine more states would follow over the next twenty years. First, a residence requirement for voting—two years in the state, one year in an election district—struck at African American tenant farmers who were in the habit of moving yearly in search of better economic opportuni-ties. Second, voters were disqualified if convicted of certain crimes that disproportionately involved blacks. Third, all taxes, including a so-called poll tax specifically for voting, had to be paid before a person could vote—a restriction that hurt both poor blacks and poor whites. Finally, all voters had to be literate, and white registrars decided who could read and who could not.

Voter intimidation and suppression

Other states added variations on the Mississippi Plan. In 1898, Louisi-ana invented the "grandfather clause," which allowed illiterate whites to vote if their fathers or grandfathers had been eligible to vote on January 1, 1867, when African Americans were still disenfranchised. By 1910, Georgia, North Carolina, Virginia, Alabama, and Oklahoma had adopted the grandfa-ther clause. Every southern state, moreover, adopted a statewide Demo-cratic primary between 1896 and 1915, and most of these primaries excluded African American voters.

When such "legal" means were not enough to ensure their political dominance, white candidates used fraud and violence to eliminate the black vote. Benjamin Tillman, the white male supremacist who served as governor of South Carolina from 1890 to 1894, provides a good example of the transformation in southern politics during the 1890s.

Tillman's election resulted from his effective use of the state's class di-visions and racial tensions. Declaring that South Carolina's farm problems were caused by white farmers renting their land to "ignorant lazy negroes," he and other political rebels gained the support of poor whites across the state to oust the Redeemers, whom he claimed had failed to help the poor whites. Tillman claimed that "I organized the majority [of voters] and put the old families out of business, and we became and are the rulers of the state." To ensure his election, Tillman and his followers eliminated the black vote. He admitted that "we have done our level best [to prevent blacks from voting]. . . . We stuffed ballot boxes. We shot them. We are not ashamed of it." The whites had gained control of the state government, he concluded, "and we intend at any and all hazards to retain it."

By the end of the nineteenth century, widespread racial discrimina-tion—segregation of public facilities, political disenfranchisement, and vigilante justice—had elevated government-sanctioned bigotry to an offi-cial way of life in the South. Benjamin Tillman bluntly declared in 1892 that blacks "must remain subordinate or be exterminated."

Mississippi Plan (1890) Series of state constitutional amend-ments that sought to disenfran-chise black voters and was quickly adopted by nine other southern states.

The efforts to suppress the black vote quickly succeeded. In 1896, Louisiana had 130,000 registered black voters. By 1900, it had only 5,320. In Alabama in 1900, 121,159 black men over twenty-one were literate, according to the census; only 3,742, however, were registered to vote. By 1900, black voting across the southern states had declined by 62 percent, the white vote by 26 percent.

The Spread of Racial Segregation

At the same time that southern blacks were being shoved out of the political arena, they were also being segregated socially. The symbolic first target was the railroad passenger car. In 1885, novelist George Washington Cable noted that in South Carolina, blacks "ride in first-class [rail] cars as a right" and "their presence excites no comment." From 1875 to 1883, in fact, any local or state law requiring racial segregation violated the federal Civil Rights Act (1875). By 1883, however, many northern whites endorsed the resegregation of southern life. In that year, the U.S. Supreme Court ruled that the Civil Rights Act of 1875 was unconstitutional. The judges explained that private individuals and organizations could engage in acts of racial discrimination because the Fourteenth Amendment specified only that "no State" could deny citizens equal protection of the law.

> **Civil Rights Act of 1875 declared unconstitutional**

The Court's interpretation of what came to be called the Civil Rights Cases (1883) left as an open question the validity of various state laws requiring racially segregated public facilities under the principle of "separate but equal," a slogan popular in the South in the late nineteenth century. In the 1880s, Tennessee and Mississippi required railroad passengers to ride in racially segregated cars.

When Louisiana followed suit in 1890, blacks challenged the law in the case of *Plessy v. Ferguson* (1896). The case originated in New Orleans when Homer Plessy, an octoroon (a person having one-eighth African ancestry), refused to leave a whites-only railroad car and was convicted of violating the law. In 1896, the Supreme Court ruled that states had a right to create laws segregating public places such as schools, hotels, and restaurants. Justice John Marshall Harlan, a Kentuckian who had once owned slaves, was the only member of the Court to dissent. He stressed that the Constitution is "color-blind, and neither knows nor tolerates classes among citizens. In respect of civil rights, all citizens are equal before the law." He feared that the Court's ruling would plant the "seeds of race hate" under "the sanction of law."

> *Plessy v. Ferguson* (1896): "separate but equal"

That is precisely what happened. The Court's ruling in the *Plessy* case legitimized the practice of racially **"separate but equal"** facilities in virtually every area of southern life, including streetcars, hotels, restaurants, hospitals, parks, sports stadiums, and places of employment. In 1900, the editor of the *Richmond Times* expressed the prevailing view throughout the white South when he insisted that racial segregation "be applied in every relation of Southern life. God Almighty drew the color line, and it cannot be

"separate but equal"
Underlying principle behind segregation that was legitimized by the Supreme Court ruling in *Plessy v. Ferguson* (1896).

obliterated. The negro must stay on his side of the line, and the white man must stay on his side, and the sooner both races recognize this fact and accept it, the better it will be for both."

The new regulations requiring racial segregation came to be called "Jim Crow" laws. The name derived from "Jump Jim Crow," an old song-and-dance caricature of African Americans performed by white actor Thomas D. Rice in blackface makeup during the 1830s. During the 1890s, the term "Jim Crow" became a satirical expression meaning "Negro." Signs reading "white only" or "colored only" above restrooms and water fountains emerged throughout the South as hallmarks of the "Jim Crow" system. Old racist customs dating back before the Civil War were revived. If whites walked along a sidewalk, blacks were expected to step aside and let them pass. There were even racially separate funeral homes, cemeteries, and churches. When a white deacon in a Mississippi Baptist church saw a black man in the sanctuary, he asked: "Boy, what you doin' in there? Don't you know this is a white church?" The black man replied: "Boss, I'm here to mop the floor." The white man paused and said, "Well, that's all right then, but don't let me catch you prayin'."

As with disenfranchisement of black voters, widespread violence accompanied the creation of Jim Crow laws. From 1890 to 1899, the United States averaged 188 lynchings per year, 82 percent of which occurred in the South. Lynchings usually involved a black man (or men) accused of a crime, often rape. White mobs would seize, torture, and kill the accused, always in ghastly ways. Racial lynchings became so common that participating whites viewed them as forms of outdoor entertainment. Large crowds, including women and children, would watch the grisly event amid a carnival-like

> "Jim Crow" laws

> Lynching

The Lynching of Henry Smith
Despite lack of evidence, Smith was convicted of murdering a white girl in Paris, Texas. A large crowd assembled to watch her family torture Smith from a platform labeled "Justice." After Smith was burned alive, the townspeople kept his charred teeth and bones as souvenirs.

atmosphere. Photographs of gruesome lynchings surrounded by crowds of laughing and smiling whites were reproduced on postcards mailed across the nation. The governor of Mississippi declared that "if it is necessary that every Negro in the state will be lynched, it will be done to maintain white supremacy."

Mob Rule in North Carolina

White supremacy was violently imposed in the thriving coastal port of Wilmington, North Carolina, then the largest city in the state, with about twenty thousand residents. In 1894 and 1896, black voters, by then a majority in the city, elected blacks to various municipal offices, infuriating the city's white elite. "We will never surrender to a ragged raffle of Negroes," warned a former congressman and Confederate colonel named Alfred Waddell, "even if we have to choke the Cape Fear River with [black] carcasses." It was not an idle threat.

On the morning of November 10, 1898, some two thousand well-armed white men and teens rampaged through the streets of Wilmington. They first destroyed the offices of the *Daily Record*, the city's black-owned newspaper, then moved into the black neighborhoods, shooting African Americans and destroying homes and businesses. Almost a hundred blacks were killed. The mob then stormed the city hall, declared that Colonel Waddell was the new mayor, and forced the African American business leaders and elected officials to board northbound trains. The new self-appointed all-white city government issued a "Declaration of White Independence" that stripped blacks of their voting rights and their jobs. Desperate black residents appealed for help to the governor as well as President William McKinley, but received none.

The Wilmington Insurrection marked the first time in history that a lawfully elected municipal government had been overthrown in the United States. Two years later, in the 1900 statewide elections, white supremacist Democrats vowed to cement their control of the political process. The night

Wilmington Insurrection

Wilmington Insurrection A mob of white supremacists pose with their rifles before the demolished printing press of the *Daily Record*, an African American newspaper.

before the election, Colonel Waddell urged supporters to use any means necessary to suppress black voting: "You are Anglo-Saxons. You are armed and prepared and you will do your duty. . . . Go to the polls tomorrow, and if you find the negro out voting, tell him to leave the polls, and if he refuses, kill him, shoot him down in his tracks. We shall win tomorrow if we have to do it with guns." The Democratic party won by a landslide.

The Black Response

African Americans responded to the resurgence of racism in various ways. Some left the South in search of greater safety, equality, and opportunity, but the vast majority stayed in their native region and tried to adjust to the brutal realities of white supremacy. "Had to walk a quiet life," explained James Plunkett, a Virginia African American. "The least little thing you would do, they [whites] would kill ya."

Yet accommodation did not mean submission. Black southerners nurtured their own culture and racial pride. A young white visitor to Mississippi in 1910 noticed that nearly every black person he met had "two distinct social selves, the one he reveals to his own people, the other he assumes among the whites."

African American churches continued to serve as hubs for black community life. Churches were used not only for worship but for social gatherings, club meetings, and political rallies. Churches enabled African Americans of all classes to interact and exercise roles denied them in the larger society. For men especially, churches offered leadership roles and political status. Serving as a deacon was often one of the most prestigious positions for an African American man.

> African American churches

Booker T. Washington

By the 1890s, Booker T. Washington, born a slave in Virginia, in 1856, the son of a black mother and a white father, had become the foremost African American orator and educator in the nation. At sixteen, he had enrolled at Hampton Normal and Agricultural Institute, one of several colleges for former slaves created during Reconstruction. Nine years later, the founder of Hampton Institute, Samuel Armstrong, a former Union general, received a request from a group in northern Alabama starting a black college called Tuskegee Institute. They needed a president of the new school. Armstrong urged them to hire Washington. Although only twenty-five, he was, according to Armstrong, "a very capable mulatto, clear headed, modest, sensible, polite, and a thorough teacher and superior man."

Young Washington was selected, and he quickly went to creating a school on a vacant lot. The first students had to help construct the first buildings, making the bricks themselves. Washington became a skilled

Booker T. Washington Founder of the Tuskegee Institute, a historically black university. He went on to become the nation's most prominent African American leader.

fundraiser, gathering substantial gifts from wealthy whites, most of them northerners. As the years passed, bustling Tuskegee Institute became celebrated as a college dedicated to discipline and vocational training. Washington's recurring message to students was the importance of "practical knowledge." In part to please his white donors, he argued that blacks should not focus on fighting racial segregation. They should instead work hard, don't complain, and don't stir up trouble. At the same time that white southerners were preventing blacks from voting and imposing Jim Crow laws, Washington was urging African Americans to begin "at the bottom," as well-educated farmers, not as social activists.

Yet Washington's conservative approach emphasizing economic self-sufficiency did not satisfy many white racists. Thomas Dixon, a prominent North Carolina Baptist minister, state legislator, and novelist, complained that Washington was teaching his students "to be masters of men, to be independent, to own and operate their own industries," all of which would "destroy the last vestige of dependence on the white man for anything."

In a famous speech in Atlanta in 1895, Washington told the African Americans in the segregated audience that fighting for "social equality" would be a huge mistake ("the extremest folly"). Instead he emphasized that they should "cast down your bucket where you are—cast it down in making friends . . . of the people of all races by whom we are surrounded. Cast it down in agriculture, mechanics, in commerce, in domestic service, and in the professions." He insisted that black southerners could succeed economically while accepting the new Jim Crow laws segregating them from whites. "In all things that are purely social," he explained, "we can be as separate as the five fingers, yet one as the hand in all things essential to mutual progress." In sum, Washington wanted to build a prosperous black community and a thriving Tuskegee Institute, and to do so he became skilled at saying what whites wanted to hear. Civil rights for blacks would have to wait. Any effort at "agitation" in the white-dominant South would, he warned, backfire on the black community. The region's heritage of racial hatred would have to subside over time.

W. E. B. Du Bois

W. E. B. Du Bois A fierce advocate for black education and civil rights.

By the start of the twentieth century, Booker T. Washington had become the most influential African American leader in the nation. Some younger black leaders, however, criticized him for sacrificing civil and political rights in his crusade for vocational education. W. E. B. Du Bois led this criticism. A native of Massachusetts, Du Bois first experienced racial prejudice as a student at Fisk University in Nashville, Tennessee. Later he became the first African American to earn a doctoral degree from Harvard (in history and sociology). In addition to promoting civil rights, he left a distinguished record as a scholar, authoring more than twenty books. Trim and dapper, Du Bois had a flamboyant personality and a combative spirit. Not long after he began teaching at Atlanta University in 1897, he launched a public assault on Booker T. Washington's strategy for improving the quality of life for African Americans.

Du Bois called Washington's 1895 speech "the **Atlanta Compromise**" and the name stuck. Du Bois refused to "surrender the leadership of this race to cowards." Washington, he argued, was so determined to please powerful whites that he "accepted the alleged inferiority of the Negro" so blacks could "concentrate all their energies on industrial education, the accumulation of wealth, and the conciliation of the South." Du Bois stressed that the priorities should be reversed—that African American leaders should adopt a strategy of "ceaseless agitation" directed at ensuring the right to vote and winning civil equality. The education of blacks, Du Bois maintained, should not be merely vocational but should develop bold leaders willing to challenge segregation and discrimination. He demanded that disenfranchisement and legalized segregation cease immediately and that the laws of the land be enforced.

For his part, Washington stressed that Du Bois never truly understood the brutal dynamics of southern racism. His militant strategy, if enacted in the South, would only have gotten more blacks lynched. Nor did Du Bois or other critics know that Washington secretly financed legal efforts to oppose the Jim Crow laws. Such "quiet efforts," he noted, were more successful and realistic than the "brass band" approach championed by Du Bois.

The dispute between Washington and Du Bois came to define the tensions that would divide the twentieth-century civil rights movement: militancy versus conciliation, separatism versus assimilation, social justice versus economic opportunities. By 1915, when Washington died, the leadership of the nation's black community was passing to Du Bois and others whose principled, yet uncompromising effort to gain true equality signaled the beginning of the civil-rights century.

The Settling of the New West

Like the South, the West is a region wrapped in myths and stereotypes. The vast land west of the Mississippi River contains remarkable geographic extremes: majestic mountains, roaring rivers, deep-sculpted canyons, blistering deserts, wide and grassy plains, and dense forests. For most western Americans, the great epics of the Civil War and Reconstruction were remote events hardly touching the lives of the Indians, Mexicans, Asians, farmers, ranchers, trappers, miners, and Mormons scattered through the plains, valleys, and mountains. There the relentless march of settlement and exploitation continued, propelled by a lust for land, a passion for profit, and a restless desire to improve one's lot in life. Between 1870 and 1900, Americans settled more land in the West than had been occupied

CORE **OBJECTIVE**
4. Describe the various groups of migrants to the West after the Civil War and the reasons they went there.

Atlanta Compromise (1895) Speech by Booker T. Washington that called for the black community to strive for economic prosperity before demanding political and social equality.

before 1870. The post–Civil War West symbolized the American emphasis on economic opportunity and personal freedom. On another level, however, the economic development of the West was a tragedy of shortsighted greed and irresponsible behavior, a story of reckless exploitation that scarred the land, decimated its wildlife, and nearly exterminated Native American culture.

The Western Landscape

After mid-century, farmers and their families began spreading west across Iowa and Kansas to the Great Plains—western Kansas, Nebraska, and Oklahoma, northern Texas, the Dakotas, and eastern Colorado, Wyoming, and Montana. From California, miners moved eastward through the mountains to Utah and Nevada, drawn by one new strike after another. From Texas, nomadic cowboys migrated northward onto the plains and across the Rocky Mountains, into the Great Basin of Utah.

The settlers in the West encountered climates and landscapes markedly different from those they had left behind. The Great Plains were dry, and the scarcity of water and timber rendered useless the familiar trappings of the pioneer—the ax, the log cabin, the rail fence—as well as the accustomed methods of tilling the soil. For a long time, the region between the Mississippi River and California had been called the Great American Desert, unfit for human habitation and therefore, in the minds of white Americans, the perfect refuge for Indians. But that view changed in the last half of the nineteenth century. The discovery of large deposits of gold, silver, copper, iron, and coal, the completion of the transcontinental railroads, the collapse of Indian resistance, and the rise of the range-cattle industry convinced many Americans that there were huge profits to be made in the West. With the use of what water was available, new techniques of "dry farming" and irrigation could make the land fruitful after all.

The Migratory Stream

During the second half of the nineteenth century, an unrelenting stream of migrants flowed into what had been the largely Indian and Hispanic West. Millions of Anglo-Americans, African Americans, Mexicans, South Americans, and European and Chinese immigrants transformed the patterns of western society and culture. Most of the settlers were relatively prosperous white, native-born farm folk. Because of the expense of transportation, land, and supplies, the very poor could not afford to relocate. Three quarters of the western migrants were men.

Canadian, Northern European, and Chinese immigrants

The largest number of foreign immigrants came from northern Europe and Canada. In the northern plains, Germans, Scandinavians, and Irish were especially numerous. In the new state of Nebraska in 1870, a quarter of the 123,000 residents were foreign born. In North Dakota in 1890, 45 percent of the residents were immigrants. Compared with European

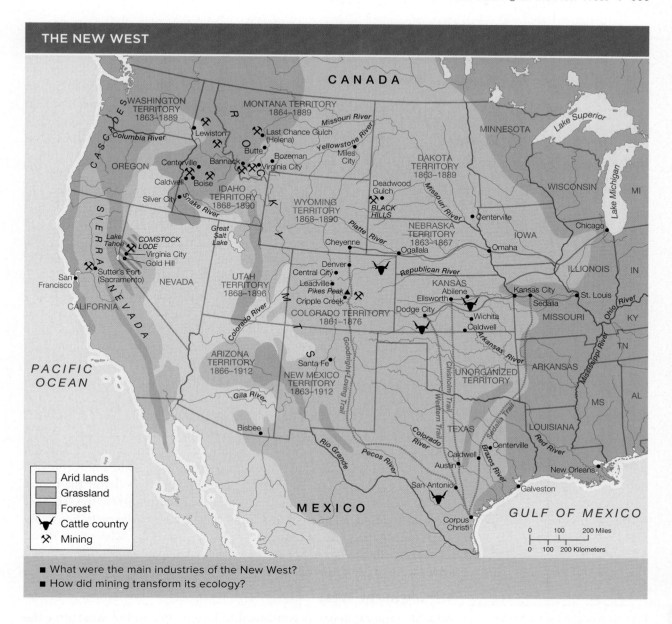

THE NEW WEST

Arid lands
Grassland
Forest
Cattle country
Mining

■ What were the main industries of the New West?
■ How did mining transform its ecology?

immigrants, those from China and Mexico were much less numerous but nonetheless significant. More than 200,000 Chinese arrived in California between 1876 and 1890, joining some seventy thousand others who had earlier come to the state to build railroads and work in the mining communities. The Chinese were frequently discriminated against and denied citizenship rights. As perpetual outsiders, they became scapegoats whenever there was an economic downturn. In 1882, Congress passed the Chinese Exclusion Act, effectively banning further immigration from China.

Nicodemus, Kansas By the 1880s, this colony had become a thriving town of Exodusters. Here, its residents are photographed in front of their First Baptist Church and general store.

The African American Migration

In the aftermath of the collapse of Radical Republican rule in the South, thousands of African Americans began migrating westward from Kentucky, Tennessee, Louisiana, Arkansas, Mississippi, and Texas. Some 6,000 southern blacks arrived in Kansas in 1879, and as many as 20,000 followed the next year. These African American migrants came to be known as **Exodusters**, because they were making their exodus from the South—in search of a haven from racism and poverty.

By the early 1880s, however, the exodus of black southerners to the West had petered out. Many of the settlers were unprepared for the living conditions on the plains. Their Kansas homesteads were not large enough to be self-sustaining, and most of the black farmers were forced to supplement their income by hiring themselves out to white ranchers. Drought, grasshoppers, prairie fires, and dust storms led to crop failures. The sudden influx of so many people taxed resources and patience. There were not enough houses, stores, or construction materials to build them, few government services, and rarely enough water. Disappointed and frustrated, many of the African American pioneers in Kansas soon abandoned their land and moved to the few cities in the state. Life on the frontier was not the "promised land" that settlers had been led to expect, though it was better than what they had experienced in the South. As an Exoduster minister stressed, "We had rather suffer and be free" in Kansas than go back to the racist South. By 1890 some 520,000 African Americans lived west of the Mississippi River. As many as 25 percent of the cowboys who participated in the Texas cattle drives were African Americans.

Mining in the West

> Prospectors and their followers

Valuable mineral deposits continued to lure people to the West after the Civil War. Every territory and state in the Far West developed a mining industry and mining culture during the second half of the nineteenth century. The miners of the 1849 California gold rush (the forty-niners) set the typical pattern, in which mobs of prospectors rushed to a new find, followed quickly by camp followers—a motley crew of peddlers, saloon keepers, prostitutes, gamblers, hustlers, and assorted desperadoes eager to "mine the miners." Lawlessness gave way first to vigilante rule as groups of miners created their own informal legal codes for the community and enforced penalties, including hangings, and, finally, to stable communities with municipal governments, sanitation, and law enforcement.

Exodusters African Americans who migrated west from the South in search of a haven from racism and poverty after the collapse of Radical Republican rule.

The drama of the 1849 gold rush was reenacted time and again in the following three decades. Along the South Platte River, not far from Pikes Peak in Colorado, a prospecting party found gold in 1858, and stories of success brought perhaps 100,000 "fifty-niners" into the area by the next year. New discoveries in Colorado kept occurring: near Central City in 1859, at Leadville in the 1870s, and at Cripple Creek in 1891 and 1894—the last important strikes in the West, again gold and silver. During those years, farming and grazing had given the economy a stable base, and Colorado, the Centennial State, entered the union in 1876.

While the early miners were crowding around Pikes Peak in Colorado, the **Comstock Lode** was discovered near Gold Hill, Nevada, on the eastern slope of the Sierra Nevada Mountains near the California border. Henry Comstock, a Canadian-born fur trapper, had drifted to the Carson River diggings, which opened in 1856. He talked his way into a share of a new discovery made by two other prospectors in 1859 and gave it his own name. The lode produced massive amounts of gold and silver. Within twenty years, it had yielded more than $300 million from shafts that reached thousands of feet into the mountainside.

The growing demand for orderly government in the West led to the hasty designation of new territories and eventually the admission of a host of new states. After Colorado's admission in 1876, however, there was a long pause because of party divisions in Congress: Democrats were reluctant to create states out of territories that were heavily Republican. After the sweeping Republican victory in the 1888 legislative races, however, Congress admitted the Dakotas, Montana, and Washington in 1889 and Idaho and Wyoming in 1890. Utah entered the Union in 1896 (after the Mormons agreed to abandon the practice of polygamy) and Oklahoma in 1907, and in 1912 Arizona and New Mexico rounded out the forty-eight contiguous states. (The final two states, Alaska and Hawaii, were added fifty years later.)

> New western states

Life in the New West

The surge of western migration had many of the romantic qualities so often depicted in novels, films, and television shows. The people who braved harsh conditions to begin new lives in the West were indeed courageous and tenacious. Cowboys and Indians, outlaws and vigilantes, farmers, ranchers, and herders, populated the plains, while miners and trappers led nomadic lives in the hills and backwoods.

But these familiar images of western life tell only part of the story. Drudgery and tragedy were as commonplace as adventure and success. Droughts, locusts, disease, tornadoes, and the erratic fluctuations of commodities markets made life relentlessly precarious. The people who settled the trans-Mississippi frontier were in fact a diverse lot: they included women as well as men, African Americans, Hispanics, Asians, and European

> CORE **OBJECTIVE**
> **5.** Explain the experiences of miners, ranchers, farmers, and women in the West.

Comstock Lode Mine in eastern Nevada acquired by Canadian fur trapper Henry Comstock that between 1860 and 1880 yielded almost $1 billion worth of gold and silver.

The original cowboys Cowboys on horseback herd cattle into a corral beside the Cimarron River in 1905.

immigrants. The feverish quest for quick profits also helped fuel a boom/bust economic cycle that injected a chronic instability into the society and politics of the region. Ultimately, the massive western migrations would take a huge toll on the Native American tribes in the region.

The Cattle Boom

When ranchers began herding cattle into the grasslands where the buffalo had roamed, the western landscape was changed forever. For many years, wild cattle had competed with buffalo in the Spanish borderlands of Texas and Arizona. Interbreeding them with Anglo-American domesticated cattle produced the Texas longhorns: lean and rangy, they were noted more for speed and endurance than for yielding a choice steak. They had little marginal value, moreover, because the largest markets for beef were too far away.

The cattle industry

That situation changed after the Civil War as railroads pushed farther west, where cattle could be driven through mostly vacant lands. Once the rail lines reached Kansas, Joseph G. McCoy, an Illinois livestock dealer, recognized the possibilities of moving Texas cattle northward to Kansas and then to the rest of the nation by rail. In 1867 in tiny Abilene, Kansas, he bought 250 acres for a stockyard and built a barn, an office building, livestock scales, a hotel, and a bank. He then sent an agent into Indian-owned areas to recruit the owners of herds bound north to go through Abilene. Once the Texas herds reached Kansas, the cattle were loaded onto rail cars and shipped to the Chicago stockyards and then (as beef) to the East Coast.

Abilene flourished as the first successful Kansas cow town. By 1871, 700,000 steers passed through it every year. The ability to ship huge numbers of western cattle by rail transformed ranching into a major national industry. Soon, other western territories and states—Colorado, Wyoming, Dakota, and Montana—followed the Kansas example and had cattle drives and railheads of their own.

The thriving cattle industry spurred rapid population growth. The population of Kansas increased from 107,000 in 1860 to 365,000 ten years later and reached almost 1 million by 1880. Nebraska witnessed similar increases. The flush times of the cow town soon passed, however, and the long cattle drives played out too, because they were economically unsound. The dangers of the trail, the wear and tear on men and cattle, the charges levied on drives across Indian territory, and the advance of farms across the trails combined to persuade cattlemen that they could function best near railroads. As railroads spread out into Texas and across the plains, the cattle business spread with them over the High Plains as far as Montana and on into Canada.

In the absence of laws governing the open range, cattle ranchers at first worked out a code of behavior largely dictated by circumstances. As cattle often wandered onto other ranchers' land, cowboys would "ride the line" to keep the animals off the adjoining ranches. In the spring they would "round up" the herds, which invariably got mixed up, and sort out ownership by identifying the distinctive ranch symbols "branded," or burned, into the cattle.

All that changed in 1873, when Joseph Glidden, an Illinois farmer, invented the first effective form of barbed wire, which ranchers used to fence off their lands at relatively low cost. People rushed to buy the new wire fencing, and soon the open range—owned by all, where a small rancher could graze his cattle anywhere—was no more. Barbed-wire fences triggered "range wars," where small ranchers, called fence cutters, fought with large ranchers to retain the open range. Fencing put a lot of ranchers out of business, and many of them became cowboys working for wages. Cattle raising, like mining, evolved from a romantic adventure into a big business dominated by large corporations. As one cowboy lamented, "times have changed."

> The end of the open range

Farming on the Plains

Farming has always been a hard life, and it was made more so on the Great Plains by the region's unforgiving environment and harsh weather. A New York newspaper publisher traveling to California described the Great Plains as a "land of starvation," "a treeless desert," scorching during daylight and "chill and piercing" cold at night. Still, people made the dangerous trek, lured by the inexpensive federal land and misleading advertisements celebrating life on the plains. One woman said she was "glad to be leaving" her

Innovative farming Powered by over a dozen horses and driven by two men, this early nineteenth-century machine boasted the ability of cutting, threshing, bagging, and weighing wheat all at the same time.

farm in Missouri: "We were going to a new land and get rich." Few did get rich, however. "In plain language," concluded a study by the Department of Agriculture: "a farmer's wife, as a general rule, is a laboring drudge."

Homesteaders

The first homesteaders in the Great Plains faced a grim struggle against danger, adversity, monotony, and loneliness. Though land was essentially free as a result of the Homestead Act (1862), horses, livestock, wagons, wells, lumber, fencing, seed, machinery, and fertilizer were not. Freight rates and interest rates on loans seemed criminally high. As in the South, declining crop prices produced chronic indebtedness, leading strapped western farmers to embrace virtually any plan to increase the money supply and thus pay off their debts with inflated currency. The virgin land itself, although fertile, resisted planting; the heavy sod woven with tough grass roots broke many a plow. Since wood and coal were rare on the prairie, pioneer families initially had to use buffalo chips (dried dung from buffaloes and cattle) for fuel.

Farm families also fought a constant battle with the elements: tornadoes, hailstorms, droughts, prairie fires, blizzards, and pests. Swarms of locusts often clouded the horizon, occasionally covering the ground six inches deep. A Wichita newspaper reported in 1878 that the grasshoppers devoured "everything green, stripping the foliage off the bark and from the tender twigs of the fruit trees, destroying every plant that is good for food or pleasant to the eyes, that man has planted." In the late 1880s, a prolonged drought forced many homesteaders on the plains to give up. Thousands left, some in wagons whose canvas coverings read: "In God we trusted, In Kansas we busted."

Commercial Farming

Eventually, as the railroads brought piles of lumber from the East, farmers could leave their houses built of sod for more comfortable frame dwellings. New farm equipment, for those who could afford to buy it, greatly improved productivity. In 1868, James Oliver, a Scottish immigrant living in Indiana, made a successful chilled-iron "sodbuster" plow that greatly eased the task of plowing the plains. Improvements and new inventions in threshing machines, hay mowers, planters, manure spreaders, cream separators, and other devices lightened the burden of farm labor but added to the farmers' capital outlay. By 1880, a steam-powered combine could do the work of twenty men. In Minnesota, the Dakotas, and central California, wealthy capitalists who could afford machinery for mass production created gigantic "bonanza farms" that became the marvels of the age. On one farm in North Dakota, 13,000 acres of wheat made a single field. Another bonanza farm employed over 1,000 migrant workers to tend 34,000 acres. Such agribusinesses were the wave of the future. Jefferson's dream of an America primarily made up of small farmers gave way to industrial agriculture.

> Bonanza farms

While the overall value of farmland and farm products increased in the late nineteenth century, small farmers did not keep up with the march of progress. Their numbers grew in size but decreased in proportion to the population at large. Wheat in the Western states, like cotton in the South, was the great export crop that spurred economic growth. For a variety of reasons, however, including an inability to afford the new machinery, few small farmers prospered. By the 1890s they were in open revolt against the "system" of corrupt processors (middlemen) and "greedy" bankers who they believed conspired against them.

Miners in the West

As ranchers and farmers settled the plains, miners played a crucial role in the economic and social development of the Far West. Throughout the region, mining camps and towns sprouted like mushrooms in the second half of the century. Initially, the miners lived in crude tents and shacks they built themselves. They worked a nine- to ten-hour day, six days a week, and usually took Sunday off. As a camp grew, it became a town with cabins, stores, and saloons providing modern services and conveniences.

> Effects of large-scale mining

The first wave of prospectors focused on "placer" (surface) mining, using iron or tin pans to sift gold dust and nuggets out of riverbeds. But once the placer deposits were exhausted, miners had to use other methods, all of which required much larger operations and investments. As mining shifted from surface digging and panning to hydraulic mining, dredging,

Small Farmers and Independence in the Coming of the Modern Age

The South and the West both underwent major changes in the late nineteenth century. Neither experienced industrialization at the rate that states in the North and Midwest did. But the economic transformation brought about by the growth of industry and Big Business reached deep into each region, profoundly affecting the lives of ordinary men and women. Both regions remained more rural and agricultural than the rest of the nation, and a large proportion of the population dreamed of sustaining an agrarian lifestyle of landownership and economic independence. But by the 1890s, these goals were harder to achieve than ever before.

Challenges	Southern Farmers	Western Farmers
Farming models	Sharecroppers or tenant farmers rented land from landowners through the **crop-lien system**, usually for the planting of cotton	**Large-scale wheat farms**, or bonanza farms, were successful, taking advantage of the cheap land, while investing in new machinery (see below)
Overproduction	Pressure to pay off debts to landowners led to excessive cotton production, which led to **lower prices and profit margins**	Pressure to pay off debts for high costs (see below) led to overproduction of wheat and **lower prices and profit margins**
High costs	■ Most farmers could not pay off debts or **high interest loans** after landowners took their share of the crops ■ Decreasing profits caused growing indebtedness, a general **decline in land ownership,** and **cash shortage**	■ Large farms often required **hired labor** ■ Farmers borrowed money at **high interest** to pay for expensive plows, threshers, and other **equipment** ■ Limited grain storage and railway transportation resulted in **high shipping costs**
Environment	■ **Infertile soil** from long-term overproduction ■ Pressure to continuously plant cotton **discouraged farming technology innovation** and **diversification of crops**	■ **Unpredictable, harsh weather** ■ **Pests, e.g., locusts** ■ **Few banks made loans more expensive**

QUESTIONS FOR ANALYSIS

1. Why was it so hard for small farmers in the South and West to profit from farming?

2. How similar was the situation of small farmers in the South and in the West?

3. What options did small farmers have for responding to the challenges they faced?

and deep-shaft "hard-rock" tunneling, mining ceased being an individual pursuit and became a big business. Only large-scale mining corporations financed by American and European investors could afford the expensive specialized power equipment and blasting dynamite needed for such operations. Many prospectors who had hoped to "strike it rich" turned into wage laborers working for mining corporations. Eventually, many of those mine workers formed unions to represent their interests in negotiations with mine owners, in part because of low pay ($3 a day) and in part because deep-shaft mining was so dangerous. In the western hard-rock mines, on-the-job accidents disabled one out of every thirty miners and killed one out of eighty. Overall, some 7,500 workers were killed and 20,000 maimed in mine accidents during the late nineteenth century.

Mining and the Environment

Hydraulicking, dredging, and shaft mining transformed vast areas of landscape and vegetation. Massive stamping mills driven by steam engines crushed enormous mountains of rock. Huge hydraulic cannons shot enormous streams of water under high pressure, stripping the topsoil and gravel from hillsides and creating steep-sloped barren canyons that could not sustain plant life. The massive amounts of dirt and debris unearthed by the water cannons covered rich farmland downstream and created sandbars that clogged rivers and killed fish. All told, some 12 billion tons of earth were blasted out of the Sierra Nevada Mountains in California and washed into local rivers.

Mining Boomtowns

Tombstone, Arizona, only thirty miles from the Mexican border, was the site of substantial silver mining in the 1870s. By only its fourth year of existence, it was the fastest-growing boomtown in the Southwest. It boasted a bowling alley, four churches, an icehouse, a school, two banks, three newspapers, and an ice cream parlor, alongside 110 saloons, 14 gambling halls, and numerous dance halls and brothels. Miners and cowboys especially enjoyed shows at the Bird Cage Theatre, the "wildest, wickedest night spot between Basin Street [in New Orleans] and the Barbary Coast [in North Africa]," open twenty-four hours a day, 365 days a year.

Some of the other largest and most famous of the mining boomtowns | Life in boomtowns
included Virginia City in Nevada, Cripple Creek and Leadville in Colorado, and Deadwood in the Dakota Territory. They were male-dominated communities with a substantial population of immigrants: Chinese, Chileans, Peruvians, Mexicans, French, Germans, Scots, Welsh, Irish, and English. In terms of ethnic diversity, the western mining cities were the most cosmopolitan communities in America.

Mining towns were also violent places. The small gold-mining town of Belleville, California, had 50 murders in one year. In 1871 a visitor to Corinne, Utah, a town only four years old with 2,000 residents, noted that the streets "are full of white men armed to the teeth, miserable-looking Indians dressed in the ragged shirts and trousers furnished by the federal government, and yellow Chinese with a business-like air and hard, intelligent faces." Ethnic prejudice was as common as violence in mining towns. The Chinese, for example, were usually prohibited from working in the mines but were allowed to operate laundries and work in boarding houses. Mexicans were often treated the worst. "Mexicans have no business in this country," a Californian insisted. "The men were made to be shot at, and the women were made for our purposes. I'm a white man—I am! A Mexican is pretty near black. I hate all Mexicans."

Most of the boomtowns, many of which were in remote mountainous areas, lasted only a few years. Once the mines played out, the people moved on, leaving ghost towns behind. In 1870, Virginia City, then called the richest city in America, hosted a population of 20,000. Today, it has fewer than 1,000 residents.

Women in the West

Pioneer Women: Greater Equality and Independence

The West remained a largely male society throughout the nineteenth century. Women in mining towns, most of whom worked as house cleaners, were as valued as gold. Many mining towns had a male-to-female ratio as high as 9 to 1. When four "respectable" women arrived in Nevada City, one of them reported that the men stood and gazed "at us with mouth and eyes wide open, every time we go out" in the streets.

In both mining towns and farming communities, women were prized as spouses, in part because farming required help. In 1900, 98 percent of the women in Nebraska were married. The women pioneers continued to face the traditional legal barriers and social prejudices prevalent in the East. A

Gathering "meadow muffins"
A pioneer woman collects dried buffalo dung to be used as fuel for cooking and warmth in the cold prairie nights.

wife could not sell property without her husband's approval, for example. Texas women could not sue except for divorce, nor could they serve on juries, act as lawyers, or witness a will.

But the constant fight for survival west of the Mississippi made men and women more equal partners than in the East. Many women who lost their mates to the deadly toil of "sod busting" thereafter assumed complete responsibility for their farms. In general, women on the prairie became more independent than women leading domestic lives back East. A Kansas woman explained "that the environment was such as to bring out and develop the dominant qualities of individual character. Kansas women of that day learned at an early age to depend on themselves—to do whatever work there was to be done, and to face danger when it must be faced, as calmly as they were able."

It was not coincidental, then, that the new western territories and states were among the first to allow women to vote in local elections and hold office. Western territories and states also hoped that by allowing women to vote they would attract more women settlers. In 1890, Wyoming was admitted to the Union as the first state that allowed women to vote in all elections. Utah, Colorado, and Idaho followed soon thereafter.

The Fate of Western Indians

As settlers spread across the continent from east and west, some 250,000 Native Americans were forced into what was supposed to be their last refuge, the Great Plains and the mountain regions of the Far West. The 1851 Fort Laramie Treaty, in which the chiefs of the Plains tribes agreed to accept definite tribal borders and allow white emigrants to travel across them on wagon trails, worked for a while. Fighting resumed, however, as the emigrants began to settle upon Indian lands rather than merely pass through them.

The Indian Wars

From the early 1860s until the late 1870s, the frontier raged with the so-called **Indian wars**. In the summer of 1862, during the Civil War, an uprising of hungry Sioux warriors killed 644 white traders, settlers, government officials, and soldiers in the Minnesota Valley. Two years later, another horrible incident occurred in Colorado, when the territorial governor persuaded Indians (mostly Cheyenne and Arapaho people) in his territory to gather at Fort Lyon, on Sand Creek in southeastern Colorado near the Kansas border, where they were promised protection. Despite that promise, at dawn on November 29, 1864, Colonel John M. Chivington's untrained militia attacked an Indian camp flying a white flag of truce, slaughtering and then mutilating 165 peaceful Indians—men, women, children, and the elderly—in what one general called the "foulest and most unjustifiable crime

CORE OBJECTIVE
6. Evaluate the impact on Native Americans of the federal government's policies in the West after the Civil War.

Sand Creek Massacre

Indian wars Bloody conflicts between U.S. soldiers and Native Americans that raged in the West from the early 1860s to the late 1870s, sparked by American settlers moving into ancestral Indian lands.

in the annals of America." Chivington had told his men to "kill all the Indians you come across." They did. But instead of pacifying the Indians, the Sand Creek Massacre led them to seek revenge. More massacres were to come, on both sides.

Further Indian Relocation

1867 Peace Commission

With other scattered battles erupting, a congressional committee in 1865 gathered evidence on the grisly Indian wars and massacres. Its 1867 "Report on the Condition of the Indian Tribes" led to the creation of an Indian Peace Commission charged with removing the causes of the Indian wars. Congress decided that this would be best accomplished by persuading Indians to move to out-of-the-way federal reservations. The Native Americans were to give up their ancestral lands, in return for peace, so that the whites could move in. In 1870, Indians outnumbered whites in the Dakota Territory by two to one; in 1880, whites outnumbered Indians by more than six to one.

In 1867, a conference at Medicine Lodge, Kansas, ended with the Kiowas, Comanches, Arapahos, and Cheyennes reluctantly accepting land in western Oklahoma. The following spring the Sioux agreed to settle within the Black Hills Reservation in Dakota Territory. But Indian resistance in the southern plains continued until the Red River War of 1874–1875, when General Philip Sheridan forced the Indians to disband in the spring of 1875. Seventy-two Indian chiefs were imprisoned for three years.

Custer and the Sioux

George A. Custer Reckless and glory-seeking Lieutenant Colonel of the U.S. Army.

Great Sioux War Conflict between Sioux and Cheyenne Indians and federal troops over lands in the Dakotas in the mid-1870s.

Meanwhile, trouble was brewing again to the north. White prospectors searching for gold were soon filtering onto the Sioux hunting grounds despite promises that the army would keep them out. In 1874, Lieutenant Colonel George Armstrong Custer, a superb horseman but a reckless, ruthless, glory-seeking officer hated by many of his men, one of whom called him a "petty tyrant," led a thousand soldiers into the Black Hills. His mission was to find the roving bands of Sioux and Cheyenne warriors and force them back onto reservations. If they resisted, his orders were to kill them. The colorful Custer stood out among his men, with long golden hair, a red kerchief around his neck, and a velveteen uniform decorated with golden braid. In 1867 he had been court-martialed for "deserting his command" and was suspended from duty for a year. Now he was in charge of an expedition to attack the wandering bands of Sioux hunting parties, even though he recognized that the Americans had caused the renewal of warfare. As Custer told newspaper reporters, "We are goading the Indians to madness by invading their hallowed [hunting] grounds."

What became the **Great Sioux War** was the largest military campaign since the end of the Civil War. The war lasted fifteen months and entailed fifteen battles in present-day Wyoming, Montana, South Dakota, and Nebraska.

Battle of Little Bighorn, 1876
Amos Bad Heart Bull, an Oglala Sioux artist and historian, painted this scene from the Battle of Little Bighorn.

In June 1876, after several indecisive encounters, the headstrong Custer found the main encampment of Sioux and their Northern Cheyenne and Arapaho allies on the Little Bighorn River in the Montana Territory. Against the advice of his experienced Indian scouts, Custer led his blue-coated men into a death trap on June 25. "Hurrah boys, we've got them," Custer shouted to his men. He assumed that Indians would always flee if confronted by a large, well-trained army unit. He was wrong. Separated from the main body of soldiers and surrounded by a thousand warriors led by the heroic chief Crazy Horse, Custer's detachment of 263 men, their ammunition exhausted, was annihilated. Afterwards, Cheyenne women pierced the dead Custer's eardrums with sewing needles because he had failed to listen to their warnings to stay out of their ancestral lands.

Instead of following up their victory, the Indians celebrated and renewed their hunting. President Ulysses Grant dispatched more troops ("Custer's Avengers") to find them. The army quickly regained the offensive. Warriors were slain, villages destroyed, and food supplies burned. Forced back onto reservations, the remaining Native Americans soon found themselves struggling to survive under harsh conditions. Many of them died of starvation or disease. When a peace commission imposed a settlement, Chief Spotted Tail said: "Tell your people that since the Great Father promised that we should never be removed, we have been moved five times. . . . I think you had better put the Indians on wheels and you can run them about wherever you wish."

The Last Resistance

In the Rocky Mountains and to the west, the same story of courageous yet hopeless resistance was repeated again and again. Indians were the last obstacle to white western expansion, and they suffered as a result. The

Chief Joseph Leader of the Nez Perce, he was widely recognized as a strong, eloquent voice against the injustices suffered by the Native Americans.

Blackfeet and Crows had to leave their homes in Montana. In a war along the California-Oregon boundary, the Modocs held out for six months in 1871–1872 before they were overwhelmed. In 1879 the Utes were forced to give up their vast territories in western Colorado. In Idaho the peaceful Nez Perce bands refused to surrender land along the Salmon River, and prolonged fighting erupted there and in eastern Oregon.

In 1877, Joseph, one of several Nez Perce chiefs, led some 650 of his people on a 1,300-mile journey through Montana in hopes of reaching safety in Canada. Just before reaching the border, they were caught by U.S. soldiers. Joseph delivered an eloquent speech of surrender that served as an epitaph to the Indians' efforts to withstand the march of American empire: "I am tired of fighting. Our chiefs are killed. . . . The old men are all dead. . . . I want to have time to look for my children, and see how many of them I can find. . . . Hear me, my chiefs! I am tired. My heart is sick and sad. From where the sun now stands I will fight no more forever." The Nez Perce asked to return to their ancestral lands in western Idaho, but they were forced to settle in the Indian Territory (Oklahoma), where many died of malaria.

A generation of Indian wars virtually ended in 1886 with the capture of Geronimo, a powerful chief of the Chiricahua Apaches, who had outridden, outwitted, and outfought the more numerous white soldiers in the Southwest for fifteen years. The fighting in Arizona and New Mexico was brutal. Once, the Apaches captured a group of settlers, tied them to their wagon wheels, and roasted them alive. U.S. Army units routinely lynched captured Apaches and treated women and children as combatants. The general in charge of the soldiers who captured Geronimo, exhausted and demoralized, called him "one of the brightest, most resolute, determined-looking men that I have ever encountered."

The Ghost Dance

Massacre at Wounded Knee

The last major clash between Indians and American soldiers occurred in 1890. Late in 1888, Wovoka (or Jack Wilson), a Paiute in western Nevada, fell ill and in a delirium imagined he had visited the spirit world, where he learned of a deliverer coming to rescue the Indians and restore their lands. To hasten their deliverance, he said, the Indians must perform a ceremonial dance that would make them bulletproof in battles with white soldiers. The Ghost Dance craze fed upon old legends of the dead reuniting with the living and bringing prosperity and peace.

Ghost Dance movement A spiritual and political movement among Native Americans whose followers performed a ceremonial "ghost dance" intended to connect the living with the dead and make the Native Americans bulletproof in battles intended to restore their homelands.

The **Ghost Dance movement** spread rapidly. In 1890 the Lakota Sioux adopted it with such passion that it alarmed white authorities. They banned the Ghost Dance on Lakota reservations, but the Indians defied the order and a crisis erupted. On December 29, 1890, a bloodbath occurred at Wounded Knee, South Dakota, after nervous soldiers fired into a group of Indians who had come to surrender. Nearly two hundred Indians and twenty-five soldiers died in the Battle of Wounded Knee. The Indian wars had ended with characteristic brutality and misunderstanding. General

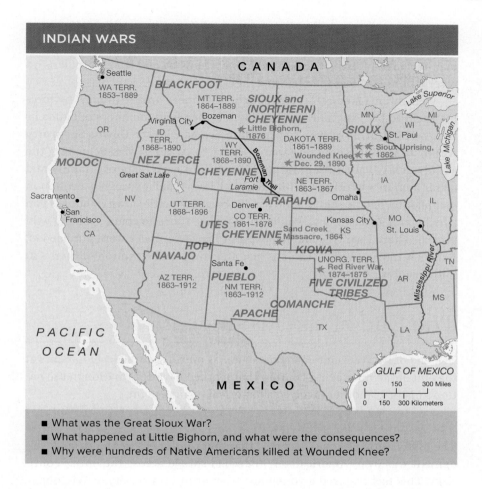

INDIAN WARS

- What was the Great Sioux War?
- What happened at Little Bighorn, and what were the consequences?
- Why were hundreds of Native Americans killed at Wounded Knee?

Philip Sheridan, the commander of U.S. troops in these conflicts, was acidly candid in summarizing how whites had treated the Indians: "We took away their country and their means of support, broke up their mode of living, their habits of life, introduced disease and decay among them, and it was for this and against this that they made war. Could anyone expect less?"

Attempts to Aid Indians

Indeed, many politicians and religious leaders scolded government officials for the persistent mistreatment of Indians. In his annual message of 1877, President Rutherford B. Hayes joined the protest: "Many, if not most, of our Indian wars have had their origin in broken promises and acts of injustice on our part." Helen Hunt Jackson, a novelist and poet, focused attention on the Indian cause in *A Century of Dishonor* (1881), a book that powerfully detailed the sad history of America's exploitation of Native Americans over the centuries.

In part as a reaction to Jackson's book, U.S. policies regarding Indians gradually improved, but they did little to improve the Indians' difficult living conditions and actually helped destroy remnants of their culture. The reservation policy inaugurated by the Peace Commission in 1867 did little more than extend a practice that dated from colonial Virginia. Partly humanitarian in motive, it also saved money: housing and feeding Indians on reservations cost less than fighting them.

Well-intentioned reformers sought to "Americanize" Indians by forcing them to become individual farmers rather than members of bands or tribes. The fruition of such reform efforts came with the **Dawes Severalty Act of 1887**. Sponsored by Senator Henry L. Dawes of Massachusetts, the act divided tribal lands, granting 160 acres to each head of a family and lesser amounts to others. White Bear, a Kiowa chief, expressed a common complaint when he said that he did "not want to settle down in houses you [the federal government] would build for us. I love to roam over the wild prairie. There I am free and happy." But his preferences were not heeded. Between 1887 and 1934, Indians lost an estimated 86 million of their 130 million acres.

CORE **OBJECTIVE**

7. Describe how the South and West had changed by 1900.

The End of the Frontier

The end of Native American resistance was one of several developments at the end of the nineteenth century that marked a transformation in the nation's history. Another involved a historical turning point.

The End of the Frontier Era?

Turner's frontier thesis

The 1890 national census reported that the frontier era in American development was over; Americans by then had spread across the entire continent. This fact inspired a young historian at the University of Wisconsin, Frederick Jackson Turner, to develop his influential "frontier thesis" which argued in 1893 that "the existence of an area of free land, its continuous recession, and the advance of American settlement westward, explain American development."

The frontier, Turner added, had shaped the national character in fundamental ways. It was

> to the frontier [that] the American intellect owes its striking characteristics. That coarseness and strength combined with acuteness and acquisitiveness; that practical, inventive turn of mind, quick to find expedients; that masterful grasp of material things, lacking in the artistic but powerful to effect great ends; that restless, nervous energy; that dominant individualism, working for good and for evil, and withal that buoyancy and exuberance which comes with freedom— these are traits of the frontier, or traits called out elsewhere because of the existence of the frontier.

Dawes Severalty Act of 1887 Federal legislation that divided ancestral Native American lands among the heads of each Indian family in an attempt to "Americanize" Indians by forcing them to become farmers working individual plots of land.

Now, however, Turner stressed, "the frontier has gone and with its going has closed the first period of American history."

Turner's frontier thesis guided several generations of scholars and students in their understanding of the distinctive characteristics of American history. His view of the frontier—as the westward-moving source of the nation's democratic politics, open society, unfettered economy, and rugged individualism—gripped the popular imagination as well.

Turner's frontier was that usually depicted in novels and films. But it left out much of the story. The frontier experience that Turner described was in many respects a self-serving myth involving only Christian white men. He virtually ignored the role of diverse women, African Americans, Native Americans, Hispanics, and Asians in shaping the human geography of the western United States. Turner's frontier was always the site of heroism, triumph, and progress. He ignored the evidence of greed, exploitation, and failure. Turner also implied that the West would be fundamentally different after 1890 because the frontier experience was essentially over. But in many respects the West has retained the qualities associated with the rush for land, gold, timber, and water rights during the post–Civil War decades. The mining frontier, as one historian has recently written, "set a mood that has never disappeared from the West: the attitude of every extractive industry—get in, get rich, get out."

Discontented Farmers

By 1900, both the South and West were quite different places from what they had been in 1865. What they had in common were dramatically changed economic conditions. In the West, the emergence of highly mechanized commercial farming ("bonanza farms") changed the nature of farming. By the end of the nineteenth century, many homesteaders had been forced to abandon their farms and become wage-earning farm laborers, often moving with the seasons to different states to harvest different crops. These migrant workers were often treated as poorly as the sharecroppers in the South. One western worker complained that the landowner "looked at me, his hired hand, as if I was just another work horse."

As discontent rose among farmers and farm workers in the South and the West, a growing number of them joined the People's party, whose followers were known as Populists, a grassroots social and political movement that was sweeping the poorest rural regions of the nation. In 1892, a Minnesota Populist named Ignatius Donnelly told Populists at their national convention that "We meet in the midst of a nation brought to the verge of moral, political, and material ruin." He affirmed that Populism sought "to restore the Government of the Republic to the hands of the 'plain people' with whom it originated." It was the Populist movement that tied the South and West together in an effort to wrest control of the political and economic systems from the East. That struggle would come to define the 1890s and determine the shape of the new twentieth century.

> The birth of the Populist party

■ **The New South** Many Southerners embraced the vision of the New South promoted by Henry Grady and others, which called for a more diverse economy with greater industrialization, wider distribution of wealth, and more vocational training. The cotton textile industry grew to surpass that of New England, iron and steel manufacturing increased, and the *American Tobacco Company* became the world's largest manufacturer of cigarettes. But agriculture—and especially the growing of cotton—still dominated the southern economy, much as it had before the Civil War. Land remained concentrated in few hands, and the crop-lien system left much of the population, both black and white, with little choice but to cultivate cotton for these large landholders.

■ **Jim Crow policies in the South** During the 1890s, Southern states disenfranchised the vast majority of African American voters and instituted a series of policies know as Jim Crow laws segregating blacks and whites in all public facilities. Starting with the *Mississippi Plan*, state governments passed a series of comprehensive measures making it impossible for most African Americans, and some poor whites, to vote through poll taxes, grandfather clauses, literacy tests, and residency requirements. Disenfranchisement was followed by legalized segregation, ruled constitutional by the Supreme Court in the 1896 *Plessy v. Ferguson* decision. African Americans who resisted were often the target of violence at the hands of whites, the worst form being organized *lynching*, or public torture, mutilation, and execution of African Americans, usually men. African Americans in the South responded by turning inward and strengthening their own social institutions, demanding the restoration of their civil rights.

■ **Western Migrants** Life in the West was often harsh and violent, but the promise of cheap land or wealth from mining drew settlers from the East.

Although most westerners were white Protestant Americans or immigrants from Germany and Scandinavia, Mexicans, African Americans (the *Exodusters*), and Chinese, as well as many other nationalities, contributed to the West's diversity. About three fourths of those who moved to the West were men.

■ **Miners, Farmers, Ranchers, and Women** Many migrants to the West were attracted to opportunities to mine, ranch, farm, or work on the railroads. Miners were drawn to the discovery of precious minerals such as silver at the *Comstock Lode* in Nevada in 1859. But most miners and cattle ranchers did not acquire wealth, because mining and raising cattle, particularly after the development of barbed wire and the end of the *open range*, became large-scale enterprises run by corporations. Because of the economic hardship and the rugged isolation of life in the West, women there achieved greater equality in everyday life, including voting rights, than did most women elsewhere in the country.

■ **Indian Wars and Policies** By 1900, Native Americans in the West were no longer free to roam the plains, as the influx of miners, ranchers, farmers, and soldiers had curtailed their traditional way of life. Instances of armed resistance, such as the *Great Sioux War*, were crushed. Initially, Indian tribes were forced to sign treaties and were confined to reservations. Beginning in 1887, with the *Dawes Severalty Act*, the American government's Indian policy shifted. It now forced Indians to relinquish their traditional culture and adopt the "American way" of individual landownership.

■ **The South and West in 1900.** In 1893, Frederick Jackson Turner, a prominent historian, declared that the frontier era was over. He argued that the western moving frontier of white settlement had been the nation's primary source of democratic politics and rugged individualism. To a certain extent, they were correct. By 1900, the West resembled the South where agricultural resources were concentrated in the hands of a few. In the 1890s, poor farmers in the West joined with tenant farmers in the South to support the People's Party or the Populist movement, which sought to wrest control of the political and economic system from the powerful East and return it to the "plain" folk. This contest would dominate the nation's politics in the 1890s and set its course for the twentieth century.

KEY TERMS

American Tobacco Company *p. 592*

Redeemers *p. 592*

crop-lien system *p. 593*

sharecroppers *p. 594*

Negrophobia *p. 596*

Mississippi Plan (1890) *p. 597*

"separate but equal" *p. 598*

Atlanta Compromise (1895) *p. 603*

Exodusters *p. 606*

Comstock Lode *p. 607*

Indian wars *p. 615*

Great Sioux War *p. 616*

Ghost Dance movement *p. 618*

Dawes Severalty Act of 1887 *p. 620*

CHRONOLOGY

1859	Comstock Lode is discovered
1862	Congress passes the Homestead Act
1864	Sand Creek Massacre in Colorado
1873	Joseph Glidden invents barbed wire
1876	Battle of Little Bighorn
1880s	Henry Grady spreads the New South idea
1886	Surrender of Geronimo marks the end of the Indian wars
1887	Congress passes the Dawes Severalty Act
1890	Battle of Wounded Knee
	James B. Duke forms the American Tobacco Company
1893	Frederick J. Turner outlines his "frontier thesis"
1900	South surpasses New England in production of cotton fabric

INQUIZITIVE

Go to InQuizitive to see what you've learned—and learn what you've missed—with personalized feedback along the way.

WET NIGHT ON THE BOWERY (1911) This scene of early twentieth-century life in New York City by John Sloan captures people of all walks of life converging on a rainy night: a smartly dressed society woman (left), a prostitute (center), and drunks stumbling about further down the block. Running overhead is the elevated train, while an electric trolley gleams from the wet street.

Society and Politics in the Gilded Age

1865–1900

Within three decades after the Civil War, American life experienced a stunning transformation. An agricultural society long rooted in the soil and little involved in global issues became an increasingly urban and industrialized nation deeply entwined in world markets and international politics. The period from the end of the Civil War to the beginning of the twentieth century was labeled the **Gilded Age** for its greed and vulgarity, as the newly rich showed off their enormous wealth that also financed widespread political and corporate corruption. Yet the Gilded Age also saw dramatic changes in other parts of society, including rural America, and in other aspects of social and cultural life.

Between 1865 and 1900, America's urban population skyrocketed from 8 million to 30 million. In 1865, there were fewer than twenty cities with populations over 50,000; by 1900 there were four times that many. Between 1865 and 1900, millions of European and Asian immigrants, as well as migrants from America's rural areas, streamed into cities, attracted by the jobs and excitements they offered. "We cannot all live in cities," cautioned Horace Greeley, the New York newspaper editor and Democratic presidential candidate in 1872, "yet nearly all seem determined to do so."

The populations of some of these cities, like Boston, New York, and Chicago, soared to sizes that many

CORE OBJECTIVES INQUIZITIVE

1. Understand the effects of urban growth during the Gilded Age, including the problems it created.

2. Describe the "new immigrants" of the late nineteenth century and how they were viewed by American society.

3. Explain how urban growth and the increasingly important role of science influenced leisure activities, cultural life, and social policy in the Gilded Age.

4. Assess how the nature of politics during the Gilded Age contributed to political corruption and stalemate.

5. Evaluate the effectiveness of politicians in developing responses to the major economic and social problems of the Gilded Age.

6. Analyze why the money supply became a major political issue during the Gilded Age and describe its impact on American politics.

Americans had never imagined, much less experienced. The growth of huge cities brought an array of problems, among them widespread poverty, unsanitary living conditions, and new forms of political corruption. How to feed, shelter, and educate the new city dwellers taxed the imaginations and resources of government officials. Even more challenging was the development of neighborhoods divided by racial and ethnic background as well as social class. By the 1890s, the largest cities had become explosive centers of unrest.

At the same time that cities were exercising a magnetic pull upon more and more people, scientific researchers were making a dazzling array of discoveries that improved human health, economic productivity, and communications. The advances of modern science stimulated public support for higher education at the graduate as well as the undergraduate level, but they also opened up a gulf of doubt about many long-accepted "truths" and religious beliefs, and led to conflicts over whether or how Charles Darwin's controversial theory of evolution could be applied to human society.

Political life during the Gilded Age was shaped by the close balance of power between Democrats and Republicans nationally and by enthusiastic public participation in politics locally, as well as the often corrupt alliance between industrial tycoons and political leaders in both parties and at all levels of government. The tradition of rewarding party supporters with government jobs drew criticism from reformers who pushed through legislation designed to limit such "patronage." Perhaps the most important underlying political issue of the Gilded Age, however, was the growing tension between city and country, industry and agriculture. In a still predominantly rural nation, millions of financially distressed farmers felt ignored or betrayed by the city-dominated political process. While industrialists and large commercial farmers prospered, small farmers in the South, Midwest, and West struggled with falling crop prices and growing indebtedness to banks, railroads, and what the farmers saw as other symbols of big-city greed and exploitation.

By the 1890s, discontented farmers had put their protest into political form and thrown themselves behind a growing movement seeking to expand ("inflate") the nation's money supply as a way to relieve economic distress. The climactic election of 1896 symbolized the central conflict of the Gilded Age: the clashing cultural and economic values of two Americas—one older, small-scale, and rural America, the other newer, bigger, and urban.

CORE **OBJECTIVE**

1. Understand the effects of urban growth during the Gilded Age, including the problems it created.

America's Move to Town

"The greater part of our population must live in cities," announced Josiah Strong, a prominent Congregationalist minister, in 1898. "There was no resisting the trend." After the Civil War, millions of Americans migrated from rural areas to cities. Many had been pushed off the land by new agricultural machinery that sharply reduced the need for farm workers. Four men could now perform the farm work that earlier had required fourteen. Others were drawn by jobs and other economic opportunities that were concentrated in cities, both old and new. By the end of the nineteenth century, much of the settlement of the West was taking an urban form, with new towns forming around mines and railroad junctions. Still other migrants, bored by rural or small-town life, moved to cities in search of a more exciting cultural life.

While the Far West had the greatest proportion of urban dwellers, concentrated in cities such as San Francisco and Denver, the Northeast and Midwest held far more people in huge cities—New York City, Boston, Philadelphia, Pittsburgh, Chicago, Cincinnati, St. Louis, and others. More and more of these city dwellers could not afford to buy a home; they had little or no money and had nothing but their labor to sell. By 1900, more than 90 percent of the residents of New York City's most densely populated borough, Manhattan, lived in rented houses or in congested, low-cost apartment buildings called **tenements**, where residents, many of them immigrants, were packed like sardines in poorly ventilated and poorly lit apartments.

Growth in All Directions

Several technological advances allowed city buildings to grow higher in order to house the surging populations. In the 1870s, heating innovations, such as steam radiators, enabled the construction of much larger apartment buildings, since coal-burning fireplaces and chimneys, expensive to build, were no longer needed in each apartment. In 1889, the Otis Elevator Company installed the first electric elevator, which made possible much taller buildings; before the 1860s, few structures had been taller than five or six stories. Now they could soar. During the 1880s, engineers developed cast-iron and steel-frame construction techniques that allowed for even taller structures—"skyscrapers."

Cities grew out as well as up, as transportation innovations like horse-drawn streetcars and commuter railways let people live at longer distances from their downtown workplaces. In 1873, San Francisco became the first city to use cable cars that clamped onto a moving underground cable driven by a central power source. Some cities ran steam-powered trains on elevated tracks, but by the 1890s electric trolleys were preferred. Mass transit received an added boost from underground subway trains built in Boston, New York City, and Philadelphia.

The new commuter trains and trolleys allowed a growing middle class of business executives and professionals (accountants, doctors, engineers, sales clerks, teachers, store managers, and attorneys) to retreat from crowded downtowns and live in quieter, tree-lined "streetcar suburbs." But the working poor, many of them immigrants or African Americans, could rarely afford to leave the inner cities. As their populations grew, cities

Skyscrapers and suburbs

Gilded Age (1860–1896)
An era of dramatic industrial and urban growth characterized by widespread political corruption and loose government oversight of corporations.

tenements Shabby, low-cost inner-city apartment buildings that housed the urban poor in cramped, un-ventilated apartments.

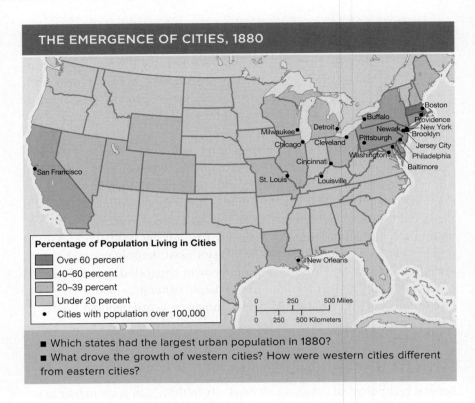

THE EMERGENCE OF CITIES, 1880

Percentage of Population Living in Cities
- Over 60 percent
- 40–60 percent
- 20–39 percent
- Under 20 percent
- • Cities with population over 100,000

■ Which states had the largest urban population in 1880?
■ What drove the growth of western cities? How were western cities different from eastern cities?

became dangerously congested and plagued with fires, violent crimes, and contagious diseases.

Crowds, Dirt, and Disease

Packed tenement housing

The wonders of big cities—their glittering new electric lights, streetcars, telephones, department stores, theaters, and many other attractions—were magnetic lures for rural youth bored by the routines of isolated farm life. In times of rural depression, thousands moved to the cities in search of economic opportunity and personal freedom. Yet in doing so they often traded one set of problems for another. In New York City in 1900, some 2.3 million people, two-thirds of the city's entire population, were living in overcrowded and often filthy tenement housing. Such rapid urban growth—much of it completely unregulated by municipal officials—affected sanitation, health, and morale. "The only trouble with New York City," said writer Mark Twain, "is that it is too large. You cannot accomplish anything in the way of business . . . without devoting a whole day to it. The distances are too great."

Tenement apartment buildings were usually six to eight stories tall, lacking elevators, and jammed so tightly against one another that most of the apartments had little or no natural light or fresh air. Such buildings

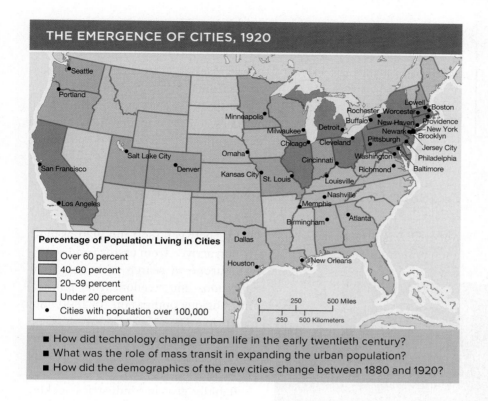

THE EMERGENCE OF CITIES, 1920

Percentage of Population Living in Cities

- Over 60 percent
- 40–60 percent
- 20–39 percent
- Under 20 percent
- • Cities with population over 100,000

■ How did technology change urban life in the early twentieth century?
■ What was the role of mass transit in expanding the urban population?
■ How did the demographics of the new cities change between 1880 and 1920?

typically housed twenty-four to thirty-two families, usually with lots of children who had few places to play except in the streets. On average, there was only one toilet (called a *privy*) for every twenty people. In one New York tenement apartment, twelve adults slept in a room only thirteen feet square.

Late-nineteenth-century cities were dirty, smelly, and disease-ridden. Streets were filled with contaminated water, horse urine and manure, and roaming pigs. Garbage and raw sewage were carelessly dumped into streets and waterways, causing epidemics of infectious diseases such as cholera, typhoid fever, and yellow fever. In one poor Chicago district at the end of the century, three of every five babies died before their first birthday.

So-called sanitary reformers—public health officials and engineers— eventually created cleaner conditions in tenements by creating regulations requiring more space per resident as well as more windows and plumbing facilities. Reformers also pushed successfully for new water and sewage systems and for regular trash collection, which by 1900 had been adopted in nearly all American cities. The many animals in cities were a huge sanitary challenge. Reformers lobbied to ban slaughterhouses as well as the raising of hogs and cattle within city limits, and to replace horse-drawn trolleys with electric-powered streetcars or trolleys.

Unsanitary conditions and "sanitary reformers"

The New Immigration

America's roaring prosperity and the promise of political and religious freedom attracted waves of new immigrants from every part of the globe in the years after the Civil War. By 1900, nearly 30 percent of the residents of major cities were foreign-born. These newcomers provided much-needed labor, but their arrival in such huge numbers sparked racial and ethnic tensions.

A Surge of Newcomers from Europe

Immigration has always been one of the most powerful forces shaping American history. This was especially true between 1860 and 1920, as more and more immigrants, most of them poor, arrived from eastern and southern Europe in search of better living conditions and freedom from political and religious oppression. In 1890, four out of five New Yorkers were foreign-born, a higher proportion than in any other city in the world. Chicago was not far behind.

Rapidly growing industries seeking low-wage workers—including mines, railroads, mills, and factories—sent recruiting agents abroad to stir up interest in migration to the United States. Under the Contract Labor Act of 1864, the federal government helped pay for immigrants' travel expenses to America. The law was repealed in 1868, but not until 1885 did the government stop companies from importing foreign laborers, a practice that put immigrant workers under the control of their employers. The tide of immigration rose from just under 3 million annually in the 1870s to more than 5 million in the 1880s. It fell to a little over 3.5 million in the 1890s before rising to its record level of nearly 9 million per year in the first decade of the twentieth century.

Ellis Island To accommodate the soaring numbers of immigrants passing through New York, Congress built a reception center on Ellis Island, near the Statue of Liberty. Pictured here is its registry room, where immigrants awaited close questioning by officials.

The so-called old immigrants who came before 1880 were mainly Protestants and Roman Catholics from northern and western Europe. This pattern began to change, however, as the proportion of immigrants from southern and eastern Europe, especially Russia, Poland, Greece, and Italy, rose sharply. After 1890, these "**new immigrants**" made up a majority of the newcomers, and by the first decade of the new century, they formed 70 percent. Their languages and cultural backgrounds were markedly

new immigrants Wave of newcomers from southern and eastern Europe, including many Jews, who became a majority among immigrants to America after 1890.

different from those of most "old immigrants" as well as most native-born Americans. The dominant religions of the new immigrants, for example, were Judaism, Eastern Orthodox, and Roman Catholicism, whereas Protestants still formed a large majority of the total U.S. population.

In 1907 Congress appointed the bipartisan Dillingham Commission to examine the changes in immigration patterns to the United States. After four years of analysis and hearings, it released a 41-volume report in 1911. The Commission concluded that the "new" immigration that emerged in the 1880s and after involved dramatic differences from previous patterns. Most who had come under the "old" immigration had "mingled freely with ...native Americans," and thus were assimilated. The new immigration that had begun around 1883, however, "was marked by an increase in transient, unskilled laborers who flocked to urban enclaves where they resisted assimilation." As a class of people, the "new" immigrants were "far less intelligent than the old, approximately one-third of all those over 14 years of age when admitted being illiterate. Racially, they are for the most part essentially unlike the British, German and other peoples who came during the prior period to 1880, and generally speaking they are actuated in coming by different ideals, for the old immigration came to be a part of the country, while the new in a large measure, comes with the intention of profiting, in a pecuniary way, by the superior advantages of the new world and then returning to the old country."

Strangers in a New Land

Once on American soil, immigrants who had not been brought over by an employer were usually desperately poor and needed to find jobs—quickly. Many were greeted at the docks by family and friends who had come over before them, others by representatives of immigrant-aid societies or by company agents offering low-paying and often dangerous jobs in mines, mills, or sweatshops and on railroads. Since most immigrants knew little if any English and nothing about American employment practices, they were easy targets for exploitation. Many unwittingly lost a healthy percentage of their wages to unscrupulous hiring agents in exchange for a bit of whiskey and a job. Other companies eager for workers gave immigrants train tickets to inland cities such as Buffalo, Pittsburgh, Cleveland, Chicago, Milwaukee, Cincinnati, and St. Louis.

> Employer exploitation of immigrants

As strangers in America, most immigrants naturally wanted to live in neighborhoods populated by people from their homeland. The largest cities had vibrant immigrant districts with names such as Little Italy, Little Hungary, and Chinatown, which served as transitional communities between the newcomers' Old World past and their New World future. In these communities, immigrants practiced their native religions and customs, and spoke as well as read newspapers in their native languages. But they paid a price for such community solidarity. When "new immigrants" moved into

> Immigrant neighborhoods

Mulberry Street, 1900 This photograph captures the many Italian immigrants who made Mulberry Street in downtown New York City their home at the turn of the century. Horse-drawn carts weave through people shopping, socializing, and people-gazing.

an area, the previous residents often moved out, taking with them whatever social prestige and political influence they had achieved. Living conditions in such neighborhoods often quickly deteriorated as housing and sanitation codes went unenforced.

The Nativist Response

Racism leads to restrictions on immigration

Then, as now, many native-born Americans saw the wave of "new immigrants" as a threat to their way of life and their jobs. Many of these **"nativists"** were also racists who believed that "Anglo-Saxon" Americans—people of British or Germanic background—were superior to the Slavic, Italian, Greek, and Jewish newcomers. A Stanford University professor, for instance, called the immigrants from southern and eastern Europe "illiterate, docile, lacking in self-reliance and initiative, and not possessing the Anglo-Teutonic conceptions of law, order, and government." Indeed, many of the new immigrants were illiterate, but others only appeared so because they could not speak or read English. Some desperate immigrants resorted to crime, encouraging suspicions that European nations were sending their criminals to America.

Throughout American history, Congress has passed laws regulating immigration that have been inconsistent in their goals and frequently rooted in racial and ethnic prejudice. During the late nineteenth century, such prejudice took an especially ugly turn against the Chinese, who suffered discrimination even beyond that leveled at the "new immigrants" from Europe. By 1880, some 75,000 Chinese formed about a ninth of the population of California. Their visible differences made them easy targets for

nativists Native-born Americans motivated by racial prejudice who blamed immigrants for social or economic problems and sought to restrict their access to America.

discrimination. They were not white, they were not Christian, and many could not read or write. Whites resented them for supposedly taking their jobs, although in many instances the Chinese were willing to do the menial work that whites refused to do. For these and other reasons, Congress in 1882 passed the **Chinese Exclusion Act**, the first federal law to restrict immigration on the basis of race. The act, which barred any more Chinese laborers from entering the country for the next ten years, was periodically renewed before being extended indefinitely in 1902. Not until 1943 were barriers to Chinese immigration finally removed.

But the Chinese were not the only group targeted. In 1891, nativists formed the Immigration Restriction League to save the Anglo-Saxon "race" from being "contaminated" by "alien" immigrants. The League sought to convince Congress to ban immigrants who were illiterate, even though illiterate immigrants from Britain and Germany had been allowed into the United States in the past. Three presidents vetoed bills banning illiterate immigrants: Grover Cleveland in 1897, William H. Taft in 1913, and Woodrow Wilson in 1915 and 1917. The last time, however, Congress overrode the veto.

Chinese Exclusion Act The Chinese caricature of John Chinaman is escorted out of America by Lady Liberty with his ironing board and opium pipe, while other accepted minorities look on.

Changes in Popular and Intellectual Culture

The flood of people into cities brought changes in patterns of recreation and leisure. Middle- and upper-class families, especially those who had moved to streetcar suburbs, often spent free time together at home, singing around a piano, reading novels, or playing games—cards, dominoes, backgammon, chess, and checkers. In congested urban areas, politics as a form of public entertainment attracted ever larger crowds, saloons became even more popular social centers for working-class men, and new forms of mass entertainment—movie theaters, music halls, vaudeville shows, art museums, symphony orchestras, and circuses—appealed to a broad cross-section of city residents.

Urbanization and technological progress also contributed to the prestige of modern science, which increased enormously during the second half of the nineteenth century. By encouraging what one writer called a "mania for facts," scientists generated changes throughout social, intellectual, and cultural life. "I tell you these are great times," the writer and social critic Henry Adams wrote to his brother in 1862. "Man has mounted science and is now run away." Scientific research led to transformational technologies

CORE **OBJECTIVE**

3. Explain how urban growth and the increasingly important role of science influenced leisure activities, cultural life, and social policy in the Gilded Age.

Chinese Exclusion Act (1882) Federal law that barred Chinese laborers from immigrating to America.

such as electrical power and lights, telephones, phonographs, motion pictures, bicycles, and automobiles.

Urban Leisure and Entertainment Options

Old and new forms of mass entertainment

Although only men could vote in most states, both men and women flocked to hear candidates speak at political party meetings. In the largest cities, membership in a political party offered many of the same benefits as belonging to a club or a college fraternity, as local political organizations provided lots of social activities in addition to promoting new candidates. As labor unions became increasingly common, they too took on social roles for working-class men.

The sheer number of city dwellers also helped generate new forms of mass entertainment, such as traveling Wild West shows, vaudeville shows featuring singers, dancers, and comedians, cycling, and spectator sports. In the last quarter of the nineteenth century, college football and basketball and professional baseball began attracting many fans. In large cities, the new streetcar transit systems helped people gather easily for sporting events, and rooting for the home

Vaudeville For as little as one cent for admission, vaudeville shows aimed to please the tastes of their wildly diverse audience with a great range of entertainment.

team helped unify a city's ethnic and racial groups and social classes. By the end of the century, sports of all kinds had become a major part of American popular culture.

The popularity of saloons

Still, the most popular leisure destinations for the urban working class were not athletic stadiums but saloons, beer gardens, and dance halls. By 1900, the United States had more saloons (over 325,000) than grocery stores and meat markets. New York City alone had 10,000 saloons, or one for every 500 residents.

The saloon served as the workingman's social club, offering fellowship to men who often worked ten hours a day, six days a week. Saloons were especially popular among male immigrants seeking companionship. In cities such as New York, Boston, Philadelphia, and Chicago, the customers were disproportionately Irish, German, and Italian Catholics, who tended to vote Democratic partly because the "temperance" organizations that tried to close down saloons were led by Protestant Republicans. Politics was often the topic of discussion in saloons; in fact, in New York City in the 1880s, saloons doubled as polling places, where patrons could cast their votes in local elections. One journalist called the saloon "the social and intellectual center of the neighborhood."

Besides drinking, socializing, and talking politics, men also went to saloons to check job postings, engage in labor union activities, cash paychecks, mail letters, read newspapers, and gossip about neighborhood affairs. Because saloons were heated and offered public restrooms, they also served as places of refuge for the homeless, especially in the winter. Patrons could play chess, billiards, darts, cards, dice, or even handball, since many saloons included gymnasiums. Although the main bar room was for men only, women and children were allowed to enter a side door to buy a pail of beer to carry home (a task called "rushing the growler"). Some saloons also provided "snugs," separate rooms for women customers. About a third of saloons, called "stall saloons," included "wine rooms" where prostitutes worked.

> Urban women and leisure

Married working-class women had even less leisure time than working-class men. Many of them were working for pay themselves, at least part-time, and even those who were not were frequently overwhelmed by housework and childrearing responsibilities. As a social worker noted, "The men have the saloons, political clubs, trade-unions or [fraternal] lodges for their recreation . . . while the mothers have almost no recreation, only a dreary round of work, day after day, with occasionally doorstep gossip to vary the monotony of their lives." Married working-class women often used the streets as their public space. Washing clothes, supervising children at play, or shopping at the local market provided opportunities for socializing with other women.

Single women, many of whom worked as domestic servants ("maids") who had more time than working mothers for leisure and recreation, flocked to dance halls, theaters, amusement parks, and picnic grounds. With the advent of movie theaters during the second decade of the twentieth century, the cinema became the most popular form of entertainment for working women. As an advertisement for a theater promised, "If you are tired of life, go to the movies. If you are sick of troubles rife, go to the picture show. You will forget your unpaid bills, rheumatism and other ills, if you stow your pills and go to the picture show."

The Impact of Darwinism

Virtually every field of thought during the Gilded Age felt the impact of English scientist Charles Darwin's controversial book *On the Origin of Species* (1859), whose first edition sold out in one day. Basing his conclusions on extensive research, Darwin argued that most organisms produce many more offspring than can survive. Those offspring with certain favorable characteristics tend to live while others die from disease or predators. This process of "natural selection" over many millions of years, Darwin said, had

Charles Darwin Darwin's scientific theories introduced and influenced more than a century of political and social debate.

led to the evolution of modern species from less complex forms of life; individuals and species that had characteristics advantageous for survival had successfully reproduced, while others fell by the wayside. Fossils revealed a natural history of conflict, pain, and species extinction. As Darwin wrote, "the vigorous, the healthy, and the happy survive and multiply."

The idea of biological evolution was shocking because most people in Europe and America still embraced a literal interpretation of the biblical creation story. Although Darwin himself had trained for the ministry and was reluctant to be drawn into religious controversy, his biological findings suggested to many, then and since, that there was no providential God controlling the universe and that people were no different from plants and animals, that they too evolved by trial and error rather than by God's purposeful hand.

These ideas—as well as the implications that people drew from them—generated heated arguments. Many Christians charged that Darwin's ideas led to atheism, a denial of the existence of God, while others found their faith severely shaken not only by evolutionary theory but also by new scientific standards of scholarly analysis that were being applied to the Bible itself. Most of the faithful, however, came to reconcile science and religion. They decided that the process of evolutionary change occurring in nature must be God's doing.

Social Darwinism

Although Darwin's complex theory of evolution applied only to biological phenomena, many drew broader implications from it, as the temptation to apply evolutionary theory to human society proved irresistible. Darwin's fellow Englishman Herbert Spencer, a leading social philosopher, was the first major prophet of what came to be called **Social Darwinism**. Spencer argued that human society and its institutions, like the organisms studied by Darwin, evolved through the same process of natural selection. The "survival of the fittest," in Spencer's chilling phrase, was the engine of social progress. By encouraging people, ideas, and nations to compete with one another for dominance, society, according to Spencer, would generate "the greatest perfection and the most complete happiness."

Darwin himself dismissed Spencer's social theories, objecting in particular to his assumption that the evolutionary process in the natural world had any relevance to human social institutions. Others, however, eagerly endorsed the notion of Social Darwinism. If, as Spencer believed, society naturally evolved for the better through "survival of the fittest," then government interference with human competition in the marketplace was a serious mistake because it would help "unfit" people survive and thereby hinder progress. Social Darwinism implied the need for hands-off, laissez-faire government policies; it argued against the regulation of business, for example, or of required minimum standards for sanitation and housing. To

Social Darwinism The application of Charles Darwin's theory of evolutionary natural selection to human society; Social Darwinists used the concept of "survival of the fittest" to justify class distinctions, explain poverty, and oppose government intervention in the economy.

Spencer and his many followers, the only acceptable charity was voluntary, and even that was of dubious value. Spencer warned that "fostering the good-for-nothing [people] at the expense of the good, is an extreme cruelty" to the health of civilization.

For Spencer and his many American supporters, successful business-men and corporations provided proof of the concept of "survival of the fittest." If the unregulated process of capitalist development led to small businesses being destroyed or acquired by huge corporate monopolies, that too was simply a necessary phase of the evolutionary process. Oil tycoon John D. Rockefeller revealed his own embrace of Social Darwinism when he told his Baptist Sunday-school class that the "growth of a large business is merely a survival of the fittest.... This is not an evil tendency in business. It is merely the working-out of a law of nature and a law of God."

Popular Science Monthly, founded in 1872, became the chief magazine for promoting Social Darwinism in the United States. That year, Spencer's chief academic disciple, William Graham Sumner, began teaching at Yale University, where he preached the gospel of natural selection. Sumner's most lasting contribution, made in his book *Folkways* (1907), was to argue that it would be a mistake for government to try to promote equality, since doing so would interfere with the "survival of the fittest."

Reform Darwinism

Sumner's efforts to use Darwinism to promote "rugged individualism" and oppose government regulation of business and efforts at social reform pro-voked strong criticism and inspired an alternative use of Darwinism in the context of human society. What came to be called Reform Darwinism found its major advocate in Lester Frank Ward, a federal government em-ployee who fought his way up from poverty and never lost his empathy for the underdog. Ward's book *Dynamic Sociology* (1883) singled out one as-pect of evolution that both Darwin and Spencer had neglected: the human brain. True, as Sumner claimed, people, like animals, compete, but as Ward explained, people also collaborate; unlike animals, people can plan for a distant future; they have minds capable of shaping and directing social change. Far from being the helpless object of irresistible evolutionary forces, Ward argued, humanity could actively control the process of social evolution through long-range planning.

Ward's Reform Darwinism thus posed a direct challenge to Sumner's conservative Social Darwinism, holding that *cooperation*, not competition, would better promote social progress. Government, in Ward's view, could contribute to social progress by pursuing two main goals: alleviating pov-erty, which impeded the development of the mind, and promoting the edu-cation of the masses. "Intelligence, far more than necessity," Ward wrote, "is the mother of invention," and "the influence of knowledge as a social factor, like that of wealth, is proportional to the extent of its distribution."

Intellect, informed by science, could foster social improvement. As the intellectual justification for social progress, Ward's concept of Reform Darwinism would prove to be one of the pillars of the "progressive" movement that would improve the quality of life in modern America during the late nineteenth century and after.

Realism in Literature and Art

Before the Civil War, romanticism had dominated American literature and painting. Romantics such as the transcendentalists in New England believed that fundamental truths rested in the unseen world of ideas and spirit. The most prominent writers and artists before the Civil War were more concerned with romantic or biblical themes than with the everyday life around them.

During the second half of the nineteenth century, however, a new generation of writers and artists calling themselves "realists" began to challenge this romantic tradition. A writer in *Putnam's Monthly* noted in 1854 a growing emphasis in American life on "the real and the practical." This emphasis on "realism" matured into a full-fledged cultural force during the late nineteenth century as more and more writers and artists focused their attention on depicting the actual aspects of urban-industrial America: scientific research and technology, factories and railroads, cities and immigrants, labor unions and social tensions.

The rise of such cultural realism resulted from a transformed social, intellectual, and moral landscape. For many Americans, the horrors of the Civil War led to a less romanticized and more realistic view of life. An editor attending an art exhibition in 1865 sensed "the greater reality of feeling developed by the war. We have grown more sober, perhaps, and less patient of romantic idealism."

Another factor contributing to the rise of realism was the impact of modern science. "This is a world of reality," admitted a romantic writer, "and romance breaks against the many hard facts." The new "scientific age," she claimed, valued only "facts that can be seen or heard or weighed or measured." The "stupendous power of Science," announced one editor, will rid American thought of "every old-time idea, every trace of old romance and art, poetry and romantic or sentimental feeling" and wash away the "ideal . . . and visionary."

Realism, as writer Fanny Bates stressed, appealed especially to people living in the busy, swarming cities, people "whose lives are crowded with a variety of interests." Money was what attracted most people to the cities, and the worship of money was the most common theme in realistic novels and short stories during the Gilded Age. In William Dean Howells's *The Rise of Silas Lapham* (1885), for example, Bromfield Corey announces that money "is the romance, the poetry of our age." Lily Bart, the heroine of Edith Wharton's novel *The House of Mirth* (1905), declares that she

***Stag at Sharkey's* (1909)** New York painter George Bellows witnessed such explosive boxing matches across the street from his studio, at the saloon of retired heavyweight boxer, "Sailor" Sharkey. Bellows is one of the most famous artists from the Ashcan School, which was committed to capturing the gritty reality of the urban scene.

"must have a great deal of money" to be happy in the fashionable circles of a large city.

City streets and parks also provided countless scenes of *real* life to depict on canvas and in words. Realistic writers and artists loved to stroll city streets, window-shopping and people-watching, consuming what the magisterial novelist Henry James called the "spectacle of the world's presence." The daily urban scene, he said, unleashed a "flood of the real" for writers and artists to study and portray. The New York City painter John Sloan chose his subjects from his habit of spying on people from his Manhattan studio. He confided in his diary that he was addicted to "*watching every bit* of human life" through his windows and along the sidewalks. Others shared his "spectatorial" sensibility. "My favorite pastime," writer Theodore Dreiser remembered, "was to walk the city streets and view the lives and activities of others." His fictional characters did the same. In Dreiser's influential novel *Sister Carrie* (1900), Carrie Meeber uses her "gift of observation" to view strangers through the open windows of shops, offices, and factories, imagining what "they deal with, how they labored, to what end it all came."

The realists' emphasis on closely observing everyday reality grew out of the scientific spirit. Just as scientists observed visible and verifiable facts and transformed them into knowledge, cultural realists studied the world around them and made it into art and literature. Like a gust of fresh air, they made Americans aware of the significance of their everyday surroundings in all their beauty and ugliness.

CORE **OBJECTIVE**

4. Explain how the nature of politics during the Gilded Age contributed to political corruption and stalemate.

Gilded Age Politics

Like William Graham Sumner, many elected officials after the Civil War believed that governments should do as little as possible, so as to allow for the natural evolution of the economy and society. The Gilded Age was an era that saw more political corruption than political innovation. As a young college graduate in 1879, future president Woodrow Wilson described the state of the political system as "No leaders, no principles." The real movers and shakers of the Gilded Age were not the men who sat in the White House or Congress but those who owned the huge corporations. These "captains of industry," labeled "robber barons" by critics, regularly used their wealth to "buy" elections and favors from both major political parties and at all levels of government. Jay Gould, one of the most aggressive railroad giants, admitted that he elected "the [New York] legislature with my own money."

> Corporate-funded corruption

The activities of "special interests," those businesses that bought favors from government officials, dominated Gilded Age politics. As President Rutherford B. Hayes confessed, the "real difficulty" with the political system of his time was "the vast wealth and power in the hands of the few and unscrupulous who represent or control capital." By the end of the nineteenth century, however, new political movements and parties were pushing reforms to deal with the many excesses and injustices created by a political system that had grown corrupt in its support for the "special interests" of Big Business.

Local Politics and Party Loyalties

> A local rather than federal focus

Perhaps the most important feature of Gilded Age politics was its local focus. Americans of the time expected little direct support from the federal government, and most political activity occurred at the state and local levels. Unlike today, the federal government was an insignificant force in the daily lives of most Americans, in part because it was so small. In 1871 the entire federal civilian workforce totaled 51,000 (most of them postal workers), of whom only 6,000 actually worked in Washington, D.C. Not until the twentieth century did the importance of the federal government begin to surpass that of local and state governments. During the Gilded Age, in fact, large cities as a group spent far more on local services than did the federal government, and three-fourths of all public employees worked for state and local governments.

> Political parties as social networks and forms of recreation

Americans during the Gilded Age were intensely loyal to their political party, which they joined as much for the social fellowship and networking connections as for its positions on issues. Attending political speeches and gatherings was a major form of public recreation, and party loyalists eagerly read newspaper coverage of political issues and joined in rallies, picnics, and parades.

Party members paid dues to join, and party leaders were so powerful in promoting their "special interests" that they demanded campaign contributions from the most powerful captains of industry and finance. Collis Huntington, a California railroad tycoon, admitted that bribery in the form of campaign contributions was regularly expected in Congress: "If you have to pay money to have the right thing done, then it is only just and fair to do it." Roscoe Conkling, a powerful Republican senator from New York, was equally candid about the role of corruption: "Of course, we do rotten things in New York. . . . Politics is a rotten business." The Democrats were no better. Horatio Seymour, a Democratic governor of New York and a presidential candidate in 1868, explained that "our people want men in office who will not steal, but who will not interfere with those who do."

In cities crowded with new immigrant voters, politics was usually controlled by "rings"—small groups of powerful insiders who shaped policy and managed the nomination and election of candidates. Each ring typically had a powerful **party "boss,"** an absolute ruler who used his "machine"—a network of neighborhood activists and officials—to govern. Bosses staged election parades, fireworks displays, and free banquets—with alcoholic beverages—for voters. They helped settle local disputes, provided aid for the needy, and distributed government jobs and contracts to loyal followers and corporate donors. Throughout most of the nineteenth century, almost every government job—local, state, and federal—was subject to the latest election results. This meant that the party in power expected government employees to become campaign workers and to do the bidding of party bosses during elections.

Party bosses, often arrogant and dictatorial in their behavior, decided who the candidates would be, often determined the party's positions on significant issues, and commanded loyalty and obedience by rewarding and punishing their members. Once in power, the bosses excelled at **patronage**, the long-standing system whereby party leaders rewarded supporters with government jobs and contracts—the so-called spoils of office. It was—and remains—a system that invited abuse and corruption. As President Ulysses S. Grant's secretary told a Republican party boss, "I only hope you will distribute the patronage in such a manner as will help the Administration."

Partisan Politics at the National Level

Several factors gave national politics during the Gilded Age its distinctive texture. First, the national political parties were much more powerful forces than they are today. Party loyalty was intense, often extending over generations in many families. A second distinctive element of Gilded Age politics at the national level was the close division between Republicans and Democrats in Congress. Both parties avoided controversial issues or bold initiatives because neither was dominant. The third important aspect of post–Civil War politics was the intensity of voter involvement at all

> Bribery, patronage, and boss rule

William "Boss" Tweed A larger-than-life political boss was New York City's William "Boss" Tweed, whose powerful connections made "no prison big enough to hold the Boss."

party "boss" A powerful political leader who controlled a "machine" of associates and operatives to promote both individual and party interests, often using informal tactics such as intimidation or the patronage system.

patronage An informal system (sometimes called the "spoils system") used by politicians to reward their supporters with government appointments or contracts.

levels—local and state as well as national. Voter turnout during the Gilded Age was commonly about 70–80 percent. (By contrast, the turnout for the 2012 presidential election was 58 percent.)

During the Gilded Age, most voters cast their ballots for the same party year after year, generation after generation, regardless of the candidates. Party loyalty was often an emotional choice. In the 1870s and 1880s, for example, people north and south continued to fight the Civil War during political campaigns. Republican candidates regularly "waved the bloody shirt," encouraging war veterans to "vote like you shot," while accusing Democrats of having caused "secession and civil war." Democrats, especially in the South, responded to such attacks by reminding voters that they stood for limited government, states' rights, and white supremacy. Republicans tended to favor high tariffs on imports, but Democrats also supported tariffs if they benefited businesses in their districts. Third parties, such as the Greenbackers, Populists, and Prohibitionists, appealed to specific interests and issues, such as currency inflation, railroad regulations, or legislation to restrict alcohol consumption.

Party loyalties reflected religious and ethnic divisions as well as geographic ones. After the Civil War, the Republican party remained strongest in the North and West and weakest in the South. It attracted mainly Protestants of British descent. As the party of Abraham Lincoln (the "Great Emancipator") and Ulysses Grant, Republicans could also rely upon the votes of African Americans in the South (until their right to vote was taken away late in the century) and of a large bloc of Union veterans of the Civil War, who were organized into a powerful national fraternal group called the Grand Army of the Republic. The Democrats, by contrast, were a more diverse and often unruly coalition of southern whites, northern immigrants, Roman Catholics, Jews, freethinkers, and those repelled by the Protestant Republican "party of morality." As one Chicago Democrat explained, "A Republican is a man who wants you t' go t' church every Sunday. A Democrat says if a man wants to have a glass of beer on Sunday he can have it."

As this quotation suggests, in the 1880s efforts to restrict or prohibit alcoholic beverages revived among Republicans, along with nativist policies designed to restrict immigration and the employment of foreigners. Among the immigrants crowded into the growing cities were many Irish, Germans, and Italians, all of whom had brought their robust drinking traditions with them into their new country. The mostly rural Republican Protestants considered saloons the central social evil around which all others revolved, and they associated these evils with the ethnic groups that frequented saloons. Carrie Nation, the most colorful member of the Women's Christian Temperance Union (WCTU), became nationally known for attacking saloons with a hatchet. Saloons, she argued, stripped a married woman of everything by turning working men into alcoholics, as had happened with Nation's first husband: "Her husband is torn from her, she is robbed of her sons, her home, her food, and her virtue."

Balanced national parties, evenly divided Congress, and intense voter involvement

National politics and party loyalties: Regional, religious, and ethnic divisions

National politics with Congress evenly divided

Between 1869 and 1913, from the first term of President Ulysses S. Grant through the election of William Howard Taft, Republicans monopolized the White House except for the two nonconsecutive terms of New York Democrat Grover Cleveland. Otherwise, however, national politics was remarkably balanced between the two major parties. Between 1872 and 1896, their strength was so closely divided that, because of support for third party candidates, *no* president won a majority of the popular vote. In each of those presidential elections, sixteen states invariably voted Republican and fourteen voted Democratic, leaving six states whose results determined the outcome. The swing-vote role played by two of those states, New York and Ohio, decided the election of eight presidents from 1872 to 1908.

No chief executive between Abraham Lincoln and Theodore Roosevelt could be described as a "strong" president. All believed that Congress, not the White House, should formulate major policies. As Senator John Sherman of Ohio stressed, "the President should merely obey and enforce the law."

Corruption and Reform: Hayes to Harrison

CORE OBJECTIVE
5. Evaluate the effectiveness of politicians in developing responses to the major economic and social problems of the Gilded Age.

Both Republicans and Democrats had their share of corrupt officials willing to buy and sell government jobs or legislative votes, yet as early as the 1870s, in response to the corruption uncovered in the Grant administration, each party also developed factions promoting honesty in government. The struggle for "clean" government became one of the foremost issues of the Gilded Age.

Hayes and Civil Service Reform

President Rutherford B. Hayes brought to the White House in 1877 both a lingering controversy over the disputed election results (critics called him "His Fraudulency") and a new style of uprightness that was in sharp contrast to the barely concealed graft of the Grant era. The son of an Ohio farmer, Hayes was wounded four times in the Civil War. He went on to serve in Congress and as governor of Ohio. Stubbornly honest and conservative, he was, said a Republican journalist, a "third-rate nonentity" whose only virtue was that he was "obnoxious to no one."

Hayes had been the compromise presidential nominee of the two factions fighting for control of the Republican party, the so-called Stalwarts and Half-Breeds, led, respectively, by Senators Roscoe Conkling of New York and James G. Blaine of Maine. The Stalwarts had been "stalwart" in their support of President Grant during the furor over the misdeeds of his cabinet members. Further, they had mastered the "spoils system" of distributing political jobs to party loyalists. The Half-Breeds were called such

Republican resistance to Hayes's reform efforts

because they supposedly were only half-loyal to Grant and half-committed to reform of the spoils system. But the two warring Republican factions existed primarily to advance the careers of Conkling and Blaine, who detested each other. Blaine once charged that Conkling and the Stalwarts were "all the desperate bad men, bent on loot and booty."

To his credit, President Hayes tried to stay above the petty political bickering. He joined the growing public outrage over political corruption, admitting that his party "must mend its ways" by focusing on Republican principles rather than fighting over the spoils of office. "He serves his party best who serves his country best," Hayes declared in announcing that it was time "for **civil service** [government jobs] **reform**." He appointed a committee to consider a "merit system" for hiring government employees, as used in some European countries, and a new practice in Britain in which civil service jobs were awarded on the basis of competitive written tests. In a dramatic gesture, Hayes also fired Chester A. Arthur, a Stalwart Republican who ran the New York Customs House, because Arthur had abused the patronage system in ways, according to Hayes, that promoted "ignorance, inefficiency, and corruption."

Hayes's commitment to cleaning up politics enraged Republican leaders. In 1879, Ohio Congressman James Garfield warned Hayes that "if he wishes to hold any influence" with fellow Republicans, he "must abandon some of his notions of Civil Service reform." For his part, Hayes confessed that he had little hope of success because he was "opposed by . . . the most powerful men in my party."

Conflict over expanding the money supply

On economic issues, Hayes held to a conservative line that would guide his successors—from both parties—for the rest of the century. His answer to the growing demands for expansion of the nation's money supply (which would become one of the leading political issues of the late nineteenth century) was to veto the Bland-Allison Act (1878), which provided for a slight increase in the supply of silver coins. (More money in circulation—inflation—was generally believed to raise farm prices and help those trying to pay off debts.) When Congress, including many Republicans, overturned Hayes's veto, the bruised president confided in his diary that he had become a president without a party. In 1879, with a year still left in his term, Hayes was ready to leave the White House. "I am now in my last year of the Presidency," he wrote a friend, "and look forward to its close as a schoolboy longs for the coming vacation."

Garfield, Arthur, and the Pendleton Act

With Hayes choosing not to pursue a second term, the Republican presidential nomination in 1880 was up for grabs. Former president Grant wanted the nomination but was unwilling to campaign for it. In the end, the party's squabbling factions selected a compromise candidate, Congressman James A. Garfield. An early foe of slavery, the tall Garfield had served as a

civil service reform An extended effort led by political reformers to end the patronage system; led to the Pendleton Act (1883), which called for government jobs to be awarded based on merit rather than party loyalty.

Union army general, like Grant and Hayes, before being elected to Congress in 1863. In an effort to please the Stalwarts and also win the crucial state of New York, Chester A. Arthur, whom Hayes had fired as head of the New York Customs House, was named the party's candidate for vice president.

The Democrats, as divided as the Republicans, selected their own compromise candidate: Winfield Scott Hancock, a retired Union general who had distinguished himself at the Battle of Gettysburg but had done little since. In large part, Hancock was chosen to help deflect the Republicans' "bloody-shirt" attacks on Democrats as the party of the Confederacy. In an election marked by widespread bribery, Garfield eked out a popular-vote plurality of only 39,000, or 48.5 percent. He won a more comfortable margin of 214 to 155 in the Electoral College.

A Presidency Cut Short

In his inaugural address, President Garfield gave an impassioned defense of civil rights, arguing that the "elevation of the negro race from slavery to the full rights of citizenship is the most important political change we have known since the adoption of the Constitution of 1787." The end of slavery, he said, "has added immensely to the moral and industrial forces of our people. It has liberated the master as well as the slave from a relation which wronged and enfeebled both." But he also confirmed that the Republicans had ended efforts to reconstruct the former Confederacy. Southern blacks were now on their own; they had been "surrendered to their own guardianship."

Garfield showed great potential as a president but had no chance to follow through. On July 2, 1881, after only four months in office, he was walking through the Washington, D.C., railroad station with James G. Blaine, now secretary of state, when he was shot twice by Charles Guiteau, a former Republican who had been turned down for a federal job. One bullet grazed the president's arm; the other went into his back. As a policeman wrestled the assassin to the ground, Guiteau shouted: "Yes! I have killed Garfield! [Chester] Arthur is President of the United States. I am a Stalwart!"—a declaration that would eventually destroy the Stalwart wing of the Republican Party. On September 19, after seventy-nine days, Garfield died of complications resulting from inept medical care. During a sensational ten-week trial, Guiteau explained that God had ordered him to kill the president. The jury refused to believe that he was insane and pronounced him guilty of murder. On June 30, 1882, Guiteau was hanged; an autopsy revealed that his brain was diseased.

The Civil Service Commission

In their grief over Garfield's death, Americans blamed Roscoe Conkling and the Stalwart Republicans for inciting Guiteau. One New York newspaper headline screamed: "MURDERED BY THE SPOILS SYSTEM!" The new president, Chester A. Arthur, who had been Conkling's trusted lieutenant,

Civil Service Commission: Merit system for government employees

surprised most political observers by distancing himself from the Stalwarts and even becoming a civil service reformer himself.

In 1883, the momentum against the "spoils system" generated by Garfield's assassination enabled George H. Pendleton, a Democratic senator from Ohio, to convince Congress to establish a Civil Service Commission, the first federal regulatory agency. Because of the Pendleton Civil Service Reform Act, a growing percentage of federal jobs would now be filled on the basis of competitive tests (the "merit system") rather than political favoritism. In addition, federal employees running for office were prohibited from receiving political contributions from other government workers.

The Pendleton Act was a limited first step in cleaning up the patronage process. It was sorely needed, in part because the federal government was expanding rapidly. By 1901, there would be 256,000 federal employees, five times the number in 1871. A growing number of these federal workers were women, who by 1890 held a third of the government's clerical jobs.

The Campaign of 1884

Chester Arthur's efforts to clean up the spoils system might have attracted voters, but they did not please Republican leaders. So in 1884 the Republicans dumped Arthur and chose as their presidential nominee James Gillespie Blaine of Maine, the handsome, colorful secretary of state, former senator, and longtime leader of the Half-Breeds, who had been at James Garfield's side three years earlier when the president was assassinated.

Corruption and a Sex Scandal

Blaine was the consummate politician. He inspired the party faithful with his electrifying speeches and knew how to wheel and deal in the backrooms, sometimes evading the law in the process. One critic charged that Blaine "wallowed in spoils like a rhinoceros in an African pool." Newspapers soon uncovered evidence of his corruption in the so-called Mulligan letters, which revealed that, as Speaker of the House, Blaine had secretly sold his votes on measures favorable to a railroad corporation. Nobody proved that he had committed any crimes, but the circumstantial evidence was powerful: his senatorial salary alone could not have built either his mansion in Washington, D.C. or his palatial home in Augusta, Maine (which has since become the state's governor's mansion). Former president Grant wrote a friend that he did not like Blaine and doubted his "reliability."

During the 1884 presidential campaign, more embarrassing letters surfaced linking Blaine to shady deal-making. For the reform element of the Republican party, this was too much, and many Republicans refused to endorse Blaine's candidacy. Party regulars scorned such critics as "goo-goos"—the good-government crowd. The editor of a New York newspaper jokingly called the anti-Blaine Republicans **Mugwumps**, after an Algonquian Indian word meaning "big chief." The Mugwumps, a self-appointed political

Mugwumps Reformers who bolted the Republican party in 1884 to support Democrat Grover Cleveland for president over Republican James G. Blaine, whose secret dealings on behalf of railroad companies had brought charges of corruption.

elite dedicated to promoting honest government, saw the election as "moral rather than political." Centered in the large cities and major universities of the northeast, they were mostly professors, editors, and writers who included in their number the most famous American of the time, Mark Twain. The Mugwumps generally opposed tariffs on imports and championed free trade. They opposed the regulation of railroads as well as efforts to inflate the money supply by coining more silver. Their foremost goal was to reform the process of appointing people to government jobs by making *all* federal jobs nonpartisan. Their break with the Republican party testified to the depth of their convictions.

The rise of the Mugwumps, as well as growing national concerns about political corruption, prompted the Democrats to nominate New Yorker Grover Cleveland, a minister's son, as a reform candidate. Cleveland had first attracted national attention in 1881, when he was elected the mayor of Buffalo on an anti-corruption platform. In 1882 he was elected governor of New York, and he continued to build a reform record by fighting New York City's corrupt Tammany Hall ring. As mayor and as governor, he repeatedly vetoed bills because in his view they served private interests at the expense of the public good. He supported civil service reform, opposed expanding the money supply, and preferred free trade to high tariffs, which tended to enrich big businesses at the expense of consumers.

Grover Cleveland As president, Cleveland made the issue of tariff reform central to the politics of the late 1880s.

Although Cleveland was known for his honesty and integrity, a juicy scandal erupted around him. A newspaper in Buffalo revealed that Cleveland, a bachelor, had befriended an attractive widow named Maria Halpin, who later named him the father of her baby born in 1874. Cleveland had discreetly provided financial support for the child.

The escapades of Blaine and Cleveland provided some of the most colorful battle cries in political history: "Blaine, Blaine, James G. Blaine, the continental liar from the state of Maine," Democrats chanted. Republicans countered with "Ma, ma, where's my pa?"

Blunders by the Blaine Campaign

Near the end of the nasty campaign, Blaine and his supporters committed two fateful blunders. The first occurred at New York City's fashionable Delmonico's restaurant, where Blaine went to a private dinner with 200 of the nation's wealthiest business leaders to ask them to help finance his campaign. Accounts of the unseemly event appeared in the newspapers for days afterwards. One headline blared: "Blaine Hobnobbing with the Mighty Money Kings!" The article explained that the banquet was intended to collect contributions for a "Republican corruption fund."

The second Blaine blunder occurred when a Protestant minister visiting Republican headquarters in New York referred to the Democrats as the party of "rum, Romanism, and rebellion [the Confederacy]." Blaine, who was present, let pass the implied insult to Catholics—a fatal oversight, since he had always cultivated Irish American support with his anti-English talk and repeated references to his mother being a Catholic. Democrats claimed that Blaine was, at heart, anti-Irish and anti-Catholic.

The two incidents may have tipped the close 1884 presidential election. The electoral vote came in at 219 to 182 in Cleveland's favor, but the popular vote ran far closer: Cleveland's plurality was fewer than 30,000 votes out of ten million cast. Cleveland won the key state of New York by only 1,149 votes out of 1,167,169 cast.

Cleveland's Reform Efforts

Democratic resistance to civil service reform

During his first few months in office, President Cleveland struggled to keep Democratic officials from reviving the patronage system. In a letter to a friend, the new president reported that he was living in a "nightmare," that "dreadful, damnable, office-seeking hangs over me and surrounds me" and that it made him "feel like resigning." Democratic newspapers heaped scorn on him for refusing to award federal jobs to his supporters. One accused Cleveland of "ingratitude" towards those who had "delivered the vote." Despite the president's best efforts to promote civil service reform, about two-thirds of the 120,000 federal jobs went to Democrats as patronage during his administration.

Cleveland also opposed federal favors to Big Business. "A public office is a public trust" was one of his favorite sayings. He held to a strictly limited view of government's role in both economic and social matters, a philosophy illustrated by his 1887 veto of a congressional effort to provide desperate Texas farmers with seeds in the aftermath of a drought. "Though the people support the government, the government should not support the people," Cleveland asserted. During his administration, he would veto more acts of Congress than any previous president.

Regulation of Railroad Rates

Creation of the Interstate Commerce Commission

For all of his genuine commitment to limited government intervention, Cleveland urged Congress to adopt an important new policy: federal regulation of the rates charged by interstate railroads (those whose tracks crossed state lines) to ship goods, crops, or livestock. He believed with many others that railroads were charging unfairly high freight rates, especially in communities served by only one railroad. States had adopted laws regulating railroads since the late 1860s, but in 1886 the Supreme Court declared in *Wabash, St. Louis, and Pacific Railroad Company v. Illinois* that no state could regulate the rates charged by railroads engaged in *interstate* traffic. Because most railroads did cross state lines, Cleveland urged Congress to close the loophole.

Interstate Commerce Commission An independent federal agency established in 1887 to oversee businesses engaged in interstate trade, especially railroads, but whose regulatory power was limited when tested in the courts.

Congress followed through, and in 1887 Cleveland signed an act creating the **Interstate Commerce Commission** (ICC), a federal regulatory agency. The law empowered the ICC's five members to ensure that railroad freight rates were "reasonable and just." The commission's actual powers proved to be weak, however, when tested in the courts. Over time, the ICC came to be ignored, and the railroads continued their practice of charging high rates while making secret pricing deals with large shippers.

Tariff Reform and the Election of 1888

President Cleveland's most dramatic challenge to the power of Big Business focused on **tariff reform**. During the late nineteenth century, the government's high-tariff policies, shaped largely by the Republican party, had favored big businesses by effectively shutting out foreign imports, thereby enabling U.S. corporations to dominate their American markets and charge higher prices for their products. In 1887, Cleveland argued that Congress should reduce both the tariff rates ("the vicious, inequitable and illogical source of unnecessary taxation . . . [and] a burden upon the poor") and the number of imported goods subject to tariffs (over 4,000 items), so as to enable European companies to compete in the American marketplace. His outspoken stance against high tariffs set the stage for his reelection campaign in 1888.

> Cleveland's anti-tariff stance

To oppose Cleveland, the Republicans, now calling themselves the GOP (Grand Old Party) to emphasize their longevity, turned to the obscure Benjamin Harrison, a Civil War veteran whose greatest attributes were his availability and the fact that he was from Indiana, a pivotal state in presidential elections. The grandson of President William Henry Harrison, he had a modest political record; he had lost a race for governor and had served one term in the U.S. Senate (1881–1887).

The Republicans accepted Cleveland's challenge to make tariffs the chief issue in the campaign. As was often the case, they enjoyed a huge advantage in campaign funding and national organization; to fend off Cleveland's efforts to reduce the tariff, business executives contributed especially generously to the Republican cause. Still, the outcome was incredibly close. Cleveland won the popular vote by the thinnest of margins—5,540,329 to 5,439,853—but Harrison carried the Electoral College by 233 to 168. "Providence," said the new president, "has given us the victory." Matthew Quay, his campaign chairman, knew better. Harrison, he muttered, "ought to know that Providence hadn't a damned thing to do with it!" It was the distribution in key states of campaign money and promises of federal government jobs that won the election for Harrison.

Republican Activism under Harrison

Harrison owed a heavy debt to Civil War veterans, whose votes had been critical to his election, and he paid it by signing the Dependent Pension Act. As a result, the number of Union war veterans (and their family members) receiving federal pensions almost doubled between 1889 and 1893. In

tariff reform Effort led by the Democratic party to reduce taxes on imported goods, which Republicans argued were needed to protect American industries from foreign competition.

"King of the World" Reformers targeted the growing power of monopolies, such as that of John D. Rockefeller's Standard Oil.

addition, the Republicans took advantage of their control of the presidency and both houses of Congress to pass a cluster of other significant legislation in 1890: the Sherman Anti-Trust Act, the Sherman Silver Purchase Act, the McKinley Tariff Act, and the admission of Idaho and Wyoming as new states, which followed the admission of North and South Dakota, Montana, and Washington in 1889.

The Sherman Anti-Trust Act, named for Ohio senator John Sherman, was the first effort in the world to limit the size of businesses by prohibiting companies from "conspiring" to establish monopolies in their industries. Though badly needed, it was rarely enforced, in large part because of its vague definitions of "trusts" and "monopolies." From 1890 to 1901, only eighteen lawsuits were instituted, four of which were filed against labor unions rather than corporations.

As for tariff policy, Republicans viewed their victory over Cleveland in 1888 as a mandate not just to maintain the tariffs protecting American companies from foreign competition, but to raise the tariff rates even higher. Piloted through Congress by Ohio representative William McKinley, the McKinley Tariff Act of 1890 raised duties on imported manufactured goods to their highest level ever. Its passage encouraged many American businesses to raise prices for their own goods, since they had no need to worry about European competitors, who were now effectively shut out of the American market.

CORE **OBJECTIVE**

6. Analyze why the money supply became a major political issue during the Gilded Age and describe its impact on American politics.

A shrinking money supply in a growing economy

Inadequate Currency and Unhappy Farmers

Even more than tariffs, trusts, and efforts to clean up political corruption, national politics during the Gilded Age was preoccupied with complex monetary issues. In 1876, several farm organizations organized the independent "Greenback" party to promote the benefits of paper money over gold and silver coins; it won fifteen seats in Congress in 1878, illustrating the significance of currency issues to voters.

Behind many of these issues lay the fact that the nation's money supply had not grown along with the expanding economy of the late nineteenth century. From 1865 to 1890, the amount of money in circulation (both coins and paper currency) actually *decreased* about 10 percent at the same time that the economy was dramatically expanding. Such currency deflation raised the cost of borrowing money as the shrinking of the money supply enabled lenders to hike interest rates on loans. Creditors—bankers and others who loaned money—supported a "sound money" policy that limited the currency supply as a means of increasing their profits. By contrast, farmers, ranchers, and others who constantly had to borrow money to make ends meet claimed that the "sound money" policy had the deflationary effect of lowering prices for their crops and herds, driving them deeper into debt.

Increasing Unrest among Farmers

The 1890 congressional elections revealed a deep-seated unrest in the farming communities of the South and on the plains of Kansas and Nebraska, as well as in the mining towns of the Rocky Mountain region. People used the term "revolution" to describe the swelling grassroots support for the Populists, a new third party focused on the needs of miners and small farmers, many of whom did not own the land they worked. In drought-devastated Kansas, Populists won five congressional seats from Republicans. In early 1891, the newly elected Populists and Democrats took control of Congress just as an acute economic crisis appeared on the horizon: farmers' debts were mounting as crop prices plummeted.

A Vicious Cycle of Depressed Prices and Debt

Since the end of the Civil War, farmers in the South and the Great Plains had suffered from worsening economic conditions. The basic source of their problems was a decline in prices earned for their crops, a deflationary trend caused by overproduction and growing international competition in world food markets as well as the inadequate money supply. The vast new lands brought under cultivation in the plains poured an ever-increasing supply of farm products into world markets, driving prices down. Meanwhile, farmers, especially small farmers in the South and West, had become increasingly indebted to "greedy" local banks or merchants who loaned them money to buy seed, fertilizer, tools, and other supplies. As prices for wheat, cotton, and corn dropped, however, so did the income the farmers received, thus preventing them from paying their debts on time. In response, most farmers had no choice but to grow even more wheat, cotton, or corn, creating a vicious cycle: as still more grains and cotton were harvested and sold, the increased supply drove down prices and farmers' incomes even further. High tariffs on imported goods also hurt farmers because they blocked foreign competition, allowing U.S. companies to raise the prices of manufactured goods needed by farm families. Farmers, however, had to sell their crops in open world markets unprotected by tariffs, where competition lowered prices.

Besides bankers, merchants, and high tariffs, struggling farmers also blamed the railroads, warehouse owners, and food processors, the so-called middle men who helped get their products to market. They especially resented that railroads, most of which had a monopoly over the shipping of grains and livestock, charged such high rates to ship their farm products.

> Indebted farmers and falling crop prices

Silver and Inflation

Among all the factors distressing farmers, the nation's inadequate money supply emerged as the source of greatest frustration. In 1873, the Republican-controlled Congress had declared that silver could no longer be used for coins, only gold. This decision (called "the Crime of '73" by critics) occurred just when silver mines in the western states had begun to increase their production. Hard-pressed farmers in the West and South demanded increased coinage of silver, which would inflate the currency and thereby raise commodity prices, providing farmers with more income with which to pay their annual debts.

The Sherman Silver Purchase Act (1890)

They found allies among legislators representing the new western states. All six states admitted to the Union in 1889 and 1890 had substantial silver mines, and their new congressional delegations—largely Republican—wanted the federal government to buy more silver for coins. The so-called silver delegates shifted the balance in Congress enough to pass the Sherman Silver Purchase Act (1890), which required the Treasury to purchase 4.5 million ounces of silver each month with new paper money. Such inflationary policies helped set the stage for the currency issue to eclipse all others during the financial panic that would sweep the country in 1893.

In the 1890 midterm elections, voters rebelled not only against the McKinley Tariff but also in support of the militant new farm protests. The result was that Democrats outnumbered Republicans in the new House of Representatives by almost three to one; in the Senate the Republican majority was reduced to eight. One of the election casualties was Congressman McKinley himself.

The Granger Movement

When the Department of Agriculture sent Oliver H. Kelley on a tour of the South in 1866, he was struck most by the social isolation of people living on small farms. To address the problem, Kelley in 1867 helped found the National Grange of the Patrons of Husbandry, better known as the Grange (an old word for places where crops were stored). In the next few years, the Granger movement mushroomed, reaching a membership of 1.5 million by 1874. It started out by offering social and educational activities for isolated farmers and their families, but as it grew, it also began to promote "cooperatives" where farmers could join together to buy, store, and sell their crops to avoid the high fees charged by brokers and other middle-men.

"Granger laws"

In five Midwest states, Grangers persuaded legislatures to pass "Granger laws" to regulate the prices charged farmers by railroads and grain warehouses (called "elevators"). Railroads and warehouses challenged the new laws, but in *Munn v. Illinois* (1877), the Supreme Court ruled that states had the right to regulate property such as grain elevators and railroads that operated in a public interest. Nine years later, however, the Court threw out the *Munn* ruling, finding in *Wabash v. Illinois* (1886) that only Congress could regulate industries involved in interstate commerce.

Farmers' Alliances

The **Granger movement** gradually fizzled out as members directed their energies into political action. In the 1880s, **Farmers' Alliances** began growing in size and significance. Like the Grange, the Farmers' Alliances (divided at the national level into Northern, Southern, and Colored branches) organized social and recreational activities for farmers and their families, but they also emphasized political action. Struggling farmers throughout the South and Midwest, where most did not own their land, saw the Alliance movement as a way to address the hardships created by chronic indebtedness, declining crop prices, and devastating droughts.

"I Feed You All!" (1875) The farmer is the cornerstone of American society, according to this Granger-inspired poster. Without the food he produces, no man in any occupation can do his job—including the very railroad magnate (left) and warehouse owners who try to exploit him.

The Alliance movement swept across the South and established strong support in Kansas and the Dakotas. In 1886, a white minister in Texas responded to the appeals of African American farmers by organizing the Colored Farmers' National Alliance. By 1890, the white Alliance movement had about 1.5 million members from New York to California, and the Colored Farmers' National Alliance claimed more than 1 million members.

In the farm states west of the Mississippi River, political activism intensified after a winter of record blizzards in 1887, which killed most of the cattle and hogs across the northern plains, and a prolonged drought two years later that destroyed millions of acres of corn, wheat, and oats. Distressed farmers lashed out against what they considered to be a powerful conspiracy of eastern financial and industrial interests, which they variously called "monopolies," "the money power," "Wall Street," or "organized wealth." The Alliance movement sponsored more than 1,000 rural newspapers and 40,000 lecturers to spread the word about the "tyrannical" forces arrayed against farmers.

New Third Parties

The Alliances, frustrated that neither Democrats nor Republicans embraced their cause, called for third-party political action to address their economic concerns. In 1890, farm radicals in Colorado joined with miners and railroad workers to form the Independent party, and Nebraska farmers formed the People's Independent party. Across the South, however, white Alliance members hesitated to leave the Democratic party, seeking instead to influence or control it. Both the third-party and the southern approaches produced startling success.

Granger movement Began by offering social and educational activities for isolated farmers and their families and later started to promote "cooperatives" where farmers could join together to buy, store, and sell their crops to avoid the high fees charged by brokers and other middlemen.

Farmers' Alliances Like the Granger movement, these organizations sought to address the issues of small farming communities; however, Alliances emphasized more political action and called for the creation of a Third Party to advocate their concerns.

Populist successes in local and state elections, and formation of a national party

In the Midwest, new third parties elected a U.S. senator and almost elected a governor under the banner of the new **People's party (Populists)** in Kansas, where a Populist won the governor's race in 1892. The Populists supported increased government intervention in the economy, for only the U.S. Congress could expand the money supply, counterbalance the power of Big Business, and provide efficient national transportation networks to support the agricultural economy. Third parties also took control of one house of the Kansas legislature and both houses in Nebraska. In the South Dakota and Minnesota legislatures, Populists won enough seats to control the balance of power between Republicans and Democrats.

In the South, the Alliance movement forced Democrats to nominate candidates pledged to its farm program and succeeded in electing four of them as governors, forty-four as congressmen, and several as U.S. senators, as well as seven state legislatures controlled by Alliance supporters. Among the most respected of the southern Alliance leaders was red-haired Thomas E. Watson of Georgia. The son of prosperous slaveholders who had lost everything after the Civil War, Watson became a successful lawyer and speaker on behalf of the Alliance cause. He took the lead in urging African American tenant farmers and sharecroppers to join white farmers in ousting the political elite. "You are kept apart," he told black and white farmers, "that you may be separately fleeced of your earnings."

In Kansas, Mary Elizabeth Lease emerged as a fiery speaker for the farm protest movement. Born in Pennsylvania, Lease migrated to Kansas, taught school, raised a family, and failed at farming in the mid-1880s. She then studied law, "pinning sheets of notes above her wash tub," and became one of the state's first female attorneys. A proud, tall, and imposing woman, she began giving public speeches on behalf of struggling farmers that drew attentive audiences. "The people are at bay," she warned in 1894; "let the bloodhounds of money beware." She urged angry farmers to obtain their goals "with the ballot if possible, but if not that way then with the bayonet." Like so many Populists, Lease viewed the urban-industrial East as the enemy. "The great common people of this country are slaves," she shouted, "and monopoly is the master. The West and South are bound and prostrate before the manufacturing East."

The Election of 1892

People's party (Populists)
Political party formed in 1892 following the success of Farmers' Alliance candidates; Populists advocated a variety of reforms, including free coinage of silver, a progressive income tax, postal savings banks, regulation of railroads, and direct election of U.S. senators.

The success of the Farmer Alliance led to the formation of yet another new political party on the national level. In 1892, Alliance leaders organized a convention of the People's Party, which opened on July 4 in Omaha, Nebraska. Delegates drafted a platform that called for unlimited coinage of silver, a "progressive" income tax whose rates would rise with personal income levels, and federal control of the railroads. The Populists also endorsed the eight-hour workday and new laws restricting immigration, for fear that foreigners were taking Americans' jobs. The party's platform turned out to be more exciting than its presidential candidate: Iowa's James

B. Weaver, a former Union army officer who had headed the Greenback party ticket twelve years earlier. To attract southern voters, the Populists nominated a former Confederate general for vice president.

The major parties renominated the same candidates who had run in 1888: Democrat Grover Cleveland and Republican Benjamin Harrison. The tariff issue monopolized their attention. Each major candidate received more than 5 million votes, but Cleveland won a majority of the Electoral College. The Populists' Weaver received more than 1 million votes and carried Colorado, Kansas, Nevada, and Idaho. Alabama was the banner Populist state of the South, with 37 percent of its vote going to Weaver.

The Depression of 1893 and the "Free Silver" Crusade

While farmers were funneling their discontent into politics during the fall of 1892, a fundamental weakness in the economy was about to cause a major collapse and a social rebellion. Just ten days before Grover Cleveland started his second presidential term, in the winter of 1893, the Philadelphia and Reading Railroad declared bankruptcy, setting off a national financial crisis, now called the **Panic of 1893**, that grew into the worst depression the nation had ever experienced.

Other overextended railroads collapsed, taking many banks with them. A quarter of unskilled urban workers lost their jobs, and by the fall of 1893 more than 600 banks had closed and 15,000 businesses had failed. Farm foreclosures soared in the South and West; between 1890 and 1894, more than 11,000 farmers lost their farms in Kansas alone. By 1900, a third of all American farmers rented their land rather than owned it. Kansans grimly joked: "In God we trusted, in Kansas we busted." By 1894, the nation's economy had reached bottom. But the depression lasted another four years, with unemployment hovering at 20 percent. In New York City, the rate was close to 35 percent, and 20,000 homeless people camped out at police stations and other makeshift shelters.

President Cleveland's response to the economic catastrophe was to convince Congress to return the nation's money supply to a solely gold standard by repealing the Sherman Silver Purchase Act of 1890, a move that only made the depression worse. The weak economy needed more money in circulation, not less. Investors rushed to exchange their silver for gold, thus further constricting the nation's money supply. A wave of violent labor unrest symbolized the fracturing of the social order; in 1894, some 750,000 workers went on strike. The depression was reshaping America's economic and political landscape.

In this climate of turmoil and anxiety, the 1894 congressional elections devastated President Cleveland and the Democrats. The Republicans gained 121 seats in the House, the largest increase ever. Only in the "Solid South"

> Repeal of the Sherman Silver Purchase Act

Panic of 1893 A major collapse in the national economy after several major railroad companies declared bankruptcy, leading to a severe depression and several violent clashes between workers and management.

did the Democrats retain their advantage. The Populists emerged with six senators and seven representatives, and they expected the festering discontent in rural areas to carry them to national power in 1896. Their hopes would be dashed, however.

Silverites versus Goldbugs

Cleveland's decision to repeal the Sherman Silver Purchase Act had created an irreparable division in his own party. One embittered pro-silver Democrat labeled the president a traitor. Politicians from western states with large silver mines increased their demands for the "unlimited" coinage of silver, presenting a strategic dilemma for Populists: should the party promote the long list of varied reforms it had originally advocated, or should it try to ride the silver issue into power? The latter seemed more likely to succeed. Although flooding the economy with silver currency would probably not have provided the benefits its advocates claimed, the "free silver" crusade had taken on powerful symbolic overtones. Over the protests of more-radical members, Populist leaders decided to hold their 1896 nominating convention after the two major-party conventions, confident that the Republicans and Democrats would at best straddle the silver issue and enable the Populists to lure away pro-silver advocates from both.

Contrary to those expectations, the major parties took opposite positions on the currency issue. The Republicans, as expected, nominated William McKinley, a former congressman and governor of Ohio, on a platform committed to gold coins as the only form of currency. After the convention, a friend told McKinley that the **"money question"** would determine the election. He was right.

Bryan's "Cross of Gold" speech

The Democratic convention in the Chicago Coliseum, the largest building in the world, was one of the great turning points in American political history. The pro-silver, largely rural delegates surprised the party leadership and the "Gold Democrats" or "goldbugs" by capturing the convention for their inflationary crusade. Thirty-six-year-old William Jennings Bryan of Nebraska gave the final speech before the balloting began. A fiery evangelical moralist, Bryan was a two-term congressman who had lost a race for the Senate in 1894, when Democrats by the dozens were swept out of office. In the months before the convention, he had traveled throughout the South and West, speaking passionately for the unlimited coinage of silver and against Cleveland's "do-nothing" response to the depression.

"money question" Late-nineteenth-century national debate over the nature of U.S. currency; supporters of a fixed gold standard were generally money lenders, and thus preferred to keep the value of money high, while supporters of silver (and gold) coinage were debtors, they owed money, so they wanted to keep the value of money low by increasing the currency supply (inflation).

Bryan was a magnetic public speaker with a booming voice, a crusading preacher in the role of a politician. At the 1896 convention, he was only a "dark horse" candidate—that is, a little-known long shot—for the presidential nomination. So he chose to take a calculated risk: he would be intentionally provocative and disruptive. In his now famous speech, Bryan claimed to speak for the "producing masses of this nation" against the eastern "financial magnates" who had "enslaved" them by manipulating the money supply to ensure high interest rates for loans. He reminded the delegates that the "man who is employed for wages is as much a business man as his employer." As his melodramatic twenty-minute speech reached its peak, Bryan fused Christian imagery with Populist anger:

> I come to speak to you in defense of a cause as holy as the cause of liberty—the cause of humanity. . . . We have petitioned, and our petitions have been scorned. . . . We have begged, and they have mocked when our calamity came. We beg no longer; we entreat no more; we petition no more. We defy them!

William Jennings Bryan His "cross of gold" speech at the 1896 Democratic Convention roused the delegates and secured him the party's presidential nomination.

Bryan then stretched his fingers across his forehead and reached his dramatic conclusion: "You shall not press down upon the brow of labor this crown of thorns. You shall not crucify mankind upon a cross of gold!"—at which point he extended his arms straight out from his sides, as if he were being crucified. It was a riveting performance that worked better than even Bryan himself had anticipated. As he walked triumphantly off the stage, the delegates erupted in wild applause. "Everybody seemed to go mad at once," reported the *New York World*. For their part, the Republicans were not at all amused by Bryan's antics. A Republican newspaper observed that no political movement had "ever before spawned such hideous and repulsive vipers."

The day after his speech, Bryan won the presidential nomination on the fifth ballot, but in the process the Democratic party was fractured. Disappointed pro-gold, pro-Cleveland Democrats dismissed Bryan as a fanatic and a socialist. They were so alienated by both his positions and his rhetoric that they walked out of the convention and nominated their own candidate, Senator John M. Palmer of Illinois. "Fellow Democrats," Palmer announced, "I will not consider it any great fault if you decide to cast your vote for [the Republican] William McKinley."

> Pro-gold Democrats and pro-silver Populists

When the Populists gathered in St. Louis for their presidential nominating convention two weeks later, they faced an impossible choice. They could name their own candidate and divide the pro-silver vote with the Democrats, or they could endorse Bryan and probably lose their identity as an independent party. In the end, they backed Bryan, but chose their own vice-presidential candidate, Thomas E. Watson, and invited the Democrats to drop their vice-presidential nominee. Bryan refused the offer.

The Election of 1896

The election of 1896 was one of the most dramatic in American history, in part because of the striking contrast between the candidates and in part because the terrible depression made the stakes so high. Bryan, the nominee of both the Democrats and the Populists, was the first major candidate since Andrew Jackson to champion the poor, the discontented, and the oppressed against the financial and industrial elite. And he was the first leader of a major party to call for the expansion of the federal government to help the working and middle classes.

National Issues of the Gilded Age

During the Gilded Age, politics was above all else a local affair. With a small federal government, an entrenched patronage system, and a highly partisan and closely divided electorate, there was little opportunity for effective national legislation. However, four issues of national political conflict did emerge: immigration, civil service and corporate reform, the "money question," and the tariff.

NATIONAL ISSUE 1 IMMIGRATION

	Supporters: Nonrestrictionists	Opponents: Nativists
Position	Few or no limits on immigration	Limit or ban on immigrants who were: ■ nonwhite (e.g., Chinese) ■ non-Anglo-Saxon (i.e., eastern and southern European) ■ non-English-speaking
Demographic	■ Democrat ■ Catholic or Jewish ■ Born outside of America	■ Republican ■ Protestant ■ Born in America
Success	President Cleveland's 1897 veto of law restricting immigration of non-English speakers	Chinese Exclusion Act of 1882 (repealed 61 years later by the Magnuson Act)

NATIONAL ISSUE 2 CIVIL SERVICE AND CORPORATE REFORM

	Supporters: Political Reformers	Opponents: Political Establishment
Position	Unskilled and semiskilled laborers had rights to safe working conditions, minimum wage, limited working day, etc.	Labor supply was a disposable commodity to be procured at the lowest possible price
Demographic	■ Democrat and Republican ■ Unskilled and semiskilled laborers ■ Female, African American, and child laborers	■ Democrat and Republican ■ Corporations ■ Political bosses and others receiving patronage from Big Businesses
Success	Pendleton Civil Service Reform Act (1883), Interstate Commerce Commission (1887), and Sherman Anti-Trust Act (1890)	Limited impact of regulatory legislation; military support in quelling strikes, e.g., the Great Railroad Strike (1877) and Haymarket Affair (1886)

NATIONAL ISSUE 3 THE "MONEY QUESTION"

	Supporters of "the Gold Standard"	Opponents: Proponents of Unlimited Silver Coinage
Position	■ Circulation of gold coinage only ■ Decrease money supply to cause deflation (lower consumer prices)	■ Circulation of silver and gold currency as well as paper money ■ Increase supply of money to cause inflation (higher prices for commodities like cotton and wheat)
Demographic	■ Creditors (money lenders), e.g., bankers ■ Veterans and others on a fixed pension ■ Primarily in North and East	■ Debtors (those who owe money) ■ Primary producers, e.g., farmers, ranchers, and miners ■ Primarily in South and West, where silver mines and/or farms were located
Success	Coinage Act (1873), Gold Standard Act (1900)	Bland-Allison Act (1878), Sherman Silver Purchase Act (1890)

NATIONAL ISSUE 4 THE TARIFF

	Supporters: Protectionists	Opponents: Proponents of Free Trade
Position	■ High tax on imported goods to benefit businesses by: 1. Protecting them from foreign competition 2. Allowing them to increase prices for their products	■ Little or no tax on imported goods to: 1. Benefit consumers by increasing price competition 2. Benefit small businesses dependent on foreign imports
Demographic	■ Majority of Republicans, some Democrats ■ Manufacturers	■ Mugwump Republicans ■ Majority of Democrats ■ Primary producers, e.g., farmers, ranchers, and miners
Success	McKinley Tariff (1890) raised rates	Wilson-Gorman Tariff (1894) lowered rates

QUESTIONS FOR ANALYSIS

1. Based on the demographic information in the tables above, which issues divided along political party lines? Which crossed them?

2. From your reading of the chapter and this feature, what role did socio-economic class and regionalism play in determining the supporters and opponents of a given issue? Explain.

3. Why did these four issues emerge at the national level, and what is the relationship among them?

Bryan's crusade for "the people"

Presidential campaign badges On the left wings of the "goldbug" and "silverite" badges are McKinley (top) and Bryan (bottom), with their running mates on the right.

McKinley defeats Bryan

Candidate Bryan crisscrossed the country like a man on a mission, delivering hundreds of impassioned speeches on behalf of the "producing masses"—workers, farmers, miners, and small-business owners. His populist crusade was for whites only, however. Like so many otherwise progressive Democratic leaders, Bryan never challenged the practices of racial segregation and violence against blacks in the solidly Democratic South.

McKinley, meanwhile, stayed at home. He knew he could not compete with Bryan as a speaker, so he conducted a "front-porch campaign," welcoming delegations of Republican supporters at his home in Canton, Ohio, and giving only prepared statements to the press. McKinley's brilliant campaign manager, Marcus "Mark" Hanna, a wealthy business executive, shrewdly portrayed Bryan as a "Popocrat," a radical whose "communistic spirit" would ruin the capitalist system and stir up a class war. Hanna convinced the Republican Party to declare that it was "unreservedly for sound money"—meaning gold coins. Theodore Roosevelt, a rising Republican star, was horrified by the thought of Bryan becoming president. "The silver craze surpasses belief," he wrote a friend. "Bryan's election would be a great calamity."

By appealing to such fears, the Republican campaign raised vast sums of money from corporations and wealthy donors to finance an army of 1,400 speakers who traveled the country in McKinley's support. It was the most sophisticated—and expensive—presidential campaign in history. McKinley promoted himself as the "advance agent of prosperity" who would provide workers with a "full dinner pail." In the end, Bryan was overwhelmed by the better-organized and better-financed Republicans. McKinley won the popular vote by 7.1 million to 6.5 million and the Electoral College vote by 271 to 176. Two million more voters cast ballots than in 1892.

Bryan carried most of the West and the South but found little support in the East. In the critical Midwest, from Minnesota and Iowa eastward to Ohio, he did not carry a single state. His evangelical Protestantism repelled many Roman Catholic voters, who were normally drawn to the Democrats. Farmers in the Northeast, moreover, were less attracted to radical reform than were farmers in the wheat and cotton belts of the West and South. In the cities, workers found it easier to identify with McKinley's focus on reviving the industrial economy than with Bryan's farm-based free-silver evangelism.

Although Bryan lost, he began the Democratic party's shift from pro-business conservatism to its eventual twentieth-century role as a party of liberal reform. The Populist party, however, virtually disintegrated. Having won a million votes in 1896, it collected only 50,000 in 1900. Conversely, McKinley's victory climaxed a generation-long struggle for the political control of an industrialized America. The Republicans would be dominant—for a while.

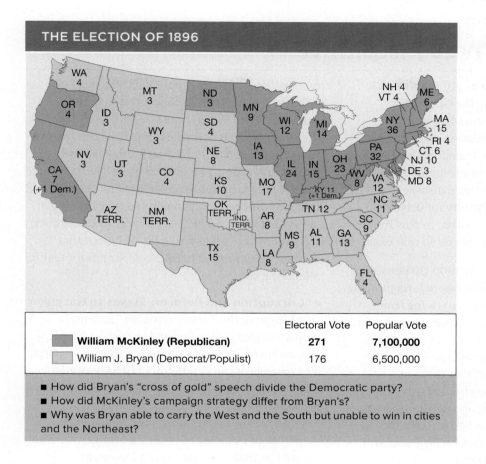

THE ELECTION OF 1896

	Electoral Vote	Popular Vote
William McKinley (Republican)	**271**	**7,100,000**
William J. Bryan (Democrat/Populist)	176	6,500,000

■ How did Bryan's "cross of gold" speech divide the Democratic party?

■ How did McKinley's campaign strategy differ from Bryan's?

■ Why was Bryan able to carry the West and the South but unable to win in cities and the Northeast?

> Economic recovery and new supplies of gold

By 1897, when McKinley was inaugurated as president, economic prosperity was returning. Part of the reason was inflation of the currency, which bore out the arguments of the Greenbackers and silverites that the money supply was inadequate. But the inflation came, in one of history's many ironies, not from more greenbacks or silver dollars issued by the federal government but from a flood of gold discovered in South Africa, northwest Canada, and Alaska. In 1900, Congress passed, and McKinley signed, a bill affirming that the United States money supply would be based only on gold.

Even though the Populist movement faded after William Jennings Bryan's defeat, most of the agenda promoted by Bryan Democrats and Populists, dismissed as too radical in 1896, would be implemented over the next two decades by a more diverse coalition of Democrats and Republicans who would call themselves "progressives."

- **America's Move to Town** America's cities grew in all directions during the *Gilded Age*. Electric elevators and new steel-frame construction allowed architects to extend buildings upward, and mass transit both above and below ground enabled the middle class to retreat to suburbs. Crowded *tenements* bred disease and crime and created an opportunity for urban political *party bosses* to gain power, in part by distributing to the poor the only relief that existed.

- **The New Immigration** By 1900, 30 percent of Americans living in major cities were foreign-born, with the majority of newcomers arriving from eastern and southern Europe rather than western and northern Europe, like most immigrants of generations past. Their languages, culture, and religion were quite different from those of native-born Americans. They tended to be Catholic, Eastern Orthodox, or Jewish rather than Protestant. Beginning in the 1880s, *nativists* advocated restrictive immigration laws and won passage of the *Chinese Exclusion Act*.

- **Changes in Culture and Thought** Many areas of American life underwent profound changes during the Gilded Age. The growth of large cities led to the popularity of vaudeville and Wild West shows and the emergence of football, baseball, and basketball as spectator sports. Saloons served as local social and political clubs for men, despite the disapproval of anti-liquor groups. Charles Darwin's *On the Origin of Species* shocked people who believed in a literal interpretation of the Bible's account of creation. Herbert Spencer and William Graham Sumner were proponents of *Social Darwinism*, which applied Darwin's theory of evolution to human society by equating economic and social success with the "survival of the fittest."

- **Gilded Age Politics** The politics of the time was dominated by huge corporations and the money they used to buy political influence. Political power was still concentrated at the state and local levels. Americans were intensely loyal to the two major parties, whose local "bosses" and "machines" won votes by distributing *patronage* jobs and contracts to members as well as charitable relief. Party loyalties reflected regional, ethnic, and religious differences. Though Republicans almost always held the presidency, the overall strength of the major parties was so closely balanced that neither party wanted to take bold stands for fear of alienating voters.

- **Corruption and Reform: Hayes to Harrison** In addition to the "*money question*," national politics in this period focused on *tariff reform,* the regulation of corporations, and *civil service reform*. The passage of the Pendleton Civil Service Reform Act in 1883 began the professionalization of federal workers. In the 1884 presidential election, Republicans favoring reform, the *Mugwumps*, helped elect Democrat Grover Cleveland. Cleveland signed the 1887 act creating the *Interstate Commerce Commission (ICC)*, intended to regulate interstate railroads. In 1890, under President Benjamin Harrison, Republicans passed the Sherman Anti-Trust Act, the Sherman Silver Purchase Act, and the McKinley Tariff Act.

- **Inadequate Currency Supply and Unhappy Farmers** Over the course of the late nineteenth century, *the "money question"* had become a central political issue. The supply of money had not increased as the economy had grown. This deflationary trend increased the value of money, which was good for bankers and creditors who could charge higher interest rates on loans, but bad for farmers who faced both more expensive mortgages and declining prices for their products. Many farmers believed that the coinage of silver, rather than simply a gold standard system, would result in inflation which in turn would effectively increase the value of their products and reduce their debts. Farmers and others unsatisfied with the Republican and Democratic parties over a host of issues formed a series of political parties and alliances, one of which, the *People's party*, briefly operated as a national third party.

KEY TERMS

CHRONOLOGY

1858	Construction of New York City's Central Park begins
1859	Charles Darwin's *On the Origin of Species* is published
1873	San Francisco begins using cable cars for mass transit
1873	Congress ends silver coinage
1877	Rutherford B. Hayes is inaugurated president
1881	President James A. Garfield is assassinated
1882	Congress passes the Chinese Exclusion Act
1883	Congress passes the Pendleton Civil Service Reform Act
1886	Supreme Court issues *Wabash, St. Louis, and Pacific Railroad Company v. Illinois* decision
1887	Interstate Commerce Commission is created
1889	Otis Elevator Company installs the first electric elevator
1890	Congress passes the Sherman Anti-Trust Act, the Sherman Silver Purchase Act, and the McKinley Tariff
1891	Basketball is invented
1892	Ellis Island opens in New York Harbor

INQUIZITIVE

Go to InQuizitive to see what you've learned—and learn what you've missed—with personalized feedback along the way.

THE CHARGE OF THE ROUGH RIDERS ON SAN JUAN HILL (1898) Before Frederic Remington pursued art professionally, he had unsuccessful forays into hunting, ranching, and even the saloon business in the West. His intimacy with the Western way of life, along with his technical skill and keen sense of observation, were not lost on Theodore Roosevelt, who invited Remington to travel with the Rough Riders during the Spanish-American War.

Seizing an American Empire

1865–1913

Throughout the nineteenth century, Americans displayed little interest in foreign affairs. The overriding priorities were at home: industrial development, western settlement, and domestic politics. After the Civil War, a mood of isolationism—a desire to stay out of conflicts elsewhere in the world, especially those among powerful European nations—dominated public opinion. America's geographic advantages encouraged this isolationist attitude: wide oceans to the east and west, and militarily weak neighbors in the Western Hemisphere. That the powerful British navy protected the shipping lanes from the United States to the British Isles gave Americans a heightened sense of security.

Yet while wanting to stay out of conflicts in Europe, a growing number of Americans during the late nineteenth century urged U.S. officials to acquire additional territory outside North America. The old idea of "manifest destiny" from the 1840s—that the United States had been blessed by God ("destined") to expand its territory westward across the North American continent—evolved during the late nineteenth century to include expanding American control over other regions of the Western hemisphere and even in the Pacific and in Asia. Armed with this concept of a destiny made manifest (revealed) to people by what they saw as the obvious superiority of their way of life, Americans embraced a new form

CORE OBJECTIVES INQUIZITIVE

1. Describe the factors that motivated America's new imperialism after the Civil War.

2. Explain why and how America expanded its influence in the Pacific before the Spanish-American War (War of 1898).

3. Explain the causes of the Spanish-American War (War of 1898), and describe its major events.

4. Analyze the consequences of the Spanish-American War (War of 1898) for American foreign policy.

5. Describe the reasons for Theodore Roosevelt's rapid rise to the presidency, and evaluate the main elements of his foreign policies.

of expansionism that sought distant territories as "colonies" with no intention of their becoming equal states. The new manifest destiny, in other words, became a justification for imperialism. "Not to advance is to recede," wrote historian Brooks Adams in *The Law of Civilization and Decay* (1895). For the United States to survive and prosper, Adams and others argued, it had to keep pushing beyond its current borders; as historian Frederick Jackson Turner had proclaimed in 1893, the American "frontier" was gone, so Americans needed new frontiers in which to exercise their "expansive character" and to spread their democratic ideals and Christian beliefs. During the late nineteenth century, manifest destiny also took on racial meaning as many Americans agreed with Theodore Roosevelt that the United States needed to expand around the world "on behalf of the *destiny* of the [Anglo-Saxon] race."

In more practical terms, prominent political and business leaders argued that America's rapid industrial development required the fast-growing nation to acquire foreign territories—by conquest if necessary—in order to gain easier access to vital raw materials such as rubber, tin, copper, palm oil, and various dyes. At the same time, American manufacturers and commercial farmers had become increasingly dependent on international trade, a dependence that required an expanded naval force to protect its merchant vessels. And a modern, steam-powered navy needed ocean bases where its ships could replenish their supplies of coal and water.

For these and other reasons, the United States during the last quarter of the nineteenth century expanded its military presence and territorial possessions both within and beyond the Western Hemisphere. Within the span of a few months in 1898, a nation born in a revolution against British colonial rule would itself become an imperial ruler of colonies around the world. Motivated by a mixture of moral and religious idealism, assumptions of "Anglo-Saxon" racial superiority, and naked greed, the expansionist push also met with strong opposition. But most Americans sided with future president Theodore Roosevelt, who in his 1896 book *The Winning of the West* declared that the conquest of the "backward peoples" of the world, like the defeat of the Indians in the American West, benefited "civilization and the interests of mankind."

CORE **OBJECTIVE**

1. Describe the factors that motivated America's new imperialism after the Civil War.

Toward the New Imperialism

The United States was a latecomer to a new surge of **imperialism** by major Western nations. Beginning in the 1880s, the British, French, Belgians, Italians, Dutch, Spanish, and Germans had conquered most of Africa and Asia. Often competing with one another for particular territories, they had established colonial governments to rule over the native populations and exploited the colonies economically. Each of the imperial nations, including the United States, dispatched missionaries to convert conquered peoples to Christianity. By 1900, some 18,000 Protestant and Catholic missionaries were scattered around the world. Writing in 1902, the British economist J. A. Hobson declared that imperialism was "the most powerful factor in the current politics of the Western world."

During the late nineteenth century, a small yet influential group of American public officials aggressively encouraged the idea of expansion beyond North America. They included powerful senators Albert J. Beveridge of Indiana and Henry Cabot Lodge of Massachusetts, as well as Theodore Roosevelt and naval captain Alfred Thayer Mahan, president of the U.S. Naval War College in Rhode Island.

> Motives behind imperialism: Economic expansion, racial superiority, Christian evangelism

In 1890, Mahan published ***The Influence of Sea Power upon History, 1660–1783***, in which he argued that the modern history of Great Britain had demonstrated that national greatness flowed from naval power. Mahan insisted that modern economic development required a powerful navy centered on huge battleships, a strong merchant marine, foreign commerce, colonies to provide raw materials and new markets for American products, and global naval bases. A self-described imperialist, he urged American leaders to "look outward" beyond the continental United States. Mahan championed America's "destiny" to control the Caribbean Sea, build a Central American canal to connect the Atlantic and Pacific oceans, and spread Western civilization across the Pacific. His ideas were widely circulated within political and military circles in the United States as well as Great Britain and Germany, and by 1896 the U.S. had built eleven new steel battleships, making America's navy the third most powerful in the world behind Great Britain and Germany.

Claims of racial superiority reinforced the new imperialist spirit. During the late nineteenth century, many Americans readily assumed that some races were dominant (Anglo-Saxons) and some inferior (Indians, Africans). Such traditional notions justifying racism were given new "scientific" authority by researchers at universities throughout Europe and America. Scholars at times went to absurd lengths to make racial distinctions—measuring facial angles, skull size, and brain weight. At the Johns Hopkins University in Baltimore, Professor James K. Hosmer claimed that "the primacy of the world will lie with us" because of the superior qualities of the Anglo-Saxon race. Prominent Americans used the arguments of Social Darwinism to justify economic exploitation and territorial conquest abroad and racial segregation at home. Among nations as among individuals, they claimed, only the strongest survive. John Fiske, a Harvard historian and popular lecturer on Darwinism, proclaimed in 1885 the superior character of "Anglo-Saxon" institutions and peoples. The English-speaking "race," he argued, was destined to dominate the globe and transform the institutions, traditions, language—even the blood—of the world's "backward" races.

imperialism The use of diplomatic or military force to extend a nation's power and enhance its economic interests, often by acquiring territory or colonies and justifying such behavior with assumptions of racial superiority.

The Influence of Sea Power upon History, 1660–1783 **(1890)** Historical work in which Rear Admiral Alfred Thayer Mahan argues that a nation's greatness and prosperity comes from the power of its navy; the book helped bolster imperialist sentiment in the United States in the late nineteenth century.

The Alaska Purchase and annexation of Hawaii

Expansion in the Pacific

For John Fiske and other American imperialists, Asia offered an especially attractive target for expansion. In 1866, Secretary of State William H. Seward had predicted that the United States must inevitably impose its economic domination "on the Pacific Ocean, and its islands and continents." Eager for American manufacturers to take advantage of the huge Asian markets, Seward believed the United States first had to remove all foreign powers from the northern Pacific coast of North America and gain access to that region's valuable ports. To that end, he tried to acquire the British colony of British Columbia, sandwiched between Russian-owned Alaska and the Washington Territory.

Late in 1866, while encouraging business leaders and civil authorities in British Columbia to consider becoming a U.S. territory, Seward learned of Russia's desire to sell Alaska. He leaped at the opportunity, in part because the purchase might influence British Columbia to join the union. In 1867, the United States bought Alaska for $7.2 million, thus removing Russia from North America as an imperial power. Critics scoffed at "Seward's folly" of buying the Alaskan "icebox," but it proved to be the biggest bargain since the Louisiana Purchase, in part because of its vast deposits of gold and oil—as well as ice.

Hawaii

Seward and other Americans promoting expanded trade with Asia also wanted the Hawaiian islands. The islands, a unified kingdom since 1795, had a sizable population of American missionaries and a single profitable crop, sugar cane. In 1875, Hawaii had signed a reciprocal trade agreement with the United States, which agreed to allow Hawaiian sugar to enter the country duty-free in exchange for Hawaii's promise that none of its territory would be leased or granted to another nation. This agreement led to a boom in sugar production based on cheap immigrant labor, mainly Chinese and Japanese, and white American sugar planters soon formed an economic elite. By the 1890s, the native Hawaiian population had been reduced to a minority by smallpox and other foreign diseases, and Asians became the most numerous ethnic group.

"Our New Senators" Mocking the Alaska Purchase, this political cartoon shows President Johnson and Seward welcoming two new senators from Alaska: an Eskimo and a penguin. That an Eskimo becoming senator is laughable reveals the racial discrimination of this period.

Beginning in 1891, Queen Liliuokalani, the Hawaiian ruler, tried to restore "Hawaii for the Hawaiians" by restricting the growing political power exercised by U.S. planters in the islands. Two years later, however, Hawaii's white population (called *haoles*) revolted and overthrew the monarchy when John L. Stevens, the U.S. ambassador, brought in marines to support the coup in January 1893. The queen surrendered "to the superior force of the United States," leading Stevens to report to the secretary of state, "The Hawaiian pear is now fully ripe, and this is the golden hour for the United States to pluck it." Within a month, a committee representing the *haoles* came to Washington, D.C., to ask the United States to annex the islands, and President Benjamin Harrison sent an annexation treaty to the Senate just as he was leaving the presidency.

To investigate the situation, new president Grover Cleveland sent a special commissioner to Hawaii, who reported that the Americans there had acted improperly and that most native Hawaiians opposed annexation. Cleveland tried to restore the queen to power but met resistance from the *haoles*. On July 4, 1894, the government they controlled created the Republic of Hawaii, which included in its constitution a provision for American annexation.

In 1897, when William McKinley became president, he was looking for an excuse to annex the islands. "We need Hawaii," he claimed, "just as much and a good deal more than we did California. It is [America's] manifest destiny." The United States took control of Hawaii in the summer of 1898, over the protests of native Hawaiians who resented their nation being annexed "without reference to the consent of the people of the Hawaiian Islands." President McKinley explained that "We need Hawaii as much as in its day we needed California. It was Manifest Destiny."

Queen Liliuokalani
The Hawaiian queen sought to preserve her nation's independence.

The Spanish-American War (War of 1898)

> CORE **OBJECTIVE**
> **3.** Explain the causes of the Spanish-American War (War of 1898), and describe its major events.

The annexation of Hawaii set in motion a series of efforts to create an American presence in Asia. Ironically, this imperialist push originated not in Asia but in Cuba, a Spanish colony ninety miles south of Florida. Even more ironically, the chief motive for American intervention in Cuba was a sense of outrage at Spain's brutal imperialism.

"Free Cuba"

Throughout the second half of the nineteenth century, Cubans had repeatedly revolted against Spanish rule, only to be ruthlessly suppressed. As one of Spain's oldest colonies, Cuba was a major export market for Spanish goods. Yet American sugar and mining companies had also invested heavily in Cuba. In fact, the United States traded more with Cuba than Spain did, and the American owners of sugar plantations in Cuba grew increasingly concerned about the security of their investments amid the rebellions.

On February 24, 1895, Cubans began another guerrilla war against Spanish troops, when uprisings erupted throughout the island. During what became the Cuban War for Independence (1895–1898), 95,000 Cuban peasants died of combat wounds as well as disease and starvation in Spanish detention camps.

Americans followed the conflict each day through the newspapers, the only source for international news. Two newspapers locked in a fierce competition for readers, William Randolph Hearst's *New York Journal* and Joseph Pulitzer's *New York World*, strove to outdo each other with sensational headlines about every Spanish atrocity in Cuba, real or invented.

The newspapers' efforts to manipulate public opinion through sensationalist reporting came to be called **yellow journalism**. Editors sent their best reporters to Cuba and encouraged them to distort and exaggerate the facts in their stories to attract more readers. In addition to boosting the *Journal*'s circulation, Hearst wanted a war against Spain to propel the United States to world-power status. Once war was declared, he took credit for it; one of his headlines blared, "HOW DO YOU LIKE THE JOURNAL'S WAR?" Many Protestant ministers and publications also campaigned for war in Cuba, in part because of antagonism toward Catholic Spain. A Catholic official in New York City criticized such "bloodthirsty preachers."

The Political Path to War

At the outset of the Cuban War for Independence in 1895, President Grover Cleveland tried to protect U.S. business interests in Cuba while avoiding military involvement. Mounting public sympathy for the rebel cause prompted acute concern in Congress, however. By concurrent resolutions on April 6, 1896, the House and Senate endorsed granting official recognition to the Cuban rebels. After his inauguration in March 1897, President William McKinley continued the policy of official neutrality but took a sympathetic stance toward the rebels. Later that year, Spain offered Cubans autonomy (self-government without formal independence) in return for ending the rebellion, but the Cubans rejected the offer.

Early in 1898, events pushed Spain and the United States into a war that neither government wanted. On January 25, the **U.S. battleship Maine** docked in the harbor of Havana, the Cuban capital, supposedly on a courtesy call. On February 9, the *New York Journal* released the text of a letter from Depuy de Lôme, Spanish ambassador to the United States, to a friend in Havana. In the **de Lôme letter**, which had been stolen from the post office by a Cuban spy, de Lôme called McKinley "weak and a bidder for the admiration of the crowd, besides being a would-be politician who tries to leave a door open behind himself while keeping on good terms with

---

Yellow journalism, the de Lôme letter, and the sinking of the *Maine*

yellow journalism A type of news reporting, epitomized in the 1890s by the newspaper empires of William Randolph Hearst and Joseph Pulitzer, that intentionally manipulates public opinion through sensational headlines, illustrations, and articles about both real and invented events.

U.S. battleship *Maine* American warship that exploded in the Cuban port of Havana on January 25, 1898; though later discovered to be the result of an accident, the destruction of the *Maine* was attributed by war-hungry Americans to Spain, contributing to the onset of the Spanish-American War.

de Lôme letter (1898) Private correspondence written by the Spanish ambassador to the U.S., Depuy de Lôme, that described President McKinley as "weak"; the letter was stolen by Cuban revolutionaries and published in the *New York Journal*, deepening American resentment of Spain and moving the two countries closer to war in Cuba.

"$50,000 Reward!" As if the news of the *Maine* sinking were not disturbing enough, the *New York Journal* sought to sensationalize the incident by offering a $50,000 reward for the perpetrator—the equivalent of $1.3 million today.

the jingoes [aggressive nationalists] of his party." De Lôme resigned to prevent further embarrassment to his government.

Six days later, on February 15, the *Maine* exploded without warning and sank in Havana Harbor, with a loss of 266 men. Although years later the sinking was ruled an accident resulting from a coal explosion, those eager for a war with Spain in 1898 saw no need to delay judgment. The headline in the *New York Journal* screamed: "Whole Country Thrills with War Fever." The thirty-nine-year-old assistant secretary of the navy, Theodore Roosevelt, called the sinking "an act of dirty treachery on the part of the Spaniards" and told a friend that he "would give anything if President McKinley would order the fleet to Havana tomorrow." The United States, he claimed, "needs a war." But McKinley, who assumed that the sinking was an accident, refused to be rushed into war. As the days passed and war did not come, Roosevelt told his friends that the president was too timid; he "has no more backbone than a chocolate éclair." With Roosevelt's encouragement, the public's outcry against Spain grew behind the saying "Remember the *Maine*!"

In the weeks following the sinking, the Spanish government agreed to virtually every demand by the American government regarding its rule over Cuba. But the weight of outraged public opinion and the influence of Republican "jingoists" such as Roosevelt and the president's closest friend, Senator Henry Cabot Lodge, eroded McKinley's neutrality. On April 11, McKinley asked Congress for authority to use armed forces in Cuba to end the fighting there. On April 20, Congress declared Cuba independent and demanded the withdrawal of Spanish forces. Upon learning of the American actions, the Spanish government broke diplomatic ties with the United States and, after U.S. ships began blockading Cuban ports, declared war. Congress then passed its own declaration of war on April 25. The **Teller Amendment**, added on the Senate floor to the war resolution, denied any U.S. intention to annex Cuba.

> A declaration of war and the Teller Amendment

Teller Amendment (1898) Addition to the congressional war resolution of April 20, 1898, which marked the U.S. entry into the war with Spain; the amendment declared that the United States' goal in entering the war was to ensure Cuba's independence, not to annex Cuba as a territory.

President McKinley signed the war resolution and called for 125,000 volunteers to supplement the 28,000 men already serving in the U.S. Army. Among the first to enlist was the man who most lusted for war: Theodore Roosevelt, who resigned from his government post and told his tailor to make him a dashing army uniform. His political opponent, Democrat William Jennings Bryan, joined the ranks as a colonel in the Third Nebraska Volunteers. Never has an American war, so casually begun and so enthusiastically supported, generated such unexpected and far-reaching consequences as did the conflict against Spain. Although McKinley had gone to war reluctantly, he soon saw it as an opportunity to acquire overseas territories. "While we are conducting war and until its conclusion," he wrote privately, "we must keep all we get; when the war is over we must keep what we want." A war to free Cuba thus became a way to gain an empire. (What had long been called the Spanish-American War has recently been renamed the War of 1898 because it involved not just Spanish and American combatants, but also Cubans, Filipinos, and Puerto Ricans.)

"A Splendid Little War"

The war with Spain lasted only 114 days. The conflict was barely underway before the U.S. Navy produced a spectacular victory in an unexpected location in the Pacific Ocean: Manila Bay in the Philippine Islands, a colony controlled by the Spanish for over 300 years. Just before war was declared, Roosevelt, who was still the assistant secretary of the navy, had ordered Commodore George Dewey, commander of the U.S. Asiatic Squadron, to engage Spanish forces in the Philippines in case of war on the other side of the world in Cuba. Dewey arrived in Manila Bay on April 30 with six modern warships, which quickly destroyed or captured the outdated Spanish vessels there. Almost 400 Spaniards were killed or wounded in the lopsided battle. One overweight American sailor died of heatstroke. An English reporter called it "a military execution rather than a real contest." However lopsided the battle, the news of Dewey's victory set off wild celebrations in the United States.

Commodore Dewey's naval victory at Manila Bay

Commodore Dewey was now in awkward possession of Manila Bay but without any soldiers to go onshore. Promised reinforcements, he stayed while German and British warships cruised offshore like watchful vultures, ready to seize the Philippines if the United States did not do so. In the meantime, Emilio Aguinaldo, the leader of the Filipino nationalist movement, declared the Philippines independent from Spain on June 12. With Aguinaldo's help, Dewey's forces entered Manila on August 13 and accepted the surrender of the Spanish troops there, who had feared revenge if they surrendered to the Filipinos. News of the American victory sent President McKinley scurrying to find a map of Asia to locate "these darned islands" now occupied by U.S. soldiers and sailors. Dewey, the first hero of the war, was promoted to admiral. Senator Lodge was delighted with the news from the Philippines: "We hold the other side of the Pacific," he announced. "We

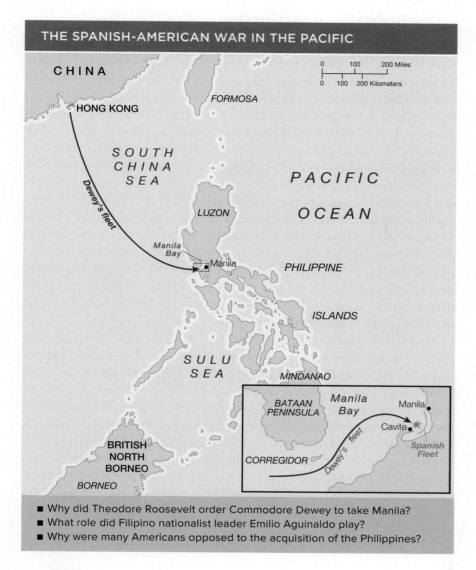

THE SPANISH-AMERICAN WAR IN THE PACIFIC

- Why did Theodore Roosevelt order Commodore Dewey to take Manila?
- What role did Filipino nationalist leader Emilio Aguinaldo play?
- Why were many Americans opposed to the acquisition of the Philippines?

must on no account let the [Philippine] Islands go." McKinley agreed, stressing that "we must keep all we get."

The Cuban Campaign

While these events were occurring halfway around the world, the fighting in Cuba reached a surprisingly quick climax. At the start of the war, the experienced Spanish army in Cuba was five times as large as the entire U.S. Army. But McKinley's call for volunteers inspired nearly a million men to enlist, far more than the military could absorb, leading to widespread

African American troops in Cuba Soldiers stand in formation wearing old wool uniforms unsuited to Cuba's tropical heat.

Rough Riders The First Volunteer Cavalry, led in the Spanish-American War by Theodore Roosevelt; victorious in their only engagement, the Battle of San Juan Hill.

confusion and mismanagement. Those new recruits had to be equipped and trained before they would be ready for battle. In the meantime, the U.S. Navy blockaded the Spanish fleet inside Santiago Harbor while some 17,000 American troops hastily assembled at Tampa, Florida. One prominent unit was the First Volunteer Cavalry, better known as the **Rough Riders**, a special regiment made up of former Ivy League athletes, ex-convicts, western cowboys, Texas Rangers, and Cherokee, Choctaw, Chickasaw, Pawnee, and Creek Indians, all of whom were "young, good shots, and good riders." The Rough Riders are best remembered because Lieutenant Colonel Theodore Roosevelt was second in command. One of the Rough Riders said that the war-hungry Roosevelt was "nervous, energetic, virile [manly]. He may wear out some day, but he will never rust out."

When the 578 Rough Riders, accompanied by a gaggle of reporters and photographers, landed on June 22, 1898, at the undefended southeastern tip of Cuba, chaos followed. Except for Roosevelt's horse, Little Texas, all their horses and mules had been mistakenly sent elsewhere, leaving them to become the "Weary Walkers." Nevertheless, land and sea battles around Santiago quickly broke Spanish resistance.

On July 1, about 7,000 U.S. soldiers took the fortified village of El Caney. While a much larger force attacked San Juan Hill, a smaller unit, led by Roosevelt and including the Rough Riders, seized nearby Kettle Hill. Four regiments of African American soldiers were the heroes of the battle. But thanks to widespread newspaper coverage, much of it exaggerated, Roosevelt became a home-front legend, the most beloved hero of the brief war. A friend of his reported to Roosevelt's wife that her husband was "reveling in victory and gore." Never inclined to humility, Roosevelt requested a Congressional Medal of Honor for his much-publicized gallop in Cuba but was unsuccessful. (President Bill Clinton finally awarded the medal posthumously in 2001.)

Colonel Roosevelt With one hand on his hip, Roosevelt rides with the Rough Riders in Cuba. Most of this regiment was culled from Arizona, New Mexico, and Texas because the Southwestern climate resembled that of Cuba.

Spanish Defeat and Concessions

On July 3, the Spanish navy trapped at Santiago made a gallant run to evade the American fleet blockading the harbor. "The Spanish ships," reported Captain John Philip, commander of the U.S. warship *Texas*, "came out as gaily as brides to the altar." But the outdated, outgunned Spanish ships were quickly destroyed by the more modern American fleet. The casualties were as one-sided as those at Manila: 474 Spaniards were killed or wounded, while only one American was killed and one wounded. Spanish officials in Santiago surrendered on July 17. On July 25 an American force moved into Spanish-held Puerto Rico, meeting only minor resistance as it took control of the island.

> American victories in Santiago and Puerto Rico

The next day, July 26, the Spanish government sued for peace. A cease-fire agreement was signed on August 12, the day before Americans entered Manila. In Cuba, the Spanish forces formally surrendered to the U.S. commander and then sailed for home; excluded from the ceremony were the Cubans, for whom the war had supposedly been fought. On December 10, the United States and Spain signed the Treaty of Paris. Under its terms, Cuba was to become independent, and the United States was to annex Puerto Rico and continue to occupy Manila, pending a transfer of power in the Philippines. With the Treaty of Paris, the Spanish empire in the Americas, initiated by the voyages of Christopher Columbus some four centuries earlier, came to a humiliating end. Now the United States was ready to create its own empire.

> Terms of the peace treaty

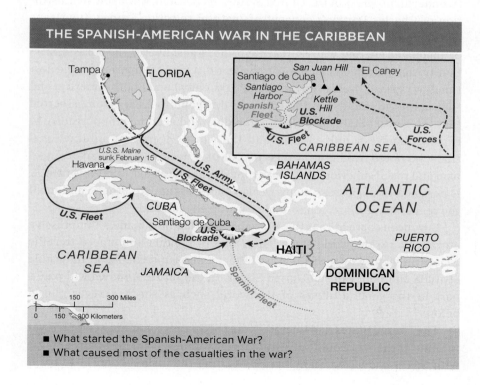

THE SPANISH-AMERICAN WAR IN THE CARIBBEAN

- What started the Spanish-American War?
- What caused most of the casualties in the war?

In all during the four-month Spanish-American War (War of 1898), more than 60,000 Spanish soldiers and sailors died of wounds or disease—mostly malaria, typhoid, dysentery, or yellow fever. Among the 274,000 Americans who served in the war, 5,462 died, but only 379 in battle; most of the rest died from unsanitary conditions in the army camps. At such a cost, the United States was launched onto the world scene as a great power, with all the benefits—and burdens—of a new colonial empire of its own.

Halfway through the conflict in Cuba, John Hay, the U.S. ambassador to Great Britain, who would soon become secretary of state, wrote a letter to Roosevelt, his close friend. In acknowledging Roosevelt's trial by fire, Hay called the conflict "a splendid little war, begun with the highest motives, carried on with magnificent intelligence and spirit, favored by that fortune which loves the brave."

CORE **OBJECTIVE**

4. Analyze the consequences of the Spanish-American War (War of 1898) for American foreign policy.

Consequences of Victory

John Hay's enthusiastic language suggests how the War of 1898 boosted American self-confidence and reinforced the self-serving belief, influenced by racism as well as Social Darwinism, that the United States had a "manifest destiny" to reshape the world in its own image. In 1885 the Reverend Josiah Strong wrote a best-selling book titled *Our Country* in which he used a Darwinian argument to strengthen the appeal of manifest destiny. The "wonderful progress of the United States," he boasted, was itself an illustration of Charles Darwin's concept of "natural selection," since Americans had demonstrated that they were the world's "superior" civilization, "a race of unequaled energy" who represented "the largest liberty, the purest Christianity, the highest civilization" in the world, a race of superior people destined to "spread itself over the earth," to Central and South America, and "out upon the islands" in the Pacific and beyond to Asia. Strong asserted that the United States had a Christian duty and economic opportunity to expand American influence around the world. A growing international trade, he noted, would grow directly out of America's missionary evangelism and racial superiority. "Can anyone doubt," he asked, "that this race . . . is destined to dispossess many weaker races, assimilate others, and mold the remainder until . . . it has Anglo-Saxonized mankind?"

America ascends to the world stage and redefines "manifest destiny"

Europeans agreed that the United States had now made an impressive entrance onto the world stage. The *Times* of London announced that the American victory over Spain must "effect a profound change in the whole attitude and policy of the United States. In the future America will play a part in the general affairs of the world such as she has never played before."

The United States had liberated most of Spain's remaining colonies, yet in some of them it would substitute its own imperialism for Spain's. If war with Spain had saved many lives by ending the insurrection in Cuba, it would also lead the United States to take many lives in suppressing another anti-colonial insurrection, in the Philippines. The acquisition of America's first imperial colonies created a host of long-lasting moral and practical problems, from the difficulties of imposing U.S. rule by force on native peoples to those of defending far-flung territories around the globe.

Annexation of the Philippines

The Treaty of Paris destroyed the Spanish empire. In Spain, the U.S. victory was called "The Disaster." But the treaty had left the political status of the Philippines unresolved. American business leaders wanted the United States to keep the islands so that they could more easily penetrate the vast markets of nearby China, with its huge population. American missionary organizations, mostly Protestant, also favored annexation, since they viewed the Philippines as a useful base from which to bring Protestant Christianity to "the little brown brother" throughout Asia.

"Well, I hardly know which to take first!" With a growing appetite for foreign territory, Uncle Sam browses his options: Cuba Steak, Puerto Rico Pig, Philippine Floating Islands, and others. An expectant President McKinley waits to take his order.

Not long after the United States took control of the Philippines, American authorities ended the Roman Catholic Church's status as the islands' official religion and made English the new official language, thus opening the door for Protestant missionaries to begin evangelical activities across the region.

These factors were among the considerations that convinced President McKinley of the need to annex "those darned islands" in the Philippines. He explained that

> American motives for annexation and further expansion in the Pacific

> . . . one night late it came to me this way—I don't know how it was, but it came: (1) that we could not give them back to Spain—that would be cowardly and dishonorable; (2) that we could not turn them over to France or Germany—our commercial rivals in the Orient—that would be bad business and discreditable; (3) that we could not leave them to themselves—they were unfit for self-government—and they would soon have anarchy and misrule over there worse than Spain's was; and (4) that there was nothing left for us to do but to take them all, and to educate the Filipinos, and uplift and civilize and Christianize them, and by God's grace do the very best we could by them, as our fellowmen for whom Christ also died. And then I went to bed, and went to sleep and slept soundly.

In this one brief statement, McKinley had summarized the motivating ideas of American imperialism: (1) national glory, (2) expanding commerce, (3) racial superiority, and (4) Christian evangelism. American negotiators in Paris finally offered Spain $20 million for the Philippines, Puerto Rico, and Guam, a Spanish-controlled island in the western Pacific between Hawaii and the Philippines.

Meanwhile, the United States took other giant steps toward imperial expansion in the Pacific. In addition to annexing Hawaii in 1898, the United States had also claimed Wake Island, between Guam and Hawaii, which would become a vital link in a future transpacific telegraph cable. Then, in 1899, Germany and the United States agreed to divide the Samoa Islands. The United States annexed the easternmost islands; Germany took the rest.

Philippines annexation

By early 1899, the Treaty of Paris ending the war with Spain had yet to be ratified in the Senate. Anti-imperialists argued that annexation of the Philippines would violate the longstanding American principle that people should be self-governing rather than colonial subjects. Opponents also noted the inconsistency of liberating Cuba and annexing the Philippines, as well as the danger that the Philippines would be impossible to defend if a foreign power such as Japan attacked. The opposition might have killed the treaty had not the most prominent national Democratic leader, William Jennings Bryan, argued that ending the war would open the way for the future independence of the Philippines. His support convinced enough Democrats to enable Senate approval of the treaty on February 6, 1899, by the narrowest of margins: only one vote more than the necessary two thirds.

President McKinley, however, had no intention of granting independence to the Philippines. Although he privately told a friend that "if old Dewey had just sailed away when he smashed that Spanish fleet, what a lot of trouble he would have saved us," he publicly insisted that the United States take control of the islands as an act of "benevolent assimilation" of the native population. But a California newspaper gave a more candid explanation. "Let us be frank," the editor exclaimed. "WE DO NOT WANT THE FILIPINOS. WE WANT THE PHILIPPINES."

Outbreak of war with Filipino nationalists

The Filipinos themselves had a different vision of their future. In January 1899, they declared their independence and named Emilio Aguinaldo the president of the first Philippine Republic. The following month, an American soldier outside Manila fired on soldiers in Aguinaldo's nationalist forces, called *insurrectos*, killing two. The next day, the U.S. army commander, without investigating the cause of the shooting, ordered his troops to assault the *insurrectos*, beginning a full-scale armed conflict that continued off and on for weeks. General Elwell S. Otis rejected Aguinaldo's proposals for a truce, saying that "fighting, having begun, must go on to the grim end." He would accept only the unconditional surrender of the Filipino forces.

On June 2, the Philippine Republic officially declared war against the United States, which now found itself in an even more costly conflict than

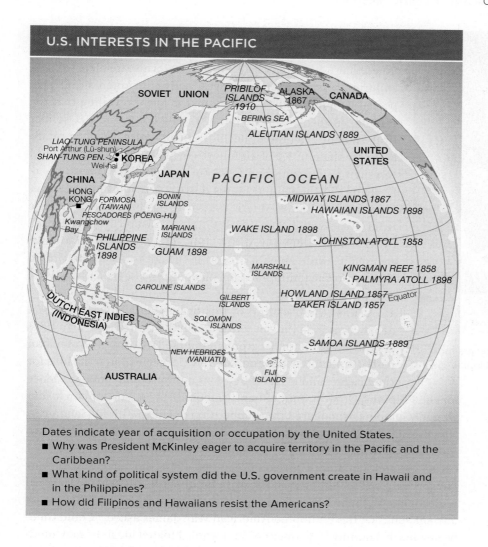

U.S. INTERESTS IN THE PACIFIC

Dates indicate year of acquisition or occupation by the United States.

- Why was President McKinley eager to acquire territory in the Pacific and the Caribbean?
- What kind of political system did the U.S. government create in Hawaii and in the Philippines?
- How did Filipinos and Hawaiians resist the Americans?

the one with Spain, this one to suppress the Filipino independence movement. Since the *insurrectos* more or less controlled the Philippines outside Manila, what followed was largely an American war of conquest at odds with the founding principle of the United States: that people have the right to govern themselves.

The Philippine-American War

The American effort to crush Filipino nationalism lasted three years, involved some 126,000 U.S. troops, and took the lives of hundreds of thousands of Filipinos (most of them civilians) and 4,234 American soldiers. It was a brutal conflict, with massacres committed by both sides and racism contributing to numerous atrocities by the Americans, many of whom referred to the Filipinos as "niggers." U.S. troops burned villages, tortured and

"The water cure" American soldiers torture a Filipino prisoner during the Philippine-American War.

executed prisoners, and imprisoned civilians in overcrowded concentration camps. A reporter for the *Philadelphia Ledger* noted that U.S. soldiers had "killed to exterminate men, women, children, prisoners and captives, active insurgents and suspected people from lads of ten up, the idea prevailing that the Filipino as such was little better than a dog." One U.S. soldier from Indiana celebrated the killing of an entire village in retaliation for the murder of an American: "I am in my glory when I can sight my gun on some dark skin and pull the trigger."

Thus did the United States destroy a revolutionary movement modeled after America's own struggle for independence from Great Britain. Organized Filipino resistance had collapsed by the end of 1899. On April 1, 1901, at a ceremony in Manila, Aguinaldo swore an oath accepting the authority of the United States over the Philippines and pledging his allegiance to the U.S. government.

Against the backdrop of this nasty guerrilla war, the great debate over imperialism continued in the United States. In 1899, several anti-imperialist groups combined to form the **American Anti-Imperialist League**. Andrew Carnegie footed the bills for the League, and even offered $20 million to buy independence for the Filipinos. Other prominent anti-imperialists included union leader Samuel Gompers, who feared the competition of cheap Filipino labor, college presidents Charles Eliot of Harvard and David Starr Jordan of Stanford, and social reformer Jane Addams. Even former presidents Grover Cleveland and Benjamin Harrison urged President McKinley to withdraw U.S. forces from the Philippines. The drive for imperialism, said the Harvard philosopher William James, had caused the United States to "puke up its ancient soul." Of the Philippine-American War, James asked, "Could there be any more damning indictment of that whole bloated ideal termed 'modern civilization'?" Senator George Frisbie Hoar, one of the few surviving founders of the Republican party, led the opposition to annexation in the Senate. Under the Constitution, he pointed out, "no power is given the Federal government to acquire territory to be held and governed permanently as colonies" or "to conquer alien people and hold them in subjugation."

Organizing the Former Spanish Territories

American Anti-Imperialist League Coalition of anti-imperialist groups united in 1899 to protest American territorial expansion, especially in the Philippine Islands; its membership included prominent politicians, industrialists, labor leaders, and social reformers.

In the end, however, the imperialists won the debate over the status of the territories acquired from Spain. Senator Albert J. Beveridge boasted in 1900: "The Philippines are ours forever. And just beyond the Philippines are China's illimitable markets. We will not retreat from either. . . . The power that rules the Pacific is the power that rules the world." He added that the American economy was producing "more than we can consume, making more than we can use. Therefore we must find new markets for our produce." And American-controlled colonies would make the best new markets. Without acknowledging it, Beveridge and others were using many of the same arguments that England had used in founding the American colonies in the seventeenth century.

On July 4, 1901, the U.S. military government in the Philippines came to an end, and Judge William Howard Taft became the civil governor. In 1902 Congress passed the Philippine Government Act which declared the islands an "unorganized territory." In 1917, the Jones Act affirmed America's intention to grant the Philippines independence eventually, but that would not happen until 1946. Closer to home, Puerto Rico had been acquired in part to serve as a U.S. outpost guarding the Caribbean Sea. On April 12, 1900, the Foraker Act established a government on the island. The president appointed a governor and eleven members of an executive council, as well as an elected House of Delegates. Residents of the island were declared citizens of Puerto Rico; they were not made citizens of the United States until 1917.

In Cuba, the United States finally fulfilled the promise of independence after restoring order, organizing schools, and improving sanitary conditions. The problem of widespread disease in Cuba prompted the work of Dr. Walter Reed, who made an outstanding contribution to health in tropical regions around the world. Named head of the Army Yellow Fever Commission in 1900, he proved that mosquitoes carried yellow fever. The commission's experiments led the way to effective control of the disease worldwide.

In 1900, on President McKinley's order, Cubans drafted a constitution modeled on that of the United States. The Platt Amendment, added to an army appropriations bill in 1901, sharply restricted the Cuban government's independence, however. The amendment required that Cuba never impair its independence by signing a treaty with a third power, that it keep its debt within the government's power to repay it out of ordinary revenues, and that it acknowledge the right of the United States to intervene in Cuba whenever it saw fit. Finally, Cuba had to sell or lease to the United States lands to be used for coaling or naval stations, a stipulation that led to a U.S. naval base at Guantánamo Bay that still exists today. American troops remained in control of the rest of Cuba until 1902 and returned several times later to suppress insurrections.

Imperial Rivalries in East Asia

While the United States was conquering the Philippines, other nations were threatening to carve up China. After Japan defeated China in the First Sino-Japanese War (1894–1895), European nations set out to exploit the weakness of the huge, virtually defenseless nation. By the end of the century, Russia, Germany, France, and Great Britain had each established spheres of influence in China, territories within it that they (rather than the Chinese government) controlled but did not formally annex. In 1898

"Open Door" policy

and again in 1899, the British asked the American government to join them in preserving the territorial integrity of China against further imperialist actions. Both times, however, the Senate rejected the request because the United States as yet had no strategic investment in the region.

The American outlook toward Asia changed with the defeat of Spain and the acquisition of the Philippines. Instead of acting jointly with Great Britain, though, the U.S. government decided to act alone. What came to be known as the **Open Door policy** was outlined in Secretary of State John Hay's Open Door Note, dispatched in 1899 to his European counterparts. Without consulting the Chinese, Hay announced that China should remain an "Open Door" to European and American trade and that other nations should not try to take control of Chinese ports or territory. As it turned out, none of the European powers except Britain accepted Hay's principles, but none rejected them, either. So Hay simply announced that all the major powers involved in China had accepted the policy.

The Open Door policy was rooted in the desire of American businesses to dominate Chinese markets. However, it also appealed to those who opposed imperialism because it pledged to keep China from being carved up by powerful European nations. But the much-trumpeted policy had little legal standing. When the Japanese became concerned about growing Russian influence in the disputed region of Manchuria in northeast China and asked how the United States intended to enforce the Open Door policy, Hay replied that America was "not prepared . . . to enforce these views." So the situation would remain for forty years, until continued Japanese military expansion in China would bring about a diplomatic dispute with America that would ignite into war in December 1941.

Open Door policy (1899)
Official U.S. insistence that Chinese trade would be open to all nations; Secretary of State John Hay unilaterally announced the policy in 1899 in hopes of protecting the Chinese market for U.S. exports.

Intervention in China After quelling the Boxer Rebellion, U.S. troops march in the Forbidden Palace, the imperial palace in the Chinese capital of Beijing.

A new Asian crisis arose in 1900 when a group of Chinese nationalists known to the Western world as Boxers (they called themselves the "Fists of Righteous Harmony") rebelled against foreign involvement in China, especially Christian missionary efforts, and laid siege to foreign embassies in Peking (now known as Beijing). An international expedition of British, German, Russian, Japanese, and American soldiers rescued the international diplomats and their staffs. Hay, fearful that the intervention might become an excuse for other nations to dismember China, took the opportunity to refine the Open Door policy. The United States, he said in a letter of July 3, 1900, sought a solution that would "preserve Chinese territorial and administrative integrity" as well as "equal and impartial trade with all parts of the Chinese Empire." Six weeks later, the foreign military expedition reached Peking and ended the Boxer Rebellion.

Theodore Roosevelt and "Big-Stick" Diplomacy

CORE OBJECTIVE

5. Describe the reasons for Theodore Roosevelt's rapid rise to the presidency, evaluate the main elements of his foreign policies, and those of his successors in relation to Latin America.

More than any other American of his time, Theodore Roosevelt transformed the role of the United States in world affairs. The nation had emerged from the War of 1898 a world power with major new international responsibilities. To ensure that Americans accepted their new global role, Roosevelt stretched both the Constitution and executive power to the limit. In the process, he pushed a reluctant nation onto the center stage of world affairs.

Rise to National Prominence

Roosevelt's "strenuous life" and early political success

Born in 1858, Roosevelt had grown up in New York City in a cultured, wealthy family. He visited Europe as a child, spoke German fluently, and graduated from Harvard with honors in 1880. From a sickly, nearsighted boy with chronic asthma, he built himself into a physical and intellectual athlete, a man of almost superhuman energy and hyperactivity who for the rest of his days lived and championed the "strenuous life." A boxer, wrestler, mountain climber, hunter, and all-around outdoorsman, he also displayed extraordinary intellectual curiosity. He became a voracious reader, a natural scientist, a bird-watcher, a historian and essayist, and a zealous moralist. He wrote thirty-eight books on a wide variety of subjects. His boundless energy and fierce competitive spirit were contagious, and he was ever eager to express an opinion on any subject. Within two years of graduating from Harvard, Roosevelt won election to the New York legislature. "I rose like a rocket," he later observed.

But with the world seemingly at Roosevelt's feet, disaster struck. In 1884, his mother, Mittie, only forty-eight years old, died of typhoid fever.

Eleven hours later, in the same house, his twenty-two-year-old wife, Alice, died in his arms of kidney failure, having recently given birth to their only child just two days earlier. The double funeral service for his wife and mother was so emotional that the officiating minister wept throughout his prayer.

In an attempt to recover from this "strange and terrible fate," Roosevelt turned his newborn daughter over to his sister, quit his political career, sold the family house, and moved west to the Dakota Territory, where he threw himself into roping and branding steers, shooting buffalo and bears, punching out bullies, capturing outlaws, fighting Indians (whom he called a "lesser race"), and reading novels by the campfire. He was, by his own admission, a poor shot, a bad roper, and an average horseman, but he loved every minute of his western life. Although his time in the West lasted only two years, he never got over being a cowboy. "I owe more than I can express to the West," he emphasized in his memoirs.

Back in New York City, Roosevelt remarried and ran unsuccessfully for mayor in 1886. He later served six years as a federal civil service commissioner and two years as New York City's police commissioner. In 1896, Roosevelt campaigned energetically for William McKinley, and the new president was asked to reward him with the position of assistant secretary of the navy. McKinley resisted at first, saying that Roosevelt was too "hot-headed," but he eventually gave in.

Roosevelt took full advantage of the celebrity he had gained with the Rough Riders in Cuba to win the governorship of New York in 1898. By then, he had become the most prominent Republican in the nation. "I have played it in bull luck this summer," the governor-elect wrote a friend about his recent streak of successes. "First, to get into the war; then to get out of it; then to get elected." Two years later, Republican leaders were urging him to become the vice presidential running mate for William McKinley, who was hoping for a second term.

From Vice President to President

In the 1900 presidential contest, the Democrats turned once again to William Jennings Bryan, who wanted to make American imperialism the "paramount issue" of the campaign. The Democratic platform condemned the Philippine conflict as "an unnecessary war" that had placed the United States "in the false and un-American position of crushing with military force the efforts of our former allies to achieve liberty and self-government."

Roosevelt's election as vice president and McKinley's assassination

The Republicans renominated McKinley and named Roosevelt, now known as "Mr. Imperialism," their candidate for vice president. Roosevelt, who despised Bryan as a dangerous "radical," criss-crossed the nation on behalf of McKinley, speaking in opposition to Bryan's "communistic and socialistic doctrines" promoting higher taxes and the unlimited coinage of silver. At one stop, Roosevelt claimed that Bryan's supporters were "all the lunatics, all the idiots, all the knaves, all the cowards." In the end, McKinley and Roosevelt won by 7.2 million to 6.4 million popular votes and 292 to 155 electoral votes. Bryan even lost Nebraska, his home state.

Less than a year later, however, McKinley's second term ended tragically. On September 6, 1901, while the president was shaking hands with well-wishers at the Pan-American Exposition in Buffalo, New York, a 28-year-old unemployed anarchist named Leon Czolgosz (pronounced *chol-gots*), the angry son of Polish immigrants, approached him with a gun concealed in a bandaged hand and fired twice at point-blank range. "I done my duty!" Czolgosz screamed. One bullet was deflected by the president's breastbone, but the other tore through his stomach and lodged in his back. As policemen wrestled the assassin to the ground, the wounded president urged them not to "hurt him."

For several days, the attending doctors issued optimistic reports about the president's condition, but after a week, McKinley knew he was dying. "It is useless, gentlemen," he told the doctors and nurses. "I think we ought to have a prayer." On September 14, McKinley died, and Theodore Roosevelt was elevated to the White House. "Now look," exclaimed Marcus "Mark" Hanna, the Ohio senator who had been McKinley's political manager, "that damned cowboy is President of the United States!" McKinley's assassination marked the end of one political era and the beginning of another.

Six weeks short of his forty-third birthday, Roosevelt was the youngest man ever to become president, but he had more experience in public affairs than most new presidents, and perhaps more vitality than any. One observer compared him to Niagara Falls—"both great wonders of nature." Even Woodrow Wilson, Roosevelt's main political opponent, described the former Rough Rider as "a great big boy" at heart, but, he added, "You can't resist the man." Roosevelt's glittering spectacles, glistening teeth, and overflowing enthusiasm were like divine gifts to political cartoonists, as was his famous motto, an old African proverb: "Speak softly, and carry a big stick."

Along with Roosevelt's boundless energy went an unshakable sense of self-righteousness, which led him to cast nearly every issue in moral and patriotic terms. He was the first truly activist president. The presidency was, as he put it, a "bully pulpit"—a wonderful platform for delivering fist-pumping speeches to the nation on the virtues of honesty, courage, and civic duty. Nowhere was President Roosevelt's forceful will more evident than in his handling of foreign affairs. Like many of his political friends and associates, he was convinced that the "civilized" and "barbarian" people of the world faced inevitable conflict, not unlike the fate of the Native Americans pushed off their ancestral lands by Americans. In 1899, Roosevelt argued that the United States, as a "great civilized power," needed to take control of other regions of the world so as to bring "law, order, and righteousness" to "backward peoples."

"A great big boy" with a "bully pulpit"

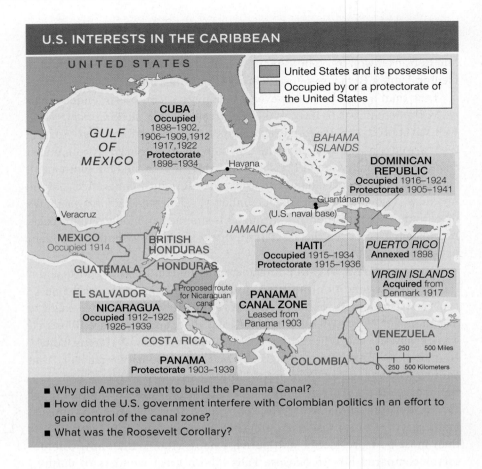

U.S. INTERESTS IN THE CARIBBEAN

UNITED STATES

☐ United States and its possessions
☐ Occupied by or a protectorate of the United States

GULF OF MEXICO

CUBA
Occupied
1898–1902,
1906–1909, 1912
1917, 1922
Protectorate
1898–1934
Havana

BAHAMA ISLANDS

DOMINICAN REPUBLIC
Occupied 1916–1924
Protectorate 1905–1941

Guantánamo
(U.S. naval base)

JAMAICA

Veracruz

MEXICO
Occupied 1914

BRITISH HONDURAS

GUATEMALA   **HONDURAS**

EL SALVADOR

Proposed route for Nicaraguan canal

NICARAGUA
Occupied 1912–1925
1926–1939

COSTA RICA

HAITI
Occupied 1915–1934
Protectorate 1915–1936

PANAMA CANAL ZONE
Leased from
Panama 1903

PUERTO RICO
Annexed 1898

VIRGIN ISLANDS
Acquired from
Denmark 1917

VENEZUELA

0   250   500 Miles

0   250   500 Kilometers

PANAMA
Protectorate 1903–1939

COLOMBIA

■ Why did America want to build the Panama Canal?
■ How did the U.S. government interfere with Colombian politics in an effort to gain control of the canal zone?
■ What was the Roosevelt Corollary?

The Panama Canal

After the War of 1898, the United States became more deeply involved in the Caribbean. One issue overshadowed every other in the region: the proposed Panama Canal. By enabling ships to travel from the Pacific Ocean to the Gulf of Mexico, such a canal would cut the travel distance between San Francisco and New York City by almost 8,000 miles. The narrow nation of Panama had first become a major concern of Americans in the late 1840s, when it became an important overland link in the sea route from the East coast to the California goldfields. Two treaties dating from that period loomed as obstacles to the construction of a canal, however. The Bidlack Treaty (1846) with Colombia (then called New Granada) guaranteed Colombia's control over Panama. In the Clayton-Bulwer Treaty (1850), the British agreed to acquire no more Central American territory, and the United States joined them in agreeing to build or fortify a canal only by mutual consent.

Taking the Panama Canal Zone

Secretary of State Hay asked the British ambassador for consent to build such a canal, and the outcome was the Hay-Pauncefote Treaty of 1901.

Other obstacles remained, however. From 1881 to 1887, a French company led by Ferdinand de Lesseps, who had engineered the Suez Canal in Egypt between 1859 and 1869, had spent nearly $300 million and some 20,000 lives to dig a canal a third of the way across Panama, which was still under the control of Colombia. The company asked that the United States purchase its partially-completed canal, which it did. Meanwhile, Secretary Hay had opened negotiations with Ambassador Tomás Herrán of Colombia. In return for acquiring a canal zone six miles wide, the United States agreed to pay $10 million. The U.S. Senate ratified the Hay-Herrán Treaty in 1903, but the Colombian senate held out for $25 million. As President Roosevelt raged against the "foolish and homicidal corruptionists in Bogotá," the Panamanians revolted against Colombian rule. Philippe Bunau-Varilla, an employee of the French canal company, assisted them and reported, after visiting Roosevelt and Hay in Washington, D.C., that U.S. warships would arrive at Colón, Panama, on November 2.

Colombian troops, who could not penetrate the overland jungle separating them from the Canal Zone, found the U.S. ships blocking the sea-lanes to the area. On November 13, the Roosevelt administration received its first ambassador from the newly independent Panama; he was Bunau-Varilla, who eagerly signed a treaty that extended the Canal Zone from six to ten miles wide. For a $10 million down payment and $250,000 a year, the United States received "in perpetuity the use, occupation and control" of the Canal Zone. The U.S. attorney general, asked to supply a legal opinion upholding Roosevelt's actions, responded wryly, "No, Mr. President, if I were you I would not have any taint of legality about it." Roosevelt later explained, "I took the Canal Zone and let Congress debate; and while the debate goes on the [construction of the] Canal does also." The Panama Canal opened on August 15, 1914, two weeks after the outbreak of the First World War in Europe.

THE BIG STICK IN THE CARIBBEAN SEA

Big Stick diplomacy President Theodore Roosevelt wields "the big stick," symbolizing his aggressive diplomacy. As he stomps through the Caribbean, he drags a string of American warships behind him.

The behavior of the United States in gaining control of the Panama Canal created ill will throughout Latin America that would last for generations. Equally upsetting to Latin Americans was constant interference by both the United States and European countries in the internal affairs of various Latin American nations. A frequent excuse for intervention in the early twentieth century was the collection of debts owed to foreign banks. The Latin Americans responded to these actions with the Drago Doctrine (1902), named after the Argentinian foreign minister Luis María Drago, which prohibited armed intervention by other countries to collect debts.

The Roosevelt Corollary to the Monroe Doctrine

In December 1902, however, German and British warships blockaded Venezuela to force repayment of debts owed to their nations' banks. Such an action defied not only the Drago Doctrine but also the Monroe Doctrine, the U.S. policy dating to 1823 that prohibited European intervention in the Western Hemisphere. Roosevelt decided that if the United States was going to keep European nations from intervening militarily in Latin America, "then sooner or later we must keep order [there] ourselves." In 1904, a crisis over the debts of the Dominican Republic prompted Roosevelt to issue what came to be known as the **Roosevelt Corollary** to the Monroe Doctrine: the principle, in short, that in certain circumstances the United States was justified in intervening in Latin American nations to prevent outsiders from doing so. "Chronic wrongdoing," Roosevelt asserted, would justify U.S. exercise of "an international police power" in the region. Thereafter, Roosevelt and other U.S. presidents repeatedly used military force to ensure that Latin American nations paid their debts to U.S. and European banks.

Relations with Japan

Negotiating an end to the Russo-Japanese War

While wielding a "big stick" in Latin America, Roosevelt was playing the role of peacemaker in East Asia. The principle of equal trading rights in East Asia represented by the Open Door policy was tested further in 1904 when the long-standing rivalry between Russia and Japan flared into warfare. The Japanese had decided that the Russians threatened Japan's ambitions to expand its influence in China and Korea. On February 8, Japanese warships devastated the Russian fleet; the Japanese then occupied the Korean peninsula and drove the Russians back into Manchuria. When the Japanese signaled that they would welcome a negotiated settlement, Roosevelt sponsored a peace conference in Portsmouth, New Hampshire. In the Treaty of Portsmouth, signed on September 5, 1905, Russia acknowledged Japan's "predominant political, military, and economic interests in Korea" (Japan would annex the kingdom in 1910), and both powers agreed to leave Manchuria.

Japan's show of strength against Russia raised concerns among U.S. leaders about the security of the Philippines. During the Portsmouth talks, Roosevelt sent William Howard Taft to meet with the Japanese foreign minister in Tokyo. The two men negotiated the Taft-Katsura Agreement of July 29, 1905, in which the United States accepted Japanese control of Korea in exchange for Japan acknowledging U.S. control of the Philippines. Three years later, the Root-Takahira Agreement, negotiated by Secretary of State Elihu Root and the Japanese ambassador to the United States,

Roosevelt Corollary (1904) President Theodore Roosevelt's revision of the Monroe Doctrine (1823) in which he argued that the United States could use military force in Central and South America to prevent European nations from intervening in the Western Hemisphere.

The American Empire: Power and Consequences

By the early twentieth century, the United States had become one of the great powers on the international stage, able to project its power abroad and influence developments far from U.S. borders. The following chart lists the motives underlying American imperialism, the territories acquired in the late nineteenth and early twentieth centuries that made up America's empire, and the broader consequences of American imperialism.

MOTIVES FOR IMPERIALISM

"Manifest Destiny" and national glory

Racial superiority, fueled by Social Darwinism

Christian evangelism

Demand for raw materials and new markets

Access to naval bases and coaling stations

To prevent other nations from acquiring colonies

TERRITORIES ACQUIRED

Pacific Region	Latin America
Purchase	**War**
Alaska, 1867, from Russia	Puerto Rico, 1899 (Spanish-American War)
Annexation	Guantanamo Bay, Cuba, 1901 (Spanish-American War)
Hawaii, 1898	**Intervention**
Wake Island, 1898	Panama Canal Zone, 1903 (Hay–Bunau-Varilla Treaty)
Eastern Samoa Islands, 1899	
War	
Guam, 1899 (Spanish-American War)	
Philippines, 1899 (Philippine-American War)	

CONSEQUENCES OF IMPERIALISM

Spanish-American War (1899)

■ End of Spain's New World empire
■ Ill will between Latin American nationalists and U.S. troops

Philippine-American War (1899–1902)

■ Exposed America's pro-colonialist leanings
■ Formation of American Anti-Imperialist League (1899)

Open Door policy in China (1899)

■ Established American presence in China

Roosevelt Corollary to the Monroe Doctrine (1904)

Taft-Katsura (1905) and Gentlemen's Agreements with Japan (1907)

Spread of American Protestant missionaries overseas

Medical breakthroughs in preventing tropical diseases

America emerges as a global power

QUESTIONS FOR ANALYSIS

1. What factors motivated American policy in creating this empire?

2. How did the United States acquire these territories?

3. What were the consequences of American imperialism?

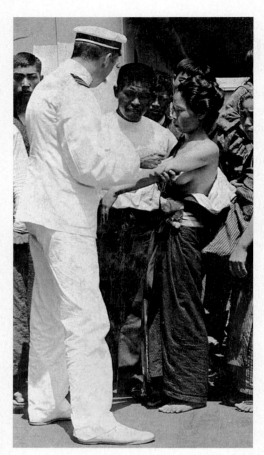

Japanese immigration Japanese immigrants are vaccinated aboard a steamship on their way to Hawaii. By 1900, about 40 percent of Hawaii's population was Japanese.

The "Great White Fleet"

reinforced the Open Door policy by supporting "the independence and integrity of China" and "the principle of equal opportunity for commerce and industry in China."

Behind the outward appearances of goodwill, however, lay mutual distrust. For many Americans, the Russian threat in East Asia now gave way to concerns about the "yellow peril" (a term apparently coined by Kaiser Wilhelm II of Germany). Racial conflict on the West Coast, especially in California, helped sour relations with Japan. In 1906, San Francisco's school board ordered students of Asian descent to attend a separate public school. When the Japanese government sharply protested, President Roosevelt persuaded the school board to change its policy, but only after making sure that Japanese authorities would stop encouraging unemployed Japanese "laborers" to go to America. This "Gentlemen's Agreement" of 1907, the precise terms of which have never been revealed, halted what had become an influx of Japanese immigrants to California and brought some relief from racial tension there.

The Great White Fleet

After Roosevelt's election to a full term as president in 1904, he celebrated America's rise as a world power with a great flourish. In 1907, he sent the entire U.S. Navy, by then second in strength only to Britain's Royal Navy, on a grand fourteen-month tour around the world, announcing that he was ready for "a feast, a frolic, or a fight." At every port of call down the Atlantic coast of South America, up the Pacific coast, out to Hawaii, and down to New Zealand and Australia, the "Great White Fleet" of sixteen gleaming battleships received a rousing welcome. The triumphal procession continued to Japan, China, and the Philippines, then Egypt through the Suez Canal and across the Mediterranean Sea before steaming back to Virginia in early 1909, just in time to close Roosevelt's presidency on a note of triumph. No sooner had the "Great White Fleet" returned than the ships were all repainted in gray.

Roosevelt believed that the United States in the twentieth century must assume a much larger role in world affairs as a result of its own international economic interests and its growing military power. America had become, he noted, the "balance of power of the whole globe."

Yet Roosevelt's success in expanding U.S. power abroad would have mixed consequences, since underlying it was a militantly racist view of the world shared by many other imperialists of the time. In their view, the world was made up of "civilized" nations such as the United States, Japan, and the nations of Europe and those they described as "barbarous," "backward," or "impotent" peoples unable to meet their basic obligations as organized societies. It was the responsibility of the "civilized" nations to exercise control of the "barbarous" peoples, by force if necessary. Roosevelt once told the graduates of the Naval War College that all "the great masterful races have been fighting races, and the minute that a race loses the hard fighting virtues . . . it has lost the right to stand as equal to the best." On another occasion he called warfare the best way to promote "the clear instinct for race selfishness" and insisted that "the most ultimately righteous of all wars is a war with savages." Such belligerent, self-righteous bigotry defied American ideals of equality and would come back to haunt the United States in world affairs.

Taft's "Dollar Diplomacy"

Republican William Howard Taft, who succeeded Roosevelt as president in 1909, continued to promote America's economic interests abroad, practicing what Roosevelt called "**dollar diplomacy**." He used the State Department to help American companies and banks to invest in foreign countries, especially East Asia and the less developed nations of Latin America and the Caribbean. To ensure the stability of those investments, Taft, like Roosevelt, did not hesitate to intervene in nations experiencing political and economic turmoil. In 1909 Taft dispatched U.S. Marines to support a revolution in Nicaragua. Once the new government was formed, Secretary of State Philander C. Knox (a corporate attorney who had helped form the giant U.S. Steel Corporation) helped U.S. banks negotiate loans to prop it up. Two years later, he again sent American troops to restore political stability. This time the soldiers stayed for more than a decade.

Taft's "dollar diplomacy"

Wilson's Interventionism

In 1913 the new Democratic president, Woodrow Wilson, attacked the "dollar diplomacy" practiced by Taft and Roosevelt, claiming that it was a form of economic imperialism. He promised to treat the Latin American nations "on terms of equality and honor." Yet Wilson, along with his secretary of state William Jennings Bryan, who called Latin Americans "our political children," dispatched American military forces to Latin America more often than Taft and Roosevelt.

Wilson's Interventionism

Wilson argued that the United States must intervene to stabilize weak governments in the Western hemisphere in order to keep European nations from doing so. He said it was "reprehensible" to allow European governments to take control of these "weak and unfortunate republics."

During his two presidential terms, the idealistic Wilson sent U.S. troops into Cuba once, Panama twice, and Honduras five times. In 1915, when the Dominican Republic on the Caribbean island of Hispaniola refused to sign a treaty that would have given the United States a "special" role in governing the island nation, Wilson sent U.S. Marines, where they established a military government and fought a nasty guerrilla war against anti-American rebels. That same year, Wilson also intervened in Haiti, next door to the Dominican Republic. He admitted that his actions were "highhanded" but justified because the "necessity for exercising control there is immediate,

"dollar diplomacy" Practice advocated by President Theodore Roosevelt in which the U.S. government fostered American investments in less developed nations and then used U.S. military force to protect those investments.

urgent, imperative." Others disagreed. As the *New York Times* charged, Wilson's frequent interventions made Taft's dollar diplomacy look like "ten cent diplomacy."

The United States in Mexico

Mexico was a much thornier problem for President Wilson's well-intentioned but misguided meddling. In 1910, long-suffering Mexicans had revolted against the long-standing dictatorship of Porfirio Diaz, who had given foreign corporations a free rein in developing the nation's economy. After revolutionary armies occupied Mexico City in 1911, the victorious rebels began squabbling among themselves. The leader of the rebellion, Francisco Madero, was himself overthrown by his chief of staff, General Victoriano Huerta, who assumed power in early 1913 and then had Madero and thirty other political opponents murdered.

Pancho Villa

Shocked by Madero's murder, President Wilson refused to recognize "a government of butchers." It was vital, he insisted, for the Latin American nations to have "fairly decent rulers." Huerta ignored Wilson's criticism and established a dictatorship. Wilson decided that Huerta must be removed. To do so, he ordered U.S. warships to halt shipments of foreign weapons to Huerta's new government. "I am going to teach the South American republics to elect good men," Wilson vowed to a British diplomat. Meanwhile, several rival revolutionary Mexican armies, the largest of which was led by a charming but ruthless bandit named Francisco Pancho Villa, began trying to unseat Huerta.

Intervention in Mexico Marines enter Veracruz, Mexico, in 1914.

On April 9, 1914, nine American sailors were arrested in Tampico, Mexico, while trying to buy supplies. Mexican officials quickly released them and apologized to the U.S. naval commander. There the incident might have ended, but the imperious U.S. admiral demanded that the Mexicans fire a 21-gun salute to the American flag. After they refused, Wilson sent U.S. troops ashore at Veracruz on April 21, 1914. They occupied the city at a cost of nineteen American lives; at least 300 Mexicans were killed or wounded.

The use of military force in Mexico played out like many previous American interventions in the Caribbean and Central America. Congress readily supported the decision because American honor was supposedly at stake, and Wilson was sure that most Mexicans would welcome U.S. intervention since his intentions were so "unselfish." But the arrival of U.S. troops in Veracruz backfired. Instead of welcoming the Americans as liberators, Mexicans viewed them as invaders. Newspapers in Mexico shouted for "Vengeance! Vengeance! Vengeance!" For seven months, the Americans governed Veracruz. They left in late 1914 after Huerta was overthrown by Venustiano Carranza.

Still, the troubles south of the border continued as various factions engaged in ongoing civil wars. In 1916, the colorful rebel leader, "Pancho" Villa, launched raids into Texas and New Mexico in a deliberate attempt to trigger U.S. intervention and to reinforce his anti-American credentials. On March 9, he and his men attacked Columbus, New Mexico, just three miles across the border. With Villa shouting "Kill all the Gringos!" his army of 500 peasant revolutionaries looted stores, burned the town, and killed seventeen Americans, men and women.

A furious Woodrow Wilson sent General John J. Pershing to Mexico with 6,000 U.S. soldiers to capture Villa and destroy his army. For nearly a year, with little success, Pershing's troops chased Villa's army through the rugged mountains of northern Mexico. As Pershing muttered, "It's like trying to chase a rat in a cornfield." In 1917, the American troops were ordered home. The elusive Villa, meanwhile, named his mule "President Wilson." By then, however, Wilson paid little notice, for he was distracted by a much greater threat: war in Europe.

■ **Toward the New Imperialism** Near the end of the nineteenth century, the popular idea that America had a "manifest destiny" to expand its territory abroad and industrialists' desire for new markets for their goods helped to fuel America's "new imperialism." The ideology of Social Darwinism was used to justify the colonization of less developed nations. American evangelical Protestants also thought they had a duty to Christianize and "uplift" people throughout the world.

■ **Expansion in the Pacific** Business leaders hoped to extend America's commercial reach across the Pacific. The United States purchased the vast Alaska territory from Russia in 1867. American planters in the Kingdom of Hawaii developed a thriving sugar industry based on Asian immigrant labor. In 1894, Hawaii's minority white population, led by planters, overthrew the native Hawaiian queen, declared a republic, and requested that Hawaii be annexed by the United States.

■ **The Spanish-American War (The War of 1898)** When Cubans revolted against Spanish colonial rule in 1895, many Americans supported their demand for independence. *Yellow journalism* publicizing the harsh Spanish suppression of the revolt, further aroused Americans' sympathy. Early in 1898, the publication of the *de Lôme letter*, in which Spain's ambassador to the United States criticized President McKinley, followed by the mysterious explosion sinking the *U.S. battleship Maine* in Havana Harbor, helped propel America into war with Spain. In its war resolution, Congress declared Cuba independent and, in the *Teller Amendment*, denied any plans to annex Cuba. Under the Treaty of Paris ending the war, Cuba became independent and the United States annexed Spain's other Caribbean possession, Puerto Rico, which it had occupied. In the Spanish colony of the Philippine Islands, America's Pacific naval fleet under Commodore George Dewey defeated the Spanish fleet in the Battle of Manila Bay at the beginning of the war and took control of the capital, Manila.

■ **Consequences of Victory** A vicious guerrilla war followed in the Philippines when Filipinos who favored independence rebelled against American control. The rebellion was suppressed, and President McKinley announced that the U.S. would annex the Philippines. This prompted a significant debate in which the *Anti-Imperialist League* and others argued that acquiring overseas territories violated American principles of self-determination and independence. But the imperialists won the debate, and Congress set up a government in the Philippines as well as in Puerto Rico. In Cuba, the United States imposed significant restrictions on the new government after U.S. forces left the island. In the Pacific region, the United States also annexed Hawaii, Guam, Wake Island, and some of the Samoa Islands during or shortly after the War of 1898. In East Asia, Secretary of State John Hay promoted the *Open Door policy* of preserving China's territorial integrity and equal access by all nations to trade with China.

■ **Theodore Roosevelt and Big-Stick Diplomacy** After succeeding to the presidency upon McKinley's assassination in 1901, Theodore Roosevelt pursued an imperialist foreign policy that confirmed the United States' new role as a world power. He helped negotiate the treaty that ended the Russo-Japanese War, oversaw diplomatic and military actions leading to the U.S. construction and control of the Panama Canal, and sent the navy's fleet of new battleships around the world as a symbol of American might. He also proclaimed the *Roosevelt Corollary* to the Monroe Doctrine, asserting that the United States would intervene in Latin America as necessary in order to prevent European intervention.

■ Taft and Wilson's Interventionism Abroad

William H. Taft and Woodrow Wilson, continued his pattern of intervening in the internal affairs of the other nations. What Roosevelt called *"dollar diplomacy"* involved the U.S. government fostering American investments in less developed nations, and then using U.S. military force to protect those investments.

KEY TERMS

imperialism *p. 667*

The Influence of Sea Power upon History, 1660–1783 (1890) *p. 667*

yellow journalism *p. 670*

U.S. battleship *Maine* *p. 670*

de Lôme letter (1898) *p. 670*

Teller Amendment (1898) *p. 671*

Rough Riders *p. 674*

American Anti-Imperialist League *p. 680*

Open Door policy (1899) *p. 682*

Roosevelt Corollary (1904) *p. 688*

"dollar diplomacy" *p. 691*

CHRONOLOGY

1867	The United States purchases Alaska from Russia
1880s	European nations create colonial empires in Asia and Africa
1890	Alfred Mahan publishes *The Influence of Sea Power upon History, 1660–1783*
1894	Republic of Hawaii is proclaimed
1895	Cuban insurrection breaks out against Spanish rule
1898	U.S. battleship *Maine* explodes in Havana Harbor
1898	The Spanish American War (War of 1898)
1898	United States annexes Hawaii
1899	U.S. Senate ratifies the Treaty of Paris, ending the Spanish-American War
1899–1902	Insurgents resist U.S. conquest of the Philippines
1903	Panamanians revolt against Colombia
1905	Russo-Japanese War
1907–1909	U.S. Great White Fleet circles the globe
1914	Panama Canal opens
1909–1917	U.S. military interventions in Mexico and Latin America

INQUIZITIVE

Go to InQuizitive to see what you've learned—and learn what you've missed—with personalized feedback along the way.

DEBATING the Annexation of the Philippines

Historians use different analytical methods to make sense of the past. Some historians focus on social and economic issues such as class conflict or who profits from a particular policy choice. Other historians focus more on culture to understand how ideas, values, and beliefs have shaped the actions of historical figures. For Part 5, *Growing Pains*, we will examine how different analytical methods result in contrasting explanations for why the United States annexed and retained the Philippines following the defeat of Spain in 1898.

For this exercise you have two tasks:

PART 1: Compare the two secondary sources on why the United States annexed the Philippines.

PART 2: Using primary sources, evaluate the arguments of the two secondary sources.

PART I Comparing Secondary Sources

Two secondary sources from very different analytical perspectives have been included for you to review. In *Standing at Armageddon: The United States, 1877–1919*, Nell Irvin Painter of Princeton University weaves together economic and foreign-policy concerns with the lives of ordinary Americans to explain the annexation of the Philippines. Kristin L. Hoganson of the University of Illinois, a gender historian, explores the question of why the United States annexed the Philippines in *Fighting for American Manhood: How Gender Politics Provoked the Spanish-American and Philippine-American Wars*. While both works contain elements of economic and cultural history, each historian emphasizes a particular analytical methodology.

Compare the views of these two scholars by answering the following questions. Be sure to find specific examples in the selections to support your answers.

■ According to each author, what problems in society did supporters of annexation think American control of the Philippines would solve?

■ Which author focuses on economic explanations, and which author focuses on cultural explanations, to explain imperialist support for annexation?

■ Do you think the authors' arguments are contradictory or complementary? In other words, can they both be correct?

Secondary Source 1

Nell Irvin Painter, "The White Man's Burden" (1989)

The foreign markets explanation sought the cause of depressions not in currency, distribution of wealth, or monopoly. The culprit, it seemed, was agricultural and industrial overproduction. Americans produced too much, it was said; it seemed to matter little that during the recent hard times thousands had run out of the very food-stuffs and manufactured goods reputedly overproduced. What was needed were new markets, especially in Asia, especially in the most populous country in the world, China. . . . While foreign markets had beckoned American businessmen for decades, this more urgent quest included the novel expectation that the government of the United States should play an active part in fostering exports. The Philippine Islands—like Hawaii—represented the perfect stepping-stones to China, stops along the way where coal burning ships bound for Asia could refuel. Expansionists saw the islands as the opportunity of the century. Manila might become an American version of Hong Kong, the British market city that tapped the markets and produce of South China. . . . For many Americans, expansion was the inevitable result of the machine age that had already filled up the continental United States and now seemed to demand the raw materials and foreign markets that overseas colonies promised. The vision of factories fuming nonstop and workers employed without interruption made this economic argument for annexation straightforward and persuasive.

Source: Painter, Nell Irvin. *Standing at Armageddon: The United States, 1877–1919.* New York: W. W. Norton & Company, 1989. 146–7.

Secondary Source 2

Kristin L. Hoganson, "The National Manhood Metaphor" (1998)

Whether they imagined the Filipinos as savages, children, or feminine figures, imperialists regarded them as a means for American men to develop their ability to govern. One adherent of imperialism summed up this belief when he averred that "the necessities involved in the unexpected annexation of strange dependencies will *call forth the governing faculty.*" The savage, childlike, and feminine stereotypes appealed to imperialists because they not only suggested the Filipinos' incapacity for self-government, but also enabled imperialists to cast themselves as civilizers and authoritative heads of household—that is, as men who wielded power. Heedful of British imperialists' claims that empire made men and interpreting colonial endeavors as unparalleled challenges, imperialists looked to the Philippines to turn white, middle- and upper-class American men into what they considered to be ideal citizens—physically powerful men who would govern unmanly subordinates with a firm hand, men accustomed to wielding authority, men who had overcome the threat of degeneracy.... In response to the accusations that their Philippine policies violated the nation's deepest convictions, imperialists brandished a national manhood metaphor. The youthful republic had become an adult, they declared, and should assume the responsibilities of a mature man. Rather than dwelling on its childish past, the nation should manfully shoulder its new obligations. . . . Imperialists implied that failing to assume responsibility for dependents would reveal an unwillingness to advance from childlike dependency to paternalistic power. In short, it would reveal a lack of manhood in the nation.

Source: Hoganson, Kristin L. *Fighting for American Manhood: How Gender Politics Provoked the Spanish-American and Philippine-American Wars.* New Haven: Yale University Press, 1998. 155, 157.

PART II Using Primary Sources to Evaluate Secondary Sources

When historians are faced with competing interpretations of the past, they often look at primary source material as part of the process of evaluating the different arguments. Four speeches follow, each by an American politician who supported annexation and rule over the Philippines. The first is from President William McKinley's State of the Union speech following U.S. annexation of the Philippines and the start of the Philippine-American War. The second is from Henry Cabot Lodge, a Republican senator from Massachusetts who was a leading supporter of American imperialism. The third speech is from Albert Beveridge, senator from Indiana, who supported Lodge's imperialist policies. And the last speech, from Vice President Theodore Roosevelt, was delivered twelve days prior to assuming the presidency following McKinley's death. While these four politicians offer very different justifications for American annexation and rule over the Philippines, they were all prominent advocates of American imperialism. Your task is to understand their arguments and see how they might be used to support the analysis of the two historians.

Carefully read each of these primary sources and answer the following questions. Decide which of the primary source documents support or refute Painter and Hoganson's analysis of the annexation of the Philippines. You may find that some documents do both but for different parts of each historian's analysis. Be sure to specify which aspects of each historian's argument the documents support or refute.

■ What arguments for U.S. retention of the Philippines does each senator offer?

■ Which of these sources would either Painter or Hoganson (or both) find most useful, and how might they use them to support their argument?

■ What might be the limitations on the usefulness of the sources for supporting their arguments?

■ After looking at the primary sources about annexation, which historian's argument do you find more compelling and why do you find it so? If you find both arguments equally compelling, how could you combine the arguments?

Primary Source 1

William McKinley, "Annual Message of the President to Congress" (December 5, 1899)

The future government of the Philippines rests with the Congress of the United States. Few graver responsibilities have ever been confided to us. If we accept them in a spirit worthy of our race and our traditions, a great opportunity comes with them. The islands lie under the shelter of our flag. They are ours by every title of law and equity. They cannot be abandoned. If we desert them we leave them at once to anarchy and finally to barbarism. We fling them, a golden apple of discord, among the rival powers, no one of which could permit another to seize them unquestioned. . . . The suggestion has been made that we could renounce our authority over the islands and, giving them independence, could retain a protectorate over them. This proposition will not be found, I am sure, worthy of your serious attention. Such an arrangement would involve at the outset a cruel breach of faith. . . .

No effort will be spared to build up the waste places desolated by war and by long years of misgovernment. We shall not wait for the end of strife to begin the beneficent work. We shall continue, as we have begun, to open the schools and the churches, to set the courts in operation, to foster industry and trade and agriculture, and in every way in our power to make these people whom Providence has brought within our jurisdiction feel that it is their liberty and not our power, their welfare and not our gain, we are seeking to enhance. Our flag has never waved over any community but in blessing. I believe the Filipinos will soon recognize the fact that it has not lost its gift of benediction in its world-wide journey to their shores.

Source: McKinley, William. "Annual Message of the President to Congress, transmitted to Congress, December 5, 1899," in *Papers Relating to the Foreign Relations of the United States with Annual Message of the President to Congress, Transmitted to Congress, December 5, 1899.* Washington, D.C.: United States Government Printing Office, 1901. L–LII.

Primary Source 2

Henry Cabot Lodge, "The Retention of the Philippine Islands," Speech in the U.S. Senate (March 7, 1900)

I believe, we shall find arguments in favor of the retention of the Philippines as possessions of great value and a source of great profit to the people of the United States which cannot be overthrown. First, as to the islands themselves. They are over a hundred thousand square miles in extent, and are of the greatest richness and fertility. From these islands comes now the best hemp in the world, and there is no tropical product which cannot be raised there in abundance. Their forests are untouched, of great extent, and with a variety of hard woods of almost unexampled value. . . . It is sufficient for me to indicate these few elements of natural wealth in the islands which only await development. . . . A much more important point is to be found in the markets which they furnish. The total value of exports and imports for 1896 amounted in round numbers to $29,000,000, and this was below the average. . . .

The Philippine Islands took from us imports to the value of only $94,000. There can be no doubt that the islands in our peaceful possession would take from us a very large proportion of their imports. Even as the islands are to-day there is opportunity for a large absorption of products of the United States, but it must not be forgotten that the islands are entirely undeveloped. The people consume foreign imports at the rate of only a trifle more than $1 per capita. With the development of the islands and the increase of commerce and of business activity the consumption of foreign imports would rapidly advance, and of this increase we should reap the chief benefit. We shall also find great profit in the work of developing the islands. . . .

Manila, with its magnificent bay, is the prize and the pearl of the East. In our hands it will become one of the greatest distributing points, one of the richest emporiums of the world's commerce. Rich in itself, with all its fertile islands behind it, it will keep open to us the markets of China and enable American enterprise and intelligence to take a master share in all the trade of the Orient!

Source: Lodge, Henry Cabot. *The Retention of the Philippine Islands, Speech of Hon. Henry Cabot Lodge of Massachusetts, in the Senate of the United States, March 7, 1900.* Washington, D.C.: United States Government Printing Office, 1900. 37, 41.

Primary Source 3

Albert Beveridge, "Our Philippine Policy," Speech in the U.S. Senate (January 9, 1900)

But, Senators, it would be better to abandon the Philippines, and count our blood and treasure already spent a profitable loss, than to apply any academic arrangement of self-government to these children [the Filipino people]. They are not yet capable of self-government. How could they be? They are not a self-governing race; they are Orientals, Malays, instructed by Spaniards in the latter's worst estate. They know nothing of practical government, except as they have witnessed the weak, corrupt, cruel, and capricious rule of Spain. What magic will anyone employ to dissolve in their minds and characters those impressions of governors and governed which three centuries of misrule has created? What alchemy will change the oriental quality of their blood, in a year, and set the self-governing currents of the American pouring through their Malay veins? How shall they, in a decade, be exalted to the heights of self-governing peoples which required a thousand years for us to reach? . . .

Self-government is no cheap boon, to be bestowed on the merely audacious. It is the degree which crowns the graduate of liberty, not the reward of liberty's infant class, which has not yet mastered the alphabet of freedom. Savage blood, oriental blood, Malay blood, Spanish example—in these do we find the elements of self-government? . . .

The men we send to administer civilized government in the Philippines must be themselves the highest examples of our civilization. I use the word examples, for examples they must be in that word's most absolute sense. They must be men of the world and of affairs, students of their fellow-men, not theorists nor dreamers. They must be brave men, physically as well as morally. They must be men whom no force can frighten, no influence coerce, no money buy. Such men come high, even here in America. But they must be had. . . . Necessity will produce them. . . . Better abandon this priceless possession, admit ourselves incompetent to do our part in the world-redeeming work of our imperial race; better now haul down the flag than to apply academic notions of self-government to these children or attempt their government by any but the most perfect administrators our country can produce. I assert that such administrators can be found.

Source: Beveridge, Albert J. "Our Philippine Policy," in *The Meaning of the Times and Other Speeches.* Indianapolis: The Bobbs-Merrill Company, 1908. 71–6.

Primary Source 4

Theodore Roosevelt, "National Duties," Speech at Minnesota State Fair (September 2, 1901)

Let me insist again, for fear of possible misconstruction, upon the fact that our duty is twofold, and that we must raise others while we are benefiting ourselves. In bringing order to the Philippines, our soldiers added a new page to the honor-roll of American history, and they incalculably benefited the islanders themselves. Under the wise administration of Governor Taft the islands now enjoy a peace and liberty of which they have hitherto never even dreamed. But this peace and liberty under the law must be supplemented by material, by industrial development. Every encouragement should be given to their commercial development, to the introduction of American industries and products; not merely because this will be a good thing for our people, but infinitely more because it will be of incalculable benefit to the people in the Philippines. We shall make mistakes; and if we let these mistakes frighten us from our work we shall show ourselves weaklings. . . . We gird up our loins as a nation, with the stern purpose to play our part manfully in winning the ultimate triumph; and therefore we turn scornfully aside from the paths of mere ease and idleness and with unfaltering steps tread the rough road of endeavor. . . .

Source: Roosevelt, Theodore. "National Duties." In *The Strenuous Life: Essays and Addresses.* New York: The Century Company, 1902. 295–97.

Modern America

The United States entered the twentieth century on a wave of unrelenting change, not all of it beneficial. In 1800, America was a rural, agrarian, Christian society largely unconcerned with international affairs. By 1900, the United States had become the world's most powerful economy, a highly industrialized urban society with a growing involvement in world politics and international commerce. In other words, the nation was on the threshold of the modern era in which the United States emerged as a leading global power.

The prospect of modernity both excited and scared Americans. Old truths and beliefs clashed with unsettling new scientific discoveries and social practices. People debated the truth of Darwinism and the Bible, the existence of God, the dangers of jazz, and proposals to prohibit the sale of alcoholic beverages. The advent of automobiles and airplanes helped shrink distance between people, and communications innovations such as radio and film helped strengthen a sense of unity or national consciousness. In the process, the United States began to emerge from its isolationist shell. Throughout most of the nineteenth century, presidents and secretaries of state had sought to isolate America from the intrigues and conflicts of the great European powers. As early as 1780, in the midst of the Revolutionary War, future president John Adams had warned Congress against involving the United States in the affairs of Europe. "Our business with them, and theirs with us," he wrote, "is commerce, not politics, much less war."

With only a few exceptions, statesmen during the nineteenth century followed such advice. Non-involvement in foreign wars and non-intervention in the internal affairs of foreign governments formed the pillars of American foreign policy until the end of the century. During the 1890s, however, expanding commercial interests around the world led Americans to broaden the horizons of their concerns. Imperialism, the acquisition by force of foreign colonies, was considered essential among the great European powers, and a growing number of American expansionists demanded that the United States join in the hunt for new territories and markets. Such motives helped spark the Spanish-American War of 1898 and helped to justify the resulting acquisition of colonies outside the continental United States.

The outbreak of the Great War in Europe in 1914 posed an even greater challenge to the tradition of isolation and nonintervention. The prospect of a German victory over the French, the British, and the Russians threatened the European balance of power, which had long ensured the security of the United States. By 1917 it appeared that Germany might emerge triumphant and begin to menace the Western Hemisphere. Woodrow Wilson's crusade to transform international affairs in accordance with his idealistic principles during the Great War severed American foreign policy from its isolationist moorings. It also started a prolonged debate about the role of the United States in world affairs, a debate that World War II would resolve for a time on the side of internationalism.

While the United States was entering the world stage as a formidable military power, it was also settling into its role as a great industrial power. Cities and factories sprouted across the landscape. An abundance of new jobs and affordable farmland served as a magnet attracting millions of immigrants from nearly every region of the world. They were not always welcomed, nor did they readily fit into American society. Ethnic and racial conflict, as well as clashes between workers and owners, increased at the turn of the century. In the midst of such social turmoil and unparalleled economic development, reformers made their first serious attempts to adapt political and social institutions to the realities of the industrial age. The worst excesses and injustices of unregulated economic development—corporate monopolies, child labor, political corruption, hazardous working conditions, urban ghettos—were finally addressed in a comprehensive way. During the Progressive Era (1890–1917), local, state, and federal governments sought to rein in the excesses of industrial capitalism and develop more rational and efficient public policies.

A conservative Republican resurgence challenged the notion of the new regulatory approaches during the 1920s. Free enterprise and corporate capitalism witnessed a dramatic revival. But the stock market crash of 1929 helped propel the United States and the world into the worst economic downturn in history. The unprecedented severity of the Great Depression renewed public demands for federal programs to protect the general welfare. "This nation asks for action," declared President Franklin Delano Roosevelt in his 1933 inaugural address. The many New Deal initiatives and agencies instituted by Roosevelt and Congressional Democrats created the framework for a welfare state that has since served as the basis for public policy.

The New Deal helped revive public confidence and put people back to work, but it did not end the Great Depression. It took a second world war to restore full employment. The necessity of mobilizing the nation in support of the war against Germany and Japan also accelerated the growth of the federal government. And the vast scope of the war helped catapult the United States into a leadership role in world politics. The use of atomic bombs to end the war against Japan ushered in a new era of nuclear diplomacy that held the fate of the world in the balance. For all of the new creature comforts associated with modern life, Americans in 1945 found themselves living amid an array of new anxieties as a chilling cold war emerged out of the world war.

"VOTES FOR <u>US</u> WHEN <u>WE</u> ARE WOMEN!" Parades organized by women's suffrage groups brought together women of all ages and classes. Here, from a patriotically outfitted automobile, some very young suffragists ask their many spectators for "votes for <u>us</u> when <u>we</u> are women."

The Progressive Era

1890–1920

T heodore Roosevelt's emergence as a national political leader coincided with the onset of what historians have labelled the Progressive Era (1890–1920), an extraordinary period of intense social activism and dramatic political innovation. Millions of "progressives" believed that America was experiencing a "crisis of democracy" that required bold action by churches, charitable organizations, experts, individuals—and an expanded role for governments. "Our country is going through a terrific period of unrest," explained Amos Pinchot, a leading progressive attorney and reformer from New York City. "Something is wrong," he said. Corruption was "destroying our respect for government, uprooting faith in political parties, and causing every precedent and convention of the old order to strain at its moorings."

Pinchot and other progressives argued that the United States had been changing so rapidly since the end of the Civil War that the nation was at risk of imploding. America had quickly become the world's fastest growing industrial economy, but prosperity was not being evenly shared. The widening gap between the rich and poor during the Gilded Age had become a major concern. Walter Weyl, a progressive economist, insisted that "we shall not advance far in working out our American ideals without striking hard at . . . inequality." Political equality, he added, "is a farce and a peril unless there is at least some measure of economic equality." The growth of new industries

CORE
OBJECTIVES INQUIZITIVE

1. Explain the varied motives of progressive reformers.

2. Explain the various sources of thought and activism that contributed to the progressive movement.

3. Identify the specific goals of progressive reformers and the ways that they advanced these public goals.

4. Describe the contributions of Presidents Theodore Roosevelt and William Howard Taft to the progressive movement, and explain how and why the two men came to disagree.

5. Describe the progressive policies of President Woodrow Wilson, and explain why and how they differed from those of Presidents Roosevelt and Taft.

like railroading, steel, coal, and oil had attracted massive waves of poor farm folk and foreign immigrants to large cities whose basic social services—food, water, housing, education, sanitation, transportation, and medical care—could not keep pace with the rate of urban growth.

Between 1890 and 1920, progressive reformers attacked the pressing problems created by unregulated industrialization, unplanned urbanization, and the increasingly unequal distribution of wealth and power. But most of all, they insisted, something must be done to control the very large, very powerful corporations that dominated America's economic life and corrupted its political life. As Amos Pinchot said, "we have permitted an uncontrolled industrial oligarchy to assume . . . tremendous and arrogant power." By the beginning of the twentieth century, progressivism had become the most dynamic social and political force in the nation. In 1910, Woodrow Wilson, then serving as president of Princeton University, told a gathering of clergymen that progressivism had generated "an extraordinary awakening in civic consciousness" over the previous twenty years.

CORE OBJECTIVE

1. Explain the varied motives of progressive reformers.

Addressing problems created by rapid urban and industrial growth

The Progressive Impulse

Progressives were liberals not revolutionaries. They wanted to reform and regulate their capitalist society, not destroy it. Most of them were civic-minded Christian moralists who felt that politics had become a contest between good and evil, honesty and corruption. What they all shared was the assumption that governments—local, state, and national—must take a more active role in addressing the huge problems created by rapid urban and industrial growth. Chicago's Jane Addams, a leading progressive reformer, reported that charities and churches were "totally inadequate to deal with the vast numbers of the city's disinherited." The "real heart of the [progressive] movement," declared another reformer, was to expand the role of government "as an agency of human welfare."

Progressivism was more a widespread impulse supported by elements of both major political parties than it was a single movement with a common agenda. The Republican Roosevelt called it the "forward movement" because its emphasis was on positive changes in society led by people "who stand for the cause of progress, for the cause of the uplift of humanity and the betterment of mankind." Progressives, he stressed, "fight to make this country a better place to live in for those who have been harshly treated by fate." Many progressives disagreed bitterly with each other over tactics and goals.

Unlike Populism, whose grassroots appeal was largely confined to poor rural regions in the South and Midwest, progressivism was a wide-ranging national movement, centered in large cities but also popular in rural areas among what came to be called populist progressives. Progressive activists, though mostly white, urban, middle-class professionals, were so numerous that they came in all stripes: men and women; Democrats, Republicans, Populists, and Socialists; labor unionists and business executives; teachers and professors; social workers and journalists; farmers and homemakers; whites and blacks; clergymen, atheists, and agnostics. Whatever their motives and methods, their combined efforts led to significant improvements at all levels of government and across all levels of society.

To make governments more responsive and "efficient" and businesses more honest and safer for workers and consumers, progressives drew upon the new "social sciences"—sociology, political science, psychology, public health, and economics—being developed at new research universities. The progressive approach to social problems was to "investigate, educate, and legislate." Florence Kelley, a tireless activist who fought to improve living conditions for the poor and to end child labor, voiced the era's widespread belief that once people knew "the truth" about social ills, "they would act upon it."

> Making government more responsive and efficient, and businesses more honest and safer places to work

Yet progressivism had its flaws and limitations, inconsistencies and hypocrisies. Progressives often armed themselves with Christian moralism, but their "do-good" perspective was limited by the racial and ethnic prejudices of the day as well as social and intellectual snobbery. The goals of white progressives rarely included racial equality; many otherwise "progressive" people, including Theodore Roosevelt and Woodrow Wilson, believed in the supremacy of the "Anglo-Saxon race." Many well-educated progressives also felt—and acted—superior to the working class they wanted to help. They assumed that modern society was too complicated for the uninformed masses to understand, much less improve, without direction by those who knew better—progressives.

The Varied Sources of Progressivism

> CORE **OBJECTIVE**
> **2.** Explain the various sources of thought and activism that contributed to the progressive movement.

During the last quarter of the nineteenth century, political progressives at the local and state levels began to attack corrupt political bosses and irresponsible corporate barons. Their goals were more honest and efficient government, more effective regulation of big businesses ("the trusts"), and better lives for the majority of Americans who worked with their hands for wages. Only by expanding the scope of local, state, and federal governments, they believed, could these goals be attained.

Depression and Populism

More than any other factor, the devastating depression of the 1890s ignited the progressive spirit of reform. The worst economic downturn in American history to that point brought massive layoffs in factories, mines, railroads,

> The depression of the 1890s and the Populists

and mills. Nearly a quarter of the adults in the workforce lost their jobs. Although the United States boasted the highest per capita income in the world, it also contained some of the highest concentrations of poverty among the industrialized nations. In 1900, an estimated 10 million of the 82 million Americans lived in desperate poverty, with annual incomes barely adequate to provide the minimum necessities of life. The devastating effects of the depression prompted many upper-middle-class urban people—lawyers, doctors, executives, social workers, teachers, professors, journalists, and college-educated women—to organize efforts to reform society.

Populism, with its roots in the rural South and West, was another thread in the fabric of progressivism. The Populist platforms of 1892 and 1896 included political reforms intended to give more power to "the people," such as the "direct" election of U.S. senators by the voters rather than by state legislatures. Although the defeat of William Jennings Bryan in the 1896 presidential campaign ended the Populist party as a serious political force, many of the reforms pushed by the Populists were implemented by progressives during the early twentieth century.

"Honest Government" Activism and Socialism

The Mugwumps and the Socialist party

The Mugwumps—"gentlemen" reformers who had fought the patronage system and insisted that government jobs be awarded on the basis of merit— supplied progressivism with another important element of its thinking: the "honest government" ideal. Over the years, the good-government movement expanded to include efforts not only to end political corruption but also to address persistent urban issues such as rising crime; access to electricity, clean water, and sewers; mass transit; and garbage collection.

Another significant "progressive" force was the growing influence of socialist ideas. In 1902, a pamphlet promoting working-class reforms claimed that "socialism is coming . . . and nothing can stop it. You can feel it in the air." The Socialist Party of America, supported mostly by militant farmers and immigrant Germans and Jews, served as the radical wing of progressivism. But unlike European socialists, who followed the economic doctrines of Karl Marx, most American socialists did not call for the government to take ownership of large corporations. They focused instead on improving working conditions in factories and mills and on closing the widening income gap between rich and poor through "progressive" taxation. In any case, most progressives were capitalist reformers, not socialist radicals. They rejected the extremes of both socialism and laissez-faire individualism, preferring instead a regulated capitalism "softened" by humanitarianism. Labor leader Samuel Gompers, for example, dismissed socialists as unrealistic: "Economically you are unsound, socially you are wrong, industrially you are an impossibility!"

Muckraking Journalism

Progressivism depended upon newspapers and magazines to inform the public about political corruption and social problems. The so-called **muckrakers** were investigative journalists whose aggressive reporting played a crucial role in educating the upper and middle classes about political and corporate wrongdoing as well as about "how the other half lives"—the title of Jacob Riis's pioneering work of photojournalism about life in the slums of New York (1890). "The rich are farther from the poor than ever before," wrote a journalist in 1886, and muckrakers saw it as the responsibility of reporters to show people in comfortable circumstances the ugly realities of poverty.

The muckrakers, who in addition to Riis included Ida Tarbell, Ray Stannard Baker, Lincoln Steffens, and William Allen White, got their nickname from Theodore Roosevelt, who said that crusading journalists were "often indispensable to . . . society, but only if they know when to stop raking the muck." By uncovering political corruption and writing about social ills in newspapers and popular monthly magazines such as *McClure's*, *Munsey's*, and *Cosmopolitan*, the muckrakers changed the face of journalism and gave it a new political role. Muckrakers challenged readers to take action against political corruption and corporate wrongdoing. "For it is OUR business," Tarbell insisted, "we, the people of the United States, and nobody else, must cure whatever is wrong" with America. Roosevelt, both as governor of New York and as president, frequently used muckrakers to drum up support for his policies; he corresponded with them, invited them to the White House, asked their advice, and used their popularity with readers to help shape public opinion.

The golden age of muckraking is sometimes dated from 1902, when Samuel S. McClure, the owner of *McClure's*, began paying idealistic journalists to root out the rampant corruption in politics and corporations. McClure was determined to make his popular magazine a "power for good"; the "vitality of democracy," he insisted, depended upon journalists educating the public about "complex questions" involving the miserable conditions in which poor Americans lived and worked.

Ida Tarbell, one of the most dedicated muckrakers, loved "the sense of vitality, of adventure, of excitement" at *McClure's*. She spent years doggedly investigating the illegal means by which John D. Rockefeller had built his gigantic Standard Oil trust. At the end of her series of nineteen *McClure's* articles reporting the results of her research, she asked readers: "And what are we going to do about it?" She stressed that it was "the people of the United States, and nobody else, [who] must cure whatever is wrong in the industrial situation." McClure told Tarbell that her campaign against monopolies had made her "the most famous woman in America."

Without the muckrakers, progressivism would never have achieved widespread popular support. During the early twentieth century, investigative

Muckrakers

Cover of *McClure's* magazine, 1902 This issue features Ida Tarbell's muckraking series on the Standard Oil Company.

muckrakers Writers who exposed corruption and abuses in politics, business, consumer safety, working conditions, and more, spurring public interest in progressive reforms.

journalism became such a powerful force for change that one editor said that Americans now had "Government by Magazine."

Religious Activism

Still another of the streams flowing into progressivism was religious activism based on social justice, the idea that society had an ethical obligation to help its poorest and most vulnerable members. A related ideal was the **social gospel**, a newer, specifically Protestant belief that religious institutions and individual Christians had an obligation to lead this effort in order to bring about the "Kingdom of God" on earth. In many respects, in fact, the progressive movement as a whole formed a new phase of Christian spiritual revival, an energetic form of public outreach also incorporating other religious (and nonreligious) groups and focusing not so much on individual conversion and salvation as on social action. "We believe," as a social gospel organization explained, "that the age of sheer individualism is past, and the age of social responsibility has arrived."

The Social Gospel

The YMCA/YWCAs and the Salvation Army

During the last quarter of the nineteenth century, a growing number of churches and synagogues began emphasizing community service and the care of the unfortunate. New organizations also made key contributions to the movement. The Young Men's Christian Association (YMCA) and a similar group for women, the YWCA, both entered the United States from England in the 1850s and grew rapidly after 1870; the Salvation Army, founded in London in 1878, came to the United States a year later. During the late nineteenth century, the YMCA and YWCA—both known as "the Y"—combined nondenominational religious evangelism with social services and fitness training in centers, segregated by race as well as gender, that were built in cities across the country. Intended to provide low-cost housing and healthful exercise in a "safe Christian environment" for young men and women from rural areas or foreign countries, the YMCA/YWCA centers often also included libraries, classrooms, and kitchens. "Hebrew" counterparts—YMHAs and YWHAs—provided many of the same facilities in cities with large Jewish populations. Salvation Army centers offered "soup kitchens" to feed the poor and day nurseries for the children of working mothers.

The major forces behind the **social gospel** movement were Protestants and Catholics who feared that Christianity had become too closely associated with the upper and middle classes and was losing its appeal to the working poor. In 1875, Washington Gladden, a prominent pastor in Springfield, Massachusetts, invited striking workers at a shoe factory to attend his church, but they refused because the factory owners and managers were members of it. Their refusal shocked Gladden, who was heartbroken that Christianity was dividing along class lines. He then wrote a pathbreaking book, *Working People and Their Employers* (1876), which argued that true Christianity was based on the principle that "thou shalt love thy neighbor as

social gospel Mostly Protestant movement that stressed the Christian obligation to address the mounting social problems caused by urbanization and industrialization.

thyself." Rejecting the view of the social Darwinists that the poor deserved their fate and should not be helped, Gladden became the first prominent American religious leader to support the rights of workers to form unions. He also spoke out against racial segregation and efforts to discriminate against immigrants.

Gladden's efforts helped launch a new era in American religious life in which churches addressed the urgent problems created by a rapidly urbanizing and industrializing society. He and other "social gospelers" reached out to the working poor who labored long hours for low wages, lived in miserable slum housing, and lacked the legal right to form unions as well as insurance coverage for on-the-job accidents. Walter Rauschenbusch, a Baptist minister serving tenement dwellers in the Hell's Kitchen neighborhood of New York City, said churches should embrace "the social aims of Jesus," for Christianity was intended to be a "revolutionary" faith, and American religious life needed the social gospel to revitalize it and make it socially relevant. Rauschenbusch became extremely influential as a public figure, serving as a presidential adviser to both Theodore Roosevelt and Woodrow Wilson.

Washington Gladden and Walter Rauschenbusch

Rauschenbusch, Gladden, and other preachers of the social gospel sought to expand the "Kingdom of God" not by giving fiery sermons but by following Christ's example and serving the poor and powerless in the streets. Rugged individualism may have been the path to wealth, they argued, but it was "Christian socialism" that offered hope for unity among all classes of Americans. "Every religious and political question," said George Herron, a religion professor at Grinnell College, "is fundamentally economic." And the solution to economic tensions was social solidarity. As the progressive economist Richard Ely put it, America could truly thrive only when it recognized that "our true welfare is not an individual matter purely, but likewise a social affair."

Settlement Houses

Among the most visible champions of the "social gospel" were those who volunteered in innovative community centers called settlement houses. At the Hull House settlement on Halsted Street in a working-class Chicago neighborhood, for instance, two women from privileged backgrounds, Jane Addams and Ellen Gates Starr, practiced social solidarity by addressing the everyday needs of the working poor, especially newly arrived European immigrants. In founding Hull House, Addams and Starr were driven by what Addams called an "impulse to share the lives of the poor" and to make social service "express the spirit of Christ." Their staff of two dozen women, most of whom lived at Hull House, served thousands of people each week. Besides a nursery for the infant children of working mothers, Hull House also sponsored health clinics, lectures, music lessons and art studios, men's clubs, an employment bureau, job training, a gymnasium, a coffeehouse, and a savings bank. By the early twentieth century, there were hundreds of settlement houses in cities across the United States, most of them in the Northeast and Midwest.

Jane Addams, Ellen Gates Starr, and the settlement house movement

While working to improve the quality of life for the powerless, the mostly white, middle-class settlement house workers saw their own lives enriched. Addams said her work at Hull House gave her the "joy of finding Christ" by joining "in fellowship" with those in need in an America that had grown "divided into two nations"—rich and poor. To her, the social gospel driving progressive reformers reflected their "yearning sense of justice and compassion."

Addams and other settlement house leaders soon realized, however, that their charitable work in the rapidly spreading immigrant slums was like bailing out the ocean with a teaspoon. They thus added political reform to their already lengthy agenda and began lobbying for new laws and regulations to ameliorate the living conditions in poor neighborhoods. As her influence in Chicago grew, Addams was appointed to prominent governmental and community boards, where she focused on improving public health and food safety, pushing for better street lighting and police protection, and reducing the use of narcotics. An ardent pacifist and outspoken advocate for suffrage (voting rights) for women, Addams would become the first American woman to win the Nobel Peace Prize.

The Woman Suffrage Movement

Jane Addams and other settlement house workers made up only a small share of the growing numbers of women working outside the home by the early twentieth century. The number of employed women tripled from 2.6 million in 1880 to 7.8 million in 1910. As women, especially college-educated women, became more involved in the public world of work and wages, the women's rights movement also grew as it tirelessly pursued the right to vote. Immediately after the Civil War, women in the movement had hoped that the Fifteenth Amendment, which guaranteed voting rights for African American men, would aid their own efforts to gain the vote. Such arguments made little impression on the majority of men, however, who still insisted that women stay out of politics, often insisting that engaging in the rough-and-tumble world of politics would corrupt the moral purity expected of women during the late nineteenth century. A Mississippi Democrat was blunt about his opposition: "I would rather die and go to hell," he claimed, "than vote for woman's suffrage."

Western states' leadership on the suffrage issue

In 1869, the year the Wyoming Territory became the first place in the United States to extend equal voting rights to women, a divisive issue broke the unity of the women's rights movement: whether it should continue to concentrate on gaining the vote or adopt a broader agenda of women's issues. Susan B. Anthony and Elizabeth Cady Stanton founded the National Woman Suffrage Association (NWSA) to promote a **woman suffrage** amendment to the Constitution, but they considered the right to vote only one among many feminist causes to be championed. For example, they also campaigned for new laws requiring higher pay for women workers and

woman suffrage Movement to give women the right to vote through a constitutional amendment, spearheaded by Susan B. Anthony and Elizabeth Cady Stanton's National Woman Suffrage Association.

East meets West San Francisco suffragists marched across the country in 1915 to deliver an amendment petition with more than 500,000 signatures to Congress in Washington, D.C. Along the way, they were warmly received by other suffragists, like those of New Jersey, pictured here.

making it easier for abused wives to get divorces. Other suffrage activists insisted that pursuing multiple issues hurt their cause. In 1869, they formed the American Woman Suffrage Association (AWSA), which focused single-mindedly on voting rights.

In 1890, after three years of negotiation, the rival groups united as the National American Woman Suffrage Association (NAWSA), the same year Wyoming was admitted as a state, the first with full voting rights for women. It was in the territories and states west of the Mississippi River that the suffrage movement had its earliest successes. In those frontier areas, where Populism found its strongest support, women were more engaged in grass-roots political activities than they were in the East. Suffrage activists in the West also emphasized getting working women engaged in the effort, and they adopted many of the tactics used by labor unions in the West. For these reasons and others, the West was more supportive of women's rights. Between 1890 and 1896, the suffrage movement won three more victories in western states—Utah, Colorado, and Idaho.

In the early twentieth century, however, the suffrage movement remained in the doldrums until proposals for voting rights at the state level easily won a Washington state referendum in 1910 and then carried California by a close majority in 1911. The following year three more western states—Arizona, Kansas, and Oregon—joined in to make a total of nine western states with full suffrage. In 1913, Illinois granted women voting rights in presidential and municipal elections. Yet not until New York acted in 1917 did a state east of the Mississippi River allow women to vote in all elections.

The advocates of women's suffrage put forth several arguments for their position. Many said that the right to vote and hold office was a matter of

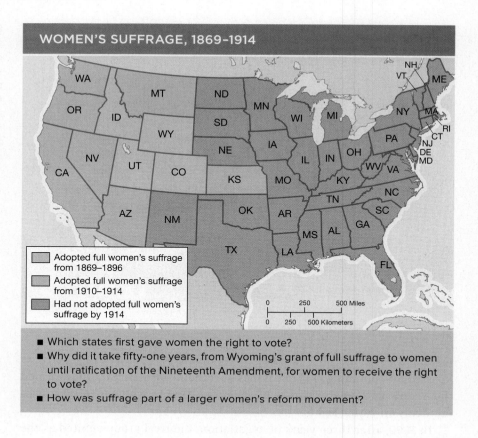

WOMEN'S SUFFRAGE, 1869–1914

Adopted full women's suffrage from 1869–1896

Adopted full women's suffrage from 1910–1914

Had not adopted full women's suffrage by 1914

■ Which states first gave women the right to vote?

■ Why did it take fifty-one years, from Wyoming's grant of full suffrage to women until ratification of the Nineteenth Amendment, for women to receive the right to vote?

■ How was suffrage part of a larger women's reform movement?

simple justice: women were just as capable as men of exercising the rights and responsibilities of citizenship. Others insisted that women were morally superior to men and therefore their participation would raise the quality of the political process and reduce the likelihood of future wars, corruption, and scandals. Women voters and politicians, advocates argued, would promote the welfare of society as a whole rather than partisan or selfish goals, so allowing women to participate in politics would create a great engine for progressive social change. One activist explicitly linked women's suffrage with the social gospel, declaring that women followed the teachings of Christ more faithfully than men; if they were elected to public office, they would "far more effectively guard the morals of society and the sanitary conditions of cities."

> The suffragists' arguments and prejudices

Yet the woman suffrage movement was not free from the social, ethnic, and racial prejudices of its time. Carrie Chapman Catt, who became president of the National American Woman Suffrage Association in 1900, echoed the fears of many middle- and upper-class women when she warned of the danger that "lies in the votes possessed by the males in the slums of the cities, and the ignorant foreign [immigrant] vote." She added that the nation with "ill-advised haste" had given "the foreigner, the Negro and the Indian" the vote but still withheld it from white women. In the South, one suffragist claimed that giving white women the vote would help "insure immediate and durable white supremacy." Throughout the country, most suffrage organizations excluded African American women.

Progressives' Aims and Achievements

CORE **OBJECTIVE**
3. Identify the specific goals of progressive reformers and the ways that they advanced toward these goals.

All of the impulses and groups comprising the progressive movement grew out of what Theodore Roosevelt called the "fierce discontent with evil" that many Americans felt at the turn of the nineteenth century. Given their great diversity, however, progressives focused on many specific goals and used many different methods. They assaulted a wide array of what they saw as social and political evils: from corrupt politicians to too-powerful corporations, from economic distress on small farms and in big cities to the general feeling that "the people" had lost control of the nation to what Roosevelt called "the special interests," selfish businesses and their leaders who were solely interested in "money-getting" at the expense of public welfare.

Reforms in the Political Process

Adoption of the direct primary, initiative, referendum, and recall

In his monthly articles in *McClure's* magazine, Lincoln Steffens, one of the leading muckrakers, regularly asked: "Will the people rule? Is democracy possible?" Steffens himself and other progressives often answered that the way to improve America's democracy was to make it even more democratic. To empower citizens to clean up a corrupt political system driven by backroom deals and rigged party conventions, Steffens and other progressives pushed for several reforms intended to make the political process more open and transparent. One was the direct primary, allowing all members of a political party to vote on the party's nominees for office, rather than the traditional practice in which an inner circle of party leaders chose the candidates. In 1896, South Carolina became the first state to adopt a statewide primary, and within twenty years nearly every state had done so.

While urging states to adopt party primaries, progressives developed other ways to increase participation in the political process. In 1898, South Dakota became the first state to adopt the *initiative* and *referendum*, procedures that allowed voters to create laws directly rather than having to wait for legislative action. Citizens could sign petitions to have a proposal put on the ballot (the initiative) and could then vote it up or down (the referendum). Still another progressive innovation was the *recall*, first adopted in Oregon in 1910, whereby corrupt or incompetent elected officials could be removed by a public petition and vote. By 1920, nearly twenty states had adopted the initiative and referendum, and nearly a dozen had added the recall procedure.

The Seventeenth Amendment: Direct election of U.S. senators

Progressives also fought to change the way that U.S. senators were elected. Under the Constitution, state legislatures elected senators, a process that was frequently corrupted by lobbyists and vote-buying. In 1900, for example, Senate investigators revealed that a Montana senator had given more than $100,000 in secret bribes to members of the legislature that chose him. In 1894, the House of Representatives passed a constitutional amendment to allow voters to elect senators directly, only to see it defeated in the Senate. In 1913, thanks to the efforts of progressives, the **Seventeenth Amendment**, providing for the direct election of senators, was ratified by enough states to become law.

Efficiency Movement in Business and Government

Taylorism in industrial management

A second major theme of progressivism was called the "gospel of efficiency." Its champion was Frederick Winslow Taylor, a Philadelphia-born engineer who during the 1890s became a celebrated business consultant, helping mills and factories operate more efficiently by practicing "scientific management." A self-described progressive who became the nation's first "efficiency expert," Taylor showed employers how to cut waste and increase productivity. By breaking down work activities (filling a wheelbarrow, driving a nail, shoveling coal) into a sequence of mechanical steps and using stopwatches to measure the time it took each worker to perform each step in a task, Taylor established detailed performance standards (and cash rewards) for each job classification, specifying how fast people doing each job should work and when they should rest. The goal of what came to be called **Taylorism** was to improve both productivity and profits for employers and also raise pay for workers; as Taylor wrote, "Men will not do an extraordinary day's work for an ordinary day's pay." There would be no need for strikes by workers in such a system, he argued.

Seventeenth Amendment (1913) Constitutional amendment that provided for the public election of senators rather than the traditional practice allowing state legislatures to name them.

Taylorism Labor system based on detailed study of work tasks, championed by Frederick Winslow Taylor, intended to maximize efficiency and profits for employers.

Many workers, however, resented Taylor's innovations, seeing them as just a tool to make people work faster. Yet Taylor's controversial system of industrial management became one of the most important contributions to capitalist economies in the twentieth century. It did bring concrete improvements in productivity. "In the future," Taylor predicted in 1911, "the system [rather than the individual workers] will be first."

Political progressives applied Taylorism to the operations of government by calling for the reorganization of state and federal agencies to eliminate overlap, the establishment of clear lines of authority, and the replacement of political appointees with trained specialists. By the early twentieth century, many complex functions of government had come to require specialists with technical expertise. As the young political scientist and future president Woodrow Wilson wrote, progressive ideals could be achieved only if government at all levels—local, state, and national—was "informed and administered by experts." Many cities set up "efficiency bureaus" to identify ways their governments were wasting money and to apply more cost-effective "best practices" from other cities.

Two Taylorist ideas for restructuring city and county governments also emerged in the first decade of the new century. One, the commission system, was first adopted in 1901 by Galveston, Texas, after the local government collapsed following a devastating hurricane and tidal wave that killed over 8,000 people, the greatest natural disaster in American history. The commission system placed ultimate authority in a board composed of a small group of commissioners who combined both legislative and executive powers in heading up city departments—commissioners of sanitation, police, utilities, and so on. Houston, Texas, created a commission system in 1906, Dallas and Des Moines, Iowa, in 1907, and Memphis in 1909.

> **The commission system and the city-manager plan**

Even more popular than the commission system was the city-manager plan, under which an appointed professional administrator ran a city or county government in accordance with policies set by the elected council and mayor. Staunton, Virginia, adopted the first city-manager plan in 1908. Five years later, the inadequate response of municipal officials to a flood led Dayton, Ohio, to become the first large city in the nation to adopt the plan.

Yet along with concrete benefits, the efforts to make local governments more "business-like" and professional had a downside. Shifting control from elected officials representing individual neighborhoods to at-large commissioners and nonpartisan specialists separated local government from party politics, which for many working-class voters had been the main way they could have a voice in how they were governed locally. In addition, running a city like a business led commissioners and managers to focus on reducing expenses rather than expanding services, even when such expansion was clearly needed.

At the statewide level, this ideal of efficient government run by nonpartisan experts was pursued most notably by progressive Republican governor Robert M. La Follette of Wisconsin between 1901 and 1906. A small, wiry man with a huge head, "Fighting Bob" La Follette declared war on "vast corporate combinations" and political corruption by creating a nonpartisan state government that would become a "laboratory for democracy." To do so, he worked closely with professors from the University of Wisconsin to establish a Legislative Reference Bureau, which provided elected officials across the state with nonpartisan research, advice, and help in the drafting of legislation. La Follette used the bureau's reports to enact such reforms as the direct primary, stronger railroad regulation, the conservation of natural resources, and workmen's compensation programs to support people injured on the job. The "Wisconsin idea" of more efficient government run by experts was widely publicized and copied by other

> **La Follette and the "Wisconsin idea"**

Friends of the working man
(*Left to right*) American labor leader Andrew Furuseth, Governor Robert M. La Follette, and muckraker Lincoln Steffens, c. 1915.

progressive governors. La Follette explained that the "Wisconsin idea" was a commitment to use government power to make "a happier and better state to live in, that its institutions are more democratic, that the opportunities of all its people are more equal, that social justice more nearly prevails."

Regulation of Business

Of all the problems facing American society at the turn of the century, one towered above all: the regulation of giant corporations, a third major theme of progressivism. The threat of corporate monopolies increased during the depression of the 1890s as struggling companies were gobbled up by larger ones. Between 1895 and 1904, 157 new holding companies gained control of 1,800 different businesses. Almost fifty of these giant holding companies controlled over 70 percent of the market in their respective industries. In 1896, fewer than a dozen companies other than railroads were worth $10 million or more. By 1903, that number had soared to 300. The explosive growth of big business changed the nature of business life. "We have come upon a very different age from any that preceded us," New Jersey governor Woodrow Wilson observed. People now worked "not for themselves" but "as employees of great corporations."

> Little success in regulating Big Business

Concerns over the concentration of economic power in "trusts" and other forms of monopolies had led Congress to pass the Sherman Anti-Trust Act in 1890, but its language about what constituted a monopoly was so vague that it proved ineffective. In addition, government agencies responsible for regulating businesses often came under the influence of those they were supposed to regulate. Retired railroad executives, for instance, were appointed to the Interstate Commerce Commission (ICC), which had been created to regulate railroads. The issue of regulating the regulators has never been fully resolved.

Promotion of Social Justice

A fourth important focus of the progressive movement was the effort to promote greater social justice for the working poor and for jobless and homeless people. In addition to their work in settlement houses and other religiously inspired efforts, many progressives formed new advocacy organizations such as the National Consumers' League, which educated consumers about harsh working conditions in factories and mills as well as companies' widespread use of child workers as a means of lowering labor costs.

Campaigns for social justice by advocacy organizations and women's clubs

Other grassroots progressive organizations such as the General Federation of Women's Clubs, founded in 1890, insisted that the nation's civic life needed the humanizing effect of female leadership. Caroline Brown started the Chicago Women's Club to help women address the "live issues of this world we live in." Women's clubs across the country sought to clean up filthy city slums by educating residents about personal and household hygiene ("municipal housekeeping"), urging construction of sewer systems, and launching public-awareness campaigns about the connection between unsanitary conditions and disease. Women's clubs also campaigned for child-care centers, kindergartens, government inspection of food processing plants, stricter housing codes, laws protecting women in the workplace, and more social services for the poor, sick, disabled, and abused. Still others addressed the widespread problems related to prostitution and alcohol abuse.

The Campaign against Drinking

Middle-class women reformers, most of them motivated by strong religious convictions, were the driving force behind grassroots progressivism. Among the most powerful campaigns organized by women to address social ills was that of the Women's Christian Temperance Union (WCTU). Founded in 1874 in Cleveland, Ohio, by 1900 the WCTU had grown into the largest women's group in the nation, boasting 300,000 members. By attacking drunkenness and closing saloons, such reformers hoped to accomplish three things: (1) prevent domestic violence by husbands and fathers, (2) reduce crime in the streets, and (3) remove one of the worst tools of corruption—free beer on election days—used by political bosses to "buy" votes among the working class. As a Boston sociologist concluded, the saloon had become "the enemy of society because of the evil results produced upon the individual."

Temperance, abstinence, and prohibition: The WCTU and the Anti-Saloon League

Initially, WCTU members met in churches to pray and then marched to nearby saloons to try to convince their owners to shut them down, often using "pray-ins" to heighten the impact. As the organization's name suggests, the Women's Christian Temperance Union advocated *temperance*—the reduction of alcohol consumption. But along with other groups, the WCTU also urged individuals to embrace *abstinence*, refusing to drink any alcoholic beverages. Members wore white ribbon bows to symbolize their commitment to the bodily purity associated with this goal.

Frances Willard, the dynamic president of the WCTU between 1879 and 1898, greatly expanded the goals and scope of the organization. Under her leadership, it moved beyond moral persuasion of saloonkeepers and drinkers and began promoting legislation to ban alcohol ("prohibition") at the local, state, and federal levels. Willard also pushed the WCTU to lobby for other progressive reforms important to women, including a nationwide eight-hour workday, the regulation of child labor, government-funded kindergartens, the right to vote for women, and federal inspections of the food industry. More than anything else, however, the WCTU stayed true to its original mission and continued to campaign against drinking.

Opposition to alcohol abuse was one of the most widely popular of the many progressive reforms. What came to be called the prohibition or temperance movement was national in scope but especially popular in the Midwest and South, where conservative Protestants were most numerous. The battle against alcoholic beverages took on new strength in 1893 with the formation of the Anti-Saloon League, an organization based in local churches that pioneered the strategy of the single-issue political pressure group. Describing itself as "the Protestant church in action against the saloon," the bipartisan League, like the WCTU, initially focused on closing down saloons rather than abolishing alcohol. Eventually, however, it decided to force the prohibition issue into the forefront of state and local elections. At its "Jubilee Convention" in 1913, the League endorsed the nineteenth amendment to the Constitution. It prohibited the manufacture, sale, and consumption of alcoholic beverages. Congress finally approved the Prohibition amendment in 1917.

Frances Willard Founder of the WCTU who lobbied for women's suffrage.

Labor Legislation

In addition to the efforts to reduce alcohol consumption, other progressive reformers pushed legislation to improve working conditions in mills, mines, and factories—and on railroads. In 1890, almost half of American wage workers toiled up to twelve hours a day—sometimes seven days a week—in unsafe, unsanitary, and unregulated conditions. Legislation to ensure better working conditions and limit child labor was perhaps the most significant reform to emerge from the drive for progressive social justice.

> Efforts to regulate children's and women's work

At the end of the nineteenth century, fewer than half of working families lived solely on the husband's earnings. Everyone in the family who could work did so. Many married women engaged in "homework"—making clothes, selling flower arrangements, preparing food for others, and taking in boarders. Parents in poor families also frequently took their children out of school in order to put them to work outside the home—in factories, shops, mines, mills, and canneries, and on farms. In 1900, some 1.75 million children between the ages of 10 and 15 were working outside the home.

Child labor Children shuck oysters in 1913 at the Varn & Platt Canning Company in Bluffton, South Carolina.

Many progressives argued that children, too, had rights in a democracy. The National Child Labor Committee, organized in 1904, led a movement to prohibit the employment of young children. Within ten years, the committee lobbied successfully for legislation in most states banning the hiring of children below a certain age (varying by state from twelve to sixteen) and limiting the hours children might work. Progressives who focused on improving the lives of children also demanded that cities build more parks and playgrounds. Further, reformers made a concerted effort to regulate the length of the workday for women, in part because some of them were pregnant and others had children at home with inadequate supervision. Spearheaded by Florence Kelley, the first president of the National Consumers' League, progressives convinced many state governments to ban work by both women and children at night or in dangerous jobs.

It took a tragic disaster to spur meaningful government regulation of dangerous workplaces. On March 25, 1911, a fire broke out at the Triangle Shirtwaist factory (called a "sweatshop" because of its cramped and unventilated work areas) in New York City. Escape routes were limited because the owner kept the stairway door locked to prevent theft, and 146 workers trapped on the upper floors of the ten-story building died in the fire or leaped to their deaths. The victims of the Triangle Shirtwaist fire were mostly young, foreign-born women in their teens, almost all of whom were Jewish, Italian, or Russian immigrants. In the aftermath of the gruesome

Response to the Triangle Shirtwaist fire

National Consumers' League exhibit To raise awareness about labor reform, everyday objects are displayed alongside descriptions of the poor working conditions and exploitation that went into their manufacture.

deaths, dozens of new city and state regulations dealing with fire hazards, dangerous working conditions, and child labor were enacted across the nation.

The Supreme Court followed an inconsistent course in its rulings on state labor laws. In *Lochner v. New York* (1905), the Court ruled that a ten-hour-workday law was unconstitutional because it violated workers' right to accept any jobs they wanted, no matter how bad the working conditions or how low the pay. Three years later, however, in *Muller v. Oregon* (1908), the Court upheld a ten-hour-workday law for women, largely on the basis of research showing the ill effects of long working hours on women's health. In *Bunting v. Oregon* (1917), the Court accepted a state law allowing no more than a ten-hour workday for both men and women. But for twenty more years, the nation's highest court held out against state laws requiring a minimum wage.

The "Progressive" Income Tax

Progressives also promoted social justice by addressing America's growing economic inequality. One way to redistribute wealth was through the creation of a "progressive" federal income tax—so called not because of the idea's association with the progressive movement, but because the tax rates are based on a sliding scale—that is, the rates "progress" or rise as income levels rise, thus forcing the rich to pay more. Such a "graduated" or "progressive" tax system was the climax of the progressive movement's commitment to a more equitable distribution of wealth.

The progressive income tax was an old idea. In 1894, William Jennings Bryan had persuaded Congress to create a 2 percent tax on annual incomes over $4,000. When millionaires responded by threatening to leave America, Bryan exclaimed, "If some of our 'best people' prefer to leave the country rather than pay the tax . . . let them depart." Soon after the tax became law, however, the Supreme Court declared it unconstitutional on a technicality.

The Sixteenth Amendment:
Authorization of an income tax

The idea of a "graduated" federal income tax refused to die, however. Progressives believed that such a tax would help slow the concentration of wealth in the hands of the richest Americans, who between 1890 and 1910 had nearly doubled their share of the national income, chiefly at the expense of the middle class. In 1907, President Theodore Roosevelt announced his support for the tax. Two years later, his successor, William Howard Taft, endorsed a constitutional amendment allowing such a tax, and Congress agreed. Finally, in 1913, this **Sixteenth Amendment** was ratified by enough states to become law.

Sixteenth Amendment (1913)
Constitutional amendment that authorized the federal income tax.

Progressivism under Roosevelt and Taft

CORE **OBJECTIVE**
4. Describe the contributions of Presidents Theodore Roosevelt and William Howard Taft to the progressive movement, and explain how and why the two men came to disagree.

In the late nineteenth century, most progressive policies originated at the state and local levels. Federal reform efforts began in earnest only when Theodore Roosevelt became president in 1901 after the assassination of William McKinley. During his rapid rise to national fame and leadership, Roosevelt had grown more progressive with each passing year. Unlike McKinley, who was patient and cautious, "T.R." was intensely energetic, and, in the words of one journalist, "impetuous, impatient, and wholly lacking in tact." He could not stand indecision or inaction. And he loved what he called "strenuosity." In the White House, the ever-boyish Roosevelt invited male guests to wrestle and box with him, or to fight with wooden swords or climb trees. "His personality," said a friend, "so crowds the room that the walls are worn thin and threaten to burst outward."

Like Andrew Jackson, Roosevelt greatly increased the power of the presidency in the process of enacting his progressive agenda. His friend and successor, William Howard Taft, continued Roosevelt's "progressive" effort to regulate corporate trusts, but he proved neither as energetic nor as wide-ranging in his role as a reformer president—a difference that led to a fateful break between the two men.

Roosevelt's Taming of Big Business

Roosevelt accomplished more by aggressive executive action than by convincing Congress to pass legislation. As president, he believed he could do anything not expressly forbidden by the Constitution. Mark Twain, the most popular writer in America, said that Roosevelt was willing to "kick the Constitution into the backyard whenever it gets in his way."

In outlining his progressive agenda, Roosevelt applauded the growth of industrial capitalism but declared war on corruption and on cronyism—the awarding of political appointments, government contracts, and other favors to politicians' personal friends and donors. He endorsed a "**Square Deal**" for "every man, great or small, rich or poor." The Square Deal program featured what was called the "Three Cs": greater government *control* of corporations; enhanced *conservation* of natural resources; and, new regulations to protect *consumers* against contaminated food and medicines. Roosevelt began by calling for more rigorous government enforcement of the Sherman Anti-Trust Act against huge corporations engaged in illegal activities. In his view, some big businesses were bad not because they were big but because their executives acted unethically or unfairly. From his youth, Roosevelt had developed a firm commitment to "fair play" in sports, in business, and in politics, and his version of progressivism centered on a commitment to equal opportunity. "A great democracy," he said, "has got to be *progressive* or it will soon cease to be great or a democracy."

Square Deal Roosevelt's progressive agenda of the "Three C's": *control* of corporations, *conservation* of natural resources, and *consumer* protection.

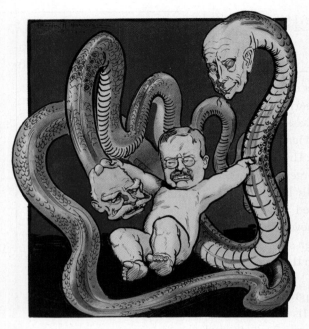

Square Deal This 1906 cartoon likens Roosevelt to the Greek legend Hercules, who as a baby strangled snakes sent from Hell to kill him. Here, the serpents are pro-corporation senator Nelson Aldrich and Standard Oil's John D. Rockefeller.

In 1902, only five months into his presidency, Roosevelt ordered the U.S. attorney general to break up the Northern Securities Company, a vast network of railroads and steamships run by J. Pierpont Morgan that monopolized transportation in several regions of the country. Shocked that Roosevelt would try to break up his corporation, Morgan rushed from New York to the White House and told the president: "If I have done anything wrong, send your man to my man and they can fix it up." But the attorney general, who was also at the meeting, told Morgan: "We don't want to 'fix it up.' We want to stop it." Turning to Roosevelt, Morgan then asked if the president planned to attack his other trusts, such as U.S. Steel and General Electric. "Certainly not," Roosevelt replied, "unless we find out that . . . they have done something wrong." In 1904, the Supreme Court ruled 5–4 that the Northern Securities Company was indeed a monopoly and must be dismantled.

Altogether, Roosevelt approved about twenty-five anti-trust suits against oversized corporations. He also sought stronger regulation of the railroads. In 1903, Congress passed the Elkins Act, making it illegal for railroads to give secret rebates (cash refunds) on freight charges to favored high-volume customers. That same year, Congress created a Bureau of Corporations to monitor the activities of big businesses. When the Standard Oil Company refused to turn over its records, the government brought an anti-trust suit that led to the breakup of the powerful company in 1911. The Supreme Court also ordered the American Tobacco Company dismantled because it had monopolized the cigarette industry.

The 1902 Coal Strike

> Roosevelt as a referee between management and labor

In everything he did, Roosevelt acted forcefully. On May 12, 1902, for example, some 150,000 members of the United Mine Workers (UMW) walked off the job at coal mines in Pennsylvania and West Virginia. The miners were seeking a 20 percent wage increase, a reduction in daily working hours from ten to nine, and official recognition of the union by the mine owners, who refused to negotiate. Instead, the owners shut down the mines to starve out the miners, many of whom were immigrants from eastern Europe. One owner expressed the ethnic prejudices shared by many other owners when he proclaimed, "The miners don't suffer—why, they can't even speak English."

By October, the lengthy shutdown had caused the price of coal to soar, and hospitals and schools reported empty coal bins as winter approached. In many northern cities, the poor had run out of coal for heating. "The country is on the verge of a vast public calamity," warned Walter Rauschenbusch. Washington Gladden led a petition drive urging Roosevelt to step in to mediate the strike. The president decided upon a bold move: he invited leaders of both sides to a conference in Washington, D.C., where he appealed to their "patriotism, to the spirit that sinks personal considerations and makes individual sacrifices for the public good." The mine owners in attendance, however, refused even to speak to the UMW leaders.

Roosevelt was infuriated by what he called the "extraordinary stupidity and temper" of the "wooden-headed" owners, saying he wanted to grab their spokesman "by the seat of his breeches" and "chuck him out" a window. Instead, he threatened to take over the mines and send in soldiers to run them. When a congressman questioned the constitutionality of such a move, Roosevelt roared, "To hell with the Constitution when the people want coal!" The threat worked: the strike ended on October 23. The miners won a reduction to a nine-hour workday and a 10 percent wage increase, but failed to gain union recognition by the owners. Roosevelt had become the first president to use his authority to referee a dispute between management and labor.

Roosevelt's Election to a Second Term

Roosevelt's forceful leadership won him the Republican nomination for election in his own right in 1904. The Democrats, having lost twice with William Jennings Bryan, turned to the more conservative and virtually unknown Alton B. Parker, chief justice of the New York Supreme Court. His only distinction was being the dullest—and most forgettable—presidential candidate in history. One journalist dubbed him "the enigma from New York." The most interesting item in Parker's official campaign biography was that he trained pigs to come when called by name.

> A reelection mandate for Roosevelt and progressivism

In the election, the Democrats suffered their worst defeat in 32 years. After sweeping to victory by a popular vote of 7.6 million to 5.1 million and an electoral vote of 336 to 140, Roosevelt told his wife that he was "no longer a political accident." He now had a popular mandate to do great things. On the eve of his inauguration in March 1905, Roosevelt announced: "Tomorrow I shall come into office in my own right. Then watch out for me!" He was ready to become the leader of the progressive movement.

Regulation of the Railroad, Food, and Drug Industries

Roosevelt launched his second term with an even stronger commitment to regulating corporations and their corrupt owners (the "criminal rich") who exploited their workers and tried to eliminate competition. In his efforts to promote the "moral regeneration of business," he took aim at the railroads first. In 1906, he persuaded Congress to pass the Hepburn Act, which for the first time gave the federal Interstate Commerce Commission the power to set maximum freight rates for the railroad industry.

> The Hepburn Act (1906) and the ICC

Under Roosevelt's Square Deal programs, the federal government also assumed oversight of key industries affecting public health: meat packers, food processors, and makers of drugs and patent medicines. Muckraking journalists had revealed all sorts of unsanitary and dangerous activities in the

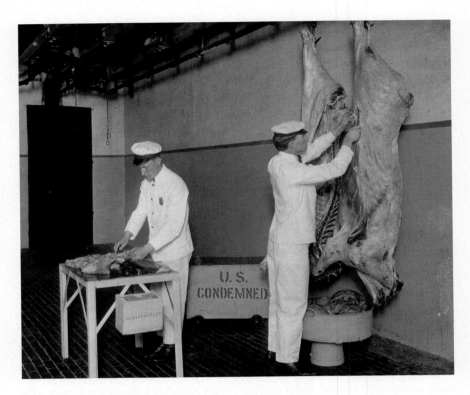

Bad meat Government inspectors closely examine tainted sides of beef at a meatpacking plant.

preparation of food and drug products by many companies. Perhaps the most powerful blow against these abuses was struck by Upton Sinclair's novel *The Jungle* (1906), which told the story of a Lithuanian immigrant working in a filthy Chicago meatpacking plant:

> It was too dark in these storage places to see well, but a man could run his hand over these piles of meat and sweep off handfuls of the dried dung of rats. These rats were nuisances, and the packers would put poisoned bread out for them, they would die, and then rats, bread, and meat would go into the hoppers [to be ground up] together.

> The Meat Inspection Act and The Pure Food and Drug Act

After reading *The Jungle* Roosevelt urged Congress to pass the Meat Inspection Act of 1906. It required the Department of Agriculture to inspect every red-meat animal whose carcass crossed state lines—both before and after slaughter. The Pure Food and Drug Act (1906), enacted the same day, required producers of food and medicines to host government inspectors, too.

Environmental Conservation

One of the most enduring legacies of Roosevelt's leadership was his energetic support for environmental conservation, one of the pillars of his Square Deal programs. Roosevelt, an avid outdoorsman, naturalist, and amateur scientist, championed efforts to manage and preserve the nation's natural resources (which he called "wild places") for the benefit of future generations. He created fifty federal wildlife refuges, approved five new national parks and fifty-one federal bird sanctuaries, and designated eighteen national monuments, including the Grand Canyon.

In 1898, Roosevelt had endorsed the appointment of his friend Gifford Pinchot, Amos's brother and the nation's first professionally trained forest manager, as the head of the U.S. Department of Agriculture's Division of Forestry. A handsome, wealthy man who devoted his life to forestry, Pinchot, like Roosevelt, was a pragmatic conservationist; he believed in economic growth as well as environmental preservation. Pinchot said that the conservation movement promoted the "greatest good for the greatest number for the longest time." Roosevelt and Pinchot used the Forest Reserve Act (1891) to protect 172 million acres of federally owned forests from being logged. Lumber companies were furious, but Roosevelt held firm, declaring, "I hate a man who skins the land." Overall, Roosevelt set aside more than 234 million acres of federal land for conservation purposes and created 45 national forests in 11 western states. As Pinchot recalled late in life, "Launching the conservation movement was the most significant achievement of the T.R. Administration, as he himself believed."

> Roosevelt and Gifford Pinchot: Preserving natural resources

Roosevelt and Race

Roosevelt's most significant failure as a progressive was his refusal to confront the movement's major blind spot: racism. Like populists, progressives worked to empower "the people" against the entrenched "special interests." In the view of most of them, however, "the people" did not include African Americans, Native Americans, or some immigrant groups. Most white progressives shared the prevailing racist attitudes of the time. They ignored or even endorsed the passage of Jim Crow laws in the South that prevented blacks from voting and subjected them to rigid racial separation in schools, housing, parks, and playgrounds. By 1901, nearly every southern state had successfully prevented almost all African Americans from voting or holding political office by disqualifying or terrorizing them. During the Progressive Era, hundreds of African Americans were lynched each year across the South, where virtually no blacks were allowed to serve on juries or work as sheriffs or policemen. A white candidate for governor in Mississippi in 1903 announced that he believed "in the divine right of the white man to rule, to do all the voting, and to hold all the offices, both state and federal." The South, wrote W. E. B. Du Bois, then a young sociologist at Atlanta University, "is simply an armed camp for intimidating black folk."

At the same time, few progressives raised objections to the many informal and private patterns of segregation and prejudice in the North and West. "The plain fact is," the muckraking journalist Ray Stannard Baker admitted in 1909, "most of us in the North do not believe in any real democracy between white and colored men."

Theodore Roosevelt himself shared such prejudices. He confided to a friend in 1906 his belief that "as a race and in the mass" African Americans "are altogether inferior to whites." Yet on occasion the president made exceptions. On October 16, 1901, soon after becoming president, Roosevelt invited Booker T. Washington, then the nation's most prominent black leader, to the White House for dinner to discuss presidential appointments in the South. Upon learning of the meeting, white Southerners exploded with fury. The *Memphis Scimitar* newspaper screamed that Roosevelt's allowing a "nigger" to dine with him was "the most damnable outrage that has ever been perpetrated by a citizen of the United States." South Carolina senator Benjamin R. Tillman was even angrier. He threatened that "a thousand niggers in the South will have to be killed to teach them 'their place' again."

Theodore Roosevelt and Booker T. Washington
Roosevelt addresses the National Negro Business League in 1900 with Washington seated to his left.

Roosevelt was stunned by the violent reaction, saying he found it "inexplicable" and insisting that he had done nothing wrong. But in the end he gave in to the criticism. Never again would he host a black leader. During a tour of the southern states in 1905, he pandered to whites by highlighting his own southern ancestry (his mother was from Georgia) and expressing his admiration for the Confederacy and Robert E. Lee. His behavior, said a black leader, was "national treachery to the Negro."

But worse was to come. The following year, 1906, witnessed a violent racial incident in Brownsville, Texas, where a dozen or so members of an African American army regiment from a nearby fort got into a shootout with whites who had been harassing them outside a saloon. One white bartender was killed and a police officer seriously wounded. Both sides claimed the other started the shooting. An investigation concluded that the soldiers were at fault, but no one could identify any of the shooters and none of the soldiers was willing to talk about the incident.

Roosevelt responded to their silence by dishonorably discharging the entire regiment of 167 soldiers, several of whom (like the president himself) had been awarded the Congressional Medal of Honor for their service in Cuba during the War of 1898. None of them was given a hearing or a trial.

Critics of Roosevelt's harsh action flooded the White House with angry telegrams. "Once enshrined in our love as our Moses" for inviting Booker T. Washington to the White House, a black minister wrote, Roosevelt "is now enshrouded in our scorn as our Judas." Secretary of War William H. Taft urged the president to reconsider his decision, but Roosevelt refused to show any mercy to "murderers, assassins, cowards, and comrades of murderers." (Sixty years later, the U.S. Army "cleared the records" of all the black soldiers.) Disheartened black leaders predicted that Roosevelt's harsh language would ignite "race hatred and violence" against innocent African Americans. "We shall oppose the re-nomination of Theodore Roosevelt," said the *Washington Bee*, a black-owned newspaper.

The Transition from Roosevelt to Taft

In fact, after his 1904 victory Roosevelt had decided he would not run for president again, in part because he did not want to be the first president to serve the equivalent of a third term. It was a noble gesture but a political blunder he would later come to regret. His personal pledge to serve only four more years would have momentous political consequences. For now, however, he urged Republicans to nominate his long-time friend and secretary of war, William Howard Taft, whom the Republican Convention endorsed on its first ballot in 1908. The Democrats decided to give William Jennings Bryan one more chance. Although Roosevelt dismissed Bryan as a "quack," he retained a faithful following, especially in the South.

Taft promised to continue Roosevelt's policies, and the Republican platform endorsed the president's progressive program. The Democratic platform echoed the Republican emphasis on needed regulation of business but called for a lower tariff. Bryan struggled to attract national support and was defeated for a third time, as Taft swept the Electoral College, 321 to 162.

William Howard Taft As the 27th president, Taft was the first president to throw the first pitch of the baseball season.

William Howard Taft had superb qualifications to be president. Born in Cincinnati in 1857, he was the son of a prominent attorney who had served in President Grant's cabinet. He had graduated second in his class at Yale, where he studied under the famous social Darwinist William Graham Sumner, and gone on to become a leading legal scholar, serving on the Ohio Supreme Court. In 1900, President McKinley had appointed him the first American governor-general of the Philippines, and three years later Roosevelt named him secretary of war.

Unlike the robust, athletic Roosevelt, Taft struggled most of his life with obesity, topping out at 332 pounds and earning the nickname "Big Bill." Roosevelt, he explained, "loves the woods, he loves hunting; he loves roughing it, and I don't." Although good-natured and easygoing, Taft as president never managed—even in his own mind—to escape the shadow of his charismatic predecessor. "When I hear someone say 'Mr. President,'" he confessed, "I look around expecting to see Roosevelt."

Taft was a cautious and conservative progressive who vowed to preserve capitalism by protecting "the right of property" and the "right of liberty." In practice, this meant that he was even more determined than Roosevelt to support "the spirit of commercial freedom" against monopolistic trusts, but he was not interested in pushing for additional reforms. Taft was no crusader; he viewed himself as a judge-like administrator, not an innovator. He said he "hated politics" and was reluctant to exercise presidential authority (after leaving the White House, he got the job he had always wanted most, chief justice of the U.S. Supreme Court).

> Taft as president: Highly qualified, judge-like administrator

Taft and Tariffs

After taking office, Taft displayed his credentials as a progressive Republican by supporting lower tariffs on imports; he even called a special session of Congress to address the matter. But he proved less skillful than Roosevelt in dealing with Congress. He discontinued Roosevelt's practice of holding weekly press conferences at which the president tried to influence Congressmen by using his "big stick through the press." Taft confessed that he did not know how to use the "bully pulpit," which Roosevelt had perfected. In the end, the Payne-Aldrich Tariff (1909) made little change in federal tariff policies. Some rates went down while others went up, but overall, tariff policies continued to favor the industrial Northeast over the rest of the nation. Taft's failure to gain real reform and his lack of a "crusading spirit" like Roosevelt's angered the progressive, pro-Roosevelt wing of the Republican party, whom Taft dismissed as "assistant Democrats."

The Ballinger–Pinchot Controversy

In 1910, the split between the conservative and progressive Republican factions was widened by what came to be called the Ballinger-Pinchot controversy, which made Taft appear to be abandoning Roosevelt's environmental conservation policies. Taft's new secretary of the interior, Richard A. Ballinger, threw open to commercial use millions of acres of federal lands that Roosevelt had ordered protected. As chief of forestry, Gifford Pinchot expressed concerns to Taft about the "giveaway," but the president refused to intervene. When Pinchot made his opposition public early in 1910, Taft fired him, labeling him a "fanatic." In doing so, Taft set in motion a feud with Roosevelt that would eventually end their friendship—and cost him his reelection.

The Taft–Roosevelt Feud

In 1909, soon after Taft became president, Roosevelt and his son Kermit sailed to Africa, where they would spend nearly a year shooting big-game animals. (When he heard about the extended safari, J. Pierpont Morgan, still angry at Roosevelt for breaking up the Northern Securities Company, expressed the hope that "every lion would do its duty.") Roosevelt had left the White House assuming that his chosen successor would continue to pursue a progressive agenda. Instead, in his view, by filling the cabinet with corporate lawyers and firing Gifford Pinchot, Taft had failed to "carry out my work unbroken." Taft means well, Roosevelt would say, "but he means well *feebly*." He was "utterly helpless as a leader."

Roosevelt's rebuke of Taft was in many ways undeserved. Taft had at least attempted tariff reform, which Roosevelt had never dared. Yes, he had fired Pinchot, but he had replaced him with other conservationists. In the end, Taft's administration preserved more federal land in four years than Roosevelt's had in nearly eight. Taft's administration also filed twice as many anti-trust suits as did Roosevelt's, including the one that led to the breakup of the Standard Oil Company in 1911.

Taft advanced other progressive causes as well. He strengthened federal control over railroad freight rates, an issue long promoted by farmers and farm organizations. In 1910, with his support, Congress passed the Mann-Elkins Act, which extended the authority of the Interstate Commerce Commission beyond railroads to telephone and telegraph companies. Taft established a federal Children's Bureau (1912) to promote children's welfare and a Bureau of Mines (1910) to oversee that huge industry. Taft also supported giving women the right to vote and workers the right to join unions.

But none of that satisfied Roosevelt. During the fall of 1910, the former president, still furious at Taft and eager to return to the political spotlight, gave a speech at Osawatomie, a small town in eastern Kansas, in which he gave a catchy name to his latest progressive principles and proposals, calling his sweeping agenda the New Nationalism. Roosevelt explained that he wanted to go beyond ensuring a "Square Deal" in which corporations were forced to "play by the rules"; he now promised to "change the rules" to force large corporations to promote social welfare and to serve the needs of working people. To save capitalism from the threat of a working-class revolution, he called for tighter federal regulation of "arrogant" corporations ("the great special business interests") that too often tried to "control and corrupt" politics, for a federal income tax (the Sixteenth Amendment had still not been ratified by the states), and for federal laws regulating child labor. It was a sweeping agenda that would greatly expand the power of the federal government over economic and political life. "What I have advocated," he explained, "is not wild radicalism. It is the highest and wisest kind of conservatism."

> Roosevelt's New Nationalism

Then, on February 24, 1912, Roosevelt abandoned his earlier pledge and announced his entry into the race for the 1912 Republican presidential nomination. He dismissed Taft as a "hopeless fathead" who had "sold the Square Deal down the river." Taft responded to his friend's attacks by calling Roosevelt a "dangerous egotist" and a "demagogue." The two former colleagues and friends now began a bitter war in which Roosevelt had the better weapons, not the least of which was his love of a good fight. Elihu Root, a Republican leader, described his friend Roosevelt as "essentially a fighter, and when he gets into a fight he is completely dominated by the desire to destroy" his opponent.

By 1912 a dozen or so "progressive" states were letting citizens vote for presidential candidates in party primaries rather than the traditional practice whereby a state's party leaders chose the nominee. Roosevelt decided that if he won big in the Republican primaries, he could claim to be "the people's choice" for the nomination. But even though he won all but two of the primaries, including the one in Taft's home state of Ohio, his personal popularity was no match for Taft's authority as party leader. In the 36 states that still chose candidates by conventions dominated by party bosses, the Taft Republicans prevailed, and at the Republican National Convention Taft was easily nominated for reelection.

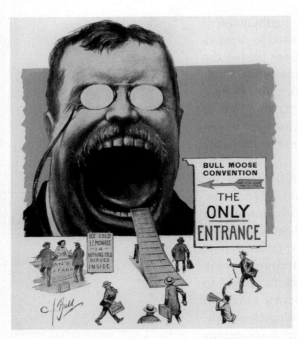

Sideshow Ted This 1912 cartoon criticizes the Bull Moose Party for being just a sideshow (with suffragists selling lemonade outside) and points out the menacing ego of Roosevelt himself.

An outraged Roosevelt denounced Taft and his supporters as thieves and walked out of the convention along with his delegates—mostly social workers, teachers, professors, journalists, and crusaders for women's suffrage, along with a few wealthy business executives who loved Roosevelt. Six weeks later the breakaway faction reconvened in Chicago to create a **Progressive party** with Roosevelt as its candidate. In his appearance before the delegates, he assured them that he felt "fit as a bull moose," leading journalists to nickname the Progressives the "Bull Moose party." When Roosevelt closed his acceptance speech by saying that "We stand at Armageddon [the climactic encounter between Christ and Satan], and we battle for the Lord," the delegates began singing the hymn "Onward, Christian Soldiers." One reporter wrote that the "Bull Moose" movement was not so much a politcal party as it was a religion.

The Progressive party platform revealed Roosevelt's growing liberalism. It supported a minimum "living wage" for hourly workers, women's suffrage, campaign finance reform, and a federal system of social insurance to protect people against sickness, unemployment, and disabilities. It also pledged to end the "boss system" governing American politics. But honesty and integrity in government was the basic theme of the new party: "To dissolve the unholy alliance between corrupt business and corrupt politics is the first task of the statesmanship of the day." Conservative critics now called Roosevelt "a socialist," a "revolutionist," and "a virtual traitor to American institutions."

Once nominated, Roosevelt repeatedly declared that Taft was not a progressive because he had tried to "undo" efforts at environmental conservation and had failed to fight either for social justice or against the "special interests." Instead, the former president charged, Taft had aligned himself with the "privileged" political and business leaders who steadfastly opposed "the cause of justice for the helpless and the wronged."

CORE **OBJECTIVE**

5. Describe the progressive policies of President Woodrow Wilson, and explain why and how they differed from those of Presidents Roosevelt and Taft.

Woodrow Wilson's Progressivism

The Republican fight between Taft and Roosevelt gave hope to the Democrats, whose presidential nominee, New Jersey governor Woodrow Wilson, had enjoyed remarkable success in his brief political career. Until his nomination and election as governor in 1910, Wilson had been a college professor and then president of Princeton University; he had never run for any other political office or worked in business. Instead, he was a man of ideas with extraordinary abilities: a keen intellect, an analytical temperament, a fertile imagination, a tireless work ethic, and an inspiring speaking style. He was convinced that he knew what was best for the nation. People often "call me an idealist," Wilson explained. "Well, that is the way I know I am an American."

Wilson's Dramatic Rise

Born in Staunton, Virginia, in 1856, the son and grandson of Presbyterian ministers, Thomas Woodrow Wilson had grown up in Georgia and the Carolinas during the Civil War and Reconstruction. Tall and slender with a long, chiselled face, he developed an unquestioning religious faith. He prayed and read the Bible daily all his life. Driven by a consuming sense that God had destined him to "serve" humanity, he often displayed an unbending self-righteousness and a fiery temper, qualities that would prove to be his undoing as president. Over the course of his presidency, he would sometimes mutter, "God save us from compromise."

Woodrow Wilson The only president to hold a Ph.D. degree to date.

Wilson graduated from Princeton in 1879. After law school at the University of Virginia, he briefly practiced law in Atlanta, but he found legal work "dreadful drudgery" and soon enrolled at Johns Hopkins University to study history and political science, earning one of the nation's first doctoral degrees. He became an expert in constitutional government and preferred the British prime-minister system over the American presidential model because it enabled a leader to accomplish more. He then taught at several colleges before being named president of Princeton in 1902. Eight years later, New Jersey Democrats offered Wilson their support for the 1910 gubernatorial nomination. He accepted the offer but already harbored higher ambitions. If he could become governor, he reflected, "I stand a very good chance of being the next President of the United States." Like Theodore Roosevelt, Wilson was an intensely ambitious and idealistic man who felt destined to preside over America's emergence as the greatest world power.

Although Wilson called himself an "amateur" politician, he proved a surprisingly effective campaigner and won a landslide victory. The professor-turned-governor then persuaded the state legislature to adopt an array of progressive reforms to curb the power of political party bosses and corporate lobbyists. "After dealing with college politicians," Wilson joked, "I find that the men who I am dealing with now seem like amateurs."

Governor Wilson soon attracted the attention of national Democratic leaders. At the 1912 Democratic convention, less than two years after beginning his political career, he faced stiff competition from several veteran party leaders for the presidential nomination, but with the support of William Jennings Bryan, he won on the forty-sixth ballot. It was, Wilson said, a "political miracle."

The Election of 1912

The 1912 presidential campaign was one of the most exciting in history. It involved four distinguished candidates: Democrat Woodrow Wilson, Republican William Howard Taft, Socialist Eugene V. Debs, and Progressive

Progressive party Political party founded by Theodore Roosevelt to support his bid to regain the presidency in 1912 after his split from the Taft Republicans.

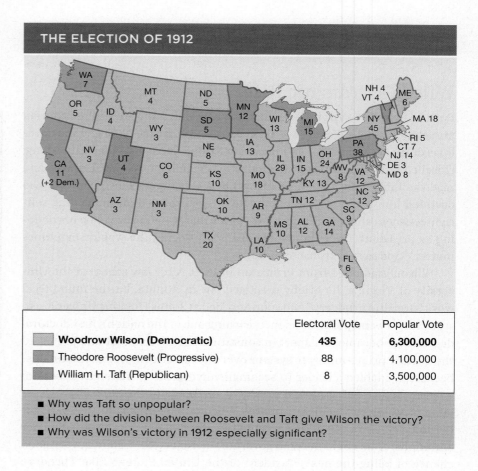

THE ELECTION OF 1912

	Electoral Vote	Popular Vote
Woodrow Wilson (Democratic)	**435**	**6,300,000**
Theodore Roosevelt (Progressive)	88	4,100,000
William H. Taft (Republican)	8	3,500,000

■ Why was Taft so unpopular?
■ How did the division between Roosevelt and Taft give Wilson the victory?
■ Why was Wilson's victory in 1912 especially significant?

Theodore Roosevelt. For all of their differences in personality and temperament, the candidates shared a basic progressive assumption that modern social problems could be resolved only through active governmental intervention.

As the contest unfolded, it settled down to a running debate between Roosevelt's New Nationalism and Wilson's **New Freedom**, a program designed by Louis D. Brandeis, a progressive Boston lawyer and future justice of the U.S. Supreme Court. The New Freedom aimed to restore competition in the economy by eliminating all trusts rather than simply regulating them. Where Roosevelt admired the power and efficiency of law-abiding corporations, no matter how large, Brandeis and Wilson were convinced that huge, "heartless" industries needed to be broken up.

On election day, Wilson won handily in the Electoral College, collecting 435 votes to 88 for Roosevelt and only 8 for Taft, the only Republican nominee for president ever to finish third. After learning of his election, the self-righteous Wilson told the chairman of his campaign committee that "I owe you nothing. God ordained that I should be the next president of the United

> The New Freedom: Eliminating rather than regulating trusts

New Freedom Program championed in 1912 by the Woodrow Wilson campaign that aimed to restore competition in the economy by eliminating all trusts rather than simply regulating them.

States. Neither you nor any other mortal could have prevented that." Had the Republicans not divided their votes between Taft and Roosevelt, however, Wilson would have lost. His was the victory of a minority candidate over a divided opposition. Since all four candidates called themselves progressives, however, the president-elect expressed his hope "that the thoughtful progressive forces of the nation may now at last unite." The election of 1912 profoundly altered the character of the Republican party. The defection of the Bull Moose Progressives had weakened the party's progressive wing. As a result, when Republicans returned to power in the 1920s, they would be more conservative in tone and temperament than Roosevelt and his progressive supporters.

The real surprise of the 1912 election, however, was the strong showing of the Socialist party candidate, Eugene V. Debs, running for the fourth time. The tall, lanky, blue-eyed idealist had devoted his adult life to fighting against the "monstrous system of capitalism" on behalf of the working class, first as a labor union official, then as a socialist promoting government ownership of railroads and other key industries and the sharing of profits with workers. Debs voiced a brand of socialism that was flexible rather than rigid, Christian rather than Marxist, democratic rather than totalitarian. He believed in political transformation, not violent revolution. As one of his supporters said, "That old man with the burning eyes actually believes that there can be such a thing as the brotherhood of man. And that's not the funniest part of it. As long as he's around I believe it myself."

Debs had become the unifying symbol of a diverse American radical movement that united West Virginia coal miners, Oklahoma sharecroppers, Pacific Northwest lumberjacks, and immigrant workers in New York City sweatshops. One newspaper highlighted "The Rising Tide of Socialism" in 1912 as some 1,150 Socialists won election to local and state offices across the nation, including eighteen mayors. To many voters, the Socialists, whose 118,000 dues-paying members in 1912 were double the number compared with the year before, offered the only real alternative to a stalemated political system in which the two major parties had few real differences. A business executive in New York City explained that he had become a Socialist "because the old parties [Democrats and Republicans] were flimflamming us all the time." But fear of socialism was also widespread during the Progressive Era. Theodore Roosevelt warned that the rapid growth of the Socialist party was "far more ominous than any Populist or similar movement in the past."

In 1912, with very few campaign funds, Debs crisscrossed the nation giving fiery speeches that frequently announced: "Comrades, this is our year!" He dismissed Roosevelt as "a fraud" whose progressive promises were nothing more than "the mouthings of a low and utterly unprincipled self-seeker and demagogue." Debs's untiring efforts brought him over 900,000 votes, an astonishing total for a Socialist, more than twice as many as he had received four years earlier.

> Eugene V. Debs and the "Rising Tide of Socialism"

A Burst of Reform Bills

On March 4, 1913, a huge crowd surrounded the Capitol in Washington, D.C., to watch Woodrow Wilson's inauguration. The new president with the long nose and spectacles declared that it was not "a day of triumph" but "a day of dedication." He promised to lower "the stiff and stupid" Republican tariffs, create a new national banking system, strengthen anti-trust laws, and establish an administration "more concerned about human rights than about property rights."

President Wilson: An expert on government, an activist, and a "fierce" reformer

Wilson worried about people comparing him to the colorful, hyperactive Roosevelt: "He appeals to their imagination; I do not. He is a real, vivid person. . . . I am a vague, conjectural [philosophical] personality, more made up of opinions and academic prepossessions than of human traits and red corpuscles." Roosevelt had been a strong president by force of personality; Wilson became a strong president by force of conviction.

For all of their differences, the two progressive presidents shared a belief that national problems demanded national solutions. Together they set in motion the modern presidency. They both shared Wilson's view that the U.S. president "is at liberty in both law and conscience to be as big as he can." Like Roosevelt, Wilson was an activist president; he was the first to speak to the nation over the radio and to host weekly press conferences. He was also unusual among presidents in that he frequently spoke to Congress and visited legislators in their offices in the Capitol. As a political scientist, Wilson was an expert at the processes of government. During his first two years, he pushed through Congress more new bills than any previous president. But like "most reformers," the president of Harvard University noted, Wilson "had a fierce and unlovely side." The new president found it hard to understand—much less work with—people who disagreed with him.

Wilson's victory, coupled with Democratic majorities in the House and Senate, gave his party effective national power for the first time since the Civil War. It also gave southerners a significant role in national politics for the first time since 1860. In addition to the president himself, five of Wilson's ten cabinet members were born in the South. At his right hand was "Colonel" Edward M. House of Texas, who held no official government position but was Wilson's most trusted adviser. The president described House as "my second personality. He is my independent self." House helped steer Wilson's proposals through a Congress in which southerners, by virtue of their seniority, held the lion's share of committee chairmanships. As a result, much of the progressive legislation of the Wilson era would bear the names of southern Democrats.

The Tariff and the Income Tax

Wilson's new administration faced its first big test on the complex issue of tariff reform. By 1913, the federal tariff included hundreds of taxes on different imported goods, from oil to nails, all designed to benefit American manufacturers. The president believed that U.S. corporations were misusing the tariff to keep out foreign competitors and create American monopolies that kept consumer prices artificially high. In order to attack high tariff rates, Wilson summoned Congress to a special session that lasted eighteen months, the longest in history, and he addressed its members in person—the first president to do so since John Adams. The new tariff bill passed the House easily. The crunch came in the Senate, the traditional graveyard of tariff reform, where swarms of industry lobbyists grew so thick, Wilson said, that "a brick couldn't be thrown without hitting one of them." The president finally won approval there by publicly criticizing the "industrious and insidious" tariff lobby.

The Underwood-Simmons Tariff (1913) lowered average tariff rates on imports—from about 40 percent to 25 percent—for the first time since the Civil War. To compensate for the government's reduced tariff revenue, the bill created the first income tax allowed under the newly ratified Sixteenth Amendment: the initial tax rates were 1 percent on income more than $3,000 ($4,000 for married couples) up to a top rate of 7 percent on annual income of $50,000 or more. Most Americans (99 percent) paid no income tax at all because they earned less than $3,000 a year.

> A lower tariff and a new income tax

The Federal Reserve Act

Before the new tariff had cleared the Senate, the administration proposed the first major banking reform since the Civil War. Ever since Andrew Jackson had killed the Second Bank of the United States in the 1830s, the nation had been without a central bank to manage its currency. Instead, the money supply was chaotically "managed" by thousands of local and state banks. Such a decentralized system produced instability and inefficiency because during financial panics fearful depositors, eager to get their money, would create "runs" that often led to the failure of smaller banks. In fact, the primary reason for a new central bank was to prevent more such panics, which had occurred five times since 1873. The most recent crisis, in 1907, had prompted the creation of a congressional commission to decide whether the United States needed a centralized banking system.

> Creation of the Federal Reserve System

By 1913, Wilson agreed that the nation's banking system needed a central reserve agency that, in a crisis, could distribute emergency cash to banks threatened by runs. But he insisted that any new national banking system must be overseen by the government rather than by bankers themselves (the "money power"). He wanted a new central bank that would benefit the entire economy, not just the large banks headquartered on Wall Street in New York City.

After much dickering, Congress finally passed the **Federal Reserve Act** on December 23, 1913. It created a new national banking system with twelve regional districts, each of which had its own Federal Reserve Bank that was owned by member banks in the district. Nationally chartered banks, which agreed to regulation by a Federal Reserve Bank in exchange for the right to issue money, had to be members of the Federal Reserve System. But state-chartered banks—essentially unregulated—did not (and, indeed, two-thirds

Federal Reserve Act (1913) Legislation passed by Congress to create a new national banking system in order to regulate the nation's currency supply and ensure the stability and integrity of member banks who made up the Federal Reserve System across the nation.

of the nation's banks chose not to become members of the Federal Reserve System). The twelve regional Federal Reserve banks were supervised by a central board of directors in Washington, D.C.

The purpose of the new Federal Reserve System was to adjust the nation's currency supply to match the needs of the economy and to ensure the stability and integrity of member banks. When banks were short of cash, they could borrow from the Federal Reserve, using their loans as collateral. Each of the new regional Federal Reserve banks issued Federal Reserve notes (currency) to member banks in exchange for their loans. By doing so, "the Fed," as the system came to be called, promoted economic growth and helped preserve the stability of banks during panics. The Federal Reserve board required member banks to have a certain percentage of their total deposits in cash on hand ("reserve") at all times.

A conservative Republican called the Federal Reserve Act "populistic, socialistic, half-baked, destructive, and unworkable." The new system soon proved its worth, however, and the criticism eased. The Federal Reserve Act was the most significant new program of Wilson's presidency.

Anti-Trust Actions

| A new Federal Trade Commission and Anti-Trust Act |

While promoting tariff and banking reforms, Wilson made "trust-busting" the central focus of his New Freedom program. Giant corporations had continued to grow despite the Sherman Anti-Trust Act and the Bureau of Corporations, the federal watchdog agency created by Theodore Roosevelt. Wilson decided to make a strong **Federal Trade Commission** (FTC) the cornerstone of his anti-trust program. Created in 1914, the five-member FTC replaced the Bureau of Corporations and assumed new powers to define "unfair trade practices" and issue "cease and desist" orders when it found evidence of such practices.

Like Roosevelt, Wilson also supported efforts to strengthen and clarify the Sherman Anti-Trust Act. Henry D. Clayton, a Democrat from Alabama, drafted an anti-trust bill in 1914. The **Clayton Anti-Trust Act** declared that labor unions were not to be viewed as "monopolies in restraint of trade," as courts had done since 1890. It also prohibited directors from serving on the boards of competing companies and further clarified the meaning of various "monopolistic" activities.

Progressives' Disappointments with Wilson

In November 1914, just two years after his election, President Wilson announced that he had accomplished the major goals of progressivism. He had fulfilled his promises to lower the tariff, create a national banking system, and strengthen the anti-trust laws. The New Freedom was now complete, he wrote. But his announcement bewildered many progressives, especially those who had long advocated additional federal social-justice legislation that Wilson had earlier supported. Herbert Croly, the influential editor of the *New Republic* magazine, was dumbfounded by Wilson's conservative

Federal Trade Commission (1914) Independent agency created by the Wilson administration that replaced the Bureau of Corporations as an even more powerful tool to combat unfair trade practices and monopolies.

Clayton Anti-Trust Act (1914) Legislation that served to enhance the Sherman Anti-Trust Act (1890) by clarifying what constituted "monopolistic" activities and declaring that labor unions were not to be viewed as "monopolies in restraint of trade."

turn. He wondered how the president could assert "that the fundamental wrongs of a modern society can be easily and quickly righted as a consequence of [passing] a few laws." Wilson's about-face, he concluded, "casts suspicion upon his own sincerity [as a progressive] or upon his grasp of the realities of modern social and industrial life."

Progressivism for Whites Only

African Americans were also disappointed by Wilson's racial conservatism. Like many other progressives, Wilson showed little interest in addressing the discrimination and violence that African Americans faced. In fact, he shared many of the racist attitudes common at the time. As a student at Princeton, he had expressed his disgust at the guarantee of voting rights for black men after the Civil War, arguing that whites must always resist domination by "an ignorant and inferior race." Later, as a politician, Wilson did court African American voters, but he rarely consulted black leaders and largely avoided associating with them in public or expressing support for them. That he refused to create a National Race Commission was a great disappointment to the black community, as were his cabinet appointments of white southerners who were outspoken racists.

Josephus Daniels, a North Carolina newspaper editor who became Wilson's secretary of the navy, was a white supremacist who wrote that "the subjection of the negro, politically, and the separation of the negro, socially, are paramount to all other considerations in the South." For Daniels and other southern progressives, "progress" was possible only if blacks were "kept in their place." Daniels and other cabinet members racially segregated the employees in their agencies; Secretary of State William Jennings Bryan supported such efforts to create separate offices, dining facilities,

> Wilson's support for racial segregation

New freedom, old rules Wilson and the First Lady ride in a carriage with African American drivers.

restrooms, and water fountains. Wilson claimed that racial segregation "is not humiliating but a benefit." He was the first president since the Civil War who openly endorsed discrimination against African Americans, arguing that segregation in government buildings was in "their best interests." His administration also reduced the number of African American appointees to federal offices.

After visiting Washington, D.C., in 1913, Booker T. Washington reported that he had "never seen the colored people so discouraged and bitter." In November 1914, a delegation of African American leaders met with Wilson in the White House to ask how a "progressive" president could adopt such "regressive" racial policies. Wilson responded that both races benefited from the policies because they eliminated "the possibility of friction." William Trotter, a Harvard-educated African American newspaper editor who had helped found the National Association for the Advancement of Colored People (NAACP), scolded the president: "Have you a 'new freedom' for white Americans, and a new slavery for 'your Afro-American fellow citizens' [a phrase Wilson had used in a speech]? God forbid." A furious Wilson then told Trotter and the other visitors to leave, saying that their unchristian "tone offends me."

The Vote for Women

Activists for women's suffrage also were disappointed in President Wilson (as they had been in President Roosevelt). Despite having two daughters who were suffragists, he insisted that the issue of women's voting rights should be left to the states rather than embodied in a constitutional amendment.

Wilson's lack of support led some leaders of the suffrage movement to revise their tactics. In 1910, Alice Paul, a New Jersey–born Quaker social worker who had earned a doctoral degree in political science from the University of Pennsylvania, returned from an apprenticeship with the militant suffragists of England, who had developed effective forms of civil disobedience as a way of generating attention and support. After Paul joined the National American Woman Suffrage Association (NAWSA), she urged activists to picket state legislatures, target and "punish" politicians who failed to endorse suffrage, chain themselves to public buildings, incite police to arrest them, and undertake hunger strikes. In March 1913, Paul organized 5,000 suffragists to march in protest at Wilson's inauguration.

Four years later, Paul, having broken with NAWSA and formed the National Woman's Party, decided that suffragists must do something even more dramatic to force Wilson to support their cause: picket the White House. Beginning on January 11, 1917, Paul and her followers took turns carrying signs there all day, five days a week, for six months, until the president ordered their arrest. Some sixty suffragists were jailed. For her leadership role, Paul was sentenced to seven months in prison. She then went on a hunger strike, leading prison officials to force-feed her through a tube inserted in

Alice Paul Sewing a suffrage flag—orange and purple, with stars—that she and other suffragists often waved at strikes and protests.

The Expanding Role of the Federal Government

Progressive reformers wanted to improve the quality of life for all Americans and believed that government should play a crucial role in doing so. Their activities led to a significant expansion in the activity of the federal government in the first two decades of the twentieth century. After the presidencies of Theodore Roosevelt, William Taft, and Woodrow Wilson, the government had gained new powers to shape the direction of the nation's economic and social well-being. The following timeline reviews many important presidential actions, legislative developments, and constitutional amendments between 1901 and 1917.

PROGRESSIVE POLICIES AT THE FEDERAL LEVEL, 1901–1917

1901–1909
Presidency of Theodore Roosevelt

1902
- The Roosevelt Administration sues the Northern Securities Company for violating the Sherman Anti-Trust Act. The Supreme Court would dissolve the corporation in 1904.
- Roosevelt intervenes in a major coal miners' strike, eventually threatening to send in federal troops to operate the mines if the owners did not negotiate with the striking workers. The owners conceded to a reduction in work hours and a 10 percent wage increase.

1903
- Congress creates the Bureau of Corporations to monitor the activities of Big Business. The Roosevelt administration sued the Standard Oil Company for violation of the Sherman Anti-Trust Act, resulting in the Supreme Court's dissolving the corporation in 1911.
- Congress passes the Elkins Act, outlawing secret rebates by railroad companies to favored customers.

1909–1913
Presidency of William Taft

1910
- Congress passes the Mann-Elkins Act, giving the Interstate Commerce Commission the power to regulate telegraph and telephone companies.

1913
- Passage of the Sixteenth Amendment to the Constitution, authorizing a federal income tax, and the Seventeenth Amendment, allowing for the direct election of U.S. senators, are ratified.

1913–1921
Presidency of Woodrow Wilson

1913
- Congress passes the Underwood-Simmons Tariff, lowering tariffs on imports and creating the nation's first progressive income tax to make up for lost federal revenue.
- Congress passes the Federal Reserve Act to oversee and regulate the nation's banking system and provide a stable currency.

1914
- Congress creates the Federal Trade Commission to replace the Bureau of Corporations in overseeing the behavior of Big Business and gives the new agency the ability to define unfair trade practices and issue cease and desist orders when it identified unfair trade practices.
- Congress passes the Clayton Anti-Trust Act, which exempted labor unions from anti-trust prosecution, prohibited corporate directors from serving on boards of competing companies, and further defined various meanings of monopolistic practices.

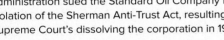

QUESTIONS FOR ANALYSIS

1. What were some of the major progressive concerns that the federal government addressed in this era?

2. What generalizations can you make about the kinds of strategies used to address these concerns?

3. What were the limits of progressivism in this period?

her nose. Under an avalanche of press coverage and public criticism, Wilson finally pardoned her and the other jailed activists.

Progressive Resurgence

By 1916, the need to create a winning political coalition in the upcoming presidential election—which required courting Republican as well as Democratic progressives—had pushed Wilson back onto the road of reform. The president scored progressive points when he nominated Louis D. Brandeis to the Supreme Court, making him the Court's first Jewish member when he was confirmed by the Senate. Wilson also won congressional approval for a broad program of legislation to help farmers and workers.

Farm Legislation

Because farmers continued to suffer from a shortage of capital available for lending, Wilson supported a proposal to set up special rural banks to provide long-term farm loans. The Federal Farm Loan Act became law in 1916. Under the control of the Federal Farm Loan Board, twelve Federal Land banks offered loans to farmers for five to forty years at low interest rates. Under the act, farmers could borrow up to 50 percent of the value of their land. At about the same time, a dream long advocated by Populists—federal loans to farmers on the security of their crops stored in warehouses—finally came to fruition when Congress passed the Warehouse Act of 1916. These crop-security loans were available to sharecroppers and tenant farmers as well as to farmers who owned the land that they worked.

Farmers were also pleased by the passage of the Smith-Lever Act of 1914 and the Smith-Hughes Act of 1917. The Smith-Lever Act provided federal programs to educate farmers about new farm machinery and new ideas related to agricultural efficiency. The Smith-Hughes Act funded agricultural and mechanical education in high schools. Farmers with the newfangled automobiles had more than a passing interest as well in the Federal Highways Act of 1916, which helped finance new highways, especially in rural areas.

Labor Legislation

The progressive resurgence of 1916 broke the logjam on workplace reforms as well. One of the long-standing goals of many progressive Democrats was a federal child-labor law. When Congress passed the Keating-Owen Act in 1916, banning products made by child workers under fourteen from being shipped across state lines, Wilson expressed doubts about its constitutionality but eventually signed it. The act was later ruled unconstitutional by the Supreme Court on the grounds that child labor was outside the bounds of Congress's authority to regulate interstate commerce. Effective action against child labor abuses had to wait until the New Deal of the 1930s.

Another landmark law was the eight-hour workday for railroad workers, a measure that the Supreme Court upheld. The Adamson Act of 1916 resulted from a threatened strike by railroad unions demanding an eight-hour day and other concessions. Wilson, who objected to some of the unions' demands, nevertheless asked Congress to approve the Adamson Act. It required time-and-a-half pay for overtime work beyond eight hours and appointed a commission to study working conditions in the railroad industry.

The Limits of Progressivism

Progressivism reached its peak during Wilson's two terms as president. People grew optimistic about the economy and an improving society. After two decades of political upheaval and social reform (three if the Populists in the 1890s are counted), Progressivism had shattered the traditional "*laissez-faire*" notion that government had no role in regulating the economy. The courage and compassion displayed by progressives of all stripes demonstrated that people of good will could make a difference in improving the quality of life for all. Progressivism awoke people to the evils and possibilities of modern urban-industrial life. Most important, progressives established the principle that governments—local, state, and federal—had a responsibility to ensure that Americans were protected from abuse by powerful businesses and corrupt politicians. As a Texas progressive said in 1910, most Americans now acknowledged that governments must protect "the weak against the encroachments of the strong."

Yet even though it had succeeded in accomplishing most of its goals—and its racial, ethnic, and class biases are more obvious today than they were at the time—on several fronts progressivism still fell short of its supporters' hopes and ideals. Child labor would not be addressed on a national level until the Great Depression in the 1930s. It would also take the shock of the Depression to lead to the passage of a national minimum wage and the creation of a government-administered pension program for retirees and disabled workers (Social Security). Like all great historic movements, too, progressivism produced unexpected consequences. For all of its efforts to give more power to "the people," voter participation actually declined during the Progressive Era. Probably the main reason for the decline of party loyalty and voter turnout was that by the twentieth century people had many more activities to distract them from politics; new forms of recreation like movies, cycling, automobiles, and spectator sports competed with politics for time and attention. But people showed less interest in political parties and public issues in part because of the progressive emphasis on government by appointed specialists and experts rather than elected politicians.

Finally, progressivism faded because international relations pushed aside domestic concerns. By 1916, the optimism of a few years earlier was being challenged by the distressing slaughter occurring in Europe in the Great War. The twentieth century, which had dawned with such bright hopes for social progress, held in store episodes of unprecedented brutality that led people to question whether governments could be trusted to serve the "public interest" or that "progress" was even possible anymore.

■ **The Progressive Impulse** Progressives believed that industrialization and urbanization were negatively affecting American life. They were mostly middle-class idealists who promoted reform and government regulation in order to ensure social justice. They also called for legislation to end child labor, promote safety in the workplace, ban the sale of alcoholic beverages, regulate or eliminate trusts and other monopolies, and grant *woman suffrage.*

■ **The Varied Sources of Progressivism** Progressivism grew out of many sources going back several decades. The depression in the 1890s led many urban middle-class people to pursue reforms to aid the working class and the poor. Many religious reformers, such as those involved in the *social gospel* movement, had urged their fellow Christians to reject social Darwinism and do more to promote a better life for the urban poor. The settlement house movement spread through urban America as educated middle-class women formed community centers in poverty-stricken neighborhoods. *Muckrakers*— investigative journalists who exposed significant political and corporate corruption—further fueled the desire of progressive reformers to address abuses of power in American society.

■ **Progressives' Aims and Achievements** To address corruption in politics, they implemented political reforms such as the direct primary; initiative, referendum, and recall at the state level; and the direct election of senators through the *Seventeenth Amendment*. They also focused on incorporating new modes of efficiency into government administration through *Taylorism.*

Many middle-class women reformers targeted what they saw as the social evils of alcohol consumption, prostitution, and poor living and working conditions. Social justice reformers also fought successfully for a progressive income tax with the passage of the *Sixteenth Amendment.*

■ **Progressivism under Roosevelt and Taft** The administrations of Theodore Roosevelt and William H. Taft increased the power of the president and the federal government to regulate corporate power. Roosevelt promoted his progressive *Square Deal* program, which included the arbitration of the 1902 coal strike, and Pure Food and Drug Acts. After severe criticism of his White House meeting with Booker T. Washington, he made no further gestures toward racial harmony or equality.

Choosing not to seek reelection in 1908, Roosevelt endorsed Taft, who easily won the election. But Taft's inability to bring about major tariff reduction with the Payne-Aldrich Tariff Act, among other failings, led Roosevelt to run again for president, promoting his New Nationalism vision. Unable to defeat Taft for the Republican nomination, Roosevelt formed a *Progressive party*. This split the Republican vote, allowing Democrat Woodrow Wilson, another progressive reformer, to win the office.

■ **Woodrow Wilson's Progressivism** Wilson's *New Freedom* program promised less federal intervention in business and a return to traditional Democratic policies like low tariffs and anti-trust regulation. He followed through on his promises with the Underwood-Simmons Tariff Act, the *Federal Reserve Act*, and to begin a rigorous anti-trust program with the passage of the *Clayton Anti-Trust Act* and the creation of the *Federal Trade Commission*. To rally Republican progressives to his side for the 1916 reelection, he endorsed greater regulation of child labor and railroad corporations, particularly through the Adamson Act. He also successfully sponsored two bills to allow farmers to get federal loans, a longtime goal of the populist movement.

KEY TERMS

CHRONOLOGY

1889	Hull House, a settlement house, opens in Chicago
1901	William McKinley is assassinated; Theodore Roosevelt becomes president
	Governor of Wisconsin Robert La Follette creates the "Wisconsin idea"
	Galveston, Texas, adopts the commission system of city government
1902	Roosevelt attempts to arbitrate a strike by coal miners
1902	Justice Department breaks up Northern Securities Company
1903	Congress passes the Elkins Act and creates the Bureau of Corporations
1904	National Child Labor Committee formed
1906	Upton Sinclair's *The Jungle* is published
1906	Congress passes the Meat Inspection Act and the Pure Food and Drug Act
1909	William Howard Taft inaugurated
1911	Triangle Shirtwaist fire
1912	Woodrow Wilson wins four-way presidential election
1913	Alice Paul and 5,000 suffragists protest Wilson's inauguration
	Sixteenth and Seventeenth Amendments ratified
	Underwood-Simmons Tariff and Federal Reserve Act passed
1914	Congress passes the Clayton Anti-Trust Act
1916	Congress passes the Adamson Act and the Keating-Owen Act

INQUIZITIVE

Go to InQuizitive to see what you've learned—and learn what you've missed—with personalized feedback along the way.

MAKE AMERICAN HISTORY In this poster for a U.S. Navy recruiting station in New York City, a sailor encourages a young man to play an active role in the Great War and gestures toward battleships in the distance.

America and the Great War

1914–1920

Throughout the nineteenth century, the Atlantic Ocean had protected America from the major land wars on the continent of Europe. During the early twentieth century, however, the nation's century-long isolation from European wars ended. Ever-expanding world trade meant that American interests were becoming deeply entwined with the economies of Europe. In addition, the development of steam-powered ships and submarines meant that foreign navies could directly threaten American security. At the same time, the election of Woodrow Wilson in 1912 brought to the White House a self-righteous moralist determined to impose his standards for proper conduct on what he saw as renegade nations. This combination of circumstances made the outbreak of the "Great War" in Europe in 1914 a profound crisis for the United States, a crisis that would become the defining event of the early twentieth century and force America to accept its role and responsibilities as a dominant world power.

Once America entered the war, mobilization called millions of men into active military duty and caused mass migrations of African Americans to northern cities and southern whites to urban centers in search of industrial work to support the war effort. With victory in hand in 1919, America would find itself as the reluctant leading world power divided over

CORE **OBJECTIVES** INQUIZITIVE

1. Describe the outbreak of the Great War and the distinctive nature of the fighting on the Western Front, and explain why the United States was drawn into the war.

2. Explain how the Wilson administration mobilized the home front, and analyze how mobilization efforts shaped American society.

3. Describe the major events of the war after U.S. entry, and explain the U.S. contribution to the defeat of the Central Powers.

4. Evaluate Wilson's efforts to promote his plans for a peaceful world order as outlined in his Fourteen Points.

5. Analyze the consequences of the war at home and abroad.

whether to approve the Treaty of Versailles while facing substantial social and economic challenges at home with the return of legions of soldiers entering the workforce.

CORE **OBJECTIVE**

1. Describe the outbreak of the Great War and the distinctive nature of the fighting on the Western Front, and explain why the United States was drawn into the war.

An Uneasy Neutrality

Woodrow Wilson once declared that he had "a first-class mind." Although lacking humility, he was indeed highly intelligent, thoughtful, principled, and courageous. Upon learning of death threats against him, for example, he refused to change his schedule of public appearances. "The country," he explained, "cannot afford to have a coward for President." For all of his accomplishments and abilities, however, Wilson had no experience or expertise in international relations before his election as president. The former college professor admitted before taking office that "it would be an irony of fate if my administration had to deal chiefly with foreign affairs"—a topic he did not even mention in his 1913 inaugural address. But from the summer of 1914, when a terrible war erupted in Europe, foreign relations increasingly overshadowed all else, including Wilson's ambitious New Freedom program of progressive reforms.

Although inexperienced in international affairs, Wilson did not lack ideas or convictions about global issues. "Sometimes people call me an idealist," he once told an audience in South Dakota. "Well, that is the way I know I'm an American." He fervently believed that the world should follow America's example of capitalist democracy and correct behavior: "America is an idea. America is an ideal, America is a vision." Wilson saw himself as directed by God to help create a new world order governed by morality and ideals rather than by selfish national interests. Both Wilson and William Jennings Bryan, his secretary of state, believed that America had a duty to promote democracy and Christianity around the world. "Every nation of the world," Wilson declared, "needs to be drawn into the tutelage [guidance] of America."

The Outbreak of War

Wilson was faced with his greatest challenge beginning in the summer of 1914, when war broke out in Europe. Most Americans were caught off guard by the news. The "dreadful conflict" erupted suddenly, like "lightning out of a clear sky," a North Carolina congressman said. And no one could have predicted the horrifying results. Lasting for more than four years, from 1914 to 1918, the conflict became known as the Great War because it would involve more nations and cause greater destruction than any previous war. The appalling slaughter would cost 20 million military and civilian deaths, and 21 million more people would be wounded. The Great War would topple monarchs and destroy empires, create new nations, and set in motion a series of events that would lead to an even greater war in 1939—one that led to the retroactive renaming of the Great War as the First World War, or World War I.

Wars are much easier to start than to control. The Great War resulted from long-simmering and extremely complex national rivalries and ethnic conflicts in central Europe that second-rate statesmen and war-hungry generals allowed to spin out of control. At the core of the tensions was the Austro-Hungarian Empire, a collection of eleven nationalities that was determined to stop the aggressive expansionism of its neighbor and long-standing enemy, Serbia, in the Balkan peninsula. At the same time, a recklessly militaristic Germany, led by Kaiser (Emperor) Wilhelm II, was eager to assert its dominance on the European continent against its old enemies, the Russian Empire and France, at the same time that it was expanding its navy to challenge the British Empire's supremacy on the seas.

War erupted just five weeks after Gavrilo Princip, a nineteen-year-old Serbian nationalist in Sarajevo (the capital of present-day Bosnia-Herzegovina), used a pistol to assassinate the heir to the Austro-Hungarian throne, 50-year-old Archduke Franz Ferdinand, and his pregnant wife Sophie, on June 28, 1914. It was a war that few wanted but nobody could stop.

> Assassination in Sarajevo

To avenge the murders, Austria-Hungary, with Germany's approval, recklessly bullied and humiliated Serbia by demanding a say in its internal affairs. Serbia gave in to virtually all of the demands, but Austria-Hungary declared war anyway. In turn, Russia mobilized its army to defend Serbia, an action that triggered chain reactions by a complex system of European military alliances: the Triple Alliance, or **Central Powers** (Germany, Austria-Hungary, and Italy), and the Triple Entente, or **Allied Powers** (France, Great Britain, and Russia).

Germany declared war on Russia on August 1, 1914, and on France two days later. Germany, hoping to defeat France before Russia could mobilize its armies in the east, invaded neutral Belgium to get at France, murdering hundreds of civilians in the process. The "rape of Belgium" brought Great Britain into the war against Germany on August 4 on the **Western Front**, the line of fighting in northern France and Belgium. Despite being a member of the Triple Alliance, Italy at first declared its neutrality in the war and then joined the Allies in return for a promise of territory taken from Austria-Hungary. On the huge Eastern Front, Russian armies would clash with German and Austro-Hungarian forces as well as those of the Turkish (Ottoman) Empire. Within five weeks of the assassination in Sarajevo, a "great war" had erupted (it would not be called the First World War until the second one came along in 1939).

An Industrial War

What started as a local conflict in the Balkans became a catastrophic war that reshaped the world. By its end, in November 1918, more than forty nations had joined the fighting, in large part because most of the warring nations had far-flung colonies around the globe. The Great War was the first

Central Powers One of the two sides during the Great War, including Germany, Austria-Hungary, the Ottoman Empire, and Bulgaria.

Allied Powers Nations fighting the Central Powers during the Great War, including France, Great Britain, and Russia; later joined by Italy and, after Russia quit the war in 1917, the United States.

Western Front Contested frontier between the Central and Allied Powers that ran along northern France and across Belgium.

WORLD WAR I IN EUROPE, 1914

Central Powers (Triple Alliance)
Allied Powers (Triple Entente)
Neutral countries

■ How did the European system of alliances spread conflict across all of Europe?
■ How was World War I different from previous wars?
■ How did the war in Europe lead to ethnic tensions in the United States?

industrial war, fought between nations using new weapons that dramatically increased the war's scope and destruction. Machine guns, submarines, aerial bombing, poison gas, flame throwers, land mines, mortars, long-range artillery, and armored tanks changed the nature of warfare and produced appalling casualties and widespread destruction, a slaughter on a scale unimaginable to this day. An average of 900 Frenchmen and 1,300 Germans died *every* day on the Western Front. It was the mechanized weaponry that made possible such mass killing on an "industrial" scale— the same scale on which items were mass-produced in an industrial economy.

Mechanized trench warfare

The early weeks of the war involved fast-moving assaults as German armies swept westward across Belgium and northeastern France. Then mistakes piled up on both sides. What began as a war of quick movement in August 1914 bogged down into a prolonged stalemate: nightmarish

Total ruin German soldiers stand before the French Fort Souville between the Battles of Verdun in September of 1916. The heavy and constant artillery fire dug craters into the land and destroyed all traces of the forest that stood there before.

trench warfare in which often inept generals sent masses of mud-streaked, steel-helmeted soldiers up and out of waterlogged, zigzagging trenches, some of them 40 feet deep and swarming with rats, that had been dug along the Western Front from the coast of Belgium some 450 miles across northeastern France to the border of Switzerland. On either side, the attackers were usually at a disadvantage as they slogged across a few muddy acres of devastated "no-man's-land" between the opposing entrenchments, soon running into webs of entangling barbed wire and fire from machine guns and high-powered rifles overlaid by constant artillery shelling. From 1914 to 1918, the opposing armies in northeastern France attacked and counterattacked, along the Western Front, hardly gaining any ground one way or another despite casualties in the millions.

It was not the kind of warfare anyone had expected or wanted. Words cannot convey the scale of the carnage. During the Battle of Verdun, in northeast France, which lasted from February to December 1916, some 32 million artillery shells streaked across the landscape—1,500 shells for *every* square yard of the battlefield. Thousands of soldiers on both sides fell victim to "shell shock," now known as post–traumatic stress disorder. "It was a horrible thing," explained a nurse. "They became quite unconscious, with violent shivering and shaking." The unprecedented firepower ravaged the land, obliterating nine villages and turning farmland and forests into cratered wastelands. Some 162,000 French soldiers died at Verdun; the Germans lost 143,000. Charles de Gaulle, a young French

trench warfare A form of prolonged combat between the entrenched positions of opposing armies, often with little tactical movement.

lieutenant who forty years later would become his nation's president, said the conflict had become a "war of extermination." Its horrific butchery seemed especially pointless, since neither side was capable of gaining the advantage. A British army chaplain described the war as a senseless "Waste of Muscle, Waste of Brain, Waste of Patience, Waste of Pain . . . Waste of Glory, Waste of God."

Muddy trench warfare in which soldiers fought, ate, slept, and often died in their dirt holes gave the Great War its lasting character. Most battles were won not by skillful maneuvers or superior generalship but by brute force. The object in such a war of attrition was not so much to gain ground as to keep inflicting death and destruction on the enemy until their manpower and resources were exhausted. In one attack at Ypres in Belgium, the British lost 13,000 men in three hours of fighting—during which time they gained 100 meaningless yards. As the war ground on, nations on both sides found themselves using up their available men, resources, courage, and cash.

> **An end to innocence about war**

There was no precedent for such a ghastly war. Throughout 1914, both sides talked about the "glory" and "glamour" of war, notions that the British poet Wilfred Owen called "the old Lie." (Owen would be killed in action in 1918, just a week before the war ended.) The old-fashioned romantic concepts of war were forever changed as masses of soldiers died like cattle in a slaughterhouse, killed often at such long distances that they never saw their opponents. Amid the senseless killing in the mucky trenches, the innocence about the true nature of warfare died, too. "Never such innocence again," wrote the English poet Phillip Larkin. "I am cured of ever wishing to be a soldier again," wrote one young veteran.

In 1917, George Barnes, a British official whose son had been killed in the war, went to speak at a military hospital in London where injured soldiers were being fitted with artificial limbs. At the appointed hour, the wounded men, in wheelchairs and on crutches, all with empty sleeves or pants legs, arrived to hear the speaker. Yet when Barnes was introduced and rose to talk, he found himself speechless—literally. As the minutes passed in awkward silence, tears rolled down his cheeks. Finally, without having said a word, he simply sat down. What the mutilated soldiers heard was not a war-glorifying speech but the muted sound of grief. The war's mindless horrors had come home. Britain's King George V called it a "horrible and unnecessary war."

Initial American Reactions

Shock in the United States over the bloodbath in Europe mingled with gratitude that a wide ocean stood between America and the killing fields. "Our isolated position and freedom from entangling alliances," said the *Literary Digest,* ensure that "we are in no peril of being drawn into the European quarrel." President Wilson maintained that the United States "was too proud to fight" in Europe's war, "with which we have nothing to do, whose causes cannot touch us." He repeatedly urged Americans to remain "neutral in thought as well as in action." Privately, however, Wilson was not neutral. He sought to provide Great Britain and France as much financial assistance and supplies as possible.

That was more easily said than done. More than a third of the nation's citizens were "hyphenated Americans"—first- or second-generation immigrants who retained strong ties to their native countries. Eight million German Americans lived in the United States in 1914, and many among the 4 million Irish Americans felt a deep-rooted hatred toward Britain, which had ruled the Irish for centuries. These groups instinctively leaned toward the Central Powers. But most other white Americans, largely of British origin, supported Britain and France.

> Ethnic divisions in American public opinion

By the spring of 1915, the Allied Powers' desperate need for food and supplies had generated an economic boom for American businesses, bankers, and farmers. U.S. exports to France and Great Britain quadrupled from 1914 to 1916. To finance their record-breaking purchases of American supplies, the Allies, especially Britain and France, needed loans from U.S. banks and "credits" from the U.S. government that would allow the Allies to pay for their American purchases later. Early in the war, Secretary of State Bryan, a strict pacifist, took advantage of Wilson's absence from Washington after the death of his wife to declare that loans and credits to any warring nation were "inconsistent with the true spirit of neutrality." Upon his return, a furious Wilson reversed Bryan's policy by removing all restrictions on loans to the warring nations ("belligerents"). American banks and other investors would eventually advance more than $2 billion to the Allies before the United States entered the war, and only $27 million to Germany.

> Official U.S. neutrality and "freedom of the seas"

Despite the disproportionate financial assistance provided to the Allies, the Wilson administration clung to its official stance of neutrality through two and a half years of warfare. Wilson tried valiantly in particular to uphold the "freedom of the seas." As a neutral nation, the United States, according to international law, should have been able to continue its trade with all the belligerents. On August 6, 1914, Secretary of State Bryan called upon the warring nations to respect the rights of all neutral nations to ship goods across the Atlantic. The Central Powers promptly accepted, but the British refused. In November 1914, the British ordered the ships of neutral nations like the United States to submit to searches to discover if cargoes were bound for Germany. A few months later, they announced that they would seize any ships carrying goods to Germany.

"The Sandwich Man" To illustrate America's hypocritical brand of neutrality, this political cartoon shows Uncle Sam wearing a sandwich board that advertises its conflicting desires.

Neutral Rights and Submarine Attacks

With the German naval fleet bottled up by a British blockade of German ports, the German government proclaimed a war zone around the British Isles. All ships in those waters would be attacked by submarines, the Germans warned, and "it may not always be possible to save crews and passengers." The German decision, based on the fact that surprise was the chief advantage of the submarine or **U-boat** (*Unterseeboot* in German), violated the long-established wartime custom of stopping an enemy vessel and allowing the passengers and crew to board lifeboats before sinking it. During 1915, German U-boats sank 227 British ships in the Atlantic Ocean and the North Sea.

> German U-boats and the sinking of the *Lusitania*

The United States called the German submarine policy "an indefensible violation of neutral rights," and Wilson warned that Germany would be held to "strict accountability" for any destruction of American lives and property. Then, on May 7, 1915, a German submarine sank an unarmed British luxury liner off the Irish coast. Only as it tipped into the waves was the German commander able to make out the name ***Lusitania*** on the ship's hull. Of the 1,198 persons on board who died, 128 were Americans.

Americans were outraged. The sinking of the *Lusitania*, asserted ex-president Theodore Roosevelt, was an act of piracy and mass murder that called for a declaration of war. Wilson at first urged patience: "There is such a thing as a man being too proud to fight. There is such a thing as a nation being so right that it does not need to convince others by force that it is right." Critics scolded Wilson for his bloodless response, with Roosevelt dismissing it as "unmanly," calling the president a "jackass," and threatening to "skin him alive if he doesn't go to war." Wilson himself privately admitted that he had misspoken. "I have a bad habit of thinking out loud," he confessed to a friend the day after his "too proud to fight" speech. The timid language, he said, had "occurred to me while I was speaking, and I let it out. I should have kept it in."

Wilson's previous demand for "strict accountability" now forced him to make a stronger response. On May 13, Secretary of State Bryan signed a letter demanding that the Germans abandon unrestricted submarine warfare and pay reparations to the families of those killed in the sinking of the *Lusitania*. The Germans responded that the ship was armed (which was false) and secretly carried a cargo of rifles and ammunition (which was true). A second letter, on June 9, repeated the American demands in stronger terms. The United States, Wilson asserted, was "contending for nothing less high and sacred than the rights of humanity."

Bryan, unwilling to risk war over the issue, resigned in protest of the president's pro-British stance, leading Edith Bolling Galt, soon to be Wilson's second wife, to shout: "Hurrah! Old Bryan is out!" She called the former secretary of state an "awful Deserter." The president confided that he, too, viewed Bryan as a "traitor." He complimented Edith on her vindictiveness: "What a dear partisan you are . . . and how you can hate, too!" Bryan's successor, Robert Lansing, signed the second "*Lusitania* Note."

U-boat German military submarine used during the Great War to attack enemy naval vessels as well as merchant ships of enemy and neutral nations.

Lusitania British ocean liner torpedoed and sunk by a German U-boat; the deaths of nearly 1,200 of its civilian passengers, including many Americans, caused international outrage.

In response to the uproar over the *Lusitania,* the German government ordered U-boat captains to avoid sinking any more passenger vessels. Despite the order, however, two Americans were killed in the sinking of the New York–bound British liner *Arabic.* The Germans paid a cash penalty to their families and offered a public assurance on September 1, 1915: "Liners will not be sunk by our submarines without warning and without safety of the lives of non-combatants, provided that the liners do not try to escape or offer resistance." This so-called *Arabic* Pledge enabled Wilson to claim victory for his neutrality policy.

During early 1916, Wilson's most trusted adviser, Colonel Edward M. House, visited London, Paris, and Berlin but found neither side ready to begin serious negotiations to end the war. On March 24, 1916, a U-boat torpedoed the French ferry *Sussex,* killing eighty passengers and injuring two Americans. When Wilson threatened to break off relations, Germany renewed its pledge that U-boats would not torpedo merchant and passenger ships. The *Sussex* Pledge was far stronger than the German promise after the *Arabic* sinking, the year before, and implied the virtual abandonment of submarine warfare.

The Debate over "Preparedness"

The sinking of the *Lusitania* and the quarrels over trading with a Europe at war contributed to a growing demand in the United States for a stronger army and navy. On December 1, 1914, champions of the "preparedness" movement, including Theodore Roosevelt, had organized the National Security League to promote more military spending. After the *Lusitania* sinking, Wilson asked the War and Navy Departments to develop plans for a $1-billion military expansion. Many Americans—pacifists, progressives, and Midwestern Republicans—opposed the "preparedness" effort, seeing it as simply a propaganda campaign to benefit businesses that made weapons and other military equipment. Some of them charged that Wilson was secretly plotting to get the nation into the war. A popular song in 1916 reflected such views: "I Didn't Raise My Boy to Be a Soldier."

Despite such opposition, Congress passed the National Defense Act in 1916, which provided for the expansion of the U.S. Army from 90,000 to 223,000 men over the next five years. While former secretary of state Bryan complained that Wilson wanted to "drag this nation into war," the reverse was actually true. Wilson told an aide that he was determined not to "be rushed into war, no matter if every damned congressman and senator stands up on his hind legs and proclaims me a coward."

Opponents of "preparedness" insisted that the financial burden of military expansion should rest upon the wealthy people who they believed were promoting it in order to profit from trade with the Allies. The income tax became their weapon. Backed by a groundswell of popular support, the Revenue Act of 1916 doubled the basic income tax rate from 1 to 2 percent, levied a 12.5 percent tax on munitions makers, and added a new tax

National Defense Act (1916) expands army

on "excessive" corporate profits. The new taxes were the capstone to the progressive legislation that Wilson supported in preparation for the upcoming presidential election.

The Election of 1916

As the 1916 election approached, Republicans hoped to reunify the party and regain the White House, and Theodore Roosevelt hoped to become their leader again. But he had committed the deadly political sin of abandoning his party to run as a Progressive in 1912. His eagerness for America to enter the European war also scared many voters. Needing a candidate who would draw Roosevelt progressives back into the fold, the Republicans turned to Supreme Court Justice Charles Evans Hughes, who had led New York as a progressive governor from 1907 to 1910.

The Democrats, staying with Wilson, adopted a platform that endorsed social-welfare legislation and prudent military preparedness. The peace theme, refined in the slogan "He kept us out of war," became the rallying cry of the Wilson campaign, although the president at the same time dismissed isolationism as outdated. The United States, he stressed, could no longer refuse to play the "great part in the world which was providentially cut out for her. . . . We have got to serve the world."

The candidates were remarkably similar. Both Wilson and Hughes were sons of preachers; both were attorneys and former professors; both had been progressive governors; both were known for their integrity. Roosevelt called the bearded Hughes a "whiskered Wilson." Wilson, however, proved to be the better campaigner—barely. By midnight on election night, Wilson went to bed assuming that he had lost. Roosevelt was so sure Hughes had won that he sent him a congratulatory telegram. At 4:00 A.M., however, the results from California were tallied, and Wilson had eked out a victory in that deciding state by only 4,000 votes, becoming the first Democrat to win a second consecutive term since Andrew Jackson in 1832.

America's Entry into the War

After his reelection, Wilson again urged the warring nations to stop fighting and negotiate a peace settlement, but to no avail. On January 31, 1917, desperate German military leaders announced the resumption of unrestricted submarine warfare in the Atlantic. All vessels from the United States headed for Britain, France, or Italy would be sunk without warning. "This was practically ordering the United States off the Atlantic," said an angry William McAdoo, Wilson's secretary of the treasury. "Freedom of the seas," said the *Brooklyn Eagle*, "will now be enjoyed [only] by icebergs and fish." The German decision, Colonel House wrote in his journal, left Wilson "sad and depressed," for the president knew it would mean war. For their part, the Germans greatly underestimated the American reaction. The United States, the German military newspaper proclaimed, "not only has no army, it has

---

> Wilson's reelection slogan: "He kept us out of war"

> Unrestricted submarine warfare, the Zimmermann telegram, and the U.S. declaration of war

Zimmermann telegram (1917) Message sent by a German official to the Mexican government urging an invasion of the United States; the telegram was intercepted by British intelligence agents and angered Americans, many of whom called for war against Germany.

no artillery, no means of transportation, no airplanes, and lacks all other instruments of modern warfare." When his advisers warned that German submarines might cause the United States to enter the war, Kaiser Wilhelm scoffed, "I don't care."

On February 3, President Wilson told a joint session of Congress that the United States had broken diplomatic relations with the German government. Three weeks later, on February 25, Wilson learned that the British had intercepted an important message from a German official, Arthur Zimmermann, to the Mexican government, urging the Mexicans to invade the United States. In exchange, Germany would give Mexico "lost territory in Texas, New Mexico, and Arizona." On March 1, news of the so-called **Zimmermann telegram** broke in the press, infuriating Americans and intensifying calls for war against the Germans, whose attacks on American vessels increased.

In March 1917, German submarines sank five U.S. ships in the North Atlantic. That was the last straw for President Wilson, who on April 2 asked Congress to declare war on Germany for its "cruel and unmanly" actions. He insisted that "the world must be made safe for democracy" and free from war. Wilson said the United States was entering the war, not so much to defend the nation or its honor as to lead a "great crusade" to end wars forever—an unattainable goal that would eventually lead to great disillusionment. For now, however, the Senate passed the war resolution by a vote of 82 to 6 on April 4. The House of Representatives followed, 373 to 50, and Wilson signed the measure on April 6.

Jeanette Rankin of Montana, the first woman elected to the House, was one of the members who voted against war. "You can no more win a war than you can win an earthquake," she explained. "I want to stand by my country, but I cannot vote for war." Wilson had doubts of his own. The president feared—accurately, as it turned out—that mobilizing the nation for war and stamping out dissent would destroy the ideals and momentum of progressivism: "Every reform we have made will be lost if we go into this war." Yet he saw no choice.

Mobilizing a Nation

In April 1917 the U.S. Army remained small and untested, armed with outdated weapons or none at all. With only 107,000 men, it was the seventeenth largest army in the world. Now the Wilson administration needed to recruit, equip, and train an army of millions and transport them across an ocean infested with German submarines. Mobilizing the nation for war led to an unprecedented expansion of federal government authority. The government drafted millions of men between the ages of 21 and 30 into the armed services, forced the conversion of industries and farms to wartime needs, took over the railroads, and in many other respects assumed control of national life.

CORE **OBJECTIVE**

2. Explain how the Wilson administration mobilized the home front, and analyze how mobilization efforts shaped American society.

Economic mobilization: The War Industries Board and the Food Administration

FOOD WILL WIN THE WAR
You came here seeking Freedom
You must now help to preserve it
WHEAT is needed for the allies
Waste nothing
UNITED STATES FOOD ADMINISTRATION

The immigrant effort This Food Administration poster emphasizes that "wheat is . . . for the allies," an important message to immigrants who hailed from Central Powers nations.

Soon after the U.S. declaration of war, President Wilson acknowledged that "it is not the army we must train and shape for war, it is a nation." He called for complete economic mobilization on the home front and created new federal agencies to coordinate this effort. The War Industries Board (WIB), established in 1917, soon became the most important of all the federal mobilization agencies. Bernard Baruch, a brilliant financier, headed the WIB, which had the authority to allocate raw materials, order construction of new factories, and set prices. Wilson appointed Republican Herbert Hoover, the celebrated engineer and business leader and future president, to head the new Food Administration, whose slogan was "Food will win the war." Its purpose was to increase agricultural production while reducing civilian food consumption, since Great Britain and France needed massive amounts of American corn and wheat. Hoover organized a huge group of volunteers who fanned out across the country to urge housewives and restaurants to participate in "Wheatless" Mondays, "Meatless" Tuesdays, and "Porkless" Thursdays and Saturdays.

Fighting in the Great War cost the U.S. government $30 billion, which was more than thirty times the entire federal budget in 1917. In addition to raising taxes to finance the war effort, the Wilson administration launched a campaign across the nation to sell "Liberty bonds," government securities in the form of paper certificates that guaranteed the purchaser a fixed rate of return. The government recruited dozens of celebrities to promote bond purchases, arguing that a Liberty bond was both a patriotic investment in the nation and a smart investment in one's own financial future. People who refused to buy bonds were branded as traitors. Even the Boy Scouts and Girl Scouts sold bonds, using advertising posters that said "Every Scout to Save a Soldier." By war's end, the government had sold over $20 billion in bonds, most of which were purchased by banks and investment houses rather than individuals.

A New Labor Force

Women's wartime work

Removing 4 million men from the workforce for service in the armed forces created an acute labor shortage across the United States during 1917. To meet it, women were encouraged to take jobs previously held mostly by men. One government poster shouted: "Women! Help America's Sons Win the War: Learn to Make Munitions." Another said, "For Every Fighter, a Woman Worker."

Initially, women had supported the war effort mostly in traditional ways. They helped organize fund-raising drives, donated canned food and war-related materials, volunteered for the Red Cross, and joined the army

At the munitions factory Women on both sides played crucial roles in the war effort, from building airplanes to cooking for soldiers overseas. Here, American women use welding torches to build bombs.

nurse corps. But as the scope of the war widened, both government and industry recruited women to work on farms, loading docks, and railway crews, as well as in the armaments industry, machine shops, steel and lumber mills, and chemical plants. "At last, after centuries of disabilities and discrimination," said a speaker at a Women's Trade Union League meeting in 1917, "women are coming into the labor [force] and festival of life on equal terms with men."

But the changes in female employment were limited and brief. About 1 million women participated in "war work," but most of them were young and single and already working outside the home, and most returned to their previous jobs once the war ended. In fact, male-dominated unions encouraged women to go back to domestic roles. The Central Federated Union of New York insisted that "the same patriotism which induced women to enter industry during the war should induce them to vacate their positions after the war."

The Great War also generated dramatic changes for many members of minority groups, both women and men. Hundreds of thousands of African American men joined or were drafted into the military, where they were required to serve in racially segregated units commanded by white officers, as in the Civil War half a century earlier. On the home front, northern businesses sent recruiting agents into the southern states, which were still largely rural and agricultural, to find workers for their factories and mills. For the first time, such efforts were directed at African Americans as well as whites. More than 400,000 southern blacks, mostly farmers, joined what came to be known as the **Great Migration** northward, a mass movement that would continue through the 1920s and change the political and social

Great Migration Mass exodus of African Americans from the rural South to the Northeast and Midwest during and after the Great War.

chemistry of northern cities such as St. Louis, Chicago, Detroit, New York, and Philadelphia. By 1930 the number of African Americans living in the North was triple that of 1910.

The Great Migration northward

Recruiting agents and newspaper editors, both black and white, portrayed the North as the "land of promise" for southern blacks suffering from their region's depressed agricultural economy and rising racial intimidation and violence. Northern factory jobs were plentiful and high-paying by southern standards, and racism was less obvious and violent—at least at first. A black migrant from Mississippi wrote home from Chicago in 1917 that he wished he had moved north twenty years earlier. "I just begin to feel like a man [here]," he explained. "It's a great deal of pleasure in knowing that you have some privilege. My children are going to the same school with the whites, and I don't have to be humble to no one."

Many Mexican Americans found similar opportunities to improve their status during the war and after. Some joined the military. David Barkley Hernandez had to drop his last name when he enlisted in San Antonio, Texas, because the local draft board was not accepting Mexicans. In 1918, just two days before the war ended, he died in France while returning from a dangerous mission behind German lines. Hernandez became the first person of Mexican descent in the U.S. Army to win the Congressional Medal of Honor.

Even more Latinos pursued economic opportunities created by the war effort. Between 1917 and 1920, some 100,000 Mexicans crossed the border into the United States. The economic expansion caused by the war enabled migrant farm workers already living in states such as Texas, New Mexico,

Segregation in the military Most black enlistees served in technical and supply units because whites believed them unfit for combat, despite black military contributions since the Revolution. Here, combat personnel of the 92nd (one of the few "colored" divisions sent overseas) march in Verdun, France.

Arizona, and California to take better jobs in factories and mills in rapidly growing cities such as Phoenix, Los Angeles, and Houston, where they moved into Spanish-speaking neighborhoods called *barrios*.

But the newcomers, whether Latinos or blacks, were often resented rather than welcomed. J. Luz Saenz, a Mexican American from Texas, noted in his diary that it took only three days after he was discharged from the army to have whites "throw us out from restaurants and deny us service as human beings." In 1917 more than forty African Americans and nine whites were killed during a riot in a weapons plant in East St. Louis, Illinois. Two years later, a Chicago race riot left twenty-three African Americans and fifteen whites dead.

A Loss of Civil Liberties

Once war was declared, patriotic emotions often took a negative turn, as Americans equated anything German with disloyalty. Many Americans quit drinking beer because most of the breweries were owned by German Americans. Symphonies refused to perform classical music by Bach and Beethoven, schools dropped German language classes, and patriots renamed *sauerkraut* as "liberty cabbage," *German measles* as "liberty measles," and *dachshunds* as "liberty pups." President Wilson had predicted as much. "Once [we] lead this people into war," he said, "they'll forget there ever was such a thing as tolerance." What Wilson did not say was that he himself would lead the effort to suppress civil liberties, for, as he claimed, subversive forces in a nation at war must be "crushed out."

The Espionage and Sedition Acts (1917–1918)

Under the Espionage and Sedition Acts, Congress outlawed criticism of government leaders and war policies. The Espionage Act of 1917 imposed penalties of up to $10,000 and twenty years in prison for anyone who gave aid to the enemy, tried to incite insubordination, disloyalty, or refusal of duty in the armed services, or tried to interfere with the war effort in other ways. To root out "vicious spies and conspirators," Wilson recruited 250,000 informers—the American Protective League—to turn in those suspected of treason. He was convinced that newly arrived immigrants had "poured the poison of disloyalty into the very arteries of our national life."

During the war, 1,055 people were convicted under the Espionage Act, not one of whom was a spy. Most of them were simply critics of the war. The Socialist leader Eugene V. Debs, a militant pacifist, was convicted under the Espionage Act simply for opposing the war and was sentenced to ten years in prison. He told the court he would always criticize wars imposed by the "master" class: "While there is a lower class, I am in it. While there is a criminal element, I am of it. While there is a soul in prison, I am not free."

Keep out of it In this 1918 war poster, the Kaiser—with his famous moustache and spiked German helmet—is characterized as a spider, spinning an invisible web to catch the stray words of Allied civilians.

The Sedition Act of 1918 extended the penalties to those who did or said anything to obstruct government sales of war bonds or to advocate cutbacks in production, and—in case something had been overlooked—for saying, writing, or printing anything "disloyal, profane, scurrilous, or abusive" about the American form of government, the Constitution, or the army and navy.

In two important decisions just after the war, the Supreme Court upheld the Espionage and Sedition Acts. *Schenck v. United States* (1919) reaffirmed the conviction of Charles T. Schenck, the head of the Socialist party, for circulating anti-draft leaflets among members of the armed forces. Justice Oliver Wendell Holmes wrote the unanimous court opinion that freedom of speech did not apply to words that represented "a clear and present danger to the safety of the country." In *Abrams v. United States* (1919), the Court upheld the conviction of a man who had distributed pamphlets opposing American military intervention in Russia to remove the Bolsheviks who had seized power in 1917. Here, justices Holmes and Brandeis dissented from the majority view. The "surreptitious publishing of a silly leaflet by an unknown man," they argued, posed no danger to government policy.

The American Role in Fighting the War

CORE OBJECTIVE

3. Describe the major events of the war after U.S. entry, and explain the U.S. contribution to the defeat of the Central Powers.

In 1917, America's war strategy focused on helping the struggling French and British armies on the Western Front. The Allied leaders stressed that they needed at least a million American troops (called "doughboys") to defeat the Germans, but it would take months to recruit, equip, and train that many new soldiers. On December 21, 1917, French premier Georges Clemenceau urged the Americans to rush their army, called the American Expeditionary Force, to France. "A terrible blow is imminent," he told an American journalist about to leave Paris. "Tell your Americans to come quickly." Clemenceau was referring to the likelihood of a massive German attack, made more probable by the end of the fighting on the Eastern Front following the Bolshevik Revolution in Russia in November 1917.

The Bolshevik Revolution

Communist revolution in Russia

Among the many casualties of the Great War, none was greater in scale than the destruction of the Russian Empire and its monarchy. On March 15, 1917, bumbling Tsar Nicholas II, having presided over terrible losses in a war that also ruined the Russian economy, had turned the nation over to the "Provisional Government" of a new Russian republic committed to continuing the war. The fall of the tsar gave Americans the illusion that all the major Allied powers were now fighting for the ideals of constitutional democracy—an illusion that was shattered after the Germans in April helped exiled radical Vladimir Lenin return to Russia from Switzerland in a secret, sealed train, hoping that he would cause turmoil in his homeland. He did much more than that.

As Lenin observed, power in war-weary Russia was lying in the streets, waiting to be picked up. To do so, Lenin mobilized the Bolsheviks, a determined group of Communist revolutionaries, who during the night of November 6–7 seized power from the Provisional Government, established a dictatorship and called for a quick end to the European war. Lenin banned both political parties and organized religions (atheism became the official belief), eliminated civil liberties and the free press, and killed or imprisoned opposition leaders, including the tsar and his family. The Bolshevik Revolution triggered a prolonged civil war throughout Russia in which the United States and its allies worked to overthrow the Communists. Wilson sent 20,000 American soldiers to Siberia to support the anti-Communist Russian forces, an effort that proved unsuccessful.

Lenin declared that the world would be freed from war only by a global revolution in which capitalism was replaced by communism. To that end, he wanted to get Russia out of the Great War as soon as possible. On March 3, 1918, Lenin signed a humiliating peace agreement with Germany, the Treaty of Brest-Litovsk. The treaty forced Russia to transfer vast territories to Germany and its ally Turkey and to recognize the independence of the Ukraine region. In addition, Russia had to pay $46 million to Germany. Lenin was willing to accept such a harsh peace because he needed to concentrate on his many internal enemies in the civil war.

Vladimir Lenin Russian communist revolutionary who led the Bolsheviks in overthrowing the monarchy and ultimately established the Soviet Union.

Crucial U.S. Contribution on the Western Front

Less than three weeks later, on March 21, the Germans, now reinforced by units from the Eastern Front made available by Russia leaving the war, began the first of several spring offensives in France and Belgium designed to win the war before the Americans arrived in force. By May, the German armies had advanced to the Marne River, within fifty miles of Paris. That was as far as they got, for in June, at the month-long Battle of Belleau Wood, U.S. forces commanded by General John J. Pershing joined the French in driving the Germans back. During the ferocious fighting, a French officer urged an American unit to retreat. In a famous exchange, U.S. Marine Captain Lloyd W. Williams refused the order, saying: "Retreat? Hell, we just got here."

The crucial American role in the fighting occurred in a great Allied offensive, begun on September 26, 1918. With the French commander urging "everyone to battle," the American troops joined British and French armies in a drive toward Sedan, France, and its strategic railroad, which supplied

American forces help repel the Germans in 1918

Meuse-Argonne Offensive
American soldiers of the 23rd Infantry, 2nd Division, fire machine guns at the Germans from what was left of the Argonne Forest in France.

the German army. With 1.2 million U.S. soldiers involved, including some 200,000 African Americans, it was the largest American action of the war, and it resulted in 117,000 U.S. casualties, including 26,000 dead. But along the entire French-Belgian front, the outnumbered Germans were in desperate retreat eastward across Belgium during the early fall of 1918. "America," wrote German General Erich Ludendorff, "became the decisive power in the war."

The End of the War

Wilson's Fourteen Points

Woodrow Wilson was determined to ensure that the Great War would be the last world war. During 1917, he appointed a group of American experts, called the Inquiry, to draft a peace plan. With their advice, Wilson developed what would come to be called the **Fourteen Points**, which he presented to a joint session of Congress on January 8, 1918, "as the only possible program" for peace. The first five points called for the open conduct of diplomacy, the recognition of neutral nations' right to continue maritime commerce in time of war ("freedom of the seas"), the removal of international trade barriers, the reduction of armaments, and the transformation of colonial empires.

Fourteen Points (1918)
President Woodrow Wilson's proposed plan for the peace agreement after the Great War that included the creation of a "league of nations" intended to keep the peace.

Most of the remaining points dealt with territorial claims: they called on the Central Powers to evacuate occupied lands and follow the difficult principle of "self-determination," allowing overlapping nationalities and ethnic groups to develop their own independent nations. Point 13 called for

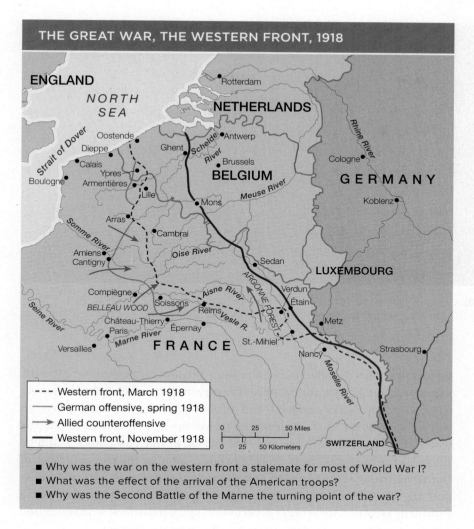

THE GREAT WAR, THE WESTERN FRONT, 1918

- --- Western front, March 1918
- —— German offensive, spring 1918
- ——▶ Allied counteroffensive
- —— Western front, November 1918

0   25   50 Miles
0   25   50 Kilometers

■ Why was the war on the western front a stalemate for most of World War I?
■ What was the effect of the arrival of the American troops?
■ Why was the Second Battle of the Marne the turning point of the war?

a new nation for the Poles, a people long dominated by the Russians on the east and the Germans on the west. Point 14, the capstone of Wilson's postwar scheme, called for the creation of a "league" of nations to preserve global peace. When the Fourteen Points were made public, African American leaders asked the president to add a fifteenth point: an end to racial discrimination. Wilson did not respond.

On October 3, 1918, a new German chancellor telegraphed President Wilson, asking for an end to the fighting on the basis of the Fourteen Points. British and French leaders accepted the Fourteen Points as a basis of negotiations, but with two significant reservations: the British insisted on the right to discuss limiting freedom of the seas, and the French demanded reparations (payments) from Germany and Austria for war damages.

Meanwhile, by the end of October 1918, Germany was on the verge of collapse. Revolutionaries rampaged through the streets. Sailors mutinied.

Armistice Night in New York **(1918)** George Luks, known for his vivid paintings of urban life, captured the unbridled outpouring of patriotism and joy that extended into the night of Germany's surrender.

Germany's allies dropped out of the war: Bulgaria on September 29, 1918, Turkey on October 30, and Austria-Hungary on November 3. On November 9, the German Kaiser resigned, and a republic was proclaimed. Then, on November 11 at 5:00 A.M., an armistice (cease-fire agreement) was signed by which the Germans were assured that Wilson's Fourteen Points would be the basis for the peace conference. Six hours later, at the eleventh hour of the eleventh day of the eleventh month, and after 1,563 days of terrible warfare, the guns fell silent. From Europe, Colonel House sent a telegram to President Wilson: "Autocracy [government by an individual with unlimited power] is dead; long live democracy and its immortal leader."

Cease-fire and celebrations

The end of fighting led to wild celebrations throughout the world as fear and grief gave way to hope. "The nightmare is over," wrote African American activist W. E. B. Du Bois. "The world awakes. The long, horrible years of dreadful night are passed. Behold the sun!" Wilson was not as joyful. The Great War, he said, had dealt a grievous injury to civilization "which can never be atoned for or repaired."

During its nineteen months in the Great War, the United States had lost 53,000 servicemen in combat. Another 63,000 died of various diseases, especially the influenza epidemic that swept through Europe and around the world in 1918. Germany's war dead totaled more than 2 million, including civilians; France lost nearly 1.4 million combatants, Great Britain 703,000, and Russia 1.7 million. The new Europe would be very different from the prewar version: much poorer, more violent, more polarized, more cynical, less sure of itself, and less capable of decisive action. The United States, for good or ill, emerged from the war as the world's dominant power.

The Fight for the Peace

In the making of a peace agreement, Woodrow Wilson showed himself both at his best and worst. His Fourteen Point peace program embodied his vision of a better world governed by fairer principles. For a glorious moment at the end of 1918, Wilson was the world's self-appointed prophet of peace. He felt guided "by the hand of God." Wilson's godlike vision of creating a peacekeeping "League of Nations" promised that henceforth all nations would live in harmony. If the diplomats gathering to draft the peace treaty failed to follow his ambitious plans to reshape the world in America's image, he warned, "there will be another world war" within a generation.

> CORE **OBJECTIVE**
> **4.** Evaluate Wilson's efforts to promote his plans for a peaceful world order as outlined in his Fourteen Points.

Wilson's Key Errors

Whatever the merits of Wilson's peace plan, his efforts to implement it proved clumsy. He made several key decisions at the war's end that would come back to haunt him. First, against the advice of his staff and of European leaders, he decided to attend the peace conference in Paris that opened on January 18, 1919. Never before had an American president visited Europe or left the nation for such a prolonged period (six months). During his months abroad, Wilson lost touch with political developments at home.

Second, in the congressional elections of November 1918, Wilson defied his advisers as well as political tradition by urging voters to elect a Democratic Congress to support his policies. Prior to that time, presidents had remained neutral during congressional elections. Republicans, who for the most part had backed Wilson's war measures, were not pleased. Nor were voters. In the elections, the Democrats lost control of both houses of Congress.

> Wilson's mistakes: Prolonged absence in Europe, disregard for Republicans at home, self-image as messiah of peace

Wilson further weakened support for his peacemaking when, in a deliberate slight, he refused to appoint Senator Henry Cabot Lodge, his arch-enemy and the leading Republican in Congress, to the American delegation to the peace conference. As chairman of the Foreign Relations Committee, Lodge was the most appropriate senator to accompany Wilson to Paris, but the president instead appointed an ineffectual Republican to join the delegation. Former president William Howard Taft groused that Wilson's real intention in going to Paris was "to hog the whole show." He almost did.

When Wilson reached Europe in December 1918, the cheering crowds in London, Paris, and Rome verged on hysteria. Millions of grateful Europeans greeted him as a hero, even a savior. An Italian mayor described Wilson's visit as the "second coming of Christ." Others hailed him as the "God of peace." Wilson privately admitted that he was now "at the apex of my glory in the hearts of these people." From such a height, there could only be a fall. Although popular with the European people, Wilson had to deal at the

peace conference with tough-minded European statesmen who shared neither his lofty goals nor his American ideals. In fact, they resented his efforts to forge a peace settlement modeled on American values. In the end, the European leaders would force him to abandon many of his objectives and become a horse trader—not a messiah.

The Paris Peace Conference

The Paris Peace Conference lasted from January to June 1919. The participants had no time to waste. The German, Austro-Hungarian, and Ottoman empires were in ruins. Across much of the European continent, food was scarce and lawlessness flourished. The threat of revolution hung over central Europe as Communists in the defeated nations threatened to take control. As the most significant world event of the era, the peace conference dealt with immensely complex and controversial issues (including creating new nations, such as Yugoslavia and Iraq, and redrawing the maps of Europe and the Middle East) that required both political statesmanship and technical expertise. The British delegation alone included almost 400 members, many of them specialists in political geography or economics. The peacemakers met daily, debating, arguing, and compromising.

The Big Four: Wilsonian idealism vs. European realism

From the start, the Paris Peace Conference was controlled by the Big Four who met 140 times: the prime ministers of Britain, France, and Italy and the president of the United States. The seventy-seven-year-old French premier Georges Clemenceau, known as "The Tiger," was a stern realist who had little patience with President Wilson's preaching. In response to Wilson's declaration that "America is the only idealistic nation in the world,"

Clemenceau grumbled that talking with the American leader was like talking to Jesus Christ. "God gave us the Ten Commandments and we broke them," the French leader sneered. "Wilson gave us the Fourteen Points—we shall see." The Big Four fought not only in private but in public as well. The French and the British, led by Prime Minister David Lloyd George, insisted that Wilson agree to their harsh provisions to weaken Germany, while Vittorio Orlando, prime minister of Italy, focused on gaining territories from defeated Austria.

Wilson, suffering from poor health, lectured them all about the need to craft a peace treaty without revenge and to embrace his beloved **League of Nations**, which he insisted must be the "keystone" of any peace settlement. Whatever compromises he might have to make and whatever mistakes might result, Wilson believed that a world peace organization would abolish war. Article X of the League of Nations charter, which Wilson called "the heart of the League," pledged member nations to impose military and economic sanctions, or penalties, against those that engaged in military aggression. The League, Wilson assumed, would exercise enormous moral influence, making military action unnecessary. These unrealistic expectations became, for Wilson, a self-defeating crusade.

On February 14, 1919, Wilson presented the finished draft of the League covenant to the Allies and left Paris for a visit home, where he faced opposition among Republicans. The League of Nations, Theodore Roosevelt complained, would revive German militarism and undermine American morale. "To substitute internationalism for nationalism," Roosevelt argued, "means to do away with patriotism." His close friend Henry Cabot Lodge, chairman of the Senate Foreign Relations Committee, also scorned Wilson and his idealism. He told Roosevelt, "I never expected to hate anyone in politics with the hatred I feel toward Wilson." Lodge dismissed the League of Nations proposed in the treaty because, he claimed, it would allow the League to involve the U.S. military in foreign conflicts without Senate approval.

The Treaty of Versailles

Back in Paris in the spring of 1919, Wilson had lost his leverage with the British and French because it was increasingly uncertain that the U.S. Senate would approve any treaty he endorsed. Wilson also gave in on many controversial issues solely to ensure that the Europeans would approve his League of Nations. In Paris, Wilson yielded to French demands that Germany transfer vast territories to France on its west and to Poland on its east and north. In other territorial matters, Wilson had to abandon his lofty but impractical and ill-defined principle of national self-determination, whereby every ethnic group would be allowed to form its own nation. As Secretary of State Robert Lansing correctly predicted, trying to allow each ethnic group in Europe to determine its own fate "will raise hopes which can never be realized." (Wilson himself later told the Senate that he wished he had never said that "all nations have a right to self-determination.")

League of Nations Organization of nations formed in the aftermath of the Great War to mediate disputes and maintain international peace; despite President Wilson's intense lobbying for the League of Nations, Congress did not ratify the Versailles treaty and the United States failed to join.

In their efforts to allow for at least some degree of ethnic self-determination in multiethnic regions, the diplomats at Versailles created the independent countries of Austria, Hungary, Poland, Yugoslavia, and Czechoslovakia in central Europe and four new nations along the Baltic Sea: Finland, Estonia, Lithuania, and Latvia. But the victorious Allies did not create independent nations out of the colonies of the defeated and now defunct European empires. Instead, they assigned the former German colonies in Africa and the Turkish colonies in the Middle East to France and Great Britain to govern while the colonies prepared themselves for independence at some undesignated point in the future, while Japan took control of the former German colonies in east Asia.

The discussion of reparations triggered especially bitter arguments among the diplomats in Paris. The British and the French (on whose soil much of the war was fought) wanted Germany to pay the entire financial cost of the war, including their veterans' pensions. On this point, Wilson made perhaps his most fateful concessions. He agreed to a clause in the peace treaty by which Germany was forced to accept responsibility for the war and its entire expense. The "war guilt" clause, written by the young American John Foster Dulles, a future secretary of state, so offended Germans that it became a major factor in the rise of the Nazi party during the 1920s. Wilson himself privately admitted that if he were a German he would refuse to sign the treaty.

> The Treaty of Versailles: Wilson's concessions on territory, reparations, and "war guilt"

On May 7, 1919, the victorious powers presented the treaty to the German delegates, who returned three weeks later with 443 pages of criticism. A few changes were made, but when the Germans still refused to sign, the French threatened to launch a new military attack. Finally, on June 28, the Germans gave up and signed the treaty in the glittering Hall of Mirrors at Versailles, the magnificent palace built by King Louis XIV in the late seventeenth century. Thereafter, it was called the **Treaty of Versailles**. When Adolf Hitler, a young German soldier, learned of the treaty's provisions, he vowed revenge. "It cannot be that two million Germans have fallen in vain," he screamed during a speech in Munich in 1922. "We demand vengeance!" Wilson and the Allies were better at winning the war than making a lasting peace.

The Debate over Treaty Ratification

On July 8, 1919, Wilson returned home to advocate the approval of the treaty by the U.S. Senate, where the Republicans now outnumbered his Democrats. Before leaving Paris, he assured a French diplomat that he would not allow any changes to the treaty. "I shall consent to nothing," he vowed. "The Senate must take its medicine." Thus began one of the most brutally partisan and bitterly personal disputes in American political history. There was only one nation strong enough to reject Wilson's dream of a League of Nations: the United States.

On July 10, Wilson became the first president to enter the Senate and deliver a treaty to be voted on. He called upon senators to accept their "great

Treaty of Versailles (1919) Peace treaty that ended the Great War, forcing Germany to dismantle its military, pay immense war reparations, and give up its colonies around the world.

EUROPE AFTER THE TREATY OF VERSAILLES, 1918

- - - - - - 1914 boundaries
New nations
Plebiscite areas
Occupied area

0   250   500 Miles
0   250   500 Kilometers

■ Why was self-determination so difficult to apply in Central Europe?
■ How did territorial concessions weaken Germany?

The U.S. Senate debate over the Treaty of Versailles

duty" and ratify the treaty, which had been guided "by the hand of God." Wilson then grew needlessly confrontational. He dismissed critics of the League of Nations as "blind and little provincial people." The whole world, Wilson claimed, was relying on the United States to sign the Versailles Treaty: "Dare we reject it and break the heart of the world?"

Yes, answered Senate Republicans who had decided that Wilson's commitment to the League was a reckless threat to America's independence. Henry Cabot Lodge denounced the treaty's "scheme of making mankind suddenly virtuous by a statute or a written constitution." Lodge's strategy was to stall approval of the treaty in hopes that public opposition to the president would grow. He took six weeks simply reading aloud the lengthy text of it to his Foreign Relations committee. He then organized a parade of expert witnesses, most of them opposed to the treaty, to appear at the committee's hearings on ratification.

In the Senate, a group of "irreconcilables," fourteen Republicans and two Democrats, refused to support U.S. membership in the League. They were mainly western and midwestern progressives, isolationists who feared that such sweeping foreign commitments would threaten domestic reforms. The irreconcilables would prove useful to Lodge's efforts to defeat the treaty, but he himself belonged to a larger group called the "reservationists," who insisted upon limiting American participation in the League in exchange for approving the treaty. The only way to get Senate approval was for Wilson to meet with Lodge and others and agree to revisions, the most important of which was the requirement that Congress authorize any American participation in a League-approved war.

As Republican senator Frank B. Kellogg of Minnesota noted, the proposed changes were crafted not by enemies of the treaty but by friends who wanted to save it. Republican senator James Watson of Indiana told Wilson that he had no choice but to accept some revisions: "Mr. President, you are licked. There is only one way you can take the United States into the League of Nations." The inflexible president, who assumed that his opponents were not just misguided but morally wrong, lashed back: "Lodge's reservations? Never!" Wilson was incapable of compromising with Lodge. He refused to negotiate or compromise, declaring that "if the Treaty is not ratified by the Senate, the War will have been fought in vain."

Wilson takes treaty to the American people

In September 1919, facing defeat after a summer of fruitless debate, an exhausted Wilson decided to bypass his Senate opponents by speaking directly to voters. On September 2, against his doctor's orders and his wife's advice, he left Washington for a grueling transcontinental railroad tour through the Midwest to the West Coast, intending to visit 29 cities. No president had ever made such a strenuous effort to win over public support. In St. Louis, Wilson said that he had returned from Paris "bringing one of the greatest documents of human history," which was now in danger of being rejected by the Senate. He pledged to "fight for a cause . . . greater than the Senate. It is greater than the government. It is as great as the cause of mankind, and I intend, in office or out, to fight that battle as long as I live."

Onward through Nebraska, South Dakota, Minnesota, North Dakota, Montana, Idaho, and Washington, Wilson traveled and spoke, sometimes as many as four times a day, despite suffering from pounding headaches. It did not help his morale to learn that his secretary of state, Robert Lansing, had said that the League of Nations was "entirely useless." By the time Wilson's train reached Spokane, Washington, the president was visibly fatigued. But he kept going, heading south through Oregon and California. Some 200,000 people greeted him in Los Angeles. In all, he had covered 10,000 miles in twenty-two days and given thirty-two major speeches.

Physical Breakdown and Political Failure

Then disaster struck. After delivering an emotional speech on September 25 in Pueblo, Colorado, Wilson collapsed from his headaches and had to admit that he could not finish the trip ("I am going to pieces"). With tears rolling down his cheeks as he looked out the train's window, he told his doctor that he had suffered the "greatest disappointment of [his] life." Back in

Washington, D.C., a week later, the president suffered a crushing stroke (cerebral hemorrhage) that almost killed him. The episode left him paralyzed on his left side; he could barely speak or see. Only his secretary, his doctor, and his wife, Edith, knew his true condition. For five months, Wilson lay flat on his back while his doctor issued reassuring medical bulletins to reporters. If a document needed Wilson's signature, his wife guided his trembling hand. Secretary of State Lansing urged the president's aides to declare him disabled and appoint the vice president in his place; they angrily refused. "I hate Lansing," Edith Wilson told Secretary of the Navy Josephus Daniels. Soon thereafter, Lansing was replaced.

The stroke made Wilson even more arrogant and stubborn. He became emotionally unstable, at times crying uncontrollably and behaving oddly. For the remaining seventeen months of his term, his protective wife, along with aides and trusted cabinet members, kept him isolated from all but the most essential business. When a group of Republican senators visited the White House, one of them said, "Well, Mr. President, we have all been praying for you." Wilson replied, "Which way, Senator?"

> Wilson's stroke and the treaty's defeat

Such presidential humor was rare, however. Wilson's hardened arteries seemed to have hardened his political judgment as well. His outspoken wife reinforced his prejudices, calling Lodge a "stinking snake." For his part, Lodge pushed through the Senate fourteen changes (the number was not coincidental) in the draft of the Versailles Treaty. Wilson rejected the proposed changes, and as a result, his supporters in the Senate were thrown into an unlikely alliance with the irreconcilables, who opposed the treaty under any circumstances. The Senate vote on Lodge's revised treaty was 39 for and 55 against. On the question of approving the original treaty without changes, the irreconcilables and the reservationists, led by Lodge, combined to defeat ratification again, with 38 for and 53 against. Lodge said that if the president "had been a true idealist, in regard to the covenant of the League of Nations, he would have . . . secured its adoption by the Senate of the United States by accepting some modification of its terms."

Woodrow Wilson's grand effort at global peacemaking had failed miserably. After refusing to ratify the treaty, Congress tried to declare an official end to American involvement in the war by a joint resolution on May 20, 1920, which Wilson vetoed in a fit of spite. It was not until July 2, 1921, four months after he had left office and almost eighteen months after the fighting had stopped, that another joint resolution ended the state of war with Germany and Austria-Hungary. Separate peace treaties with Germany, Austria, and Hungary were ratified on October 18, 1921, but by then Warren G. Harding was president of the United States.

The failure of the United States to ratify the Versailles Treaty and exercise strong world leadership would have long-range consequences. With Great Britain and France too exhausted and too timid to keep Germany weak and isolated, a dangerous power vacuum would emerge in Europe during the 1920s which Adolf Hitler and the Nazis would fill.

CORE **OBJECTIVE**
5. Analyze the consequences of the war at home and abroad.

Lurching from War to Peace

The Versailles Treaty, for all the time the Senate spent on it, was but one of many issues demanding attention in the turbulent period after the war. The year 1919 began with joyous victory parades and congressional approval of women's suffrage, but celebration soon gave way to widespread labor unrest, socialist and Communist radicalism, race riots, terrorist bombings, and government crackdowns. With millions of servicemen returning to civilian life, war-related industries shutting down, and wartime price controls ending, unemployment and prices for consumer goods spiked. President Wilson's leadership was missing during the postwar crisis. Bedridden by his stroke, the president became increasingly grim, distant, and depressed. Wilson, observed David Lloyd George, the British prime minister, was "as much a victim of the war as any soldier who died in the trenches."

The Spanish Flu

Beginning in 1918, many Americans confronted an infectious enemy that produced far more casualties than the war itself. It became known as the Spanish flu (although its geographic origins are debated), and its contagion spread around the globe, transformed modern medicine, and altered the course of world history. The disease appeared suddenly in the spring of 1918, and its initial outbreak lasted a year and killed millions of people worldwide, twice as many as died in the war. In the United States alone it accounted for 675,000 deaths, over ten times the number of U.S. combat deaths in France. A fifth of the nation's population caught the flu, so many that the public health system was strained to the breaking point. Hospitals ran out of beds, and funeral homes ran out of coffins. By the spring of 1919, the pandemic had finally run its course, ending as suddenly—and as inexplicably—as it had begun. Although another outbreak occurred in the winter of 1920, people had grown more resistant to it. No disease in human history had killed so many people, and no war, famine, or natural catastrophe had killed so many people in such a short time.

Suffrage at Last

Women's suffrage: Ratification of the Nineteenth Amendment

As the first outbreak of the Spanish flu was ending, American women finally gained a Constitutional guarantee of their right to vote. After six months of delay, debate, and failed votes, Congress finally passed the **Nineteenth Amendment** in the spring of 1919 and sent it to the states for ratification. Tennessee's legislature was the last of thirty-six state assemblies to approve the amendment, and it did so in dramatic fashion. The initial vote was 48–48. Then a twenty-four-year-old Republican legislator named Harry T. Burn changed his vote to yes at the insistence of

Nineteenth Amendment (1920)
Constitutional amendment that granted women the right to vote.

his mother. The Nineteenth Amendment became official on August 18, 1920, making the United States the twenty-second nation in the world to allow women's suffrage. It was a climactic achievement of the Progressive Era. Suddenly, 9.5 million women were eligible to vote in national elections; in the 1920 presidential election, they would make up 40 percent of the electorate.

Their first votes Women of New York City's East Side vote for the first time in the presidential election of 1920.

The Economic Transition

As consumer prices continued to rise, discontented workers, released from wartime controls on wages, grew more willing to go out on strike for their demands. In 1919, more than 4 million hourly wage workers, 20 percent of the total in the U.S. workforce, participated in 3,600 strikes against management. Most of them wanted nothing more than higher wages and shorter workweeks, but their critics linked striking workers with the worldwide Communist movement. After a general strike in Seattle, the mayor, Ole Hanson, claimed the strikers were seeking a "revolution" under Bolshevik influence, and a Seattle newspaper declared that "this is America—not Russia." Such charges of a Communist conspiracy were greatly exaggerated. In 1919, fewer than 70,000 Americans nationwide belonged to the Communist party. The Seattle strike lasted only five days, but public resentment of the strikers damaged the cause and image of unions across the country.

> A surge of labor strikes and public reaction against them

The most controversial postwar labor dispute was in Boston, where most of the police went on strike on September 9, 1919. Massachusetts governor Calvin Coolidge was furious and mobilized the National Guard. After four days, the striking policemen offered to return, but instead they were all fired. When labor leaders appealed for their reinstatement, Coolidge responded in words that made him an instant national hero: "There is no right to strike against the public safety by anybody, anywhere, any time."

Racial Friction

The summer of 1919 also sparked a wave of deadly race riots across the nation. As more and more African Americans, including many of the 367,000 who were war veterans, moved out of the rural South to different parts of the country, developed successful careers, and asserted their civil

> "Red Summer" of race riots

Safe, briefly Escorted by a police officer, an African American family moves its belongings from their home, likely destroyed by white rioters, and into a protected area of Chicago.

rights in the face of deeply embedded segregationist practices, resentful whites reacted with an almost hysterical racism. One newspaper headline accused civil rights activists of being guided by Communists: "REDS TRY TO STIR NEGROES TO REVOLT!"

What African American leader James Weldon Johnson called the Red Summer (*red* signifying blood) began in July, when a mob of whites invaded the black neighborhood in Longview, Texas, angry over rumors of interracial dating. They burned shops and houses and ran several African Americans out of town. A week later, in Washington, D.C., exaggerated or even false reports of black assaults on white women stirred up white mobs, and gangs of white and black rioters waged a race war in the streets until soldiers and driving rains ended the fighting. The worst was yet to come. In late July, 38 people were killed and 537 injured in five days of race rioting in Chicago, where some 50,000 blacks, mostly from the rural South, had moved during the war, leading to tensions with local whites over jobs and housing. White unionized workers especially resented blacks who were hired as strikebreakers. Altogether, twenty-five race riots erupted in 1919, and there were eighty lynchings of African Americans, eleven of them war veterans.

The Red Scare

The Red Scare

With so much of the public convinced that the strikes and riots were inspired by Communists and anarchists (two very different groups who shared a hatred for capitalism), a New York journalist reported that Americans were "shivering in their boots over Bolshevism, and they are far more scared of Lenin than they ever were of the [German] Kaiser. We seem to be the most frightened victors the world ever saw." Fears of revolution in America were fueled by the violent actions of a few scattered militants. In early 1919, the Secret Service discovered a plot by Spanish anarchists to kill President Wilson and other government officials. In April 1919, postal workers intercepted nearly forty homemade mail bombs addressed to government officials. One slipped through and blew off the hands of a Georgia senator's maid. In June another bomb destroyed the front of U.S. Attorney General A. Mitchell Palmer's house in Washington, D.C. Palmer, who had ambitions to succeed Wilson as president, concluded that a "Red Menace," a Communist "blaze of revolution," was "sweeping over every American institution of law and order." In August 1919, Palmer appointed a twenty-four-year-old attorney named J. Edgar Hoover to lead a new government division created to collect information on radicals. Hoover and others in the Justice Department worked with a network of 250,000 informers in 600 cities, all of them members of the American Protective League, which was founded during the war to root out "traitors" and labor radicals.

On November 7, 1919, while Wilson lay incapacitated in the White House, federal agents rounded up 450 alien "radicals," most of whom were recent, law-abiding Russian immigrants looking for work. All were deported to Russia without a court hearing. On January 2, 1920, police raids in dozens of cities swept up 5,000 more suspects, many taken from their homes without arrest warrants.

What came to be called the **First Red Scare** (after another outbreak of anti-Communist hysteria occurred in the 1950s) represented one of the largest violations of civil liberties in American history. In 1919, novelist Katharine Fullerton Gerould announced in *Harper's Magazine* that, as a result of the government crackdown, America "is no longer a free country in the old sense." Civil liberties that had long been protected were being violated with abandon.

J. Edgar Hoover Fresh out of law school, Hoover joined the Justice Department and rose the ranks to become the first director of the FBI.

Panic about possible foreign terrorists erupted in communities across the nation as vigilantes took matters into their own hands. At a patriotic pageant in Washington, D.C., a sailor shot a spectator who refused to rise for "The Star-Spangled Banner"; the crowd cheered. In Hammond, Indiana, a jury took only two minutes to acquit a man who had murdered an immigrant for yelling "To hell with the U.S." In Waterbury, Connecticut, a salesman was sentenced to six months in jail for saying that Vladimir Lenin was "one of the brainiest" of the world's leaders.

By the summer of 1920, the Red Scare had begun to subside. Although Attorney General Palmer kept predicting more foreign-inspired terrorism, it never came. Bombings tapered off; the wave of strikes and race riots receded. By September 1920, when a bomb at the corner of Broad and Wall Streets in New York City killed thirty-eight people, Americans were ready to take it for what it was: the work of a crazed mind and not the start of a revolution. The Red Scare nonetheless left a lasting mark on American life. It strengthened the conservative crusade for "100 percent Americanism" and new restrictions on immigration.

Effects of the Great War

The extraordinary turbulence in 1919 and 1920 was an unmistakable indication of how the Great War had changed the shape of modern history: the world war was a turning point after which little was the same. It had destroyed old Europe—not only many of its cities, people, empires, and

First Red Scare Outbreak of anti-Communist hysteria that included the arrest without warrants of thousands of suspected radicals, most of whom (especially Russian immigrants) were deported.

The Great War

The Great War had a profound impact on the United States. Among other things, it significantly changed the nation's relationship with the rest of the world, the scale and scope of government involvement in the economy and society, the geographical and racial demographics of the population, the economic and political roles of women, and public attitudes toward the labor movement, African Americans, and immigrants. As you review the following list of facts, consider how participation in the war affected the role of the federal government in the United States; the position of women, African Americans, and immigrant communities in American society; and Americans' perceptions of themselves and their role in the world.

EFFECTS OF THE GREAT WAR ON THE UNITED STATES

FACT 1	FACT 2	FACT 3	FACT 4
The United States participated in a European war for the first time.	Millions of men were drafted into the military.	Industries and farms were converted to serve wartime needs through new federal agencies such as the War Industries Board and the Food Administration.	The Espionage and Sedition Acts severely curbed freedom of speech, making it a crime to speak out against American participation in the war or policies supporting the war effort.

FACT 5	FACT 6
Four hundred thousand African Americans migrated from the South to urban industrial centers in the North. Their arrival sparked racial tensions that often resulted in riots, particularly during the Red Summer of 1919. More African Americans would migrate in the next decade.	One million women participated in types of "war work" that had traditionally been reserved for men, particularly in industry. Most were young and single and, when the war ended, returned to previous jobs more commonly held by women at that time.

economies, but also its self-image as the admired center of civilized Western culture. Winston Churchill, the future British prime minister, called postwar Europe "a crippled, broken world." Peace did not bring stability; the trauma of the war lingered long after the shooting stopped. Most Germans and Austrians believed they were the victims of a harsh peace, and many wanted revenge, especially a hate-filled German war veteran named Adolf Hitler. At the same time, the war had hastened the already simmering Bolshevik Revolution that caused Russia to exit the war and abandon its western European allies and, in 1922, to reemerge on the world stage as the Union of Soviet Socialist Republics (USSR). Thereafter, Soviet communism would be one of the most powerful forces shaping the twentieth century.

FACT 7

Congress passed and President Wilson approved the Nineteenth Amendment to the Constitution, which gave women the right to vote. With the ratification of enough states, the amendment went into effect in time for the 1920 election.

FACT 8

To negotiate the Treaty of Versailles that officially ended the war, Wilson became the first president to travel overseas for a prolonged period while in office. At the Paris Peace Conference, he was unable to achieve many of his most important goals. Although the victorious Allies agreed to form a League of Nations, they imposed harsh reparations on Germany, stirring resentment in the defeated nation that would feed the growth of Nazism.

FACT 9

The U.S. Senate refused to ratify the Treaty of Versailles; and the United States, clearly the world's leading economic and military power after the war, did not join the new League of Nations.

FACT 10

During the summer of 1919, the nation experienced a red scare, a sudden fear that a radical revolution like the one in which communists had seized power in Russia during the war was sweeping across the nation. These fears were heightened by numerous strikes related to the difficult transition from the wartime to a peacetime economy and by incidents of domestic terrorism. The Justice Department responded by arresting and deporting many radicals, most of whom were recent immigrants.

QUESTIONS FOR ANALYSIS

1. How did participation in the war transform the role of the federal government in the United States?

2. How did participation in the war change the position of women, African Americans, and immigrant communities in American society?

3. How did the war affect Americans' perceptions of themselves and their role in the world?

Postwar America was a much different story. For the first time, the United States had decisively intervened in a major European war. The American economy had emerged from the conflict largely unscathed, and bankers and business executives were eager to fill the vacuum created by the destruction of the major European economies. The United States was now the world's dominant power. In 1928, ten years after the end of the Great War, a British official in London explained that Great Britain now faced "a phenomenon for which there is no parallel in our modern history." The United States, he added, was "twenty-five times as wealthy, three times as populous, twice as ambitious, almost invulnerable, and at least our equal in prosperity, vital energy, technical equipment, and industrial strength." What came to be called the "American Century" was at hand.

- **An Uneasy Neutrality** In 1914, a system of military alliances divided Europe in two. Britain, France, and the Russian Empire had formed the Triple Entente, later called the *Allied Powers*. The Triple Alliance, later called the *Central Powers*, comprised Germany and Austria-Hungary along with Italy (which in 1915 would switch sides and join the Allied Powers). In the summer of 1914, the assassination of the heir to the Austro-Hungarian throne by a Serbian nationalist triggered a chain reaction involving these alliances that erupted into the Great War. On the *Western Front*, troops primarily engaged in *trench warfare*. New weapons such as machine guns, long-range artillery, and poison gas resulted in unprecedented casualties.

  The Wilson administration declared the nation neutral but allowed American businesses to extend loans to the Allies. Americans were outraged by the German *U-boat* warfare, especially after the 1915 sinking of the British passenger liner *Lusitania*. In 1917, the publication of the *Zimmermann telegram* led the United States to enter the Great War.

- **Mobilizing a Nation** The Wilson Administration drafted millions of young men and created new agencies, such as the War Industries Board and the Food Administration, to coordinate industrial and agricultural production. As white workers left their factory jobs to join the army, hundreds of thousands of African Americans migrated from the rural South to the urban North, known as the *Great Migration*. Many southern whites and Mexican Americans also migrated to industrial centers. One million women worked in defense industries. The federal government severely curtailed civil liberties during the war. The Espionage and Sedition Acts of 1917 and 1918 criminalized public opposition to the war.

- **The American Role in Fighting the War** In 1918, the arrival of millions of fresh American troops turned the tide of the war, rolling back a final desperate German offensive. German leaders sued for peace, and an armistice was signed on November 11, 1918.

  Woodrow Wilson insisted that the war aim of the United States was the emergence of a new, democratic Europe. His *Fourteen Points (1918)* speech outlined his ideas for smaller, ethnically based nation-states to replace the empires. A League of Nations would promote peaceful resolutions to future conflicts.

- **The Fight for the Peace** At the Paris Peace Conference, Wilson was only partially successful in achieving his goals. The *Treaty of Versailles (1919)* did create the *League of Nations* but included a "war guilt" clause that forced Germany to pay massive reparations for war damages to France and Britain. In the United States, the fight for Senate ratification of the treaty pitted supporters and those who wanted certain revisions against those who feared that involvement in a league of nations would hinder domestic reforms and require U.S. participation in future wars. Wilson's refusal to compromise and alienation of Republican senators resulted in the failure of Senate ratification.

- **Lurching from War to Peace** The Bolsheviks established a Communist regime in the old Russian Empire in 1917. The German and Austro-Hungarian empires were dismantled and replaced by smaller nation-states. The "war guilt" clause fostered German bitterness and contributed to the subsequent rise of the Nazis.

  The United States struggled with its new status as the leading world power and with changes at home. As wartime industries shifted to peacetime production, wartime wage and price controls were ended, and millions of former soldiers reentered the workforce. Unemployment rose and consumer prices increased, provoking labor unrest in many cities. Many Americans believed the labor strikes were part of a Bolshevik plot to gain power in the United States. Several incidents of domestic terrorism fueled these fears and provoked the *First Red Scare.* Race riots broke out as resentful white mobs tried to stop African Americans from exercising their civil rights. The summer of 1919 also saw the ratification of the *Nineteenth Amendment,* which gave women throughout the country the right to vote.

KEY TERMS

Central Powers *p. 749*
Allied Powers *p. 749*
Western Front *p. 749*
trench warfare *p. 751*
U-boat *p. 754*

Lusitania *p. 754*
Zimmermann telegram (1917) *p. 756*
Great Migration *p. 759*
Fourteen Points (1918) *p. 764*

League of Nations *p. 769*
Treaty of Versailles (1919) *p. 770*
Nineteenth Amendment (1920) *p. 774*
First Red Scare (1919–1920) *p. 777*

CHRONOLOGY

1914	The Great War (World War I) begins in Europe
1915	The British liner *Lusitania* is torpedoed by a German U-boat; 128 Americans are killed
1916	Congress passes the National Defense Act and the Revenue Act
April 1917	United States enters the Great War
January 1918	Woodrow Wilson delivers his Fourteen Points
November 11, 1918	Representatives of warring nations sign armistice
1919	Paris Peace Conference convenes
	Germany signs the Treaty of Versailles
	Race riots break out across America during the Red Summer
	First Red Scare leads to arrests and deportations of suspected radicals
	Boston police strike ends with firing of all strikers
1920	Senate rejects the Treaty of Versailles
	Nineteenth Amendment is ratified

INQUIZITIVE

Go to InQuizitive to see what you've learned—and learn what you've missed—with personalized feedback along the way.

NIGHTCLUB (1933) With all its striking sights and sounds, the roar of the twenties subsided for some at the heart of it all. In this painting by American artist Guy Pène du Bois, flappers and their dates crowd into a fashionable nightclub, yet their loneliness amidst the excitement is utterly palpable.

A Clash of Cultures

1920–1929

The 1920s was perhaps the most dynamic decade in American history, a legendary era bounded on both ends by tragedies: the butchery of the Great War and the miseries of the Great Depression. It was a contradictory and conflict-ridden decade of rapid urbanization, technological innovation, widespread prosperity, unparalleled social freedom, cultural upheaval, and political conservatism. As the disruptive innovations associated with "modernism" clashed with the entrenched certainties of traditionalism, old and new values confronted each other in a cultural civil war that continues today. The decade's two most popular labels—the Jazz Age and the Roaring Twenties—describe a turbulent period that was, as a writer in the *New York Times* declared in 1923, "the greatest era of transition the human race has ever known. Old institutions are crumbling, old ideals are being battered into dust; the shock of the most cataclysmic war in history has left the world more disorganized than ever."

Among the most obvious changes during the twenties was an economic boom fueled by the spread of transformational new technologies (automobiles, trucks, tractors, airplanes, radios, movies, electrical appliances, indoor plumbing) that greatly reshaped and improved the standard of living for most Americans. At the same time, major social and political changes signaled what many people called a "New Era"

CORE
OBJECTIVES INQUIZITIVE

1. Describe the consumer culture that emerged in America during the 1920s, and explain the factors that contributed to its growth.

2. Describe other major new social and cultural trends and movements that became prominent during the twenties, and explain how they challenged traditional standards and customs.

3. Explain what "modernism" means in intellectual and artistic terms and how the modernist movement influenced American culture in the early twentieth century.

4. Identify important examples of reactionary conservatism in the decade, and analyze their impact on government policies.

5. Trace the Republican party's dominance of the federal government during the twenties, and analyze the extent to which its policies were a rejection of progressivism.

in American life. Women were at last allowed to vote in all states (although most African American women—and men—in the South were limited from doing so) and to experience many freedoms previously limited to men. The Eighteenth Amendment outlawed alcoholic beverages ("Prohibition"), setting off an epidemic of lawbreaking. Another disruptive force was growing public awareness of the scientific discoveries of Albert Einstein in physics and Sigmund Freud in psychology, findings that undermined many traditional assumptions about God, the universe, and human behavior while profoundly affecting social and cultural life. Such sweeping and speedy changes created what one historian called a "nervous generation" of Americans "groping for what certainty they could find."

Much of the cultural conflict during the 1920s grew out of tension between rural and urban ways of life. For the first time, more Americans lived in cities than in rural areas. While urban Americans generally prospered, farmers suffered from the end of the wartime boom in food exports to Europe. As the rural economy remained depressed throughout the twenties, 4 million people moved from farms to cities. Amid this population shift, bitter fights erupted between supporters and opponents of evolutionary theory, Prohibition, and the increasing ethnic and religious diversity of America, among other issues.

In the political arena, both major parties still included "progressive" wings, but they were shrinking. Woodrow Wilson's losing fight with the Republican-led Senate over the Treaty of Versailles, coupled with his administration's savage crackdown on dissenters and socialists during and after the war, had weakened an already fragmented progressive movement. As the tireless reformer Amos Pinchot bitterly observed, President Wilson had "put his enemies in office and his friends in jail." By 1920, many progressives had withdrawn from public life. The prominent reformer Jane Addams lamented that the twenties, dominated politically by a Republican party devoted to the interests of business, were "a period of political and social sag."

CORE **OBJECTIVE**

1. Describe the consumer culture that emerged in America during the 1920s, and explain the factors that contributed to its growth.

A "New Era" of Consumption

During the twenties, the U.S. economy became the envy of the world. Following the brief postwar recession in 1920–1921, Americans benefited from the fastest economic growth rate in history to that point. Jobs were plentiful, inflation was low, and income rose throughout the decade. The nation's total wealth almost doubled between 1920 and 1930, while wage workers enjoyed a whopping 30 percent increase in income, the sharpest rise in history to that point. By 1929, the United States had the highest standard of living in the world.

Construction led the way. The war had caused people to postpone building offices, plants, homes, and apartments. By 1921, however, a building boom was underway that would last the rest of the decade. At the same time, the remarkable growth of the automotive industry created an immediate need for roads and highways helped to stimulate other industries such as steel, concrete, and furniture. Technology also played a key role in the prosperity of the twenties by making manufacturing a more mechanical, assembly-line process. New machines (electric motors, steam turbines, dump trucks, tractors, bulldozers, steam shovels) and more efficient ways of operating farms, factories, plants, mines, and mills generated dramatic increases in production.

In the late nineteenth century, the U.S. economy had been driven by commercial agriculture and large-scale industrial production—the building of railroads and bridges, the manufacturing of steel, and the construction of housing and businesses in cities. During the twenties, such industrial production continued, but the dominant aspect of the economy involved an explosion of new consumer goods.

A Growing Consumer Culture

Perhaps the most visible change during the twenties was the emergence of a powerful, urban-dominated "**consumer culture**" in which the mass production and consumption of nationally advertised products came to dictate much of social life and social status. A 1920 newspaper editorial insisted that, with the war over, the American's "first importance to his country is no longer that of citizen but that of consumer. Consumption is a new necessity." The United States economy had entered what many called a "New Era" in which the consumption of goods became a national obsession. To keep factory production humming required converting people into carefree shoppers. "People may ruin themselves by saving instead of spending," warned one economist.

In the twenties, old virtues of hard work, plain living, and frugal money management were challenged by a new system of values celebrating leisure, self-expression, and self-indulgence, all achieved through the purchase of "name brand" products. "During the war," a journalist noted in 1920, "we accustomed ourselves to doing without, to buying carefully, to using economically. But with the close of the war came reaction. A veritable orgy of extravagant buying is going on. Reckless spending takes the place of saving, waste replaces conservation." Writing in *Nation's Business* in 1926, journalist William A. Feather proclaimed that the ideal American was unashamedly believed "in the doctrine of selfishness" and was proudly "rich, fat, arrogant, [and] superior."

> Rise of mass culture: New emphasis on spending, advertising, credit, and conveniences

To keep people buying, business executives focused their attention and resources on two crucial innovations: marketing and advertising campaigns to increase consumer demand and new ways for buyers to finance purchases over time ("layaway") rather than have to pay cash up front. Installment buying promised instant gratification for consumers ("Buy Now, Pay

consumer culture A society in which mass production and consumption of nationally advertised products comes to dictate much of social life and status.

Later"). As paying with cash and staying out of debt came to be seen as needlessly "old-fashioned" practices, consumer debt almost tripled during the twenties. By 1929, almost 60 percent of American purchases were made on the installment plan.

Mass advertising, first developed in the late nineteenth century, grew into a huge enterprise essential to the success of the mass-production/mass-consumption economy. Popular new weekday radio programs, for example, were often sponsored by national companies trying to sell laundry detergent and hand soap—hence the term "soap operas." Because women purchased two-thirds of consumer goods during the twenties, advertisers aimed at them especially. An ad in *Photoplay* magazine targeted the "woman of the house" because "she buys most of the things which go to make the home happy, healthful, and beautiful. Through her slim, safe fingers goes most of the family money."

Zelda Sayre Fitzgerald, the writer and wife of the wildly popular young novelist F. Scott Fitzgerald, recalled that "we grew up founding our dreams on the infinite promises of American advertising." Men were by no means ignored by advertisers, however. In his best-selling novel *Babbitt* (1922), Sinclair Lewis described George F. Babbitt, a frustrated real estate salesman, as a true believer in the benefits of the new consumer culture: "Just as he was an Elk, a Booster, and a member of the chamber of commerce, just as the priests of the Presbyterian Church determined his every religious belief . . . so did the large national advertisers fix the surface of his life, fix what he believed to be his individuality."

A modern home This 1925 Westinghouse advertisement urges homemakers to buy its "Cozy Glow, Jr." heater and "Sol-Lux Luminaire" lamp, among other electrical appliances that would "do anything for you in return."

Perhaps no decade in American history witnessed such dramatic changes in everyday life as a result of the consumer culture. The huge jump in the use of electricity during the twenties was a revolutionary new force. In 1920, only 35 percent of homes had electricity; by 1930 the number was 68 percent. Similar increases occurred in the number of households with indoor plumbing, washing machines, and automobiles. Moderately priced creature comforts and conveniences, such as flush toilets, electric irons and fans, handheld cameras, wristwatches, cigarette lighters, vacuum cleaners, and linoleum floors, became more widely available, especially among the urban middle class.

The Rise of Mass Culture

The powerful new consumer culture helped create a national marketplace of retail stores and brands in which local and regional businesses were squeezed out by giant "chain" corporations. By the 1920s, Woolworth's, for example, had 1,500 stores scattered across the country. Large national retailers bought goods in such large quantities that they were able to get discounted prices that they passed on to consumers. Mass advertising and marketing campaigns increasingly led to a mass culture: more and more Americans now not only saw and heard the same advertisements and shopped at the same companies' stores but also read the same magazines, listened to the same radio programs, and watched the same movies. Through these media, they could follow the lives and careers of the nation's first celebrities and superstars. At the same time, Americans were increasingly on the move: automobiles enabled more people to travel easily, exposing them to new values and different viewpoints. America in the twenties, explained the celebrated New York journalist Walter Lippmann, was experiencing "a vast dissolution of ancient habits" as more and more Americans embraced the "New Era."

A Love Affair with Movies

In 1896, a New York City audience viewed the first moving-picture show. By 1924, there were 20,000 movie theaters (the largest of which were called "motion picture palaces") across the nation, showing 700 new "silent" films a year that used captions to show the dialogue. Hollywood, California, became the international center of movie production, grinding out Westerns, crime dramas, and comedies. By 1930, even most small towns had theaters, and movies had become the nation's chief form of mass entertainment. Movie attendance during the 1920s averaged 80 million people a week, more than half the national population, and attendance surged even more after 1928, when "talking" movies appeared. Americans spent ten times as much on movies as they did on tickets to baseball and football games.

Charlie Chaplin An English-born actor who rose to international fame as the "Tramp," pictured above in the 1921 silent film *The Kid.*

The Effects of Radio

Radio broadcasting experienced even more spectacular growth. In 1920, station WWJ in Detroit began transmitting news bulletins, and KDKA in Pittsburgh began broadcasting regularly scheduled programs. The first radio commercial aired in New York in 1922. By the end of that year, there were 508 stations and some 3 million radios in use. In 1926, the National Broadcasting Company (NBC), a subsidiary of the Radio Corporation of America (RCA), began linking stations into a national network; the Columbia Broadcasting System (CBS) entered the field the next year.

The widespread ownership of radios changed the patterns of everyday life. At night after dinner, families gathered around the radio to listen to music, speeches, news broadcasts, weather forecasts, and comedy shows. One ad claimed that the radio "is your theater, your college, your newspaper, your library." Calvin Coolidge became the first president to address the nation by radio, and he did so monthly, paving the way for Franklin Delano Roosevelt's influential "fireside chats" a decade later.

Taking to the Air

> Charles Lindbergh's and Amelia Earhart's boost to the new aviation industry

Advances in transportation were as significant as the impact of radio and movies. In 1903, Wilbur and Orville Wright, owners of a bicycle shop in Dayton, Ohio, had built and flown the first airplane at Kitty Hawk, North Carolina. But airplane technology advanced slowly until the outbreak of war in 1914, after which Europeans rapidly adapted the airplane as a military weapon. When the United States entered the war, it had no combat planes—American pilots flew British or French planes. An American aircraft industry arose during the war but collapsed in the postwar demobilization. Under the Kelly Act of 1925, however, the federal government began to subsidize the industry through the awarding of airmail contracts. The Air Commerce Act of 1926 provided federal funds for the advancement of air transportation and navigation, including the construction of airports.

The aviation industry received a huge psychological boost in 1927 when twenty-six-year-old Charles A. Lindbergh Jr. made the first *solo* transatlantic flight, traveling from New York City to Paris in thirty-three and a half hours. The heroic feat, which won him $25,000 and a Congressional Medal of Honor, was truly dramatic: already exhausted from lack of sleep when he took off, Lindbergh flew through severe storms as well as a dense fog for part of the way that forced him to descend to within ten feet of the ocean's surface. When he landed in France, 100,000 people greeted him with thunderous cheers, and a New York City parade celebrating Lindbergh's accomplishment surpassed even the celebration of the armistice ending World War I. Youngsters developed a new dance step in his honor, called the Lindy Hop. Five years after Lindbergh's famous flight, New York City celebrated another pioneering aviator—Amelia Earhart, a former stunt pilot at air shows who became the first woman to fly solo across the Atlantic.

The Car Culture

By far the most significant economic and social development of the early twentieth century was the widespread ownership of automobiles. The first motorcar had been manufactured for sale in 1895, but the founding of the Ford Motor Company in 1903 revolutionized the infant industry. Henry Ford vowed "to democratize the automobile." "When I'm through," he predicted, "everybody will be able to afford one, and about everyone will have one." Ford's Model T, the celebrated "Tin Lizzie," cheap and long-lasting, came out in 1908 at a price of $850 (about $22,000 at today's prices). By

Amelia Earhart The pioneering aviator would tragically disappear in her 1937 attempt to fly around the world.

1924, as a result of Ford's increasingly efficient production techniques, the same car sold for $290 (less than $4000 today). The Model T changed little from year to year, and it came in only one color: black. Ford ads assured buyers that they "could have any color you want, as long as it is black."

In 1916, the total number of cars in the United States passed 1 million; by 1920 more than 8 million were registered, and in 1929 there were more than 23 million. The automobile revolution was in part propelled by the discovery of vast oil fields in Texas, Oklahoma, Wyoming, and California. By 1920, the United States produced two-thirds of the world's oil and gasoline.

> Henry Ford and the automotive revolution

The automobile industry became the leading example of modern mass-production techniques and efficiency. Ford's Highland Park plant outside Detroit was designed to increase output dramatically by creating a moving assembly line rather than having a crew of workers assemble each car in a fixed position. With conveyors pulling the parts along feeder lines and the chassis down an assembly line, each worker performed a single particular task, such as installing a fender or a wheel. This system could produce a new car in ninety-three minutes.

Such efficiency enabled Ford to lower the price of his cars, thereby increasing the number of people who could afford them and enabling him to pay his workers the highest wages in the industry. For the workers, however, producing cars this way made for a monotonous, mind-numbing experience, especially since Ford prohibited them from talking, sitting, smoking, or singing on the job. But his methods accomplished his goal. During the twenties, the United States built ten times more automobiles than all of Europe.

Just as the railroad helped transform the pace and scale of American life in the second half of the nineteenth century, the mass production of automobiles changed social life during the twentieth century. During the 1920s, Americans literally developed a love affair with cars. In the words of one man, young people viewed the car as "an incredible engine of escape" from parental control and a safe place to "take a girl and hold hands, neck,

Ford Motor Company's Highland Park plant, 1913 Gravity slides and chain conveyors contributed to the mass production of automobiles.

pet, or . . . go the limit." In 1923–1924, nineteen women in Muncie, Indiana, were arrested for "sex crimes" in automobiles.

Cars enabled people to live farther away from their workplaces, thus encouraging suburban sprawl. Cars also helped fuel the economic boom of the 1920s by creating tens of thousands of new jobs and a huge demand for steel, rubber, leather, oil, and gasoline. The ever-expanding car culture stimulated road construction (financed in large part by a gasoline tax), sparked a real estate boom in Florida and California, and dotted the landscape with gasoline stations, traffic lights, billboards, and motor hotels ("motels"). By 1929, the federal government was constructing 10,000 miles of paved highways each year.

Spectator Sports

> Mass popularity of baseball, football, and boxing

The widespread ownership of automobiles as well as rising incomes changed the way people spent their leisure time. City dwellers could easily drive into the countryside, visit friends and relatives, and go to ballparks, stadiums, or boxing rings to see baseball or football games and prizefights. During the 1920s, Americans fell in love with mass spectator sports.

Created in the 1870s in rural areas, baseball had, by the 1920s, gone urban and earned its label of "the national pastime." With larger-than-life heroes such as New York Yankee stars George Herman "Babe" Ruth Jr. and Henry Louis "Lou" Gehrig, professional baseball teams attracted intense loyalties and huge crowds. In 1920, more than a million spectators attended Yankees' games. Two years later, the Yankees built a new stadium, called the "house that Ruth built," and they went on to win World Series championships in 1923, 1927, and 1928. More than 20 million people attended professional baseball games in 1927, the year that Ruth, the "Sultan of Swat," set a record by hitting sixty home runs. Because baseball was still a segregated sport, so-called Negro leagues were organized at the amateur, semiprofessional, and professional levels for African Americans to play in and watch.

Football, especially at the college level, also attracted huge crowds, usually more affluent than baseball spectators. It, too, benefited from superstars such as Harold Edward

Babe Ruth This star pitcher and outfielder won the hearts of Americans with the Boston Red Sox, New York Yankees, and finally the Boston Braves. Here, he autographs bats and balls for military training camps.

"Red" Grange, the phenomenal running back for the University of Illinois and the first athlete to appear on the cover of *Time* magazine. In a game against the University of Michigan, the "Galloping Ghost" scored a touchdown each of the first four times he carried the ball; after Illinois won, students carried Grange on their shoulders for two miles across the campus. When Grange signed a contract with the Chicago Bears in 1926, he single-handedly made professional football competitive with baseball as a spectator sport.

What Ruth and Grange were to their sports, William Harrison "Jack" Dempsey was to boxing. In 1919, he won the world heavyweight title from Jess Willard, a giant of a man weighing 300 pounds and standing six and a half feet tall. Dempsey knocked him down seven times in the first round. After Willard, his face bruised and bloodied, threw in the towel in the fourth round, Dempsey became a national celebrity and a wealthy man. Like Babe Ruth, the brawling Dempsey was especially popular with working-class men, for he too had been born poor and had worked with his hands for wages. In 1927, when James Joseph "Gene" Tunney defeated Dempsey, more than 100,000 people attended, including a thousand reporters, ten state governors, and numerous Hollywood celebrities. Some 60 million people listened to the fight over the radio.

The "Jazz Age"

While most Americans of all ages became devoted to spectator sports, radio programs, and movies during the twenties, many young people focused their energies on social and cultural rebellion. F. Scott Fitzgerald, a boyishly handsome Princeton University dropout, was labeled "the voice of his generation" after his first novel, *This Side of Paradise* (1920), became a best seller with its account of student life at Princeton. Fitzgerald fastened upon the **"Jazz Age"** as a label for the spirit of rebelliousness and spontaneity he saw welling up among many young Americans.

The Birth of Jazz

Fitzgerald's term referred to the raging popularity of jazz music, a dynamic blend of several musical traditions. It had first emerged as piano-based "ragtime" at the end of the nineteenth century. Thereafter, African American musicians such as Jelly Roll Morton, Duke Ellington, Louis Armstrong, and Bessie Smith (the "Empress of the Blues") combined the energies of ragtime with the emotions of the blues to create *jazz*, originally an African American slang term meaning sexual intercourse. With its constant improvisations and variations and its sensual spontaneity, jazz

> CORE **OBJECTIVE**
> **2.** Describe other major new social and cultural trends and movements that became prominent during the twenties, and explain how they challenged traditional standards and customs.

> The craze for jazz music and dancing

Jazz Age Term coined by writer F. Scott Fitzgerald to characterize the spirit of rebellion and spontaneity among young Americans in the 1920s, a spirit epitomized by the hugely popular jazz music of the era.

F. Scott Fitzgerald Author known for his depictions of the youthful, boisterous spirit of the roaring twenties in *This Side of Paradise* (1920) and *The Great Gatsby* (1925).

appealed to many people of all ethnicities and ages because it was all about pleasure and immediacy, letting go and enjoying the freedom of the moment. In 1925 an African American journalist announced that jazz had "absorbed the national spirit of go and nervousness, lack of conventionality and boisterous good nature characteristic of the American, black or white."

The culture of jazz quickly spread from its origins in New Orleans, Kansas City, Memphis, and St. Louis to the African American neighborhoods of Harlem in New York City and Chicago's South Side. Large dance halls were built to meet the swelling demand for jazz music and the dance craze that accompanied it, including new dances like the Charleston and the Black Bottom whose sexually provocative movements shocked traditionalists. Affluent whites flocked to dance halls as well as to "black" nightclubs and "jazz joints." During the 1920s, people commonly spoke of—"jazzing something up" (enlivening it) or "jazzing around" (acting youthfully and energetically).

Many Americans, however, were not fans of jazz. Several prominent women's rights leaders dismissed both ragtime and jazz as dangerously sensual music that encouraged rape. In 1921 the *Ladies' Home Journal* discouraged jazz dancing because of its "direct appeal to the body's sensory centers," and Princeton professor Henry van Dyke dismissed jazz as "merely an irritation of the nerves of hearing, a sensual teasing of the strings of physical passion." Such shortsighted criticism, however, failed to stem the frenzied popularity of jazz, which swept across Europe as well as America.

Duke Ellington and his band
Jazz emerged in the 1920s as an especially American expression of the modernist spirit. African American artists bent musical conventions to give freer rein to improvisation and sensuality.

A Revolution in Manners and Morals

"Flaming youth," Freud, and flappers

Much of the shock to old-timers during the Jazz Age came from the revolution in manners and morals among young people, especially those on college campuses. From novels such as *This Side of Paradise* as well as dozens of magazine articles, middle-class Americans learned about the hidden world of "flaming youth" (the title of another popular novel): wild parties, free love, speakeasies, skinny-dipping, and the uses to which automobiles were put on lovers' lanes. A promotional poster for the 1923 silent film *Flaming Youth* asked: "How Far Can a Girl Go?" Other ads claimed the movie appealed especially to "neckers, petters, white kisses, red kisses, pleasure-mad daughters, [and] sensation-craving mothers."

The increasingly frank treatment of sex during the twenties resulted in part from the spreading influence of Sigmund Freud, the founder of modern psychoanalysis. Freud, an Austrian who was trained as a physician, changed the way people understood their behavior and feelings by insisting that the mind is essentially and mysteriously "conflicted" by often unconscious efforts to control or repress powerful irrational impulses and sexual desires ("libido"). In 1899, he had published his pathbreaking book *The Interpretation of Dreams*, which stressed the crucial role of the subconscious, that dark swamp of our irrational minds, in shaping behavior and moods. Dreams, he said, revealed "repressed" sexual yearnings deep in the psyche, many of which resulted from early childhood experiences.

Sigmund Freud Founder of modern psychoanalysis, in 1926.

By 1909, when Freud first visited the United States to lecture at Clark University in Massachusetts, he was surprised to find himself famous "even in prudish America." It did not take long for his ideas to penetrate society at large. Psychoanalysis soon became the most celebrated—and controversial—technique for helping troubled people come to grips with their demons. Through "talk therapy," patients discussed their inner frustrations and revealed their repressed fears and urges. By 1916, there were some 500 psychoanalysts in New York City alone.

Freud's emphasis on unruly sexual desires swirling about in the subconscious fascinated some people and scared others. For many young Americans especially, Freud seemed to provide scientific justification for rebelling against social conventions and indulging in sex. Some oversimplified his theories by claiming that sexual pleasure was essential for emotional health, that all forms of sexual activity were good, and that all inhibitions—feelings of restraint—about sex were bad. In his novel *Dark Laughter* (1925), Sherwood Anderson contrasted the sexual puritanism of white Americans with what he saw as the unrepressed sensuality of African Americans: "If there is anything that you do not understand in life," one of the characters advises, "consult the works of Dr. Freud." Traditionalists, on the other hand, were shocked at the behavior of rebellious young women who claimed to be acting out Freud's theories. "One hears it said," complained a Baptist magazine, "that the girls are actually tempting the boys more than the boys do the girls, by their dress and conversation."

As such remarks suggest, new fashions in clothing reflected the rebellion against traditional female roles. The emancipated "new woman" of the twenties eagerly discarded the confining wardrobe of the nineteenth and early twentieth centuries—pinched-in corsets, layers of petticoats, and floor-length dresses. In 1919 skirts were typically six inches above the ground; by 1927 they were at the knee. The shortest ones were worn by the so-called **flappers**, young women who—in defiance of proper prewar standards—drove automobiles, "bobbed" their hair (cut it short, requiring the invention of the "bobby pin"), and wore minimal underclothing, gauzy fabrics, sheer stockings, and plenty of makeup, especially rouge and lipstick. They also often joined young men in smoking cigarettes, (illegally) drinking and gambling, and dancing to jazz music—not to mention even more sensual activities.

Self-consciously outrageous and outlandish, flappers wanted more out of life than marriage and motherhood. Their carefree version of feminism was fun-loving, defiant, and self-indulgent. F. Scott Fitzgerald claimed that his rebellious wife, Zelda, was the "First American Flapper." The wayward daughter of a strict Alabama judge, Zelda was wild to the point of exhaustion. Emboldened by alcohol, she loved to do what she called "crazy things" such as dancing in New York City fountains and stripping off her clothes in the middle of Grand Central Station. Many were appalled by the flappers. A Catholic priest in Brooklyn complained that the feminism of the 1920s had provoked a "pandemonium of powder, a riot of rouge, and a moral anarchy of dress." In discussing the flapper phenomenon, a newspaper columnist reported that "the world is divided into those who delight in her, those who fear her, and those who try pathetically to take her as a matter of course."

The beautiful and the damned In an outfit typical of flappers, Zelda Fitzgerald poses with her husband on the Riviera in 1926.

Women in the 1920s

Most women in the 1920s, even most young, college-educated women, were not flappers, however. Lillian Symes, a longtime activist in the women's movement, stressed that her "generation of feminists" had little in common with the "spike-heeled, over-rouged flapper of today. We grew up before the postwar disillusionment engulfed the youth of the land." Although more middle-class women attended college in the 1920s than ever before, a higher percentage of them married soon after graduation than had been the case in the nineteenth century.

flappers Young women of the 1920s whose rebellion against prewar standards of femininity included wearing shorter dresses, bobbing their hair, dancing to jazz music, driving cars, smoking cigarettes, and indulging in illegal drinking and gambling.

The conservative political mood of the twenties helped to steer women back into their traditional roles as homemakers, and college curricula began to shift accordingly. At Vassar College in New York, an all-women's school, students took courses such as "Husband and Wife," "Motherhood," and "The Family as an Economic Unit." At the same time, fewer college-educated women pursued careers: the proportion of physicians who were women fell from 6 to 4 percent during the twenties, with similar reductions among dentists, architects, and chemists. A student at all-female Smith College expressed frustration "that a woman must choose between a home and her work, when a man may have both. There must be a way out, and it is the problem of our generation to find the way."

A return to more "traditional" domestic roles for most women

As before, most women who worked outside the home labored in un-skilled, low-wage jobs. Only 4 percent of working women in the 1920s were salaried professionals; the vast majority worked for hourly wages. Some women moved into new vocations created by the growing consumer culture, such as accounting assistants and department store clerks. The number of beauty shops soared from five thousand in 1920 to forty thousand in 1930, creating new jobs for hair stylists, manicurists, and cosmeticians.

The majority of women, however, were still either full-time wives and mothers or household servants. Fortunately, the advent of electricity and electrical appliances—vacuum cleaners, toasters, stoves, washing machines, irons—made housework quicker and easier than it had been for their mothers and grandmothers. African American and Mexican American women faced the greatest challenges. As a New York City newspaper observed, they were forced to do "work which white women will not do." Women of color usually worked as maids, laundresses, or seamstresses or on farms.

The Harlem Renaissance

As their Great Migration from the South continued into the twenties, African Americans found new freedom of speech and action in northern settings; they also gained leverage as voters by settling in states with many electoral votes. With these new opportunities came a bristling spirit of protest that became known as the **Harlem Renaissance**, the nation's first self-conscious black literary and artistic movement.

The Harlem Renaissance

The movement started among the fast-growing African American community in the Harlem neighborhood of northern Manhattan in New York City. In 1890, one in seventy people in Manhattan had been African American; by 1930 it was one in nine. The "great, dark city" of Harlem, as poet Langston Hughes's called it, contained more blacks per square mile than any other urban neighborhood in the nation. Their dense concentration there generated a sense of common identity, growing power, and distinctive

Harlem Renaissance The nation's first self-conscious black literary and artistic movement; centered in New York City's Harlem district, which had a largely black population in the wake of the Great Migration from the South.

Augusta Savage The sculptor, shown with her statue *Realization* (1938), found success in America and abroad, though after much struggle with racism.

self-expression that soon made Harlem the cultural capital of African American life. Dotted with raucous nightclubs where writers and painters discussed literature and art while listening to jazz and drinking bootleg alcohol, Harlem became what journalists called the "Nightclub Capital of the World."

The Harlem Renaissance writers celebrated African Americans' heritage as well as their more recent contributions to American culture, including jazz and the blues. As Langston Hughes wrote, "I am a Negro—and beautiful. . . . The night is beautiful. So [are] the faces of my people." He loved Africa and its cultural heritage, but declared, "I was not Africa. I was Chicago and Kansas City and Broadway and Harlem." The Harlem group promoted a racially integrated society. James Weldon Johnson coined the term "Aframerican" to designate Americans with African ancestry, whom he called "conscious collaborators" in the creation of American society and culture. By 1930 the Harlem Renaissance writers had produced dozens of novels and volumes of poetry, several Broadway plays, and a flood of short stories, essays, and films. A people capable of producing such great art and literature, Johnson declared, should never again be "looked upon as inferior."

Garveyism

The celebration of black culture also found expression in what came to be called Negro nationalism, which promoted black separatism from mainstream American life. Its leading spokesman was the flamboyant Marcus Garvey. In 1916, Garvey brought to Harlem the headquarters of the Universal Negro Improvement Association (UNIA), which he had started in his native Jamaica two years before.

Garvey insisted that blacks had nothing in common with whites—and that was a good thing. He therefore called for racial separation to integration. In passionate speeches and in editorials in his newspaper, the *Negro World*, Garvey urged African Americans to separate themselves from the surrounding white culture. He saw every white person as a "potential Klansman" and endorsed the "social and political separation of all peoples to the extent that they promote their own ideals and civilization."

The UNIA grew rapidly amid the racial tensions of the postwar years. By 1923, Garvey claimed to have as many as 4 million UNIA members served by 800 offices. The UNIA became the largest black political organization in the twentieth century. Garvey's goal was to build an all-black empire in Africa: "We will let white men have America and Europe, but we are going to have Africa." To that end, he began calling himself the "Provisional President of Africa," raising funds to send Americans to Africa, and expelling any UNIA member who married a white.

Garvey's message of black nationalism and racial solidarity appealed to many African Americans living in slums in northern cities, but it appalled other black leaders. W. E. B. Du Bois, for example, labeled Garvey "the most dangerous enemy of the Negro race.... He is either a lunatic or a traitor." An African American newspaper pledged to help "drive Garvey and Garveyism in all its sinister viciousness from the American soil."

Garvey's crusade collapsed in 1923 when he was convicted of mail fraud related to overselling shares of stock in a steamship corporation intended to transport American blacks to Africa. Sentenced to five years in prison, in 1927 he was pardoned by President Calvin Coolidge on the condition that he be deported to Jamaica. One of the largest crowds in Jamaican history greeted him upon his return to his native country. Garvey died in obscurity in 1940, but the memory of his movement kept alive an undercurrent that would re-emerge in the 1960s under the slogan "black power."

Marcus Garvey Founder of the Universal Negro Improvement Association and leading spokesman for "Negro nationalism" in the 1920s.

The NAACP

A more lasting force for racial equality during the twenties was the **National Association for the Advancement of Colored People (NAACP)**, founded in 1910 by black activists and white progressives. Black NAACP leaders came mainly from the Niagara Movement, a group that had met each year since 1905 at places associated with the anti-slavery movement (Niagara Falls; Oberlin, Ohio; Boston; Harpers Ferry) and issued defiant statements against discrimination. Within a few years, the NAACP had become a broad-based national organization. It embraced the progressive idea that the solution to social problems begins with education, by informing people about social problems. W. E. B. Du Bois became the organization's director of publicity and research and the editor of its journal, *Crisis*.

Politically, the NAACP's main strategy focused on legal action to bring the Fourteenth and Fifteenth Amendments back to life. One early victory came with *Guinn v. United States* (1915), in which the Supreme Court struck down Oklahoma's efforts to deprive African Americans of the vote. In *Buchanan v. Warley* (1917) the Court invalidated a residential segregation ordinance in Louisville, Kentucky. In 1919, the NAACP launched a national campaign against lynching, still a common form of vigilante racist violence. An anti-lynching bill to make mob murder a federal crime passed the House in 1922 but lost to a filibuster by southerners in the Senate.

The NAACP: Progressive interracial activism on racial issues

National Association for the Advancement of Colored People (NAACP) Organization founded in 1910 by black activists and white progressives that promoted education as a means of combating social problems and focused on legal action to secure the civil rights supposedly guaranteed by the Fourteenth and Fifteenth Amendments.

CORE **OBJECTIVE**

3. Explain what "modernism" means in intellectual and artistic terms and how the modernist movement influenced American culture in the early twentieth century.

The Modernist Revolt

The dramatic changes in society and the economy during the twenties were spurred by transformations in science and the arts that marked the onset of a "modernist" sensibility. Modernists were rebellious intellectuals, writers, and artists who believed that the start of the twentieth century was a historical hinge opening the way for a new world view that rejected traditional notions of reality and values (progress, reason, and even God) and adopting radical new forms of artistic expression. As the celebrated American writer Willa Cather declared, "The world broke in two in 1922 or thereabouts." She meant that during the twenties a civil war erupted between cultural modernists and their traditionalist critics. In 1922 the Irish modernist James Joyce published his pathbreaking novel *Ulysses* and the Anglo-American poet T.S. Eliot wrote "The Waste Land." Critics charged that Eliot, Joyce, and others were "ruining" literature. One said that Eliot's impenetrable writing was "a gash at the root of our poetry." Modernists fought back, claiming that as apostles of radical change they were simply acknowledging the arrival of an unsettling new way of viewing life and expressing its raucous energies.

Of course, modernism, as much a state of mind as a movement, did not simply drop out of the sky in 1922. It had been years in the making. During the early twentieth century, people were both inspired and terrified by an explosion of new scientific and technical knowledge that unveiled troubling mysteries of the universe. Since the eighteenth-century Enlightenment, conventional wisdom had held that the universe was governed by basic underlying laws of time and energy, light and motion. This rational world of order and certainty disintegrated in the early twentieth century, thanks to the discoveries of European physicists.

Science and Modernism: Einstein and Relativity

In the first decade of the century, Albert Einstein, a young German physicist, published several research papers that changed science forever while at times defying common sense. The first paper, for which he was later awarded the Nobel Prize, described how light was not only a wave of energy but also a stream of particles, called quanta or photons. This wave-particle duality became the foundation of what is known as quantum physics and would later provide the theoretical basis for such developments as television, laser beams, and semiconductors used to make computers. The second paper confirmed the existence of molecules and atoms by showing statistically how their random collisions explained the jerky motion of tiny particles in water.

Important as both of these papers were, it was Einstein's third paper that truly upended traditional notions of the universe. It grew out of one of

Albert Einstein One of the most influential scientists of the twentieth century, Einstein was awarded a Nobel Prize in 1921.

his favorite thought experiments: if you could travel at the speed of light, what would a light wave look like? If you were in a train that neared the speed of light, would you see time and space differently? Einstein's conclusions to those questions led him to create the special theory of relativity (1905), which explains that no matter how fast one is moving toward or away from a source of light, the speed of that light beam will appear the same, a constant 186,000 miles per second. But space and time will appear relative. As a train accelerates to near the speed of light, time on the train will slow down from the perspective of a stationary observer, and the train will get shorter and heavier.

The most important of Einstein's ideas was his general theory of relativity (1916), which maintained that the fundamental concepts of space, time, matter, and energy were not distinct, independent things with continuous dimensions, as Sir Isaac Newton had assumed in the eighteenth century, but instead were interacting elements.

Nothing is fixed or absolute in Einstein's bewildering universe; everything is *relative* to the location and motion of the observer and the effects of gravity, which warps space and time. Things are big or little, long or short, slow or fast, light or heavy only by comparison to something else. So, for example, the particular spot on earth on which we are positioned at any given moment is not fixed but is, relative to the sun, moving through space at 18.5 miles per second. Einstein also revealed that objects shrink as they approach the speed of light, that beams of light are bent by gravity, and that all matter is simply stored energy.

Einstein's new vision of the universe revolutionized the way people understood time, space, and light. Although few understood the details of his theories, many began to embrace the idea that there were no absolute standards or fixed points of reference in the world. During the twenties, the idea of "relativity" gradually emerged in popular discussions of decidedly nonscientific topics such as sexuality, the arts, and politics; there was less faith in absolutes, not only of time and space but also of truth and morality. Just as Darwinism became not just a biological theory but also a social, economic, and political one, so too did relativity shape many of the intellectual, cultural, and social currents of the twentieth century. In 1920, the year before Einstein was awarded the Nobel Prize, an American journalist said that his theories had moved physics into the region of "metaphysics, where paradox and magic take the place of solid fact . . . and common sense." The farther scientists reached out into the universe and into the microscopic world of the atom, the more Western certainty dissolved.

> Modernism and science: Einstein's breakthroughs and impact

Modernist Art and Literature

The scientific breakthroughs associated with Freud, Einstein, and others helped to inspire a "modernist" cultural revolution among intellectuals and creative artists. **Modernism** as a recognizable movement in the arts and ideas had appeared first in the capitals of Europe—London, Paris,

modernism An early-twentieth-century cultural movement that rejected traditional notions of reality and adopted radical new forms of artistic expression.

Berlin, and Vienna—in the 1890s. By the second decade of the twentieth century, it had spread to the United States, especially New York City and Chicago. It arose out of a widespread recognition that Western civilization was entering an era of bewildering change as new technologies, modes of transportation and communication, and startling scientific discoveries combined to transform the nature of everyday life and the way people "saw" the world.

Modernism as a cultural movement

The shocking horrors of the Great War accelerated and expanded the appeal of modernism—and helped explain why modernists cared little for established standards of good taste or for history. To be "modern" in the early twentieth century was to break free of tradition, by taking chances, violating artistic rules and moral restrictions, and behaving in deliberately shocking ways, including treating sexuality with a startling frankness. "Art," said a modernist painter, "is meant to disturb."

As an experimental cultural impulse, full of astonishing energy and contradictions, surprise and scandal, modernism was loosely based on three unsettling assumptions: (1) God did not exist; (2) "reality" was not rational, orderly, or obvious; and, in the aftermath of the Great War, (3) social progress could no longer be taken for granted. These modernist premises challenged writers, painters, musicians, dancers, and architects to risk poverty and humiliation by rudely rebelling against good taste, old-fashioned morals, and old-time religion. In its simplest sense, modernism was a disrespectful war of new values against old ones. Experimental poet Ezra Pound provided the slogan for modernism: "Make It New!"

Like many previous cultural movements, modernism also involved a new way of *seeing* the world by a new intellectual and cultural elite determined to capture and express the hidden realm of imagination and dreams. Doing so, however, often made their experimental writing, art, music, and dance vague and obscure, famously difficult to understand, interpret, or explain. "The pure modernist is merely a snob," explained a British writer. For many modernists, being misunderstood by the general public was a badge of honor. The American experimentalist writer Gertrude Stein, for example, declared that a novel "which tells about what happens is of no interest." Instead of depicting "real" life or telling recognizable stories, she was interested in playing with language. Words, not people, are the characters in her writings.

Much about modernism provoked, perplexed, and upset people. Until the twentieth century, most writers and artists had taken for granted an accessible "real" world that could be readily observed, scientifically explained, and accurately represented in words or paint or even music. The young generation of modernists, however, applied Einstein's ideas about relativity to a world in which "reality" no longer had an objective or recognizable basis. They agreed wholeheartedly with Freud that reality was something deeply personal and even unrecognizable by others, something to be imagined and expressed by one's innermost being rather than observed in and reproduced from the visible world. Walter Pach, an early

***Russian Ballet* (1916)** Jewish American artist Max Weber's painting is a modernist take on a traditional subject. Splicing the scene of the performance into planes of jarring colors, this painting exemplifies the impact of psychoanalysis and the theory of relativity on the arts.

American champion of modern art, explained that modernism resulted from the discovery by Freud and others of "the role played by the unconscious in our lives."

For modernists such as the Spanish painter Pablo Picasso and the Irish writer James Joyce, then, their work required an unpredictable journey into the realm of individual fantasy and dreams, exploring and expressing the personal, the unknown, the primitive, the abstract. Paul Cezanne, one of the earliest French modernists, insisted that a painting "should represent nothing but color." American artist Marsden Hartley reported from Paris that his reading of Freud and other "new psychologists" had led him to quit painting objects from "real life" and instead paint "intuitive abstractions." In the early twentieth-century art world, modernists discarded literal representation of recognizable subjects in favor of vibrant color masses, simplified forms, or geometric shapes.

The Armory Show

The crusade to bring European-inspired modernism to the United States reached a climax in the Armory Show of 1913, the most scandalous event in the history of American art. Mabel Dodge, one of the organizers, wrote that the exhibition would cause "a riot and revolution and things will never be the same afterwards."

Modernism and art: The Armory Show of 1913

To house the 1,200 modernist works of art collected from more than 300 painters and sculptors in America and Europe, the two dozen young painters who organized the show leased the vast 69th Regiment Armory in New York City. The Armory Show, officially known as the International Exhibition of Modern Art, opened on February 17, 1913. As Dodge had predicted, it created an immediate sensation. For many, modern art became the thing that they loved to hate. Modernism, growled a prominent art critic, "is nothing else than the total destruction of the art of painting." The *New York Times* warned visitors who shared the "old belief in reality" that they would enter "a stark region of abstractions" at the "lunatic asylum" show that was "hideous to our unaccustomed eyes." The experimentalist ("*avant-garde*") artists whose works were on display (including paintings by Vincent Van Gogh, Paul Gaugin, and Henri Matisse as well as Cezanne and Picasso) were "in love with science but not with objective reality," the *Times* critic complained, adding that they had produced paintings "revolting in their inhumanity." Former president Theodore Roosevelt dismissed the show as "repellent from every standpoint"—an indication of the gap separating political progressivism from artistic modernism.

Yet the Armory Show also generated excitement. "A new world has arisen before our eyes," announced an American art magazine. "To miss modern art," a critic stressed, "is to miss one of the few thrills that life holds." From New York, the show went on to Chicago and Boston, where it aroused similarly strong responses and attracted comparable crowds. A quarter million people viewed the exhibition in the three cities.

After the Avmovy Show, modern art became one of the nation's favorite topics of debate. Many adjusted to the shock of modernism and found a new faith in the disturbing powers of art. "America in its newness," predicted Walt Kuhn, a painter who helped organize the exhibition, "is destined to become the coming center" of modernism. Indeed, the Museum of Modern Art, founded in New York City in 1929, came to house the world's most celebrated collection of avant-garde paintings and sculpture.

The "Lost Generation"

Modernism and literature: The Lost Generation

In addition to modernism, the arts and literature of the twenties were also greatly influenced by the horrors of the Great War. F. Scott Fitzgerald wrote in *This Side of Paradise* that the younger generation of Americans, the "sad young men" who had fought in Europe to "make the world safe for democracy," had "grown up to find all Gods dead, all wars fought, all faiths in man shaken." Cynicism had displaced idealism in the wake of the war's horrific senselessness. As Fitzgerald asserted, "There's only one lesson to be learned from life anyway. . . . That there's no lesson to be learned from life." Frederic Henry, a character in Ernest Hemingway's novel *A Farewell to Arms* (1929), declares that "abstract words such as *glory, honor, courage* . . . were obscene" in the context of the war's colossal casualties.

Fitzgerald, Hemingway, and other self-conscious young modernists of the era came to be labeled the Lost Generation—those who had lost faith in the values and institutions of Western civilization and were frantically looking for new gods to worship. It was Gertrude Stein who in 1921 told

Hemingway that he and his friends who had served in the war were "a lost generation." When Hemingway objected, she held her ground. "You are [lost]. You have no respect for anything. You drink yourselves to death."

In his first novel, *The Sun Also Rises* (1926), Hemingway used the phrase "lost generation" as the book's opening quotation. The novel centers on Jake Barnes, a young American journalist castrated by a war injury. His despairing impotence leads him to wander the cafes and nightclubs of postwar Europe with his unhappy friends, who acknowledge that they are all wounded and sterile in their own way: they have lost their innocence, their illusions, and their motivation to do anything with their lives.

Fitzgerald, the earliest chronicler of the "lost generation," blazed up brilliantly and then quickly flickered out like many of the sad young characters in his novels. He wrote about self-indulgent and self-destructive people like him who drank and partied too much before zooming around in their sleek cars. In Fitzgerald's fiction, automobiles function not only as stylish symbols of wealth and power and freedom but also as modern engines of death and destruction. A friend and fellow writer called Fitzgerald "our darling, our genius, our fool." What gave depth to the best of his work was what a character in *The Great Gatsby* (1925), his finest novel, called "a sense of the fundamental decencies" amid all the surface gaiety—and almost always a sense of impending doom in a world that had lost its meaning through the disorienting discoveries of modern science and the horrors of world war.

The Reactionary Twenties

The self-indulgent excesses of the "lost generation" made little sense to the vast majority of Americans during the twenties, many of whom aggressively defended established values, old certainties, and the comfort of past routines. The reactionary conservatism of the twenties fed on the energies provided by militant traditional Protestantism and a revival of **nativism**.

Nativism

The Red Scare of 1919 and a renewal of the large-scale immigration that had been cut off during the war helped generate a renewed surge of anti-immigrant hysteria. From June 1920 to June 1921, more than 800,000 people immigrated to the United States, 65 percent of them from southern and eastern Europe. In the early 1920s, more than half of the white men and a third of the white women working in mines, mills, and factories were European immigrants, some of whom had brought with them to America a passion for socialism or anarchism. The foreign connections of so many political radicals triggered efforts to close the door to immigrants. Many nativists also tried to stir up hatred of immigrants already in the United States and of their "un-American" religions and ideas.

CORE **OBJECTIVE**
4. Identify important examples of reactionary conservatism in the decade, and analyze their impact on government policies.

nativism Reactionary conservative movement characterized by heightened nationalism, anti-immigrant sentiment, and laws setting stricter regulations on immigration.

Sacco and Vanzetti

The Sacco and Vanzetti case and new immigration limits

The most celebrated criminal case of the 1920s reinforced the connection between European immigrants and political radicalism. On May 5, 1920, two Italian immigrants who described themselves as revolutionary anarchists eager to topple the American government, shoemaker Nicola Sacco and fish peddler Bartolomeo Vanzetti, were arrested outside Boston, Massachusetts. They were charged with stealing $16,000 from a shoe factory payroll and killing the paymaster and a guard. Both men were armed with loaded pistols when arrested, both lied to police about their activities, and both were identified by eyewitnesses. But the stolen money was never found.

The **Sacco and Vanzetti case** occurred at the height of Italian immigration to the United States and against the backdrop of numerous terror attacks by anarchists, some of which Sacco and Vanzetti had participated in. Such a charged atmosphere ensured that their 1921 trial would become a huge public spectacle. The presiding judge was openly biased, referring to the defendants as "anarchist bastards." Sacco and Vanzetti were convicted and sentenced to death: their appeals lasted seven years before they were executed on August 23, 1927, still claiming their innocence. To millions around the world, Sacco and Vanzetti had become martyrs, victims of American injustice. The case remains passionately disputed today.

Immigration Restriction

Concerns about an invasion of foreign radicals led Congress to pass the Emergency Immigration Act of 1921, which restricted immigration from each European country each year to 3 percent of the total number of that nationality represented in the 1910 census. The **Immigration Act of 1924** reduced the number to 2 percent and changed the standard to the 1890 census, which had included fewer "new" immigrants from southern and eastern Europe. The law also set a permanent overall limitation, effective in 1929, of slightly over 150,000 new arrivals per year. The purpose of the new quotas was clear: to favor immigrants from northern and western Europe and reduce those from southern and eastern Europe. A Kansas congressman expressed the prejudices felt by many rural American Protestants: "On the one side is beer, bolshevism, unassimilating settlements and perhaps many flags—on the other side is constitutional government; one flag, stars and stripes."

The new immigration laws excluded anyone from Japan or China. On the other hand, the Immigration Act of 1924 left the gate open to new arrivals from countries in the Western Hemisphere, so that an unintended result of it was a substantial increase in the Hispanic Catholic population of the United States. People of Latin American descent (chiefly Mexicans, Puerto Ricans, and Cubans) became the fastest-growing ethnic minority in the country.

Sacco and Vanzetti case (1921) Trial of two Italian immigrants that occurred at the height of Italian immigration and against the backdrop of numerous terror attacks by anarchists; despite a lack of clear evidence, the two defendants, both self-professed anarchists, were convicted of murder and were executed.

Immigration Act of 1924 Federal legislation intended to favor northern and western European immigrants over those from southern and eastern Europe by restricting the number of immigrants from any one European country to 2 percent of the total number of immigrants per year, with an overall limit of slightly over 150,000 new arrivals per year.

The New Klan

The most violent of the reactionary movements during the twenties were A revived Ku Klux Klan the members of a revived Ku Klux Klan, the infamous post–Civil War group of anti-black racists that had recreated itself in 1915. The old Klan had died out in the 1870s once white Democrats regained control of the former Confederate states after Reconstruction. No longer simply a southern group intent on terrorizing African Americans, the new Klan was a nation-wide organization devoted to "100 percent Americanism"; only "natives"— white Protestants born in the United States—could be members.

With its secret signs and codes, weird rituals, and its costumes featuring white sheets and spooky hats, the Klan called for strict personal morality, opposed bootleg liquor, and preached hatred against not only African Americans but Roman Catholics, Jews, immigrants, Communists, atheists, prostitutes, and adulterers. The United States was no melting pot, shouted Imperial Wizard William J. Simmons, a traveling salesman turned Methodist preacher: "It is a garbage can! . . . When the hordes of aliens walk to the ballot box and their votes outnumber yours, then that alien horde has got you by the throat." The new Klan included a women's auxiliary group called the Kemellia, and whole families attended Klan gatherings, "klasping" hands while listening to inflammatory speeches, watching fireworks, and burning crosses.

The reborn Klan, headquartered in Atlanta and calling itself the "Invisible Empire," grew rapidly in cities and small towns across the nation. During the twenties, 40 percent of members were in three Midwestern states (Illinois, Indiana, and Ohio) and Connecticut had more Klan members than Mississippi. Recruiters, called Kleagles, were told to "play upon whatever prejudices were most acute in a particular area." In Texas, the Klan fed on prejudice against Mexicans. In California, it focused on Japanese

Ku Klux Klan rally In 1925 the KKK held an expansive march down Pennsylvania Avenue in Washington, D.C.

Americans, and in New York, the enemy was primarily Jews and Catholics. Most Klan members were small farmers, sharecroppers, or wage workers, but the organization also attracted doctors, lawyers, accountants, business leaders, teachers, and even politicians. As a prominent southern journalist observed, the new Klan was "anti-Negro, anti-alien, anti-red, anti-Catholic, anti-Jew, anti-Darwin, anti-Modern, anti-Liberal; Fundamentalist, vastly Moral, militantly Protestant." African Americans grew increasingly concerned as the ranks of the new Klan mushroomed. The Chicago *Defender*, the black newspaper with the widest circulation in the nation, urged its readers to fight back against Klansmen trying to "win what their fathers [in the Civil War] lost by fire and sword."

By 1923, the Klan had more than 4 million members, including judges, mayors, sheriffs, state legislators, six governors, and three U.S. senators. The Grand Dragon of Indiana, a con man named David C. Stephenson, grew so influential in electing local and state officials (the "kluxing" of America, as he called it) that he boasted "I am the law in Indiana!" Klan-endorsed candidates won the Indiana governorship and controlled the state legislature. At the 1924 Republican State Convention, Stephenson patrolled the aisles with a pistol and later confessed that he "purchased the county and state officials." Stephenson, who had grown wealthy by skimming from the dues he collected from Klan members as well as selling robes and hoods, planned to run for president of the United States.

But the Klan's influence, both in Indiana and nationwide, crumbled after Stephenson was sentenced to life in prison in 1925 for kidnapping and raping a twenty-eight-year-old woman who then committed suicide. At the same time, several states passed anti-Klan laws and others banned the wearing of masks. By 1930, nationwide membership had dwindled to 100,000, mostly southerners. Yet the impulse underlying the Klan lived on, fed by deep-seated fears and hatreds that have yet to disappear.

Fundamentalism

While the Klan saw a threat mainly in the "alien menace," many defenders of "old-time religion" felt threatened by ideas circulating in "progressive" Protestant churches, especially the idea that the Bible should be studied in the light of modern scholarship (the "higher criticism") or that it should accommodate Darwinian theories of biological evolution. In response to such "modern" notions, conservative Protestants embraced a militant new fundamentalism, which was distinguished less by a shared faith than by a posture of hostility toward "liberal" beliefs and its insistence on the literal truth of the Bible.

Fundamentalist hostility toward Darwinism: The Scopes trial

Among national leaders, only the "Great Commoner," William Jennings Bryan, the former congressman, secretary of state, and three-time presidential candidate, had the support, prestige, and eloquence to transform fundamentalism into a popular crusade. Bryan remained a firm believer in the literal truth of the Bible, from the snake forced to spend eternity on its belly for tempting Eve to the looming Apocalypse predicted in the Book of Revelation. In 1921, Bryan backed new state laws banning the teaching of evolution in public schools. He passionately denounced Charles Darwin's theory of evolution, which suggested that human beings over millions of years had evolved from monkeys and apes. Anti-evolution bills were introduced in numerous state legislatures, but the only victories came in the South. Governor Miriam "Ma" Ferguson of Texas outlawed school textbooks that included sections on Darwinism. "I am a Christian mother," she declared, "and I am not going to let that kind of rot go into Texas schoolbooks."

The dramatic climax of the fundamentalist war on Darwinism came in Tennessee, where in 1925 the legislature outlawed the teaching of evolution in public schools and colleges. In the tiny mining town of Dayton, in eastern Tennessee, civic leaders eager for publicity persuaded John T. Scopes, a twenty-four-year-old high-school science teacher and part-time football coach, to become a test case against the new law. Scopes used a textbook that taught Darwinian evolution, and he was duly arrested for doing so. The town boosters succeeded beyond their wildest hopes: the **Scopes Trial** received worldwide publicity—but it was not flattering to Dayton.

Before the start of the twelve-day "monkey trial" on July 10, 1925, the streets of Dayton swarmed with evangelists, atheists, hot-dog and soda-pop peddlers, and hundreds of newspaper and radio reporters. A man tattooed with Bible verses preached on a street corner while a monkey was paraded about town.

The stars of the show pitting science against fundamentalism were both national celebrities: Bryan, who had offered his services to the prosecution, and Clarence Darrow, the nation's most famous trial lawyer, a tireless defender of hopeless causes who championed the rights of the working class, who had volunteered to defend Scopes and evolution.

Bryan insisted that the trial was not about Scopes but about a state's right to determine what was taught in the public schools, and he announced that the "contest between evolution and Christianity is a duel to the death." Darrow countered: "Scopes is not on trial. Civilization is on trial." His goal, Darrow thundered, was to prevent "bigots and ignoramuses from controlling the education of the United States" by proving that America was "founded on liberty and not on narrow, mean, intolerable and brainless prejudice of soulless religio-maniacs."

On July 20, the defense called Bryan as an "expert" witness on biblical interpretation. Under Darrow's aggressive cross-examination, Bryan repeatedly revealed his ignorance of biblical history and scholarship and gradually conceded that he had never worried that many of the Bible's stories conflicted with common sense and basic scientific truths. At one point, he claimed that Darrow was insulting Christians. Darrow, his thumbs clasping his colorful suspenders, shot back: "You insult every man of science and learning in the world because he does not believe in your fool religion." At one point, Darrow and Bryan, their patience exhausted in the broiling summer heat, lunged at each other, prompting the judge to adjourn court.

Scopes Trial (1925) Highly publicized trial of a high school teacher in Tennessee for violating a state law that prohibited the teaching of evolution; the trial was seen as the climax of the fundamentalist war on Darwinism.

Monkey trial In this snapshot of the courtroom, Scopes (*far left*) clasps his face in his hands and listens to his attorney (*second from right*). Darrow (*far right*), too, listens on, visibly affected by the sweltering weather.

As the trial ended, the judge ruled that the only issue before the jury was whether John T. Scopes had taught evolution, and no one had denied that he had done so. Eager to get on with their lives and get the peach harvest in, the jurors did not even sit down before deciding that Scopes was guilty. But the Tennessee Supreme Court, while upholding the anti-evolution law, waived Scopes's $100 fine on a technicality. Both sides claimed victory.

Five days after the trial ended, Bryan died of a heart condition aggravated by heat and fatigue. Scopes left Dayton to study geology at the University of Chicago; he became a petroleum engineer. Meanwhile, the Scopes Trial only sharpened the national debate between fundamentalism and evolution. The debate continues today.

Prohibition

Challenges and side effects of banning booze

William Jennings Bryan died knowing that one of his other crusades had succeeded: alcoholic beverages had been outlawed nationwide. The movement to prohibit beer, wine, and liquor forged an unusual alliance between rural and small-town Protestants and urban political progressives— between believers in "old-time religion," who considered drinking sinful, and social reformers, mostly women, who were convinced that **Prohibition** would reduce prostitution, spousal abuse, and other alcohol-related violence. What connected the two groups to each other and to nativist movements were the ethnic and social prejudices that many members shared. The head of the Anti-Saloon League, for example, declared that

Prohibition (1920–1933)
National ban on the manufacture and sale of alcohol, though the law was widely violated and proved too difficult to enforce effectively.

German Americans "eat like gluttons and drink like swine." For many anti-alcohol crusaders, in fact, the primary goal of Prohibition seemed to be policing the behavior of the foreign-born, the working class, and the poor.

During the Great War, both houses of Congress had finally responded to the efforts of the Anti-Saloon League and the Women's Christian Temperance Union. The wartime need to use grain for food rather than for making booze, combined with a grassroots backlash against beer brewers because of their German background, transformed the cause of Prohibition into a virtual test of American patriotism. On December 18, 1917, Congress sent to the states the Eighteenth Amendment. Ratified on January 16, 1919, it banned "the manufacture, sale, and transportation of intoxicating liquors," effective one year later.

Prohibition was thus the law—but it was not widely followed. As the most ambitious social reform ever attempted in the United States, it proved to be a colossal and costly failure. It was too sweeping for the government to enforce and too frustrating for most Americans to respect, and it had many consequences not widely foreseen. The loss of liquor taxes cost the federal government 10 percent of its annual revenue. The closing of breweries, distilleries, and saloons eliminated thousands of jobs. Even more troubling were the huge number of Americans who got into the habit of regular law-breaking and the huge boost that Prohibition during the twenties gave to police corruption and to organized crime.

The Volstead Act (1919), which outlined the rules and regulations needed to enforce the Eighteenth Amendment, had so many loopholes that it virtually guaranteed failure. For example, individuals and organizations were allowed to keep and use any liquor owned on January 16, 1919. Not surprisingly, people stocked up before the law took effect. The Yale Club in Manhattan stored enough liquor to supply itself for the entire thirteen years that Prohibition was enforced.

An even greater weakness of Prohibition was that Congress never supplied adequate funding to enforce it. In 1920, the United States had only 1,520 federal agents in the Prohibition Bureau. Given

All fair in drink and war Torpedoes filled with malt whiskey were discovered in the New York harbor in 1926, an elaborate attempt by bootleggers to smuggle alcohol during Prohibition. Each "torpedo" had an air compartment so it could be floated to shore.

the public thirst for alcohol and the profits to be made in making and selling it illegally, called "bootlegging," it would have taken armies of agents to police the nation. Even so, more than half a million people were jailed for violating

Cultural Clash in the 1920s

After the Great War, patterns of where and how Americans lived, how they entertained themselves, and how they saw their position in society changed dramatically. In many cases, these trends had begun before the war, but they exploded afterward, challenging traditional values and assumptions. During the 1920s, many Americans experimented with new kinds of freedom, new sources of information, and new forms of expression. But these new cultural patterns often clashed with older ones, provoking strong reactions from millions of Americans. The nation saw heated and sometimes violent debates emerge about what it meant to be American and "modern" and about what place racial and ethnic minorities and women should occupy within American society. Many aspects of this debate continued throughout the twentieth century and still have strong echoes today. After you read through the chart below of new developments in American culture after the Great War and the reactions to them, answer the Questions for Analysis that follow.

NEW CULTURAL DEVELOPMENTS AFTER WORLD WAR I

REACTIONS TO THESE CULTURAL DEVELOPMENTS

"The New Immigrants"

Until the 1950s, the immigration trends from the early twentieth century continued. Of the 800,000 immigrants who entered the country in 1920 and 1921, two thirds were from eastern and southern Europe. Two thirds of white workers in mines, mills, and factories were immigrants.

Nativism

Nativists associated the New Immigrants with radical ideas such as socialism, communism, and anarchism. Many political radicals did have foreign connections or came from regions in Europe where these ideas were popular. The Sacco and Vanzetti case reinforced these associations among millions of Americans. Congress severely reduced immigration from eastern and southern Europe through the Immigration Act of 1924.

The Great Migration and "the New Negro"

The migration of African Americans from the rural South to the urban North continued after the war. By 1930, roughly one million had migrated. In northern cities, African Americans developed a sense of common identity, growing political and economic power, and distinctive cultural expression, resulting in the coining of the phrase "the New Negro." Assertions of African American pride and influence on the broader society were seen in the Harlem Renaissance; the spreading popularity of jazz music beyond African American communities; the popularity of the Garveyism movement, which preached black nationalism and separatism; and the activism of the NAACP, which began organizing legal challenges to racial discrimination across the country.

The Klan

The Klan became a national organization that defined American identity as white and Protestant, anti-modern and anti-radical. The group's renewed popularity extended beyond the South. Membership soared in small towns and cities in the North, particularly the Midwest, including poorly educated farmers and middle-class professionals. The Klan continued its reign of terror against African Americans, and became highly influential in politics, electing numerous candidates to office.

New Technologies and the Growth of a Consumer Economy

During the 1920s, the mass production and consumption of automobiles, radios, motion pictures, and other new technologies produced unprecedented prosperity for much of the nation. Mass media and advertising created the world's first consumer culture, as millions of Americans indulged themselves with spectator sports, department-store shopping on installment plans, and media coverage of celebrities in the entertainment industry and elsewhere.

Modernism

Modernists were intellectuals, artists, and academics who called into question traditional notions of reality and human nature. They based their ideas and activities on new scientific discoveries and radical forms of artistic expression that had first appeared in 1900s–1910s.

Fundamentalists

Fundamentalists opposed applying modern scholarship to Biblical studies because they believed that every word in the Bible was literally true. In particular, they waged a campaign against biological theories of evolution and backed state laws that would ban the teaching of evolution in public schools. These efforts succeeded only in a few southern states. The movement lost its momentum after the nationwide coverage of the 1925 Scopes Trial that was largely unfavorable to the fundamentalists.

Flappers, or "the New Women"

Many women rebelled against traditional ideas about female sexuality and appropriate female behavior. They abandoned long skirts and corsets for loose-fitting clothing that showed their legs. They also cut their hair short, drank and smoked in public, and acted in a more brazen way than before the war. They were more likely to seek personal fulfillment outside marriage and motherhood.

Prohibition

By 1920, Prohibition—one of the great crusades of the Progressive Era—had become the law of the land. In banning the sale, manufacture, and transportation of almost all intoxicating beverages, the law united many social reformers who viewed alcohol as a major source of spousal abuse, crime, and prostitution with Protestants who considered its consumption immoral. The law proved tough to enforce, however, as Congress never provided enough funds to employ enough federal agents to police the nation. Prohibition was widely violated as millions of Americans found ways to consume alcohol, often provided to them through organized crime, which many Americans associated with new immigrant communities.

QUESTIONS FOR ANALYSIS

1. How did urbanization, new technologies, and the growth of a consumer-centered economy challenge older American values and ways of life? Why might some Americans have been disturbed by these changes?

2. How did the "new immigrants," "New Negro," "New Women," and modern artists and intellectuals challenge traditional assumptions about the American social order? What groups of Americans might have been most disturbed by these changes, and why?

3. How were nativism, the Klan, fundamentalism, and Prohibition related? What did they have in common, in terms of their causes, supporters, public expressions, and effects? What differences were there between them?

the Volstead Act. Many of the activities associated with the Roaring Twenties were fueled by bootleg liquor supplied by organized crime and sold in illegal saloons called "speakeasies," which were often ignored by local policemen corrupted by bribes. New York City's police commissioner estimated that there were 32,000 speakeasies in the city in 1929, compared to 15,000 saloons in 1919. President Harding regularly drank and served bootleg liquor in the White House, explaining that he was "unable to see this as a great moral issue," and the largest bootlegger in Washington, D.C., reported that "a majority of both houses" of Congress were regular customers. Although total national alcohol consumption did decrease, in many parts of the nation drinking actually *increased* during Prohibition. As the popular humorist Will Rogers quipped, "Prohibition is better than no liquor at all."

Prohibition supplied organized crime with a source of enormous new income. The most celebrated Prohibition-era gangster was "Scarface" Al Capone. In 1927, his Chicago-based bootlegging, prostitution, and gambling empire involved 700 gangsters and brought in $60 million. Capone insisted that he was merely giving the public the goods and services it demanded: "They say I violate the Prohibition law. Who doesn't?" He neglected to add that he had also beaten to death several police officers and ordered the execution of dozens of rival criminals. Law-enforcement officials led by FBI agent Eliot Ness began to smash Capone's bootlegging operations in 1929, but the charges finally pinned on him were for tax evasion. Tried in 1931, Capone was sentenced to eleven years in prison.

CORE OBJECTIVE

5. Trace the Republican party's dominance of the federal government during the twenties, and analyze the extent to which its policies were a rejection of progressivism.

Republican Resurgence

In national politics, the small-town backlash against modern city life—whether represented by immigrants plotting revolution, liberal churches accepting evolution, or jazzed-up flappers swilling cocktails—was mirrored by a Republican resurgence determined to reverse the progressivism of Theodore Roosevelt and Woodrow Wilson. By 1920, the progressive political coalition that had reelected Wilson in 1916 had fragmented. The growing middle class had become preoccupied less with reform than with enjoying the general prosperity based on mass production and consumption. Progressivism did not simply disappear, of course. The impulse for honest, efficient government and regulation of business remained strong, especially at the state and local levels, where movements for better roads, education, public health, and social-welfare programs gained momentum. At the national level, however, Republican conservatives returned to power.

Harding and "Normalcy"

After the Great War, most Americans had grown weary of Wilson's crusading idealism and were suspicious of any leader who promoted sweeping reforms. Wilson himself recognized the shifting public mood. "It is only once in a generation," he remarked, "that a people can be lifted above material things. That is why conservative government is in the saddle two-thirds of the time."

The Election of 1920

In 1920, Republican party leaders, unable to settle on a nationally prominent figure as their presidential candidate, turned in the end to Warren G. Harding, an easy-going, silver-haired senator from Ohio. Another Republican senator explained that Harding was selected not for his abilities or experience (which were not extensive) but because he was available and looked presidential. Harding, he said, was "the best of the second-raters."

Harding set the conservative tone of his campaign when he told a Boston audience that it was time to end Wilsonian progressivism: "America's present need is not heroics, but healing; not nostrums, but normalcy; not revolution, but restoration; not agitation, but adjustment; not surgery, but serenity; not the dramatic, but the dispassionate." In contrast to Wilson's grandiose internationalism, Harding promised to "safeguard America first . . . to exalt America first, to live for and revere America first."

Harding's vanilla promise of a **"return to normalcy"** reflected his unexceptional background and personality. A farmer's son and newspaper editor, he described himself as "just a plain fellow" who was "old-fashioned and even reactionary in matters of faith and morals." In his personal life, however, Harding secretly drank liquor in the White House, smoked and chewed tobacco, loved twice-weekly poker games with his buddies in the White House library, and had numerous extramarital affairs and even fathered children with women other than his austere wife, Florence, whom he called "the Duchess." One of the women tried to blackmail him, demanding money for her silence—which she received. The public, however, was unaware of Harding's escapades. Voters saw him as a handsome, charming politician who looked the part of a leader yet recognized his own limitations. "I am not fit for this office and should never have been here," he once admitted. "I cannot hope to be one of the great presidents, but perhaps I may be remembered as one of the best loved."

The Democrats, meanwhile, had to contend with the breakup of the Wilsonian coalition and the conservative postwar mood. At the 1920 Democratic convention, another Ohioan, James Cox, a former newspaper publisher and former governor of the state, won the nomination of his increasingly divided party on the forty-fourth ballot. For vice president, the convention chose New Yorker Franklin Delano Roosevelt, only thirty-eight years old, who as assistant secretary of the navy occupied the same position his Republican cousin Theodore Roosevelt had once held.

The country voted overwhelmingly for Harding's promised "return to normalcy." Harding polled 16 million votes to 9 million for Cox, who won no state outside the South. The Republican majority in both houses of Congress increased. Franklin Roosevelt predicted that his party could not hope to return to national power until the Republicans led the nation "into a serious period of depression and unemployment." He was right.

> Harding's victorious "return to normalcy"

"return to normalcy"
Campaign promise of Republican presidential candidate Warren G. Harding in 1920, meant to contrast with Woodrow Wilson's progressivism and internationalism.

Harding's Associates and Personality

Harding in office had much in common with Ulysses S. Grant. His cabinet, like Grant's, mixed some of the "best minds" in the party, whom he had promised to seek out, with some of its worst characters. Charles Evans Hughes, like Grant's Hamilton Fish, became a distinguished secretary of state. Herbert Hoover in the Commerce Department, Andrew W. Mellon in the Treasury Department, and Henry C. Wallace in the Agriculture Department were dedicated public servants. Other cabinet members and Harding appointees, however, were not so conscientious. The secretary of the interior landed in prison, and the attorney general narrowly escaped serving time.

Harding loved hobnobbing and "bloviating" (a favorite word of his, meaning "speaking in a pompous, long-winded way") at public events and joking around with his political buddies behind the scenes. As president, however, he was in over his head and knew it. "I don't think I'm big enough for the Presidency," he confided to a friend. He much preferred to relax with the "Ohio gang," his closest friends, who shared his taste for whiskey, poker, and women. Still, Harding and his social friends did have a political agenda.

Andrew Mellon and the Economy

The Harding administration inherited a slumping economy still burdened by high wartime taxes and a national debt that had ballooned from $1 billion in 1914 to $27 billion in 1920 because of the expenses associated with the war. Unemployment was at nearly 12 percent. To address these challenges, the new president established a pro-business tone, vetoing a bill to provide war veterans with a cash bonus, arguing that it would increase the federal budget deficit.

> The Mellon Plan: Economic growth through low taxes and spending and high tariffs

To generate economic growth, Secretary of the Treasury Andrew Mellon, the third richest man in the world behind John D. Rockefeller and Henry Ford, developed a plan to reduce federal spending and lower tax rates. Mellon persuaded Congress to pass the landmark Budget and Accounting Act of 1921, which created a Bureau of the Budget to streamline the process of preparing an annual federal budget. The bill also created a General Accounting Office to audit spending by federal agencies. This act fulfilled a long-held progressive desire to bring greater efficiency and non-partisanship to the budget preparation process.

The brilliant but cold Mellon (his son described him as a "thin-voiced, thin-bodied, shy and uncommunicative man") also proposed a series of tax reductions. By 1918, the tax rate on the highest income bracket had risen to 73 percent because of the extraordinary expense of the war. Mellon believed that such high rates were pushing wealthy Americans to avoid paying taxes by investing their money in foreign countries or in tax-free government bonds. Throughout the twenties, with the support of Congress and

Presidents Harding and Coolidge, Mellon's policies systematically reduced tax rates while increasing tax revenues. The top tax rate was cut from 73 percent in 1921 to 24 percent in 1929. Rates for the people with the lowest annual incomes were also cut substantially, helping the working poor.

The Mellon Plan worked. By 1926, 65 percent of federal income tax revenue came from people with incomes of $300,000 or more. In 1921, less than 20 percent had come from this group. During this same period, the overall income tax burden on those with incomes of less than $10,000 dropped from $155 million to $32.5 million. By 1929, barely 2 percent of American workers had to pay any income tax at all.

At the same time, Mellon helped Harding reduce the federal budget. Government expenditures fell, as did the national debt, and the economy soared. Unemployment plummeted to 2.4 percent in 1923. Mellon's admirers tagged him the greatest secretary of the Treasury since Alexander Hamilton in the late eighteenth century. In addition to tax cuts, Mellon, who had earlier built huge empires in the steel, oil, shipbuilding, coal, banking, and aluminum industries, promoted the long-standing Republican policy of high tariffs on imported goods. The Fordney-McCumber Tariff of 1922 increased rates on chemical and metal products to help prevent the revival of German corporations that had dominated those industries before the Great War. To please commercial farmers, who historically had benefited little from tariffs, the new act further extended duties on agricultural imports.

Reduced Regulation and Racial Progressivism

The Republican economic program of the 1920s also featured reduced regulation of corporations. Neither Harding nor his successor, Calvin Coolidge, could dismantle the federal regulatory agencies created during the Progressive Era, but they named as commissioners of those agencies people who generally promoted regulation "friendly" to business interests. Progressive Republican senator George W. Norris characterized Harding's appointments as "the nullification of federal law by a process of boring from within." His conservative colleague Henry Cabot Lodge agreed, boasting that "we have torn up Wilsonism by the roots."

In addition, Harding's four Supreme Court appointments were all conservatives, including Chief Justice William Howard Taft, the former president, who announced that he had been "appointed to reverse a few decisions." During the 1920s, the Taft court struck down a federal child-labor law and a minimum-wage law for women and issued numerous injunctions against striking unions as well as rulings limiting the powers of federal regulatory agencies.

In one area, however, Harding proved to be more progressive than Woodrow Wilson. He reversed the Wilson administration's policy of excluding African Americans from federal government jobs and spoke out against the vigilante racism that had flared up across the country during

> Commission and court appointments friendly to business; policies and speeches opposed to racism

and after the war. In his first speech to Congress in 1921, Harding insisted that the nation deal with the "race question." He attacked the Ku Klux Klan for fomenting "hatred and prejudice and violence" and urged Congress "to wipe the stain of barbaric lynching from the banners of a free and orderly, representative democracy." Southern Democrats in the Senate, however, stopped an anti-lynching bill from becoming law.

Setbacks for Unions

> A corporate campaign against organized labor

Organized labor suffered under Republican rule in the 1920s. Although President Harding endorsed collective bargaining and tried to reduce the twelve-hour workday and the six-day workweek to give the working class "time for leisure and family life," he ran into stiff opposition in Congress. After the war, the Red Scare and strikes of 1919 had created fears that unions promoted radical socialism. The brief postwar depression further weakened the unions, and in 1921 business groups in Chicago designated the **open shop** to be the "American plan" of employment. Although the open shop in theory implied only an employer's right to hire anyone, whether a union member or not, in practice it meant discrimination against unionists and a refusal by companies to negotiate with unions even when most of the workers belonged to one. A labor organizer identified another reason for his movement's weakness: "The Ford car has done an awful lot of harm to the unions. . . . As long as men have enough money to buy a second-hand Ford and tires and gasoline, they'll be out on the road and paying no attention to union meetings."

To suppress unions, employers often required workers to sign "yellow-dog" contracts, which forced them to agree not to join a union. Owners also used labor spies, blacklists, and intimidation to keep their workers from organizing unions. Some employers, such as Henry Ford, tried to kill the unions with kindness by introducing programs of "industrial democracy" guided by company-sponsored unions or various schemes of "welfare capitalism," such as profit sharing, bonuses, pensions, health programs, recreational activities, and the like. All these efforts paid off. Union membership dropped from about 5 million in 1920 to 3.5 million in 1929. But the anti-union movement, led by businesses that wanted to keep wages low, helped to create a "purchasing crisis" whereby the working poor were not making enough money to buy the huge volume of goods being churned out by America's ever more productive industries.

Isolationism in Foreign Affairs

In addition to the Senate's rejection of American membership in the League of Nations, the postwar spirit of isolation from world affairs found other expressions: the Red Scare, the higher tariff rates on imports, and the restrictive immigration laws with which the nation all but shut the door to newcomers. George Jean Nathan, a drama critic, expressed the sentiments of many Americans when he announced that the "great problems of the

open shop Business policy of not requiring union membership as a condition of employment; such a policy, where legal, has the effect of weakening unions and diminishing workers' rights.

world—social, political, economic and theological—do not concern me in the slightest.... What concerns me alone is myself, and the interests of a few close friends."

Yet the desire to stay out of foreign wars did not mean that the United States could ignore its own expanding global interests. American businesses now had worldwide connections. As a result of the Great War, the United States had become the world's chief banker, and American investments and loans enabled foreigners to purchase U.S. exports.

Isolationist foreign policy and expanding global economic interests

Probably nothing did more to heighten American isolationism—or anti-American feeling in Europe—than the complex challenge facing America's recent military allies: paying off their huge war debts to the United States. Beginning in 1917, when France and Great Britain ran out of money for military supplies, the U.S. government had advanced them massive loans, first for the war effort and then, after the war, for reconstruction projects. Most Americans, including Treasury Secretary Mellon, expected the debts to be repaid, but the Europeans thought otherwise. The British noted that after the American Revolution, the newly independent United States had refused to pay old debts to British merchants. The French likewise pointed out that they had never been repaid for helping the Americans win the Revolutionary War.

But the most difficult challenges in the 1920s were the practical problems of repayment. To get U.S. dollars to use to pay their war-related debts, European nations had to sell their goods to the United States. However, rising American tariff rates made imported European goods more expensive and less competitive with U.S. products, thus making it even harder for the Allies to repay their war-related debts. The French and British insisted that they could repay only by collecting the $33 billion in war reparations from defeated Germany, whose economy was devastated after the war by hyperinflation of consumer prices. Twice during the 1920s, the financial strain on the German economy forced American bankers to intervene with more loans so that Germany could pay its reparations to Britain and France, thereby enabling them to pay their debts to the United States.

Attempts at Disarmament

After the Great War, many Americans decided that excessive armed forces and weaponry had been the principal causes of the terrible conflict. The best way to keep the peace, they argued, was to limit the size of armies and navies. The United States had no intention of maintaining a large army after 1920, but under the shipbuilding program begun in 1916, it had constructed a powerful navy second only to that of Great Britain. Although neither the British nor the Americans wanted a naval armaments race, both were worried about the growth of Japanese power.

To address the problem, President Harding in 1921 invited diplomats from eight nations to a conference in Washington, D.C., at which Secretary of State Charles Evans Hughes made a blockbuster proposal. The only way

The Five-Power Treaty provides for naval disarmament

to avoid an expensive naval arms race, he declared, "is to end it now" by eliminating scores of existing warships and prohibiting the construction of new ones. It was one of the most dramatic moments in diplomatic history. In less than fifteen minutes, one journalist reported, Hughes had destroyed more warships "than all the admirals of the world have sunk in a cycle of centuries." His daring proposal was greeted by a "tornado of cheering" among the delegates.

Following Hughes's lead, delegates from the United States, Britain, Japan, France, and Italy signed the Five-Power Treaty (1922), which limited the size of their nations' navies. It was the first disarmament treaty in history. The five major powers also agreed to refrain from strengthening their military forces in the Pacific. The agreement in effect partitioned the world: U.S. naval power became supreme in the Western Hemisphere, Japanese power in the western Pacific, and British power from the North Sea to Singapore.

With these agreements in hand, Harding could boast of what seemed to be a brilliant diplomatic coup that relieved citizens of the need to pay for an enlarged navy and prevented potential conflicts in the Pacific. But the treaty set limits only on "capital" ships (battleships and aircraft carriers); the race to build cruisers, destroyers, submarines, and other smaller craft continued. Japan withdrew from the agreement in 1934, and by then the Soviet Union and Germany, which had been excluded from the conference, were building up their navies as well. Thus, twelve years after the Washington Naval Conference, the dream of naval disarmament died.

The Harding Scandals

Teapot Dome, other scandals, and Harding's death and historical reputation

Republican conservatives such as Henry Cabot Lodge, Andrew W. Mellon, Calvin Coolidge, and Herbert Hoover operated out of a philosophical conviction that was intended to benefit the nation. Members of Harding's Ohio gang, however, used their White House connections to line their own pockets. Early in 1923, for example, Harding learned that the head of the Veterans Bureau was systematically looting medical and hospital supplies. A few weeks later, the legal adviser to the bureau committed suicide. Not long afterward, a close friend of Attorney General Harry M. Daugherty, who had set up an office in the Justice Department from which he illegally sold paroles, pardons, and judgeships, was found shot dead in a hotel room after he had threatened to "quit the racket." Finally, the attorney general himself was implicated in the fraudulent handling of German assets seized after the war. These were but the most visible of the many scandals that touched federal agencies under Harding.

One major scandal rose above all, however. The "**Teapot Dome**," like "Watergate" fifty years later, would become the catchphrase for the climate of corruption surrounding a presidential administration. The Teapot Dome was a government-owned oil field in Wyoming that had been set aside as an oil reserve to ensure a supply of fuel for warships. After Harding moved administrative control of the field from the Department of the Navy to the

Teapot Dome (1923) Harding administration scandal in which Secretary of the Interior Albert B. Fall profited from secret leasing of government oil reserves in Wyoming to private oil companies.

Department of the Interior, Interior Secretary Albert B. Fall, deeply in debt and eight years overdue in paying his taxes, began signing overly generous federal contracts with close friends who were executives of petroleum companies that wanted access to the field. It turned out that he had taken bribes of about $400,000 (which came in "a little black bag") from an oil tycoon. Fall was convicted of conspiracy and bribery and sentenced to a year in prison, the first former cabinet official to serve time as a result of misconduct in office.

How much Harding knew of the scandals was unclear, but he knew enough to be troubled. "My God, this is a hell of a job!" he confided to a journalist. "I have no trouble with my enemies; I can take care of my enemies all right. But my damn friends, my God-damn friends. . . . They're the ones that keep me walking the floor nights!" In 1923, Harding left on what would be his last journey, a speaking tour to the West Coast and a trip to the Alaska Territory. He suffered an attack of food poisoning in Seattle, recovered briefly, then died in a San Francisco hotel. He was fifty-seven years old.

Because of Harding's sexual misbehavior and his corrupt associates, his administration came to be viewed as one of the worst in history. Even Herbert Hoover, his loyal secretary of commerce, admitted that Harding was not "a man with either the experience or the intellectual quality that the position needed" and that he was unable to admit or resolve the "terrible corruption by his playmates." More recent assessments suggest, however, that the scandals obscured Harding's accomplishments. He led the nation out of the turmoil of the postwar years and helped create the remarkable economic boom of the 1920s. He also promoted diversity and civil rights, appointing Jews to key federal positions and becoming the first president to criticize racial segregation in a speech before a white audience in the South. No previous president had promoted women's rights as forcefully as he did. Like Hoover, though, even Harding's foremost scholarly defender admits that he lacked good judgment and "probably should never have been president."

Coolidge Conservatism

The news of Harding's death reached Vice President Calvin Coolidge when he was visiting his father in the isolated mountain village of Plymouth Notch, Vermont, his birthplace. There, at 2:47 A.M. on August 3, 1923, by the light of a kerosene lamp, Colonel John Coolidge, a farmer and merchant, administered the presidential oath of office to his son. Calvin Coolidge, born on the Fourth of July in 1872, was a throwback to an earlier era. A puritan in his personal life, he was, unlike Harding, horrified by the jazzed-up Roaring Twenties, whose rebellious social and cultural forces he could not understand. But he sincerely believed in the ideals of personal integrity and devotion to public service. He was also a virtuous evangelist for capitalism who would bring stability to the White House and prosperity to the economy.

A Modest, Upright, and Tight-Lipped Evangelist for Capitalism

Although Coolidge had won every political race he had entered, beginning in 1898, he had never loved the limelight. Shy and awkward, he was a man of famously few words—hence, his nickname, "Silent Cal." After being reelected president of the Massachusetts State Senate in 1916, he gave a four-sentence inaugural address that concluded with "above all things, be brief." Voters liked Coolidge's uprightness, his straight-talking style, and his personal humility. He was a simple, direct man of strong principles and intense patriotism who championed self-discipline and hard work.

As a Massachusetts state senator, Coolidge had often aligned himself with Republican progressives. He voted for women's suffrage, a state income tax, a minimum wage for female workers, and salary increases for public school teachers. By the time he entered the White House, however, he had abandoned most of those causes.

Coolidge was determined *not* to be an activist president. Unlike Theodore Roosevelt and Woodrow Wilson, he had no exaggerated sense of self-importance; he knew he was "not a great man." Nor did he have an ambitious program to push through Congress. "Four-fifths of our troubles," Coolidge believed, "would disappear if we would sit down and keep still." Following his own logic, he insisted on twelve hours of sleep *and* an afternoon nap. The irreverent journalist H. L. Mencken claimed that Coolidge "slept more than any other president."

Calvin Coolidge "Silent Cal" was so reticent that when he died in 1933, American humorist Dorothy Parker remarked, "How could they tell?"

Even more than Harding, Coolidge linked the nation's welfare with the success of big business. "The chief business of the American people is business," he preached. "The man who builds a factory builds a temple. The man who works there worships there." Where Harding had tried to balance the interests of labor, agriculture, and industry, Coolidge focused on promoting industrial development. He reduced federal regulations of business and, with the help of Treasury Secretary Mellon and Republican Congresses, continued to lower income tax rates.

Coolidge was also "obsessed" with reducing spending, even to the point of issuing government workers only one pencil at a time—and only after they turned in the stub of the old pencil. "I am for economy" in government spending, he stressed. "After that, I am for more economy." When a South African mayor sent the president two lion cubs as a present, Coolidge named them "Tax Reduction" and "Budget Bureau." His fiscal frugality and pro-corporate stance led the *Wall Street Journal* to rejoice: "Never before, here or anywhere else, has a government been so completely fused with business."

America also had too many laws, Coolidge insisted, and it was "much more important to kill bad bills than to pass good ones." True to his word, he vetoed fifty acts of Congress. As a journalist said, "In a great day of yes-men, Calvin Coolidge was a no-man."

> Coolidge: "The chief business of the American people is business."

The Election of 1924

A man of honesty, a good administrator who had restored the dignity of the presidency while speaking out against racial prejudice and capably managing the various Republican factions, Coolidge easily gained the party's 1924 presidential nomination. Meanwhile, the Democrats again fell to fighting among themselves, prompting humorist Will Rogers's classic statement that "I am a member of no organized political party. I am a Democrat." The party's fractiousness illustrated the deep divisions between urban and rural America during the 1920s. It took the Democrats 103 ballots to decide on a presidential candidate: John W. Davis, a corporate lawyer from West Virginia who could nearly outdo Coolidge in his conservatism.

While the Democrats bickered, rural populists and urban progressives again decided to abandon both major parties, as they had done in 1912. Reorganizing the old Progressive party, they nominated Robert M. "Fighting Bob" La Follette for president. The sixty-nine-year-old Republican Wisconsin senator (and former governor) had voted against the 1917 declaration of war against Germany. Now, in addition to the Progressives, he won the support of the Socialist party and the American Federation of Labor.

In the 1924 campaign, the voters preferred to "Keep Cool with Coolidge," who decisively swept both the popular and the electoral votes. Davis took only the solidly Democratic South, and La Follette carried only Wisconsin. The popular vote went 15.7 million for Coolidge, 8.4 million for Davis, and 4.8 million for La Follette—the largest vote ever for a third-party candidate up to that time.

> Coolidge landslide: The height of postwar conservatism

Coolidge's landslide victory represented the height of postwar political conservatism. The Democratic party was in disarray, and the Republicans were triumphant. Business executives interpreted the Republican victory as an endorsement of their leading influence on government, and Coolidge saw the economy's surging prosperity as confirmation of his aggressive support of the interests of business. In fact, the prosperity and technological achievements of the New Era did have much to do with Coolidge's victory.

The Rise of Herbert Hoover

> Hoover and Republicans as champions of industrial efficiency

During the twenties, the drive for industrial efficiency, which had been a prominent theme among progressives, powered the wheels of mass production and consumption and became a cardinal belief of Republican leaders. Herbert Hoover, who served as secretary of commerce in the Harding and Coolidge cabinets, was himself a remarkable success story.

Born into an Iowa farm family in 1874, Hoover was a shy but industrious "loner" who had become a world-renowned mining engineer, oil tycoon, financial wizard, and multimillionaire before the age of forty. His meteoric success and genius for managing difficult tasks bred a self-confidence that bordered on conceit. Famously short-tempered and quick to take offense, Hoover had to have complete control of any project he managed. "I have insisted on having my own way," he admitted, and, in his twenties, he was already planning to be the president of the United States.

Hoover the "Wonder Boy"

After applying his managerial skills to the Food Administration during the Great War, Hoover served with the U.S. delegation at the Versailles peace conference. He idolized Woodrow Wilson and supported American membership in the League of Nations. A young Franklin Roosevelt, then assistant secretary of the navy, was dazzled by Hoover, the man he would eventually defeat in the presidential election of 1932. In 1920, Roosevelt said that Hoover was "certainly a wonder [boy], and I wish we could make him President of the United States."

Hoover soon disappointed Roosevelt, however, by declaring himself a Republican "progressive conservative." In a book entitled *American Individualism* (1922), Hoover promoted an "ideal of *service*" that went beyond "rugged individualism." He wanted government to encourage business leaders to forgo "cutthroat competition" and called instead for them to engage in "voluntary cooperation" by forming trade associations that would share information and promote standardization and efficiency.

As secretary of commerce during the 1920s, Hoover transformed the small Commerce Department into the government's most dynamic agency. He looked for new markets for business, created a Bureau of Aviation to promote the new airline industry, and established the Federal Radio Commission.

The 1928 Election: Hoover versus Smith

On August 2, 1927, while on vacation in the Black Hills of South Dakota, President Coolidge suddenly announced, "I do not choose to run for President in 1928." His choice surprised the nation and cleared the way for Hoover to win the 1928 Republican nomination. The party's platform took credit for the nation's longest period of sustained prosperity, the government's cost cutting, debt and tax reduction, and the high tariffs ("as vital to American agriculture as . . . to manufacturing") designed to "protect" American businesses from foreign competition.

The Democratic nomination went to four-term New York governor Alfred E. Smith, the "Happy Warrior." The two candidates presented sharply different images: Hoover, the successful businessman and bureaucratic manager from an Iowa farm, versus Smith, a professional politician from a Lower East Side neighborhood of New York City. To working-class Democrats in northern cities, Smith was a hero, the poor grandson of Irish immigrants who had worked himself up to being governor of the most populous state. His outspoken criticism of Prohibition also endeared him to the Irish, Italians, and others in the North.

> A third straight Republican presidential landslide

On the other hand, as the first Roman Catholic nominated for president by a major party, a product of big-city machine politics, and a "wet" on Prohibition (in direct opposition to his party's platform), Smith represented all that was hateful to southern and western rural Democrats—as well as most rural and small-town Republicans. A powerful Kansas newspaper editor declared that the "whole puritan civilization, which has built a sturdy, orderly nation, is threatened by Smith." The Ku Klux Klan issued a "Klarion Kall for a Krusade" against him, mailing thousands of postcards proclaiming that "Alcohol" Smith, the Catholic New Yorker, was the Antichrist. While Hoover stayed above the fray, reminding Americans of their unparalleled prosperity, Smith was forced to deal with constant criticism. He denounced his opponents for injecting "bigotry, hatred, intolerance and un-American sectarian division" into the campaign. But it did little good.

On Election Day, Hoover won in the third consecutive Republican presidential landslide, with 21 million popular votes to Smith's 15 million and an Electoral College majority of 444 to 87. Hoover even cracked the Democrats' Solid South, leaving Smith only six Deep South states plus Massachusetts and Rhode Island. Republicans kept control of both houses of Congress. The election was a clear indication that voters appreciated the prosperity generated during the Harding and Coolidge administrations. Coolidge, however, was skeptical that Hoover could sustain the good times. He quipped that the "Wonder Boy" had offered him "unsolicited advice for six years, all of it bad." Coolidge's skepticism about Hoover's political abilities would prove all too accurate, as the talented new president would soon be struck by an economic earthquake that would test all of his skills—and more.

■ **A "New Era" of Consumption** During the 1920s, the American economy grew at the fastest rate in history, while consumer debt tripled. Innovations in production, advertising, and financing, combined with a jump in the use of electricity, enabled and encouraged millions of Americans to purchase automobiles, radios, and other electrical household appliances. The new *consumer culture,* valued leisure, self-expression, and self-indulgence. More and more Americans purchased national brand-name items from retail chain stores, listened to the same radio shows and watched the same movies.

■ **The Jazz Age** New social and cultural movements challenged the traditional order. The carefree attitude of the 1920s, perhaps best represented by the frantic rhythms of jazz music, led writer F. Scott Fitzgerald to call the decade the *Jazz Age*. Though *flappers* emerged to challenge gender norms, the majority of women remained full-time housewives or domestic servants. As the Great Migration continued, African Americans in northern cities felt freer to speak out against racial injustice and express pride in their race. The *Harlem Renaissance* gave voice to African American literature and arts. Racial separatism and black nationalism grew popular under Marcus Garvey, while the *National Association for the Advancement of Colored People (NAACP)* made efforts to undo racism through education and legislation.

■ **The Modernist Revolt** Many artists and intellectuals were attracted to *modernism*, which drew upon Einstein's theory of relativity and Freud's psychological explorations. For modernists, the world was no longer governed by reason, but rather something created and expressed through one's highly individual consciousness. To be "modern" meant to break free of tradition, to violate restrictions, and to shock and confuse the public.

■ **The Reactionary Twenties** Retaliating against to these challenges to convention, various movements fought to uphold their traditional ideas of what America was and how it should remain. In reaction to a renewed surge of immigration after the Great War and the Red Scare, nativists persuaded Congress to restrict future immigration with the *Immigration Act of 1924*. A revived Ku Klux Klan gained a large membership and considerable political influence across the nation. Fundamentalist Protestants campaigned against teaching evolution in public schools, arguing instead for the literal truth of the Bible. Their efforts culminated in the 1925 *Scopes Trial*. Progressive reformers and conservative Protestants supported the nationwide *Prohibition* of alcoholic beverages that started in 1920. Union membership declined as businesses adopted new techniques like *open shop*.

■ **Republican Resurgence** Disillusionment with the Great War turned the public against progressivism, and in favor of disarmament and isolationism. The Republican Party benefited from this shift in the public mood. Warren G. Harding's call for a *"return to normalcy"* brought about his landslide presidential victory in 1920. His administration followed the Mellon Plan, which succeeded in reviving the economy. The progressive goal of efficiency through better management remained a part of many Republican initiatives, such as the Budget and Accounting Act.

KEY TERMS

CHRONOLOGY

1903   Wright Brothers fly first motorized airplane

Ford Motor Company is founded

1905   First movie house opens

1910   National Association for the Advancement of Colored People
(NAACP) is founded

1913   Armory Show introduces Americans to modern art

1916   Marcus Garvey brings Universal Negro Improvement Association to
New York

1920   Prohibition begins

Warren G. Harding is elected president

1921   Sacco and Vanzetti Trial

Washington Naval Conference and Five-Power Treaty

Congress passes Emergency Immigration Act

1922   First radio commercial

1923   Teapot Dome scandal

1924   Congress passes Immigration Act

Calvin Coolidge is reelected president

1925   Scopes "monkey trial"

1927   Charles A. Lindbergh Jr. makes first solo transatlantic airplane flight

Sacco and Vanzetti are executed

1928   Herbert Hoover is elected president

INQUIZITIVE

Go to InQuizitive to see what you've learned—and learn what you've missed—with personalized feedback along the way.

CONSTRUCTION OF A DAM (1939), DETAIL One of the most famous and controversial of the artists commissioned by the New Deal's Works Progress Administration was William Gropper, who painted this mural in the Department of the Interior building in Washington, D.C. Based on his observations of dam construction on the Columbia and Colorado Rivers, Gropper illustrates the triumph and brotherhood that emerged from America's grand undertakings during the Great Depression.

New Deal America

1929–1939

The milestone year 1929 dawned with high hopes. Rarely had a new president entered office with greater expectations. In fact, Herbert Hoover was worried that people viewed him as "a superman; that no problem is beyond my capacity." Hoover was right to be concerned. People did consider him a superman—"the man who had never failed"—a dedicated public servant whose engineering genius and business savvy would ensure continued prosperity. At the time, more Americans were working than ever before and earning record levels of income. But that was about to change.

The Great Depression, which began at the end of 1929, brought with it widespread human misery. No other business slump had been so deep, so long, or so painful. One out of four Americans in 1932 was unemployed; in many large cities, nearly half of the adults were out of work. Some 500,000 people had lost homes or farms because they could not pay their mortgages. Thousands of banks had failed; millions of people lost their life savings. What made the Great Depression so severe and so enduring was its global nature. In 1929, the economies of Europe were still reeling from the First World War. Once the American economy tumbled, it sent shock waves throughout Europe and elsewhere.

The suffering was worldwide when Franklin Delano Roosevelt was elected in 1932 to lead an anxious nation mired in the third year of an unprecedented economic downturn. Within days of becoming president,

CORE OBJECTIVES INQUIZITIVE

1. Identify the major causes of the Great Depression.

2. Describe the impact of the Great Depression on the American people.

3. Explain the response of the Hoover administration to the Great Depression.

4. Assess the goals and accomplishments of the early New Deal.

5. Analyze the major criticisms of the early New Deal.

6. Evaluate the ways the New Deal evolved and how it transformed the role of federal government.

Roosevelt took dramatic steps that forever transformed the scope and role of the federal government. He and a supportive Congress adopted bold measures to relieve the human suffering and promote economic recovery. Roosevelt was not an ideologue; rather, he was a pragmatist willing to try different approaches. As he once explained, "Take a method and try it. If it fails, admit it frankly and try another." Roosevelt's program for recovery, the New Deal, was therefore a series of trial-and-error actions rather than a comprehensive scheme. None of these well-intentioned but often poorly planned initiatives worked perfectly, and in fact some of them failed miserably. But their combined effect was to restore hope and energy to a nation paralyzed by fear and uncertainty.

CORE OBJECTIVE

1. Identify the major causes of the Great Depression.

The Causes of the Great Depression

Herbert Hoover's election in 1928 boosted the hopes of investors in what had come to be called "the Great Bull Market." Since 1924, the prices of stock shares invested in U.S. companies had steadily risen. Beginning in 1927, prices soared further on wings of reckless speculation. In 1929, President Hoover voiced concern about the "orgy of mad speculation" in the stock market, and he urged investors to be more cautious—but to no avail. Treasury Secretary Andrew W. Mellon's tax reductions had given people more money to spend or invest, much of which went into the stock market. The nation's foremost economist, Irving Fisher of Yale University, assured investors in 1929 that "stock prices have reached what looks like a permanently high plateau."

The Stock Market during the Twenties

Margin loans, reckless stock speculation, and slowing economy

What made it so easy for hundreds of thousands of people to invest in stocks during the twenties was the common practice of buying stock "on margin"—that is, an investor could make a small cash down payment (the "margin") on shares of stock and borrow the rest from a stockbroker, who held the stock certificates as security in case the stock price plummeted. If stock prices rose, as they did in 1927, 1928, and most of 1929, the investor made enough profits to pay for the "margin loan" and reinvest the rest. But if the stock price declined and the buyer failed to meet a "margin call" for cash to pay off the broker's loan, the broker could sell the stock at a much lower price to cover the loan. By August 1929, stockbrokers were lending investors more than two-thirds of the face value of the stocks they were buying. Yet few people seemed concerned, and stock prices kept rising.

But despite the soaring stock market, there were signs that the economy was weakening. By 1927, steel production, residential construction, and automobile sales were slowing, as was the rate of consumer spending. By mid-1929, industrial production, employment, and other measures of economic activity were also declining. Still, the stock market rose.

Then, in early September 1929, the speculative bubble burst when the stock market fell sharply. By the middle of October, world markets were in a steep decline. Still, most investors remained bullish. On October 22, 1929, a leading bank president assured reporters that there was "nothing fundamentally wrong with the stock market or with the underlying business and credit structure."

The Crash

The next week, however, stock market values tumbled, triggering a wild scramble as terrified investors tried to sell stocks whose values were falling. Then, on Black Tuesday, October 29—the worst day in the stock market's history to that point—widespread panic set in. Stock prices went into free fall. By the end of the month, stocks on the New York Stock Exchange had dropped an average of 37 percent. An atmosphere of gloom settled over the financial community. "Life would no longer be, ever again, all fun and games" the comedian Harpo Marx sighed, as he anticipated the onset of the worst depression in history.

After the catastrophic drop in the stock market, fear and uncertainty spread like a virus across the nation and around the world. Investors who had borrowed heavily to buy stocks were now forced to sell their holdings at huge losses in order to pay their debts. Several stockbrokers and investors who had lost everything committed suicide. The president of a cigar company that had gone bankrupt jumped off the ledge of a New York hotel. A Seattle man shot himself. Two men, business partners, joined hands and jumped to their deaths from the Ritz Hotel in New York City. Room clerks in Manhattan hotels began asking guests at registration if they wanted a room for jumping or sleeping.

During 1930, the national economy sputtered and stumbled. Some 26,355 businesses shut down; even more failed the following year. Half of the textile workers in New England mills were jobless. The resulting slowdown in economic growth, called a *recession*, became so severe and long-lasting that it came to be called the **Great Depression**. The collapse of the stock market did not *cause* the Great Depression. Rather, it revealed that the prosperity of the 1920s had been built on weak foundations.

Of course, the stock market crash had the added effect of creating a psychological panic that accelerated the economic decline. Frightened that they were at risk of losing everything, people rushed to get their money out of banks and out of the stock market. Such panicky behavior only made things worse. By 1932, more than 9,000 banks had closed their doors. The nation's formerly robust economy experienced a shocking collapse that would last over ten years.

Black Tuesday

Financial panic

Great Depression (1929–1941) Worst economic downturn in American history; it was spurred by the stock market crash in the fall of 1929 and lasted until the Second World War.

Why the Economy Collapsed

Stagnant wages, slow consumer spending, drop in GDP, and widespread unemployment

What were the underlying *causes* of the Great Depression? Economists still debate the relative importance of the various factors, but most scholars emphasize a combination of interrelated elements that triggered the profound economic downturn. The economy had actually begun to fall into a recession in the summer of 1929, months *before* the stock market crash. Too many business owners during the twenties had taken large profits while denying wage increases to employees. And by plowing profits into business expansion, executive salaries, and stock dividends rather than wage increases for hourly workers, employers created a growing imbalance: factories and mills were producing more goods but the purchasing power of consumers was declining because of stagnant wages. During the twenties, industrial productivity had increased 43 percent, but the wages of factory workers had gone up only 11 percent, in part because labor unions had declined in power and had lost their ability to ensure that wages for their workers were fair. In 1920, there were 5 million union members in the United States; by 1929, there were only 3.4 million. Two-thirds of American families in 1929 earned less than $2,000 in annual income, an amount said by economists to provide "only basic necessities." In essence, the economy was producing more and more products that consumers could not afford to buy, and too many people had been borrowing too much money for unproductive purposes, such as speculating in the stock market.

Factories cut back production or shut down altogether. From 1929 to 1933, U.S. economic output (called *gross domestic product*, or GDP) dropped almost 27 percent. By 1932, one-quarter of the workforce was out of work. Businesses posted signs that read, "We are Firing, not Hiring."

Weak agricultural sector worsens

At the same time that the financial and industrial sectors were collapsing in the early 1930s, the farm sector remained feeble. Increasing production during the twenties had led to lower prices for grains and livestock, in part because the spreading use of tractors to replace horses and mules made farmers much more productive. As more corn and wheat were grown, however, the prices farmers earned for their crops began a relentless decline. To make matters worse, record harvests in the summer and fall of 1929 caused prices for corn, wheat, and cotton to fall even faster, pinching the income of struggling farmers. A bushel of wheat that brought a farmer $2.94 in 1920 brought only 30 cents by 1932.

Government Actions and the Economy

Government policies: High tariffs, shrinking trade, and an inadequate money supply

Government policies also contributed to the Depression. High tariffs hurt the economy by reducing foreign trade. Like most Republican presidents, Herbert Hoover supported Congressional efforts to raise tariffs on imported goods in order to keep out foreign competition. The Smoot-Hawley Tariff of 1930, authored by two leading Republicans, Reed Owen Smoot and Willis C. Hawley, was intended to help the farm sector by raising tariff barriers on farm products imported into the United States. But a swarm of corporate lobbyists convinced Congress to add hundreds of new imported manufactured items to the tariff bill. More than 1,000 economists urged Hoover to veto the tariff bill because its logic was flawed: by trying to "protect" American farmers from foreign competition, the bill would actually raise prices on most raw materials and consumer products by impeding imports. Hoover signed the bill anyway, causing another steep drop in the stock market. The new Smoot-Hawley Tariff also prompted other countries to retaliate by passing tariffs of their own, thereby making it more difficult for American farms and businesses to sell their products abroad. U.S. exports plummeted, worsening the depression.

Another factor contributing to the Great Depression was the stance of the Federal Reserve (known as "the Fed"), the government agency responsible for serving as a "central bank" by managing the nation's money supply and interest rates. Instead of expanding the nation's money supply in an effort to generate growth, the Federal Reserve did the reverse, reducing the money supply out of concern for possible inflation in consumer prices. Between 1929 and 1932, the nation's money supply shrank by a third, leading almost 10,000 small banks to close their doors and, in turn, taking millions of their depositors with them into bankruptcy.

Bank run As news of the Great Crash spread across the world, people rushed to their banks to withdraw their deposits. The line for this Millbury, Massachusetts, savings bank wraps around the building.

The Impact of Europe's Economy

A final cause of the Depression was the chaotic state of the European economy, which had never fully recovered from the shock of the Great War. During the late 1920s, nations such as Great Britain, France, Spain, and Italy slowed their purchases of American goods as their shattered economies, slowly recovering from the devastation of the war, were finally able to produce more goods of their own. Meanwhile, the important German economy continued to flounder. A related factor was the continuing inability of European nations to pay their debts to each other—and to the United States—that they had incurred during the war. The American government insisted that the $11 billion it loaned to the Allies be repaid, but nations such as Great Britain and France had no money to send to Washington, D.C. They were forced to borrow huge sums ($5 billion) from U.S. banks, which only increased their overall indebtedness. After the stock market crash in

European nations default on paying war debts

October 1929, American banks could no longer prop up the European economies. The Federal Reserve's tighter monetary policy also drastically slowed the amount of American capital (money) going abroad. The economies of nations like Germany, which had grown dependent on loans from American banks during the twenties, were devastated as American money dried up. Then the Smoot-Hawley Tariff made it even more difficult for European nations to sell their products in the United States, which meant that those countries had less money with which to buy American goods. So as the European economy sputtered, it dragged the American economy deeper into depression.

CORE **OBJECTIVE**
2. Describe the impact of the Great Depression on the lives of the American people.

The Human Toll of the Depression

The Depression of the 1930s came to be called "Great" because its effects were so severe and long-lasting. It generated record levels of unemployment and widespread human distress. By 1932, perhaps a quarter of the entire population could not afford housing or adequate food. The carefree optimism of the twenties disappeared as the suffering spread. Grassroots protests erupted as the Depression worsened. In many cities, hungry people looted grocery stores. Angry mobs stopped local sheriffs from foreclosing on farms; others threatened to lynch judges at bankruptcy hearings. In Harlan, Kentucky, coal miners went on strike to protest a cut in their wages. The mine owners called in the National Guard, which routed the union. In 1931, Socialists recruited 45,000 people to join the Unemployed Citizens' League in Seattle, Washington, which helped people avoid eviction and bankruptcy, found them part-time jobs, and lobbied for more government assistance. Some people talked of revolution. "Folks are restless," Mississippi governor Theodore Bilbo told reporters in 1931. "Communism is gaining a foothold. . . . In fact, I'm getting a little pink myself." Yet for all the radical talk, few Americans embraced communism during the early 1930s. "There was anger and rebellion among a few," recounted an Iowa farmer but most people lived in "helpless despair and submission."

Unemployment and "Relief"

As the economy spiraled downward between 1930 and 1933, growing numbers of workers were fired or saw their wages cut. National unemployment soared to 4 million in 1930, 8 million in 1931, and 12 million by 1932. Some 6,000 jobless New Yorkers sold apples on street corners.

Many struggling business executives and professionals—lawyers, doctors, dentists, accountants, stockbrokers, teachers, nurses, and engineers—

Soaring unemployment, spreading poverty, failure of local efforts at "relief" went without food and stopped going to doctors and dentists in order to save money and to avoid the humiliation of "going on relief." A dentist in New York City and his wife committed suicide, explaining in a note that "we want to get out of the way before we are forced to accept relief money." The sense of shame cut across class lines. In *The Grapes of Wrath* (1939), John Steinbeck's best-selling novel about the Depression, a poor but proud woman is disgraced by accepting "charity" from the Salvation Army: "We was hungry. They made us crawl for our dinner. They took our dignity."

The Grapes of Wrath **(1939)**
First edition of John Steinbeck's bestseller, adapted into an acclaimed film in 1940.

Hunger

Hard-pressed families went without fruit and most vegetables, eating mostly beans and soup. Surveys of children in the nation's public schools in 1932 showed that one quarter suffered from malnutrition. In a rural school in Appalachia, a teacher told a sickly child to go home and get something to eat. "I can't," she replied. "It's my sister's turn to eat." In 1931, New York City hospitals reported about 100 cases of actual starvation, where people died solely from the lack of food. Hungry people by the millions lined up at soup kitchens where minimal amounts of food and water were distributed; others rummaged through trash cans behind restaurants. In Detroit, "we saw the city at its worst," wrote Louise V. Armstrong. "One vivid, gruesome moment of those dark days we shall never forget. We saw a crowd of some fifty men fighting over a barrel of garbage which had been set outside the back door of a restaurant. American citizens fighting over scraps of food like animals!"

Homelessness

The contraction of the economy especially squeezed debtors, who had monthly mortgages or installment debts to pay. A thousand Americans per day lost their homes to foreclosure. At first, the poor made homeless by the Depression were usually placed in *poorhouses* or *workhouses*. By 1933, however, the numbers of homeless overwhelmed the small number of public facilities. People were forced to live under bridges, on park benches, and in doorways and police stations. To make matters worse, the poor were degraded as a class of outsiders and subject to frequent abuse and arrest. The constitutions of fourteen states even banned paupers from voting.

Millions of homeless people, mostly men, simply took to living on the road or the rails. These hobos, or tramps, as they were called, walked, hitchhiked in cars, or sneaked onto empty railway cars and rode from town to town. One railroad, the Missouri Pacific, counted 200,000 people living in its empty boxcars in 1931. The following year, the Southern Pacific Railroad reported that it had evicted 683,457 people from its freight trains. A black military veteran recalled life as a freight train hobo: "Black and white, it didn't make any difference who you were, 'cause everybody was poor. . . . They didn't have no mothers or sisters, they didn't have no home;

they were dirty, they had overalls on, they didn't have no food, they didn't have anything."

Desperate Responses

As always, those hardest hit were the most disadvantaged groups—immigrants, women, farmers, the urban unemployed, Native Americans, and African Americans. Desperate conditions did lead desperate people to do desperate things. Crime soared during the 1930s, as did street-corner begging, homelessness, and prostitution. A Pennsylvania man wrote the governor in 1931, explaining that he did not "want to steal, but I won't let my wife and boy cry for something to eat. . . . How long is this going to keep up? I cannot stand it any longer."

> Families in distress: Crime, desertion, and declining birth rates

Although the divorce rate dropped during the decade, in part because couples could not afford to live separately or pay the legal fees to obtain a divorce, many jobless husbands simply deserted their wives and children. Some 1.5 million husbands left home during the thirties. "You don't know what it's like when your husband's out of work," a woman told a reporter. "He's gloomy and unhappy all the time. Life is terrible. You must try all the time to keep him from going crazy." With their future so uncertain, married couples often decided not to have children; birth rates plummeted during the 1930s. Many struggling parents sent their children to live with relatives or friends. Some 900,000 children simply left home and joined the growing army of homeless tramps. During the Great Depression, for the first time ever, more people left the United States than arrived as immigrants.

The Plight of Married Working Women

Women were placed in a peculiar position by the Depression. By 1932, 20 percent of working women were unemployed, a slightly lower percentage than men. On the one hand, because women held a disproportionate number of the lowest-paying jobs, they were often able to keep their jobs as employers laid off the higher-paid men. Even if they kept their jobs, however, many women also had the added burden of keeping their families together emotionally when their husbands lost jobs. Many magazines during the thirties published articles about the challenge of maintaining households when the husband had been "unmanned" by losing his job as breadwinner. One of the most famous Broadway show tunes during the early thirties was "Remember My Forgotten Man."

> Discrimination against married women and minorities in hiring and assistance

As the Depression deepened, however, married women in the workforce became the primary targets of layoffs. Some 26 states passed laws prohibiting the employment of married women. The reasoning behind such laws was that a married woman—who presumably had a husband to take care of her—should not "steal" a job from a man. It was acceptable for single women to find jobs because these were usually lower-paying jobs considered "women's work": sales clerks, beauticians, schoolteachers, secretaries, and nurses. The job market for African American women was even more restricted, with most black women working as maids, cooks, or laundresses. In a desperate attempt to create jobs for unemployed men, many employers adopted policies barring married women from employment. For example, three-fourths of the public school systems across the nation during the Great Depression fired women teachers who got married. As a legislator commented, the working woman in Depression-era America was "the first orphan in the storm."

African Americans, Mexicans, and Asians

Most African Americans during the Depression still lived in the eleven southern states of the former Confederacy, where the southern economy, still farm-dominated, was already depressed. Most African Americans who lived in the South earned their livelihood from farming as tenants and sharecroppers. Pervasive racial discrimination kept blacks out of the few labor unions in the South and consigned them to the most-menial, lowest-paying jobs. Most blacks were still excluded from voting, segregated from whites in public places like hotels and trains, and limited mostly to farm work. Already living in poverty, they were among the hardest hit by the Depression. As a blues song called "Hard Times Ain't Gone Nowhere" revealed, "Hard times don't worry me; I was broke when it first started out." Some 3 million rural blacks in the South lived in cramped cabins without electricity, running water, or bathrooms.

Just dropping off a resume In October 1938, the government opened six custodian positions and 15,000 African American women started lining up overnight to turn in their applications. Pictured here is a policeman leaping over a hedge to administer some crowd control.

In many mills, factories, mines, and businesses, the philosophy of "last hired, first fired" meant that the people who could least afford to be jobless were fired first. Blacks who had left the poverty-stricken South to take factory jobs in the North were among the first to be laid off. Blacks across the nation had the highest rate of joblessness in the early years of the Great Depression. "At no time in the history of the Negro since slavery," reported the Urban League, "has his economic and social outlook seemed so discouraging." Churches and other charity organizations gave aid, but some only assisted whites and refused to provide support for blacks, Mexicans, and Asians.

Impoverished whites found themselves competing with local Hispanics and Asians for seasonal farm work in the cotton fields or orchards of large corporate farms. Many Chinese, Japanese, and Filipino farm laborers moved to cities. Mexicans were also mostly migrant farm workers, traveling from farm to farm to work during harvest and planting seasons of different crops. They settled in California, New Mexico, Arizona, Colorado, Texas, and the midwestern states. As economic conditions worsened, government

> Deportation of Mexican-born Americans

officials called for the deportation of Mexican-born Americans in order to avoid the cost of providing them with public services. By 1935, over 500,000 Mexican Americans and their American-born children were deported to Mexico. The state of Texas alone returned over 250,000 people.

Dust Bowl Migrants

Black blizzards and Dust Bowl refugees

In the southern plains of the Midwest and the Mississippi Valley, a terrible drought during the 1930s created a catastrophe known as the **Dust Bowl**. Colorado, New Mexico, Kansas, Nebraska, Texas, Arkansas, and Oklahoma were the states hardest hit. Crops withered and income plummeted. Strong winds swept across the treeless plains, scooping up millions of tons of parched topsoil into billowing dark clouds that floated east across entire states, engulfing farms and towns in what were called black blizzards. By 1938, over 25 million acres of prairie land had lost their topsoil.

Okies on the run A sharecropping family reaches its destination of Bakersfield, California, in 1935, after "we got blowed out in Oklahoma."

Human misery paralleled the environmental devastation. Parched farmers could not pay their debts, and banks foreclosed on their property. Suicides soared. With each year, millions of people abandoned their farms. Many uprooted farmers and their families from the South and the Midwest headed toward California, where jobs were said to be plentiful. So off they went on a cross-country trek in pursuit of new opportunities. Frequently lumped together as "Okies" or "Arkies," most of the dust bowl refugees were from cotton belt communities in Arkansas, Texas, Missouri, and Oklahoma. During the 1930s and 1940s, some 800,000 people, mostly whites, left those four states and headed to the Far West in a migration powerfully described in Steinbeck's *The Grapes of Wrath* as well as in the folk songs of Woody Guthrie, a musician who traveled the nation during the thirties, singing about people down on their luck.

Most people uprooted by the dust bowl went to California's urban areas—Los Angeles, San Diego, or San Francisco. Others moved into the San Joaquin Valley, the agricultural heartland of California. There they discovered that rural California was no paradise. Only a few of the dust bowl migrants could afford to buy land. Living in tents or crude cabins and frequently on the move, the migrant workers suffered from exposure to the elements, poor sanitation, and social abuse. As an Okie reported, when the big farmers "need us they call us *migrants*, and when we've picked their crop, we're *bums* and we got to get out."

Dust Bowl Vast area of the Midwest where windstorms blew away millions of tons of topsoil from parched farmland after a long drought in the 1930s, causing great social distress and a massive migration of farm families.

From Hooverism to the New Deal

CORE **OBJECTIVE**
3. Explain the response of the Hoover administration to the Great Depression.

The initial response of government officials to the Great Depression was denial: there was no crisis, they insisted. All that was needed, President Hoover and others argued, was to let the sick economy cure itself. The best policy, Treasury Secretary Andrew Mellon advised, would be to "liquidate labor, liquidate stocks, liquidate the farmers, liquidate real estate." Letting events run their course, he insisted, would "purge the rottenness out of the system. High costs of living and high living will come down. People will work harder, live a more moral life." Mellon's do-nothing approach did not work, however. Falling wages and declining land and home values made it harder for farmers, businesses, and households to pay their debts. With so many people losing jobs and income, consumers and businesses simply could not buy enough goods and services to get the economy growing again.

Hoover's Efforts at Recovery

President Hoover was less willing than Andrew Mellon to sit by and let events take their course. As the "Great Engineer," he in fact did more than any president had ever done before in such dire economic circumstances. Hoover, for example, invited business, labor, government, and agricultural leaders to a series of White House conferences in which the president urged companies to maintain employment and wage levels, asked union leaders to end strikes, and pleaded with states to follow through on planned construction projects. None of these efforts worked. Unemployment continued to rise, and wage levels continued to fall.

Hoover's efforts to end the Depression: Government construction projects and private cooperation

In speech after speech, Hoover became a cheerleader for American capitalism. He asked people to keep up hope. In early May 1930, the president told the U.S. Chamber of Commerce that he was "convinced we have passed the worst and with continued effort we shall rapidly recover." A few weeks later, Hoover assured a group of bankers that the "depression is over." The Hoover administration also circulated upbeat slogans such as "Business IS Better" and "Keep Smiling." But uplifting words were not enough. More and more people kept losing their jobs and homes.

Short-Sighted Tax Increases

The Great Depression was the greatest national emergency since the Civil War, and the nation was woefully unprepared to deal with it. As personal income plummeted, so too did government tax revenues. Despite the Depression, President Hoover insisted on trying to balance the federal budget. To do so, he pushed through Congress the Revenue Act of 1932, the largest—and most poorly timed—peacetime tax increase in American history. By taking money out of consumers' pockets, the higher taxes accelerated the economic slowdown. People had less money to spend when what the depressed economy most needed was increased consumer spending.

The Revenue Act of 1932

Hooverville *Left:* Of the many Hoovervilles set up in Seattle alone, this particular shantytown near the shipyards was the largest and lasted nine years. *Right:* A toddler begs for change in one of the Bonus Army camps.

Hoover's Reaction to the Social Crisis

By the fall of 1930, many city governments were buckling under the strain of lost revenue and growing human distress. The federal government had no programs to deal with homelessness and joblessness. State and local governments cut spending, worsening the economic situation. All across the country, shantytowns sprouted in vacant lots where people erected shacks out of cardboard and scrap wood and metal. There they shivered and suffered, calling their makeshift villages *Hoovervilles* in criticism of the president. To keep warm during the winter, the homeless wrapped themselves in newspapers, calling them *Hoover blankets.* As the numbers rose, more and more people called for governments to step in to deal with the emergency of homeless, starving people. Frustrated by his critics, Hoover dismissed the concerns of "calamity mongers and weeping men."

> Hoover rejects federal intervention

President Hoover refused to provide any federal programs to help the needy for fear that the nation would be "plunged into socialism" if the government provided direct support to the poor. His governing philosophy, rooted in America's mythic commitment to rugged individualism, self-reliance, and free enterprise, set firm limits on emergency government action, and he was unwilling to set that philosophy aside even to meet an unprecedented national emergency. The president still trumpeted the virtues of "self-reliance" and individual initiative, claiming that government assistance would be the very worst thing for a nation in crisis, for it would rob people of the desire to help themselves.

> Voluntarism

Hoover hoped that the "natural generosity" of the American people and local charitable organizations would be sufficient to handle the crisis, and he believed that volunteers (the backbone of local charity organizations) would relieve the social distress caused by the Depression. But Hoover's faith in traditional "voluntarism" was misplaced. Although most Americans tried to get jobs to earn a living, there simply were no jobs, even for industrious people. The local and state relief agencies were overwhelmed by the magnitude of the social crisis. Churches and charitable organizations like the Salvation Army and the Red Cross were also swamped with needy people.

Rising Criticism of Hoover

As always, a depressed economy hurt the political party in power—and its president. The *New York Times* reported in the summer of 1930 that public opinion "is turning rather heavily against the Hoover administration." The Democrats shrewdly exploited Hoover's predicament. In November 1930, the Democrats gained their first national election victory since 1916, winning a majority in the House and a near majority in the Senate. Hoover refused to see the elections as a warning signal. Instead, he grew more resistant to calls for federal intervention in the struggling economy. By 1932, almost 25 percent of the workforce—15 million people—were unemployed. Still, Hoover resisted calls for federal assistance. The *New York Times* concluded that Hoover had "failed as a party leader. He has failed as an economist. . . . He has failed as a business leader. . . . He has failed as a personality because of [his] awkwardness of manner and speech and lack of mass magnetism."

Congressional Initiatives

With a new Congress in session in 1932, demands for federal action forced Hoover to do more. That year, the new Congress set up the **Reconstruction Finance Corporation** (RFC) to make emergency loans to struggling banks, life-insurance companies, and railroads. Yet if the federal government could help huge banks and railroads, asked New York Democratic senator Robert F. Wagner, why not "extend a helping hand to that forlorn American, in every village and every city of the United States, who has been without wages since 1929?" Democrats like Wagner called for federal help for the people hit hardest by the economic collapse. But Hoover held back and only signed the Emergency Relief Act (1932), which authorized the RFC to make loans to the states for construction projects.

Reconstruction Finance Corporation (RFC)

Farmers and Veterans in Protest

Meanwhile, desperate farmers across the nation took matters into their own hands. The average *annual* income of families working the land during the early 1930s was $240. Prices for agricultural products fell so low that farmers lost money if they took them to market. Thousands of Midwestern farmers joined the Farmers' Holiday Association to protest the low prices by dumping milk, vegetables, and fruits on the highways.

Reconstruction Finance Corporation (1932) Federal program established under President Hoover to loan money to banks and other corporations to help them avoid bankruptcy.

Fears of organized revolt arose when thousands of unemployed military veterans converged on the nation's capital in the spring of 1932. The **Bonus Expeditionary Force**, made up of veterans of the American Expeditionary Force (AEF) that fought in Europe in the Great War, pressed Congress to pay the cash bonus owed to nearly 4 million veterans. The House passed a bonus bill, but when the Senate voted it down to avoid a tax increase, most of the veterans went home. The rest, along with their wives and children, having no place to go, camped in vacant federal buildings and in a shanty-town at Anacostia Flats, within sight of the nation's Capitol building.

Eager to remove the homeless veterans, Hoover persuaded Congress to pay for their train tickets home. More left, but others stayed even after Congress adjourned, hoping at least to meet with the president. Late in July, President Hoover ordered the government buildings cleared. In doing so, a policeman panicked, fired into the crowd, and killed two veterans. The secretary of war then dispatched seven hundred soldiers to remove the "Bonus Army." Using horses, tanks, tear gas, and bayonets, the soldiers dispersed the unarmed veterans and their families and burned their makeshift camp. Fifty-five veterans were injured and 135 arrested. The Democratic governor of New York was horrified as he read newspaper accounts of the army's violent assault on the unemployed military veterans. "Well," Franklin Roosevelt told an aide, "this elects me" as the next president. (The military veterans of the war were finally paid their "bonus" in 1936).

The disheartened, angry mood of the Bonus Army matched the sour mood of the country, as well as that of President Hoover himself. He worked hard, seven days a week, but the stress of dealing with the Great Depression sapped his health and morale. "I am so tired," he said, "that every bone in my body aches." When aides urged Hoover to be more of a public leader, he replied, "I have no Wilsonian qualities." The man who in 1928 had seemed to be an organizational genius and had promised Americans "permanent prosperity" was now the laughingstock of the nation. *Time* magazine reported that "two years have destroyed the Hoover legend." In the end, Hoover's efforts to restore prosperity were simply not enough, in large part because he never understood or acknowledged the seriousness of the economic problems that he and the nation faced.

The 1932 Election

In June 1932, glum Republicans gathered in Chicago to nominate Hoover for a second presidential term. The delegates went through the motions in a mood of defeat but felt they had no choice. By contrast, the Democrats arrived in Chicago for their nominating convention a few weeks later confident that they would nominate the next president. Fifty-year-old New York governor Franklin Delano Roosevelt won the nomination on the fourth ballot. In a bold gesture, Roosevelt flew for nine hours to Chicago to accept the nomination in person instead of awaiting formal notification. No nominee had ever done so. Roosevelt had broken with tradition, he told the delegates, because the stakes were so high. Hoover and the Republicans, he

Bonus Expeditionary Force (1932) Protest march on Washington, D.C. by thousands of military veterans and their families, calling for immediate payment of their service bonus certificates; violence ensued when President Herbert Hoover ordered their tent villages cleared.

stressed, had failed to address the terrible economic disaster. "I pledge you, I pledge myself to a *new deal* for the American people" that would "break foolish traditions" and create a new government "of competence and courage." But first he would have to defeat Herbert Hoover. His race against the Republican president would be "more than a political campaign; it is a call to arms." It was a vague but self-assured and uplifting message of hope at a time when many people were slipping into despair. Roosevelt's upbeat personality communicated joy, energy, and confidence. His campaign song was "Happy Days Are Here Again."

Throughout the campaign, Roosevelt blamed the Great Depression on the Republicans. He attacked Hoover for his "extravagant government spending," and repeatedly promised a "New Deal" for the American people. Like Hoover, Roosevelt pledged to balance the federal budget, but he was willing to create short-term deficits to prevent starvation and revive the economy. Perhaps most important, he recognized that a revitalized economy would require new ideas and aggressive action. "The country needs, and, unless I mistake its temper, the country demands bold, persistent experimentation," he said. "Above all, try something."

In contrast to Roosevelt, the bewildered Hoover lacked vitality and vision. Roosevelt's proposals, he warned, "would destroy the very foundations of our American system." The election, he stressed, was a battle "between two philosophies of government" that would decide "the direction our nation will take over a century to come." On Election Day, Hoover lost that battle. Voters swept Roosevelt into office with 23 million votes to Hoover's 16 million.

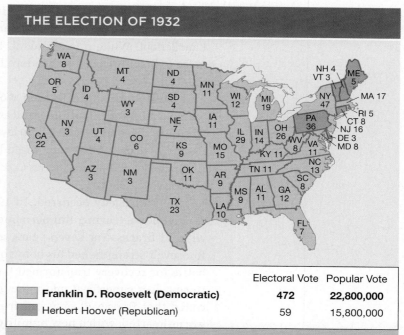

THE ELECTION OF 1932

		Electoral Vote	Popular Vote
	Franklin D. Roosevelt (Democratic)	472	22,800,000
	Herbert Hoover (Republican)	59	15,800,000

■ Why did Roosevelt appeal to voters struggling during the Depression?
■ What were Hoover's criticisms of Roosevelt's New Deal?
■ What policies defined Roosevelt's New Deal during the presidential campaign?

Roosevelt's New Deal

Roosevelt had promised voters a "New Deal," and within hours of being inaugurated he and his aides set about changing the role of government in American life. The new president had seemingly been in a hurry all his life.

Born in 1882, the adored only child of wealthy, aristocratic parents, young Franklin Roosevelt had enjoyed a pampered life. He was educated by

> CORE **OBJECTIVE**
> **4.** Assess the goals and accomplishments of the early New Deal.

tutors at Hyde Park, his father's Hudson River estate north of New York City. Young Roosevelt attended Harvard College and Columbia University Law School. While a law student, he married Anna Eleanor Roosevelt, a niece of his fifth cousin, Theodore Roosevelt, then president of the United States.

In 1910, Franklin Roosevelt won a Democratic seat in the New York State Senate. Tall, handsome, and athletic, blessed with a sparkling personality and infectious smile, Roosevelt seemed destined for greatness. In 1913, Woodrow Wilson appointed him assistant secretary of the navy. In 1920, Roosevelt became James Cox's vice presidential running mate on the Democratic ticket.

Then a tragedy occurred. In 1921, at age thirty-nine, Roosevelt contracted polio, leaving him permanently disabled, unable to stand or walk without braces. For seven years, aided by his remarkable wife, Eleanor, Roosevelt strengthened his body to compensate for his disability. The long battle for recovery transformed the young aristocrat. He became less arrogant, less superficial, more focused, and more interesting. A friend recalled that Roosevelt emerged from his struggle with polio "completely warm-hearted, with a new humility of spirit" that led him to identify with the poor and the suffering. In 1928 and 1930, Roosevelt won the governorship of New York. The aristocrat had developed the common touch as well as a great talent for public relations, but he also was vain and calculating, a clever manipulator of others. In other words, he was a master politician.

Launching the New Deal

Roosevelt was neither an efficient administrator nor a deep thinker. One of his closest aides said the president never "read a serious book." But Roosevelt had courage, a charming personality, strong instincts, unrelenting optimism, and a willingness to experiment with different ways to address problems. He would support a balanced budget and complain about a "bloated bureaucracy," for example, only to incur more budget deficits than all his predecessors combined and dramatically expand the scope of federal government. His inconsistencies reflected his distinctively flexible personality as he launched his presidency and the New Deal.

The 1933 Inauguration

Inaugurated as president in March 1933, Franklin Delano Roosevelt assumed leadership during one of the greatest crises in modern history, a crisis that threatened the very fabric of American capitalism. No other business slump had been so deep, so long, or so painful as the Great Depression. "The situation is critical, Franklin," the prominent journalist Walter Lippmann warned President-elect Roosevelt. "You may have to assume dictatorial powers"—as had already happened in Germany, Italy, and the Soviet Union.

Roosevelt did not become a dictator, but he did take extraordinary steps to address the Depression while assuring Americans "that the only thing we have to fear is fear itself." Roosevelt confessed in his inaugural address that he did not have all the answers, but he did know that "this nation asks for action, and action now." To deal with the crisis, he asked Congress for "a broad Executive power to wage a war against the emergency" just as "if we were in fact invaded by a foreign foe." Roosevelt's uplifting speech won rave reviews. Nearly 500,000 Americans wrote letters to the new president after his inauguration.

The First Hundred Days

In March 1933, President Roosevelt confronted four major challenges: reviving the industrial economy, relieving the widespread human misery, rescuing the ravaged farm sector and its desperate families, and reforming those aspects of the capitalist system that had helped cause the Depression. His goal in providing "relief, recovery, and reform" was to save the nation's capitalist system, not destroy it, while also providing help to those in great distress. The new president admitted that he planned to try several different "experiments" to solve the Great Depression. Eleanor Roosevelt said her husband and his top advisers were "going at it blindly, because we're in a tremendous stream, and none of us knows where we are going to land." To advise him about options, the new president assembled a "brain trust" of brilliant specialists, many of them college professors, who feverishly developed fresh ideas to address the nation's urgent problems.

> New Deal goals: Relief, recovery, and reform

Roosevelt and his advisers initially settled on a three-pronged strategy to revive the economy. First, they addressed the immediate money crisis and provided short-term emergency relief for the jobless. Second, the New Dealers encouraged agreements between management and unions. Third, they attempted to raise depressed commodity prices by paying farmers "subsidies" to shrink the size of their crops and herds. By reducing the supply of grain, cattle, and pigs, prices would rise and thereby increase farm income. From March 9 to June 16, the so-called First Hundred Days, a cooperative Congress approved fifteen major pieces of legislation proposed by the president. Several of these programs comprised what came to be called the **First New Deal** (1933–1935).

Shoring Up the Financial System

Money is the lubricant of capitalism, and money was fast disappearing from circulation by 1933. Ever since the stock market crash of 1929, panicky depositors had been withdrawing their money from banks and the stock market for fear that the banks and corporations would fail. Taking so much money out of circulation, however, worsened the Depression and brought the banking system to the brink of collapse.

First New Deal (1933–1935)
Franklin D. Roosevelt's ambitious first-term cluster of economic and social programs designed to combat the Great Depression.

Banking Regulation

Emergency Banking Relief Act
and "fireside chats"

On his second day in office, March 9, 1933, Roosevelt called Congress into special session to pass the Emergency Banking Relief Act, which declared a four-day bank holiday to allow the financial panic to subside. (Herbert Hoover called it a "move to gigantic socialism.") For the first time in history, all banks closed their doors to stop the panic. "All business came to a complete halt," an Ohio woman reported. Roosevelt's financial experts worked all night drafting a bill to restore confidence in the nation's banks. On March 12, in the first of his radio-broadcast "fireside chats" to the American people, the president assured the 60 million listeners that it was safer to "keep your money in a reopened bank than under the mattress." His reassurances soothed a nervous nation. The following day, people took their money back to their banks. "Capitalism was saved in eight days," said one of Roosevelt's advisers.

A few weeks later, on June 16, 1933, Roosevelt signed the Banking Act of 1933, part of which created the **Federal Deposit Insurance Corporation** (FDIC), which guaranteed customer saving accounts in banks up to $2,500, thus reducing the likelihood of future panics. In addition to insuring savings accounts, the Glass-Steagall Act, which was actually another section of the Banking Act of 1933, called for the separation of commercial banking from investment banking in order to prevent conventional banks from investing the savings of depositors in the risky stock market; only banks that specialized in investment could invest in the stock market after 1933. In addition, the Federal Reserve Board was given more authority to intervene in future financial emergencies. The banking crisis had ended, and the new administration was ready to get on with a broader program of economic recovery.

Franklin Delano Roosevelt
Preparing to deliver the first of his popular "fireside chats." This message focused on measures to reform the American banking system.

Regulating Wall Street

Before the Great Crash in 1929, there was very little government oversight of the securities (stocks and bonds) industry, popularly known as "Wall Street," the financial district in Manhattan where the largest banks and brokerage houses were centered. In 1933, the Roosevelt administration developed two important pieces of legislation intended to regulate the operations of the stock market to eliminate fraud and abuses. The first, the Securities Exchange Act of 1933, was the first major federal legislation to regulate the sale of stocks and bonds. It required corporations that issued stock for public sale to "disclose" all relevant information about the operations and management of the company so that purchasers could know what they were buying. The second bill, the Securities Exchange Act of 1934, established the **Securities and Exchange Commission**, a federal agency created to enforce the new laws and regulations governing the issuance and trading of stocks and bonds. The Act also required that all stock brokers be licensed.

Federal Deposit Insurance Corporation (1933) Independent government agency, established to prevent bank panics, that guarantees the safety of deposits in citizens' savings accounts.

Securities and Exchange Commission (1934) Federal agency established to regulate the issuance and trading of stocks and bonds in an effort to avoid financial panics and stock market "crashes."

The Federal Budget

Roosevelt next convinced Congress to pass an Economy Act (1933) allowing him to cut government workers' salaries, reduce payments to military veterans for non-service-connected disabilities, and reorganize federal agencies in order to reduce government expenses. Roosevelt then took the dramatic step of ending Prohibition, in part because it was being so widely violated, in part because most Democrats wanted it ended, and in part because he wanted to regain the federal tax revenues from the sale of alcoholic beverages. The Twenty-First Amendment was ratified on December 5, 1933. The "noble experiment" of Prohibition was over.

> Economy Act and end of Prohibition

Helping the Unemployed and Homeless

Another urgent priority in 1933 was relieving the widespread human distress caused by the Great Depression. Herbert Hoover had stubbornly refused to help the unemployed and homeless, since he assumed that individual acts of charity (what he called *voluntarism*) and the efforts of local organizations (churches and charities) would be sufficient to get people clothed, fed, and housed. In dealing with the needs of millions of jobless and homeless Americans, the Roosevelt administration had a much greater sense of urgency than Hoover had displayed. As Roosevelt's aide Harry Hopkins said, "Hunger is not debatable." He and Roosevelt, from their experiences in New York state government, knew that the scope of the problem greatly exceeded the "voluntarism" that Hoover promoted. The new president was much more flexible, pushing through a series of new programs that created what came to be called the "welfare state." He did not believe that individuals should be given cash by the government (called a "dole"), but he did want the government to help people get jobs. For the first time, the federal government took primary responsibility for assisting the most desperate Americans, because the number of people in need far exceeded the capacity of charitable organizations and local government agencies.

> Creation of the welfare state

Putting People to Work

The Federal Emergency Relief Administration (FERA), headed by Harry Hopkins, was Roosevelt's first major effort to deal with unemployment. It sent money to the states to spend on the unemployed and homeless. After the state-sponsored programs funded by the FERA proved inadequate, Congress created the Civil Works Administration (CWA) in November 1933. It was the first large-scale *federal* experiment with work relief, hiring people directly on the government payroll at competitive wages. Several states had done so before, but never the national government. The CWA provided 4 million federal jobs to those unable to find work during the winter of 1933–1934. The agency organized a variety of useful projects:

> Federal work relief

repairing 500,000 miles of roads, laying sewer lines, constructing or improving more than a thousand airports and 40,000 public schools, and providing 50,000 teaching jobs that helped keep small rural public schools open. As the number of people employed by the CWA soared, however, the program's costs skyrocketed to over $1 billion. Roosevelt balked at such high costs and worried that the people hired would become dependent upon federal jobs. So in the spring of 1934, he ordered the CWA dissolved. By April, some 4 million workers were again unemployed.

The CCC

The most successful of the New Deal programs to provide jobs to the unemployed was the Civilian Conservation Corps (CCC), managed by the War Department. It built 2,500 camps around the nation to house 3 million unemployed, unmarried young men aged eighteen to twenty-five to work as "soil soldiers" in national forests, parks, and recreational areas and on soil-conservation projects. The CCC also recruited 150,000 unemployed military veterans and 85,000 Native Americans, housing them in separate camps. CCC workers built roads, bridges, campgrounds, fire towers, fish hatcheries, and 800 parks; planted 3 *billion* trees; taught farmers how to control soil erosion; and fought fires. The enrollees, who were supervised by soldiers, were given shelter, clothing, and food, as well as a small wage of $30 a month ($25 of which had to be sent home to their families). The CCC workers could also earn high-school diplomas at their camps.

Saving Homes

Federal Housing Administration (FHA) and the National Industrial Recovery Act (NIRA)

During 1933, a thousand homes or farms were being foreclosed upon each day. Roosevelt's Home Owners' Loan Act established the Home Owners' Loan Corporation, which helped home owners refinance their mortgages at lower interest rates and avoid bankruptcy. In 1934, Roosevelt created the Federal Housing Administration (FHA), which offered Americans much longer home mortgages (twenty years) in order to reduce their monthly payments.

Reviving the Industrial Sector

National Recovery Administration (1933) Controversial federal agency that brought together business and labor leaders to create "codes of fair competition" and "fair labor" policies, including a national minimum wage.

The centerpiece of the New Deal's efforts to revive the industrial economy was the National Industrial Recovery Act (NIRA) of 1933. One of its two major sections dealt with economic recovery by creating massive public-works construction projects funded by the federal government. The NIRA created the Public Works Administration (PWA), granting $3.3 billion for the construction of government buildings, highways, bridges, dams, port facilities, and sewage plants.

The second, and more controversial, part of the NIRA created the **National Recovery Administration** (NRA), headed by Hugh S. Johnson, a retired army general. Its primary purpose was to promote economic growth by temporarily waiving the anti-trust laws and allowing large corporations to create detailed "codes of fair competition" among themselves for 500 different industries, including the setting of prices on an array of products. At the same time, the NRA codes also included "fair labor" policies long sought by unions and social progressives: a national forty-hour work week, minimum weekly wages of $13 ($12 in the South, where living costs were lower), and a ban on the employment of children under the age of sixteen. The NRA also included a provision (Section 7a) that guaranteed the right of workers to organize unions.

These were landmark changes in working conditions and union rights, and, for a time, the downward spiral of wages and prices subsided. But as soon as economic recovery began, small business owners complained that the larger corporations dominated the NRA, whose price-fixing robbed small producers of the chance to compete. And because the NRA wage codes excluded agricultural and domestic workers (at the insistence of southern Democrats), three out of every four African Americans derived no direct benefit from the program. By 1935, the NRA had developed more critics than friends. When it died, in May 1935, struck down by the Supreme Court as unconstitutional, few paused to mourn.

Yet the NRA experiment had left an enduring mark. The NRA codes set new workplace standards, such as the forty-hour workweek, a minimum wage, and the abolition of child labor. The NRA's endorsement of collective bargaining between workers and owners spurred the growth of unions. Yet as 1934 ended, economic recovery was still nowhere in sight.

> The National Recovery Act (NRA): Creation of fair labor standards and recognition of the right to unionize

Agricultural Assistance

In addition to rescuing the banks and providing jobs to the unemployed, Roosevelt and his advisers promoted the long-term recovery of agriculture during the Hundred Days in the spring of 1933. Roosevelt created the Farm Credit Administration to help farmers deal with their crushing debts. Like the Home Owners' Loan Corporation, the Farm Credit Administration helped farmers lower their mortgage payments to avoid bankruptcy.

> Farm Credit Association and the Agricultural Adjustment Act (1933)

The **Agricultural Adjustment Act** of 1933 created a new federal agency, the Agricultural Adjustment Administration (AAA), which sought to raise prices for crops and herds by paying farmers to cut back production. The money for such payments came from a tax levied on the "processors" of certain basic commodities—cotton gins, flour mills, and slaughterhouses. By the time the AAA was created, however, the spring growing season was already under way. The prospect of another bumper cotton crop forced the AAA to sponsor a "plow-under" program in which farmers were paid to kill the sprouting seeds in their fields. To destroy a growing crop was a "shocking commentary on our civilization," Agriculture Secretary Henry A. Wallace admitted. "I could tolerate it only as a cleaning up of the wreckage from the old days of unbalanced production."

Agricultural Adjustment Act (1933) Legislation that paid farmers to produce less in order to raise crop prices for all; the AAA was later declared unconstitutional by the U.S. Supreme Court in the case of *United States v. Butler* (1936).

Norris Dam The massive dam in Tennessee, completed in 1936, was essential to creating jobs and expanding power production under the TVA.

Moreover, in an effort to raise pork prices, some 6 million baby pigs were slaughtered and buried. By the end of 1934, the AAA efforts had worked: wheat, cotton, and corn production had declined and prices for those commodities had risen. Farm income increased by 58 percent between 1932 and 1935.

Regional Planning: The TVA

One of the most innovative programs of the First New Deal created the Tennessee Valley Authority (TVA), an ambitious venture designed to bring electrical power, flood control efforts, and jobs to Appalachia, the desperately poor mountainous region including West Virginia, western Virginia and North Carolina, Kentucky, eastern Tennessee, and northern Georgia and Alabama. By 1940, the TVA, a multipurpose public corporation, had constructed twenty-one electricity-generating dams which created the "Great Lakes of the South." The agency, moreover, dredged rivers to allow for boat and barge traffic, promoted soil conservation and scientific forestry management, experimented with fertilizers, drew new industries to the region, encouraged the formation of labor unions, improved schools and libraries, and provided electricity to the depressed region. The TVA provided 1.5 million farms with access to electricity and indoor plumbing for the first time.

During Roosevelt's first year in office, his programs and his personal charm generated widespread support. A former CCC worker remembered that Roosevelt "restored a sense of confidence and morale and hope—hope being the greatest of all." The First New Deal programs—as well as Roosevelt's leadership—had given Americans a sense of renewed faith in the future. Voters showed their appreciation in the congressional elections of 1934: the Democrats increased their dominance in Congress with an almost unprecedented midterm victory for a party in power.

Eleanor Roosevelt

One of the reasons for Franklin Roosevelt's popularity was his energetic wife, Eleanor Roosevelt, who had become an enormous political asset and would prove to be one of the most influential leaders of the time. Born in 1884 in New York City, the niece of Theodore Roosevelt, Eleanor married her distant cousin Franklin in 1905. During the 1920s, Eleanor Roosevelt began a lifelong crusade on behalf of women, blacks, and youth. Her tireless compassion resulted in part from the loneliness she had experienced as she was growing up and in part from the sense of betrayal she felt upon learning in 1918 that her husband had fallen in love with Lucy Mercer, her personal secretary. "The bottom dropped out of my own particular world," she recalled. Eleanor and Franklin decided to maintain their marriage, but as their son James said, it became an "armed truce." Eleanor later observed that she could "forgive, but never forget." Alice Roosevelt Longworth—the daughter of Theodore Roosevelt, and a cousin of Eleanor's—actually nurtured the affair, hosting Mercer and Franklin for dinner several times. She later explained that Roosevelt "deserved a good time . . . he was married to Eleanor."

Eleanor Roosevelt redefined the role of the First Lady. She was not content just to host social events in the White House. Instead, she became an outspoken activist: the first woman to address a national political convention, to write a nationally-syndicated newspaper column, and to hold regular press conferences. The tireless Eleanor crisscrossed the nation, speaking in support of the New Deal, meeting with African American leaders, supporting women's causes and organized labor, and urging Americans to live up to their humanitarian ideals. In 1933, she convened a White House conference on the emergency needs of women which urged the Federal Emergency Relief Administration (FERA) to ensure that it "pay particular attention to see that women are employed wherever possible." Within six months, some 300,000 women were at work on various federal government projects.

A popular joke in Washington claimed that President Roosevelt's nightly prayer was: "Dear God, please make Eleanor a little tired." But he was in fact deeply dependent on his industrious wife. She was the agitator dedicated to what *should* be done; he was the practical politician concerned with what *could* be done.

Eleanor Roosevelt Intelligent, principled, and a political figure in her own right, she is pictured here addressing the Red Cross Convention in 1934.

The New Deal under Fire

By 1934, Franklin Roosevelt had become the best loved and most hated president of the twentieth century. Although a child of wealth and prestige, he was loved because he believed in and fought for the common people, for the "forgotten man" (and woman). And he was loved for what one French leader called his "glittering personality." Roosevelt radiated personal charm, joy in his work, courage in a crisis, and optimism for the future. "Meeting him," said the British prime minister Winston Churchill, "was like uncorking a bottle of champagne."

But Roosevelt was hated too, especially by business leaders and political conservatives who believed the New Deal and the higher taxes it required were moving America toward socialism. Others, on the Left, hated Roosevelt for not doing enough to end the Depression. By the mid-1930s, the early New Deal programs had helped stop the economy's downward slide, but prosperity remained elusive. "We have been patient and long suffering," said a farm leader. "We were promised a New Deal. . . . Instead, we have the same old stacked deck."

CORE **OBJECTIVE**
5. Analyze the major criticisms of the early New Deal.

New Deal criticized by those on the Left and Right

Continuing Hardships

Although the programs making up the so-called First New Deal helped ease the devastation caused by the Depression, they did not restore prosperity or end the widespread human suffering. The Depression continued to exact a terrible toll on Americans as the shattered economy slowly worked its way back to health. As late as 1939, some 9.5 million workers (17 percent of the labor force) remained unemployed. Critics stressed that the economy, while stabilized, remained mired in the Depression.

African Americans and the New Deal

However progressive Franklin Delano Roosevelt was on social issues, he showed little interest in the plight of African Americans, even as black voters, by 1936, were shifting from the Republicans (the "party of Lincoln") to the Democrats. President Roosevelt, like Woodrow Wilson before him, failed to address long-standing patterns of racism and segregation in the South for fear of angering conservative southern Democrats in Congress.

New Deal discrimination, the NAACP, and the "Black Cabinet"

As a result, many of the New Deal programs discriminated against blacks. As Mary White Ovington, the treasurer of the National Association for the Advancement of Colored People (NAACP), stressed, the racism in any agency "varies according to the white people chosen to administer it, but always there is discrimination." For example, the payments from the AAA to farm owners to take land *out* of production in an effort to raise the prices for farm products forced hundreds of thousands of tenant farmers and sharecroppers, both blacks and whites, off the land. Meanwhile, the FHA refused to guarantee mortgages on houses purchased by blacks in white neighborhoods. In addition, both the CCC and the TVA practiced racial segregation. The NAACP waged an energetic legal campaign against racial prejudice throughout the 1930s, but a major setback occurred in the Supreme Court ruling on *Grovey v. Townsend* (1935), which upheld the Texas Democrats' whites-only election primary.

Latinos and the New Deal When Mexican migrant workers went on strike against California cotton growers in 1933, local authorities prohibited relief agencies from giving food to strikers and their families. Here, Mexican women and children picket for government aid in Pixley, California.

Thanks to relentless pressure from Eleanor Roosevelt, the president did appoint more African Americans to government positions than ever before. One of the most visible of the new appointees was Mary McLeod Bethune, the child of former slaves from South Carolina, who had founded

Bethune-Cookman College in Florida and had served as the head of the NAACP in the 1920s. In 1935, Roosevelt approved her appointment as the director of the Division of Negro Affairs within the National Youth Administration, an agency that provided jobs to unemployed young Americans. Bethune worked with other blacks in New Deal agencies to form an informal "Black Cabinet" to ensure that African Americans across the country had equal access to federal programs.

Court Cases and Civil Liberties

The continuing prejudice against blacks in the South was vividly revealed in a controversial case in Alabama. In 1931, an all-white jury, on flimsy evidence, hastily convicted nine black boys, ranging in age from thirteen to twenty-one, of raping two young white women while riding a freight train. Eight of the "Scottsboro Boys" were sentenced to death before cheering whites who packed the courtroom. In his award-winning novel *Native Son* (1940), the African American writer Richard Wright recalled the "mob who surrounded the Scottsboro jail with rope and kerosene" after the Scottsboro boys' initial conviction.

The "Scottsboro boys"

The injustice of the Scottsboro case sparked protests throughout the nation and around the world. The two white girls, it turned out, had been selling sex to white and black boys on the train. One of the girls eventually recanted the rape charges and began appearing at rallies on behalf of the black defendants.

No case in American legal history had ever produced as many trials, appeals, reversals, and retrials as the much-publicized Scottsboro case. Further, it prompted two important legal interpretations. In *Powell v. Alabama* (1932), the U.S. Supreme Court overturned the original convictions in the case because the judge had not ensured that the accused were provided adequate defense attorneys. The Court ordered new trials. In another case, *Norris v. Alabama* (1935), the Court ruled that the systematic

Scottsboro case Heywood Patterson (center), one of the defendants in the case, is seen here with his attorney, Samuel Liebowitz (left) in Decatur, Alabama, in 1933.

exclusion of African Americans from Alabama juries had denied the Scottsboro defendants equal protection under the law—a principle that had widespread impact on state courts by opening up juries to blacks. Eventually, but too late to help the defendants, whose lives were ruined, the state of Alabama dropped the charges against the four youngest of the "Scottsboro boys" and granted paroles to the others; the last one was released from prison in 1950.

Native Americans and the Depression

The "Indian New Deal"

The Great Depression also ravaged Native Americans. They were initially encouraged by Roosevelt's appointment of John Collier as the commissioner of the Bureau of Indian Affairs (BIA). Collier steadily increased the number of Native Americans employed by the BIA and ensured that Native Americans gained access to the various federal relief programs. Collier's primary objective, however, was passage of the Indian Reorganization Act. Designed to reinvigorate Native American cultural traditions by restoring land to tribes, the proposed law would grant them the right to start businesses and establish self-governing constitutions, and provide federal funds for vocational training and economic development. The act that Congress finally passed, however, was a much-diluted version of Collier's original proposal, and the "Indian New Deal" brought only a partial improvement to the lives of Native Americans. Yet it did spur the various tribes to revise their constitutions so as to give women the right to vote and hold office.

Critics Assault the New Deal

For all of their criticisms of the inadequacy of New Deal programs, Native Americans and African Americans still voted in large majorities for Franklin Roosevelt. Other New Deal critics, however, hated Roosevelt as much as his policies.

Huey Long

The most potent threat to Roosevelt came from Louisiana's Democratic senator Huey P. Long. A short, colorful man with wild curly hair, Long, known as the "Kingfish," was a theatrical political performer (a demagogue) who appealed to the raw emotions of the masses. The swaggering son of a backwoods farmer, he sported pink suits and pastel shirts, red ties, and two-toned shoes. He claimed to serve the poor, arguing that his Louisiana would be a place where "every man [is] a king, but no one wears a crown." First as Louisiana's governor, then as its most powerful U.S. senator, Long viewed the state as his personal empire. Reporters called him the "dictator of Louisiana." True, he reduced state taxes, improved roads and schools, built charity hospitals, and provided better public services, but in the process, he became a bullying dictator who used bribery, intimidation, and blackmail to get his way.

Huey Long As the powerful governor of Louisiana, Long was a shrewd lawyer and consummate politician.

In 1933, Senator Long arrived in Washington as a supporter of Roosevelt and the New Deal, but he quickly grew suspicious of the NRA's efforts to cooperate with big business. Having developed his own presidential aspirations, he had also grown jealous of "Prince Franklin" Roosevelt's popularity. To launch his own presidential candidacy, Long devised a simplistic plan for dealing with the Great Depression that he called the Share-the-Wealth Society. Long wanted to raise taxes on the wealthiest Americans and redistribute the money to "the people"—giving every poor family $5,000 and every worker an annual income of $2,500, providing pensions to retirees, reducing working hours, paying bonuses to military veterans, and enabling every qualified student to attend college.

Huey Long's Share-the-Wealth Society

It did not matter that Long's plan would have spent far more dollars than would have been raised by his proposed taxes. As he told a group of Iowa farmers, "Maybe somebody says I don't understand it [government finance]. Well, you don't have to. Just shut your damn eyes and believe it. That's all." By early 1935, the outspoken Long claimed to have enough support to unseat Roosevelt. "I can take him," he bragged. "He's a phony. . . . He's scared of me. I can outpromise him, and he knows it. People will believe me, and they won't believe him."

The Townsend Plan

Another popular critic of Roosevelt was a retired California doctor, Francis E. Townsend. Outraged by the sight of three elderly women digging through garbage cans for food scraps, Townsend began promoting the Townsend Recovery Plan in 1934. It called for the federal government to pay $200 a month to every American over sixty who agreed to quit working. The recipients had to spend the money each month; it could not be saved. Townsend claimed that his plan would create new jobs for young people by forcing older people to retire, and it would energize the economy by enabling retirees to buy more products every month.

The Townsend Plan and Father Coughlin

Like Huey Long's "Share Our Wealth" scheme, the numbers in Townsend's crackpot scheme did not add up: the Townsend Plan, which would serve only 9 percent of the population, would have paid those retirees more than half the total national income. Yet Townsend, like Long, didn't care about the numbers adding up. "I'm not in the least interested in the cost of the plan," he blandly told a Congressional committee. Not surprisingly, however, the Townsend Plan attracted great support among Americans 60 years of age and older. Thousands of Townsend Clubs sprang up across the nation, and advocates of the plan flooded the White House with letters urging Roosevelt to enact it.

Father Coughlin

A third outspoken critic of Roosevelt was Father Charles E. Coughlin, the Roman Catholic "radio priest" in Detroit who founded the National Union for Social Justice in 1935. In fiery weekly broadcasts over the CBS radio network that attracted as many as 40 million listeners, he assailed Roosevelt as "anti-God" and claimed that the New Deal was a Communist conspiracy. During the 1930s, Coughlin became increasingly anti-Semitic, claiming that Roosevelt was a tool of "international Jewish bankers" and relabeling the New Deal the "Jew Deal." He praised Hitler and the Nazis for killing Jews because he believed that all Jews were Communists who must be hunted down. "When we get through with the Jews in America," the thuggish Coughlin bragged, "they'll think the treatment they received in Germany was nothing."

Coughlin, Townsend, and Long were Roosevelt's most prominent critics. Of the three, Long had the largest political following. A 1935 survey showed that he could draw over 5 million votes as a third-party candidate for president in 1936, perhaps enough to prevent Roosevelt's reelection. Roosevelt decided to "steal the thunder" from his most vocal critics by instituting an array of new programs. "I'm fighting Communism, Huey Longism, Coughlinism, Townsendism," Roosevelt told a reporter in early 1935. He needed to fight even harder "to save our system, the capitalist system," from such "crackpot ideas."

Opposition from the Court

The opposition to the New Deal came from all directions. Among the most powerful was the Supreme Court. By the mid-1930s, businesses were filing law suits against various elements of the New Deal, and some of them made their way to the Supreme Court.

The Supreme Court vs. The New Deal

Supreme Court overturns some New Deal programs

On May 27, 1935, the U.S. Supreme Court killed the National Industrial Recovery Act (NIRA) by a unanimous vote. In *Schechter Poultry Corporation v. United States*, the justices ruled that Congress had given too much of its authority to the president when the NIRA created the National Recovery Administration and gave it the power to bring business and labor leaders together to create "codes of fair competition" for their industries. In a press conference soon after the Court announced its decision, Roosevelt fumed: "We have been relegated to the horse-and-buggy definition of interstate commerce."

But by 1935, the NRA had developed more critics than friends. While the NRA had worked for a time, and the downward spiral of wages and prices subsided, as soon as economic recovery began, small business owners complained that the larger corporations dominated the NRA, whose price-fixing robbed small producers of the chance to compete. And because the NRA wage codes excluded agricultural and domestic workers (at the insistence of southern Democrats), three out of every four African Americans derived no direct benefit from the program.

Then, on January 6, 1936, in *United States v. Butler*, the Supreme Court declared the Agricultural Adjustment Act's tax on the companies that processed food crops and commodities like cotton, unconstitutional. In response to the Court's decision, the Roosevelt administration passed the Agricultural Adjustment Act of 1938, which reestablished the earlier crop-reduction payment programs but left out the tax on processors. Although the AAA helped boost the overall farm economy, conservatives criticized its sweeping powers. By the end of its 1936 term, the Supreme Court had ruled against New Deal programs in seven of nine major cases. The same line of conservative judicial reasoning, Roosevelt warned, might endanger other New Deal programs—if he did not act swiftly to prevent it.

The Second New Deal

To rescue his legislative program from such judicial and political challenges, Roosevelt in January 1935 launched the second, more radical phase of the New Deal, explaining that "social justice, no longer a distant ideal, has become a definite goal" of his administration. In his effort "to steal Huey Long's thunder," the president called on Congress to pass a cluster of what he designated as his "must" legislation that included a new federal construction program to employ the jobless, banking reforms, increased taxes on the wealthy, and programs to protect people during unemployment, old age, and illness. Roosevelt's closest aide, Harry L. Hopkins, told the cabinet: "Boys—this is our hour. We've got to get everything we want—a [public] works program, social security, wages and hours, everything—now or never."

The WPA

In the first three months of 1935, dubbed the Second Hundred Days, Roosevelt used all of his considerable political skills to convince the Democratic-controlled Congress to pass most of the **Second New Deal**'s "must" legislation. The results changed the face of American life. The first major initiative, the $4.8-billion Emergency Relief Appropriation Act, sailed through the new Congress. Roosevelt called it the "Big Bill" because it was the largest peacetime spending bill in history up to that point. It included an array of federal job programs managed by a new government agency, the **Works Progress Administration** (WPA).

The WPA quickly became the nation's largest employer, hiring an average of 2 million people annually over four years. Federal WPA workers built New York's LaGuardia Airport, restored the St. Louis riverfront, and managed the bankrupt city of Key West, Florida. The WPA also employed a wide range of talented writers, artists, actors, and musicians in new cultural programs: the Federal Theatre Project, the Federal Art Project, the Federal Music Project, and the Federal Writers' Project. The National

> **CORE OBJECTIVE**
> **6.** Evaluate the ways the New Deal changed and how it transformed the role of federal government.

> Second New Deal: Works Progress Administration (WPA)

Second New Deal (1935–1938) Expansive cluster of legislation proposed by President Roosevelt that established new regulatory agencies, strengthened the rights of workers to organize unions, and laid the foundation of a federal social welfare system through the creation of Social Security.

Works Progress Administration (1935) Government agency established to manage several federal job programs created under the New Deal; it became the largest employer in the nation.

Federal Art Project A group of WPA artists at work on *Building the Transcontinental Railroad*, a mural celebrating the contributions of immigrants that appears in the immigrants' dining hall on Ellis Island.

Youth Administration (NYA), also under the WPA, provided part-time employment to students and aided jobless youths. Twenty-seven-year-old Lyndon B. Johnson directed an NYA program in Texas, and Richard M. Nixon, a struggling Duke University law student, found work through the NYA at 35¢ an hour. Although the WPA took care of only 3 million of some 10 million jobless at any one time, in all it helped some 9 million people weather desperate circumstances before it expired in 1943.

The Wagner Act

Second New Deal: Wagner Act and unions

Another major element of the Second New Deal was the National Labor Relations Act, often called the **Wagner Act** in honor of the New York senator, Robert Wagner, who drafted it and convinced Roosevelt to support it. The Wagner Act was one of the most important pieces of labor legislation in history, guaranteeing workers the right to organize unions and bargain directly with management about wages and other issues. It also prohibited employers from interfering with union activities. The Wagner Act created a National Labor Relations Board to oversee union activities across the nation.

Social Security

Wagner Act (1935) Legislation that guaranteed workers the right to organize unions, granted them direct bargaining power, and barred employers from interfering with union activities.

Social Security Act (1935) Legislation enacted to provide federal assistance to retired workers through tax-funded pension payments and benefit payments to the unemployed and disabled.

As Francis Townsend stressed, the Great Depression hit the oldest Americans and those with disabilities especially hard. To address the problems faced by the old, blind, and disabled, Roosevelt proposed the **Social Security Act** of 1935. Social Security was, he announced, the "cornerstone" and "supreme achievement" of the New Deal. The basic concept of government assistance to the elderly was not new. Progressives during the early 1900s had proposed a federal system of social security for the aged, poor, disabled, and unemployed. Other nations had already enacted such programs, but not the United States. The hardships caused by the Great Depression revived the idea of a social security program, however, and Roosevelt masterfully guided the legislation through Congress.

The Social Security Act, designed by Secretary of Labor Frances Perkins, the first woman cabinet member in history, included three major provisions. Its centerpiece was a self-financed federal retirement fund for people over sixty-five. Beginning in 1937, workers and employers contributed payroll taxes to establish the fund. Most of the collected taxes were spent on pension payments to retirees; whatever was left over went into a trust fund for the future. Roosevelt stressed that Social Security was not intended to guarantee everyone a comfortable retirement. Rather, it was meant to supplement other sources of income and protect the elderly from some of the "hazards" of life. Only during the 1950s did voters and politicians come to view Social Security as the *primary* source of retirement income for working-class Americans.

The Social Security Act also set up a shared federal-state unemployment-insurance program, financed by a payroll tax on employers. In addition, the new legislation committed the national government to a broad range of social-welfare activities based upon the assumption that "unemployables"—people who were unable to work—would remain a state responsibility while the national government would provide work relief for the able-bodied. To that end, the Social Security Act provided federal funding for three state-administered public-assistance programs—old-age assistance, aid to dependent children, and aid for the blind—and further aid for maternal, child-welfare, and public health services.

When compared with similar programs in Europe, the new U.S. Social Security system was conservative. It was the only government-managed retirement program in the world financed by taxes on the earnings of workers; most other countries funded such programs out of general government revenues. The Social Security payroll tax was also a regressive tax because it used a single withholding tax *rate* for everyone, regardless of income level. It thus pinched the poor more than the rich, and it also hurt Roosevelt's efforts to revive the economy because it removed from circulation a significant amount of money: the new Social Security tax took money out of workers' pockets and placed it into a retirement fund, worsening the shrinking money supply that was one of the main causes of the Depression. In addition, the Social Security system, at the insistence of southern Democrats determined to maintain white supremacy in the region, excluded 9.5 million workers who most needed the new program: farm laborers, domestic workers (maids and cooks), and the self-employed, a disproportionate percentage of whom were African Americans.

Roosevelt regretted the limitations of the Social Security Act, but he knew that they were necessary compromises in order to gain Congressional approval and to withstand court challenges. As he replied to an aide who criticized funding the pension program out of employee contributions:

> I guess you're right on the economics, but those taxes were never a problem of economics. They are politics all the way through. We put those payroll contributions there so as to give the contributors a moral, legal, and political right to collect their pensions and their unemployment benefits. With those taxes in there, no damn politician can ever scrap my Social Security program.

Roosevelt also preferred workers to fund their own Social Security pensions because he wanted Americans to view their retirement checks not as a welfare payment but as an *entitlement*—as something that they had paid for, something they deserved. On the other hand, conservatives condemned the Social Security Act as tyrannical. Former president Herbert Hoover was among a few Americans who refused to apply for a Social Security card because of his opposition to the "radical" program. He received a Social Security number anyway.

Taxing the Rich

Another major bill making up the second phase of the New Deal was the Revenue Act of 1935, sometimes called the "Wealth-Tax Act" but popularly known as the "soak-the-rich" tax. The Revenue Act raised tax rates on annual income above $50,000, in part because of stories that many wealthy Americans were not paying taxes. The powerful banker J. P. Morgan confessed to a Senate committee that he had created fictitious sales of stock to his wife that enabled him to pay no taxes. Morgan and other business leaders fumed over Roosevelt's tax and spending policies. The newspaper editor William Randolph Hearst growled that the wealth tax was "essentially communism." Roosevelt countered by stressing that "I am fighting communism. . . . I want to save our system, the capitalistic system." Yet he added that saving capitalism and "rebalancing" its essential elements required a more equal "distribution of wealth." Like his cousin Theodore, Franklin Roosevelt did not hate capitalism; he hated capitalists who engaged in "unfair" or illegal behavior.

A New Direction for Unions

The New Deal helped revive the labor union movement. When the National Industrial Recovery Act (NIRA) demanded that every industry code affirm workers' rights to organize, alert unionists quickly translated it to mean "the president wants you to join the union." John L. Lewis, head of the United Mine Workers (UMW), was among the first to capitalize upon the pro-union spirit of the NIRA. He rebuilt the UMW from 150,000 members to 500,000 within a year. Spurred by Lewis's success, Sidney Hillman

Second New Deal: Social Security and the Wealth-Tax Act

of the Amalgamated Clothing Workers and David Dubinsky of the International Ladies Garment Workers organized workers in the clothing industry. As leaders of industrial unions (composed of all types of workers in a particular industry, skilled or unskilled), which were in the minority by far, they found the smaller, more restrictive craft unions (composed of skilled male workers only, with each union serving just one trade) to be obstacles to organizing workers in the country's basic industries.

In 1935, with the passage of the Wagner Act, industrial unionists formed a Committee for Industrial Organization (CIO), and craft unionists (skilled workers) began to fear submergence by the mass unions made up mainly of unskilled workers. Jurisdictional disputes divided them, and in 1936 the American Federation of Labor (AFL) expelled the CIO unions, which then formed a permanent structure, called after 1938 the Congress of Industrial Organizations (also known by the initials CIO). The rivalry spurred both groups to recruit more members.

The CIO's major organizing drives in the automobile and steel industries began in 1936, but until the Supreme Court upheld the Wagner Act in 1937, companies failed to cooperate with its pro-union provisions. Employers used various forms of intimidation to fight the efforts of workers to form unions. Early in 1937 automobile workers spontaneously adopted a new tactic, the "sit-down strike," in which workers refused to leave a workplace until employers had granted collective-bargaining rights to their union.

> "Sit-down strikes"

Led by the fiery young autoworker and union organizer Walter Reuther, thousands of employees at the General Motors assembly plants in Flint, Michigan, occupied the factories and stopped all production. Female workers supported their male counterparts by picketing at the plant entrances. Company officials called in police to harass the strikers, sent spies to union meetings, and threatened to fire the workers. They also pleaded with President Roosevelt to dispatch federal troops. He refused, while expressing his displeasure with the sit-down strike, which the courts later declared illegal. The standoff lasted over a month. Then, on February 11, 1937, the company relented and signed a contract recognizing the fledgling United Automobile Workers (UAW) as a legitimate union.

Labor union violence This 1935 photograph captures unionized strikers fighting "scabs," or nonunion replacement employees, as the scabs attempt to pass the picket line and enter the factory.

Combating the Great Depression

The federal government's efforts to combat the Great Depression changed over time. The following charts explore the first three phases of the federal government's response to the Great Depression, those of the Hoover administration (1929–1933), the Roosevelt administration during the First New Deal (1933–1935), and finally the Roosevelt administration during the Second New Deal (1935–1938). In each phase, the federal government had a particular strategy to end the Depression, each targeting a different set of problems to be solved, and each employing a different set of tactics and programs.

PHASE I Hoover Administration (1929–1933)

Overall Strategy to end the Depression: The economy will cure itself if left alone.

Problems the administration thought needed to be solved: "High costs of living and high living"; foreign competition; poor economic morale

Tactics and Programs:

- Increased taxes to balance the budget
- Smoot-Hawley Tariff of 1930 to keep out foreign goods
- Reconstruction Finance Corporation to make loans to major industries and to states for limited public works projects
- Upbeat slogans
- Dismissed critics as "calamity mongers and weeping men"

Results: The Great Depression worsened and spread globally.

PHASE II Roosevelt Administration during the First New Deal (1933–1935)

Overall Strategy to end the Depression: "Bold, persistent experimentation"

Problems the administration thought needed to be solved: Bank crisis; unemployment and homelessness; low wages and prices

Tactics and Programs:

- "Bank holiday," "fireside chats," and FDIC to insure deposits in order to stop bank runs
- Mortgage and foreclosure reform through Home Owners' Loan Corporation, and Federal Housing Administration
- Funding of state and federal work relief programs like the Civil Conservation Corps and Public Works Administration
- Agricultural Adjustment Administration (AAA) payments to farmers to cut production
- National Recovery Administration (NRA)—mandated increases of wages and prices
- Tennessee Valley Authority (TVA) development of the rural mountain South through flood control, electrification, and other projects

Results: In the First New Deal, FDR was able to use regulation to mitigate the banking crisis and begin resolving the housing crisis. Rural America received electricity and other regional improvements, but the work relief programs—many of which barred minorities from participation—failed to resolve the unemployment crisis, and the Great Depression continued.

Roosevelt's Second Term

On June 27, 1936, Franklin Delano Roosevelt accepted the Democratic Party's nomination for a second term. The Republicans chose Governor Alfred M. Landon of Kansas, a progressive Republican who had endorsed many New Deal programs. The Republicans hoped that the followers of Long, Coughlin, Townsend, and other Roosevelt critics would combine to

PHASE III Roosevelt Administration during the Second New Deal (1935–1938)

Overall Strategy to end the Depression: "Social justice, no longer a distant ideal, has become a definite goal."

Problems the administration thought needed to be solved: Continued high unemployment; opposition from both populist critics and the Supreme Court; poverty among the elderly and disabled; weak unions; economic inequality

Tactics and Programs:

- Works Project Administration created to employ many millions of Americans in construction and cultural projects
- Wagner Act passed to guarantee workers the right to unionize and to collectively bargain with management; created the National Labor Relations Board
- Social Security created to provide a government social safety net for the disabled and people over sixty-five
- Wealth-Tax Act passed to raise taxes on those earning more than $50,000

Results: The Second New Deal strengthened the power of unions, expanded federal work relief programs, engaged in redistributive taxation, and initiated the first federal social welfare programs through social security. While programs like the WPA created some jobs, the Great Depression persisted until America mobilized for World War II.

QUESTIONS FOR ANALYSIS

1. How and why did the overall approach employed by the federal government to combat the Depression change between the Hoover administration and the Roosevelt administration during the First New Deal?

2. What problems created by the Depression was the federal government able to resolve, and which problems continued?

3. How did the role of the federal government change as a result of these developments?

draw enough Democratic votes away from Roosevelt to throw the election to them. But that possibility faded when an assassin, the son-in-law of a Louisiana judge whom Huey Long had sought to remove, shot and killed the forty-two-year-old senator in 1935.

In the 1936 election, Roosevelt carried every state except Maine and Vermont, with a popular vote of 27.7 million to Landon's 16.7 million, the largest margin of victory up to that point. Democrats would also dominate Republicans in the new Congress, by 77 to 19 in the Senate and 328 to 107 in the House.

In winning another landslide election, Roosevelt forged in 1936 a new electoral coalition that would affect national politics for years to come. While holding the support of most traditional Democrats, North and South, the president made strong gains in the West among beneficiaries of New Deal agricultural programs. In the northern cities, he held on to the ethnic groups helped by New Deal welfare policies. Many middle-class voters whose property had been saved by New Deal measures flocked to support Roosevelt, as did intellectuals stirred by the ferment of new ideas coming from the government. The revived labor union movement threw its support to Roosevelt. And in the most profound departure of all, African American voters for the first time cast the majority of their ballots for a Democratic president. "My friends, go home and turn Lincoln's picture to the wall," a Pittsburgh journalist told black voters. "That debt has been paid in full."

The Court-Packing Plan

Roosevelt's landslide victory led him to bolder, and at times reckless, efforts to end the Great Depression. In his second inaugural address, delivered on January 20, 1937, he promised even greater reforms. The challenge to democracy, he maintained, was that millions lacked "the necessities of life. . . . I see one-third of a nation ill-housed, ill-clad, ill-nourished." Roosevelt argued that his re-election demonstrated that the nation wanted even more extensive government action to revive the economy. The three-to-one Democratic majorities in Congress ensured that he could pass new legislation. Yet one major roadblock stood in the way: the conservative Supreme Court.

Suits challenging the constitutionality of the Social Security and Wagner acts were pending. Given the conservative bent of the Court, the Second New Deal seemed in danger of being nullified by judges, just as much of the original New Deal had been.

For that reason, Roosevelt hatched a plan to change the Court's conservative stance by increasing its members. Congress, not the Constitution, determines the size of the Supreme Court, which over the years had numbered between six and ten justices. In 1937, the number was nine. On February 5, 1937, Roosevelt, without consulting Congressional leaders or even his own advisers, asked Congress to name up to six new Supreme Court justices, explaining that the aging justices then on the Court were falling behind in their work and needed help.

"Court-packing" plan

But the "Court-packing" plan, as opponents labeled the president's scheme, backfired. It was too manipulative and far too political. A leading journalist said that Roosevelt had become "drunk with power." Roosevelt's plan aroused fears even among Democrats that the president was seeking dangerous new powers.

As it turned out, unforeseen events blunted Roosevelt's clumsy effort to change the Court. A sequence of Court decisions during the spring of 1937 surprisingly upheld disputed provisions of the Wagner and Social Security acts. In addition, a conservative justice resigned, and Roosevelt replaced him with one of the most consistent New Dealers, Senator Hugo Black of Alabama. Despite criticism from both parties, however, Roosevelt insisted on forcing his Court-packing bill through the Congress. On July 22, 1937, the Senate overwhelmingly voted it down. It was the biggest political blunder and humiliation of Roosevelt's career. The episode fractured the Democratic party and damaged the president's prestige. For the first time, Democrats in large numbers, especially southerners, opposed him, and the momentum of his 1936 landslide victory was lost. As Secretary of Agriculture Henry A. Wallace later remarked, "The whole New Deal really went up in smoke as a result of the Supreme Court fight."

A Slumping Economy

During the years 1935 and 1936, the depressed economy was finally showing signs of revival. By the spring of 1937, industrial output had moved above the 1929 level. In 1937, however, Roosevelt, worried about federal budget deficits and rising inflation, ordered sharp cuts in government spending. The result was that the economy suddenly stalled and then slid into a business slump deeper than that of 1929. In only three months, unemployment rose by 2 million people. When the spring of 1938 failed to bring economic recovery, Roosevelt asked Congress to adopt a new large-scale federal spending program, and Congress voted $3.3 billion in new expenditures. The increase in government spending reversed the economy's decline, but only during World War II would employment reach pre-1929 levels.

> "Roosevelt's recession" in 1937

The Court-packing fight, the sit-down strikes, and the 1937 recession all undercut Roosevelt's prestige and power. When the 1937 congressional session ended, the only major New Deal initiatives were the Wagner-Steagall National Housing Act and the Bankhead-Jones Farm Tenant Act. The Housing Act, developed by Senator Robert F. Wagner, set up the federal Housing Authority which extended long-term loans to cities for public housing projects in blighted low-income neighborhoods. The agency also subsidized rents for poor people. Later, during World War II, it financed housing for workers in new defense plants.

The Farm Tenant Act addressed the epidemic of rural poverty. It created a new agency, the Farm Security Administration (FSA), which provided loans to keep farm owners from losing their land to bankruptcy. It also made loans to tenant farmers to enable them to purchase their own farms. In the end, however, the FSA proved to be little more than another relief operation that tided a few farmers over during difficult times. A more effective answer to the problem eventually arrived in the form of national mobilization for war, which landed many struggling tenant farmers in military service or the defense industry, broadened their horizons, and taught them new skills.

In 1938, the Democratic Congress also enacted the Fair Labor Standards Act. It replaced many of the provisions that had been in the NIRA, which had been declared unconstitutional. The federal government established a minimum wage of 40¢ an hour and a maximum workweek of forty hours. The act, which applied only to businesses engaged in *interstate* commerce, also prohibited the employment of children under the age of sixteen.

Setbacks for the President

> Democrats divided over New Deal

During the late 1930s, the Democrats in Congress increasingly split into two factions, with conservative southerners on one side and liberal northerners on the other. Many white southern Democrats balked at the national party's growing dependence on the votes of northern labor unions and African Americans. Senator Ellison "Cotton Ed" Smith of South Carolina, the powerful chair of the Committee on Agriculture, and several other southern delegates walked out of the 1936 Democratic party convention, with Smith declaring that he would not support any party that views "the Negro as a political and social equal." Other critics believed that Roosevelt was exercising too much power and spending too much money. Some disgruntled southern Democrats began to work with conservative Republicans to veto any additional New Deal programs.

Roosevelt now headed a divided party, and the congressional elections of November 1938 handed the administration another setback when the Democrats lost 7 seats in the Senate and 80 in the House. In his State of the Union message in 1939, Roosevelt for the first time proposed no new reforms but spoke of the need "to *preserve* our reforms." The conservative coalition of Republicans and southern Democrats had stalemated the once unstoppable Roosevelt. As one observer noted, the New Deal "has been reduced to a movement with no program, with no effective political organization, with no vast popular party strength behind it."

A Halfway Revolution

The New Deal's political momentum petered out in 1939 just as a new world war was erupting in Europe and Asia. Many of the New Deal programs had failed or were poorly conceived and implemented, victims of bureaucratic infighting and inefficient management, but others were changing American life for the better: Social Security, the federal regulation of stock markets and banks, minimum wage levels for workers, federally insured bank accounts, the right to join labor unions. Roosevelt had also transformed the nation's political dynamics, luring black voters in large numbers to the Democratic party. A self-proclaimed "preacher President," Roosevelt raised the nation's spirits through his relentless optimism.

In addition, Roosevelt changed the role of the federal government in national life. During the 1930s, for the first time, the federal government assumed responsibility for planning and managing the economy and intervening to ensure social stability. By the end of the 1930s, the power and scope of the national government were vastly larger than in 1932. Landmark laws expanded the powers of the national government by establishing regulatory agencies and laying the foundation of a social welfare system. Most important of all, however, the New Deal restored a sense of hope to many people who had grown discouraged and desperate. The enduring reforms of the New Deal entailed more than just a bigger federal government and revived public confidence; they also constituted a significant change from the progressivism of Theodore Roosevelt and Woodrow Wilson. Those reformers had assumed that the function of progressive government was to use aggressive *regulation* of industry and business to ensure that people had an equal opportunity to pursue the American Dream.

> **Foundation for social welfare system**

Franklin Roosevelt and the New Dealers went beyond the progressive concept of regulated capitalism by insisting that the government provide at least a minimal level of support for all Americans. The enduring protections afforded by bank-deposit insurance, unemployment benefits, a minimum hourly wage, the Wagner Act, and Social Security pensions provided people with a sense of security as well as a safeguard for the nation against future economic crises (there has not been a similar "depression" since the 1930s).

> **Federal regulation of business and banking**

The greatest failure of the New Deal was its inability to restore prosperity and end record levels of unemployment. In 1939, 10 million Americans—nearly 17 percent of the workforce—remained jobless. Only the prolonged crisis of the Second World War would finally produce full employment—in the military as well as in factories making things for the military.

Roosevelt's energetic pragmatism was his greatest strength—and weakness. He was flexible in developing new policies and programs; he kept what worked and discarded what failed. The result was both revolutionary and conservative. Roosevelt sharply increased the regulatory powers of the federal government and laid the foundation for what would become an expanding system of social welfare programs. Roosevelt, however, was no socialist, as Republican critics charged; he sought to preserve the basic capitalist economic structure while providing protection to the nation's most vulnerable people. In this sense, the New Deal represented a "halfway revolution" that permanently altered the nation's social and political landscape. In a time of peril, Roosevelt created for Americans a more secure future.

■ **The Great Depression** The 1929 stock market crash revealed the structural flaws in the economy, but it was not the only cause of the *Great Depression (1929–1941)*. During the twenties, business owners did not provide adequate wage increases for workers, resulting in the overproduction of many goods by the end of the decade. The nation's agricultural sector also suffered from overproduction. Government policies—such as high tariffs and the reduction of the nation's money supply as a means of dealing with the financial panic—further reduced the nation's overall consumption and exacerbated the emerging economic depression.

■ **The Human Toll of the Depression** Thousands of banks and businesses closed, while millions of homes and jobs were lost. By the early 1930s, many people were homeless and hopeless. The *Dust Bowl* of the 1930s compounded the hardship for rural Americans living on the southern Great Plains. Many state laws and business practices discouraged the employment of married women. Discrimination against African Americans, Native Americans, Hispanics, and Asian Americans in hiring was widespread.

■ **Hoover's Failure** The first phase of federal response to the Great Depression included President Hoover's attempts at increasing public works and exhorting unions, businesses, and farmers to revive economic growth. His philosophy of voluntary self-reliance prevented him from using federal intervention to relieve the human suffering. In March 1933, the economy was shattered. Millions more Americans were without jobs, basic necessities, and hope.

■ **The First New Deal** During his early months in office, Congress and President Roosevelt enacted the *First New Deal (1933–1935)*, which propped up the banking industry with the *Federal Deposit Insurance Corporation (1933)*, provided short-term emergency work relief promoted industrial recovery with the *National Recovery Administration (1933)*, and raised agricultural prices with the *Agricultural Adjustment Act (1933)*. In this second phase of the federal response, most of the early New Deal programs helped end the economy's downward spiral but still left millions unemployed and mired in poverty.

■ **New Deal under Fire** The Supreme Court ruled that several of the First New Deal programs were unconstitutional violations of private property and states' rights. Many conservatives criticized the New Deal for expanding the scope and reach of the federal government so much that it was steering the nation toward socialism. By contrast, other critics did not think the New Deal went far enough. African American critics decried the widespread discrimination in New Deal policies and agencies.

■ **The Second New Deal and the New Deal's Legacy** Roosevelt responded to the criticism and the continuing economic hardship with a third phase, the *Second New Deal (1935–1938)*, which sought to reshape the nation's social structure by expanding the role of the federal government. Many of its programs, such as the *Works Progress Administration (1935)*, *Social Security (1935)*, and the *Wagner Act (1935)*, aimed to achieve greater social justice by establishing new regulatory agencies and laying the foundation of a federal social welfare system. The Second New Deal reformed business, industry, and banking with provisions such as unemployment pay, a minimum hourly wage, old-age pensions, and bank-deposit insurance. The New Deal established the idea that the federal government should provide a baseline quality of life for all Americans.

KEY TERMS

Great Depression (1929–1941)
  p. 829
Dust Bowl *p. 836*
Reconstruction Finance
  Corporation (1932) *p. 839*
Bonus Expeditionary Force (1932)
  p. 840
First New Deal (1933–1935) *p. 843*

Federal Deposit Insurance
  Corporation (1933) *p. 844*
Securities and Exchange
  Commission (1934) *p. 844*
National Recovery
  Administration (1933)
  p. 846

Agricultural Adjustment Act
  (1933) *p. 847*
Second New Deal (1935–1938)
  p. 855
Works Progress Administration
  (1935) *p. 855*
Wagner Act (1935) *p. 856*
Social Security Act (1935) *p. 856*

CHRONOLOGY

1929	Hoover inaugurated as president in March, and stock market crashes in late October
1930	Congress passes the Hawley-Smoot Tariff
1932	Congress sets up the Reconstruction Finance Corporation
1932	Bonus Expeditionary Force heads to Washington, D.C.
1932	Franklin D. Roosevelt is elected President
March–June 1933	First One Hundred Days of Roosevelt's presidency
December 1933	Twenty-First Amendment repeals Prohibition
May 1935	Supreme Court finds National Industrial Recovery Act unconstitutional
1935	Roosevelt creates the Works Progress Administration
1935	Congress passes the Wagner Act
1936	President Roosevelt is reelected in a landslide
1937	Social Security goes into effect
1937	Roosevelt attempts Court-packing scheme

INQUIZITIVE

Go to InQuizitive to see what you've learned—and learn what you've missed—with personalized feedback along the way.

RAISING THE FLAG ON IWO JIMA (February 23, 1945) Five members of the United States Marine Corps raise the flag on Mount Suribachi, during the Battle of Iwo Jima. Three of these Marines would die within days of this photograph, which later earned photographer Joe Rosenthal the Pulitzer Prize. A bronze statue of this scene is the centerpiece of the Marine Corps War Memorial in Virginia.

The Second World War

1933–1945

When Franklin Roosevelt became president in 1933, he shared with most Americans a determination to stay out of international disputes. His focus was on combating the Great Depression. While the United States had become deeply involved in global trade during the twenties, it had remained aloof from global conflicts. So-called isolationists insisted that there was no justification for America to become embroiled in international affairs. With each passing year during the thirties, however, Germany, Italy, and Japan threatened the stability of Europe and Asia.

Roosevelt strove mightily to keep the United States out of what he called the "spreading epidemic of world lawlessness," as brutal fascist dictatorships in Germany and Italy and ultranationalist militarists in Japan violated international law by invading neighboring countries. By the end of the decade, Roosevelt had decided that the only way for the United States to avoid fighting in another war was to offer all possible assistance to its allies, Great Britain and France. His efforts to make the United States the "arsenal of democracy" ignited a fierce debate between isolationists and interventionists, a debate which ended with shocking suddenness on December 7, 1941, when Japan staged a surprise attack against U.S. military bases at Pearl Harbor in Hawaii. The second world war that Americans had struggled for years to avoid had arrived at last. It would become the most significant event of the twentieth century, engulfing five continents and leaving few people untouched.

The Japanese attack unified the American people as never before. Men and women rushed to join the armed forces. Eventually, 16.4 million Americans would serve in the military during the war, including 350,000 women. To win the war against Japanese imperialism and German and Italian fascism, the United States would have to mobilize all of its economic resources; total war required massive government spending that boosted industrial production and wrenched the economy out of the Great Depression.

Four years after the Japanese attack on Pearl Harbor, the United States and its allies emerged victorious in the costliest and most destructive war in history. Whole cities were destroyed, nations dismembered, and societies transformed. More than 50 million people were killed in the war between 1939 and 1945—perhaps 60 percent of them civilians, including millions of Jews and other ethnic minorities murdered in Nazi death camps and Soviet concentration camps.

The global scope and scale of the Second World War transformed America's role in the world by ending the tradition of isolationism. By 1945 America was the world's most powerful nation, with new international interests and global responsibilities. The war left in its wake power vacuums in Europe and Asia that the Soviet Union and the United States sought to fill in order to protect their military, economic, and political interests. Instead of bringing peace, the end of the war led to a new "cold war" between two former allies, the United States and the Soviet Union. As the *New Yorker* magazine asked, "If you do not know that your country is now entangled beyond recall with the rest of the world, what do you know?"

CORE **OBJECTIVE**

1. Assess how German and Japanese actions led to the outbreak of war in Europe and in Asia.

The Rise of Fascism in Europe

In 1917, Woodrow Wilson had led the United States into the First World War in order to make the world "safe for democracy." In fact, though, democracy was in retreat after 1919. Soviet Communism was on the march during the twenties and thirties. So, too, was its ideological opponent, **fascism**, a radical form of totalitarian government in which a dictator uses propaganda and brute force to seize absolute control of all aspects of national life—the economy, the armed forces, the legal and educational systems, and the press. Fascism in Germany and Italy thrived on a violent ultranationalist patriotism and almost hysterical emotionalism built upon claims of racial superiority and the simmering resentments that grew out of defeat in the First World War. At the same time, halfway around the world, the Japanese government fell under the control of militarist expansionists eager to conquer China and all of south Asia. Japanese leaders were convinced that they were a "master race" with a "mission" to conquer and lead a resurgent Asia, just as Hitler claimed that Germany's "mission" as home of the superior

fascism A radical form of totalitarian government that emerged in 1920s Italy and Germany in which a dictator uses propaganda and brute force to seize control of all aspects of national life.

"Aryan" race was to dominate Europe. By 1941, there would be only a dozen or so democratic nations left on earth.

Italy and Germany

In 1922, political journalist Benito Mussolini and his black-shirted supporters had seized control in Italy, taking advantage of a paralyzed political system incapable of dealing with widespread unemployment and runaway inflation. By 1925, he was wielding dictatorial power as "Il Duce" (the Leader). All opposition political parties were eliminated, and several political opponents were murdered. "Mussolini Is Always Right," screamed propaganda posters. Indeed, there was something comical about the strutting, chest-thumping Mussolini, who claimed that "my animal instincts are always right." Italy, after all, was a declining industrial power whose pitiful performance in the First World War was a national embarrassment.

Germany was another matter, however. There was nothing amusing about Mussolini's German counterpart, the Austrian-born Adolf Hitler, whom Mussolini privately described as "an aggressive little man . . . probably a liar, and certainly mad." Hitler's remarkable transformation during the 1920s from social misfit to head of the National Socialist German Workers' (Nazi) party startled the world. Hitler and the Nazis claimed that they represented a German ("Aryan") master race whose "purity and strength" were threatened by liberals, Jews, Communists, homosexuals, Gypsies, and other "inferior" peoples. Hitler promised to make Germany strong again by uniting all the German-speaking peoples of Europe into a vast empire that would give fast-growing Germany "living space" to expand, dominate the "lesser" races, and rid the continent of Jews.

Hitler had little patience with conventional political processes. He urged that "democracy must be destroyed." To enforce his rise to power, Hitler recruited 2 million street-brawling thugs called "storm troopers" to intimidate his opponents. "We are barbarians!" Hitler shouted. "We want to be barbarians! It is an honorable title. We shall rejuvenate the world!" Hitler also urged Germany to defy the restrictions on its armed forces imposed by the hated Versailles Peace Treaty after the First World War.

Hitler portrayed himself as Germany's savior from the humiliation of defeat in the First World War and the widespread suffering caused by the Great Depression. Appointed chancellor on January 30, 1933, five weeks before Franklin Roosevelt was first inaugurated, Hitler, like Mussolini, declared himself absolute leader, or *Führer*, banned all political parties except the Nazis, created a secret police force known as the *Gestapo*, and stripped people of voting rights. There would be no more elections, labor unions, or strikes. During the mid-1930s, Hitler's brutal Nazi police state cranked up the engines of tyranny and terrorism, propaganda and censorship. Brown-shirted Nazi "storm troopers" fanned out across the nation, burning books and persecuting, imprisoning, and murdering Communists, Jews, and their sympathizers.

Fascist propaganda Mussolini's headquarters in Rome's Palazzo Braschi, which bore an oversized reproduction of his leering face and 132 *si*'s (Italian for "yes") in 1934.

Mussolini seizes power in Italy (1922); Hitler becomes head of Nazi party in Germany

Hitler becomes German chancellor, creates Nazi police state (1933)

Adolf Hitler Hitler performs the Nazi salute at a rally. The majestic banners, triumphant music, powerful oratory, and expansive military parades were both hypnotic and alluring to the public.

The Expanding Axis

> Japan occupies Manchuria (1932) and begins military build-up (1934)

As the 1930s unfolded, a catastrophic series of events in Asia and Europe sent the world hurtling toward disaster. In 1931–1932, some ten thousand Japanese troops had occupied Manchuria, a weakly defended province in northeast China blessed with valuable deposits of iron ore and coal. At the time, China was fragmented by civil war between Communists led by Mao Zedong and Nationalists led by Chiang Kai-shek. The Japanese took advantage of China's weakness to proclaim Manchuria's independence, renaming it "The Republic of Manchukuo." This was the first major step in Japan's eventual effort to control all of China. In 1934, Japan began an aggressive military buildup in anticipation of conquering all of East Asia.

The next year, Mussolini launched Italy's reconquest of Ethiopia, a weak nation in eastern Africa that Italy had controlled until 1896 (Mussolini dismissed it as "a country without a trace of civilization"). When the League of Nations branded Mussolini as an aggressor and imposed economic sanctions on Italy, the racist Italian leader expressed surprise that European leaders would prefer a "horde of barbarian Negroes" in Ethiopia over Italy, the "mother of civilization."

> Mussolini conquers Ethiopia (1935), German soldiers enter the Rhineland (1936) and the Spanish Civil War (1936)

In 1935, Hitler, in flagrant violation of the Versailles Treaty, began rebuilding Germany's armed forces. The next year, 1936, he sent 35,000 soldiers into the Rhineland, the demilitarized buffer zone between France and Germany. In a staged vote, 99 percent of the Germans living in the Rhineland approved Hitler's action. The failure of France and Great Britain to enforce the Versailles Treaty convinced Hitler that the western democracies were weak and frightened.

The year 1936 also witnessed the outbreak of the Spanish Civil War, which began when Spanish troops loyal to General Francisco Franco, with the support of the Roman Catholic Church, revolted against the fragile new republican government. Hitler and Mussolini rushed troops ("volunteers"), warplanes, and massive amounts of military and financial aid to support Franco's fascist insurgency.

While peace in Europe was unraveling, the Japanese government fell under the control of aggressive militarists. In 1937, a government official announced that the "tide has turned against the liberalism and democracy that once swept over the nation." On July 7, 1937, Japanese and Chinese soldiers clashed at China's Marco Polo Bridge, west of Beijing. The incident quickly developed into a full-scale conflict, the Sino-Japanese War. From Beijing, the Japanese army swept northward toward Nanjing, home of the Nationalist Chinese government. In 1937, Japan joined Germany and Italy in establishing the Rome-Berlin-Tokyo **"Axis" alliance**. Hitler and Mussolini vowed to create a "new order in Europe" that would end the domination of Great Britain and France, while the Japanese imperialists pursued their "divine right" to control all of East Asia by creating what they called the Greater East Asia Co-Prosperity Sphere.

Anschluss and the Munich Pact (1938)

Hitler was equally aggressive. In March 1938, he forced the *Anschluss* (union) of Austria with Germany. German armies marched into Austria, followed by Hitler, whose triumphant return to his native Austria was greeted by pro-German crowds waving Nazi flags and tossing flowers. When Mussolini congratulated Hitler for his bold action, the German dictator told his Italian partner that he would "never forget him for this. Never, never, never—whatever happens." A month later, after arresting over 70,000 opponents of the Nazis, German leaders announced that a remarkable 99.75 percent of Austrian voters had "approved" the forced annexation by Hitler's Germany (in fact, some 400,000 Austrians, mostly liberals and Jews, were prevented from voting). Again, no nation stepped up to oppose Hitler's aggressive actions, and soon the new Nazi government in Austria began adopting Hitler's policies of arresting or murdering opponents and imprisoning or exiling Jews, including the famed psychiatrist Sigmund Freud.

Hitler then declared his intention to annex the Sudeten territory (or Sudetenland), a mountainous region in western Czechoslovakia along the German border where more than 3 million ethnic Germans lived. Paralyzed by fear of another world war, British and French leaders tried to "appease" Hitler, hoping that if they agreed to his demands for the Sudeten territory he would stop his aggressions. On September 30, 1938, the British prime minister, Neville Chamberlain, the French prime minister, Édouard Daladier, Italian dictator Benito Mussolini, and Hitler signed the notorious Munich Pact, which transferred the Sudetenland to Germany, leading the

Germany annexes Austria (1938) and takes control of Czechoslovakia (1938-1939)

"Axis" alliance Military alliance formed in 1937 by the three major fascist powers: Germany, Italy, and Japan.

Czechoslovakian president to resign in protest. Chamberlain returned to London claiming that the Munich treaty provided "peace for our time. Peace with honor." Winston Churchill, a member of the British Parliament who would himself become prime minister in May 1940, strongly disagreed. In a speech to the House of Commons, Churchill claimed that "England has been offered a choice between war and shame. She has chosen shame, and will get war." The Munich Pact, he predicted, would not end Hitler's advances. "This is only the beginning of the reckoning."

Churchill was right. Hitler, in fact, had already confided to aides that he had no intention of abiding by the Munich Pact: "That piece of paper is of no further significance whatever." Although Hitler had promised that the Sudetenland would be his last territorial demand, he violated his pledge in March 1939, when he sent German tanks and soldiers to conquer the remainder of the Czech Republic. The European democracies, having shrunk their armies after the First World War, continued to cower in the face of Hitler's ruthless behavior and seemingly unstoppable military forces.

After Hitler's troops seized all of Czechoslovakia on March 15, 1939, the German leader announced it was "the greatest day of my life." President Roosevelt was not amused. He decided that Hitler and Mussolini were "madmen" who "respect force and force alone." Throughout late 1938 and 1939, he tried to convince Americans, as well as British and French leaders, that the growing menace of fascism would only respond to force, not words. He also persuaded Congress to increase military spending in anticipation of a possible war.

The Conquest of Poland

Later in 1939, the insatiable Hitler turned his sights to Poland, Germany's eastern neighbor. In part he wanted to regain German territory taken to form Poland after the First World War, but he also wanted to conquer Poland so as to give the German army a clear path to invade the Soviet Union. To ensure that the Soviets did not interfere with his plans, Hitler camouflaged his virulent anticommunism on August 23, 1939, when he signed the Nazi-Soviet Non-Aggression Pact with the antifascist Soviet premier, Josef Stalin. The announcement of the treaty stunned a world that had understood fascism and communism to be eternal enemies. By the terms of the treaty, the two tyrants secretly agreed to divide northern and eastern Europe between them. Just nine days later, at dawn on September 1, 1939, 1.5 million German troops invaded Poland from the north, south, and west. Hitler ordered his armies "to kill without mercy men, women, and children of the Polish race or language." The German leader also ordered all terminally ill patients in German hospitals killed to make room for soldiers wounded in Poland.

This was the final straw for the western democracies. Having allowed Austria and Czechoslovakia to be seized by Hitler's war machine, the leaders of Great Britain and France now did an about-face. On September 3,

Josef Stalin Leader of the Soviet Union who rose to power in the mid-1920s after the death of Vladimir Lenin.

1939, they honored their commitment to defend Poland. Europe, the world's smallest continent, was again embroiled in what would soon become another world war. The nations making up the British Empire and Commonwealth around the world—Canada, India, Australia, New Zealand—joined the war against Nazi Germany.

Sixteen days after German troops stormed across the Polish border, the Soviet Union invaded Poland from the east. Pressed from all sides by its old enemies, 700,000 poorly equipped Polish soldiers (many Poles fought on horseback) surrendered, having suffered seventy thousand deaths and many more wounded. On October 6, 1939, the Nazis and Soviets divided conquered Poland between them and then set about systematically destroying it. Hitler's goal was to obliterate Polish civilization, especially the Jews, and Germanize the country. For his part, Stalin wanted to recapture Polish territory lost by Russia during the First World War. Over the next five years, the Nazis and Soviets arrested, deported, enslaved, or murdered millions of Poles.

In late November 1939, the Soviets invaded neighboring Finland, leading President Roosevelt to condemn Russia's "wanton disregard for law." Outnumbered five to one, Finnish troops held off the Soviet invaders for three months but were forced to negotiate a surrender in March 1940 that gave the Soviet Union a tenth of Finland.

The Outbreak of War in Europe

After the quick German conquest of Poland, the war on the ground in Europe settled into a three-month stalemate during early 1940 that was called "the phony war," as Hitler's generals waited out the winter. Then, in the early spring, Germany suddenly attacked again. At dawn on April 9, without warning, Nazi armies occupied Denmark and landed along the Norwegian coast. German paratroopers, the first ever used in warfare, seized Norway's airports. Denmark fell in a day, Norway within a few weeks. On May 10, German forces invaded the Low Countries—Belgium, Luxembourg, and the Netherlands (Holland). Luxembourg fell the first day, the Netherlands four days later. Belgium lasted until May 28.

A few days later, German tanks roared into northern France. "The fight beginning today," Hitler declared, "decides the fate of the German nation for the next thousand years!" Hitler's brilliant **blitzkrieg** ("lightning war") strategy centered on speed. Fast-moving columns of tanks, motorized artillery, and truck-borne infantry, all supported by warplanes and paratroopers, moved so fast that they paralyzed their stunned opponents.

A British army sent to help the Belgians and the French was forced along with French troops to make a frantic retreat to the English Channel coast, with the Germans in hot pursuit. On May 26, while the German *Panzer* divisions (made up of tanks and other armored vehicles) followed Hitler's surprising order to rest and refuel, Great Britain was able to organize a desperate week-long evacuation of battle-weary British and French soldiers

blitzkrieg (1940) The German "lightning war" strategy characterized by swift, well-organized attacks using infantry, tanks, and warplanes.

Winston Churchill Prime Minister of Great Britain who led the nation during the Second World War.

from the beaches at Dunkirk, on the northern French coast near the border with Belgium. Despite attacks from German warplanes, some 338,000 soldiers escaped to England on more than a thousand ships and small boats, barges, and ferries, leaving behind vast stockpiles of vehicles, weaponry, and ammunition. "Wars are not won by evacuations," observed Prime Minister Churchill, "but there was a victory inside this deliverance."

While the miraculous evacuation at Dunkirk was unfolding, German forces decimated the remaining French armies. The crumbling French war effort prompted Italy's dictator, Mussolini, to declare war on France and Great Britain, which he dismissed as "the reactionary democracies of the West." Roosevelt characterized Mussolini's action as a "stab in the back."

On June 14, 1940, German soldiers marched unopposed into the streets of Paris. Eight days later, French leaders surrendered the entire nation. The rapid fall of France stunned the world. The war was but ten months old, yet Germany ruled most of Europe. The Germans then established a puppet

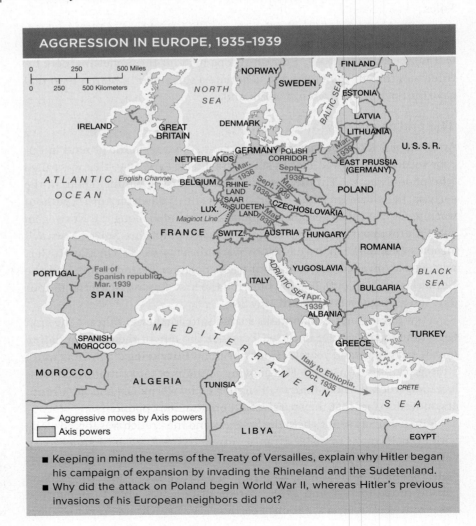

AGGRESSION IN EUROPE, 1935-1939

→ Aggressive moves by Axis powers
▨ Axis powers

■ Keeping in mind the terms of the Treaty of Versailles, explain why Hitler began his campaign of expansion by invading the Rhineland and the Sudetenland.
■ Why did the attack on Poland begin World War II, whereas Hitler's previous invasions of his European neighbors did not?

French fascist government in the city of Vichy to manage the conquered nation and implement its own anti-Jewish policies. A Free French movement made up of exiles and soldiers rescued at Dunkirk organized in London to aid the Allies. Great Britain now stood alone facing Hitler's relentless military power. "The war is won," an ecstatic Hitler bragged to Mussolini. "The rest is only a matter of time." He spoke too soon.

The United States: From Isolationism to Intervention

During the 1930s, most Americans responded to the mounting crises in Europe and Asia by deepening their commitment to isolationism. In his 1933 inaugural address, President Roosevelt announced that he would continue the efforts of Herbert Hoover to promote what he called "the good neighbor policy" in the Western Hemisphere, declaring that no nation "has the right to intervene in the internal or external affairs of another." True to his word, he withdrew U.S. troops from Nicaragua and Haiti.

The nation's deeply rooted isolationist mood was reinforced by a prominent Senate inquiry into the role of bankers and businesses in the American decision to enter World War I. Chaired by Senator Gerald P. Nye of North Dakota, the "Nye Committee" began its hearings in 1934 and lasted until early 1936. The Committee concluded that weapons makers and bankers (the "merchants of death") had spurred U.S. intervention in the European conflict in 1917 and were continuing to "help frighten nations into military activity."

U.S. Neutrality

In 1935, in response to Italy's invasion of Ethiopia and the Nye Committee hearings, President Roosevelt signed the first of several "neutrality laws" intended to avoid the mistakes that had led the nation into the First World War. However, the president did not, as Woodrow Wilson had done in 1914, ask Americans to remain neutral in their hearts because "even a neutral has a right to take account of the facts," which in his view, unlike in 1914, made it clear to all that Germany was the aggressor. The Neutrality Act of 1935 prohibited Americans from selling weapons or traveling on ships owned by nations at war. Public opinion surveys showed that most Americans were determined to stay out of Europe's conflicts. As a Minnesota senator declared in 1935, "To hell with Europe and the rest of those nations!" In 1936, Congress revised the Neutrality Act by banning loans to warring nations.

Roosevelt, however, was not so sure that the United States could or should remain neutral in a world of growing conflict. In October 1937, he delivered a speech in Chicago, the heartland of isolationism, in which he

CORE **OBJECTIVE**
2. Explain how President Roosevelt and Congress responded to the outbreak of wars in Europe and Asia between 1933 and 1941.

1937 Neutrality Act: Nonmilitary goods for warring nations

called for international cooperation to "quarantine the aggressors," who were responsible for disturbing world peace, especially the Japanese who had assaulted China. But his appeal for a more active American role in world affairs fell flat in Congress and across the nation. The Neutrality Act of 1937 allowed the president to require that nonmilitary American goods bought by warring nations be sold on a cash-and-carry basis (that is, a nation would have to pay cash and then carry the American-made goods away in its own ships). This was intended to preserve America's profitable trade with warring nations without running the risk of being drawn into the fighting.

In September 1939, Roosevelt decided that the United States must do more to help stop "aggressor" nations. He summoned Congress into special session to revise the Neutrality Act. "I regret the Congress passed the Act," the president said. "I regret equally that I signed the Act." After six weeks of debate, the Congress passed the Neutrality Act of 1939, which allowed Britain and France to send their own ships to the United States to bring back American military supplies. It was, said Roosevelt, the best way "to keep us out of war." Public opinion supported such measures as long as other nations did the actual fighting. "What the majority of the American people want," wrote the editors of the *Nation*, "is to be as un-neutral as possible without getting into war."

Preparing America for War

As Hitler's armies continued their conquest of Europe, the United States found itself in no condition to wage war. After the First World War, the U.S. Army was reduced to a small force; by 1939, it numbered only 175,000. By contrast, Germany had almost 5 million soldiers. In promoting "military preparedness," President Roosevelt in May 1940 called for increasing the size of the army and producing 50,000 combat planes in 1942, a seemingly outlandish goal, since Germany was producing only 15,000 warplanes that year. Roosevelt also increased military aid to Great Britain, promising to provide all possible "aid to the Allies short of war."

German submarines were now destroying many of the ships carrying desperately needed supplies from America to Great Britain. To address the challenge, Roosevelt and Prime Minister Churchill, whose mother was an American, negotiated a trade on September 2, 1940, called the Destroyers for Bases Agreement, by which fifty old U.S. warships went to the British Royal Navy in return for allowing the U.S. to build military bases on British island colonies in the Caribbean. Two weeks later, on September 16, 1940, Roosevelt made an even more controversial decision, opposed even by his wife Eleanor, by pushing through a reluctant Congress the first peacetime conscription (military draft) in American history, requiring the registration of all 16 million men aged twenty-one to thirty-five.

The world crisis transformed Roosevelt. Having been stalemated for much of his second term by congressional opposition to the New Deal, he

1939 Neutrality Act: Military supplies for Britain and France

U.S military buildup and increased aid to Great Britain and peacetime conscription

The Manhattan Project

was revitalized by the urgent need to stop the spread of Nazism across Europe. Adding to Roosevelt's concerns was the possibility that Germany might have a secret weapon. The famous physicist Albert Einstein, a Jewish Austrian refugee from Nazism, had alerted Roosevelt in the fall of 1939 that the Germans were trying to create atomic bombs. In June 1940, the president set up the National Defense Research Committee to coordinate military research, including a top-secret effort to develop an atomic bomb—the Manhattan Project—before the Germans did. Almost 200,000 people worked on the Manhattan Project, including Dr. J. Robert Oppenheimer, who led the team of distinguished scientists scattered among several secret facilities across the country. The Manhattan Project was so secret that Vice President Harry Truman knew nothing about it.

U-Boat After the Treaty of Versailles set limits on the size of the German navy, Germany developed military submarines of unprecedented size and power. Here, a row of Nazi U-boats are on display in the German port of Kiel in 1938.

The Battle of Britain

Having conquered western Europe, Hitler began planning the invasion of Great Britain ("Operation Sea Lion"). The late summer of 1940 witnessed the desperate Battle of Britain, as the Germans first sought to destroy Britain's Royal Air Force (RAF) before invading the island nation. The Nazis deployed some 2,500 warplanes, outnumbering the RAF two to one. "Never has a nation been so naked before its foes," Prime Minister Winston Churchill admitted. Churchill became the symbol of Britain's determination to stop Hitler. With his bulldog face, ever-present cigar, and "V for Victory" gesture, he urged the British citizenry to make the war "their finest hour." He breathed defiance while preparing the nation for a German invasion. The British, he pledged, would confront Hitler's invaders with "blood, toil, tears, and sweat." They would "never surrender."

In July and August, 1940, the German air force (*Luftwaffe*) launched day and night bombing raids against military targets—ships and naval bases, warplanes and airfields—across southeast England. The Royal Air Force, with the benefit of radar, a secret new technology, surprised the world by fending off the German assault. Hitler then ordered his bombers to target civilians and cities (especially London) in nighttime raids designed to terrorize British civilians. In what came to be called "the Blitz" during September and October of 1940, the Germans caused massive destruction in Britain's major cities.

German bombers attack Great Britain: The Blitz

The London "Blitz" An aerial photograph of London set aflame by the heavy German bombing raids in 1940. Winston Churchill responded, "We shall never surrender."

The air raids killed some 43,000 British civilians, wounded thousands more, and left 2 million homeless. But the Blitz enraged rather than demoralized the British people. A London newspaper headline summarized the nation's defiant mood: "Is That the Best You Can Do, Adolf?" At the same time, British fighter pilots were destroying 1,300 German warplanes. The British success in the air proved to be a decisive turning point in the war, for in October 1940, Hitler gave up his planned invasion of the British Isles. It was the first battle he had lost.

Debate over America's Role

During 1940, Roosevelt began a long, urgent, and eloquent campaign to convince Americans that isolationism was impractical and even dangerous. His actions to aid Great Britain and prepare America for war outraged isolationists. A prominent Democrat remembered that the dispute between isolationists and so-called interventionists during the late 1930s was "the most savage political debate during my lifetime." Isolationists, mostly midwestern and western Republicans who believed that Roosevelt was systematically drawing the United States into another European war, formed the America First Committee to oppose "military preparedness." Charles Lindbergh, the first man to fly solo across the Atlantic ocean, led the isolationist effort. To Lindbergh, Roosevelt's efforts to help Britain were driven primarily by Jews who owned "our motion pictures, our press, our radio, and our government." Lindbergh assured Americans that Britain was doomed; they should join hands with Hitler.

Roosevelt's Third Term

Roosevelt reelected (1940)

Lindbergh and the other isolationists sought to make the 1940 presidential campaign a debate about the European war. In June, just as France was falling to Germany, the Republicans nominated a dark-horse candidate, Wendell L. Willkie of Indiana, a plainspoken corporate lawyer who as a former Democrat had voted for Roosevelt in 1932 and had remained registered as a Democrat until 1938. In his acceptance speech, Willkie clumsily referred to "you Republicans." Once the campaign started, Willkie warned that Roosevelt was a "warmonger" and predicted that "if you reelect him you may expect war in April, 1941." Roosevelt responded that he had "said this before, but I shall say it again and again and again: Your boys are not going to be sent into any foreign wars." In November 1940, Roosevelt won an unprecedented third term by a comfortable margin of 27 million votes to Willkie's 22 million and by an even more decisive margin, 449 to 82, in the Electoral College.

The Lend-Lease Bill

Once reelected, Roosevelt found an ingenious way to provide even more military aid to Britain, whose cash was running out. The **Lend-Lease Bill**, introduced in Congress on January 10, 1941, allowed the president to lend or lease military equipment to "any country whose defense the President deems vital to the defense of the United States." It was a bold challenge to the isolationists, prompted by Roosevelt's conviction that "no nation can appease the Nazis. No man can turn a tiger into a kitten by stroking it." The United States, he added, would provide everything the British needed to fend off a German invasion while doing the same for China in its war against Japan. "We must be the great arsenal of democracy," Roosevelt explained. Between 1941 and 1945, the Lend-Lease program would ship $50 billion worth of supplies to Great Britain, the Soviet Union, France, China, and other Allied nations. Lend-Lease was Roosevelt's most emphatic effort to move America from isolationism to interventionism in the growing wars in Europe and Asia. Winston Churchill called it the most generous "act in the history of any nation."

> The Lend-Lease Bill (1941)

Germany Invades the Soviet Union

While Americans continued to debate Roosevelt's efforts to help Great Britain, the European war expanded. In the spring of 1941, German troops joined Italian forces in Libya, forcing the British army in North Africa to withdraw to Egypt. In April 1941, Nazi forces overwhelmed Yugoslavia and Greece. With Hungary, Romania, and Bulgaria also part of the Axis, Hitler controlled nearly all of Europe. But his ambition was unbounded. On June 22, 1941, without warning, massive German armies suddenly invaded their supposed ally, the Soviet Union, in "Operation Barbarossa." Hitler's objective in turning on Stalin was his long-standing dream to destroy communism, enslave the vast population of the Soviet Union, and exploit its considerable natural resources.

Hitler's decision to attack the Soviet Union was the defining moment of the European war, for the Germans would eventually be worn down and thrown back by the Soviets. At first, however, the largest invasion in history seemed a great success as the German armies raced across the vast plains of western Russia; entire Soviet armies and cities were surrounded and destroyed. During the second half of 1941, 3 million Soviet soldiers were captured, many of whom were then murdered or starved to death. For four months, the Soviet armies retreated in the face of the German blitzkrieg. By December, 1941, German units had reached the suburbs of Moscow, a thousand miles east of Berlin.

Lend-Lease Bill (1941) Legislation that allowed the president to lend or lease military equipment to any country whose own defense was deemed vital to the defense of the United States.

U.S. sends massive aid to Soviet Union

To American isolationists, Germany's invasion of Russia confirmed that America should stay out of the war and let two dreadful dictatorships bleed each other to death. Roosevelt, however, insisted on including the Soviet Union in the Lend-Lease agreement, for, along with Winston Churchill, he was determined to keep the Soviets fighting Hitler rather than see them surrender. In 1941 alone, America sent thousands of trucks, tanks, guns, and warplanes to the Soviet Union, along with food (especially Spam), and enough cotton, blankets, shoes, and boots to clothe the entire Russian army.

Gradually, Stalin used his dictatorial powers to slow the Nazi advance by forcing people to fight—or be killed by their own Soviet troops. During the Battle of Moscow, Russian defenders showed their pitiless resolve by executing eight thousand civilians charged with "cowardice." Slowly, the tide started to turn against the once unbeatable Germans. By the winter of 1941–1942, Hitler's generals were learning the same bitter lesson that the Russians had taught Napoleon and the French army in 1812. Invading armies must contend not only with Russia's ferocious fighters and enormous population but also vast distances, deep snow, and subzero temperatures.

The Atlantic Charter

The Atlantic Charter (1941) and German U-boats

By the late summer of 1941, the United States was no longer a "neutral" nation. In August, Roosevelt and Churchill met on a U.S. warship off the Canadian coast, where they drew up a joint statement of "common principles" known as the **Atlantic Charter**. The agreement pledged that after the "final destruction of the Nazi tyranny" the victors would promote certain common values: the self-determination of all peoples, economic cooperation, freedom of the seas, and a new system of international security to be called the United Nations. Within weeks, eleven anti-Axis nations, including the Soviet Union, had endorsed the idealistic principles of the Atlantic Charter.

No sooner had Roosevelt signed the Atlantic Charter than U. S. ships in the North Atlantic were attacked. On October 17, 1941, a German submarine ("U-boat") sank the American warship *Kearny*. Eleven seamen were killed. Two weeks later, the destroyer *Reuben James* went down, with a loss of 115 seamen. The sinkings spurred Congress to change the 1939 Neutrality Act by allowing merchant vessels to be armed and to enter combat zones and the ports of nations at war ("belligerents"). Roosevelt ordered U.S. warships to "shoot on sight" any German submarines. Step by step, the United States had given up neutrality and begun to engage in naval warfare against Nazi Germany. Still, Americans hoped to avoid taking the final step into all-out war.

The Storm in the Pacific

Atlantic Charter (1941) Joint statement crafted by Franklin D. Roosevelt and British prime minister Winston Churchill that listed the war goals of the Allied Powers.

Hitler's efforts to conquer Great Britain and the Soviet Union had stalled by late 1941, but U.S. relations with Japan were worsening. In 1940, Japan and the United States began a series of moves that pushed them closer to war. Japan forced the helpless Vichy French government, under German

WORLD WAR II MILITARY ALLIANCES, 1942

Legend:
- Axis
- Axis-controlled
- Allies
- Neutral

- What was the Atlantic Charter?
- Compare and contrast the alliances in the First World War with those in the Second World War.
- How were the Germans able to seize most of Europe so quickly?

control, to permit the construction of Japanese airfields in French-controlled northern Indochina and to cut off the railroad into south China. The United States responded with the Export Control Act of July 2, 1940, which authorized President Roosevelt to restrict the export of military supplies and other strategic materials crucial to Japan. By 1940, Japan was spending half of its annual government budget on military expansion.

Japanese in Indochina and the Export Control Act (1940)

The Tripartite Pact

On September 27, 1940, the Tokyo government signed a Tripartite Pact with Germany and Italy, by which each pledged to declare war on any nation that attacked any of them. In July 1941, Japan announced that it was taking complete control of French Indochina in its effort to expand the "Empire of the Rising Sun." Roosevelt responded by freezing all Japanese financial assets in the United States and restricting oil exports to Japan (the United States was then producing half of the world's oil). He also closed the Panama Canal to Japanese shipping and merged the Filipino army with the U.S. Army. *Time* magazine claimed that Roosevelt was

The Tripartite Pact (1940), Japan takes control of French Indochina, and United States freezes its assets

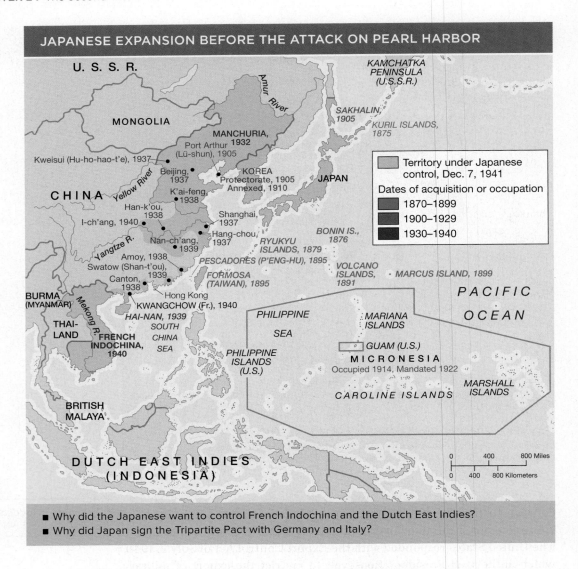

JAPANESE EXPANSION BEFORE THE ATTACK ON PEARL HARBOR

- Why did the Japanese want to control French Indochina and the Dutch East Indies?
- Why did Japan sign the Tripartite Pact with Germany and Italy?

"waging the first great undeclared war in U.S. history." Without access to American oil, iron, steel, and other products, Japan found that its expansionist plans were stalled, for Japan bought more than half its imports from the United States. Japanese military leaders responded to the American embargo by deciding to conquer areas in Southeast Asia such as French Indochina and the Dutch East Indies that could provide the much-needed strategic raw materials cut off by the United States.

The Attack on Pearl Harbor

On October 16, 1941, War Minister Hideki Tōjō became the Japanese prime minister. Viewing war with the United States as inevitable, he ordered a powerful fleet of Japanese warships to prepare for war. The Japanese naval commander, Admiral Isoroku Yamamoto, knew that his country could not defeat the United States in a long war; its only hope was "to decide the fate of the war on the very first day" by launching a "fatal attack" on the U.S. Navy.

On November 5, 1941, the Japanese asked the Roosevelt administration to end its embargo of oil and other products or "face conflict." The American secretary of state, Cordell Hull, responded on November 26 that Japan must remove all of its troops from China before the United States would lift its embargo. The Japanese had no intention of leaving China. Instead, they secretly ordered a fleet of warships to begin steaming toward Hawaii. By this time, political and military leaders on both sides considered war inevitable, and some even deemed it desirable.

The U.S. Navy Department in Washington, D.C., sent an urgent message to all of its commanders in the Pacific: "Negotiations with Japan . . . have ceased, and an aggressive move by Japan is expected within the next few days." For his part, Roosevelt staked his desperate hope for a peaceful solution on a last-minute message sent to Japan's emperor Hirohito. "Both of us," Roosevelt said, "have a sacred duty to restore traditional amity [cooperation] and prevent further death and destruction in the world."

By the time Roosevelt's message reached the emperor, Japanese warplanes were already in the air headed for U.S. bases in Hawaii. On the early morning of Sunday, December 7, 1941, 360 Japanese planes began bombing the unsuspecting U.S. fleet at **Pearl Harbor**. Of the eight American battleships, all were sunk or disabled, along with eleven other ships. Japanese bombers also destroyed 180 American warplanes. The raid, which lasted less than two hours, killed more than 2,400 American servicemen (mostly sailors) and civilians, and wounded nearly 1,200 more. At the same time that the Japanese were attacking Pearl Harbor, they were also assaulting U.S. military facilities in the Philippines and on Guam and Wake Islands in the Pacific, as well as British bases in Singapore, Hong Kong, and Malaysia.

The surprise attack fulfilled the dreams of its Japanese planners, but it fell short of military success in two important ways. First, the bombers ignored the maintenance facilities and oil storage tanks in Hawaii that supported the U.S. fleet, without which the surviving ships might have been forced back to the West Coast. Second, the Japanese bombers missed the U.S. aircraft carriers that had luckily left port a few days earlier. In the naval war to come, aircraft carriers, not battleships, would prove to be the decisive weapon. In a larger sense, the Japanese attack on Pearl Harbor was a spectacular miscalculation, for the surprise attack aroused the Americans to wage total, vengeful war and brought the isolationist movement to an abrupt end. "Lick the hell out of them," advised one formerly isolationist senator. Even the Japanese admiral who planned the attack had misgivings amid his officers' celebrations: "I fear that we have only succeeded in awakening a sleeping tiger."

On December 8, President Roosevelt, composed and determined, delivered his war message to Congress: "Yesterday, December 7, 1941—a date which will live in infamy—the United States of America was suddenly and

Hideki Tōjō Prime Minister and War Minister of Japan simultaneously until 1944, one year before Japan's unconditional surrender.

> Pearl Harbor attacked, United States enters the war

Pearl Harbor (1941) Surprise Japanese attack on the U.S. fleet at Pearl Harbor on December 7, which prompted the immediate American entry into the war.

Explosion of the USS *Shaw*
The destroyer exploded after Japanese warplanes pummeled it with three bombs. The *Shaw* was repaired shortly thereafter and went on to earn eleven battle stars in the Pacific campaign.

deliberately attacked by naval and air forces of the Empire of Japan." Three days later, on December 11, Germany and Italy declared war on what Hitler called the "half Judaized and the other half Negrified" United States, which he insisted "was not dangerous to us." The separate wars raging in Asia, Europe, and Africa had now become one global conflict. President Roosevelt told the American people in a radio address that "We are going to win, and we are going to win the peace that follows."

CORE **OBJECTIVE**
3. Analyze the effects of the Second World War on American society.

War Powers Act (1941)

Mobilization at Home

Waging war against Germany and Japan required all of America's immense industrial capacity. On December 18, 1941, Congress passed the War Powers Act, which gave the president far-reaching authority to reorganize government agencies and create new ones, regulate business and industry, and even censor mail and other forms of communication. With the declaration of war, men between the ages of eighteen and forty-five were drafted. Some 16 million men and several hundred thousand women served in the military during the war. Many teens lied about their age in order to enlist. The average American soldier or sailor in the Second World War was 26 years old, stood five feet eight, and weighed 144 pounds, an inch taller and eight pounds heavier than the typical recruit in the First World War. Only one in ten had attended college and only one in four had graduated from high school.

Arsenal of Democracy

In 1940, Adolf Hitler had scoffed at the idea that the United States could produce 50,000 warplanes a year, claiming that America was nothing but "beauty queens, millionaires, and Hollywood." His ignorance of America's industrial potential proved fatal to Germany's war plans. By the end of 1942, U.S. war production had already exceeded the *combined* output of Germany, Japan, and Italy. At an Allied planning conference in Iran in 1943, Josef Stalin raised a glass to toast "American production, without which this war would have been lost."

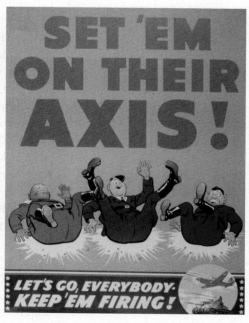

The **War Production Board**, created by Roosevelt in 1942, directed the conversion of industries to war production. In 1941, more than 3 million automobiles were manufactured in the United States; only 139 were built during the next four years. Instead of cars, automobile plants began making huge numbers of tanks, jeeps, trucks, and warplanes. "Something is happening that Hitler doesn't understand," announced *Time* magazine in 1942. "It is the miracle of production."

In making the United States the "great arsenal of democracy," the Roosevelt administration transformed the economy into the world's most efficient military machine. By 1945, the year the war ended, the United States would be manufacturing many of them running twenty-four hours a day, seven days a week, produced 300,000 warplanes, 89,000 tanks, 3 million machine guns, and 7 million rifles.

War Production Board This 1942 poster features caricatures of Mussolini, Hitler, and Tōjō, who—according to the poster—will fall on their "axis" if American civilians continue their relentless wartime production.

Financing the War

To cover the war's huge cost (some $3 trillion in today's values), Congress passed the Revenue Act of 1942 (also called the Victory Tax). It raised tax rates and increased the number of taxpayers. Where in 1939 only about 4 million people (about 5 percent of the workforce) filed tax returns, the new act made most workers (75 percent) taxpayers. By the end of war, 90 percent of workers were paying income tax. Tax revenues covered about 45 percent of military costs from 1939 to 1946; the government borrowed the rest, mostly through a massive promotional campaign that sold $185 billion worth of government war bonds, which paid interest to purchasers. In all, by the end of the war, the national debt was six times what it had been at the start.

The size of the federal government soared during the war. Over a dozen new federal agencies were created to manage the shift to a war economy. The number of civilian federal workers quadrupled, from 1 million to 4 million. Jobs were suddenly plentiful as millions of people quit work to join the military. The nation's unemployment rate plummeted from 14 percent in 1940 to 2 percent in 1943. People who had long lived on the margins of the economic system, especially women, were now brought fully into the labor

> American industry shifts to the manufacture of armaments

> U.S. employment soars

War Production Board Federal agency created by Roosevelt in 1942 that converted America's industrial output to war production.

force. Stubborn pockets of poverty did not disappear, but for most civilians, especially those who had earlier lost their jobs and homes in the Depression, the war spelled a better life than ever before. Some 24 million Americans moved during the war to take advantage of new job opportunities. Many of them headed to the states along the West Coast, where shipyards and airplane factories were hiring nonstop.

Economic Controls

Office of Price Administration (1942)

The need for the United States not only to equip and feed its own military forces but also provide massive amounts of food, clothing, and weapons to its allies created shortages of many consumer goods. Such shortages caused sharp price increases for many items. In 1942, Congress responded to such price inflation by authorizing the Office of Price Administration to set price ceilings. With prices frozen, basic goods had to be allocated through rationing, with coupons doled out for limited amounts of sugar, coffee, gasoline, automobile tires, and meat. The government promoted patriotic conservation with a massive public relations campaign that circulated posters with slogans such as "Use it up, wear it out, make it do, or do without." Businesses and workers often grumbled about the wage and price controls. On occasion the government seized industries threatened by strikes. Despite these problems, however, the government effort to stabilize wages and prices succeeded. By the end of the war, consumer prices had risen about 31 percent, a record far better than the World War I rise of 62 percent.

A Conservative Backlash

Smith-Connally War Labor Disputes Act (1943)

For all of the patriotism inspired by the war effort, criticism of government actions such as rationing increased with each passing year. In the 1942 congressional elections, Republicans gained forty-six seats in the House and nine in the Senate. During the 1940s, a coalition of conservatives from both parties dismantled "nonessential" New Deal agencies such as the Work Projects Administration (originally the Works Progress Administration), the National Youth Administration, and the Civilian Conservation Corps. Organized labor, despite substantial gains in membership and power during the war, felt the impact of the conservative trend. In the spring of 1943, when 400,000 coal miners went on strike demanding a $2-a-day wage increase, conservatives in Congress passed, over Roosevelt's veto, the Smith-Connally War Labor Disputes Act, which authorized the government to seize plants and mines and keep them operating if workers went on strike.

The War at Home

As a total war, the Second World War transformed life at home as it was being fought abroad. The dramatic changes required by the conflict also caused unexpected changes in many areas of social life, the impact of which would last long after the war's end.

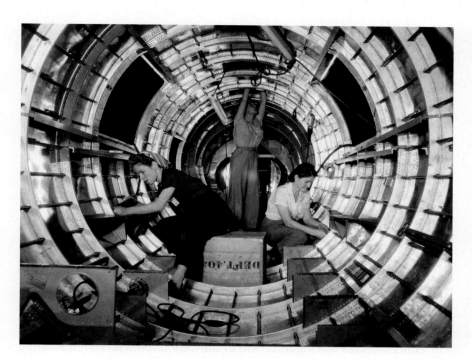

Women of the workforce, 1942 At the Douglas Aircraft Company in Long Beach, California, three women assemble the tail fuselage of a Boeing B-17 Flying Fortress bomber.

Women in the War

The war marked a watershed in the status of women. With millions of men going into military service, the demand for civilian workers shook up old prejudices about gender roles in the workplace—and in the military. During the war, nearly 200,000 women served in the **Women's Army Corps** (WAC) and the navy's equivalent, Women Accepted for Volunteer Emergency Service (WAVES). Others joined the Marine Corps, the Coast Guard, and the Army Air Force.

Sidney Hillman, appointed by Roosevelt to find workers for the defense plants, announced that "war is calling on the women of America for production skills." More than 6 million women entered the civilian workforce during the war, an increase of more than 50 percent overall (110 percent in manufacturing alone). To help recruit women to take traditionally male jobs in industry, the government launched a promotional campaign featuring the story of "Rosie the Riveter," a woman named Rosina Bonavita, who excelled as a riveter at an airplane factory.

Many men opposed the surge of women taking traditionally male jobs. A disgruntled male legislator asked who would handle traditional household tasks if women flocked to factories: "Who will do the cooking, the washing, the mending, the humble homey tasks to which every woman has devoted herself; who will rear and nurture the children?" Many women, however, were eager to escape the bland routines of domestic life and earn good wages. A female welder remembered that her wartime job "was the first time I had a chance to get out of the kitchen and work in industry and make a few bucks. This was something I had never dreamed would happen."

> Millions of women join workforce and the military

Women's Army Corps Women's branch of the United States Army; by the end of the Second World War, nearly 150,000 women had served in the WAC.

African Americans

While President Roosevelt focused on military strategy, his wife Eleanor focused on organizing the home front. She insisted that the government's wartime partnership with business not neglect the needs of workers, argued that America could not fight racism abroad while tolerating it at home, and championed the mass influx of women into the once-male workforce during the war.

African Americans move West

More than a half million African Americans left the South for better opportunities during the war years, and more than a million blacks nationwide joined the industrial workforce for the first time. Lured by jobs and higher wages in new military-related plants and factories, African Americans from Texas, Oklahoma, Arkansas, and Louisiana headed west, where the dramatic expansion of defense-related jobs had significant effects on the region's population. During the war years, the number of African Americans rose sharply in western cities such as Seattle, Portland, and Los Angeles.

Rural poor take manufacturing jobs

At the same time, the construction of military bases and the influx of new personnel provided a boon to southern textile mills responding to the war effort through the manufacture of military uniforms. Manufacturing jobs led tens of thousands of "dirt poor" sharecroppers and tenant farmers, many of them African Americans, to leave the land for steady work in new mills and factories. Sixty of the hundred new army camps created during the war were in southern states, further transforming local economies. Throughout the United States during the Second World War, the rural population decreased by 20 percent.

Racial Tension at Home

Racial discrimination and race riots at home

Although Americans found themselves fighting against the racial bigotry promoted by fascism and Nazism, the war did not end racism in the United States. The Red Cross, for example, initially refused to accept blood donated by blacks, and the president of North American Aviation announced that "we will not employ Negroes." Blacks who were hired were often limited to the lowest-paid, lowest-skilled jobs.

Some courageous black leaders refused to accept these racist practices. In 1941, A. Philip Randolph, head of the Brotherhood of Sleeping Car Porters, planned a march on Washington, D.C., to demand an end to racial discrimination in defense industries. To fend off the march, the Roosevelt administration struck a bargain. Randolph called off the demonstration in return for a presidential order calling for equal treatment in the hiring of workers.

Throughout the war, African Americans noted the irony of the United States fighting against racism abroad while tolerating it at home. "The army is about to take me to fight for democracy," a black Detroit draftee said, "but I would [rather] fight for democracy right here." During the summer of 1943 alone, there were 274 race-related incidents in almost 50

Home front versus frontlines *Left*: Though tasked with protecting the African American man from further violence in the Detroit Riots of 1943, the police officers do nothing when a member of the white mob reaches out to strike him. *Right*: The Tuskegee Airmen were the first African American military pilots. Here, the first graduates are reviewed at Tuskegee, Alabama, in 1941.

cities. In Detroit, growing racial tensions escalated into a full-fledged riot. Fighting raged for two days until federal troops arrived. By then, twenty-five blacks and nine whites had been killed, and more than 700 people had been injured.

African Americans in Uniform

The most volatile social issue ignited by the war was African American participation in the military. Although the armed forces were still racially segregated in 1941, African Americans rushed to enlist after the Japanese attack on Pearl Harbor. As African American Joe Louis, the world heavyweight boxing champion, put it, "Lots of things [are] wrong with America, but Hitler ain't going to fix them." Black soldiers and sailors, assigned to racially segregated units, were initially excluded from combat units. Black officers could not command white soldiers or sailors. Henry L. Stimson, the secretary of war, claimed that "leadership is not embedded in the negro race." Every army camp and navy base had segregated facilities—and experienced frequent racial "incidents."

Altogether, about a million African Americans—men and women—served in the armed forces during the war. Among the most famous African American servicemen were some 600 pilots trained in Tuskegee, Alabama. The so-called **Tuskegee Airmen** ended up flying more than 15,000 missions during the war. Their unquestionable excellence spurred military and civilian leaders to desegregate the armed forces after the war.

> African Americans serve in segregated military units

Tuskegee Airmen U.S. Army Air Corps unit of African American pilots whose combat success spurred military and civilian leaders to desegregate the armed forces after the war.

Off to court Latinos dressed in zoot suits are chained and escorted onto a Los Angeles County Sheriff's bus for a court appearance in June of 1943.

Mexicans and Mexican Americans

As rural dwellers moved to western cities, many farm counties experienced a labor shortage. In an ironic about-face, local and federal government authorities who before the war had forced migrant laborers back across the Mexican border now recruited them to harvest crops on American farms. The Mexican government would not consent to provide the needed workers, however, until the United States promised to ensure decent working and living conditions for the migrant workers. The result was the creation of the **bracero program** in 1942, whereby Mexico agreed to provide seasonal farm workers on year-long contracts. Under the bracero program, some 200,000 Mexican farm workers entered the western United States. At least that many more crossed the border as undocumented workers.

The rising tide of Mexican Americans in Los Angeles prompted a stream of anti-Mexican editorials and ugly racial incidents. Even though some 300,000 Mexican Americans served in the war and earned a higher percentage of Congressional Medals of Honor than any other minority group, racial prejudices still prevailed. In southern California there was constant conflict between Anglo servicemen and Mexican American gang members and teenage "zoot-suiters" (zoot suits were flamboyant clothing worn by some young Mexican American men). In 1943 several thousand off-duty sailors and soldiers, joined by hundreds of local whites, rampaged through the streets of Los Angeles, assaulting Hispanics, African Americans, and Filipinos. The weeklong violence came to be called the "Zoot Suit Riots."

Native Americans in the Military

Indians supported the war effort more fully than any other group in American society. Almost a third of eligible Native American men served in the armed forces. Many others worked in defense-related industries, and thousands of Indian women volunteered as nurses or joined the WAVES.

bracero program (1942)
System that permitted seasonal farm workers from Mexico to work in the United States on year-long contracts.

"war relocation camps"
Detention camps housing thousands of Japanese Americans from the West Coast who were forcibly interned from 1942 until the end of the Second World War.

As was the case with African Americans, Indians benefited from the experiences afforded by the war. Those who left reservations to work in defense plants or to join the military gained new vocational skills as well as a greater awareness of mainstream society and how to succeed within it.

Why did so many Native Americans fight for a nation that had stripped them of their land and ravaged their heritage? Some felt that they had no choice. Mobilization for the war effort ended many New Deal programs that had provided Indians with jobs. At the same time, many viewed the Nazis and the Japanese warlords as threats to their own homeland. Whatever their motivations, Indians distinguished themselves in the military. Unlike their African American counterparts, Indian servicemen were integrated into regular units with whites. Perhaps their most distinctive role was serving as "code talkers": every military branch used Indians, especially Navajos, to encode and decipher messages using Indian languages unknown to the Germans and Japanese.

Navajo code talkers
The complex makeup of the Navajo language made it impossible for the Axis Powers to decode American messages. Here, a code talker relays messages for the Marines in the Battle of Bougainville in the South Pacific in 1943.

Discrimination against Japanese Americans

The attack on Pearl Harbor ignited a hunger for vengeance against the Nisei—people of Japanese descent living in the United States. As Idaho's governor declared, "A good solution to the Jap problem would be to send them all back to Japan, then sink the island." Such hysteria helps explain why the U.S. government sponsored one of the worst violations of civil liberties during the twentieth century when more than 112,000 Nisei were forcibly removed from their homes along the West Coast and transported to ten **"war relocation camps."**

President Roosevelt initiated the removal of Japanese Americans (whom he called "Japs") when he issued Executive Order 9066 on February 19, 1942. More than 60 percent of the internees were U.S. citizens; a third were under the age of nineteen. Forced to sell their farms and businesses at great loss within 48 hours, the internees lost not only their property but also their liberty. Few if any were disloyal (in fact, 39,000 Japanese-Americans served in the armed forces during the war), but all were victims of fear and racial prejudice. Not until 1983 did the government acknowledge the injustice of the internment policy. Five years later it granted those Nisei still living $20,000 each in compensation, a tiny amount relative to what they had lost during four years of confinement.

A farewell to civil rights American troops escorted Japanese Americans by gunpoint to remote internment camps, many of which were horse racing tracks, whose stables served as housing.

CORE **OBJECTIVE**

4. Explain the major factors that enabled the United States and its allies to win the war in Europe.

The Allied Drive toward Berlin

By mid-1942, the "home front" was hearing good news from the war in Europe. U.S. naval forces had been increasingly successful at destroying German U-boats off the Atlantic coast. This was all the more important because the Grand Alliance—Great Britain, United States, and the Soviet Union—called for the defeat of Germany first. Defeating the Japanese in the Pacific could wait.

War Aims and Strategy

The Russian Front

A major consideration for Allied military strategy was the fighting on the vast Eastern Front in the Soviet Union, where, in fact, the outcome of the war against Hitler was largely decided. During 1941–1942, the Nazis and the Soviets waged colossal battles against each other. The Soviet population—by far—bore the brunt of the war against the Nazis, leading Josef Stalin to insist that the Americans and British relieve the pressure on his troops by attacking the Germans in western Europe, thereby forcing Hitler to pull units away from the Russian Front.

Meanwhile, with most of the German army deployed on the Russian Front, the British and American air forces, flying from bases in England, would bomb military and industrial targets in German-occupied western Europe, and especially in Germany itself, while American and British generals prepared plans to attack Nazi troops in North Africa, Italy, and France.

Roosevelt and Churchill agreed that they needed to create a second front in western Europe, but they could not agree on the timing or the location of an attack on German forces. U.S. military planners wanted to attack the Germans in France before the end of 1942. The British, however, were wary of moving too fast. An Allied defeat on the French coast, Churchill warned, was "the only way in which we could possibly lose this war." Finally, Roosevelt told U.S. military planners to accept Churchill's compromise proposal for a joint Anglo-American invasion of North Africa, which was occupied by German and Italian armies.

The North Africa Campaign

Allied armies take North Africa

On November 8, 1942, British and American forces landed in Morocco and Algeria on the North African coast ("Operation Torch"). They were led by a little-known U.S. general, Dwight D. Eisenhower, who was as untested in battle as were his troops. Farther east, British armies were pushing the Germans and Italians back across Libya. The American soldiers and their commanders were beaten badly in early battles. During the winter and spring of 1943, however, Eisenhower, soon known universally by his nickname, "Ike," found a brilliant field commander in General George Patton. Armed with ivory-handled pistols and brimming with bravado, he showed American troops how to fight a war of speed and daring in an exotic landscape. Corporal Morris Zimmerman wrote his mother from North Africa, "This is your son reporting from the land of Arabs and wine, sticky flies and red sand. I have always wanted to cross an ocean to see what was on the other side and darned if I didn't." Hammered from all sides and unable to retreat, some 250,000 Germans and Italians surrendered on May 12, 1943, leaving all of North Africa in Allied control.

The Casablanca Conference

Five months earlier, in January 1943, Roosevelt, Churchill, and the Anglo-American military chiefs met at Casablanca, the largest city in Morocco. It was a historic occasion. No U.S. president had ever flown abroad while in office, and none had ever visited Africa. Stalin chose to stay in the Soviet Union, but he sent a message which again urged the Allies to invade Nazi-controlled western Europe in order to relieve the pressure on the Russians.

At the Casablanca Conference, Churchill and Roosevelt made several key decisions. After intense debates, the British convinced the Americans that they should follow up the anticipated victory in North Africa with an assault on German and Italian forces on the Italian island of Sicily before then attacking Italy itself. Roosevelt and Churchill also decided to step up the bombing of Germany and to increase shipments of military supplies to the Soviet Union and the Nationalist Chinese forces fighting the Japanese.

Before leaving the Casablanca conference, Roosevelt announced, with Churchill's blessing, that the war would end only with the "unconditional surrender" of all enemy nations. This decision was designed to quiet Soviet suspicions that the Western Allies might negotiate separately with Hitler to end the war in western Europe. The announcement also reflected Roosevelt's determination that "every person in Germany should realize that this time Germany is a defeated nation."

The Battle of the Atlantic

While fighting raged in North Africa, the Battle of the Atlantic reached its climax. Great Britain desperately needed more food and military supplies from the United States, but German submarines were sinking the British vessels transporting American goods faster than British shipyards could replace them. Also, there could be no invasion of German-occupied France until the U-boat menace was defeated. By July 1942, some 230 Allied ships and almost 5 million tons of war supplies had been lost. "The only thing that ever frightened me during the war," recalled Churchill, "was the U-boat peril."

> New military technologies: Sonar and radar

By the end of 1942, however, the British and Americans discovered ways to defeat the U-boats. A key breakthrough occurred when British experts cracked the German naval radio codes, enabling Allied convoys to steer clear of U-boats or to hunt them down with long-range warplanes (called "subchasers") and new anti-submarine weapons deployed on warships. New technology also helped. Sonar and radar allowed Allied ships to track submarines. Yet the best tactic against U-boats was to group cargo vessels

Contributions and Impacts of World War II

World War II had a profound impact on American society. Women, African Americans, Mexican Americans, Japanese Americans, and Native Americans were just some of the groups whose wartime experiences were both essential to Allied victory and transformative at home. The chart below outlines some of the contributions that these groups made toward the American war effort, and some of the ways the war impacted them.

WOMEN

Contributions to the War	Impacts from the War
Hundreds of thousands of women volunteered to serve in the Women's Army Corps (WAC), Women Accepted for Volunteer Emergency Service (WAVES), and other service branches. Millions of women worked in war-related industries or for the federal government.	6 million more women entered the civilian workforce during the war. The valuable experience, education, and income from women's exposure to nontraditional roles set the stage for the women's movements of the 1960s and 1970s.

AFRICAN AMERICANS

Contributions to the War	Impacts from the War
Approximately 1 million African Americans served in the armed forces in segregated units, including 600 fighter pilots who served as Tuskegee Airmen. Millions of African Americans worked in industries to produce materials for the war effort.	Forced de-segregation of defense industries. About 500,000 more African Americans left the South. Almost 1 million more African Americans joined the industrial workforce; African American migration to cities increased. African American population of the West Coast increased greatly. African Americans faced increasing racial violence. Laid the foundation for the desegregation of the armed forces and civil rights movement of the fifties and sixties.

MEXICAN AMERICANS AND MEXICAN IMMIGRANTS

Contributions to the War	Impacts from the War
About 300,000 Mexican Americans served in the military. Mexicans and Mexican Americans worked in war industries and in production of needed food, having been recruited as farm laborers through the bracero program.	Hundreds of thousands of Mexican farm workers came to the United States through the bracero program. Mexican Americans faced increased racial violence in cities like Los Angeles. Set the stage for the Mexican American civil rights movement following the war.

JAPANESE AMERICANS

Contributions to the War	Impacts from the War
Large numbers of Japanese Americans served in the U.S. military during the war, including many who had faced internment.	Over 112,000 Japanese Americans living on the West Coast were forcibly placed in "war relocation camps." Many internees had to sell their property, such as farms and businesses.

NATIVE AMERICANS

Contributions to the War	Impacts from the War
One-third of all eligible Native Americans served in the armed forces. "Code talkers" sent and received encoded messages for the military using Native American languages. Many Native Americans left reservations to work in war industries.	Some Native Americans gained new skills and greater exposure to American society outside of Indian reservations. Set the stage for the "red power" movement of the 1960s and 1970s.

QUESTIONS FOR ANALYSIS

1. What were some of the ways that these groups contributed to the American war effort?

2. How did the war shape the way different groups of people lived? Do any patterns emerge?

3. How did the war impact these groups economically?

together into tightly bunched convoys so that warships could protect them more effectively. In May 1943, the Allies destroyed forty-one U-boats. Thereafter, the U-boats were on the defensive, and Allied shipping losses fell significantly.

Sicily and Italy

Allied forces reclaim Sicily and Italy: Mussolini flees

On July 10, 1943, following the Allied victory in North Africa, about 250,000 British and American troops landed on the coast of Sicily in the first effort to reclaim European territory since the war began. The entire island was in Allied hands by August 17, bringing to an end Benito Mussolini's twenty years of fascist rule in Italy. On July 25, 1943, the Italian king had dismissed Mussolini as prime minister and had him arrested. The new Italian government startled the Allies when it offered not only to surrender but also to switch sides in the war. To prevent them from doing so, Hitler sent German armies into Italy. Mussolini, plucked from prison by a daring German airborne raid, became head of a puppet fascist government in northern Italy as Allied forces took control of the rest of the country. On June 4, 1944, the U.S. Fifth Army entered Rome.

The Tehran Conference

Late in the fall of 1943, in Tehran, Iran, Churchill and Roosevelt had their first joint meeting with Josef Stalin. Their discussions focused on the planned invasion of Nazi-controlled France and a simultaneous Russian offensive westward across eastern Europe. The three leaders agreed to create an international organization—the United Nations—to maintain peace after the war. Upon arriving back in the United States, Roosevelt confided to Churchill his distrust of Stalin, stressing that it was a "ticklish" business keeping the "Russians cozy with us" because of the tension between communism and capitalism. As General Eisenhower stressed, however, the fate of Britain and the U.S. depended on the Soviets' survival as an ally against Nazi Germany. "The prize we seek," he said in 1942, "is to keep 8 million Russians [soldiers] in the war."

The Strategic Bombing of Europe

Allied air supremacy over Europe

Behind the long-anticipated Allied invasion of German-occupied France lay months of preparation. While waiting for D-day (the day the invasion would begin), the U.S. Army Air Force tried to pound Germany into submission with long-range bombers such as the B-17 "Flying Fortress" and the B-24 "Liberator." The American and British air campaign against Germany, carried out night and day, killed some 350,000 civilians (by comparison, the entire Blitz on Britain cost 43,000 lives) and frightened many others. A German girl in Berlin reported that "bombs belonged to my life." Yet the strategic air offensive failed to shatter either German morale or war production; many bombs missed their targets because of thick clouds, high winds, and inaccurate navigational systems, and many Allied planes were shot down by German fighter planes and anti-aircraft batteries. The massive Allied bombing campaign, however, did force the Germans to commit precious resources to air-raid defense and eventually wore down their air force. With Allied air supremacy over Europe assured by 1944, the much-anticipated invasion of Hitler's "Fortress Europe" could move forward.

Planning an Invasion

In early 1944, General Dwight D. Eisenhower arrived in London with a new title: Supreme Commander of the Allied Expeditionary Force (AEF) that would invade Nazi-controlled western Europe. Eisenhower faced enormous challenges. Not only did he have to create an effective command structure for the combined U.S. and British armed services, but he was also forced to handle disagreements between President Roosevelt and Prime Minister Churchill. He also faced the daunting task of planning Operation Overlord, the daring assault on Hitler's "Atlantic Wall," a formidable array of fortifications, mines, machine guns, barbed wire, and jagged beach obstacles along the French coastline. An attack by sea against heavily fortified defenders was the toughest of military operations. The planned invasion of France gave Churchill nightmares: "When I think of the beaches . . . choked with the flower of American and British youth . . . I see the tides running red with their blood. I have my doubts. I have my doubts."

For months, Eisenhower dedicated himself to planning the risky invasion and managing the complex political and military rivalries among the Allied leaders. He was a perfectionist, impatient with his staff, and at times unleashing a volcanic temper. Awake before dawn and asleep only after midnight, he drank fifteen cups of coffee and smoked four packs of cigarettes a day as he attended to every detail.

As D-day approached in early June 1944, Eisenhower's chief of staff predicted only a 50–50 chance of success. The seaborne invasion was the greatest gamble and most complex military operation in history. "I am very uneasy about the whole operation," admitted Sir Alan Brooke, the head of British forces. "It may well be the most ghastly disaster of the whole war." Eisenhower was so concerned about the invasion that he carried in his wallet a note which was to be circulated if the Allies failed. It read: "If any blame or fault attaches to the attempt, it is mine alone."

General Dwight D. Eisenhower Eisenhower instructing paratroopers before they launch the D-day assault in Operation Overlord.

D-day and After

Operation Overlord succeeded in part because it surprised the German defenders. The Allies made elaborate efforts—including the positioning of British decoy troops and making misleading public statements—to fool the Nazis into believing that the invasion would come at Pas-de-Calais, on the French-Belgian border, where the English Channel was narrowest. Instead, the landings would occur along fifty miles of shoreline in northern Normandy, a French coastal region almost 200 miles south.

On the evening of June 5, General Eisenhower visited some of the 16,000 American paratroopers preparing to drop behind the German lines in France at night to seize key bridges and roads. The tough soldiers, many of

Operation Overlord

their faces blackened by burnt cork and heads shaved to resemble Indian warriors, noticed Eisenhower's concern and tried to lift his spirits. "Now quit worrying, General," one of them said, "we'll take care of this thing for you." Another said, "We ain't worried. It's Hitler's turn to worry." After the planes took off, Eisenhower returned to his car with tears in his eyes. "Well," he said quietly to his driver, "it's on."

As the planes carrying the paratroopers arrived over France, thick clouds and German anti-aircraft fire disrupted the formations. Some soldiers were dropped miles from their landing sites, some were dropped far out at sea, some were dropped so low that their parachutes never opened. Yet the U.S. 82nd and 101st Airborne Divisions, although badly scattered, outfought three German divisions during the chaotic night and prepared the way for the main invasion by destroying bridges and capturing artillery positions and key road junctions.

The Normandy Landings

D-day: The Normandy Landings

As the gray, misty light of dawn broke on D-day morning, June 6, 1944, the biggest invasion fleet in history—some 5,300 Allied ships carrying 370,000 soldiers and sailors—filled the horizon off the Normandy coast. Sleepy German soldiers guarding the beaches awoke to see Allied ships of every size. A French boy said he saw "more ships than sea."

Major battles often depend on luck. For several hours on D-day, the local German commanders misinterpreted the Normandy landings as merely a diversion for the "real" attack at Pas-de-Calais. (It helped that the German commander, Field Marshal Erwin Rommel, assuming that the weather was too foul for an invasion, had gone home to Germany to celebrate his wife's birthday.) "How stupid of me," Rommel said when he heard the news. "How stupid of me!"

When Hitler learned of the Allied landings, he boasted that "the news couldn't be better. As long as they [the Allied armies] were in Britain, we couldn't get at them. Now we have them where we can destroy them." In the United States, word that the long-anticipated liberation of Nazi Europe had begun captured the nation's attention. Businesses closed, church bells tolled, and traffic was stopped so that people could pray in the streets. Churchill called the D-day invasion "undoubtedly the most complicated and difficult" military operation in history.

Resilience and creativity are crucial virtues amid the confusion of battles (the "fog of war"), which rarely go according to plan, and despite Eisenhower's meticulous preparations, the huge operation almost failed. During the first day of the Normandy landings, many Allied planes dropped their bombs too far inland, often on Allied troops as they moved off the beaches. Rough seas caused injuries and nausea and capsized dozens of landing craft. Indeed, many of them never managed to land at all, and over a thousand men, weighed down by their packs and equipment, drowned as they stepped off landing craft into water over their heads. Some of the landing craft delivered their often seasick troops to the wrong locations. "We

The landing at Normandy D-day, June 6, 1944. Before they could huddle under a seawall and begin to root out the region's Nazi defenders, soldiers on Omaha Beach had to cross a fifty-yard stretch that exposed them to machine guns housed in concrete bunkers.

have landed in the wrong place," shouted Brigadier General Theodore Roosevelt Jr. (son of the former president), who would receive the Medal of Honor for his courage that day. "But we will start the war from here." The noise was deafening as shells exploded across the beach and in the surf. The bodies of the killed, wounded, and drowned piled up amid wrenching cries for help. "As our boat touched sand and the ramp went down," Private Harry Parley remembered, "I became a visitor to Hell."

The first U.S. units ashore at Omaha Beach, beneath 130-foot-tall cliffs defended by German machine guns and mortars, lost more than 90 percent of their men. In one company, 197 of the 205 men were killed or wounded within ten minutes. Officers struggled to rally the exhausted, bewildered men pinned down on the beach. "Two kinds of men are staying on this beach," shouted Colonel George Taylor on Omaha Beach. "The dead and those who are going to die. Get up! Move in! Goddammit! Move in and die!" Inch by inch, backed up by waves of reinforcements, the U.S. soldiers pushed across the beach and up the cliffs. By nightfall, 156,000 Allied soldiers—57,000 of them Americans—were scattered across fifty miles of Normandy coastline. So too were the bodies of some 5,000 dead or wounded Allied soldiers.

On June 13, a week after the Normandy landings, Erwin Rommel, the German commander, told his wife that the "battle is not going at all well for us." Within three weeks, the Allies had landed more than 1 million troops, 566,000 tons of supplies, and 171,000 vehicles. "Whether the enemy can still be stopped at this point is questionable," German headquarters near Paris warned Hitler. "The enemy air superiority is terrific and smothers almost every one of our movements. . . . Losses in men and equipment are extraordinary."

Operation Overlord was the greatest seaborne invasion in the annals of warfare, but it was small when compared with the offensive launched by the Soviets in Russia a few weeks after D-day. Between June and August 1944, the Soviet Army killed, wounded, or captured more German soldiers (350,000) than were stationed in all of western Europe.

Still, the Normandy invasion was a turning point in the war. With the beachhead secured, the Allied leaders knew that victory was in their grasp. "What a plan!" Churchill exclaimed to the British Parliament. For all of the Allied success, however, Eisenhower privately struggled with the daily casualty reports. "How I wish this cruel business of war could be completed quickly," he wrote his wife. "War demands real toughness of fiber—not only in the soldiers [who] must endure, but in the homes that must sacrifice their best."

The Liberation of Paris

It would take seven more weeks and 37,000 more lives for the Allied troops to gain control of Normandy; the Germans lost more than twice as many. Some 19,000 French civilians were killed in the carnage. Then, on July 25, 1944, American armies broke out from Normandy and headed east toward Paris. On August 15, a joint American-French invasion force landed on the French Mediterranean coast and raced up the Rhone Valley in eastern France.

The path to victory in France was anything but smooth; German resistance collapsed only after ten weeks of ferocious fighting. A division of the Free French Resistance, aided by American units, had the honor of liberating Paris on August 25. As American soldiers marched through the city's cheering crowds, a reporter said that he had never "seen in any place such joy as radiated from the people of Paris this morning." One American soldier wrote home: "I was kissed at least by five million girls—and I mean beautiful girls."

By mid-September, most of France and Belgium had been cleared of German troops; meanwhile, the Soviet army moved relentlessly westward along a twelve-hundred-mile front, pushing the fleeing Germans out of Russia. Between D-day until the end of the war in Europe a year later, 1.2 million Germans were killed and wounded on the western and eastern fronts. Only 572 German warplanes were still operable, compared to 14,000 planes flown by American and British pilots.

Roosevelt's Fourth Term

Roosevelt elected to fourth term (1944)

In 1944, war or no war, the calendar required another presidential election. This time the Republicans turned to New York governor Thomas E. Dewey as their candidate. Dewey did not propose to dismantle Roosevelt's popular

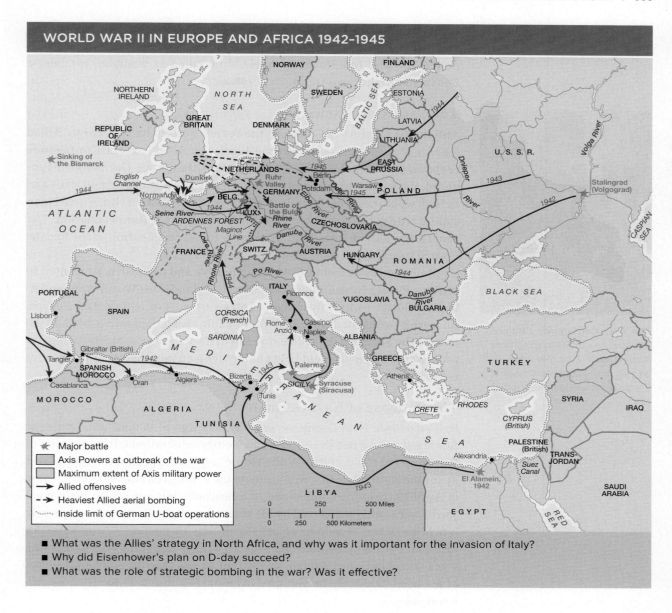

WORLD WAR II IN EUROPE AND AFRICA 1942–1945

- What was the Allies' strategy in North Africa, and why was it important for the invasion of Italy?
- Why did Eisenhower's plan on D-day succeed?
- What was the role of strategic bombing in the war? Was it effective?

New Deal programs but argued that it was time for a younger man to replace the "tired" Democratic leader. Nevertheless, on November 7, 1944, Franklin Roosevelt was elected yet again, this time by a popular vote of 25.6 million to 22 million and an electoral vote of 432 to 99.

The End of the War in the European Theatre

By the time Roosevelt was reelected, Allied armies were approaching the German border from the east and west. Churchill worried that if the Soviets arrived first in shattered Berlin, the German capital, Stalin would control the postwar map of Europe. He urged Eisenhower to beat the Soviets to Berlin. But Eisenhower decided it was not worth the estimated 100,000 Americans who would be killed or wounded to liberate Berlin before the Soviets did.

The Yalta Conference

Anticipating victory in Germany, the Soviets hosted the "Big Three" Allied leaders at a seaside resort on the Black Sea for the **Yalta Conference** (February 4–11, 1945). The leaders agreed that, once Germany surrendered, the Soviets would control eastern Germany, and the Americans and British would control the industrial areas of the west. Berlin, the German capital within the Soviet zone, would be subject to joint occupation. The Americans and British later created a fourth occupation zone for the French to administer.

Stalin's goals at Yalta were both defensive and expansive: he wanted to retrieve former Russian territory ceded to Poland after World War I and to impose Soviet control over the countries of eastern and central Europe. Roosevelt, exhausted and in failing health, was cooperative because he needed the Soviets to help defeat Japan in northeast Asia. Military analysts estimated that Japan could hold out for eighteen months after the defeat of Germany.

The Collapse of Nazi Germany

By early 1945, Nazi Germany was on the verge of defeat. But President Roosevelt would not live to join the victory celebrations. In the spring of 1945, he went to the "Little White House" in Warm Springs, Georgia, to rest up for the conference that would create the United Nations. On the morning of April 12, 1945, he complained of a headache but seemed to be in good spirits, pleasantly distracted by his beloved stamp collection. It was nearly lunchtime when he said to an artist painting his portrait, "Now we've got just about 15 minutes more to work." Then, as she watched him reading some documents, he groaned, saying that he had "terrific pain" in the back of his head. Suddenly he slumped over and fell into a coma. He died two hours later.

On hand to witness the president's death was Lucy Mercer Rutherford, the woman with whom Roosevelt had had an affair in 1916–1918. Eleanor Roosevelt was in Washington, D.C. when Franklin died, unaware of the president's guest. Although Franklin had promised in 1918 to end all communications with Mercer, he had in fact secretly stayed in touch, even enabling her to attend his presidential inauguration in 1933.

Roosevelt's death shocked and saddened people all over the world. Even his sharpest critics were devastated. Ohio Senator Robert Taft, known as "Mr. Republican," called Roosevelt's death one of the worst tragedies in American history. "The President's death removes the greatest figure of our time at the very climax of his career. . . . He dies a hero of the war, for he

The Yalta Conference Churchill, Roosevelt, and Stalin (with their respective foreign ministers behind them) confer on plans for the postwar world in February 1945.

Yalta Conference (1945) Meeting of the "Big Three" Allied leaders, Franklin D. Roosevelt, Winston Churchill, and Joseph Stalin, to discuss how to divide control of postwar Germany and eastern Europe.

literally worked himself to death in the service of the American people." By contrast, a desperate Adolf Hitler saw in Roosevelt's death a "great miracle" for the besieged Germans. "The war is not lost," he told an aide. "Read it. Roosevelt is dead!"

Hitler's shrinking Nazi empire collapsed less than a month later. In Berlin, as Soviet troops prepared to enter the city, Adolf Hitler married his mistress, Eva Braun, in an underground bunker on the last day of April. She then poisoned herself, and he killed himself with a pistol shot. On May 2, Berlin fell. Five days later, on May 7, the chief of staff of the German armed forces signed a treaty agreeing to unconditional surrender. So ended Nazi domination of Europe, little more than twelve years after Hitler had come to power proclaiming his "Thousand-Year Reich."

On May 8, V-E Day (Victory in Europe) generated massive celebrations. In Paris, an American bomber pilot flew his plane through the Eiffel Tower. In New York City, 500,000 people celebrated in the streets. But the elation was tempered by the ongoing war against Japan and the immense challenges of helping war-torn Europe rebuild. The German economy had to be revived, a new democratic government had to be formed, and the Germans and millions of other Europeans had to be clothed, housed, and fed.

> Soviet troops enter Berlin:
> Germany surrenders

The Holocaust

The end of the war in Europe revealed the horrific extent of the **Holocaust**, Hitler's systematic efforts to destroy the Jews of Europe. Reports of the Nazis' methodical slaughter of Jews had appeared as early as 1942, but the ghastly stories seemed beyond belief until the Allied armies liberated the death camps in central and eastern Europe where the Germans had imposed their "Final Solution" to what Hitler called the "Jewish problem": the wholesale extermination of some 6 million Jews, along with more than 1 million other captured peoples.

Holocaust survivors American troops encounter survivors of the Mauthausen concentration camp in their barracks in May of 1945. The Nazis tattooed their prisoners with identification numbers on their wrists or chests, as seen on the man at left.

In 1945, the Allied troops were horrified at what they discovered in the concentration camps. Bodies were piled as high as buildings; survivors were virtually skeletons. General Eisenhower reported to his wife that the evidence of "starvation, cruelty, and bestiality were so overpowering as to leave me a bit sick."

American officials, even some Jewish leaders, had dragged their feet in acknowledging the Holocaust during the war for fear that relief efforts for

Holocaust Systematic efforts by the Nazis to exterminate the Jews of Europe, resulting in the murder of over 6 million Jews and more than a million other "undesirables."

Jewish refugees might stir up anti-Semitism at home. Under pressure, President Roosevelt had set up a War Refugee Board early in 1944. It managed to rescue about 200,000 European Jews and some 20,000 others. Overall, however, the Allied response to the Nazi atrocities was inept at best and disgraceful at worst. In 1944, Churchill called the Holocaust the "most horrible crime ever committed in the history of the world."

CORE **OBJECTIVE**

5. Describe how the Japanese were defeated in the war in the Pacific.

Fighting in the Pacific

For months after the attack on Pearl Harbor, the news from the Pacific was "all bad," as President Roosevelt confessed. The Japanese captured numerous territories in Asia, including the British colonies of Hong Kong, Burma, Malaysia, and Singapore, as well as the French colony of Indochina. "Everywhere in the Pacific," said Winston Churchill, "we were weak and naked." In the Philippines, U.S. forces and their Filipino allies, outmanned, outgunned, and malnourished, surrendered in the early spring of 1942. Soon, Japan had seized control of a vast new Pacific empire and was on the verge of assaulting Australia.

Coral Sea and Midway

Battles of Coral Sea and Midway (1942)

During the spring of 1942, U.S. forces finally had some success in two key naval battles. The Battle of the Coral Sea (May 7–8, 1942) stopped a Japanese fleet headed toward the enormous island of New Guinea. Planes from the *Lexington* and the *Yorktown* sank one Japanese carrier, damaged another, and destroyed several smaller ships. American losses were greater, but the Japanese threat against Australia was stopped.

Less than a month later, Admiral Yamamoto steered his main Japanese battle fleet toward Midway, the westernmost of Hawaii's inhabited islands, from which he hoped to strike again at Pearl Harbor. This time it was the Japanese who were taken by surprise. Americans had broken the Japanese military radio code, allowing Admiral Chester Nimitz, commander of the U.S. central Pacific fleet, to learn where Yamamoto's fleet was heading. Nimitz was able to reinforce the American air base at tiny Midway Island with planes and aircraft carriers.

The first Japanese attack against Midway, on June 4, 1942, severely damaged the island's defenses, but at the cost of about a third of the Japanese planes. American bombers then struck back. In the strategic Battle of Midway, U.S. warplanes sank three Japanese aircraft carriers and crippled a fourth that was later sunk by a torpedo; it was the first major defeat for the Japanese navy in 350 years and the turning point of the Pacific war. The American victory at Midway blunted Japan's military momentum, eliminated the threat to Hawaii, and bought time for the United States to organize its massive industrial productivity for a wider war. Japanese hopes for a short, decisive war were dashed.

MacArthur's Pacific Strategy

American and Australian forces were under the command of General Douglas MacArthur, a self-infatuated military genius who constantly irritated his superiors in Washington with his "unpleasant personality" and his relentless efforts to embellish his image as a hero. Yet MacArthur was indeed a brilliant strategist. In 1942, his forces began to dislodge the Japanese from islands in the southwest Pacific.

After first pushing the Japanese back in New Guinea, on August 7, 1942, 19,000 U.S. Marines landed on Guadalcanal Island, only 1,200 miles from Australia, where the Japanese had built an air base. The American commander was optimistic that his undersupplied troops could defeat the entrenched Japanese even though, he said, there were "a hundred reasons why this operation should fail." But it did not fail. The savage fighting on Guadalcanal lasted through February 1943, but resulted in the Japanese army's first defeat, a loss of 20,000 men compared to 1,752 Americans.

The Japanese were skilled defensive fighters who rarely surrendered, and they controlled most of the islands in the Pacific. Their suicidal intensity in battles in New Guinea and on Guadalcanal led MacArthur and American military planners to adopt a brilliant "leapfrogging" strategy whereby they focused on the most important islands and used airpower and seapower to bypass the others, leaving the isolated Japanese bases to "wither on the vine," as Admiral Nimitz put it. For example, when U.S. warplanes destroyed the Japanese airfield at Rabaul in eastern New Guinea, 135,000 Japanese troops were left stranded on the island, cut off from resupply by air or by sea. What the Allies did to the Japanese garrison on Rabaul set the pattern for the remainder of the "island-hopping" war in the Pacific.

> Guadalcanal (1943) and Pacific Leapfrogging

Battles in the Central Pacific

On June 15, 1944, just days after the D-day invasion, U.S. forces liberated Tinian, Guam, and Saipan, three Japanese-controlled islands in the Mariana Islands. Saipan was strategically important because it allowed the new American B-29 "Superfortress" bombers to strike Japan itself. With New Guinea and the Mariana Islands all but liberated, General MacArthur's forces invaded the Japanese-held Philippines on October 20. The Japanese, knowing that the loss of the Philippines would cut them off from essential raw materials, brought in warships from three directions to battle the U.S. fleet.

The four sea battles that were fought in the Philippine Sea from October 23 to October 26, 1944, came to be known collectively as the Battle of Leyte Gulf, the largest naval engagement in history and the worst Japanese defeat of the war. By the end of the day, thirty-six Japanese warships, including four aircraft carriers, had been destroyed. The battle included the first Japanese *kamikaze* ("divine wind") attacks—suicide pilots deliberately crashing their bomb-laden planes into American warships.

> Battle of Leyte Gulf (1944)

General Douglas MacArthur
MacArthur theatrically coming ashore at the island of Leyte in the Philippines, October 1944.

As General MacArthur waded ashore with the U.S. troops liberating the Philippines, he reminded reporters of his 1942 pledge to return when he was evacuated from the islands in the face of the Japanese invasion. Now the U.S. commander announced with great fanfare: "People of the Philippines, I have returned! The hour of your redemption is here. . . . Rally to me."

A Grinding War against Japan

Iwo Jima (1945)

The closer the Allied forces got to Japan itself, the fiercer the resistance they encountered. While fighting continued in the Philippines, 30,000 U.S. Marines landed on Japanese-held Iwo Jima island, a speck of volcanic rock 760 miles from Tokyo that the Americans needed as a base for fighter planes to escort bombers over Japan. It took nearly six weeks to secure the tiny island at a cost of nearly 7,000 American lives.

Battle of Okinawa

Battle of Okinawa (1945)

The fight for the Japanese island of Okinawa, which began on Easter Sunday, April 1, was even bloodier. Okinawa was strategically important because it would serve as the staging area for the planned Allied invasion of Japan. The conquest of Okinawa was the largest amphibious operation of the Pacific war, involving some 300,000 troops, and almost three months of brutal fighting. More than 110,000 Japanese were killed; the remaining 7,871 were either captured or surrendered.

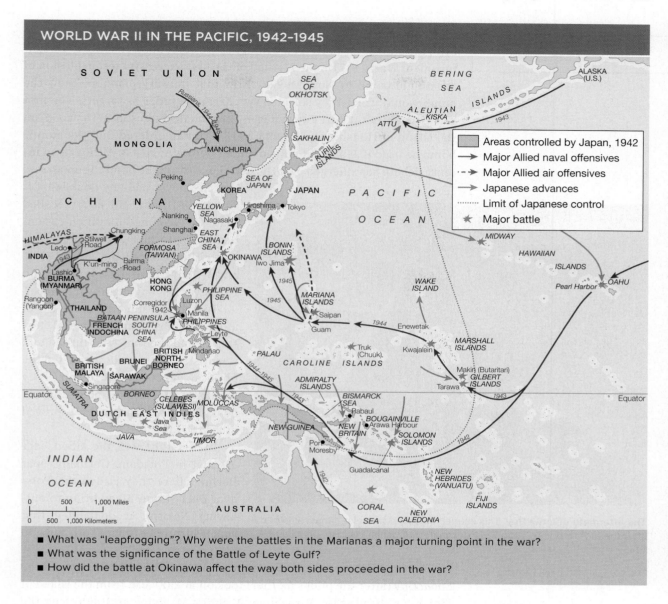

WORLD WAR II IN THE PACIFIC, 1942–1945

Areas controlled by Japan, 1942
→ Major Allied naval offensives
⇢ Major Allied air offensives
→ Japanese advances
······ Limit of Japanese control
✶ Major battle

- What was "leapfrogging"? Why were the battles in the Marianas a major turning point in the war?
- What was the significance of the Battle of Leyte Gulf?
- How did the battle at Okinawa affect the way both sides proceeded in the war?

Preparations for the Invasion of Japan

Even as the fighting still raged on Okinawa, Allied commanders began planning Operation Downfall—the invasion of Japan itself. To weaken the Japanese defenses, destroy many of their war-related industries, and erode civilian morale, the Allied command launched massive bombing raids over Japan in the summer of 1944. In early 1945, General Curtis Lemay, head of the U.S. Bomber Command, ordered devastating "firebomb" raids over Japan upon Japanese cities. On March 9, for example, some 300 B-29 bombers dropped napalm bombs on Tokyo, incinerating sixteen square miles of the city and killing 85,000 people.

Allies firebomb Tokyo

Atomic bomb dropped on Hiroshima

The Atomic Bomb

Still, the Japanese showed no willingness to surrender. In early 1945, new president Harry S. Truman learned of the first successful test explosion of an atomic bomb in New Mexico. Now that military planners knew the bomb would work, they selected two Japanese cities as targets. The first was **Hiroshima**, a port city and army headquarters in southern Japan, on the island of Honshu. On July 25, 1945, Truman ordered that the atomic bomb be used if Japan did not surrender before August 3. Although an intense debate has emerged over the decision to drop the bomb, Truman said that he "never had any doubt that it should be used." He later recalled that "we faced half a million casualties trying to take Japan by land. It was either that or the atom bomb, and I didn't hesitate a minute, and I've never lost any sleep over it since."

To Truman and others, the use of atomic bombs seemed a logical next step to end the war. As it turned out, scientists greatly underestimated the physical effects of the bomb. They predicted that 20,000 people would be killed, an estimate that proved much too low.

In mid-July 1945, the Allied leaders met in Potsdam, Germany, near Berlin. There they issued the Potsdam Declaration. In addition to outlawing Nazism, it demanded that Japan surrender or face "prompt and utter destruction."

The aftermath of Little Boy This image shows the wasteland that remained after the atomic bomb "Little Boy" decimated Hiroshima, Japan, on August 6, 1945.

The deadline passed, and on August 6, 1945, a B-29 bomber named the *Enola Gay* (after the pilot's mother) took off at 2:00 A.M. from the island of Tinian and headed for Hiroshima. At 8:15 A.M., flying at 31,600 feet, the *Enola Gay* released the five-ton, ten-foot-long uranium bomb nicknamed "Little Boy." Forty-three seconds later, as the *Enola Gay* turned sharply to avoid the blast, the bomb tumbled to an altitude of 1,900 feet where it exploded, creating a blinding flash of light followed by a fireball towering to 40,000 feet. The tail gunner on the *Enola Gay* described the scene: "It's like bubbling molasses down there . . . the mushroom is spreading out . . . fires are springing up everywhere . . . it's like a peep into hell."

Hiroshima (1945) Japanese port city that was the first target of the newly developed atomic bomb on August 6, 1945. Most of the city was destroyed.

The powerful bomb's shock wave and firestorm killed some 78,000 people, including thousands of Japanese soldiers and twenty-three American prisoners of war housed in the city. By the end of the year, the death toll would reach 140,000, as more people died of injuries or radiation poisoning. In addition, 70,000 buildings were destroyed, and four square miles of the city turned to rubble.

President Truman was aboard the battleship *Augusta* returning from the Potsdam Conference when news arrived that the atomic bomb had been dropped. "This is the greatest thing in history!" he exclaimed. In the United States, Americans greeted the news with similar joy. To them, the atomic bomb promised a quick end to the long nightmare of war. "No tears of sympathy will be shed in America for the Japanese people," the *Omaha World-Herald* predicted. "Had they possessed a comparable weapon at Pearl Harbor, would they have hesitated to use it?" Others reacted more soberly when they considered the implications of atomic warfare. "Yesterday," journalist Hanson Baldwin wrote in the *New York Times*, "we clinched victory in the Pacific, but we sowed the whirlwind."

Two days after the Hiroshima bombing, an opportunistic Soviet Union, hoping to share in the spoils of victory, hastened to enter the war in the Pacific by sending Russian troops into Japanese-occupied Manchuria along the border between China and the Soviet Union. Truman and his aides, frustrated by the stubborn refusal of Japanese leaders to surrender and fearful that the Soviet Union's entry would complicate negotiations, ordered a second atomic bomb ("Fat Man") to be dropped on Japan. On August 9, the city of Nagasaki, a shipbuilding center on the island of Kyushu, experienced the same nuclear devastation that had destroyed Hiroshima. Five days later, on August 14, 1945, the Japanese emperor finally accepted the terms of surrender.

Bombing of Nagasaki A 20,000-foot tall mushroom cloud swallowed the city of Nagasaki after the atomic bombing on August 9, 1945

A New Age Is Born

Thus ended the largest and costliest war in human history. The Soviet Union suffered 20 million deaths, China 10 million, Germany 5.6 million, and Japan 2.3 million. The Second World War (1939–1945) was more costly for the United States than any other foreign war: 292,000 battle deaths and 114,000 noncombat deaths; a million Americans were wounded, half of them seriously disabled. But in proportion to its population, the United States suffered far fewer losses than did the other major Allies or their enemies, and American territory escaped the devastation suffered in so many other parts of the world. For every American killed in the Second World War, for example, some 59 Soviets died.

The Second World War was the pivotal event of the twentieth century; it reshaped entire societies and transformed international relations. German and Italian fascism as well as Japanese militarism were destroyed. The colonial empires in Africa and Asia governed by European nations rapidly crumbled as the changes wrought by the war unleashed independence

CORE **OBJECTIVE**

6. Evaluate the efforts of President Roosevelt and the Allies to shape the postwar world.

The end of colonial empires and the emergence of the Soviet Union as a global power movements. In 1947, for example, the new nations of India and Pakistan liberated themselves from British control. The Soviet Union emerged from the war as a new global superpower, while the United States, as Winston Churchill told the House of Commons, stood "at the summit of the world."

Why Did the Allies Win?

Many factors contributed to the Allied victory in the Second World War. The American and British leaders—Roosevelt and Churchill—were better at coordinating military efforts and maintaining national morale than were Hitler, Mussolini, and the Japanese emperor, Hirohito. By 1944, Hitler had grown increasingly unstable and unpredictable in his decision making and more withdrawn from the German people, especially after a failed attempt by high-ranking officers to assassinate him in July.

In the end, however, what turned the tide of war was the awesome productivity of American industry and the ability of the Soviet Union to absorb the massive German invasion and then push back all the way to Berlin. By the end of the war, Japan had run out of food and Germany had run out of fuel. By contrast, the United States was churning out more of everything at war's end. As early as 1942, just a few weeks after the Japanese attack on Pearl Harbor, Fritz Todt, a Nazi engineer, told Hitler that the war against the United States was already lost because of America's ability to outproduce all the other warring nations combined.

Yalta's Legacy and the Postwar World

The United Nations (1945)

Franklin Roosevelt viewed the Yalta meeting as a test of whether the wartime alliance between the United States and the Soviet Union would survive once the conflict ended. Roosevelt staked his hopes for postwar cooperation on the creation of a new international peacekeeping organization, the United Nations. At Yalta, the "Big Three" agreed to hold organizational meetings in the United States beginning on April 25, 1945. Like Woodrow Wilson before him, Roosevelt was determined to replace America's "outdated" isolationism of the 1920s and 1930s with an engaged internationalism. But the creation of the United Nations came at a high price. In order to get Stalin's approval of the United Nations, Roosevelt gave in to Stalin's demands for territory held by Japan in northeast Asia.

Soviet domination of eastern Europe

Stalin also signed the Yalta Declaration of Liberated Europe, which called for free and open elections in the liberated nations of eastern Europe. Nevertheless, the wily Stalin would fail to live up to the promises he made at Yalta. When the Red Army "liberated" Hungary, Romania, Bulgaria, Czechoslovakia, Poland, and eastern Germany, it plundered and sent back to Russia anything of economic value, dismantling thousands of factories and mills and rebuilding them in the Soviet Union. To ensure control over the nations of eastern Europe, the Soviets shipped off to prisons anyone who questioned the new communist governments they created.

Republicans later savagely attacked Roosevelt for "giving" eastern Europe over to Soviet domination at Yalta. Some blamed his behavior on his declining health (he would die in a few weeks). But even a robust Roosevelt could not have dislodged the Soviet army from its control of eastern Europe. The course of the war shaped the outcome at Yalta, not Roosevelt's failed diplomacy. The United States had no real leverage when it came to eastern Europe; the huge Soviet army controlled Poland and its neighbors. As a U.S. diplomat admitted, "Stalin held all the cards" at Yalta.

The Transformation of American Life

Wars often have far-reaching societal effects. This was especially true of the Second World War. The war changed many Americans from being isolationists, often proudly ignorant of and indifferent to the rest of the world, into internationalists aware that they now had profound responsibilities for the stability and security of the entire world.

The war also transformed American life by ending the Great Depression and launching a period of unprecedented prosperity. Big businesses during the war grew into gigantic corporations as a result of huge government contracts for military weapons and supplies. New technologies and products developed for military purposes—radar, computers, electronics, plastics and synthetics, jet engines, rockets, atomic energy—began to transform the private sector, as did new consumer products that were generated from war-related innovations. And new opportunities for women as well as for African Americans, Mexican Americans, and other minorities set in motion major social changes that would culminate in the civil rights movement of the 1960s and the feminist movement of the 1970s.

> The post-war United States: New technologies, bustling industries, social change, and opportunities for women and minorities

The expansion of the federal government spurred by the war effort continued after 1945. Presidential authority increased enormously at the expense of congressional and state power. The isolationist sentiment in foreign relations that had been so powerful in the 1920s and 1930s evaporated, as the United States assumed new global responsibilities and economic interests.

> The post-war United States: Global superpower

In August 1945, President Truman told the nation that the United States had "emerged from this war the most powerful nation in this world—the most powerful nation, perhaps, in all history." But the Soviet Union, despite its profound human losses and physical destruction, had gained much new territory, built massive armed forces, and enhanced its international influence, making it the greatest power in Europe and Asia. A little over a century after Frenchman Alexis de Tocqueville had predicted that Europe would eventually be overshadowed by the United States and Russia, his prophecy had come to pass.

Reviewing the
CORE OBJECTIVES | INQUIZITIVE

■ **Fascism and the Start of the War** In Italy, Benito Mussolini assumed control by promising law and order. Adolf Hitler rearmed Germany in defiance of the Treaty of Versailles and aimed to unite all German speakers in a "Greater Germany." Civil war in Spain and the growth of the Soviet Union under Josef Stalin contributed to a precarious balance of power in Europe. By March 1939, Nazi Germany had annexed Austria and seized Czechoslovakia. Hitler then sent troops to invade Poland with the *blitzkrieg* strategy in September 1939, after signing a non-aggression pact with the Soviet Union. At last, the British and French governments declared war.

■ **America Goes to War** The United States issued "neutrality laws" to keep it out of war, but with the fall of France, Roosevelt accelerated military aid to Great Britain through the *Lend-Lease Bill.* In 1941, the United States and Great Britain signed the *Atlantic Charter,* announcing their aims in the war. After Japan joined with Germany and Italy to form the *"Axis" alliance* and Japan announced its intention to take control of French Indochina, President Roosevelt froze Japanese assets in the United States and restricted oil exports to Japan. The frustrated Japanese decided to launch a surprise attack at *Pearl Harbor,* Hawaii, in hopes of destroying the U.S. Pacific Fleet.

■ **The Second World War and American Society** The war had profound effects on American society. Americans migrated west to take jobs in defense factories, making unemployment a thing of the past. Farmers, too, recovered from hard times, supported by Mexican labor through the *bracero program.* The federal government, through agencies like the *War Production Board,* took control of managing the economy for the war effort. Many women took nontraditional jobs, some in the *Women's Army Corps.* About 1 million African Americans served in the military in segregated units such as the *Tuskegee Airmen.* More than 100,000 Japanese Americans were forcibly interned in *"war relocation camps."*

■ **Road to Allied Victory in Europe** By 1943, the Allies had defeated the German and Italian armies occupying North Africa then launched attacks on Sicily and the mainland of Italy. Stalin demanded an Allied attack on the Atlantic coast of France, but Operation Overlord was delayed until 1944. Invaded from the west and the east, German resistance slowly crumbled. Allied leaders Roosevelt, Churchill, and Stalin met at the *Yalta Conference* in February 1945, where they decided to divide a conquered Germany into four occupation zones. In May, Soviet forces captured Berlin and Germany surrendered. After the war, Allied forces discovered the extent of the *Holocaust*—the Nazis' systematic attempt to exterminate the Jews.

■ **The Pacific War** The Japanese advance across the Pacific was halted in June 1942 when the U.S. Navy destroyed much of the Japenese fleet in the Battle of Midway. The United States fought costly battles in New Guinea and Guadalcanal before dislodging the Japanese from the Philippines in 1944. Fierce Japanese resistance at Iwo Jima and Okinawa and refusal to surrender led the new president, Harry S. Truman, to drop atomic bombs on the Japanese cities of *Hiroshima* and Nagasaki.

■ **Postwar World** The Soviet Union and the United States emerged from the war as global superpowers. The United States possessed the world's strongest economy. Military production had brought America out of the Great Depression, and new military technologies changed industrial and private life. The opportunities for women and minorities during the war also increased their aspirations and would contribute to the emergence of the civil rights and feminist movements.

KEY TERMS

CHRONOLOGY

1933	Hitler becomes chancellor of Germany
1935	Italy invades Ethiopia
1936–1939	Spanish Civil War
1937	War between China and Japan begins
1938	Hitler forces the *Anschluss* (union) of Austria and Germany
1939	Soviet Union agrees to a non-aggression pact with Germany
September 1939	German troops invade Poland
1940	Battle of Britain
September 1940	Germany, Italy, and Japan sign the Tripartite Pact
June 1941	Germany invades Soviet Union
August 1941	United States and Great Britain sign the Atlantic Charter
December 7, 1941	Japanese launch surprise attack at Pearl Harbor, Hawaii
June 1942	Battle of Midway
July 1943	Allied forces land on Sicily
June 6, 1944	D-day
February 1945	Yalta Conference
May 8, 1945	Nazi Germany surrenders unconditionally; V-E Day
August 1945	Atomic bombs dropped on Hiroshima and Nagasaki
September 2, 1945	Japan surrenders; V-J Day

INQUIZITIVE

Go to InQuizitive to see what you've learned—and learn what you've missed—with personalized feedback along the way.

DEBATING the United States' Response to the Holocaust

One of the more difficult tasks that historians face is assessing the actions and beliefs of historical figures within an ethical framework. Should individuals be judged by the standards of their own time or by those of today? Should we hold celebrated historical figures to a higher ethical standard? How should we assess a nation's priorities in a time of crisis and war? For Part 6, *Modern America*, President Franklin D. Roosevelt's and the U.S. government's response to the Holocaust during the Second World War demonstrate how historians can disagree when they attempt to evaluate historic individuals from an ethical perspective.

For this exercise you have two tasks:

PART 1: Compare the two secondary sources on the United States and Holocaust.
PART 2: Using primary sources, evaluate the arguments of the two secondary sources.

PART I Comparing Secondary Sources

Secondary sources from two scholars are included for you to review. The first is from David Wyman, formerly of the University of Massachusetts at Amherst and currently chairman of the David S. Wyman Institute of Holocaust Studies. Wyman is one of the most influential historians on the American response to the Holocaust. The second is from Holocaust historian Richard Breitman, editor of the scholarly journal *Holocaust and Genocide Studies*, and historian Allan J. Lichtman. Both teach at American University. In the following selections, these scholars explore President Franklin Delano Roosevelt's response to the challenges posed by the Holocaust.

Compare the views of these two scholars by answering the following questions. Be sure to find specific examples in the selections to support your answers.

■ How do the authors characterize the American response to the Holocaust, and what explanation(s) do they give for that conduct?

■ What role in America's response to the Holocaust does each author ascribe to Franklin D. Roosevelt?

■ How does each author assess the morality of the response to the Holocaust of both the U.S. government and President Roosevelt? What ethical standards do the authors use in making their assessments?

■ What ethical standard would you use to evaluate the conduct of President Roosevelt and the U.S. government?

Secondary Source 1

David S. Wyman, *The Abandonment of the Jews* (1985)

Why did America fail to carry out the kind of rescue effort that it could have?

The American State Department . . . had no intention of rescuing large numbers of European Jews. On the contrary, they continually feared that Germany or other Axis nations might release tens of thousands of Jews into Allied hands. Any such exodus would have placed intense pressure on Britain to open Palestine and on the United States to take in more Jewish refugees, a situation the two great powers did not want to face. Consequently, their policies aimed at obstructing rescue possibilities and dampening public pressures for government action.

Authenticated information that the Nazis were systematically exterminating European Jewry was made public in the United States in November 1942. President Roosevelt did nothing about the mass murder for fourteen months, then moved only because he was confronted with political pressures he could not avoid and because his administration stood on the brink of a nasty scandal over its rescue policies. The War Refugee Board, which the President then established to save Jews and other victims of the Nazis, received little power, almost no cooperation from Roosevelt or his administration, and grossly inadequate government funding.

Strong popular pressure for action would have brought a much fuller government commitment to rescue and would have produced it sooner. Several factors hampered the growth of public pressure. Among them were anti-Semitism and anti-immigration attitudes, both widespread in American society in that era. . . . In 1944 the United States War Department rejected several appeals to bomb the Auschwitz gas chambers and the railroads leading to Auschwitz, claiming that such actions would divert essential airpower from decisive operations elsewhere. . . . Franklin Roosevelt's indifference to so momentous an historical event as the systematic annihilation of European Jewry emerges as the worst failure of his presidency.

Source: Wyman, David S. *The Abandonment of the Jews: America and the Holocaust, 1941–1945.* New York: The New Press, 1985. xiv–xv.

Secondary Source 2

Richard Breitman and Allan J. Lichtman, *FDR and the Jews* (2013)

Some scholars have condemned Franklin Delano Roosevelt, the president of the United States from 1933 to 1945, for callously standing by while Hitler persecuted German Jewry and then exterminated nearly two-thirds of Europe's Jews. . . . Others claim that Roosevelt did everything feasible to rescue European Jews and saved millions of potential victims by orchestrating the defeat of Nazi Germany in World War II. . . . For most of his presidency Roosevelt did little to aid the imperiled Jews of Germany and Europe. He put other policy priorities well ahead of saving Jews and deferred to fears of an anti-Semitic backlash at home. He worried that measures to assist European Jews might endanger his political coalition at home and then a wartime alliance abroad. FDR usually avoided singling out the Jews in public. When he engaged Jewish issues, he maneuvered, often behind the scenes. When he hesitated, other American officials with far less sympathy for Jews set or carried out policies. Still, at times Roosevelt acted decisively to rescue Jews, often withstanding contrary pressures from the American public, Congress, and his own State Department. Oddly enough, he did more for the Jews than any other world figure, even if his efforts seem deficient in retrospect. He was a far better president for Jews than any of his political adversaries would have been. Roosevelt defied most Republican opponents and some isolationist Democrats to lead political and military opposition to Nazi Germany's plans for expansion and world domination. . . . Unlike other authors, we examine FDR's decision-making as president from the perspective of his life experiences and full political career. Roosevelt's handling of the crisis of European Jewry may offer the best opportunity to understand the political dynamics of American responses to persecution and genocide in foreign lands. FDR was a man of faith. He recognized both moral issues across the globe and the practical concerns of governing a great nation. . . . How he responded, and why, reveals much about the strengths and limitations of the American presidency. The story of FDR and the Jews is ultimately a tragic one that transcends the achievements and failures of any one leader. Even if FDR had been more willing to override domestic opposition and twist arms abroad, he could not have stopped the Nazis' mass murder of some six million Jews. For Hitler and his followers, the annihilation of Jews was not a diversion from the war effort, but integral to its purpose. For America and Britain, the rescue of Jews, even if practical, was ultimately subordinate to the overriding priorities of total war and unconditional surrender of the enemy. "Action expresses priorities," Mahatma Gandhi said while engaged in a freedom struggle of his own.

Source: Breitman, Richard, and Allan J. Lichtman. *FDR and the Jews.* Cambridge, Mass.: The Belknap Press of Harvard University Press, 2013. 2, 6–7.

PART II Using Primary Sources to Evaluate Secondary Sources

When historians are faced with competing interpretations of the past, they often look at primary source material as part of the process of evaluating the different arguments. A selection of primary source materials relating to the United States and the Holocaust follows. The first document is a 1942 letter to the president from the leaders of the American Jewish community soon after the public revelation of the holocaust. The second selection comes from a State Department memorandum to the British government regarding refugees from Nazi-occupied territories. The third document is from a letter from Secretary of State Cordell Hull to the president regarding the Bermuda conference of April 1943, in which the United States and Great Britain discuss the issue of Jewish refugees. The fourth document is a 1944 memorandum written by John Pehle, an assistant to Treasury Secretary Henry Morgenthau Jr., following a meeting with President Roosevelt. Morgenthau was the highest-ranking Jewish member of FDR's cabinet and the leading advocate for U.S. intervention in stopping the Holocaust. The fifth document is a draft of a statement by FDR regarding crimes against humanity that was distributed to Axis forces in Europe in 1944. The final document is a July 4, 1944, letter from Assistant Secretary of War John J. McCloy to John W. Pehle outlining reasons why the War Department rejected Pehle's request to bomb the rail lines used to transport Jews and other prisoners to the Nazi death camps.

Carefully read each of the primary sources and answer the following questions. Which of the primary source documents support or refute Wyman's or Breitman and Lichtman's arguments about the U.S. response to the Holocaust. You may find that some documents do both, but for different parts of each historian's interpretation. Be sure to identify which specific components of each historian's argument the documents support or refute.

■ Based on these primary sources, how would you characterize the U.S. government's response to the Holocaust?

■ Judging from these primary sources, what role did FDR play in formulating U.S. policy toward the Holocaust?

■ Which of the primary sources do you think Wyman or Breitman and Lichtman would find most useful, and how might they use them to support their argument?

■ Which of the secondary sources do you think is best supported by the primary source evidence?

■ Based on the ethical standard you would use to evaluate the conduct of President Roosevelt and the U.S. government (see the previous questions for comparing secondary sources), how do you assess what these primary sources reveal about the U.S. government's and FDR's response to the Holocaust?

Primary Source 1

Representatives of the Jewish Community of the United States, "Letter to the President" (December 8, 1942)

Dear Mr. President:

We come to you as representatives of all sections of the Jewish community of the United States. Within recent months all Americans have been horrified by the verification of reports concerning the barbarities against the inhabitants of countries over-run by Hitler's forces. To these horrors has now been added the news of Hitler's edict calling for the extermination of all Jews in the subjugated lands.

Already almost two million Jews, men, women and children, have been cruelly done to death, and five million more Jews live under the threat of a similar doom.

The record of these heinous crimes against the Jews in East Europe is detailed in the attached memorandum.

. . .

In the midst of their suffering, however, the peoples of Europe are sustained by a hope that the victory of the Democracies will destroy the Nazi scourge and restore freedom to the world. European Jews share that hope. But will they live to see the dawn of this day of freedom? Unless action is taken immediately, the Jews of Hitler's Europe are doomed.

In this hour of deepest anguish and despair we turn to you, Mr. President. . . .

We ask you now once again to raise your voice—in behalf of the Jews of Europe. We ask you once again to warn the Nazis that they will be held to strict accountability for their crimes. We ask you to employ every available means to bring solemn protest and warning to the peoples of the Axis countries so that they may be deterred from acting as the instruments of the monstrous designs of their mad leaders.

Maurice Wertheim, President, American Jewish Committee

Dr. Stephen Wise, President, American Jewish Congress

Adolph Held, President, American Jewish Labor Committee

Henry Monsky, President, B'nai B'rith

Israel Goldstein, President, Synagogue Council of America

Rabbi Israel Rosenberg, Chairman, Union of Orthodox Rabbis in the United States

Source: Wertheim, Maurice, Adolph Held, Israel Goldstein, Stephen Wise, Henry Honsky, and Rabbi Israel Rosenberg. "Letter to the President, December 8, 1942." Selected Digitized Documents Related to the Holocaust and Refugees, 1933–1945. Official File 76—Church Matters: 76c—Jewish, October–December 1942. Franklin D. Roosevelt Presidential Library & Museum. Accessed at the *FRANKLIN, FDR Library's Digital Collections*: www.fdrlibrary.marist.edu/_resources/images/hol/hol00023.pdf#search=>.

Primary Source 2

U.S. Department of State, Response to British Embassy on Assisting Jewish refugees (February 25, 1943)

Since the entry of the United States into the war, there have been no new restrictions placed by the Government of the United States upon the number of aliens of any nationality permitted to proceed to this country under existing laws, except for the more intensive examination of aliens required for security reasons. . . . In affording asylum to refugees, however, it is and must be bound by legislation enacted by Congress [in] determining the immigration policy of the United States.

Source: United States Department of State. "Refugees from Nazi-Occupied Territory: Reception in the United Kingdom and British Colonial Territory [February 25, 1943]." President's Secretary's File, Box 71, State Department—Summary of Consular Reports Relating to Conditions in Occupied Countries, January 1942–May 1943, July 8, 1941. Franklin D. Roosevelt, Papers as President: The President's Secretary's File (PSF), 1933–1945. Franklin D. Roosevelt Presidential Library & Museum. Accessed at *FRANKLIN, FDR Library's Digital Collections*: <http://www.fdrlibrary.marist.edu/_resources/images/psf/b-psfc000198.pdf#search=>.

Primary Source 3

Secretary of State and the President's Correspondence, Abstract (May 7, 1943)

Writes at length to the President re the recent Bermuda Conference on Refugees, and in this connection encloses a copy of the summary or outline of the recommendations, which have been unanimously made by the American and British Delegates. . . . the most important of the items recommended at Bermuda concerns the evacuation of some 5,000 persons from Bulgaria via Turkey to Palestine, another important recommendation requires action by the U.S. Government as well as by the British Government relates to the movement of some 20,000 refugees from Spain to North Africa, "not only to relieve the Spanish authorities of the present burden, but also to make it possible for Spain to receive more and more refugees who in turn may be evacuated to North Africa." . . . The President made certain suggestions . . . as follows: that we do not give unlimited promise but that we undertake with Britain to share the cost of financing from time to time any specific cases—in connection with the providing for refugees; that we can do nothing but comply strictly with the present immigration laws. . . . he agrees that we cannot open the question of our immigration laws, and he agrees with Sec'y. Hull as to bringing in temporary visitors, stating: "We have already brought in a large number." The President returned the above-mentioned cablegram with his O.K.

Source: "Abstract, Letter to President Franklin Delano Roosevelt from Secretary of State Cordell Hull, May 7, 1943." Selected Digital Documents Related to the Holocaust and Refugees, 1933–1945. Series 1, Official File 76—Church Matters: 76c—Jewish—Abstracts, 1943–1945. Franklin D. Roosevelt Presidential Library & Museum. Accessed at *FRANKLIN, FDR Library's Digital Collections*: <http://www.fdrlibrary.marist.edu/_resources/images/hol/hol00029.pdf#search=>.

Primary Source 4

U.S. State Department's Efforts to Rescue European Jews, Memorandum (January 16, 1944)

Secretary Morgenthau advised the President that he was deeply disturbed about the failure of the State Department to take any effective action to save the remaining Jews in Europe. He explained that the Treasury Department . . . had uncovered evidence indicating that not only were the people in the State Department inefficient in dealing with this problem, but that they were actually taking action to prevent the rescue of the Jews. . . . The President listened attentively and seemed to grasp the significance of the various points. . . . The President said he agreed that some effective action could be taken. . . . The President seemed disinclined to believe that Long [Assistant Secretary of State Breckinridge Long] wanted to stop effective action from being taken, but said that Long had been somewhat soured on the problem when Rabbi Wise got Long to approve a long list of people being brought into this country, many of whom turned out to be bad people. Secretary Morgenthau reminded the President that at a Cabinet meeting Biddle [identify] had indicated that only three Jews of those entering the United States during the war had turned out to be undesirable. The President said that he had been advised that the figure was considerably larger. In any event he felt that Long was inclined to be soured on the situation. . . . The Secretary told Mr. Stettinius in plain words that he was convinced that people in the State Department, particularly Breckinridge Long, were deliberately obstructing the execution of any plan to save the Jews and that forthright immediate action was necessary if this Government was not going to be placed in the same position as Hitler and share the responsibility for exterminating all the Jews of Europe. . . .

Source: Pehle, John. "Memorandum for the Secretary's Files, January 16, 1944." Eleanor Roosevelt Papers—Henry Morgenthau Jr. Diary, Vol. 694: Acquiescence Memo, Personal Report to the President, and related documents, January 13–16, 1944. Selected Digitized Documents Related to the Holocaust and Refugees, 1933–1945. Franklin D. Roosevelt Presidential Library & Museum. Accessed at *FRANKLIN, FDR Library's Digital Collections*: <http://www.fdrlibrary.marist.edu/_resources/images/hol/hol00521.pdf#search=morgenthau>.

Primary Source 5

Franklin D. Roosevelt, "The Blackest Crimes of All History" (April 3, 1944)

[O]ne of the blackest crimes of all history—begun by the Nazis in the days of peace, and multiplied by them a hundred fold in time of war—the wholesale systematic murder of the Jews of Europe—goes on unabated every hour.

It is therefore fitting that we should again proclaim our determination that none who participate in any of these acts of savagery shall go unpunished. The United Nations have made it clear that they will pursue the guilty and deliver them up in order that justice be done. That warning applies not only to the leaders but also to their functionaries and subordinates in Germany and in the satellite countries. All who knowingly take part in the deportation of Jews to their death in Poland, or Norwegians and French to their death in Germany, are equally guilty with the executioner. All who share the guilt shall share the punishment.

Source: "Draft Press Release, Statement by the President re: the Holocaust, April 3, 1944." Series 1: Franklin D. Roosevelt Significant Documents, Box 1, FDR-63. Significant Documents Collection. Franklin D. Roosevelt Presidential Library & Museum. Accessed at *FRANKLIN, FDR Library's Digital Collections*: <http://www.fdrlibrary.marist.edu/_resources/images/sign/fdr_60.pdf#search=>.

Primary Source 6

U.S. War Department to Treasury Department, On Bombing Death Camp Railways (July 4, 1944)

I refer to your letter of June 29 . . . proposing that certain sections of railway lines between Hungary and Poland be bombed to interrupt the transportation of Jews from Hungary. The War Department is of the opinion that the suggested air operation is impracticable. It could be executed only by the diversion of considerable air support essential to the success of our forces now engaged in decisive operations and would in any case be of such very doubtful efficacy that it would not amount to a practical project. The War Department fully appreciates the humanitarian motives which prompted the suggested operation, but for the reasons stated above, the operation suggested does not appear justified.

Source: McCloy, John J. "Letter, John J. McCloy to John W. Pehle re: bombing of railway lines transporting Jews to death camps, July 4, 1944." Series 1: Franklin D. Roosevelt Significant Documents, Box 1, FDR-63. Significant Documents Collection. Franklin D. Roosevelt Presidential Library & Museum. Accessed at *FRANKLIN, FDR Library's Digital Collections*: <http://www.fdrlibrary.marist.edu/_resources/images/sign/fdr_63.pdf#search=john%20j.%20mccloy>.

The American Age

PART

7

As the Second World War was coming to an end in 1945, President Franklin D. Roosevelt staked his hopes for a peaceful future on a new international organization, the United Nations. On April 25, 1945, two weeks after Roosevelt's death and two weeks before the German surrender, delegates from fifty nations at war with Germany and Japan met in San Francisco to draw up the Charter of the United Nations. The UN Security Council was given "primary responsibility for the maintenance of international peace and security." The Security Council included five *permanent* members: the United States, the Soviet Union (replaced by the Russian Federation in 1991), Great Britain, France, and the Republic of China (replaced by the People's Republic of China in 1971). Each permanent member could *veto* any proposed action by the United Nations. Not long after the United Nations was created, however, it became evident that two members of the Security Council, the United States and the Soviet Union, had such intense differences of opinion about international policies that the United Nations was largely impotent in dealing with the cold war that dominated postwar politics.

The United States emerged from the Second World War as the world's preeminent military and economic power, the only nation in possession of atomic weapons. While much of Europe and Asia struggled to recover from the human misery and physical devastation of the war, including an acute shortage of

923

men, the United States was virtually unscathed, its economic infrastructure intact and operating at peak efficiency. Jobs that had been scarce in the 1930s were now available for the taking. By 1955 the United States, with only 6 percent of the world's population, was producing half of the world's goods. American capitalism became a dominant cultural force around the world, too. In Europe, Japan, South Korea, and elsewhere, American products, fashion, and forms of entertainment attracted excited attention. Henry Luce, the publisher of *Time* and *Life* magazines, proclaimed that the twentieth century had become the "American century."

Yet a deepening "cold war" between the democratic and Communist nations cast a cloud of concern over the postwar world. The tense ideological contest with the Soviet Union produced numerous foreign crises and sparked a domestic witch hunt for Communists in the United States. After 1945, Republican and Democratic presidents aggressively sought to "contain" the spread of communism around the world. This bedrock assumption embroiled the United States in costly wars in Korea and in Southeast Asia. A backlash against the Vietnam War (1964–1973) also inflamed a rebellious "countercultural" movement at home in which young idealists not only opposed the war but also provided much of the energy for many overdue social reforms, including racial equality, gay rights, feminism, and environmentalism. The anti-war movement destroyed Lyndon Johnson's presidency in 1968 and provoked a conservative counterattack. President Richard Nixon's paranoid reaction to his critics led to the Watergate affair and the destruction of his presidency.

Through all of this turmoil, however, the expanding role of the federal government that Franklin Roosevelt and his New Deal programs had initiated remained essentially intact. With only a few exceptions, both Republicans and Democrats after 1945 acknowledged that the federal government must assume greater responsibility for the welfare of individuals. Even President Ronald Reagan, a sharp critic of federal social-welfare programs during the 1980s, recognized the need for the government to provide a "safety net" for those who could not help themselves.

Yet this fragile consensus on public policy and the cold war had largely broken down by the late 1980s amid stunning international developments and social changes at home. The surprising collapse of the Soviet Union in 1989 and the disintegration of European communism left the United States the only superpower. After forty-five years, U.S. foreign policy was no longer focused on a single adversary. During the early 1990s, East and West Germany reunited, racial segregation (*apartheid*) in South Africa ended, and Israel and the Palestinians, long-standing foes, signed a treaty ending hostilities—at least for a while.

The end of the cold war and the dissolution of the Soviet Union into fifteen separate nations lowered the threat of nuclear war and reduced public interest in foreign affairs. Yet numerous ethnic, nationalist, and separatist conflicts brought constant tensions and instability at the end of the twentieth century and into the twenty-first. The United States found itself drawn into political and military crises in faraway lands such as Bosnia, Somalia, Afghanistan, Iraq, Ukraine, and Syria.

Throughout the 1990s, the United States waged a difficult struggle against many groups engaged in organized terrorism. The challenges facing intelligence agencies in tracking the movements of foreign terrorists became tragically evident in 2001. At 8:46 on the morning of September 11, 2001, the world watched in horror as a hijacked commercial airplane slammed into the North Tower of the World Trade Center in New York City. Seventeen minutes later, a second hijacked plane hit the South Tower. While the catastrophe was unfolding in New York City, a third hijacked airliner crashed into the Pentagon in Washington, D.C., while a fourth, headed for the White House, missed its mark when passengers assaulted the terrorists, sending the plane out of control and crashing to the ground near Shanksville, Pennsylvania, killing all on board.

Within hours of the hijackings, officials identified the nineteen hijackers as members of Al Qaeda (Arabic for "The Base"), a well-financed worldwide network of Islamic terrorists, led by a wealthy Saudi renegade, Osama bin

Laden. The new president, Republican George W. Bush, responded by declaring a "war on terror." With the passage of the so-called Patriot Act, Congress gave the president new authority to track down and imprison terrorists at home and abroad. The "war on terror" began with assaults first on terrorist bases in Afghanistan and then on Saddam Hussein's dictatorship in Iraq ("Operation Iraqi Freedom"). Yet terrorism proved to be an elusive and resilient foe, and the war in Iraq and the ensuing U.S. military occupation was much longer, more expensive, and less successful than Americans had expected.

The 9/11 terror attacks generated a wave of patriotism in the United States but divisive issues remained. A huge federal debt, rising annual budget deficits, and soaring health-care costs threatened to bankrupt an America that was becoming top-heavy with retirees as the baby boom generation born during and after the Second World War entered its sixties. The "graying of America" had profound social and political implications. It made the tone of political debate more conservative (because older people tend to be more conservative) and exerted increasing stress on health-care costs, nursing-home facilities, and the Social Security system.

The surprising victory of Barack Obama in the 2008 presidential election resulted from people embracing his theme of "hope and change." He pledged to end the wars in Iraq and Afghanistan, unite a divided nation, and provide jobs to the growing numbers of unemployed. As the first African American president, Obama symbolized the societal changes transforming national life in the twenty-first century. Yet no sooner was Obama inaugurated than he inherited the worst economic slowdown since the Great Depression of the 1930s. What came to be called the Great Recession has dominated the Obama presidency and, indeed, much of American life, bringing with it a prolonged sense of uncertainty and insecurity. For all of its economic power and military might, the United States in the twenty-first century has not eliminated the threat of terrorism or unlocked the mystery of sustaining prosperity in an era of globalization.

DUCK AND COVER The familiar duck-and-cover drill that is practiced in many schools across the country was first implemented in 1949, when the Soviet Union set off its first nuclear explosive and the cold war arms race. Pictured above are American schoolchildren practicing ducking and covering in February 1951.

The Cold War and the Fair Deal

1945–1952

No sooner did the Second World War end than a prolonged "cold war" began. The awkward wartime alliance between the capitalist United States and the communist Soviet Union collapsed during the spring and summer of 1945. With the elimination of their common enemy, Nazism, the two strongest nations to emerge from the war became intense rivals who could not bridge their ideological differences over basic issues such as human rights, individual liberties, democratic elections, and religious freedom. Mutual suspicion and a race to gain influence over the "non-aligned" nations of the world in Asia, Africa, the Middle East, and Central and South America further distanced the two former allies. The defeat of Japan and Germany had created power vacuums in Europe and Asia that sucked the Soviet Union and the United States into an unrelenting war of words fed by clashing strategic interests and political ideologies.

The postwar era also saw an eruption of anti-colonial liberation movements in Asia, Africa, and the Middle East that would soon strip Great Britain, France, the Netherlands, and the United States of their global empires. The Philippines, for example, gained its independence from America in 1946. The next year, Great Britain withdrew from Hindu-dominated India after carving out two new Islamic nations, Pakistan and

CORE OBJECTIVES INQUIZITIVE

1. Explain why and how the cold war between the United States and the Soviet Union developed after the Second World War.

2. Analyze the impact of American efforts to contain the Soviet Union and the expansion of communism during Truman's presidency.

3. Describe Truman's efforts to expand the New Deal, and evaluate the effectiveness of his own "Fair Deal" agenda.

4. Assess the major international developments during 1949–1950, including the outbreak of the Korean War, and explain how they altered U.S. foreign policy.

5. Examine the emergence of the Red Scare, after the Second World War, and explain its impact on American politics and society.

Bangladesh (originally called East Pakistan). The emergence of Communist China (the People's Republic) in 1949 further complicated global politics and the dynamics of the cold war.

The postwar world was thus an unstable one in which international tensions shaped domestic politics as well as foreign relations. The advent of atomic weapons was both a blessing and curse. Such weapons of mass destruction made the very idea of warfare unthinkably horrific, which in turn made national leaders more cautious to avoid letting disputes get out of hand. But even the mere possibility of nuclear holocaust cast a cloud of anxiety over the postwar era.

CORE OBJECTIVE

1. Explain why and how the cold war between the United States and the Soviet Union developed after the Second World War.

The Cold War

Less than three months after Harry S. Truman had begun his new role as vice president, Eleanor Roosevelt calmly told him, "Harry, the President is dead." When Truman asked what he could do to help her, the First Lady replied: "Is there anything we can do for *you*? For you are the one in trouble now."

Truman was a clumsy public speaker, frequently stumbling over big words and long sentences. He lacked Roosevelt's dash and charm, his brilliance and creativity. But the plain-speaking man from Missouri had virtues of his own. Truman resembled Andrew Jackson in his decisiveness, bluntness, folksy manner—and raw courage. A common man who became president at an uncommon time, Truman was a feisty leader who rose above his limitations to do extraordinary things. In his two presidential terms, Truman made many important decisions with long-term consequences. His challenges were enormous: he was expected to lead America out of the Second World War and into a postwar era complicated by the cold war against communism and the need to rebuild a devastated Europe and Asia. And Truman was supposed to do all of that while managing the complex conversion to peacetime at home. He ended up doing better than anyone expected. While visiting Truman at the end of his presidency in 1952, the British leader Winston Churchill confessed that he initially "held you in very low regard. I loathed your taking the place of Franklin Roosevelt. I misjudged you badly. Since that time, you, more than any other man, have saved Western civilization."

Origins of the Cold War

Historians have long debated the unanswerable question: Was the United States or the Soviet Union more responsible for the onset of the cold war? The conventional view argues that the Soviets, led by Josef Stalin, a ruthless Communist dictator ruling a traditionally insecure nation, set out to dominate the globe after 1945. The United States had no choice but to stand firm in defense of democratic capitalist values. By contrast, "revisionist" historians insist that President Truman was the primary culprit. Instead of

Harry S. Truman The successor to Franklin Roosevelt who led the United States out of World War II.

continuing Roosevelt's efforts to collaborate with Stalin and the Soviets, Truman's aggressive, confrontational foreign policy aggravated the tensions between the two countries. Yet such an interpretation fails to recognize that President Truman inherited a deteriorating relationship with the Soviets. East and West in the postwar world were captives of a nuclear nightmare of fear, suspicion, and posturing.

In retrospect, the onset of the cold war seems to have been inevitable. America's traditional commitment to capitalism, political self-determination, and religious freedom conflicted dramatically with the Soviet Union's preference for controlling its neighbors, enforcing ideological conformity, and prohibiting religions. Insecurity, as much as Communist ideology, drove much of Soviet behavior after the Second World War. Russia, after all, had been invaded by Germany twice in the first half of the twentieth century, and Soviet leaders wanted loyal nations on their borders for protection. As had often happened before, the peoples of Eastern Europe were caught in the middle.

> U.S.–Soviet fears and suspicions; conflicting visions for postwar Europe

Differences with the Soviets

The wartime military alliance against Nazism disintegrated after 1945 as the Soviet Union violated the promises it had made at the Yalta Conference and imposed its military control and Communist political system on the nations of Eastern Europe. On May 12, 1945, four days after victory in Europe, Winston Churchill asked Truman: "What is to happen about Europe? An **iron curtain** is drawn down upon [the Russian] front. We do not know what is going on behind [it]." Churchill and Truman wanted to lift the "iron curtain" created by Soviet military occupation in Eastern Europe and help those nations develop democratic governments. They still hoped that the Yalta agreements would be carried out, but events during the second half of 1945 dashed those expectations and made compromise and conciliation more difficult.

> Iron curtain

As early as the spring of 1945 and continuing for the next two years, the Soviet Union installed new "puppet" governments in Central and Eastern Europe (Bulgaria, Czechoslovakia, East Germany, Poland, Romania, and Yugoslavia). In each nation, one by one, the Soviets eliminated all political parties except the Communists, created secret police forces, took control of intellectual and cultural life, including the mass media (especially the radio networks), undermined the Roman Catholic Church, and organized a process of "ethnic cleansing" whereby millions of Germans, as well as Poles and Hungarians, were relocated from Eastern Europe, usually to West Germany or to prisons. Europeans who opposed the new Soviet regime were exiled, silenced, executed, or imprisoned. The postwar reign of terror unleashed by Stalin was intended to make people better Communists by locking up or killing the ones who refused to be Communists.

> Soviets establish Communist regimes in central and Eastern Europe

Stalin's promises at the Yalta Conference to allow open elections in the nations of Eastern Europe controlled by Soviet armies had turned out to be

iron curtain Term coined by Winston Churchill to describe the cold war divide between Western Europe and the Soviet Union's Eastern European satellite nations.

lies. U.S. secretary of state James F. Byrnes tried to use America's monopoly on atomic bombs as leverage to pressure the Soviets to abide by the Yalta accords. In April 1945, he had suggested to President Truman that nuclear weapons "might well put us in position to dictate our own terms [with the Soviets] at the end of the war." But the Soviets had paid little notice to such "atomic diplomacy," in part because their spies had kept them informed of what American scientists had been doing and in part because they were quickly developing their own atomic bombs.

Throughout the spring of 1945, the Soviets created new "friendly governments" in Eastern Europe, arguing that the United States had done the same in Italy and Japan after those nations had surrendered. The difference was the Soviets violated their pledges at the Yalta Conference by preventing noncommunists from participating in the political process in Poland and Bulgaria.

A few days before the opening of the San Francisco conference to organize the United Nations in April, Truman met with Soviet foreign minister Vyacheslav Molotov at the White House. The Soviets had just put in place a pro-Communist government in Poland in violation of Stalin's pledge at Yalta to allow free elections. Truman directed Molotov to tell Stalin that the United States expected the Soviet leader to live up to his agreements. "I have never been talked to like that in my life," Molotov angrily replied. "Carry out your agreements," Truman snapped, "and you won't get talked to like that."

Later, in July 1945, when President Truman first met Stalin at the Potsdam Conference, he wrote his mother that he had never seen "such pigheaded people as are the Russians." He described himself as "an innocent idealist" surrounded by wolves. He later acknowledged that the Soviets broke their promises to him "as soon as the unconscionable Russian Dictator [Stalin] returned to Moscow!" Truman added, with a note of embarrassment, "And I liked the little son of a bitch."

CORE **OBJECTIVE**

2. Analyze the impact of American efforts to contain the Soviet Union and the expansion of communism during Truman's presidency.

George Kennan's "Long Telegram" and containment policy

The Containment Policy

By the beginning of 1947, relations with the Soviet Union had grown ice cold. A year before, in February 1946, Stalin had declared that peace was impossible "under the present capitalist development of the world economy." His provocative statement led the State Department to ask for an analysis of Soviet communism from forty-two-year-old George F. Kennan, the best-informed expert on the Soviet Union working in the U.S. embassy in Moscow.

Kennan responded on February 22, 1946, with a famous 8,000-word "Long Telegram" in which he sketched the roots of Russian history, the pillars of Soviet policy, Stalin's "neurotic view of world affairs," and Russia's historic determination to protect its western border with Europe. In his extensive analysis, Kennan explained that the Soviet Union was founded on a rigid ideology (Marxism–Leninism) that saw a fundamental conflict between the communist and capitalist nations. Stalin and other Soviet leaders, he added, could not imagine "permanent peaceful coexistence" with the capitalist nations. The Soviet goal was to build military strength while promoting tensions between the capitalist democracies and subverting their stability by all possible means. The best way for the United States to deal with such an ideological foe, Kennan advised, was not military confrontation. Instead, he called for patient, persistent, and firm "strategic" efforts to "contain" Soviet expansionism over the long term, without resorting to war. Creating such "unalterable counterforce," he predicted, would eventually cause "either the breakup or the gradual mellowing of Soviet power" because communism, in Kennan's view, was an inherently unstable system that would eventually collapse if Americans were patient and helped postwar Europe rebuild its economies.

New secretary of state George C. Marshall, who had commanded all of America's military forces during the war, was so impressed by Kennan's analysis that he put him in charge of the State Department's Policy Planning office. No other American diplomat at the time forecast so accurately what would in fact happen to the Soviet Union some forty years later.

In its broadest dimensions, Kennan's call for the "firm and vigilant **containment** of Russian expansive tendencies" echoed the outlook of Truman and his advisers and would guide U.S. foreign policy for decades. Kennan's careful analysis, however, remained vague on several key issues: How exactly were the United States and its allies to "contain" the Soviet Union's expansionist tendencies? How should the United States respond to specific acts of Soviet aggression around the world?

Kennan was an analyst, not a policymaker. He left the task of "containing" communism to President Truman and his advisers, most of whom, unlike Kennan, viewed containment as a *military* doctrine rather than a *political* strategy. In 1946, civil war broke out in Greece between an undemocratic, authoritarian government backed by the British and a Communist-led insurgency supported by the Soviets that held the northern part of the nation.

> The Communist threat abroad: Civil war in Greece

On February 21, 1947, the British informed the U.S. government that they could no longer provide economic and military aid to Greece; they would withdraw in five weeks. Truman quickly conferred with congressional leaders, one of whom, Republican senator Arthur Vandenberg of Michigan, warned the president that he would need to "scare the hell out of the American people" about the urgent necessity to stop the menace of spreading communism in order to gain public support for his aid program. Truman was eager to do so, for he had grown tired of "babying the Russians."

containment U.S. cold war strategy to exert political, economic, and, if necessary, military pressure on global Soviet expansion as a means of combating the spread of communism.

The Truman Doctrine

On March 12, 1947, President Truman gave a national radio speech in which he asked Congress for $400 million to assist Greece and Turkey. More important, the president announced what came to be known as the **Truman Doctrine**. He declared that since the Communist challenge was worldwide, it had to be confronted everywhere around the globe. Like a row of dominoes, he predicted, the fall of Greece to communism would spread to the other nations of the Middle East, then to Western Europe. To prevent such a catastrophe, he said, the United States must "support free peoples who are resisting attempted subjugation by armed minorities or by outside pressures." In this single sentence, the president established the foundation of U.S. foreign policy for the next forty years. In Truman's view, shared by later presidents, the assumptions of the "domino theory" made an aggressive "containment" strategy against communism a necessity.

At the State Department, George Marshall thought the "flamboyant anticommunism" in Truman's speech was unnecessarily provocative, and George F. Kennan cringed at the president's "grandiose" commitment to "contain" communism *everywhere*. In his view, Truman's "militarized view of the cold war" was foolish. Efforts to "contain" communism needed to be selective rather than universal, political and economic rather than military in nature. All crises, Kennan insisted, were not equally significant. For all of its power, he noted, the United States could not intervene in every "hot spot" around the world. Kennan saw no need to provide military aid to Turkey, where no Communist threat existed. And he preferred that economic assistance, not weapons, be provided to Greece. In his view, the Soviet threat was primarily political, not military, in nature.

Truman and his advisers rejected Kennan's concerns. In 1947, Congress approved the president's request for economic and military assistance to Greece and neighboring Turkey. The Truman Doctrine marked the beginning of a contest that the former presidential adviser Bernard Baruch named in a 1947 speech to the legislature of South Carolina: "Let us not be deceived—today we are in the midst of a *cold war*." Only a few observers at the time questioned the implications of the Truman Doctrine. Walter Lippmann, the nation's leading political journalist, characterized Truman's new policy as a "strategic monstrosity" that would entangle the United States in endless international disputes and force it to partner with right-wing dictatorships—as turned out to be the case.

The Marshall Plan

In the spring of 1947, most of postwar Europe remained broke, shattered, and desperate. Factories had been bombed to rubble, railroads and bridges had been destroyed. People were starving for food and for jobs, and political unrest was growing. By 1947, socialist and communist parties were emerging in many European nations struggling to recover after the war,

The Truman Doctrine

Truman Doctrine (1947)
President Truman's program of "containing" communism in Eastern Europe and providing economic and military aid to any nations at risk of Communist takeover.

including Italy, France, and Belgium. The crisis in postwar Europe required bold action.

The Marshall Plan

While giving a graduation speech at Harvard University in May, Secretary of State George C. Marshall, building upon suggestions given to him by George Kennan and other members of the State Department, called for massive financial and technical assistance to rescue war-ravaged Europe, including the Soviet Union. What came to be known as the **Marshall Plan** was "directed not against country or doctrine, but against hunger, poverty, desperation, and chaos." It was intended to reconstruct the European economy, neutralize communist insurgencies, and build up secure foreign markets for American products. As Truman said, "the American [capitalist] system can survive only if it is part of a world system." But the Marshall Plan was about more than economics. It was also part of Truman's effort to contain the expansionist tendencies of the Soviet Union by building up a strong Western Europe. The Americans, said a British official, "want an integrated Europe looking like the United States of America."

In December 1947, Truman submitted Marshall's proposal to a special session of Congress. Initially, Republican critics dismissed it as "New Dealism" for Europe. However, two months later, on February 25, 1948, a Communist-led coup in Czechoslovakia, the last nation in eastern Europe with a democratic government, ensured congressional passage of the Marshall Plan, for it seemed to confirm the immediate Communist threat to Western Europe.

From 1948 until 1951, the Marshall Plan provided $13 billion to sixteen European nations to help revive their war-ravaged economies. The Soviet Union, however, refused to participate, calling it "dollar imperialism."

The Marshall Plan worked as hoped; prosperity returned to Europe. The British foreign minister called the plan "a lifeline to sinking men." By 1951, Western Europe's industrial production had soared to 40 percent above prewar levels, and its farm output was larger than ever. The Marshall Plan also snatched the initiative in the cold war away from the Soviet Union. England's *Economist* magazine called the Marshall Plan "an act without peer in history."

Divided Germany

The Marshall Plan drew the nations of Western Europe closer together, but it increased tensions with the Soviet Union, for Stalin saw the American effort to rebuild the European economy as a way to weaken Soviet influence in the region. The breakdown of the wartime alliance between the United States and the Soviet Union also left the problem of postwar Germany unsettled. In 1945 Berlin, the German capital, had been divided into four sectors or zones, each governed by one of the four principal allied nations, the United States, France, Great Britain, and the Soviet Union. The German economy languished, requiring the U.S. Army to provide food and basic

Marshall Plan (1948) Secretary of State George C. Marshall's post–World War II program providing massive U.S. financial and technical assistance to war-torn European countries.

Family reunion A girl gives her grandmother a kiss through the barbed wire fence that divides the Dutch-German frontier in 1947, while the British border guards turn a blind eye.

necessities to millions of civilians. Slowly, the Allied occupation zones evolved into functioning governments. In 1948, the British, French, and Americans united their three administrative zones into one and developed a common currency to be used in West Germany as well as in West Berlin. The West Germans also organized state governments and began drafting a federal constitution.

> Soviet blockade of Berlin and the Berlin Airlift

The political unification of West Germany infuriated Stalin, who was determined to keep Germany weak. And the status of divided Berlin, located deep inside the Soviet occupation zone (East Germany), had become a powder keg. In March 1948, Stalin forced the issue of Berlin's status by preventing the new West German currency from being delivered into the city. Then, on June 23, Stalin decided that there was nothing to be gained by continuing to pretend that the Soviet Union and the United States were anything but enemies. He ordered the Soviet army occupying eastern Germany to stop all road and rail traffic into West Berlin, hoping the blockade would force the United States and its allies to leave the divided city.

The Americans interpreted Stalin's aggressive blockade as a tipping point in the cold war. "When Berlin falls," predicted General Lucius D. Clay, the iron-willed U.S. army commander in Germany, "western Germany will be next. Communism will run rampant." The United States thus faced a dilemma fraught with dangers: risk a third world war by using force to break the Soviet blockade or begin a humiliating retreat from West Berlin, leaving the residents to be swallowed up by communism.

Truman, who prided himself on his decisiveness, made clear his stance when he declared: "We stay in Berlin—period." In response to the Soviet blockade, the United States announced an embargo against all goods exported from Soviet-controlled eastern Germany, and it began organizing a massive airlift to provide needed food and supplies to West Berliners.

By October 1948, the U.S. and British air forces were landing cargo planes every few minutes at the Berlin airport, flying in 7,000 tons of food, fuel, medicine, coal, and equipment each day to keep the 2.25 million Berliners alive. To support the Berlin airlift and prepare for a possible war, thousands of former military pilots were called back into service, Truman revived the military draft, and Congress provided emergency funds to increase military spending.

Through the iron curtain German children greet a United States cargo plane with waves and cheers as it flies over West Berlin to drop off much-needed food and supplies.

At times it seemed that the two superpowers were on the verge of warfare in Berlin. President Truman confided in his diary that he had a "terrible feeling" that "we are very close to war." For all the threats and harsh words, however, the **Berlin airlift** went on daily for eleven months without any shots being fired. Finally, on May 12, 1949, the Soviets lifted the blockade, in part because bad Russian harvests made them desperate for food grown in western Germany.

The Berlin airlift was the first major "victory" for the West in the cold war. The unprecedented efforts of the United States and Great Britain to supply West Berliners transformed most of them from defeated adversaries into devoted allies. In May 1949, as the Soviet blockade was ending, the Federal Republic of Germany (West Germany) was founded. Six months later, in October, the German Democratic Republic (East Germany) came into being.

Forming Alliances

The Soviet blockade of Berlin convinced the United States and its allies that they needed to act together to stop further communist expansion into Western Europe. On April 4, 1949, a month before the Berlin Blockade ended, the North Atlantic Treaty was signed by twelve nations: the United States, Great Britain, France, Belgium, the Netherlands, Luxembourg, Canada, Denmark, Iceland, Italy, Norway, and Portugal. Greece and Turkey joined the alliance in 1952, West Germany in 1955, and Spain in 1982.

The **North Atlantic Treaty Organization (NATO)**, the largest collective defense alliance in the world, declared that an attack against any one of the members would be considered an attack against all. The creation of

Berlin airlift (1948) Effort by the United States and Great Britain to fly massive amounts of food and supplies into West Berlin in response to the Soviet land blockade of the city.

North Atlantic Treaty Organization (NATO) Defensive political and military alliance formed in 1949 by the United States, Canada, and ten Western European nations to deter Soviet expansion in Europe.

THE OCCUPATION OF GERMANY AND AUSTRIA

- How did the Allies divide Germany and Austria at the Yalta Conference?
- What was the "iron curtain"?
- Why did the Allies airlift supplies to Berlin?

NATO marked the high point of efforts to "contain" the Soviets from expanding into Western Europe. In 1949, Congress provided $1 billion in military equipment to NATO members. By joining NATO, the United States—for the first time since its alliance with France during the Revolutionary War—committed itself to go to war on behalf of its allies. Isolationism was dead.

Reorganizing the Military

The onset of the cold war and the emergence of nuclear weapons led Truman to restructure the way the U.S. armed forces were managed. In 1947, Congress passed the **National Security Act**, which centralized the National Military Establishment. It created a Department of Defense to oversee the three separate military branches—the Army, Navy, and Air Force—and the National Security Council (NSC), a group of the government's top specialists in international relations who advised the president. The act made

National Security Act (1947)
Congressional legislation that created the Department of Defense, the National Security Council, and the Central Intelligence Agency.

permanent the Joint Chiefs of Staff, a wartime innovation bringing together the leaders of the branches of the armed forces, and it established the Central Intelligence Agency (CIA) to coordinate global intelligence-gathering activities. In 1952 Truman created the National Security Agency (NSA) within the Defense Department, charged with the mission to "encrypt" government communications to ensure their privacy and to intercept the communications of other nations. The NSA also provided surveillance of individuals targeted by other agencies as potential threats.

A New Jewish Nation: Israel

At the same time that the United States was helping to form new alliances, it was also helping to form a new nation. Palestine, the biblical Holy Land, had been a British protectorate since 1919. For hundreds of years, Jews throughout the world had dreamed of returning to their ancestral homeland of Israel and its ancient capital Zion, a part of Jerusalem. Many Zionists, Jews who wanted a separate Jewish nation, had migrated there. More arrived during and after the Nazi persecution of European Jews, and they received energetic support from American Jews and worldwide Jewish organizations. Hitler's gruesome effort to kill millions of Jews convinced many that their only hope for a secure future was to create their own nation.

Late in 1947, the United Nations voted to divide ("partition") Palestine into separate Jewish and Arab states. The Jews readily agreed, but the Arabs fiercely opposed the UN partition. Palestine was their ancestral home, too. Jerusalem was as holy to Muslims as it was to Jews and Christians. Arabs viewed the creation of a Jewish nation in Palestine as an act of war, and they attacked Israelis in early 1948. Hundreds of people were killed before the Haganah (Jewish militia) won control of most of Palestine. When the British administration of Palestine officially expired on May 14, 1948, David Ben-Gurion, the Jewish leader in Palestine, soon to be elected prime minister, proclaimed the independence of Israel. President Truman, who had been in close touch with American Jewish leaders, officially recognized the new Israeli state within minutes, as did the Soviet Union.

One million Jews, most of them European immigrants, now had their own nation. Early the next morning, however, the Arab League nations—Lebanon, Syria, Iraq, Jordan, and Egypt—invaded Israel, beginning a period of nearly constant warfare in the Holy Land. UN mediators gradually worked out a truce agreement, restoring an uneasy peace by May 11, 1949, when Israel joined the United Nations. Israel got to keep all its conquered territories, including the whole Palestine coast. The Palestinian Arabs lost everything. Most of them became stateless refugees who scattered into the neighboring nations of Lebanon, Jordan, and Egypt. But stored-up resentments and sporadic warfare between Israel and the Arab states have festered ever since, complicating U.S. foreign policy, which has tried to maintain friendship with both sides but has usually tilted toward Israel.

> Israel joins the United Nations

CORE **OBJECTIVE**

3. Describe Truman's efforts to expand the New Deal, and evaluate the effectiveness of his own "Fair Deal" agenda.

Expanding the New Deal

For the most part, Republicans and Democrats in Congress cooperated with President Truman on issues related to the cold war. They were not as unified in dealing with domestic policies. The cost-cutting Republicans in Congress hoped that they could end the New Deal as the war itself ended. As a brand-new president, Truman thought otherwise as he guided the nation's "complicated and difficult" transition from war to peace.

From War to Peace

Conversion to a peacetime economy

With the end of the wars in Europe and Asia, Truman in September 1945 called Congress into a special emergency session at which he presented a twenty-one-point program to guide the nation's "reconversion" effort from wartime back to peacetime. Massive government spending during the war had ended the Great Depression and brought about full employment, but Truman's postwar challenge was to ensure that the peacetime economy absorbed the millions of men and women who had served in the armed forces and were now seeking civilian jobs. During the second half of 1945 and throughout 1946, some 700,000 people in uniform, mostly men, returned to civilian life. By 1947, the total armed forces had shrunk from 12 million to 1.5 million.

Truman's program to ensure a smooth transition to a peacetime economy included proposals for unemployment insurance to cover more workers, a higher minimum wage, the construction of massive low-cost public housing projects, regional development projects modeled on the Tennessee Valley Authority to put military veterans to work, and much more. A powerful Republican congressman named Joseph W. Martin was stunned by the scope of Truman's proposals. "Not even President Roosevelt," he gasped, "ever asked for so much at one sitting."

Truman's primary goal was to "prevent prolonged unemployment" while avoiding the "bitter mistakes" made after the First World War that had produced a wild inflation in prices and a recession. To do so, he also wanted to retain, for a while, the wartime controls on wages, prices, and rents as well as the rationing of scarce food items. Most of all, Truman wanted to minimize unemployment as workers in defense plants were laid off and millions of military veterans went looking for civilian jobs.

Congress responded by approving the Employment Act of 1946, which authorized Truman and the federal government "to promote maximum employment, production, and purchasing power." But Republicans and conservative southern Democrats in Congress balked at most of Truman's efforts to revive or expand New Deal programs. One called Truman's proposals "creeping socialism." The Great Depression was over, critics stressed. Different times demanded different programs—or none at all.

Peacetime: Women return home, the GI Bill, and a "baby boom"

The end of the war caused short-term economic problems but not the postwar depression that many had feared. Many women who had been recruited to work in defense industries were shoved out as men took off uniforms and looked for jobs. At a shipyard in California, the foreman gathered all the women workers and told them to go welcome the troop ships as they pulled into port. "We were thrilled. We all waved," recalled one of the women. Then, the next day, all of the women working at the shipyard were let go to make room for male veterans.

Still, several shock absorbers cushioned the economic impact of demobilization: federal unemployment insurance and other Social Security benefits; the Servicemen's Readjustment Act of 1944, known as the GI Bill of Rights, under which the federal government spent $13 billion on military veterans for education, vocational training, medical treatment, unemployment insurance, and loans for building houses and starting new businesses.

With the war over, military veterans eagerly returned to schools, jobs, wives, and babies. Marriage rates soared at war's end. So, too, did population growth, which had dropped off sharply in the 1930s. Americans born during this postwar period (roughly 1946–1964) composed what came to be known as the "baby-boom generation," a disproportionately large group that would shape the nation's social and cultural life throughout the second half of the twentieth century and after.

Wages, Prices, and Labor Unrest

The most acute economic problem Truman faced was the postwar spike in prices for consumer goods. During the war, the government had frozen all wages and prices—and banned strikes by labor unions. When wartime economic controls on the economy were removed, prices for high-demand consumer items shot up, which led labor unions to demand pay increases for workers. When such raises were not given, a series of postwar strikes erupted across the nation in 1945–1946.

> Inflation spikes after the war

Major labor disputes developed in the coal and railroad industries. Like Theodore Roosevelt before him, Truman grew frustrated with the stubbornness of both management and labor leaders. He took federal control of the coal mines, whereupon the mine owners agreed to union demands. Truman also seized control of the railroads and won a five-day postponement of a strike. But when the union leaders refused to make further concessions, the president lashed out against their "obstinate arrogance" and threatened to draft striking railroad workers into the armed forces. A few weeks later, the unions backed down and returned to work, having won healthy improvements in wages and benefits. But by taking such a hard line, Truman had damaged his relationship with a key constituency within the Democratic party coalition: unionists.

> Widespread union strikes

Political Cooperation and Conflict

As Congressional elections approached in the fall of 1946, Republicans used a simple campaign slogan: "Had Enough? Vote Republican!" Public discontent ran high, especially among the 5 million workers who had gone out on strike during that single year. A union leader tagged Truman "the No. 1 Strikebreaker," while much of the public, upset at the unions, price increases, and food shortages, blamed the strikes on the White House. Labor unions emerged from the war with more power than ever before. Some 14.5 million workers, over a third of the workforce, were unionized. Members had tended to vote Democratic, but not in the 1946 elections, which gave Republicans majorities in both houses of Congress for the first time since 1928. "The New Deal is kaput," one newspaper editor crowed—prematurely, as it turned out.

The new Republican Congress reflected the discontent of middle-class Americans and business executives with striking unions. It curbed the power of unions by passing the **Taft-Hartley Labor Act** of 1947 (officially called the Labor-Management Relations Act), which prohibited "unfair labor practices" such as the "closed shop" (in which nonunion workers could not be hired by a unionized company). The Taft-Hartley Act also required union leaders to take "loyalty oaths" declaring that they were not members of the Communist party. The Taft-Hartley act also banned strikes by federal employees and imposed a "cooling-off" period of eighty days on any strike that the president deemed dangerous to the public welfare. Yet the most troubling element of the new bill was a provision that allowed state legislatures to pass "right-to-work" laws which ended the practice of forcing all wage workers at a company to join a union once a majority voted to unionize.

In a show of support for organized labor, whose members tended to vote Democratic, Truman vetoed the Taft-Hartley bill, which unions called "the slave-labor act." He denounced the "shocking" bill as "unworkable," "burdensome," and "disruptive." Working-class Democrats were delighted. Many blue-collar unionists who had gone over to the Republicans in 1946 returned to the Democrats as a result of Truman's stance. Congress, however, overturned the president's veto of the Taft-Hartley Act, and it became law. By 1954, fifteen states, mainly in the South and West, had used the Taft-Hartley Act to enact "right-to-work" laws forbidding union shops. Those states thereafter recruited industries to relocate because of their low wages and "nonunion" policies.

Civil Rights during the 1940s

Another of Truman's challenges in postwar labor relations was the bigotry faced by returning African American soldiers. When one black soldier arrived home in a uniform decorated with combat medals, he was welcomed by a white neighbor who said: "Don't you forget . . . that you're still a nigger."

But the Second World War had changed America's racial landscape. As a *New York Times* editorial explained in early 1946, "This is a particularly good time to campaign against the evils of bigotry, prejudice, and race

---

Taft-Hartley Labor Act (1947)

Taft-Hartley Labor Act (1947)
Congressional legislation that banned "unfair labor practices" by unions, required union leaders to sign anti-Communist "loyalty oaths," and prohibited federal employees from going on strike.

hatred because we have witnessed the defeat of enemies who tried to found a mastery of the world upon such cruel and fallacious policy." African American veterans had fought in large numbers to overthrow the Nazi regime of government-sponsored racism, and returning veterans were unwilling to put up with continuing racial abuse at home. The cold war confrontation with the Soviet Union also gave political leaders added incentive to improve race relations. In the ideological contest with communism for influence among the newly emerging nations of Africa, the Soviets often compared racism in the South to the Nazis' treatment of the Jews.

Black veterans who spoke out against racial bigotry often risked their lives. In 1946, two African American couples in rural Georgia were gunned down by a white mob. One of the murderers explained that George Dorsey, one of the victims, was "a good nigger" until he went into the army. "But when he came out, he thought he was as good as any white people."

In the fall of 1946, a delegation of civil rights activists urged President Truman to condemn the Ku Klux Klan and the lynching of African Americans. The delegation graphically described incidents of torture and intimidation against blacks in the South.

Such horrific racial incidents so shocked Truman that he appointed a Committee on Civil Rights to investigate violence against African Americans. On July 26, 1948, Truman took a bolder step when he banned racial discrimination in the federal government. Four days later, he issued an executive order ending racial segregation in the armed forces. The air force and navy quickly complied, but the army dragged its feet until the early 1950s. By 1960, however, the armed forces were the most racially integrated of all national organizations. Desegregating the military was, Truman claimed, "the greatest thing that ever happened to America."

Fight for desegregation Demonstrators led by activist A. Philip Randolph (left) picket the Democratic National Convention on July 12, 1948, calling for racial integration of the armed forces.

Jackie Robinson

Meanwhile, racial segregation was being dismantled in a much more public field of endeavor: professional baseball. In April 1947, as the baseball season opened, the Brooklyn Dodger roster included the first African American to play major league baseball: Jackie Robinson. He was selected in part because of his baseball abilities and in part because of his personality: he was a strong, quiet warrior of incomparable courage who was capable of not fighting back when provoked. And he was often provoked. During his first season with the Dodgers, teammates and opposing players viciously baited Robinson, pitchers threw at him, base runners spiked him, and spectators booed him, even as he led the team to win the National League championship. Hotels refused him rooms, and restaurants denied him service. Hate mail arrived by the bucketful. One sportswriter called the trailblazing

Jackie Robinson Robinson's unfaltering courage and skill diversified the baseball stands, drawing African American and Latino spectators to the games. Here, he greets his Dominican fans at Trujillo High School in Santo Domingo.

Robinson "the loneliest man I have ever seen in sports." On the other hand, black spectators were electrified by Robinson's courageous example; they turned out in droves to watch him play. As time passed, Robinson won over many fans and players with his courage, wit, and talent. Other teams soon began signing black players. Racial attitudes were changing—slowly.

Mexican Americans

In the Far West, Mexican Americans (often grouped together with other Spanish-speaking immigrants as *Hispanics* or *Latinos*) continued to experience ethnic prejudice after the war. Schools in Arizona, New Mexico, Texas, and California routinely segregated Mexican American children from whites. After the war, the 500,000 Latino veterans were especially frustrated that their efforts in the armed forces were not rewarded with equality at home. "We had paid our dues," said one war veteran, yet nothing had changed. Latinos were frequently denied access to the educational, medical, and housing benefits made available to white servicemen. In fact, some mortuaries even denied funeral services to Mexican Americans killed in combat. As a funeral director in Texas explained, "the Anglo people would not stand for it."

To fight such prejudicial treatment, Mexican American war veterans led by Dr. Hector Perez Garcia, a decorated U.S. Army major who had served as a combat surgeon, organized the American GI Forum in Texas in 1948. Soon there were branches throughout Texas and across the nation. Garcia, born in Mexico in 1914 and raised in Texas, stressed the importance of formal education to Mexican Americans. The new organization's motto read: "Education Is Our Freedom and Freedom Should Be Everybody's Business." At a time when Mexican Americans in Texas averaged no more than a third-grade education, Garcia and five of his siblings were exceptional, each having completed medical school and become physicians. Yet upon Major Garcia's return from the war, he encountered "discrimination everywhere. We had no opportunities. We had to pay [poll taxes] to vote. We had segregated schools. We were not allowed to go into public places."

Garcia and the GI Forum initially focused on veterans' issues but soon expanded the organization's scope to include fostering equal opportunities and equal treatment for all people. The GI Forum lobbied to end poll taxes, sued for the right of Latinos to serve on juries, and developed schools for jobless veterans. In 1984, President Ronald Reagan presented Garcia with the Presidential Medal of Freedom, the nation's highest civilian honor.

Shaping the Fair Deal

By early 1948, after three years in the White House, Truman had yet to shake the widespread impression that he was not up to the job. Most political analysts assumed that the president would lose his reelection effort in November. The Democratic party was about to split in two: southern conservatives resented Truman's outspoken support of civil rights, while the left wing of the party resented his firing of Secretary of Commerce Henry A. Wallace in September 1946 for openly criticizing the administration's anti-Soviet policies in a speech at Madison Square Garden in New York City. "Getting tough [with the Soviet Union]," Wallace argued, "never brought anything real and lasting—whether for schoolyard bullies or world powers. The tougher we get, the tougher the Russians will get." Wallace added that the United States had "no more business in the *political affairs* of Eastern Europe than Russia has in the *political affairs* of Latin America." The secretary of state and other leaders of the State Department were so outraged by Wallace's comments that Truman felt he had no choice but to get rid of him.

The gloomy predictions of a Truman defeat in 1948 did not faze the combative president, however. He mounted an intense reelection campaign. His first step was to shore up the major elements of the New Deal coalition of working-class voters: farmers, labor unionists, and African Americans. In his 1948 State of the Union message, Truman announced that the programs that he would later call his "**Fair Deal**" (to distinguish his new domestic program from Roosevelt's New Deal) would build upon the New Deal by offering something to nearly every group the Democrats hoped to attract as voters. The first goal, Truman said, was to ensure civil rights for all Americans. He added proposals to increase federal aid to education, expand

Truman's "Fair Deal"

Fair Deal (1949) President Truman's proposals to build upon the New Deal with national health insurance, the repeal of the Taft-Hartley Act, new civil rights legislation, and other initiatives; most were rejected by the Republican-controlled Congress.

unemployment and retirement benefits, create a comprehensive system of national health insurance, enable more rural people to connect to electricity, and increase the minimum wage.

The Election of 1948

The Republican-controlled Congress dismissed Truman's proposals, an action it would later regret. At the Republican Convention, New York governor Thomas E. Dewey won the presidential nomination on the third ballot. The platform endorsed most of the New Deal reforms and approved the administration's bipartisan foreign policy; Dewey promised to run things more efficiently, however. In July, a glum Democratic Convention gathered in Philadelphia. But delegates who expected to do little more than go through the motions were doubly surprised: first by the battle on the convention floor over civil rights and then by President Truman's acceptance speech. Liberal Democrats called on Congress to take more aggressive steps to end segregation in the South and commended Truman "for his courageous stand on the issue of civil rights." White segregationist delegates from Alabama and Mississippi walked out of the convention in protest.

On July 17, a group of rebellious southern Democrats met in Birmingham, Alabama. While waving Confederate flags and singing "Dixie," they nominated South Carolina's segregationist governor, Strom Thurmond, on a States' Rights Democratic ticket, quickly dubbed the "Dixiecrat party." The **Dixiecrats** denounced Truman's "infamous" civil rights initiatives and championed states' rights against any federal efforts to change the tradition of white supremacy in the South.

Birth of the Dixiecrats Alabama delegates stand to boo Truman's announcement of his civil rights platform before walking out of the 1948 Democratic National Convention.

A few days later, on July 23, the left wing of the Democratic party gathered in Philadelphia to form a new Progressive party and nominate for president Henry A. Wallace, Roosevelt's former secretary of agriculture and vice president—whom Truman had fired as secretary of commerce. One Democratic leader asked Truman to withdraw from the race to help the party's chances. He replied: "I was not brought up to run from a fight."

The splits in the Democratic ranks seemed to spell the final blow to Truman, but the feisty president pledged to "win this election and make the Republicans like it!" He then set out on a 31,000-mile "whistle-stop" train tour, making ten speeches a day scolding the "do-nothing" Eightieth Congress. Friendly audiences loved his fighting spirit and dogged courage, shouting, "Pour it on, Harry!" and "Give 'em hell, Harry." Truman responded: "I don't give 'em hell. I just tell the truth and they think it's hell."

Dixiecrats Breakaway faction of white southern Democrats who defected from the national Democratic party in 1948 to protest the party's increased support for black civil rights and to nominate their own segregationist candidates for elective office.

The polls predicted a sure win for Dewey and the Republicans, but on election day Truman won the biggest upset in history, taking 24.2 million votes (49.5 percent) to Dewey's 22 million (45.1 percent) and winning a thumping margin of 303 to 189 in the Electoral College. Thurmond and Wallace each received more than 1 million votes, but the revolt of right and left had worked to Truman's advantage. The Dixiecrat rebellion backfired by angering black voters, who turned out in droves to support Truman, while the Progressive party's radicalism made it hard for Republicans to tag Truman as soft on communism. Thurmond carried four southern states (South Carolina, Mississippi, Alabama, and Louisiana).

The Fair Deal Rejected

Truman viewed his surprising victory as a mandate for expanding the social welfare programs established by Franklin Roosevelt. His State of the Union message in early 1949 repeated the agenda he had set forth the year before. "Every segment of our population and every individual," he declared, "has a right to expect from our government a *fair deal*." Truman's Fair Deal proposals promised "greater economic opportunity for the mass of the people."

Most of Truman's Fair Deal proposals that gained Congressional approval were extensions or enlargements of earlier New Deal programs: a higher minimum hourly wage, expansion of Social Security coverage to 10 million workers not included in the original 1935 bill, and a sizable slum-clearance and public-housing program for 800,000 poor Americans. Despite enjoying Democratic majorities in Congress, however, Truman ran up against the same alliance of conservative southern Democrats and Republicans who had allied against Roosevelt in the late 1930s. The bipartisan conservative coalition nixed most of Truman's new Fair Deal programs. Congress rejected several civil rights bills, national health insurance, federal aid to education, and a new approach to subsidizing farmers. Congress also turned down Truman's requested repeal of the anti-union Taft-Hartley Act. Yet the Fair Deal was not a complete failure. It laid the foundation for programs that the next generation of reformers would promote in the sixties and after.

> Congress rejects Fair Deal legislation

THE ELECTION OF 1948

	Electoral Vote	Popular Vote
Harry S Truman (Democrat)	**303**	**24,200,000**
Thomas E. Dewey (Republican)	189	22,000,000
J. Strom Thurmond (States' Rights Democrat)	39	1,200,000

- Why did the political pundits predict a Dewey victory?
- Why was civil rights a divisive issue at the Democratic Convention?
- How did the candidacies of Thurmond and Wallace help Truman?

CORE **OBJECTIVE**

4. Assess the major international developments during 1949–1950, including the outbreak of the Korean War, and explain how they altered U.S. foreign policy.

Communist victory in China

Mao Zedong Chairman of the Chinese Communist Party and founder of the People's Republic of China.

H-bomb

NSC-68 (1950) Top-secret policy paper approved by President Truman that outlined a militaristic approach to combating the spread of global communism.

The Cold War Heats Up

As was true during Truman's first term, global concerns during his second term would again distract the president's attention from domestic issues. In his 1949 inaugural address, President Truman called for a vigilant anti-Communist foreign policy resting on three pillars: the United Nations, the Marshall Plan, and NATO. None of those pillars could help resolve the civil war in China, however.

"Losing" China

One of the thorniest postwar problems, the Chinese civil war, was fast coming to a head in 1949. The Chinese Nationalists, led by Chiang Kai-shek, had been fighting Mao Zedong and the Communists since the 1920s. After the Second World War, the Nationalists were put on the defensive as the Communists won over most of the peasants. By the end of 1949, the Nationalist government was forced to flee to the island of Formosa, which it renamed Taiwan. Truman's critics—mostly Republicans—now asked bitterly, "Who lost China to communism?" What they did not explain in attacking Truman was how he could have prevented a Communist victory without a massive U.S. military intervention, which would have been risky, unpopular, and expensive. After 1949, the United States continued to recognize the Nationalist government on Taiwan as the official government of China, delaying formal relations with "Red China" (the People's Republic of China) for thirty years.

The Soviets Develop Atomic Bombs

As the Communists were gaining control of China, the Soviets were heightening American concerns by developing atomic bombs of their own. News that the Soviets had detonated a nuclear weapon in 1949 frightened people around the world and led Truman to speed up the construction of a hydrogen "superbomb," a weapon far more powerful than the atomic bombs dropped on Japan. That the Soviets now possessed atomic weapons greatly heightened every cold war confrontation between East and West. "There is only one thing worse than one nation having an atomic bomb," said Nobel Prize–winning physicist Harold C. Urey. "That's two nations having it." Now, the fear of nuclear annihilation joined the fear of communism in deepening the Red Scare.

NSC-68

In January 1950 President Truman, concerned about the Soviets possessing atomic weapons, asked the National Security Council to assess America's changing role in the cold war world. Four months later, the Council submitted to the president a top-secret report called **NSC-68**. The document, officially approved by Truman in September, laid out in alarmist tones the major assumptions of U.S. foreign policy for the next twenty years: "The

Shelter for sale On display in a 1950s showroom is a basement bomb fallout shelter, complete with a television, library, and exercise bike.

issues that face us are momentous, involving the fulfillment or destruction not only of this Republic but of civilization itself." NSC-68 endorsed George Kennan's "containment" strategy, but where he had focused on political and economic counterpressure against the Soviets, its tone was global and militaristic, calling for "a policy of calculated and gradual coercion" against Soviet expansionism—everywhere.

Hawkish Paul Nitze, Kennan's successor as director of policy planning for the State Department, was the NSC-68's primary author. He claimed that the Soviets, driven by their "fanatical faith" in their destiny to impose their will "on the rest of the world," were becoming increasingly "reckless" in their international behavior and would invade Western Europe by 1954, by which time they would have enough nuclear weapons to destroy the United States.

By signing NSC-68, Truman endorsed its assumptions about a perpetual struggle with Soviet communism in which there could be only victory or defeat. "It meant," he said, "doubling or tripling the budget, increasing taxes heavily, and imposing various kinds of economic controls. It meant a great change in our normal peacetime way of doing things." NSC-68 became the guidebook for future American policy, especially as the United States became involved in an unexpected war in Korea that ignited into open combat the smoldering animosity between East and West, communism and capitalism.

War in Korea

By mid-1950, tensions between the United States and the Soviet Union in Europe had temporarily eased into a stalemate as a result of the "balance of terror" created by both sides having atomic weapons. In Asia, however, the situation remained turbulent. The Communists had gained control of mainland China and were threatening to destroy the Chinese Nationalists, who had taken refuge on the island of Taiwan. Japan, meanwhile, was

Fight and flight American soldiers brush shoulders with Korean refugees as they march into the Nakdong River region in the south.

experiencing a dramatic recovery from the devastation of defeat and the destruction caused by U.S. bombing raids during the Second World War. Douglas MacArthur showed deft leadership as the consul in charge of U.S.-occupied Japan. He oversaw the disarming of the Japanese military, the drafting of a democratic constitution, and the nation's economic recovery, all of which were turning Japan into America's friend.

To the east of Japan, however, tensions between North Korea and South Korea threatened to erupt into civil war. The Japanese had occupied the Korean peninsula since 1910, and after their defeat and withdrawal in 1945 the victorious Allies had faced the difficult task of creating a new independent Korean nation. Complicating that effort was the presence of Soviet troops in northern Korea. They had accepted the surrender of Japanese forces above the 38th parallel, which divides the Korean peninsula, while U.S. forces had overseen the Japanese surrender south of that line. The Soviets quickly organized a Communist government, the Democratic People's Republic of Korea (North Korea) in the industrial north, just as they were doing in eastern Europe. The Americans countered by helping to establish a democratic government in the agricultural and more populous south, the Republic of Korea (South Korea). By the end of 1948, separate regimes had appeared in the two sectors, Soviet and American forces had withdrawn, and some 2 million North Koreans had fled to South Korea.

On June 25, 1950, with the encouragement of the Soviet Union and Communist China, the Soviet-equipped North Korean People's Army invaded the Republic of South Korea and drove the South Korean army down the peninsula in a headlong retreat. Within three days of fighting, Seoul, the South Korean capital, was captured and only 22,000 of the 100,000 South Korean soldiers were still capable of combat. When asked how he would respond to the invasion, President Truman declared: "By God, I'm going to let them have it!" He assumed, correctly, that the North Korean attack had been encouraged by the Soviets. "There's no telling what they'll do if we don't put up a fight right now," Truman predicted. He then made a critical decision: without consulting the Joint Chiefs of Staff or Congress, he decided to wage war through the backing of the United Nations rather than seeking a declaration of war from Congress.

An emergency meeting of the UN Security Council in New York City in late June 1950 quickly censured the North Korean "breach of peace." By sheer coincidence, the Soviet delegate, who held a veto power, was at the time boycotting the council because it would not seat Communist China in place of Nationalist China. On June 27, the Security Council took advantage of his absence to call on UN members to "furnish such assistance to the Republic of Korea as may be necessary to repel the armed attack and to restore international peace and security in the area." Truman ordered U.S. air, naval, and ground forces into action. He then appointed 70-year-old Douglas MacArthur as the supreme commander of the UN forces.

The Korean conflict was the first military action authorized by the United Nations, only five years old, and some twenty other nations participated. The United States provided the largest contingent of non-Korean forces by far, some 330,000 troops. The American military defense of South Korea set a worrisome precedent: war by order of a president rather than by a vote of Congress, which the U.S. Constitution requires. Truman dodged the constitutional issue by officially calling the conflict in Korea a "police action" rather than a war. Critics labeled it "Mr. Truman's War."

> U.S. "police action" in Korea

Turning the Tables

For the first three months, the fighting in Korea went badly for the Republic of Korea (ROK) and the UN forces. By September 1950, the decimated South Korean troops were barely hanging on to the southeast corner of the Korean peninsula. Then, in a brilliant maneuver on September 15, General MacArthur staged a surprise amphibious landing behind the North Korean lines at Inchon, the port city for Seoul. UN troops drove a wedge through the North Korean army; only a quarter of the North Koreans, some 25,000 soldiers, managed to flee across the border. Days later, South Korean troops recaptured Seoul.

At that point, MacArthur became overconfident and persuaded Truman to allow the U.S. troops to push north into North Korea and seek to reunify Korea. Containment of communism was no longer enough; MacArthur now hatched a grandiose plan to rid North Korea of the "red menace," even if this meant expanding the war into China in order to prevent the Chinese from resupplying their North Korean allies.

The Chinese Intervene

By October 1950, UN forces were about to capture the North Korean capital, Pyongyang. President Truman, concerned that MacArthur's move into North Korea would provoke Communist China to enter the war, flew seven

> Chinese intervention in Korea

thousand miles to Wake Island for a conference with MacArthur on October 15 (the haughty general had refused to travel to the United States). At his meeting with Truman, MacArthur dismissed Chinese threats to intervene, even though they had massed troops on the Korean border. That same day, the Communist government in Beijing announced that China "cannot stand idly by" as their North Korean allies were humiliated. On October 20, UN forces entered the North Korean capital, and on October 26, advance units had reached Ch'osan, on the Yalu River, North Korea's border with China.

MacArthur predicted total victory by Christmas. On the night of November 25, however, some 300,000 Chinese "volunteers" vowing to "liberate Korea" and drive "warmonger MacArthur into the sea" counterattacked, sending the U.S. forces in desperate retreat just at the onset of winter. By January 15, the Communist Chinese and North Koreans had recaptured Seoul, the South Korean capital. "We ran like antelopes," said one American soldier. "We lost everything we had."

MacArthur Pushes the Limit

The Chinese intervention caught MacArthur wholly unprepared. It had become "an entirely new war," he said. The U.S. commander of UN forces asked for thirty-four atomic bombs and proposed air raids on China. MacArthur's plans to use nuclear weapons and attack China horrified the military leadership in Washington, D.C. It would be, explained General Omar Bradley, chairman of the Joint Chiefs of Staff, "the wrong war at the wrong place at the wrong time with the wrong enemy." Truman agreed, saying that MacArthur's plan would lead the United States into the "gigantic booby trap" of war with China.

In late 1950, the UN forces rallied. By January 1951, they finally secured their lines below Seoul and then launched a counterattack. When Truman began negotiations with the North Koreans to restore the prewar boundary, General MacArthur undermined the president by issuing an ultimatum for China to make peace or suffer an attack on their own country. On April 5, on the floor of Congress, the Republican minority leader read a letter from General MacArthur that criticized the president and said that "there is no substitute for victory." Such a reckless act of open insubordination left Truman only two choices: he could either accept MacArthur's aggressive demands or fire him.

Sacking a Hero

MacArthur controversy

On April 11, 1951, with civilian control of the military at stake, Truman removed the brilliant but bullheaded MacArthur (Truman called him "Mr. Prima Donna") and replaced him with jut-jawed General Matthew B. Ridgway. "I believe that we must try to limit the war to Korea," Truman explained. "A number of events have made it evident that General MacArthur did not agree with that policy. I have therefore considered it essential to

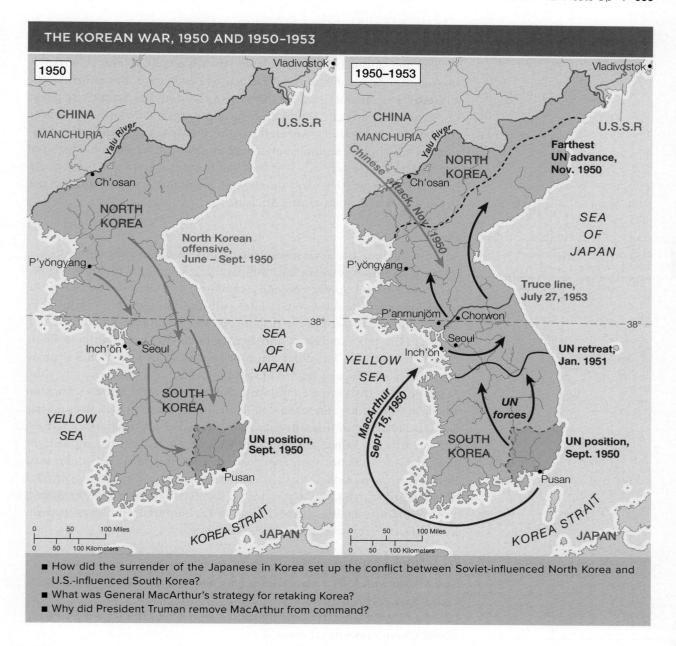

THE KOREAN WAR, 1950 AND 1950–1953

1950

CHINA

MANCHURIA

Yalu River

U.S.S.R

Vladivostok

Ch'osan

NORTH KOREA

North Korean offensive, June – Sept. 1950

P'yŏngyang

38°

Inch'ŏn • Seoul

SEA OF JAPAN

SOUTH KOREA

YELLOW SEA

UN position, Sept. 1950

Pusan

KOREA STRAIT   JAPAN

0   50   100 Miles
0   50   100 Kilometers

1950–1953

CHINA

MANCHURIA

Yalu River

Chinese attack, Nov. 1950

U.S.S.R

Vladivostok

NORTH KOREA

Ch'osan

Farthest UN advance, Nov. 1950

SEA OF JAPAN

P'yŏngyang

P'anmunjŏm • Chorwon

Truce line, July 27, 1953

Seoul

Inch'ŏn

38°

YELLOW SEA

MacArthur Sept. 15, 1950

UN retreat, Jan. 1951

UN forces

SOUTH KOREA

UN position, Sept. 1950

Pusan

KOREA STRAIT   JAPAN

0   50   100 Miles
0   50   100 Kilometers

■ How did the surrender of the Japanese in Korea set up the conflict between Soviet-influenced North Korea and U.S.-influenced South Korea?

■ What was General MacArthur's strategy for retaking Korea?

■ Why did President Truman remove MacArthur from command?

relieve General MacArthur so that there would be no doubt or confusion as to the real purpose and aim of our policy."

Truman's sacking of MacArthur, the Army's only five-star general, divided a shocked nation into two emotional camps. *Time* magazine reported that "seldom had a more unpopular man fired a more popular one." Senator Joseph McCarthy called the president a "son of a bitch" for sacking MacArthur. In his diary, Truman noted the ferocious backlash against him: "Quite an explosion. . . . Letters of abuse by the dozens." Sixty-six percent of Americans initially opposed Truman's relieving MacArthur of command.

The man Truman fired was a larger-than-life military hero, idolized by most Americans, and greeted by adoring crowds upon his return to the United States. Republicans in Congress protested MacArthur's removal, but Truman stood firm, claiming the decision was an obvious one: "I fired him because he wouldn't respect the authority of the President. I didn't fire him because he was a dumb son of a bitch, although he was, but that's not against the law for generals. If it was, half to three-quarters of them would be in jail." The fact that all of the top military leaders supported Truman's decision deflated much of the criticism.

A Cease-Fire

38th parallel divided North and South Korea

On June 24, 1951, the Soviet representative at the United Nations proposed a cease-fire in Korea along the 38th parallel, the original dividing line between North and South. Secretary of State Dean Acheson accepted the cease-fire (armistice) a few days later with the consent of the United Nations. China and North Korea responded favorably. Truce talks started on July 10, 1951, at Panmunjom, only to drag on for two years while sporadic fighting continued. The chief snags were exchanges of prisoners (many captured North Korean and Chinese soldiers did not want to go home) and South Korea's insistence on unification of the two rival Koreas. Syngman Rhee, the South Korean leader, explained that "an armistice without national unification [is] a death sentence without protest." By the time a truce agreement was reached, on July 27, 1953, Truman had retired and Dwight D. Eisenhower was president. No peace treaty was ever signed, and Korea, like Germany, remained divided. The inconclusive war cost the United States more than 33,000 battle deaths and 103,000 wounded or missing. South Korean casualties, all told, were about 2 million, and North Korean and Chinese casualties an estimated 3 million.

The Impact of the Korean War

The Korean War influenced U.S. foreign policy in significant ways. To most Americans, the North Korean attack on South Korea provided concrete proof that there was an international Communist conspiracy guided by the Soviet Union to control the world.

U.S. military buildup worldwide

Truman's assumption that Stalin and the Soviets were behind the invasion of South Korea prompted three far-reaching decisions. First, Truman mistakenly viewed the Korean conflict as actually a diversion for a Soviet invasion of Western Europe, so he ordered a major expansion of U.S. military forces in Europe—and around the world. Second, the president increased assistance to French troops fighting a Communist independence movement in the French colony of Indochina (which included Vietnam), starting America's deepening military involvement in Southeast Asia. Third, the Korean War demonstrated how important a role Japan would play in America's military presence in Asia.

Another Red Scare

The Korean War excited another Red Scare at home, as in 1919, as people grew fearful that Soviet-directed Communists were infiltrating American society. Since 1938 the **House Committee on Un-American Activities (HUAC)** had kept up a drumbeat of accusations about supposed Communist agents in the federal government. On March 21, 1947, just nine days after he announced the Truman Doctrine, the president signed an executive order (also known as the Loyalty Order) requiring federal government workers to go through a background investigation to ensure they were not Communists or even associated with Communists (as well as other "subversive" groups).

The president knew that the "loyalty program" violated the civil liberties of government workers, but he felt he had no choice. He was responding to pressure from FBI director J. Edgar Hoover and Attorney General Tom Clark, both of whom were convinced that there were numerous spies working inside the federal government. Truman was also eager to blunt criticism by Republicans that he was not doing enough to ensure that Soviet sympathizers were working in government.

The president himself thought that all of the fear about Communist subversives was misplaced. "People are very much wrought up about the communist 'bugaboo,'" he wrote to Pennsylvania governor George Earle, "but I am of the opinion that the country is perfectly safe so far as Communism is concerned." By early 1951, the federal Civil Service Commission had cleared over 3 million people, while only 378 had been dismissed for doubtful loyalty. Others, however, had resigned for fear they would be dismissed. In 1953, President Dwight D. Eisenhower revoked the Loyalty Order.

The Hollywood Ten

In May 1947, charges that Hollywood was a "hotbed of communism" led the House Committee on Un-American Activities to launch a full-blown investigation of the motion-picture industry. The HUAC subpoenaed dozens of prominent actors, producers, and directors to testify at its hearings, held in Los Angeles in October. Ten witnesses refused to answer questions about their political activities, arguing that such questions violated their First Amendment rights. When asked if he were a member of the Communist party, screenwriter Ring Lardner Jr. replied: "I could answer, but I would hate myself in the morning." Another member of the so-called Hollywood Ten, screenwriter Dalton Trumbo, shouted as he left the hearings, "This is the beginning of an American concentration camp." All ten were cited for contempt, given prison terms, and blacklisted (banned) from the film industry.

The witch hunt launched by the HUAC inspired playwright Arthur Miller, who himself was blacklisted, to write *The Crucible* (1953), a dramatic

CORE OBJECTIVE
5. Examine the emergence of the Red Scare after the Second World War and explain its impact on American politics and society.

House Committee on Un-American Activities (HUAC) Committee of the U.S. House of Representatives formed in 1938; originally tasked with investigating Nazi subversion during the Second World War and later focused on rooting out Communists in the government and the motion-picture industry.

The verge of verdict A few courageous movie stars attended the HUAC hearings to support their friends and colleagues who were being accused of being Communists. *Left to right*: Danny Kaye, June Havoc, Humphrey Bogart, and Lauren Bacall (seated).

account of the notorious witch trials in Salem, Massachusetts, at the end of the seventeenth century, intended to alert readers about the dangers of the anti-Communist hysteria.

Alger Hiss

The spy case most damaging to the Truman administration involved Alger Hiss, president of the Carnegie Endowment for International Peace, who had earlier served in several government agencies, including the State Department. Whittaker Chambers, a former Soviet spy and later an editor of *Time* magazine, told the HUAC in 1948 that Hiss had given him secret documents ten years earlier, when Chambers was spying for the Soviets and Hiss was working in the State Department. Hiss sued for libel, and Chambers produced microfilms of the State Department documents that he said Hiss had passed to him. Hiss denied the accusation, whereupon he was indicted and, after one mistrial, convicted in 1950. The charge was perjury, but he was convicted of lying about espionage, for which he could not be tried because the statute of limitations on that crime had expired.

More cases of Communist infiltration surfaced. In 1949, eleven top leaders of the Communist party of the United States were convicted under the Smith Act of 1940, which outlawed any conspiracy to advocate the overthrow of the government. The Supreme Court upheld the law under the doctrine of a "clear and present danger," which overrode the right to free speech.

Atomic Spying

Julius and Ethel Rosenberg

In 1950, the F.B.I. unearthed the existence of a British-American spy network that had secretly passed information about the development of the atomic bomb to the Soviet Union. These disclosures led to the widely publicized arrest of Klaus Fuchs, a German-born English nuclear physicist who had worked in the United States during the war, helping to develop the atomic bomb.

As it turned out, a New York couple, former Communists Julius and Ethel Rosenberg, were part of the same Soviet spy ring. Their claims of innocence were undercut by the confession of Ethel's brother, who admitted he was a spy along with his sister and brother-in-law.

The convictions of Fuchs and the Rosenbergs fueled Republican charges that Truman's administration was not doing enough to hunt down Communist agents who were stealing American military secrets. The Rosenberg case, called the crime of the century by J. Edgar Hoover, also served to heighten American fears that a vast Soviet network of spies and sympathizers was operating in the United States—and now had "given" Stalin the secret of building atomic weapons. Irving Kaufman, the federal judge who sentenced the Rosenbergs to death in the electric chair, explained that "plain, deliberate murder is dwarfed . . . by comparison with the crime you have committed." They were the first Americans ever executed for spying.

McCarthy's Witch Hunt

Evidence of Soviet spying in the United States encouraged politicians to exploit the public's fears of the Communist menace at home. Early in 1950, a little-known Republican senator, Joseph R. McCarthy of Wisconsin, suddenly surfaced as the most ruthless manipulator of the nation's anti-Communist anxieties.

An intelligent, determined, but unethical man eager to attract media attention, McCarthy took up the cause of anti-Communism with a fiery speech to a women's Republican club in Wheeling, West Virginia, on February 9, 1950, in which he charged that the State Department was infested with Communists—and he claimed to have their names, although he never provided them.

"Joe" McCarthy's reckless charges created a media sensation and, over the next four years, led the senator to make more reckless accusations, initially against Democrats, whom he attacked as "dupes" or "fellow travelers" of the "Commies," then against just about everyone, including the U.S. Army.

Truman privately denounced McCarthy as "just a ballyhoo artist who has to cover up his shortcomings with wild charges," but McCarthy was not so easily dismissed. He enjoyed the backing of fellow Republicans eager to hurt Democrats in the 1950 Congressional elections by claiming they were "soft on Communism." Senator Lyndon B. Johnson of Texas said McCarthy was "the sorriest senator" in Washington. "But he's riding high now, he's got people scared to death. . . ."

By the summer of 1951, what had come to be called **McCarthyism** had gotten out of control. McCarthy's excesses were revealed for all to see when he outrageously accused George Marshall, the former secretary of state and war hero, of making "common cause with Stalin." Concerns about the truth or fair play did not faze him. He refused to answer critics or provide evidence; his focus was on creating a reign of terror by groundless accusations.

Despite his outlandish claims and boorish bullying, McCarthy's witch hunt for Communists never uncovered a single Communist agent in the government. But his smear campaign, which tarnished many lives and

Joseph R. McCarthy The senator with a mission to sweep the Communists from the government and beyond, 1954.

McCarthyism Anti-Communist hysteria led by Senator Joseph McCarthy's "witch hunts" attacking the loyalty of politicians, federal employees, and public figures, despite a lack of evidence.

The Cold War and the Rise of the National Security State

The federal government had assumed a commitment to improving the lives of millions of Americans through the New Deal during the Great Depression, and continued to do so after World War II. The demands of the war effort further expanded the role of the federal government in the nation's life. Immediately after World War II, President Truman worked to demilitarize the nation but soon reversed course as he became alarmed at the Soviet threat around the world, developing an aggressive policy to "contain" the Soviets in both Europe and Asia. The emergence of the cold war—an intense, bitter, and all-consuming rivalry between the Soviet Union and the United States—fundamentally altered the federal government and laid the foundation for a National Security State. After you review the historical developments, consider the questions further below.

FEBRUARY 1946

Kennan's "Long Telegram"

After witnessing Soviet-U.S. tensions in Germany, Korea, and East Europe, state official George Kennan declares in his famous telegram that Marxist-Leninist philosophy presumed a fundamental conflict between the communist and capitalist worlds. Kennan urged persistent and firm containment of Soviet expansion.

MARCH 1947

Truman Doctrine

Truman announces the U.S. commitment to "support free peoples who are resisting subjugation . . . by outside pressures." Congress approved U.S. economic and military assistance to non-communist forces in the Greek civil war and the Turkish government.

MARCH 1947

Loyalty Order

Truman orders all federal government employees to undergo background checks in response to growing fears that communists had infiltrated the U.S. government.

MAY 1947

Marshall Plan

Secretary of State George Marshall announces the program that would ultimately provide $13 billion in financial assistance to European nations struggling to restore their economies and to fend off communism.

JULY 1947

National Security Act

Congress authorizes the creation of a Department of Defense, a National Security Council, and a Central Intelligence Agency.

OCTOBER 1948–MAY 1949

Berlin airlift

The United States organizes an airlift of supplies to the Western-controlled sections of Berlin in response to the Soviet blockade.

APRIL 1949	1949–1950	JANUARY–APRIL 1950
North Atlantic Treaty Organization (NATO)	**Hydrogen bomb (H-bomb)**	**NSC-68 Report**
The United States and 12 other North American and Western European nations form a defensive political and military alliance.	The Soviet Union detonates a nuclear weapon. In response, Truman speeds up the development of an H-bomb, far more powerful than the atomic bomb.	The National Security Council report calls for "a policy of calculated and gradual coercion against Soviet expansionism—everywhere." This promotion of struggle against communism, according to Truman, would require "doubling or tripling the budget" and "a great change in our normal peacetime way of doing things."

EARLY 1950s	JUNE 1950	SEPTEMBER 1950	1950–1952
McCarthy's Second Red Scare	**"Police Action" in Korea**	**McCarran International Security Act**	**United States expands involvement to global scale**
Senator Joseph McCarthy takes up the anti-communist cause with a series of charges accusing many U.S. government officials of being Soviet spies or covering up for alleged spies within the U.S. government.	The United States receives the United Nations Security Council's blessing to lead a "police action" to combat North Korean aggression.	The act made it unlawful "to conspire . . . to perform any act which would substantially contribute to . . . the establishment of a totalitarian dictatorship."	In response to the Korean War, Truman orders the expansion of U.S. military presence in Western Europe and increases U.S. assistance of French troops fighting a communist insurgency in Vietnam, a French colony in Southeast Asia.

QUESTIONS FOR ANALYSIS

1. What new policies and institutions did Truman and Congress initiate to contain Soviet expansion?

2. Why did Truman build a stronger military presence in Europe and Asia?

3. How did cold war tensions affect U.S. military spending?

4. In what ways did the cold war affect civil liberties in the United States?

5. How did the emergence of the cold war shape the size and role of the federal government?

reputations, went largely unchallenged until the end of the Korean War. During the Red Scare, thousands of left-wing Americans were "blacklisted" from employment because of past political associations, real or rumored. Movies with titles like "I Married a Communist" fed the hysteria, and stories in popular magazines warned of "a Red under every bed."

McCarran Internal Security Act

Fears of Soviet spies in the United States working with American sympathizers led Congress in 1950 to pass the McCarran Internal Security Act over President Truman's veto, making it unlawful "to combine, conspire, or agree with any other person to perform any act which would substantially contribute to . . . the establishment of a totalitarian dictatorship." Communist organizations had to register with the attorney general. Would-be immigrants who had belonged to totalitarian parties in their home countries were barred from admission to the United States. And during any future national emergencies, American Communists were to be herded into concentration camps. The McCarran Internal Security Act, Truman said in his veto message, would "put the government into the business of thought control."

Assessing the Red Scare and the Cold War

Violations of civil liberties and overstretched foreign policy

Playing upon the fears of the American public did not make for good policy in 1919, nor did it work well in the early fifties. Both Red Scares ended up violating the civil liberties of innocent people. If international events had set the stage for the cold war and the Red Scare, the actions of political leaders and thinkers set events in motion. Hindsight is always clearer than foresight, and President Truman may have erred in 1947 by creating a government loyalty program that aggravated the anti-Communist hysteria. Truman's own attorney general, Tom Clark, contended that there were "so many Communists in America" that they "were everywhere—in factories, offices, butcher shops, on street corners, in private businesses—and each carries with him the germs of death for society." Truman also overstretched American resources when he pledged to "contain" communism everywhere. Containment itself proved hard to contain amid the ideological posturing of Soviet and American leaders. Its chief theorist, George F. Kennan, later confessed that he was partly to blame because he had failed at the outset to spell out the limits of the containment policy and to stress that the United States needed to prioritize its responses to Soviet adventurism.

Creation of the "military-industrial complex"

The years after the Second World War were unlike any other postwar period in American history. Having taken on global burdens, the nation became committed to a permanently large national military establishment, along with the attendant creation of shadowy new government agencies such as the National Security Council (NSC), the National Security Agency (NSA), and the Central Intelligence Agency (CIA). The federal government—and the presidency—continued to grow larger, more powerful, and more secretive during the cold war, fueled by the actions of both major political parties as well as by the intense lobbying efforts of what Dwight D. Eisenhower would later call the *military-industrial complex*.

Fears of communism at home grew out of legitimate concerns about a Soviet spy network in the United States but mushroomed into politically motivated paranoia. As had been true during the First Red Scare, after the First World War, long-standing prejudices against Jews fed the anti-Communist hysteria; indeed, many Communist sympathizers were Jews from eastern Europe. The Red Scare also provided a powerful tool for Republicans eager to attack the Truman administration and the Democratic party, claiming that the Democrats were "soft on Communism." One of the worst effects of the Red Scare was to encourage widespread conformity of thought and behavior in the United States. By 1950, it had become dangerous to criticize anything associated with the American way of life.

On March 30, 1952, Harry Truman announced he would not seek another presidential term, in part because it was unlikely he could win. Less than 25 percent of voters surveyed said that he was doing a good job, the lowest presidential approval rating in history. Although Americans applauded Truman's integrity and courage, they were disheartened that members of his administration were inept and even corrupt. The unrelenting war against communism, at home and abroad, led people to question Truman's strategy. Negotiations to end the war in Korea had bogged down for many months, the "red-baiting" of McCarthyism was expanding across the nation, and conservative southern Democrats, members of Truman's own party, had defeated most of the president's Fair Deal proposals in Congress. The war in Korea had brought higher taxes and higher prices for American consumers, many of whom blamed Truman for their frustrations. Only years later would people (and historians) fully appreciate how effective Truman had been in dealing with so many complex problems.

To the end of his presidency, Truman, a plainspoken man who made decisions based on his "gut-feeling" about what was "right," viewed himself as an ordinary person who had been given opportunities to do extraordinary things. "I have tried my best to give the nation everything I have in me," Truman told reporters at one of his last press conferences. "There are a great many people . . . who could have done the job better than I did it. But I had the job and had to do it." And it was not a simple job, by any means. At the end of one difficult day in the White House, Truman growled while sipping a bourbon and water: "They [his critics] talk about the power of the President, how I can just push a button to get things done. Why, I spend most of my time kissing somebody's . . . [butt]."

By the time a frustrated Truman left the White House in early 1953, the cold war against Communism had become an accepted part of the American way of life. But fears of Soviet and Chinese communism on the march around the world were counterbalanced by the joys of unexpected prosperity. Toward the end of Truman's presidency, during the early fifties, the economy began to grow at what would become the fastest rate in history, transforming social and cultural life, and becoming the marvel of the world. The booming economy brought with it the "nifty" fifties.

Reviewing the
CORE OBJECTIVES | INQUIZITIVE

■ **The Cold War** The cold war was an ideological contest between the Western democracies (especially the United States) and the Communist countries (especially the Soviet Union). At the end of the Second World War, the Soviet Union established "friendly" governments in the Eastern European countries it occupied behind an *iron curtain*, violating promises that Stalin had made at the Yalta Conference. The United States and the Soviet Union, former allies, came to differ openly on issues of human rights, individual liberties, self-determination, and religious freedoms. As mutual hostility emerged, the two nations and their allies competed to shape the postwar order around the globe.

■ **Containment** President Truman responded to the Soviet occupation of Eastern Europe with *containment*, a policy to halt the spread of communism by opposing it wherever it emerged around the world. With the *Truman Doctrine (1947)*, he proposed giving economic and military aid to countries facing Communist insurgencies, such as Greece and Turkey. The *National Security Act* reorganized the U.S. armed forces and created the Central Intelligence Agency. The *Marshall Plan* offered postwar redevelopment aid to all European nations. In 1948, the United States withstood a Soviet blockade of supplies to West Berlin with the *Berlin airlift and,* in 1949, became a founding member of the *North Atlantic Treaty Organization (NATO)*.

■ **Truman's Fair Deal** The *Fair Deal* proposed to preserve and expand the New Deal in the face of intense Republican opposition in Congress. While he could not stop the Republican-backed, anti-union *Taft-Hartley Labor Act*. Truman successfully expanded Social Security, desegregated the military, and banned racial discrimination in the hiring of federal employees. In his second term, he proposed new laws such as a civil rights bill, national health insurance, federal aid to education, and new farm subsidies. However, conservative majorities of Republicans and southern Democrats (*Dixiecrats*) were able to defeat these initiatives in domestic policy.

■ **The Korean War** While containment policies halted Soviet expansion in Europe, they proved less effective in East Asia as Communists won a long civil war in China in 1949 and ignited a war in Korea. In response, Truman authorized *NSC-68*, which called for a dramatic increase in military spending and nuclear arms. When North Korean troops invaded South Korea in June 1950, Truman considered this an attempt by the Soviet Union to distract the U.S. from Western Europe, so he quickly decided to go to war under the auspices of the United Nations, thus bypassing Congress's authority to declare war. After three years of war, a truce established a demilitarized zone in Korea on either side of the 38th parallel. Truman also began assisting French efforts to subdue a Communist insurgency in its Southeast Asian colony of Indochina.

■ **The Red Scare** The onset of the cold war inflamed another Red Scare. After the Second World War, investigations by the *House Committee on Un-American Activities (HUAC)* sought to find "subversives" within the federal government. Starting in 1950, Senator Joseph R. McCarthy exploited American fears of Soviet infiltration of the U.S. government. *McCarthyism* flourished in the short term because the threat of a world dominated by Communist governments seemed all too real to many Americans.

KEY TERMS

CHRONOLOGY

1944	Congress passes the GI Bill of Rights
April 1945	Fifty Allied nations sign the United Nations Charter
	Soviet Union begins installing "puppet" Communist regimes in Eastern Europe
February 1946	State Department official George Kennan issues his "Long Telegram"
March 1947	President Truman announces the Truman Doctrine
May 1947	Secretary of State George Marshall proposes the Marshall Plan
June 1947	Congress passes the Taft-Hartley Labor Act
July 1947	National Security Council (NSC) is established
May 1948	Israel is proclaimed an independent nation
July 1948	Truman issues an executive order ending segregation in the U.S. armed forces
August 1948	Alger Hiss accused of having been a Soviet spy before the HUAC
October 1948	Berlin airlift
April 1949	NATO is created
October 1949	China "falls" to communism
	Soviet Union tests an atomic bomb
February 1950	Second Red Scare begins
June 1950–July 1953	The Korean War

InQUIZITIVE

Go to InQuizitive to see what you've learned—and learn what you've missed—with personalized feedback along the way.

THE ART OF CONSUMERISM The United States experienced tremendous prosperity after the Second World War, giving many Americans the unprecedented opportunity of carefree consumption in the 1950s—and personal indebtedness. The Pop Art movement tapped into this era's affluence and anxiety. Its artists made use of the newly mass-produced and advertised American landscape to comment on consumer culture. One such artist was Tom Wesselman, a detail of whose 1962 collage *Untitled* (*Still-Life No. 22*) is shown above.

Affluence and Anxiety in the Atomic Age

1950–1959

I n the summer of 1959, two newlyweds spent their honeymoon in an underground bomb shelter in the backyard of their home. *Life* magazine showed the couple in their twenty-ton, steel and concrete bunker stocked with enough food and water to survive an atomic attack. The image of the newlyweds seeking sheltered security in a new age of nuclear terror symbolized how America in the 1950s was awash in contrasting emotions. The deepening cold war with the Soviet Union cast a frightening shadow over the nation's traditional sunny optimism. In 1959, two out of three Americans listed the possibility of atomic war as the nation's most urgent threat. Despite the fears of nuclear destruction, however, Americans emerged from the Second World War proud of their military strength, international stature, and industrial might. It was a time rich with possibilities, and people were eager to seize their destinies. As the editors of *Fortune* magazine proclaimed in 1946, "This is a dream era . . . The Great American Boom is on."

So it was, at least for the growing number of white middle-class Americans. During the late 1940s and throughout the 1950s, the United States enjoyed unprecedented economic growth that created a dazzling array of new consumer products. Amid the insecurities of the cold war, most Americans were remarkably content with the improving quality of their lives. Divorce

CORE OBJECTIVES INQUIZITIVE

1. Explain President Eisenhower's political philosophy and priorities.

2. Identify the factors that contributed to postwar prosperity, and analyze to what extent all Americans benefited from it.

3. Examine the criticism of postwar American society and culture, and describe the various forms of dissent and anxiety.

4. Evaluate the goals, strategies, and impact of the civil rights movement that emerged in the 1950s.

5. Assess President Eisenhower's priorities in conducting the nation's foreign policy and his influence on global affairs.

and homicide rates fell and people lived longer, on average, thanks in part to miraculous medical breakthroughs such as new antibiotics and the vaccine invented by Dr. Jonas Salk that ended the menace of polio. The "happy days" image of America in the fifties as an innocent, prosperous nation awash in good times and enlivened by teenage energies has a kernel of truth, but life in the fifties was much more complicated than that, hugely varied and even contradictory and hypocritical at times, with many Americans worried about an uncontrollable future.

CORE **OBJECTIVE**

1. Explain President Eisenhower's political philosophy and priorities.

Moderate Republicanism—
The Eisenhower Years

Dwight David Eisenhower dominated the political landscape during the 1950s. The military hero of World War II was a model of moderation, stability, and optimism. Eisenhower's commitment to what he called **moderate Republicanism** promised to restore the authority of state and local governments, and restrain the federal government from engaging in any more political and social "engineering." In the process, he sought to renew traditional virtues and inspire Americans with a vision of a brighter future despite the continuing cold war.

"Time for a Change"

By 1952, the Truman administration had piled up a heavy burden of political liabilities. Its bold stand in Korea had resulted in a bloody stalemate in the war, renewed wage and price controls at home, and the embarrassing exposure of corrupt lobbyists who rigged military contracts. The disclosure of corruption within several federal agencies led Truman to fire nearly 250 employees of the Internal Revenue Service, but doubts lingered that the president would ever finish the housecleaning.

It was, Republicans claimed, "time for a change," and public sentiment turned their way as the 1952 election approached. Beginning in the late 1940s, both Republican and Democratic leaders, including President Truman, recruited General Eisenhower to be their presidential candidate. Born in Texas but raised in Kansas, the affable Eisenhower, known as "Ike," had displayed remarkable organizational and diplomatic abilities in coordinating the Allied invasion of Nazi-controlled Europe. In 1952, after serving as president of Columbia University, he had moved to Paris to become the supreme commander of NATO forces in Europe. His decision to run for president as a Republican was wildly popular. Bumper stickers announced simply: "I Like Ike."

Eisenhower won the nomination on the first ballot. Republican leaders then tried to reassure conservatives by balancing the ticket with a youthful, fiercely ambitious running mate: Richard M. Nixon, a thirty-nine-year-old California senator whose dogged insistence on pursuing the Alger Hiss

Dwight D. Eisenhower His many supporters wore "I Like Ike" hats, pins, and even nylon stockings, speaking to consumer culture's impact on politics.

moderate Republicanism Promise to curb federal government and restore state and local government authority, spearheaded by President Eisenhower.

spying case in Congressional hearings had brought him national prominence. Nixon built his early political career as an anti-Communist bent on exposing left-wing "subversives" holding government posts in the Truman administration. The Republican party platform declared that the Democratic emphasis on "containing" communism was a "negative, futile, and misguided" form of appeasement. The Eisenhower administration, if elected, would roll back the Communist threat by bringing "genuine independence" to the "captive peoples" of Eastern Europe.

Rolling back communism

The Election of 1952

The 1952 presidential campaign matched two contrasting personalities. Eisenhower, though a political amateur, had been in the public eye for a decade. Illinois governor Adlai Stevenson, the Democratic candidate, was hardly known outside his home state. Eisenhower pledged to clean up "the mess in Washington." To this he added a promise to secure "an early and honorable" end to the conflict in Korea.

An end to the Korean War

Stevenson was outmatched. Although a brilliant man whose witty speeches charmed liberals, he came across to most voters as too aloof and intellectual. The Republicans labeled him an "egghead" (meant to suggest a balding professor with more intellect than common sense). Even Truman questioned Stevenson's decisiveness, grumbling that the Democratic candidate "was too busy making up his mind whether he had to go to the bathroom or not."

On election night, Eisenhower triumphed in a landslide, gathering nearly 34 million votes to Stevenson's 27 million. The electoral vote was much more lopsided: 442 to 89. The hapless Stevenson even failed to win his home state of Illinois.

More important, the election marked a turning point in Republican fortunes in the South. For the first time in more than a century, the Democratic "Solid South" was moving toward a two-party system. By winning four Democratic southern states, Eisenhower had made it respectable, even fashionable, to vote for a Republican presidential candidate in the South.

Voters liked Eisenhower's folksy charm and battle-tested poise better than they liked his political party. In the 1952 election, Democrats retained most of the governorships,

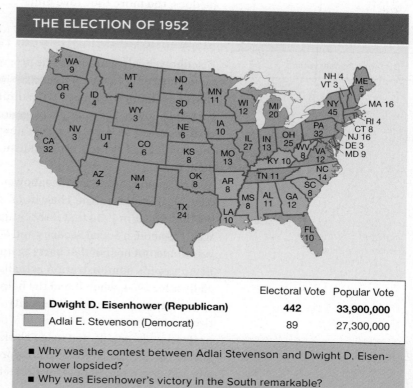

THE ELECTION OF 1952

	Electoral Vote	Popular Vote
Dwight D. Eisenhower (Republican)	442	33,900,000
Adlai E. Stevenson (Democrat)	89	27,300,000

- Why was the contest between Adlai Stevenson and Dwight D. Eisenhower lopsided?
- Why was Eisenhower's victory in the South remarkable?

lost control of the House by only eight seats, and broke even in the Senate, where only the vote of the vice president gave Republicans the slimmest possible majority. The congressional elections two years later would further weaken the Republican grip on Congress, and Eisenhower would have to work with a Democratic Congress throughout his second term.

A "Middle Way" Presidency

Consensus and compromise

Eisenhower was the first professional soldier elected president since Ulysses S. Grant in 1868, and the last president born in the nineteenth century. He promised to pursue a "middle way between untrammelled freedom of the individual and the demands of the welfare of the whole nation." He saw no need to dismantle all of the Democrats' New Deal and Fair Deal programs. Instead, he wanted to end the "excesses" that had resulted from twenty years of Democratic control of the White House. He pledged to reduce the federal bureaucracy and make it more efficient while restoring the balance between the executive and legislative branches of government. Eisenhower's cautious personality and genial public face fit perfectly with the prevailing mood of most voters. He was a unifier, not a divider; he inspired trust and sought consensus and compromise; he avoided confrontation. Eisenhower also championed the nineteenth-century view that Congress should make policy and the president should carry it out. A journalist noted in 1959 that "the public loves Ike. The less he does, the more they love him."

"Dynamic Conservatism" at Home

"Dynamic conservatism"

Eisenhower called his domestic program "dynamic conservatism," by which he meant being "conservative when it comes to money and liberal when it comes to human beings." His administration set out to reduce defense spending, lower tax rates, weaken government regulation of business, and restore power to the states. The new president warned repeatedly against the dangers of "creeping socialism," "huge bureaucracies," and budget deficits.

In the end, however, Eisenhower kept intact the basic structure of the New Deal, much to the chagrin of conservative Republicans. He told his brother Edgar in 1954 that if the "stupid" right wing of the Republican party tried "to abolish Social Security and eliminate labor laws and farm programs, you would not hear of that party again in our political history." In some ways, Eisenhower's administration actually expanded New Deal programs, especially after 1954, when it had the help of Democratic majorities in Congress. Amendments to the Social Security Act in 1954 and 1956 extended the retirement program to millions of workers formerly excluded: white-collar professionals, maids and sales clerks, farm workers, and members of the armed forces. Eisenhower also approved increases in the minimum wage and additional public housing projects for low-income occupants.

Under Eisenhower, the federal government launched two massive construction projects: the St. Lawrence Seaway and the Interstate Highway System, both of which resembled the huge public works projects constructed under the New Deal during the 1930s. The St. Lawrence Seaway project (in partnership with Canada) opened the Great Lakes to oceangoing ships.

The **Federal-Aid Highway Act** (1956) created a national network of interstate highways to serve the needs of commerce and defense, as well as the convenience of citizens. The interstate highway system, funded by gasoline taxes, took twenty-five years to construct and was the largest federal project in history. It stretched for 47,000 miles and required 55,512 bridges. The vast project created jobs, stimulated the economy, and spurred the tourism, motor hotel ("motel"), and long-haul trucking industries. Interstate highways transformed the way people traveled and where they lived, and it even created a new form of middle-class leisure, the family vacation by car.

The second great age of the automobile had arrived after the war. In 1948, only 60 percent of families owned a car; by 1955, 90 percent owned a car and many households had two. "The American," the Mississippi writer William Faulkner observed in 1948, "really loves nothing but his automobile." Americans had always cherished personal freedom and mobility, rugged individualism and masculine

> The Federal-Aid Highway Act (1956)

Drive in, cash in Founded by brothers Maurice and Richard McDonald in southern California, this hugely successful fast food chain started as a carhop drive-in and did not have customer seating until the 1960s.

force, and automobiles embodied all these qualities and more. Thanks to the new highway system, explained President Eisenhower, cars would provide "greater convenience, greater happiness, and greater standards of living." Cars in the fifties were much more than a form of transportation; they provided social status and personal freedom. They were the means of personal democracy, acting as a social leveling force, granting more and more people a wider range of personal choices—where to travel, where to work and live, where to seek personal pleasure and social recreation. The "car culture" soon transformed social behavior, prompting the creation of "convenience stores," drive-in movies, and fast-food restaurants.

The End of McCarthyism

Republicans thought their presidential victory in 1952 would curb the often unscrupulous efforts of Wisconsin senator Joseph R. McCarthy to ferret out Communist spies in the federal government. Instead, the

Federal-Aid Highway Act (1956) Largest federal project in U.S. history that created a national network of interstate highways.

publicity-seeking senator grew even more outlandish in his behavior. McCarthy finally overreached when he made the absurd charge that the U.S. Army itself was "soft" on communism. On December 2, 1954, the Senate voted 67 to 22 to "condemn" the crusading senator for his reckless tactics. Soon thereafter, his political influence collapsed. His savage crusade against Communists in government had catapulted him into the limelight and captured the nation's attention, but in the process he had trampled upon civil liberties. McCarthy's political demise helped the Democrats capture control of both houses of Congress in the 1954 elections. In 1957, at the age of forty-eight, he died of a liver inflammation brought on by years of alcohol abuse.

A People of Plenty

CORE **OBJECTIVE**
2. Identify the factors that contributed to post-war prosperity, and analyze to what extent all Americans benefited from it.

What most distinguished the United States from the rest of the world after the Second World War was what one journalist called America's "screwball materialism." After a brief postwar recession in 1945–1946, the economy soared to record heights as businesses shifted from wartime production to the construction of new housing and the manufacture of an array of mass-produced consumer goods. In 1953, Eisenhower's first year in office, the United States, with 6 percent of the world's population, was producing two-thirds of the world's manufactured goods. In 1957, *U.S. News and World Report* magazine declared that "never had so many people, anywhere, been so well off." By 1960, over 75 percent of American families owned a car and 87 percent had a television set.

Postwar Prosperity

Global arms race

Several factors created the nation's tremendous prosperity. First, huge federal expenditures during the Second World War and the Korean War catapulted the economy out of the Great Depression. High government spending at all levels—federal, state, and local—continued in the 1950s, thanks to the global arms race unleashed by the cold war and the relentless construction of new highways, bridges, airports, and ports. The still-large military budget after 1945 represented the single most important stimulant to the economy.

Robust manufacturing and dramatic new technologies

The superior productivity of American industries also contributed to dramatic economic growth. No sooner was the war over than the federal government turned over to civilian owners many of its war-related plants, giving them a boost as they retooled for peacetime manufacturing. Military-related research also helped stimulate new glamour industries: chemicals (including plastics), electronics, and aviation. By 1957, the aircraft industry was the nation's largest employer. The extraordinary increase in productivity benefited from new technologies, including the first generation of computers. Factories and industries became increasingly "automated." At the same time, the oil boom in Texas, Wyoming, and Oklahoma continued to provide the United States with low-cost fuel to heat buildings and drive cars and trucks.

Another reason for the record-breaking growth of the U.S. economy was the lack of foreign competition. Most of the other major industrial nations—Great Britain, France, Germany, Japan, and the Soviet Union—had been physically devastated during the Second World War, leaving American manufacturers with a virtual monopoly on international trade that lasted well into the 1950s.

U.S. dominance in international trade

The Consumer Culture

The major catalyst in promoting economic expansion after 1945, however, was the unleashing of pent-up consumer demand from the Depression and the war years, when civilians had been forced to conserve and do without. What differentiated the postwar era from earlier periods of prosperity was the large number of people who shared in the rising standard of living—not just corporate executives and salaried managers but also hourly wage workers. Between 1947 and 1960, the average income for the working class increased by as much as it had in the previous *fifty* years. More and more blue-collar Americans, especially automotive and steel workers, moved into the middle class. George Meany, the leading union spokesman during the 1950s, declared in 1955 that his members "never had it so good." That same year, three out of every four American adults categorized themselves as "middle class."

Increased income across classes

Americans had money to spend during the fifties, and they did so with gusto, becoming famous around the world for their carefree consumption. In 1955, a marketing consultant stressed that the nation's "enormously productive economy demands that we make *consumption* a way of life, that we convert the buying and use of goods into [religious] rituals, that we seek our spiritual satisfaction, our ego satisfaction, in consumption." The consumer culture, he explained, demanded that things be "consumed, burned up, worn out, replaced, and discarded at an ever-increasing rate."

Americans engaged in a prolonged buying spree aided by financing innovations that made it easier to buy things. The first credit card appeared in 1949; by the end of the decade, "buying with plastic" had become the new norm for tens of millions of people. Personal indebtedness doubled during the fifties, in part because people were so confident about their economic future. Frugality became unpatriotic. As television personality Hugh Downs remembered, "those were exciting days . . . of hope and optimism . . . when the sky was the limit."

Increased consumer spending: Credit cards, home ownership, and television

A Buying Spree

What most Americans wanted to buy after the Second World War was a new house. In 1945, only 40 percent of Americans owned homes; by 1960, the number had increased to 60 percent. And those new homes featured the latest electrical appliances—refrigerators, dishwashers, washing machines, vacuum cleaners, electric mixers, carving knives, even shoe polishers.

Your DINE/OUT carton . . . carries _your_ reputation!

Family, modified The fantasy of the American family changed with the onslaught of new, affordable products. In this 1959 advertisement for TV dinners, the family eats out of disposable containers in front of the television.

The use of electricity tripled during the decade, in part because of the popularity of television. Watching television quickly displaced listening to the radio or going to the movies as the most popular way to spend free time. Between 1948 and 1952, the number of homes with TV sets jumped from 172,000 to 15.3 million. In 1954, grocery stores began selling frozen "TV dinners" to be heated and consumed while watching popular shows such as *Father Knows Best*, *I Love Lucy*, and *The Adventures of Ozzie and Harriet*, all of which idealized the child-centered world of suburban white families. In 1955, *U.S. News and World Report* magazine noted that the "biggest of the new forces in American life today is television. There has been nothing like it in the postwar decade, or in many decades before that—perhaps not since the invention of the printing press. Even radio, by contrast, was a placid experience."

The popularity of television provided a powerful new medium for advertisers to promote a powerful new phase of the consumer culture that reshaped the contours of postwar life: the nature of work, where people lived and traveled, how they interacted, and what they valued. It also affected class structure, race relations, and gender roles. Jack Metzgar, the son of a Pennsylvania steelworker, remembered that in 1946 "we did not have a car, a television set, or a refrigerator. By 1952, we had all those things."

The GI Bill of Rights

GI Bill of Rights (1944) Provided unemployment, education, and financial benefits for World War II veterans to ease their transition back to the civilian world.

In 1944, as Americans grew confident that the war would soon be won, fears that the sudden influx of war veterans into the civilian workforce would disrupt the economy and produce widespread unemployment led Congress to pass the Servicemen's Readjustment Act of 1944, nicknamed the **GI Bill of Rights** ("GI" meaning "government issue," a phrase stamped on military uniforms and equipment that became slang for "serviceman").

Between 1944 and 1956, the GI Bill boosted upward social mobility in postwar America. It included a package of crucial benefits to veterans: unemployment pay for one year, preference to those applying for federal government jobs, loans for home construction or starting a business, access to government hospitals, and generous subsidies for education. Some 5 million veterans bought new homes with the assistance of GI Bill mortgage loans, which required no down payment. Almost 8 million veterans took advantage of $14.5 billion in GI Bill benefits to attend college or enroll in job-training programs. Before the Second World War, approximately 160,000 Americans had graduated from college each year. By 1950, the figure had risen to 500,000. In 1949, veterans accounted for 40 percent of college enrollments, and the United States could boast the world's best-educated workforce, largely because of the GI Bill. To cite but one example: Joe Shi, a decorated Army veteran from Macon, Georgia, was able to attend graduate school in business at the University of Pennsylvania because of the financial aid provided by the GI Bill.

Overall, the GI Bill was one of the most successful federal programs in history. Many African American veterans, however, could not take advantage of many of its benefits. Most colleges and universities remained racially segregated and refused to admit blacks. Those that enrolled blacks often discriminated against them. African Americans attending white colleges or universities were barred from playing on athletic teams, attending social events, and joining fraternities or sororities. Black veterans were also often prevented from buying homes in white neighborhoods. Although women veterans were eligible for GI Bill benefits, there were so few of them that the program had the unintended effect of widening the income gap between men and women.

The Suburban Frontier

The second half of the twentieth century witnessed a mass migration to a new frontier—the suburbs. The acute housing shortage after the war (98 percent of cities reported shortages of houses and apartments in 1945) sparked the suburban revolution. Of the 13 million homes built between 1948 and 1958, 11 million were in suburbs. Rural America continued to lose population during the 1950s (and after), as many among the exploding middle-class white population moved to what were called the Sunbelt states—California, Arizona, Florida, Texas, and the southeast region, where rapid population growth generated an economic boom. As air conditioning became a common household fixture in the Sunbelt states, it greatly enhanced the appeal of living in warmer climates.

Suburbia met an acute need—affordable housing—and fulfilled a common dream—personal freedom and familial security within commuting distance of cities. In the half century after the Second World War, the suburban good life for middle-class white families included a big home with a big yard on a big lot accessed by a big car—or two. The widespread

GI Bill

Sunbelt migration, suburban development, and the car culture

suburbia Communities formed from mass migration of middle-class whites from urban centers.

Levittown Identical mass-produced houses in Levittown, New York, and other suburbs across the country provided veterans and their families with affordable homes.

Suburbia, Levittowns, and racial segregation

ownership of cars enabled the suburban revolution during the fifties. Nine of ten suburban families in the 1950s owned a car, compared to six of ten urban households. During the 1950s, suburbs grew six times as fast as cities, and by 1970 more people lived in suburbs than in cities.

A brassy New York real estate developer, William Levitt, led the suburban revolution. Between 1947 and 1951, on 6,000 acres of Long Island farmland near New York City, he built 17,447 small, look-alike homes (essentially identical in design) to house more than 82,000 people. The planned community, called Levittown, included schools, swimming pools, shopping centers, and playing fields. Levitt encouraged and even enforced uniformity and conformity in Levittown. The houses all sold for the same price—$6,900, with no down payments for veterans—and featured the same floor plan and accessories. Each had a picture window, a living room, a bathroom, a kitchen, and two bedrooms. Trees were planted every twenty-eight feet in the former potato fields, and homeowners were required to cut their grass once a week.

Levitt soon built three more Levittowns in Pennsylvania, New Jersey, and Puerto Rico. They and other planned suburban communities benefited greatly from government assistance. Federal and state tax codes favored homeowners over renters, and local governments paid for the infrastructure required by new Levittown-style suburban subdivisions: roads, water and sewer lines, fire and police protection. By insuring loans for up to 95 percent of the value of a house, the Federal Housing Administration (FHA) made it easy for builders to construct low-cost homes and for people to buy them.

Levitt and other suburban developers created lily-white communities. Initially, the contracts for houses in Levittown specifically excluded "members of other than the Caucasian race," since Levitt believed that whites would not want to buy a house in Levittown if blacks were living there. As he explained, "We can solve a housing problem or we can try to solve a racial problem. But we can't combine the two." A year later, however, the U.S. Supreme Court ruled in *Shelley v. Kraemer* (1948) that such racial restrictions were illegal. The court ruling, however, did not end segregated housing practices; it simply made them more discreet. In 1953, when Levittown's population reached 70,000, it was the largest community in the nation without a single African American resident. Although Jewish himself, Levitt also discouraged Jews from living in his communities. "As a Jew," he explained, "I have no room in my heart for racial prejudice. But the plain fact is that most whites prefer not to live in mixed communities. This attitude may be wrong morally, and someday it may change. I hope it will."

Other developers across the country soon mimicked Levitt's efforts, building suburban communities with rustic names such as Lakewood, Streamwood, Elmwood, Cedar Hill, Park Forest, and Deer Park. In 1955, *House and Garden* magazine could declare that suburbia had become the "national way of life." By 1960, however, only 5 percent of African Americans lived in suburbs.

Minorities on the Move

African Americans were not part of the initial wave of suburban development, but they began moving in large numbers after 1945. The mass migration of rural southern blacks to the urban North, Midwest, and West after the Second World War was much larger than the similar trend after the First World War, and its social consequences were even more dramatic. After 1945, more than 5 million southern blacks formed a new "great migration" out of the South in search of better jobs, higher wages, decent housing, and greater civil rights.

A new "great migration"

By 1960, for the first time in history, more African Americans were living in urban areas than in rural areas. As blacks moved into northern cities, many white residents moved to the suburbs, leaving behind racial ghettos. Nine of the nation's ten largest cities lost population to the suburbs during the 1950s. Between 1950 and 1960, some 3.6 million whites left the nation's largest cities for new suburban neighborhoods while 4.5 million blacks moved into those same cities, most of them coming from the rural South.

Deeply entrenched racial attitudes outside the South forced blacks to organize their own efforts to counter the hostility they confronted in communities across the nation. Through organizations such as the National Association for the Advancement of Colored People (NAACP), the Congress of Racial Equality (CORE), and the National Urban League, they sought to change the hearts and minds of their white neighbors. However, for all of the varied forms of racism that black migrants to the North and West encountered, most of them found their new lives preferable to the enforced segregation and often violent racism that they had left behind in the South. Southern blacks still faced voting discrimination and segregation in theaters, parks, schools, colleges, hospitals, buses, cinemas, libraries, restrooms, beaches, bars, and prisons. By the late 1950s, local black leaders had convinced most northern states to adopt some form of anti-discrimination legislation.

Anti-discrimination legislation in the North

Just as African Americans were on the move, so, too, were Mexicans and Puerto Ricans. Congress renewed the bracero program, begun during the Second World War, which enabled Mexicans to work as wage laborers in the United States, often as migrant workers moving from farm to farm as needed for the planting and harvest seasons. Mexicans streamed across the nation's southwest border, and by 1960 Los Angeles had the largest concentration of Mexican Americans in the nation. Like African Americans who served in the war, Mexican Americans, Puerto Ricans, and other Hispanic/Latino minorities benefited from the GI Bill. Between 1940 and 1960, nearly a million Puerto Ricans, mostly small farmers and agricultural workers, moved into mainland American cities, especially New York City. In fact, by

Hispanic migration to the United States

Fountains of truth An Alabama day-hotel offers its white clientele chilled water from a cooler, while its African American guests must use a rudimentary drinking fountain.

the late 1960s more Puerto Ricans lived in New York City than in San Juan, the capital of Puerto Rico. The popular Broadway musical drama *West Side Story* (1957) highlighted the tensions generated by the influx of Puerto Ricans into traditionally white neighborhoods.

Shifting Women's Roles

During the Second World War, millions of women had responded to patriotic appeals and assumed traditionally male jobs in factories and mills to help the war effort. After the war, those same working women were encouraged to return to their traditional roles as loving wives, caring mothers, and happy homemakers. A 1945 article in *House Beautiful* magazine lectured women on their domestic duties. The returning war veteran, it said, was "head man again. . . . Your part in the remaking of this man is to fit his home to him, understanding why he wants it this way, forgetting your own preferences."

"The happy homemaker"

Advertisements in popular magazines often targeted middle-class women, depicting them happily bound to the house, at work in the kitchen in dresses adorned with jewelry (usually pearl necklaces) and high heels, conversing with children, serving dinner, cleaning, and otherwise displaying the joy of a clean home or the latest kitchen appliance. The prevailing images of middle-class life in the fifties featured tree-lined suburban streets, kids riding their bikes through beautiful neighborhoods, and women as devoted servants to their husbands. Idealized images of "the happy homemaker" and middle-class suburban life in popular television programs like *The Donna Reed Show* or *Leave It to Beaver* also supported the cold war campaign to portray the superiority of capitalism, democracy, freedom, and religion over life under Soviet communism; Russian women, by contrast, were depicted toiling in drudgery as manual laborers in drab factories or on government farms.

During the fifties, the U.S. marriage rate reached an all-time high, and the average age of marriage for women plummeted to nineteen. There was enormous social pressure on teen-aged girls to get married quickly; if a woman wasn't engaged or married by her early twenties, she was in danger of becoming an "old maid." Getting married during high school or while in college became the norm. In 1956, one-fourth of all white college women wed while still enrolled in school, and most dropped out before receiving a degree. A common joke of the time was that women went to college to get an "M.R.S. degree"—that is, a husband.

Female college students were encouraged to take courses to prepare them for home life—home economics, interior decoration, and family finance. Lynn White, president of Mills College, argued that "the curriculum for female students should prepare women to foster the intellectual and emotional life of her family and community." Although women had other aspirations in life, the celebration of marriage and motherhood in the culture and media promoted the idea that getting a husband was far more important for a young woman than earning a college degree.

Despite this modern version of the nineteenth century's "cult of domesticity," in which women's roles were largely confined to the home and family duties, many women did work outside the home during the fifties, usually out of necessity. In 1950, women comprised 29 percent of the work force, and that percentage rose steadily throughout the decade. Some 70 percent of employed women worked in clerical positions—secretaries, bank tellers, or sales clerks—or worked on assembly lines in factories or in the service industry (waitresses, laundresses, maids). Less than 15 percent of women were employed in a professional capacity (teachers, nurses, accountants, social workers). Women represented only 3.5 percent of attorneys and 6 percent of physicians. African American and other minority women had even fewer vocational choices, mostly low-paying domestic service jobs as maids and cooks.

The Child-Centered Fifties

The fifties witnessed a record number of marriages—and births. The decade was an ideal time to be a child. The horrors of the Second World War were over, the economy was surging, and social life became centered on the needs of children—because there were so many of them. Between 1946 and 1964, the birth of 76 million Americans reversed a century-long decline in the nation's birth rate and created a demographic upheaval whose

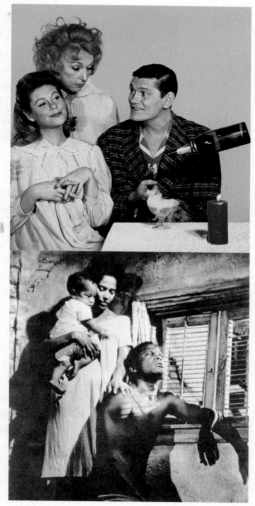

Hollywood homemakers TV shows and films were outlets for homemakers' anxieties and fantasies. *Left*: *Bewitched* was a popular comedy about a witch-turned-homemaker even though her family has bigger dreams for her. *Right*: Domestic bliss was never in reach for African American female characters. In *Porgy and Bess* (1959), Dorothy Dandridge plays an addict so lost in the vice of New Orleans that even her self-sacrificing disabled lover (Sidney Poitier) cannot save her.

repercussions are still being felt. The "**baby boom**" peaked in 1957, when a record 4.3 million births occurred, one every seven seconds. A majority of brides during the fifties were pregnant within seven months of their wedding, and they didn't just stop at one child. Large families were typical. From 1940 to 1960, the number of families with three children doubled and the number of families having a fourth child quadrupled. Dr. Benjamin Spock's *The Common Sense Book of Baby and Child Care* sold more than a million copies a year during the fifties.

The unusually large baby boom generation has since shaped social history and economic development. Postwar babies initially created a surge in demand for diapers, washing machines, and baby food, then required the construction of thousands of new schools—and the hiring of teachers to staff them. As the so-called baby boomers became children and then adolescents, their needs drove much of the economy's growth, creating a huge market for toys, candy, gum, records, clothes, and other items. In 1958, *Life* magazine reported that the nation's four-year-olds were creating a "backlog of business orders that will take two decades to fulfill."

The powerful forces promoting conformity in American social life during the cold war influenced the role of women. A special issue of *Life* magazine in 1956 featured the "ideal" middle-class woman: a thirty-two-year-old "pretty and popular" white suburban housewife, mother of four, who had married at age sixteen. She was described as an excellent wife, mother, volunteer, and "home manager" who preferred marriage and childrearing to a career outside the home. She made her own clothes, hosted dozens of dinner parties each year, sang in her church choir, and was devoted to her husband. "In her daily round," *Life* reported, "she attends club or charity meetings, drives the children to school, does the weekly grocery shopping, makes ceramics, and is planning to study French." The soaring birth rate reinforced the deeply embedded notion that a woman's place was in the home. "Of all the accomplishments of the American woman," the *Life* cover story proclaimed, "the one she brings off with the most spectacular success is having babies."

A Religious Nation

After the Second World War, Americans, unlike Europeans, joined churches and synagogues in record numbers. In 1940, less than half the adult population belonged to a church; by 1960, over 65 percent were members of churches or synagogues. Sales of Bibles soared, as did the demand for books, movies, and songs with religious themes. The cold war provided a direct stimulant to Christian evangelism. Communism, explained the Reverend Billy Graham, the most famous evangelist of the fifties, was "a great sinister anti-Christian movement masterminded by Satan" that must be fought wherever it emerged around the world.

President Eisenhower promoted a patriotic religious crusade during the fifties. "Recognition of the Supreme Being," he declared, "is the first, the

> Demands of a "baby boom"

baby boom Markedly high birth rate in the years following World War II, leading to the biggest demographic "bubble" in U.S. history.

most basic, expression of Americanism. Without God, there could be no American form of government, nor an American way of life." In 1954, Congress added the phrase "one nation under God" to the Pledge of Allegiance and in 1956 made the statement "In God We Trust" the nation's official motto. Eisenhower ordered that the motto be displayed on all currency. A godly nation, it was widely assumed, would better withstand the march of "godless" communism.

The prevailing tone of the popular religious revival of the 1950s was upbeat and soothing. As the Protestant Council of New York City explained to its radio and television presenters, their on-air broadcasts "should project love, joy, courage, hope, faith, trust in God, goodwill. Generally avoid condemnation, criticism, controversy. In a very real sense we are 'selling' religion, the good news of the Gospel."

The best salesman for this gospel of reassuring "good news" was the Reverend Norman Vincent Peale, the champion of feel-good religion. No speaker was more in demand during the 1950s, and no writer was more widely read. Peale's book *The Power of Positive Thinking* (1952) was a phenomenal best

Roadside service Drive-in churches offered its members the comfort of listening to Sunday Mass from their cars. Here, the pastor of New York's Tremont Methodist Church greets a member of his car-centered congregation.

seller throughout the decade—and for good reason. It offered a simple how-to course in personal happiness. "Flush out all depressing, negative, and tired thoughts," Peale advised. "Start thinking faith, enthusiasm, and joy." By following this simple formula for success, he pledged, each American could become "a more popular, esteemed, and well-liked individual."

Cracks in the Picture Window

CORE **OBJECTIVE**
3. Examine the criticism of postwar American society and culture, and describe the various forms of dissent and anxiety.

In contrast to Peale's feel-good religion, the fifties also experienced growing anxiety, dissent, and diversity. In *The Affluent Society* (1958), for example, economist John Kenneth Galbraith attacked the prevailing notion that sustained economic growth was solving chronic social problems. He reminded readers that for all of America's vaunted prosperity, the nation had yet to eradicate poverty, especially among minorities in inner cities, female-led households, Mexican American migrant farm workers, Native Americans, and rural southerners, both black and white.

Poverty amid Prosperity

Chronic poverty; income gap widens between whites and minorities

Uncritical praise for the "throwaway" culture of consumption during the 1950s masked the chronic poverty amid America's mythic plenty. In 1959, a quarter of the population had *no* financial assets, and more than half had no savings accounts or credit cards. Poverty afflicted nearly half of the African American population, compared to only a quarter of whites. True, by 1950 blacks were earning on average more than four times their 1940 wages. But African Americans and members of other minority groups lagged well behind whites in their *rate* of improvement, and the gap between the average yearly income of whites and minorities widened. At least 40 million people remained "poor" during the 1950s, but their plight was largely ignored amid the wave of middle-class white consumerism.

Racial tensions

The "promised land" in the North where many minorities moved was not perfect. Because those who moved out of the South were often undereducated, poor, and black, they were regularly denied access to good jobs, good schools, and good housing. Although states in the North, Midwest, and Far West did not have the same blatant forms of racial discrimination as the South, African Americans still encountered racial prejudice and discrimination in workplace hiring, in housing, in schools, and in social life. Outside the South, blacks and whites typically lived in separate neighborhoods and led unequal lives. When a black family tried to move into Levittown, Pennsylvania, white residents greeted them by throwing rocks. Between 1945 and 1954, Chicago witnessed nine race riots.

Literature

Many social critics, writers, and artists were alarmed by America's worship of consumerism during the fifties. One of the most striking aspects of the decade was the sharp contrast between the happy public mood and the increasingly bitter social criticism coming from intellectuals, theologians, novelists, playwrights, poets, and artists. A growing number of writers and artists questioned the prevailing complacency about the goodness and superiority of the American way of life. Writer Norman Mailer, for instance, said the 1950s was "one of the worst decades in the history of man."

Mailer was one of many social critics who challenged what they viewed as the decade's moral complacency and bland conformity. For all of America's mythic devotion to rugged individualism, the nation during the cold war celebrated conformity. As novelist John Updike observed, he and other writers felt estranged "from a government that extolled business and mediocrity." The most enduring novels of the postwar period emphasized the individual's struggle for survival amid the smothering forces of mass society. The characters in books such as James Jones's *From Here to Eternity* (1951), Ralph Ellison's *Invisible Man* (1952), Saul Bellow's *Seize the Day* (1956), J. D. Salinger's *Catcher in the Rye* (1951), William Styron's *Lie Down in Darkness* (1951), and Updike's *Rabbit, Run* (1961) are restless, tormented souls who can find neither contentment nor respect in an uninterested world.

The upper-middle-class white suburbs and the culture of comfortable conformity they created were frequent literary targets during the fifties. Writer John Cheever located most of his often brilliant short stories in suburban neighborhoods outside of New York City—"cesspools of conformity" where life was mindless and hollow. The typical suburban dweller, as one critic charged in 1956, did everything like the neighbors: "buys the right car, keeps his lawn like his neighbor's, eats crunchy breakfast cereal, and votes Republican."

In his vicious satire of affluent suburbia, *The Crack in the Picture Window* (1956), John Keats charged that "miles of identical boxes are spreading like gangrene" across the nation, producing a runaway consumerism, "haggard" businessmen, "tense and anxious" housewives, and "the gimme kids" who, after unwrapping the last Christmas gift, "look up and ask whether that is all." He dismissed the Levittowns of America as residential "developments conceived in error, nurtured by greed, corroding everything they touch. They destroy established cities and trade patterns, pose dangerous problems for the areas they invade, and actually drive mad myriads of housewives shut up in them."

> **Social criticism:** Complacency and conformity in the suburbs

The Beats

A small but highly visible and controversial group of young writers, poets, painters, and musicians rejected the materialism of the consumer culture as well as the traditional expectations and responsibilities of middle-class life. They were known as the **Beats**, a term with multiple meanings: to be "beat" was likened to being "upbeat" and even "beatific," as well as being "on the beat" in "real cool" jazz music. But the rebellious Beats also liked the name because it implied "weariness," being "exhausted" or "beaten down," qualities which none of them actually exhibited.

> **The Beats (bohemians) reject middle-class values**

Jack Kerouac, Allen Ginsberg, William Burroughs, Neal Cassady, Gary Snyder, and other Beats were cultural outlaws who rebelled against conventional literary and artistic expression and excelled at outrageous behavior. Intensely self-absorbed, they celebrated, even embodied, lives of breathtaking risk and originality, fueled by spontaneity and energy. They pursued rebellious and reckless lives of alcohol- and drug-induced ecstasies and sexual excesses (many of them were gay or bi-sexual during an era when homosexuality was viewed as a form of deviance requiring psychotherapy). The mostly male Beats viewed women as second-class accessories; Carolyn Cassady said her husband Neal's approach to making love was "rape." She added that Neal and the "boys didn't know where they were going. . . . They just knew they wanted to *go*."

Beats Group of bohemian writers, artists, and musicians who flouted convention in favor of liberated forms of self-expression.

Art ache The Beat community fostered in its members a frenzied desire to create. In this 1959 photograph, poet Tex Kleen reads in a bathtub at Venice Beach, California, while artist Mad Mike paints trash cans.

The Beat hipsters grew out of the bohemian underground in New York City's Greenwich Village. Undisciplined and often unkempt, they were essentially apolitical and more interested in transforming themselves than in reforming the world. They sought personal rather than social solutions to their needs and anxieties; they wanted their art and literature to change consciousness rather than address social ills. As Kerouac insisted in his remarkable novel *On the Road* (1957), the first draft of which was typed almost nonstop onto a continuous roll of butcher paper during three feverish weeks, his rootless, reckless friends were not beat in the sense of beaten down; they were "mad to live, mad to talk, mad to be saved, desirous of everything at the same time, the ones who never yawn or say a commonplace thing, but burn, burn, burn like fabulous yellow roman candles exploding like spiders across the stars."

The Beats nursed an urge to "go, go, go" and not stop until they got there, wherever "there" might be. Their road to salvation lay in hallucinogenic drugs and lots of alcohol, casual sex, petty crime, gratuitous violence, a passion for uptempo jazz ("bebop"), fast cars, the street life of urban ghettos, an affinity for Buddhism, and a restless, vagabond spirit that took them racing back and forth across the country between San Francisco and New York. At heart, the Beats were romantics searching for an authentic sense of self in a nation absorbed in consumerism, conformism, and anticommunism. The tortured rebelliousness of the Beats set the stage for the more widespread youth revolt of the 1960s.

Rock 'n' Roll

Youth culture and juvenile delinquency

The millions of children making up the first wave of the baby boomers born during and just after the Second World War became adolescents in the 1950s. A distinctive teen subculture began to emerge, and a wave of juvenile delinquency swept across middle-class society. By 1956, over a million teens were being arrested each year. One contributing factor was access to automobiles, which enabled teens to escape parental control and, in the words of one journalist, provided "a private lounge for drinking and for petting [embracing and kissing] or sex episodes."

Rebellion, sexual suggestion, and new forms of music

Many concerned observers blamed teen delinquency on rock 'n' roll, a new form of music that emerged during the 1950s. Alan Freed, a Cleveland disc jockey, coined the term rock 'n' roll in 1951. He had noticed that white teenagers buying rhythm and blues (R&B) records preferred the livelier recordings by African Americans and Hispanic Americans. Freed began playing R&B records on his radio show, but he called the music "rock 'n' roll" (a phrase used in African American communities to refer to dancing and sex). Freed's popular program helped bridge the gap between "white" and "black" music. African American singers such as Chuck Berry, Little Richard, and Ray Charles, as well as Hispanic American performers such as Ritchie Valens (Richard Valenzuela), captivated young, white, middle-class audiences eager to claim their own cultural style.

At the same time, Elvis Presley, the lanky son of a poor Mississippi farm family who moved to a public housing project in Memphis, Tennessee, began experimenting with "rockabilly" music, a unique blend of gospel, country-and-western, and R&B. At the same time, Sam Phillips, a local radio disk jockey, was searching for a particular type of pop singer. "If I could find a white man with a Negro sound," Phillips said, "I could make a billion dollars."

Then he found Elvis. In 1956, the twenty-one-year-old Presley, by then a

Elvis Presley Hysterical girls grab at him from all angles, but the "King of Rock and Roll" stays cool, crooning into the camera while performing in Miami, 1956.

regional star famous for his long, unruly hair, his sensual sneer, and his wildly swiveling hips, released his smash-hit recording "Heartbreak Hotel." Over the next two years, he emerged as the most popular musician in American history. Presley's gyrating, sensual stage performances (his nickname was "Elvis the Pelvis") and his incomparably rich and raw baritone voice drove teenagers (a word that came into use during the fifties) wild and earned him millions of fans around the world. His movements, said one music critic, "suggest, in a word, sex."

Cultural conservatives were outraged by Presley's antics. Critics urged parents to destroy his records because they promoted "a pagan concept of life." A Roman Catholic official denounced Presley as a vile symptom of a teenage "creed of dishonesty, violence, lust and degeneration." Patriotic groups claimed that rock 'n' roll music was part of a Communist plot to corrupt America's youth. Writing in the *New York Times*, a psychiatrist characterized rock 'n' roll as a "communicable disease." A U.S. Senate sub-committee investigating juvenile delinquency warned that Elvis was threatening "to rock-n-roll the juvenile world into open revolt against society. The gangster of tomorrow is the Elvis Presley type of today."

Yet rock 'n' roll flourished amid such opposition, in part because it was so controversial. It gave teenagers a self-conscious sense of belonging to a tribal social group. More important, it brought together, on equal terms, musicians (and their audiences) of varied races and backgrounds. In doing so, it helped dispel the racial prejudices that conflicted with the nation's ideals.

CORE **OBJECTIVE**

4. Evaluate the goals, strategies, and impact of the civil rights movement that emerged in the 1950s.

The Early Years of the Civil Rights Movement

Soon after the cold war began, Soviet diplomats began to use America's racial discrimination against African Americans as a propaganda tool to illustrate the supposed defects of the American way of life. Under the Jim Crow system in the southern states, blacks still risked being lynched if they registered to vote. They were forced to use separate facilities in public—water fountains, restrooms, hotels, theaters, parks—and to attend segregated schools. In the North, discrimination was not as "official," but it was equally real, especially in housing and employment. During the mid-1950s, the ongoing tragedy of race relations in the United States offered President Eisenhower an opportunity to exercise transformational leadership; his unwillingness to do so was his greatest failure. As *Time* magazine noted in 1958, Eisenhower "overlooked the fact that the U.S. needed [his] moral leadership in fighting segregation."

Eisenhower and Race

Eisenhower had entered the White House committed to civil rights in principle, and he pushed for improvements in some areas. During his first three years as president, for example, public facilities (parks, playgrounds, libraries, restaurants) in Washington, D.C., were desegregated, and he intervened to end discrimination at military bases in Virginia and South Carolina. The president also appointed the first African American to an executive office: E. Frederic Morrow, who was named Administrative Officer for Special Projects. Beyond that, however, Eisenhower refused to make civil rights for African Americans a moral crusade. Pushing too hard against segregation in the South, he believed, would "raise tempers and increase prejudices," doing more harm than good.

Eisenhower's civil rights record

Two aspects of Eisenhower's political philosophy limited his commitment to racial equality: his preference for state or local action over federal involvement and his doubt that laws could change attitudes. "I don't believe you can change the hearts of men with laws or decisions," he insisted. His passive attitude toward racial issues meant that governmental leadership on civil rights would come from the judiciary more than from the executive or legislative branch.

In 1953, Eisenhower appointed former Republican governor Earl Warren of California as chief justice of the U.S. Supreme Court, a decision he later said was the "biggest damn fool mistake I ever made." Warren, who had seemed safely conservative while in elected office, displayed a social conscience and a streak of libertarianism that was shared by another Eisenhower appointee to the Court, William J. Brennan Jr. Under Warren's leadership (1953–1969), the Supreme Court became one of the most powerful forces for social and political change through the 1960s.

African American Activism

However, the most crucial leaders of the civil rights movement came from the long-suffering people whose rights were most often violated: African Americans, Hispanic Americans, Asian Americans, and other minorities. Rural and urban, young and old, male and female, courageous blacks led what would become the most important social movement in twentieth-century American history. With brilliance, bravery, and dignity, they fought on all fronts—in the courts, at the ballot box, and in the streets—against the deeply entrenched system of racial segregation and discrimination. Although many African Americans moved to the North and West during and after the Second World War, a majority remained in the South, where they were forced to attend segregated public schools, to accept the least desirable jobs, and to operate within a rigidly segregated society that restricted their civil rights. In the 1952 presidential election, for example, only 20 percent of eligible African Americans were registered to vote.

In the mid-1930s, the National Association for the Advancement of Colored People (NAACP) challenged the **separate-but-equal** judicial doctrine that had upheld racial segregation since the *Plessy* decision by the Supreme Court in 1896. Yet it took almost fifteen years to convince the courts that racial segregation must end. Finally, in *Sweatt v. Painter* (1950), the Supreme Court ruled that a separate black law school in Texas was *not* equal in quality to the state's whites-only schools. The Court ordered the state to remedy the situation. It was the first step toward dismantling America's tradition of racial segregation.

> NAACP's legal efforts

The *Brown* Decision

By the early 1950s, challenges to state laws mandating racial segregation in the public schools were rising through the court system. Five such cases, from Kansas, Delaware, South Carolina, Virginia, and the District of Columbia—usually cited by reference to the first, **Brown v. Board of Education** of Topeka, Kansas—came to the Supreme Court for joint argument by NAACP attorneys in 1952. President Eisenhower told the attorney general that he hoped the justices would postpone dealing with the explosive case "until the next Administration took over." When it became obvious that the Court was moving forward, Eisenhower invited Earl Warren to a White House dinner during which he urged the chief justice to side with segregationists. Warren was not swayed: "You mind your business," he told the president, "and I'll mind mine."

Warren himself wrote the pathbreaking opinion, handed down on May 17, 1954, in which a unanimous Court declared that "in the field of public education the doctrine of 'separate but equal' has no place." In support of its opinion, the Court cited sociological and psychological findings demonstrating that even if racially separate schools were equal in quality, the very practice of separating students by race caused feelings of inferiority among

> *Brown v. Board of Education*: The separate-but-equal doctrine overturned

separate-but-equal Principle that formed the basis for legal racial segregation.

Brown v. Board of Education **(1952)** Landmark Supreme Court case that struck down racial segregation in public schools and declared "separate-but-equal" unconstitutional.

black children. A year later, the Court directed that the process of racial *integration* should move "with all deliberate speed."

Eisenhower refused to endorse or enforce the Court's ruling. Privately, he grumbled "that the Supreme Court decision set back progress in the South at least fifteen years." Anyone who thinks "you can do these things by force is just plain nuts," he said. While token racial integration began as early as 1954 in Kentucky and Missouri, hostility mounted in the Lower South and Virginia. The Alabama State Senate and the Virginia legislature both passed resolutions "nullifying" the Supreme Court's decision.

Opponents of court-ordered integration of schools and other public places were defiant. In 1956, 101 members of Congress signed a Declaration of Constitutional Principles ("Southern Manifesto") denouncing the Supreme Court's decision in the *Brown* case as "a clear abuse of judicial power" that had created an "explosive and dangerous condition" in the South. Only three southern Democrats in Congress refused to sign. One of them, Senator Lyndon B. Johnson of Texas, would become president seven years later. In six southern states at the end of 1956, two years after the *Brown* ruling, not a single black child attended school with whites.

The Montgomery Bus Boycott

The *Brown* case did much more than mobilize white resistance in the South. It inspired many blacks (and white activists) by suggesting that the federal government was finally beginning to confront racial discrimination. Yet the essential role played by the NAACP and the courts in providing a legal lever for the civil rights movement often overshadows the courageous contributions of individual African Americans who took great personal risks to challenge segregation in their communities.

For example, in Montgomery, Alabama, on December 1, 1955, Mrs. Rosa Parks, a forty-two-year-old black seamstress, civil rights activist, and secretary of the local NAACP chapter, refused to give up her seat on a city bus to a white man. Like many southern communities, Montgomery, the "Cradle of the Confederacy," required blacks to sit in the rear seats of buses or trains. They could sit in the front seats designated for whites only if there were empty seats. If a white rider asked for a black to move, they were expected to go "to the back of the bus." Parks, however, was "tired of giving in" to the humiliating practice. When the bus driver told her that "niggers must move back" or he would have her arrested, she replied, with quiet courage and fierce determination, "You may do that." Police then arrested her. The next night, black community leaders met in the Dexter Avenue Baptist Church to organize a long-planned boycott of the city's bus system, 75 percent of whose riders were African Americans. Student and faculty volunteers from Alabama State University stayed up all night to distribute 35,000 flyers denouncing the arrest of Rosa Parks and urging support for the **Montgomery bus boycott**.

Montgomery bus boycott

Montgomery bus boycott
Boycott of bus system in Montgomery, Alabama, organized by civil rights activists after the arrest of Rosa Parks in 1955.

Martin Luther King's nonviolent resistance

In the Dexter Avenue church's twenty-six-year-old pastor, Martin Luther King Jr., the boycott movement found a brave and charismatic leader. Born in Atlanta, the grandson of a slave and son of a prominent minister, the short, stocky King was intelligent and courageous. He also was an eloquent and passionate speaker. "We must use the weapon of love," King told his supporters. "We must realize so many people are taught to hate us that they are not totally responsible for their hate." To his foes, the self-controlled King warned, "We will soon wear you down by our capacity to suffer, and in winning our freedom we will so appeal to your heart and conscience that we will win you in the process." King preached **nonviolent civil disobedience**, the tactic of defying unjust laws through peaceful actions, but he also valued militancy, for without confrontation with those in power there would be no negotiation or progress.

The Montgomery bus boycott achieved remarkable unity. For 381 days, African Americans, women and men, used carpools, called black-owned taxis, hitchhiked, or simply walked. White supporters also provided rides. A few boycotters rode horses or mules to work. The unprecedented mass protest infuriated many whites; police harassed and ticketed black carpools, and white thugs attacked black pedestrians. Ku Klux Klan members burned black churches and bombed houses owned by King and other boycott leaders. King himself was arrested twice. In trying to calm an angry black crowd eager for revenge against their white tormentors, he urged restraint: "Don't get panicky. Don't get your weapons. We want to love our enemies."

On December 20, 1956, the Montgomery boycotters won a federal case they had initiated against racial segregation on public buses. The Supreme Court affirmed that "the separate but equal doctrine can no longer be safely followed as a correct statement of the law." The next day, King and other African Americans boarded the buses. The success of the boycott showed

nonviolent civil disobedience Tactic of defying unjust laws through peaceful actions championed by Dr. Martin Luther King, Jr.

that well-coordinated, nonviolent black activism could trigger major changes in public policy. Among African Americans, hope replaced resignation during the bus boycott, and action supplanted passivity. The boycott also catapulted King into the national spotlight. And what of Rosa Parks? She and her husband lost their jobs, and hate mail as well as death threats forced them to leave Alabama. They moved to Detroit, where they remained fully engaged in the evolving civil rights movement.

The Civil Rights Acts of 1957 and 1960

Civil Rights Acts (1957, 1960)

President Eisenhower's timidity in the field of race relations emerged again when he was asked to protect the right of African Americans to vote. In 1956, hoping to exploit divisions between northern and southern Democrats and to reclaim some of the black vote for Republicans, congressional leaders agreed to support what became the Civil Rights Act of 1957. The first civil rights law passed since 1875, it finally got through the Senate, after a year's delay, with the help of majority leader Lyndon B. Johnson, a Texas Democrat who knew that he could never be elected president if he was viewed as just another racist white southerner. The bill was intended to ensure that all Americans, regardless of their race or ethnicity, were allowed to vote. Although Johnson believed that the civil rights bill was just and necessary, he won southern acceptance of the bill by watering down its enforcement provisions. Eisenhower reassured Johnson that the final version represented "the mildest civil rights bill possible."

The Civil Rights Act established the Civil Rights Commission and a new Civil Rights Division in the Justice Department intended to prevent interference with the right to vote. Yet by 1959, the Civil Rights Act had not resulted in a single southern black voter being added to the rolls. Neither did the Civil Rights Act of 1960, which provided for federal courts to register African Americans to vote in districts around the country where there was a "pattern and practice" of racial discrimination. This bill, too, lacked teeth and depended upon vigorous presidential enforcement to achieve any tangible results.

Desegregation in Little Rock

Eisenhower sends federal troops to Little Rock

A few weeks after the Civil Rights Act of 1957 was passed, Arkansas's Democratic governor, Orval Faubus, a rabid segregationist eager to win a third term, called out the state's National Guard to prevent nine black students from entering Little Rock's Central High School under a federal court order. The National Guard commander's orders were explicit: "No niggers in the building." When one of the students, fifteen-year-old Elizabeth Eckford, tried to enter the school, a surging mob of jeering whites shrieked, "Lynch her! Lynch her!" Local authorities removed the students from the school in an effort to protect them, and the mayor frantically called the White House to request federal troops to stop the violence. At that point, President Eisenhower reluctantly dispatched a thousand Army paratroopers to

Little Rock to protect the brave black students as they entered the school. It was the first time since the 1870s that federal troops had been sent to the South to protect the rights of African Americans. Dunbar Ogden, a Presbyterian minister in Little Rock, found a ray of hope in the ugly confrontation: "This may be looked back upon by future historians as the turning point—for good—of race relations in this country."

The soldiers stayed in Little Rock through the school year. Unyielding southern segregationists lashed out at the president, charging that Eisenhower was violating states' rights. In 1954 Virginia senator and former governor, Harry F. Byrd, supplied a rallying cry for white diehards when he called for "**massive resistance**" against federal efforts to enforce integration in the South. Senator Richard Russell of Georgia said the paratroopers in Little Rock were be-

"Lynch her!" Fifteen-year-old Elizabeth Eckford endures the hostile screams of future classmates as she enters Central High School in Little Rock.

having like "Hitler's storm troopers." Eisenhower was quick to deny that he was making any moral judgment about the situation in Little Rock. He stressed that his use of federal troops had little to do with "the integration or segregation question" and everything to do with maintaining law and order. Martin Luther King Jr., who had earlier criticized Eisenhower's tepid support of civil rights, now told the president that the "overwhelming majority of southerners, Negro and white, stand behind your resolute action to restore law and order in Little Rock." Southern politicians had a different view. Many called for the president's impeachment and removal.

In the summer of 1958, Governor Faubus, supported by the state legislature, closed the Little Rock high schools rather than allow racial integration. The governor of Virginia did the same in his state. Their actions led Jonathan Daniels, editor of the Raleigh, North Carolina, *News & Observer*, to write that closing public schools is "something beyond secession from the Union; [it] is secession from civilization." Court proceedings in Arkansas dragged into 1959 before the schools were reopened. Resistance to integration in Virginia collapsed when both state and federal courts struck down state laws that had cut off funds to integrated public schools. Thereafter, massive resistance to racial integration was confined mostly to the Lower South, where five states—from South Carolina westward through

massive resistance White rallying cry for disrupting federal efforts to enforce racial integration in the South.

Louisiana—still opposed even token integration. Faubus went on to serve six terms as governor of Arkansas.

Southern Christian Leadership Conference

After the confrontation at Little Rock, progress toward greater civil rights seemed agonizingly slow. Frustrated African Americans began blaming the NAACP for relying too much on the courts to end segregation. "The Negro masses are angry and restless, tired of prolonged legal battles that end in paper decrees," reported black journalist Louis Lomax. "The organizations that understand this unrest and rise to lead it will survive; those that do not will perish."

The widespread sense of disappointment after the Little Rock incident gave Martin Luther King's nonviolent civil rights movement even greater visibility. As King explained, "We were confronted with blasted hopes, and the dark shadow of a deep disappointment settled upon us. So we had no alternative except that of preparing for direct action, whereby we would present our very bodies as a means of laying our case before the conscience of the local and national community."

On January 10, 1957, following the Montgomery bus boycott victory and consultations with Bayard Rustin, Ella Baker, and others, Dr. King invited about 60 black ministers and leaders to Ebenezer Church in Atlanta. Their goal was to form an organization to coordinate and support nonviolent direct action as a method of desegregating bus systems across the South. In addition to Rustin and Baker, the Reverend Fred Shuttlesworth of Birmingham, the Reverend Joseph Lowery of Mobile, the Reverend Ralph Abernathy of Montgomery, and the Reverend C. K. Steele of Tallahassee all played key roles in this meeting.

On February 15, a follow-up meeting was held in New Orleans. Out of these two meetings came the creation of a new organization called the **Southern Christian Leadership Conference (SCLC)**, with Dr. King as its president. Unlike the NAACP, which recruited individual members, SCLC coordinated activities on behalf of a cluster of organizations, mostly individual churches or community groups such as the Montgomery Improvement Association. Because Dr. King pushed SCLC and its member churches to take direct action against the segregated white South, only a few African American ministers were initially willing to affiliate with SCLC, for fear of a white backlash.

King persisted, however, and over time SCLC grew into a powerful organization at the center of the growing civil rights movement. The civil rights activists knew that violence awaited them. Roy Wilkins, the head of the NAACP, noted that "the Negro citizen has come to the point where he is not afraid of violence. He no longer shrinks back. He will assert himself, and if violence comes, so be it." Thus began the second phase of the civil rights movement, a phase that would come to fruition in the 1960s as King and other African American activists showed the nation the courage to resist

Southern Christian Leadership Conference (SCLC)

Southern Christian Leadership Conference (SCLC) Civil rights organization formed by Dr. Martin Luther King, Jr., that championed nonviolent direct action as a means of ending segregation.

injustice, the power to love everyone, and the strength to endure discouragement and opposition.

Foreign Policy in the 1950s

CORE **OBJECTIVE**
5. Assess President Eisenhower's priorities in conducting the nation's foreign policy and his influence on global affairs.

The Truman administration's commitment to "contain" communism focused on the Soviet threat to Western Europe. During the 1950s, the Eisenhower administration, especially Secretary of State John Foster Dulles, expanded America's objective in the cold war. "Containment" was no longer enough; communism must be "rolled back" around the world. The Eisenhower administration soon discovered, however, that the complexities of world affairs and the realities of Soviet and Communist Chinese power made the commitment to manage the destiny of the world unrealistic—and costly.

Concluding an Armistice

To break the stalemate in the Korean peace talks, Eisenhower took the bold step in mid-May 1953 of intensifying the aerial bombardment of North Korea. The president let it be known that he would use nuclear weapons if a truce were not forthcoming. Thereafter, negotiations moved quickly toward a ceasefire agreement (called an armistice) on July 26, 1953, affirming the established border between the two Koreas just above the 38th parallel. Other factors in bringing about the armistice were China's rising military losses in the conflict and the spirit of uncertainty and caution felt by the Soviet Communists after the death of Joseph Stalin on March 5, 1953, six weeks after Eisenhower's inauguration.

A truce in Korea (1953)

Dulles and Massive Retaliation

The architect of the Eisenhower administration's efforts to "roll back" communism was Secretary of State John Foster Dulles. Like Woodrow Wilson, Dulles was a minister's son, a self-righteous and humorless statesman, and a man of immense energy and intelligence who believed that the United States was "born with a sense of destiny and mission" to lead the world. His British counterparts, however, were not impressed with his sermonizing speeches, calling them "dull, duller, Dulles."

Dulles insisted that the Democratic policy of "containing" communism was "immoral" because it did nothing to free people from oppression. America, he argued, should instead work toward the "liberation" of the "captive peoples" of Eastern Europe and China. When George F. Kennan, the leading Soviet analyst in the State Department who had first suggested the containment doctrine, dismissed such hollow rhetoric as lunacy, Dulles fired him. Eisenhower was quick to explain that the "liberation" doctrine would not involve military force. He would promote the removal of Communist control "by every peaceful means, but only by peaceful means."

Eisenhower's "liberation" doctrine

The threat of nuclear war and brinkmanship

Dulles and Eisenhower knew that the United States could not win a ground war against the Soviet Union or Communist China, both of whose armies had millions more soldiers than the United States. Nor could the administration afford—politically or financially—to sustain military expenditures at the levels required during the Korean War. So in an effort to get "more bang for the buck," Dulles and Eisenhower crafted a new strategy growing out of the Korean experience. It came to be called "**massive retaliation**," which meant using the threat of nuclear warfare ("massive retaliatory power") to prevent Communist aggression. The massive retaliation strategy, Eisenhower, Dulles, and the military chiefs argued, would provide a "maximum deterrent at bearable cost."

The strategy of promising "massive retaliation" had major weaknesses, however. By the mid-1950s, both the United States and the Soviet Union had developed hydrogen bombs, which were 750 times as powerful as the atomic bombs dropped on Japan in 1945. A single hydrogen bomb would have a devastating global impact, yet war planners envisioned using hundreds of them. "The necessary art," Dulles explained, was in the brinksmanship, "the ability to get to the verge without getting into war. . . . If you are scared to go to the brink, you are lost."

The CIA and Foreign Interventions

At the same time that Eisenhower and Dulles were publicly promoting the "liberation" of Communist nations in Europe and Asia and "massive retaliation" as a strategy against the Soviets, they were secretly using the new **Central Intelligence Agency (CIA)** to influence world politics.

CIA intervention in the Middle East and Latin America

The anti-colonial independence movements unleashed by the Second World War placed the United States in the awkward position of watching nationalist groups around the globe revolt against British and French rule. In Iran in May 1951, the parliament seized control of the nation's British-run oil industry. The following year, a newly elected prime minister, European-educated Mohammed Mossadegh, cut all diplomatic ties with Great Britain. Dulles predicted that Iran was on the verge of falling under Communist control. The CIA and the British intelligence service, MI6, then launched Operation Ajax, designed, in the words of the agency's head, Allen Dulles (the secretary of state's brother), to "bring about the fall of Mossadegh."

The CIA bribed Iranian army officers and hired Iranian agents to arrest Mossadegh, who was convicted of high treason. He was imprisoned for three years, then put under house arrest until his death in 1967. In return for access to Iranian oil, the U.S. government thereafter provided massive support for the anti-Communist and increasingly authoritarian regime of the shah (king) of Iran, Mohammad Reza Pahlavi, who was able to consolidate power after the removal of Mossadegh.

The success of the CIA-engineered coup in Iran emboldened Eisenhower to authorize other secret operations designed to undermine

massive retaliation Strategy that used the threat of nuclear warfare as a means of combating the global spread of communism.

Central Intelligence Agency (CIA) Intelligence-gathering government agency founded in 1947; under President Eisenhower's orders, secretly undermined elected governments deemed susceptible to communism.

"unfriendly" government regimes. In 1954, the target was Guatemala, a desperately poor Central American country led by Colonel Jacobo Arbenz Guzman. Arbenz's decision to take over U.S.-owned property and industries in Guatemala convinced John Foster Dulles that Guatemala was falling victim to "international communism." He persuaded Eisenhower to approve a CIA operation to organize a secret Guatemalan army in Honduras. On June 18, 1954, aided by CIA-piloted warplanes, the 150 paid "liberators" crossed the border into Guatemala and forced Arbenz Guzman into exile in Mexico. The United States then installed a new ruler in Guatemala who eliminated all political opposition.

The CIA operations revealed that the United States was secretly overthrowing elected governments around the world to ensure that they did not join the Soviet bloc. The illegal operations succeeded in toppling rulers, but in doing so they destabilized Iran and Guatemala and created problems in the Middle East and Central America that would come back to haunt the United States decades later.

Indochina: Background to America's Longest War

During the fifties, the United States also became embroiled in the complex region of Southeast Asia. Indochina, created by French imperialists in the nineteenth century out of the old kingdoms of Cambodia, Laos, and Vietnam, offered a distinctive case of anti-colonial nationalism. During the Second World War, after Japanese troops occupied the region, the Viet Minh (League for the Independence of Vietnam) waged a guerrilla resistance movement. They were led by Ho Chi Minh, a seasoned revolutionary and passionate nationalist. Mild-mannered and soft-spoken, "Uncle Ho," a wispy man weighing barely a hundred pounds, worked sixteen hours each day toward a single goal: independence for his country. "You must give the people an example of poverty, misery, and denial," he explained. At the end of the war against Japan, the Viet Minh controlled part of northern Vietnam. On September 2, 1945, Ho Chi Minh proclaimed the creation of a Democratic Republic of Vietnam, with its capital in Hanoi.

The French, like the Americans would later, underestimated the determination of Ho and the Vietnamese nationalists to maintain their independence. In 1946, the First Indochina War began when Ho's fighters resisted French efforts to restore the colonial regime. French forces quickly regained control of the cities, while the Viet Minh controlled the countryside. When the Korean War ended, the United States continued its efforts to strengthen French control of Vietnam. By the end of 1953, the Eisenhower administration was paying nearly 80 percent of the cost of the French military effort, and the United States found itself at the brink of military intervention.

In December 1953, some 12,000 French soldiers parachuted into **Dien Bien Phu**, a cluster of villages in a valley ringed by mountains in northern Vietnam near the Laotian border. The French military plan, which

Ho Chi Minh Though a ruthless leader, he cultivated a humble, proletarian version of himself as Uncle Ho, a man of the people.

Dien Bien Phu Cluster of Vietnamese villages and site of a major Vietnamese victory over the French in the First Indochina War.

Dien Bien Phu Viet Minh soldiers march French captives to a prisoner camp in Dien Bien Phu on May 7, 1954.

Eisenhower deemed foolish, was to build a well-fortified base to lure Viet Minh guerrillas into the open and then overwhelm them with superior firepower. The French assumed that the surrounding forested hills were impassable. But slowly, in single file, over 55,000 Viet Minh fighters equipped with Chinese Communist weapons took up positions atop the ridges overlooking the French military base. They laboriously dismantled cannons and carried them in pieces up the hills, then dug trenches and tunnels down into the valley. By March 1954, the French found themselves surrounded.

As the weeks passed, the French government pleaded with the United States to use its warplanes to relieve the pressure on Dien Bien Phu, which a French journalist called "Hell in a very small place." The National Security Council—Dulles, Vice President Nixon, and the chairman of the Joint Chiefs of Staff—urged Eisenhower to use atomic bombs to aid the trapped French force. Eisenhower snapped back: "You boys must be crazy. We can't use those awful things against Asians for the second time in less than ten years. My God!" The president opposed any U.S. intervention unless the British joined the effort. When they refused, Eisenhower told the French that U.S. military action in Vietnam was "politically impossible." As Eisenhower stressed, "No one could be more bitterly opposed to ever getting the U.S. involved in a hot war in that region than I am." On May 7, 1954, the Viet Minh fighters overwhelmed the last French resistance at Dien Bien Phu. The catastrophic defeat signaled the end of French colonial rule in Asia.

On July 20, 1954, representatives of France, Britain, the Soviet Union, the People's Republic of China, and the Viet Minh signed the Geneva Accords. The complex agreement gave Laos and Cambodia their independence and divided Vietnam in two at the 17th parallel. The Geneva Accords gave the Viet Minh Communists control in the North; the French would remain south of the line until nationwide elections in 1956 reunified all of Vietnam. American and South Vietnamese representatives refused to sign the Geneva Accords, arguing that the treaties legitimized the Communist victory. After 1954 Ho Chi Minh took complete control of the government in North Vietnam, executing thousands of Vietnamese he deemed opponents.

The Geneva Accords, South Vietnam, and the Viet Cong

In South Vietnam, power gravitated to a new premier chosen by the French at American urging: Ngo Dinh Diem, a Catholic nationalist who had opposed both the French and the Viet Minh. In 1954, Eisenhower began

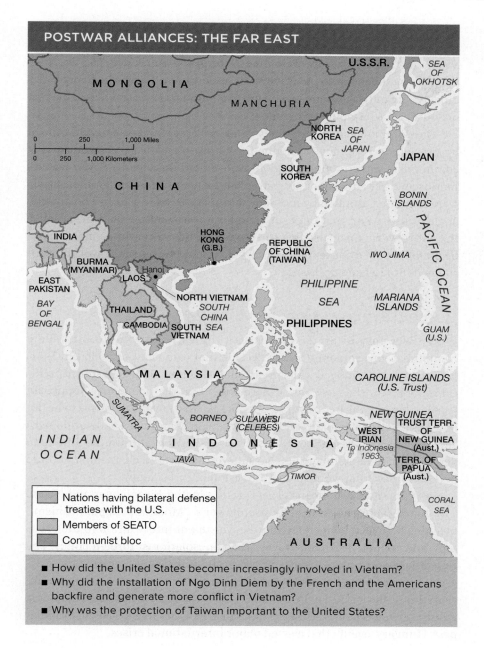

POSTWAR ALLIANCES: THE FAR EAST

Legend:
- Nations having bilateral defense treaties with the U.S.
- Members of SEATO
- Communist bloc

■ How did the United States become increasingly involved in Vietnam?

■ Why did the installation of Ngo Dinh Diem by the French and the Americans backfire and generate more conflict in Vietnam?

■ Why was the protection of Taiwan important to the United States?

providing military and economic aid to Diem. The president remained opposed to the use of U.S. combat troops, believing that military intervention would lead to a costly stalemate—as indeed it eventually did. Diem's autocratic efforts to eliminate all opposition played into the hands of the Communists, who found eager recruits among the discontented South Vietnamese. By 1957, Communist guerrillas known as the **Viet Cong** were launching attacks on the Diem government. As the warfare intensified, the Eisenhower administration concluded that its only option was to "sink or swim with Diem."

Viet Cong Communist guerrillas in South Vietnam who launched attacks on the Diem government.

In 1954, Eisenhower had used what he called the **"falling domino" theory** to explain why the United States needed to fight communism in Vietnam: "You have a row of dominos set up, you knock over the first one, and what will happen to the last one is the certainty that it will go over very quickly." If South Vietnam were to fall to communism, he predicted, the rest of Southeast Asia would soon follow.

The domino analogy, originally used by President Truman and echoed by presidents Eisenhower, Kennedy, Johnson, and Nixon, assumed that communism was a monolithic global movement directed by Soviet leaders in Moscow. Yet anti-colonial insurgencies such as those in Southeast Asia were animated as much by nationalist motives as by ideology. The domino analogy also meant that the United States was assuming that it must police the entire world to ensure that the dominoes, no matter how small, did not begin falling. As a consequence, every insurgency around the world mushroomed into a strategic crisis.

Reelection and Foreign Crises

While Secretary of State John Foster Dulles was trying to intimidate communist governments, a new presidential campaign unfolded in 1956. Eisenhower still enjoyed widespread public support. James Reston, a political reporter for the *New York Times*, noted that the president's popularity "has got beyond the bounds of reasonable calculation and will have to be put down as a national phenomenon, like baseball." Americans had developed a "love affair" with Eisenhower. But the president's health was beginning to deteriorate. In September 1955, he suffered a heart attack, the first of three major illnesses that would affect the rest of his presidency.

In 1956, the Republicans eagerly renominated Eisenhower and Nixon. The party platform endorsed Eisenhower's "Moderate Republicanism," meaning balanced budgets, reduced government intervention in the economy, and an internationalist rather than an isolationist foreign policy. The Republicans promised "peace, progress, and prosperity," crowing that "everything's booming but the guns." The Democrats turned again to the liberal Illinois leader, Adlai Stevenson. During the last week of the campaign, fighting erupted along the Suez Canal in Egypt and in the streets of Budapest, Hungary, events that caused major international crises.

Repression in Hungary

Soviets crush Hungarian revolt

On October 23, 1956, Hungarian nationalists, encouraged by American propaganda broadcasts through Radio Free Europe, revolted against Communist troops in Budapest. The Soviets responded by sending 500,000 soldiers and 4,000 tanks into Hungary, where they killed thousands of Hungarian "freedom fighters" before installing a new puppet government.

Eisenhower offered his sympathy for the Hungarian people, but nothing more. His strategy in dealing with such crises was, as he later said, "Take a hard line—and bluff." Although he avoided war over the Soviet

falling domino theory Theory that if one country fell to communism, its neighboring countries would necessarily follow suit.

suppression of democracy in Hungary, Eisenhower had allowed administration officials, especially Secretary of State Dulles, to make reckless pledges about "rolling back" communism and "liberating" the nations of Eastern Europe. "To all those suffering under Communist slavery," Dulles promised, "let us say you can count on us."

In Hungary, the Soviets called the Eisenhower administration's bluff. The Hungarian freedom fighters, having been led to expect U.S. support, paid with their lives. Vice President Richard Nixon cynically reassured Eisenhower that the Soviet crackdown on the rebellion would be beneficial in showing the world the ruthlessness of communism. The president, however, felt pangs of guilt, telling Dulles that "we have excited Hungarians for all these years," and are "now turning our backs on them when they are in a jam." Dulles showed little concern, reminding the president that "we always have been against violent rebellion."

The Suez War

Eisenhower was more successful in handling an unexpected international crisis in Egypt, which occurred at the same time as the revolt in Hungary. In 1952, an Egyptian army officer, Gamal Abdel Nasser, had overthrown King Farouk. Once in power, Nasser set out to become the leader of the entire Arab world. To do so, he promised to destroy the new Israeli nation, created in 1948. Nasser, with Soviet support, first sought control of the Suez Canal, the crucial international waterway in Egypt connecting the Mediterranean and Red Seas. The canal had opened in 1869 as a joint French-Egyptian venture, and from 1882 on, British troops protected the canal as the British Empire's "lifeline" to India and its other Asian colonies. When Nasser's nationalist regime pressed for the withdrawal of the British forces, Eisenhower and Dulles supported the demand. In 1954, an Anglo-Egyptian treaty provided for British withdrawal within twenty months.

In 1955, Nasser, adept at playing both sides in the cold war, announced a huge arms deal with the Soviet Union. The United States countered by offering to help Egypt finance a massive hydroelectric dam at Aswan on the Nile River. In 1956, when Nasser increased trade with the Soviet bloc and recognized the People's Republic of China, Dulles abruptly cancelled the offer to fund the Aswan Dam.

Unable to retaliate directly against the United States, Nasser seized control of the Suez Canal Company and denied access to Israel-bound ships. The British and French were furious. On October 29, 1956, while Hungarian rebels were battling Soviet tanks, Israeli, British, and French forces invaded Egypt. Nasser responded by sinking all forty of the international ships then in the Suez Canal. A few days later, Anglo-French commandos and paratroopers took control of the canal.

The attack on Egypt by Britain, France, and Israel almost destroyed the NATO alliance. Eisenhower saw the military action as a revival of the "old-fashioned gunboat diplomacy" associated with colonial imperialism: "How could we possibly support Britain and France," he asked, "if in doing so we

Cease-fire in Suez crisis

lose the whole Arab world?" Eisenhower adopted a bold stance. He demanded that the British and French withdraw from the Suez Canal and that the Israelis evacuate the Sinai peninsula—or face severe economic sanctions. That the three aggressor nations grudgingly complied with a cease-fire agreement on November 7 testified to Eisenhower's strength, influence, and savvy in dealing with military matters.

The **Suez crisis** and the Hungarian revolt led Adlai Stevenson to declare the administration's foreign policy "bankrupt." Most voters, however, reasoned that the foreign turmoil spelled a poor time to switch leaders, and they handed Eisenhower an even more lopsided victory than the one in 1952. In carrying Louisiana, Eisenhower became the first Republican to win a Lower South state since Reconstruction; nationally, he carried all but seven states and won the electoral vote by 457 to 73. Eisenhower's decisive victory, however, failed to swing a congressional majority for his party in either house.

Reactions to Sputnik

Sputnik (1957)

On October 4, 1957, the Soviets launched the first communications satellite, called *Sputnik 1*. NBC News reported that it was "the most important story of the century." Americans panicked at the news. The Soviet success in space dealt a severe blow to the prestige of American science and technology, which had seemed unquestionably preeminent since the Second World War. It also changed the military balance of power. If the Soviets were so advanced in rocketry, many people reasoned, then perhaps they could hit U.S. cities with nuclear missiles. Democrats charged that the Soviets had "humiliated" the United States; they launched a congressional investigation to assess the new threat to the nation's security.

"*Sputnik* mania" led the United States to increase defense spending and establish a crash program to enhance science education. In 1958, Congress created the National Aeronautics and Space Administration (NASA) to coordinate research and development related to outer space. The same year, Congress, with Eisenhower's support, enacted the National Defense Education Act (NDEA), which authorized massive federal grants to colleges and universities to enhance education and research in mathematics, science, and modern languages, as well as for student loans and fellowships. The NDEA provided more financial aid to higher education than any other previous legislation.

The Eisenhower Doctrine

In the aftermath of the Suez crisis, Eisenhower decided that the United States must replace Great Britain and France as the guarantor of Western interests in the Middle East. In 1958, Congress approved what came to be called the Eisenhower Doctrine, a resolution that promised to extend economic and military aid to Arab nations and to use armed force if necessary to assist any such nation against Communist aggression. When

Suez crisis (1956) British, French, and Israeli attack on Egypt after Nasser's seizure of the Suez Canal; President Eisenhower interceded to demand the withdrawal of the British, French, and Israeli forces from the Sinai peninsula and the strategic canal.

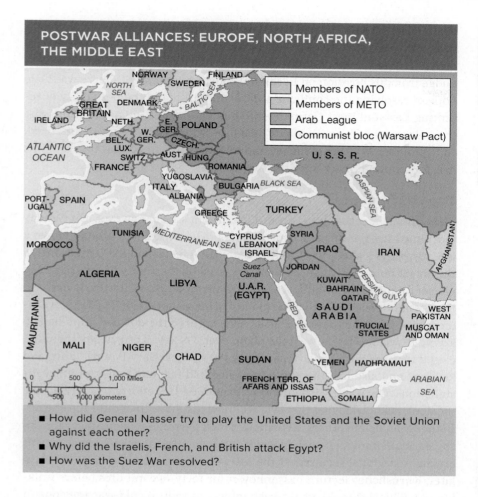

POSTWAR ALLIANCES: EUROPE, NORTH AFRICA, THE MIDDLE EAST

Legend:
- Members of NATO
- Members of METO
- Arab League
- Communist bloc (Warsaw Pact)

- How did General Nasser try to play the United States and the Soviet Union against each other?
- Why did the Israelis, French, and British attack Egypt?
- How was the Suez War resolved?

Lebanon appealed to the United States to help fend off an insurgency, Eisenhower ordered 5,000 marines into the country. In October 1958, once the situation had stabilized, U.S. forces (up to 15,000 at one point) withdrew.

Crisis in Berlin

The unique problem of West Berlin, an island of Western capitalism deep in Soviet-controlled East Germany, boiled over in the late 1950s. Since the Second World War, West Berlin had served as a "showplace" of Western democracy and prosperity, a listening post for Western intelligence gathering, and a funnel through which news and propaganda from the West penetrated what British leader Winston Churchill had labeled "the iron curtain." Although East Germany had sealed its western frontiers, refugees could still pass from East to West Berlin. On November 10, 1958, however, Nikita Khrushchev, the unpredictable Soviet leader who had earlier boasted that "history is on our side. We will bury you," threatened to give East Germany control of East Berlin and of the air lanes into West Berlin. After the

Nikita Khrushchev The Soviet premier speaks on the problem of the divided city of Berlin, 1959.

U.S.–Soviet setback: The U-2 conflict; diplomatic relations with Cuba suspended

deadline he set (May 27, 1959), Western occupation authorities would have to deal with the Soviet-controlled East German government, in effect recognizing it, or face the possibility of another blockade. Eisenhower refused to budge from his position on Berlin but sought a settlement. There was little hope of resolving the conflicting views on Berlin and the possibility of re-uniting East and West Germany into one nation, but the negotiations distracted attention from the May 27 deadline, which passed almost unnoticed. In September 1959, Khrushchev and Eisenhower agreed that the time was ripe for a summit meeting of the two leaders.

The U-2 Summit

The summit meeting blew up in Eisenhower's face, however. On Sunday morning, May 1, 1960, he learned that a Soviet rocket had brought down a U.S. spy plane (called the U-2) flying at 70,000 feet some 1,200 miles inside the Soviet border. Khrushchev, embarrassed by the ability of American spy planes to enter Soviet airspace, sprang a trap on Eisenhower. At first the Soviets announced only that the plane had been shot down. The U.S. government, not realizing that the Soviets had captured the downed pilot, lied by saying it was missing a weather plane over Turkey. Khrushchev then disclosed that the Soviets had American pilot Francis Gary Powers "alive and kicking" and also had the photographs he had taken of Soviet military installations. On May 11, Eisenhower abandoned U.S. efforts to cover up the incident, acknowledging that "we will now just have to endure the storm." Rather than blame others, Eisenhower took personal responsibility for the spying, explaining that such illegally obtained intelligence information was crucial to national security. At the testy summit meeting in Paris five days later, Khrushchev lectured Eisenhower for forty-five minutes before walking out. The U-2 incident set back efforts to reduce cold war tensions in Berlin and worldwide. Later, in 1962, Francis Gary Powers would be exchanged for a captured Soviet spy.

Castro's Cuba

Of all of Eisenhower's crises in foreign affairs, the greatest embarrassment was Fidel Castro's new communist regime in Cuba, which came to power on January 1, 1959, after two years of guerrilla warfare against the U.S.-supported dictator, Fulgencio Batista. Castro readily embraced Soviet support, leading a CIA agent to predict, "We're going to take care of Castro just like we took care of Arbenz [in Guatemala]." The Soviets warned that any American intervention in Cuba would trigger a military response. One of Eisenhower's last acts as president, on January 3, 1961, was to suspend diplomatic relations with Castro's Cuba. Eisenhower also authorized a secret CIA operation to train a force of Cuban refugees to oust Castro. But the final decision on the use of the anti-Castro invasion force would rest with the next president, John F. Kennedy.

Fidel Castro Castro (center) became Cuba's Communist premier in 1959 after three years of guerrilla warfare.

Assessing the Eisenhower Presidency

During President Eisenhower's second term, Congress added Alaska and Hawaii as the forty-ninth and fiftieth states (1959), while the nation experienced its worst economic slump since the Great Depression. Volatile issues such as civil rights, defense policy, and corrupt aides, including White House chief of staff Sherman Adams, Eisenhower's most trusted and influential adviser, compounded the administration's troubles. The president's desire to avoid divisive issues and maintain public goodwill led him at times to value harmony and popularity over justice. One observer called the Eisenhower years "the time of the great postponement," during which the president left domestic and foreign policies "about where he found them in 1953."

Opinion of Eisenhower's presidency has improved with time, however. After all, Eisenhower presided with steady self-confidence over a nation content with a leader whose essential virtue was prudence. He fulfilled his pledge to end the war in Korea, refused to intervene militarily in Indochina, and maintained the peace in the face of explosive global tensions. Eisenhower's greatest decisions were the wars he chose to avoid. After the truce in Korea, not a single American soldier died in combat during his two administrations, something no president since has achieved. For the most part, he acted with poise, restraint, and intelligence in managing an increasingly complex cold war that he predicted would last for decades. If Eisenhower did little to address social and racial problems, he did balance the budget while sustaining the major reforms of the New Deal. If he tolerated unemployment of as much as 7 percent, he saw to it that inflation remained minimal. Even Adlai Stevenson, defeated twice by Eisenhower, admitted that Ike's victory in 1952 had been good for America. "I like Ike, too," he said.

Eisenhower's January 17, 1961, farewell address to the American people focused on a topic never before addressed by a public official: the threat posed to government integrity by "an immense military establishment and a large arms industry." As a much-celebrated military leader, it was all the more striking for Eisenhower to highlight the dangers of a large "military-industrial complex" exerting "unwarranted influence" in Congress and the White House. "The potential for the disastrous rise of misplaced power exists and will persist," he warned. Eisenhower confessed that his greatest disappointment was that he could affirm only that "war has been avoided," not that "a lasting peace is in sight." Despite the combative language of Secretary of State John Foster Dulles, Eisenhower never promoted warfare as an instrument of foreign policy. Instead, he pledged to "do anything to achieve peace within honorable means. I'll travel anywhere. I'll talk to anyone." His successors were not as successful in keeping war at bay.

Political Consensus after World War II

President Dwight D. Eisenhower's policies and personality symbolized American politics in the 1950s. As the first Republican president since Herbert Hoover, he inherited a federal government whose roles, responsibilities, and institutions had expanded profoundly since the 1920s. An advocate of "moderate Republicanism," he did not seek to undo most of the programs created by the New Deal and Fair Deal of Presidents Roosevelt and Truman, although he complained about their expense. In comparing Eisenhower's policies and positions to those of his Democratic predecessor, Harry Truman, broad patterns of agreement are evident, reflecting a postwar consensus among the American electorate. As you review the following chart comparing the two presidents' positions on domestic policies, foreign affairs, and civil rights, consider the questions at the end of this exercise.

	Harry Truman, 1945–1953	Dwight Eisenhower, 1953–1961
Domestic Policy: "Expansion of the New Deal"	Truman's Fair Deal called for national health insurance and an expansion of many popular New Deal programs (however, most of his proposals were rejected by a conservative Congress): 1. expansion of social security coverage 2. farm subsidies 3. a higher minimum wage 4. federal aid to education 5. increased public housing 6. public works construction projects 7. opposition to the Taft-Hartley legislation	Eisenhower called for an end to "political and social engineering from the federal government" and opposed national health insurance, but he favored sustaining and expanding other popular New and Fair Deal programs: 1. expansion of social security coverage 2. support for existing farm programs 3. a higher minimum wage 4. increased spending on science education 5. increased public housing 6. major public works projects: St. Lawrence seaway and the interstate highway system 7. support for existing labor laws

	Harry Truman, 1945–1953	Dwight Eisenhower, 1953–1961
Foreign Affairs: "Policies and Strategies to Contain Communism"	**1.** Initiated a global containment strategy (the Truman Doctrine) to block Soviet expansionism after World War II. **2.** The United States joined NATO and began stationing troops in Western Europe. **3.** Committed U.S. military forces to defend noncommunist South Korea from communist North Korean aggression. **4.** Promoted military and financial assistance to nations resisting communism. Increased assistance to French forces fighting a communist independence movement in Vietnam. **5.** Sustained high defense spendings to wage the cold war and authorized the development of the hydrogen bomb.	**1.** Committed to containing the Soviet Union but also spoke of "rolling back" communism. **2.** Supported NATO and expanded American alliances to wage the cold war through covert C.I.A. operations rather than troops. **3.** Negotiated an end to the Korean War and resisted calls for military intervention in Vietnam. **4.** Empowered the CIA to covertly work to overthrow leftist regimes in Iran, Guatemala, and Cuba but did not use force to support the Hungarian revolt against Soviet Russia. Committed the United States to fighting communism in the Middle East (the Eisenhower Doctrine). Committed the United States to upholding an independent noncommunist South Vietnam. **5.** Reduced overall military spending, expanding the cold war instead through threats of nuclear retaliation.
Civil Rights: "Desegregation" and "Voting Rights"	**1.** Proposed a major civil rights bill to Congress. **2.** Through executive orders, desegregated the armed forces and banned racial discrimination in federal employment.	**1.** Supported Civil Rights Acts in 1957 and 1960 which committed the federal government to protect the voting rights of African Americans, but gave federal authorities no real power to enforce the commitment. **2.** Sent federal troops to enforce the desegregation of a high school in Little Rock in the *Brown* decision, but he never pushed Southern states to comply with the law.

QUESTIONS FOR ANALYSIS

1. How did each president view the reforms of the New Deal period and what did each believe was the role of the federal government in the nation's economic life?

2. How did Truman and Eisenhower differ in their strategies towards containing Soviet expansion abroad?

3. What role did Truman and Eisenhower believe they should play as president in addressing racial inequality?

4. In what areas do their presidencies suggest broad agreement among the American voters after World War II? Where was there less consensus?

■ **Eisenhower's Dynamic Conservatism**
As president, Dwight Eisenhower promoted what he called *moderate Republicanism* or "dynamic conservatism." While critical of excessive government spending on social programs, he also expanded Social Security coverage and launched ambitious public works programs, such as the *Federal-Aid Highway Act* that constructed the Interstate Highway System. He opposed large budget deficits, however, and cut spending on national defense and an array of domestic programs.

■ **Growth of the U.S. Economy** High levels of federal government spending, begun before the war, continued during the postwar period. The *GI Bill of Rights* boosted home buying and helped many veterans attend college and enter the middle class. Consumer demand for homes, cars, and household goods that had been unavailable during the war fueled the economy, as did buying with new credit cards as well as demand created by the *baby boom*. After the Second World War, with the growth of *suburbia*, corporations, and advertising, America's mass culture displayed what critics called a bland sameness. A large majority of Americans, including many in the working class, experienced unprecedented rising living standards during the 1950s. But discrimination in the work force continued against African Americans, Hispanics, and women who were relegated to lower paying jobs. African Americans were largely excluded from the new suburbs, and women experienced enormous social pressure to marry and raise children as opposed to pursuing careers.

■ **Critics of Mainstream Culture**
The *Beats* rebelled against what they claimed was the suffocating conformity of middle-class life in the fifties, as did many other writers and artists. Adolescents rebelled through acts of juvenile delinquency and a new form of sexually provocative music called rock 'n' roll. Pockets of chronic poverty persisted despite record-breaking economic growth, and minorities did not prosper to the extent that white Americans did.

■ **Civil Rights Movement** During the early 1950s, the NAACP mounted legal challenges in federal courts to states requiring racially segregated public schools. In the most significant case, *Brown v. Board of Education (1954)*, the U.S. Supreme Court nullified the *separate-but-equal* doctrine. Many white southerners adopted a strategy of *massive resistance* against court-ordered desegregation. In response, civil rights activists, both blacks and whites, used *nonviolent civil disobedience* to force local and state officials to allow integration, as demonstrated in the *Montgomery bus boycott* in Alabama and the forced desegregation of public schools in Little Rock, Arkansas. Martin Luther King organized the *Southern Christian Leadership Conference (SCLC)* to rally civil rights opposition after white violence against activists in Little Rock. In 1957, the U.S. Congress passed a Civil Rights Act intended to stop discrimination against black voters in the South, but it was rarely enforced.

■ **American Foreign Policy in the 1950s**
Eisenhower's first major foreign-policy accomplishment was to end the fighting in Korea. Thereafter, Eisenhower kept the nation out of war. Instead, he relied on secret *Central Intelligence Agency (CIA)* intervention, financial and military aid, and threats of *massive retaliation* to stem the spread of communism. Though American aid was not enough to save the French at *Dien Bien Phu*, Eisenhower's belief in the *falling domino theory* deepened U.S. support for the government in South Vietnam in its war with North Vietnam and the communist *Viet Cong* insurgents. He came closest to ordering military intervention in the *Suez crisis*, but was able to mediate a solution. Closer to home, however, he approved a secret CIA operation to overthrow Fidel Castro, Cuba's communist leader.

KEY TERMS

moderate Republicanism *p. 966*

Federal-Aid Highway Act (1956) *p. 969*

GI Bill of Rights (1944) *p. 972*

suburbia *p. 973*

baby boom *p. 978*

Beats *p. 981*

separate-but-equal *p. 985*

Brown v. Board of Education (1954) *p. 985*

Montgomery bus boycott *p. 986*

nonviolent civil disobedience *p. 987*

massive resistance *p. 989*

Southern Christian Leadership Conference (SCLC) *p. 990*

massive retaliation *p. 992*

Central Intelligence Agency (CIA) *p. 992*

Dien Bien Phu *p. 993*

Viet Cong *p. 995*

falling domino theory *p. 996*

Suez crisis (1956) *p. 998*

CHRONOLOGY

1949	The first credit card is introduced
1952	Eisenhower wins the presidency
July 1953	Armistice is reached in Korea
	CIA organizes the overthrow of Mohammed Mossadegh in Iran and Jacobo Arbenz Guzman in Guatemala
1954	*Brown v. Board of Education*
July 1954	Geneva Accords adopted
December 1955	Montgomery, Alabama, bus boycott begins
1956	Elvis Presley releases "Heartbreak Hotel"
	Congress passes the Federal-Aid Highway Act
	Soviets suppress Hungarian revolt
	In Suez War, Israel, Britain, and France attack Egypt
1957	Desegregation of Central High School in Little Rock, Arkansas
	Soviet Union launches *Sputnik 1* satellite
	Baby boom peaks
1959	Fidel Castro seizes power in Cuba
1960	The U-2 incident

INQUIZITIVE

Go to InQuizitive to see what you've learned—and learn what you've missed—with personalized feedback along the way.

SKYWAY (1964) With new frontiers came new fears. Artist Robert Rauschenberg's collage encapsulates the turbulence of the sixties: the stark collisions of the old and the new, and the total disorder of it all. John F. Kennedy, early manned space flights, and the Vietnam War are suspended within the childish form of the collage, making Rauschenberg's message all the more foreboding.

New Frontiers

1960–1968

For those who considered the social and political climate of the fifties dull, the following decade provided a striking contrast. The sixties were years of extraordinary social turbulence and liberal activism, tragic assassinations and painful trauma. Assassins killed four of the most important leaders of the time: John F. Kennedy, Malcolm X, Martin Luther King, and Robert F. Kennedy. The "politics of expectation" that a British journalist said shone brightly in Kennedy's short tenure as president did not die with the president in November 1963. Instead, Kennedy's idealistic commitment to improving America's quality of life—for everyone—was given new meaning and energy by his very different successor, Texan Lyndon B. Johnson, whose War on Poverty and Great Society programs outstripped Franklin Roosevelt's New Deal in their scope and promises.

Johnson's remarkable energy and legislative savvy resulted in a blizzard of new federal programs. At the same time, many social issues that had been ignored or postponed for decades—civil rights for minorities, equality for women, gay rights, federal aid to the poor—forced their way to the forefront of national concerns. In the end, however, Lyndon Johnson promised too much. The elaborate Great Society programs fell victim to unrealistic hopes, poor execution, and the nation's expanding involvement with the war in Vietnam. The deeply entrenched assumptions of the cold war against global communism led the nation into the longest, most controversial, and least successful war in its history to that point.

CORE OBJECTIVES INQUIZITIVE

1. Assess President John F. Kennedy's efforts to contain communism abroad and pursue civil rights and other social programs at home.

2. Describe the strategies and achievements of the civil rights movement in the 1960s, and explain the divisions that emerged among its activists during the decade.

3. Analyze Lyndon B. Johnson's War on Poverty and Great Society initiatives, and evaluate their impact on American society.

4. Explain Presidents Kennedy and Johnson's motivations for deepening America's military involvement in the Vietnam War and appraise their efforts to preserve a noncommunist South Vietnam.

5. Examine the presidential election of 1968 and explain the issues that propelled Richard Nixon to victory.

The New Frontier

In his 1960 speech accepting the Democratic presidential nomination, John F. Kennedy showcased the muscular language that would stamp the rest of his campaign and his presidency: "We stand today on the edge of a **New Frontier**—the frontier of unknown opportunities and perils—a frontier of unfulfilled hopes and threats." Kennedy and his staff fastened upon the frontier metaphor as the label for their proposed domestic program because they believed that Americans had always been adventurers, eager to conquer and exploit new frontiers. Kennedy promised that if elected he would get the country "moving again" and be a more aggressive cold warrior than Eisenhower.

Kennedy versus Nixon

In 1960, the presidential election pitted two candidates—Vice President Richard M. Nixon and Massachusetts senator John F. Kennedy (JFK)—of similar ages but contrasting personalities and backgrounds. As the popular Eisenhower's partner over successive terms, Nixon was assured the Republican nomination for president in 1960. A native of California, he had fought tenaciously to be a success, first as an attorney, then as a congressman. He had come to Washington eager to reverse the tide of New Deal liberalism. His visibility among Republicans benefited from his leadership of the anti-Communist hearings in Congress during the McCarthy hysteria.

New Frontier Proposed domestic program championed by the incoming Kennedy administration in 1961 that aimed to jump-start the economy and trigger social progress.

All his life, Nixon had had to claw and struggle to the top. Now he had the presidency within his grasp. But Nixon, graceless, awkward, and stiff, proved to be one of the most complicated and most interesting political figures in American history.

By 1960, Vice President Nixon had developed the reputation for being a cunning deceiver, the "Tricky Dick" who concealed his real ideas and bigoted attitudes. Kennedy told an aide that "Nixon doesn't know who he is . . . so every time he makes a speech he has to decide which Nixon he is, and that will be very exhausting."

The forty-three-year-old Kennedy had not distinguished himself in the House or the Senate, but he was handsome and charming, and he had the energy and wit to match his grace and ambition. He also had a bright, agile mind, a quick wit, a Harvard education, a record of heroism in the

The Kennedy–Nixon debates Nixon's decision to debate his less prominent opponent on television backfired.

Second World War, a rich and powerful Roman Catholic family, and a beautiful, accomplished, and young wife, only 32 years-old. In the words of a southern senator, Kennedy combined "the best qualities of Elvis Presley and Franklin D. Roosevelt"—a combination that played well in the first-ever televised presidential debate. Some 70 million people tuned in and saw an obviously uncomfortable Nixon, still weak from a recent illness, perspiring heavily and looking pale, haggard, and even sinister before the camera. Kennedy, on the other hand, appeared tanned and calm, projected a cool poise, and offered crisp answers that made him seem Nixon's equal, if not superior, in his fitness for the nation's highest office.

John Kennedy's political rise owed much to the effective public relations campaign engineered by his father, Joseph Kennedy, a self-made tycoon with a genius for promotion. "Can't you get it into your head," the elder Kennedy told John, "that it's not important what you *really* are? The only important thing is what people *think* you are." To ensure that people thought well of his son, the elder Kennedy hired writers to produce his son's two books, paid a publisher to print them, purchased thousands of copies to make them "best sellers," and helped engineer his son's elections to the Congress and Senate.

Yet much of the glamour surrounding Kennedy was cosmetic. Despite his athletic interests and robust appearance, he suffered from lifelong health problems: Addison's disease (a debilitating disorder of the adrenal glands), venereal disease, chronic back pain, and fierce fevers. He took powerful prescription medicines daily, sometimes hourly. Like Franklin D. Roosevelt, he and his aides and family members masked from the public his physical ailments—as well as his reckless sexual forays.

The momentum that Kennedy gained from the first debate with Nixon was not enough to ensure his victory. The Democratic candidate became a relentless campaigner— traveling 65,000 miles, visiting 25 states, and making over 350 speeches— including an address to Protestant ministers in Texas in which he neutralized concerns about his being a Roman Catholic by stressing that the pope in Rome would never "tell the President—should he be a Catholic—how to

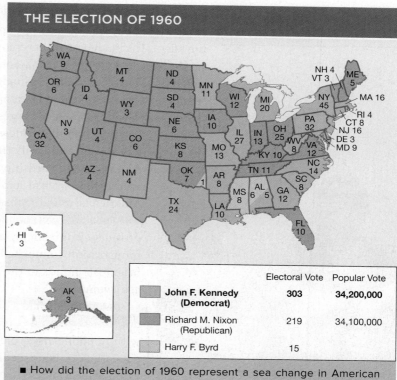

THE ELECTION OF 1960

	Electoral Vote	Popular Vote
John F. Kennedy (Democrat)	303	34,200,000
Richard M. Nixon (Republican)	219	34,100,000
Harry F. Byrd	15	

- How did the election of 1960 represent a sea change in American presidential politics?
- What three events shaped the campaign?
- How did John F. Kennedy win the election in spite of winning fewer states than Richard M. Nixon?

act." Kennedy also worked to increase the registration of African American voters across the nation, and he won the hearts of many black voters by helping to get Martin Luther King Jr. out of a Georgia jail after he had been convicted of "trespassing" in an all-white restaurant. "I've got a suitcase of votes," explained King's appreciative father, "and I'm going to take them to Mr. Kennedy and dump them in his lap." On the Sunday before election day, a million leaflets about Kennedy's enabling King's release from prison were distributed in African American churches across the nation.

When the votes were counted, Kennedy and his running mate, the powerful Texas senator Lyndon B. Johnson, had won the closest presidential election since 1888. The winning margin was only 118,574 votes out of more than 68 million cast. Nixon had carried more states than Kennedy, sweeping most of the West and holding four of the six southern states that Eisenhower had carried in 1956. But Kennedy won 70 percent of the black vote, which proved decisive in at least three key states.

A Vigorous New Administration

Kennedy's New Frontier

John F. Kennedy was the youngest person and first Roman Catholic elected president. His inauguration ceremony on a cold, clear, blustery January day set the tone of youthful elegance, charm, and energy that would come to be called the *Kennedy style*. In his inaugural speech, the president quite intentionally spoke as the leader of "a new generation of Americans," implying that Eisenhower had come to represent older Americans. Kennedy dazzled listeners with uplifting words: "Let every nation know, whether it wishes us well or ill, that we shall pay any price, bear any burden, meet any hardship, support any friend, oppose any foe, to assure the survival and success of liberty. And so, my fellow Americans: ask not what your country can do for you—ask what *you* can do for your country." Such inspiring language heralded a presidency of fresh promise and new beginnings, an activist administration committed to bringing together the "best and the brightest" minds in the nation to fashion a new era in political achievement.

Yet Kennedy had a difficult time launching his New Frontier domestic program. Conservative southern Democrats joined with Republicans to block his efforts to increase federal aid to education, provide medical insurance for the aged, and create a cabinet-level department of urban affairs and housing to address poverty in the inner cities. Legislators did approve the Peace Corps, created in 1961 to recruit idealistic young volunteers who would provide educational and technical service abroad, and also the Alliance for Progress, a financial assistance program to Latin American countries intended to blunt the appeal of communism in those nations. The Kennedy administration further persuaded Congress to increase the minimum wage

Jack and Jackie Young, refined, and fabulous, the Kennedys were instant celebrities. Women teased their hair into the First Lady's famous hairdo, while men craved JFK's effortless cool.

and pass a Housing Act that earmarked nearly $5 billion for new public housing projects in poverty-stricken inner-city areas. Kennedy also won support for an accelerated space program with the audacious goal of landing astronauts on the moon before the end of the decade.

Kennedy and Civil Rights

The most important development in domestic life during the sixties occurred in civil rights. Throughout the South, racial segregation remained firmly in place. Signs outside public restrooms distinguished between "Whites" and "Colored"; restaurants declared "Colored Not Allowed," or "Colored Served Only in Rear." Stores prohibited African Americans from trying on clothes before buying them. Witnesses in courtrooms were sworn in with their hands placed on different Bibles, depending on their race. Despite the *Brown v. Board of Education* ruling in 1954, many public schools across the South remained segregated and unequal in quality.

Like Franklin D. Roosevelt, John F. Kennedy celebrated racial equality but did little to promote it until events forced him to do so. He was reluctant to challenge conservative southern Democrats on the explosive issue of segregation. Both he and his brother Robert ("Bobby"), the attorney general as well as the president's closest adviser, had to be dragged unwillingly into actively supporting the civil rights movement.

Catastrophe in Cuba

Kennedy's record in foreign relations, as in domestic affairs, was mixed, but more spectacularly so. Although he had told a reporter that he wanted to "break out of the confines of the Cold War," he quickly found himself reinforcing its confining assumptions. While still a senator, Kennedy had blasted Eisenhower for not being tough enough with the Soviets and for allowing Fidel Castro and his Communist followers to take over Cuba in 1959.

Walk of shame Captured anti-Castro Cubans at the Bay of Pigs.

Soon after his inauguration, Kennedy learned that a secret CIA operation, approved by Eisenhower, was training 1,500 anti-Castro Cubans for an invasion of their homeland. U.S. military leaders assured Kennedy that the invasion plan (Operation Trinidad) was feasible; CIA analysts predicted that news of the invasion would inspire anti-Castro Cubans to rebel against their Communist dictator. In reality, the covert operation had little chance of succeeding. When the ragtag force, transported on American ships, landed at the **Bay of Pigs** on Cuba's south shore on April 17, 1961, it was

Bay of Pigs (1961) Failed CIA operation that deployed Cuban rebels to overthrow Fidel Castro's Communist regime.

Severed ties Two West Berliners climb the newly constructed Berlin Wall to communicate with a family member at an open window.

quickly defeated. Kennedy panicked when he realized the operation was failing and refused desperate pleas from the Cuban rebels for "promised" support from U.S. warplanes. A *New York Times* columnist reported that the Americans involved in the botched invasion "looked like fools to our friends, rascals to our enemies, and incompetents to the rest." The clumsy effort to overthrow the Cuban government humiliated the new American president. To his credit, Kennedy admitted that the Bay of Pigs invasion was a "colossal mistake" and "the worst experience of my life."

The Vienna Summit

Berlin Wall

Just six weeks after the Bay of Pigs fiasco, Kennedy, heavily medicated because of chronic back pain, met Soviet premier Nikita Khrushchev at a summit conference in Vienna, Austria. Khrushchev bullied the young president and threatened to limit American access to Berlin, the divided city inside Communist East Germany. Kennedy, desperate not to appear weak, responded by calling up Army Reserve and National Guard units to protect West Berlin. Then on August 13, 1961, the Soviets decided to stop all traffic between East and West Berlin by erecting the twenty-seven-mile-long **Berlin Wall**, made of concrete and topped with barbed wire. For the United States, the wall became a powerful propaganda weapon. As Kennedy said, "Freedom has many difficulties and democracy is not perfect, but we have never had to put up a wall to keep our people in."

The Berlin Wall demonstrated the Soviets' willingness to challenge American resolve in Europe. Kennedy and Secretary of Defense Robert McNamara responded by embarking upon the most intensive arms race in history, increasing the number of nuclear missiles fivefold, adding 300,000 men to the armed forces, and creating the U.S. Special Forces

Berlin Wall Twenty-seven-mile-long concrete wall constructed in 1961 by East German authorities to stop the flow of East Germans fleeing to West Berlin.

(Green Berets), an elite group of commandos specializing in guerrilla warfare who could provide a "more flexible response" than nuclear weapons to "hotspots" around the world and enable the United States to wage small wars in faraway lands.

> Green Berets

The Cuban Missile Crisis

In the fall of 1962, Nikita Khrushchev and the Soviets posed another challenge to Kennedy, this time only ninety miles off the Florida coast. To protect Communist Cuba from another American-backed invasion, Khrushchev approved the secret installation of Soviet missiles on the island nation. The Soviets felt they were justified in doing so because the United States had earlier installed missiles with nuclear warheads in Turkey, along the Soviet border.

> Soviet missiles in Cuba

On October 16, 1962, photos taken by U.S. spy planes revealed the Soviet missile sites in Cuba. Although the Soviet actions violated no law or treaty, Kennedy decided that the forty or so missiles had to be removed. But how? As the air force chief of staff told Kennedy, "You're in a pretty bad fix, Mr. President."

Over the next thirteen days, perhaps the most dangerous two weeks in history, Kennedy and the National Security Council (NSC) discussed several possible responses, ranging from doing nothing to invading Cuba. The commander of the Marines at one point reminded the group that the missiles in Cuba were not a true threat. The Soviet Union "has a hell of a lot better way to attack us than to attack us from Cuba." Yet the group insisted that the missiles be removed for symbolic reasons.

> Naval quarantine of Cuba

At that point, the world came closer to a war involving the exchange of nuclear weapons than it ever has before or since. Kennedy and the NSC discussed in some detail the unthinkable possibility of a nuclear war, even estimating the damage that atomic bombs might inflict on major cities. Eventually, however, the group narrowed the options to a choice between a "surgical" air strike on the missiles and a naval blockade of Cuba. Although the military advisers urged bombing the missile sites followed by an invasion of the island, Kennedy chose the naval blockade, which was carefully disguised by calling it a *quarantine*, since a *blockade* is technically an act of war.

On Monday night, October 22, President Kennedy delivered a solemn speech to the world, announcing that the U.S. Navy was establishing a naval quarantine of Cuba to prevent Soviet ships from delivering the goods and weapons that the island nation depended on. He urged the Soviets to "move the world back from the abyss of destruction."

Tensions grew as Khrushchev replied that Soviet ships would ignore the quarantine. He accused Kennedy of "an act of aggression propelling humankind into the abyss of a world nuclear-missile war." Despite such rhetoric, however, on Wednesday, October 24, five Soviet ships, presumably with more missiles aboard, stopped well short of the quarantine line.

> Soviets remove missiles under nuclear threat

Two days later, Khrushchev, knowing that the U.S. still enjoyed a 5 to 1 advantage in nuclear weapons, offered a deal. The Soviets would remove the missiles in return for a *public* pledge by the United States not to invade Cuba—and a *secret* agreement to remove U.S. missiles from Turkey. Kennedy agreed. Secretary of State Dean Rusk stressed to a newscaster, "Remember, when you report this, [say] that eyeball to eyeball, they [the Soviets] blinked first."

In the aftermath of the **Cuban missile crisis**, tensions between the United States and the Soviet Union subsided, in part because of several symbolic steps: an agreement to sell the Soviet Union surplus American wheat, the installation of a "hotline" telephone between Washington and Moscow to provide instant contact between the heads of government, and the removal of aging U.S. missiles from Turkey, Italy, and Britain.

Controlling Atomic Weapons

Test Ban Treaty: Bans testing of nuclear weapons in the atmosphere

Going to the edge of nuclear war over Soviet missiles in Cuba led Kennedy and others in the administration to soften their cold war rhetoric and pursue other ways to reduce the threat of atomic warfare. As Kennedy told his advisers at a White House meeting, "It is insane that two men, sitting on opposite sides of the world, should be able to decide to bring an end to civilization." In June 1963, the president began discussions with the Soviets to reduce the risk of nuclear war. "If we cannot end our differences," he said, "at least we can help make the world a safe place for diversity." After two months of difficult negotiations, those discussions resulted in the Test Ban Treaty with the Soviet Union and Great Britain, ratified in September 1963, which banned the testing of nuclear weapons in the atmosphere. It was an important move toward improved relations with the Soviet Union. As Kennedy put it, using an ancient Chinese proverb, "A journey of a thousand miles begins with one step."

Kennedy and Vietnam

Military advisers in Vietnam

As tensions with the Soviet Union eased, a new crisis was growing in Southeast Asia, where events were moving toward what would eventually become the greatest American foreign-policy calamity of the century. The situation in South Vietnam had worsened under the corrupt leadership of Premier Ngo Dinh Diem and his family. He had backed away from promised social and economic reforms, and his repressive tactics, directed not only against Communists but also against the Buddhist majority and other critics, played into the hands of his enemies. Kennedy continued to dispatch military "advisers" to South Vietnam in the hope of stabilizing the situation (they were called advisers to avoid the impression that U.S. troops were doing the fighting). When he took office, the United States had 2,000 troops in Vietnam; by the end of 1963, there were 16,000, all of whom were officially classified as advisers rather than combatants.

Cuban missile crisis (1962) Thirteen-day U.S.-Soviet standoff sparked by the discovery of Soviet missile sites in Cuba; closest the world has come to nuclear war since 1945.

By 1963, Kennedy was receiving sharply conflicting reports from South Vietnam. U.S. military analysts expressed confidence in the Army of the Republic of Vietnam. On-site journalists, however, predicted civil turmoil as long as Diem remained in power. By midyear, frequent Buddhist demonstrations against Diem ignited widespread discontent. The spectacle of Buddhist monks setting themselves on fire in public squares to protest government tyranny stunned Americans. By the fall of 1963, the Kennedy administration had decided that the autocratic Diem was "out of touch with his people" and had to go. On November 1, army generals seized the South Vietnamese government but then took a step that Kennedy had neither intended nor expected: they murdered Diem and his brother. The rebel generals, however, provided no more political stability than had Diem, and successive coups set the fragile country spinning from one military leader to another.

United States backs coup in South Vietnam

By September 1963, Kennedy seemed to have developed doubts about the ability of the United States to prop up the South Vietnamese government. When asked about the South Vietnamese effort to hold off Communist insurgents, he replied: "In the final analysis it's their war. They're the ones who have to win it or lose it. We can help them as advisers but they have to win it."

Kennedy's Assassination

By the fall of 1963, John F. Kennedy had matured a great deal as president. Not only had he come to understand the urgency and momentum of the civil rights movement, he also had come to see the cold war as a more complex issue than he had believed during his first year in office. In October 1963, he announced his intention to withdraw U.S. forces from South Vietnam by the end of 1965.

What Kennedy would have done thereafter in Vietnam has remained a matter of endless discussion, because on November 22, 1963, while riding in an open car through Dallas, Texas, he was shot and killed by Lee Harvey Oswald, a twenty-four-year-old ex-Marine turned Communist who worked in the Texas School Book Depository, from which he fired at Kennedy with a rifle. Debate still swirls about whether Oswald acted alone or was part of a conspiracy to assassinate the president, in part because Oswald did not live long enough to tell his story. As Oswald was being transported to a court hearing, Jack Ruby, a Dallas nightclub owner distraught over Kennedy's death, shot and killed a handcuffed Oswald as a nationwide television audience watched.

Kennedy's shocking assassination and his heartrending funeral enshrined the young president in the public imagination as a martyred leader cut down in the prime of his life. His short-lived but drama-filled presidency had flamed up and out like a comet hitting the earth's atmosphere. Americans wept in the streets, and the world was on edge as the wounded nation welcomed a new and very different president.

CORE **OBJECTIVE**

2. Describe the strategies and achievements of the civil rights movement in the 1960s, and explain the divisions that emerged among its activists during the decade.

Expansion of the Civil Rights Movement

After the Montgomery bus boycott of 1955–1956, Martin Luther King Jr.'s philosophy of militant nonviolence stirred others to challenge the deeply entrenched patterns of racial segregation in the South. The civil rights movement had challenged the complacent prosperity of the fifties, and many young adults were inspired by Kennedy's direct appeals to youthful idealism. Thousands enrolled in the Peace Corps and others joined African Americans in the fight for civil rights.

Sit-Ins

The Greensboro Four: Lunch counter "sit-ins"

The civil rights movement gained added momentum when four polite, well-dressed black college students sat down and ordered coffee and doughnuts at an "all-white" Woolworth's lunch counter in Greensboro, North Carolina, on February 1, 1960. The clerk refused to serve them, explaining that blacks had to eat standing up or take their food outside. The Greensboro Four, as the students came to be called, waited for forty-five minutes and then returned the next day with two dozen more students. Along with others, they returned every day for a week, patiently tolerating being jeered at, jostled, and spat upon by white hooligans.

The "sit-in" movement spread quickly to six more towns in the state, and within two months similar sit-ins—involving 50,000 blacks and whites, men and women, young and old—had occurred in over a hundred cities in thirteen states. Some 3,600 people had been arrested. By the end of July 1960, officials in Greensboro lifted the whites-only policy at the Woolworth's lunch counter. The civil rights movement had found an effective new tactic: nonviolent sit-ins against segregation.

In April 1960, some 200 college student activists, black and white, had converged in Raleigh, North Carolina, to form the **Student Nonviolent Coordinating Committee** (**SNCC**—pronounced "snick"). The goal of what they came to call "the movement" was to intensify the effort to dismantle segregation. SNCC broadened the sit-ins, which began at restaurants, to include "kneel-ins" at all-white churches and "wade-ins" at segregated public swimming pools. In many communities, demonstrators were pelted with rocks, burned with cigarettes, subjected to unending verbal abuse, and even killed by white racists. As a Florida hog farmer named Holstead "Hoss" Manucy explained to a journalist, "I ain't got no bad habits. Don't smoke. Don't cuss. My only bad habit is fightin' niggahs."

Freedom Rides

Student Nonviolent Coordinating Committee (SNCC) Interracial organization formed in 1960 with the goal of intensifying the effort to end racial segregation.

In 1961, civil rights leaders decided to put "the movement on wheels" by integrating public transportation: buses and trains. Their larger goal was to force the Kennedy administration to engage the cause of civil rights in the Democratic South. On May 4, the New York–based Congress of Racial

Civil rights and its peaceful warriors *Left*: The Greensboro Four—(*listed from left*) Joseph McNeil, Franklin McCain, Billy Smith, and Clarence Henderson—await service on day two of their sit-in at the Woolworth's. *Right*: On May 14, 1961, a white mob assaulted a Freedom Bus, flinging fire bombs into its windows and beating the activists as they emerged. Here, the surviving Freedom Riders sit outside the burnt shell of their bus.

Equality (CORE), led by James Farmer, sent a courageous group of eighteen black and white **Freedom Riders**, as they were called, on two public buses from Washington, D.C., through the Lower South to New Orleans. They wanted to test a federal court ruling that banned racial segregation on buses and trains, and in terminals. Farmer warned Attorney General Robert F. Kennedy that the bus riders would probably be attacked as they traveled through the South.

The warning was well founded, for on May 14, a mob of white racists in rural Alabama, many of them members of the Ku Klux Klan, surrounded the Greyhound bus carrying the Freedom Riders. After throwing a firebomb into the bus, angry whites barricaded the bus's door. "Burn them alive," one of them yelled. "Fry the damned niggers." After the gas tank exploded, the riders were able to escape the burning bus, only to be battered by metal pipes, chains, and clubs.

A few hours later, Freedom Riders on a second bus were beaten by whites armed with bats and chains after entering whites-only waiting rooms at the bus terminal in Birmingham. The police, as it turned out, had encouraged the beatings. Alabama's governor complained that the Freedom Riders were violating "our law and customs." The next day, the Freedom Riders wanted to continue their trip, but the bus drivers refused.

When Diane Nash, a fearless black college student and SNCC leader in Nashville, Tennessee, heard about the violence in Birmingham, she recruited new riders. On May 17, Nash and ten students took a bus to Birmingham, where they were arrested. While in jail, the students sang

Freedom Riders

Freedom Riders Activists who, beginning in 1961, traveled by bus through the South to test federal court rulings that banned segregation on buses and trains.

"freedom songs": "We'll Never Turn Back," "Ain't Gonna Let Nobody Turn Me Around," "We Shall Overcome." Eugene "Bull" Connor, the notoriously racist police chief, grew so frustrated at their joyous rebelliousness that he drove them in the middle of the night to the Tennessee state line and dropped them off to walk, saying, "I couldn't stand your singing." Instead of going to Nashville, however, the gutsy students returned to Birmingham.

President Kennedy was not inspired by the courageous Freedom Riders, in part because he was preoccupied with the crisis with the Soviet Union over Berlin. The president and his brother dismissed the Freedom Riders as "publicity seekers."

The demonstrators persisted, finally forcing the president to provide another bus which enabled them to renew the journey to New Orleans. When the new group of Freedom Riders reached Montgomery, the capital of Alabama, they were attacked. The next night, civil rights activists gathered at a Montgomery church to honor the Freedom Riders, but their meeting was interrupted by a rampaging mob of whites armed with rocks and fire bombs. Ministers made frantic appeals to the White House. President Kennedy responded by urging the Alabama governor to intervene. After midnight, National Guardsmen arrived to disperse the mob. The Freedom Riders continued into Mississippi, where they were imprisoned. They never made it to New Orleans.

> **Integration of interstate transportation facilities**

Still, they succeeded in their larger goal. The courage and principled resistance of the Freedom Riders—and of federal judges across the nation whose rulings supported integration efforts—led the Interstate Commerce Commission (ICC) in September 1961 to order that all interstate transportation facilities be integrated. The Freedom Riders had worked and were a turning point in the civil rights movement. Widespread media coverage showed the nation that the nonviolent protesters were prepared to die for their rights rather than continue to endure racist assaults on their dignity.

James Meredith

> **Desegregating the University of Mississippi**

In the fall of 1962, James Meredith, an African American student and Air Force veteran whose grandfather had been a slave, tried to enroll at the all-white University of Mississippi in Oxford. Ross Barnett, the governor of Mississippi, refused to allow Meredith to register for classes. Robert F. Kennedy then dispatched federal marshals to enforce the law. When the marshals were assaulted by a white mob shouting "Go to Hell, JFK," President Kennedy sent National Guard troops (all white). The arrival of soldiers on the campus ignited rioting that left two dead and dozens injured. Once the violence subsided, however, James Meredith was registered at the university. "Only in America," a reporter noted, "would the federal government send thousands of troops to enforce the right of an otherwise obscure citizen to attend a particular university."

Birmingham

Several months later, in early 1963, in conjunction with the celebration of the hundredth anniversary of Abraham Lincoln's Emancipation Proclamation, Martin Luther King Jr. announced that he and other civil rights activists were fed up "with tokenism and gradualism and see-how-far-you've-comeism. We can't wait any longer. Now is the time." He then defied the wishes of President Kennedy by organizing a massive series of demonstrations against segregation in Birmingham, Alabama, a state presided over by a feisty new racist governor—George Wallace—who had vowed to protect "segregation now, segregation tomorrow, segregation forever!" King knew that demonstrations in Birmingham would likely provoke violence, but a hard-won victory there, he felt, would build national support and "break the back of segregation all over the nation."

As King and other activists led demonstrations through Birmingham streets in April, the all-white police force led by Bull Connor used snarling dogs, tear gas, electric cattle prods, and fire hoses on the protesters. Millions of Americans across the nation were outraged when they saw the ugly confrontations on television. "The civil

> Nonviolent civil disobedience: King's "Letter from Birmingham City Jail"

rights movement," President Kennedy observed, "owes Bull Connor as much as it owes Abraham Lincoln." It also owed a lot to the power of television, which brought the savagery of racism into millions of American homes.

More than 3,000 demonstrators were arrested in Birmingham, including Dr. King. While in jail, he wrote a "Letter from Birmingham City Jail," a stirring defense of **"nonviolent civil disobedience"** that has since become a classic document of the civil rights movement. "One who breaks an unjust law," King stressed, "must do so openly, lovingly, and with a willingness to *accept the penalty*." King's efforts prevailed when Birmingham

Bull's dogs Eugene "Bull" Connor ordered Birmingham police to unleash their dogs on civil rights demonstrators in May of 1963.

officials finally agreed to end their segregationist practices. White racists did not change overnight, however. One angry Alabaman sent a letter to King: "This isn't a threat but a promise—your head will be blown off as sure as Christ made green apples."

Throughout the Lower South, whites defied efforts at racial integration. On June 11, 1963, Alabama governor George Wallace personally blocked the door at the University of Alabama as African American students tried to register for classes. Wallace finally stepped aside in the face of insistent

nonviolent civil disobedience The principled tactic that Martin Luther King Jr. advocated: peaceful lawbreaking as a means of ending segregation.

federal marshals and army troops. That night President Kennedy told the nation that he was urging Congress to pass a major new civil rights bill. Four hours later, an African American civil rights activist, Medgar Evers, was shot to death in his driveway in Jackson, Mississippi. Such violence aroused the nation's indignation and elevated civil rights as America's most pressing social issue. Yet southern Democrats in Congress blocked Kennedy's civil rights bill.

"I Have a Dream!"

Nonviolent civil disobedience: March on Washington

The standoff in Congress led African American leaders to take a bold step. On August 28, some 250,000 blacks and whites of all ages, many of them schoolchildren brought on buses for the occasion, marched arm-in-arm down the Mall in Washington, D.C., chanting "Equality Now!" and singing "We Shall Overcome."

The **March on Washington** for Jobs and Freedom was the largest political demonstration in American history. The organizers, primarily civil rights veterans Bayard Rustin and A. Philip Randolph, never imagined that so many people would participate. "When you looked at the crowd," remembered a U.S. Park Service ranger, "you didn't see blacks or whites. You saw America." Prominent entertainers Mahalia Jackson, Marian Anderson, Joan Baez, Bob Dylan, Odetta, and Peter, Paul, and Mary sang protest songs, and civil rights activists gave speeches calling for racial justice.

Then something remarkable happened. Standing on the steps of the Lincoln Memorial, 34-year-old Martin Luther King Jr., who in recent years had been attacked four times, had seen his home bombed three times, and had been arrested fourteen times, spoke to the huge crowd. He began awkwardly. Noticing his nervousness, someone on stage urged him to "tell 'em about the dream." As if suddenly inspired, King set aside his prepared remarks and delivered an extraordinary speech. He started slowly and picked up speed, as if he were speaking at a revival, giving poetic voice to the hopes of millions as he stressed the "fierce urgency of now" and the unstoppable power of "meeting physical force with soul force." President Kennedy, who earlier had tried to convince organizers to call off the march, was watching King's speech on TV at the White House, just a mile away. As King spoke, the president told an aide that "he's damn good."

Dr. King then shared his dream of an America in which the ideal of equality would be realized:

In spite of the difficulties and frustrations of the moment, I still have a *dream*. It is a *dream* deeply rooted in the American dream. I have a *dream* that one day this nation will rise up and live out the true meaning of its creed: 'We hold these truths to be self-evident; that all men are created equal.' I have a *dream* that one day . . . the sons of former slaves and the sons of former slaveowners will be able to sit together at the table of brotherhood.

March on Washington (1963)
Civil rights demonstration on the National Mall, where Martin Luther King, Jr. gave his famous "I Have a Dream" speech.

As if at a massive church service, many in the crowd began shouting "Amen!" as King summoned a flawed nation to justice: "So let freedom ring!" he shouted, for "when we allow freedom to ring from every town and every hamlet, from every state and every city, we will be able to speed up the day when *all* God's children—black men and white men, Jews and Gentiles, Protestants and Catholics—will be able to join hands and sing in the words of the old Negro spiritual, *"Free at last, free at last, thank God Almighty, we are free at last!"* As King finished, there was a startling hush, then a deafening ovation. The crowd spontaneously began singing "We Shall Overcome," holding hands and swaying as if at a prayer meeting.

King's dream of ending racial violence remained just that—a dream. Eighteen days after the March on Washington, four Klansmen in Birmingham detonated a bomb in a black church, killing four young girls. The awful murders sparked indignation across the country—and around the world. The editors of the *Milwaukee Sentinel* stressed that the Birmingham bombing "should serve to goad the conscience. The deaths . . . in a sense are on the hands of each of us."

The Warren Court

The civil rights movement depended as much on the courts as it did on the leadership of Dr. King and others, and federal judges kept forcing states and localities to integrate schools and other public places. Under Chief Justice Earl Warren, the U.S. Supreme Court also made landmark decisions in other areas of American life.

> Federal Courts force integration in schools and public places

In 1962, the Court ruled that a school prayer adopted by the New York State Board of Regents violated the constitutional prohibition against government-supported religion. In *Gideon v. Wainwright* (1963), the Court required that every felony defendant be provided a lawyer regardless of the defendant's ability to pay. In 1964, the Court ruled in *Escobedo v. Illinois* that a person accused of a crime must be allowed to consult a lawyer before being interrogated by police. Two years later, in *Miranda v. Arizona*, the Court issued a bitterly criticized ruling when it ordered that an accused person in police custody be informed of certain basic rights: the right to remain silent; the right to know that anything said to authorities can be used against the individual in court; and the right to have a defense attorney present during interrogation; since then, these requirements have been known as "Miranda rights." In addition, the Court established rules for police to follow in informing suspects of their legal rights before questioning could begin.

Freedom Summer

During late 1963 and throughout 1964, in the aftermath of President Kennedy's assassination, the civil rights movement grew in scope, visibility, and power. Racism, however, remained entrenched in the Lower South. Blacks continued to be excluded from the political process. For example, in

1963 only 6.7 percent of Mississippi blacks were registered to vote, the lowest percentage in the nation. White officials in the South kept African Americans from voting through a variety of means: charging them expensive poll taxes, forcing them to take difficult literacy tests, making the application process inconvenient, and intimidating them through the use of arson, beatings, and lynchings.

African American voter registration drives

In early 1964, Harvard-educated Robert "Bob" Moses, a thin, bespectacled, black New Yorker who had resigned from Martin Luther King's SCLC to head up the Student Nonviolent Coordinating Committee (SNCC) office in Mississippi, decided it would take "an army" to force the state to give voting rights to blacks. So he set about recruiting an army of black and white volunteers who would live with rural African Americans, teach them in "freedom schools," and help them register to vote.

Most of the recruits for what came to be called "Freedom Summer" were idealistic white college students, and many were Jewish. Mississippi's white leaders prepared for "the nigger-communist invasion" by doubling the state police force and stockpiling tear gas, electric cattle prods, and shotguns. The famous writer Eudora Welty reported from her hometown of Jackson, Mississippi, that she had heard that "this summer all hell is going to break loose."

"Freedom schools"

It did. In mid-June, the volunteer activists met at an Ohio college to learn about southern racial history, nonviolent civil disobedience, and the likely abuses they would suffer. On the final evening of the training session, Moses pleaded with anyone who feared heading to Mississippi to go home; several of them did. The next day, the remaining volunteers boarded buses and headed south, fanning out across the state. In all, forty-one "freedom schools" that summer taught thousands of children math, writing, and history. They also tutored black adults about the complicated process of voter registration.

Forty-six-year-old Fannie Lou Hamer was one of the local blacks who worked with the SNCC volunteers during Freedom Summer. The youngest in a household of twenty children, she had spent most of her life working on local cotton plantations. During the Freedom Summer of 1963 and after, she led gatherings of volunteers in freedom songs and excelled as a lay preacher. "God is not pleased," she said, "at all the murdering, and all of the brutality, and all the killings for no reason at all. God is not pleased at the Negro children in the State of Mississippi, suffering from malnutrition. God is not pleased because we have to go raggedy each day. God is not pleased because we have to go to the field and work from ten to eleven hours for three lousy dollars."

In response to Freedom Summer, the Ku Klux Klan, local police, and other white racists harassed, arrested, and assaulted many of the young volunteers. Hamer was brutally beaten by jail guards in Winona. Then, in June 1964, Klan members abducted and murdered three young civil rights workers: James Earl Chaney, Andrew Goodman, and Michael "Mickey" Schwerner. Their decomposed bodies were found two months later in a cattle pond. In the process of searching for the missing men, authorities found the bodies of eight black males in rivers and swamps. The murders, said one volunteer, were "the end of innocence," after which "things could never be the same."

From Civil Rights to Black Power

Racism was never limited solely to the South. In retrospect, it was predictable that the civil rights movement would shift its focus from the rural South to the very different plight of urban blacks. By the mid-sixties, about 70 percent of the nation's African Americans were living in urban areas, most of them in central-city ghettos bypassed by prosperity. Though the majority of African Americans continued to identify with the nonviolent, Christian-centered integration movement promoted by Martin Luther King Jr. and organizations such as the NAACP, SCLC, CORE, and the Urban League, King and others acknowledged privately that many young blacks, especially those in large cities, were losing faith in the strategy of nonviolence.

White terror Young men cruise through a riot zone in Chicago in 1966, brandishing a Confederate flag and racist signs.

The fragmentation of the civil rights movement was tragically evident on August 11, 1965, when Watts, the largest black ghetto in Los Angeles, exploded in a frenzy of rioting and looting. When the uprising ended, thirty-four were dead, almost 4,000 were in jail, and property damage exceeded $35 million. Chicago and Cleveland, along with forty other American cities, experienced similar race riots in the summer of 1966. The following summer, Newark, New Jersey, and Detroit, Michigan, burst into flames. Between 1965 and 1968, nearly 300 racial uprisings shattered the peace of urban America.

> Race riots

The racial violence in northern cities revealed the civil war within the civil rights movement. As Gil Scot-Heron, a black musician, sang: "We are tired of praying and marching and thinking and learning / Brothers want to start cutting and shooting and stealing and burning." What came to be called "Black Power" began to compete with the integrationist, nonviolent philosophy espoused by Dr. King and the SCLC.

> Black power movement

The most articulate spokesman for the **black power movement** was Malcolm X (formerly Malcolm Little, the X denoting his lost African family name). His parents were courageous supporters of Marcus Garvey's 1920s crusade for black nationalism, and his childhood home in Lansing, Michigan, was burned to the ground by white racists. Malcolm quit school during ninth grade and began to display what would become a lifelong ability to reinvent himself. By age nineteen, now known as Detroit Red, he had become a thief, drug dealer, and pimp. He spent seven years in Massachusetts prisons, where he experienced a conversion and joined a small Chicago-based religious sect, the Nation of Islam (NOI), whose members were called Black Muslims. The organization had little to do with Islam and everything to do with its domineering leader, Elijah Muhammad, and the cultlike devotion he required. Muhammad dismissed whites as "devils"

black power movement Militant form of civil rights protest focused on urban communities in the North that emerged as a response to impatience with the nonviolent tactics of Martin Luther King, Jr.

Malcolm X The black power movement's most influential spokesman.

Malcolm X assassinated; Black Panther party

and championed black nationalism, racial pride, self-respect, and self-discipline. By 1953, a year after leaving prison, Malcolm X was a full-time NOI minister famous for his electrifying speeches attacking white racism and black powerlessness.

Malcolm X dismissed mainstream civil rights leaders such as Martin Luther King Jr. as being "nothing but modern Uncle Toms" who "keep you and me in check, keep us under control, keep us passive and peaceful and nonviolent." His militant speeches inspired thousands of mostly urban blacks to join NOI. "Yes, I'm an extremist," Malcolm acknowledged in 1964. "The black race in the United States is in extremely bad shape. You show me a black man who isn't an extremist and I'll show you one who needs psychiatric attention." More than most black leaders, Malcolm X expressed the emotions and frustrations of the inner-city African American working poor. Yet at the peak of his influence, Malcolm X became embroiled in a conflict with Elijah Muhammad that proved fatal; NOI assassins killed Malcolm X in Manhattan on February 21, 1965.

Black militancy did not die with Malcolm X, however. By 1966, "black power" had become a rallying cry for young extremists. When Stokely Carmichael, a twenty-five-year-old graduate of Howard University, became head of the Student Nonviolent Coordinating Committee (SNCC), he enforced the separatist philosophy of black power by ousting whites from the organization. "When you talk of black power," Carmichael shouted, "you talk of bringing this country to its knees, of building a movement that will smash everything Western civilization has created."

Where Dr. King spoke to white America's moral conscience, Carmichael spoke to the seething rage of the young black underclass impatient with nonviolent protest. Soon he would move on to the Black Panther party, a group of leather-jacketed black revolutionaries founded in Oakland, California, attracting recruits with its incendiary strategies. H. Rap Brown, who succeeded Carmichael as head of SNCC in 1967, was equally committed to a strategy of violence. He urged blacks to "get you some guns" and "kill the honkies [whites]."

Black Power in Retrospect

Although widely covered in the media, the black power movement never attracted more than a small minority of African Americans. Dr. King dismissed black separatism and the promotion of violent social change, reminding his followers that "we can't win violently."

Still, the emphasis on black power had two positive effects upon the civil rights movement. First, black power advocates forced King and other mainstream black leaders and organizations to shift their focus from the rural South to poverty-stricken inner-city ghettos in the North and West. Legal access to restaurants, schools, and other public accommodations, King pointed out, meant little to people mired in chronic poverty. They needed jobs and decent housing as much as they needed access to all-white facilities. To this end, King began to emphasize the economic needs of the black urban underclass, launching his own war on poverty. The time had come, he declared while launching his "Poor People's Campaign" in December 1967, for radical new measures "to provide jobs and income for the poor." Yet as King and others stressed, the hugely expensive war in Vietnam was taking funds away from federal programs serving the poor, and black soldiers were dying in disproportionate numbers in Southeast Asia.

Second, the controversial black power movement also motivated African Americans to take greater pride in their racial heritage by pushing for black studies programs in schools and colleges, the celebration of African cultural and artistic traditions, the organizing of inner-city voters to elect black mayors, laws forcing landlords to treat blacks fairly, and the creation of grassroots organizations and community centers in black neighborhoods. It was Malcolm X who insisted that blacks call themselves *African Americans* as a symbol of pride in their roots and as a spur to learn more about their history. As the popular singer James Brown urged, "Say it loud—I'm black and I'm proud."

Panther power Black Panthers throw up the black power salute outside of a San Francisco Liberation School, where activists raised awareness and appreciation of African American history, a topic ignored by white, mainstream curriculum.

Lyndon B. Johnson and the Great Society

CORE **OBJECTIVE**
3. Analyze Lyndon B. Johnson's War on Poverty and Great Society initiatives, and evaluate their impact on American society.

Growing federal support for civil rights came from an unlikely source: a drawling white Texan who succeeded John F. Kennedy in the White House. Lyndon B. Johnson, the towering Texan, took the presidential oath of office on board the plane that brought Kennedy's body back to Washington from Dallas. Fifty-five years old, six feet four inches tall, Johnson had spent twenty-six years in Washington and served nearly a decade as perhaps the most powerful Democratic leader ever in the Senate. Now he was the first southern president since Woodrow Wilson, a legislative magician who had excelled as Senate majority leader. His transition to the presidency was not easy. The Kennedy brothers despised Johnson, and he felt the same about them. They had excluded him from key decisions, often dismissing the rural Texan with the deep southern drawl as "Rufus Cornpone."

Johnson brought to the White House a dramatically different personality and style from that of his predecessor. Unlike Kennedy, who was born to

The oath of office Less than an hour and a half after Kennedy's death, Johnson took the presidential oath aboard Air Force One between his wife, Lady Bird (left), and Jacqueline Kennedy (right), before flying out of Dallas for Washington, D.C.

great wealth, Johnson was a rags-to-riches story. With almost superhuman energy and crushing ambition, he had worked his way out of poverty during the Great Depression to become one of the Senate's most dominating figures. LBJ had none of the Kennedy elegance. His ego and insecurities were as massive as his vanity and ambition; he insisted on being the center of attention wherever he went. Ruthless and often bullying, needy and warmhearted, he was a whirlwind of energy and dreams, a crude idealist and a brutal optimist. Yet he was also compassionate and generous toward the poor. Johnson yearned to be loved and respected as a transformational leader. Like Kennedy, he displayed a lifelong weakness for attractive women. (His wife, Lady Bird, acknowledged that "Lyndon loved the human race, and half of the human race are women.")

Those who viewed Johnson as a stereotypical southern conservative failed to appreciate his long-standing admiration for Franklin D. Roosevelt, the depth of his concern for the poor, and his bold support for the cause of civil rights (in part because he needed to win over the northern wing of the Democratic party). "I'm going to be the best friend the Negro ever had," Johnson bragged to a member of the White House staff soon after becoming president. His commitment to civil rights was in part motivated by politics and in part by his desire to bring the South into the mainstream of American life.

Unlike the politically cautious Kennedy, Johnson had Texas-sized ambitions. Few presidents had ever dreamed as big as Lyndon Johnson. He wanted to be the greatest American president, the one who did the most good for the most people. He promised to "help every child get an education, to help every Negro and every American citizen have an equal opportunity, to help every family get a decent home, and to help bring healing to the sick and dignity to the old."

Politics and Poverty

> LBJ's first legislation: The Revenue Act (1964), Civil Rights Act (1964), and Economic Opportunity Act (1964)

Johnson managed legislation through Congress better than any president in history, including Franklin Roosevelt, his idol. He was the consummate wheeler-dealer. "It is the politician's task," Johnson asserted, "to pass legislation, not to sit around saying principled things." In 1964 he set about doing just that, taking advantage of widespread public support to push through Congress Kennedy's stalled measures for tax reductions and civil rights. He later said that he wanted to take Kennedy's incomplete program "and turn it into a martyr's cause." The Revenue Act of 1964 provided a 20 percent reduction in tax rates (the top rate was then a whopping 91 percent, compared to 39.6 today). It was intended to give consumers more money to spend so as to boost economic growth and create new jobs, and it worked as planned. Unemployment fell from 5.2 percent in 1964 to 4.5 percent in 1965, and 3.8 percent in 1966.

Civil Rights Act of 1964

Long thwarted by southern Democrats who had held it up in Congress, the **Civil Rights Act of 1964** finally became law on July 2 after eighty days of Congressional debate. President Johnson played a crucial role in its passage. A son of the South, he used his experience as a power broker in the Senate to launch his own risky crusade for racial justice as president. One senator who survived the "Johnson treatment," as it came to be called, said that the president would "twist your arm off at the shoulder and beat your head with it" if you did not agree to vote as he wanted.

Soon after becoming president, Johnson hosted his close friend and arch-segregationist, Senator Richard Russell of Georgia, for lunch at the White House and warned him that "you've got to get out of my way. I'm going to run over you" in order to pass the Civil Rights Act. "You may do that," Russell replied. "But by God, it's going to cost you the South and cost you the election of 1964." Johnson answered: "If that's the price I've got to pay, I'll pay it gladly." Soon thereafter, Johnson told Congress that "we have talked long enough in this country about equal rights. . . . It is time now to write the next chapter, and to write it in the book of law."

Many others (called the "coalition of conscience" by labor leader Walter Reuther) helped Johnson convince Congress to pass the Civil Rights Act—Congressional committee chairs, both Republicans and Democrats, labor unions, church leaders, and civil rights organizations. Their collective efforts produced what is arguably the single most important piece of legislation created in the twentieth century. The passage of the Civil Rights Act after more than a year of Congressional delays marked one of those extraordinary moments when the ideals of democracy, equal opportunity, and human dignity are affirmed by action.

Civil Rights Act of 1964 Legislation that outlawed discrimination in public accommodations and employment, passed at the urging of President Lyndon B. Johnson.

Down with segregation A worker removes a sign from a Greensboro, North Carolina bus that reads: "White Patrons Please Seat from Front. Colored Patrons Please Seat from Rear."

The Civil Rights Act of 1964 dealt a major blow to the deeply entrenched system of racial segregation. It banned racial segregation in public places such as bus terminals, restaurants, theaters, and hotels. It also gave new powers to the federal government to bring lawsuits against organizations or businesses that violated constitutional rights, and it established the Equal Employment Opportunities Commission to ensure that employers treated job applicants equally, regardless of race, gender, or national origin. On the night after signing the pathbreaking Civil Rights Act, Johnson knew that many conservative white southerners would be outraged. He correctly predicted that "we have just delivered the South to the Republican party for a long time to come."

The War on Poverty

Johnson's War on Poverty

In addition to fulfilling Kennedy's legislative priorities that had been stalled in Congress, Johnson launched a much more elaborate legislative program of his own by declaring "unconditional war on poverty in America." Americans had "rediscovered" poverty in 1962 when the social critic Michael Harrington published a powerful exposé, *The Other America*. Harrington revealed that more than 40 million people were mired in an invisible "culture of poverty" that held them hostage in a vicious cycle. Poverty led to poor housing conditions, which in turn led to poor health, poor attendance at school or work, alcohol and drug abuse, unwanted pregnancies, single-parent families, and so on. Harrington added that poverty was much more extensive in the United States than people realized because much of it was hidden from view in isolated rural areas or inner-city slums. He urged the United States to launch a "comprehensive assault on poverty."

President Kennedy had read Harrington's book and had asked his advisers in the fall of 1963, just before his assassination, to investigate the poverty problem and suggest solutions. Upon taking office as president, Johnson announced that he wanted an anti-poverty legislative package that was "big and bold, that would hit the nation with real impact." Money for the program would come from the tax revenues generated by corporate profits made possible by the tax reduction of 1964, which had led to one of the longest sustained economic booms in history. By the mid-sixties, unemployment had dropped, consumer spending had increased, and corporate profits were soaring.

Economic Opportunity Act of 1964

Economic Opportunity Act (1964) Key legislation in President Johnson's "War on Poverty" that created the Office of Economic Opportunity and programs like Head Start and the work-study financial-aid program for low-income college students.

The **Economic Opportunity Act of 1964** was the primary weapon in Johnson's much-trumpeted "War on Poverty." It created an Office of Economic Opportunity (OEO) to administer eleven new community-based programs, many of which still exist. They included a Job Corps training program for inner-city youths aged sixteen to twenty-one; a Head Start educational program for disadvantaged pre-schoolers; a Legal Services Corporation to provide legal assistance for low-income Americans;

work-study financial-aid programs for low-income college students; grants to small farmers and rural businesses; loans to businesses that hired the chronically unemployed; the Volunteers in Service to America program (VISTA) that recruited volunteers to combat inner-city poverty; and the Community Action Program, which would allow the poor "maximum feasible participation" in organizing and directing their own neighborhood programs designed for their benefit. In 1964, Congress also approved the Food Stamp Act, a program run by the Department of Agriculture to help poor people afford to buy groceries.

The Election of 1964

Johnson's successes in creating an array of new federal social-welfare programs triggered a Republican counterattack. Arizona senator Barry Goldwater, a wealthy department-store owner, emerged as the blunt-talking leader of the growing conservative wing of the Republican party. In his best-selling book *The Conscience of a Conservative* (1960), Goldwater had called for ending the income tax and drastically reducing federal entitlement programs such as Social Security. Conservatives controlled the Republican Convention when it gathered in San Francisco in the early summer of 1964, and they ensured Goldwater's nomination. "I would remind you," Goldwater told the delegates, "that extremism in the defense of liberty is no vice." He later explained that his objective was like that of Calvin Coolidge in the 1920s: "to reduce the size of government. Not to pass laws, but repeal them."

In his memoirs, Goldwater admitted that he knew he had no chance to win the presidency: "I just wanted the conservatives to have a real voice in the country." As a candidate, he frightened many voters when he urged wholesale bombing of North Vietnam and even suggested using atomic weapons. He criticized Johnson's War on Poverty as a waste of money, told students that the federal government should not provide any assistance for education, and opposed the nuclear test ban treaty and the Civil Rights Act of 1964, having been one of only six Republican senators to vote against it. To Republican campaign buttons that claimed, "In your heart, you know he's right," Democrats responded, "In your guts, you know he's nuts."

Johnson portrayed himself as a responsible centrist in contrast to Goldwater's "extreme" conservatism. He chose as his running mate Hubert H. Humphrey of Minnesota, a prominent liberal senator who had long promoted civil rights. In contrast to Goldwater's aggressive rhetoric on Vietnam, Johnson pledged that he was "not about to send American boys nine or ten thousand miles from home to do what Asian boys ought to be doing for themselves."

The result was a landslide. Johnson polled 61 percent of the vote; Goldwater carried only Arizona and five states in the Lower South. Johnson won the electoral vote by a whopping 486 to 52. In the Senate, the Democrats increased their majority by two (68 to 32) and in the House by thirty-seven (295 to 140). Goldwater's success in the Lower South, however, accelerated the region's shift to the Republican party, and his candidacy proved to be a turning point in the development of the national conservative movement, inspiring a generation of young activists and the formation of conservative organizations that would transform the dynamics of American politics during the 1970s and 1980s. Their success would culminate in the presidency of Ronald Reagan, the Hollywood actor who co-chaired the California for Goldwater campaign in 1964.

The Great Society

> Johnson's Great Society program

Lyndon Johnson made a classical mistake by misreading his lopsided victory as a mandate for massive changes. He knew, however, that his popularity could quickly fade. "Every day I'm in office," he told his aides, "I'm going to lose votes. I'm going to alienate somebody. . . . We've got to get this legislation fast. You've got to get it during my honeymoon."

As Johnson's War on Poverty gathered momentum, his already-outsized ambitions grew even more. In May 1964, he announced his intention to create an array of new programs intended to create a "Great Society" that would end poverty and racial injustice and provide "abundance and liberty for all." That was a magisterial goal, but it "was just the beginning," Johnson insisted, given that the United States had the resources to do much more than assault poverty. "We have the opportunity to move not only toward the rich society and the powerful society, but upward to the Great Society." He did not explain precisely what he meant by a "great society," but it soon became clear that Johnson viewed the federal government as the magical lever for raising the quality of life for all Americans—rich and poor. He would surpass his hero Franklin Roosevelt in expanding the goals and scope of the federal government to ensure that Americans were a people of plenty.

When Johnson became president in November 1963, Social Security was America's only nationwide social program. That soon changed. In 1965, Johnson began flooding Congress with waves of Great Society legislation that he said would end poverty, revitalize decaying cities, provide every young person the chance to attend college, protect the health of the elderly, enhance the arts and humanities, clean up the nation's polluted air and water, and make the highways safer and prettier. The scope of Johnson's Great Society programs exceeded Franklin D. Roosevelt's New Deal, in part because of the nation's extraordinary prosperity during the mid-1960s. "This country," Johnson proclaimed, "is rich enough to do anything it has the guts to do and the vision to do and the will to do." That proved *not* to be the case, however.

Health Insurance, Housing, and Higher Education

Johnson's first priority was federal health insurance and aid to help young people pursue higher education, "liberal" proposals that had languished since President Truman had proposed them in 1945. For twenty years, the

War on Poverty In 1964, Johnson visited Tom Fletcher, a father of eight children living in a tar-paper shack in rural Kentucky. Fletcher became a "poster father" for the War on Poverty, though, as it turned out, his life improved little from its programs.

steadfast opposition of the physicians making up the American Medical Association (AMA) had stalled a comprehensive medical-insurance program. Now that Johnson and the Democrats had the votes to pass the measure, however, the AMA joined Republicans in supporting a bill serving those over age sixty-five. The act that finally emerged went well beyond the original proposal. It created not just a **Medicare** health-insurance program for the elderly but also a **Medicaid** program of federal grants to states to help cover medical expenses for the poor. Johnson signed the bill on July 30, 1965, in Independence, Missouri, with eighty-one-year-old Harry Truman looking on.

The Higher Education Act of 1965 increased federal grants to universities, created scholarships for low-income students, provided low-interest loans for students, and established a National Teachers Corps. "Every child," Johnson asserted, "must be encouraged to get as much education as he has the ability to take."

The momentum generated by the Higher Education and Medicare acts helped carry 435 more Great Society bills through Congress. Among them was the Appalachian Regional Development Act of 1966, which allocated $1 billion for programs in remote mountain areas that had long been pockets of desperate poverty. The Housing and Urban Development Act of 1965 provided $3 billion for urban renewal projects. Funds to help low-income families pay their rent followed in 1966, and the same year a new Department of Housing and Urban Development appeared, headed by Robert C. Weaver, the first African American cabinet member.

In implementing his Great Society programs, Lyndon Johnson had, in the words of one Washington reporter, "brought to harvest a generation's backlog of ideas and social legislation." People were amazed by Johnson's

> Johnson's Great Society: Medicare and Medicaid (1965), the Higher Education Act (1965), and the Housing and Urban Development Act (1965)

Medicare and Medicaid Health-care programs designed to aid the elderly and disadvantaged, respectively, as part of President Johnson's Great Society initiative.

energy, drive, and legislative skills. He never seemed to stop or slow down. A woman in Hawaii noted that Johnson "is a mover of men. Kennedy could inspire men, but he couldn't move them."

The Immigration Act

Little noticed in the stream of Great Society legislation was a major new immigration bill, the **Immigration and Nationality Services Act of 1965**, which Johnson signed in a ceremony held on Liberty Island in New York Harbor. In his speech, he stressed that the law would redress the wrong done to those "from southern and eastern Europe" and the "developing continents" of Asia, Africa, and Latin America. It abolished the discriminatory annual quotas based upon an immigrant's national origin and treated all nationalities and races equally. In place of nationality quotas, it created hemispheric ceilings on visas issued: 170,000 for persons from outside the Western Hemisphere, 120,000 for persons from within. It also stipulated that no more than 20,000 people could come from any one country each year. During the sixties, Asians and Latin Americans became the largest contingent of new Americans.

Voting Rights Legislation

Building upon the successes of "Freedom Summer," Martin Luther King Jr. organized an effort in early 1965 to register the 3 million unregistered African American voters in the South. In Selma, Alabama, where only 250 of the 15,000 blacks of voting age were registered voters, 8,000 black and white civil rights protesters began a march to Montgomery, about forty miles away, only to be assaulted by 500 state troopers using clubs, tear gas, and bullwhips. A federal judge agreed to allow the marchers to continue, and President Johnson provided troops for their protection. Still, two white marchers—a mother of five from Detroit and a Boston minister—were murdered. By March 25, when the demonstrators reached Montgomery, some 25,000 people were with them, and Dr. King delivered a rousing address on the steps of the state capitol in which he said, "the battle is in our hands. And we can answer with creative nonviolence the call to higher ground to which the new directions of our struggle summons us."

Several days earlier, Johnson had urged Congress to "overcome the crippling legacy of bigotry and injustice" by making the cause of civil rights "our cause too." He then concluded by slowly speaking the words of the movement's hymn: "And we *shall* overcome."

The resulting **Voting Rights Act of 1965** ensured all citizens the right to vote. It authorized the attorney general to send federal officials to register voters in areas that had long experienced racial discrimination. In states or counties where fewer than half the adults had voted in 1964, the act banned the various ways, like literacy tests, that local officials used to keep blacks and Hispanics from voting. By the end of the year, some 250,000 African Americans were newly registered to vote in several southern states. By

Immigration and Nationality Services Act of 1965
Legislation that abolished discriminatory quotas based upon immigrants' national origin and treated all nationalities and races equally.

Voting Rights Act of 1965
Legislation ensuring that all Americans were able to vote; ended literacy tests and other means of restricting voting rights.

1968, 53 percent of blacks in Alabama were registered to vote compared to only 14 percent in 1960. In this respect, the Voting Rights Act was even more important than the Civil Rights Act because it empowered black voters in the South, thereby transforming the white-dominated politics in the region and enabling, for the first time, the election of black public officials.

Assessing the Great Society

As an accidental president following a tragic assassination, Lyndon B. Johnson sought to give Americans a sense of forward movement in troubled times and show them that he could overcome their fears of a divided America and create a "Great Society" whereby people would be "more concerned with the quality of their goals than the quantity of their goods."

Yet the Great Society and War on Poverty programs never lived up to Johnson's grandiose goals, in part because the Vietnam War soon took priority and siphoned away funding and in part because neither Johnson nor his Congressional supporters understood the stubborn complexity of chronic poverty. The Great Society did include several triumphs for low-income Americans, however. Infant mortality has dropped, college completion rates have soared, malnutrition has virtually disappeared, and far fewer elderly Americans are living below the poverty line. The federal guarantee of civil rights and voting rights remains in place to this day. Medicare and Medicaid have become two of the most appreciated government programs. Consumers now have a federal agency protecting them. Head Start programs providing preschool enrichment activities for poor students have produced long-term benefits. The federal food stamp program has improved the nutrition and health of children living in poverty. Finally, the scholarships provided to low-income college students have been immensely valuable in enabling young people to gain access to higher education.

Several of Johnson's most ambitious programs, however, were ill-conceived, others were vastly underfunded, and many were mismanaged and even corrupt. Some of the problems they were meant to address actually worsened. As Joseph Califano, one of Johnson's senior aides, confessed: "Did we legislate too much? Were mistakes made? Plenty of them." Medicare, for example, removed incentives for hospitals to control costs, so medical bills skyrocketed—for everyone. In addition, food stamp fraud soared as people took advantage of a program intended to ensure healthy nutrition.

Overall, Great Society programs helped reduce the percentage of people living in poverty from 19 in 1964 to 10 in 1973, but it did so largely by providing federal welfare payments, not by finding people decent jobs. By 1966, middle-class resentment over the cost and excesses of the Great Society programs had generated a conservative backlash that fueled a Republican resurgence in Congress. By then, however, the Great Society had transformed public expectations of the power and role of federal government. Its greatest successes were the civil rights acts of 1964 and 1965.

Conservative backlash

CORE **OBJECTIVE**

4. Explain Presidents Kennedy and Johnson's motivations for deepening America's military involvement in the Vietnam War and appraise their efforts to preserve a noncommunist South Vietnam.

The Tragedy of Vietnam

In foreign affairs, Lyndon Johnson was, like Woodrow Wilson, a novice. And, again like Wilson, his presidency would become a victim of his crusading idealism. As racial violence erupted in America's cities, the war in Vietnam reached new levels of intensity and destruction. With weapons supplied by China and the Soviet Union, North Vietnam provided massive support to the Viet Cong (VC), the Communist guerrillas fighting in South Vietnam to overthrow the U.S.-backed government and unify the divided nation under Communist control.

When he became president, Johnson inherited a long-standing U.S. commitment to prevent a Communist takeover in Vietnam. Beginning with Harry S. Truman, U.S. presidents had done just enough to avoid being charged with having "lost" Vietnam to communism. Johnson initially sought to do the same, fearing that any other course of action would undermine his political influence and jeopardize his Great Society programs in Congress. His path, however, took the United States into a deeper military commitment in Southeast Asia.

In November 1963, when President Kennedy was assassinated, there were 16,000 U.S. military "advisers" in South Vietnam. Early in his presidency, Johnson doubted that Vietnam was worth more extensive military involvement. In May 1964, he told his national security adviser, McGeorge Bundy, that he had spent a sleepless night worrying about Vietnam: "It looks to me like we are getting into another Korea. . . . I don't think it's worth fighting for. And I don't think we can get out. It's just the biggest damned mess that I ever saw."

Yet Johnson's fear of appearing weak abroad outweighed his misgivings. By the end of 1965, there were 184,000 U.S. troops in Vietnam; in 1966 there were 385,000; and by 1969, at the height of the American war effort, 542,000.

Escalation in Vietnam

The official justification for the military "escalation"—a Defense Department term favored in the Vietnam era—was the **Tonkin Gulf Resolution**, passed by the Senate on August 7, 1964. On that day, President Johnson told a national television audience that on August 2 and 4, North Vietnamese torpedo boats had attacked two destroyers, the U.S.S. *Maddox* and the U.S.S. *C. Turner Joy,* in the Gulf of Tonkin, off the coast of North Vietnam. Johnson's description was later shown to be false and misleading; the U.S. ships had actually fired first. They had been supporting South Vietnamese attacks against two North Vietnamese islands—attacks planned by American advisers.

The Tonkin Gulf Resolution authorized the president to "take all necessary measures to repel any armed attack against the forces of the United States and to prevent further aggression." Senator Wayne Morse of Oregon, who had learned that Johnson's account of the incident in the Tonkin Gulf

U.S. air strikes Sustained bombing of Vietnam left 30–50-foot wide craters that can still be seen today.

Tonkin Gulf Resolution (1964) Congressional action that granted the president unlimited authority to defend U.S. forces abroad, after an allegedly unprovoked attack on American warships off the coast of North Vietnam.

was false, argued that American warships were in fact engaged in "acts of war rather than acts of defense." His efforts to oppose Johnson failed, however. Only Morse and one other senator voted against the Tonkin Gulf Resolution, which Johnson thereafter interpreted as equivalent to a congressional declaration of war.

Soon after his landslide victory over Goldwater in November 1964, Johnson made the crucial decisions that committed the United States to a full-scale war in Vietnam. On February 5, 1965, Viet Cong (VC) guerrillas killed 8 and wounded 126 at a U.S. base near Pleiku, in South Vietnam. More attacks later that week led Johnson to order Operation Rolling Thunder, the first sustained bombing of North Vietnam, which was intended to stop the flow of soldiers and supplies into the south. Thereafter, there were essentially two fronts in the expanding war: one, in North Vietnam, where U.S. warplanes continued a massive bombing campaign, and the other, in South Vietnam, where nearly all the ground combat occurred.

In March 1965, the new U.S. commander in Vietnam, General William C. Westmoreland, greeted the first American combat troops in Vietnam. By the summer, U.S. forces were engaged in "search and destroy" operations against VC guerrillas throughout South Vietnam. It was a frustrating war for the Americans. The Viet Cong, made up of both men and women, wore no uniforms and dissolved by day into the villages, hiding among Vietnamese civilians. Their elusiveness exasperated American soldiers, most of whom were not trained for such unconventional warfare in dense jungles and intense heat and humidity.

Hidden A Vietnamese mother hides her son and herself in the bushes near the village of Le My in 1965 after U.S. Marines clear the area of Viet Cong forces.

As combat operations increased, so did casualties (the number of killed, wounded, and missing) announced each week on the nightly television news, along with the "body count" of alleged VC dead. "Westy's war," although fought with helicopter gunships, chemical defoliants (Agent Orange), and highly flammable napalm, became like the trench warfare of World War I—a war of attrition, whereby each side hoped to outlast the other by causing so much loss of life as to force a surrender. "We will not be defeated," Johnson told the nation in April. "We will not grow tired. We will not withdraw."

The Context for Policy

President Johnson's decision to "Americanize" the Vietnam War, so mistaken in retrospect, was consistent with the foreign-policy principles pursued by all presidents after the Second World War. The idea of "containing" communism, articulated first in the Truman Doctrine, endorsed

> Commitment to "containing" communism

VIETNAM, 1966

CHINA

NORTH VIETNAM

Red River

•Dien Bien Phu   •Hanoi   •Haiphong

GULF OF TONKIN   HAI-NAN

Mekong R.

•Vinh

LAOS

Vientiane•

Demarcation Line of 1954

SOUTH CHINA SEA

■ Udon Thani   Hue•

Ho Chi Minh Trail

■ Da Nang

THAILAND   Chu Lai■   ■ My Lai

Mekong River   ■ Quang Ngai

■ Ubon Ratchathani   •Kon Tum

■ An Khe

■ Pleiku   ■ Qui Nhon

■ Ta Khli   SOUTH VIETNAM

•Bangkok   CAMBODIA   ■ Nha Trang

■ Cam Ranh Bay

■ Bien Hoa

Phnom Penh•   •Saigon

Tan Son Nhut■

GULF OF THAILAND   Can Tho■   SOUTH CHINA SEA

■ Major U.S. military bases

0   50   100 Miles
0   50 100 Kilometers

■ Why was there an American military presence in South Vietnam?
■ What was the Ho Chi Minh Trail?
■ What was the Tet offensive?

by President Eisenhower, and reaffirmed by President Kennedy, included a pledge to oppose the advance of communism anywhere in the world. "Why are we in Vietnam?" Johnson asked during a speech at Johns Hopkins University in 1965. "We are there because we have a promise to keep. . . . To leave Vietnam to its fate would shake the confidence of all these people in the value of American commitment." Military intervention was thus a logical culmination of the assumptions that had long been shared by the foreign-policy establishment and the leaders of both political parties.

At the same time, Johnson and his advisers believed that military efforts in Vietnam must not reach levels that would cause the Chinese or Soviets to become involved—which meant, in effect, that a military victory was never possible. As a practical matter, the United States was not fighting to "win" the war, but to prevent the North Vietnamese and the Viet Cong from winning and, eventually, thereby, force them to sign a negotiated settlement. This meant that the United States would have to maintain a military presence as long as the enemy retained the will to fight.

The Vietnam War was the defining event for the baby boomers, the largest generation of Americans ever, and it divided that generation in lasting ways. As it turned out, American support for the war eroded faster than the will of the North Vietnamese leaders to tolerate devastating casualties and destruction.

Widespread opposition to the war on college campuses began in 1965 with "teach-ins" at the University of Michigan. The following year, Senator J. William Fulbright of Arkansas, chairman of the Senate Foreign

Relations Committee, began congressional investigations into American policy in Vietnam. George F. Kennan, the author of the containment doctrine, told the committee that the doctrine was appropriate for Europe but not for Southeast Asia, a region that was not essential to U.S. security. In addition, a respected military leader testified that America's strategy had no chance of achieving victory.

By 1967, anti-war demonstrations were attracting massive support, and Americans were dividing themselves into "hawks" who supported the war and "doves" who opposed it. Nightly television accounts of the fighting—Vietnam was the first war to receive extended television coverage and hence was dubbed the "living-room war"—called into question the accuracy of statements by military and government officials claiming the Americans were winning. By May 1967, even Secretary of Defense Robert McNamara was wavering: "The picture of the world's greatest superpower killing or injuring 1,000 civilians a week, while trying to pound a tiny backward nation into submission on an issue whose merits are hotly disputed, is not a pretty one." Between 1965 and 1968, U.S. warplanes dropped more bombs on Vietnam than had fallen on all enemy targets in the Second World War.

> Mounting opposition to the Vietnam War

Johnson and his advisers badly underestimated the strength of the North Vietnamese and Viet Cong commitment to unify Vietnam and expel American forces. While the United States fought a limited war for limited objectives, the Vietnamese Communists, aided by the Soviets and Chinese, fought an all-out war for their very survival. Just as General Westmoreland was assuring Johnson and the public in early 1968 that his troops were on the verge of gaining the upper hand, the Communists organized widespread assaults that jolted American confidence and resolve.

The Turning Point

On January 31, 1968, the first day of the Vietnamese New Year (Tet), the Viet Cong defied a holiday truce by launching well-coordinated assaults on American and South Vietnamese forces throughout South Vietnam. The old capital city of Hué fell to the Communists, and VC fighters temporarily occupied the U.S. embassy in Saigon, the capital of South Vietnam. Within a few days, however, superior American firepower turned the tables. General Westmoreland proclaimed the **Tet offensive** a major defeat for the Viet Cong, and most military strategists later agreed with him.

> Tet Offensive

The Viet Cong had hoped the Tet offensive would ignite a general uprising in the countryside. In that, they failed. Yet while VC casualties were enormous, the *political* impact of the surprise attack was dramatic, for it decisively turned Americans against the war. The scope and intensity of the Tet offensive contradicted upbeat claims by U.S. commanders that the war had been going well. "What the hell is going on?" CBS newscaster Walter Cronkite demanded when he heard about the offensive. "I thought we were

Tet offensive (1968) Surprise attack by Viet Cong guerrillas and the North Vietnamese army on U.S. and South Vietnamese forces that shocked the American public and led to widespread sentiment against the war.

winning this war." *Time* and *Newsweek* magazines soon ran anti-war editorials urging the withdrawal of U.S. forces. President Johnson's popularity plummeted.

Civil rights leaders and social activists felt betrayed as they saw federal funds earmarked for the War on Poverty gobbled up by the ever-expanding war. By 1967, the United States was spending some $2 billion each month in Vietnam, about $322,000 for every VC killed; anti-poverty programs at home received only $53 per person. As Martin Luther King Jr. pointed out, "the bombs in Vietnam explode at home—they destroy the hopes and possibilities for a decent America."

President Johnson, under constant assault by critics of "Johnson's War," grew increasingly embittered and isolated. He suffered from depression and bouts of paranoia as he realized that the Vietnam War ("that bitch of a war") was a never-ending stalemate dividing the nation and undermining his Great Society programs. Clark Clifford, Johnson's new secretary of defense, reported in early 1968 that a task force of prominent soldiers and civilians saw no prospect for a military victory.

Robert F. Kennedy, now a New York Senator, was considering a run for the presidency to challenge Johnson's Vietnam policy. Senator Eugene McCarthy of Minnesota had already decided to oppose Johnson. With anti-war students rallying to his "Dump Johnson" candidacy, McCarthy polled a stunning 42 percent of the vote to Johnson's 48 percent in New Hampshire's March Democratic primary. It was a remarkable showing for a little-known senator. Each presidential primary now promised to become a referendum on Johnson's Vietnam policy. In Wisconsin, the scene of the next primary, the president's political advisers forecast a humiliating defeat.

On March 31, 1968, Johnson appeared on national television to announce a limited halt to the bombing of North Vietnam and renewed efforts for a negotiated cease-fire. Then he added a shocking postscript: "I shall not seek, and I will not accept, the nomination of my party for another term as your President." As his daughter explained, the "agony of Vietnam" had engulfed her father.

Johnson, a flawed giant, had promised far more than he could accomplish, raising false hopes and stoking violent resentments. He ended up losing two wars—the one in Vietnam and the one against poverty. Although U.S. troops would remain in Vietnam for five more years, the quest for military victory ended with Johnson's presidency. America had tried to fight a "limited war" in Vietnam. The problem with such a strategy was that the Vietnamese Communists fought an absolute war. Among other things, Johnson's presidency revealed that the resources of the United States, including its military power, were limited; the nation could not do everything it wanted, which was a disheartening realization for many Americans used to getting their way.

Lyndon Johnson under siege

Whose war? Johnson lowers his head in disappointment as he listens to a commander's report from Vietnam in 1968.

Sixties Crescendo

By the late 1960s, traditional notions of authority were everywhere under attack. An angry spirit of rebelliousness among disaffected youth who were "beyond your command," according to singer Bob Dylan, expanded into a multidimensional attack, not only on the Johnson administration and the war in Vietnam but on virtually every aspect of mainstream life, including the family, the middle-class work ethic, universities, religion, and the integrationist philosophy underpinning the nonviolent civil rights movement led by Martin Luther King Jr. Many alienated young Americans during the sixties, often lumped together as "hippies," felt that they were part of "the Revolution," a magical force of history that would overthrow a corrupt and outdated way of life.

A Traumatic Year

Change moved at a fearful pace throughout the sixties, but 1968, another election year, was the most traumatic year of all, filled with chaos punctuated by tragedy. As *Time* magazine reported, "Nineteen sixty-eight was a knife blade that severed past from future." On April 4, only four days after Lyndon Johnson's shocking withdrawal from the presidential race, a white racist named James Earl Ray shot and killed Martin Luther King Jr. as he stood on the second-floor balcony of the Lorraine Motel in a black neighborhood of Memphis, Tennessee.

King's murder set off a wave of violence. The prominent African American writer James Baldwin said that whites would never understand the depth of black grief. Riots occurred in over a hundred cities. Forty-six people died, all but five of them black. Some 20,000 Army troops and 34,000 National Guardsmen were mobilized to stop the violence across the country. On April 15 Chicago's Mayor Daley ordered his police to shoot to kill arsonists and to shoot to maim looters.

The night that Martin Luther King died, Senator Robert Kennedy was in Indianapolis, Indiana. Upon hearing the sad news, he stood on a flatbed truck to speak to a grieving crowd of African Americans. "Those of you who are black can be filled with hatred, with bitterness and a desire for revenge," he said. "We can move toward further polarization. Or we can make an effort, as Dr. King did, to understand, to reconcile ourselves and to love."

Love was hard to find in 1968. Two months after King's death, after midnight on June 6, 1968, Robert Kennedy appeared at the Ambassador Hotel in Los Angeles to celebrate his victory over Senator Eugene McCarthy in the California Democratic presidential primary. Kennedy closed his remarks by pledging that "we can end the divisions within the United States, end the violence."

> **CORE OBJECTIVE**
>
> **5.** Examine the presidential election of 1968 and explain the issues that propelled Richard Nixon to victory.

> Martin Luther King assassinated

Robert F. Kennedy assassinated

After the applause subsided, he walked through the kitchen on his way to the press room for interviews. Along the way, a Jordanian Arab named Sirhan Sirhan, resentful of the senator's strong support of Israel, shot Kennedy in the head. He died the next day.

Only forty-two years old, the father of ten children with another on the way, Kennedy was buried beside his brother John in Arlington National Cemetery outside of Washington, D.C. The assassinations of Robert Kennedy, Martin Luther King, Malcolm X, and John Kennedy came to frame the sixties. With their deaths, a wealth of idealism died too—the idealism that Bobby Kennedy had hoped would put a fragmented America back together again. A growing number of young people felt orphaned from the political system. Having lost the leading voices for real change in the political process, many of them lost hope in democracy and turned to radicalism and violence.

Chicago and Miami

Riots at the 1968 Democratic National Convention

In the summer of 1968, the social unrest in the nation came to a head at the Democratic National Convention. In August, delegates gathered inside a Chicago convention hall to nominate Johnson's faithful vice president, Hubert H. Humphrey, as the party's contender for the presidency.

Outside, almost 20,000 police officers, National Guard troops, and television reporters stood watch over a large gathering of scruffy, passionate anti-war protesters herded together miles away in a public park, their youthful energy having been converted to electrical fury as they taunted the police with obscenities. Richard J. Daley, Chicago's gruff Democratic mayor, warned that he would not tolerate disruptions. Nonetheless, ugly riots broke out and were televised nationwide. It was war in the streets. As police used tear gas and clubs to pummel anti-war demonstrators, others chanted, "The whole world is watching." As the *New York Times* reported, "Those were our children in the streets, and the Chicago police beat them up."

Nixon and the "silent majority"

Three weeks before the Chicago riots, the Republicans had gathered in Miami Beach to nominate Richard Nixon. Only six years earlier, after he had lost the California governor's race, Nixon had vowed never again to run for public office. By 1968, however, he had changed his mind and become a self-appointed spokesman for the values of "middle America." He and the Republicans offered a vision of stability ("law and order") that appealed to what Nixon called the **"silent majority"** of Americans. In accepting the nomination, Nixon promised to listen to "the voice of the great majority of Americans, the forgotten Americans, the non-shouters, the non-demonstrators, that are not racists or sick, that are not guilty of the crime that plagues the land."

George Wallace, the governor of Alabama and an outspoken segregationist, dismissed both Democrats and Republicans as too liberal ("owned by the Eastern Establishment") and ran on the American Independent party ticket,

silent majority Term popularized by President Richard Nixon to describe the great majority of American voters who did not express their political opinions publicly— "the non-demonstrators."

a party he formed to defend racial segregation. Wallace promised to get tough on "scummy anarchists" and bring stability to the nation. He appealed even more forcefully than Nixon to voters' concerns about antiwar protesters, the mushrooming federal welfare system, the growth of the federal government, forced racial integration, and rioting in urban ghettos. He displayed a savage wit on the campaign trail, once saying that the "only four-letter words that hippies did not know were w-o-r-k and s-o-a-p." Wallace predicted that on Election Day, the nation would realize that "there are a lot of rednecks in this country." His candidacy generated considerable appeal outside his native South, especially among white working-class communities, where resentment of Johnson's Great Society liberalism flourished. Although never likely to win, Wallace hoped to deny Humphrey and Nixon an electoral majority and thereby throw the choice into the House of Representatives, which would have provided a fitting climax to a chaotic year.

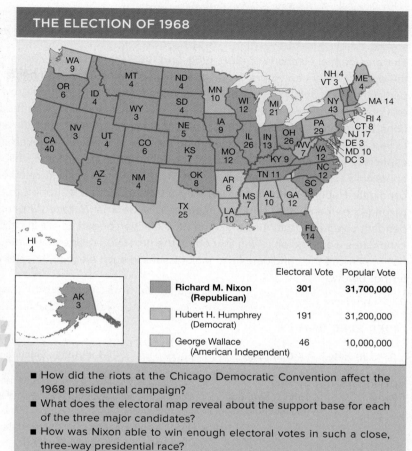

THE ELECTION OF 1968

		Electoral Vote	Popular Vote
	Richard M. Nixon (Republican)	**301**	**31,700,000**
	Hubert H. Humphrey (Democrat)	191	31,200,000
	George Wallace (American Independent)	46	10,000,000

- How did the riots at the Chicago Democratic Convention affect the 1968 presidential campaign?
- What does the electoral map reveal about the support base for each of the three major candidates?
- How was Nixon able to win enough electoral votes in such a close, three-way presidential race?
- What was Wallace's appeal to 10 million voters?

Nixon Triumphant

It did not happen that way. Richard Nixon and Governor Spiro Agnew of Maryland, his acid-tongued running mate, eked out a narrow victory of about 500,000 votes, a margin of about 1 percentage point. The electoral vote was more decisive: 301 for Nixon, 191 for Hubert Humphrey. George Wallace received 10 million votes, 13.5 percent of the total, while all but one of Wallace's 46 electoral votes were from the Lower South. Nixon swept all but four of the states west of the Mississippi. By contrast, Humphrey's support came almost exclusively from the Northeast.

Nixon elected (1968)

So at the end of a turbulent year, near the end of a traumatic decade, a society divided between sharply hostile points of view on the right and left looked to combative Richard Nixon to bring "peace with honor" in Vietnam and to "bring us together" as a nation.

Presidential Elections in the Sixties

The presidential elections of 1960, 1964, and 1968 show the tumultuous 1960s through the eyes of American voters. Issues that divided the country—civil rights, the cold war, particularly U.S. military engagement in Vietnam and the continued growth of the federal government—were key factors in each election. Democrats won the first two elections, but faltered in the third. Democratic candidates Kennedy, Johnson, and Humphrey, to various degrees, supported expanding the role of the federal government at home, especially when it came to securing civil rights for all Americans, while aggressively containing communist expansion abroad. By 1968, voters strongly rejected Democratic candidate Hubert Humphrey, giving over 55 percent of their support to either Richard Nixon (43 percent), the Republican nominee, or George Wallace (13 percent), an independent candidate from Alabama. The 1968 election began an era in which Republican candidates would go on to win four out of the next five presidential contests. When you have reviewed the candidates and major issues in each election, answer the questions further below.

1960 ELECTION

Political Party	Candidate	Issues in the Election	Results
Democratic Party	Senator John F. Kennedy (Massachusetts)	■ Promised new domestic programs to get the country "moving again" and more aggressive cold war efforts than under Eisenhower ■ First Roman Catholic to run for president since Alfred E. Smith, the Democratic nominee in 1928 ■ Dynamic and comfortable in the nation's first televised presidential debates ■ Influenced the release of civil rights activist Martin Luther King Jr., in jail for "trespassing" on a whites-only restaurant	Kennedy won the closest election since 1888 by a margin of 118,574 votes out of 68 million cast. Kennedy's margin in the electoral college was 303 to 219, even though Nixon won more states. Kennedy won 70 percent of the African American vote.
Republican Party	Vice President Richard Nixon (California)	■ Popular with the Republican Party ■ Vice President for the previous eight years under Eisenhower ■ Cunning and deceptive reputation, earning him the nickname "Tricky Dick"	

1964 ELECTION

Political Party	Candidates	Issues in the Election	Results
Democratic Party	President Lyndon Johnson (Texas)	■ Touted his success at passing Kennedy's stalled legislation: the Civil Rights Act, major tax reduction, and the Economic Opportunity Act ("War on Poverty") ■ Pledged to build a "Great Society" to eradicate poverty and racial discrimination in America ■ Campaigning as a foreign policy centrist, pledged not to send U.S. troops to South Vietnam	Johnson won in a landslide, polling 61 percent of the votes. Johnson won the electoral college by 486 to 52. Goldwater won six states in the South, signaling the conservative region's continued shift to the Republican party. Goldwater's candidacy inspired many young conservative activists to reshape the Republican party in the 1970s and 1980s.
Republican Party	Senator Barry Goldwater (Arizona)	■ Opposed the Civil Rights Act ■ Pledged to limit the federal government's size and reach by cutting income tax and federal entitlement programs ■ Urged a more aggressive foreign policy in Vietnam	

1968 ELECTION

Political Party	Candidates	Issues in the Election	Results
Democratic Party	Vice President Hubert Humphrey (Minnesota)	■ Deeply divided over the Vietnam War ■ Promised to try new ways of ending the Vietnam War	Nixon won a narrow victory of 500,000 votes, a margin of only 1 percent of all votes cast. Nixon won the electoral college 301 to 191. Wallace received 13.5 percent of the vote and 46 electoral votes, all but one from the Lower South.
Republican Party	Former Vice President Richard Nixon (California)	■ Self-appointed spokesman for "Middle America" ■ Promised to represent the majority of Americans disturbed by the lawlessness of antiwar protests and urban riots ■ Pledged to end the Vietnam War	
American Independent Party	Former Governor of Alabama George Wallace	■ Savagely criticized antiwar protestors and "hippies" ■ Opposed the growth of the federal government and its welfare system ■ Denounced forced racial integration and rioting blacks in urban ghettos ■ Targeted white working-class communities outside of the South	

QUESTIONS FOR ANALYSIS

1. How did the issue of race influence the outcomes of these elections?

2. How did voters respond to Lyndon Johnson's term in office?

3. What kind of voter did George Wallace appeal to in 1968 and how did his successes challenge the Democratic party?

■ **Kennedy's New Frontier** President John F. Kennedy promised a *"New Frontier"* in 1961, but many of his domestic policies stalled in Congress. He inherited a CIA plan to topple Fidel Castro's regime in Cuba that resulted in the *Bay of Pigs* fiasco. Soviet premiered Nikita Khrushchev tested American resolve by erecting the *Berlin Wall* and installing missiles in Cuba, provoking the *Cuban missile crisis*. Determined to stand up to the Soviet Union, Kennedy ordered a naval "quarantine" of Cuba and succeeded in forcing Khrushchev to withdraw the missiles. During his presidency, Kennedy also deepened America's anticommunist commitment in Vietnam.

■ **Civil Rights' Achievements** At the beginning of the decade, growing numbers of African Americans and whites staged acts of *nonviolent civil disobedience* to protest discrimination in the South. In 1960, student activists formed the *Student Nonviolent Coordinating Committee (SNCC)* to intensify efforts to dismantle segregation. In 1961, courageous *Freedom Riders* attempted to integrate Southern bus and train stations. Martin Luther King, Jr. delivered his famous "I Have a Dream" speech at the *March on Washington* (1963). But King and other leaders did little to address the concerns of the inner cities, where 70 percent of the nation's African American population lived and experienced frequent discrimination in housing, education, and employment. The *black power movement*, emphasized militancy, black nationalism, separatism, and, often, violence.

■ **Johnson's Great Society** Early in his presidency, Johnson shepherded the *Civil Rights Act of 1964* and, as part of his "war" on poverty, the *Economic Opportunity Act* through Congress. After his resounding presidential victory in 1964, he pushed his vision for a Great Society through Congress—hundreds of initiatives that expanded federal social welfare programs, such as the *Voting Rights Act, Medicare,* and *Medicaid.* It also ended national quotas in immigration law through the *Immigration and Nationality Services Act of 1965.*

■ **1968 Presidential Election** Johnson shockingly chose not to seek reelection in early 1968. Anti-war Democrats rallied around Senators Eugene McCarthy and Robert Kennedy. In April, Martin Luther King Jr. was assassinated, setting off a series of violent riots in urban ghettos across the country. Robert Kennedy himself was assasinated in June. Ultimately, the Democrats selected Johnson's loyal vice president, Hubert Humphrey, as their nominee, provoking angry protests by anti-war demonstrators at the 1968 Chicago Democratic Party Convention. The Republicans nominated former candidate Richard Nixon who claimed to represent the *"silent majority."* The segregationist former governor of Alabama, George Wallace, ran as an independent candidate and also appealed to the "silent majority." In the end, Nixon narrowly beat Humphrey and Wallace who made one of the best showings ever by a third-party candidate.

KEY TERMS

New Frontier *p. 1008*
Bay of Pigs (1961) *p. 1011*
Berlin Wall *p. 1012*
Cuban missile crisis (1962)
p. 1014
Student Nonviolent Coordinating
Committee (SNCC) *p. 1016*
Freedom Riders *p. 1017*

nonviolent civil disobedience
p. 1019
March on Washington (1963)
p. 1020
black power movement *p. 1023*
Civil Rights Act of 1964 *p. 1027*
Economic Opportunity Act
(1964) *p. 1028*

Medicare and Medicaid *p. 1031*
Immigration and Nationality
Services Act of 1965 *p. 1032*
Voting Rights Act of 1965 *p. 1032*
Tonkin Gulf Resolution (1964)
p. 1034
Tet offensive (1968) *p. 1037*
silent majority *p. 1040*

CHRONOLOGY

February 1960	Greensboro Four stage a sit-in
April 1960	Student Nonviolent Coordinating Committee (SNCC) formed
November 1960	John F. Kennedy elected president
April 1961	Bay of Pigs invasion fails
May 1961	Freedom Rides begin
August 1961	Soviets erect the Berlin Wall
October 1962	Cuban missile crisis
August 1963	March on Washington for Jobs and Freedom
November 1963	John F. Kennedy assassinated in Dallas, Texas
June 1964	Congress passes the Civil Rights Act
August 1964	Congress passes the Tonkin Gulf Resolution
November 1964	Lyndon B. Johnson elected to a full term
February 1965	Malcolm X assassinated
June–August 1965	Congress passes immigration reform, Medicare and Medicaid, the Voting Rights Act
August 1965	Race riots in Watts, California
January 1968	Viet Cong stage the Tet offensive
April 1968	Martin Luther King Jr. assassinated
June 1968	Robert Kennedy assassinated
November 1968	Richard Nixon elected president

INQUIZITIVE

Go to InQuizitive to see what you've learned—and learn what you've missed—with personalized feedback along the way.

REBELS WITH A CAUSE Established in 1967, the Vietnam Veterans Against the War (VVAW) grew quickly during the sixties and seventies. Here, a former Marine throws his service uniform jacket and medals onto the steps of the Capitol on April 23, 1971, as part of a five-day protest against the U.S. invasion of Laos.

Rebellion and Reaction

The 1960s and 1970s

As Richard M. Nixon entered the White House in early 1969, he took charge of a nation whose social fabric was in tatters. Everywhere, it seemed, institutions and notions of authority were under attack. The traumatic events of 1968 had been like a knife blade cutting the past away from the future, revealing how deeply divided America had become and how difficult a task Nixon faced in carrying out his campaign pledge to restore social harmony.

In the end, the stability and harmony he promised proved elusive. His controversial policies and his combative temperament heightened rather than reduced societal tensions. Ironically, many of the same forces that had enabled the complacent prosperity of the fifties—the baby boom, the cold war, and the growing consumer culture—helped generate the social upheaval of the sixties and early seventies. The civil rights movement promoting equality for African Americans inspired efforts to ensure equal treatment for other minorities—women, gays, Native Americans, Hispanics, and others. It was one of the most turbulent and significant periods in American history—exciting, threatening, explosive, and transformative.

Despite President Nixon's promise to restore the public's faith in the integrity of government leaders, he ended up aggravating the growing cynicism about the motives and methods of government officials. During 1973 and 1974, the Watergate scandal resulted in the greatest constitutional crisis since the impeachment of President Andrew Johnson in 1868, and it ended with the first resignation in history of a U.S. president.

CORE OBJECTIVES InQuizitive

1. Analyze the origins of the youth revolt and compare the responses of the New Left and the counterculture.

2. Assess the influence of the youth revolt and the early civil rights movement on other protest movements and how new protest movements affected social attitudes and public policy.

3. Analyze how Richard Nixon's election strategy and domestic policies were affected by the political environment of the late sixties.

4. Analyze how and why Richard Nixon and Henry Kissinger changed military and political strategies to end America's involvement in the Vietnam War.

5. Examine the world order that evolved after the Vietnam War from Richard Nixon's and Henry Kissinger's diplomacy and foreign policies.

6. Explain how the Watergate scandal unfolded, and assess its political significance.

"Forever Young": The Youth Revolt

The Greensboro sit-ins in 1960 not only launched a decade of civil rights activism but also signaled an end to the carefree inertia that had enveloped many college campuses and much of social life during the fifties. Rennie Davis, a sophomore at Ohio's Oberlin College in 1960, remembered that the young Greensboro civil rights advocates inspired him and many others to become political and social activists. "Here were four students from Greensboro who were suddenly all over *Life* magazine. There was a feeling that they were us and we were them, and a recognition that they were expressing something we were feeling as well."

Youth disillusionment with the U.S. government and "authority"

The sit-ins, marches, protests, ideals, and sacrifices associated with the civil rights movement inspired other minority groups—women, Native Americans, Hispanics, gays, and the disabled—to demand justice, freedom, and equality as well. As Bob Dylan sang in 1963, "How many times can a man turn his head / Pretending he just doesn't see." He and many other idealistic young people decided that they could no longer turn a blind eye to the growing evidence of injustice and inequality staining the American dream.

A full-fledged youth revolt erupted during the mid-sixties. "Your sons and your daughters are beyond your command," sang Dylan in "The Times They Are a-Changin'." By 1970, more than half of Americans were under thirty years of age, and almost 8 million of them were attending college. The baby boomers, who unlike their parents had experienced neither an economic depression nor a major war during their young lifetimes, were now attending colleges and universities in record numbers; enrollment quadrupled between 1945 and 1970. Many universities had become gigantic institutions dependent upon huge research contracts from corporations and the federal government, especially the Defense Department. As these "multiversities" grew larger and more bureaucratic, they became targets for a generation of students wary of involvement in what President Dwight D. Eisenhower had labeled "the military-industrial complex." As criticism of U.S. military involvement in Vietnam mounted, young people disillusioned with the government and "authority" of all kinds flowed into two distinct yet frequently overlapping movements: the New Left and the counterculture.

The New Left

Students for a Democratic Society (SDS)

The political arm of the youth revolt originated in 1960 when Tom Hayden and Alan Haber, two University of Michigan students, formed Students for a Democratic Society (SDS), a campus-based organization influenced by the tactics and successes of the civil rights movement. In 1962, Hayden and Haber called a meeting of sixty young men and women activists at Port

Huron, Michigan. Their goal was ambitious: to design a strategy to remake the United States into a more democratic society. Hayden drafted an impassioned document known as the Port Huron Statement. It began: "We are the people of this generation, bred in at least moderate comfort, housed in universities, looking uncomfortably to the world we inherit." Only by giving power to "the people," the manifesto insisted, could America restore its founding principles. Hayden called for political reforms, racial equality, and workers' rights. Inspired by the example of African American civil rights activists in the South, Hayden declared that college students should engage in "participatory democracy" by snatching "control of the educational process from the administrative bureaucracy."

Hayden and others adopted the term **New Left** to distinguish their efforts at grassroots democracy from those of the Old Left of the thirties, which had embraced an orthodox Marxism. "We have no sure formulas, no closed theories," Hayden explained. The New Left was determined to let the people decide what form the new society would take. SDS grew quickly during the sixties, forming chapters on over a thousand campuses.

In the fall of 1964, students at the University of California at Berkeley took Hayden's New Left program to heart. Several had returned to the campus after spending the summer working with the Student Nonviolent Coordinating Committee's (SNCC) voter-registration project in Mississippi, where three volunteers had been killed and many others arrested or harassed. Their idealism and activism had been aroused, and they were eager to bring changes to campus life as well. When the university's chancellor announced that political demonstrations would no longer be allowed on campus, thousands of students staged a sit-in. After a tense thirty-two-hour standoff, the administration relented. Student groups then formed the free-speech movement (FSM).

> Student free-speech movement (FSM)

Led by Mario Savio, a philosophy major who had participated in Freedom Summer in Mississippi, the FSM initially protested on behalf of students' rights, but it quickly mounted a more general criticism of the university and what Savio called the "depersonalized, unresponsive bureaucracy" smothering American life. In 1964, Savio led hundreds of students into UC Berkeley's administration building and organized a sit-in. They were not welcomed by the president. In the early-morning hours, 600 policemen, dispatched by the governor, arrested the protesters. But their example lived on.

Anti-War Protests

The goals and tactics of FSM and SDS soon spread to colleges across the country. By 1965, however, the growing U.S. involvement in Vietnam changed the rebellious students' agenda. With the dramatic expansion of the war after 1965, millions of young men during the late sixties faced the grim prospect of being drafted to fight in an increasingly unpopular

New Left Term coined by the Students for a Democratic Society to distinguish their efforts at grassroots democracy from those of the 1930s Old Left, which had embraced orthodox Marxism and admired the Soviet Union under Stalin.

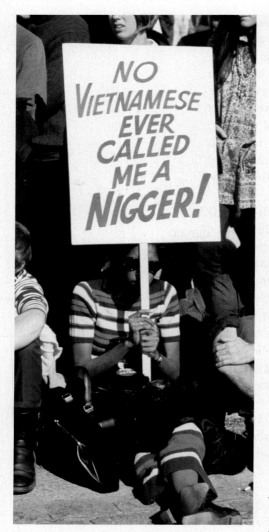

All that rises must converge This protester's sign at a Washington, D.C. demonstration bridged the civil rights and anti-war movements, which called for many of the same racial and political reforms.

conflict. In fact, however, the Vietnam War, like virtually every other, was primarily a poor man's fight. Most college students were able to postpone military service until they received their degree or reached the age of twenty-four; in 1965–1966, college students made up only 2 percent of all military inductees. African Americans and Hispanics were twice as likely to be drafted as whites.

As the war dragged on, Americans divided into two bitter factions, hawks and doves, those who supported the war and those who opposed it. Some 200,000 young men ignored their draft notices during the sixties, and some 4,000 served prison sentences for doing so. Another 56,000 qualified for conscientious objector status during the Vietnam War, compared with only 7,600 during the Korean conflict. Others ceremoniously burned their draft cards in front of television cameras. Still others fled the United States altogether—several thousand moved to Canada or Sweden—to avoid military service. The most popular way to escape the draft was to use a variety of creative ways to flunk the physical examination. Whatever the preferred method, many college students succeeded in avoiding military service. Of the 1,200 men in Harvard's class of 1970, only 56 served in the military, and just 2 of them went to Vietnam.

Rising Violence

Throughout 1967 and 1968, the anti-war movement grew more violent as inner-city ghettos in Cleveland, Detroit, Newark, and other large cities were exploding in flames fanned by racial injustice. Frustration over deeply entrenched patterns of discrimination in employment and housing, as well as staggering rates of joblessness among inner-city African American youths, ignited rage in scores of urban ghettos. "There was a sense everywhere, in 1968," journalist Garry Wills wrote, "that things were giving way. That man had not only lost control of his history, but might never regain it."

During the eventful spring of 1968—when Lyndon Johnson announced that he would not run for reelection and Martin Luther King Jr. and Robert F. Kennedy were assassinated—campus unrest boiled over across the country. The turmoil reached a climax at Columbia University, where SDS student radicals and black militants occupied the president's office and classroom buildings. The administration was forced to cancel classes and call in the New York City police.

The events at Columbia inspired similar clashes among students, administrators, and police at Harvard, Cornell, and San Francisco State, among others. Vice President Spiro Agnew dismissed the anti-war protesters as "impudent snobs who characterize themselves as intellectuals."

The Counterculture

Looking back over the 1960s, Tom Hayden, the founder of SDS, recalled that most rebellious young Americans did not join SDS. They "were not narrowly political. Most were not so interested in attaining [elected] office but in changing lifestyles. They were not interested in being opinion makers as in changing the climate of opinion." Hayden acknowledged that the shocking events of 1968 led disaffected young rebels—so-called hippies—to abandon conventional political activism and embrace the **counterculture**, an unorganized rebellion against mainstream institutions, values, and behavior that at times overlapped with the New Left but more often was focused on cultural rebellion rather than political activism. Hippies focused on changing lifestyles rather than changing political policies. In pursuing personal liberation, they rejected the pursuit of wealth and careers and instead embraced plain living, authenticity, friendship, peace, and, especially, *freedom*.

Counterculture: Hippies and Yippies and communes

Columbia riots Mark Rudd, leader of SDS at Columbia University, speaks to the media during student protests in April 1968.

The counterculture and the New Left both fiercely rejected the status quo in American society, but most of the hippies preferred to "drop out" rather than try to change the political system. Their preferred anti-war slogan was "Make Love, Not War." Like the Beats of the fifties, hippies celebrated personal freedom from virtually all traditional constraints. In all their technicolor variety, they were at once defiant, innocent, optimistic, and indulgent as they rejected the authority of the nation's core institutions: the family, government, political parties, corporations, the military, and colleges and universities.

The colorful lifestyle of those embracing the counterculture included an array of popular ideals and activities: peace, love, harmony, rock music, mystical religions, mind-altering drugs, casual sex, and communal living arrangements. Many hippies practiced meditation and yoga. Hippie fashion featured defiantly long hair for both women and men (prompting the label *long hairs*), flowing cotton dresses, ragged bell-bottom blue jeans, tie-dyed T-shirts, love beads, peace symbols, and sandals. Young men grew beards and women discarded makeup as badges of difference (or indifference, as it were).

The countercultural rebels were primarily middle-class whites alienated by the Vietnam War, racism, political corruption, and parental authority. In their view, a superficial materialism had settled over urban and suburban life, and they were determined to break out of conventional behavior by

counterculture Unorganized youth rebellion against mainstream institutions, values, and behavior that more often focused on cultural radicalism rather than political activism.

Flower power *Left*: Hippies let loose at a 1967 love-in, gatherings that celebrated peace, free love, and non-theological spirituality, often as a gesture of protest. *Right*: Author Ken Kesey and his posse, the Merry Pranksters, held Acid Test Graduation parties throughout the San Francisco, California, area that celebrated the psychedelic drug LSD (also known as "acid").

embracing the tactics recommended by the drug-promoting former Harvard psychology professor Timothy Leary: "Tune in, turn on, drop out." Illegal drugs—marijuana, amphetamines, cocaine, peyote, hashish, heroin, and LSD—were commonplace within the counterculture. Said Todd Gitlin, a former SDS president, "More and more, to get access to youth culture" in the late 1960s, "you had to get high." The Byrds sang about getting "Eight Miles High," and singer/songwriter Bob Dylan proclaimed that "everybody must get stoned!"

In fact, getting stoned was one of the principal purposes of the 1967 "Summer of Love" centered in San Francisco when over 100,000 hippies ("flower children") from around the country converged on the city's hip Haight-Ashbury district and other enclaves around northern California. The loosely organized "Council for the Summer of Love" intended the gathering to be the first step in a grassroots revolution celebrating alternative lifestyles, especially those "of compassion, awareness, and love, and the revelation of unity for all mankind." That same summer, the Beatles issued one of their all-time best-selling songs, "All You Need Is Love"—a number-one hit worldwide.

The countercultural alternative to SDS and the New Left was the zany Youth International Party, better known as the Yippie movement, founded by two irreverent pranksters, Jerry Rubin and Abbie Hoffman. Often calling themselves Groucho Marxists, the Yippies were countercultural comedians, wacky mischief-makers bent on thumbing their noses at conventional laws and behavior and mocking capitalism as well as the consumer culture. Abbie Hoffman, a founding Yippie, explained that their "conception of revolution is that it's fun." The Yippies were the jokesters in the generational revolution, a clownish force of history that, they believed, would overthrow the power structure. Rubin claimed that the widespread use of "psychedelic" drugs among young Americans "signifies the total end of the Protestant ethic: screw work, we want to know ourselves," and that meant rejecting America's "sick notion of work, success, reward, and status."

The anarchistic Yippies specialized in scandalous theatrical gestures and pranks intended to generate media coverage. They organized marijuana "smoke-ins," threw pies in the faces of political figures, nominated a pig named Pigasus for the presidency, urged voters to cast their ballots for "None of the Above," and threatened to put LSD in the city of Chicago's water supply during the Democratic National Convention in 1968. When asked what being a Yippie meant, Hoffman replied: "Energy–fun–fierceness–exclamation point!" He had no interest in making the Yippies a traditional political organization. "We shall not defeat *Amerika* by organizing a political party," he declared. "We shall do it by building a new nation—a nation as rugged as the marijuana leaf."

For some, the counterculture involved experimenting with alternative living arrangements, especially "intentional communities" or "communes." Communal living in urban areas such as San Francisco's Haight-Ashbury district, New York's Greenwich Village, Chicago's Uptown, and Atlanta's 14th Street neighborhood were popular for a time, as were rural communes. Thousands of inexperienced hippie romantics flocked to the countryside during the late 1960s, eager to liberate themselves from parental and institutional restraints, live in harmony with nature, and coexist in an atmosphere of love and openness.

The participants in the back-to-the-land movement, as it became known, were seeking a path to more authentic living that would deepen their sense of self and forge authentic community ties. "Out here," one of the rural communalists reflected, "we've got the earth and ourselves and God above. . . . We came for simplicity and to rediscover God."

Yet all but a handful of the back-to-the-land experiments collapsed within a few months or years. Almost none of those attracted by rural life actually knew how to farm. And in many cases they were not willing to do the hard work that living off the land required. "The hippies will not change America," a journalist predicted, "because change means pain, and the hippie subculture is rooted in the pleasure principle." In a candid reflection, a young hippie confessed that "we are so stupid, so unable to cope with anything practical." A resident of Paper Farm in northern California, which started in 1968 and collapsed a year later, said of its participants: "They had no commitment to the land—a big problem. All would take food from the land, but few would tend it. . . . We were entirely open. We did not say no [to anyone]. We felt this would make for a more dynamic group. But we got a lot of sick people."

The sixties counterculture thrived on music—initially folk "protest" songs and later psychedelic or "acid rock" music. During the early sixties, Pete Seeger, Joan Baez, Peter, Paul, and Mary, and Bob Dylan, among others, produced powerful songs of social reform. In Dylan's "The Times They Are A-Changin'," first sung in 1963, he warns: "There's a battle outside and

Bob Dylan Born Robert Allen Zimmerman, Dylan came to the New York folk music scene by way of northern Minnesota, penning the anti-war movement anthem "Blowin' in the Wind."

it's ragin' / It'll soon shake your windows and rattle your walls / For the times, they are a-changin'." Within a few years, however, the hippies' favorite performers were those under the influence of mind-altering drugs, especially the San Francisco–based "acid rock" bands: Jefferson Airplane, Big Brother and the Holding Company (Janis Joplin), and The Grateful Dead.

The Woodstock Festival (1969)

Huge outdoor music concerts were wildly popular events among the counterculture. The largest of these was the sprawling Woodstock Music and Art Fair ("Aquarian Exposition"). In mid-August 1969, more than 400,000 mostly young people converged on a 600-acre farm near the tiny rural town of Bethel, New York, for what was called the world's "largest happening," three days "of peace and music." The powerful lure of the festival was the all-star cast of musicians: Jimi Hendrix, the Jefferson Airplane, Janis Joplin, Santana, The Who, Joan Baez, and Crosby, Stills & Nash, among many others. For three days amid summer heat, rain storms, and rivers of mud, the assembled "flower children" "grooved" on good music, beer and booze, cheap marijuana, and casual sex. Drug use was rampant, but there were no robberies, assaults, or rapes. Reflecting on the scene, a long-haired teen said: "People are finally getting together."

The carefree "spirit of love" that blossomed at the Woodstock festival was short-lived, however. Just four months later, when other concert promoters tried to replicate the "Woodstock Nation" experience at the Altamont Speedway Free Festival near San Francisco, the counterculture fell victim to the criminal culture. The Rolling Stones hired the Hells Angels motorcycle gang to provide "security" for their show. During the band's performance of "Under My Thumb," a drunken Hells Angel stabbed to death an eighteen-year-old African American man wielding a gun in front of the stage. Three other spectators were accidentally killed that night, and much of the vitality and innocence of the counterculture died with them. After 1969, the hippie phenomenon began to fade as the counterculture became counterproductive. The spirit of liberation ran up against the hard realities of growing poverty, drug addiction, crime, and mental and physical illness among the "flower children."

Decline of the New Left

At the same time, the New Left was also self-destructing as an organized political movement. In large measure, SDS had committed suicide by abandoning the pacifist principles that had originally inspired participants and given the movement moral legitimacy. The Weathermen, a violent SDS splinter group named for a line in a Bob Dylan song, took to the streets of Chicago in October 1969 to assault police and trash the city. Almost 300 were arrested. During the so-called Days of Rage between September 1969 and May 1970, there were 250 bombings of draft board offices, ROTC buildings on university campuses, federal government facilities, and corporate headquarters. In March 1970, three Weathermen died when a bomb they were making in New York City exploded prematurely.

SDS and other radical groups were also plagued by internal disputes and were forced underground by the aggressive efforts of federal law enforcement agencies. The energy behind the youth revolt waned as the Vietnam War began to wind down. There would be a resurgent wave of student protests against the Nixon administration in 1970–1971, but thereafter campus unrest diminished as Nixon ended the military draft and withdrew U.S. troops from Vietnam, which greatly defused the resistance movement.

Social Activism Spreads

The same liberationist ideals that prompted young people to revolt against mainstream American values and to protest against the Vietnam War also led many of them to embrace other causes. The success of the civil rights movement inspired other groups to demand equal opportunities and equal rights as well—women; Mexican Americans, Native Americans, and other ethnic groups; gays; the elderly; and the physically and mentally disabled. Still others joined the emerging environmental movement or groups working on behalf of consumers, led by the crusading Ralph Nader.

The New Feminism

Like the New Left, the new feminism drew much of its inspiration and many of its tactics from the civil rights movement. The women's movement in the late nineteenth and early twentieth centuries had focused on gaining the right to vote. The feminist movement of the sixties and seventies was much more comprehensive in its goals, seeking equal rights in virtually every area of life. Its aim was to challenge the conventional ideal of female domesticity and ensure that women were treated equally in the workplace.

Most women in the early sixties, however, did not yet view gender equality as possible or even desirable. In 1962, more than two-thirds of women surveyed agreed that the most important family decisions "should be made by the man of the house." Although the Equal Pay Act of 1963 had made it illegal to pay women less than men for doing the same job, varied forms of discrimination and harassment continued in the workplace and throughout society. Women, who were 51 percent of the nation's population in the sixties and held 37 percent of the jobs, earned overall salaries that were 42 percent less than those for men.

Betty Friedan, a forty-two-year-old journalist and mother of three from Peoria, Illinois, emerged as the leader of the **women's movement** during the mid-sixties. Her influential book *The Feminine Mystique* (1963) helped launch the new phase of female protest. Friedan claimed that "something was very wrong with the way American women are trying to live their lives today." Her generation of white, college-educated women (she did not discuss working-class or African American women) had actually lost ground after the Second World War, when many left wartime employment and settled in suburbia as full-time wives and mothers, only to

CORE OBJECTIVE

2. Assess the influence of the youth revolt and the early civil rights movement on other protest movements and how new protest movements affected social attitudes and public policy.

The Feminine Mystique (1963)

women's movement Wave of activism sparked by Betty Friedan's *The Feminine Mystique* (1963); it argued for equal rights for women and fought against the cult of domesticity that limited women's roles to the home as wife, mother, and homemaker.

Betty Friedan Author of *The Feminine Mystique* and the first president of NOW.

National Organization for Women (NOW)

Roe v. Wade **(1973)** Landmark Supreme Court decision striking down state laws that banned abortions during the first trimester of pregnancy.

suffer from the "happy homemaker" syndrome which undermined their intellectual capacity and public aspirations while tying them to household duties. "A century earlier," she wrote, "women had fought for higher education; now girls went to college to get a husband." Friedan blamed a massive propaganda campaign by advertisers and women's magazines for brainwashing women to embrace the "feminine mystique" of blissful domesticity in which fulfillment came only with marriage and motherhood. Underemployed women, Friedan claimed, "were being duped into believing homemaking was their natural destiny."

The Feminine Mystique, an immediate best seller, forever changed American society by defining "the problem that has no name." Friedan's analysis of the "feminine mystique" that limited women's lives to being bored housewives and tired mothers inspired many well-educated, unfulfilled middle- and upper-class white women who felt trapped by a suffocating suburban ideal of household drudgery. Moreover, Friedan discovered that there were far more women working outside the home (a third of the workforce) than she had assumed. Many of these working women were frustrated by the demands of holding "two full-time jobs instead of just one—underpaid clerical worker and unpaid housekeeper." Perhaps most important, Friedan helped the emerging women's movement to focus on empowering women to achieve their "full human capacities"—in the home, in schools, in offices, on college campuses, and in politics.

In 1966, Friedan and other activists founded the National Organization for Women (NOW). They chose the acronym NOW because it was part of a popular civil rights chant: "What do you want?" protesters yelled. "FREEDOM!" "When do you want it?" "NOW!"

Initially, NOW sought to end gender discrimination in the workplace and went on to spearhead efforts to legalize abortion and obtain federal and state support for child-care centers. In August 1970, Friedan organized a march for women's equality in New York City that involved 50,000 people walking down Fifth Avenue. Change came slowly, however. By 1970, there was still only one woman in the U.S. Senate, ten in the House of Representatives, and none on the Supreme Court or in the president's cabinet.

In the early seventies, members of Congress, the Supreme Court, and NOW advanced the cause of gender equality. Title IX of the Educational Amendments of 1972 barred discrimination on the basis of sex in any "education program or activity receiving federal financial assistance." Most notably applied to athletics, Title IX has allowed for female participation in high school sports to increase nearly tenfold and almost double at the college level. Congress also overwhelmingly approved an equal-rights amendment (ERA) to the federal constitution, which, if ratified by the states, would have required equal treatment for women throughout society and politics. By mid-1973, twenty-eight states had approved the amendment, still ten short of the thirty-eight states needed for approval.

In 1973, the Supreme Court, in its *Roe v. Wade* decision, made history by striking down state laws forbidding abortions during the first three months of pregnancy. The majority on the Court ruled that women have a fundamental "right to choose" whether to bear a child or not, since pregnancy necessarily affects a woman's health and well-being. The *Roe v. Wade* decision and the ensuing success of NOW's efforts to liberalize local and state abortion laws generated a powerful conservative backlash, especially among Roman Catholics and evangelical Protestants, who mounted a potent "right-to-life" crusade that helped fuel the conservative political resurgence in the seventies and thereafter.

Meanwhile, all-male colleges, including Yale, Princeton, and the U.S. Military Academy, led a movement for coeducation that swept the country. "If the 1960s belonged to blacks," said one feminist, "the next ten years are ours."

Radical Feminism

During the late sixties, a new wave of younger and more radical feminists emerged to challenge everything from women's economic, political, and legal status to sexual double standards for men and women. They sought "women's liberation" from all forms of "sexism" (also called "male chauvinism" or "male oppression"), not simply equality in the workplace.

The new generation of feminists, often called "women's libbers," was more militant than Betty Friedan and others who had established NOW. Many younger feminists were veterans of the civil rights movement and the anti-war crusade who had come to realize that male revolutionaries could be sexists too. They began meeting in small groups to discuss their opposition to the war and racism, only to discover at such "consciousness-raising" sessions that what bound them together were their shared grievances as women operating in a "man's world."

To gain true liberation, many of them decided, required exercising "sexual politics" whereby women would organize themselves into a political movement based on women's common problems and goals. The writer Robin Morgan captured this newly politicized feminism in the slogan, "The personal is political," a radical notion that Betty Friedan rejected. When lesbians demanded a public role in the women's movement, Friedan deplored the "lavender menace" of lesbianism as a divisive distraction that would only enrage their opponents. By 1973, however, NOW had endorsed gay rights.

Friedan, however, could not dampen or deflect the younger generation of women activists, just as Martin Luther King, Jr. had failed to control the Black Power movement. The goal of the women's liberation movement, said Susan Brownmiller, a self-described "radical feminist," was to "go beyond a simple concept of equality. NOW's emphasis on legislative change left the radicals cold." She dismissed Friedan as "hopelessly bourgeois." For women to be truly equal, Brownmiller and others believed, required transforming *every* aspect of society: child rearing, entertainment, domestic duties, business, and the arts. Lesbianism, she and others argued, should be celebrated rather than hidden.

> Radical feminism: Direct action and social transformation

What women want *Left*: The Women's Strike for Equality brought tens of thousands of women together on August 26, 1970 to march for gender equality and celebrate the 50th anniversary of the Nineteenth Amendment. *Right*: The antifeminist campaign, STOP ERA ("Stop Taking Our Privileges, Equal Rights Amendment"), found its most outspoken activist in Phyllis Schlafly, a constitutional lawyer and staunch conservative.

Like civil rights activists, feminists also demanded that their "hidden history," the story of women's rights advocates over the centuries, be taught in schools and colleges. Radical feminists also took direct action, such as picketing the 1968 Miss America Pageant, burning copies of *Playboy* and other men's magazines, tossing their bras and high-heeled shoes into "freedom cans," and assaulting gender-based discrimination in all of its forms. They also formed militant organizations like WITCH (Women's International Terrorist Conspiracy from Hell), WRAP (Women's Radical Action Project), Keep on Truckin' Sisters, and the Redstockings, whose manifesto proclaimed that they were tired of being exploited by men "as sex objects, breeders, domestic servants, and cheap labor." Members sported buttons proclaiming their collective nickname: "Uppity Women."

Fractured Feminism

Successes and failures of feminism: Gains in education, employment, and politics; conservative backlash; and failure of the ERA

By the end of the seventies, sharp disputes between moderate and radical feminists had fractured the women's movement in ways similar to the fragmentation experienced by civil rights organizations a decade earlier. The movement's failure to broaden its appeal much beyond the confines of the white middle class also caused reform efforts to stall. Ratification of the Equal Rights Amendment, which had once seemed a straightforward assertion of equal opportunity ("Equality of rights under the law shall not be denied or abridged by the United States or by any State on account of sex"), was stymied in several state legislatures by the organized opposition of conservative groups, many of which used the possibility of women having to serve in combat roles in the armed services as reason enough to oppose the ERA. By 1982, it had finally died, three states short of passage. The defeat of the ERA was seen as a triumph by the surging conservative movement that drew its strength, in part, from the backlash against changing social attitudes about women's roles.

Yet the successes of the women's movement endured. Whether young or old, conventional or radical, those women fighting for equal rights focused on several basic issues during the sixties and seventies: gender discrimination in the workplace, equal pay for equal work, an equal chance at jobs traditionally reserved for men, the availability of high-quality, government-subsidized child-care centers, and easier access to birth control devices, prenatal care, and abortion. Feminists helped win improvements in divorce laws and gained easier access for women seeking clinical abortions.

It was also the feminist movement that called attention to issues long hidden or ignored in American society. In 1970, for example, 36 percent of the nation's "poor" families were headed by women, as were most urban families dependent on federal welfare services. Nearly 3 million poor children needed access to day-care centers but there were only places for 530,000. It was the feminist movement that helped women achieve mass entry into the labor market and enjoy steady improvements towards equal pay and treatment in the workplace. In 1960, some 38 percent of women were working outside the home; by 1980, 52 percent were doing so.

A growing presence in the labor force brought women a greater share of economic and political influence. By 1976, more than half of married women, and nine of ten female college graduates, were employed outside the home, a development that one economist called "the single most outstanding phenomenon of this century." Women also enrolled in graduate and professional schools in record numbers. During the 1970s, women began winning elected offices at the local, state, and national levels.

The Sexual Revolution and the Pill

The feminist movement coincided with the so-called sexual revolution, a much-discussed loosening of traditional restrictions on social behavior. During the sixties and after, Americans became more tolerant of premarital sex, and women became more sexually active. Between 1960 and 1975, the number of college women engaging in sexual intercourse doubled, from 27 percent to 50 percent. Enabling this change, in large part, was a scientific breakthrough in contraception: the birth-control pill, approved for public use by the Food and Drug Administration in 1960.

> Birth control and changing sexual attitudes

Widespread access to the pill fundamentally changed social life by giving women a greater sense of sexual freedom. The pill also led to more open discussion of birth control, reproduction, and sexuality in general. By 1990, the world would have 400 million fewer people as a result of the pill. Although the birth control pill also contributed to a rise in sexually transmitted diseases, many women viewed it as a godsend—an inexpensive, nonintrusive way for them to gain better control over their bodies and their futures. "It was a savior," recalled Eleanor Smeal, president of the Feminist Majority Foundation. "The whole country was waiting for it. I can't even describe to you how excited people were."

Hispanic Rights

The activism of student revolts, the civil rights movement, and the crusade for women's rights soon spread to various ethnic minority groups. The word *Hispanic*, referring to people who trace their ancestry to Spanish-speaking Latin America or Spain, came into increasing use after 1945 in conjunction with growing efforts to promote economic and social justice. (Although frequently used as a synonym for Hispanic, the term *Latino* technically refers only to people of Latin American descent.) Labor shortages during the Second World War had led defense industries to offer Hispanic Americans their first significant access to skilled-labor jobs. And as was the case with African Americans, service in the military during the war years helped to heighten an American identity among Hispanic Americans, increasing their desire for equal rights and social opportunities.

Social equality, however, remained elusive for Hispanics who were wanted in the United States for their labor but not for their race and culture. After the Second World War, Hispanic Americans still faced widespread discrimination in hiring, housing, and education. Poverty was rampant. In 1960, for example, the median income of a Mexican American family was only 62 percent of the national average. Hispanic American activists denounced segregation, called for improved public schools serving their children, and struggled to increase Hispanic political influence, economic opportunities, and visibility in the curricula of schools and colleges.

Hispanic civil rights leaders faced an awkward dilemma: What should they do about the continuing stream of undocumented Mexican immigrants flowing across the border into the United States? Many Mexican Americans argued that their hopes for economic advancement and social equality were put at risk by the daily influx of Mexican laborers willing to accept low-paying jobs. Mexican American leaders thus helped end the bracero program in 1964 (which trucked in contract day-laborers from Mexico during harvest season).

United Farm Workers (UFW)

In the early sixties, Mexican American workers formed their own civil rights organization, the **United Farm Workers (UFW)**. The founder of the UFW was the charismatic Cesar Chavez. Born in 1927 in Yuma, Arizona, the son of Mexican immigrants, Chavez moved with his family to California in 1939. There they joined thousands of other poor migrant farmworkers moving from job to job, living in tents, cars, or ramshackle cabins. After serving in the U.S. Navy during the Second World War and then working as a migrant laborer, Chavez first became a community organizer focused on registering Latinos to vote.

United Farm Workers (UFW)
Organization formed in 1962 to represent the interests of Mexican American migrant workers.

Cesar Chavez The usually energetic Chavez is visibly weakened from what would be a 25-day hunger strike in support of the United Farm Workers Union in March of 1968. Robert F. Kennedy, a great admirer of Chavez, is seated to his right.

Then, along with Dolores Huerta, a talented organizer, Chavez created UFW, a union for migrant lettuce workers and grape pickers, many of them undocumented immigrants who could be deported at any time. Up and down California, Chavez led nonviolent mass protest marches that had the energy of religious pilgrimages; he staged hunger strikes like those of his hero, India's Mahatma Gandhi; and he managed nationwide boycotts.

> Nonviolent Protest: Marches, boycotts, and *la huelga* (strike against California grape growers)

The United Farm Workers gained national attention in September 1965 when the union organized a strike ("*la huelga*") against the corporate grape growers in California's San Joaquin Valley. As Huerta explained, "We have to get farmworkers the same type of benefits, the same type of wages, and the respect that they deserve because they do the most sacred work of all. They feed our nation every day."

Chavez's relentless energy and deep Catholic faith, his insistence upon nonviolent tactics, his reliance upon college-student volunteers, his skillful alliance with organized labor and religious groups, and the life of poverty he chose for himself—all combined to attract media interest and popular support.

However, the chief strength of the Hispanic rights movement lay less in the tactics of sit-ins and protest marches than in the rapid growth of the Hispanic American population. In 1970, Hispanics in the United States numbered 9 million (4.8 percent of the total population); by 2000 their numbers had increased to 35 million (12.5 percent); and in 2012, they numbered 53 million, making them the nation's largest minority group (17 percent). The voting power of Hispanics and their concentration in states with key electoral votes has helped give the Hispanic point of view significant political clout.

Native American Rights

American Indians—many of whom had begun calling themselves *Native Americans*—also emerged as a political force in the late sixties. Two conditions combined to make Indian rights a priority. First, many whites felt guilty for the destructive actions of their ancestors toward a people who had, after all, been here first. Second, the plight of Native Americans was more desperate than that of any other group in the country. Indian unemployment was ten times the national rate, life expectancy was twenty years lower than the national average, and the suicide rate was a hundred times higher than the rate for whites.

Although President Lyndon Johnson attempted to funnel federal anti-poverty-program funds into reservations, militants within the Indian community grew impatient with the pace of change. Those promoting "**Red Power**" organized protests and demonstrations against local, state, and federal agencies. On November 20, 1969, fourteen Red Power activists occupied Alcatraz Island near San Francisco, which until 1963 had hosted a federal prison. Over the next several months, they were joined by hundreds of others, mostly students. The Nixon administration responded by cutting off electrical service and telephone lines. Stranded without electrical power and fresh water, most of the protesters left the island. Finally, on June 11, 1971, the government removed the remaining fifteen Native Americans from the island.

In 1968, the year before the Alcatraz occupation, two Chippewas (or Ojibwas) living in Minneapolis, George Mitchell and Dennis Banks, founded the American Indian Movement (AIM). In October 1972 AIM organized the Trail of Broke Treaties caravan which traveled by bus and car across the nation from the West coast to Washington, D.C., drawing attention to the history of the federal government's broken treaties and promises. When officials in the Nixon administration refused to meet with the protesters, they occupied the federal Bureau of Indian Affairs on November 3. The sit-in ended when federal negotiators agreed to renew discussions of Native American grievances about the administration of government programs intended to improve their quality of life.

In 1973, AIM led 200 Sioux in the occupation of the tiny village of Wounded Knee, South Dakota, where the U.S. Seventh Cavalry had massacred a Sioux village in 1890. Outraged by the light sentences given a group of local whites who had killed a Sioux in 1972, the organizers sought to draw attention to the plight of the Indians

"Red Power" and the occupation of Wounded Knee

Red Power Activism by militant Native American groups to protest living conditions on Indian reservations through demonstrations, legal action, and, at times, violence.

Standoff at Wounded Knee After occupying Wounded Knee and taking eleven hostages, members of the American Indian Movement and the Oglala Sioux stand guard outside of the town's Sacred Heart Catholic Church.

living on the reservation there. After the militants took eleven hostages, federal marshals and FBI agents surrounded the encampment. The occupation at Wounded Knee captured more media attention in its first few days than the Indian rights movement had received in the decade up to that point. For ten weeks the two sides engaged in a tense standoff. When AIM leaders tried to bring in food and supplies, a shoot-out erupted, with one Indian killed and another wounded. Soon thereafter, the confrontation ended with a government promise to reexamine Indian treaty rights.

Indian protesters subsequently discovered a more effective tactic than direct action and sit-ins: they went into federal courts armed with copies of old treaties and demanded that the documents become the basis for financial restitution for the lands taken from them over the centuries. In Alaska, Maine, South Carolina, and Massachusetts, they won substantial settlements that officially recognized their tribal rights and awarded monetary compensation at levels that upgraded the standard of living on several reservations.

> Legal recognition of historic Native American treaties and tribal rights

Gay Rights

The liberationist impulses of the sixties also encouraged homosexuals to assert their right to equal treatment. Throughout the sixties, gay men and lesbians continued to be treated frequently with disgust, cruelty, and violence. On Saturday night, June 28, 1969, New York City vice police raided the Stonewall Inn, a popular gay bar in Greenwich Village, because it lacked a liquor license. Instead of dispersing, the diverse patrons fought back, and the struggle spilled into the streets. Hundreds of other gays and their supporters joined the fracas.

> Stonewall riots (1969)

The **Stonewall riots** lasted throughout the weekend, during which the Stonewall Inn caught fire and burned down. When the turmoil ended, gays had forged a new sense of solidarity embodied in two new organizations, the Gay Liberation Front and the Gay Activists' Alliance, both of which focused on ending discrimination and harassment against gays and transvestites. "Gay is good for all of us," proclaimed one of its members. "The artificial categories 'heterosexual' and 'homosexual' have been laid on us by a sexist society."

As news of the Stonewall rebellion spread, the gay rights movement grew in its numbers and its demands. By 1973, almost 800 gay organizations had been formed across the country, and every major city had a visible gay community and cultural life. That year, the American Psychiatric Association removed homosexuality from its official manual of "mental illnesses." Colleges and universities began offering courses and majors in "Gay Studies" (also called Queer Studies), and grassroots movements as well as national organizations began pushing for official government recognition of same-sex marriages. As was the case with the civil rights and women's movements, however, the campaign for gay rights soon suffered from internal divisions and a conservative counterattack.

Stonewall riots (1969) Violent clashes between police and gay patrons of New York City's Stonewall Inn, seen as the starting point of the modern gay rights movement.

The Movements of the 1960s and 1970s

The struggles and successes of the African American civil rights that began in the fifties and evolved into a powerful political force in the sixties inspired many other groups and individuals in American society. The 1950s also saw the beginning of a student movement and an emerging counterculture, but by the sixties and seventies these had grown into a more general youth rebellion that often focused on opposing the Vietnam War as well as promoting a more democratic society. Other civil rights movements also emerged. Marginalized Americans such as women, homosexuals, Hispanics, and Native Americans demanded a more equitable role in American society. The following chart describes some of these movements.

Movement	Causes	Main Organizations (year founded)	Origins & Influences	Significant Events
Student Movement	Create a more democratic society through political reforms, racial equality, and workers' rights; later, anti-war causes	Students for a Democratic Society (SDS) (1960), The Weathermen faction (1969)	Inspired by the civil rights movement Founded by Michigan students Tom Hayden and Alan Haber in 1960	■ Free Speech Movement (FSM) founded (1964) ■ Emergence of the New Left (1960s) ■ Columbia riots (1968) ■ Kent State and Jackson State anti-war protests and shootings (1970)
Counterculture Movement	Refusing conventional consumerism and embracing alternative, more authentic social arrangements	Hippies, Youth International Party (Yippie movement) (1967), back-to-land movement (1960s–1970s)	Associated with anti-war cause Music: rock, folk, psychedelic or "acid rock" Mysticism, mind-altering drugs, casual sex, communal living	■ Summer of Love (1967) ■ Woodstock Music and Art Fair (1969)
Women's Movement	Challenge social assumptions of women's domesticity Fight against gender discrimination and for reproductive rights	National Organization for Women (NOW) (1963), WITCH (1968) and other radical feminist organizations	*The Feminine Mystique* (1963) by Betty Freidan Inspired by the civil rights movement	■ Title IX of the Educational Amendments passed (1972) ■ *Roe v. Wade* (1973) ■ Failure of the Equal Rights Amendment (1982) ■ Internal divisions and conservative opposition slowed reforms (1970s)

Movement	Causes	Main Organizations (year founded)	Origins & Influences	Significant Events
Hispanic American Rights Movement	Combat racial segregation and lack of economic opportunity for Hispanic Americans	United Farm Workers (UFW) (1962)	World War II labor shortages and military service provided first significant access to skilled labor jobs and military service, increasing demand for equal rights Inspired by the civil rights movement	■ End of the bracero program (1964) ■ Increase in political power with dramatic population growth
Red Power Movement	Reform of state and federal Native American policies to improve conditions on reservations	American Indian Movement (AIM) (1963)	Lacking opportunities and funds from government agencies, as one of the nation's most disenfranchised groups Inspired by the civil rights movement	■ Occupation at Alcatraz Island (1963) ■ AIM's standoff at Wounded Knee (1972) ■ Native American enforcement of historic treaties in federal court
Gay Rights Movement	Equal treatment and social acceptance for homosexuals; gay solidarity	Gay Liberation Front (1969), Gay Activists' Alliance (1969)	Sparked by Stonewall riots in New York City (1969)	■ Stonewall riots (1969) ■ Removal of "homosexuality" from official U.S. mental illness manual (1973) ■ Internal divisions and conservative opposition slowed reforms (1970s)

QUESTIONS FOR ANALYSIS

1. What similarities were there in the origins and goals of these movements?

2. What patterns do you see among these movements' successes and failures?

3. What role did the African American civil rights movement play in the development of these other movements?

CORE **OBJECTIVE**

3. Analyze how Richard Nixon's election strategy and domestic policies were affected by the political environment of the late sixties.

Nixon and the Revival of Conservatism

By the end of the sixties, Americans were engaged in a cultural civil war. The turmoil of the sixties spawned a cultural backlash among what Richard Nixon called the "great silent majority" of middle-class Americans that propelled him to a narrow election victory in November 1968, in large part because he promised to bring "law and order" to a nation overflowing with "violence, lawlessness, and permissiveness." Nixon was no friend of the civil rights movement, the youth revolt, or spreading social activism. He had been elected president as the representative of middle America, those voters fed up with liberal politics, countercultural hippies, radical feminism, and **affirmative-action** programs giving preferential treatment to minorities and women to atone for past injustices.

The Conservative Backlash

Alabama's Democratic governor, George Wallace, led the conservative counterattack. "Liberals, intellectuals, and long hairs," he shouted, "have run the country for too long." Wallace repeatedly lashed out at "welfare queens," unmarried women who he claimed "were breeding children as a cash crop" in order to receive federal child-support checks. Wallace's support was not limited to the South. He became the popular voice for many working-class whites across the nation fed up with political liberalism and social radicalism.

All in the Family, the most popular TV show in the 1970s, was created to showcase the decade's cultural wars. In the much-celebrated sitcom (situation comedy), the Bunker family lived in a state of perpetual conflict in a working-class suburb outside of New York City. Semi-literate Archie Bunker (played by Carroll O'Connor), a Polish-American loading-dock worker, was the gruff but lovable head of the family, a proud Republican, Nixon supporter, and talkative member of the "silent majority" who was a bundle of racial, ethnic, and political prejudices. Enthroned in his easy chair, he railed each week against blacks, Jews, Italians, gays, feminists, hippies, and liberals (including his live-in daughter and her hippie husband, both "bleeding-heart" liberals). At one point, Archie says: "I ain't no bigot. I'm the first guy to say, 'It ain't your fault that youse are colored.'" The producer of the series, Norman Lear, intended Archie's raging intolerance as a satire to provoke viewers to question their own prejudices. In fact, however, many of the 50 million people watching each Saturday night identified *with* the narrow-minded values of Archie Bunker, who in 1973 was "the most recognized face in America."

At a grassroots level, conservatives in the early seventies fought back in the courts against preferential treatment for historically disadvantaged groups, arguing that government-mandated affirmative-action programs were neither fair nor efficient ways to address the problems of historic

The "silent majority"

affirmative action Programs designed to give preferential treatment to women and minorities as compensation for past injustices.

inequality. Others sought to combat the counterculture by creating new rules and regulations to enforce old values. In Louisville, Kentucky, for instance, the Fire Department announced that "beards, goatees, or any other extraneous facial hair will not be permitted." In supporting such efforts, Nixon appealed to the working- and middle-class whites who feared that America was being corrupted by permissiveness, anarchy, and the tyranny of the rebellious minority. He promised to return "law and order" to a nation on the verge of chaos.

In 1952, the powerful Senator Robert A. Taft of Ohio, known as "Mr. Republican," had characterized young Senator Richard Nixon as a "little man in a big hurry" with "a mean and vindictive streak." A grocer's son from Whittier, California, Nixon was a humorless man of fierce ambition and extraordinary perseverance. Raised in a family that struggled with poverty, he had to claw and struggle to the top his whole life, and he nursed a deep resentment of people who had an easier time of it (the "moneyed class").

Nixon was much more than persistent, however. He was also smart, shrewd, cunning, and doggedly determined to succeed in politics. Republican senator Barry Goldwater described Nixon as "the most complete loner I've ever known." Throughout his career, Nixon displayed violent mood swings punctuated by raging temper tantrums, vulgar profanity, and anti-Semitic outbursts. He was nicknamed "Tricky Dick" because he was a good liar. In his speech accepting the Republican nomination in 1968, Nixon pledged "to find the truth, to speak the truth, and live with the truth." In fact, however, he often did not speak the truth. One of his presidential aides admitted that "we did often lie, mislead, deceive, try to use [the media], and to con them."

Nixon's Appointments

In his first term, Nixon selected for his cabinet and White House staff only white men who would carry out his orders with blind obedience. John Mitchell, the gruff attorney general who had been a senior partner in Nixon's New York law firm, was the new president's closest confidant. H. R. (Bob) Haldeman, a former advertising executive, served as chief of staff. As Haldeman explained, "Every President needs a son of a bitch, and I'm Nixon's. I'm his buffer, I'm his bastard." John Ehrlichman, a Seattle attorney and college schoolmate of Haldeman, served as Nixon's chief domestic-policy adviser. John W. Dean III, an associate deputy in the office of the U. S. Attorney General, became the White House legal counsel.

Nixon tapped as secretary of state his old friend William Rogers, who had served as attorney general under Dwight D. Eisenhower, but Nixon had no intention of making Rogers the nation's chief diplomat. Instead, the president virtually ignored Rogers and the State Department in the process of forging an unlikely partnership with Dr. Henry Kissinger, a brilliant German-born Harvard political scientist who had become the nation's leading foreign-policy expert. His thick German accent, owlish appearance, and outsized ego had helped to make him an international celebrity, courted by presidents of both parties. In 1969 Nixon named Kissinger his National Security Advisor, and in 1973 Kissinger became secretary of state.

Nixon and Kissinger, the politician and the professor, formed an odd but effective diplomatic team. Both were loners and outsiders who preferred operating in secret; both were insecure and even paranoid at times; and both mistrusted and envied the other's power and prestige. Nixon would eventually grow tired of Kissinger's efforts at self-promotion and his frequent threats to resign if he did not get his way. For his part, Kissinger lavished praise on Nixon in public, while in private he was less supportive, dismissing the president's "meatball mind" and criticizing his excessive drinking. Yet for all of their differences, they worked well together, in part because they both loved secrecy and intrigue, power politics and diplomatic flexibility, and in part because of their shared vision of a new multipolar world order beginning to replace the bipolar cold war as the United States slowly withdrew its military forces from Vietnam.

The Southern Strategy

A major reason for Nixon's election victories in 1968 and 1972 was his shrewd southern strategy, designed to win over white southern Democrats upset by the civil rights revolution. Of all the nation's regions, the South had long been the most conservative. The majority of white southern voters were religious and patriotic, fervently anti-Communist and anti-union, and skeptical of social-welfare programs. For a century, whites in the "Solid South" had steadfastly voted for Democrats in national elections. Their doing so reflected lingering southern resentments, dating back to the Civil War and Reconstruction, that demonized Abraham Lincoln and his Republican successors for imposing northern ways of life on the South, including racial integration. During the late sixties and seventies, however, a surging economy and a spurt of population growth transformed the South. The region's warm climate, low cost of living, absence of labor unions, low taxes, and government incentives for economic development convinced waves of businesses, workers, professionals, and retirees to relocate to the region.

Between 1970 and 1990, the South's population grew by 40 percent, more than twice the national average. During the seventies, job growth in the South was seven times greater than in New York and Pennsylvania. In the sixties and seventies, southern "redneck" culture suddenly became all the rage, as people across the nation embraced stock car racing, cowboy boots, pickup trucks, barbecue, and country music. As Alabama's George Wallace had claimed while campaigning for president in 1968, "For 100 years, both parties have looked down their noses and called us rednecks down here in this part of the country. I'm sick and tired of it, and on November 5, they're goin' to find out there are a lot of rednecks in this country."

Rapid population growth—and the continuing spread of air-condition-ing—brought the Sunbelt states of the South, the Southwest, and California more congressional seats and more electoral votes. Every president elected between 1964 and 2008 had roots in the Sunbelt, the region that spear-headed the backlash against sixties radicalism. Nixon's favorite singer, country star Merle Haggard, crooned in his smash hit, "Okie from Musk-ogee": "We don't smoke marijuana in Muskogee / We don't take our trips on LSD / We don't burn our draft cards down on Main Street / We like livin' right and bein' free." Haggard's conservative working-class fans bristled at anti-war protesters, hippies, rising taxes, social-welfare programs, and civil rights activism. The alienation of many blue-collar whites from the liberal-ism of the Democratic party, as well as the demographic changes transform-ing Sunbelt states and the white backlash against court-ordered integration, created a welcome opportunity for the Republican party to exploit, which Richard Nixon eagerly seized.

In the 1968 presidential campaign, Nixon's southern strategy took ad-vantage of the backlash against liberalism and civil rights in the region to win over traditionally Democratic white voters. Nixon shrewdly "played the race card," assuring white conservatives that he would appoint justices to the Supreme Court who would undermine federal enforcement of civil rights laws such as mandatory school busing to achieve racial integration and affirmative action that gave minorities priority in hiring decisions and the awarding of government contracts. Nixon also appealed to the economic concerns of middle-class southern whites by promising lower tax rates and less government regulation. Finally, like George Wallace, he specialized in hard-hitting, polarizing rhetoric in which he pledged to restore "law and order" in the streets of America.

> Political realignment in a conservative South

In the 1972 election, it was Nixon's southern strategy that won the day: he carried every southern state by whopping majorities. The Republican takeover of the once "solid" Democratic South was the greatest realignment in American politics since Franklin D. Roosevelt's election in 1932.

Nixon's Domestic Agenda

As president, Nixon was less a rigid conservative ideologue than he was a crafty politician forced to deal with a Congress controlled by Democrats. He therefore chose his battles carefully and showed surprising flexibility, lead-ing political journalist Tom Wicker to describe him as "at once liberal and conservative, generous and begrudging, cynical and idealistic, choleric and calm, resentful and forgiving."

> New Federalism and Democratic legislation

Nixon's focus during his first term was developing policies and programs that would gain him reelection in 1972. To please conservative Republicans and recruit conservative Democrats, he touted his New Federalism whereby he sent federal monies to the states and local governments for them to spend as they saw fit. He also disbanded the core agency of Lyndon John-son's War on Poverty program—the Office of Economic Opportunity—and cut funding to several Great Society programs. At the same time, the Democrats in Congress passed significant new legislation that Nixon did sign: the right of eighteen-year-olds to vote in national elections (1970) and in all elections under the Twenty-Sixth Amendment (1971); increases in Social Security benefits and food-stamp funding; the Occupational Safety and Health Act (1970) to ensure safer workplace environments; and the Federal Election Campaign Act (1971), which modified the rules governing corporate financial donations to political campaigns.

Nixon and Civil Rights

During his first term, President Nixon followed through on his campaign pledges to conservative white southerners to blunt the momentum of the civil rights movement. He appointed no African Americans to his cabinet, and refused even to meet with the all-Democratic Congressional Black Caucus. "We've had enough social programs: forced integration, education, housing," he told his chief of staff. "People don't want more [people] on welfare. They don't want to help the working poor, and our mood needs to be harder on this, not softer."

Off to school Because of violent protests against desegregation, school buses in South Boston are escorted by police in October of 1974.

Nixon also launched a concerted effort to block congressional renewal of the Voting Rights Act of 1965 and to delay implementation of federal court orders requiring the racial desegregation of school districts in Mississippi. Sixty-five lawyers in the U.S. Justice Department signed a letter protesting Nixon's stance. The Democratic-controlled Congress then extended the Voting Rights Act over Nixon's veto.

The Supreme Court also thwarted Nixon's efforts to slow desegregation. Above the entrance to the Supreme Court building in Washington, D.C., are inscribed four words: "Equal justice under law." In its first decision under the new chief justice, Warren Burger—a Nixon appointee—the Court ordered the racial integration of the Mississippi public schools in *Alexander v. Holmes County Board of Education* (1969). During Nixon's first term, more schools were desegregated under court orders than in all the Kennedy-Johnson years combined.

Nixon's efforts to block desegregation in urban areas were also failures. The Burger Court ruled unanimously in *Swann v. Charlotte-Mecklenburg Board of Education* (1971) that school systems must bus students out of their neighborhoods if necessary to achieve racially integrated schools. Protests over busing desegregation thereafter erupted in the North, the Midwest, and the Southwest, as white families in Boston, Denver, and other cities denounced the destruction of "the neighborhood school." Angry white parents in Pontiac, Michigan, were so determined to stop mandatory busing to achieve racial integration that they firebombed empty school buses.

Nixon and Environmental Protection

Dramatic increases in the price of oil and gasoline during the seventies fueled a major energy crisis in the United States. Natural resources grew limited—and increasingly precious. Bowing to pressure from both parties, as well as polls showing that 75 percent of voters supported stronger environmental protections, President Nixon told an aide to "keep me out of trouble on environmental issues"—he was "bored" by them. Yet he recognized that the public mood had shifted in favor of greater federal environmental protections, especially after two widely publicized environmental events in 1969.

The first was a massive oil spill off the coast of Santa Barbara, California. Within ten days, an enormous slick of crude oil contaminated 200 miles of California beaches, killing thousands of sea birds and marine animals. Six months later, on June 22, 1969, the Cuyahoga River, an 80-mile-long stream that slices through the center of Cleveland, Ohio, spontaneously caught fire. Fouled with oil and grease, bubbling with subsurface gases, and littered with debris, the chocolate-colored river ignited and burned for five days, its flames leaping fifty feet into the air. Like the Santa Barbara oil spill, the images of the burning river became an important catalyst in the raising of environmental awareness across the nation. A 1969 survey of college campuses by the *New York Times* revealed that many young people were transferring their attention and idealism from the anti-war movement to the environmental movement.

President Nixon knew that if he vetoed legislative efforts to improve environmental quality, the Democratic majorities in Congress would overrule him, so he chose not to stand in the way. In late 1969, Nixon signed the amended Endangered Species Preservation Act and the National Environmental Policy Act. The latter became effective on January 1, 1970, the year that environmental groups established an annual Earth Day celebration that would involve millions nationwide. In 1970, Nixon by executive order created two new federal environmental agencies, the **Environmental Protection Agency (EPA)** and the National Oceanic and Atmospheric Administration (NOAA). The same year, he signed the Clean Air Act to reduce air pollution on a national level. Two years later, however, Nixon vetoed a new clean water act, only to see Congress override his effort. He also undermined many of the new environmental laws by refusing to spend money appropriated by Congress to fund them.

> Nixon approves Environmental Protection Agency (EPA)

"Stagflation"

The major domestic development during the Nixon administration was a floundering economy. The accumulated expense of the Vietnam War and the Great Society programs helped quadruple the annual inflation rate from 3 percent in 1967 to 12 percent in 1974. Meanwhile, unemployment, at a low

Environmental Protection Agency (EPA) (1970) Federal environmental agency created by Nixon to appease the demands of congressional Democrats for a federal environmental watchdog agency.

"The Nixon Recession": Federal deficits, international competition, new workers, and an oil crisis

of 3.3 percent when Nixon took office, nearly doubled to 6 percent by the end of 1970. Economists coined the term **stagflation** to describe the unprecedented situation of stalled economic growth (stagnation), rising inflation, and high unemployment all occurring at the same time. Consumer prices usually rose with a rapidly growing economy and rising employment. Now it was just the reverse, and there were no easy ways to fight the unusual combination of recession and inflation.

Stagflation had at least three deep-rooted causes. First, the Johnson administration had financed both the Great Society social-welfare programs and the Vietnam War without a major tax increase, thereby generating larger federal deficits, a major expansion of the money supply, and price inflation. Second, and more important, U.S. companies were now facing stiff international competition from West Germany, Japan, and other emerging industrial powers around the world. The technological and economic superiority that the U.S. had enjoyed since the Second World War was no longer unchallenged. Third, America's prosperity since 1945 had resulted in part from the ready availability of cheap sources of energy. No other nation was more dependent than the United States upon the automobile and the automobile industry, and no other nation was more wasteful in its use of fossil fuels in factories and homes. During the seventies, however, oil and gasoline became scarcer and costlier. High energy prices and oil shortages took their toll on the economy.

Just as domestic petroleum reserves began to dwindle and dependence upon foreign sources increased, the Organization of Petroleum Exporting Countries (OPEC) decided to use its huge oil supplies as a political and economic weapon. In 1973, the United States sent massive aid to Israel after a devastating Syrian-Egyptian attack that was launched on Yom Kippur, the holiest day on the Jewish calendar. OPEC responded by announcing that it would not sell oil to nations supporting Israel in the so-called Yom Kippur War and that it was raising its oil prices by 400 percent. The Arab oil embargo, called an "economic Pearl Harbor," caused gasoline shortages and skyrocketing prices. American motorists suddenly faced mile-long lines at gas stations, and factories cut production because of spiking energy costs. The environmental movement received a boost from the effects of the OPEC oil embargo as growing numbers of concerned Americans envisioned a future based on energy conservation, renewable energy, and simpler living.

Oil crisis, 1973 The scarcity of oil forced the rationing of gasoline. Gas stations, such as this one in Colorado, closed on Sundays to conserve supplies.

Another condition leading to stagflation was the flood of new workers—mainly baby boomers and women—into the labor market. From 1965 to 1980, the workforce grew by almost 30 million workers, a number greater than the total labor force of France or West Germany. The number of new jobs could not keep up with the growth of the workforce, leaving many unemployed.

The Nixon administration responded erratically and ineffectively to stagflation, trying old remedies for a new problem. First, the president

stagflation Term coined by economists during the Nixon presidency to describe the unprecedented situation of stagnant economic growth and consumer price inflation occurring at the same time.

sought to reduce the federal deficit by raising taxes and cutting the budget. When the Democratic Congress refused to cooperate, he encouraged the Federal Reserve Board to reduce the nation's money supply by raising interest rates. The stock market immediately nose-dived, and the economy plunged into the "Nixon recession."

A sense of desperation about the stagnant economy seized the White House. In 1969, when asked about the possibility of imposing government caps on wages and prices, Nixon had been clear: "Controls. Oh, my God, no! . . . We'll never go to controls." In 1971, however, he reversed himself. He froze all wages and prices for ninety days. Still, the economy remained sluggish.

"Peace with Honor": Ending the Vietnam War

By the time Nixon entered the White House in January 1969, he and Henry Kissinger had developed a comprehensive vision of a new world order. The result of their collaboration was a dramatic transformation of U.S. foreign policy. Since 1945, the United States had lost its monopoly on nuclear weapons, its overwhelming economic dominance, and much of its geopolitical influence. The rapid rise of competing power centers in Europe, China, and Japan complicated the cold war as well as international relations in general.

Nixon and Kissinger envisioned defusing the cold war by pursuing peaceful coexistence with the Soviets and Chinese. After a "period of confrontation," Nixon explained in his 1969 inaugural address, "we are entering an era of negotiation." Preoccupied with secrecy, Nixon and Kissinger bypassed the State Department, including Secretary of State Rogers, and the Congress in their efforts to take advantage of quickly shifting world events.

The immediate task for Nixon and Kissinger was ending the war in Vietnam, which one presidential aide called a "bone in the nation's throat." Until the war was ended and all troops had returned home, the nation would find it difficult to achieve the social harmony that President Nixon had promised. Privately, he had decided that "there's no way to win the war" in Vietnam, so instead he sought what he called "peace with honor." That is, the United States could not simply cut and run; it needed to withdraw in a way that upheld the credibility of its military alliances around the world. Peace, however, was long in coming, not very honorable, and shockingly brief.

Gradual Withdrawal

The Vietnam policy implemented by Nixon and his national security adviser Henry Kissinger moved along three fronts. First, U.S. negotiators in Paris demanded the withdrawal of Viet Cong forces from South Vietnam and the preservation of the U.S.-backed government of President Nguyen

> CORE **OBJECTIVE**
> **4.** Analyze how and why Richard Nixon and Henry Kissinger changed military and political strategies to end America's involvement in the Vietnam War.

"Peace with honor"

Van Thieu. The North Vietnamese and Viet Cong negotiators, for their part, insisted on retaining a Communist military presence in the south and re-unifying the Vietnamese people under a government dominated by the Communists. There was no common ground. Hidden from public aware-ness and from America's South Vietnamese allies were secret meetings be-tween Kissinger and the North Vietnamese.

"Vietnamization" and ending the military draft

On the second front, Nixon tried to quell domestic unrest. He labeled the anti-war movement a "brotherhood of the misguided, the mistaken, the well-meaning, and the malevolent." He sought to defuse the anti-war move-ment by reducing the number of U.S. troops in Vietnam, justifying the re-duction as the natural result of "**Vietnamization**"—the equipping and training of South Vietnamese soldiers and pilots to assume the burden of combat. From a peak of 560,000 troops in 1969, U.S. combat forces were withdrawn by Nixon at a steady pace. By 1973, only 50,000 troops remained in Vietnam.

In 1969, Nixon also established a draft lottery whereby the birthdates of nineteen-year-old men were randomly selected and assigned a number be-tween 1 and 365 in order of their selection. Those with low lottery numbers would be the first drafted into military service. The lottery system elimi-nated many inequities and clarified the likelihood of being drafted. Four years later, in 1973, the president did away with the draft altogether by cre-ating an all-volunteer military. Those initiatives, coupled with the troop withdrawals from Vietnam, defused the anti-war movement. Opinion polls showed strong public support for Nixon's policies related to the Vietnam War. "We've got those liberal bastards on the run now," the president gloated, "and we're going to keep them on the run." Nixon had much less success in forcing concessions from the North Vietnamese negotiators.

On the third front, while steadily reducing the number of U.S. combat troops in Southeast Asia, Nixon and Kissinger greatly expanded the bomb-ing of North Vietnam in hopes of pressuring the Communist leaders to end the war. Kissinger felt that "a fourth-rate power" like North Vietnam must have a "breaking point" at which it would decide it was suffering too much damage. Nixon agreed, suggesting that they let the North Vietnamese lead-ers know that he was so "obsessed about Communism" that he might use the "nuclear button" if necessary.

Three fronts: Negotiation, troop reduction, and airstrikes

In March 1969, the United States began a fourteen-month-long bombing campaign aimed at Communist forces that were using neighboring Cambo-dia as a base for raids into South Vietnam. Congress did not learn of the se-cret airstrikes until 1970, although the total tonnage of bombs dropped was four times that dropped on Japan during the Second World War. Still, Hanoi's leaders did not flinch; they decided to wait and let Nixon's domestic critics undermine his presidency. Then, on April 30, 1970, Nixon announced an "incursion" into "neutral" Cambodia by U.S. troops to "clean out" hidden Vietnamese Communist military bases. Privately, Nixon told Kissinger, who strongly endorsed the decision to extend the fighting into Cambodia, "If this doesn't work, it'll be your ass, Henry." Nixon knew that sending

Vietnamization Nixon-era pol-icy of equipping and training South Vietnamese forces to take over the burden of combat from U.S. troops.

troops into Cambodia would reignite the anti-war movement. Secretary of State William Rogers predicted that "this will make the [anti-war] students puke."

Divisions at Home

Just as Nixon had expected, the escalation of the air war in Vietnam and the extension of the war into Cambodia triggered widespread anti-war demonstrations. In the fall of 1969, two massive day-long demonstrations in hundreds of cities across the nation and around the world brought millions of protesters into the streets. Nixon, however, was unmoved. "As far as this kind of activity is concerned," he gruffly explained, "we expect it; however, under no circumstances will I be affected whatever by it." Nixon later referred to student protesters as "bums."

Escalation of anti-war riots over the invasion of Cambodia

In the spring of 1970, news of the secret Cambodian "incursion" by U.S. forces breathed new life into the anti-war movement and set off explosive demonstrations on college campuses and across the nation. At Kent State University, the Ohio National Guard was called in to control campus rioting. The poorly trained guardsmen panicked and opened fire on the rock-throwing demonstrators, killing four student bystanders.

The killings at Kent State added new fury to the anti-war and anti-Nixon movement. That spring, demonstrations occurred on more than 350 campuses. A presidential commission charged with investigating the shootings concluded that they were "unnecessary and unwarranted." Eleven days after the Kent State tragedy, on May 15, Mississippi highway patrolmen riddled a dormitory at Jackson State College with bullets, killing two students who were protesting the war. In New York City, anti-war demonstrators who gathered to protest the student deaths and the invasion of Cambodia were attacked by conservative "hard-hat" construction workers, who forced the protesters to disperse and then marched on City Hall to raise the U.S. flag, which had been lowered to half-staff in mourning for the Kent State victims.

Shooting at Kent State Mary Ann Vecchio, a teenage runaway participating in the anti-war demonstration, decries the murder of a Kent State student after the National Guard fired into the crowd.

The following year, in June 1971, the *New York Times* began publishing excerpts from *The History of the U.S. Decision-Making Process of Vietnam Policy*, a secret Defense Department study commissioned by Robert McNamara before his resignation as Lyndon Johnson's secretary of defense in 1968. The so-called Pentagon Papers, leaked to the press by Daniel Ellsberg, a former Defense Department official, confirmed what many critics of the war had long suspected: Congress and the public had not received the

The Pentagon Papers published (1971)

full story on the Gulf of Tonkin incident of 1964, and contingency plans for U.S. entry into the war were being drawn up even as President Johnson was promising that combat troops would never be sent to Vietnam. Although the Pentagon Papers dealt with events only up to 1965, the Nixon administration blocked their publication, arguing that release of the classified information would endanger national security and would prolong the war. By a vote of 6 to 3, the Supreme Court ruled against the government. Newspapers throughout the country began publishing the controversial documents the next day.

War without End

During 1972, mounting social divisions at home and the approach of the presidential election influenced the negotiations in Paris between the United States and representatives of North Vietnam. In the summer of 1972, Henry Kissinger renewed private meetings with the North Vietnamese negotiators, and he now dropped his insistence upon the removal of all North Vietnamese troops from South Vietnam before the withdrawal of the remaining U.S. troops. On October 26, only a week before the U.S. presidential election, Kissinger announced that "Peace is at hand."

Christmas bombings of North Vietnam (1972)

As it turned out, however, this was a cynical ploy to win votes. Several days earlier, the Thieu regime in South Vietnam had rejected the Kissinger plan for a cease-fire, fearful that allowing North Vietnamese troops to remain in the south would virtually guarantee a Communist victory. The Paris peace talks broke off on December 16, and two days later the newly reelected Nixon ordered massive bombings of Hanoi and Haiphong, the two largest cities in North Vietnam. "The bastards have never been bombed like they're going to be bombed this time," Nixon pledged. These so-called Christmas bombings and the simultaneous U.S. mining of North Vietnamese harbors aroused worldwide protest.

Paris Peace Accords (1973)

Yet the bombings also made the North Vietnamese more willing to negotiate. The air strikes stopped on December 29, and the talks in Paris soon resumed. On January 27, 1973, the United States, North and South Vietnam, and the Viet Cong signed an "agreement on ending the war and restoring peace in Vietnam," known as the Paris Peace Accords. In fact, it was a carefully disguised surrender that enabled the United States to end its combat role. While Nixon and Kissinger claimed that the bombings had brought North Vietnam to its senses, in truth the North Vietnamese never altered their basic stance; they kept 150,000 troops in South Vietnam and remained committed to the reunification of Vietnam under one government.

What had changed was the willingness of the South Vietnamese, who were never allowed to participate in the negotiations, to accept the agreement, however reluctantly, on the basis of Nixon's promise that the United States would respond "with full force" to any Communist violation of the agreement. Kissinger had little confidence that the treaty provisions would enable South Vietnam to survive on its own. He told a White House staffer, "If they're lucky, they can hold out for a year and a half."

By the time the Paris Peace Accords were signed in 1973, another 20,000 Americans had died since Nixon had taken office in 1969, the morale of the U.S. military had been shattered, millions of Southeast Asians had been killed or wounded, and fighting soon broke out again in both Vietnam and Cambodia. In the end, Nixon and Kissinger's diplomatic efforts gained nothing the president could not have accomplished in 1969 by ending the war on similar terms.

The Collapse of South Vietnam

On March 29, 1973, the last U.S. combat troops left Vietnam. The same day, almost 600 American prisoners of war, most of them downed pilots, were released from Hanoi. Within months of the U.S. withdrawal, however, the cease-fire in Vietnam collapsed, the war between North and South resumed, and the Communist forces gained the upper hand. In Cambodia (renamed the Khmer Republic after a 1970 military coup) and Laos, where fighting had been more sporadic, a Communist victory also seemed inevitable.

In 1975, the North Vietnamese launched a full-scale invasion, sending the South Vietnamese army into headlong panic, followed by ragged columns of terrified civilians. South Vietnamese president Nguyen Van Thieu desperately appealed to Washington for the promised U.S. assistance to which he was entitled by the Paris Peace Accords—and to which South Vietnam had grown addicted. But the U.S. Congress, long since weary of spending more dollars and lives in Vietnam, refused. On April 21, Thieu resigned and flew to Taiwan, carrying with him three and a half tons of gold to ease his sorrow.

"Peace with honor" had proven to be, in the words of one CIA official, only a "decent interval"—enough time for the United States to remove itself before the collapse of the South Vietnamese government. On April 30, 1975, Americans watched on television as North Vietnamese tanks rolled into Saigon, soon to be renamed Ho Chi Minh City, and military helicopters lifted desperate U.S. embassy and South Vietnamese officials and their families to warships waiting offshore.

The longest, most controversial, and least successful war in American history up to that point was finally over, leaving a bitter legacy. During the period of U.S. involvement, almost 2 million combatants and civilians were killed on both sides. North Vietnam absorbed incredible losses—some 600,000 soldiers and countless civilians killed. South Vietnam lost 240,000 soldiers, and over 500,000 Vietnamese became refugees in the United States. More than 58,000 Americans died in Vietnam, 300,000 were wounded, 2,500 were declared missing, and almost 100,000 returned missing one or more limbs. The United States spent over $158 billion on the war.

The Vietnam War was the defining life event for the "baby boomers," the largest generation of Americans ever, the generation that provided most of the U.S. troops in Vietnam as well as most of the anti-war protesters. The war divided that generation in ways that would be felt for years. The "loss"

Leave with honor Hundreds of thousands of South Vietnamese tried to flee the Communist forces with evacuating Americans. Here U.S. official punches a Vietnamese man attempting to join his family in an overflowing airplane at Nha Trang.

of the war, combined with news of atrocities committed by American soldiers, eroded respect for the military so thoroughly that many young people came to regard military service as corrupting and dishonorable.

The Vietnam combat veterans (average age 19, compared to 26, the average age of servicemen in the Second World War) faced a unique ordeal. They had "lost" a war in which their country had lost interest. When they returned to America, many of them found that even their families were unwilling to talk about what they had experienced, or were embarrassed about it. "I went over there thinking I was doing something right and came back a bum," said Larry Langowski from Illinois. "I came back decked with medals on my uniform, and I got spit on by a hippie girl."

The Vietnam War, initially described as a crusade on behalf of democratic ideals, instead revealed that democracy was not easily transferable to regions of the world that lacked any historical experience with democratic government. Fought to show that the United States would be steadfast in containing the spread of communism, the war instead sapped the national will and fragmented the national consensus that had governed foreign affairs since 1947, when President Truman developed policies to "contain" Communism around the world. It also changed the balance of power in domestic politics.

As opposition to the war undermined Lyndon B. Johnson's presidency, it also created enduring fractures within the Democratic party. Said George McGovern, the anti-war senator and 1972 Democratic presidential nominee, "The Vietnam tragedy is at the root of the confusion and division of the Democratic party. It tore up our souls."

Not only had a decade of American effort in Vietnam proved futile, but the Khmer Rouge, the insurgent Cambodian Communist movement, had also won a resounding victory over the government of the U.S.-backed Khmer Republic, plunging that country into a bloodbath. The maniacal Khmer Rouge leaders renamed the country Kampuchea and organized a genocidal campaign to destroy all of their opponents, killing almost a third of the total population.

The Nixon Doctrine and a Thawing Cold War

CORE **OBJECTIVE**
5. Examine the world order that evolved after the Vietnam War from Richard Nixon's and Henry Kissinger's diplomacy and foreign policies.

Despite the frustrations associated with his efforts to end the Vietnam War, Richard Nixon, like John F. Kennedy, greatly preferred foreign policy over domestic policy (which he compared to building "sewer projects"), and his greatest successes were in international relations. Nixon was an expert in foreign affairs and had traveled abroad frequently as Eisenhower's vice president during the 1950s, and he benefited greatly from the expertise and strategic vision of Henry Kissinger. Their grand design for U.S. foreign policy after the Vietnam War centered on developing friendly relations with the Soviet Union and Communist China. Kissinger said they wanted to "improve the possibilities of accommodations with each as we increase our options with both," enabling all three superpowers to reduce the cost of the arms race while minimizing the possibility of nuclear war. Kissinger pressed for a return to an Eisenhower-era approach to foreign policy that entailed using the Central Intelligence Agency (CIA) to pursue America's strategic interests covertly and reducing large-scale military interventions.

The CIA in Chile

Ever since Fidel Castro and his Communist supporters gained control of Cuba in 1959, American presidents had been determined to prevent any more Communist insurgencies in the Western Hemisphere. In 1970, Salvador Allende, a Marxist, a Socialist party leader, and a friend of Fidel Castro, was a leading presidential candidate in Chile, a thousand-mile-long nation on the southwest coast of South America. Allende's candidacy caused President Nixon and Henry Kissinger great concern, for they knew that, if elected, Allende planned to "nationalize" Chilean industries, including those owned by U.S. corporations. They did not want "another Castro" in Latin America.

In September 1970, Nixon told the head of the CIA that an Allende government in Chile was "unacceptable," and he authorized $10 million to prevent an Allende presidency, urging the CIA to do anything "your

U.S. foreign policy in Latin America: Anti-communism and the CIA imagination can conjure" up to stop Allende. Nevertheless, although CIA agents provided campaign funds to Allende's opponents, he was elected on October 24, 1970. The CIA then encouraged Chilean military leaders to oust him. In September 1973, the army took control, Allende either committed suicide or was murdered, and General Augusto Pinochet, a ruthless military dictator supposedly friendly to the United States, declared himself the head of the government.

After Pinochet assumed power, Kissinger, now secretary of state, told Nixon that the CIA "didn't do it," but "we helped them" by creating the conditions that made the coup possible. In consolidating control over Chile, Pinochet executed thousands of people. It was yet another example of the United States being so obsessed by anti-communism and protecting American business interests that it was willing to interfere in the democratic process of other nations and help remove elected officials through covert operations.

The Nixon Doctrine

The Nixon Doctrine and détente

In July 1969, while trying to get America out of the war in Vietnam, President Nixon revealed the negative effects of the lengthy war at a press conference on Guam island in the Pacific. There, while announcing the first U.S. troop withdrawals, he unveiled what came to be called the Nixon Doctrine, a new approach to America's handling of international crises. Unlike John F. Kennedy, who had declared that the United States would "pay any price, bear any burden" to win the cold war, Nixon explained that "America cannot—and will not—conceive *all* the plans, design *all* the programs, execute *all* the decisions, and undertake *all* the defense of the free nations of the world." Those nations experiencing Communist insurgencies must in the future assume primary responsibility for their own defense. The United States would provide weapons and money but not soldiers.

At the same time that Nixon was reducing the likelihood of U.S. military interventions, he announced that the United States would pursue partnerships with Communist countries in areas of mutual interest. That Nixon, a Republican with a history of rabid anti-communism, would pursue such a policy of **détente** (a French word meaning "easing of relations") with America's Communist archenemies shocked many observers and demonstrated yet again his pragmatic flexibility.

The People's Republic of China

détente Period of improving relations between the United States and Communist nations, particularly China and the Soviet Union, during the Nixon administration.

Nixon had a genius for surprise, an exquisite gift for defying expectations. In 1971, without even informing Secretary of State Rogers, Nixon sent Henry Kissinger on a secret trip to Beijing to explore the possibility of U.S. recognition of Communist China. Since 1949, when Mao Zedong's revolutionary movement established control in China, the United States had refused to recognize the People's Republic of China, preferring to regard Chiang Kai-shek's exiled regime on the island of Taiwan as the legitimate Chinese government. But now the time seemed ripe for a bold renewal of ties. Both the United States and Communist China were exhausted from intense domestic strife (anti-war protests in America, the Cultural Revolution in China), and both were eager to resist Soviet expansionism.

Nixon's bombshell announcement on July 15, 1971, that Kissinger had just returned from Beijing and that the president himself would be going to China the following year sent shock waves around the world. Nixon became the first U.S. president to use the term *People's Republic of China*, an important symbolic step in his efforts to normalize relations with the most populous nation in the world. The Nationalist Chinese on Taiwan felt betrayed, and the Japanese, historic enemies of China, were furious at the American news. What they called "Nixon shock" was a major factor in the collapse of the Japanese government. In October 1971, the United Nations voted to admit the People's Republic of China and expel Taiwan.

> Nixon recognizes Communist China (1972)

On February 21, 1972, during the "week that changed the world," Americans who had lived amid the intense anti-Communist atmosphere of the cold war were stunned to turn on their televisions and see President Nixon shake hands and drink toasts in Beijing with Prime Minister Zhou Enlai and Communist Party Chairman Mao Zedong. In one simple but astonishing stroke, Nixon and Kissinger had ended two decades of diplomatic isolation of the People's Republic of China. They had seen a geopolitical opportunity and seized it.

During the president's week-long visit, the two nations agreed to scientific and cultural exchanges, steps toward the resumption of trade, and the eventual reunification of Taiwan with the mainland. A year after Nixon's visit, "liaison offices" that served as unofficial embassies were established in Washington and Beijing, and in 1979, diplomatic recognition was formalized. As a conservative anti-Communist, Nixon had accomplished a diplomatic feat that his Democratic predecessors could not have attempted for fear of being branded "soft on Communism." Nixon and Kissinger's bold move in China had the added benefit of giving them leverage with the Soviet Union, which was understandably nervous about a U.S.-Chinese alliance.

Nixon goes to China President Nixon and Chinese premier Zhou Enlai raise a toast to each other at the lavish farewell banquet in Shanghai that rounded off the historic visit.

Embracing the Soviet Union

In truth, China welcomed the breakthrough in relations with the United States because of tensions with its neighbor, the Soviet Union, with which it shared a long but contested border. By 1972, the Chinese leadership had become more fearful of the Soviet Union than the United States. The Soviet leaders, in turn troubled by the agreements between China and the United States, were also eager to ease tensions with the Americans. Once again, President Nixon surprised the world by announcing that he would visit

> The Moscow summit: Trade agreements, arms reductions, and the easing of cold war tensions

Moscow in 1972 for discussions with Leonid Brezhnev, the Soviet premier. The high drama of the China visit was repeated in Moscow, with toasts and elegant dinners attended by world leaders who had previously regarded each other as incarnations of evil.

What became known as détente with the Soviets offered the promise of less intense competition between the superpowers. Nixon and Brezhnev signed the pathbreaking **Strategic Arms Limitation Treaty (SALT I)**, which negotiators had been working on since 1969. The SALT agreement did not end the nuclear arms race, but it did limit the number of missiles with nuclear warheads and prohibited the construction of missile-defense systems. The Moscow summit also produced new trade agreements, including an arrangement whereby the United States sold almost a quarter of its wheat crop to the Soviets at a favorable price (critics called it the Great Grain Robbery).

The Moscow summit resulted in the dramatic easing of tensions between the two cold war superpowers. As Nixon told Congress upon his return, "never before have two adversaries, so deeply divided by conflicting ideologies and political rivalries, been able to limit the armaments upon which their survival depends." For Nixon and Kissinger, the agreements with China and the Soviet Union represented monumental changes in the global order that would have lasting consequences. Over time, the détente policy with the Soviet Union would help end the cold war altogether by lowering Soviet hostility to Western influences penetrating their closed society, which in turn slowly eroded Communist rule from the inside.

Shuttle Diplomacy

U.S.-negotiated cease-fire in the Middle East

The Nixon-Kissinger initiatives in the Middle East were less dramatic and less conclusive than the agreements with China and the Soviet Union, but they did show that the United States at long last recognized the legitimacy of Arab interests in the region and its own dependence upon Middle Eastern oil, even though the Arab nations were adamantly opposed to the existence of Israel. In the Six-Day War of 1967, Israeli forces had routed the armies of Egypt, Syria, and Jordan, and seized territory from all three nations. Moreover, the number of Palestinian refugees, many of them homeless since the creation of Israel in 1948, increased after the Israeli victory.

The Middle East remained a tinderbox of tensions. On October 6, 1973, the Jewish holy day of Yom Kippur, Syria and Egypt, backed by money from Saudi Arabia and armed with Soviet weapons, attacked Israel, igniting what became the Yom Kippur War. It created the most dangerous confrontation between the United States and the Soviet Union since the Cuban missile crisis. When the Israeli army, with weapons supplied by the United States, launched a fierce counterattack that appeared likely to overwhelm Egypt, the Soviets threatened to intervene militarily. Nixon, whose presidency was at risk because of the ongoing Watergate investigations, was bedridden because he was drunk, according to Henry Kissinger and other aides, so

Strategic Arms Limitation Treaty (SALT I) (1972) Agreement signed by President Nixon and Secretary Brezhnev prohibiting the development of missile defense systems in the United States and Soviet Union and limiting the quantity of nuclear warheads for both.

Kissinger, as secretary of state, presided over a National Security Council meeting that placed America's military forces on full alert to keep the Soviets out of the Middle Eastern war. On October 20, Kissinger flew to Moscow to meet with Soviet premier Leonid Brezhnev. Kissinger skillfully negotiated a cease-fire agreement and exerted pressure on the Israelis to prevent them from taking additional Arab territory. In an attempt to broker a lasting settlement, Kissinger made numerous flights among the capitals of the Middle East. His "shuttle diplomacy" won acclaim from all sides, though he failed to find a comprehensive formula for peace. He did, however, lay the groundwork for an important treaty between Israel and Egypt in 1977.

Watergate

> CORE **OBJECTIVE**
> **6.** Explain how the Watergate scandal unfolded, and assess its political significance.

Nixon's foreign policy achievements allowed him to stage the presidential campaign of 1972 as a triumphal procession. Early on, the main threat to his reelection came from George Wallace, who had the potential as a third-party candidate to deprive the Republicans of conservative southern votes and thereby throw the election to the Democrats. That threat ended, however, on May 15, 1972, when Wallace was shot in an assassination attempt. Although he survived, he was left paralyzed below the waist and had to withdraw from the campaign.

Meanwhile, the Democrats nominated Senator George McGovern of South Dakota, an anti-war liberal. A poor campaigner who was viewed by many Americans as a left-wing extremist, he never had a chance of winning. In the 1972 election, Nixon won the greatest victory of any Republican presidential candidate in history, capturing 520 electoral votes to only 17 for McGovern. The popular vote was equally decisive: 46 million to 28 million, a proportion of the total vote (60.8 percent) that was second only to Lyndon Johnson's victory over Barry Goldwater in 1964. After his landslide victory, Nixon planned to promote the "more conservative values and beliefs of the New Majority throughout the country and use my power to put some teeth in my new American Revolution."

For all of his abilities and accomplishments, however, Nixon was a chronically insecure person. More than most presidents, he nursed grudges and took politics personally, and he could be ruthless in attacking his opponents. As president, he began keeping a secret "enemies list" and launched numerous efforts to embarrass and punish those on the list. Little did he know that such behavior would bring his second term crashing down around him.

"Dirty Tricks"

By the spring of 1972, senior Nixon aide John Ehrlichman was overseeing a secret team of agents who performed various acts of sabotage against leading Democrats, such as falsely accusing Senators Hubert H. Humphrey and

Henry Jackson of sexual improprieties, forging press releases, setting off stink bombs at Democratic campaign events, and planting spies on McGovern's campaign plane.

During the campaign, McGovern had complained about the numerous "dirty tricks" orchestrated by members of the Nixon administration. Nixon, it turned out, had ordered illegal wiretaps on his opponents (as well as on his own aides), tried to coerce the Internal Revenue Service to intimidate Democrats, and told his chief of staff, Bob Haldeman, to break into the safe at the Brookings Institution, a Washington research center with Democratic ties. "Goddamnit," he told Haldeman, "get in and get those files. Blow the safe and get it."

The Watergate break-in (1972)

McGovern was especially disturbed by an incident on June 17, 1972, when five burglars were caught breaking into the Democratic National Committee headquarters in the exclusive **Watergate** apartment and office complex in Washington, D.C. The burglars were former CIA agents, and one, James W. McCord, worked for the Nixon reelection campaign. At the time, McGovern's complaints about the Watergate break-in seemed like sour grapes from a candidate running far behind in the polls. Nixon and his staff ignored the news of the "third-rate burglary." The president said that no one cares "when somebody bugs somebody else," and he denied any involvement in this "very bizarre incident." Privately, however, he and his senior aides began feverish efforts to cover up the Watergate affair. They secretly provided $400,000 in "hush money" to the jailed burglars to buy their silence and tried to keep the FBI out of the investigation. They also discussed using the CIA to derail the Justice Department's investigation of the burglary.

Uncovering the Cover-up

CREEP: Committee to Re-Elect the President

During the trial of the accused Watergate burglars in January 1973, the relentless questioning of federal judge John J. Sirica led one of the accused to tell the full story of the Nixon administration's involvement. James W. McCord, security chief of the Committee to Re-Elect the President (CREEP), was the first in what would become a long line of informers to reveal the systematic efforts of Nixon and his aides to create an "imperial presidency" above the law. By the time of the Watergate break-in, the money to finance "dirty tricks" was being illegally collected through CREEP and controlled by the White House staff.

The Watergate cover-up

The trail of evidence pursued first by Judge Sirica, then by a grand jury, and then by a Senate committee headed by Democrat Samuel J. Ervin Jr. of North Carolina, led directly to what the White House legal counsel John Dean called a "cancer close to the Presidency." Nixon was personally involved in the cover-up of the Watergate incident, using his presidential powers to discredit and block the investigation. He ordered the CIA to keep the FBI off the case and even coached his aides how to lie under oath. Most alarming, as it turned out, the Watergate burglary was merely one small part

Watergate (1972–1974)
Scandal that exposed the criminality and corruption of the Nixon administration and ultimately led to President Nixon's resignation in 1974.

of a larger pattern of corruption and criminality sanctioned by the Nixon White House.

The Watergate cover-up crumbled as various people, including John Dean, began to cooperate with prosecutors. At the same time, two reporters for the *Washington Post*, Carl Bernstein and Bob Woodward, relentlessly pursued the story, eventually making it a compelling topic of national conversation.

The cover-up unraveled further in 1973 when L. Patrick Gray, acting director of the FBI, resigned after confessing that he had destroyed several incriminating documents. On April 30, Ehrlichman and Haldeman resigned (they would later serve time in prison), as did Attorney General Richard Kleindienst. A few days later, Nixon nervously assured the public in a television address, "I am not a crook." Then Dean, whom Nixon had dismissed because of his cooperation with prosecutors, shocked the nation by testifying before the Ervin committee that there had been a White House–led cover-up approved by the president.

Nixon thereafter became preoccupied with frantic efforts at self-defense and survival. He refused to provide Senator Ervin's committee with documents it requested, citing "executive privilege" to protect national security. In another shocking disclosure, a White House aide told the Ervin committee that Nixon had installed a secret taping system in the White House, and that many of the conversations about the Watergate burglary and cover-up had been recorded.

The bombshell news about the recording system in the Oval Office set off a yearlong legal battle for the "Nixon tapes." Harvard law professor Archibald Cox, whom Nixon's new attorney general, Elliot Richardson, had appointed as special prosecutor to investigate the Watergate case, took the president to court in October 1973 to obtain the tapes. Nixon refused to release the recordings and ordered Cox fired. On October 20, in what became known as the "Saturday Night Massacre," Richardson and Deputy Attorney General William Ruckelshaus resigned rather than fire the special prosecutor. (Solicitor General Robert Bork finally fired Cox.) Nixon's dismissal of Cox produced a firestorm of public indignation. Numerous newspaper and magazine editorials, as well as a growing chorus of legislators, called for the president to be impeached for obstructing justice. A Gallup poll revealed that Nixon's approval rating had plunged to 17 percent, the lowest level any president had ever received.

The "Nixon tapes" and the Saturday Night Massacre

Cox's dismissal failed to end Nixon's legal troubles. The new special prosecutor, Leon Jaworski, also took the president to court. In March 1974, the Watergate grand jury indicted John Ehrlichman, Bob Haldeman, and former Attorney General John Mitchell for obstruction of justice and named Nixon an "unindicted co-conspirator." On April 30, Nixon, still refusing to turn over the actual tapes, released 1,254 pages of transcribed recordings that he had edited himself, often substituting the phrase "expletive deleted" for the vulgar language and anti-Semitic rants he had

Calls for Nixon's impeachment

frequently unleashed ("People said my language was bad," Nixon later rationalized, "but Jesus, you should have heard LBJ!"). At one point in the transcripts, the president told his aides that they should have frequent memory lapses when testifying about the cover-up.

The transcripts provoked widespread anger and disgust, for they revealed a president who behaved in disgracefully unpresidential ways. His Oval Office conversations were so petty, self-serving, bigoted, and profane that they degraded the stature of the presidency—"shabby, disgusting, immoral," said Republican senator Hugh Scott. The transcripts only fueled the growing demands for Nixon to resign.

By the summer of 1974, Nixon was under intense pressure and in full retreat. He became alternately combative, melancholy, and petty. During White House visits, Henry Kissinger found him increasingly unstable and drinking heavily. Nixon's efforts to orchestrate the cover-up obsessed him, unbalanced him, and unhinged him. After meeting with the president, Senator Barry Goldwater reported that Nixon "jabbered incessantly, often incoherently." He seemed "to be cracking."

United States v. Richard M. Nixon (1974)

The Watergate drama transfixed Americans, who watched the daily Ervin committee hearings as if they were episodes in a soap opera. On July 24, 1974, the Supreme Court ruled unanimously, in *United States v. Richard M. Nixon*, that the president must surrender *all* of the tape recordings. A few days later, the House Judiciary Committee voted to recommend three articles of impeachment: obstruction of justice through the payment of "hush money" to witnesses and the withholding of evidence; abuse of power through the use of federal agencies to deprive citizens of their constitutional rights; and defiance of Congress by withholding the tapes.

Before the House of Representatives could meet to vote on impeachment, Nixon grudgingly handed over the complete set of White House tapes. The drama continued, however, when investigators learned that sections of certain recordings were missing, including eighteen minutes of a key conversation in June 1972 during which Nixon first mentioned the Watergate burglary. The president's loyal secretary took the blame for the erasure, claiming that she had accidentally pushed the wrong button, but technical experts later concluded that the missing segments had been intentionally deleted. The other White House tape recordings, however, provided more than enough evidence of Nixon's involvement in the cover-up. At one point, the same president who had been the architect of détente with the Soviet Union and the recognition of Communist China had yelled at aides who were asking what they and others should say to Watergate investigators, "I don't give a shit what happens. I want you all to stonewall it, let them plead the Fifth Amendment, cover up or anything else."

Nixon the first president to resign in office

The evidence in the tape recordings led Republican leaders to urge Nixon to quit rather than face an impeachment trial in the Senate. On August 9, 1974, the embattled president resigned from office, the only president ever to do so. In 1969, he had begun his presidency hoping to heal America, to "bring people together." Now he left the White House to begin a self-imposed exile at his home in San Clemente, California, having deeply wounded the nation. Nixon was one of the strangest, most complicated, and most interesting political figures in American history. He never understood why the Watergate affair could have ended his presidency; in his view, his only mistake was getting caught. Nixon claimed that a president's actions could not be "illegal." He was wrong. The Watergate affair's clearest lesson was that not even a president is above the law.

Watergate and the Presidency

If there was a silver lining in the dark cloud of Watergate, it was the vigor and resilience of the institutions that had brought a rogue president to justice—the press, Congress, the courts, and aroused public opinion.

Congress responded to the Watergate revelations with several pieces of legislation designed to curb executive power. Already nervous about possible efforts to renew American military assistance to South Vietnam, the Democratic Congress passed the **War Powers Act** (1973), which requires a president to inform Congress within forty-eight hours if U.S. troops are deployed in combat abroad and to withdraw troops after sixty days unless Congress specifically approves their stay. In an effort to correct abuses in the use of campaign funds, Congress enacted legislation in 1974 that set new ceilings on political contributions and expenditures. And in reaction to the Nixon claim of "executive privilege" as a means of withholding evidence, Congress strengthened the 1966 Freedom of Information Act to require prompt responses to requests for information from government files and to place on government agencies the burden of proof for classifying information as secret.

V for "victory" Before boarding the White House helicopter following his resignation, Nixon flashes a bright smile and his trademark V-sign to the world on August 9, 1974.

An Unelected President

During Richard Nixon's last year in office, the Watergate crisis so dominated national politics that major domestic and foreign problems received little attention. Vice President Spiro Agnew had himself been forced to resign in October 1973 for accepting bribes from contractors before and during his term in office. The vice president at the time of Nixon's resignation was Gerald Ford, a congenial former House minority leader from Michigan whom Nixon had appointed to succeed Agnew under the provisions of the Twenty-Fifth Amendment, which was ratified in 1967. On August 9, 1974, Ford was sworn in as the nation's first politically appointed chief executive, the only person in history to serve as both vice president and president without having been elected to those offices.

Gerald Ford assumes presidency (1974)

War Powers Act (1973) Legislation requiring the president to inform Congress within 48 hours of the deployment of U.S. troops abroad and to withdraw them after 60 days unless Congress approves their continued deployment.

Gerald Ford The 38th president listens apprehensively to news of rising rates of unemployment and inflation in 1974.

President Ford reassured the nation that "our long nightmare is over," but restoring public confidence in elected leaders was not easy. Only a month after taking office, Ford reopened the wounds of Watergate by issuing a "full, free, and absolute pardon" to Richard Nixon. Many Americans were not in a forgiving mood when it came to Nixon, and Ford's pardon unleashed a storm of controversy. "Jail Ford!" yelled many protesters outside the White House. Ford was grilled by a House subcommittee wanting to know whether Nixon had made a secret deal with Ford for the pardon. Ford vigorously denied the charge, adding that nothing was to be gained by putting Nixon in prison. But the pardon hobbled Ford's presidency. His approval rating plummeted from 71 percent to 49 percent in one day, the steepest drop ever recorded. Even Ford's press secretary resigned in protest of his boss's decision. The president never fully recovered the public's confidence.

The Ford Years

As president, Gerald Ford soon adopted the posture he had developed as the minority leader in the House of Representatives: naysaying leader of the opposition who believed that the federal government exercised too much power. In his first fifteen months as president, Ford vetoed thirty-nine bills passed by Congress, thereby outstripping Herbert Hoover's all-time veto record in less than half the time.

By far the most important development during Ford's brief presidency was the struggling economy. During the fall of 1974, the nation had entered the deepest recession since the Great Depression. Unemployment jumped to 9 percent in 1975, the annual rate of inflation reached double digits, and the federal deficit soon hit a record. President Ford announced that inflation had become "Public Enemy No. 1," but instead of taking bold action, he launched a timid public relations campaign featuring lapel buttons that simply read WIN, symbolizing the administration's determination to "Whip Inflation Now."

The WIN buttons became a national joke and a symbol of Ford's ineffectiveness in the fight against stagflation. He himself later admitted that it was a failed "gimmick." Ford initially supported increased taxes on corporations and individuals to fight inflation, only to reverse himself. By 1975, when Ford delivered his State of the Union address, he lamely conceded that "the state of the union is not good." In March 1975, Ford signed a tax reduction bill that failed in its goal of stimulating economic growth. Instead it was the federal budget deficit that grew from $53 billion in 1975 to $74 billion in 1976.

In foreign policy, Ford retained Henry Kissinger as secretary of state (while stripping him of his dual role as national security adviser) and pursued Nixon's goals of stability in the Middle East, friendly relations with China, and détente with the Soviet Union. In addition, Kissinger's tireless

Middle East diplomacy produced an important agreement: Israel promised to return to Egypt most of the Sinai territory captured in the 1967 War, and the two nations agreed to rely upon negotiations rather than force to settle future disagreements. These limited but significant achievements should have enhanced Ford's image, but they were drowned in the sea of criticism over the collapse of the South Vietnamese government in the face of the North Vietnamese invasion.

The Election of 1976

Both political parties were in disarray as they prepared for the 1976 presidential election. At the Republican Convention, Gerald Ford had to fend off a powerful challenge from the darling of the party's growing conservative wing, Ronald Reagan, a former two-term California governor and Hollywood actor.

The Democrats chose James Earl Carter Jr., who had served one term as governor of Georgia. A former naval officer and engineer turned peanut farmer, Carter was one of several Democratic southern governors who sought to move their party away from its traditional "tax and spend" liberalism. Carter insisted that he was neither a liberal nor a conservative but a pragmatic "engineer" who would be able to get the "right thing" done in the "right ways." He capitalized on post-Watergate cynicism by promising that he would "never tell a lie to the American people." He also trumpeted his status as a political "outsider" whose inexperience in Washington politics would be an asset. Carter was certainly different from conventional candidates. Political reporters covering the campaign marveled at a Southern Baptist candidate who was a "born again" Christian.

Ford made a crucial mistake during a televised debate with Carter when he mistakenly claimed that "there is no Soviet domination of Eastern Europe, and there never will be under a Ford administration." To the surprise of many, the little-known Carter revived the New Deal voting alliance of southern whites, blacks, urban labor unionists, and ethnic groups like Jews and Hispanics to eke out a narrow win, receiving 41 million votes to Ford's 39 million. A heavy turnout of African Americans in the South enabled Carter to sweep every state in the region except Virginia. He also benefited from the appeal of Walter F. Mondale, his liberal running mate and a favorite among blue-collar workers and the urban poor.

The significant story of the election was not so much Carter or Ford but the low voter turnout. "Neither Ford nor Carter won as many votes as Mr. Nobody," said one reporter, commenting on how almost half the eligible voters, apparently alienated by Watergate, the stagnant economy, and the two lackluster candidates, chose to sit out the election. It was not a good omen for a new Democratic president about to begin his term.

■ **Youth Revolt** Civil rights activism inspired a heightened interest in a number of social causes during the sixties, especially among the youth. Students for a Democratic Society (SDS) embodied the *New Left* ideology, and helped spur the free-speech movement (FSM) starting at the University of California, Berkeley, and spreading to many campuses across the nation. By 1970, a distinctive *counterculture* also emerged among disaffected youth and attracted hippies many of whom used mind-altering drugs, lived on rural communes, and refused conventional life, which they viewed as corrupt and constricting.

■ **The Inspirational Effects of the Civil Rights Movement** The energy, ideals, tactics, and courage of the civil rights movement inspired many other social reform movements, including the *women's movement*, the *"Red Power"* movement and the *United Farm Workers (UFW)*. The 1969 *Stonewall riots* marked a militant new era in the crusade for gay rights.

■ **Reaction and Domestic Agenda** Richard Nixon took advantage of the backlash against these liberal politics and cultural movements to win election in 1968. His "southern strategy" drew large numbers of conservative southern white Democrats into the Republican party for the first time. As president, he sought to slow the momentum of the civil rights movement with *affirmative action* programs and vetoed the extension of the Voting Rights Act of 1968, though with no success. Nixon did grudgingly support important new federal environmental policies like the *Environmental Protection Agency (EPA)*. Both the Nixon and Ford administrations were unable to overcome *stagflation*.

■ **End of the Vietnam War** In his 1968 campaign, Nixon pledged to secure "peace with honor" in Vietnam, but years would pass before the war ended. He did change the military strategy in Vietnam by implementing *Vietnamization:* increasing aid to South Vietnam and aggressively bombing North Vietnam, while attempting to negotiate a cease-fire with North Vietnam. The Pentagon Papers and the intense bombing of North Vietnam in December 1972 sparked worldwide protests. But a month into the bombings, North and South Vietnam agreed to a cease-fire called the Paris Peace Accords. In 1975 the South Vietnamese government collapsed after a massive North Vietnamese invasion. The Communist victors forcibly reunited the North and South.

■ **Détente** Nixon's greatest accomplishments were in foreign policy. As an aggressive anti-Communist, he shocked the world by opening diplomatic relations with Communist China and pursuing *détente* with the Soviet Union, focusing on areas of shared agreement with SALT I. He and Henry Kissinger eased tensions in the Middle East, while aggravating anti-American feelings in countries like Chile with covert CIA operations to overthrow governments with Communist ties.

■ **Watergate** During the 1972 presidential campaign, the Committee to Re-Elect the President (CREEP) was implicated in a break-in of the Democratic campaign's Watergate headquarters. In *United States v. Richard M. Nixon* (1974), the Supreme Court ruled that Nixon had to surrender the recordings of White House meetings dealing with the scandal. Nixon resigned in 1974 to avoid impeachment. He was succeeded by Vice President Gerald Ford, whose presidency was undermined by continued economic struggles, international incidents, and his controversial decision to pardon Nixon.

KEY TERMS

CHRONOLOGY

1960	Students for a Democratic Society (SDS) founded
1962	United Farm Workers (UFW) established
1963	Betty Friedan's *The Feminine Mystique* published
1965	Forced integration of Mississippi schools
1966	National Organization for Women (NOW) founded
1967–1968	Inner-city riots; student sit-ins on college campuses
1968	Riots at the Democratic National Convention
	American Indian Movement (AIM) founded
March 1969	U.S. warplanes bomb Cambodia
June 1969	Stonewall riots in New York City
August 1969	Woodstock music festival attracts 400,000 people
1970	Kent State and Jackson State shootings
1971	*Pentagon Papers* published
1972	Nixon visits China and U.S.S.R., signs SALT I
1972–1974	Watergate scandal unfolds
1973	Sioux occupation of Wounded Knee, South Dakota
	U.S. troop withdrawal from Vietnam begins
	Roe v. Wade
1974	Nixon resigns; Gerald Ford becomes president
April 1975	Saigon falls to the North Vietnamese

INQUIZITIVE

Go to InQuizitive to see what you've learned—and learn what you've missed—with personalized feedback along the way.

FEELS GOOD TO BE RIGHT This proud Republican and Reagan supporter lets his cowboy hat adorned with campaign buttons speak for him at the 1980 Republican National Convention. Held in Detroit, Michigan, the convention nominated former California governor Ronald Reagan, who promised to "make America great again."

Conservative Revival

1977–1990

During the seventies, the United States lost much of its self-confidence. The failed Vietnam War, the sordid revelations of the Watergate scandal, and the spike in oil prices, interest rates, and consumer prices revealed the limits of the nation's power, prosperity, and virtue. Surveys showed that Americans felt defensive and dispirited about their nation and its prospects in what journalists were calling an "age of limits." For a nation long accustomed to economic growth and spreading prosperity, the frustrating persistence of stagflation and gasoline shortages undermined national optimism. At the same time, a fast-growing environmental movement criticized the widespread pollution of the nation's air, water, and wetlands caused by unregulated economic development. Even in July 1976, as the United States celebrated the bicentennial of its independence, many people were downsizing their expectations of the American Dream.

Jimmy Carter took office promising a government that would be "competent" as well as "decent, open, fair, and compassionate." After four years as president, however, Carter had little to show for his efforts. The economy remained sluggish, consumer prices continued to increase at historic levels, and failed efforts to free Americans held hostage in Iran prompted critics, including Democrats, to denounce the administration as being indecisive and inept. In the end, Carter's inability to mobilize national support for his ill-fated energy program and his call for "a time of

CORE
OBJECTIVES INQUIZITIVE

1. Analyze why Jimmy Carter had such limited success as America's thirty-ninth president.

2. Identify the factors that led to the election of Ronald Reagan, the rise of the conservative movement, and the resurgence of the Republican party.

3. Define "Reaganomics" and evaluate its effects on American society and economy.

4. Explain how Reagan's Soviet strategy helped end the Cold War .

5. Characterize the social and economic issues and innovations that emerged during the 1980s.

6. Appraise the impact of the end of the cold war and the efforts of President George H. W. Bush to create a post–cold war foreign policy.

national austerity" revealed both his ineffective legislative skills and his misreading of the public mood.

The Republicans capitalized on public frustration by electing Ronald Reagan president in 1980. Where Jimmy Carter had denounced the evils of unregulated capitalism, Reagan promised to unleash the capitalist spirit, restore national pride, and regain international respect. He did all of that and more. During his two-term presidency in the 1980s, he transformed the political landscape. Reagan accelerated the conservative resurgence in politics, helped restore prosperity, and set in motion the forces that would cause the collapse of the Soviet Union and the end of the Cold War.

CORE OBJECTIVE

1. Analyze why Jimmy Carter had such limited success as America's thirty-ninth president.

The Carter Presidency

James (Jimmy) Earl Carter Jr. won the close 1976 election because he convinced voters that he was an incorruptible political "outsider," a common man of pure motives who would restore integrity and honesty to the presidency in the aftermath of the Watergate scandal (his campaign slogan was "I'll never tell a lie"). He also promised that he was not a "tax and spend" liberal. Instead he represented a new generation of "moderate" southern Democratic leaders who were committed to restrain "big government" spending. In his 1977 inaugural address, Carter highlighted America's limitations rather than its power: "We have learned that 'more' is not necessarily 'better,' that even our great nation has its recognized limits, and that we can neither answer all questions nor solve all problems." That may have been true, but it was not what many Americans wanted to hear.

Jimmy Who?

Like Gerald Ford before him, Jimmy Carter was an honest, forthright man. Yet his charming modesty in public masked a complex and at times contradictory personality. "Jimmy's a hard person to get to know," admitted his top aide Hamilton Jordan. No modern president was as openly committed to his Christian faith as Carter was. At the same time, few other presidents were as tough on others as Carter, who once called the lovable Democratic leader Hubert Humphrey "a loser." The former governor of Georgia who came out of nowhere to win the presidential campaign ("Jimmy Who?") was both blessed and cursed by a surplus of self-confidence. All his life he had displayed a fierce determination to succeed and expected those around him to show the same tenacity. "I am pretty rigid," Carter admitted. As he entered the White House in early 1977, Carter, the former naval officer, nuclear engineer, efficiency expert, and business executive stressed that he wanted to be a "strong, aggressive president" who would reshape the federal government to run more smoothly at less expense to the taxpayers by eliminating waste and providing expert management.

In 1977 Carter needed to summon all of his intelligence and conviction ("I like to run things," he said), for he faced difficult economic problems and formidable international challenges. He was expected to cure the stubborn economic recession and reduce inflation at a time when all industrial economies around the world were struggling. Carter was also expected to restore U.S. stature abroad and lift the national spirit through a set of political institutions in which many people had lost faith as a result of the Watergate scandal.

Early Success

During the first two years of his presidency, Carter enjoyed several successes, both symbolic and real. In a sign of his commitment to efficiency, he reduced the size of the White House staff by a third and told cabinet officers to give up their government cars and drive their own. His new administration included more African Americans and women than any before. He fulfilled a controversial campaign pledge by offering amnesty (forgiveness) to the thousands of young men who had fled the country rather than serve with the U.S. military in Vietnam. He reorganized the executive branch and reduced government red tape by slowing burdensome new regulations and creating two new cabinet-level agencies, the Departments of Energy and Education. He also pushed through Congress several significant environmental initiatives, including stricter controls over the strip-mining of coal, the creation of a $1.6-billion "Superfund" to clean up toxic chemical waste sites, and a bill protecting more than 100 million acres of Alaskan land from development. At the end of his first hundred days in office, Carter enjoyed a 75 percent public approval rating.

The Carters After his inauguration, President Jimmy Carter forgoes the traditional limousine and walks down Pennsylvania Avenue with his wife, Rosalynn.

Carter's Limitations

Carter's successes were short-lived, however. By nature, he was less a leader than a bureaucrat, a compulsive micromanager (he even insisted on scheduling the use of the White House tennis court) who failed to establish a compelling vision for the nation's future. Instead of focusing on a few priorities, Carter tried to do too much too fast, and his inexperienced team of senior aides, most of whom he had brought with him from Georgia, was often more a burden than a blessing. The "outsider" president saw little need to consult with Democratic leaders in Congress, which helps explain why many of his legislative requests were voted down.

Ultimately, however, it was Carter's mismanagement of the economy that crippled his presidency. Stagflation continued to defy easy solutions. Carter first tried to attack unemployment, authorizing some $14 billion in federal spending to trigger job growth while cutting taxes by $34 billion. His actions helped generate new jobs but in doing so caused a spike in inflation.

A deepening recession

Annual inflation (increases in consumer prices) jumped from 5 percent when he took office to as much as 13 percent during 1980. The result was a deepening recession, rising unemployment, and growing criticism of the president.

The "energy crisis"

What made Carter's efforts to restore prosperity more challenging was the worsening "energy crisis." Since the Arab oil embargo in 1973, the price of imported oil had doubled, while U.S. dependence on foreign oil had grown from 35 percent to 50 percent of its annual needs. In April 1977, Carter presented Congress with a comprehensive energy proposal designed to cut oil consumption, but legislators defeated most of the bill's specific measures, in part because of Carter's poor relationship with Democratic leaders. The final energy bill, the National Energy Act of 1978, was so gutted by oil, gas, and automobile industry lobbyists that one presidential aide said it looked like it had been "nibbled to death by ducks."

In 1979, the energy crisis grew even more troublesome when Islamic fundamentalists took over the government in oil-rich Iran. The revolution shut off the supply of Iranian oil to the United States, creating shortages of gasoline and much higher prices. Warning that the "growing scarcity in energy" would paralyze the U.S. economy, Carter asked Congress for a new and much more comprehensive energy bill, but again the legislators turned down its most important provisions for energy conservation intended to reduce America's dependence on foreign oil.

A "Crisis of Confidence"

Loss of congressional support and public confidence

By July 1979, Carter had grown so discouraged by his inability to lead the nation out of the doldrums that he took an unusual step: for two weeks he holed up at Camp David, the presidential retreat in the Maryland mountains. There he met privately with leaders from all walks of life—business, labor, education, religion, even psychiatry. Then, on July 15, the president returned to the White House and delivered a televised speech in which he claimed that a "crisis of confidence" was paralyzing the nation and that the people had lost confidence in his leadership. He then made a crucial mistake when he seemingly blamed the American people for the problems facing the nation. "All the legislation in the world can't fix what's wrong with America," Carter stressed in a tone more appropriate to an angry preacher than an uplifting president. People had become preoccupied with "owning and consuming things" at the expense of "hard work, strong families, close-knit communities, and our faith in God." The nation was at a crossroads, he concluded. Americans could choose continued self-indulgence and political stalemate, or they could revive traditional values such as thrift, mutual aid, simple living, and spirituality. "We can take the first step down that path as we begin to solve our energy problem. Energy will be the immediate test of our ability to unite this nation."

But Carter failed that test. Many Americans felt the president's "sad and worried" speech had blamed them for his own failures of leadership. An

Arizona newspaper said that "the nation did not tune in Carter to hear a sermon. It wanted answers. It did not get them." Carter's new energy proposals got nowhere in Congress, in part because many members resented the president's abrupt decision to fire half of his cabinet members and transfer several others. The sudden firings seemed an act of self-serving desperation. By the end of the summer of 1979, Carter's negative ratings in public polls were the highest in history.

Carter's Foreign Policy

Carter's crowning achievement, which even his most bitter critics applauded, was his dogged effort to work out a 1978 peace agreement between Prime Minister Menachem Begin of Israel and President Anwar Sadat of Egypt. It was the first time that an Arab nation (Egypt) had officially recognized the existence of Israel. However, this historic agreement, dubbed the **Camp David Accords** for the presidential retreat where the negotiations took place, created only a "framework for peace," not a true settlement of differences. In the wake of the Camp David Accords, most Arab nations condemned Sadat as a traitor, and Islamic extremists assassinated him in 1981. Still, Carter's high-level diplomacy made an all-out war between Israel and the Arab world less likely.

> Carter's foreign policy controversies: Human rights, the Panama Canal Treaty, responses to the Soviet invasion of Afghanistan

Human Rights

Carter also got caught in a political crossfire when he vowed that "the soul of our foreign policy" should be an absolute "commitment to human rights" abroad, drawing a direct contrast between his international "idealism" and the geopolitical "realism" practiced by Richard Nixon and Henry Kissinger. Carter created an Office of Human Rights within the State Department and selectively cut off financial assistance to some repressive governments around the world (Chile, El Salvador, Rhodesia, and South Africa) while maintaining support of brutal governments in places like Argentina, Ethiopia, Pakistan, and Uruguay. Carter's inconsistent moralism led critics on the right to argue that he was sacrificing America's national interests in order to promote an impossible standard of international moral purity, while critics on the left highlighted his seeming hypocrisy in pursuing human rights in a few nations but not everywhere.

Panama Canal

Similarly, Carter's controversial decision to turn over control of the Panama Canal Zone to the Panamanian government aroused intense criticism. The president argued that Panama's deep resentment of America's having taken control of the Canal Zone during the presidency of Theodore Roosevelt left him no choice but to transfer management of the canal to Panama. Conservatives blasted Carter for surrendering U.S. control of such a

Camp David Accords (1978) Peace agreement facilitated by President Carter between Prime Minister Menachem Begin of Israel and President Anwar Sadat of Egypt, the first Arab head of state to officially recognize the state of Israel.

strategic asset. Ronald Reagan claimed the canal was America's forever: "We bought it, we paid for it, it's ours."

Afghanistan

In 1979, Carter faced another crisis when the Soviet army invaded Afghanistan, where a faltering Communist government was being challenged by Islamist *jihadis* ("holy warriors") and ethnic warlords. Carter responded with a series of steps, some of which provoked intense criticism: he refused to sign a new Strategic Arms Limitation Talks treaty with the Soviets (SALT II), suspended grain shipments to the Soviet Union, began supplying Afghan "freedom fighters" with weapons smuggled through Pakistan, requested large increases in military spending, required all nineteen-year-old men to register for the military draft, and called for an international boycott of the 1980 Olympic Games, which were to be held that summer in Moscow.

The Soviet invasion of Afghanistan also prompted Carter to announce what came to be called the Carter Doctrine, in which the president threatened to use military force to prevent any nation from gaining control of the Persian Gulf waterways, through which most of the oil from the Middle East made its way to foreign ports, including American cities.

A king's ransom An Iranian militant holds a group of U.S. embassy staff members hostage in Tehran, Iran, in 1979.

Crisis in Iran

Then came the **Iranian hostage crisis**, a series of dramatic events that illustrated the inability of the United States to control world affairs. In January 1979, Islamic revolutionaries in Iran had ousted the pro-American government led by the shah of Iran, Mohammad Reza Pahlavi, who owed his rule to secret CIA intervention in 1953. The turmoil in Iran led to a sharp drop in oil production, driving gasoline prices up. By the spring of 1979, Americans were again waiting in long lines to pay record prices for limited amounts of gas.

In October, the United States allowed the deposed shah to receive medical treatment at an American hospital. This "humanitarian" decision enraged Iranian revolutionaries. On November 4, 1979, a frenzied mob of Iranian youths stormed the U.S. embassy in Tehran and seized sixty-six diplomats and staff, including fifty-two American citizens. The Iranian leader, Ayatollah Ruhollah Khomeini, endorsed the mob action and demanded the return of the hated shah of Iran from the United States (along with all his wealth) in exchange for the release of the hostages. Nightly

Iranian hostage crisis (1979) Storming of the U.S. embassy in Tehran by Iranian revolutionaries, who held fifty-two Americans hostage for 444 days, despite President Carter's appeals for their release and a botched rescue attempt.

television coverage of the taunting Iranian rebels generated among viewers a near obsession with the fate of the hostages and the falling stature of the United States.

Angry Americans, including many in Congress, demanded a military response to the kidnappings in Iran. Carter, however, believed his options were limited to avoid the hostages being killed. He appealed to the United Nations, but Khomeini scoffed at UN requests for release of the hostages. Carter then froze all Iranian financial assets in America and asked Europe to join the United States in a trade embargo of Iran, including its oil. The trade restrictions were only partially effective because America's allies were not willing to lose access to Iranian oil. As the hostage crisis continued and gasoline prices rose to record levels, a frustrated Carter authorized a risky rescue attempt by U.S. commandos on April 24, 1980 (his decision caused his secretary of state, Cyrus Vance, to resign in protest). The raid had to be cancelled when three of the eight helicopters developed mechanical problems; it ended with eight U.S. deaths when a helicopter collided with a transport plane at a remote staging site in the Iranian desert.

For fourteen months, the frustrating Iranian hostage crisis paralyzed Carter's ability to lead the nation. Like a black cloud, it loomed over every decision he made. For many, the prolonged standoff with Iran became a symbol of his failed presidency. "For the first time in its history," *Business Week* magazine's editors observed, "the United States is no longer growing in power and influence among the nations of the world." The hostage crisis finally ended after 444 days, on January 20, 1981, when Carter, just hours before leaving office, released several billion dollars of Iranian assets to ransom the hostages.

Ayatollah Khomeini Religious figure and leader of the Iranian Revolution that overthrew the Iranian monarchy in 1979.

The Rise of Ronald Reagan

No sooner had Carter been elected in 1976 than conservative Republicans (the "New Right") began working to ensure that he would not win a second term. Their plans for a Republican revival centered on the popularity of tall, square-shouldered, plain-speaking Ronald Reagan, the Hollywood actor, two-term California governor, and prominent political commentator. Reagan was not a deep thinker, but he was a superb reader of the public mood, an outspoken emotional patriot, and a committed champion of conservative principles.

CORE **OBJECTIVE**

2. Identify the factors that led to the election of Ronald Reagan, the rise of the conservative movement, and the resurgence of the Republican party.

The Actor Turned President

Born in the drab prairie town of Tampico, Illinois, in 1911, the son of an often-drunk shoe salesman and a devout, Bible-quoting mother, Ronald Reagan graduated from tiny Eureka College in 1932 during the depths of the Great Depression. He first worked as a radio sportscaster before starting a

Ronald Reagan The "Great Communicator" flashes his charming, trademark smile.

movie career in Hollywood in 1937. He served three years in the army during the Second World War, making training films. At that time, as Reagan recalled, he was a Democrat, "a New Dealer to the core" who voted for Franklin D. Roosevelt four times. After the war, Reagan became president of the acting profession's union, the Screen Actors Guild (SAG), where he honed his negotiating skills and fended off Communist efforts to infiltrate the union. Reagan supported Democrat Harry S. Truman in the 1948 presidential election, but during the fifties he decided that federal taxes were too high. In 1960 he campaigned as a Democrat for Richard Nixon, and two years later he abandoned the Democrats and joined the Republican party. Reagan achieved political stardom in 1964 when he delivered a rousing speech on national television on behalf of Barry Goldwater's presidential candidacy. Soon thereafter, wealthy admirers convinced him to run for governor of California in 1966, and he won by a landslide.

Now, as the Republican presidential nominee in 1980, Reagan set about drawing a vivid contrast between his optimistic vision of America's future and Jimmy Carter's bleak outlook. Unlike Carter, Reagan insisted that there was "nothing wrong with the American people" and that there were "simple answers" to the complex problems facing the United States, though they were not *easy* answers. He pledged to reverse the social-welfare programs that had grown so dramatically during and after Lyndon Johnson's presidency, increase military spending to "win" the Cold War, dismantle the "bloated" federal bureaucracy, restore states' rights, reduce taxes and government regulations of business ("get the government off our backs"), and appoint conservative judges to the Supreme Court and federal courts across the nation. He also promised to affirm old-time religious values by banning abortions and reinstituting prayer in public schools. (He ended up doing neither.)

Reagan's popularity resulted from his remarkable skill as a public speaker (journalists dubbed him the "Great Communicator") and his steadfast commitment to a few basic principles and simple themes. Blessed with a baritone voice and a wealth of entertaining stories, he charmed audiences. Reagan rejected Carter's assumption that Americans needed "to start getting along with less, to accept a decline in our standard of living." He instead promised boundless economic expansion. By reducing taxes and easing government regulations of businesses, he pledged, the engine of capitalism would spread prosperity to everyone.

The Rise of the "New Right"

Population growth in conservative Sunbelt states

By 1980, social developments had made Reagan's anti-liberal stance a major asset. An increase in the number of senior citizens, a group that tends to be more politically and socially conservative, and the steady migration of people—especially older Americans—to the conservative Sunbelt states was shifting the political balance of power toward Reagan's philosophy. Fully 90 percent of the nation's total population growth during the eighties occurred in southern or western Sunbelt states, while the Northeast and industrial states of the Midwest—Ohio, Michigan, and Illinois (called the "rust belt")— experienced economic decline and population losses. The population shifts forced a massive redistricting of the House of Representatives, with Florida, California, and Texas gaining seats and northern states such as New York losing them.

A related development during the seventies was a growing grassroots tax revolt spurred by prolonged inflation. As consumer prices and the value of houses rose, so too did property taxes. In California, Ronald Reagan's home state, skyrocketing property taxes threatened to force many working-class people from their homes. This led to grassroots efforts to cut back on the size and cost of state government to enable reductions in property taxes. In June 1978, tax rebels in California, with Reagan's support, succeeded in putting an initiative known as Proposition 13 on the state ballot. An overwhelming majority of voters—both Republicans and Democrats—approved the measure, which slashed property taxes by 57 percent and amended the state constitution to make it more difficult for local and state governments to raise taxes. The "Prop 13" tax revolt in California soon spread across the nation, leading the *New York Times* to call it a "modern Boston Tea Party."

| Tax revolts |

The Religious Right

The California tax revolt fed into a national conservative resurgence led by the rapidly growing "**religious right**." Religious conservatives pushing a faith-based political agenda formed the strongest grassroots movement of the late twentieth century. By the eighties, Catholic conservatives and Protestant evangelicals owned powerful television and radio stations, operated their own schools and universities, and organized "mega-churches" from which such "televangelists" as the Reverend Jerry Falwell launched a cultural crusade against the "demonic" forces of liberalism at home and communism abroad.

| A crusade against liberalism, feminism, and abortion |

In 1979, Falwell formed a group he called the Moral Majority (later renamed the Liberty Alliance) to campaign for the major political and social goals of the religious right: the economy should operate without "interference" by the government, which should be reduced in size; the Supreme Court decision in *Roe v. Wade* (1973) legalizing abortion should be reversed; Darwinian evolution should be replaced in school textbooks by the biblical story of creation; prayer should return to public schools; women should submit to their husbands; and Soviet communism should be opposed as a form of pagan totalitarianism.

That Ronald Reagan became the hero of the religious right was a tribute to the candidate's political skills, for he himself rarely attended church

religious right Christian conservatives with a faith-based political agenda that includes prohibition of abortion and allowing prayer in public schools.

Look on the Right side The rise of the religious right saw protests against Supreme Court rulings that reinforced the separation of church and state. Here, in a 1984 protest organized by the Moral Majority, students chant "Kids want to pray!" in support of an amendment to reinstate prayer in public schools.

services and had no strong religious affiliations. However, white evangelical Christians—alienated by the liberal social agenda of the Democratic party, especially policies regarding abortions and endorsement of gay rights—became a crucial element in Reagan's electoral strategy.

Anti-Feminist Backlash

By the late seventies, a well-organized and well-financed backlash against the feminist movement reinforced the rise of the "New Right." Anti-feminist activists like Phyllis Schlafly, a conservative Catholic attorney and Republican activist from Alton, Illinois, campaigned successfully to keep the ERA from being ratified by the required thirty-eight states. Schlafly's STOP (Stop Taking Our Privileges) ERA organization, founded in 1972, warned that the ERA would allow husbands to abandon their wives, force women into military service, and give gay "perverts" the right to marry. She and others also stressed that the gender equality promised by the proposed amendment violated biblical teachings about women's "God-given" roles as nurturers and helpmates. By the late seventies, the national effort to gain ratification of the ERA had failed, largely because no states in the conservative South and West had ratified it.

Many of Schlafly's anti-ERA supporters also participated in the growing anti-abortion, or "pro-life," movement. The National Right to Life Committee, supported by the National Conference of Catholic Bishops, denounced abortion as murder, and the emotional intensity of the issue made it a powerful political force. Reagan highlighted his support for traditional "family values," gender roles, and the "rights" of the unborn, which helped persuade many northern Democrats—mostly working-class Catholics—to switch parties and support Reagan.

Financing Conservatism

The business community as well had become a source of revitalized conservative activism. In 1972, the leaders of the nation's largest corporations formed the Business Roundtable to promote business interests in Congress. Within a few years, many of those corporations had created political action committees (PACs) to distribute money to pro-business political candidates. Corporate donations also helped fund conservative "think tanks," such as the American Enterprise Institute, the Cato Institute, and the Heritage Foundation, all of which opposed "liberal" legislation. By 1980, the national conservative insurgency had become a powerful political force with substantial financial resources, carefully crafted ideas, and grassroots energy, all of which helped to explain Ronald Reagan's presidential victory.

The Election of 1980

Reagan's supporters during the 1980 campaign loved his simple solutions, upbeat personality, and folksy humor, and they responded passionately to his recurring question at campaign stops: "Are you better off than you were four years ago?" Their answer was a resounding "No!" On election day, Reagan swept to a lopsided victory, with 489 electoral votes to 49 for Carter, who carried only six states. The popular vote was 44 million (51 percent) for Reagan to Carter's 35 million (41 percent), with 7 percent going to John Anderson, a moderate Republican who ran on an independent ticket. Reagan's thumping of Carter signaled a major realignment of voters in which many so-called Reagan Democrats—conservative white southern Protestants and blue-collar northern Catholics crossed over to the Republican party.

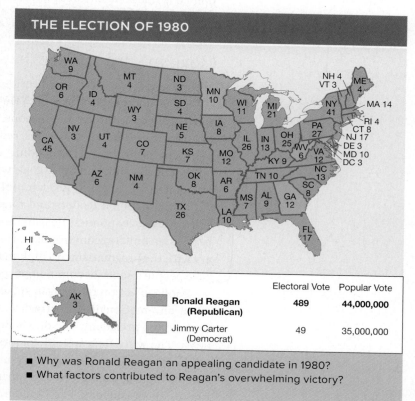

THE ELECTION OF 1980

	Electoral Vote	Popular Vote
Ronald Reagan (Republican)	**489**	**44,000,000**
Jimmy Carter (Democrat)	49	35,000,000

■ Why was Ronald Reagan an appealing candidate in 1980?
■ What factors contributed to Reagan's overwhelming victory?

The Reagan Revolution

Those Democrats who dismissed 69-year-old Ronald Reagan, the oldest man to assume the presidency, as a third-rate actor and mental lightweight famously inattentive to the details of policy and management, underrated his many virtues, including the importance of his years in front of a

> **CORE OBJECTIVE**
> **3.** Define "Reaganomics" and evaluate its effects on American society and economy.

camera. Politics is a performing art, all the more so in the age of television, and few people, if any, in public life had Reagan's stage presence—or confidence. He may have been a mediocre actor, but no one played the part of president better than Reagan. His remarkable ability to make Americans again believe in the greatness of their country won him two presidential elections, in 1980 and 1984, and ensured the victory of his chosen successor, Vice President George H. W. Bush, in 1988. Just how revolutionary the "Reagan Era" was remains a subject of intense debate, but what cannot be denied is that Reagan's actions and beliefs set the tone for the decade's political and economic life.

Reagan's First Term

"Fellow conservatives," new-president Ronald Reagan said in a speech in 1981, "Our moment has arrived." He succeeded as president where Jimmy Carter failed for three main reasons. First, Reagan focused on a few essential priorities (lowering tax rates, reducing the scope of the federal government, increasing military spending, and conducting an anti-Soviet foreign policy), and he pursued those goals with what an aide called a "warmly ruthless" intensity. Second, Reagan, unlike Carter, was skilled at negotiating with congressional leaders and foreign heads of state. A true believer in conservative economics, Reagan also recognized early on that politics is a profession built on compromises. He combined the passion of a revolutionary with the pragmatism of a diplomat. Third, Reagan's infectious optimism gave people a sense of common purpose and renewed confidence.

Public affection for Reagan spiked just two months into his presidency when an emotionally-disturbed young man eager for notoriety fired six shots at the president, one of which punctured a lung and lodged near his heart. The witty Reagan told doctors as they prepared for surgery: "Please tell me you're Republicans." Reagan's gritty response to the assassination and his injuries created an outpouring of support that gave added momentum to his presidency. The Democratic Speaker of the House, Tip O'Neill, told colleagues that Reagan "has become a hero. We can't argue with a man as popular as he is."

Reaganomics

Economic Recovery Tax Act (1981)

On August 1, 1981, the president signed the Economic Recovery Tax Act (ERTA), which cut personal income taxes by 25 percent, lowered the maximum rate from 70 to 50 percent for 1982, and offered a broad array of other tax concessions. The tax-cut bill was the centerpiece of what Reagan called his "common sense" economic plan. While theorists called the philosophy behind the plan "supply-side economics," journalists dubbed the president's proposals **Reaganomics**.

Simply put, Reaganomics argued that the stagflation of the seventies had resulted from excessive taxes, which weakened incentives for individuals and businesses to increase productivity, save money, and reinvest in

Reaganomics President Reagan's "supply-side" economic philosophy combining tax cuts with the goals of decreased government spending, reduced regulation of business, and a balanced budget.

economic expansion. The "supply-side" or Reaganomics solution to stagflation was to slash tax rates on companies and individuals, especially on the wealthy, in the belief that they would spend their tax savings on business expansion and consumer goods (the "supply side" of the economy). By generating economic growth, Reaganomics promised to generate enough new tax revenues from rising corporate profits and personal incomes to pay for the cuts in tax rates. In the short term, however, ERTA did not work as planned. The federal budget deficit grew rather than shrank. By November 1981, the economy was officially in recession, "a slight one," explained the president.

Budget Cuts

To offset the loss of government tax revenues, David Stockman, Reagan's budget director, proposed sharp reductions in federal spending, including Social Security and Medicare, the two most expensive—and most popular— federal social programs. Liberal Democrats howled at efforts to dismantle social-welfare programs. Reagan responded that he was committed to maintaining the "safety net" of government services for the "truly needy." When the president told Stockman that there would be no cuts to Social Security, the budget director knew that there was no hope to balance the federal budget.

Failure to curb "liberal" social-welfare programs

For all of Reagan's bold talk about shrinking the government, he was not a true revolutionary in that regard. It was much easier to promise to reduce the scope of federal government while a candidate than as president. In the end, the president and Congress agreed to cut "food stamps" (government subsidies to help poor people buy groceries) only 4 percent from what the Carter administration had planned to spend. The Reagan administration

A miss for Reaganomics
A throng of more than 5,000 senior citizens staged a demonstration in downtown Detroit against Reagan's decision to cut federal budgets for Social Security and other programs to aid the elderly in 1982.

also continued huge federal subsidies to corporations and agribusinesses—what critics called "welfare for the rich." In the end, Reagan never dismantled the major federal social programs that he savagely criticized.

Within a year, David Stockman realized that the cuts in domestic spending approved by Reagan had fallen far short of what would be needed to balance the budget in four years, as the president had promised. Massive increases in military spending greatly complicated the situation. In essence, Reagan gave the Defense Department a blank check, telling the secretary of defense to "spend what you need." Over the next five years, the administration would spend some $1.2 *trillion* on military expenses. Something had to give.

| A growing federal deficit |

In the summer of 1981, Stockman warned the president that "we're heading for a crash landing on the budget. We're facing potential deficit numbers so big that they could wreck the president's entire economic program." The fast-growing federal budget deficit, which helped trigger the worst economic recession since the 1930s, was Reagan's greatest failure, as he himself admitted. During 1982, there were 10 million Americans unable to find jobs. "The stench of failure hangs over Ronald Reagan's White House," declared the *New York Times*.

Stockman and other worried aides finally convinced the president that the government needed "revenue enhancements" (tax increases). With Reagan's support, Congress passed a tax increase bill in 1982 that would raise almost $100 billion, but the economic slump persisted for a time, with unemployment standing at 10.4 percent. In the 1982 Congressional midterm elections, Democrats picked up twenty-six seats in the House of Representatives.

| Increased military spending, lower interest rates and lower tax rates |

But Reagan's determination to "stay the course" in pursuing his economic program began to pay off. By the summer of 1983, a major economic recovery was under way, in part because of increased government spending and lower interest rates and in part because of lower tax rates. Inflation subsided along with unemployment and "deregulation" of business, as Reagan appointed pro-business conservatives to head regulatory agencies.

Reaganomics, however, was not helping to balance the budget: in fact, the annual federal deficits had grown larger—so much so that the president, who in 1980 had pledged to balance the federal budget by 1983, had in fact run up an accumulated federal debt larger than that of all his predecessors combined. Reagan was willing to tolerate the growing budget deficits in part because he believed that they would force more responsible spending behavior in Congress, and in part because he was so committed to increased military spending as a way to intimidate the Soviets.

Reagan's Anti-Liberalism

| Setbacks for unions |

During Reagan's presidency, organized labor suffered severe setbacks, even though Reagan himself had been a union leader. In 1981, Reagan fired members of the Professional Air Traffic Controllers Organization who had participated in an illegal strike intended to shut down air travel. Even more important, Reagan's actions broke the political power of the American Federation of Labor–Congress of Industrial Organizations (AFL-CIO), the national confederation of labor unions that traditionally supported Democratic candidates. His criticism of unions reflected a general trend in public opinion. Although record numbers of new jobs were created during the eighties, union membership steadily dropped. By 1987, unions represented only 17 percent of the nation's full-time workers, down from 24 percent in 1979.

Reagan also went on the offensive against feminism and the enforcement of civil rights. Echoing Phyllis Schlafly, he opposed the Equal Rights Amendment, legal abortion, and proposals to require equal pay for jobs of comparable worth. He did name Sandra Day O'Connor as the first woman Supreme Court justice, but critics labeled it a token gesture rather than a reflection of genuine commitment to gender equality. Reagan also cut funds for civil rights enforcement and the Equal Employment Opportunity Commission, and he opposed renewal of the Voting Rights Act of 1965 before being overruled by Congress.

Sandra Day O'Connor Her Supreme Court confirmation hearing in September 1981 was picketed by conservatives who decried her pro-abortion stance.

The Election of 1984

By 1983, prosperity had returned, the stock market was soaring, and Reagan's "supply-side" economic program was at last working as advertised—except for the growing budget deficits. By 1984, reporters had begun to speak of the "Reagan Revolution." The economy surged with new energy. The slogan at the Republican National Convention was "America is back and standing tall." The Democrats' presidential nominee, Jimmy Carter's vice president, Walter Mondale, struggled to present a competing vision. Endorsed by the AFL-CIO, the National Organization for Women (NOW), and many prominent African Americans, Mondale was viewed as the candidate of liberal special-interest groups. He set a precedent by choosing as his running mate Geraldine Ferraro, a New York congresswoman, who was quickly placed on the defensive by the need to explain her husband's complicated business dealings.

A bit of frankness in Mondale's acceptance speech ended up hurting his campaign. "Mr. Reagan will raise taxes, and so will I," he told the convention. "He won't tell you. I just did." Reagan responded by vowing never to approve another tax increase (a promise he could not keep) and by chiding Mondale for his stance. Reagan also repeated a theme he had used against Jimmy Carter: the future, according to Mondale and the Democrats, was "dark and getting darker." Reagan's vision of America's future, however, was bright with optimism and hope. As his campaign ads claimed, "It's morning again in America," and record numbers of Americans were headed to work. In the end, Reagan took 59 percent of the popular vote and lost only Minnesota (Mondale's home state) and the District of Columbia.

Reagan's Second Term

Tax Reform Act (1986)

Spurred by his overwhelming victory, Reagan called for "a Second American Revolution of hope and opportunity." He dared Democrats to raise taxes; his veto pen was ready. "Go ahead and make my day," he said, echoing a popular line from a Clint Eastwood movie. Through much of 1985, the president drummed up support for a tax-simplification plan. After vigorous debate that ran nearly two years, Congress passed a comprehensive Tax Reform Act that the president signed in 1986. The measure reduced the number of federal tax brackets from fourteen to two and reduced rates from the maximum of 50 percent to 15 and 28 percent—the lowest since Calvin Coolidge was president in the twenties.

Reagan's Half-Hearted Revolution

Ronald Wilson Reagan was the first president since Dwight Eisenhower to complete two full terms in office. Although in 1981 he had proclaimed his intention to "curb the size and influence of the federal establishment," he did not, in part because the Democrats controlled the House of Representatives throughout his presidency. The number of federal employees actually *grew* during the Reagan presidency. Neither the Social Security system nor Medicare, the two largest federal social programs, were overhauled during Reagan's two-term presidency. And the federal agencies that Reagan had threatened to abolish, such as the Department of Education, not only survived but saw their budgets grow. The federal budget deficit almost tripled during his two terms.

Reagan and his aides repeatedly blamed Congress for the problem, "since only Congress can spend money," but in fact the legislators essentially approved the budgets that Reagan had submitted to them (and he never submitted a balanced budget). The cost of Social Security, the most expensive government "entitlement" program, grew by 27 percent, as some 6,000 Americans each day turned 65. Moreover, Reagan failed to fulfill his campaign promises to the religious right, such as reinstituting daily prayer in public schools and a ban on abortions. But he did follow through on his pledge to reshape the federal court system. During his two terms, Reagan was much more successful in transforming the judicial system than in ending the welfare state. He appointed 368 mostly conservative judges, three of whom were added to the U.S. Supreme Court: Sandra Day O'Connor (the Court's first woman justice), Antonin Scalia, and Anthony Kennedy.

"The Great Expansion"

Martin Anderson, Reagan's domestic policy adviser, stressed that it was "a mistake to think that there ever was a Reagan Revolution, or that Reagan gave it life." It was the grassroots conservative revolution that "caused Reagan—and the same forces will continue to the end of the century." What Reagan, the half-hearted revolutionary on the right, did accomplish was to end the prolonged period of economic "stagflation" and set in motion what economists called "The Great Expansion," an unprecedented, twenty-year-long burst of productivity and prosperity. True, Reagan's presidency left the nation with a massive debt burden that would eventually cause major problems, but the "Great Communicator" who defined America as "a sunrise every day—fresh new opportunities, dreams to build," also renewed the nation's strength, self-confidence, and soaring sense of possibilities.

Over his two terms, Ronald Reagan became a transformational president. In the process of restoring the stature of the presidency and reviving the economy, he transformed political life by accelerating the nation's shift toward conservatism and by revitalizing the Republican party after the Watergate scandal. He put the Democratic party on the defensive and forced conventional New Deal "liberalism" into a panicked retreat. For the next twenty years or so, Reagan's anti-government, anti-tax conservative agenda would dominate the national political landscape.

An Anti-Communist Foreign Policy

> CORE **OBJECTIVE**
> **4.** Explain how Reagan's Soviet strategy helped end the Cold War.

On a flight to Detroit, Michigan, to accept the Republican party's presidential nomination in the summer of 1980, Ronald Reagan was asked why he wanted to be president. He answered: "To end the Cold War." A few years earlier, he had offered a simple formula for success against what he described as the international Communist conspiracy directed by the Soviet Union: "We win, they lose." As president, Reagan systematically worked to make that happen by promoting what he called his "peace through strength" strategy. Through a series of bold steps, he would build up U.S. military strength to the point it would overwhelm the Soviet Union, both financially and militarily. At the same time, Reagan launched a widespread "war of ideas" against communism by charging that the Soviet Union (the "evil empire") was "the focus of evil in the modern world."

> "War of ideas" and the Reagan Doctrine

What came to be called the Reagan Doctrine revived and expanded the old notion of "containment" by pledging to combat Soviet adventurism throughout the world, even if it meant partnering with brutal dictatorships to do so. Reagan believed that aggressive CIA-led efforts to stalemate Soviet expansionism would eventually cause the unstable Soviet system to implode "on the ash heap of history."

A Massive Defense Buildup

> The arms race and bankrupting the Soviet Union

Reagan's conduct of foreign policy reflected his belief that trouble in the world stemmed mainly from Moscow, the capital of what he called the "evil empire." Reagan had long believed that former Republican presidents Nixon and Ford—following the advice of Henry Kissinger—had been too soft on the Soviets. Kissinger's emphasis on détente, he said, had been a "one-way street" favoring the Soviets.

By contrast, Reagan first wanted to reduce the risk of nuclear war by convincing the Soviets that they could not win such a conflict. To do so, he and Secretary of Defense Caspar Weinberger embarked upon a major buildup of nuclear and conventional weapons. During Reagan's two presidential terms, defense spending came to represent a fourth of all federal government expenditures. Reagan claimed that such expensive defense allocations had another purpose: it was also intended to bankrupt the Soviets by forcing them to spend much more on their own military budgets. To critics who complained about the money being spent on expensive new U.S. weapons systems, Reagan replied, "It will break the Soviets first." It did.

In 1983, Reagan escalated the nuclear arms race by authorizing the Defense Department to develop the controversial **Strategic Defense Initiative (SDI)**, featuring a complex anti-missile defense system positioning satellites with laser weapons in outer space to "intercept and destroy" Soviet missiles in flight. Despite skepticism among the media, many scientists, and even government officials that such a defense system (dubbed "Star Wars" by the media) could ever be built (Secretary of State George Shultz called it "lunacy"), Congress approved the first stage of funding, which in turn forced the Soviets to launch an expensive research and development effort of their own to keep pace.

The Americas

Fighting the Communist threat in Central America

Reagan's foremost international concern, however, was Central America, where he detected the most serious Communist threat. The tiny nation of El Salvador, caught up since 1980 in a brutal struggle between Communist-supported revolutionaries and right-wing militants, received U.S. economic and military assistance. Critics argued that U.S. involvement ensured that the revolutionary forces would gain public support by capitalizing on "anti-Yankee" sentiment. Supporters countered that allowing a Communist victory in El Salvador would lead all of Central America into the Communist camp (a new "domino" theory). By 1984, however, the U.S.-backed government of President José Napoleón Duarte had brought some stability to El Salvador.

Even more troubling to Reagan was the situation in Nicaragua. The State Department claimed that the Cuban-sponsored Sandinista socialist government, which had seized power in 1979, was sending Soviet and Cuban arms to leftist Salvadoran rebels. In response, the Reagan administration ordered the CIA to train anti-Communist Nicaraguans, or Contras (short for *contrarevolucionarios*, or counterrevolutionaries), who staged attacks on Sandinista bases from sanctuaries in Honduras.

In supporting these "freedom fighters," Reagan sought not only to impede the traffic in arms to Salvadoran rebels but also to replace the Sandinistas with a democratic government in Nicaragua. Critics accused the Contras of being mostly right-wing fanatics who killed indiscriminately. They also feared that the United States might eventually commit its own combat forces, leading to a Vietnam-like intervention. Reagan warned that if the Communists prevailed in Central America, "our credibility would collapse, our alliances would crumble, and the safety of our homeland would be jeopardized."

Strategic Defense Initiative (SDI) (1983) Ronald Reagan's proposed space-based anti-missile defense system, dubbed "Star Wars" by the media, that aroused great controversy and escalated the arms race between the United States and the Soviet Union.

The Iran-Contra Affair

During the fall of 1986, Democrats regained control of the Senate with a 55 to 45 majority. They also picked up 6 seats in the House to increase their already comfortable margin to 259 to 176. Those results had less to do with Reagan's popularity than with the qualities of the particular candidates and local and state issues. Whatever the reason, the 1986 elections meant that Reagan would face an oppositional Congress during the last two years of his presidency.

What was worse, reports surfaced in late 1986 that the United States had been secretly selling arms to U.S.-hating Iran (which Reagan had called an "outlaw state") in the hope of securing the release of American hostages held in Lebanon by extremist groups sympathetic to Iran. Such action contradicted Reagan's repeated insistence that his administration would never negotiate with terrorists. The disclosures angered America's allies as well as many Americans who vividly remembered the 1979 Iranian takeover of the embassy in Tehran. Over the next several months, revelations reminiscent of the Watergate affair disclosed a complicated series of covert activities carried out by administration officials.

At the center of what came to be called the **Iran-Contra affair** was Marine lieutenant colonel Oliver North, a swashbuckling aide to the National Security Council who specialized in counterterrorism. Working from the basement of the White House, North had been secretly selling military supplies to Iran and using the proceeds to support the Contra rebels fighting in Nicaragua at a time when Congress had voted to ban such aid.

North's illegal activities, it turned out, had been approved by national security adviser Robert McFarlane; McFarlane's successor, Admiral John Poindexter; and CIA director William Casey. Both Secretary of State George Shultz and Secretary of Defense Caspar Weinberger criticized the arms sale to Iran, but their objections were ignored, and they were thereafter kept in the dark about what was going on. On three occasions, Shultz threatened to resign over the "pathetic" scheme. After information about the secret dealings surfaced in the press, North and others erased incriminating computer files and destroyed documents. McFarlane attempted suicide, Poindexter resigned, and North was fired. Casey, who denied any connection to the clumsy operation, left the CIA for health reasons and died shortly thereafter from a brain tumor.

Iran-Contra hearings Admiral John Poindexter listens to a question from the investigation committee with apprehension on July 21, 1987.

Under increasing criticism, Reagan appointed a three-member commission, led by former Republican senator John Tower, to investigate the scandal. The Tower Commission issued a devastating report early in 1987 that placed much of the responsibility for the bungled Iran-Contra affair on Reagan's loose management style. When asked if he had known of Colonel North's illegal actions, the president simply replied: "I don't remember." He was stunned that "for the first time in my life, people didn't believe me."

Iran-Contra affair (1987) Reagan administration scandal over the secret, unlawful U.S. sale of arms to Iran in partial exchange for the release of hostages in Lebanon; the arms money in turn was used illegally to aid Nicaraguan right-wing insurgents, the Contras.

During the spring and summer of 1987, a joint House-Senate committee began holding hearings into the Iran-Contra affair. The televised sessions revealed a tangled web of inept financial and diplomatic transactions, the illegal shredding of incriminating government documents, crass profiteering, and misguided patriotism.

The investigations of the independent counsel led to six indictments in 1988. A Washington jury found Oliver North guilty of three relatively minor charges but innocent of nine more serious counts, apparently reflecting the jury's reasoning that he acted as an agent of higher-ups. His conviction was later overturned on appeal. Of those involved in the affair, only John Poindexter received a jail sentence—six months for obstructing justice and lying to Congress.

A Historic Treaty

The most positive achievement at the end of Reagan's second term was a surprising arms-reduction agreement with the Soviet government. Under Mikhail Gorbachev, who came to power in 1985, the Soviets pursued renewed détente so that they could reduce military spending related to the Cold War and focus on more pressing problems, especially a notoriously inefficient economy and a losing war in Afghanistan.

In October 1986 Reagan and Gorbachev met in Reykjavik, Iceland, to discuss ways to reduce the threat of nuclear war. At one point during ten hours of intense negotiations, Reagan shocked the Soviets by saying, "It would be fine with me if we eliminated all nuclear weapons." Equally shocking was Gorbachev's reply: "We can do that." By the end of the meeting, however, the two sides remained so far apart on the details that they had given up.

The logjam in the disarmament negotiations with the Soviet Union suddenly broke in 1987, when Gorbachev announced that he was willing to consider mutually reducing nuclear weaponry. After nine months of strenuous negotiations, Reagan and Gorbachev met amid much fanfare in Washington, D.C., on December 9, 1987, and signed the **Intermediate-Range Nuclear Forces (INF) Treaty**, an agreement to eliminate intermediate-range (300- to 3,000-mile) missiles. Reagan's steadfast show of strength against the Soviets and a new kind of Soviet leader in Mikhail Gorbachev combined to produce the most sweeping reduction in nuclear weaponry in history.

The INF treaty marked the first time that the two nations had agreed to destroy a whole class of weapons systems. Under the terms of the treaty, the United States would destroy 859 missiles, and the Soviets would eliminate 1,752. Still, the reductions represented only 4 percent of the total nuclear-missile count on both sides.

Gorbachev's successful efforts to liberalize Soviet domestic life and improve East-West relations cheered Americans. The Soviets suddenly began stressing cooperation with the West in dealing with hot spots around

Mikhail Gorbachev Deputy Chairman, and later President, of the Soviet Union in 1988.

Intermediate-Range Nuclear Forces (INF) Treaty (1987) Agreement signed by U.S. president Ronald Reagan and Soviet premier Mikhail Gorbachev to eliminate the deployment of intermediate-range missiles with nuclear warheads.

the world. In the Middle East, they urged the Palestine Liberation Organization, founded in 1964 to represent the Palestinian people, to recognize Israel's right to exist and advocated a greater role for the United Nations in the volatile Persian Gulf. Perhaps the most dramatic symbol of a thawing cold war was the phased withdrawal of 115,000 Soviet troops from Afghanistan, which began in 1988.

Reagan's Global Legacy

Reagan achieved the unthinkable by helping to end the Cold War. Although his massive defense buildup almost bankrupted the United States, it did bankrupt the Soviet Union and force it to the bargaining table. By negotiating the nuclear disarmament treaty and lighting the fuse of democratic freedom in Soviet-controlled Eastern Europe, he set in motion events that would cause the collapse of the Soviet Union. In June 1987, Reagan visited the huge concrete and barbed wire Berlin Wall and, in a dramatic speech, called upon the Soviet Union to allow greater freedom within the countries under its control. "General Secretary Gorbachev, if you seek peace, if you seek prosperity for the Soviet Union and Eastern Europe, if you seek liberalization: Come here to this gate! Mr. Gorbachev, open this gate! Mr. Gorbachev, tear down this wall!"

The Changing Economic and Social Landscape

During the eighties, profound changes transformed American life. The economy went through a wrenching transformation in adapting to an increasingly interconnected global marketplace. The nations that had been devastated by the Second World War—France, Germany, the Soviet Union, Japan, and China—had by the eighties developed formidable economies with higher levels of productivity than the United States. More and more American manufacturing companies shifted their production overseas, thereby accelerating the transition of the economy from its once-dominant industrial base to a more services-oriented economy. Driving all of these changes was the impact of the computer revolution and the development of the Internet.

The Computer Revolution

The idea of a programmable machine that would rapidly perform mental tasks had been around since the eighteenth century, but it took the Second World War to marshal the intellectual and financial resources needed to create such a "computer." In 1946, a team of engineers at the University of Pennsylvania created ENIAC (electronic numerical integrator and computer), the first all-purpose, all-electronic digital computer.

> **CORE OBJECTIVE**
> **5.** Characterize the social and economic issues and innovations that emerged during the 1980s.

The Reagan Revolution

The election of Ronald Reagan in 1980 was a turning point in American political history—in many ways a reaction against the previous two decades in politics. Reagan and the "New Right" political movement he embodied helped shift the focus of American politics away from the New Deal "liberalism" that had dominated the domestic agenda since 1932. While Reagan did not put an end to the federal welfare state (as some of his supporters fervently hoped), he did slow its expansion. In foreign policy, Reagan also broke with past presidents by taking a more confrontational stance against the Soviet Union. As you examine the ways in which "The Reagan Revolution" reshaped the political landscape, consider the questions below.

FACTORS CONTRIBUTING TO REAGAN'S ELECTION	REAGAN'S GOVERNING PHILOSOPHY
Economic Distress of the 1970s: High inflation and economic stagnation increased the appeal of Reagan's "supply-side" economic message over the New Deal "liberalism" of Carter and other past presidents, spawning tax revolts among some working- and middle-class property owners, who joined anti-tax and anti–big government movements.	**"Supply-Side" Economics:** Cut taxes to incentivize individuals and businesses to increase productivity, invest, and spend.
Growth of the Sunbelt: Population growth of southern and western states increased the electoral influence of older and more conservative voters.	**Anti–Big Government:** Shrink the federal bureaucracy, empower states' rights, reduce regulation of business, and reduce the role of the federal government generally.
Rise of the Religious Right and Anti-Feminism: Religious conservatives mobilized against abortion rights and restrictions on school prayer, leading to greater organization and political power; anger at the feminist movement over abortion rights, as well as challenges to traditional gender roles, moved many culturally conservative Democrats, especially working-class Roman Catholics, toward Reagan.	**Social Conservatism:** Support traditional "family values," gender roles, and the "rights" of the unborn; oppose feminism, abortion rights, gay rights, and secularism.
Resentment of Protest Movements: Reagan attracted voters alienated by protests over the Vietnam War and civil rights, and promised a "renewed" America and a return to more traditional values.	**Hard-line Anti-Communism:** Take a tougher stance against communism and the Soviet Union, and support anti-Communist efforts across the globe.
Iran Hostage Crisis: The seizure of the American embassy in Tehran made President Carter appear weak and ineffective.	

The next major breakthrough was the invention in 1971 of the **microprocessor**—virtually a tiny computer on a silicon chip. The functions that had once been performed by huge computers that took up an entire room could now be performed by a microchip circuit the size of a postage stamp.

The microchip made possible the personal computer. In 1975, an engineer named Ed Roberts developed the Altair 8800, the prototype of the personal computer. Its potential excited a Harvard sophomore named Bill

microprocessor An electronic circuit printed on a tiny silicon chip; a major technological breakthrough in 1971, it paved the way for the development of the personal computer.

EFFECTS OF REAGAN'S DOMESTIC POLICIES

Tax Cuts for High Income Earners and Investors: Increased economic growth and consumerism; increased budget deficit and national debt.

Deregulation: Relaxed government price controls on oil and natural gas led to a decline in energy prices that helped stimulate economic growth.

Efforts to Weaken the Power of Labor Unions: Decline in union membership and the power of unions.

Slowed Growth of Social Welfare Programs: Slowed expansion of federal welfare state; increased income inequality.

Criticism of Feminist, Civil Rights, and Environmental Movements: Increased influence of the "New Right" conservative movement in American politics.

EFFECTS OF REAGAN'S FOREIGN POLICY

Increased Anti-Communist Rhetoric: Energized anti-Soviet movements in Eastern Europe.

Increased Anti-Communist Activities in Central America: Military assistance to anti-Communist forces; Iran-Contra affair.

Increased Military Spending: Increased budget deficit and national debt; economic pressure of arms race contributed to economic and political collapse of Soviet Union; arms-reduction treaty with Soviets.

QUESTIONS FOR ANALYSIS

1. How was Reagan's governing philosophy different from that of recent presidents?

2. How did the events and trends of the sixties and seventies help lead to Reagan's election in 1980?

3. What were the effects of Reagan's domestic policy?

4. How did Reagan's foreign policy reshape the Cold War?

Gates, who improved the software of the Altair 8800, dropped out of college, and formed a company called Microsoft to sell the new system. By 1977, Gates and others had helped transform the personal computer into a mass consumer product. The development of the Internet, electronic mail (e-mail), and cell-phone technology during the eighties and nineties allowed for instantaneous communication, thereby accelerating the globalization of the economy and dramatically increasing productivity in the workplace.

Debt and the Stock Market Plunge

Black Monday A 508-point plunge devastated Wall Street on October 19, 1987 and sent traders on the floor of the New York Stock Exchange into a panic-selling frenzy.

During the eighties, Ronald Reagan lowered tax rates so that people would have more money to spend and thereby accelerate the growth of the economy. Americans had little trouble going on a spending spree. During the "Reagan Era," marketers and advertisers celebrated instant gratification at the expense of the future. Michelob beer commercials promised that "you can have it all," and many people went on self-indulgent spending sprees. The more they bought, the more they wanted. Compulsive shoppers donned T-shirts proclaiming: "Born to Shop." Money—lots of it—came to define the American Dream. In the hit movie *Wall Street* (1987), the high-flying land developer and corporate raider Gordon Gekko, played by actor Michael Douglas, announced that "greed . . . is good. Greed is right."

The Poor

Increased homelessness

The eighties were years of vivid contrast. Despite unprecedented prosperity, growing numbers of underclass Americans were without hope. Widespread homelessness became the most acute social issue.

A variety of causes had led to a shortage of low-cost housing. The government had given up on building public housing, urban-renewal programs had demolished blighted residential areas but provided no housing for those who were displaced, and owners had abandoned unprofitable buildings in poor neighborhoods or converted them into expensive condominiums, a process called *gentrification*. In addition, after new medications allowed for the release of some mentally ill patients from institutions, many of them ended up on the streets because the promised mental-health services failed to materialize. Drug and alcohol abuse were rampant among the homeless, mostly unemployed single adults. A quarter of them had spent time in mental institutions; some 40 percent had spent time in jail; a third were delusional.

The AIDS Epidemic

HIV/AIDS Human immunodeficiency virus (HIV) transmitted via the bodily fluids of infected persons to cause acquired immunodeficiency syndrome (AIDS), an often-fatal disease of the immune system when it appeared in the 1980s.

Still another group of outcasts in the eighties included those suffering from a newly identified disease called AIDS (acquired immunodeficiency syndrome). At the beginning of the eighties, public health officials had reported that gay men and intravenous drug users were especially at risk for developing AIDS. People contracted the human immunodeficiency

AIDS Memorial Quilt Composed of more than 48,000 panels, the quilt was first conceptualized by gay rights and AIDS activist Cleve Jones to commemorate those who died of AIDS-related causes. It continues to grow to this day.

virus (HIV), by coming into contact with the blood or bodily fluids of an infected person. Those infected with the virus that causes AIDS showed signs of extreme fatigue, developed a strange combination of infections, and soon died.

The Reagan administration showed little interest in AIDS in part because it was initially viewed as a "gay" disease. Patrick Buchanan, the conservative spokesman who served as Reagan's director of communications, said that homosexuals had "declared war on nature, and now nature is extracting an awful retribution." Buchanan and others convinced Reagan not to engage the **HIV/AIDS** issue. By 2000, AIDS had claimed almost 300,000 American lives and was spreading among a larger segment of the population. Nearly 1 million Americans were carrying the deadly virus, and it had become the leading cause of death among men ages twenty-five to forty-four.

> AIDS becomes leading cause of death for young men

The Presidency of George H. W. Bush

Reagan's two-term vice president, George H. W. Bush, won the Republican presidential nomination in 1988. Born into a prominent New England family, the son of a U.S. senator, he enlisted at the age of eighteen in the U.S. Navy at the start of the Second World War, becoming America's youngest combat pilot. After his distinguished service in the war, Bush graduated

> **CORE OBJECTIVE**
> **6.** Appraise the impact of the end of the Cold War and the efforts of President George H. W. Bush to create a post–cold war foreign policy.

George H. W. Bush His son, George W. Bush, would also serve as president, making them the second father-son presidential duo in history (the first was John Adams and John Quincy Adams).

from Yale University, having also been captain of the baseball team. Bush and his family moved to west Texas, where he became a wealthy oil executive before entering government service, first as a member of the U.S. House of Representatives, then as U.S. ambassador to the UN, a diplomat in China, and head of the CIA before becoming vice president in 1981.

In all of those roles, Bush had displayed intelligence, integrity, and courage. But he lacked Reagan's charm and speaking skills. One Democrat described him as a man born "with a silver foot in his mouth." Bush was a centrist Republican who had never embraced right-wing conservatism. He promised to use the White House to fight bigotry, illiteracy, and homelessness. "I want a kinder, gentler nation," Bush said in his speech accepting the Republican nomination. His most memorable line in the speech, though, was a defiant statement ruling out any tax increases to deal with the massive budget deficits created during the Reagan years: "The Congress will push me to raise taxes, and I'll say no, and they'll push, and I'll say no, and they'll push again. And I'll say to them: Read my lips. No new taxes."

Meanwhile, Massachusetts governor Michael Dukakis won the Democratic nomination, but it did little good. In the end, Bush won a decisive victory. Dukakis carried only ten states plus the District of Columbia, with clusters of support in the Northeast, Midwest, and Northwest. Bush carried the rest, with a margin of about 54 percent to 46 percent in the popular vote and 426 to 111 in the Electoral College, but the Democrats retained control of the House and Senate.

George H. W. Bush sought to reinforce the initiatives that Reagan had put in place rather than launch his own array of programs and policies. "We don't need to remake society," he announced. As an example of his "gentler, kinder" conservatism, Bush supported the Democratic-proposed Americans with Disabilities Act (1990), which strengthened the civil rights of the physically or mentally disabled in areas such as employment, public transportation, and housing. The act also required organizations (for-profit, non-profit, and governmental) to ensure that people with disabilities could access facilities by providing mechanized doors, wheelchair ramps, and elevators.

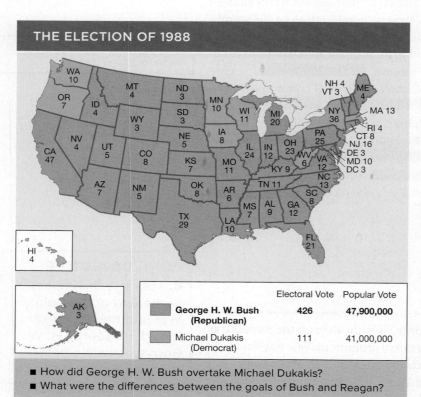

THE ELECTION OF 1988

	Electoral Vote	Popular Vote
George H. W. Bush (Republican)	426	47,900,000
Michael Dukakis (Democrat)	111	41,000,000

■ How did George H. W. Bush overtake Michael Dukakis?
■ What were the differences between the goals of Bush and Reagan?

The Federal Debt and Recession

The biggest problem facing the Bush administration was the huge national debt, which stood at $2.6 trillion in 1989, nearly three times its 1980 level. Bush's pledge not to increase taxes (especially income taxes) made it more difficult to reduce the annual deficit or trim the long-term debt. Likewise, Bush was not willing to make substantial cutbacks in spending on defense or social welfare programs like Social Security, Medicare, and food stamps. As a result, by 1990 the country faced "a fiscal mess."

During the summer of 1990, Bush agreed with Congressional Democrats to approve "tax revenue increases," which he had sworn to avoid. His decision to support tax increases set off a revolt among conservative Republicans, from which he never recovered. The increase in the top tax rate from 28 to 31 percent raised federal revenue but eroded Bush's political support among conservative Republicans. The economy barely grew at all during the first three years of the Bush administration—the worst record since the end of the Second World War.

The Democracy Movement Abroad

George H. W. Bush entered the White House with more foreign-policy experience than most presidents, and, like Nixon before him, preferred to deal with international relations rather than domestic issues such as the deficit, drug abuse, and the problems of the inner cities. In the Soviet Union, amazing changes were underway. With the economy failing, Mikhail Gorbachev responded with policies of *perestroika* (economic restructuring) and *glasnost* (openness), a loosening of centralized economic planning and censorship of the press. His foreign policy sought harmony and trade with the West. Early in 1989, Soviet troops left Afghanistan after nine years. Gorbachev then renounced the right of the Soviet Union to intervene in the internal affairs of other Communist countries. Soon thereafter, the old Communist regimes in Eastern Europe fell with surprisingly little bloodshed. Communist rule enforced by the Soviet Union ended first in Poland and Hungary, then in Czechoslovakia and Bulgaria. In Romania, the year of peaceful revolution ended in a bloodbath when the people joined the army in a bloody uprising against Nicolae Ceaușescu, the country's brutal dictator. He and his wife were captured, tried, and then executed on Christmas Day.

> The end of the Soviet empire; the reunification of East and West Germany

The End of the Berlin Wall

The most spectacular event in the collapse of the Soviet Empire came on November 9, 1989, when Germans—using hand tools and even their bare hands—tore down the Berlin Wall, the chief symbol of the Cold War. With the borders to the West now fully open, the Communist government of East Germany collapsed, and a freely elected government came to power. On October 3, 1990, the five states of East Germany were united with West

perestroika Russian term for "economic restructuring"; applied to Mikhail Gorbachev's series of political and economic reforms that included shifting a centrally planned Commmunist economy to a mixed economy allowing for capitalism.

glasnost Russian term for "openness"; applied to the loosening of censorship in the Soviet Union under Mikhail Gorbachev.

A hammer to the Soviet Empire A West German demonstrator pounds away at the Berlin Wall on November 11, 1989, while East Berlin border guards look on. Two days later, all the crossings between East and West Germany were opened.

U.S. recognition of the new Soviet government and the independent Baltic republics

Germany. The reform impulse that Gorbachev helped unleash in the Eastern-bloc countries sped out of control within the Soviet Union itself, however. Gorbachev had proven unusually adept at political restructuring, yielding the Communist monopoly of government but building a new presidential system that gave him, if anything, increased powers. His skills, however, could not salvage an antiquated economy that resisted change.

Communist Coup Fails

Gorbachev's popularity shrank in the Soviet Union even as it grew abroad. Communist hard-liners saw in his reforms the unraveling of their bureaucratic and political empire. Once the genie of freedom was released from the Communist lamp, however, it took on a momentum of its own. On August 18, 1991, a group of political and military leaders tried to seize the reins of power. They accosted Gorbachev at his vacation retreat in Crimea and demanded that he proclaim a state of emergency and transfer his powers to them. He replied, "Go to hell," whereupon he was placed under house arrest.

The coup was doomed from the start, however. Poorly planned and clumsily implemented, it lacked effective coordination. The plotters failed to arrest popular leaders such as Boris Yeltsin, the president of the Russian republic. They also neglected to close the airports or cut off telephone and television communications, and they were opposed by key elements of the military and KGB (the secret police).

On August 20, President Bush responded favorably to Yeltsin's request for support and persuaded other world leaders to join him in refusing to recognize the legitimacy of the new Soviet government. The next day, word began to seep out that the plotters had given up and were fleeing. Several committed suicide, and a newly released Gorbachev ordered the others arrested.

Yet things did not go back to the way they had been. Although Gorbachev reclaimed the title of president, he was forced to resign as head of the Communist party and admit that he had made a grave mistake in appointing the men who had turned against him. Boris Yeltsin emerged as the most popular political figure in the country.

So what had begun as a reactionary coup turned into a powerful accelerant for astonishing changes in the Soviet Union, or the "Soviet Disunion," as one journalist termed it. Most of the fifteen republics proclaimed their independence from Russia, with the Baltic states of Latvia, Lithuania, and Estonia regaining the status of independent nations. The Communist party was dismantled, prompting celebrating crowds to topple statues of Lenin and other Communist heroes.

Reducing the Nuclear Threat

The collapse of the Soviet Union accelerated efforts to reduce their stockpiles of nuclear weapons. In late 1991, President Bush announced that the United States would destroy all its tactical nuclear weapons in Europe and Asia. Bush explained that the prospect of a Soviet invasion of Western Europe was "no longer a realistic threat," and that this transformation provided an unprecedented opportunity for reducing the threat of nuclear holocaust. President Gorbachev responded by announcing similar Soviet cutbacks. The sudden end of the Cold War led many to believe that the United States could greatly reduce the vast global military responsibilities it had developed over four decades of anti-Communism.

> The end of the Soviet "threat"

Panama

The end of the Cold War did not spell the end of international tensions and conflict, however. Indeed, before the end of 1989, U.S. troops were engaged in battle in Panama, where a petty tyrant provoked the first of America's military engagements under George H. W. Bush. In 1983, General Manuel Noriega had become leader of the Panamanian Defense Forces, which made him the head of the government in fact if not in title.

In 1988, federal grand juries in Miami and Tampa indicted Noriega and fifteen others on charges of drug trafficking. The next year, the Panamanian president tried to fire Noriega, but the National Assembly ousted the president instead and named Noriega "maximum leader." The legislators then declared Panama "in a state of war" with the United States. On December 16, 1989, a U.S. marine in Panama was killed, whereupon President Bush ordered an invasion of Panama to capture Noriega and install a government to be headed by Guillermo Endara, who had won the presidency in a recent election that was then nullified by Noriega.

> Panama–U.S. "war"

In the early morning of December 20, U.S. troops struck at strategic targets in the country. Within hours, Noriega had surrendered. Twenty-three U.S. servicemen were killed in the action, and estimates of Panamanian casualties, including many civilians, were as high as 4,000. In April 1992, Noriega was convicted in the United States on eight counts of racketeering and drug distribution.

The Gulf War

Months later, Saddam Hussein, dictator of Iraq, focused U.S. attention back upon the Middle East when his army suddenly invaded its tiny neighbor, Kuwait, on August 2, 1990. Kuwait had recently increased its production of oil, contrary to agreements with the Organization of the Petroleum Exporting Countries (OPEC). The resulting drop in global oil prices offended the Iraqi regime, which was deeply in debt and heavily dependent upon oil revenues.

> First Gulf War

President Bush condemned Iraq's "naked aggression" and dispatched planes and troops to Saudi Arabia on a "wholly defensive" mission: to protect

Operation Desert Storm Allied soldiers patrol the southern Iraqi town of Salman on February 27, 1991. On the side of a building is a propaganda mural of dictator Saddam Hussein in military uniform.

Saudi Arabia. British forces soon joined in, as did Arab units from Egypt, Morocco, Syria, Oman, the United Arab Emirates, and Qatar. A flurry of negotiations failed, as Iraq refused to yield, leading Congress on January 12, 1991, to authorize the use of U.S. armed forces. Four days later, more than thirty nations, including ten Islamic countries, launched **Operation Desert Storm** against Iraq. The swift-moving allied ground assault began on February 24 and lasted only four days. Iraqi soldiers surrendered by the thousands.

On February 28, six weeks after the fighting began, President Bush called for a cease-fire. The Iraqis accepted, and the shooting ended. There were 137 American fatalities. The lowest estimate of Iraqi deaths, civilian and military, was 100,000. The coalition forces occupied about a fifth of Iraq, but Hussein's tyrannical regime was intact. What came to be called the First Gulf War was thus a triumph without victory. Hussein had been defeated, but he was allowed to escape and foster greater mischief. The consequences of the brief but intense First Gulf War, the "mother of all battles," in Saddam Hussein's words, would be played out in the future in ways that no one had predicted. Arabs who felt humiliated by the lopsided American triumph began plotting revenge that would spiral into a new war of terrorism.

Bush's "New World Order"

For months after the First Gulf War in 1991, George H. W. Bush seemed unbeatable; his public approval rating soared to 91 percent. Yet the aftermath of Desert Storm was mixed, with Saddam Hussein's iron grip on Iraq still

Operation Desert Storm (1991) Assault by American-led multinational forces that quickly defeated Iraqi forces under Saddam Hussein in the First Gulf War, ending the Iraqi occupation of Kuwait.

intact. The Soviet Union meanwhile stumbled on to its surprising end. On December 25, 1991, the Soviet flag over the Kremlin was replaced by the flag of the Russian Federation. The Cold War had ended with the dismemberment of the Soviet Union and its fifteen republics. As a result, the United States had become the world's only dominant military power.

"Containment" of the Soviet Union, the bedrock of U.S. foreign policy for more than four decades, had suddenly become irrelevant. For all of its potential horrors, the Cold War brought stability because the two superpowers, the United States and the Soviet Union, had restrained themselves from an all-out war that may well have involved the use of nuclear weapons. Now the world would witness a growing number of unresolved political crises and unstable regimes, some of which had access to weapons of mass destruction—nuclear as well as chemical and biological weapons. Bush struggled to interpret the fluid new international scene. He spoke of a "new world order" but never defined it, admitting that he had trouble with "the vision thing." By the end of 1991, the euphoria of the Gulf War victory had worn off and a listless Bush faced a challenge in the Republican primary from the feisty conservative commentator and former White House aide Patrick Buchanan, who adopted the slogan "America First" and called on Bush to "bring home the boys."

> Bush's "New World Order"

The excitement over the allied victory in the Gulf War quickly gave way to anxiety over the depressed economy. In addressing the recession, Bush tried a clumsy balancing act, on the one hand acknowledging that "people are hurting" while on the other telling Americans that "this is a good time to buy a car." By 1991, the public approval rating of his economic policy had plummeted to 18 percent.

The Election of 1992

At the 1992 Republican Convention, Patrick Buchanan, who had won about a third of the votes in the party's primaries, blasted Bush for breaking his pledge not to raise taxes and for becoming the "biggest spender in American history." As the 1992 election unfolded, Bush's real problem was not Pat Buchanan and the conservative wing of the Republican party, however. What threatened his reelection was his own failed effort to improve the economy. A popular bumper sticker reflected the growing public frustration with the economic policies of the Bush administration: "Saddam Hussein still has his job. What about you?"

In contrast to the divided Republicans, the Democrats at their 1992 convention presented an image of centrist or moderate forces in control. For several years, the Democratic Leadership Council, led by Arkansas governor William Jefferson Clinton, had been pushing the party from the liberal left to the center of the political spectrum. Clinton called for a "third way" positioned between conservatism and liberalism.

The 1992 campaign also featured a third-party candidate, Texan H. Ross Perot, a puckish billionaire who found a large audience for his criticism of

Reaganomics as "voodoo economics" (a phrase originally used in the 1980 Republican primary by then-contender George H. W. Bush before he was named the vice-presidential candidate on the Reagan presidential ticket) and his warnings about the impending crisis posed by the huge federal debt.

Born in 1946 in Hope, Arkansas, Bill Clinton never knew his biological father, a traveling salesman who died in a car crash a few months before his son was born. Even as a teen, Clinton yearned to be a political leader on a national scale. He attended Georgetown University in Washington, D.C., won a Rhodes Scholarship to Oxford University, and then earned a law degree from Yale University, where he met his future wife, Hillary Rodham. Clinton returned to Arkansas and won election as the state's attorney general. By 1979, at age thirty-two, Bill Clinton was the youngest governor in the country. He served three more terms as Arkansas governor and in the process emerged as a dynamic young leader of the "**New Democrats**" committed to winning back the middle-class whites ("Reagan Democrats") who had voted Republican during the 1980s.

Bill Clinton and Al Gore The hopeful Democratic candidates round out their presidential campaign in Clinton's hometown of Little Rock, Arkansas on November 3, 1992.

A self-described moderate seeking the Democratic presidential nomination, Clinton promised to cut the defense budget, provide tax relief for the middle class, and create a massive economic aid package for the former republics of the Soviet Union to help them forge democratic societies. Witty, intelligent, and charismatic, with an in-depth knowledge of public policy, Clinton was a superb campaigner; he projected energy, youth, and optimism, reminding many political observers of John F. Kennedy, Clinton's boyhood hero.

But beneath Clinton's charisma and public-policy expertise lurked several flaws. Self-absorbed and self-indulgent, he, like Lyndon Johnson, yearned to be loved. The *New York Times* explained that Clinton was "emotionally needy, indecisive, and undisciplined." Even more enticing to the media were charges that Clinton was a chronic adulterer. Clinton's evasive denials of both allegations could not dispel a lingering mistrust of his character.

After a series of bruising party primaries, Clinton won the Democratic presidential nomination in the summer of 1992, promising to restore the "hopes of the forgotten middle class." He chose Senator Albert "Al" Gore Jr. of Tennessee as his running mate. Gore described himself as a "raging moderate." So the Democratic candidates were two Southern Baptists from adjoining states, Arkansas and Tennessee. Flushed with their convention victory and sporting a ten-point lead over Bush in the polls, the Clinton-Gore team hammered Bush on economic issues to win over working-class voters. Clinton pledged that, if elected, he would cut the federal budget deficit in half in four years while cutting taxes on middle-class Americans.

New Democrats Centrist ("moderate") Democrats led by President Bill Clinton that emerged in the late 1980s and early 1990s to challenge the "liberal" direction of the party.

Such promises helped Clinton win the election with 370 electoral votes and about 43 percent of the vote; Bush received 168 electoral votes and 39 percent of the vote; and, Perot garnered 19 percent of the popular vote, more than any other third-party candidate since Theodore Roosevelt in 1912. As 1992 came to an end, Bill Clinton, the "New Democrat," prepared to lead the United States through the last decade of the twentieth century. "The urgent question of our time," he said, "is whether we can make change our friend and not our enemy." During his eight years as president, Clinton would embrace many unexpected changes while ushering America into the twenty-first century.

■ **The Carter Presidency** Jimmy Carter had notable achievements, such as the *Camp David Accords*. Yet, his administration suffered from legislative inexperience, a deepening economic recession, soaring inflation, and the *Iranian hostage crisis*. His sermonizing about the need for Americans to lead simpler lives compounded the public's loss of faith in his presidency.

■ **The Rise of Conservatism** Ronald Reagan's charm, coupled with the public's disillusionment over Carter's presidency, won Reagan the election in 1980. The Republican insurgency, characterized in part by a cultural backlash against the feminist movement, was dominated by the *religious right*. Sunbelt voters, many of whom were older transplants to southern and western states, were socially conservative and favored lower taxes and a smaller, less intrusive federal government. California passed a property-tax-lowering referendum, Proposition 13, which led to a nationwide tax revolt.

■ **Reaganomics** Reagan introduced a "supply-side" economic philosophy, commonly called *Reaganomics*, that championed tax cuts for the rich, reduced government regulation, cuts to social-welfare programs, and increased defense spending. In practice, however, Reagan was unable to cut domestic spending significantly, and the tax cuts failed to pay for themselves as promised. The result was a dramatic increase in the national debt. Reagan also did much to weaken unions and the feminist movement, and to shift the political landscape away from the New Deal liberalism that had dominated American politics since 1932.

■ **The End of the Cold War** Reagan's massive military buildup, including preliminary development of the *Strategic Defense Initiative*, brought the Soviets to agreement on the *Intermediate-Range Nuclear Forces (INF) Treaty*—the beginning of the end of the Cold War. But Reagan's foreign policy was badly tarnished by the *Iran-Contra affair*: members of his administration had illegally sold U.S. armaments to Iran to secure the release of American hostages. The proceeds were then secretly funneled to Nicaraguan Contras (despite a congressional ban on such aid). Reagan's loose management style, an independent commission determined, had allowed these illegal activities to flourish.

■ **America in the 1980s** The eighties brought not only unprecedented prosperity but also rising poverty and homelessness. The prevailing conservative mood condemned *HIV/AIDS* as a "gay" disease. The *microprocessor* ignited the computer revolution, which dramatically increased productivity and communications while generating new industries. Consumerism flourished all too well, resulting in massive public and private debt as well as the stock market collapse of 1987.

■ **A New World Order** In the late 1980s, democratic political movements erupted, failing in Communist China but succeeding in Eastern Europe. Gorbachev's steps to restructure the Soviet Union's economy (*perestroika*) and promote more open policies (*glasnost*) ultimately led to the collapse of the Soviet empire. Iraq, led by Saddam Hussein, invaded Kuwait in 1990. The U.S. led allied forces in *Operation Desert Storm*; the Iraqis soon surrendered. Despite the success of the first Gulf War, the sluggish economy led to Bush's defeat by the *"New Democrats"* under Bill Clinton.

KEY TERMS

Camp David Accords (1978) *p. 1097*
Iranian hostage crisis (1979) *p. 1098*
religious right *p. 1101*
Reaganomics *p. 1104*
Strategic Defense Initiative (SDI)
    (1983) *p. 1110*

Iran-Contra affair (1987) *p. 1111*
Intermediate-Range Nuclear Forces
    (INF) Treaty (1987) *p. 1112*
microprocessor *p. 1114*
HIV/AIDS *p. 1116*

perestroika *p. 1119*
glasnost *p. 1119*
Operation Desert Storm
    (1991) *p. 1122*
"New Democrats" *p. 1124*

CHRONOLOGY

1971	Microprocessor developed
1975	First personal computer, the Altair 8800, produced
1978	Camp David Accords
	Tax revolt in California leads to the passage of Proposition 13
1979	Jerry Falwell organizes the Moral Majority
November 1979	Iranian hostage crisis
1980	Ronald Reagan elected president
1981	Reagan enacts major tax cuts
1983	Strategic Defense Initiative (SDI) authorized
1987	Tower Commission issues report on Iran-Contra affair
	Reagan delivers Berlin Wall speech
October 1987	Stock market plunges 23 percent on "Black Monday"
1988	George H. W. Bush elected president
November 1989	Berlin Wall torn down
December 1989	U.S. troops invade Panama and capture Manuel Noriega
August 1990–1991	First Gulf War
	Soviet Union dissolves
1992	Bill Clinton elected president

INQUIZITIVE

Go to InQuizitive to see what you've learned—and learn what you've missed—with personalized feedback along the way.

YOUTH SPEAKS The Occupy Wall Street movement was born when thousands of protestors, many of them unemployed young adults, "occupied" Wall Street in downtown Manhattan to protest the "tyrannical" financial industry. The grassroots movement soon spread across the nation, then the world. Here, members of the movement stage a protest outside of the New York Stock Exchange in September 2011.

Twenty-First–Century America

1993–Present

The United States entered the final decade of the twentieth century triumphant. American persistence in fighting and financing the Cold War had contributed to the shocking collapse of the Soviet Union and the birth of democracy and capitalism in Eastern Europe. By the end of the twentieth century, the United States was the only superpower.

During the 1990s, the U.S. economy became the marvel of the world as remarkable gains in productivity enabled by new "digital" technologies created the greatest period of prosperity in modern history.

Yet no sooner did the century come to an end than America's sense of physical security and material comfort was shattered by surprise terrorist attacks in 2001 on New York City and Washington, D.C., attacks that killed thousands, plunged the economy into recession, and raised profound questions about national security and personal safety.

The United States led the fight against global terrorism, which embroiled the nation in long, costly, and controversial wars in Iraq and Afghanistan. Opposition to the conduct of those wars would provide much of the momentum for Democrat Barack Obama to win election in 2008 as the nation's first African American president. Obama entered the White House at the same time that the United States was experiencing the Great Recession, a sharp, prolonged economic downturn that almost destroyed the global banking system, caused widespread unemployment, and ignited growing social unrest and political tensions at home and abroad.

CORE OBJECTIVES INQUIZITIVE

1. Describe the major population trends (demographics) in the United States during the twenty-first century, and assess their impact on the nation's politics.

2. Evaluate the accomplishments and setbacks of Bill Clinton's presidency.

3. Summarize the impact of global terrorism on the United States during the presidency of George W. Bush, and evaluate the effectiveness of his "war on terror."

4. Assess the issues and developments during Bush's second term that helped lead to Barack Obama's historic victory in the 2008 presidential election.

5. Identify President Obama's priorities at home and abroad, and assess his efforts to pursue them.

CORE **OBJECTIVE**

1. Describe the major population trends (demographics) in the United States during the twenty-first century, and assess their impact on the nation's politics.

America's Changing Population

The United States at the end of the twentieth century and the beginning of the twenty-first century witnessed dramatic social changes. By the end of 2014, there were more than 320 million Americans, over 80 percent of whom lived in cities or suburbs.

Even more important, the nation's racial and ethnic composition was changing rapidly. The majority white population continued to decline as a proportion of the total population while the proportion represented by minority groups soared. Hispanics/Latinos represented 18 percent of the population, African Americans 13 percent, Asians about 5 percent, and Native Americans 1 percent. The rate of increase among those four groups was twice as fast as it had been during the 1980s. In 2005, Hispanics surpassed African Americans as the nation's largest minority group. Yet the fastest-growing group in the nation were the nearly 10 million who described themselves as "multiracial," representing over 3 percent of the entire population.

Population growth among Hispanics, African Americans, Asians, and Native Americans

The primary cause of this dramatic change in the nation's ethnic mix during the twenty-first century was a surge of immigration. In 1992, the Republican presidential candidate Pat Buchanan warned that the United States was experiencing "the greatest invasion in its history, a migration of millions of illegal aliens a year from Mexico." While Buchanan and others wanted to close the border with Mexico, many others believed that embracing immigrants remained one of the nation's essential ideals.

In 2014, the United States had more foreign-born residents than ever before, more than 45 million Americans, 11 million of whom were undocumented immigrants (formerly classified as "illegal aliens"). In the first decade of the twenty-first century, the United States became home to more than twice as many immigrants as *all* other countries in the world combined. For the first time in the nation's history, the majority of immigrants came not from Europe but from other parts of the world: Asia, Latin America, and Africa. Mexicans made up the largest share of Hispanics, followed by Puerto Ricans, and Cubans. (Americans now consume more salsa than ketchup each year.)

Rising immigration from Asia, Latin America, and Africa

The changing ethnic composition of American society has had an increasingly significant impact on social life. In 1980, Hispanic Americans lived mainly in five states: California, Arizona, New Mexico, Texas, and Florida. By 2014, *every* state had a rapidly growing Hispanic population. "These are big demographic changes," said Mark Mather, a population analyst. "There is going to be some culture shock, especially in communities that haven't had high numbers of immigrants or minorities in the past."

Immigration also had significant political effects. In 1980, there were six Hispanic Americans serving in the U.S. Congress. By 2010, there were more than five times as many. In 1992, Hispanics constituted only 2 percent of American voters; by 2014 they were 10 percent. Asian Americans increased

Over the quota, under the radar
Increasing numbers of Chinese people were willing to risk their lives to gain entry to the United States. A freighter carrying undocumented immigrants ran aground near Rockaway Beach, New York, in June 1993, forcing its undocumented passengers to swim ashore.

their numbers at a faster rate than any other ethnic group, largely because of a surge in Chinese immigrants. Such new voters represented an increasing share of America's future, and politicians could no longer ignore them, as had often happened in the past.

Like Hispanics, African Americans and Asian Americans tend to vote for Democrats, in large part because minority groups benefit more from affirmative-action programs and government-funded social services frequently under attack from Republicans. As the population was becoming more racially and ethnically diverse, the Republican party nationwide was becoming a party dominated by white men. In 2012 the Pew Research Center reported that the Republican party was 87 percent white—virtually the same as it was thirty years before. That was not a problem in 1980, when 86 percent of the voters were white. By 2012, however, only 72 percent of voters were white. A Republican campaign consultant recognized that "we need to do better in minority communities." The rapidly changing ethnic and racial mix of the nation's population would become a major factor in the shifting social and political life of the twenty-first century.

The Clinton Presidency

Clinton's inexperience in international affairs and congressional maneuvering led to several missteps in his first year as president. Like George H. W. Bush before him, he reneged on several campaign promises. In a bruising battle with Congress, he was forced to abandon his proposed middle-class tax cut in order to keep another campaign promise, to reduce the federal

CORE **OBJECTIVE**
2. Evaluate the accomplishments and setbacks of Bill Clinton's presidency.

deficit. Then he dropped his promise to allow gays to serve in the armed forces after military commanders expressed strong opposition. Instead, he later announced an ambiguous new policy concerning gays in the military that came to be known as "don't ask, don't tell" (DADT), which allowed gays, lesbians, and bisexuals to serve in the military but only if they kept their sexual orientation secret. "I got the worst of both worlds," Clinton later confessed. "I lost the fight, and the gay community was highly critical of me for the compromise." In Clinton's first two weeks in office, his approval rating dropped 20 percent. Throughout his presidency, however, Clinton displayed a remarkable ability to manage crises and rebound from adversity.

> Early setbacks: "Don't ask, don't tell" (DADT) and abandonment of middle-class tax relief

The Economy

> Successes: NAFTA, higher taxes for the wealthy, and an economic stimulus package

As a candidate, Clinton had pledged to reduce the federal deficit without damaging the economy or hurting the nation's most vulnerable people. To this end, the new president proposed $241 billion in higher taxes for corporations and for the wealthiest individuals (the top rate rising from 33 to 39.6 percent) over four years and $255 billion in spending cuts over the same period. The hotly contested bill finally passed by 218 to 216 in the House and 51 to 50 in the Senate, with Vice President Al Gore providing the tie-breaking vote. For virtually the first time since 1945, Congress had passed a major bill without a single Republican vote, a troubling indication of the nation's growing partisan divide. Clinton's deficit-reduction effort worked as planned, however. It led to lower interest rates which, along with low energy prices, helped spur dramatic economic growth throughout the nineties.

Equally difficult was gaining congressional approval of the **North American Free Trade Agreement (NAFTA)**, which the Bush administration had already negotiated with Canada and Mexico. Clinton urged approval of NAFTA, which would make North America the largest free-trade zone in the world. Opponents of the bill favored tariffs to discourage the importation of cheaper foreign products, especially from Mexico. Yet Clinton prevailed with solid Republican support while losing a sizable minority of Democrats, mostly labor unionists and southerners, who feared that many textile mills would lose business (and millions of jobs) to "cheap labor" countries—as they did.

Health-Care Reform

> Failed health-care reform

Clinton's major public-policy initiative was an ambitious plan to overhaul the nation's health-care system. "If I don't get health care," he declared, "I'll wish I didn't run for president." Public support for government-administered health insurance spread as annual medical costs skyrocketed and some 37 million Americans, most of them poor or unemployed, went without any medical insurance at all. The Clinton administration argued that making medical insurance available to everyone, regardless of income, would reduce the costs of health care to the nation as a whole, but critics in Congress questioned the savings as well as the ability of the federal government to manage such a huge program efficiently. The plan called for all

North American Free Trade Agreement (NAFTA) (1994) Agreement eliminating trade barriers that was signed in 1994 by the United States, Canada, and Mexico, making North America the largest free-trade zone in the world.

large businesses to pay for most of the medical insurance expenses of their employees, and required small businesses to form "health alliances" so that they, too, could provide subsidized health insurance to their workers. By the summer of 1994, Clinton's 1,364-page health-insurance plan, developed by a task force headed by the First Lady, Hillary Rodham Clinton, rather than congressional leaders, was doomed, in part because the president opposed any changes to his wife's plan and in part because the thousand-page report was impossibly complicated. Strenuously opposed by Republicans and health-care interest groups, especially the pharmaceutical and insurance industries, Clinton's prized health-care bill was voted down by Congress in August 1994.

Landslide Republican Victory

The health-care bill disaster influenced the 1994 midterm elections, when the Democrats, the world's oldest political party, suffered a humbling defeat. It was the first election since 1952 in which Republicans captured both houses of Congress at the same time. The Republicans also won 32 governorships, including the largest states of California, New York, and Texas, where George W. Bush, the son of the former president and a future president himself, won handily.

> Midterm Elections: Republicans win the majority in the House and the Senate

The Republican victory was led by a feisty Georgia conservative named Newton ("Newt") Leroy Gingrich. In early 1995, he became the first Republican Speaker of the House in forty-two years. Gingrich, a former history professor with a lust for controversy and an unruly ego, was a superb tactician who had helped mobilize religious and social conservatives associated with the Christian Coalition. The Christian Coalition, organized by television evangelist Pat Robertson in 1989 to replace Jerry Falwell's Moral Majority (which had disbanded that year), chose the Republican party as the best vehicle for promoting its pro–school prayer, anti-abortion, anti-feminist, and anti–gay rights positions. In addition to celebrating "traditional family values," it urged politicians to "radically downsize" government. Ralph Reed, a born-again Christian political activist who would head the Christian Coalition, declared that Christians needed "to take back this country." In many respects, the religious right did take control of the political and social landscape in the nineties.

> Republican opposition: Contract with America

In 1994, Gingrich and the Republican candidates for Congress rallied conservative voters by promising a **Contract with America**, a pledge to dismantle the "corrupt liberal welfare state" created by Democrats eager to serve the undeserving poor. The ten-point, anti-big-government "contract" featured less regulation of businesses, less environmental protection, term limits for members of Congress, reductions in social welfare programs, and a constitutional amendment requiring a balanced budget. As Texan Tom DeLay, a leading Republican in the House of Representatives, explained, "You've got to understand, we are ideologues. We have an agenda. We have a philosophy." Republicans were determined to change how America was governed.

Contract with America (1994) List of conservative promises in response to the supposed liberalism of the Clinton administration; drafted by Speaker of the House Newt Gingrich and other congressional Republicans as a campaign tactic for the 1994 midterm elections.

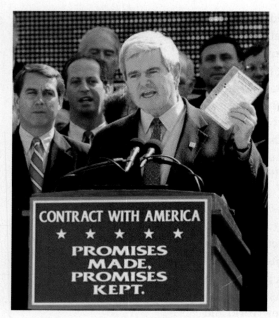

Newt Gingrich Joined by 160 of his fellow House Republicans, Gingrich promotes the Contract with America in April of 1995.

Yet the much-trumpeted Contract with America quickly fizzled. The conservatives pushed their agenda too hard and too fast, realizing only too late that their slim majority in Congress could not launch a Republican revolution. Even with their control of Congress, the Republicans were only able to pass four of the most minor elements of their "Contract." Gingrich's heavy-handed methods contributed to the disintegration of the Contract with America. Republican senator Bob Dole said Gingrich was "a one-man band who rarely took advice." He was too ambitious, too abrasive, too divisive. When Clinton refused to go along with Republican demands for a balanced-budget pledge, Gingrich twice shut down the federal government during the fall of 1995. The tactic backfired. By 1996, Gingrich had higher negative ratings in public surveys than the president.

The Supreme Court and Race

The conservative mood during the mid-nineties also revealed itself in Supreme Court rulings that undermined affirmative-action programs created by colleges in the sixties to give African American students special consideration in admissions and financial aid awards. Between 1970 and 1977, as a result of such programs, African American enrollment in colleges and universities doubled, even as white students and their parents complained about "reverse discrimination" against them.

In 1996, two major steps were taken against affirmative action in college admissions. In *Hopwood v. Texas*, a federal court ruled that race could not be used as a consideration for admission. Later that year, the state of California passed Proposition 209, an initiative that ruled out any preferential treatment based on race, sex, ethnicity, or national origin. Similar complaints were directed against affirmative-action programs that awarded government contracts to minority-owned businesses. In 1995, the Court in *Adarand Constructors v. Peña* declared that affirmative-action programs had to be "narrowly tailored" to serve a "compelling national interest." The implication of such vague language was clear: the Court had come to share the growing public suspicion of the value and legitimacy of race-based benefit programs.

Legislative Breakthrough

Welfare reform

After the surprising 1994 Republican takeover of Congress, Bill Clinton shrewdly resolved to save his presidency by reinforcing his claim that he was a "centrist," not a liberal. He co-opted much of the energy of the growing conservative movement by announcing that "the era of big government is over" and by reforming the federal system of welfare payments to the poor, created during the 1930s under the New Deal.

Late in the summer of 1996, the Republican Congress passed a comprehensive welfare-reform measure that Clinton signed after some revisions. The **Personal Responsibility and Work Opportunity Act of 1996 (PRWOA)** illustrated Clinton's efforts to move the Democratic party away from the old liberalism it had promoted since the 1930s. PRWOA abolished the Aid to Families with Dependent Children (AFDC) program, which provided poor families with almost $8,000 a year in support, and replaced it with the Temporary Assistance for Needy Families program, which limited the duration of welfare payments to two years in an effort to encourage unemployed people to get jobs. Liberal Democrats bitterly criticized Clinton's "welfare reform" deal with Republicans. Yet the new federal approach to supporting the poor was a statistical success. The number of welfare recipients and poverty rates both declined during the late nineties, leading the editors of the left-leaning *The New Republic* to report that the PRWOA had "worked much as its designers had hoped."

The 1996 Campaign

The Republican takeover of Congress in 1994 gave them hope that they could prevent Clinton's reelection. After clinching the Republican presidential nomination in 1996, Senate majority leader Bob Dole resigned his seat in order to devote his attention to defeating Bill Clinton. Clinton, however, maintained a large lead in the polls. With an improving economy and no major foreign-policy crises, cultural and personal issues again surged into prominence. Concern about Dole's age (seventy-three) and his gruff public personality, as well as tensions within the Republican party between economic conservatives and social conservatives over volatile issues such as abortion and gun control, hampered Dole's efforts to generate widespread support, especially among the growing number of independent voters who identified with neither party.

On November 5, 1996, Clinton won a second term as president, with an electoral vote victory of 379 to 159 and 49 percent of the popular vote. Dole received only 41 percent of the popular vote, and third-party candidate Ross Perot got 8 percent.

The "New Economy"

Bill Clinton's presidency benefited from a prolonged period of unprecedented prosperity. During his last three years in office (1998–2000), the federal government generated unheard-of budget *surpluses*. At the end of the twentieth century, what came to be called the **"new economy"** featured high-flying electronics, computer, software, telecommunications (cellular phones, cable TV, etc.), and e-commerce Internet firms called "dot-com" companies. These dynamic new enterprises helped the economy set records in every area: low inflation, low unemployment, and dizzying corporate profits and personal fortunes. The stock-market value of U.S. companies nearly tripled during the nineties. People began to claim that the new

Personal Responsibility and Work Opportunity Act of 1996 (PRWOA) Comprehensive welfare-reform measure aiming to decrease the size of the "welfare state" by limiting the amount of government unemployment aid to encourage its recipients to find jobs.

"new economy" Period of sustained economic prosperity during the nineties marked by federal budget surpluses, the explosion of dot-com industries, low inflation, and low unemployment.

economy defied the boom-and-bust cycles of the previous hundred years. Alan Greenspan, the Federal Reserve Board chairman, suggested "that we have moved 'beyond history' "—into an economy that seemed only to grow. He would be proven wrong.

Globalization

Another major feature of the new economy in the nineties was **globalization**. The end of the Cold War and the disintegration of the Soviet Union opened up many new opportunities for U.S. companies in international trade. In addition, new globe-spanning communication technologies and massive new container-carrying ships and cargo jets shortened time and distance, enabling United States–based multinational companies to conduct a growing business abroad as more and more nations lowered trade barriers.

Bill Clinton accelerated the process of globalization. "The global economy," he said, "is giving more of our own people, and billions around the world, the chance to work and live and raise their families with dignity." He especially welcomed the World Wide Web, which opened the Internet up not just to the elite community of scientists but to everyone, and, by doing so, greatly accelerated U.S. dominance of the international economy.

By 2000, over a third of the production of U.S. multinational companies was occurring abroad, compared with only 9 percent in 1980. In 1970, there were 7,000 American multinational companies; by 2000, the number had soared to 63,000. Many U.S. multinational companies pursued controversial "outsourcing" strategies by which they moved their production "offshore" to nations such as Mexico and China to take advantage of lower labor costs and fewer workplace and environmental regulations. At the same time, many European and Asian companies, especially automobile manufacturers, built large plants in the United States to reduce the shipping expenses required to get their products to American markets. The U.S. economy had become internationalized to such a profound extent that global concerns exercised an ever-increasing influence on domestic and foreign policies.

> "Outsourcing" jobs abroad and foreign manufacturers at home

Foreign Policy in the Nineties

Unlike his predecessor George H. W. Bush, Bill Clinton had little interest in global politics. "Foreign policy is not what I came here to do," he admitted. Untrained and inexperienced in international relations, he had hoped that the post–cold war era would be focused on creating opportunities around the world for U.S. business expansion. Yet as the international analyst Leslie Gelb cautioned the new president, "A foreign economic policy is not a foreign policy, and it is not a national security strategy."

globalization An important and controversial transformation of the world economy led by the growing number of multinational companies and the Internet, whereby an international marketplace for goods and services was created.

Haiti

Events soon forced Clinton to intervene to help nations in crisis. In 1990, the politically unstable Caribbean island nation of Haiti, the hemisphere's poorest country, had installed its first democratically elected president, a popular Catholic priest named Jean-Bertrand Aristide. When Haitian army officers ousted Aristide the following year, he and thousands of his supporters took up exile in America, most of them settling in south Florida, which upset many Floridians.

In 1994 President Clinton announced his intention to restore Aristide to power, in part to return the exiled "boat people" to their homeland. With drawn-out negotiations leading nowhere, Clinton asked in July for a UN resolution authorizing military intervention in Haiti. At that juncture, former president Jimmy Carter volunteered to help negotiate a last-minute settlement, and he convinced the military leaders to relinquish their control of the government and leave the nation. Clinton sent 20,000 U.S. troops to ensure a peaceful transfer of power. Aristide returned to Haiti on October 15, and on March 31, 1995, the U.S. peacekeeping troops left as a UN force commanded by an American general took over. But neither Aristide nor his successors were able to generate prosperity or stability.

> Restoration of democratic rule in Haiti

The Middle East

President Clinton continued George H. W. Bush's policy of orchestrating patient negotiations between the Arabs and the Israelis. A new development was the inclusion of the Palestinian Liberation Organization (PLO) in the negotiations. In 1993, secret talks between Israeli and Palestinian representatives in Oslo, Norway, resulted in a draft agreement between Israel and the PLO. This agreement provided for the restoration of Palestinian self-rule in the occupied Gaza Strip and in Jericho, on the West Bank, in a "land for peace" exchange as provided in UN Security Council resolutions. A formal signing occurred at the White House on September 13, 1993. With President Clinton presiding, Israeli prime minister Yitzhak Rabin and PLO leader Yasir Arafat exchanged handshakes, and their foreign ministers signed the agreement.

> Arab-Israeli peace negotiations

The Middle East peace process suffered a terrible blow in early November 1995, however, when Prime Minister Rabin was assassinated by an Israeli zealot who resented Rabin's efforts to negotiate with the Palestinians. Some observers feared that the assassin had killed the peace process as well when seven months later conservative hard-liner Benjamin Netanyahu narrowly defeated the United States–backed Shimon Peres in the Israeli national elections. Yet in October 1998, Clinton brought Arafat, Netanyahu, and King Hussein of Jordan together at a conference in Maryland, where they reached an agreement. Under the Wye River Accords, Israel agreed to surrender land in return for security guarantees by the Palestinians.

The Balkans

Clinton also felt compelled to address violent turmoil in the Eastern European nations that had freed themselves from Soviet domination. In 1991, Yugoslavia had disintegrated into ethnic warfare as four of its six

> U.S.-NATO intervention in the Balkans

multiethnic republics declared their independence. Serb minorities, backed by the new Republic of Serbia, stirred up civil wars in neighboring Croatia and Bosnia. In Bosnia, the conflict involved systematic efforts to eliminate Muslims. Clinton decided that the situation was "intolerable" because the massacres of tens of thousands of people "tore at the very fabric" of human decency. He ordered food and medical supplies sent to besieged Bosnian Muslims and dispatched warplanes to stop the massacres.

In 1995, U.S. negotiators finally persuaded the foreign ministers of Croatia, Bosnia, and Yugoslavia (by then only a loose federation of the republics of Serbia and Montenegro) to agree to a comprehensive peace plan. Bosnia would remain a single nation but would be divided into two states: a Muslim-Croat federation controlling 51 percent of the territory and a Bosnian-Serb republic controlling the remaining 49 percent. Basic human rights would be restored and free elections would be held to appoint a parliament and joint president. To enforce the agreement, 60,000 NATO peacekeeping troops were dispatched to Bosnia.

McRubble Pro-Milošević residents of Belgrade, Yugoslavia, destroy the storefront of a McDonald's fast-food restaurant in 1999 to protest NATO and the United States' airstrikes on their homeland.

In 1998, the Balkan tinderbox flared up again, this time in the Yugoslav province of Kosovo, which had long been considered sacred ground by Christian Serbs, although 90 percent of the 2 million Kosovars were in fact Albanian Muslims. In 1998, Yugoslav president Slobodan Milošević began a program of "**ethnic cleansing**," whereby Yugoslav forces burned Albanian villages, murdered men, raped women, and displaced hundreds of thousands of Muslim Kosovars.

On March 24, 1999, NATO, relying heavily upon U.S. military resources and leadership, launched air strikes against Yugoslavian military targets. "Ending this tragedy is a moral imperative," explained President Clinton. After seventy-two days of bombardment, Milošević sued for peace on NATO's terms, in part because his Russian allies had finally abandoned him. An agreement was reached on June 3, 1999. President Clinton pledged extensive U.S. aid in helping the Yugoslavs rebuild their war-torn economy.

ethnic cleansing Systematic removal of an ethnic group from a territory through violence or intimidation in order to create a homogeneous society; the term was popularized by the Yugoslav policy brutally targeting Albanian Muslims in Kosovo.

The Scandal Machine

For a time, Clinton's preoccupation with foreign crises helped deflect public attention from a growing number of investigations into his personal conduct. During his first term, the president was dogged by old charges revolving around investments that he and his wife Hillary had made in Whitewater, a planned resort development in Arkansas. The project turned out to be a fraud and a failure, and the Clintons were accused of conspiring with the developer. In 1994, Kenneth Starr, a former judge and a conservative Republican, was appointed as independent counsel to investigate the Whitewater case.

Starr did not uncover any evidence that the Clintons were directly involved in the Whitewater fraud, but in the course of another investigation he happened upon evidence of a White House sex scandal.

Between 1995 and 1997, Clinton had engaged in a sexual affair with a twenty-two-year-old White House intern, Monica Lewinsky. Even more disturbing, he had pressed her to lie about their relationship, even under oath. Clinton initially denied the charges, telling the nation in late January 1998 that "I did not have sexual relations with that woman, Miss Lewinsky." Yet the scandal would not disappear.

For the next thirteen months, the media circus surrounding the "Monicagate" or "Zippergate" affair captured public attention. In August, however, the bottom fell out of Clinton's denials when Lewinsky agreed to provide a federal grand jury with a detailed account of her relationship with the president.

Soon thereafter, Clinton became the first president in history to testify before a grand jury. On August 17, the self-pitying, defiant president admitted having had "inappropriate, intimate physical contact" with Lewinsky but insisted that he had done nothing illegal.

The Impeachment of President Clinton

On September 9, 1998, Starr, the special prosecutor, submitted to Congress thirty-six boxes of documents that included a lengthy, disturbingly graphic account of the Lewinsky episode, claiming that there was "substantial and creditable" evidence of presidential wrongdoing (committing perjury, obstructing justice, and abusing his presidential powers). The Starr Report led the Republican-dominated House of Representatives on October 8 to begin a wide-ranging impeachment inquiry of the president. Thirty-one Democrats joined the Republicans in supporting the investigation.

> The Starr Report

On December 19, 1998, William Jefferson Clinton was impeached (charged with "high crimes and misdemeanors") by the House of Representatives. The House officially approved two articles of impeachment, charging Clinton with lying under oath to a federal grand jury and obstructing justice.

> President Clinton impeached and acquitted

The Senate impeachment trial of President Clinton began on January 7, 1999. Five weeks later, on February 12, Clinton was acquitted, largely on a party-line vote. A majority of senators, both Democrats and a few Republicans (55–45), decided that Clinton's adultery and lies were not the "high crimes and misdemeanors" required to remove a president from office. The president was acquitted—much to the regret of many Republicans.

A New Century

The United States—and the world—greeted with great fanfare the new century, in a new millennium. Wild celebrations ushered in the year 2000, but the joyous mood did not last. Powerful new forces were emerging to destabilize the post–cold war world, the most dangerous of which were global networks of menacing high-tech terrorists eager to disrupt and destroy Western values and institutions. As Americans decided on a new president in the fall of 2000, none suspected that the United States would soon experience the first major foreign attack on American soil since the Japanese bombed Pearl Harbor in December 1941.

A Disputed Election

The presidential election of 2000 proved to be one of the closest and most controversial in history. The two major-party candidates for president, Vice President Albert Gore Jr., the Democrat, and Texas governor George W. Bush, the son of the former Republican president, offered contrasting views on the role of the federal government, tax cuts, environmental policies, and the best way to preserve Social Security and Medicare.

Gore, a Tennessee native and Harvard graduate whose father had been a prominent senator, favored an active federal government that would do much more to protect the environment.

Bush, on the other hand, campaigned on a theme of "compassionate conservatism" at home, promising to restore "honor and dignity" to the White House and proposing, as previous Republican presidents had done, to transfer power from the federal government to the states. A "born-again" Christian with degrees from Yale University and Harvard Business School, Bush also urged a more "humble" foreign policy, one that would end U.S. efforts to install democratic governments in undemocratic societies ("nation building").

The bitter tone of party politics (called *polarization*) continued to inspire candidates at the extremes to run as third-party candidates. Two independent candidates added zest to the 2000 presidential campaign: the colorful conservative commentator Patrick Buchanan, and the liberal consumer activist Ralph Nader, representing the Green party.

The November election created high drama. The television networks initially reported that Gore had narrowly won the state of Florida and its decisive twenty-five electoral votes. Later in the evening, however, the networks reversed themselves, saying that Florida was too close to call. In the chaotic early-morning hours, the networks declared that Bush had been elected president. The final tally in Florida showed Bush with a razor-thin lead, but state law required a recount. For the first time in 125 years, the results of a presidential election remained in doubt for weeks after the voting.

The recount In yet another recount on November 24, 2000, Judge Robert Rosenberg examines a ballot with a magnifying glass. That Florida's voting machines had limited accuracy introduced a great margin of doubt in a close election.

As a painstaking hand count of ballots proceeded in Florida, supporters of Bush and Gore sparred in the Florida courts and the U.S. Supreme Court; each side accused the other of trying to steal the election. The political drama lasted for five weeks. At last, on December 12, 2000, a bitterly divided Supreme Court handed down its decision in the case known as *Bush v. Gore*, with a bare 5–4 majority ruling that the recount in Florida was to be halted. Bush was declared the winner in Florida by only 537 votes. Although Gore had amassed a 540,000-vote lead nationwide, he lost in the Electoral College by two votes when he lost Florida. Although Al Gore "strongly disagreed" with the Supreme Court's decision, he asked voters to rally around President-elect Bush and move forward. "Partisan rancor," he urged, "must be put aside."

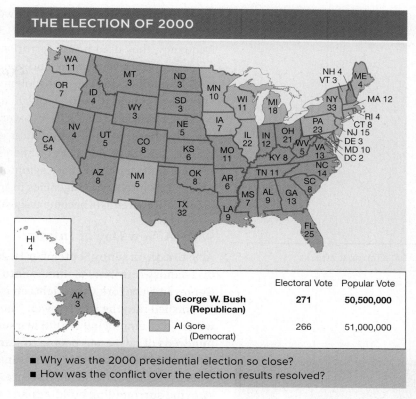

THE ELECTION OF 2000

	Electoral Vote	Popular Vote
George W. Bush (Republican)	**271**	**50,500,000**
Al Gore (Democrat)	266	51,000,000

■ Why was the 2000 presidential election so close?
■ How was the conflict over the election results resolved?

A Change of Direction

George W. Bush had promised during the campaign to cut taxes for the wealthy, increase military spending, oppose strict environmental regulations, and "privatize" Social Security by investing workers' retirement pension funds in the stock market.

First, however, the new president had to deal with a sputtering economy and a falling stock market. By March 2001, the economy was in recession for the first time in over a decade. Bush decided that cutting taxes was the best way to boost economic growth. On June 7, 2001, he signed the Economic Growth and Tax Relief Act, which cut $1.35 trillion in taxes—even more than the famous Reagan tax cuts. Instead of paying for themselves in renewed economic growth, however, the Bush tax cuts like those pushed by Ronald Reagan, led to a sharp drop in federal revenue, producing in turn a fast-growing budget deficit as the Clinton surpluses were quickly used up. Huge increases in the costs of Medicare and Medicaid, the federal health-care programs, resulting from the aging of the baby-boom generation, contributed to the soaring budget deficits, as did unexpected military expenditures resulting from an unexpected war.

As had happened so often with presidents during the twentieth century, President Bush soon found himself distracted by global issues and foreign crises. Islamic militants around the world bitterly resented what they viewed as the "imperial" globalization of U.S. culture and power. With increasing frequency, they used brutal terrorism, including suicide bombings, to gain notoriety, exact vengeance, and generate fear and insecurity, making the world vulnerable to chaos and violence. Throughout the nineties, the United States had fought a losing struggle against global terrorist groups, in part because terrorism thrives in impoverished nations with weak governments overwhelmed by rapid population growth, scarce resources, widespread poverty, and huge numbers of unemployed young men; there were lots of nations suffering from those symptoms around the world. The ineffectiveness of U.S. intelligence agencies in tracking the movements and intentions of militant extremists became tragically evident in the late summer of 2001.

9/11—A New Day of Infamy

9/11: Terrorist attacks

At 8:45 A.M. on sunny September 11, 2001, an airliner that had been hijacked by Islamist terrorists slammed into the north tower of the World Trade Center in New York City. Eighteen minutes later, a second hijacked jumbo jet crashed into the south tower. The twin towers, 110 stories tall and filled with offices employing 50,000 workers, burned fiercely, the inferno forcing hundreds of desperate people to jump to their deaths as thousands more, on floors below the points of impact, struggled to evacuate the skyscrapers. Quickly, though, the steel structures collapsed from the intense heat, destroying surrounding buildings and killing nearly 3,000 people, including more than 400 firefighters and police officers who had rushed into the burning towers. The southern end of Manhattan—"ground zero"—became a hellish scene of twisted steel, suffocating smoke, wailing sirens, and panicked people.

While the catastrophic drama in New York City was unfolding, a third hijacked plane crashed into the Pentagon in Washington, D.C. A fourth airliner, probably headed for the White House, missed its mark when passengers—who had heard reports of the earlier hijackings via their cell phones—assaulted the hijackers in order to prevent the plane from being used as a weapon. During the struggle in the cockpit, the plane went out of control and plummeted into the ground near Shanksville, Pennsylvania, killing all aboard.

Within hours of the hijackings, officials had identified the nineteen dead terrorists as members of al Qaeda (Arabic for "the Base"), a well-financed network of Islamic extremists led by a wealthy Saudi renegade, Osama bin Laden. Years before, bin Laden had declared *jihad* (holy war) on the United States, Israel, and the Saudi monarchy in his effort to create a single Islamist *caliphate* (global empire). To foster his clash of civilizations by organizing global Islamist terrorism, he used remote bases in Sudan and war-torn Afghanistan as training centers for *jihadist* fighters. Collaborating with bin Laden's terrorist network was Afghanistan's ruling Taliban, a coalition of ultraconservative Islamists who provided bin Laden with a safe haven.

September 11th Smoke pours out of the north tower of the World Trade Center as the south tower bursts into flames after being struck by a second hijacked airplane. Both would collapse within an hour.

The "War on Terror"

The 9/11 assault on the United States, like the Japanese attack on Pearl Harbor on December 7, 1941, changed the course of modern life. The falling World Trade Center towers symbolized the shocking collapse of one era and the start of a new one. Numbed by the terrible events, people were initially paralyzed by grief, fear, and anger. The U.S. economy, already in decline, went into free fall. President Bush was thrust into the role of commander in chief of a wounded nation eager for vengeance. The new president told the world that he was going to launch a global **war on terror** "to answer these attacks and rid the world of evil," as if he were launching a religious crusade, warning other nations that "either you are with us or you are with the terrorists." A wave of patriotic fervor rolled across the nation. "United We Stand"

War fever President George W. Bush addresses the Special Forces in July 2002 as part of an appeal to Congress to increase defense spending after the September 11th attacks.

became the motto for people determined to rebuild what had been lost in the rubble of the fallen towers and to defeat the heartless fanatics who had caused such destruction and suffering. People formed long lines to donate blood while others signed up for military service.

Bush demanded that Afghanistan's Taliban government surrender the al Qaeda terrorists or risk military attack. On October 7, 2001, after the Taliban refused to turn over bin Laden, the United States and its allies launched a military campaign—called Operation Enduring Freedom—to punish terrorists or "those harboring terrorists." American and British cruise missiles and bombers destroyed Afghan military installations and al Qaeda training camps, followed by an American-led invasion by ground troops from the United States and some of its NATO allies who, working with Afghan opponents of the Taliban, routed Taliban forces in just two months. On December 9, the Taliban regime collapsed. The war in Afghanistan then transitioned into a high-stakes manhunt for the elusive Osama bin Laden, who escaped into the mountains of Pakistan along with a large number of al Qaeda and Taliban fighters.

> War on terror abroad: Operation Enduring Freedom in Afghanistan (2001)

The "War on Terror" at Home

While the military campaign continued in Afghanistan, officials in Washington worried that terrorists might attack the United States with biological, chemical, or even nuclear weapons. To address the threat and to help restore public confidence, President Bush created a new federal agency, the Office of Homeland Security. Another new federal agency, the Transportation Security Administration, assumed responsibility for screening airline passengers for weapons and bombs. At the same time, President Bush and a supportive Congress created the **USA Patriot Act**, which gave government

war on terror Global crusade to root out anti-Western and anti-American Islamist terrorist cells launched by President George W. Bush as a response to the 9/11 attacks.

USA Patriot Act (2001) Wide-reaching Congressional legislation, triggered by the War on Terror, which gave government agencies the right to eavesdrop on confidential conversations between prison inmates and their lawyers and permitted suspected terrorists to be tried in secret military courts.

War on terror at home: Homeland Security and the USA Patriot Act

agencies the right to eavesdrop on confidential conversations between prison inmates and their lawyers and permitted suspected terrorists to be tried in secret military courts. Civil liberties groups voiced grave concerns that the measures jeopardized constitutional rights and protections, but the superheated atmosphere after 9/11 led most people to support these extraordinary steps.

What the public did not know was that Vice President Cheney, Secretary of Defense Donald Rumsfeld, and others convinced the president to authorize the use of torture ("enhanced interrogation techniques") in the CIA and FBI's treatment of captured terrorist suspects, tactics that violated international law and compromised the human rights ideals that had always been America's greatest strength. When asked about such activities, the shadowy Cheney scoffed that America sometimes had to work "the dark side": "We've got to spend time in the shadows in the intelligence world. . . ."

The Bush Doctrine

Bush Doctrine: Preemptive military action

In the fall of 2002, President Bush unveiled a dramatic new national security policy. The **Bush Doctrine** said that the growing menace posed by "shadowy networks" of terrorist groups and unstable rogue nations with "weapons of mass destruction" required that the United States at times must abandon diplomacy and use preemptive military action. "If we wait for threats to fully materialize," or wait for allies to join America, he explained, "we will have waited too long. In the world we have entered, the only path to safety is the path of action. And this nation will *act*."

The Second Iraq War

War on terror abroad: United States invades Iraq (2003)

During 2002 and 2003, Iraq emerged as the focus of the Bush administration's new policy of "preemptive" military action. Three of the president's most influential advisers, Vice President Cheney, Secretary of Defense Rumsfeld, and Deputy Defense Secretary Paul Wolfowitz convinced Bush that the dictatorial regime of Saddam Hussein and his loyal Sunni faction of Muslims, who lorded over the Shiite majority and the ethnic Kurds in the north, represented a "grave and gathering danger" because of its supposed possession of biological and chemical weapons of mass destruction.

On March 17, 2003, President Bush, eager to finish what his father had started, issued an ultimatum to Saddam Hussein: he and his sons must leave Iraq within forty-eight hours or face a United States–led invasion. Hussein refused. Two days later, on March 19, American and British forces attacked Iraq. Despite U.S. diplomatic attempts to assemble an international coalition similar to that of the First Gulf War a decade earlier, France and Germany refused to participate in what they viewed as unnecessary American aggression.

"Operation Iraqi Freedom" began with a massive bombing campaign intended to provoke "shock and awe," followed by a fast-moving invasion across the Iraqi desert from bases in Kuwait. Some 250,000 American

Bush Doctrine National security policy launched in 2002 by which the Bush administration claimed the right to launch preemptive military attacks against perceived enemies, particularly outlaw nations or terrorist organizations believed to possess weapons of mass destruction.

soldiers, sailors, and marines were joined by 50,000 British troops. On April 9, after three weeks of intense fighting amid sweltering heat and blinding sandstorms, U.S. forces captured Baghdad, the capital of Iraq. Saddam Hussein's regime and his inept, demoralized army collapsed a week later.

The six-week war came at a cost of fewer than 200 combat deaths among the 300,000 allied troops. Over 2,000 Iraqi soldiers were killed; civilian casualties numbered in the tens of thousands. President Bush donned a pilot's flight suit to stage a celebration on a U.S. aircraft carrier at which he announced victory in Iraq under a massive banner proclaiming "MISSION ACCOMPLISHED." But he declared victory much too soon; the initial military triumph carried with it the seeds of disappointment and disaster, for no weapons of mass destruction were to be found in Iraq. Bush later said that the absence of WMDs in Iraq left him with a "sickening feeling," for he knew that his primary justification for the war had evaporated.

Rebuilding Iraq

It proved far easier to win the brief war than to rebuild Iraq in America's image. Unprepared U.S. officials faced the daunting task of restoring order and installing a democratic government in an Iraq fractured by ancient religious feuds and ethnic tensions—made worse by the breakdown in law and order caused by the allied invasion. Looting and violence immediately engulfed the war-torn country, large parts of which fell under the control of local warlords and criminal gangs. Within weeks, vengeful Islamic radicals from around the world streamed into the crippled nation to wage a merciless campaign of terror, sabotage, and suicide bombings against the U.S. forces. Bush's macho reaction to the insurgency in Iraq—"Bring 'em on!"—revealed how uninformed he was about the fast-deteriorating situation. The leader of the new Iraqi government, Prime Minister Nouri al-Maliki, quickly imposed his own authoritarian, Shiite-dominated regime which discriminated against the Sunnis, the Kurds, and other ethnic and religious minorities.

Ignoring the advice of Defense Department analysts and some of his top generals, Secretary Rumsfeld greatly underestimated the difficulty and expense of occupying, pacifying, and reconstructing postwar Iraq. By the fall of 2003, President Bush admitted that substantial numbers of American troops (around 150,000) would have to remain in Iraq much longer than anticipated. He also said that rebuilding the splintered nation amid its religious and ethnic civil wars would take years and cost almost a *trillion* dollars. The investigative reporter James Fallows concluded that the U.S. "occupation in Iraq is a debacle not because the government did no planning but because a vast amount of expert planning was willfully ignored by the people in charge."

Victory on the battlefields of Iraq did not bring victory in the "war on terrorism." Militant Islamist groups seething with hatred towards the United States remained a constant global threat. Among Americans, the

> Growing insurgency in Iraq

Freedom for whom? The American torture of Iraqi prisoners in Abu Ghraib only exacerbated the anger and humiliation that Iraqis experienced since the First Gulf War. In response to America's incessant promises of peace and autonomy, a Baghdad mural fires back: "That Freedom For B[u]sh."

thrill of a quick battlefield victory turned to dismay as the number of casualties and the expense of the military occupation in Iraq soared. Americans grew more alienated when journalists revealed graphic pictures of U.S. soldiers abusing and torturing Arab detainees in the infamous Abu Ghraib prison near Baghdad. "When you lose the moral high ground," an army general sadly observed, "you lose it all."

In the face of mounting criticism, President Bush urged Americans to "stay the course," insisting that a democratic Iraq would bring stability to the volatile Middle East and thereby blunt the momentum of Islamic terrorism. Although Saddam Hussein was captured in December 2003 and later hanged by the new Iraqi authorities, Iraq now seemed less secure than ever to anxious Americans worried about the rising cost of an unending occupation. By the beginning of 2004, a thousand Americans had died in the conflict and more than 10,000 had been wounded. And the ethnic and religious tensions embroiling Iraq only worsened as violent Sunni *jihadists* allied with al Qaeda to undermine the new Iraqi government and assault U.S. forces.

The Election of 2004

Growing public concern about Iraq complicated George W. Bush's campaign for a second presidential term in 2004. The Democratic nominee, Senator John Kerry of Massachusetts, condemned the Bush administration for misleading the nation about weapons of mass destruction in Iraq and for its slipshod handling of the reconstruction of postwar Iraq. Kerry also highlighted the record budget deficits occurring under the Republican administration. Bush countered that the tortuous efforts to create a democratic government in Iraq would enhance America's long-term security.

On election day, November 2, 2004, the exit polls suggested a Kerry victory, but in the end the election hinged on the crucial swing state of Ohio. No Republican had ever lost Ohio and still won the presidency. Despite early returns from Ohio indicating a Kerry victory there, late returns appeared to tip the balance slightly toward Bush, even as rumors of electoral "irregularities" began to circulate. Nevertheless, Kerry conceded the election. "The outcome," he stressed, "should be decided by voters, not a protracted legal battle."

By narrowly winning Ohio, Bush captured 286 electoral votes to Kerry's 251. Yet in some respects the close election was not so close. Bush received 3.5 million more votes nationwide than Kerry, and Republicans increased their majority control of both houses of Congress.

THE ELECTION OF 2004

	Electoral Vote	Popular Vote
George W. Bush (Republican)	286	60,700,000
John Kerry (Democrat)	251	57,400,000

■ How did the war in Iraq polarize the electorate?
■ In what ways did the election of 2004 give Republicans a mandate?

A Resurgent Democratic Party

George Bush stumbled in his second term as he was beset by thorny political problems, a sluggish economy, and continuing turmoil and violence in Iraq. In 2005, he pushed through Congress an energy bill and a Central American Free Trade Act. But his effort to privatize Social Security retirement accounts, enabling individuals to invest their accumulated pension dollars themselves, went nowhere, and soaring budget deficits made many fiscal conservatives feel betrayed by the supposedly "conservative" Bush. The editors of the *Economist*, an influential conservative newsmagazine, declared that Bush had become "the least popular re-elected president since Richard Nixon."

Hurricane Katrina

In 2005, President Bush's eroding public support suffered another blow, this time when a natural disaster turned into a political crisis. In late August, a killer hurricane named Katrina slammed into the Gulf coast, devastating large areas of Alabama, Mississippi, and Louisiana. Katrina's awful wake left over a thousand people dead in the three states and millions homeless and hopeless, especially in New Orleans. Local political officials and the Federal Emergency Management Agency (FEMA) were caught

CORE **OBJECTIVE**

4. Assess the issues and developments during Bush's second term that helped lead to Barack Obama's historic victory in the 2008 presidential election.

Bush's stalled presidency

Hurricane Katrina and Democrats win control of the House

The aftermath of Katrina Two men paddle through high water with wooden planks in a devastated New Orleans.

Nancy Pelosi The Speaker of the House at a news conference on Capitol Hill.

unprepared as the catastrophe unfolded. Disaster plans were incomplete; confusion and incompetence abounded. In the face of blistering criticism, President Bush accepted responsibility for the balky federal response to the disaster and accepted the resignation of the FEMA director. Rebuilding the Gulf coast would take a long time and a lot of money.

In the November 2006 congressional elections, the Democrats capitalized on widespread public disapproval of the Bush administration to win control of the House of Representatives, the Senate, and a majority of governorships and state legislatures. Former Texas Republican congressman Dick Armey said that "the Republican Revolution of 1994 officially ended" with the 2006 election. "It was a rout." The transformational election also included a significant milestone: Californian Nancy Pelosi, the leader of the Democrats in the House of Representatives, became the highest-ranking woman in the history of the U.S. Congress upon her election as House Speaker in January 2007.

The "Surge" in Iraq

George W. Bush bore the brunt of public indignation over the bungled federal response to the Katrina disaster and the continuing cost and casualties of the war in Iraq. Senator Chuck Hagel, a Nebraska Republican, declared in 2005 that "we're losing in Iraq." Throughout the fall of 2006, the violence in Iraq spiraled upward. Bush eventually responded to declining public and political support for the Iraq War by creating the Iraq Study Group, a bipartisan task force whose final report recommended that the United States withdraw its combat forces from a "grave and deteriorating Iraq" by the spring of 2008.

President Bush disagreed with the Study Group and others, including key military leaders, who urged a phased withdrawal. On January 10, 2007, he announced that he was sending a "surge" of 20,000 (eventually 30,000) additional troops to Iraq, bringing the total to almost 170,000. From a military perspective, the "surge" strategy succeeded. By the fall of 2008, the convulsive violence in Iraq had declined dramatically, and the United States–supported Iraqi government had grown in stature and confidence. Still, by 2008, over 60 percent of Americans said that the war in Iraq had been a mistake.

The "Surge" in Iraq

Economic Shock

After the intense but brief 2001 recession, the boom/bust capitalist economy had begun another period of prolonged expansion. Between 1997 and 2006, home prices in the United States, especially in the fast-growing Sunbelt states, rose 85 percent, leading to a frenzy of irresponsible mortgage lending for the purchase of homes—and a debt-financed consumer spending spree. Tens of millions of people bought houses they could not afford, refinanced their mortgages, or tapped home-equity loans to make discretionary purchases. The irrational confidence in soaring housing prices also led government regulatory agencies and mortgage lenders to ease credit restrictions so that unqualified people could buy homes.

Financial collapses typically follow real estate bubbles, rising indebtedness, and prolonged budget deficits. The housing bubble burst in 2007, when home values and housing sales began a sharp decline. During 2008, the loss of trillions of dollars in home values set off a seismic shock across the economy. Record numbers of borrowers defaulted on their mortgage payments. Foreclosures and bankruptcies soared. Banks lost billions, first on the shaky mortgages, then on most other categories of debt: credit cards, car loans, student loans, and an array of commercial mortgage-backed securities.

The sudden contraction of corporate spending and consumer purchases pushed the economy into a deepening recession in 2008. The scale and suddenness of the slump caught economic experts and business leaders by surprise. Some of the nation's most prestigious banks, investment firms, and insurance companies went belly-up. The price of

Rio Vista, California With an $816,000 deficit, this northern California city filed for bankruptcy and pulled the plug on its massive, 750-home housing development in November 2008. Here, model homes stand eerily in a blank landscape of sidewalks and cul-de-sacs.

food and gasoline spiked. Unemployment soared. What had begun as a sharp decline in home prices became a panicky global economic meltdown. No investment seemed safe.

The economic crisis demanded decisive action to stem the panic and restore confidence. On October 3, 2008, just before the presidential election, President Bush signed into law a bank bailout fund called the **Troubled Asset Relief Program (TARP)**, which called for the Treasury Department to spend $700 billion to keep big banks and other large financial institutions from collapsing. Yet the passage of the bill did little to restore confidence. In early October, stock markets around the world began to crash with the onset of what came to be called the **Great Recession**, which technically lasted from December 2007 to January 2009, and forced almost 9 million people out of work. But its effects would last long thereafter. The economic recovery that began in June 2009 would be the weakest since the end of the Second World War. "The Age of Prosperity is over," announced the prominent Republican economist Arthur Laffer in 2008.

> The Great Recession

Great Recession (2007–2009)
Massive, prolonged economic downturn sparked by the collapse of the housing market and the financial institutions holding unpaid mortgages; resulted in 9 million Americans losing their jobs.

A Historic New Presidency

George Bush's unpopularity excited Democrats about regaining the White House in the 2008 election. The early front-runner for the Democratic nomination was New York senator Hillary Rodham Clinton, the spouse of ex-president Bill Clinton. Like her husband, she displayed an impressive command of policy issues and mobilized a well-funded campaign team. And, as the first woman with a serious chance of gaining the presidency, she had widespread support among voters eager for female leadership. In the end, however, an overconfident Clinton was upset in the Democratic primaries and caucuses by little-known first-term senator Barack Obama of Illinois. Young, handsome, and intelligent, Obama was an inspiring speaker who attracted huge crowds by promising a "politics of hope." He mounted an innovative Internet-based campaign directed at grassroots voters, donors, and volunteers. In early June 2008, he gained enough delegates to secure the Democratic nomination alongside Senator Joseph Biden of Delaware as his vice presidential running mate.

Obama was the first African American presidential nominee of either party, the gifted biracial son of a white mother from Kansas and a black Kenyan father who left the household and returned to Africa when Barack was a toddler. Obama made the most of his abilities, eventually graduating from Columbia University in New York before earning a law degree from Harvard. The forty-seven-year-old senator presented himself to voters as a deal-maker who could inspire and unite a diverse people and forge bipartisan collaborations. Obama radiated poise,

Barack Obama The president-elect and his family wave to the crowd of supporters in Chicago's Grant Park.

confidence, and energy. By contrast, his Republican opponent, seventy-two-year-old Arizona senator John McCain, was the oldest presidential candidate in history. As a twenty-five-year veteran of Congress, a leading Republican senator, and a candidate for the Republican presidential nomination in 2000, he had developed a reputation as a bipartisan "maverick" willing to work with Democrats to achieve key legislative goals.

On November 4, 2008, Barack Obama made history by becoming the nation's first person of color to be elected president. He won the popular vote by 53 percent to 46 percent. His margin in the Electoral College was even more impressive: 365 to 173. Obama also helped the Democrats win solid majorities in both houses of Congress. Within days of his victory, Obama adopted a bipartisan approach in selecting his new cabinet members.

THE ELECTION OF 2008

	Electoral Vote	Popular Vote
Barack Obama (Democrat)	365	69,500,000
John McCain (Republican)	173	59,900,000

■ How did the economic crisis affect the outcome of the election?
■ What are the similarities and differences between the map of the 2004 election and the map of the 2008 election?

He appointed Hillary Clinton secretary of state, retained Republican Robert Gates as secretary of defense, selected retired general James Jones, who had campaigned for McCain, as his national security adviser, and appointed Eric Holder as the nation's first African American attorney general. But picking a bipartisan cabinet proved easier than forging a bipartisan presidency.

New Priorities at Home and Abroad

CORE **OBJECTIVE**
5. Identify President Obama's priorities at home and abroad, and assess his efforts to pursue them.

The new Obama administration inherited two unpopular wars, in Iraq and Afghanistan, and the worst economic stumble in eighty years. His most pressing challenge was to keep the Great Recession from becoming a prolonged depression. Unemployment in early 2009 had passed 8 percent and was still rising. The financial sector remained paralyzed. And public confidence plummeted.

Obama's First Term

To enable banks to start lending again, the new administration continued the implementation of the TARP program created by the outgoing Bush administration, providing massive government bailouts to save the largest

Wall Street bank bailouts

banks and financial institutions. The big bank bailouts were highly controversial, attacked by both the left and the right as deeply unfair to most struggling Americans. As Treasury secretary Timothy Geithner later explained, "We had to do whatever we could to help people feel their money was safe in the [banking] system, even if it made us unpopular." Had they not saved the big banks, Obama and Geithner argued, the whole economy would have crashed. Geithner admitted that we saved "the economy, but we lost the country doing it."

Preserving the banking system did not create new jobs, however. To do so, in mid-February 2009, after a prolonged debate, Congress passed, and Obama signed, an $832-billion economic stimulus bill called the **American Recovery and Reinvestment Act**. The bill included cash distributions to the states for construction projects to renew the nation's infrastructure (roads, bridges, levees, government buildings, and the electricity grid), money for renewable-energy systems, and $212 billion in tax reductions for individuals and businesses, as well as additional funds for food stamps and unemployment benefits. It was the largest government infusion of cash into the economy in history. In the end, however, it was not large enough to generate a robust economic recovery.

| Economic Stimulus: American Recovery and Reinvestment Act (2009) |

Health-Care Reform

| A national health care program: The Affordable Care Act (2010) |

The economic crisis merited Obama's full attention, but he chose as his top legislative priority a controversial federal health-insurance program that had been one of his key campaign pledges. From his first day in office, Obama stressed his intention to reform a health-care system so broken that it was "bankrupting families, bankrupting businesses, and bankrupting our government at the state and federal level." The United States, home to the world's costliest health system, was spending 18 percent of its total economic resources on health care. Great Britain, Norway, and Sweden each spent half as much, but their citizens lived longer. America was the only rich nation without a national health-care program. Since 1970, the proportion of uninsured people had been steadily rising along with health care costs. In 2010 roughly 50 million Americans, 16 percent of the population, had no health insurance, most of them being either poor or young, or people of color.

The president's goal in creating the Patient Protection and **Affordable Care Act (ACA)**, which many people refer to as "Obamacare," was to make health insurance more affordable and make health care accessible for everyone, regardless of income. The $940-billion health-care law, proposed in 2009 and debated bitterly for a year, centered on the so-called *individual mandate*, which required uninsured adults to purchase an approved *private* insurance policy made available through state-run exchanges (websites where people could shop for insurance) or pay a tax penalty. Lower-income Americans would be provided with federal subsidies to help pay for their coverage. Insurance companies could no longer deny coverage to people

Affordable Care Act (ACA) (2010) Vast health-care reform initiative championed by President Obama and widely criticized by Republicans that aimed to make health insurance more affordable and make health care accessible to everyone, regardless of income or prior medical conditions.

with pre-existing illnesses. Employers who did not offer health insurance would also have to pay higher taxes, and drug companies as well as manufacturers of medical devices would have to pay annual government fees. Everyone, but especially the wealthy, would pay higher Medicare payroll taxes to help fund the changes.

All of the many efforts at providing national health insurance over the previous sixty years had been controversial. The ACA was no exception. The individual mandate was designed to ensure that all Americans had health insurance so as to reduce the skyrocketing costs of hospitals providing "charity care" for the uninsured poor. The ACA did not change the American tradition of using employment-based health insurance provided by private companies as the basic vehicle for financing medical care. But the idea of forcing people to buy such insurance flew in the face of the principle of individual freedom and personal responsibility. Critics questioned not only the individual mandate but also the administration's projections that the new program would reduce federal expenditures over the long haul.

Republicans quickly mobilized to defeat the ACA. "If we're able to stop Obama on this it will be his Waterloo. It will break him," predicted South Carolina senator Jim DeMint. Despite heated Republican opposition, however, the ACA was passed with narrow party-line majorities in both houses of Congress and signed into law by President Obama on March 23, 2010. Its complex provisions, implemented over a four-year transition period, would bring health insurance to 32 million people, half of whom would be covered by expanded Medicaid, and the other half covered by the individual mandate. In its scope and goals, the ACA was a landmark law in the history of health and social welfare—as well as the expansion of the federal government.

Obamacare and the Courts

No sooner had Obama pushed his controversial health-care plan through Congress than Republican opponents began challenging its constitutionality. On June 28, 2012, the Supreme Court issued its much-awaited decision in the case of *National Federation of Independent Business v. Sebelius*. The landmark 5–4 ruling surprised Court observers by declaring most of the new federal law to be constitutional. Even more surprising was that the deciding vote was cast by the chief justice, John G. Roberts, a philosophical conservative who had never before voted with the four "liberal" justices on the Court. Roberts upheld the ACA's individual mandate that required people to buy private health insurance or else pay a tax, arguing that it was within the Congress's power to impose taxes as outlined in Article 1 of the Constitution. Many conservatives, including the four dissenting justices, felt betrayed by Roberts's unexpected decision. The unexpected verdict led the *New York Times* to predict that the ruling "may secure Obama's place in history."

Regulating Wall Street

Wall Street Reform and
Consumer Protection Act (2010)

The near collapse of the nation's financial system beginning in 2008 prompted calls for overhauling the financial regulatory system. On July 21, 2010, Obama signed the Wall Street Reform and Consumer Protection Act, also called the Dodd-Frank bill after its two congressional sponsors. It was the most comprehensive reform of the financial system since the New Deal in the thirties. The 2,319-page law required government agencies to exercise greater oversight over complex new financial transactions and protected consumers from unfair practices in loans and credit cards by establishing a new consumer financial-protection agency. President Obama predicted that the bill, despite its complexity, would "lift our economy," give "certainty to everybody" about the technical rules governing banking, and end "tax-funded bailouts—period." By 2010, however, the economy had not been "lifted" and many bankers remained confused about the new rules regulating the financial industry.

The Obama Doctrine and Iraq

The Obama Doctrine

President Obama had more success in dealing with foreign affairs than in reviving the American economy. His foremost concern was the overextension of U.S. power abroad. What journalists came to call the Obama Doctrine was very much like the Nixon Doctrine (1970), stressing that the United States could not afford to continue to be the world's principal policeman. Yet it would not be easy to lower the nation's posture abroad, for the fate of America's economy and security was entangled more than ever with the fate of an unstable and often violent world.

The Obama Doctrine grew out of the fact that the president was trying to end two complex and expensive wars, one in Iraq and the other in Afghanistan. On February 27, 2009, Obama announced that all 142,000 U.S. troops would be withdrawn from Iraq by the end of 2011, as had been agreed to by the Iraqi government and the Bush administration in 2008. True to his word, the last U.S. combat troops left Iraq in December 2011. Their exit marked the end of a bitterly divisive war that had raged for nearly nine years.

The U.S. intervention in Iraq had cost over 4,500 American lives, 30,000 wounded (many grievously so), more than 110,000 Iraqi lives, and $2 trillion. Perhaps the greatest embarrassment was that the government that the U.S. left behind in Iraq was inept and not even friendly to American interests.

A "Surge" in Afghanistan

End of U.S. military presence in
Iraq and Afghanistan

At the same time that President Obama was reducing U.S. military involvement in Iraq, he dispatched 21,000 additional troops to Afghanistan in what was called a "surge." While doing so, however, he narrowed the focus of the U.S. mission to suppressing terrorists rather than "nation building"— the idea of transforming strife-torn Afghanistan into a stable capitalist democracy. The military surge worked as hoped. By the summer of 2011, President Obama announced that the "tide of war was receding" and that the United States had largely achieved its goals in Afghanistan, setting in motion a substantial withdrawal of forces beginning in 2011 and lasting until 2014. In April 2014, despite threats by the Taliban to kill voters, Afghans turned out in huge numbers to choose a new president to lead them into the post-American era. But it was an expensive outcome for America's longest war. In the thirteen years since the United States invaded Afghanistan in 2001, America had spent over a trillion dollars there and had lost 2,300 servicemen.

The Death of Osama Bin Laden

The crowning achievement of Obama's anti-terrorism efforts was the discovery, at long last, of Osama bin Laden's hideout. Ever since the attacks of 9/11, bin Laden had eluded an intensive manhunt after crossing the Afghan border into Pakistan. His luck ran out in August 2011, however, when U.S. intelligence analysts discovered his sanctuary in a walled residential compound outside of Abbottabad, Pakistan. On May 1, 2011, without alerting the Pakistani government, President Obama authorized a daring night raid by a U.S. Navy SEAL team of two dozen specially trained commandos transported by helicopters from Afghanistan. After a brief firefight, the Navy SEAL team killed bin Laden and then dropped his body into the sea. Bin Laden's death was a watershed moment, but it did not spell the end of Islamist terrorism.

> Death of Osama bin Laden (2011)

The "Arab Awakening"

In late 2010 and early 2011, spontaneous democratic uprisings erupted throughout much of the Arab world, as long-oppressed peoples rose up against authoritarian regimes. One by one, corrupt Arab tyrants were forced out of power by a new generation of young activists inspired by democratic ideals and connected by social media on the Internet. What was soon dubbed "the Arab Awakening" sent waves of unrest rippling across Tunisia, Algeria, Bahrain, Jordan, Morocco, Egypt, Oman, Yemen, Libya, Saudi Arabia, and Syria during what came to be called the Arab Spring of 2011. The remarkable uprisings heralded a new era in the history of the Middle East struggling to be born.

For all the excitement about "people power" emerging in the Middle East, however, the work of building new democratic governments proved much harder than expected. Grassroots democratic movements in most Arab nations stumbled and stalled by 2014, lurching

Arab Awakening Thousands of protesters converge in Cairo's Tahrir Square to call for an end to Moubarak's rule.

from crisis to crisis usually triggered by their unwillingness to allow for freedom of religion.

Libya Ousts Gaddafi

The pro-democracy turmoil in North Africa engulfed oil-rich Libya, long governed by the mercurial dictator Colonel Muammar Gaddafi, the Arab world's most violent despot. Anti-government demonstrations began on February 15, 2011, prompting Gaddafi to order Libyan soldiers and mercenaries (paid foreign soldiers) to suppress the rebellious "rats." By the end of February, what began as a peaceful pro-democratic uprising had turned into a full-scale civil war that provided the first real test of the Obama Doctrine. True to his word, the president refused to act alone in helping the Libyan rebels. Instead, he encouraged European allies to take the lead. On March 19, France and Great Britain, with American support, launched a bombing campaign against Gaddafi's military strongholds. In late August, rebel forces captured the capital of Tripoli, scattering Gaddafi's government and marking the end of his forty-two-year dictatorship. On October 20, rebel fighters captured and killed Gaddafi. But the rebel militias that removed Gaddafi soon started shooting at each other, and stability remained elusive by the end of 2014.

Polarized Politics

At the same time that Arabs were rebelling against entrenched political elites, grassroots rebellions were occurring in the United States as well. Barack Obama had campaigned in 2008 on the promise of bringing dramatic change to the federal government in an evenhanded way that would reduce the partisan warfare between the two national parties.

By the end of Obama's first year in office, however, a Gallup poll found that he had become the most polarizing president in modern history. It was not solely his fault. His Republican opponents had no interest in negotiating compromises with him. American political culture in the twenty-first century suffered from a crisis of mutual resentment, so polarized that it resembled two separate nations. Each had its own political party, its own cable-news station and rabidly partisan commentators, its own newspapers, its own think tanks, and its own billionaire activists.

And both "nations"—blue and red, liberal and conservative—had their own factions committed to a politics of rage. No sooner was Obama sworn in than anti-government conservatives mobilized against him and the "tax-and-spend" liberalism he represented in their eyes. In January 2009, a New York stock trader named Graham Makohoniuk sent an e-mail message urging people to send tea bags to their congressional representatives to symbolize the famous Boston Tea Party of 1773 when American colonists protested against British tax policies.

Within a year or so, the tax revolt had become a national **Tea Party** movement, with groups spread across the fifty states. The Tea Party is not

> Polarized politics: Conservative resurgence (the Tea Party)

Tea Party Right-wing populist movement, largely made up of middle-class, white male conservatives, that emerged as a response to the expansion of the federal government under the Obama administration.

so much a cohesive political organization as it is a mood, an attitude, and an ideology, a diverse collection of self-described "disaffected," "angry," and "very conservative" activists, mostly white, male, married middle-class Republicans over forty-five, boiling mad at the massive government bailouts of huge banks and corporations that had come in the wake of the 2008 economic meltdown. To the grassroots anti-tax rebels, the federal bailouts ordered by Bush and Obama were a form of "crony capitalism" whereby elected officials of both parties (the "elite") rewarded the big companies that had funded their campaigns. Tea Party members demanded a radically smaller federal government (although most of them supported Social Security and Medicare, the two most expensive federal social programs). Democrats, including President Obama, initially dismissed the Tea Party as a fringe group of extremists, but the 2010 election results proved them wrong.

Democratic House and Senate candidates (as well as moderate Republicans), including many long-serving leaders, were defeated in droves when conservative Republicans, many of them aligned with the Tea Party, gained sixty-three seats to recapture control of the House of Representatives and won a near majority in the Senate as well. It was the most lopsided midterm election since 1938. "We've come to take our government back," declared one Republican congressional winner. Thereafter, Obama and the Republican-dominated House of Representatives engaged in a harsh sparring match. With each side refusing to negotiate or compromise, the bickering between both parties prevented meaningful action on the languishing economy, chronic joblessness, and the runaway federal budget deficit.

The emergence of the Tea Party was mirrored on the far left wing of the political spectrum by the Occupy Wall Street (OWS) movement, mobilized in the fall of 2011 when a call went out over the Internet to "Occupy Wall Street. Bring tent." Dozens, then hundreds, then thousands of people, mostly young adults, many of them unemployed, converged on Zuccotti Park in lower Manhattan. They formed tent villages and gathered in festive groups to "occupy" Wall Street, protesting the "tyrannical" power of Wall Street banks and investment companies. The protesters described themselves as the voice of the 99 percent of Americans who were being victimized by the 1 percent

Occupy Wall Street The Manhattan-born grassroots movement grew rapidly from rallies to massive marches in financial districts nationwide, like this demonstration in downtown Los Angeles.

of the wealthiest and most politically connected Americans. Unlike the Tea Party, however, OWS did not have staying power. Within a year, its energies and visibility had waned, in part because of mass arrests, in part because it was an intentionally "leaderless" movement more interested in saying what it was *against* than explaining what it was *for*.

American politics has always been chaotic and combative; its raucous energy is one of the strengths of a democracy. But during Obama's presidency, the emergence of the Tea Party and Occupy Wall Street symbolized how political combat had become so fierce that *compromise* and *moderation* had become dirty words. Rarely before had Democrats and Republicans viewed each other with greater venom and less respect.

> Failure of bipartisanship

Bold Decisions

For all of the angry political sniping and Congressional stalemate, however, attitudes toward "hot-button" cultural values were slowly changing. In December 2010, Congress took a significant step toward equal treatment for gays when it repealed the "don't ask, don't tell" (DADT) military policy that, since 1993, had resulted in some 9,500 men and women being discharged from the armed forces. A year after the repeal was enacted, a report by army officers concluded that the repeal of DADT "has had no overall negative impact on military readiness or its component dimensions, including cohesion, recruitment, retention, assaults, harassment, or morale."

In May 2012 President Obama jumped headfirst into the nation's simmering cultural wars by announcing his support for the right of gay and lesbian couples to marry. That his statement came a day after the state of North Carolina legislature voted to ban all rights for gay couples illustrated how incendiary the issue was around the country. While asserting that it was the "right" thing to do, Obama also knew that endorsing **same-sex marriage** had powerful political implications. The gay community would play an energetic role in the 2012 presidential election, and the youth vote—the under-30 electorate who among all the voting-age groups most supported gay marriage—would be equally crucial to Obama's reelection chances. No sooner had Obama made his pathbreaking announcement than polls showed that American voters for the first time split half and half on the charged issue, with Democrats and independent voters providing the bulk of support for Obama's pro-same-sex-marriage position.

The following month, in June 2012, Obama again made waves by issuing an executive order (soon labeled the DREAM Act) that allowed 1.5 million undocumented immigrants who had been brought to the United States as children to remain in the country as citizens. His unanticipated decision thrilled Hispanic supporters who had lost heart over his failure to convince Congress to support a more comprehensive reform of immigration laws. Republicans in Congress steadfastly opposed giving the estimated 12 million undocumented immigrants, 80 percent of whom were Latinos, a "pathway

same-sex marriage Legal right for gay and lesbian couples to marry; the most divisive issue in the culture wars of the early 2010s as increasing numbers of court rulings affirmed this right across the United States.

Refugees from gangland
Braving hundreds of miles on foot, Honduran and Salvadorian children are sent off by their parents for a better life in the United States, away from the drugs and violence of Central America. Here, border guards stop a group of child refugees in Granjeno, Texas.

to citizenship," as Obama proposed, without first ensuring that the U.S.-Mexican border was secured.

The DREAM Act, however, had unexpected consequences. It excited the dreams of masses of Central Americans willing to endure enormous risks to live in America. Panicked parents in El Salvador, Guatemala, and Honduras, worried about widespread drug-related gang violence, started sending their children on a dangerous journey through Mexico to the United States in hopes of connecting with relatives and being granted citizenship. During 2014, some 57,000 young migrants were caught along the nearly 2,000 mile-long border with Mexico, and communities across the United States rushed to find families to "sponsor" the unaccompanied children.

At the same time, the Obama administration was deporting record numbers of undocumented immigrants (over 2 million by the end of 2014), some of whom had been working in the nation for decades while others were Central American gang members, in what was called the "great expulsion." Obama, called the "Deporter in Chief" by critics, claimed that he was only following the laws written by anti-immigration Republicans. Others suggested that the president's harsh deportation policy was part of his "grand strategy" to force Congress to pass a comprehensive immigration reform bill. Either way, it was the immigrants who were caught in the middle.

The Supreme Court in the Twenty-First Century

The Supreme Court surprised observers in 2013 by overturning the Defense of Marriage Act (DOMA) of 1996, signed by President Bill Clinton, which had denied gay and lesbian couples who married in states allowing such unions the right to federal benefits. In *United States v. Windsor* (2013), the Court by a 5-4 vote ruled that the federal government could not withhold

Supreme Court overturns the Defense of Marriage Act (DOMA) (2013)

spousal benefits from same-sex couples who had been legally married. While restoring federal benefits, the Court did not rule that same-sex marriage is a *right* guaranteed under the U.S. Constitution. Each state, therefore, decided whether to allow such marriages. During 2014, however, federal courts repeatedly overturned state laws banning same-sex marriages, arguing that the right to marry was guaranteed by the Constitution.

Supreme Court dismantles the 1965 Voting Rights Act (2013)

While the Supreme Court disappointed social conservatives with its ruling in the *Windsor* case, the five conservatives on the Supreme Court continued to make rulings intended to restrict the powers of the federal government. In June 2013, in *Shelby County v. Holder* (2013), the Court gutted key provisions of the 1965 Voting Rights Act (VRA). The majority opinion declared that in five of the six southern states originally covered by the VRA, black voter turnout now exceeded white turnout. To the judges, this seemed to prove that there was no evidence of continuing racial discrimination. Soon after the Court's ruling, counties and states in the South pushed through new laws that had the effect of making it more difficult for minorities and poor people to vote by reducing voting hours or requiring that driver's licenses be shown on voting days.

The 2012 Election

As the November 2012 presidential election approached, one thing was certain: it would be the most expensive election ever, in part because the U.S. Supreme Court ruled in *Citizens United v. Federal Elections Committee* (2010) that corporations could spend as much as they wanted in support of candidates.

But if spending on the campaign was certain to be a record, it remained to be seen whether President Obama could shift the focus of voters from the sluggish economy to cultural politics and social issues. After a divisive battle in the primaries that included twenty televised debates with nearly a dozen other candidates, Mitt Romney won the Republican presidential nomination primarily because he promised, as a former corporate executive and Massachusetts governor, to accelerate economic growth.

Two things injured Romney's candidacy toward the end of the most expensive campaign in history ($6 billion). First was his decision to please right-wing voters by opposing immigration reforms that might allow undocumented immigrants a pathway to citizenship. The second was the disclosure late in the campaign that Romney had privately told a group of wealthy contributors that he "did not care" about the 47 percent of Americans who failed "to take personal responsibility and care for their lives." It was not his job "to worry about" those who did not pay federal income taxes because they were dependent on federal government programs. The Obama campaign seized on the impolitic statement, demonizing the wealthy Romney as an uncaring elitist. On Election Day, the president won with 66 million votes to Romney's 61 million, and 332 electoral votes to 206.

Embedded in the election returns were some striking statistics. Nearly 60 percent of white voters chose Romney. But the nation's fastest growing groups—Hispanics, Asian Americans, and African Americans—voted overwhelmingly for Obama, as did college-educated women, white and non-white. In the aftermath of Romney's defeat, David Frum, a prominent Republican speechwriter and columnist, confessed that his party was becoming "increasingly isolated and estranged from modern America."

> Obama elected to a second term (2012)

Obamacare on the Defensive

President Obama's proudest achievement, the Affordable Care Act, was so massive in its scope and complicated in its implementation that it took four years of preparation before it was ready to "roll out." In the fall of 2013, the federal online health insurance "exchange" where people without insurance, mostly the working poor, could sign up, opened with great fanfare. Obama assured Americans that using the new online registration system would be "real simple." It was not. On October 1, millions tried to sign up for Obamacare online; few succeeded. As it turned out, the government website had never been properly tested, and it was hobbled with technical glitches. At the same time, it became evident that Obama had misled the nation about key elements of his health-care plan. In campaigning for its passage in 2010, he had repeatedly told voters that if they liked their current health insurance plan, they could, under Obamacare, "keep that insurance. Period. End of story." As it turned out, however, many saw their policies canceled by insurers.

Democrats had little time to celebrate, however. By November 2013, 57 percent of voters said they opposed Obamacare, in part because the program benefited only a quarter of the population, the uninsured and the underinsured, and Obama's job approval ratings had plunged. It had taken the president weeks to acknowledge the botched roll-out of Obamacare: "We created this problem we didn't need to create," he said to aides. "And it's our own doing, and it's our most important initiative," and "nobody is madder than me."

A frantic effort to repair the ACA website bore fruit. By August 2014, over 9 million people, well above the original target number, had signed up for the new health insurance. "The Affordable Care Act is here to stay," President Obama assured a nation still uncertain of its benefits. Yet Republican critics of Obamacare were so angry over its implementation that they filed a lawsuit against the president and some even talked of impeaching him.

New Global Challenges in an Age of Insecurity

In 2013 the United States held its first high-level talks with Iran since 1979, when Iranian militants in Tehran stormed the U.S. embassy and took its employees hostage. On November 23, Secretary of State John Kerry,

> A limited nuclear negotiation with Iran

who succeeded Hillary Clinton in that role that year, reached a multinational agreement with Iran to scale back its nuclear development program for six months as a first step toward a more comprehensive agreement not to develop nuclear weapons that might threaten Israel or Iran's Arab neighbors.

Russians avert U.S. intervention in Syria

At the same time that the United States was trying to reduce Iran's nuclear threat, an increasingly bloody civil war in Syria that had so far claimed 150,000 lives was beginning to have major international repercussions. In 2013, U.S. intelligence analysts confirmed that the Syrian government on August 21 had used chemical weapons to kill 1,400 people, many of them children. President Obama had repeatedly warned that the use of such weapons of mass destruction was a "red line" that would trigger international military intervention. In late August, he (and the French government) hesitantly began preparations for a military strike, although a war-fatigued Congress and most Americans opposed such action. On September 9, Secretary of State John Kerry defused the crisis by signing an agreement with Russia to dispose of Syria's chemical weapons. By the end of October, all the chemical weapon stockpiles at twenty-three locations had been destroyed or dismantled, but the ferocious civil war raged on. Obama's reluctance to use force in Syria illustrated his reluctance to order another U.S. military intervention in the fractious and complex Middle East, especially after twelve years of inconclusive warfare in Iraq and Afghanistan.

As the Syrian civil war continued, a civil uprising occurred in Ukraine, the former Soviet republic of 46 million people that had gained its independence in 1991. For years, Russian president Vladimir Putin, who viewed the humiliating disintegration of the Soviet Union as the "greatest geopolitical catastrophe of the century," had been trying to exert economic and political control over the republics of the former Soviet Union.

Vladimir Putin President of Russia and former Soviet secret service agent.

On February 27, Putin sent troops into the Crimea, a disputed part of the Ukraine. A week later, the Crimean parliament voted to become part of the Russian Federation. Putin, claiming that Crimea had "always been an inseparable part of Russia" even as he lied about the role of Russian troops in Crimea, quickly made the illegal annexation official.

The speed and ruthlessness with which Putin seized control of Crimea, mobilized 40,000 Russian troops on the Ukrainian border, and cut off Ukraine's crucial access to natural gas surprised President Obama and European leaders. It may not have been the start of a new cold war, but it put an end to hope that Russia would become a sincere partner of the Western democracies. The United States and the European Union refused to recognize the legitimacy of Russia's annexation of Crimea, warned Russia not to invade eastern Ukraine, and announced economic sanctions against Russia while pledging financial assistance to struggling Ukraine. "If Russia continues to interfere in Ukraine, we stand ready to impose further sanctions," Obama said. By a vote of 100–11, the UN General Assembly also opposed Russia's annexation of Crimea.

In April 2014, heavily armed pro-Russian separatists, as many as a third of whom were in fact Russian soldiers and agents, seized control of several cities in eastern Ukraine. They declared a "people's republic" and called for secession from Ukraine.

Pressure mounted on the United States and Europe to impose even more sanctions against Russia when a Malaysian passenger jet flying across eastern Ukraine was shot down by a Russian-made rocket in July 2014, killing all 298 on board, most of them Dutch citizens. The missile launcher was quickly spirited back into Russia. The U.S. and its allies slammed Russia with more severe economic sanctions, but the coldly calculating Putin showed no sign of backing away from his adventurism in Ukraine.

> Sanctions over Russian aggression in Ukraine

Events overseas during the summer of 2014 gave Obama the opportunity to take decisive action. In June, the volatile Middle East took a sudden turn for the worse when Sunni jihadists from around the world (including the United States and Great Britain) who had been fighting in the civil war in Syria against the Assad government invaded northern Iraq and announced the creation of their own nation ("caliphate"), called the Islamic State (IS or ISIS). The Islamic State had become the largest, best equipped, and most brutal of the many Islamist terrorist groups, financing its far-flung operations and 40,000 fanatical fighters by selling oil and ransoming hostages.

In the face of the IS advance, many Iraqi government soldiers that the United States had spent billions of dollars training and equipping simply fled, leaving to IS their valuable weapons and vehicles. The blood-thirsty IS fighters seized huge tracts of territory in Syria and Iraq while gleefully enslaving, terrorizing, raping, massacring, crucifying, or beheading thousands who refused to embrace their ruthless version of the Sunni faith. In August 2014, after IS terrorists gruesomely beheaded two captured Americans, President Obama ordered "systematic" airstrikes in Iraq—and later Syria—to prevent genocide as well-armed and financed IS fighters assaulted Christians, Yazidis, and Kurds in the region. The U.S. president scored a diplomatic coup by building a broad coalition of Arab and European partners to avoid "going it alone" against the "cancer" of the Islamic State, but there was no doubt that American warplanes would bear the brunt of the action. Obama assured Americans that he would not "get dragged into another ground war."

Although some criticized Obama's actions, he characterized the effort to stop the mass murder and mayhem by the Islamic State as "American leadership at its best." Preventing genocide is not simply a burden of great power, it is an obligation.

A Fading American Dream?

When Barack Obama won the Democratic nomination for president in 2008, he and his supporters touted him as an uplifting example of the American Dream at work, a biracial man who had defied the odds and won great success. His inspiring story echoed one of the most powerful themes in the nation's history: America as a mythic land of unique opportunities for people from around the world. In 1811, former president John Adams marveled at the growth and prosperity of the young American republic: "There is no people on earth so ambitious as the people of America . . . because the lowest [poorest] can aspire [to wealth] as freely as the highest."

The ideal of equal opportunity has always been the engine of American distinctiveness. By the early twenty-first century, though, that ideal seemed increasingly out of reach to millions of disenchanted Americans. The most striking change in modern life since the 1970s was the *widening* inequality of income and wealth between the powerful groups making up the economic elite and the rest of society. Modern America had become a tale of two very different societies in which "the rich get richer and the poor get poorer," to quote a famous song. America at the end of 2014 had never experienced more income inequality or less social mobility. "Today," reported the Nobel Prize–winning economist Joseph Stiglitz in 2012, "the United States has less equality of opportunity than almost any other advanced industrial country." The American dream of the poor having an equal chance to succeed, he said, had become more of a myth than ever before. America had grown much better at encouraging innovation then spreading opportunity.

By 2014, the richest 1 percent controlled more than 20 percent of total income. The 46 million Americans living *below* the official poverty line in 2014 ($11,702 annual income for an individual, or $23,850 for a family of four) was the highest in history. One out of every five children lives in poverty. And at the other extreme, corporate executives were reaping an ever-higher percentage of national wealth. In 1993 the disparity in pay between corporate leaders and the average U.S. worker was 195 to 1; in 2012, it had almost doubled to 360 to 1. "Increasingly," as journalist Hedrick Smith reported in 2012, America is becoming a society in which "privilege sustains privilege; poverty begets poverty," resulting in the "slow, poisonous polarization and disintegration of our great democracy."

A growing inequality gap

What caused the widening economic inequality, the shrinking of the middle class, and the new culture of poverty? Some argued that capitalism, by its vary nature, produced violent extremes of poverty and wealth. Others suggested that the United States had developed a "high-poverty economy" in which widespread poverty was simply the price to be paid for a highly competitive and largely deregulated high-tech economy in which the undereducated and unskilled were relegated to minimum-wage jobs. The globalization of the economy and the computer/Internet revolution paid huge dividends for the wealthiest and best-educated Americans while undercutting middle-class job opportunities. At the same time, economic inequality over time produces political inequality, as the role of "big money" in determining elections has steadily increased. Candidates have grown dependent on rich donors and corporate contributions, so that once elected, they often reciprocate by cutting taxes on the wealthy and reducing regulations of businesses.

Whatever its causes, what came to be called the "great divide" between the "1 percent" and the "99 percent" had profound social and political consequences as well as problematic moral dimensions. A nation founded on the ideal of equal opportunity ("All men are created equal") had become fabulously richer but less equal and less socially mobile than other advanced industrial nations. The true test of a capitalist democracy is not how wealthy the richest citizens are, but the quality of life of the average citizen. As Theodore Roosevelt had pledged in 1903, he would ensure a "Square Deal" for "every man, great or small, rich or poor."

What the two extremes of the political spectrum—the Tea Party and the Occupy Wall Street movement—agreed upon in the new century was that economic and political elites had come to rule America at the expense of the citizenry. Al Gore's slogan during the 2000 presidential campaign—"the people versus the powerful"—came to define the political dynamics of the twenty-first century.

Unlike many nations in the past, the United States has so far survived its growing economic inequalities and social strife without serious upheavals. For all its growing diversity and deepening divisions, the nation remains united under a common government and political system, something that few societies can claim. For centuries, Americans have also displayed a distinctively self-critical temperament, especially noticeable to foreign visitors. In the early nineteenth century, the English writer Charles Dickens said that the American "always is depressed, and always is stagnated, and always is at an alarming crisis, and never was otherwise."

Perhaps that is why the nation has always overcome its greatest crises: Americans have high expectations and eventually address their urgent problems. The nation has always displayed a remarkable genius for self-renewal, a confident ability to maneuver itself through the most difficult threats and challenges, emerging not only intact but stronger. It needs such innovative resilience today, for unless the entwined ideals of equal opportunity and fair reward are addressed, Americans may lose what has always united the republic and informed the nation's sense of purpose: the widely shared hope, even expectation, of a better future—for all—based on hard work, ingenuity, and sacrifice. As President Obama declared in 2014, growing income inequality had become a "fundamental threat to the American Dream, our way of life, and what we stand for around the globe."

U.S. Foreign Policy Post-Cold War

As the twentieth century came to an end, the United States' relationship with the rest of the world entered a new era. "Containment" of the Soviet Union had become less crucial, but regional conflicts and other issues of national security did not disappear, and American leaders—no longer locked in a fierce nuclear rivalry with the Soviet Union—struggled to define America's role in an unstable post-Cold War era. U.S. military forces would intervene in regions and conflicts unimaginable a few decades earlier and not always successfully or with clear purpose.

Two key issues have shaped post-Cold War policies. On September 11, 2001, the United States suffered its worst attack since the Japanese bombing of Pearl Harbor. Terrorists linked to al Qaeda, a worldwide network of Islamic extremists, crashed hijacked commercial airliners into the World Trade Center in New York City and the Pentagon in Washington, D.C., killing thousands. Then, in 2008, the nation plunged into the Great Recession, the worst economic crisis since the Great Depression of the 1930s. Review the following foreign policy highlights from the first three "post-Cold War" presidents and answer the questions further below.

Foreign Policy Highlights from the Clinton Presidency, 1993–2001

1993 Congress passes the North American Free Trade Agreement (NAFTA).

American negotiators broker an agreement between Israel and the Palestinian Liberation Organization (PLO) that restored Palestinian self-rule in parts of Israeli-occupied territory in the Gaza Strip and West Bank.

1994 President Clinton, with United Nations authorization, intervenes to restore the democratically-elected President of Haiti, Jean-Bertrand Aristide, after a military coup.

1995 American negotiators broker a peace settlement in Bosnia. After declaring its independence from Yugoslavia in 1991, Bosnia quickly became embroiled in an ethnic and religious civil war. The peace plan divided the country into two states and committed 60,000 NATO troops to enforce the agreement.

1998 President Clinton negotiates a deal among leaders of Israel, Jordan, and the PLO, by which Israel agreed to surrender land in return for security guarantees by the Palestinians.

1999 NATO forces, relying heavily on the U.S. military, launch airstrikes against Serbia that end its attempts to assert control over Kosovo by brutalizing its ethnic Albanian population.

Foreign Policy Highlights from the Bush Presidency, 2001–2009

October 2001 U.S. forces lead "Operation Enduring Freedom," an international coalition into Afghanistan, after the Taliban government refused to turn over Osama bin Laden, mastermind of al Qaeda and the 9/11 attacks. After the collapse of the Taliban in December, American-led international forces continued to occupy the country searching for bin Laden and support a new internationally recognized government.

Congress passes the USA Patriot Act.

Bush Presidency, 2001–2009, continued

November 2002 Congress creates the Office of Homeland Security.

Fall of 2002 Bush announces the "Bush Doctrine."

March 2003 The U.S. and its allies invade Iraq and overthrow its dictator, Saddam Hussein, based on the Bush administration's claim that the regime possessed chemical and biological weapons of mass destruction, weapons that were never found by occupying forces.

Fall of 2003 President Bush announces that 150,000 U.S. troops would remain in Iraq and that rebuilding the fracturing country would take years and be very expensive.

Foreign Policy Highlights from the Obama Presidency, 2009–2014

2009 President Obama announces that U.S. troops would be withdrawn from Iraq by the end of 2011. The U.S. intervention in Iraq had cost over 4,500 American lives, 30,000 wounded, over 100,000 Iraqi lives, and $2 trillion.

President Obama transfers 21,000 additional troops to Afghanistan but confines their mission to suppressing terrorists, not nation building.

Late 2010–2011 An "Arab Awakening" emerges as spontaneous democratic uprisings break out in several Arab countries dominated by authoritarian leaders. Demonstrators toppled regimes in Egypt, Libya, and Tunisia, but failed to establish stable democracies in their place. President Obama exercised restraint in responding to these developments.

2011 President Obama announces that the military surge in Afghanistan had worked and American forces would be withdrawn from the country by the end of 2014.

March 2011 President Obama supports a British and French bombing campaign against dictator Colonel Muammar Gaddafi and in support of the rebellion against him. The rebels eventually overthrew Gaddafi and killed him in October.

May 1, 2011 A U.S. Navy Seal Team kills Osama bin Laden in a secret compound in Pakistan.

2013 The United States holds its first high-level talks with Iranian officials since 1979. Iran agrees to scale back its nuclear development program.

August 2013 President Obama and French officials organize a military strike against the Syrian government after it used chemical weapons in its civil war. Before Congress could vote on the measure, Syria agreed to dispose of its remaining chemical weapons, thus diffusing the crisis.

September 2014 President Obama orders U.S. airstrikes against IS forces operating in Iraq and Syria.

QUESTIONS FOR ANALYSIS

1. How did Presidents Clinton and Bush differ in their use of military force to intervene abroad?

2. Out of all three presidents in the new millennia, which president seemed most willing to use military force to promote his objectives and which seemed least? What events and developments shaped their decisions?

3. Why do you think each president focused so much attention on the Middle East?

■ **Changing Demographics** From 1980 to 2010, the U.S. population grew by 25 percent, to 306 million, and was more racially and ethnically diverse. Because of a wave of immigration from Latin America, Hispanics surpassed African Americans as the nation's largest minority. The rate at which the nonwhite population increased had quadrupled since the 1970s. By 2012, the U.S. population included more foreign-born and first-generation residents than ever before.

■ **Divided Government** Just two years into the presidency of "New Democrat" Bill Clinton, Republican Speaker of the House Newt Gingrich crafted his *Contract with America* against the "corrupt liberal welfare state" and achieved, a Republican landslide in the 1994 midterm elections. The *North American Free Trade Act (NAFTA)* (1994) and the *Personal Responsibility and Work Opportunity Act of 1996* were bipartisan successes. The prosperous high-tech *"new economy"* thriving on the *globalization* of commerce helped Clinton balance the federal budget. Yet, Clinton's personal scandals tarnished his presidency even though he was ultimately acquitted. He later intervened in the Balkans to stop *ethnic cleansing* and brokered the Wye River Accords in the Middle East.

■ **Global Terrorism** The 9/11 terrorist attacks led President George W. Bush to declare a *war on terror*. The U.S. invaded Afghanistan (Operation Enduring Freedom) to capture the 9/11 attack's mastermind, Osama bin Laden, destroy his terrorist organization, al Qaeda, and oust the Islamist Taliban government that harbored it. Congress also authorized the Office of Homeland Security and the *USA Patriot Act*. In 2003, the Bush administration invoked the *Bush Doctrine* against Saddam Hussein, the leader of Iraq. The Second Iraq War succeeded in removing Hussein from power but turned up no weapons of mass destruction. The administration was unprepared to establish order in postwar Iraq, which was soon wracked by sectarian violence. Americans became bitterly divided over the war and whether the Bush Doctrine enhanced U.S. security.

■ **A Historic Election** The 2008 presidential campaigns featured Democrats Senator Hillary Clinton and Senator Barack Obama, the first female and African American candidates, respectively; The Republicans nominated Senator John McCain, the oldest candidate in history. Obama won the popular vote and a landslide victory in the electoral college, becoming the nation's first African American president. His victory resulted from public dismay about the *Great Recession* and weariness with Bush's policies. His Internet- and grassroots-based campaign excelled at fundraising and voter turnout. He won much of the nonwhite vote, a rapidly increasing share of the electorate.

■ **Obama's Priorities** Obama's first priority was shoring up the failing economy through controversial Wall Street bailouts and a huge economic stimulus package: the American Recovery and Reinvestment Act. Economic recovery remained sluggish and unequal, widening the economic divide and spawning the Occupy Wall Street movement. Obama's legacy legislation, the *Affordable Care Act (ACA),* incited bitter opposition from the *Tea Party,* which leveraged its control over the House of Representatives to shut down the federal government for sixteen days. Obama reduced U.S. military abroad, removing all combat troops from Iraq in 2011, downsizing their presence in Afghanistan, refusing to make broad military commitments in the Arab Awakening. Obama also endorsed *same-sex marriage* and a path to citizenship for undocumented residents.

KEY TERMS

North American Free Trade Agreement (NAFTA) (1994) *p. 1132*

Contract with America (1994) *p. 1133*

Personal Responsibility and Work Opportunity Act of 1996 (PRWOA) *p. 1135*

"new economy" *p. 1135*

globalization *p. 1136*

ethnic cleansing *p. 1138*

war on terror *p. 1143*

USA Patriot Act (2001) *p. 1143*

Bush Doctrine *p. 1144*

Great Recession (2007–2009) *p. 1150*

Affordable Care Act (ACA) (2010) *p. 1152*

Tea Party *p. 1156*

same-sex marriage *p. 1158*

CHRONOLOGY

1991	Ethnic conflict explodes in Yugoslavia
1992	Bill Clinton elected president
1993	Congress passes NAFTA
1995	Contract with America
1996	Congress passes welfare reform
1998	President Clinton impeached
2000	Supreme Court issues *Bush v. Gore* decision
September 11, 2001	9/11 Terrorist attacks
October 2001	Operation Enduring Freedom begins
2003–2011	Second Iraq War begins
August 2005	Hurricane Katrina
2007–2009	Great Recession begins
2009	Barack Obama elected president
	Tea Party movement begins
2010	Congress passes the Affordable Care Act
2011	Occupy Wall Street, Arab Awakening
August 2011	Osama bin Laden killed
2013	Defense of Marriage Act overturned
2014	Islamic State of Iraq and Syria (ISIS) established

INQUIZITIVE

Go to InQuizitive to see what you've learned—and learn what you've missed—with personalized feedback along the way.

DEBATING Contemporary Immigration and the Uses of History

One of the reasons that the study of history is so important is that it informs the way we think about society today. Comparisons with the past are an essential part of how policy makers and citizens debate the key issues of the day. For instance, one of the most controversial issues in American society today is immigration, and many arguments hinge on comparisons to past generations of immigrants and how they were perceived at the time. For Part Seven, *The American Age*, the issue of Latino immigration demonstrates how history influences contemporary political debates. For this exercise, you will be taking on the role of historian, and thus you should focus on evaluating the uses of history, not current immigration policy.

For this exercise you have two tasks:

PART 1: Compare the ways that history is used in two secondary sources discussing contemporary Latino immigration.

PART 2: Using primary sources, evaluate how history is used in these secondary sources.

PART I Comparing Secondary Sources

Each of the secondary sources that is included here is written by a scholar of contemporary immigration politics. In these selections, the authors draw comparisons between the issues surrounding past generations of immigrants and the issues surrounding immigrants today. The first is from Dr. Jason Richwine, a contributing writer at the National Review and former Senior Policy Analyst, Heritage Foundation. The second text is from Leo Chavez, a professor of anthropology at the University of California, Irvine. While Richwine is interested in assimilation, immigration, and national culture, Chavez is concerned with how immigrant groups are represented in contemporary discourse.

Compare the views of these two scholars by answering the following questions. Be sure to find specific examples in the selections to support your answers.

■ What issues that surround Latino immigration to America does each author address?

■ What comparisons does each author make to historical immigration groups?

■ In what ways might these authors respond to each other's work?

■ Based on what you have learned, what examples from American history can you think of that would support or refute each author's argument?

Secondary Source 1
Jason Richwine, on Assimilation (2009)

They're not just like the Irish—or the Italians or the Poles, for that matter. The large influx of Hispanic immigrants after 1965 represents a unique assimilation challenge for the United States. Many optimistic observers have assumed—incorrectly, it turns out—that Hispanic immigrants will follow the same economic trajectory European immigrants did in the early part of the last century. Many of those Europeans came to America with no money and few skills, but their status steadily improved. Their children outperformed them, and their children's children were often indistinguishable from the "founding stock." The speed of economic assimilation varied somewhat by ethnic group, but three generations were typically enough to turn "ethnics" into plain old Americans.

This would be the preferred outcome for the tens of millions of Hispanic Americans, who are significantly poorer and less educated on average than native whites. When immigration skeptics question the wisdom of importing so many unskilled people into our nation at one time, the most common response cites the remarkable progress of Europeans a century ago. "People used to say the Irish or the Poles would always be poor, but look at them today!" For Hispanics, we are led to believe, the same thing will happen.

But that claim isn't true. Though about three-quarters of Hispanics living in the U.S. today are either immigrants or the children of immigrants, a significant number have roots here going back many generations. We have several ways to measure their intergenerational progress, and the results leave little room for optimism about their prospects for assimilation . . . .

First, the second generation still does not come close to matching the socioeconomic status of white natives. Even if Hispanics were to keep climbing the ladder each generation, their assimilation would be markedly slower than that of other groups. But even that view is overly optimistic, because of the second, larger problem with Hispanic assimilation: It appears to stall after the second generation. We see little further ladder-climbing from the grandchildren of Hispanic immigrants. They do not rise out of the lower class . . . .

So why do Hispanics, on average, not assimilate? Theories abound. Popular explanations from the left include the legacy of white racism, labor-market discrimination, housing segregation, and poor educational opportunities. Those on the right tend to cite enforced multiculturalism, ethnic enclaves, and a self-perpetuating culture of poverty. . . . [T]he lack of Hispanic assimilation is likely to create ethnic tensions that threaten our cultural core. Human beings are a tribal species, and this makes ethnicity a natural fault line in any society. Intra-European ethnic divisions have been largely overcome through economic assimilation—Irish and Italian immigrants may have looked a bit different from natives, but by the third generation their socioeconomic profiles were similar. Hispanic Americans do not have that benefit.

Persistent ethnic disparities in socioeconomic status add to a sense of "otherness" felt by minorities outside the economic mainstream. Though it is encouraging that Hispanics often profess a belief in the American creed, an undercurrent of this "otherness" is still apparent. For example, a Pew Hispanic Center Survey in 2002 asked American-born Hispanics "which terms they would use first to describe themselves." Less than half (46 percent) said "American," while the majority said they primarily identified either with their ancestral country or as simply Hispanic or Latino. . . .

It is difficult to see how a unifying national culture can be preserved and extended in that environment.

Source: Jason Richwine, "The Congealing Pot," *National Review* 61 no. 15 (August 24, 2009): 37–39.

Secondary Source 2
Leo Chavez, on Illegal Aliens (2008)

This book grew out of my attempt to unpack the meanings of . . . [negative] views about Latinos. Rather than considering them in isolation, I began to see them as connected, as part of a larger set of concerns over immigration, particularly from Mexico and other parts of Latin America; the meaning of citizenship; and the power of media spectacles in contemporary life. The Latino Threat Narrative provides the raw material that weaves these concerns together.

The Latino Threat Narrative posits that Latinos are not like previous immigrant groups, who ultimately became part of the nation. According to the assumptions and taken-for-granted "truths" inherent in this narrative, Latinos are unwilling or incapable of integrating, of becoming part of the national community. Rather, they are part of an invading force from south of the border that is bent on reconquering land that was formerly theirs (the U.S. Southwest) and destroying the American way of life. . . .

The contemporary Latino Threat Narrative has its antecedents in U.S. history: the German language threat, the Catholic threat, the Chinese and Japanese immigration threats, and the southern and eastern European threat. In their day, each discourse of threat targeted particular immigrant groups and their children. Each was pervasive and defined "truths" about the threats posed by immigrants that, in hindsight, were unjustified or never materialized in the long run of history. And each of these discourses generated actions, such as alarmist newspaper stories (the media of the day), anti-immigrant riots, restrictive immigration laws, forced internments, and acrimonious public debates over government policies. In this sense, the Latino Threat Narrative is part of a grand tradition of alarmist discourse about immigrants and their perceived negative impacts on society. . . .

Latinos have been in what is now the United States since the late sixteenth and early seventeenth centuries, actually predating the English colonies. Since the Mexican-American War, immigration from Mexico and other Latin countries has waxed and waned, building in the early twentieth century, diminishing in the 1930s, and building again the post-1965 years. These migrations paralleled those of other immigrant groups. But Mexicans in particular have been represented as the quintessential "illegal aliens," which distinguishes them from other immigrant groups. Their social identity has been plagued by the mark of illegality, which in much public discourse means that they are criminals and thus illegitimate members of society undeserving of social benefits, including citizenship. Latinos are an alleged threat because of this history and social identity, which supposedly make their integration difficult and imbue them, particularly Mexicans, with a desire to remain socially apart as they prepare for a reconquest of the U.S. Southwest.

Source: Leo Chavez, *The Latino Threat: Constructing Immigrants, Citizens, and the Nation* (Redwood City, CA: Stanford University Press, 2008), 3–4.

PART II Using Primary Sources to Evaluate Secondary Sources

When historians are faced with competing interpretations of the past, they often look at primary source material as part of the process of evaluating the different arguments. Below is a selection of primary source materials relating to some of the historical issues relating to immigration and assimilation brought up by the two authors. The first document is excerpted from a short essay, one of the first works on demography, by Benjamin Franklin in 1751. The second document is an 1878 statement from the California State Senate to the U.S. Congress requesting that immigration to the United States from China be restricted. The third document is an article by Republican Senator Henry Cabot Lodge of Massachusetts, a leading immigration restrictionist who was instrumental in the passage of such legislation in the 1920s. The final document is from the 1963 book, *Beyond the Melting Pot: The Negroes, Puerto Ricans, Jews, Italians, and Irish of New York City*, by sociologist Nathan Glazer and future U.S. senator Daniel Patrick Moynihan. This book appeared just prior to the liberalization of U.S. immigration policy in 1965 and explores the assimilation of various ethnic groups in New York City.

Carefully read each of the following primary sources and answer the following questions.

■ How does each document address the issue of assimilation and identity?

■ Based on these documents, what pattern do you see in how Americans historically have responded to the arrival of new immigrant groups?

■ Which of the primary sources do you think Richwine and Chavez would find most useful, and how might they use them to support their arguments?

■ Which of the secondary sources do you think is best supported by the primary source evidence?

Primary Source 1

Benjamin Franklin, on the Germans (1755)

And since detachments of English from Britain sent to America, will have their places at home so soon supply'd and increase so largely here; why should the Palatine Boors [Germans] be suffered to swarm into our settlements, and by herding together establish their languages and manners to the exclusion of ours? Why should Pennsylvania, founded by the English, become a colony of Aliens, who will shortly be so numerous as to Germanize us instead of our Anglifying them, and will never adopt our language or customs, any more than they can acquire our complexion? Which leads me to add one remark: That the number of purely white people in the world is proportionally very small. All Africa is black or tawny. Asia chiefly tawny. America (exclusive of the new comers) wholly so. And in Europe, the Spaniards, Italians, French, Russians, and Swedes are generally of what we call a swarthy complexion; as are the Germans also, the Saxons only excepted, who with the English make the principal body of white people on the face of the earth. I could wish their numbers were increased. And while we are, as I may call it, scouring our planet, by clearing America of woods, and so making this side of our globe reflect a brighter light to the eyes of inhabitants in Mars or Venus, why should we in the sight of superior beings, darken its people? Why increase the sons of Africa, by planting them in America, where we have so fair an opportunity, by excluding all blacks and tawneys, of increasing the lovely white and red? But perhaps I am partial to the complexion of my Country, for such kind of partiality is natural to Mankind.

Source: Benjamin Franklin, *Observations Concerning the Increase of Mankind, Peopling of Countries, etc.* (Boston, MA: Printed and Sold by S. Kneeland in Queen Street, 1755), 224.

Primary Source 2

Senate of California to the Congress, on Chinese Immigration (1878)

The State of California has a population variously estimated at from seven hundred thousand to eight hundred thousand, of which one hundred and twenty-five thousand are Chinese. The additions to this class have been very rapid since the organization of the State, but have been caused almost entirely by immigration, and scarcely at all by natural increase....

The pious anticipations that the influence of Christianity upon the Chinese would be salutary, have proved unsubstantial and vain. Among one hundred and twenty-five thousand of them, with a residence here beneath the elevating influences of Christian precept and example, and with the zealous labors of earnest Christian teachers, and the liberal expenditure of ecclesiastical revenues, we have no evidence of a single genuine conversion to Christianity, or of a single instance of an assimilation with our manners, or habits of thought or life.... Neither is there any possibility that in the future education, religion, or the other influences of our civilization can effect any change in this condition of things....

Above and beyond these considerations, however, we believe, and the researches of those who have most attentively studied the Chinese character confirm us in the consideration, that the Chinese are incapable of adaptation to our institutions. The national intellect of China has become decrepit from sheer age. It has long since passed its prime and is waning into senility.... Their code of morals, their forms of worship, and their maxims of life are those of the remotest antiquity. In this aspect they stand a barrier against which the elevating tendency of a higher civilization exerts itself in vain. And, in an ethnological point of view, there can be no hope that any contact with our people, however long continued, will ever conform them to our institutions, enable them to comprehend or appreciate our form of government, or to assume the duties or discharge the functions of citizens.

During their entire settlement in California they have never adapted themselves to our habits, modes of dress, or our educational system, have never learned the sanctity of an oath, never desired to become citizens, or to perform the duties of citizenship, never discovered the difference between right and wrong, never ceased the worship of their idol gods, or advanced a step beyond the musty traditions of their native hive. Impregnable to all the influences of our Anglo-Saxon life, they remain the same stolid Asiatics that have floated on the rivers and slaved in the fields of China for thirty centuries of time.

We thus find one-sixth of our entire population composed of Chinese coolies, not involuntary, but, by the unalterable structure of their intellectual being, voluntary slaves. This alien mass, constantly increasing by Immigration, is injected into a republic of freemen, eating of its substance, expelling free white labor, and contributing nothing to the support of the government. All of the physical conditions of California are in the highest degree favorable to their influx. Our climate is essentially Asiatic in all its aspects. And the Federal Government by its legislation and treaties fosters and promotes the immigration. What is to be the result? Does it require any prophetic power to foretell? Can American statesmen project their vision forward for a quarter of a century and convince themselves that this problem will work out for itself a wise solution? In that brief period, with the same ratio of increase, this fair State will contain a Chinese population outnumbering its free men. White labor will be unknown, because unobtainable, and then how long a period will elapse before California will, nay must, become essentially . . . lesser Asia, with all its deathly lethargy?

Source: "Memorial of the Senate of California to the Congress of the United States," *Chinese Immigration; Its Social, Moral, and Political Effect. Report to the California State Senate of Its Special Committee on Chinese Immigration* (Sacramento: State Office, F. P. Thompson, Supt. State Printing, 1878), 60, 62–4.

Primary Source 3

Henry Cabot Lodge, "The Restriction of Immigration" (1891)

The nations of Europe which chiefly contributed to the upbuilding of the original thirteen colonies were the English, the Scotch-Irish, so called, the Dutch, the Germans, and the Huguenot French. With the exception of the last they were practically all people of the same stock. During this century and until very recent years these same nations, with the addition of Ireland and the Scandinavian countries, have continued to furnish the chief component parts of the immigration which has helped to populate so rapidly the territory of the United States. Among all these people, with few exceptions, community of race or language, or both, has facilitated the work of assimilation. In the last ten years, however, as appears from the figures just given, new and wholly different elements have been introduced into our immigration, and what is more important still the rate of immigration of these new elements has risen with much greater rapidity than that of those which previously had furnished the bulk of the population of the country. The mass of immigration, absolutely speaking, continues, of course, to come from the United Kingdom and from Germany, but relatively the immigration from these two sources is declining rapidly in comparison with the immigration from Italy and from the Slavic countries of Russia, Poland, Hungary, and Bohemia, the last of which appears under the head of Austria. . . .

Thus it is proved, first, that immigration to this country is increasing, and, second, that it is making its greatest relative increase from races most alien to the body of the American people and from the lowest and most illiterate classes among those races. In other words, it is apparent that, while our immigration is increasing, it is showing at the same time a marked tendency to deteriorate in character. . . . As one example of the practical effect of unrestricted immigration the committee [of the Fiftieth Congress to investigate immigration] cite the case of the coal-mining country: "Generally speaking, the class of immigrants who have lately been imported and employed in the coal regions of this country are not such, in the opinion of the committee, as would make desirable inhabitants of the United States. They are of a very low order of intelligence. They do not come here with the intention of becoming citizens; their whole purpose being to accumulate by parsimonious, rigid, and unhealthy economy a sum of money and then return to their native land. They live in miserable sheds like beasts; the food they eat is so meagre, scant, unwholesome, and revolting that it would nauseate and disgust an American workman, and he would find it difficult to sustain life upon it. Their habits are vicious, their customs are disgusting, and the effect of their presence here upon our social condition is to be deplored. . . . [I]n the opinion of the committee, no amount of effort would improve their morals or 'Americanize' this class of immigrants."

Source: Henry Cabot Lodge, "The Restriction of Immigration," *North American Review* 152, no. 410 (Jan. 1891), 28, 30, 32–33.

Primary Source 4

Nathan Glazer and Daniel Patrick Moynihan, on the Nonexistent "American" (1963)

Perhaps the meaning of ethnic labels will yet be erased in America. But it has not yet worked out this way in New York. It is true that immigrants to this country were rapidly transformed, in comparison with immigrants to other countries, that they lost their language and altered their culture. It was reasonable to believe that a new American type would emerge, a new nationality in which it would be a matter of indifference whether a man was of Anglo-Saxon or German or Italian or Jewish origin, and in which indeed, because of the diffusion of populations through all parts of the country and all levels of the social order, and because of the consequent close contact and intermarriage, it would be impossible to make such distinctions. This may still be the most likely result in the long run. After all, in 1960 almost half of New York City's population was still foreign-born or the children of foreign-born. Yet it is also true that it is forty years since the end of mass immigration, and new processes, scarcely visible when our chief concern was with the great masses of immigrants and the problems of their "Americanization," now emerge to surprise us. The initial notion of an American melting pot did not, it seems, quite grasp what would happen in America. At least it did not grasp what would happen in the short run, and since this short run encompasses at least the length of a normal lifetime, it is not something we can ignore.

It is true that language and culture are very largely lost in the first and second generations, and this makes the dream of "cultural pluralism"—of a new Italy or Germany or Ireland in America, a League of Nations established in the New World—as unlikely as the hope of a "melting pot." But as the groups were transformed by influences in American society, stripped of their original attributes, they were recreated as something new, but still as identifiable groups. Concretely, persons think of themselves as members of that group, with that name; they are thought of by others as members of that group, with that name; and most significantly, they are linked to other members of the group by new attributes that the original immigrants would never have recognized as identifying their group, but which nevertheless serve to mark them off, by more than simply name and association, in the third generation and even beyond.

The assimilating power of American society and culture operated on immigrant groups in different ways, to make them, it is true, something they had not been, but still something distinct and identifiable. The impact of assimilating trends on the groups is different in part because the groups are different—Catholic peasants from Southern Italy were affected differently, in the same city and the same time, from urbanized Jewish workers and merchants from Eastern Europe. . . .

Conceivably the fact that one's origins can become only a memory suggests the general direction for ethnic groups in the United States—toward assimilation and absorption into a homogeneous American mass. And yet, as we suggested earlier, it is hard to see in the New York of the 1960s just how this comes about. Time alone does not dissolve the groups if they are not close to the Anglo-Saxon center. Color marks off a group, regardless of time; and perhaps most significantly, the "majority" group, to which assimilation should occur, has taken on the color of an ethnic group, too. To what does one assimilate in modern America? The "American" in abstract does not exist, though some sections of the country, such as the Far West, come closer to realizing him than does New York City.

Source: Nathan Glazer and Daniel Patrick Moynihan, *Beyond the Melting Pot: The Negroes, Puerto Ricans, Jews, Italians, and Irish of New York City* (Cambridge, MA: Massachusetts Institute of Technology Press and Harvard University Press, 1963), 12–14, 20.

Glossary

36°30′ According to the Missouri Compromise, any part of the Louisiana Purchase north of this line (Missouri's southern border) was to be excluded from slavery.

54th Massachusetts Regiment After President Abraham Lincoln's Emancipation Proclamation, the Union army organized all black military units, which white officers led. The 54th Massachusetts Regiment was one of the first of such units to be organized.

Abigail Adams (1744–1818) As the wife of John Adams, she endured long periods of separation from him while he served in many political roles. During these times apart, she wrote often to her husband, and their correspondence has provided a detailed portrait of life during the Revolutionary War.

abolition In the early 1830s, the anti-slavery movement shifted its goal from the gradual end of slavery to the immediate end or abolition of slavery.

abolitionism Movement that called for an immediate end to slavery throughout the United States.

John Adams (1735–1826) He was a signer of the Declaration of Independence and a delegate to the First and Second Continental Congresses. A member of the Federalist Party, he served as the first vice president and the second president of the United States. As president, he passed the Alien and Sedition Acts and endured a stormy relationship with France, which included the XYZ affair.

John Quincy Adams (1767–1848) As secretary of state, he urged President Monroe to issue the Monroe Doctrine, which incorporated his belief in an expanded use of federal powers. As the sixth president, Adams's nationalism and praise of European leaders caused a split in his party, causing some Republicans to leave and form the Democrat party.

Samuel Adams (1722–1803) A genius of revolutionary agitation, he believed that English Parliament had no right to legislate for the colonies. He organized the Sons of Liberty as well as protests in Boston against the British.

Jane Addams (1860–1935) She founded and ran of one of the best known settlement houses, the Hull House. Active in the peace and suffragist movements, she established child care for working mothers, health clinics, job training, and other social programs.

affirmative action Programs designed to give preferential treatment to women and minorities as compensation for past injustices.

Affordable Care Act (ACA) (2010) Vast health-care reform initiative signed into law and championed by President Obama, and widely criticized by Republicans, that aims to make health insurance more affordable and make health care accessible to everyone, regardless of income or prior medical conditions.

Agricultural Adjustment Act (1933) Legislation that paid farmers to produce less in order to raise crop prices for all; the AAA was later declared unconstitutional by the U.S. Supreme Court in the case of *United States v. Butler* (1936).

Emilio Aguinaldo (1869?–1964) He was a leader in the Filipino struggle for independence. During the war of 1898, Commodore George Dewey brought Aguinaldo back to the Philippines from exile to help fight the Spanish. However, after the Spanish surrendered to Americans, America annexed the Philippines and Aguinaldo fought against the American military until he was captured in 1901.

Alamo, Battle of the Siege in the Texas War for Independence of 1836, in which the San Antonio mission fell to the Mexicans. Davy Crockett and Jim Bowie were among the courageous defenders.

Albany Plan of Union A failed proposal by the seven northern colonies in anticipation of the French and Indian War, urging the unification of the colonies under one Crown-appointed president.

Alien and Sedition Acts of 1798 Four measures passed during the undeclared war with France that limited the freedoms of speech and press and restricted the liberty of non-citizens.

Allied Powers The nations fighting the Central Powers during the First World War, including France, Great Britain, and Russia; later joined by Italy and, after Russia quit the war in 1917, the United States.

American Anti-Imperialist League Coalition of anti-imperialist groups united in 1899 to protest American territorial expansion, especially in the Philippine Islands; its membership included prominent politicians, industrialists, labor leaders, and social reformers.

American Colonization Society Established in 1817, an organization whose mission was to return freed slaves to Africa.

American Federation of Labor Founded in 1881 as a national federation of trade unions made up of skilled workers.

American Indian Movement (AIM) Fed up with the poor conditions on Indian reservations and the federal government's unwillingness to help, Native Americans founded the American Indian Movement (AIM) in 1963. In 1973, AIM led 200 Sioux in the occupation of Wounded Knee. After a ten-week standoff with the federal authorities, the government agreed to reexamine Indian treaty rights and the occupation ended.

American Recovery and Reinvestment Act Hoping to restart the weak economy, President Obama signed this $787-billion economic stimulus bill in February of 2009. The bill included cash distributions to states, funds for food stamps, unemployment benefits, construction projects to renew the nation's infrastructure, funds for renewable-energy systems, and tax reductions.

American System Economic plan championed by Henry Clay of Kentucky that called for federal tariffs on imports, a strong national bank, and federally-financed internal improvements—roads, bridges, canals—all intended to strengthen the national economy and end American dependence on Great Britain.

American Tobacco Company Business founded in 1890 by North Carolina's James Buchanan Duke, who combined the major tobacco manufacturers of the time, ultimately controlling 90 percent of the country's cigarette production.

Anaconda Plan The Union's primary war strategy calling for a naval blockade of major southern seaports and then dividing the Confederacy by gaining control of the Tennessee, Cumberland, and Mississippi Rivers.

Annapolis Convention In 1786, all thirteen colonies were invited to a convention in Annapolis to discuss commercial problems, but only representatives from five states attended. However, the convention was not a complete failure because the delegates decided to have another convention in order to write the constitution.

Battle of Antietam (1862) Turning-point battle near Sharpsburg, Maryland, leaving over 20,000 soldiers dead or wounded, in which Union forces halted a Confederate invasion of the North.

anti-Federalists Opponents of the Constitution as an infringement on individual and states' rights, whose criticism led to the addition of a Bill of Rights to the document.

Many anti-Federalists later joined Thomas Jefferson's Democratic-Republican party.

Anti-Masonic party This party grew out of popular hostility toward the Masonic fraternal order and entered the presidential election of 1832 as a third party. It was the first party to run as a third party in a presidential election as well as the first to hold a nomination convention and announce a party platform.

Appomattox Court House Virginia village where Confederate general Robert E. Lee surrendered to Union general Ulysses S. Grant on April 9, 1865.

Arab Awakening A wave of spontaneous democratic uprisings that spread throughout the Arab world beginning in 2011, in which long-oppressed peoples demanded basic liberties from generations-old authoritarian regimes.

Benedict Arnold (1741–1801) A traitorous American commander who planned to sell out the American garrison at West Point to the British; his plot was discovered before it could be executed and he joined the British army.

Articles of Confederation The first form of government for the United States, ratified by the original thirteen states in 1781; weak in central authority, it was replaced by the U.S. Constitution in 1789.

The Atlanta Compromise A speech by Booker T. Washington that called for the black community to strive for economic prosperity before attempting political and social equality.

Atlantic Charter (1941) Joint statement crafted by Franklin D. Roosevelt and British prime minister Winston Churchill that listed the war goals of the Allied Powers.

Aztec Empire A network of more than 300 city-states and upward of 30 provinces, established in the fourteenth century under the imperialistic Mexica, or Aztecs, in the valley of Mexico.

Crispus Attucks (1723–1770) During the Boston Massacre, he was supposedly at the head of the crowd of hecklers who baited the British troops. He was killed when the British troops fired on the crowd.

Stephen F. Austin (1793–1836) He established the first colony of Americans in Texas, which eventually attracted 2,000 people.

"Axis" alliance Military alliance formed in 1937 by the three major fascist powers: Germany, Italy, and Japan.

Aztec Empire Mesoamerican people who were conquered by the Spanish under Hernando Cortés, 1519–1528.

baby boom Markedly high birth rate in the years following World War II, leading to the biggest demographic "bubble" in U.S. history.

Bacon's Rebellion Unsuccessful 1676 revolt led by planter Nathaniel Bacon against Virginia governor William Berkeley's administration, which, Bacon charged, had failed to protect settlers from Indian raids.

Bank of the United States (1791) National bank responsible for holding and transferring federal government funds, making business loans, and issuing a national currency.

The Bank War Political struggle in the early 1830s between President Jackson and financier Nicholas Biddle over the renewing of the Second Bank's charter.

Barbary pirates North Africans who waged war (1801–1805) on the United States after President Thomas Jefferson refused to pay tribute (a bribe) to protect American ships.

Bay of Pigs Failed CIA operation that, in April 1961, deployed a band of Cuban rebels to overthrow Fidel Castro's Communist regime.

Battle of the Bulge On December 16, 1944, the German army launched a counterattack against the Allied forces, which pushed them back. However, the Allies were eventually able to recover and break through the German lines. This defeat was a great blow to the Nazi's morale and their army's strength. The battle used up the last of Hitler's reserve units and opened a route into Germany's heartland.

Bear Flag Republic On June 14, 1846, a group of Americans in California captured Sonoma from the Mexican army and declared it the Republic of California whose flag featured a grizzly bear. In July, the commodore of the U.S. Pacific Fleet landed troops on California's shores and declared it part of the United States.

Beats Group of bohemian, downtown New York writers, artists, and musicians who flouted convention in favor of liberated forms of self-expression.

beatnik A name referring to almost any young rebel who openly dissented from the middle-class life. The name itself stems from the Beats.

Berlin airlift (1948) Effort by the United States and Great Britain to deliver massive amounts of food and supplies flown to West Berlin in response to the Soviet land blockade of the city.

Berlin Wall Twenty-seven-mile-long concrete wall constructed in 1961 by East German authorities to stop the flow of East Germans fleeing to West Berlin.

Bessemer converter Apparatus that blasts air through molten iron to produce steel in very large quantities.

Nicholas Biddle (1786–1844) He was the president of the second Bank of the United States. In response to President Andrew Jackson's attacks on the bank, Biddle curtailed the bank's loans and exchanged its paper currency for gold and silver. In response, state banks began printing paper without restraint and lent it to speculators, causing a binge in speculating and an enormous increase in debt.

Bill of Rights First ten amendments to the U.S. Constitution, adopted in 1791 to guarantee individual rights and to help secure ratification of the Constitution by the states.

Osama bin Laden (1957–2011) The Saudi-born leader of al Qaeda, whose members attacked America on September 11, 2001. Years before the attack, he had declared *jihad* (holy war) on the United States, Israel, and the Saudi monarchy. In Afghanistan, the Taliban leaders gave bin Laden a safe haven in exchange for aid in fighting the Northern Alliance, who were rebels opposed to the Taliban. Following the Taliban's refusal to turn over bin Laden to the United States, America and a multinational coalition invaded Afghanistan and overthrew the Taliban. In May 2011, bin Laden was shot and killed by American special forces during a covert operation in Pakistan.

birth rate Proportion of births per 1,000 of the total population.

black codes Laws passed in southern states to restrict the rights of former slaves; to combat the codes, Congress passed the Civil Rights Act of 1866 and the Fourteenth Amendment and set up military governments in southern states that refused to ratify the amendment.

black power movement Militant form of civil rights protest focused on urban communities in the North and led by Malcolm X that grew as a response to impatience with the nonviolent tactics of Martin Luther King, Jr.

James Gillepsie Blaine (1830–1893) As a Republican congressman from Maine, he developed close ties with business leaders, which contributed to him losing the presidential election of 1884. He later opposed President Cleveland's efforts to reduce tariffs, which became a significant issue in the 1888 presidential election. Blaine served as secretary of state under President Benjamin Harrison.

Bleeding Kansas (1856) A series of violent conflicts in the Kansas territory between anti-slavery and pro-slavery factions over the status of slavery.

blitzkrieg (1940) The German "lightning war" strategy characterized by swift, well-organized attacks using infantry, tanks, and warplanes.

Bolsheviks Under the leadership of Vladimir Lenin, this Marxist party led the November 1917 revolution against the newly formed provisional government in Russia. After seizing control, the Bolsheviks negotiated a peace treaty with Germany, the Treaty of Brest-Litovsk, and ended their participation in World War I.

Bonus Expeditionary Force (1932) Protest march in Washington, D.C. by thousands of World War I veterans and their families, calling for immediate payment of their service bonuses certificates; violence ensued when President Herbert Hoover ordered their tent villages cleared.

boomtown Town, often in the West, that developed rapidly due to the sudden influx of wealth and work opportunities; often male-dominated with a substantial immigrant population.

Daniel Boone (1734–1820) He found and expanded a trail into Kentucky, which pioneers used to reach and settle the area.

John Wilkes Booth (1838?–1865) He assassinated President Abraham Lincoln at the Ford's Theater on April 14, 1865. He was pursued and killed.

Boston Massacre Violent confrontation between British soldiers and a Boston mob on March 5, 1770, in which five colonists were killed.

Boston Tea Party Demonstration against the Tea Act of 1773 in which the Sons of Liberty, dressed as Indians, dumped hundreds of chests of British-owned tea into Boston Harbor.

Bourbons In post–Civil War southern politics, the opponents of the Redeemers were called Bourbons. They were known for having forgotten nothing and learned nothing from the ordeal of the Civil War.

***bracero* program (1942)** System created in 1942 that permitted seasonal farm workers from Mexico to work in the United States on year-long contracts.

Joseph Brant (1742?–1807) Mohawk leader who led the Iroquois against the Americans in the Revolutionary War.

brinksmanship Secretary of State John Foster Dulles believed that communism could be contained by bringing America to the brink of war with an aggressive Communist nation. He believed that the aggressor would back down when confronted with the prospect of receiving a mass retaliation from a country with nuclear weapons.

John Brown (1800–1859) In response to a pro-slavery mob's sacking of the free-state town of Lawrence, Kansas, Brown went to the pro-slavery settlement of Pottawatomie, Kansas, which led to a guerrilla war in the Kansas territory. In 1859, he attempted to raid the federal arsenal at Harpers Ferry, hoping to use the stolen weapons to arm slaves, but he was captured and executed.

***Brown v. Board of Education* (1952)** Landmark Supreme Court case that struck down racial segregation in public schools and declared "separate-but-equal" unconstitutional.

William Jennings Bryan (1860–1925) He delivered the pro-silver "cross of gold" speech at the 1896 Democratic Convention and won his party's nomination for president. Disappointed pro-gold Democrats chose to walk out of the convention and nominate their own candidate, which split the Democratic party and cost them the White House. Bryan's loss also crippled the Populist movement that had endorsed him.

"Bull Moose" Progressive party *See* Progressive party

Bull Run, Battles of (First and Second Manassas) First land engagement of the Civil War took place on July 21, 1861, at Manassas Junction, Virginia, at which surprised Union troops quickly retreated; one year later, on August 29–30, Confederates captured the federal supply depot and forced Union troops back to Washington.

Martin Van Buren (1782–1862) During President Jackson's first term, he served as secretary of state and minister to London. In 1836, Van Buren was elected president, and he inherited a financial crisis. He believed that the government should not continue to keep its deposits in state banks and set up an independent Treasury, which was approved by Congress after several years of political maneuvering.

General John Burgoyne (1722–1792) He was the commander of Britain's northern forces during the Revolutionary War. He and most of his troops surrendered to the Americans at the Battle of Saratoga.

burial mounds A funeral tradition, practiced in the Mississippi and Ohio Valleys by the Adena-Hopewell cultures, of erecting massive mounds of earth over graves, often in the designs of serpents and other animals.

burned-over district Area of western New York strongly influenced by the revivalist fervor of the Second Great Awakening; Disciples of Christ and Mormons are among the many sects that trace their roots to the phenomenon.

Aaron Burr (1756–1836) Even though he was Thomas Jefferson's vice president, he lost favor with Jefferson's Republican supporters. He sought to work with the Federalists and run as their candidate for the governor of New York. Alexander Hamilton opposed Burr's candidacy and his stinging remarks on the subject led to Burr challenging him to duel in which Hamilton was killed.

George H. W. Bush (1924–) He served as vice president during the Reagan administration and then won the presidential election of 1988. His presidency was marked by raised taxes in the face of the federal deficit, the creation of the Office of National Drug Control Policy, and military activity abroad, including the invasion of Panama and Operation Desert Storm in Kuwait. He lost the 1992 presidential election to Bill Clinton.

George W. Bush (1946–) In the 2000 presidential election, Texas governor George W. Bush won as the Republican nominee against Democratic nominee Vice President Al Gore. After the September 11 terrorist attacks, he launched his "war on terrorism." President Bush adopted the Bush Doctrine, and United States invaded Afghanistan and Iraq with unclear outcomes leaving the countries divided. In September 2008, the nation's economy nose-dived as a credit crunch spiraled into a global economic meltdown. Bush signed into law the bank bailout fund called Troubled Asset Relief Program (TARP), but the economy did not improve.

Bush v. Gore (2000) The close 2000 presidential election came down to Florida's decisive twenty-five electoral votes. The final tally in Florida gave Bush a slight lead, but it was so small that a recount was required by state law. While the votes were being recounted, a legal battle was being waged to stop the recount. Finally, the case, *Bush v. Gore*, was presented to the Supreme Court who ruled 5–4 to stop the recount and Bush was declared the winner.

Bush Doctrine National security policy launched in 2002 by which the Bush administration claimed the right to launch preemptive military attacks against perceived enemies, particularly outlaw nations or terrorist organizations believed to possess weapons of mass destruction.

buying (stock) on margin The investment practice of making a small down payment (the "margin") on a stock and borrowing the rest of the money needed for the purchase from a broker who held the stock as security against a down market. If the stock's value declined and the buyer failed to meet a margin call for more funds, the broker could sell the stock to cover his loan.

Cahokia The largest chiefdom and city of the Mississippian Indian culture located in present-day Illinois, and the site of a sophisticated farming settlement that supported up to 15,000 inhabitants.

John C. Calhoun (1782–1850) He served in both the House of Representatives and the Senate for South Carolina before becoming secretary of war under President Monroe and then John Quincy Adams's vice president. Though he started his political career as an advocate of a strong national government, he eventually believed that states' rights, limited central government, and the power of nullification were necessary to preserve the Union.

California Gold Rush (1849) A massive migration of gold hunters, mostly men, who transformed the economy of California after gold was discovered in the foothills of northern California.

Camp David Accords (1978) Peace agreement between Prime Minister Menachem Begin of Israel and President Anwar Sadat of Egypt, the first Arab head of state to officially recognize the state of Israel.

"Scarface" Al Capone (1899–1947) The most successful gangster of the Prohibition era whose Chicago-based criminal empire included bootlegging, prostitution, and gambling.

Andrew Carnegie (1835–1919) A steel magnate who believed that the general public benefited from big business even if these companies employed harsh business practices. This philosophy became deeply ingrained in the conventional wisdom of some Americans. After retiring, he devoted himself to philanthropy in hopes of promoting social welfare and world peace.

Carnegie Steel Company Corporation under the leadership of Andrew Carnegie that came to dominate the American steel industry.

Carolina colonies English proprietary colonies comprised of North and South Carolina, whose semitropical climate made them profitable centers of rice, timber, and tar production.

carpetbaggers Northern emigrants who participated in the Republican governments of the reconstructed South.

Jimmy Carter (1924–) Elected president in 1976, Jimmy Carter was an outsider to Washington. He created the departments of Energy and Education and signed into law several environmental initiatives. In 1978, he successfully brokered a peace agreement between Israel and Egypt called the Camp David Accords. However, his unwillingness to make deals with legislators caused other bills to be either gutted or stalled in Congress. His administration was plagued with a series of crises: a recession and increased inflation, a fuel shortage, the Soviet invasion of Afghanistan, and the overthrow of the Shah of Iran, leading to the Iran Hostage Crisis. Carter struggled to get the hostages released and was unable to do so until after he lost the 1980 election to Ronald Reagan. He was awarded the Nobel Peace Prize in 2002 for his efforts to further peace and democratic elections around the world.

Jacques Cartier (1491–1557) He led the first French effort to colonize North America and explored the Gulf of St. Lawrence, reaching as far as present day Montreal on the St. Lawrence River.

Fidel Castro (1926–) In 1959, his Communist regime came to power in Cuba after two years of guerrilla warfare against the dictator Fulgenico Batista. He enacted land redistribution programs and nationalized all foreign-owned property. The latter action as well as his political trials and summary executions damaged relations between Cuba and America. Castro was turned down when he asked for loans from the United States. However, he did receive aid from the Soviet Union.

Central Intelligence Agency (CIA) Intelligence-gathering government agency founded in 1947; under President Eisenhower's orders, secretly undermined elected governments deemed susceptible to communism.

Central Powers One of the two sides during the First World War, including Germany, Austria-Hungary, the Ottoman Empire (Turkey), and Bulgaria.

Carrie Chapman Catt (1859–1947) She was a leader of a new generation of activists in the women's suffrage movement who carried on the work started by Elizabeth Cady Stanton and Susan B. Anthony.

Cesar Chavez (1927–1993) He founded the United Farm Workers (UFW) in 1962 and worked to organize migrant farm workers. In 1965, the UFW joined Filipino farm workers striking against corporate grape farmers in California's San Joaquin Valley. In 1970, the strike and a consumer boycott on grapes compelled the farmers to formally recognize the UFW. As the result of Chavez's efforts, wages and working conditions improved for migrant workers. In 1975, the California state legislature passed a bill that required growers to bargain collectively with representatives of the farm workers.

child labor The practice of sending children to work in mines, mills, and factories, often in unsafe conditions; widespread among poor families in the late nineteenth century.

Chinese Exclusion Act (1882) Federal law that barred Chinese laborers from immigrating to America.

Church of Jesus Christ of Latter-day Saints / Mormons Founded in 1830 by Joseph Smith, the sect was a product of the intense revivalism of the burned-over district of New York; Smith's successor Brigham Young led 15,000 followers to Utah in 1847 to escape persecution.

Winston Churchill (1874–1965) The British prime minister who led the country during the Second World War. Along with Roosevelt and Stalin, he helped shape the post-war world at the Yalta Conference. He also coined the term "iron curtain," which he used in his famous "The Sinews of Peace" speech.

citizen-soldiers Part-time non-professional soldiers, mostly poor farmers or recent immigrants who had been indentured servants, who played an important role in the Revolutionary War.

"city machines" Local political party officials used these organizations to dispense patronage and favoritism amongst voters and businesses to ensure their loyal support to the political party.

Civil Rights Act of 1957 First federal civil rights law since Reconstruction; established the Civil Rights Commission and the Civil Rights Division of the Department of Justice.

Civil Rights Act of 1964 Legislation that outlawed discrimination in public accommodations and employment, passed at the urging of President Lyndon B. Johnson.

civil service reform An extended effort led by political reformers to end the patronage system; led to the Pendleton Act (1883), which called for government positions to be awarded based on merit rather than party loyalty.

Henry Clay (1777–1852) In the first half of the nineteenth century, he was the foremost spokesman for the American system. As Speaker of the House in the 1820s, he promoted economic nationalism, "market revolution," and the rapid development of western states and territories. A broker of compromise, he formulated the "second" Missouri Compromise and the Compromise of 1850. In 1824, Clay supported John Quincy Adams, who won the presidency and appointed Clay to secretary of state. Andrew Jackson claimed that Clay had entered into a "corrupt bargain" with Adams for his own selfish gains.

Clayton Anti-Trust Act (1914) Legislation that served to enhance the Sherman Anti-Trust Act (1890) by clarifying what constituted "monopolistic" activities and declaring that labor unions were not to be viewed as "monopolies in restraint of trade."

Bill Clinton (1946–) The governor of Arkansas won the 1992 presidential election against President George H. W. Bush. In his first term, he pushed through Congress a tax increase, an economic stimulus package, the adoption of the North America Free Trade Agreement, welfare reform, a raise in the minimum wage, and improved public access to health insurance. His administration also negotiated the Oslo Accord and the Dayton Accords. After his re-election in 1996, he was involved in two high-profile scandals: his investment in the fraudulent Whitewater Development Corporation (but no evidence was found of him being involved in any wrongdoing) and his sexual affair with a White House intern. His attempt to cover up the affair led to a vote in Congress on whether or not to begin an impeachment inquiry. The House of Representatives voted to impeach Clinton, but the Senate found him not guilty.

Hillary Rodham Clinton (1947–) In the 2008 presidential election, Senator Hillary Clinton, the spouse of former President Bill Clinton, initially was the front-runner for the Democratic nomination, which made her the first woman with a serious chance to win the presidency. However, Senator Barack Obama's Internet-based and grassroots-orientated campaign garnered him enough delegates to win the nomination. After Obama became president, she was appointed secretary of state.

clipper ships Tall, slender, mid-nineteenth-century sailing ships that were favored over older merchant ships for their speed, but ultimately gave way to steamships because they lacked cargo space.

Coercive Acts Four parliamentary measures of 1774 that required the colonies to pay for the Boston Tea Party's damages, imposed a military government, disallowed colonial trials of British soldiers, and forced the quartering of troops in private homes.

coffin ships Irish immigrants fleeing the potato famine had to endure a six-week journey across the Atlantic to reach America. During these voyages, thousands of passengers died of disease and starvation, which led to the ships being called "coffin ships."

Columbian Exchange The transfer of biological and social elements, such as plants, animals, people, diseases, and cultural practices, among Europe, the Americas, and Africa in the wake of Christopher Columbus's voyages to the "New World."

Christopher Columbus (1451–1506) The Italian sailor who persuaded King Ferdinad and Queen Isabella of Spain to fund his expedition across the Atlantic to discover a new trade route to Asia. Instead of arriving at China or Japan, he reached the Bahamas in 1492.

Committee of Correspondence Group organized by Samuel Adams in retaliation for the *Gaspée* incident to address American grievances, assert American rights, and form a network of rebellion.

Committee on Public Information During the First World War, this committee produced war propaganda that conveyed the Allies' war aims to Americans as well as attempted to weaken the enemy's morale.

Committee to Re-elect the President (CREEP) During Nixon's presidency, his administration engaged in a number of immoral acts, such as attempting to steal information and falsely accusing political appointments of sexual improprieties. These acts were funded by money illegally collected through CREEP.

Common Sense Popular pamphlet written by Thomas Paine attacking British principles of hereditary rule and monarchical government, and advocating a declaration of American independence.

Compromise of 1850 A package of five bills presented to the Congress by Henry Clay intended to avoid secession or civil war by reducing tensions between North and South over the status of slavery.

Compromise of 1877 Deal made by a special congressional commission on March 2, 1877, to resolve the disputed presidential election of 1876; Republican Rutherford B. Hayes, who had lost the popular vote, was declared the winner in exchange for the withdrawal of federal troops from the South, marking the end of Reconstruction.

Comstock Lode Mine in eastern Nevada acquired by Canadian fur trapper Henry Comstock that between 1860 and 1880 yielded almost $1 billion worth of gold and silver.

Conestoga wagons These large horse-drawn wagons were used to carry people or heavy freight long distances, including from the East to the western frontier settlements.

conquistadores Spanish term for "conquerors," applied to Spanish and Portuguese soldiers who conquered lands held by indigenous peoples in central and southern America as well as the current states of Texas, New Mexico, Arizona, and California.

consumer culture A society in which mass production and consumption of nationally advertised products comes to dictate much of social life and status.

containment U.S. cold war strategy that sought to prevent global Soviet expansion and influence through political, economic, and, if necessary, military pressure as a means of combating the spread of communism.

Continental army Army authorized by the Continental Congress, 1775–1784, to fight the British; commanded by General George Washington.

Contract with America (1994) A list of conservative promises in response to the supposed liberalism of the Clinton administration, that was drafted by Speaker of the House Newt Gingrich and other congressional Republicans as the GOP platform for the 1994 midterm elections. More a campaign tactic than a practical program, few of its proposed items ever became law.

contrabands Slaves who sought refuge in Union military camps or who lived in areas of the Confederacy under Union control.

Contras The Reagan administration ordered the CIA to train and supply guerrilla bands of anti-Communist Nicaraguans called Contras. They were fighting the Sandinista government that had recently come to power in Nicaragua. The State Department believed that the Sandinista government was supplying the leftist Salvadoran rebels with Soviet and Cuban arms. A cease-fire agreement between the Contras and Sandinistas was signed in 1988.

Calvin Coolidge (1872–1933) After President Harding's death, his vice president, Calvin Coolidge, assumed the presidency. Coolidge believed that the nation's welfare was tied to the success of Big Business, and he worked to end government regulation of business and industry as well as reduce taxes. In particular, he focused on the nation's industrial development.

Copperhead Democrats Democrats in northern states who opposed the Civil War and argued for an immediate peace settlement with the Confederates; Republicans labeled them "Copperheads," likening them to venomous snakes.

Hernán Cortés (1485–1547) The Spanish conquistador who conquered the Aztec Empire and set the precedent for other plundering conquistadores.

General Charles Cornwallis (1738–1805) He was in charge of British troops in the South during the Revolutionary War. His surrender to George Washington at the Battle of Yorktown ended the Revolutionary War.

Corps of Discovery Meriwether Lewis and William Clark led this group of men on an expedition of the newly purchased Louisiana territory, which took them from Missouri to Oregon. As they traveled, they kept detailed journals and drew maps of the previously unexplored territory. Their reports attracted traders and trappers to the region and gave the United States a claim to the Oregon country by right of discovery and exploration.

"corrupt bargain" Scandal in which presidential candidate and Speaker of the House Henry Clay secured John Quincy Adams's victory over Andrew Jackson in the 1824 election, supposedly in exchange for Clay being named secretary of state.

cotton gin Hand-operated machine invented by Eli Whitney in the late eighteenth century that quickly removed seeds from cotton bolls, enabling the mass production of cotton in nineteenth-century America.

cotton kingdom Cotton-producing region, relying predominantly on slave labor, that spanned from North Carolina west to Louisiana and reached as far north as southern Illinois.

cotton White fibers harvested from cotton plants, spun into yarn, and woven into textiles that made comfortable, easy-to-clean products, especially clothing; the most valuable cash crop driving the economy in the United States and Great Britain during the nineteenth century.

the counterculture "Hippie" youth culture of the 1960s, which rejected the values of the dominant culture in favor of illicit drugs, communes, free sex, and rock music.

counterculture Unorganized youth rebellion against mainstream institutions, values, and behavior that more often focused on cultural rather than political activism.

court-packing plan President Franklin D. Roosevelt's failed 1937 attempt to increase the number of U.S. Supreme Court justices from nine to fifteen in order to save his Second New Deal programs from constitutional challenges.

covenant theory A Puritan concept that believed true Christians could enter a voluntary union for the common worship of God. Taking the idea one step further, the union could also be used for the purposes of establishing governments.

crop-lien system Credit system used by sharecroppers and share tenants who pledged a portion ("share") of their future crop to local merchants or land owners in exchange for farming supplies and food.

"Cross of Gold" Speech In the 1896 election, the Democratic Party split over the issue of whether to use gold or silver to back American currency. Significant to this division was the pro-silver "Cross of Gold" speech that William Jennings Bryan delivered at the Democratic convention, which was so well received that Bryan won the nomination to be their presidential candidate. Disappointed pro-gold Democrats chose to walk out of the convention and nominate their own candidate.

Cuban missile crisis Thirteen-day U.S.-Soviet standoff in October 1962, sparked by the discovery of Soviet missile sites in Cuba; the crisis was the closest the world has come to nuclear war since 1945.

cult of domesticity A pervasive nineteenth-century ideology that urged women to celebrate their role as manager of the household and nurturer of the children.

George A. Custer (1839–1876) He was a reckless and glory-seeking Lieutenant Colonel of the U.S. Army who fought the Sioux Indians in the Great Sioux War. In 1876, he and his detachment of soldiers were entirely wiped out in the Battle of Little Bighorn.

***Dartmouth College v. Woodward* (1819)** Supreme Court ruling that enlarged the definition of *contract* to put corporations beyond the reach of the states that chartered them.

Daughters of Liberty Colonial women who protested the British government's tax policies by boycotting British products, such as clothing, and who wove their own fabric, or "homespun."

Dawes Severalty Act of 1887 Federal legislation that divided ancestral Native American lands among the heads of each Indian family in an attempt to "Americanize" Indians by forcing them to become farmers working individual plots of land.

D-day June 6, 1944, when an Allied amphibious assault landed on the Normandy coast and established a foothold in Europe from which Hitler's defenses could not recover.

Jefferson Davis (1808–1889) He was the president of the Confederacy during the Civil War. When the Confederacy's defeat seemed invitable in early 1865, he refused to surrender. Union forces captured him in May of that year.

Bartolomé de Las Casas (1484–1566) A Catholic missionary who renounced the Spanish practice of coercively converting Indians and advocated their better treatment. In 1552, he wrote *A Brief Relation of the Destruction of the Indies*, which described the Spanish's cruel treatment of the Indians.

death rate Proportion of deaths per 1,000 of the total population; also called *mortality rate*.

Eugene V. Debs (1855–1926) Founder of the American Railway Union, which he organized against the Pullman Palace Car Company during the Pullman strike. Later he organized the Social Democratic party, which eventually became the Socialist Party of America. In the 1912 presidential election, he ran as the Socialist party's candidate and received more than 900,000 votes.

Declaration of Independence Formal statement, principally drafted by Thomas Jefferson and adopted by the Second Continental Congress on July 4, 1776, that officially announced the thirteen colonies' break with Great Britain.

Declaration of Sentiments Document based on the Declaration of Independence that called for gender equality, written primarily by Elizabeth Cady Stanton and signed by Seneca Falls Convention delegates in 1848.

Declaratory Act Following the repeal of the Stamp Act in 1766, Parliament passed this act which asserted Parliament's full power to make laws binding the colonies "in all cases whatsoever."

Deism Enlightenment thought applied to religion, emphasizing reason, morality, and natural law rather than scriptural authority or an ever-present God intervening in human life.

détente Period of improving relations between the United States and Communist nations, particularly China and the Soviet Union, during the Nixon administration.

George Dewey (1837–1917) On April 30, 1898, Commodore George Dewey's small U.S. naval squadron defeated the Spanish warships in Manila Bay in the Philippines. This quick victory aroused expansionist fever in the United States.

John Dewey (1859–1952) He is an important philosopher of pragmatism. However, he preferred to use the term *instrumentalism*, because he saw ideas as instruments of action.

Ngo Dinh Diem (1901–1963) Following the Geneva Accords, the French, with the support of America, forced the Vietnamese emperor to accept Dinh Diem as the new premier of South Vietnam. President Eisenhower sent advisors to train Diem's police and army. In return, the United States expected Diem to enact democratic reforms and distribute land to the peasants. Instead, he suppressed his political opponents, did little or no land distribution, and let corruption grow. In 1956, he refused to participate in elections to reunify Vietnam. Eventually, he ousted the emperor and declared himself president.

Distribution Act (1836) Law requiring the distribution of the federal budget surplus to the states, creating chaos among state banks that had become dependent on such federal funds.

Dorothea Lynde Dix (1802–1887) She was an important figure in increasing the public's awareness of the plight of the mentally ill. After a two-year investigation of the treatment of the mentally ill in Massachusetts, she presented her findings and won the support of leading reformers. She eventually convinced twenty states to reform their treatment of the mentally ill.

Dixiecrats Breakaway faction of southern Democrats who defected from the national Democratic party in 1948 to protest the party's increased support for civil rights and to nominate their own segregationist candidates for elective office.

"dollar diplomacy" practice advocated by President Theodore Roosevelt in which the U.S. government fostered American investments in less developed nations and then used U.S. military force to protect those investments

Donner party Forty-seven surviving members of a group of migrants to California were forced to resort to cannibalism to survive a brutal winter trapped in the Sierra Nevadas, 1846–1847; highest death toll of any group traveling the Overland Trail.

Stephen A. Douglas (1812–1861) As a senator from Illinois, he authored the Kansas-Nebraska Act. Running for senatorial reelection in 1858, he engaged Abraham Lincoln in a series of public debates about slavery in the territories. Even though Douglas won the election, the debates gave Lincoln a national reputation.

Frederick Douglass (1818–1895) He escaped from slavery and become an eloquent speaker and writer against the institution. In 1845, he published his autobiography entitled *Narrative of the Life of Frederick Douglass* and two years later he founded an abolitionist newspaper for blacks called the *North Star*.

dot-coms In the late 1990s, the stock market soared to new heights and defied the predictions of experts that the economy could not sustain such a performance. Much of the economic success was based on dot-com enterprises, which were firms specializing in computers, software, telecommunications, and the internet. However, many of the companies' stock market values were driven higher and higher by speculation instead of financial success. Eventually the stock market bubble burst.

***Dred Scott v. Sandford* (1857)** U.S. Supreme Court ruling that slaves were not U.S. citizens and therefore could not sue for their freedom and that Congress could not prohibit slavery in the western territories.

W. E. B. Du Bois (1868–1963) He criticized Booker T. Washington's views on civil rights as being accommodationist. He advocated "ceaseless agitation" for civil rights and the immediate end to segregation and an enforcement of laws to protect civil rights and equality. He promoted an education for African Americans that would nurture bold leaders who were willing to challenge discrimination in politics.

John Foster Dulles (1888–1959) As President Eisenhower's secretary of state, he institutionalized the policy of containment and introduced the strategy of deterrence. He believed in using brinkmanship to halt the spread of communism. He attempted to employ it in Indochina, which led to the United States' involvement in Vietnam.

Dust Bowl Vast area of the Midwest where windstorms blew away millions of tons of topsoil from parched farmland after a long drought in the 1930s, causing great social distress and a massive migration of farm families.

Eastern Woodlands Peoples Various Native American peoples, particularly the Algonquian, Iroquoian, and Muskogean regional groups, who once dominated the Atlantic seaboard from Maine to Louisiana.

Peggy Eaton (1796–1879) The wife of John Eaton, President Jackson's secretary of war, was the daughter of a tavern owner with an unsavory past. Supposedly her first husband had committed suicide after learning that she was having an affair with

John Eaton. The wives of members of Jackson's cabinet snubbed her because of her lowly origins and past, resulting in a scandal known as the Eaton Affair.

Economic Opportunity Act Key legislation in President Johnson's "War on Poverty" which created the Office of Economic Opportunity and programs like Head Start and work-study.

Jonathan Edwards (1703–1758) New England Congregationalist minister who began a religious revival in his Northampton church and was an important figure in the Great Awakening.

election of 1800 Presidential election between Thomas Jefferson and John Adams; resulted in the first Democratic-Republican victory after the Federalist administrations of George Washington and John Adams.

1864 Election Abraham Lincoln's successful re-election campaign, capitalizing on Union military successes in Georgia, to defeat Democratic opponent, former general George B. McClellan, who ran on a peace platform.

election of 1912 The presidential election of 1912 featured four candidates: Wilson, Taft, Roosevelt, and Debs. Each candidate believed in the basic assumptions of progressive politics, but each had a different view on how progressive ideals should be implemented through policy. In the end, Taft and Roosevelt split the Republican party votes and Wilson emerged as the winner.

Queen Elizabeth I of England (1533–1603) The protestant daughter of Henry VIII, she was Queen of England from 1558–1603 and played a major role in the Protestant Reformation. During her long reign, the doctrines and services of the Church of England were defined and the Spanish Armada was defeated.

General Dwight D. Eisenhower (1890–1969) During the Second World War, he commanded the Allied Forces landing in Africa and was the supreme Allied commander as well as planner for Operation Overlord. In 1952, he was elected president on his popularity as a war hero and his promises to clean up Washington. His administration sought to cut the nation's domestic programs and budget, ended the fighting in Korea, and institutionalized the policies of containment and deterrence. He established the Eisenhower doctrine, which promised to aid any nation against aggression by a Communist nation.

Ellis Island Reception center in New York Harbor through which most European immigrants to America were processed from 1892 to 1954.

Emancipation Proclamation (1863) Military order issued by President Abraham Lincoln that freed slaves in areas still controlled by the Confederacy

Embargo Act (1807) A law promoted by President Thomas Jefferson prohibiting American ships from leaving for foreign ports, in order to safeguard them from British and French attacks. This ban on American exports proved disastrous to the U.S. economy.

Ralph Waldo Emerson (1803–1882) As a leader of the transcendentalist movement, he wrote poems, essays, and speeches that discussed the sacredness of nature, optimism, self-reliance, and the unlimited potential of the individual. He wanted to transcend the limitations of inherited conventions and rationalism to reach the inner recesses of the self.

encomienda A land-grant system under which Spanish army officers (*conquistadores*) were awarded large parcels of land taken from Native Americans.

Enlightenment A revolution in thought begun in Europe in the seventeenth century that emphasized reason and science over the authority and myths of traditional religion.

enumerated goods According to the Navigation Act, these particular goods, like tobacco or cotton, could only be shipped to England or other English colonies.

Environmental Protection Agency (EPA) (1970) Federal environmental agency created by Nixon to appease the demands of congressional Democrats for a federal environmental watchdog agency.

Erie Canal Most important and profitable of the barge canals of the 1820s and 1830s; stretched from Buffalo to Albany, New York, connecting the Great Lakes to the East Coast and making New York City the nation's largest port.

ethnic cleansing The systematic removal of an ethnic group from a territory through violence or intimidation in order to create a homogenous society; the term was popularized by the Yugoslav policy brutally targeting Albanian Muslims in Kosovo.

exodusters African Americans who migrated west from the South in search of a haven from racism and poverty after the collapse of Radical Republican rule.

The Fair Deal (1949) President Truman's proposals to build upon the New Deal with national health insurance, the repeal of the Taft-Hartley Act, new civil rights legislation, and other initiatives; most were rejected by the Republican-controlled Congress.

Fair Employment Practices Commission Created in 1941 by executive order, the FEPC sought to eliminate racial discrimination in jobs; it possessed little power but represented a step toward civil rights for African Americans.

falling domino theory Theory that if one country fell to communism, its neighboring countries would follow suit.

Farmers' Alliances Like the Granger Movement, these organizations sought to address the issues of small farming communities; however Alliances emphasized more political action and called for the creation of a Third Party to advocate their concerns.

fascism A radical form of totalitarian government that emerged in Italy and Germany in the 1920s in which a dictator uses propaganda and brute force to seize control of all aspects of national life.

field hands Slaves who toiled in the cotton or cane fields in organized work gangs.

Federal-Aid Highway Act (1956) Largest federal project in U.S. history that created a national network of interstate highways and was the largest federal project in history.

Federal Deposit Insurance Corporation (1933) Independent government agency, established to prevent bank panics, that guarantees the safety of deposits in citizens' savings accounts.

Federal Reserve Act (1913) Legislation passed by Congress to create a new national banking system in order to regulate the nation's currency supply and ensure the stability and integrity of member banks who made up the Federal Reserve System across the nation.

Federal Trade Commission (1914) Independent agency created by the Wilson administration that replaced the Bureau of Corporations as an even more powerful tool to combat unfair trade practices and monopolies.

Federal Writers' Project During the Great Depression, this project provided writers, such as Ralph Ellison, Richard Wright, and Saul Bellow, with work, which gave them employment and a chance to develop as artists.

federalism Concept of dividing governmental authority between the national government and the states.

The Federalist Papers Collection of eighty-five essays, published widely in newspapers in 1787 and 1788, written by Alexander Hamilton, James Madison, and John Jay in support of adopting the proposed U.S. Constitution.

Federalists Proponents of a centralized federal system and the ratification of the Constitution. Most Federalists were relatively young, educated men who supported a broad interpretation of the Constitution whenever national interest dictated such flexibility. Notable Federalists included Alexander Hamilton and John Jay.

Geraldine Ferraro (1935–) In the 1984 presidential election, Democratic nominee, Walter Mondale, chose her as his running mate. As a member of the U.S. House of Representatives from New York, she was the first woman to be a vice-presidential nominee for a major political party. However, she was placed on the defensive because of her husband's complicated business dealings.

Fifteenth Amendment This amendment forbids states to deny any person the right to vote on grounds of "race, color or pervious condition of servitude." Former Confederate states were required to ratify this amendment before they could be readmitted to the Union.

"final solution" The Nazi party's systematic murder of some 6 million Jews along with more than a million other people including, but not limited to, gypsies, homosexuals, and handicap individuals.

First New Deal (1933–1935) Franklin D. Roosevelt's ambitious first-term cluster of economic and social programs designed to combat the Great Depression.

First Red Scare Outbreak of anti-Communist hysteria that included the arrest without warrants of thousands of suspected radicals, most of whom (mainly Russian immigrants) were deported.

flappers Young women of the 1920s whose rebellion against prewar standards of femininity included wearing shorter dresses, bobbing their hair, dancing to jazz music, driving cars, smoking cigarettes, and indulging in illegal drinking and gambling.

Food Administration After America's entry into World War I, the economy of the home front needed to be reorganized to provide the most efficient means of conducting the war. The Food Administration was a part of this effort. Under the leadership of Herbert Hoover, the organization sought to increase agricultural production while reducing civilian consumption of foodstuffs.

The "Force Bill" (1833) Legislation, sparked by the Nullification Crisis in South Carolina, that authorized the president's use of the army to compel states to comply with federal law.

Gerald Ford (1913–2006) He was appointed to the vice presidency under President Nixon after the resignation of Spiro Agnew, and assumed the presidency after President Nixon's resignation. He resisted congressional pressure to both reduce taxes and increase federal spending, which sent the American economy into the deepest recession since the Great Depression. Ford retained Kissinger as his secretary of state and continued Nixon's foreign policy goals. He was heavily criticized following the collapse of South Vietnam.

Fort Laramie Treaty (1851) Restricted the Plains Indians from using the Overland Trail and permitted the building of government forts.

Fort Necessity After attacking a group of French soldiers, George Washington constructed and took shelter in this fort from vengeful French troops. Washington eventually surrendered to them after a day-long battle. This conflict was a significant event in igniting the French and Indian War.

Fort Sumter First battle of the Civil War, in which the federal fort in Charleston (South Carolina) Harbor was captured by the Confederates on April 14, 1861, after two days of shelling.

"forty-niners" Speculators who went to northern California following the discovery of gold in 1848; the first of several years of large-scale migration was 1849.

Fourteen Points President Woodrow Wilson's proposed plan for the peace agreement after the First World War that included the creation of a "league of nations" intended to keep the peace.

Fourteenth Amendment (1868) Guaranteed rights of citizenship to former slaves, in words similar to those of the Civil Rights Act of 1866.

alliance with France Critical diplomatic, military, and economic alliance between France and the newly independent United States, codified by the Treaty of Amity and Commerce and the Treaty of Alliance (1778).

Franciscan Missions In 1769, Franciscan missioners accompanied Spanish soldiers to California and over the next fifty years established a chain of missions from San Diego to San Francisco. At these missions, friars sought to convert Indians to Catholicism and make them members of the Spanish empire. The friars stripped the Indians of their native heritage and used soldiers to enforce their will.

Benjamin Franklin (1706–1790) A Boston-born American, who epitomized the Enlightenment for many Americans and Europeans, Franklin's wide range of interests led him to become a publisher, inventor, and statesman. As the latter, he contributed to the writing of the Declaration of Independence, served as the minister to France during the Revolutionary War, and was a delegate to the Constitutional Convention.

Free-Soil Party A political coalition created in 1848 that opposed the expansion of slavery into the new western territories.

Freedmen's Bureau Reconstruction agency established in 1865 to protect the legal rights of former slaves and to assist with their education, jobs, health care, and landowning.

Freedom Riders Activists who, beginning in 1961, traveled by bus through the South to test federal court rulings that banned segregation on buses and trains.

John C. Frémont "the Pathfinder" (1813–1890) He was an explorer and surveyor who helped inspire Americans living in California to rebel against the Mexican government and declare independence.

French and Indian War (Seven Years' War) The last—and most important—of four colonial wars fought between England and France for control of North America east of the Mississippi River.

French Revolution Revolutionary movement beginning in 1789 that overthrew the monarchy and transformed France into an unstable republic before Napoleon Bonaparte assumed power in 1799.

Sigmund Freud (1865–1939) He was the founder of psychoanalysis, which suggested that human behavior was motivated by unconscious and irrational forces. By the 1920s, his ideas were being discussed more openly in America.

frontier revivals Religious revival movement within the Second Great Awakening, that took place in frontier churches in western territories and states in the early nineteenth century.

Fugitive Slave Act (1850) Part of the Compromise of 1850, a provision that authorized federal officials to help capture and then return escaped slaves to their owners without trials.

fundamentalism Anti-modernist Protestant movement started in the early twentieth century that proclaimed the literal truth of the Bible; the name came from *The Fundamentals*, published by conservative leaders.

William Lloyd Garrison (1805–1879) In 1831, he started the anti-slavery newspaper *Liberator* and helped start the New England Anti-Slavery Society. Two years later, he assisted Arthur and Lewis Tappan in the founding of the American Anti-Slavery Society. He and his followers believed that America had been thoroughly corrupted and needed a wide range of reforms, embracing abolition, temperance, pacifism, and women's rights.

Marcus Garvey (1887–1940) He was the leading spokesman for Negro Nationalism, which exalted blackness, black cultural expression, and black exclusiveness. He called upon African Americans to liberate themselves from the surrounding white culture and create their own businesses, cultural centers, and newspapers. He was also the founder of the Universal Negro Improvement Association.

Citizen Genet (1763–1834) As the ambassador to the United States from the new French Republic, he engaged American privateers to attack British ships and conspired with frontiersmen and land speculators to organize an attack on Spanish Florida and Louisiana. His actions and the French radicals excessive actions against their enemies in the new French Republic caused the French Revolution to lose support among Americans.

Geneva Accords In 1954, the Geneva Accords were signed, which ended French colonial rule in Indochina. The agreement created the independent nations of Laos and Cambodia and divided Vietnam along the 17th parallel until an election in 1956 would reunify the country.

Battle of Gettysburg (1863) A monumental three-day battle in southern Pennsylvania, widely considered a turning point in the war, in which Union forces successfully countered a second Confederate invasion of the North.

Ghost Dance movement A spiritual and political movement among Native Americans whose followers performed a ceremonial "ghost dance" intended to connect the living with the dead and make the Indians bulletproof in battles to restore their homelands.

GI Bill of Rights (1944) Provided unemployment, education, and financial benefits for World War II veterans to ease their transition back to the civilian world.

***Gibbons v. Ogden* (1824)** Supreme Court case that gave the federal government the power to regulate interstate commerce.

Newt Gingrich (1943–) He led the Republican insurgency in Congress in the mid 1990s through mobilizing religious and social conservatives. Along with other Republican congressmen, he created the Contract with America, which was a ten-point anti-big government program. However, the program fizzled out after many of its bills were not passed by Congress.

Gilded Age (1860–1896) An era of dramatic industrial and urban growth characterized by widespread political corruption and loose government oversight of corporations.

The Gilded Age Mark Twain and Charles Dudley Warner's 1873 novel, the title of which became the popular name for the period from the end of the Civil War to the turn of the century.

glasnost Russian term for "openness"; applied to the loosening of censorship in the Soviet Union under Mikhail Gorbachev.

globalization An important, and controversial, transformation of the world economy whereby the Internet helped revolutionize global commerce by creating an international marketplace for goods and services. Led by the growing number of multinational companies and the Americanization of many foreign consumer cultures, with companies like McDonald's and Starbucks appearing in all of the major cities of the world.

Glorious Revolution Successful 1688 coup, instigated by a group of English aristocrats, which overthrew King James II and instated William of Orange and Mary, his English wife, to the British throne.

Barry Goldwater (1909–1998) A leader of the Republican right whose book, *The Conscience of a Conservative*, was highly influential to that segment of the party. He proposed eliminating the income tax and overhauling Social Security. In 1964, he ran as the Republican presidential candidate and lost to President Johnson. He campaigned against Johnson's war on poverty, the tradition of New Deal, the nuclear test ban and the Civil Rights Act of 1964 and advocated the wholesale bombing of North Vietnam.

Samuel Gompers (1850–1924) He served as the president of the American Federation of Labor from its inception until his death. He focused on achieving concrete economic gains such as higher wages, shorter hours, and better working conditions.

"good neighbor" policy Proclaimed by President Franklin D. Roosevelt in his first inaugural address in 1933, it sought improved diplomatic relations between the United States and its Latin American neighbors.

Mikhail Gorbachev (1931–) In the late 1980s, Soviet leader Mikhail Gorbachev attempted to reform the Soviet Union through his programs of *perestroika* and *glasnost* and pursued a renewal of détente with America, signing new arms-control agreements with President Reagan. Gorbachev allowed the velvet revolutions of Eastern Europe to occur without outside interference. Eventually the political, social, and economic upheaval he had unleashed would lead to the break-up of the Soviet Union.

Albert Gore Jr. (1948–) He served as a senator of Tennessee and then as President Clinton's vice president. In the 2000 presidential election, he was the Democratic candidate against Governor George W. Bush. The close election came down to Florida's electoral votes. While the votes were being recounted as required by state law, a legal battle was being waged to stop the recount. Finally, the case, *Bush v. Gore*, was presented to the Supreme Court who ruled 5–4 to stop the recount and Bush was declared the winner.

Jay Gould (1836–1892) As one of the biggest railroad robber barons, he was infamous for buying rundown railroads, making cosmetic improvements and then reselling them for a profit. He used corporate funds for personal investments and to bribe politicians and judges.

gradualism This strategy for ending slavery involved promoting the banning of slavery in the new western territories and encouraging the release of slaves from slavery. Supporters of this method believed that it would bring about the gradual end of slavery.

Granger Movement Began by offering social and educational activities for isolated farmers and their families and later started to promote "cooperatives" where farmers could join together to buy, store, and sell their crops to avoid the high fees charged by brokers and other middle-men.

Ulysses S. Grant (1822–1885) After distinguishing himself in the western theater of the Civil War, he was appointed general in chief of the Union army in 1864. Afterward, he defeated General Robert E. Lee through a policy of aggressive attrition. Lee surrendered to Grant on April 9th, 1865 at the Appomattox Court House. His presidential tenure suffered from scandals and fiscal problems, including the debate on whether or not greenbacks, paper money, should be removed from circulation.

Great Awakening Fervent religious revival movement that swept the thirteen colonies from the 1720s through the 1740s.

Great Compromise (Connecticut Compromise) Mediated the differences between the New Jersey and Virginia delegations to the Constitutional Convention by providing for a bicameral legislature, the upper house of which would have equal representation and the lower house of which would be apportioned by population.

Great Depression (1929–1941) Worst economic downturn in American history; it was spurred by the stock market crash in the fall of 1929 and lasted until the Second World War.

Great Migration Mass exodus of African Americans from the rural South to the Northeast and Midwest during and after the First World War.

Great Railroad Strike of 1877 A series of demonstrations, some violent, held nationwide in support of striking railroad workers in Martinsburg, West Virginia, who refused to work due to wage cuts.

Great Recession (2007–2009) Massive, prolonged economic downturn sparked by the collapse of the housing market and the financial institutions holding unpaid mortgages; it lasted from December 2007 to January 2009 and resulted in 9 million Americans losing their jobs.

Great Sioux War Conflict between Sioux and Cheyenne Indians and federal troops over lands in the Dakotas in the mid-1870s.

Great Society Term coined by President Lyndon B. Johnson in his 1965 State of the Union address, in which he proposed legislation to address problems of voting rights, poverty, diseases, education, immigration, and the environment.

Horace Greeley (1811–1872) In reaction to Radical Reconstruction and corruption in President Ulysses S. Grant's administration, a group of Republicans broke from the party to form the Liberal Republicans. In 1872, the Liberal Republicans chose Horace Greeley as their presidential candidate who ran on a platform of favoring civil service reform and condemning the Republican's Reconstruction policy.

greenbacks Paper money issued during the Civil War. After the war ended, a debate emerged on whether or not to remove the paper currency from circulation and revert back to hard-money currency (gold coins). Opponents of hard-money feared that eliminating the greenbacks would shrink the money supply, which would lower crop prices and make it more difficult to repay long-term debts. President Ulysses S. Grant, as well as hard-currency advocates, believed that gold coins were morally preferable to paper currency.

Greenback party Formed in 1876 in reaction to economic depression, the party favored issuance of unsecured paper money to help farmers repay debts; the movement for free coinage of silver took the place of the greenback movement by the 1880s.

General Nathanael Greene (1742–1786) He was appointed by Congress to command the American army fighting in the South during the Revolutionary War. Using his patience and his skills of managing men, saving supplies, and avoiding needless risks, he waged a successful war of attrition against the British.

Sarah Grimké (1792–1873) and **Angelina Grimké (1805–1879)** These two sisters gave anti-slavery speeches to crowds of mixed gender that caused some people to condemn them for engaging in unfeminine activities. In 1840, William Lloyd Garrison convinced the Anti-Slavery Society to allow women equal participation in the organization.

Half-Way Covenant Allowed baptized children of church members to be admitted to a "halfway" membership in the church and secure baptism for their own children in turn, but allowed them neither a vote in the church, nor communion.

Alexander Hamilton (1755–1804) His belief in a strong federal government led him to become a leader of the Federalists. As the first secretary of the Treasury, he laid the foundation for American capitalism through his creation of a federal budget, funded debt, a federal tax system, a national bank, a customs service, and a coast guard. His "Reports on Public Credit" and "Reports on Manufactures" outlined his vision for economic development and government finances. He died in a duel against Aaron Burr.

Alexander Hamilton's economic reforms Various measures designed to strengthen the nation's economy and generate federal revenue through the promotion of new industries, the adoption of new tax policies, the payment of war debts, and the establishment of a national bank.

Warren G. Harding (1865–1923) In the 1920 presidential election, he was the Republican nominee who promised Americans a "return to normalcy." Once in office, Harding's administration dismantled many of the social and economic components of progressivism and pursued a pro-business agenda. Harding appointed four pro-business Supreme Court Justices, cut taxes, increased tariffs, and promoted a lenient attitude towards regulation of corporations. However, he did speak out against racism and ended the exclusion of African Americans from federal positions.

Harlem Renaissance The nation's first self-conscious black literary and artistic movement; it was centered in New York City's Harlem district, which had a largely black population in the wake of the Great Migration from the South.

Hartford Convention A series of secret meetings in December 1814 and January 1815 at which New England Federalists protested American involvement in the War of 1812 and discussed several constitutional amendments, including limiting each president to one term, designed to weaken the dominant Republican Party.

Haymarket Riot (1886) Violent uprising in Haymarket Square, Chicago, where police clashed with labor demonstrators in the aftermath of a bombing.

headright A land-grant policy that promised fifty acres to any colonist who could afford passage to Virginia, as well as fifty more for any accompanying servants. The headright policy was eventually expanded to include any colonists—and was also adopted in other colonies.

Patrick Henry (1736–1799) He inspired the Virginia Resolves, which declared that Englishmen could only be taxed by their elected representatives. In March of 1775, he met with other colonial leaders to discuss the goals of the upcoming Continental Congress and famously declared "Give me liberty or give me death." During the ratification process of the U.S. Constitution, he became one of the leaders of the anti-federalists.

Hiroshima (1945) Japanese port city that was the first target of the newly developed atomic bomb on August 6, 1945. Most of the city was destroyed.

Alger Hiss (1904–1996) During the second Red Scare he had served in several government departments and was accused of being a spy for the Soviet Union and was convicted of lying about espionage. The case was politically damaging to the Truman administration because the president called the charges against Hiss a "red herring."

Adolph Hitler (1889–1945) The leader of the Nazis who advocated a violent anti-Semitic, anti-Marxist, pan-German ideology. He started World War II in Europe and orchestrated the systematic murder of some 6 million Jews along with more than a million others.

HIV/AIDS Human immunodeficiency virus (HIV) transmitted via the bodily fluids of infected persons to cause acquired immunodeficiency syndrome (AIDS), an often-fatal disease of the immune system when it appeared in the 1980s.

holding company A corporation established to own and manage other companies' stock rather than to produce goods and services itself.

Holocaust Systematic racist attempt by the Nazis to exterminate the Jews of Europe, resulting in the murder of over 6 million Jews and more than a million other "undesirables."

Homestead Act (1862) Legislation granting "homesteads" of 160 acres of government-owned land to settlers who agreed to work the land for at least five years.

Homestead steel strike (1892) Labor conflict at the Homestead steel mill near Pittsburgh, Pennsylvania, culminating in a battle between strikers and private security agents hired by the factory's management.

Herbert Hoover (1874–1964) Prior to becoming president, Hoover served as the secretary of commerce in both the Harding and Coolidge administrations. As president during the Great Depression, he believed that the nation's business structure was sound and sought to revive the economy through boosting the nation's confidence. He also tried to restart the economy with government constructions projects, lower taxes and new federal loan programs, but nothing worked.

horizontal integration The process by which a corporation acquires or merges with its competitors.

horse A tall, four-legged mammal (*Equus caballus*), domesticated and bred since prehistoric times for carrying riders and pulling heavy loads. The Spanish introduced horses to the Americas, eventually transforming many Native American cultures.

House Committee on Un-American Activities (HUAC) Committee of the U.S. House of Representatives formed in 1938; it was originally tasked with investigating Nazi subversion during the Second World War and later shifted its focus to rooting out Communists in the government and the motion-picture industry.

Sam Houston (1793–1863) During Texas's fight for independence from Mexico, Sam Houston was the commander in chief of the Texas forces, and he led the attack that captured General Antonio López de Santa Anna. After Texas gained its independence, he was named its first president.

Jacob Riis' *How the Other Half Lives* Jacob Riis was an early muckraking journalist who exposed the slum conditions in New York City in his book *How the Other Half Lives*.

General William Howe (1729–1814) As the commander of the British army in the Revolutionary War, he seized New York City from Washington's army, but failed to capture it. He missed several more opportunities to quickly end the rebellion, and he resigned his command after the British defeat at Saratoga.

Saddam Hussein (1937–2006) The former dictator of Iraq who became the head of state in 1979. In 1980, he invaded Iran and started the eight-year-long Iran-Iraq War. In 1990, he invaded Kuwait, which caused the Gulf War of 1991. In 2003, he was overthrown and captured when the United States invaded. He was sentenced to death by hanging in 2006.

Anne Hutchinson (1591–1643) The articulate, strong-willed, and intelligent wife of a prominent Boston merchant, who espoused her belief in direct divine revelation. She quarreled with Puritan leaders over her beliefs; and they banished her from the colony.

Immigration Act of 1924 Federal legislation intended to favor northern and western European immigrants over those from southern and eastern Europe by restricting the number of immigrants from any one European country to 2 percent of the total number of immigrants per year, with an overall limit of slightly over 150,000 new arrivals per year.

Immigration and Nationality Services Act of 1965 Legislation that abolished discriminatory quotas based upon immigrants' national origin and treated all nationalities and races equally.

imperialism The use of diplomatic or military force to extend a nation's power and enhance its economic interests, often by acquiring territory or colonies and justifying such behavior with assumptions of racial superiority.

impressment The British navy used press-gangs to kidnap men in British and colonial ports who were then forced to serve in the British navy.

indentured servitude A defined period of labor (often four to seven years) which settlers consented to in exchange for having their passage to the New World paid by their "master."

Independent Treasury Act (1840) System created by President Martin Van Buren and approved by Congress in 1840 whereby the federal government moved its funds from favored state banks to the U.S. Treasury, whose financial transactions could only be in gold or silver coins of paper currency backed by gold or silver.

"Indian New Deal" This phrase refers to the reforms implemented for Native Americans during the New Deal era. John Collier, the commissioner of the Bureau of Indian Affairs (BIA), increased the access Native Americans had to relief programs and employed more Native Americans at the BIA. He worked to pass the Indian Reorganization Act. However, the version of the act passed by Congress was a much-diluted version of Collier's original proposal and did not greatly improve the lives of Native Americans.

Indian Removal Act (1830) Law permitting the forced relocation of Indians to federal lands west of the Mississippi River in exchange for the land they occupied in the East and South.

Indian wars Bloody conflicts between U.S. soldiers and Native Americans that raged in the West from the early 1860s to the late 1870s, sparked by American settlers moving into ancestral Indian lands.

Indochina This area of Southeast Asia consists of Laos, Cambodia, and Vietnam and was once controlled by France as a colony. After the Viet Minh defeated the French, the Geneva Accords were signed, which ended French colonial rule. The agreement created the independent nations of Laos and Cambodia and divided Vietnam along the 17th parallel until an election would reunify the country. Fearing a Communist take over, the United States government began intervening in the region during the Truman administration, which led to President Johnson's full-scale military involvement in Vietnam.

Industrial Revolution Major shift in the nineteenth century from hand-made manufacturing to mass production in mills and factories using water-, coal-, and steam-powered machinery.

industrial war A new concept of war enabled by industrialization that developed from the early 1800s through the Atomic Age. New technologies, including automatic weaponry, forms of transportation like the railroad and airplane, and communication technologies such as the telegraph and telephone, enabled nations to equip large, mass-conscripted armies with chemical and automatic weapons to decimate opposing armies in a "total war."

Industrial Workers of the World (IWW) A radical union organized in Chicago in 1905, nicknamed the Wobblies; its opposition to World War I led to its destruction by the federal government under the Espionage Act.

infectious diseases Also called contagious diseases, illnesses that can pass from one person to another by way of invasive biological organisms able to reproduce in the bodily tissues of their hosts. Europeans unwittingly brought many such diseases to the Americas, devastating the Native American peoples.

Intermediate-Range Nuclear Forces (INF) Treaty (1987) Agreement signed by U.S. president Ronald Reagan and Soviet premier Mikhail Gorbachev to eliminate the deployment of intermediate-range missiles with nuclear warheads.

internal improvements Construction of roads, bridges, canals, harbors, and other infrastructural projects intended to facilitate the flow of goods and people.

internationalists Prior to the United States' entry in World War II, internationalists believed that America's national security depended on aiding Britain in its struggle against Germany.

Interstate Commerce Commission An independent federal agency established in 1887 to oversee businesses engaged in interstate trade, especially railroads, but whose regulatory power was limited when tested in the courts.

interstate highway system In the late 1950s, construction began on a national network of interstate superhighways for the purpose of commerce and defense. The interstate highways would enable the rapid movement of military convoys and the evacuation of cities after a nuclear attack.

Iran-Contra affair (1987) Reagan administration scandal over the secret, unlawful U.S. sale of arms to Iran in partial exchange for the release of hostages in Lebanon; the arms money in turn was used illegally to aid Nicaraguan right-wing insurgents, the Contras.

Iranian hostage crisis (1979) Storming of the U.S. embassy in Tehran by Iranian revolutionaries, who held fifty-two Americans hostage for 444 days, despite President Carter's appeals for their release as well as a botched rescue attempt.

Irish Potato Famine In 1845, an epidemic of potato rot brought a famine to rural Ireland that killed over 1 million peasants and instigated a huge increase in the number of Irish immigrating to America. By 1850, the Irish made up 43 percent of the foreign-born population in the United States; and in the 1850s, they made up over half the population of New York City and Boston.

iron curtain Term coined by Winston Churchill to describe the cold war divide between western Europe and the Soviet Union's Eastern European satellites.

Iroquois League An alliance of the Iroquois tribes, originally formed sometime between 1450 and 1600, that used their combined strength to pressure Europeans to work with them in the fur trade and to wage war across what is today eastern North America.

Andrew Jackson (1767–1837) As a major general in the Tennessee militia, he had a number of military successes. As president, he worked to enable the "common man" to play a greater role in the political arena. He vetoed the re-chartering of the Second National Bank and reduced federal spending. When South Carolina nullified the Tariffs of 1828 and 1832, Jackson requested that Congress pass a "force bill" that would authorize him to use the army to compel the state to comply with the tariffs. He forced eastern Indians to move west of the Mississippi River so their lands could be used by white settlers. Groups of those who opposed Jackson come together to form a new political party called the Whigs.

Thomas "Stonewall" Jackson (1824–1863) A Confederate general who was known for his fearlessness in leading rapid marches, bold flanking movements, and furious assaults. He earned his nickname at the Battle of the First Bull Run for standing courageously against Union fire. During the battle of Chancellorsville, his own men accidentally mortally wounded him.

William James (1842–1910) He was the founder of Pragmatism and one of the fathers of modern psychology. He believed that ideas gained their validity not from their inherent truth, but from their social consequences and practical application.

Jay's Treaty (1794) Agreement between Britain and the United States, negotiated by Chief Justice John Jay, that settled disputes over trade, prewar debts owed to British merchants, British-occupied forts in American territory, and the seizure of American ships and cargo.

Jazz Age Term coined by writer F. Scott Fitzgerald to characterize the spirit of rebellion and spontaneity among young Americans in the 1920s, a spirit epitomized by the hugely popular jazz music of the era.

Thomas Jefferson (1743–1826) He was a plantation owner, author, the drafter of the Declaration Independence, ambassador to France, leader of the Republican party, secretary of state, and the third president of the United States. As president, he purchased the Louisiana territory from France, withheld appointments made by President Adams leading to *Marybury v. Madison*, outlawed foreign slave trade, and was committed to a "wise and frugal" government.

Jeffersonian Republicans Political party founded by Thomas Jefferson in opposition to the Federalist Party led by Alexander Hamilton and John Adams; also known as the Democratic-Republican Party.

Jesuits A religious order founded in 1540 by Ignatius Loyola. They sought to counter the spread of Protestantism during the Protestant Reformation and spread the Catholic faith through work as missionaries. Roughly 3,500 served in New Spain and New France.

"Jim Crow" laws In the New South, these laws mandated the separation of races in various public places that served as a way for the ruling whites to impose their will on all areas of black life.

Andrew Johnson (1808–1875) He was elevated to the presidency after Abraham Lincoln's assassination. In order to restore the Union after the Civil War, he issued an amnesty proclamation and required former Confederate states to ratify the Thirteenth Amendment. After disagreements over the power to restore states rights, the Radical Republicans attempted to impeach Johnson but fell short on the required number of votes needed to remove him from office.

Lyndon B. Johnson (1908–1973) Former member of the House of Representatives and the former Majority Leader of the Senate, Vice President Lyndon B. Johnson assumed the presidency after President Kennedy's assassination. During his presidency, he passed the Civil Rights Act of 1964, declared a "war on poverty" promoting his own social program called the Great Society, and signed the Immigration and Nationality Service Act of 1965. Johnson greatly increased America's role in Vietnam.

joint-stock companies Businesses owned by investors, who purchase shares of companies' stocks and share all the profits and losses.

Kansas-Nebraska Act (1854) Controversial legislation that created two new territories taken from Native Americans, Kansas and Nebraska, where residents would vote to decide whether slavery would be allowed (popular sovereignty).

Florence Kelley (1859–1932) As the head of the National Consumer's League, she led the crusade to promote state laws to regulate the number of working hours imposed on women who were wives and mothers.

George F. Kennan (1904–2005) While working as an American diplomat, he devised the strategy of containment, which called for the halting of Soviet expansion. It became America's choice strategy throughout the cold war.

John F. Kennedy (1917–1963) He was elected president in 1960. Despite the difficulties he had in getting his legislation through Congress, he established the Alliance for Progress programs to help Latin America, the Peace Corps, the Trade Expansion Act of 1962, and funding for urban renewal projects and the space program. His foreign political involvement included the failed Bay of Pigs invasion and the missile crisis in Cuba, as well as support of local governments in Indochina. In 1963, he was assassinated by Lee Harvey Oswald in Dallas, Texas.

Kent State During the spring of 1970, students on college campuses across the country protested the expansion of the Vietnam War into Cambodia. At Kent State University, the National Guard attempted to quell the rioting students. The guardsmen panicked and shot at rock-throwing demonstrators. Four student bystanders were killed.

Kentucky and Virginia Resolutions (1798–1799) Passed in response to the Alien and Sedition Acts, the resolutions advanced the state-compact theory that held states could nullify an act of Congress if they deemed it unconstitutional.

Francis Scott Key (1779–1843) During the War of 1812, he watched British forces bombard Fort McHenry, but fail to take it. Seeing the American flag still flying over the fort at dawn inspired him to write "The Star-Spangled Banner," which became the American national anthem.

Martin Luther King, Jr. (1929–1968) A central leader of the civil rights movement, he urged people to use nonviolent civil disobedience to demand their rights and bring about change. He successfully led the Montgomery Bus Boycott. While in jail for his role in demonstrations, he wrote his famous "Letter from Birmingham City Jail," in which he defended his strategy of nonviolent protest. In 1963, he delivered his famous "I Have a Dream Speech" from the steps of the Lincoln Memorial as a part of the March on Washington. A year later, he was awarded the Nobel Peace Prize. In 1968, he was assassinated.

King Philip's War A bloody, three-year war in New England (1675–1678), resulting from the escalation of tensions between Indians and English settlers; the defeat of the Indians led to broadened freedoms for the settlers and their dispossessing the region's Indians of most of their land.

King William's War (War of the League of Augsburg) First (1689–1697) of four colonial wars between England and France.

Henry Kissinger (1923–) He served as the secretary of state and national security advisor in the Nixon administration. He negotiated with North Vietnam for an end to the Vietnam War, but the cease-fire did not last; South Vietnam fell to North Vietnam. He helped organize Nixon's historic trips to China and the Soviet Union. In the Middle East, he negotiated a cease-fire between Israel and its neighbors following the Yom Kippur War and solidified Israel's promise to return to Egypt most of the land it had taken during the 1967 war.

Knights of Labor A national labor organization with a broad reform platform; reached peak membership in the 1880s.

Know-Nothing party Nativist, anti-Catholic third party organized in 1854 in reaction to large-scale German and Irish immigration.

Ku Klux Klan Organized in Pulaski, Tennessee, in 1866 to terrorize former slaves who voted and held political offices during Reconstruction; a revived organization in the 1910s and 1920s stressed white, Anglo-Saxon, fundamentalist Protestant supremacy; the Klan revived a third time to fight the civil rights movement of the 1950s and 1960s in the South.

Marquis de Lafayette (1757–1834) A wealthy French idealist excited by the American cause, he offered to serve in Washington's army for free in exchange for being named a major general. He overcame Washington's initial skepticism to become one of his most trusted aides.

laissez-faire An economic doctrine holding that businesses and individuals should be able to pursue their economic interests without government interference.

Land Ordinance of 1785 Directed surveying of the Northwest Territory into townships of thirty-six sections (square miles) each, the sale of the sixteenth section of which was to be used to finance public education.

League of Nations Organization of nations formed in the aftermath of the First World War to mediate disputes and maintain international peace; despite President Wilson's intense lobbying for the League of Nations, Congress did not ratify the treaty and the United States failed to join.

Mary Elizabeth Lease (1850–1933) She was a leader of the farm protest movement who advocated violence if change could not be obtained at the ballot box. She believed that the urban-industrial East was the enemy of the working class.

Robert E. Lee (1807–1870) Even though he had served in the United States Army for thirty years, he chose to fight on the side of the Confederacy. Lee was excellent at using his field commanders and his soldiers respected him. However, General Ulysses S. Grant eventually wore down his army, and Lee surrendered to Grant at the Appomattox Court House on April 9, 1865.

Lend-Lease Bill (1941) Legislation that allowed the president to lend or lease military equipment to any country whose own defense was deemed vital to the defense of the United States.

Levittown First low-cost, mass-produced development of suburban tract housing built by William Levitt on Long Island, New York, in 1947.

Lewis and Clark Expedition (1804) Led by Meriwether Lewis and William Clark, a mission to the Pacific coast commissioned for the purposes of scientific and geographical exploration

Lexington and Concord, Battle of The first shots fired in the Revolutionary War, on April 19, 1775, near Boston; approximately 100 Minutemen and 250 British soldiers were killed.

Liberator William Lloyd Garrison started this anti-slavery newspaper in 1831 in which he renounced gradualism and called for abolition.

Queen Liliuokalani (1838–1917) In 1891, she ascended to the throne of the Hawaiian royal family and tried to eliminate white control of the Hawaiian government. Two years later, Hawaii's white population revolted and seized power with the support of American Marines.

Abraham Lincoln (1809–1865) Shortly after he was elected president in 1860, southern states began seceding from the Union, and in April of 1861 he declared war on the seceding states. On January 1, 1863, Lincoln signed the Emancipation Proclamation. At the end of the war, he favored a reconstruction strategy for the former Confederate states that did not radically alter southern social and economic life. He was assassinated by John Wilkes Booth at Ford's Theater on April 14, 1865.

Lincoln-Douglas Debates (1858) In the Illinois race between Republican Abraham Lincoln and Democrat Stephen A. Douglas for a seat in the U.S. Senate, a series of seven dramatic debates focusing on the issue of slavery in the territories.

John Locke (1632–1704) An English philosopher whose ideas were influential during the Enlightenment. He argued in his *Essay on Human Understanding* (1690) that humanity is largely the product of the environment, the mind being a blank tablet, *tabula rasa*, on which experience is written.

Henry Cabot Lodge (1850–1924) He was the chairman of the Senate Foreign Relations Committee who favored limiting America's involvement in the League of Nations' covenant and sought to amend the Treaty of Versailles.

de Lôme letter Private correspondence written in 1898 by the Spanish ambassador to the U.S., Depuy de Lôme, that described President McKinley as "weak"; the letter was stolen by Cuban revolutionaries and published in the *New York Journal*, deepening American resentment of Spain and moving the two countries closer to war in Cuba.

Lone Star Republic After winning independence from Mexico, Texas became its own nation that was called the Lone Star Republic. In 1836, Texans drafted a constitution, legalized slavery, banned free blacks, named Sam Houston president, and voted for the annexation to the United States. However, quarrels over adding a slave state and fears of instigating a war with Mexico delayed Texas's entrance into the Union until December 29, 1845.

Huey P. Long (1893–1935) He began his political career in Louisiana where he developed a reputation for being an unscrupulous reformer. As a U.S. senator, he became a critic of President Roosevelt's New Deal Plan and offered his alternative called the Share-the-Wealth program. He was assassinated in 1935.

Louisiana Purchase (1803) President Thomas Jefferson's purchase of the Louisiana Territory from France for $15 million, doubling the size of U.S. territory.

The Lowell system Model New England factory communities that during the first half of the nineteenth century provided employees, mostly young women, with meals, a boardinghouse, and moral discipline, as well as educational and cultural opportunities.

Loyalists Colonists who remained loyal to Great Britain before and during the Revolutionary War.

Lusitania British ocean liner torpedoed and sunk by a German U-boat; the deaths of nearly 1,200 of its civilian passengers, including many Americans, caused international outrage.

Martin Luther (1483–1546) A German monk who founded the Lutheran church. He protested abuses in the Catholic Church by posting his Ninety-five Theses, which began the Protestant Reformation.

General Douglas MacArthur (1880–1964) During World War II, he and Admiral Chester Nimitz dislodged the Japanese military from the Pacific Islands they had occupied. Following the war, he was in charge of the occupation of Japan. After North Korea invaded South Korea, Truman sent the U.S. military to defend South Korea under the command of MacArthur. Later in the war, Truman expressed his willingness to negotiate the restoration of prewar boundaries which MacArthur attempted to undermine. Truman fired MacArthur for his open insubordination.

James Madison (1751–1836) He participated in the Constitutional Convention during which he proposed the Virginia Plan. He believed in a strong federal government and was a leader of the Federalists. However, he also presented to Congress the Bill of Rights and drafted the Virginia Resolutions. As secretary of state, he withheld a commission for William Marbury, which led to the landmark *Marbury v. Madison* decision. During his presidency, he declared war on Britain in response to violations of American shipping rights, which started the War of 1812.

Alfred Thayer Mahan, *The Influence of Sea Power upon History, 1660–1783* (1890) Historical work in which Rear Admiral Alfred Thayer Mahan argues that a nation's greatness and prosperity comes from the power of its navy; the book helped bolster imperialist sentiment in the United States in the late nineteenth century.

U.S. battleship *Maine* American warship that exploded in the Cuban port of Havana on January 25, 1898; though later discovered to be the result of an accident, the destruction of the *Maine* was attributed by war-hungry Americans to Spain, contributing to the onset of the War of 1812.

maize (corn) The primary grain crop in Mesoamerica yielding small kernels often ground into cornmeal. Easy to grow in a broad range of conditions, it enabled a global population explosion after being brought to Europe, Africa, and Asia.

Malcolm X (1925–1964) The most articulate spokesman for black power. Originally the chief disciple of Elijah Muhammad, the black Muslim leader in the United States, Malcolm X broke away and founded his own organization committed to establishing relations between African Americans and the nonwhite peoples of the world. Near the end of his life, he began to preach a biracial message of social change. In 1964, he was assassinated by members of a rival group of black Muslims.

Manchuria incident The northeast region of Manchuria was an area contested between China and Russia. In 1931, the Japanese claimed that they needed to protect their extensive investments in the area and moved their army into Manchuria. They quickly conquered the region and set up their own puppet empire. China asked both the United States and the League of Nations for help and neither responded.

Manifest Destiny The widespread belief that America was "destined" by God to expand westward across the continent into lands claimed by Native Americans as well as European nations.

Horace Mann (1796–1859) He believed the public school system was the best way to achieve social stability and equal opportunity. As a reformer of education, he sponsored a state board of education, the first state-supported "normal" school for training teachers, a state association for teachers, the minimum school year of six months, and led the drive for a statewide school system.

Marbury v. Madison **(1803)** First Supreme Court decision to declare a federal law—the Judiciary Act of 1801—unconstitutional.

March on Washington Civil rights demonstration on August 28, 1963, on the National Mall, where Martin Luther King, Jr. gave his famous "I Have a Dream" speech.

market economy Large-scale manufacturing and commercial agriculture that emerged in America during the first half of the nineteenth century, displacing much of the pre-market subsistence and barter-based economy and producing boom-and-bust cycles while raising the American standard of living.

George C. Marshall (1880–1959) As the chairman of the Joint Chiefs of Staff, he orchestrated the Allied victories over Germany and Japan in the Second World War. In 1947, he became President Truman's secretary of state and proposed the massive reconstruction program for western Europe called the Marshall Plan.

Chief Justice John Marshall (1755–1835) During his long tenure as chief justice of the supreme court (1801–1835), he established the foundations for American jurisprudence, the authority of the Supreme Court, and the constitutional supremacy of the national government over states.

Marshall Plan (1948) Secretary of State George C. Marshall's post–World War II program providing massive U.S. financial and technical assistance to war-torn European countries.

Massachusetts Bay Colony English colony founded by English Puritans in 1630 as a haven for persecuted Congregationalists.

massive resistance White rallying cry disrupting federal efforts to enforce racial integration in the South.

massive retaliation Strategy that used the threat of nuclear warfare as a means of combating the global spread of communism.

Mayflower Compact A formal agreement signed by the Separatist colonists aboard the *Mayflower* in 1620 to abide by laws made by leaders of their own choosing.

Senator Joseph R. McCarthy (1908–1957) In 1950, this senator became the shrewdest and most ruthless exploiter of America's anxiety of communism. He claimed that the United States government was full of Communists and led a witch hunt to find them, but he was never able to uncover a single communist agent.

McCarthyism Anti-Communist hysteria led by Senator Joseph McCarthy's "witch hunts" attacking the loyalty of politicians, federal employees, and public figures, despite a lack of evidence.

George B. McClellan (1826–1885) In 1861, President Abraham Lincoln appointed him head of the Army of the Potomac and, later, general in chief of the U.S. Army. He built his army into well trained and powerful force. After failing to achieve a decisive victory against the Confederacy, he was removed from command in 1862.

Cyrus Hall McCormick (1809–1884) In 1831, he invented a mechanical reaper to harvest wheat, which transformed the scale of agriculture. By hand a farmer could only harvest a half an acre a day, while the McCormick reaper allowed two people to harvest twelve acres of wheat a day.

McCormick reaper Mechanical reaper invented by Cyrus Hall McCormick in 1831 that dramatically increased the production of wheat.

William McKinley (1843–1901) As a congressman, he was responsible for the McKinley Tariff of 1890, which raised the duties on manufactured products to their highest level ever. Voters disliked the tariff and McKinley, as well as other Republicans, lost his seat in Congress the next election. However, he won the presidential election of 1896 and raised the tariffs again. In 1898, he annexed Hawaii and declared war on Spain. The war concluded with the Treaty of Paris, which gave America control over Puerto Rico, Guam, and the Philippines. Soon America was fighting Filipinos, who were seeking independence for their country. In 1901, McKinley was assassinated.

Robert McNamara (1916–) He was the secretary of defense for both President Kennedy and President Johnson and a supporter of America's involvement in Vietnam.

Medicare and Medicaid Health-care programs designed to aid the elderly and disadvantaged, respectively, as part of President Johnson's Great Society initiative.

Andrew W. Mellon (1855–1937) As President Harding's secretary of the Treasury, he sought to generate economic growth through reducing government spending and lowering taxes. However, he insisted that the tax reductions mainly go to the rich because he believed the wealthy would reinvest their money. In order to bring greater efficiency and nonpartisanship to the government's budget process, he persuaded Congress to created a new Bureau of the Budget and a General Accounting Office.

mercantilism Policy of Great Britain and other imperial powers of regulating the economies of colonies to benefit the mother country.

James Meredith (1933–) In 1962, the governor of Mississippi defied a Supreme Court ruling and refused to allow James Meredith, an African American, to enroll at the University of Mississippi. Federal marshals were sent to enforce the law which led to clashes between a white mob and the marshals. Federal troops intervened and two people were killed and many others were injured. A few days later, Meredith was able to register at the university.

Merrimack* (ship renamed the *Virginia*) and the *Monitor First engagement between ironclad ships; fought at Hampton Roads, Virginia, on March 9, 1862.

Metacomet (?–1676) or King Philip The chief of the Wampanoages, who the colonists called King Philip. He resented English efforts to convert Indians to Christianity and waged a war against the English colonists in which he was killed.

Mexica Otherwise known as "Aztecs," a Mesoamerican people of northern Mexico who founded the vast Aztec Empire in the fourteenth century, later conquered by the Spanish under Hernán Cortés in 1521.

microprocessor An electronic circuit printed on a small silicon chip; a major technological breakthrough in 1971, it paved the way for the development of the personal computer.

Middle Passage The hellish and often deadly middle leg of the transatlantic "Triangular Trade" in which European ships carried manufactured goods to Africa, then transported enslaved Africans to the Americas and the Caribbean, and finally conveyed American agricultural products back to Europe; from the late sixteenth to the early nineteenth centuries, some 12 million Africans were transported via the Middle Passage, unknown millions more dying en route.

militant nonviolence After the success of the Montgomery bus boycott, people were inspired by Martin Luther King, Jr.'s use of this nonviolent form of protest. Throughout the civil rights movement, demonstrators used this method of protest to challenge racial segregation in the South.

Militia Act (1862) Congressional measure that permitted freed slaves to serve as laborers or soldiers in the United States Army.

Ho Chi Minh (1890–1969) He was the Vietnamese communist resistance leader who drove the French and the United States out of Vietnam. After the Geneva Accords divided the region into four countries, he controlled North Vietnam, and ultimately became the leader of all of Vietnam at the conclusion of the Vietnam War.

minstrelsy A form of entertainment that was popular from the 1830s to the 1870s. The performances featured white performers who were made up as African Americans or blackface. They performed banjo and fiddle music, "shuffle" dances and lowbrow humor that reinforced racial stereotypes.

Minutemen Special units organized by the militia to be ready for quick mobilization.

Miranda v. Arizona (1966) U.S. Supreme Court decision required police to advise persons in custody of their rights to legal counsel and against self-incrimination.

The Mississippi Plan Series of state constitutional amendments in 1890 which sought to severely disenfranchise black voters and were quickly adopted by other southern states.

Missouri Compromise (1820) Legislative decision to admit Missouri as a slave state and abolish slavery in the area west of the Mississippi River and north of the parallel 36°30′.

Model T Ford Henry Ford developed this model of car so that it was affordable for everyone. Its success led to an increase in the production of automobiles which stimulated other related industries such steel, oil, and rubber. The mass use of automobiles increased the speed goods could be transported, encouraged urban sprawl, and sparked real estate booms in California and Florida.

moderate Republicanism Promise to curb federal government and restore state and local government authority, spearheaded by President Eisenhower.

modernism An early-twentieth-century intellectual and artistic movement that rejected traditional notions of reality and adopted radical new forms of artistic expression.

monopoly A corporation so large that it effectively controls the entire market for its products or services.

the "money question" Late-nineteenth-century national debate over the nature of U.S. currency; supporters of a fixed gold standard were generally money lenders, and thus preferred to keep the value of money high, while supporters of silver (and gold) coinage were debtors, they owed money, so they wanted to keep the value of money low by increasing the currency supply (inflation).

James Monroe (1758–1831) He served as secretary of state and war under President Madison and was elected president. As the latter, he signed the Transcontinental Treaty with Spain which gave the United States Florida and expanded the Louisiana territory's western border to the Pacific coast. In 1823, he established the Monroe Doctrine. This foreign policy proclaimed the American continents were no longer open to colonization and America would be neutral in European affairs.

Monroe Doctrine (1823) U.S. foreign policy that barred further colonization in the Western Hemisphere by European powers and pledged that there would be no American interference with any existing European colonies.

Montgomery bus boycott Boycott of bus system in Montgomery, Alabama, organized by civil rights activists after the arrest of Rosa Parks.

Moral Majority Televangelist Jerry Falwell's political lobbying organization, the name of which became synonymous with the religious right—conservative evangelical Protestants who helped ensure President Ronald Reagan's 1980 victory.

J. Pierpont Morgan (1837–1913) As a powerful investment banker, he would acquire, reorganize, and consolidate companies into giant trusts. His biggest achievement was the consolidation of the steel industry into the United States Steel Corporation, which was the first billion-dollar corporation.

J. Pierpont Morgan and Company An investment bank under the leadership of J. Pierpont Morgan that bought or merged unrelated American companies, often using capital acquired from European investors.

Mormons Members of the Church of Jesus Christ of Latter-day Saints, which dismissed other Christian denominations, emphasizing universal salvation and a modest lifestyle; Mormons were often persecuted for their secrecy and clannishness.

Morrill Land Grant Act (1862) Federal statute that allowed for the creation of land-grant colleges and universities, which were founded to provide technical education in agriculture, mining, and industry.

Samuel F. B. Morse (1791–1872) In 1832, he invented the telegraph and revolutionized the speed of communication.

mountain men Inspired by the fur trade, these men left civilization to work as trappers and reverted to a primitive existence in the wilderness. They were the first white people to find routes through the Rocky Mountains, and they pioneered trails that settlers later used to reach the Oregon country and California in the 1840s.

muckrakers Writers who exposed corruption and abuses in politics, business, consumer safety, working conditions, and more, spurring public interest in progressive reforms.

Mugwumps Reformers who bolted the Republican party in 1884 to support Democratic Grover Cleveland for president over Republican James G. Blaine, whose secret dealings on behalf of railroad companies had brought charges of corruption.

mulattoes Mixed-race people who constituted most of the South's free black population.

Benito Mussolini (1883–1945) The Italian founder of the Fascist party who came to power in Italy in 1922 and allied himself with Adolf Hitler and the Axis powers during the Second World War.

National Association for the Advancement of Colored People (NAACP) Organization founded in 1910 by black activists and white progressives that promoted education as a means of combating social problems and focused on legal action to secure the civil rights supposedly guaranteed by the Fourteenth and Fifteenth Amendments.

North American Free Trade Agreement (NAFTA) (1994) Agreement eliminating trade barriers that was signed in 1994 by the United States, Canada, and Mexico, making North America the largest free-trade zone in the world.

North Atlantic Treaty Organization (NATO) Defensive political and military alliance formed in 1949 by the United States, Canada, and ten Western European nations to deter Soviet expansion in Europe.

National Industrial Recovery Act (1933) Passed on the last of the Hundred Days; it created public-works jobs through the Federal Emergency Relief Administration and established a system of self-regulation for industry through the National Recovery Administration, which was ruled unconstitutional in 1935.

National Labor Union A federation of labor and reform leaders established in 1866 to advocate for new state and local laws to improve working conditions.

National Recovery Administration (1933) Controversial federal agency that brought together business and labor leaders to create "codes of fair competition" and "fair labor" policies, including a national minimum wage.

National Security Act Congressional legislation passed in 1947 that created the Department of Defense, the National Security Council, and the Central Intelligence Agency.

National Socialist German Workers' Party (Nazi) Founded in the 1920s, this party gained control over Germany under the leadership of Adolf Hitler in 1933 and continued in power until Germany's defeat at the end of the Second World War. It advocated a violent anti-Semitic, anti-Marxist, pan-German ideology. The Nazi party perpetrated the Holocaust.

National Trades' Unions Formed in 1834 to organize all local trade unions into a stronger national association, only to be dissolved amid the economic depression during the late 1830s.

nativism Reactionary conservative movement characterized by heightened nationalism, anti-immigrant sentiment, and the enactment of laws setting stricter regulations on immigration.

natural rights An individual's basic rights that should not be violated by any government or community.

Navigation Acts Restrictions passed by the British Parliament between 1650 and 1775 to control colonial trade and bolster the mercantile system.

Negrophobia A violent new wave of racism that spread in the late nineteenth century largely spurred by white resentment for African American financial success and growing political influence.

new conservatism The political philosophy of those who led the conservative insurgency of the early 1980s. This brand of conservatism was personified in Ronald Reagan who believed in less government, supply-side economics, and "family values."

First New Deal Franklin D. Roosevelt's campaign promise, in his speech to the Democratic National Convention of 1932, to combat the Great Depression with a "new deal for the American people;" the phrase became a catchword for his ambitious plan of economic programs.

New Democrats Centrist ("moderate") Democrats led by President Bill Clinton that emerged in the late 1980s and early 1990s to challenge the "liberal" direction of the party.

"new economy" Period of sustained economic prosperity during the nineties marked by budget surpluses, the explosion of dot.com industries, low inflation, and low unemployment.

New France The name used for the area of North America that was colonized by the French. Unlike Spanish or English colonies, New France had a small number of colonists, which forced them to initially seek good relations with the indigenous people they encountered.

New Freedom Program championed in 1912 by the Woodrow Wilson campaign that aimed to restore competition in the economy by eliminating all trusts rather than simply regulating them.

New Frontier Proposed domestic program championed by the incoming Kennedy administration in 1961 that aimed to jump-start the economy and trigger social progress.

"new immigrants" Wave of newcomers from southern and eastern Europe, including many Jews, who became a majority among immigrants to America after 1890.

New Jersey Plan The delegations to the Constitutional Convention were divided between two plans on how to structure the government: New Jersey wanted one legislative body with equal representation for each state.

New Left Term coined by the Students for a Democratic Society to distinguish their efforts at grassroots democracy from those of the 1930s Old Left, which had embraced orthodox Marxism.

New Mexico A U.S. territory and later a state in the American Southwest, originally established by the Spanish, who settled there in the sixteenth century, founded Catholic missions, and exploited the region's indigenous peoples.

New Nationalism Platform of the Progressive party and slogan of former President Theodore Roosevelt in the presidential campaign of 1912; stressed government activism, including regulation of trusts, conservation, and recall of state court decisions that had nullified progressive programs.

"New Negro" In the 1920s, a slow and steady growth of black political influence occurred in northern cities where African Americans were freer to speak and act. This political activity created a spirit of protest that expressed itself culturally in the Harlem Renaissance and politically in "new Negro" nationalism.

New Netherland Dutch colony conquered by the English in 1667 and out of which four new colonies were created—New York, New Jersey, Pennsylvania, and Delaware.

Battle of New Orleans (1815) Final major battle in the War of 1812, in which the Americans under General Andrew Jackson unexpectedly and decisively countered the British attempt to seize the port of New Orleans, Louisiana.

New South *Atlanta Constitution* editor Henry W. Grady's 1886 term for the prosperous post–Civil War South: democratic, industrial, urban, and free of nostalgia for the defeated plantation South.

William Randolph Hearst's *New York Journal* In the late 1890s, the *New York Journal* and its rival, the *New York World*, printed sensationalism on the Cuban revolution as part of their heated competition for readership. The *New York Journal* printed a negative letter from the Spanish ambassador about President McKinley and inflammatory coverage of the sinking of the *Maine* in Havana Harbor. These two events roused the American public's outcry against Spain.

Joseph Pulitzer's *New York World* In the late 1890s, the *New York World* and its rival, *New York Journal*, printed sensationalism on the Cuban revolution as part of their heated competition for readership.

Admiral Chester Nimitz (1885–1966) During the Second World War, he was the commander of central Pacific. Along with General Douglas MacArthur, he dislodged the Japanese military from the Pacific Islands they had occupied.

Nineteenth Amendment Constitutional amendment that granted women the right to vote in 1920.

Richard M. Nixon (1913–1994) He first came to national prominence as a congressman involved in the investigation of Alger Hiss, and later served as vice president during the Eisenhower administration. After being elected president in 1968, he slowed the federal enforcement of civil rights and appointed pro-Southern justices to the Supreme Court. He began a program of Vietnamization of the war. In 1973, America, North and South Vietnam, and the Viet Cong agreed to end the war and the United States withdrew. However, the cease-fire was broken, and the South Vietnam fell to North Vietnam. In 1970, Nixon declared that America was no longer the world's policeman and he would seek some partnerships with Communist countries, historically traveling to China and the Soviet Union. In 1972, he was reelected, but the Watergate scandal erupted shortly after his victory; he resigned the presidency under threat of impeachment.

No Child Left Behind President George W. Bush's education reform plan that required states to set and meet learning standards for students and make sure that all students were "proficient" in reading and writing by 2014. States had to submit annual reports of students' standardized test scores. Teachers were required to be "proficient" in their subject area. Schools who failed to show progress would face sanctions. States criticized the lack of funding for remedial programs and noted that poor school districts would find it very difficult to meet the new guidelines.

nonviolent civil disobedience Tactic of defying unjust laws through peaceful actions championed by Dr. Martin Luther King, Jr.

Lord North (1732–1792) The first minister of King George III's cabinet whose efforts to subdue the colonies only brought them closer to revolution. He helped bring about the Tea Act of 1773, which led to the Boston Tea Party. In an effort to discipline Boston, he wrote, and Parliament passed, four acts that galvanized colonial resistance.

North Atlantic Treaty Organization (NATO) Defensive alliance founded in 1949 by ten western European nations, the United States, and Canada to deter Soviet expansion in Europe.

Northwest Ordinance (1787) Land policy for new western territories in the Ohio valley that established the terms and conditions for self-government and statehood while also banning slavery from the region.

NSC-68 (1950) Top-secret policy paper approved by President Truman that outlined a militaristic approach to combating the spread of global communism.

nullification The right claimed by some states to veto a federal law deemed unconstitutional.

Nuremberg trials At the site of the annual Nazi party rallies, twenty-one major German offenders faced an international military tribunal for Nazi atrocities. After a ten-month trial, the court acquitted three and sentenced eleven to death, three to life imprisonment, and four to shorter terms.

Barack Obama (1961–) In the 2008 presidential election, Senator Barack Obama mounted an innovative Internet based and grassroots orientated campaign. As the nation's economy nose-dived in the fall of 2008, Obama linked the Republican economic philosophy with the country's dismal financial state and promoted a message of "change" and "politics of hope," which resonated with voters. He decisively won the presidency and became America's first person of color to be elected president.

Occupy Wall Street A grassroots movement protesting a capitalist system that fostered social and economic inequality. Begun in Zuccotti Park, New York City, during 2011, the movement spread rapidly across the nation, triggering a national conversation about income inequality and protests of the government's "bailouts" of the banks and corporations allegedly responsible for the Great Recession.

Sandra Day O'Connor (1930–) She was the first woman to serve on the Supreme Court of the United States and was appointed by President Reagan. Reagan's critics charged that her appointment was a token gesture and not a sign of any real commitment to gender equality.

Ohio gang In order to escape the pressures of the White House, President Harding met with a group of people, called the "Ohio gang," in a house on K Street in Washington D.C. Members of this gang were given low-level positions in the American government and they used their White House connection to "line their pockets" by granting government contracts without bidding, which led to a series of scandals, most notably the Teapot Dome Scandal.

The Old Southwest Region covering western Georgia, Alabama, Mississippi, Louisiana, Arkansas, and Texas, where low land prices and fertile soil attracted hundreds of thousands of settlers after the American Revolution.

Frederick Law Olmsted (1822–1903) In 1858, he constructed New York's Central Park, which led to a growth in the movement to create urban parks. He went on to design parks for Boston, Brooklyn, Chicago, Philadelphia, San Francisco, and many other cities.

Open Door policy Official U.S. insistence that Chinese trade would be open to all nations; Secretary of State John Hay unilaterally announced the policy in 1899 in hopes of protecting the Chinese market for U.S. exports.

open shop Business policy of not requiring union membership as a condition of employment; such a policy, where legal, has the effect of weakening unions and diminishing workers' rights.

open range Informal system of governing property on the frontier in which small ranchers could graze their cattle anywhere on unfenced lands; brought to an end by the introduction of barbed wire, a low-cost way to fence off one's land.

Operation Desert Shield After Saddam Hussein invaded Kuwait in 1990, President George H. W. Bush sent American military forces to Saudi Arabia on a strictly defensive mission. They were soon joined by a multinational coalition. When the coalition's mission changed to the retaking of Kuwait, the operation was renamed Desert Storm.

Operation Desert Storm (1991) Assault by American-led multinational forces that quickly defeated Iraqi forces under Saddam Hussein in the First Gulf War, ending the Iraqi occupation of Kuwait.

Operation Overlord The Allies' assault on Hitler's "Atlantic Wall," a seemingly impregnable series of fortifications and minefields along the French coastline that German forces had created using captive Europeans for laborers.

J. Robert Oppenheimer (1904–1967) He led the group of physicists at the laboratory in Los Alamos, New Mexico, who constructed the first atomic bomb.

Oregon Country The Convention of 1818 between Britain and the United States established the Oregon Country as being west of the crest of the Rocky Mountains and the two countries were to jointly occupy it. In 1824, the United States and Russia signed a treaty that established the line of 54°40′ as the southern boundary of Russia's territorial claim in North America. A similar agreement between Britain and Russia finally gave the Oregon Country clearly defined boarders, but it remained under joint British and American control.

"Oregon Fever" The lure of fertile land and economic opportunities in the Oregon Country that drew thousands of settlers westward, beginning in the late 1830s.

Osceola (1804?–1838) He was the leader of the Seminole nation who resisted the federal Indian removal policy through a protracted guerilla war. In 1837, he was treacherously seized under a flag of truce and imprisoned at Fort Moultrie, where he was left to die.

Overland Trails Trail routes followed by wagon trains bearing settlers and trade goods from Missouri to the Oregon Country, California, and New Mexico, beginning in the 1840s.

A. Mitchell Palmer (1872–1936) As the attorney general, he played an active role in the government's response to the Red Scare. After several bombings across America, including one at Palmer's home, he and other Americans became convinced that there was a well-organized Communist terror campaign at work. The federal government launched a campaign of raids, deportations, and collecting files on radical individuals.

Panic of 1819 A financial panic that began a three-year-long economic crisis triggered by a reduced demand of American imports, declining land values, and reckless practices by local and state banks.

Panic of 1837 A financial calamity in the United States brought on by a dramatic slowdown in the British economy and exacerbated by falling cotton prices, failed crops, high inflation, and reckless state banks.

Panic of 1893 A major collapse in the national economy after several major railroad companies declared bankruptcy, leading to a severe depression and several violent clashes between workers and management.

panning A method of mining that used a large metal pan to sift gold dust and nuggets from riverbeds during the California gold rush of 1849.

Rosa Parks (1913–2005) In 1955, she refused to give up her seat to a white man on a city bus in Montgomery, Alabama, which a local ordinance required of blacks. She was arrested for disobeying the ordinance. In response, black community leaders organized the Montgomery bus boycott.

Parliament Legislature of Great Britain, composed of the House of Commons, whose members are elected, and the House of Lords, whose members are either hereditary or appointed.

party "boss" A powerful political leader who controlled a "machine" of associates and operatives to promote both individual and party interests, often using informal tactics such as intimidation or the patronage system.

paternalism A moral position developed during the first half of the nineteenth century which claimed that slaves were deprived of liberty for their own "good." Such a rationalization was adopted by some slave owners to justify slavery.

Patriots Colonists who rebelled against British authority before and during the Revolutionary War.

patronage An informal system (sometimes called the "spoils system") used by politicians to reward their supporters with government appointments or contracts.

Alice Paul (1885–1977) She was a leader of the women's suffrage movement and head of the Congressional Committee of National Women Suffrage Association. She instructed female suffrage activists to use more militant tactics, such as picketing state legislatures, chaining themselves to public buildings, inciting police to arrest them, and undertaking hunger strikes.

Norman Vincent Peale (1898–1993) He was a champion of the upbeat and feel-good theology that was popular in the 1950s religious revival. He advocated getting rid of any depressing or negative thoughts and replacing them with "faith, enthusiasm and joy," which would make an individual popular and well liked.

Pearl Harbor (1941) Surprise Japanese attack on the U.S. fleet at Pearl Harbor on December 7, which prompted the immediate American entry into the war.

"peculiar institution" A phrase used by whites in the antebellum South to refer to slavery without using the word slavery.

Pennsylvania English colony founded by William Penn in 1681 as a Quaker commonwealth, though it welcomed people of all religions.

Pentagon Papers Informal name for the Defense Department's secret history of the Vietnam conflict; leaked to the press by former official Daniel Ellsberg and published in the *New York Times* in 1971.

People's Party (Populists) Political party largely made up of farmers from the South and West that struggled to gain political influence from the East. Populists advocated a variety of reforms, including free coinage of silver, a progressive income tax, postal savings banks, regulation of railroads, and direct election of U.S. senators.

Pequot War Massacre in 1637 and subsequent dissolution of the Pequot Nation by Puritan settlers, who seized the Indians' lands.

perestroika Russian term for "economic restructuring"; applied to Mikhail Gorbachev's series of political and economic reforms that included shifting a centrally planned Commmunist economy to a mixed economy allowing for capitalism.

Commodore Matthew Perry (1794–1858) In 1854, he negotiated the Treaty of Kanagawa, which was the first step in starting a political and commercial relationship between the United States and Japan.

John J. Pershing United States general sent by President Wilson to put down attacks on the Mexican border led by Francisco "Pancho" Villa.

Personal Responsibility and Work Opportunity Act of 1996 (PRWOA) Comprehensive welfare-reform measure, passed by a Republican Congress and signed by President Clinton, that aimed to decrease the size of the "welfare state" by limiting the amount of government aid provided the unemployed so as to encourage recipients to find jobs.

"pet banks" During President Andrew Jackson's fight with the national bank, Jackson resolved to remove all federal deposits from it. To comply with Jackson's demands, Secretary of the Treasury Taney continued to draw on government's accounts in the national bank, but deposit all new federal receipts in state banks. The state banks that received these deposits were called "pet banks."

Pilgrims Puritan Separatists who broke completely with the Church of England and sailed to the New World aboard the *Mayflower*, founding Plymouth Colony on Cape Cod in 1620.

King Philip (?–1676) or **Metacomet** The chief of the Wampanoages, who the colonists called King Philip. He resented English efforts to convert Indians to Christianity and waged a war against the English colonists in which he was killed.

Dien Bien Phu Cluster of Vietnamese villages and site of a major Vietnamese victory over the French in the First Indochina War.

Gifford Pinchot (1865–1946) As the head of the Division of Forestry, he implemented a conservation policy that entailed the scientific management of natural resources to serve the public interest. His work helped start the conservation movement.

Elizabeth Lucas Pinckney (1722? –1793) One of the most enterprising horticulturists in colonial America, she began managing her family's three plantations in South Carolina at the age of sixteen. She had tremendous success growing indigo, which led to many other plantations growing the crop as well.

Pinckney's Treaty Treaty with Spain negotiated by Thomas Pinckney in 1795; established United States boundaries at the Mississippi River and the 31st parallel and allowed open transportation on the Mississippi.

Francisco Pizarro (1478?–1541) In 1531, he lead his Spanish soldiers to Peru and conquered the Inca Empire.

"plain white folk" Yeoman farmers who lived and worked on their own small farms, growing a food and cash crops to trade for necessities.

plantation mistress Matriarch of a planter's household, responsible for supervising the domestic aspects of the estate.

planters Owners of large farms in the South that were worked by twenty or more slaves and supervised by overseers.

political "machine" A network of political activists and elected officials, usually controlled by a powerful "boss," that attempts to manipulate local politics

James Knox Polk "Young Hickory" (1795–1849) As president, his chief concern was the expansion of the United States. Shortly, after taking office, Mexico broke off relations with the United States over the annexation of Texas. Polk declared war on Mexico and sought to subvert Mexican authority in California. The United States defeated Mexico; and the two nations signed the Treaty of Guadalupe Hidalgo in which Mexico gave up any claims on Texas north of the Rio Grande River and ceded New Mexico and California to the United States.

Pontiac's Rebellion An Indian attack on British forts and settlements after France ceded to the British its territory east of the Mississippi River, as part of the Treaty of Paris in 1763, without consulting France's Indian allies.

"Popular Sovereignty" Legal concept by which the white male settlers in a new U.S. territory would vote to decide whether or not to permit slavery.

Populist/People's party Political success of Farmers' Alliance candidates encouraged the formation in 1892 of the People's party (later renamed the Populist party); active until 1912, it advocated a variety of reform issues, including free coinage of silver, income tax, postal savings, regulation of railroads, and direct election of U.S. senators.

Pottawatomie Massacre In retaliation for the "sack of Lawrence," John Brown and his abolitionist cohorts hacked five men to death in the pro-slavery settlement of Pottawatomie, Kansas, on May 24, 1856, triggering a guerrilla war in the Kansas Territory that cost 200 settler lives.

The Powhatan Confederacy An alliance of several powerful Algonquian tribes under the leadership of Chief Powhatan, organized into thirty chiefdoms along much of the Atlantic coast in the late sixteenth and early seventeenth centuries.

Chief Powhatan Wahunsonacock He was called Powhatan by the English after the name of his tribe, and was the powerful, charismatic chief of numerous Algonquian-speaking towns in eastern Virginia representing over 10,000 Indians.

pragmatism William James founded this philosophy in the early 1900s. Pragmatists believed that ideas gained their validity not from their inherent truth, but from their social consequences and practical application.

Proclamation of 1763 Proclamation drawing a boundary along the Appalachian Mountains from Canada to Georgia in order to minimize occurrences of settler–Indian violence; colonists were forbidden to go west of the line.

professions Occupations requiring specialized knowledge of some field; the Industrial Revolution and its new organization of labor created an array of professions in the nineteenth century.

Progressive party In the 1912 election, Theodore Roosevelt was unable to secure the Republican nomination for president. He left the Republican party and formed his own party of progressive Republicans, called the "Bull Moose" party (later Progressive Party). Roosevelt and Taft split the Republican vote, which allowed Democrat Woodrow Wilson to win.

Prohibition National ban on the manufacture and sale of alcohol that lasted from 1920 to 1933, though the law was widely violated and proved too difficult to enforce effectively.

proprietary colonies A colony owned by an individual, rather than a joint-stock company.

Protestant Reformation Sixteenth-century religious movement initiated by Martin Luther, a German monk whose public criticism of corruption in the Roman Catholic Church, and whose teaching that Christians can communicate directly with God, gained a wide following.

public schools Elementary and secondary schools funded by the state and free of tuition.

pueblos The Spanish term for the adobe cliff dwellings of the indigenous people of the southwestern United States.

Pullman strike (1894) A national strike by the American Railway Union, whose members shut down major railways in sympathy with striking workers in Pullman, Illinois; ended with intervention of federal troops.

Puritans English religious dissenters who sought to "purify" the Church of England of its Catholic practices.

Quakers George Fox founded the Quaker religion in 1647. They rejected the use of formal sacraments and ministry, refused to take oaths and embraced pacifism. Fleeing persecution, they settled and established the colony of Pennsylvania.

race-based slavery Institution that uses racial characteristics and myths to justify enslaving a people.

Radical Republicans Senators and congressmen who, strictly identifying the Civil War with the abolitionist cause, sought swift emancipation of the slaves, punishment of the rebels, and tight controls over the former Confederate states after the war.

railroad Steam-powered vehicles that improved passenger transportation, quickened western settlement, and enabled commercial agriculture in the nineteenth century.

Raleigh's Roanoke Island Colony English expedition of 117 settlers, including Virginia Dare, the first English child born in the New World; colony disappeared from Roanoke Island in the Outer Banks sometime between 1587 and 1590.

A. Philip Randolph (1889–1979) He was the head of the Brotherhood of Sleeping Car Porters who planned a march on Washington D.C. to demand an end to racial discrimination in the defense industries. To stop the march, the Roosevelt administration negotiated an agreement with the Randolph group. The demonstration would be called off and an executive order would be issued that forbid discrimination in defense work and training programs and set up the Fair Employment Practices Committee.

range wars In the late 1800s, conflicting claims over land and water rights triggered violent disputes between farmers and ranchers in parts of the western United States.

Ronald Reagan (1911–2004) In 1980, the former actor and governor of California was elected president. In office, he reduced social spending, cut taxes, and increased defense spending. During his presidency, the federal debt tripled, the federal deficit rose, programs such as housing and school lunches were cut, and the HIV/AIDS crisis grew to prominence in the United States. He signed an arms-control treaty with the Soviet Union in 1987, authorized covert CIA operations in Central America, and in 1986 the Iran-Contra scandal was revealed.

Reaganomics President Reagan's "supply-side" economic philosophy combining tax cuts with the goals of decreased government spending, reduced regulation of business, and a balanced budget.

Reconstruction Finance Corporation (1932) Federal program established under President Hoover to loan money to banks and other corporations to help them avoid bankruptcy.

Red Power Activism by militant Native American groups to protest living conditions on Indian reservations through demonstrations, legal action, and, at times, violence.

First Red Scare Fear among many Americans after the First World War of Communists in particular and noncitizens in general, it was a reaction to the Russian Revolution, mail bombs, strikes, and riots.

Redeemers Post–Civil War Democratic leaders who supposedly saved the South from Yankee domination and preserved the primarily rural economy.

Dr. Walter Reed (1851–1902) His work on yellow fever in Cuba led to the discovery that the fever was carried by mosquitoes. This understanding helped develop more effective controls of the worldwide disease.

Reform Darwinism A social philosophy developed by Lester Frank War that challenged the ruthlessness of Social Darwinism by asserting that humans were not passive pawns of evolutionary forces. Instead, people could actively shape the process of evolutionary social development through cooperation, innovation, and planning.

Reformation European religious movement that challenged the Catholic Church and resulted in the beginnings of Protestant Christianity. During this period, Catholics and Protestants persecuted, imprisoned, tortured, and killed each other in large numbers.

religious right Christian conservatives with a faith-based political agenda that includes prohibition of abortion and allowing prayer in public schools.

reparations As a part of the Treaty of Versailles, Germany was required to confess its responsibility for the First World War and make payments to the victors for the entire expense of the war. These two requirements created a deep bitterness among Germans.

Alexander Hamilton's Report on Manufactures First Secretary of the Treasury Alexander Hamilton's 1791 analysis that accurately foretold the future of American industry and proposed tariffs and subsidies to promote it.

Republican ideology Political belief in representative democracy in which citizens govern themselves by electing representatives, or legislators, to make key decisions on the citizens' behalf.

Republican simplicity Deliberate attitude of humility and frugality, as opposed to monarchical pomp and ceremony, adopted by Thomas Jefferson in his presidency.

Republicans First used during the early nineteenth century to describe supporters of a strict interpretation of the Constitution, which they believed would safeguard individual freedoms and states' rights from the threats posed by a strong central government. The idealist Republican vision of sustaining an agrarian-oriented union was developed largely by Thomas Jefferson.

"return to normalcy" Campaign promise of Republican presidential candidate Warren G. Harding in 1920, meant to contrast with Woodrow Wilson's progressivism and internationalism.

Paul Revere (1735–1818) On the night of April 18, 1775, British soldiers marched toward Concord to arrest American Revolutionary leaders and seize their depot of supplies. Paul Revere famously rode through the night and raised the alarm about the approaching British troops.

Roaring Twenties The 1920s, an era of social and intellectual revolution in which young people experimented with new forms of recreation and sexuality. The Eastern, urban cultural shift clashed with conservative and insular Midwestern America, which increased the tensions between the two regions.

Jackie Robinson (1919–1972) In 1947, he became the first African American to play major league baseball. He won over fans and players and stimulated the integration of other professional sports.

rock-and-roll music Alan Freed, a disc jockey, noticed white teenagers were buying rhythm and blues records that had been only purchased by African Americans and Hispanic Americans. Freed began playing these records, but called them rock-and-roll records as a way to overcome the racial barrier. As the popularity of the music genre increased, it helped bridge the gap between "white" and "black" music.

John D. Rockefeller (1839–1937) In 1870, he founded the Standard Oil Company of Ohio, which was his first step in creating his vast oil empire. He perfected the idea of a holding company.

***Roe v. Wade* (1973)** Landmark Supreme Court decision striking down state laws that banned abortions during the first trimester of pregnancy.

Roman Catholicism The Christian faith and religious practices of the Roman Catholic Church, which exerted great political, economic, and social influence on much of Western Europe and, through the Spanish and Portuguese Empires, on the Americas.

Romanticism Philosophical, literary, and artistic movement of the nineteenth century that was largely a reaction to the rationalism of the previous century; Romantics valued emotion, mysticism, and individualism.

Eleanor Roosevelt (1884–1962) She redefined the role of the presidential spouse and was the first woman to address a national political convention, write a nationally syndicated column and hold regular press conferences. She travelled throughout the nation to promote the New Deal, women's causes, organized labor, and meet with African American leaders.

Franklin Delano Roosevelt (1882–1945) Elected during the Great Depression, Roosevelt sought to help struggling Americans through his New Deal programs that created employment and social programs, such as Social Security. After the bombing of Pearl Harbor, he declared war on Japan and Germany and led the country through most of the Second World War before dying of cerebral hemorrhage.

Theodore Roosevelt (1858–1919) As the assistant secretary of the navy, he supported expansionism, American imperialism, and war with Spain. He led the Rough Riders in Cuba during the war of 1898 and used the notoriety of this military campaign for political gain. As President McKinley's vice president, he succeeded McKinley after his assassination. His forceful foreign policy became known as "big stick diplomacy." Domestically, his policies on natural resources helped start the conservation movement. Unable to win the Republican nomination for president in 1912, he formed his own party of progressive Republicans called the "Bull Moose" party.

Roosevelt Corollary President Theodore Roosevelt's 1904 revision of the Monroe Doctrine (1823) in which he argued that the United States could use military force in Central and South American nations to prevent European nations from intervening in the Western Hemisphere.

Rough Riders The First U.S. Volunteer Cavalry, led in the War of 1898 by Theodore Roosevelt; they were victorious in their only engagement, the Battle of San Juan Hill near Santiago, Cuba, and Roosevelt was celebrated as a national hero, bolstering his political career.

Nicola Sacco (1891–1927) In 1920, he and Bartolomeo Vanzetti were Italian immigrants who were arrested for stealing $16,000 and killing a paymaster and his guard. Their trial took place during a time of numerous bombings by anarchists and their judge was openly prejudicial; many liberals and radicals believe that their conviction was based on their political ideas and ethnic origin rather than the evidence against them.

Sacco and Vanzetti case 1921 trial of two Italian immigrants that occurred at the height of Italian immigration and against the backdrop of numerous terror attacks by anarchists; despite a lack of clear evidence, the two defendants, both self-professed anarchists, were convicted of murder and were executed in 1927.

saloons Bars or taverns where mostly men would gather to drink, eat, relax, play games, and, often, to discuss politics.

salutary neglect Informal British policy during the first half of the eighteenth century that allowed the American colonies considerable freedom to pursue their economic and political interests in exchange for colonial obedience.

same-sex marriage The legal right for gay and lesbian couples to marry; it became the most divisive issue in the culture wars of the early 2010s as more and more court rulings affirmed this right in states and municipalities across the United States.

Sandinista Cuban-sponsored government that came to power in Nicaragua after toppling a corrupt dictator. The State Department believed that the Sandinistas were supplying the leftist Salvadoran rebels with Cuban and Soviet arms. In response, the Reagan administration ordered the CIA to train and supply guerrilla bands of anti-Communist Nicaraguans called Contras. A cease-fire agreement between the Contras and Sandinistas was signed in 1988.

Sandlot Incident Violence occurring during the Great Railroad Strike of 1877, when mobs of frustrated working-class whites in San Francisco attacked Chinese immigrants, blaming them for economic hardship.

General Antonio López de Santa Anna (1794–1876) In 1834, he seized political power in Mexico and became a dictator. In 1835, Texans rebelled against him and he led his army to Texas to crush their rebellion. He captured the mission called the Alamo and killed all of its defenders, which inspired Texans to continue resistance and Americans to volunteer to fight for Texas. The Texans captured Santa Anna during a surprise attack and he bought his freedom by signing a treaty recognizing Texas's independence.

battles of Saratoga Decisive defeat of 5,000 British troops under General John Burgoyne in several battles near Saratoga, New York, in October 1777; the American victory helped convince France to enter the war on the side of the Patriots.

scalawags White southern Republicans—some former Unionists—who served in Reconstruction governments.

Phyllis Schlafly (1924–) A right-wing Republican activist who spearheaded the anti-feminism movement. She believed feminists were "anti-family, anti-children, and pro-abortion." She worked against the equal-rights amendment for women and civil rights protection for gays.

Scopes Trial Highly publicized 1925 trial of a high school teacher in Tennessee for violating a state law that prohibited the teaching of evolution; the trial was seen as the climax of the fundamentalist war on Darwinism.

Winfield Scott (1786–1866) During the Mexican War, he was the American general who captured Mexico City, which ended the war. Using his popularity from his military success, he ran as a Whig party candidate for President.

Sears, Roebuck and Company By the end of the nineteenth century, this company dominated the mail-order industry and helped create a truly national market. Its mail-order catalog and low prices allowed people living in rural areas and small towns to buy products that were previously too expensive or available only to city dwellers.

secession Shortly after President Abraham Lincoln was elected, southern states began dissolving their ties with the United States because they believed Lincoln and the Republican party were a threat to slavery.

Second Bank of the United States Established in 1816 after the first national bank's charter expired; it stabilized the economy by creating a sound national currency, by making loans to farmers, small manufacturers, and entrepreneurs, and by regulating the ability of state banks to issue their own paper currency.

Second Great Awakening Religious revival movement that arose in reaction to the growth of secularism and rationalist religion; spurred the growth of the Baptist and Methodist churches.

Second Industrial Revolution Beginning in the late nineteenth century, a wave of technological innovations, especially in iron and steel production, steam and electrical power, and telegraphic communications, all of which spurred industrial development and urban growth.

Second New Deal (1935–1938) Expansive cluster of legislation proposed by President Roosevelt that established new regulatory agencies, strengthened the rights of workers to organize unions, and laid the foundation of a federal social welfare system through the creation of Social Security.

Securities and Exchange Commission (1934) Federal agency established to regulate the issuance and trading of stocks and bonds in an effort to avoid financial panics and stock market "crashes."

Seneca Falls Convention (1848) Convention organized by feminists Lucretia Mott and Elizabeth Cady Stanton to promote women's rights and issue the pathbreaking Declaration of Sentiments.

"separate but equal" Principle underlying legal racial segregation, which was upheld in *Plessy v. Ferguson* (1896) and struck down in *Brown v. Board of Education* (1954).

separation of powers Strict division of the powers of government among three separate branches (executive, legislative, and judicial) which, in turn, check and balance each other.

September 11 On September 11, 2001, Islamic terrorists, who were members of the al Qaeda terrorist organization, hijacked four commercial airliners. Two were flown into the World Trade Center, a third into the Pentagon, and a fourth plane was brought down in Pennsylvania. In response, President George W. Bush launched his "war on terrorism." His administration assembled an international coalition to fight terrorism, which invaded Afghanistan after the country's government would not turn over Osama bin Laden. Bush and Congress passed the U.S.A. Patriot Act, which allowed government agencies to try suspected terrorists in secret military courts and eavesdrop on confidential conversations.

settlement houses Product of the late nineteenth-century movement to offer a broad array of social services in urban immigrant neighborhoods; Chicago's Hull House was one of hundreds of settlement houses that operated by the early twentieth century.

Seventeenth Amendment (1913) Constitutional amendment that provided for the direct election of senators rather than the traditional practice allowing state legislatures to name them.

Shakers Founded by Mother Ann Lee Stanley in England, the United Society of Believers in Christ's Second Appearing settled in Watervliet, New York, in 1774 and subsequently established eighteen additional communes in the Northeast, Indiana, and Kentucky.

share tenants Poor farmers who rented land to farm in exchange for a substantial share of the crop, though they would often have their own horse or mule, tools, and line of credit with a nearby store.

sharecroppers Poor, mostly black farmers who would work an owner's land in return for shelter, seed, fertilizer, mules, supplies, and food, as well as a substantial share of the crop produced.

Share-the-Wealth program Huey Long offered this program as an alternative to the New Deal. The program proposed to confiscate large personal fortunes, which would be used to guarantee every poor family a cash grant of $5,000 and every worker an annual income of $2,500. This program promised to provide pensions, reduce working hours, pay veterans' bonuses, and ensures a college education to every qualified student.

Shays's Rebellion Storming of the Massachusetts federal arsenal in 1787 by Daniel Shays and 1,200 armed farmers seeking debt relief from the state legislature through issuance of paper currency and lower taxes.

Sherman's "March to the Sea" The Union army's devastating march through Georgia from Atlanta to Savannah led by General William T. Sherman, intended to demoralize civilians and destroy the resources the Confederate army needed to fight.

silent majority Term popularized by President Richard Nixon to describe the great majority of American voters who did not express their political opinions publicly—"the non-demonstrators."

Sixteenth Amendment (1913) Constitutional amendment that authorized the federal income tax.

slave codes Ordinances passed by a colony or state to regulate the behavior of slaves, often including brutal punishments for infractions.

Alfred E. Smith (1873–1944) In the 1928 presidential election, he won the Democratic nomination, but failed to win the presidency. Rural voters distrusted him for being Catholic and the son of Irish immigrants as well as his anti-Prohibition stance.

Captain John Smith (1580–1631) A swashbuckling soldier of fortune with rare powers of leadership and self-promotion, he was appointed to the resident council to manage Jamestown.

Joseph Smith (1805–1844) In 1823, he claimed that the Angel Moroni showed him the location of several gold tablets on which the Book of Mormon was written. Using the Book of Mormon as his gospel, he founded the Church of Jesus Christ of Latter-day Saints, or Mormons. In 1839, they settled in Commerce, Illinois, to avoid persecution. In 1844, Joseph and his brother were arrested and jailed for ordering the destruction of a newspaper that opposed them. While in jail, an anti-Mormon mob stormed the jail and killed both of them.

Social Darwinism The application of Charles Darwin's theory of evolutionary natural selection to human society; Social Darwinists used the concept of "survival of the fittest" to justify class distinctions, explain poverty, and oppose government intervention in the economy.

social gospel Protestant movement that stressed the Christian obligation to address the mounting social problems caused by urbanization and industrialization.

social justice An important part of the Progressive's agenda, social justice sought to solve social problems through reform and regulation. Methods used to bring about social justice ranged from the founding of charities to the legislation of a ban on child labor.

Social Security Act (1935) Legislation enacted to provide federal assistance to retired workers through tax-funded pension payments and benefit payments to the unemployed and disabled.

Sons of Liberty First organized by Samuel Adams in the 1770s, groups of colonists dedicated to militant resistance against British control of the colonies.

Hernando de Soto (1500?–1542) A conquistador who explored the west coast of Florida, western North Carolina, and along the Arkansas river from 1539 till his death in 1542.

Southern Christian Leadership Conference (SCLC) Civil rights organization formed by Dr. Martin Luther King, Jr., that championed nonviolent direct action as a means of ending segregation.

"southern strategy" This strategy was a major reason for Richard Nixon's victory in the 1968 presidential election. To gain support in the South, Nixon assured southern conservatives that he would slow the federal enforcement of civil rights laws and appoint pro-southern justices to the Supreme Court. As president, Nixon fulfilled these promises.

Spanish Armada A massive Spanish fleet of 130 warships that was defeated at Plymouth in 1588 by the English navy during the reign of Queen Elizabeth I.

Spanish flu Unprecedentedly lethal influenza epidemic of 1918 that killed more than 22 million people worldwide.

Herbert Spencer (1820–1903) As the first major proponent of social Darwinism, he argued that human society and institutions are subject to the process of natural selection and that society naturally evolves for the better. He was against any form of government interference with the evolution of society, like business regulations, because it would help the "unfit" to survive.

spirituals Songs with religious messages sung by slaves to help ease the strain of field labor and to voice their suffering at the hands of their masters and overseers.

spoils system The term—meaning the filling of federal government jobs with persons loyal to the party of the president—originated in Andrew Jackson's first term; the system was replaced in the Progressive Era by civil service.

Square Deal Roosevelt's progressive agenda of the "Three C's": control of corporations, conservation of natural resources, and consumer protection.

stagflation Term coined by economists during the Nixon presidency to describe the unprecedented situation of stagnant economic growth and consumer price inflation occurring at the same time.

Joseph Stalin (1879–1953) The Bolshevik leader who succeeded Lenin as the leader of the Soviet Union in 1924 and ruled the country until his death. During his totalitarian rule of the Soviet Union, he used purges and a system of forced labor camps to maintain control over the country, and claimed vast areas of Eastern Europe for Soviet domination.

Stalwarts Conservative Republican party faction during the presidency of Rutherford B. Hayes, 1877–1881; led by Senator Roscoe B. Conkling of New York, Stalwarts opposed civil service reform and favored a third term for President Ulysses S. Grant.

Stamp Act Act of Parliament requiring that all printed materials (e.g., newspapers, bonds, and even playing cards) in the American colonies use paper with an official tax stamp in order to pay for British military protection of the colonies.

Stamp Act Congress Twenty-seven delegates from nine of the colonies met from October 7 to 25, 1765 and wrote a Declaration of the Rights and Grievances of the Colonies, a petition to the King and a petition to Parliament for the repeal of the Stamp Act.

Standard Oil Company Corporation under the leadership of John D. Rockefeller that attempted to dominate the entire oil industry through horizontal and vertical integration.

Elizabeth Cady Stanton (1815–1902) A prominent reformer and advocate for the rights of women, she helped organize the Seneca Falls Convention to discuss women's rights. The convention was the first of its kind and produced the Declaration of Sentiments, which proclaimed the equality of men and women.

staple crop A profitable market crop, such as cotton, tobacco, or rice that predominates in a given region.

state constitutions Charters that define the relationship between the state government and local governments and individuals, and also protects their rights from violation by the national government.

steamboats Ships and boats powered by wood-fired steam engines. First used in the early nineteenth century, they made two-way traffic possible in eastern river systems, creating a transcontinental market and an agricultural empire.

Thaddeus Stevens (1792–1868) As one of the leaders of the Radical Republicans, he argued that the former Confederate states should be viewed as conquered provinces, which were subject to the demands of the conquerors. He believed that all of Southern society needed to be changed, and he supported the abolition of slavery and racial equality.

Adlai E. Stevenson (1900–1965) In the 1952 and 1956 presidential elections, he was the Democratic nominee who lost to Dwight Eisenhower. He was also the U.S. Ambassador to the United Nations and is remembered for his famous speech in 1962 before the UN Security Council that unequivocally demonstrated that the Soviet Union had built nuclear missile bases in Cuba.

Stono Rebellion A 1739 slave uprising in South Carolina that was brutally quashed, leading to executions as well as a severe tightening of the slave code.

Stonewall Riots (1969) Violent clashes between police and gay patrons of New York City's Stonewall Inn, seen as the starting point of the modern gay rights movement.

Strategic Arms Limitation Treaty (SALT I) (1972) Agreement signed by President Nixon and Secretary Brezhnev prohibiting the development of missile defense systems in the United States and Soviet Union and limiting the quantity of nuclear warheads for both.

Strategic Defense Initiative (SDI) (1983) Ronald Reagan's proposed space-based anti-missile defense system, dubbed "Star Wars" by the media, that aroused great controversy and escalated the arms race between the United States and the Soviet Union.

Levi Strauss (1829–1902) A Jewish tailor who followed miners to California during the gold rush and began making durable work pants that were later dubbed blue jeans or Levi's.

Student Nonviolent Coordinating Committee (SNCC) Interracial organization formed in 1960 with the goal of intensifying the effort to end racial segregation.

Students for a Democratic Society (SDS) Major organization of the New Left, founded at the University of Michigan in 1960 by Tom Hayden and Al Haber.

suburbia Communities formed from mass migration of middle-class whites from urban centers.

Suez crisis (1956) British, French, and Israeli attack on Egypt after Nasser's seizure of the Suez Canal; President Eisenhower interceded to demand the withdrawal of the British, French, and Israeli forces from the Sinai peninsula and canal.

Sunbelt The label for an arc that stretched from the Carolinas to California. During the postwar era, much of the urban population growth occurred in this area.

the "surge" In early 2007, President Bush decided he would send a "surge" of new troops to Iraq and implement a new strategy. U.S. forces would shift their focus from offensive operations to the protection of Iraqi civilians from attacks by terrorist insurgents and sectarian militias. While the "surge" reduced the violence in Iraq, Iraqi leaders were still unable to develop a self-sustaining democracy.

Taft-Hartley Labor Act (1947) Congressional legislation that banned "unfair labor practices" by labor unions, required union leaders to sign anti-Communist "loyalty oaths," and prohibited federal employees from going on strike.

Taliban A coalition of ultraconservative Islamists who rose to power in Afghanistan after the Soviets withdrew. The Taliban leaders gave Osama bin Laden a safe haven in their country in exchange for aid in fighting the Northern Alliance, who were rebels opposed to the Taliban. After they refused to turn bin Laden over to the United States, America invaded Afghanistan.

Tammany Hall The "city machine" used by "Boss" Tweed to dominate politics in New York City until his arrest in 1871.

tariff A tax on goods imported from other nations, typically used to protect home industries from foreign competitors and to generate revenue for the federal government.

Tariff of 1816 A cluster of taxes on imports passed by Congress to protect America's emerging iron and textile industries from British competition.

Tariff of 1832 This tariff act reduced the duties on many items, but the tariffs on cloth and iron remained high. South Carolina nullified it along with the tariff of 1828. President Andrew Jackson sent federal troops to the state and asked Congress to grant him the authority to enforce the tariffs. Henry Clay presented a plan of gradually reducing the tariffs until 1842, which Congress passed and ended the crisis.

"Tariff of Abominations" (1828) Tax on imported goods, including British cloth and clothing, that strengthened New England textile companies but hurt southern consumers, who experienced a decrease in British demand for raw cotton grown in the South.

tariff reform Effort led by the Democratic party to reduce taxes on imported goods, which Republicans argued were needed to protect American industries from foreign competition.

Troubled Asset Relief Program (TARP) In 2008 President George W. Bush signed into law the bank bailout fund called Troubled Asset Relief Program (TARP), which required the Treasury Department to spend $700 billion to keep banks and other financial institutions from collapsing.

Zachary Taylor (1784–1850) During the Mexican War, he scored two quick victories against Mexico, which made him very popular in America. He used his popularity from his military victories to be elected president as a member of the Whig party, but died before he could complete his term.

Taylorism Labor system based on detailed study of work tasks, championed by Frederick Winslow Taylor, intended to maximize efficiency and profits for employers.

Tea Party Right-wing populist movement, largely made up of middle-class, white male conservatives, that emerged as a response to the expansion of the federal government under the Obama administration.

Teapot Dome Harding administration scandal in which Secretary of the Interior Albert B. Fall profited from secret leasing of government oil reserves in Wyoming to private oil companies.

Tecumseh (1768–1813) He was a leader of the Shawnee tribe who tried to unite all Indians into a confederation that could defend their hunting grounds. He believed that no land cessions could be made without the consent of all the tribes since they held the land in common. His beliefs and leadership made him seem dangerous to the American government and they waged war on him and his tribe. He was killed at the Battle of the Thames.

Tecumseh's Indian Confederacy A group of Native Americans under leadership of Shawnee leader Tecumseh and his prophet brother Tenskwatawa; its mission of fighting off American expansion was thwarted in the Battle of Tippecanoe (1811), when the confederacy fell apart.

Tejanos Texas settlers of Spanish or Mexican descent.

telegraph system System of electronic communication invented by Samuel F. B. Morse that could be transmitted instantaneously across great distances (first used in the 1840s).

Teller Amendment Addition to the congressional war resolution of April 20, 1898, which marked the U.S. entry into the war with Spain; the amendment declared that the United States' goal in entering the war was to ensure Cuba's independence, not to annex Cuba as a territory.

temperance A widespread reform movement, led by militant Christians, focused on reducing the use of alcoholic beverages.

tenements Shabby, low-cost inner-city apartment buildings that housed the urban poor in cramped, unventilated apartments.

Tenochtitlán The capital city of the Aztec Empire. The city was built on marshy islands on the western side of Lake Tetzcoco, which is the site of present-day Mexico City.

Tet offensive Surprise attack by Viet Cong guerrillas and the North Vietnamese army on U.S. and South Vietnamese forces in 1968 that shocked the American public and led to widespread sentiment against the war.

The Texas Revolution (1835–1836) Conflict between Texas colonists and the Mexican government that resulted in the creation of the separate Republic of Texas in 1836.

textile industry Commercial production of thread, fabric, and clothing from raw cotton in mills in New England during the first half of the nineteenth century, and later in the South in the late nineteenth century.

Thirteenth Amendment (1865) Amendment to the U. S. Constitution that freed all slaves in the United States.

Battle of Tippecanoe (1811) Battle in northern Indiana between U.S. troops and Native American warriors led by Tenskwatawa, the brother of Tecumseh, who had organized an anti-American Indian confederacy to fight American efforts to settle on Indian lands.

tobacco A cash crop grown in the Caribbean as well as the Virginia and Maryland colonies, made increasingly profitable by the rapidly growing popularity of smoking in Europe after the voyages of Columbus.

Gulf of Tonkin incident On August 2 and 4 of 1964, North Vietnamese vessels attacked two American destroyers in the Gulf of Tonkin off the coast of North Vietnam. President Johnson described the attacks as unprovoked. In reality, the U.S. ships were monitoring South Vietnamese attacks on North Vietnamese islands that America advisors had planned. The incident spurred the Tonkin Gulf resolution.

Tonkin Gulf Resolution Congressional action that granted the president unlimited authority to defend U.S. forces abroad, passed in August 1964 after an allegedly unprovoked attack on American warships off the coast of North Vietnam.

Tories Term used by Patriots to refer to Loyalists, or colonists who supported the Crown after the Declaration of Independence.

Townshend Acts Parliamentary measures to extract more revenue from the colonies; the Revenue Act of 1767, which taxed tea, paper, and other colonial imports, was one of the most notorious of these policies.

"Trail of Tears" The Cherokees' eight-hundred mile journey (1838–1839) from the southern Appalachians to Indian Territory (in present-day Oklahoma); four thousand died people along the way.

transcendentalism Philosophy of a small group of New England writers and thinkers who advocated personal spirituality, self-reliance, social reform, and harmony with nature.

Transcontinental railroad First line across the continent from Omaha, Nebraska, to Sacramento, California, established in 1869 with the linkage of the Union Pacific and Central Pacific railroads at Promontory, Utah.

Transcontinental Treaty (1819) (Adams-Onís Treaty) Treaty between Spain and the United States that clarified the boundaries of the Louisiana Purchase and arranged the transfer of Florida to the United States in exchange for cash.

triangular trade A network of trade in which exports from one region were sold to another region, which sent its exports to a third region, which exported its own goods back to the first country or colony.

Treaty of Ghent (1814) Agreement between Great Britain and the United States that ended the War of 1812, signed on December 24, 1814.

The Treaty of Guadeloupe Hidalgo (1848) Treaty between United States and Mexico that ended the Mexican-American War.

Treaty of Paris Settlement between Great Britain and France that ended the French and Indian War.

Treaty of Versailles Peace treaty that ended the First World War, forcing Germany to dismantle its military, pay immense war reparations, and give up its colonies around the world.

trench warfare A form of prolonged combat between the entrenched positions of opposing armies, often with little tactical movement.

Harry S. Truman (1884–1972) As President Roosevelt's vice president, he succeeded him after his death near the end of the Second World War. After the war, Truman wrestled with the inflation of both prices and wages, worked with Congress to pass the National Security Act, and banned racial discrimination in the hiring of federal employees and ended racial segregation in the armed forces. In foreign affairs, he established the Truman Doctrine to contain communism, developed the Marshall Plan to rebuild Europe, and sent the U.S. military to defend South Korea after North Korea invaded.

Truman Doctrine (1947) President Truman's program of "containing" communism in Eastern Europe and providing economic and military aid to any nations at risk of Communist takeover.

trust A business arrangement that gives a person or corporation (the "trustee") the legal power to manage another person's money or another company without owning those entities outright.

Sojourner Truth (1797?–1883) She was born into slavery, but New York State freed her in 1827. She spent the 1840s and 1850s travelling across the country and speaking to audiences about her experiences as slave and asking them to support abolition and women's rights.

Harriet Tubman (1820–1913) She was born a slave, but escaped to the North. She then returned to the South nineteen times and guided 300 slaves to freedom.

Frederick Jackson Turner An influential historian who authored the "Frontier Thesis" in 1893, arguing that the existence of an alluring frontier and the experience of persistent westward expansion informed the nation's democratic politics, unfettered economy, and rugged individualism.

Nat Turner (1800–1831) He was the leader of the only slave revolt to get past the planning stages. In August of 1831, the revolt began with the slaves killing the members of Turner's master's household. Then they attacked other neighboring farmhouses and recruited more slaves until the militia crushed the revolt. At least fifty-five whites were killed during the uprising and seventeen slaves were hanged afterwards.

Nat Turner's Rebellion (1831) Insurrection in rural Virginia led by black overseer Nat Turner, who killed slave owners and their families; in turn, federal troops indiscriminately killed hundreds of slaves in the process of putting down Turner and his rebels.

Tuskegee Airmen U.S. Army Air Corps unit of African American pilots whose combat success spurred military and civilian leaders to desegregate the armed forces after the war.

Mark Twain (1835–1910) Born Samuel Langhorne Clemens in Missouri, he became a popular humorous writer and lecturer and established himself as one of the great American satirists and authors. His two greatest books, *The Adventures of Tom Sawyer* and *The Adventures of Huckleberry Finn*, drew heavily on his childhood in Missouri.

"Boss" Tweed (1823–1878) An infamous political boss in New York City, Tweed used his "city machine," the Tammany Hall ring, to rule, plunder and sometimes improve the city's government. His political domination of New York City ended with his arrest in 1871 and conviction in 1873.

Twenty-first Amendment (1933) Repealed prohibition on the manufacture, sale, and transportation of alcoholic beverages, effectively nullifying the Eighteenth Amendment.

two-party system Domination of national politics by two major political parties, such as the Whigs and Democrats during the 1830s and 1840s.

Underground Railroad A secret system of routes and safe houses through which runaway slaves were led to freedom in the North.

Unitarians Members of the liberal New England Congregationalist offshoot, often well-educated and wealthy, who profess the oneness of God and the goodness of rational man.

United Farm Workers (UFW) Organization formed in 1962 to represent the interests of Mexican American migrant workers.

United Nations Security Council A major agency within the United Nations which remains in permanent session and has the responsibility of maintaining international peace and security. Originally, it consisted of five permanent members, (United States, Soviet Union, Britain, France, and the Republic of China), and six members elected to two-year terms. After 1965, the number of rotating members was increased to ten. In 1971, the Republic of China was replaced with the People's Republic of China and the Soviet Union was replaced by the Russian Federation in 1991.

Universalists Members of a New England religious movement, often from the working class, who believed in a merciful God and universal salvation.

USA Patriot Act (2001) Wide-reaching Congressional legislation, triggered by the War on Terror, which gave government agencies the right to eavesdrop on confidential conversations between prison inmates and their lawyers and permitted suspected terrorists to be tried in secret military courts.

U-boat German military submarine (*Unterseeboot*) used during the First World War to attack enemy naval vessels as well as merchant ships of enemy and neutral nations.

utopian communities Ideal communities that offered innovative social and economic relationships to those who were interested in achieving salvation.

Valley Forge American military encampment near Philadelphia, where more than 3,500 soldiers deserted or died from cold and hunger in the winter of 1777–1778.

Cornelius Vanderbilt (1794–1877) In the 1860s, he consolidated several separate railroad companies into one vast entity, New York Central Railroad.

Bartolomeo Vanzetti (1888–1927) In 1920, he and Nicola Sacco were Italian immigrants who were arrested for stealing $16,000 and killing a paymaster and his guard. Their trial took place during a time of numerous bombings by anarchists and their judge was openly prejudicial. Many liberals and radicals believe that their conviction was based on their political ideas and ethnic origin rather than the evidence against them.

vertical integration The process by which a corporation gains control of all aspects of the resources and processes needed to produce and sell a product.

Amerigo Vespucci (1455–1512) Italian explorer who reached the New World in 1499 and was the first to suggest that South America was a new continent. Afterward, European mapmakers used a variant of his first name, America, to label the New World.

Battle of Vicksburg (1863) A protracted battle in northern Mississippi in which Union forces under Ulysses Grant besieged the last major Confederate fortress on the Mississippi River, forcing the inhabitants into starvation and then submission.

Viet Cong Communist guerrillas in Vietnam who launched attacks on the Diem government.

Vietnamization Nixon-era policy of equipping and training South Vietnamese forces to take over the burden of combat from U.S. troops.

Vikings Norse people from Scandinavia who sailed to Newfoundland about A.D. 1001.

Francisco Pancho Villa (1877–1923) While the leader of one of the competing factions in the Mexican civil war, he provoked the United States into intervening. He hoped attacking the United States would help him build a reputation as an opponent of the United States, which would increase his popularity and discredit Mexican President Carranza.

Virginia Company A joint stock enterprise that King James I chartered in 1606. The company was to spread Christianity in the New World as well as find ways to make a profit in it.

Virginia Plan The delegations to the Constitutional Convention were divided between two plans on how to structure the government: Virginia called for a strong central government and a two-house legislature apportioned by population.

Virginia Statute of Religious Freedom A Virginia law, drafted by Thomas Jefferson in 1777 and enacted in 1786, that guarantees freedom of, and from, religion.

virtual representation The idea that the American colonies, although they had no actual representative in Parliament, were "virtually" represented by all members of Parliament.

Voting Rights Act of 1965 Legislation ensuring that all Americans were able to vote; the law ended literacy tests and other means of restricting voting rights.

Wagner Act (1935) Legislation that guaranteed workers the right to organize unions, granted them direct bargaining power, and barred employers from interfering with union activities.

George Wallace (1919–1998) An outspoken defender of segregation. As the governor of Alabama, he once attempted to block African American students from enrolling at the University of Alabama. He ran as the presidential candidate for the American Independent party in 1968, appealing to voters who were concerned about rioting anti-war protestors, the welfare system, and the growth of the federal government.

war hawks In 1811, congressional members from the southern and western districts who clamored for a war to seize Canada and Florida were dubbed "war hawks."

War of 1812 Conflict fought in North America and at sea between Great Britain and the United States, 1812–1815, over American shipping rights and British efforts to spur Indian attacks on American settlements. Canadians and Native Americans also fought in the war.

war on terror Global crusade to root out anti-American, anti-Western Islamist terrorist cells launched by President George W. Bush as a response to the 9/11 attacks.

War Powers Act (1973) Legislation requiring the president to inform Congress within 48 hours of the deployment of U.S. troops abroad and to withdraw them after 60 days unless Congress approves their continued deployment.

War Production Board Federal agency created by President Roosevelt in 1942 that converted America's industrial output to war production.

"war relocation camps" Detention camps housing thousands of Japanese Americans from the West Coast who were forcibly interned from 1942 until the end of the Second World War.

Warren Court The U.S. Supreme Court under Chief Justice Earl Warren, 1953–1969, decided such landmark cases as *Brown v. Board of Education* (school desegregation), *Baker v. Carr* (legislative redistricting), and *Gideon v. Wainwright* and *Miranda v. Arizona* (rights of criminal defendants).

Booker T. Washington (1856–1915) He founded a leading college for African Americans in Tuskegee, Alabama, and become the foremost black educator in America by the 1890s. He believed that the African American community should establish an economic base for its advancement before striving for social equality. His critics charged that his philosophy sacrificed educational and civil rights for dubious social acceptance and economic opportunities.

George Washington (1732–1799) In 1775, the Continental Congress named him the commander in chief of the Continental Army which defeated the British in the American Revolution. He had previously served as an officer in the French and

Indian War. In 1787, he was the presiding officer over the Constitutional Convention, but participated little in the debates. In 1789, the Electoral College chose Washington to be the nation's first president. Washington faced the nation's first foreign and domestic crises, maintaining the United States' neutrality in foreign affairs. After two terms in office, Washington chose to step down; and the power of the presidency was peacefully passed to John Adams.

Watergate (1972–1974) Scandal that exposed the criminality and corruption of the Nixon administration and ultimately led to President Nixon's resignation in 1974.

Daniel Webster (1782–1852) As a representative from New Hampshire, he led the New Federalists in opposition to the moving of the second national bank from Boston to Philadelphia. Later, he served as representative and a senator for Massachusetts and emerged as a champion of a stronger national government. He also switched from opposing to supporting tariffs because New England had built up its manufactures with the understanding tariffs would protect them from foreign competitors.

Webster-Ashburton Treaty Settlement in 1842 of U.S.–Canadian border disputes in Maine, New York, Vermont, and in the Wisconsin Territory (now northern Minnesota).

Webster-Hayne debate U.S. Senate debate of January 1830 between Daniel Webster of Massachusetts and Robert Hayne of South Carolina over nullification and states' rights.

Western Front The contested frontier between the Central and Allied Powers that ran along northern France and across Belgium.

Whig party Political party founded in 1834 in opposition to the Jacksonian Democrats; Whigs supported federal funding for internal improvements, a national bank, and high tariffs on imported goods.

Whigs Another name for revolutionary Patriots.

Whiskey Rebellion (1794) Violent protest by western Pennsylvania farmers against the federal excise tax on corn whiskey, put down by a federal army.

Eli Whitney (1765–1825) He invented the cotton gin which could separate cotton from its seeds. One machine operator could separate fifty times more cotton than worker could by hand, which led to an increase in cotton production and prices. These increases gave planters a new profitable use for slavery and a lucrative slave trade emerged from the coastal South to the Southwest.

Wilderness Road Originally an Indian path through the Cumberland Gap, it was used by over 300,000 settlers who migrated westward to Kentucky in the last quarter of the eighteenth century.

Roger Williams (1603–1683) Puritan who believed that the purity of the church required a complete separation between church and state and freedom from coercion in matters of faith. In 1636, he established the town of Providence, the first permanent settlement in Rhode Island and the first to allow religious freedom in America.

Wendell L. Willkie (1892–1944) In the 1940 presidential election, he was the Republican nominee who ran against President Roosevelt. He supported aid to the Allies and criticized the New Deal programs. Voters looked at the increasingly dangerous world situation and chose to keep President Roosevelt in office for a third term.

Wilmot Proviso (1846) Proposal by Congressman David Wilmot, a Pennsylvania Democrat, to prohibit slavery in any land acquired in the Mexican-American War.

Woodrow Wilson (1856–1924) In the 1912 presidential election, Woodrow Wilson ran under the slogan of New Freedom, which promised to improve of the banking system, lower tariffs, and break up monopolies. At the beginning of the First World War, Wilson kept America neutral, but provided the Allies with credit for purchases of supplies; however, the sinking of U.S. merchant ships and the Zimmerman telegram caused him to ask Congress to declare war on Germany. Wilson supported the entry of America into the League of Nations and the ratification of the Treaty of Versailles, but Congress would not approve the entry or ratification.

John Winthrop Puritan leader and Governor of the Massachusetts Bay Colony who resolved to use the colony as a refuge for persecuted Puritans and as an instrument of building a "wilderness Zion" in America.

woman suffrage Movement to give women the right to vote through a constitutional amendment, spearheaded by Susan B. Anthony and Elizabeth Cady Stanton's National Woman Suffrage Association.

Women Accepted for Voluntary Emergency Services (WAVES) During the Second World War, the increased demand for labor shook up old prejudices about gender roles in the workplace and in the military. Nearly 200,000 women served in the Women's Army Corps or its naval equivalent, Women Accepted for Volunteer Emergency Service (WAVES).

Women's Army Corps Women's branch of the United States Army; by the end of the Second World War nearly 150,000 women had served in the WAC.

women's movement Wave of activism sparked by Betty Friedan's *The Feminine Mystique* (1963); it argued for equal rights for women and fought against the cult of domesticity of the 1950s that limited women's roles to the home as wife, mother, and housewife.

women's work The traditional term referring to routine tasks in the house, garden, and fields performed by women. The sphere of women's occupations expanded in the colonies to include medicine, shopkeeping, upholstering, and the operation of inns and taverns.

Woodstock In 1969, roughly a half a million young people converged on a farm near Bethel, New York, for a three-day music festival that was an expression of the flower children's free spirit.

Works Progress Administration (1935) Government agency established to manage several federal job programs created under the New Deal; it became the largest employer in the nation.

Wounded Knee, Battle of Last incident of the Indians Wars took place in 1890 in the Dakota Territory, where the U.S. Cavalry killed over 200 Sioux men, women, and children who were in the process of surrender.

XYZ affair French foreign minister Tallyrand's three anonymous agents demanded payments to stop French plundering of American ships in 1797; refusal to pay the bribe led to two years of sea war with France (1798–1800).

Yalta Conference (1945) Meeting of the "Big Three" Allied leaders, Franklin D. Roosevelt, Winston Churchill, and Joseph Stalin, to discuss how to divide control of postwar Germany and eastern Europe

yellow journalism A type of news reporting, epitomized in the 1890s by the newspaper empires of William Randolph Hearst and Joseph Pulitzer, that intentionally manipulates public opinion through sensational headlines, illustrations, and articles about both real and invented events.

yeomen Small landowners (the majority of white families in the South) who farmed their own land and usually did not own slaves.

Battle of Yorktown Last major battle of the Revolutionary War; General Cornwallis along with over 7,000 British troops surrendered to George Washington at Yorktown, Virginia, on October 17, 1781.

Brigham Young (1801–1877) Following Joseph Smith's death, he became the leader of the Mormons and promised Illinois officials that the Mormons would leave the state. In 1846, he led the Mormons to Utah and settled near the Salt Lake. After the United States gained Utah as part of the Treaty of Guadalupe Hidalgo, he became the governor of the territory and kept the Mormons virtually independent of federal authority.

youth culture The youth of the 1950s had more money and free time than any previous generation which allowed a distinct youth culture to emerge. A market emerged for products and activities that were specifically for young people such as transistor radios, rock records, *Seventeen* magazine, and Pat Boone movies.

Zimmermann telegram Message sent by a German official to the Mexican government in 1917 urging an invasion of the United States; the telegram was intercepted by British intelligence agents and angered Americans, many of whom called for war against Germany.

Appendix

The Declaration of Independence (1776)

When in the Course of human events, it becomes necessary for one people to dissolve the political bands which have connected them with another, and to assume among the powers of the earth, the separate and equal station to which the Laws of Nature and of Nature's God entitle them, a decent respect to the opinions of mankind requires that they should declare the causes which impel them to the separation.

We hold these truths to be self-evident, that all men are created equal, that they are endowed by their Creator with certain unalienable Rights, that among these are Life, Liberty and the pursuit of Happiness. —That to secure these rights, Governments are instituted among Men, deriving their just powers from the consent of the governed, —That whenever any Form of Government becomes destructive of these ends, it is the Right of the People to alter or to abolish it, and to institute new Government, laying its foundation on such principles and organizing its powers in such form, as to them shall seem most likely to effect their Safety and Happiness. Prudence, indeed, will dictate that Governments long established should not be changed for light and transient causes; and accordingly all experience hath shewn, that mankind are more disposed to suffer, while evils are sufferable, than to right themselves by abolishing the forms to which they are accustomed. But when a long train of abuses and usurpations, pursuing invariably the same Object evinces a design to reduce them under absolute Despotism, it is their right, it is their duty, to throw off such Government, and to provide new Guards for their future security.— Such has been the patient sufferance of these Colonies; and such is now the necessity which constrains them to alter their former Systems of Government. The history of the present King of Great Britain is a history of repeated injuries and usurpations, all having in direct object the establishment of an absolute Tyranny over these States. To prove this, let Facts be submitted to a candid world.

He has refused his Assent to Laws, the most wholesome and necessary for the public good.

He has forbidden his Governors to pass Laws of immediate and pressing importance, unless suspended in their operation till his Assent should be obtained; and when so suspended, he has utterly neglected to attend to them.

He has refused to pass other Laws for the accommodation of large districts of people, unless those people would relinquish the right of Representation in the Legislature, a right inestimable to them and formidable to tyrants only.

He has called together legislative bodies at places unusual, uncomfortable, and distant from the depository of their public Records, for the sole purpose of fatiguing them into compliance with his measures.

He has dissolved Representative Houses repeatedly, for opposing with manly firmness his invasions on the rights of the people.

He has refused for a long time, after such dissolutions, to cause others to be elected; whereby the Legislative powers, incapable of Annihilation, have returned to the People at large for their exercise; the State remaining in the mean time exposed to all the dangers of invasion from without, and convulsions within.

He has endeavoured to prevent the population of these States; for that purpose obstructing the Laws for Naturalization of Foreigners; refusing to pass others to encourage their migrations hither, and raising the conditions of new Appropriations of Lands.

He has obstructed the Administration of Justice, by refusing his Assent to Laws for establishing Judiciary powers.

He has made Judges dependent on his Will alone, for the tenure of their offices, and the amount and payment of their salaries.

He has erected a multitude of New Offices, and sent hither swarms of Officers to harrass our people, and eat out their substance.

He has kept among us, in times of peace, Standing Armies without the Consent of our legislatures.

He has affected to render the Military independent of and superior to the Civil power.

He has combined with others to subject us to a jurisdiction foreign to our constitution, and unacknowledged by our laws; giving his Assent to their Acts of pretended Legislation:

For quartering large bodies of armed troops among us:

For protecting them, by a mock Trial, from punishment for any Murders which they should commit on the Inhabitants of these States:

For cutting off our Trade with all parts of the world:

For imposing Taxes on us without our Consent:

For depriving us in many cases, of the benefits of Trial by Jury:

For transporting us beyond Seas to be tried for pretended offences

For abolishing the free System of English Laws in a neighbouring Province, establishing therein an Arbitrary government, and enlarging its Boundaries so as to render it at once an example and fit instrument for introducing the same absolute rule into these Colonies:

For taking away our Charters, abolishing our most valuable Laws, and altering fundamentally the Forms of our Governments:

For suspending our own Legislatures, and declaring themselves invested with power to legislate for us in all cases whatsoever.

He has abdicated Government here, by declaring us out of his Protection and waging War against us.

He has plundered our seas, ravaged our Coasts, burnt our towns, and destroyed the lives of our people.

He is at this time transporting large Armies of foreign Mercenaries to compleat the works of death, desolation and tyranny, already begun with circumstances of Cruelty & perfidy scarcely paralleled in the most barbarous ages, and totally unworthy the Head of a civilized nation.

He has constrained our fellow Citizens taken Captive on the high Seas to bear Arms against their Country, to become the executioners of their friends and Brethren, or to fall themselves by their Hands.

He has excited domestic insurrections amongst us, and has endeavoured to bring on the inhabitants of our frontiers, the merciless Indian Savages, whose known rule of warfare, is an undistinguished destruction of all ages, sexes and conditions.

In every stage of these Oppressions We have Petitioned for Redress in the most humble terms: Our repeated Petitions have been answered only by repeated injury. A Prince whose character is thus marked by every act which may define a Tyrant, is unfit to be the ruler of a free people.

Nor have We been wanting in attentions to our Brittish brethren. We have warned them from time to time of attempts by their legislature to extend an unwarrantable jurisdiction over us. We have reminded them of the circumstances of our emigration and settlement here. We have appealed to their native justice and magnanimity, and we have conjured them by the ties of our common kindred to disavow these usurpations, which, would inevitably interrupt our connections and correspondence. They too have been deaf to the voice of justice and of consanguinity. We must, therefore, acquiesce in the necessity, which denounces our Separation, and hold them, as we hold the rest of mankind, Enemies in War, in Peace Friends.

We, therefore, the Representatives of the united States of America, in General Congress, Assembled, appealing to the Supreme Judge of the world for the rectitude of our intentions, do, in the Name, and by Authority of the good People of these Colonies, solemnly publish and declare, That these United Colonies are, and of Right ought to be Free and Independent States; that they are Absolved from all Allegiance to the British Crown, and that all political connection between them and the State of Great Britain, is and ought to be totally dissolved; and that as Free and Independent States, they have full Power to levy War, conclude Peace, contract Alliances, establish Commerce, and to do all other Acts and Things which Independent States may of right do. And for the support of this Declaration, with a firm reliance on the protection of divine Providence, we mutually pledge to each other our Lives, our Fortunes and our sacred Honor.

Georgia
Button Gwinnett
Lyman Hall
George Walton

North Carolina
William Hooper
Joseph Hewes
John Penn

South Carolina
Edward Rutledge
Thomas Heyward, Jr.
Thomas Lynch, Jr.
Arthur Middleton

Massachusetts
John Hancock

Maryland
Samuel Chase
William Paca
Thomas Stone
Charles Carroll
    of Carrollton

Virginia
George Wythe
Richard Henry Lee
Thomas Jefferson
Benjamin Harrison
Thomas Nelson, Jr.
Francis Lightfoot Lee
Carter Braxton

Pennsylvania
Robert Morris
Benjamin Rush
Benjamin Franklin
John Morton
George Clymer
James Smith
George Taylor
James Wilson
George Ross

Delaware
Caesar Rodney
George Read
Thomas McKean

New York
William Floyd
Philip Livingston
Francis Lewis
Lewis Morris

New Jersey
Richard Stockton
John Witherspoon
Francis Hopkinson
John Hart
Abraham Clark

New Hampshire
Josiah Bartlett
William Whipple

Massachusetts
Samuel Adams
John Adams
Robert Treat Paine
Elbridge Gerry

Rhode Island
Stephen Hopkins
William Ellery

Connecticut
Roger Sherman
Samuel Huntington
William Williams
Oliver Wolcott

New Hampshire
Matthew Thornton

Articles of Confederation (1787)

To all to whom these Presents shall come, we the undersigned Delegates of the States affixed to our Names send greeting.

Whereas the Delegates of the United States of America in Congress assembled did on the fifteenth day of November in the Year of our Lord One Thousand Seven Hundred and Seventy-seven, and in the Second Year of the Independence of America agree to certain articles of Confederation and perpetual Union between the States of Newhampshire, Massachusetts-bay, Rhodeisland and Providence Plantations, Connecticut, New York, New Jersey, Pennsylvania, Delaware, Maryland, Virginia, North-Carolina, South-Carolina and Georgia in the Words following, viz.

Articles of Confederation and perpetual Union between the States of Newhampshire, Massachusetts-bay, Rhodeisland and Providence Plantations, Connecticut, New-York, New-Jersey, Pennsylvania, Delaware, Maryland, Virginia, North-Carolina, South-Carolina and Georgia.

ARTICLE I. The stile of this confederacy shall be "The United States of America."

ARTICLE II. Each State retains its sovereignty, freedom and independence, and every power, jurisdiction and right, which is not by this confederation expressly delegated to the United States, in Congress assembled.

ARTICLE III. The said States hereby severally enter into a firm league of friendship with each other, for their common defence, the security of their liberties, and their mutual and general welfare, binding themselves to assist each other, against all force offered to, or attacks made upon them, or any of them, on account of religion, sovereignty, trade or any other pretence whatever.

ARTICLE IV. The better to secure and perpetuate mutual friendship and intercourse among the people of the different States in this Union, the free inhabitants of each of these States, paupers, vagabonds and fugitives from justice excepted, shall be entitled to all privileges and immunities of free citizens in the several States; and the people of each State shall have free ingress and regress to and from any other State, and shall enjoy therein all the privileges of trade and commerce, subject to the same duties, impositions and restrictions as the inhabitants thereof respectively, provided that such restrictions shall not extend so far as to prevent the removal of property imported into any State, to any other State of which the owner is an inhabitant; provided also that no imposition, duties or restriction shall be laid by any State, on the property of the United States, or either of them.

If any person guilty of, or charged with treason, felony, or other high misdemeanor in any State, shall flee from justice, and be found in any of the United States, he shall upon demand of the Governor or Executive power, of the State from which he fled, be delivered up and removed to the State having jurisdiction of his offence.

Full faith and credit shall be given in each of these States to the records, acts and judicial proceedings of the courts and magistrates of every other State.

ARTICLE V. For the more convenient management of the general interests of the United States, delegates shall be annually appointed in such manner as the legislature of each State shall direct, to meet in Congress on the first Monday in November, in every year, with a power reserved to each State, to recall its delegates, or any of them, at any time within the year, and to send others in their stead, for the remainder of the year.

No State shall be represented in Congress by less than two, nor by more than seven members; and no person shall be capable of being a delegate for more than three years in any term of six years; nor shall any person, being a delegate, be capable of holding any office under the United States, for which he, or another for his benefit receives any salary, fees or emolument of any kind.

Each State shall maintain its own delegates in a meeting of the States, and while they act as members of the committee of the States.

In determining questions in the United States, in Congress assembled, each State shall have one vote.

Freedom of speech and debate in Congress shall not be impeached or questioned in any court, or place out of Congress, and the members of Congress shall be protected in their persons from arrests and imprisonments, during the time of their going to and from, and attendance on Congress, except for treason, felony, or breach of the peace.

ARTICLE VI. No State without the consent of the United States in Congress assembled, shall send any embassy to, or receive any embassy from, or enter into any conference, agreement, alliance or treaty with any king, prince or state; nor shall any person holding any office of profit or trust under the United States, or any of them, accept of any present, emolument, office or title of any kind whatever from any king, prince or foreign state; nor shall the United States in Congress assembled, or any of them, grant any title of nobility.

No two or more States shall enter into any treaty, confederation or alliance whatever between them, without the consent of the United States in Congress assembled, specifying accurately the purposes for which the same is to be entered into, and how long it shall continue.

No State shall lay any imposts or duties, which may interfere with any stipulations in treaties, entered into by the United States in Congress assembled, with any king, prince or state, in pursuance of any treaties already proposed by Congress, to the courts of France and Spain.

No vessels of war shall be kept up in time of peace by any State, except such number only, as shall be deemed necessary by the United States in Congress assembled, for the defence of such State, or its trade; nor shall any body of forces be kept up by any State, in time of peace, except such number only, as in the judgment of the United States, in Congress assembled, shall be deemed requisite to garrison the forts necessary for the defence of such State; but every State shall always keep up a well regulated and disciplined militia, sufficiently armed and accoutred, and shall provide and constantly have ready for use, in public stores, a due number of field pieces and tents, and a proper quantity of arms, ammunition and camp equipage.

No State shall engage in any war without the consent of the United States in Congress assembled, unless such State be actually invaded by enemies, or shall have received certain advice of a resolution being formed by some nation of Indians to invade such State, and the danger is so imminent as not to admit of a delay, till the United States in Congress assembled can be consulted: nor shall any State grant commissions to any ships or vessels of war, nor letters of marque or reprisal, except it be after a declaration of war by the United States in Congress assembled, and then only against the kingdom or state and the subjects thereof, against which war has been so declared, and under such regulations as shall be established by the United States in Congress assembled, unless such State be infested by pirates, in which case vessels of war may be fitted out for that occasion, and kept so long as the danger shall continue, or until the United States in Congress assembled shall determine otherwise.

ARTICLE VII. When land-forces are raised by any State of the common defence, all officers of or under the rank of colonel, shall be appointed by the Legislature of each State respectively by whom such forces shall be raised, or in such manner as such State shall direct, and all vacancies shall be filled up by the State which first made the appointment.

ARTICLE VIII. All charges of war, and all other expenses that shall be incurred for the common defence or general welfare, and allowed by the United States in Congress assembled, shall be defrayed out of a common treasury, which shall be supplied by the several States, in proportion to the value of all land within each State, granted to or surveyed for any person, as such land and the buildings and improvements thereon shall be estimated according to such mode as the United States in Congress assembled, shall from time to time direct and appoint.

The taxes for paying that proportion shall be laid and levied by the authority and direction of the Legislatures of the several States within the time agreed upon by the United States in Congress assembled.

ARTICLE IX. The United States in Congress assembled, shall have the sole and exclusive right and power of determining on peace and war, except in the cases mentioned in the sixth article—of sending and receiving ambassadors—entering into treaties and alliances, provided that no treaty of commerce shall be made whereby the legislative power of the respective States shall be restrained from imposing such imposts and duties on foreigners, as their own people are subjected to, or from prohibiting the exportation or importation of and species of goods or commodities whatsoever—of establishing rules for deciding in all cases, what captures on land or water shall be legal, and in what manner prizes taken by land or naval forces in the service of the United States shall be divided or appropriated—of granting letters of marque and reprisal in times of peace—appointing courts for the trial of piracies and felonies committed on the high seas and establishing courts for receiving and determining finally appeals in all cases of captures, provided that no member of Congress shall be appointed a judge of any of the said courts.

The United States in Congress assembled shall also be the last resort on appeal in all disputes and differences now subsisting or that hereafter may arise between two or more States concerning boundary, jurisdiction or any other cause whatever; which authority shall always be exercised in the manner following. Whenever the legislative or executive authority or lawful agent of any State in controversy with another shall present a petition to Congress, stating the matter in question and praying for a hearing, notice thereof shall be given by order of Congress to the legislative or executive authority of the other State in controversy, and a day assigned for the appearance of the parties by their lawful agents, who shall then be directed to appoint by joint consent, commissioners or judges to constitute a court for hearing and determining the matter in question: but if they cannot agree, Congress shall name three persons out of each of the United States, and from the list of such persons each party shall alternately strike out one, the petitioners beginning, until the number shall be reduced to thirteen; and from that number not less than seven, nor more than nine names as Congress shall direct, shall in the presence of Congress be drawn out by lot, and the persons whose names shall be so drawn or any five of them, shall be commissioners or judges, to hear and finally determine the controversy, so always as a major part of the judges who shall hear the cause shall agree in the determination: and if either party shall neglect to attend at the day appointed, without reasons, which Congress shall judge sufficient, or being present shall refuse to strike, the Congress shall proceed to nominate three persons out of each State, and the Secretary of Congress shall strike in behalf of such party absent or refusing; and the judgment and sentence of the court to be appointed, in the manner before prescribed, shall be final and conclusive; and if any of the parties shall refuse to submit to the authority of such court, or to appear or defend their claim or cause, the court shall nevertheless proceed to pronounce sentence, or judgment, which shall in like manner be final and decisive, the judgment or sentence and other proceedings being in either case transmitted to Congress, and lodged among the acts of Congress for the security of the parties concerned: provided that every commissioner, before he sits in judgment, shall take an oath to be administered by one of the judges of the supreme or superior court of the State where the case shall be tried, "well and truly to hear and determine the matter in question, according to the best of his judgment, without favour, affection or hope of reward:" provided also that no State shall be deprived of territory for the benefit of the United States.

All controversies concerning the private right of soil claimed under different grants of two or more States, whose jurisdiction as they may respect such lands, and the states which passed such grants are adjusted, the said grants or either of them being at the same time claimed to have originated antecedent to such settlement of jurisdiction, shall on the petition of either party to the Congress of the United States, be finally determined as near as may be in the same manner as is before prescribed for deciding disputes respecting territorial jurisdiction between different States.

The United States in Congress assembled shall also have the sole and exclusive right and power of regulating the alloy and value of coin struck by their own authority, or by that of the respective States—fixing the standard of weights and measures throughout the United States—regulating the trade and managing all affairs with the Indians, not members of any of the States, provided that the legislative right of any State within its own limits be not infringed or violated—establishing and regulating post-offices from one State to another, throughout all of the United States, and exacting such postage on the papers passing thro' the same as may be requisite to defray the expenses of the said office—appointing all officers of the land forces, in the service of the United States, excepting regimental officers—appointing all the officers of the naval forces, and commissioning all officers whatever in the service of the United States—making rules for the government and regulation of the said land and naval forces, and directing their operations.

The United States in Congress assembled shall have authority to appoint a committee, to sit in the recess of Congress, to be denominated "a Committee of the States," and to consist of one delegate from each State; and to appoint such other committees and civil officers as may be necessary for managing the general affairs of the United States under their direction—to appoint one of their number to preside, provided that no person be allowed to serve in the office of president more than one year in any term of three years; to ascertain the necessary sums of money to be raised for the service of the United States, and to appropriate and apply the same for defraying the public expenses—to borrow money, or emit bills on the credit of the United States, transmitting every half year to the respective States an account of the sums of money so borrowed or emitted,—to build and equip a navy—to agree upon the number of land forces, and to make requisitions from each State for its quota, in proportion to the number of white inhabitants in such State; which requisition shall be binding, and thereupon the Legislature of each State shall appoint the regimental officers, raise the men and cloath, arm and equip them in a soldier like manner, at the expense of the United States; and the officers and men so cloathed, armed and equipped shall march to the place appointed, and within the time agreed on by the United States in Congress assembled: but if the United States in Congress assembled shall, on consideration of circumstances judge proper that any State should not raise men, or should raise a smaller number of men than the quota thereof, such extra number shall be raised, officered, cloathed, armed and equipped in the same manner as the quota of such State, unless the legislature of such State shall judge that such extra number cannot be safely spared out of the same, in which case they shall raise officer, cloath, arm and equip as many of such extra number as they judge can be safely spared. And the officers and men so cloathed, armed and equipped, shall march to the place appointed, and within the time agreed on by the United States in Congress assembled.

The United States in Congress assembled shall never engage in a war, nor grant letters of marque and reprisal in time of peace, nor enter into any treaties or alliances, nor coin money, nor regulate the value thereof, nor ascertain the sums and expenses necessary for the defence and welfare of the United States, or any of them, nor emit bills, nor borrow money on the credit of the United States, nor appropriate money, nor agree upon the number of vessels to be built or purchased, or the number of land or sea forces to be raised, nor appoint a commander in chief of the army or navy, unless nine States assent to the same: nor shall a question on any other point, except for adjourning from day to day be determined, unless by the votes of a majority of the United States in Congress assembled.

The Congress of the United States shall have power to adjourn to any time within the year, and to any place within the United States, so that no period of adjournment be for a longer duration than the space of six months, and shall publish the journal of their proceedings monthly, except such parts thereof relating to treaties, alliances or military operations, as in their judgment require secresy; and the yeas and nays of the delegates of each State on any question shall be entered on the Journal, when it is desired by any delegate; and the delegates of a State, or any of them, at his or their request shall be furnished with a transcript of the said journal, except such parts as are above excepted, to lay before the Legislatures of the several States.

ARTICLE X. The committee of the States, or any nine of them, shall be authorized to execute, in the recess of Congress, such of the powers of Congress as the United States in Congress assembled, by the consent of nine States, shall from time to time think expedient to vest them with; provided that no power be delegated to the said committee, for the exercise of which, by the articles of confederation, the voice of nine States in the Congress of the United States assembled is requisite.

ARTICLE XI. Canada acceding to this confederation, and joining in the measures of the United States, shall be admitted into, and entitled to all the advantages of this Union: but no other colony shall be admitted into the same, unless such admission be agreed to by nine States.

ARTICLE XII. All bills of credit emitted, monies borrowed and debts contracted by, or under the authority of Congress, before the assembling of the United States, in pursuance of the present confederation, shall be deemed and considered as a charge against the United States, for payment and satisfaction whereof the said United States, and the public faith are hereby solemnly pledged.

ARTICLE XIII. Every State shall abide by the determinations of the United States in Congress assembled, on all questions which by this confederation are submitted to them. And the articles of this confederation shall be inviolably observed by every State, and the Union shall be perpetual; nor shall any alteration at any time hereafter be made in any of them; unless such alteration be agreed to in a Congress of the United States, and be afterwards confirmed by the Legislatures of every State.

And whereas it has pleased the Great Governor of the world to incline the hearts of the Legislatures we respectively represent in Congress, to approve of, and to authorize us to ratify the said articles of confederation and perpetual union. Know ye that we the undersigned delegates, by virtue of the power and authority to us given for that purpose, do by these presents, in the name and in behalf of our respective constituents, fully and entirely ratify and confirm each and every of the said articles of confederation and perpetual union, and all and singular the matters and things therein contained: and we do further solemnly plight and engage the faith of our respective constituents, that they shall abide by the determinations of the United States in Congress assembled, on all questions, which by the said confederation are submitted to them. And that the articles thereof shall be inviolably observed by the States we respectively represent, and that the Union shall be perpetual.

In witness thereof we have hereunto set our hands in Congress. Done at Philadelphia in the State of Pennsylvania the ninth day of July in the year of our Lord one thousand seven hundred and seventy-eight, and in the third year of the independence of America.

The Constitution of the United States (1787)

We the People of the United States, in Order to form a more perfect Union, establish Justice, insure domestic Tranquility, provide for the common defence, promote the general Welfare, and secure the Blessings of Liberty to ourselves and our Posterity, do ordain and establish this Constitution for the United States of America.

Article. I.

Section. 1. All legislative Powers herein granted shall be vested in a Congress of the United States, which shall consist of a Senate and House of Representatives.

Section. 2. The House of Representatives shall be composed of Members chosen every second Year by the People of the several States, and the Electors in each State shall have the Qualifications requisite for Electors of the most numerous Branch of the State Legislature.

No Person shall be a Representative who shall not have attained to the Age of twenty five Years, and been seven Years a Citizen of the United States, and who shall not, when elected, be an Inhabitant of that State in which he shall be chosen.

Representatives and direct Taxes shall be apportioned among the several States which may be included within this Union, according to their respective Numbers, which shall be determined by adding to the whole Number of free Persons, including those bound to Service for a Term of Years, and excluding Indians not taxed, three fifths of all other Persons. The actual Enumeration shall be made within three Years after the first Meeting of the Congress of the United States, and within every subsequent Term of ten Years, in such Manner as they shall by Law direct. The Number of Representatives shall not exceed one for every thirty Thousand, but each State shall have at Least one Representative; and until such enumeration shall be made, the State of New Hampshire shall be entitled to chuse three, Massachusetts eight, Rhode-Island and Providence Plantations one, Connecticut five, New-York six, New Jersey four, Pennsylvania eight, Delaware one, Maryland six, Virginia ten, North Carolina five, South Carolina five, and Georgia three.

When vacancies happen in the Representation from any State, the Executive Authority thereof shall issue Writs of Election to fill such Vacancies.

The House of Representatives shall chuse their Speaker and other Officers; and shall have the sole Power of Impeachment.

Section. 3. The Senate of the United States shall be composed of two Senators from each State, chosen by the Legislature thereof for six Years; and each Senator shall have one Vote.

Immediately after they shall be assembled in Consequence of the first Election, they shall be divided as equally as may be into three Classes. The Seats of the Senators of the first Class shall be vacated at the Expiration of the second Year, of the second Class at the Expiration of the fourth Year, and of the third Class at the Expiration of the sixth Year, so that one third may be chosen every second Year; and if Vacancies happen by Resignation, or otherwise, during the Recess of the Legislature of any State, the Executive thereof may make temporary Appointments until the next Meeting of the Legislature, which shall then fill such Vacancies.

No Person shall be a Senator who shall not have attained to the Age of thirty Years, and been nine Years a Citizen of the United States, and who shall not, when elected, be an Inhabitant of that State for which he shall be chosen.

The Vice President of the United States shall be President of the Senate, but shall have no Vote, unless they be equally divided.

The Senate shall chuse their other Officers, and also a President pro tempore, in the Absence of the Vice President, or when he shall exercise the Office of President of the United States.

The Senate shall have the sole Power to try all Impeachments. When sitting for that Purpose, they shall be on Oath or Affirmation. When the President of the United States is tried, the Chief Justice shall preside: And no Person shall be convicted without the Concurrence of two thirds of the Members present.

Judgment in Cases of Impeachment shall not extend further than to removal from Office, and disqualification to hold and enjoy any Office of honor, Trust or Profit under the United States: but the Party convicted shall nevertheless be liable and subject to Indictment, Trial, Judgment and Punishment, according to Law.

Section. 4. The Times, Places and Manner of holding Elections for Senators and Representatives, shall be prescribed in each State by the Legislature thereof; but the Congress may at any time by Law make or alter such Regulations, except as to the Places of chusing Senators.

The Congress shall assemble at least once in every Year, and such Meeting shall be on the first Monday in December, unless they shall by Law appoint a different Day.

Section. 5. Each House shall be the Judge of the Elections, Returns and Qualifications of its own Members, and a Majority of each shall constitute a Quorum to do Business; but a smaller Number may adjourn from day to day, and may be authorized to compel the Attendance of absent Members, in such Manner, and under such Penalties as each House may provide.

Each House may determine the Rules of its Proceedings, punish its Members for disorderly Behaviour, and, with the Concurrence of two thirds, expel a Member.

Each House shall keep a Journal of its Proceedings, and from time to time publish the same, excepting such Parts as may in their Judgment require Secrecy; and the Yeas and Nays of the Members of either House on any question shall, at the Desire of one fifth of those Present, be entered on the Journal.

Neither House, during the Session of Congress, shall, without the Consent of the other, adjourn for more than three days, nor to any other Place than that in which the two Houses shall be sitting.

Section. 6. The Senators and Representatives shall receive a Compensation for their Services, to be ascertained by Law, and paid out of the Treasury of the United States. They shall in all Cases, except Treason, Felony and Breach of the Peace, be privileged from Arrest during their Attendance at the Session of their respective Houses, and in going to and returning from the same; and for any Speech or Debate in either House, they shall not be questioned in any other Place.

No Senator or Representative shall, during the Time for which he was elected, be appointed to any civil Office under the Authority of the United States, which shall have been created, or the Emoluments whereof shall have been encreased during such time; and no Person holding any Office under the United States, shall be a Member of either House during his Continuance in Office.

Section. 7. All Bills for raising Revenue shall originate in the House of Representatives; but the Senate may propose or concur with Amendments as on other Bills.

Every Bill which shall have passed the House of Representatives and the Senate shall, before it become a Law, be presented to the President of the United States; If he approve he shall sign it, but if not he shall return it, with his Objections to that House in which it shall have originated, who shall enter the Objections at large on their Journal, and proceed to reconsider it. If after such Reconsideration two thirds of that House shall agree to pass the Bill, it shall be sent, together with the Objections, to the other House, by which it shall likewise be reconsidered, and if approved by two thirds of that House, it shall become a Law. But in all such Cases the Votes of both Houses shall be determined by yeas and Nays, and the Names of the Persons voting for and against the Bill shall be entered on the Journal of each House respectively. If any Bill shall not be returned by the President within ten Days (Sundays excepted) after it shall have been presented to him, the Same shall be a Law, in like Manner as if he had signed it, unless the Congress by their Adjournment prevent its Return, in which Case it shall not be a Law.

Every Order, Resolution, or Vote to which the Concurrence of the Senate and House of Representatives may be necessary (except on a question of Adjournment) shall be presented to the President of the United States; and before the Same shall take Effect, shall be approved by him, or being disapproved by him, shall be repassed by two thirds of the Senate and House of Representatives, according to the Rules and Limitations prescribed in the Case of a Bill.

Section. 8. The Congress shall have Power To lay and collect Taxes, Duties, Imposts and Excises, to pay the Debts and provide for the common Defence and general Welfare of the United States; but all Duties, Imposts and Excises shall be uniform throughout the United States;

To borrow Money on the credit of the United States;

To regulate Commerce with foreign Nations, and among the several States, and with the Indian Tribes;

To establish an uniform Rule of Naturalization, and uniform Laws on the subject of Bankruptcies throughout the United States;

To coin Money, regulate the Value thereof, and of foreign Coin, and fix the Standard of Weights and Measures;

To provide for the Punishment of counterfeiting the Securities and current Coin of the United States;

To establish Post Offices and post Roads;

To promote the Progress of Science and useful Arts, by securing for limited Times to Authors and Inventors the exclusive Right to their respective Writings and Discoveries;

To constitute Tribunals inferior to the supreme Court;

To define and punish Piracies and Felonies committed on the high Seas, and Offences against the Law of Nations;

To declare War, grant Letters of Marque and Reprisal, and make Rules concerning Captures on Land and Water;

To raise and support Armies, but no Appropriation of Money to that Use shall be for a longer Term than two Years;

To provide and maintain a Navy;

To make Rules for the Government and Regulation of the land and naval Forces;

To provide for calling forth the Militia to execute the Laws of the Union, suppress Insurrections and repel Invasions;

To provide for organizing, arming, and disciplining, the Militia, and for governing such Part of them as may be employed in the Service of the United States, reserving to the States respectively, the Appointment of the Officers, and the Authority of training the Militia according to the discipline prescribed by Congress;

To exercise exclusive Legislation in all Cases whatsoever, over such District (not exceeding ten Miles square) as may, by Cession of particular States, and the Acceptance of Congress, become the Seat of the Government of the United States, and to exercise like Authority over all Places purchased by the Consent of the Legislature of the State in which the Same shall be, for the Erection of Forts, Magazines, Arsenals, dock-Yards, and other needful Buildings;—And

To make all Laws which shall be necessary and proper for carrying into Execution the foregoing Powers, and all other Powers vested by this Constitution in the Government of the United States, or in any Department or Officer thereof.

Section. 9. The Migration or Importation of such Persons as any of the States now existing shall think proper to admit, shall not be prohibited by the Congress prior to the Year one thousand eight hundred and eight, but a Tax or duty may be imposed on such Importation, not exceeding ten dollars for each Person.

The Privilege of the Writ of Habeas Corpus shall not be suspended, unless when in Cases of Rebellion or Invasion the public Safety may require it.

No Bill of Attainder or ex post facto Law shall be passed.

No Capitation, or other direct, Tax shall be laid, unless in Proportion to the Census or enumeration herein before directed to be taken.

No Tax or Duty shall be laid on Articles exported from any State.

No Preference shall be given by any Regulation of Commerce or Revenue to the Ports of one State over those of another; nor shall Vessels bound to, or from, one State, be obliged to enter, clear, or pay Duties in another.

No Money shall be drawn from the Treasury, but in Consequence of Appropriations made by Law; and a regular Statement and Account of the Receipts and Expenditures of all public Money shall be published from time to time.

No Title of Nobility shall be granted by the United States: And no Person holding any Office of Profit or Trust under them, shall, without the Consent of the Congress, accept of any present, Emolument, Office, or Title, of any kind whatever, from any King, Prince, or foreign State.

Section. 10. No State shall enter into any Treaty, Alliance, or Confederation; grant Letters of Marque and Reprisal; coin Money; emit Bills of Credit; make any Thing but gold and silver Coin a Tender in Payment of Debts; pass any Bill of Attainder, ex post facto Law, or Law impairing the Obligation of Contracts, or grant any Title of Nobility.

No State shall, without the Consent of the Congress, lay any Imposts or Duties on Imports or Exports, except what may be absolutely necessary for executing it's inspection Laws: and the net Produce of all Duties and Imposts, laid by any State on Imports or Exports, shall be for the Use of the Treasury of the United States; and all such Laws shall be subject to the Revision and Controul of the Congress.

No State shall, without the Consent of Congress, lay any Duty of Tonnage, keep Troops, or Ships of War in time of Peace, enter into any Agreement or Compact with another State, or with a foreign Power, or engage in War, unless actually invaded, or in such imminent Danger as will not admit of delay.

Article. II.

Section. 1. The executive Power shall be vested in a President of the United States of America. He shall hold his Office during the Term of four Years, and, together with the Vice President, chosen for the same Term, be elected, as follows:

Each State shall appoint, in such Manner as the Legislature thereof may direct, a Number of Electors, equal to the whole Number of Senators and Representatives to which the State may be entitled in the Congress: but no Senator or Representative, or Person holding an Office of Trust or Profit under the United States, shall be appointed an Elector.

The Electors shall meet in their respective States, and vote by Ballot for two Persons, of whom one at least shall not be an Inhabitant of the same State with themselves. And they shall make a List of all the Persons voted for, and of the Number of Votes for each; which List they shall sign and certify, and transmit sealed to the Seat of the Government of the United States, directed to the President of the Senate. The President of the Senate shall, in the Presence of the Senate and House of Representatives, open all the Certificates, and the Votes shall then be counted. The Person having the greatest Number of Votes shall be the President, if such Number be a Majority of the whole Number of Electors appointed; and if there be more than one who have such Majority, and have an equal Number of Votes, then the House of Representatives shall immediately chuse by Ballot one of them for President; and if no Person have a Majority, then from the five highest on the List the said House shall in like Manner chuse the President. But in chusing the President, the Votes shall be taken by States, the Representation from each State having one Vote; A quorum for this purpose shall consist of a Member or Members from two thirds of the States, and a Majority of all the States shall be necessary to a Choice. In every Case, after the Choice of the President, the Person having the greatest Number of Votes of the Electors shall be the Vice President. But if there should remain two or more who have equal Votes, the Senate shall chuse from them by Ballot the Vice President.

The Congress may determine the Time of chusing the Electors, and the Day on which they shall give their Votes; which Day shall be the same throughout the United States.

No Person except a natural born Citizen, or a Citizen of the United States, at the time of the Adoption of this Constitution, shall be eligible to the Office of President; neither shall any Person be eligible to that Office who shall not have attained to the Age of thirty five Years, and been fourteen Years a Resident within the United States.

In Case of the Removal of the President from Office, or of his Death, Resignation, or Inability to discharge the Powers and Duties of the said Office, the Same shall devolve on the Vice President, and the Congress may by Law provide for the Case of Removal, Death, Resignation or Inability, both of the President and Vice President, declaring what Officer shall then act as President, and such Officer shall act accordingly, until the Disability be removed, or a President shall be elected.

The President shall, at stated Times, receive for his Services, a Compensation, which shall neither be increased nor diminished during the Period for which he shall have been elected, and he shall not receive within that Period any other Emolument from the United States, or any of them.

Before he enter on the Execution of his Office, he shall take the following Oath or Affirmation:—"I do solemnly swear (or affirm) that I will faithfully execute the Office of President of the United States, and will to the best of my Ability, preserve, protect and defend the Constitution of the United States."

Section. 2. The President shall be Commander in Chief of the Army and Navy of the United States, and of the Militia of the several States, when called into the actual Service of the United States; he may require the Opinion, in writing, of the principal Officer in each of the executive Departments, upon any Subject relating to the Duties of their respective Offices, and he shall have Power to grant Reprieves and Pardons for Offences against the United States, except in Cases of Impeachment.

He shall have Power, by and with the Advice and Consent of the Senate, to make Treaties, provided two thirds of the Senators present concur; and he shall nominate, and by and with the Advice and Consent of the Senate, shall appoint Ambassadors, other public Ministers and Consuls, Judges of the supreme Court, and all other Officers of the United States, whose Appointments are not herein otherwise provided for, and which shall be established by Law: but the Congress may by Law vest the Appointment of such inferior Officers, as they think proper, in the President alone, in the Courts of Law, or in the Heads of Departments.

The President shall have Power to fill up all Vacancies that may happen during the Recess of the Senate, by granting Commissions which shall expire at the End of their next Session.

Section. 3. He shall from time to time give to the Congress Information of the State of the Union, and recommend to their Consideration such Measures as he shall judge necessary and expedient; he may, on extraordinary Occasions, convene both Houses, or either of them, and in Case of Disagreement between them, with Respect to the Time of Adjournment, he may adjourn them to such Time as he shall think proper; he shall receive Ambassadors and other public Ministers; he shall take Care that the Laws be faithfully executed, and shall Commission all the Officers of the United States.

Section. 4. The President, Vice President and all civil Officers of the United States, shall be removed from Office on Impeachment for, and Conviction of, Treason, Bribery, or other high Crimes and Misdemeanors.

Article III.

Section. 1. The judicial Power of the United States shall be vested in one supreme Court, and in such inferior Courts as the Congress may from time to time ordain and establish. The Judges, both of the supreme and inferior Courts, shall hold their Offices during good Behaviour, and shall, at stated Times, receive for their Services a Compensation, which shall not be diminished during their Continuance in Office.

Section. 2. The judicial Power shall extend to all Cases, in Law and Equity, arising under this Constitution, the Laws of the United States, and Treaties made, or which shall be made, under their Authority;—to all Cases affecting Ambassadors, other public Ministers and Consuls;—to all Cases of admiralty and maritime Jurisdiction;—to Controversies to which the United States shall be a Party;—to Controversies between two or more States;— between a State and Citizens of another State,—between Citizens of different States,—between Citizens of the same State claiming Lands under Grants of different States, and between a State, or the Citizens thereof, and foreign States, Citizens or Subjects.

In all Cases affecting Ambassadors, other public Ministers and Consuls, and those in which a State shall be Party, the supreme Court shall have original Jurisdiction. In all the other Cases before mentioned, the supreme Court shall have appellate Jurisdiction, both as to Law and Fact, with such Exceptions, and under such Regulations as the Congress shall make.

The Trial of all Crimes, except in Cases of Impeachment, shall be by Jury; and such Trial shall be held in the State where the said Crimes shall have been committed; but when not committed within any State, the Trial shall be at such Place or Places as the Congress may by Law have directed.

Section. 3. Treason against the United States, shall consist only in levying War against them, or in adhering to their Enemies, giving them Aid and Comfort. No Person shall be convicted of Treason unless on the Testimony of two Witnesses to the same overt Act, or on Confession in open Court.

The Congress shall have Power to declare the Punishment of Treason, but no Attainder of Treason shall work Corruption of Blood, or Forfeiture except during the Life of the Person attainted.

Article. IV.

Section. 1. Full Faith and Credit shall be given in each State to the public Acts, Records, and judicial Proceedings of every other State. And the Congress may by general Laws prescribe the Manner in which such Acts, Records and Proceedings shall be proved, and the Effect thereof.

Section. 2. The Citizens of each State shall be entitled to all Privileges and Immunities of Citizens in the several States.

A Person charged in any State with Treason, Felony, or other Crime, who shall flee from Justice, and be found in another State, shall on Demand of the executive Authority of the State from which he fled, be delivered up, to be removed to the State having Jurisdiction of the Crime.

No Person held to Service or Labour in one State, under the Laws thereof, escaping into another, shall, in Consequence of any Law or Regulation therein, be discharged from such Service or Labour, but shall be delivered up on Claim of the Party to whom such Service or Labour may be due.

Section. 3. New States may be admitted by the Congress into this Union; but no new State shall be formed or erected within the Jurisdiction of any other State; nor any State be formed by the Junction of two or more States, or Parts of States, without the Consent of the Legislatures of the States concerned as well as of the Congress.

The Congress shall have Power to dispose of and make all needful Rules and Regulations respecting the Territory or other Property belonging to the United States; and nothing in this Constitution shall be so construed as to Prejudice any Claims of the United States, or of any particular States.

Section. 4. The United States shall guarantee to every State in this Union a Republican Form of Government, and shall protect each of them against Invasion; and on Application of the Legislature, or of the Executive (when the Legislature cannot be convened), against domestic Violence.

Article. V.

The Congress, whenever two thirds of both Houses shall deem it necessary, shall propose Amendments to this Constitution, or, on the Application of the Legislatures of two thirds of the several States, shall call a Convention for proposing Amendments, which, in either Case, shall be valid to all Intents and Purposes, as Part of this Constitution, when ratified by the Legislatures of three fourths of the several States, or by Conventions in three fourths thereof, as the one or the other Mode of Ratification may be proposed by the Congress; Provided that no Amendment which may be made prior to the Year One thousand eight hundred and eight shall in any Manner affect the first and fourth Clauses in the Ninth Section of the first Article; and that no State, without its Consent, shall be deprived of its equal Suffrage in the Senate.

Article. VI.

All Debts contracted and Engagements entered into, before the Adoption of this Constitution, shall be as valid against the United States under this Constitution, as under the Confederation.

This Constitution, and the Laws of the United States which shall be made in Pursuance thereof; and all Treaties made, or which shall be made, under the Authority of the United States, shall be the supreme Law of the Land; and the Judges in every State shall be bound thereby, any Thing in the Constitution or Laws of any State to the Contrary notwithstanding.

The Senators and Representatives before mentioned, and the Members of the several State Legislatures, and all executive and judicial Officers, both of the United States and of the several States, shall be bound by Oath or Affirmation, to support this Constitution; but no religious Test shall ever be required as a Qualification to any Office or public Trust under the United States.

Article. VII.

The Ratification of the Conventions of nine States, shall be sufficient for the Establishment of this Constitution between the States so ratifying the Same.

The Word, "the," being interlined between the seventh and eighth Lines of the first Page, the Word "Thirty" being partly written on an Erazure in the fifteenth Line of the first Page, The Words "is tried" being interlined between the thirty second and thirty third Lines of the first Page and the Word "the" being interlined between the forty third and forty fourth Lines of the second Page.

Attest William Jackson Secretary

Done in Convention by the Unanimous Consent of the States present the Seventeenth Day of September in the Year of our Lord one thousand seven hundred and Eighty seven and of the Independance of the United States of America the Twelfth In witness whereof We have hereunto subscribed our Names,

G°. Washington
Presidt and deputy from Virginia

Delaware	Geo: Read Gunning Bedford jun John Dickinson Richard Bassett Jaco: Broom	New Hampshire	John Langdon Nicholas Gilman
Maryland	James McHenry Dan of St Thos. Jenifer Danl. Carrol	Massachusetts	Nathaniel Gorham Rufus King
Virginia	John Blair James Madison Jr.	Connecticut	Wm. Saml. Johnson Roger Sherman
North Carolina	Wm. Blount Richd. Dobbs Spaight Hu Williamson	New York	Alexander Hamilton
South Carolina	J. Rutledge Charles Cotesworth Pinckney Charles Pinckney Pierce Butler	New Jersey	Wil: Livingston David Brearley Wm. Paterson Jona: Dayton
Georgia	William Few Abr Baldwin	Pennsylvania	B Franklin Thomas Mifflin Robt. Morris Geo. Clymer Thos. FitzSimons Jared Ingersoll James Wilson Gouv Morris

Amendments to the Constitution

The Bill of Rights: A Transcription

The Preamble to The Bill of Rights

Congress of the United States
begun and held at the City of New-York, on
Wednesday the fourth of March, one thousand seven hundred and eighty nine.

THE Conventions of a number of the States, having at the time of their adopting the Constitution, expressed a desire, in order to prevent misconstruction or abuse of its powers, that further declaratory and restrictive clauses should be added: And as extending the ground of public confidence in the Government, will best ensure the beneficent ends of its institution.

RESOLVED by the Senate and House of Representatives of the United States of America, in Congress assembled, two thirds of both Houses concurring, that the following Articles be proposed to the Legislatures of the several States, as amendments to the Constitution of the United States, all, or any of which Articles, when ratified by three fourths of the said Legislatures, to be valid to all intents and purposes, as part of the said Constitution; viz.

ARTICLES in addition to, and Amendment of the Constitution of the United States of America, proposed by Congress, and ratified by the Legislatures of the several States, pursuant to the fifth Article of the original Constitution.

Note: The first ten amendments to the Constitution were ratified December 15, 1791, and form what is known as the "Bill of Rights."

Amendment I

Congress shall make no law respecting an establishment of religion, or prohibiting the free exercise thereof; or abridging the freedom of speech, or of the press; or the right of the people peaceably to assemble, and to petition the Government for a redress of grievances.

Amendment II

A well regulated Militia, being necessary to the security of a free State, the right of the people to keep and bear Arms, shall not be infringed.

Amendment III

No Soldier shall, in time of peace be quartered in any house, without the consent of the Owner, nor in time of war, but in a manner to be prescribed by law.

Amendment IV

The right of the people to be secure in their persons, houses, papers, and effects, against unreasonable searches and seizures, shall not be violated, and no Warrants shall issue, but upon probable cause, supported by Oath or affirmation, and particularly describing the place to be searched, and the persons or things to be seized.

Amendment V

No person shall be held to answer for a capital, or otherwise infamous crime, unless on a presentment or indictment of a Grand Jury, except in cases arising in the land or naval forces, or in the Militia, when in actual service in time of War or public danger; nor shall any person be subject for the same offence to be twice put in jeopardy of life or limb; nor shall be compelled in any criminal case to be a witness against himself, nor be deprived of life, liberty, or property, without due process of law; nor shall private property be taken for public use, without just compensation.

Amendment VI

In all criminal prosecutions, the accused shall enjoy the right to a speedy and public trial, by an impartial jury of the State and district wherein the crime shall have been committed, which district shall have been previously ascertained by law, and to be informed of the nature and cause of the accusation; to be confronted with the witnesses against him; to have compulsory process for obtaining witnesses in his favor, and to have the Assistance of Counsel for his defence.

Amendment VII

In Suits at common law, where the value in controversy shall exceed twenty dollars, the right of trial by jury shall be preserved, and no fact tried by a jury, shall be otherwise re-examined in any Court of the United States, than according to the rules of the common law.

Amendment VIII

Excessive bail shall not be required, nor excessive fines imposed, nor cruel and unusual punishments inflicted.

Amendment IX

The enumeration in the Constitution, of certain rights, shall not be construed to deny or disparage others retained by the people.

Amendment X

The powers not delegated to the United States by the Constitution, nor prohibited by it to the States, are reserved to the States respectively, or to the people.

Amendment XI

Passed by Congress March 4, 1794. Ratified February 7, 1795.

Note: Article III, section 2, of the Constitution was modified by amendment 11.

The Judicial power of the United States shall not be construed to extend to any suit in law or equity, commenced or prosecuted against one of the United States by Citizens of another State, or by Citizens or Subjects of any Foreign State.

Amendment XII

Passed by Congress December 9, 1803. Ratified June 15, 1804.

Note: A portion of Article II, section 1 of the Constitution was superseded by the 12th amendment.

The Electors shall meet in their respective states and vote by ballot for President and Vice-President, one of whom, at least, shall not be an inhabitant of the same state with themselves; they shall name in their ballots the person voted for as President, and in distinct ballots the person voted for as Vice-President, and they shall make distinct lists of all persons voted for as President, and of all persons voted for as Vice-President, and of the number of votes for each, which lists they shall sign and certify, and transmit sealed to the seat of the government of the United States, directed to the President of the Senate; — the President of the Senate shall, in the presence of the Senate and House of Representatives, open all the certificates and the votes shall then be counted; — The person having the greatest number of votes for President, shall be the President, if such number be a majority of the whole number of Electors appointed; and if no person have such majority, then from the persons having the highest numbers not exceeding three on the list of those voted for as President, the House of Representatives shall choose immediately, by ballot, the President. But in choosing the President, the votes shall be taken by states, the representation from each state having one vote; a quorum for this purpose shall consist of a member or members from two-thirds of the states, and a majority of all the states shall be necessary to a choice. [And if the House of Representatives shall not choose a President whenever the right of choice shall devolve upon them, before the fourth day of March next following, then the Vice-President shall act as President, as in case of the death or other constitutional disability of the President. —]* The person having the greatest number of votes as Vice-President, shall be the Vice-President, if such number be a majority of the whole number of Electors appointed, and if no person have a majority, then from the two highest numbers on the list, the Senate shall choose the Vice-President; a quorum for the purpose shall consist of two-thirds of the whole number of Senators, and a majority of the whole number shall be necessary to a choice. But no person constitutionally ineligible to the office of President shall be eligible to that of Vice-President of the United States.

Superseded by section 3 of the 20th amendment.

Amendment XIII

Passed by Congress January 31, 1865. Ratified December 6, 1865.

Note: A portion of Article IV, section 2, of the Constitution was superseded by the 13th amendment.

Section 1.
Neither slavery nor involuntary servitude, except as a punishment for crime whereof the party shall have been duly convicted, shall exist within the United States, or any place subject to their jurisdiction.

Section 2.
Congress shall have power to enforce this article by appropriate legislation.

Amendment XIV

Passed by Congress June 13, 1866. Ratified July 9, 1868.

Note: Article I, section 2, of the Constitution was modified by section 2 of the 14th amendment.

Section 1.
All persons born or naturalized in the United States, and subject to the jurisdiction thereof, are citizens of the United States and of the State wherein they reside. No State shall make or enforce any law which shall abridge the privileges or immunities of citizens of the United States; nor shall any State deprive any person of life, liberty, or property, without due process of law; nor deny to any person within its jurisdiction the equal protection of the laws.

Section 2.
Representatives shall be apportioned among the several States according to their respective numbers, counting the whole number of persons in each State, excluding Indians not taxed. But when the right to vote at any election for the choice of electors for President and Vice-President of the United States, Representatives in Congress, the Executive and Judicial officers of a State, or the members of the Legislature thereof, is denied to any of the male inhabitants of such State, being twenty-one years of age,* and citizens of the United States, or in any way abridged, except for participation in rebellion, or other crime, the basis of representation therein shall be reduced in the proportion which the number of such male citizens shall bear to the whole number of male citizens twenty-one years of age in such State.

Section 3.
No person shall be a Senator or Representative in Congress, or elector of President and Vice-President, or hold any office, civil or military, under the United States, or under any State, who, having previously taken an oath, as a member of Congress, or as an officer of the United States, or as a member of any State legislature, or as an executive or judicial officer of any State, to support the Constitution of the United States, shall have engaged in insurrection or rebellion against the same, or given aid or comfort to the enemies thereof. But Congress may by a vote of two-thirds of each House, remove such disability.

Section 4.

The validity of the public debt of the United States, authorized by law, including debts incurred for payment of pensions and bounties for services in suppressing insurrection or rebellion, shall not be questioned. But neither the United States nor any State shall assume or pay any debt or obligation incurred in aid of insurrection or rebellion against the United States, or any claim for the loss or emancipation of any slave; but all such debts, obligations and claims shall be held illegal and void.

Section 5.

The Congress shall have the power to enforce, by appropriate legislation, the provisions of this article.

Changed by section 1 of the 26th amendment.

Amendment XV

Passed by Congress February 26, 1869. Ratified February 3, 1870.

Section 1.

The right of citizens of the United States to vote shall not be denied or abridged by the United States or by any State on account of race, color, or previous condition of servitude—

Section 2.

The Congress shall have the power to enforce this article by appropriate legislation.

Amendment XVI

Passed by Congress July 2, 1909. Ratified February 3, 1913.

Note: Article I, section 9, of the Constitution was modified by amendment 16.

The Congress shall have power to lay and collect taxes on incomes, from whatever source derived, without apportionment among the several States, and without regard to any census or enumeration.

Amendment XVII

Passed by Congress May 13, 1912. Ratified April 8, 1913.

Note: Article I, section 3, of the Constitution was modified by the 17th amendment.

The Senate of the United States shall be composed of two Senators from each State, elected by the people thereof, for six years; and each Senator shall have one vote. The electors in each State shall have the qualifications requisite for electors of the most numerous branch of the State legislatures.

When vacancies happen in the representation of any State in the Senate, the executive authority of such State shall issue writs of election to fill such vacancies: *Provided,* That the legislature of any State may empower the executive thereof to make temporary appointments until the people fill the vacancies by election as the legislature may direct.

This amendment shall not be so construed as to affect the election or term of any Senator chosen before it becomes valid as part of the Constitution.

Amendment XVIII

Passed by Congress December 18, 1917. Ratified January 16, 1919. Repealed by amendment 21.

Section 1.
After one year from the ratification of this article the manufacture, sale, or transportation of intoxicating liquors within, the importation thereof into, or the exportation thereof from the United States and all territory subject to the jurisdiction thereof for beverage purposes is hereby prohibited.

Section 2.
The Congress and the several States shall have concurrent power to enforce this article by appropriate legislation.

Section 3.
This article shall be inoperative unless it shall have been ratified as an amendment to the Constitution by the legislatures of the several States, as provided in the Constitution, within seven years from the date of the submission hereof to the States by the Congress.

Amendment XIX

Passed by Congress June 4, 1919. Ratified August 18, 1920.

The right of citizens of the United States to vote shall not be denied or abridged by the United States or by any State on account of sex.

Congress shall have power to enforce this article by appropriate legislation.

Amendment XX

Passed by Congress March 2, 1932. Ratified January 23, 1933.

Note: Article I, section 4, of the Constitution was modified by section 2 of this amendment. In addition, a portion of the 12th amendment was superseded by section 3.

Section 1.
The terms of the President and the Vice President shall end at noon on the 20th day of January, and the terms of Senators and Representatives at noon on the 3rd day of January, of the years in which such terms would have ended if this article had not been ratified; and the terms of their successors shall then begin.

Section 2.

The Congress shall assemble at least once in every year, and such meeting shall begin at noon on the 3d day of January, unless they shall by law appoint a different day.

Section 3.

If, at the time fixed for the beginning of the term of the President, the President elect shall have died, the Vice President elect shall become President. If a President shall not have been chosen before the time fixed for the beginning of his term, or if the President elect shall have failed to qualify, then the Vice President elect shall act as President until a President shall have qualified; and the Congress may by law provide for the case wherein neither a President elect nor a Vice President shall have qualified, declaring who shall then act as President, or the manner in which one who is to act shall be selected, and such person shall act accordingly until a President or Vice President shall have qualified.

Section 4.

The Congress may by law provide for the case of the death of any of the persons from whom the House of Representatives may choose a President whenever the right of choice shall have devolved upon them, and for the case of the death of any of the persons from whom the Senate may choose a Vice President whenever the right of choice shall have devolved upon them.

Section 5.

Sections 1 and 2 shall take effect on the 15th day of October following the ratification of this article.

Section 6.

This article shall be inoperative unless it shall have been ratified as an amendment to the Constitution by the legislatures of three-fourths of the several States within seven years from the date of its submission.

Amendment XXI

Passed by Congress February 20, 1933. Ratified December 5, 1933.

Section 1.

The eighteenth article of amendment to the Constitution of the United States is hereby repealed.

Section 2.

The transportation or importation into any State, Territory, or Possession of the United States for delivery or use therein of intoxicating liquors, in violation of the laws thereof, is hereby prohibited.

Section 3.

This article shall be inoperative unless it shall have been ratified as an amendment to the Constitution by conventions in the several States, as provided in the Constitution, within seven years from the date of the submission hereof to the States by the Congress.

Amendment XXII

Passed by Congress March 21, 1947. Ratified February 27, 1951.

Section 1.

No person shall be elected to the office of the President more than twice, and no person who has held the office of President, or acted as President, for more than two years of a term to which some other person was elected President shall be elected to the office of President more than once. But this Article shall not apply to any person holding the office of President when this Article was proposed by Congress, and shall not prevent any person who may be holding the office of President, or acting as President, during the term within which this Article becomes operative from holding the office of President or acting as President during the remainder of such term.

Section 2.

This article shall be inoperative unless it shall have been ratified as an amendment to the Constitution by the legislatures of three-fourths of the several States within seven years from the date of its submission to the States by the Congress.

Amendment XXIII

Passed by Congress June 16, 1960. Ratified March 29, 1961.

Section 1.

The District constituting the seat of Government of the United States shall appoint in such manner as Congress may direct:

A number of electors of President and Vice President equal to the whole number of Senators and Representatives in Congress to which the District would be entitled if it were a State, but in no event more than the least populous State; they shall be in addition to those appointed by the States, but they shall be considered, for the purposes of the election of President and Vice President, to be electors appointed by a State; and they shall meet in the District and perform such duties as provided by the twelfth article of amendment.

Section 2.

The Congress shall have power to enforce this article by appropriate legislation.

Amendment XXIV

Passed by Congress August 27, 1962. Ratified January 23, 1964.

Section 1.

The right of citizens of the United States to vote in any primary or other election for President or Vice President, for electors for President or Vice President, or for Senator or Representative in Congress, shall not be denied or abridged by the United States or any State by reason of failure to pay poll tax or other tax.

Section 2.

The Congress shall have power to enforce this article by appropriate legislation.

Amendment XXV

Passed by Congress July 6, 1965. Ratified February 10, 1967.

Note: Article II, section 1, of the Constitution was affected by the 25th amendment.

Section 1.
In case of the removal of the President from office or of his death or resignation, the Vice President shall become President.

Section 2.
Whenever there is a vacancy in the office of the Vice President, the President shall nominate a Vice President who shall take office upon confirmation by a majority vote of both Houses of Congress.

Section 3.
Whenever the President transmits to the President pro tempore of the Senate and the Speaker of the House of Representatives his written declaration that he is unable to discharge the powers and duties of his office, and until he transmits to them a written declaration to the contrary, such powers and duties shall be discharged by the Vice President as Acting President.

Section 4.
Whenever the Vice President and a majority of either the principal officers of the executive departments or of such other body as Congress may by law provide, transmit to the President pro tempore of the Senate and the Speaker of the House of Representatives their written declaration that the President is unable to discharge the powers and duties of his office, the Vice President shall immediately assume the powers and duties of the office as Acting President.

Thereafter, when the President transmits to the President pro tempore of the Senate and the Speaker of the House of Representatives his written declaration that no inability exists, he shall resume the powers and duties of his office unless the Vice President and a majority of either the principal officers of the executive department or of such other body as Congress may by law provide, transmit within four days to the President pro tempore of the Senate and the Speaker of the House of Representatives their written declaration that the President is unable to discharge the powers and duties of his office. Thereupon Congress shall decide the issue, assembling within forty-eight hours for that purpose if not in session. If the Congress, within twenty-one days after receipt of the latter written declaration, or, if Congress is not in session, within twenty-one days after Congress is required to assemble, determines by two-thirds vote of both Houses that the President is unable to discharge the powers and duties of his office, the Vice President shall continue to discharge the same as Acting President; otherwise, the President shall resume the powers and duties of his office.

Amendment XXVI

Passed by Congress March 23, 1971. Ratified July 1, 1971.

Note: Amendment 14, section 2, of the Constitution was modified by section 1 of the 26th amendment.

Section 1.
The right of citizens of the United States, who are eighteen years of age or older, to vote shall not be denied or abridged by the United States or by any State on account of age.

Section 2.
The Congress shall have power to enforce this article by appropriate legislation.

Amendment XXVII

Originally proposed Sept. 25, 1789. Ratified May 7, 1992.

No law, varying the compensation for the services of the Senators and Representatives, shall take effect, until an election of representatives shall have intervened.

PRESIDENTIAL ELECTIONS

Year	Number of States	Candidates	Parties	Popular Vote	% of Popular Vote	Electoral Vote	% Voter Participation
1789	11	**GEORGE WASHINGTON**	No party designations			69	
		John Adams				34	
		Other candidates				35	
1792	15	**GEORGE WASHINGTON**	No party designations			132	
		John Adams				77	
		George Clinton				50	
		Other candidates				5	
1796	16	**JOHN ADAMS**	Federalist			71	
		Thomas Jefferson	Democratic-Republican			68	
		Thomas Pinckney	Federalist			59	
		Aaron Burr	Democratic-Republican			30	
		Other candidates				48	
1800	16	**THOMAS JEFFERSON**	Democratic-Republican			73	
		Aaron Burr	Democratic-Republican			73	
		John Adams	Federalist			65	
		Charles C. Pinckney	Federalist			64	
		John Jay	Federalist			1	
1804	17	**THOMAS JEFFERSON**	Democratic-Republican			162	
		Charles C. Pinckney	Federalist			14	

Year	Number of States	Candidates	Parties	Popular Vote	% of Popular Vote	Electoral Vote	% Voter Participation
1808	17	JAMES MADISON	Democratic-Republican			122	
		Charles C. Pinckney	Federalist			47	
		George Clinton	Democratic-Republican			6	
1812	18	JAMES MADISON	Democratic-Republican			128	
		DeWitt Clinton	Federalist			89	
1816	19	JAMES MONROE	Democratic-Republican			183	
		Rufus King	Federalist			34	
1820	24	JAMES MONROE	Democratic-Republican			231	
		John Quincy Adams	Independent			1	
1824	24	JOHN QUINCY ADAMS	Democratic-Republican	108,740	30.5	84	26.9
		Andrew Jackson	Democratic-Republican	153,544	43.1	99	
		Henry Clay	Democratic-Republican	47,136	13.2	37	
		William H. Crawford	Democratic-Republican	46,618	13.1	41	
1828	24	ANDREW JACKSON	Democratic	647,286	56.0	178	57.6
		John Quincy Adams	National-Republican	508,064	44.0	83	

Year	Number of States	Candidates	Parties	Popular Vote	% of Popular Vote	Electoral Vote	% Voter Participation
1832	24	**ANDREW JACKSON**	Democratic	688,242	54.5	219	55.4
		Henry Clay	National-Republican	473,462	37.5	49	
		William Wirt	Anti-Masonic	101,051	8.0	7	
		John Floyd	Democratic			11	
1836	26	**MARTIN VAN BUREN**	Democratic	765,483	50.9	170	57.8
		William H. Harrison	Whig	739,795	49.1	73	
		Hugh L. White	Whig			26	
		Daniel Webster	Whig			14	
		W. P. Mangum	Whig			11	
1840	26	**WILLIAM H. HARRISON**	Whig	1,274,624	53.1	234	80.2
		Martin Van Buren	Democratic	1,127,781	46.9	60	
1844	26	**JAMES K. POLK**	Democratic	1,338,464	49.6	170	78.9
		Henry Clay	Whig	1,300,097	48.1	105	
		James G. Birney	Liberty	62,300	2.3		
1848	30	**ZACHARY TAYLOR**	Whig	1,360,967	47.4	163	72.7
		Lewis Cass	Democratic	1,222,342	42.5	127	
		Martin Van Buren	Free Soil	291,263	10.1		
1852	31	**FRANKLIN PIERCE**	Democratic	1,601,117	50.9	254	69.6
		Winfield Scott	Whig	1,385,453	44.1	42	
		John P. Hale	Free Soil	155,825	5.0		
1856	31	**JAMES BUCHANAN**	Democratic	1,832,955	45.3	174	78.9
		John C. Frémont	Republican	1,339,932	33.1	114	
		Millard Fillmore	American	871,731	21.6	8	

Year	Number of States	Candidates	Parties	Popular Vote	% of Popular Vote	Electoral Vote	% Voter Participation
1860	33	**ABRAHAM LINCOLN**	Republican	1,865,593	39.8	180	81.2
		Stephen A. Douglas	Democratic	1,382,713	29.5	12	
		John C. Breckinridge	Democratic	848,356	18.1	72	
		John Bell	Constitutional Union	592,906	12.6	39	
1864	36	**ABRAHAM LINCOLN**	Republican	2,206,938	55.0	212	73.8
		George B. McClellan	Democratic	1,803,787	45.0	21	
1868	37	**ULYSSES S. GRANT**	Republican	3,013,421	52.7	214	78.1
		Horatio Seymour	Democratic	2,706,829	47.3	80	
1872	37	**ULYSSES S. GRANT**	Republican	3,596,745	55.6	286	71.3
		Horace Greeley	Democratic	2,843,446	43.9	66	
1876	38	Rutherford B. Hayes	Republican	4,036,572	48.0	185	81.8
		Samuel J. Tilden	Democratic	4,284,020	51.0	184	
1880	38	**JAMES A. GARFIELD**	Republican	4,453,295	48.5	214	79.4
		Winfield S. Hancock	Democratic	4,414,082	48.1	155	
		James B. Weaver	Greenback-Labor	308,578	3.4		
1884	38	**GROVER CLEVELAND**	Democratic	4,879,507	48.5	219	77.5
		James G. Blaine	Republican	4,850,293	48.2	182	
		Benjamin F. Butler	Greenback-Labor	175,370	1.8		
		John P. St. John	Prohibition	150,369	1.5		
1888	38	**BENJAMIN HARRISON**	Republican	5,477,129	47.9	233	79.3
		Grover Cleveland	Democratic	5,537,857	48.6	168	
		Clinton B. Fisk	Prohibition	249,506	2.2		
		Anson J. Streeter	Union Labor	146,935	1.3		

Year	Number of States	Candidates	Parties	Popular Vote	% of Popular Vote	Electoral Vote	% Voter Participation
1892	44	GROVER CLEVELAND	Democratic	5,555,426	46.1	277	74.7
		Benjamin Harrison	Republican	5,182,690	43.0	145	
		James B. Weaver	People's	1,029,846	8.5	22	
		John Bidwell	Prohibition	264,133	2.2		
1896	45	WILLIAM MCKINLEY	Republican	7,102,246	51.1	271	79.3
		William J. Bryan	Democratic	6,492,559	47.7	176	
1900	45	WILLIAM MCKINLEY	Republican	7,218,491	51.7	292	73.2
		William J. Bryan	Democratic; Populist	6,356,734	45.5	155	
		John C. Wooley	Prohibition	208,914	1.5		
1904	45	THEODORE ROOSEVELT	Republican	7,628,461	57.4	336	65.2
		Alton B. Parker	Democratic	5,084,223	37.6	140	
		Eugene V. Debs	Socialist	402,283	3.0		
		Silas C. Swallow	Prohibition	258,536	1.9		
1908	46	WILLIAM H. TAFT	Republican	7,675,320	51.6	321	65.4
		William J. Bryan	Democratic	6,412,294	43.1	162	
		Eugene V. Debs	Socialist	420,793	2.8		
		Eugene W. Chafin	Prohibition	253,840	1.7		
1912	48	WOODROW WILSON	Democratic	6,296,547	41.9	435	58.8
		Theodore Roosevelt	Progressive	4,118,571	27.4	88	
		William H. Taft	Republican	3,486,720	23.2	8	
		Eugene V. Debs	Socialist	900,672	6.0		
		Eugene W. Chafin	Prohibition	206,275	1.4		

Year	Number of States	Candidates	Parties	Popular Vote	% of Popular Vote	Electoral Vote	% Voter Participation
1916	48	**WOODROW WILSON**	Democratic	9,127,695	49.4	277	61.6
		Charles E. Hughes	Republican	8,533,507	46.2	254	
		A. L. Benson	Socialist	585,113	3.2		
		J. Frank Hanly	Prohibition	220,506	1.2		
1920	48	**WARREN G. HARDING**	Republican	16,143,407	60.4	404	49.2
		James M. Cox	Democratic	9,130,328	34.2	127	
		Eugene V. Debs	Socialist	919,799	3.4		
		P. P. Christensen	Farmer–Labor	265,411	1.0		
1924	48	**CALVIN COOLIDGE**	Republican	15,718,211	54.0	382	48.9
		John W. Davis	Democratic	8,385,283	28.8	136	
		Robert M. La Follette	Progressive	4,831,289	16.6	13	
1928	48	**HERBERT C. HOOVER**	Republican	21,391,993	58.2	444	56.9
		Alfred E. Smith	Democratic	15,016,169	40.9	87	
1932	48	**FRANKLIN D. ROOSEVELT**	Democratic	22,809,638	57.4	472	56.9
		Herbert C. Hoover	Republican	15,758,901	39.7	59	
		Norman Thomas	Socialist	881,951	2.2		
1936	48	**FRANKLIN D. ROOSEVELT**	Democratic	27,752,869	60.8	523	61.0
		Alfred M. Landon	Republican	16,674,665	36.5	8	
		William Lemke	Union	882,479	1.9		
1940	48	**FRANKLIN D. ROOSEVELT**	Democratic	27,307,819	54.8	449	62.5
		Wendell L. Willkie	Republican	22,321,018	44.8	82	
1944	48	**FRANKLIN D. ROOSEVELT**	Democratic	25,606,585	53.5	432	55.9
		Thomas E. Dewey	Republican	22,014,745	46.0	99	

Year	Number of States	Candidates	Parties	Popular Vote	% of Popular Vote	Electoral Vote	% Voter Participation
1948	48	**HARRY S. TRUMAN**	Democratic	24,179,345	49.6	303	53.0
		Thomas E. Dewey	Republican	21,991,291	45.1	189	
		J. Strom Thurmond	States' Rights	1,176,125	2.4	39	
		Henry A. Wallace	Progressive	1,157,326	2.4		
1952	48	**DWIGHT D. EISENHOWER**	Republican	33,936,234	55.1	442	63.3
		Adlai E. Stevenson	Democratic	27,314,992	44.4	89	
1956	48	**DWIGHT D. EISENHOWER**	Republican	35,590,472	57.6	457	60.6
		Adlai E. Stevenson	Democratic	26,022,752	42.1	73	
1960	50	**JOHN F. KENNEDY**	Democratic	34,226,731	49.7	303	62.8
		Richard M. Nixon	Republican	34,108,157	49.5	219	
1964	50	**LYNDON B. JOHNSON**	Democratic	43,129,566	61.1	486	61.9
		Barry M. Goldwater	Republican	27,178,188	38.5	52	
1968	50	**RICHARD M. NIXON**	Republican	31,785,480	43.4	301	60.9
		Hubert H. Humphrey	Democratic	31,275,166	42.7	191	
		George C. Wallace	American Independent	9,906,473	13.5	46	
1972	50	**RICHARD M. NIXON**	Republican	47,169,911	60.7	520	55.2
		George S. McGovern	Democratic	29,170,383	37.5	17	
		John G. Schmitz	American	1,099,482	1.4		

Year	Number of States	Candidates	Parties	Popular Vote	% of Popular Vote	Electoral Vote	% Voter Participation
1976	50	**JIMMY CARTER**	Democratic	40,830,763	50.1	297	53.5
		Gerald R. Ford	Republican	39,147,793	48.0	240	
1980	50	**RONALD REAGAN**	Republican	43,901,812	50.7	489	52.6
		Jimmy Carter	Democratic	35,483,820	41.0	49	
		John B. Anderson	Independent	5,719,437	6.6		
		Ed Clark	Libertarian	921,188	1.1		
1984	50	**RONALD REAGAN**	Republican	54,451,521	58.8	525	53.1
		Walter F. Mondale	Democratic	37,565,334	40.6	13	
1988	50	**GEORGE H. W. BUSH**	Republican	47,917,341	53.4	426	50.1
		Michael Dukakis	Democratic	41,013,030	45.6	111	
1992	50	**BILL CLINTON**	Democratic	44,908,254	43.0	370	55.0
		George H. W. Bush	Republican	39,102,343	37.4	168	
		H. Ross Perot	Independent	19,741,065	18.9		
1996	50	**BILL CLINTON**	Democratic	47,401,185	49.0	379	49.0
		Bob Dole	Republican	39,197,469	41.0	159	
		H. Ross Perot	Independent	8,085,295	8.0		
2000	50	**GEORGE W. BUSH**	Republican	50,455,156	47.9	271	50.4
		Al Gore	Democrat	50,997,335	48.4	266	
		Ralph Nader	Green	2,882,897	2.7		
2004	50	**GEORGE W. BUSH**	Republican	62,040,610	50.7	286	60.7
		John F. Kerry	Democrat	59,028,444	48.3	251	
2008	50	**BARACK OBAMA**	Democrat	69,456,897	52.92%	365	63.0
		John McCain	Republican	59,934,814	45.66%	173	

Candidates receiving less than 1 percent of the popular vote have been omitted. Thus the percentage of popular vote given for any election year may not total 100 percent.

Before the passage of the Twelfth Amendment in 1804, the electoral college voted for two presidential candidates; the runner-up became vice president.

ADMISSION OF STATES

Order of Admission	State	Date of Admission	Order of Admission	State	Date of Admission
1	Delaware	December 7, 1787	26	Michigan	January 26, 1837
2	Pennsylvania	December 12, 1787	27	Florida	March 3, 1845
3	New Jersey	December 18, 1787	28	Texas	December 29, 1845
4	Georgia	January 2, 1788	29	Iowa	December 28, 1846
5	Connecticut	January 9, 1788	30	Wisconsin	May 29, 1848
6	Massachusetts	February 7, 1788	31	California	September 9, 1850
7	Maryland	April 28, 1788	32	Minnesota	May 11, 1858
8	South Carolina	May 23, 1788	33	Oregon	February 14, 1859
9	New Hampshire	June 21, 1788	34	Kansas	January 29, 1861
10	Virginia	June 25, 1788	35	West Virginia	June 30, 1863
11	New York	July 26, 1788	36	Nevada	October 31, 1864
12	North Carolina	November 21, 1789	37	Nebraska	March 1, 1867
13	Rhode Island	May 29, 1790	38	Colorado	August 1, 1876
14	Vermont	March 4, 1791	39	North Dakota	November 2, 1889
15	Kentucky	June 1, 1792	40	South Dakota	November 2, 1889
16	Tennessee	June 1, 1796	41	Montana	November 8, 1889
17	Ohio	March 1, 1803	42	Washington	November 11, 1889
18	Louisiana	April 30, 1812	43	Idaho	July 3, 1890
19	Indiana	December 11, 1816	44	Wyoming	July 10, 1890
20	Mississippi	December 10, 1817	45	Utah	January 4, 1896
21	Illinois	December 3, 1818	46	Oklahoma	November 16, 1907
22	Alabama	December 14, 1819	47	New Mexico	January 6, 1912
23	Maine	March 15, 1820	48	Arizona	February 14, 1912
24	Missouri	August 10, 1821	49	Alaska	January 3, 1959
25	Arkansas	June 15, 1836	50	Hawaii	August 21, 1959

POPULATION OF THE UNITED STATES

Year	Number of States	Population	% Increase	Population per Square Mile
1790	13	3,929,214		4.5
1800	16	5,308,483	35.1	6.1
1810	17	7,239,881	36.4	4.3
1820	23	9,638,453	33.1	5.5
1830	24	12,866,020	33.5	7.4
1840	26	17,069,453	32.7	9.8
1850	31	23,191,876	35.9	7.9
1860	33	31,443,321	35.6	10.6
1870	37	39,818,449	26.6	13.4
1880	38	50,155,783	26.0	16.9
1890	44	62,947,714	25.5	21.1
1900	45	75,994,575	20.7	25.6
1910	46	91,972,266	21.0	31.0
1920	48	105,710,620	14.9	35.6
1930	48	122,775,046	16.1	41.2
1940	48	131,669,275	7.2	44.2
1950	48	150,697,361	14.5	50.7
1960	50	179,323,175	19.0	50.6
1970	50	203,235,298	13.3	57.5
1980	50	226,504,825	11.4	64.0
1985	50	237,839,000	5.0	67.2
1990	50	250,122,000	5.2	70.6
1995	50	263,411,707	5.3	74.4
2000	50	281,421,906	6.8	77.0
2005	50	296,410,404	5.3	77.9
2010	50	308,745,538	9.7	87.4

IMMIGRATION TO THE UNITED STATES, FISCAL YEARS 1820–2011

Year	Number	Year	Number	Year	Number	Year	Number
1820–1989	**55,457,531**	**1871–80**	**2,812,191**	**1921–30**	**4,107,209**	**1971–80**	**4,493,314**
1820	8,385	1871	321,350	1921	805,228	1971	370,478
1821–30	**143,439**	1872	404,806	1922	309,556	1972	384,685
1821	9,127	1873	459,803	1923	522,919	1973	400,063
1822	6,911	1874	313,339	1924	706,896	1974	394,861
1823	6,354	1875	227,498	1925	294,314	1975	386,914
1824	7,912	1876	169,986	1926	304,488	1976	398,613
1825	10,199	1877	141,857	1927	335,175	1976 TQ	103,676
1826	10,837	1878	138,469	1928	307,255	1977	462,315
1827	18,875	1879	177,826	1929	279,678	1978	601,442
1828	27,382	1880	457,257	1930	241,700	1979	460,348
1829	22,520	**1881–90**	**5,246,613**	**1931–40**	**528,431**	1980	530,639
1830	23,322	1881	669,431	1931	97,139	**1981–90**	**7,338,062**
1831–40	**599,125**	1882	788,992	1932	35,576	1981	596,600
1831	22,633	1883	603,322	1933	23,068	1982	594,131
1832	60,482	1884	518,592	1934	29,470	1983	559,763
1833	58,640	1885	395,346	1935	34,956	1984	543,903
1834	65,365	1886	334,203	1936	36,329	1985	570,009
1835	45,374	1887	490,109	1937	50,244	1986	601,708
1836	76,242	1888	546,889	1938	67,895	1987	601,516
1837	79,340	1889	444,427	1939	82,998	1988	643,025
1838	38,914	1890	455,302	1940	70,756	1989	1,090,924
1839	68,069	**1891–1900**	**3,687,564**	**1941–50**	**1,035,039**	1990	1,536,483
1840	84,066	1891	560,319	1941	51,776	**1991–2000**	**9,090,857**
1841–50	**1,713,251**	1892	579,663	1942	28,781	1991	1,827,167
1841	80,289	1893	439,730	1943	23,725	1992	973,977
1842	104,565	1894	285,631	1944	28,551	1993	904,292
		1895	258,536	1945	38,119	1994	804,416
		1896	343,267	1946	108,721		

Year	Number	Year	Number	Year	Number	Year	Number
1843	52,496	1897	230,832	1947	147,292	1995	720,461
1844	78,615	1898	229,299	1948	170,570	1996	915,900
1845	114,371	1899	311,715	1949	188,317	1997	798,378
1846	154,416	1900	448,572	1950	249,187	1998	660,477
1847	234,968					1999	644,787
1848	226,527	1901–10	8,795,386	1951–60	2,515,479	2000	841,002
1849	297,024	1901	487,918	1951	205,717	2001–10	10,501,053
1850	369,980	1902	648,743	1952	265,520	2001	1,058,902
		1903	857,046	1953	170,434	2002	1,059,356
1851–60	2,598,214	1904	812,870	1954	208,177	2003	705,827
1851	379,466	1905	1,026,499	1955	237,790	2004	957,883
1852	371,603	1906	1,100,735	1956	321,625	2005	1,122,373
1853	368,645	1907	1,285,349	1957	326,867	2006	1,266,129
1854	427,833	1908	782,870	1958	253,265	2007	1,052,415
1855	200,877	1909	751,786	1959	260,686	2008	1,107,126
1856	200,436	1910	1,041,570	1960	265,398	2009	1,130,818
1857	251,306					2010	1,042,625
1858	123,126	1911–20	5,735,811	1961–70	3,321,677	2011	1,062,040
1859	121,282	1911	878,587	1961	271,344		
1860	153,640	1912	838,172	1962	283,763		
		1913	1,197,892	1963	306,260		
1861–70	2,314,824	1914	1,218,480	1964	292,248		
1861	91,918	1915	326,700	1965	296,697		
1862	91,985	1916	298,826	1966	323,040		
1863	176,282	1917	295,403	1967	361,972		
1864	193,418	1918	110,618	1968	454,448		
1865	248,120	1919	141,132	1969	358,579		
1866	318,568	1920	430,001	1970	373,326		
1867	315,722						
1868	138,840						
1869	352,768						
1870	387,203						

Source: U.S. Department of Homeland Security.

IMMIGRATION BY REGION AND SELECTED COUNTRY OF LAST RESIDENCE, FISCAL YEARS 1820–2011

Region and country of last residence	1820 to 1829	1830 to 1839	1840 to 1849	1850 to 1859	1860 to 1869	1870 to 1879	1880 to 1889	1890 to 1899
Total	128,502	538,381	1,427,337	2,814,554	2,081,261	2,742,137	5,248,568	3,694,294
Europe	99,272	422,771	1,369,259	2,619,680	1,877,726	2,251,878	4,638,677	3,576,411
Austria-Hungary	—	—	—	—	3,375	60,127	314,787	534,059
Austria	—	—	—	—	2,700	54,529	204,805	268,218
Hungary	—	—	—	—	483	5,598	109,982	203,350
Belgium	28	20	3,996	5,765	5,785	6,991	18,738	19,642
Bulgaria	—	—	—	—	—	—	—	52
Czechoslovakia	—	—	—	—	—	—	—	—
Denmark	173	927	671	3,227	13,553	29,278	85,342	56,671
Finland	—	—	—	—	—	—	—	35,616
France	7,694	39,330	75,300	81,778	35,938	71,901	48,193	35,616
Germany	5,753	124,726	385,434	976,072	723,734	751,769	1,445,181	579,072
Greece	17	49	17	32	51	209	1,807	12,732
Ireland	51,617	170,672	656,145	1,029,486	427,419	422,264	674,061	405,710
Italy	430	2,225	1,476	8,643	9,853	46,296	267,660	603,761
Netherlands	1,105	1,377	7,624	11,122	8,387	14,267	52,715	29,349
Norway-Sweden	91	1,149	12,389	22,202	82,937	178,823	586,441	334,058
Norway	—	—	—	—	16,068	88,644	185,111	96,810
Sweden	—	—	—	—	24,224	90,179	401,330	237,248
Poland	19	366	105	1,087	1,886	11,016	42,910	107,793
Portugal	177	820	196	1,299	2,083	13,971	15,186	25,874
Romania	—	—	—	—	—	—	5,842	6,808
Russia	86	280	520	423	1,670	35,177	182,698	450,101
Spain	2,595	2,010	1,916	8,795	6,966	5,540	3,995	9,189
Switzerland	3,148	4,430	4,819	24,423	21,124	25,212	81,151	37,020
United Kingdom	26,336	74,350	218,572	445,322	532,956	578,447	810,900	328,759
Yugoslavia	—	—	—	—	—	—	—	—
Other Europe	3	40	79	4	9	590	1,070	145

Region / Country								
Asia	34	55	121	36,080	54,408	134,128	71,151	61,285
China	3	8	32	35,933	54,028	133,139	65,797	15,268
Hong Kong		—	—	42	50	166	247	102
India	9	38	33	—	—	—	—	102
Iran	—	—	—	—	—	—	—	—
Israel	—	—	—	—	—	—	—	—
Japan	—	—	—	—	138	193	1,583	13,998
Jordan	—	—	—	—	—	—	—	—
Korea	—	—	—	—	—	—	—	—
Philippines	—	—	—	—	—	—	—	—
Syria	—	—	—	—	—	—	—	—
Taiwan	—	—	—	—	—	—	—	—
Turkey	19	8	45	94	129	382	2,478	27,510
Vietnam	—	—	—	—	—	—	—	—
Other Asia	3	1	11	11	63	248	1,046	4,407
America	9,655	31,905	50,516	84,145	130,292	345,010	524,826	37,350
Canada and Newfoundland	2,297	11,875	34,285	64,171	117,978	324,310	492,865	3,098
Mexico	3,835	7,187	3,069	3,446	1,957	5,133	2,405	734
Caribbean	3,061	11,792	11,803	12,447	8,751	14,285	27,323	31,480
Cuba	—	—	—	—	—	—	—	—
Dominican Republic	—	—	—	—	—	—	—	—
Haiti	—	—	—	—	—	—	—	—
Jamaica	—	—	—	—	—	—	—	—
Other Caribbean	3,061	11,792	11,803	12,447	8,751	14,285	27,323	31,480
Central America	57	94	297	512	70	173	279	649
Belize	—	—	—	—	—	—	—	—
Costa Rica	—	—	—	—	—	—	—	—
El Salvador	—	—	—	—	—	—	—	—
Guatemala	—	—	—	—	—	—	—	—
Honduras	—	—	—	—	—	—	—	—
Nicaragua	—	—	—	—	—	—	—	—
Panama	—	—	—	—	—	—	—	—
Other Central America	57	94	297	512	70	173	279	649
South America	405	957	1,062	3,569	1,536	1,109	1,954	1,389
Argentina	—	—	—	—	—	—	—	—
Bolivia	—	—	—	—	—	—	—	—

Region and country of last residence	1820 to 1829	1830 to 1839	1840 to 1849	1850 to 1859	1860 to 1869	1870 to 1879	1880 to 1889	1890 to 1899
Brazil	—	—	—	—	—	—	—	—
Chile	—	—	—	—	—	—	—	—
Colombia	—	—	—	—	—	—	—	—
Ecuador	—	—	—	—	—	—	—	—
Guyana	—	—	—	—	—	—	—	—
Paraguay	—	—	—	—	—	—	—	—
Peru	—	—	—	—	—	—	—	—
Suriname	—	—	—	—	—	—	—	—
Uruguay	—	—	—	—	—	—	—	—
Venezuela	—	—	—	—	—	—	—	—
Other South America	405	957	1,062	3,569	1,536	1,109	1,954	1,389
Africa	—	—	—	—	—	—	—	—
Egypt	15	50	61	84	407	371	763	432
Ethiopia	—	—	—	—	4	29	145	51
Liberia	1	8	5	7	43	52	21	9
Morocco	—	—	—	—	—	—	—	—
South Africa	—	—	—	—	35	48	23	9
Other Africa	14	42	56	77	325	242	574	363
Oceania	3	7	14	166	187	9,996	12,361	4,704
Australia	2	1	2	15	—	8,930	7,250	3,098
New Zealand	1	6	12	151	187	1,027	5,090	1,594
Other Oceania	—	—	—	—	—	39	21	12
Not Specified	19,523	83,593	7,366	74,399	18,241	754	790	14,112

Total	8,202,388	6,347,380	4,295,510	699,375	856,608	2,499,268	3,213,749	6,244,379
Europe	7,572,569	4,985,411	2,560,340	444,399	472,524	1,404,973	1,133,443	668,866
Austria-Hungary	2,001,376	1,154,727	60,891	12,531	13,574	113,015	27,590	20,437
Austria	532,416	589,174	31,392	5,307	8,393	81,354	17,571	15,374
Hungary	685,567	565,553	29,499	7,224	5,181	31,661	10,019	5,063
Belgium	37,429	32,574	21,511	4,013	12,473	18,885	9,647	7,028
Bulgaria	34,651	27,180	2,824	1,062	449	97	598	1,124
Czechoslovakia	—	—	101,182	17,757	8,475	1,624	2,758	5,678
Denmark	61,227	45,830	34,406	3,470	4,549	10,918	9,797	4,847
Finland	—	—	16,922	2,438	2,230	4,923	4,310	2,569
France	67,735	60,335	54,842	13,761	36,954	50,113	46,975	32,066
Germany	328,722	174,227	386,634	119,107	119,506	576,905	209,616	85,752
Greece	145,402	198,108	60,774	10,599	8,605	45,153	74,173	37,729
Ireland	344,940	166,445	202,854	28,195	15,701	47,189	37,788	22,210
Italy	1,930,475	1,229,916	528,133	85,053	50,509	184,576	200,111	55,562
Netherlands	42,463	46,065	29,397	7,791	13,877	46,703	37,918	11,234
Norway-Sweden	426,981	192,445	170,329	13,452	17,326	44,224	36,150	13,941
Norway	182,542	79,488	70,327	6,901	8,326	22,806	17,371	3,835
Sweden	244,439	112,957	100,002	6,551	9,000	21,418	18,779	10,106
Poland	—	—	223,316	25,555	7,577	6,465	55,742	63,483
Portugal	65,154	82,489	44,829	3,518	6,765	13,928	70,568	42,685
Romania	57,322	13,566	67,810	5,264	1,254	914	2,339	24,753
Russia	1,501,301	1,106,998	61,604	2,463	605	453	2,329	33,311
Spain	24,818	53,262	47,109	3,669	2,774	6,880	40,793	22,783
Switzerland	32,541	22,839	31,772	5,990	9,904	17,577	19,193	8,316
United Kingdom	469,518	371,878	341,552	61,813	131,794	195,709	220,213	153,644
Yugoslavia	—	—	49,215	6,920	2,039	6,966	17,990	16,267
Other Europe	514	6,527	22,434	9,978	5,584	11,756	6,845	3,447
Asia	299,836	269,736	126,740	19,231	34,532	135,844	358,605	2,391,356
China	19,884	20,916	30,648	5,874	16,072	8,836	14,060	170,897
Hong Kong	—	—	—	—	—	13,781	67,047	112,132
India	3,026	3,478	2,076	554	1,692	1,850	18,638	231,649
Iran	—	—	208	198	1,144	3,195	9,059	98,141
Israel	—	—	—	—	98	21,376	30,911	43,669

Region and country of last residence	1900 to 1909	1910 to 1919	1920 to 1929	1930 to 1939	1940 to 1949	1950 to 1959	1960 to 1969	1980 to 1989
Japan	139,712	77,125	42,057	2,683	1,557	40,651	40,956	44,150
Jordan	—	—	—	—	83	4,899	9,230	28,928
Korea	—	—	—	391	4,099	4,845	27,048	322,708
Philippines	—	—	5,307	2,188	1,179	17,245	70,660	502,056
Syria	—	—	—	—	—	1,091	2,432	14,534
Taiwan	—	—	—	—	—	721	15,657	119,051
Turkey	127,999	160,717	40,450	1,327	754	2,980	9,464	19,208
Vietnam	—	—	—	—	—	290	2,949	200,632
Other Asia	9,215	7,500	5,994	6,016	7,854	14,084	40,494	483,601
America	277,809	1,070,539	1,591,278	230,319	328,435	921,610	1,674,172	2,695,329
Canada and Newfoundland	123,067	708,715	949,286	162,703	160,911	353,169	433,128	156,313
Mexico	31,188	185,334	498,945	32,709	56,158	273,847	441,824	1,009,586
Caribbean	100,960	120,860	83,482	18,052	46,194	115,661	427,235	790,109
Cuba	—	—	12,769	10,641	25,976	73,221	202,030	132,552
Dominican Republic	—	—	—	1,026	4,802	10,219	83,552	221,552
Haiti	—	—	—	156	823	3,787	28,992	121,406
Jamaica	—	—	—	—	—	7,397	62,218	193,874
Other Caribbean	100,960	120,860	70,713	6,229	14,593	21,037	50,443	120,725
Central America	7,341	15,692	16,511	6,840	20,135	40,201	98,560	339,376
Belize	77	40	285	193	433	1,133	4,185	14,964
Costa Rica	—	—	—	431	1,965	4,044	17,975	25,017
El Salvador	—	—	—	597	4,885	5,094	14,405	137,418
Guatemala	—	—	—	423	1,303	4,197	14,357	58,847
Honduras	—	—	—	679	1,874	5,320	15,078	39,071
Nicaragua	—	—	—	405	4,393	7,812	10,383	31,102
Panama	—	—	—	1,452	5,282	12,601	22,177	32,957
Other Central America	7,264	15,652	16,226	2,660	—	—	—	—

South America	15,253	39,938	43,025	9,990	19,662	78,418	250,754	399,862
Argentina	—	—	—	1,067	3,108	16,346	49,384	23,442
Bolivia	—	—	—	50	893	2,759	6,205	9,798
Brazil	—	—	4,627	1,468	3,653	11,547	29,238	22,944
Chile	—	—	—	347	1,320	4,669	12,384	19,749
Colombia	—	—	—	1,027	3,454	15,567	68,371	105,494
Ecuador	—	—	—	244	2,207	8,574	34,107	48,015
Guyana	—	—	—	131	596	1,131	4,546	85,886
Paraguay	—	—	—	33	85	576	1,249	3,518
Peru	—	—	—	321	1,273	5,980	19,783	49,958
Suriname	—	—	—	25	130	299	612	1,357
Uruguay	—	—	—	112	754	1,026	4,089	7,235
Venezuela	—	—	—	1,155	2,182	9,927	20,758	22,405
Other South America	15,253	39,938	—	4,010	7	17	28	61
Other America	—	—	—	25	25,375	60,314	22,671	83
Africa	6,326	8,867	38,398	2,120	6,720	13,016	23,780	141,990
Egypt	—	—	29	781	1,613	1,996	5,581	26,744
Ethiopia	—	—	6,362	10	28	302	804	12,927
Liberia	—	—	1,063	35	37	289	841	6,420
Morocco	—	—	—	73	879	2,703	2,880	3,471
South Africa	—	—	—	312	1,022	2,278	4,360	15,505
Other Africa	6,326	8,867	5,299	909	3,141	5,448	9,314	76,923
Oceania	12,355	12,339	9,860	3,306	14,262	11,353	23,630	41,432
Australia	11,191	11,280	8,404	2,260	11,201	8,275	14,986	16,901
New Zealand	—	—	935	790	2,351	1,799	3,775	6,129
Other Oceania	1,164	1,059	521	256	710	1,279	4,869	18,402
Not Specified	33,493	488	930	—	135	12,472	119	305,406

Region and country of last residence	1990 to 1999	2000 to 2009	2010	2011
Total	9,775,398	10,299,430	1,042,625	1,062,040
Europe	1,348,612	1,349,609	95,429	90,712
Austria-Hungary	27,529	33,929	4,325	4,703
Austria	18,234	21,151	3,319	3,654
Hungary	9,295	12,778	1,006	1,049
Belgium	7,077	8,157	732	700
Bulgaria	16,948	40,003	2,465	2,549
Czechoslovakia	8,970	18,691	1,510	1,374
Denmark	6,189	6,049	545	473
Finland	3,970	3,970	414	398
France	35,945	45,637	4,339	3,967
Germany	92,207	122,373	7,929	7,072
Greece	25,403	16,841	966	1,196
Ireland	65,384	15,642	1,610	1,533
Italy	75,992	28,329	2,956	2,670
Netherlands	13,345	17,351	1,520	1,258
Norway-Sweden	17,825	19,382	1,662	1,530
Norway	5,211	4,599	363	405
Sweden	12,614	14,783	1,299	1,125
Poland	172,249	117,921	7,391	6,634
Portugal	25,497	11,479	759	878
Romania	48,136	52,154	3,735	3,679
Russia	433,427	167,152	7,502	8,548
Spain	18,443	17,695	2,040	2,319
Switzerland	11,768	12,173	868	861
United Kingdom	156,182	171,979	14,781	13,443
Yugoslavia	57,039	131,831	4,772	4,611
Other Europe	29,087	290,871	22,608	20,316

Asia	2,859,899	3,470,835	410,209	438,580
China	342,058	591,711	67,634	83,603
Hong Kong	116,894	57,583	3,263	3,149
India	352,528	590,464	66,185	66,331
Iran	76,899	76,755	9,078	9,015
Israel	41,340	54,081	5,172	4,389
Japan	66,582	84,552	7,100	6,751
Jordan	42,755	53,550	9,327	8,211
Korea	179,770	209,758	22,022	22,748
Philippines	534,338	545,463	56,399	55,251
Syria	22,906	30,807	7,424	7,983
Taiwan	132,647	92,657	6,785	6,206
Turkey	38,687	48,394	7,435	9,040
Vietnam	275,379	289,616	30,065	33,486
Other Asia	637,116	745,444	122,320	122,417
America	5,137,743	4,441,529	426,981	423,277
Canada and Newfoundland	194,788	236,349	19,491	19,506
Mexico	2,757,418	1,704,166	138,717	142,823
Caribbean	1,004,687	1,053,357	139,389	133,012
Cuba	159,037	271,742	33,372	36,261
Dominican Republic	359,818	291,492	53,890	46,036
Haiti	177,446	203,827	22,336	21,802
Jamaica	177,143	172,523	19,439	19,298
Other Caribbean	181,243	113,773	10,352	9,615
Central America	610,189	591,130	43,597	43,249
Belize	12,600	9,682	997	933
Costa Rica	17,054	21,571	2,306	2,230
El Salvador	273,017	251,237	18,547	18,477
Guatemala	126,043	156,992	10,263	10,795
Honduras	72,880	63,513	6,381	6,053

Region and country of last residence	1990 to 1999	2000 to 2009	2010	2011
Nicaragua	80,446	70,015	3,476	3,314
Panama	28,149	18,120	1,627	1,447
Other Central America	—	—	—	—
South America	570,624	856,508	85,783	84,687
Argentina	30,065	47,955	4,312	4,335
Bolivia	18,111	21,921	2,211	2,113
Brazil	50,744	115,404	12,057	11,643
Chile	18,200	19,792	1,940	1,854
Colombia	137,985	236,570	21,861	22,130
Ecuador	81,358	107,977	11,463	11,068
Guyana	74,407	70,373	6,441	6,288
Paraguay	6,082	4,623	449	501
Peru	110,117	137,614	14,063	13,836
Suriname	2,285	2,363	202	167
Uruguay	6,062	9,827	1,286	1,521
Venezuela	35,180	82,087	9,497	9,229
Other South America	28	2	1	2
Other America	37	19	4	—
Africa	346,416	759,734	98,246	97,429
Egypt	44,604	81,564	9,822	9,096
Ethiopia	40,097	87,207	13,853	13,985
Liberia	13,587	23,316	2,924	3,117
Morocco	15,768	40,844	4,847	4,249
South Africa	21,964	32,221	2,705	2,754
Other Africa	210,396	494,582	64,095	64,228
Oceania	56,800	65,793	5,946	5,825
Australia	24,288	32,728	3,077	3,062
New Zealand	8,600	12,495	1,046	1,006
Other Oceania	23,912	20,570	1,823	1,757
Not Specified	25,928	211,930	5,814	6,217

— Represents zero or not available.

PRESIDENTS, VICE PRESIDENTS, AND SECRETARIES OF STATE

	President	*Vice President*	*Secretary of State*
1.	George Washington, Federalist 1789	John Adams, Federalist 1789	Thomas Jefferson 1789 Edmund Randolph 1794 Timothy Pickering 1795
2.	John Adams, Federalist 1797	Thomas Jefferson, Dem.-Rep. 1797	Timothy Pickering 1797 John Marshall 1800
3.	Thomas Jefferson, Dem.-Rep. 1801	Aaron Burr, Dem.-Rep. 1801 George Clinton, Dem.-Rep. 1805	James Madison 1801
4.	James Madison, Dem.-Rep. 1809	George Clinton, Dem.-Rep. 1809 Elbridge Gerry, Dem.-Rep. 1813	Robert Smith 1809 James Monroe 1811
5.	James Monroe, Dem.-Rep. 1817	Daniel D. Tompkins, Dem.-Rep. 1817	John Q. Adams 1817
6.	John Quincy Adams, Dem.-Rep. 1825	John C. Calhoun, Dem.-Rep. 1825	Henry Clay 1825
7.	Andrew Jackson, Democratic 1829	John C. Calhoun, Democratic 1829 Martin Van Buren, Democratic 1833	Martin Van Buren 1829 Edward Livingston 1831 Louis McLane 1833 John Forsyth 1834
8.	Martin Van Buren, Democratic 1837	Richard M. Johnson, Democratic 1837	John Forsyth 1837
9.	William H. Harrison, Whig 1841	John Tyler, Whig 1841	Daniel Webster 1841

President	Vice President	Secretary of State
10. John Tyler, Whig and Democratic 1841	None	Daniel Webster 1841 Hugh S. Legaré 1843 Abel P. Upshur 1843 John C. Calhoun 1844
11. James K. Polk, Democratic 1845	George M. Dallas, Democratic 1845	James Buchanan 1845
12. Zachary Taylor, Whig 1849	Millard Fillmore, Whig 1848	John M. Clayton 1849
13. Millard Fillmore, Whig 1850	None	Daniel Webster 1850 Edward Everett 1852
14. Franklin Pierce, Democratic 1853	William R. King, Democratic 1853	William L. Marcy 1853
15. James Buchanan, Democratic 1857	John C. Breckinridge, Democratic 1857	Lewis Cass 1857 Jeremiah S. Black 1860
16. Abraham Lincoln, Republican 1861	Hannibal Hamlin, Republican 1861 Andrew Johnson, Unionist 1865	William H. Seward 1861
17. Andrew Johnson, Unionist 1865	None	William H. Seward 1865
18. Ulysses S. Grant, Republican 1869	Schuyler Colfax, Republican 1869 Henry Wilson, Republican 1873	Elihu B. Washburne 1869 Hamilton Fish 1869
19. Rutherford B. Hayes, Republican 1877	William A. Wheeler, Republican 1877	William M. Evarts 1877

	President	*Vice President*	*Secretary of State*
20.	James A. Garfield, Republican 1881	Chester A. Arthur, Republican 1881	James G. Blaine 1881
21.	Chester A. Arthur, Republican 1881	None	Frederick T. Frelinghuysen 1881
22.	Grover Cleveland, Democratic 1885	Thomas A. Hendricks, Democratic 1885	Thomas F. Bayard 1885
23.	Benjamin Harrison, Republican 1889	Levi P. Morton, Republican 1889	James G. Blaine 1889 John W. Foster 1892
24.	Grover Cleveland, Democratic 1893	Adlai E. Stevenson, Democratic 1893	Walter Q. Gresham 1893 Richard Olney 1895
25.	William McKinley, Republican 1897	Garret A. Hobart, Republican 1897 Theodore Roosevelt, Republican 1901	John Sherman 1897 William R. Day 1898 John Hay 1898
26.	Theodore Roosevelt, Republican 1901	Charles Fairbanks, Republican 1905	John Hay 1901 Elihu Root 1905 Robert Bacon 1909
27.	William H. Taft, Republican 1909	James S. Sherman, Republican 1909	Philander C. Knox 1909
28.	Woodrow Wilson, Democratic 1913	Thomas R. Marshall, Democratic 1913	William J. Bryan 1913 Robert Lansing 1915 Bainbridge Colby 1920
29.	Warren G. Harding, Republican 1921	Calvin Coolidge, Republican 1921	Charles E. Hughes 1921
30.	Calvin Coolidge, Republican 1923	Charles G. Dawes, Republican 1925	Charles E. Hughes 1923 Frank B. Kellogg 1925

	President	Vice President	Secretary of State
31.	Herbert Hoover, Republican 1929	Charles Curtis, Republican 1929	Henry L. Stimson 1929
32.	Franklin D. Roosevelt, Democratic 1933	John Nance Garner, Democratic 1933 Henry A. Wallace, Democratic 1941 Harry S. Truman, Democratic 1945	Cordell Hull 1933 Edward R. Stettinius, Jr. 1944
33.	Harry S. Truman, Democratic 1945	Alben W. Barkley, Democratic 1949	Edward R. Stettinius, Jr. 1945 James F. Byrnes 1945 George C. Marshall 1947 Dean G. Acheson 1949
34.	Dwight D. Eisenhower, Republican 1953	Richard M. Nixon, Republican 1953	John F. Dulles 1953 Christian A. Herter 1959
35.	John F. Kennedy, Democratic 1961	Lyndon B. Johnson, Democratic 1961	Dean Rusk 1961
36.	Lyndon B. Johnson, Democratic 1963	Hubert H. Humphrey, Democratic 1965	Dean Rusk 1963
37.	Richard M. Nixon, Republican 1969	Spiro T. Agnew, Republican 1969 Gerald R. Ford, Republican 1973	William P. Rogers 1969 Henry Kissinger 1973
38.	Gerald R. Ford, Republican 1974	Nelson Rockefeller, Republican 1974	Henry Kissinger 1974
39.	Jimmy Carter, Democratic 1977	Walter Mondale, Democratic 1977	Cyrus Vance 1977 Edmund Muskie 1980

	President	Vice President	Secretary of State
40.	Ronald Reagan, Republican 1981	George H. W. Bush, Republican 1981	Alexander Haig 1981 George Schultz 1982
41.	George H. W. Bush, Republican 1989	J. Danforth Quayle, Republican 1989	James A. Baker 1989 Lawrence Eagleburger 1992
42.	William J. Clinton, Democratic 1993	Albert Gore, Jr., Democratic 1993	Warren Christopher 1993 Madeleine Albright 1997
43.	George W. Bush, Republican 2001	Richard B. Cheney, Republican 2001	Colin L. Powell 2001 Condoleezza Rice 2005
44.	Barack Obama, Democratic 2009	Joseph R. Biden, Democratic 2009	Hillary Rodham Clinton 2009 John Kerry 2013

Further Readings

Chapter 1

A fascinating study of pre-Columbian migration is Brian M. Fagan's *The Great Journey: The Peopling of Ancient America*, rev. ed. (2004). Alice B. Kehoe's *North American Indians: A Comprehensive Account*, 2nd ed. (1992), provides an encyclopedic treatment of Native Americans. See also Charles Mann's *1491: New Revelations of the Americas before Columbus* (2005) and *1493: Uncovering the New World that Columbua Created* (2011), and Daniel K. Richter, *Before the Revolution: America's Ancient Pasts* (2011). On North America's largest Native American city, see Timothy R. Pauketat, *Cahokia* (2010).

The conflict between Native Americans and Europeans is treated well in James Axtell's *The Invasion Within: The Contest of Cultures in Colonial North America* (1986) and *Beyond 1492: Encounters in Colonial North America* (1992). Colin G. Calloway's *New Worlds for All: Indians, Europeans, and the Remaking of Early America* (1997) explores the ecological effects of European settlement.

Laurence Bergreen examines the voyages of Columbus in *Columbus: The Four Voyages* (2011). For sweeping overviews of Spain's creation of a global empire, see Henry Kamen's *Empire: How Spain Became a World Power, 1492–1763* (2003) and Hugh Thomas's *Rivers of Gold: The Rise of the Spanish Empire, from Columbus to Magellan* (2004). David J. Weber examines Spanish colonization in *The Spanish Frontier in North America* (1992). For the French experience, see William J. Eccles's *France in America*, rev. ed. (1990). For an insightful comparison of Spanish and English modes of settlement, see J. H. Elliott, *Empires of the Atlantic World: Britain and Spain in America, 1492–1830* (2006).

Chapter 2

Two excellent surveys of early American history are Peter C. Hoffer's *The Brave New World: A History of Early America,* 2nd ed. (2006), and William R. Polk's *The Birth of America: From before Columbus to the Revolution* (2006).

Bernard Bailyn's *The Barbarous Years: The Peopling of British North America: The Conflict of Civilizations, 1600-1675* (2013) tells the often brutal story of British settlement in America during the seventeenth century. Jack P. Greene offers a brilliant synthesis of British colonization in *Pursuits of Happiness: The Social Development of Early Modern British Colonies and the Formation of American Culture* (1988). The best overview of the colonization of North America is Alan Taylor's *American Colonies: The Settling of North America* (2001). On the interactions among Indian, European, and African cultures, see Gary B. Nash's *Red, White, and Black: The Peoples of Early North America*, 5th ed. (2005).

A good overview of the founding of Virginia and Maryland is Jean and Elliott Russo's *The Early Chesapeake in British North America* (2012). For information regarding the Puritan settlement of New England, see David D. Hall's *A Reforming People: Puritanism and the Transofrmaiton of Public Life in New England* (2013). The best biography of John Winthrop is Francis J. Bremer's *John Winthrop: America's Forgotten Founding Father* (2003). On Roger Williams, see John M. Barry's *Roger Williams and the Creation of the American Soul* (2012)

The pattern of settlement in the middle colonies is illuminated in Barry Levy's *Quakers and the American Family: British Settlement in the Delaware Valley* (1988).

On the early history of New York, see Russell Shorto's *The Island at the Center of the World: The Epic Story of Dutch Manhattan and the Forgotten Colony That Shaped America* (2004). Settlement of the areas along the Atlantic in the South is traced in James Horn's *Adapting to a New World: English Society in the Seventeenth-Century Chesapeake* (1994).

On shifting political life in England, see Steve Pincus, *1688: The First Modern Revolution* (2009). For a study of race and the settlement of South Carolina, see Peter H. Wood's *Black Majority: Negroes in Colonial South Carolina from 1670 through the Stono Rebellion* (1974). On the flourishing trade in captive Indians, see Alan Gallay's *The Indian Slave Trade: The Rise of the English Empire in the American South, 1670–1717* (2002). On the Yamasee War, see Steven J. Oatis's *A Colonial Complex: South Carolina's Frontiers in the Era of the Yamasee War, 1680–1730* (2004).

Chapter 3

The diversity of colonial societies may be seen in David Hackett Fischer's *Albion's Seed: Four British Folkways in America* (1989). John Frederick Martin's *Profits in the Wilderness: Entrepreneurship and the Founding of New England Towns in the Seventeenth Century* (1991) indicates that economic concerns rather than spiritual motives were driving forces in many New England towns.

Bernard Rosenthal challenges many myths concerning the Salem witch trials in *Salem Story: Reading the Witch Trials of 1692* (1993). Mary Beth Norton's *In the Devil's Snare: The Salem Witchcraft Crisis of 1692* (2002) emphasizes the role of Indian violence.

Discussions of women in the New England colonies can be found in Laurel Thatcher Ulrich's *Good Wives: Image and Reality in the Lives of Women in Northern New England, 1650–1750* (1980), and Mary Beth Norton, *Separated by Their Sex: Women in Public and Private in the Colonial Atlantic World* (2011). On women and religion, see Susan Juster's *Disorderly Women: Sexual Politics and Evangelicalism in Revolutionary New England* (1994). John Demos describes family life in *A Little Commonwealth: Family Life in Plymouth Colony*, new ed. (2000).

For an excellent overview of Indian relations with Europeans, see Colin G. Calloway's *New Worlds for All: Indians, Europeans, and the Remaking of Early America* (1997). For analyses of Indian wars, see Alfred A. Cave's *The Pequot War* (1996) and Jill Lepore's *The Name of War: King Philip's War and the Origins of American Identity* (1998). The story of the Iroquois is told well in Daniel K. Richter's *The Ordeal of the Longhouse: The Peoples of the Iroquois League in the Era of European Colonization* (1992). Indians in the southern colonies are the focus of James Axtell's *The Indians' New South: Cultural Change in the Colonial Southeast* (1997). On the fur trade, see Eric Jay Dolan, *Fur, Fortune, and Empire: The Epic Story of the Fur Trade in America* (2010).

For the social history of the southern colonies, see Allan Kulikoff's *Tobacco and Slaves: The Development of Southern Cultures in the Chesapeake, 1680–1800* (1986). On the interaction of the cultures of blacks and whites, see Mechal Sobel's *The World They Made Together: Black and White Values in Eighteenth-Century Virginia* (1987). On the slave trade, see William St. Clair's *The Door of No Return* (2007). African Americans during colonial settlement are the focus of Timothy H. Breen and Stephen Innes's *"Myne Owne Ground": Race and Freedom on Virginia's Eastern Shore, 1640–1676*, new ed. (2004). David W. Galenson's *White Servitude in Colonial America: An Economic Analysis* (1981) looks at the indentured labor force.

Henry F. May's *The Enlightenment in America* (1976) and Donald H. Meyer's *The Democratic Enlightenment* (1976) examine intellectual trends in eighteenth-century America. On the Great Awakening, see Frank Lambert's *Inventing the "Great Awak-*

ening" (1999), and Thomas S. Kidd's *The Great Awakening: The Roots of Evangelical Christianity in Colonial America* (2007). The best biography of Edwards is Phillip F. Gura's *Jonathan Edwards: A Life* (2003).

Chapter 4

A good introduction to the imperial phase of the colonial conflicts is Douglas Edward Leach's *Arms for Empire: A Military History of the British Colonies in North America, 1607–1763* (1973). Also useful is Brendan Simms's *Three Victories and a Defeat: The Rise and Fall of the Fiurst British Empire* (2008). Fred Anderson's *Crucible of War: The Seven Years' War and the Fate of Empire in British North America, 1754–1766* (2000) is the best history of the Seven Years' War. For the implications of the British victory in 1763, see Colin G. Calloway's *The Scratch of a Pen: 1763 and the Transformation of North America* (2006). On the French colonies in North America, see Allan Greer's *The People of New France* (1997).

For a narrative survey of the events leading to the Revolution, see Edward Countryman's *The American Revolution,* rev. ed. (2003). For Great Britain's perspective on the imperial conflict, see Ian R. Christie's *Crisis of Empire: Great Britain and the American Colonies, 1754–1783* (1966). Also see Jeremy Black's *George III: America's Last King* (2007).

The intellectual foundations of revolt are traced in Bernard Bailyn's *The Ideological Origins of the American Revolution* (1992). To understand how these views were connected to organized protest, see Jon Butler's *Becoming America: The Revolution before 1776* (2000) and Kevin Phillips's *1775: A Good Year for a Revolution* (2012). On the first major battle, see Nathaniel Philbrick's *Bunker Hill: A Siege, a Revolution* (2013).

On the efforts of colonists to boycott the purchase of British goods, see T. H. Breen's *The Marketplace of Revolution: How Consumer Politics Shaped American Independence* (2004). For the events during the summer of 1776, see Joseph J. Ellis's *Revolutionary Summer: The Birth of American Independence.* Pauline Maier's *American Scripture: Making the Declaration of Independence* (1997) remains the best analysis of the framing of that document. The best analysis of why Americans supported independence is Thomas Slaughter's *Independence: The Tangled Roots of the American Revolution* (2014).

Chapter 5

Military affairs in the early phases of the Revolutionary War are handled in John W. Shy's *Toward Lexington: The Role of the British Army in the Coming of the American Revolution* (1965). The Revolutionary War is the subject of Gordon S. Wood's *The Radicalism of the American Revolution* (1991) and Jeremy Black's *War for America: The Fight for Independence, 1775–1783* (1991). John Ferling's *Setting the World Ablaze: Washington, Adams, Jefferson, and the American Revolution* (2000) highlights the roles played by key leaders.

On the social history of the Revolutionary War, see John W. Shy's *A People Numerous and Armed: Reflections on the Military Struggle for American Independence,* rev. ed. (1990). Colin G. Calloway tells the neglected story of the Indian experiences in the Revolution in *The American Revolution in Indian Country: Crisis and Diversity in Native American Communities* (1995).

Why some Americans remained loyal to the Crown is the subject of Thomas B. Allen's *Tories: Fighting for the King in America's First Civil War* (2010) and Maya

Jasanoff's *Liberty's Exiles: American Loyalists in the Revolutionary War* (2011). A superb study of African Americans during the Revolutionary era is Douglas R. Egerton's *Death or Liberty: African Americans and Revolutionary America* (2009).

Carol Berkin's *Revolutionary Mothers: Women in the Struggle for America's Independence* (2005) documents the role that women played in securing independence. A superb biography of Revolutionary America's most prominent woman is Woody Holton's *Abigail Adams* (2010). A fine new biography of America's commander in chief is Ron Chernow's *Washington: A Life* (2010). The best analysis of the British side of the war is Andrew Jackson O'Shuaghnessy's *The Men Who Lost America: British Leadership, the American Revolution, and the Fate of Empire* (2013).

Chapter 6

A good overview of the Confederation period is Richard B. Morris's *The Forging of the Union, 1781–1789* (1987). Another useful analysis of this period is Richard Buel Jr.'s *Securing the Revolution: Ideology in American Politics, 1789–1815* (1972). David P. Szatmary's *Shays's Rebellion: The Making of an Agrarian Insurrection* (1980) covers that fateful incident. For a fine account of cultural change during the period, see Joseph J. Ellis's *After the Revolution: Profiles of Early American Culture* (1979).

An excellent overview of post-Revolutionary life is Joyce Appleby's *Inheriting the Revolution: The First Generation of Americans* (2000). On the political philosophies contributing to the drafting of the Constitution, see Ralph Lerner's *The Thinking Revolutionary: Principle and Practice in the New Republic* (1987). For the dramatic story of the framers of the Constitution, see Richard Beeman's *Plain, Honest Men: The Making of the American Constituion* (2009). Woody Holton's *Unruly Americans and the Origins of the Constitution* (2007) emphasizes the role of taxes and monetary policies in the crafting of the Constitution. The complex story of ratification is well told in Pauline Maier's *Ratification: The People Debate the Constitution, 1787-1788* (2010).

The best introduction to the early Federalists remains John C. Miller's *The Federalist Era, 1789–1801* (2011). Other works analyze the ideological debates among the nation's first leaders. Richard Buel Jr.'s *Securing the Revolution: Ideology in American Politics, 1789–1815* (1972), Joyce Appleby's *Capitalism and a New Social Order: The Republican Vision of the 1790s* (1984), and Stanley Elkins and Eric McKitrick's *The Age of Federalism: The Early American Republic, 1788–1800* (1993) trace the persistence and transformation of ideas first fostered during the Revolutionary crisis. The best study of Washington's political career is John Ferling's *The Ascent of George Washington: The Hidden Political Genius of an American Icon* (2009).

The 1790s may also be understood through the views and behavior of national leaders. See the following biographies: Richard Brookhiser's *Founding Father: Rediscovering George Washington* (1996), *Alexander Hamilton, American* (1999), and *James Madison* (2013), and Joseph J. Ellis's *Passionate Sage: The Character and Legacy of John Adams* (1993).

On the formation of the federal government and its economic policies, see Thomas K. McCraw's *The Founders and Finance* (2012). Federalist foreign policy is explored in Jerald A. Comb's *The Jay Treaty: Political Battleground of the Founding Fathers* (1970) and William Stinchcombe's *The XYZ Affair* (1980).

Chapter 7

Marshall Smelser's *The Democratic Republic, 1801–1815* (1968) presents an overview of the Republican administrations. Even more comprehensive is Gordon S. Wood's

Empire of Liberty: A History of the Early Republic, 1789-1815 (2010). The best treatment of the election of 1800 is Edward J. Larson's *A Magnificent Catastrophe: The Tumultuous Election of 1800* (2008).

The standard biography of Jefferson is Joseph J. Ellis's *American Sphinx: The Character of Thomas Jefferson* (1996). On the life of Jefferson's friend and successor, see Drew R. McCoy's. *The Last of the Fathers: James Madison and the Republican Legacy* (1989). Joyce Appleby's *Capitalism and a New Social Order: The Republican Vision of the 1790s* (1984) minimizes the impact of Republican ideology.

Linda K. Kerber's *Federalists in Dissent: Imagery and Ideology in Jeffersonian American* (1970) explores the Federalists while out of power. The concept of judicial review and the courts can be studied in Cliff Sloan and David McKean's *The Great Decision: Jefferson, Adams, Marshall, and the Battle for the Supreme Court* (2009). Liff Sloan and David McKean's *The Great Decision: Jefferson, Adams, Marshall, and the Battle for the Supreme Court* (2009). Milton Lomask's two volumes, *Aaron Burr: The Years from Princeton to Vice President, 1756–1805* (1979) and *The Conspiracy and the Years of Exile, 1805–1836* (1982) trace the career of that remarkable American.

For the Louisiana Purchase, consult Jon Kukla's *A Wilderness So Immense: The Louisiana Purchase and the Destiny of America* (2003). For a captivating account of the Lewis and Clark expedition, see Stephen Ambrose's *Undaunted Courage: Meriwether Lewis, Thomas Jefferson, and the Opening of the American West* (1996).

Burton Spivak's *Jefferson's English Crisis: Commerce, Embargo, and the Republican Revolution* (1979) discusses Anglo-American relations during Jefferson's administration; Clifford L. Egan's *Neither Peace Nor War: Franco-American Relations, 1803–1812* (1983) covers America's relations with France. An excellent revisionist treatment of the events that brought on war in 1812 is J. C. A. Stagg's *Mr. Madison's War: Politics, Diplomacy, and Warfare in the Early American Republic, 1783–1830* (1983). The war itself is the focus of Donald R. Hickey's *The War of 1812: A Forgotten Conflict* (1989). See also Alan Taylor's award-winnning *The Civil War of 1812: American Citizens, British Subjects, Irish Rebels, and Indian Allies* (2011).

Chapter 8

The best overview of the second quarter of the nineteenth century is Daniel Walker Howe, *What Hath God Wrought: The Transformation of America, 1815-1845* (2007). The classic study of transportation and economic growth is George Rogers Taylor's *The Transportation Revolution, 1815–1860* (1951). A more recent treatment is Sarah H. Gordon's *Passage to Union: How the Railroads Transformed American Life, 1829–1929* (1996). On the Erie Canal, see Carol Sheriff's *The Artificial River: The Erie Canal and the Paradox of Progress, 1817–1862* (1996). See also John Lauritz Larson's *Internal Improvement: National Public Works and the Promise of Popular Government in the Early United States* (2001).

Several books focus on social issues of the post-Revolutionary period, including *Keepers of the Revolution: New Yorkers at Work in the Early Republic* (1992), edited by Paul A. Gilje and Howard B. Rock; Ronald Schultz's *The Republic of Labor: Philadelphia Artisans and the Politics of Class, 1720–1830* (1993); and Peter Way's *Common Labor: Workers and the Digging of North American Canals, 1780–1860* (1993).

On the industrial revolution, see Charles R. Morris's *The Dawn of Innovation: The First American Industrial Revolution* (2013. The impact of technology is traced in David J. Jeremy's *Transatlantic Industrial Revolution: The Diffusion of Textile Technologies between Britain and America, 1790–1830s* (1981). On the invention of the telegraph, see Kenneth Silverman's *Lightning Man: The Accursed Life of Samuel*

F. B. Morse (2003). For the story of steamboats, see Andrea Sutcliffe's *Steam: The Untold Story of America's First Great Invention* (2004).

The outlook of the working class during this time of transition is surveyed in Edward E. Pessen's *Most Uncommon Jacksonians: The Radical Leaders of the Early Labor Movement* (1967). Detailed case studies of working communities include Anthony F. C. Wallace's *Rockdale: The Growth of an American Village in the Early Industrial Revolution* (1978), Thomas Dublin's *Women at Work: The Transformation of Work and Community in Lowell, Massachusetts, 1826–1860* (1979), and Sean Wilentz's *Chants Democratic: New York and the Rise of the American Working Class, 1788–1850* (1984).

For a fine treatment of urbanization, see Charles N. Glaab and A. Theodore Brown's *A History of Urban America* (1967). On immigration, see Jay P. Dolan's *The Irish Americans* (2008) and John Kelly's *The Graves Are Walking: The Great Famine and the Saga of the Irish People* (2012).

Chapter 9

The standard overview of the Era of Good Feelings remains George Dangerfield's *The Awakening of American Nationalism, 1815–1828* (1965). A classic summary of the economic trends of the period is Douglass C. North's *The Economic Growth of the United States, 1790–1860* (1961). An excellent synthesis of the era is Charles Sellers's *The Market Revolution: Jacksonian America, 1815–1846* (1991).

On diplomatic relations during James Monroe's presidency, see William Earl Weeks's *John Quincy Adams and American Global Empire* (1992). For relations after 1812, see Ernest R. May's *The Making of the Monroe Doctrine* (1975). The campaign that brought Andrew Jackson to the White House is analyzed in Robert Vincent Remini's *The Election of Andrew Jackson* (1963).

Chapter 10

The best comprehensive surveys of politics and culture during the Jacksonian era are Daniel Walker Howe's *What Hath God Wrought: The Transformation of America, 1815–1848* (2007) and David S. Reynolds's *Waking Giant: America in the Age of Jackson* (2008). A more political focus can be found in Harry L. Watson's *Liberty and Power: The Politics of Jacksonian America* (1990). On the rise of urban political machines, see Terry Golway's *Machine Made: Tammany Hall and the Creation of Modern American Politics* (2014).

For an outstanding analysis of women in New York City during the Jacksonian period, see Christine Stansell's *City of Women: Sex and Class in New York, 1789–1860* (1986). In *Chants Democratic: New York City and the Rise of the American Working-Class, 1788–1850* (1984), Sean Wilentz analyzes the social basis of working-class politics. More recently, Wilentz has traced the democratization of politics in *The Rise of American Democracy: Jefferson to Lincoln* (2009).

The best biography of Jackson remains Robert Vincent Remini's three-volume work: *Andrew Jackson: The Course of American Empire, 1767–1821* (1977), *Andrew Jackson: The Course of American Freedom, 1822–1832* (1981), and *Andrew Jackson: The Course of American Democracy, 1833–1845* (1984). A more critical study of the seventh president is Andrew Burstein's *The Passions of Andrew Jackson* (2003).

On Jackson's successor, consult John Niven's *Martin Van Buren: The Romantic Age of American Politics* (1983) and Ted Widmer's *Martin Van Buren* (2005). Studies of other major figures of the period include John Niven's *John C. Calhoun and the Price of Union: A Biography* (1988), Merrill D. Peterson's *The Great Triumvirate: Webster, Clay, and Calhoun* (1987), and Robert Vincent Remini's *Henry Clay: Statesman for the Union* (1991) and *Daniel Webster: The Man and His Time* (1997).

The political philosophies of Jackson's opponents are treated in Michael F. Holt's *The Rise and Fall of the American Whig Party: Jacksonian Politics and the Onset of the Civil War* (1999) and Harry L. Watson's *Andrew Jackson vs. Henry Clay: Democracy and Development in Antebellum America* (1998). The outstanding book on the nullification issue remains William W. Freehling's *Prelude to Civil War: The Nullification Controversy in South Carolina, 1816–1836* (1965). John M. Belohlavek's *"Let the Eagle Soar!": The Foreign Policy of Andrew Jackson* (1985) is a thorough study of Jacksonian diplomacy. A. J. Langguth's *Driven West: Andrew Jackson and the Trail of Tears to the Civil War* (2010) analyzes the controversial relocation policy.

Chapter 11

Russel Blaine Nye's *Society and Culture in America, 1830–1860* (1974) provides a wide-ranging survey of the Romantic movement. On the reform impulse, consult Ronald G. Walter's *American Reformers, 1815–1860*, rev. ed. (1997). Revivalist religion is treated in Nathan O. Hatch's *The Democratization of American Christianity* (1989), Christine Leigh Heyrman's *Southern Cross: The Beginnings of the Bible Belt* (1997), and Ellen Eslinger's *Citizens of Zion: The Social Origins of Camp Meeting Revivalism* (1999). On the Mormons, see Alex Beam's *American Crucifixition: The Murder of Joseph Smith and the Fate of the Mormon Church* (2014).

The best treatments of transcendentalist thought are Paul F. Boller's *American Transcendentalism, 1830–1860: An Intellectual Inquiry* (1974) and Philip F. Gura's *American Transcendentalism: A History* (2007). For the war against alcohol, see W. J. Rorabaugh's *The Alcoholic Republic: An American Tradition* (1979) and Barbara Leslie Epstein's *The Politics of Domesticity: Women, Evangelism, and Temperance in Nineteenth-Century America* (1981). On prison reform and other humanitarian projects, see David J. Rothman's *The Discovery of the Asylum: Social Order and Disorder in the New Republic*, rev. ed. (2002), and Thomas J. Brown's biography *Dorothea Dix: New England Reformer* (1998).

Useful surveys of abolitionism include Seymour Drescher's *Abolition: A History of Slavery and Antislavery* (2009), James Brewer Stewart's *Holy Warriors: The Abolitionists and American Slavery*, rev. ed. (1997), and Julie Roy Jeffrey's *The Great Silent Army of Abolitionism: Ordinary Women in the Antislavery Movement* (1998). For the pro-slavery argument as it developed in the South, see Larry E. Tise's *Proslavery: A History of the Defense of Slavery in America, 1701–1840* (1987) and James Oakes's *The Ruling Race: A History of American Slaveholders* (1982). The problems southerners had in justifying slavery are explored in Kenneth S. Greenberg's *Masters and Statesmen: The Political Culture of American Slavery* (1985).

Chapter 12

Three efforts to understand the mind of the Old South and its defense of slavery are Eugene D. Genovese's *The Slaveholders' Dilemma: Freedom and Progress in Southern Conservative Thought, 1820–1860* (1992), William W. Freehling's *The Road to Disunion: Secessionists Triumphant, 1854–1861* (2007), and Walter Johnson's *River of Dark Dreams: Slavery and Empire in the Cotton Kingdom* (2013). Stephanie

McCurry's *Masters of Small Worlds: Yeoman Households, Gender Relations, and the Political Culture of the Antebellum South Carolina Low Country* (1995) describes southern households, religion, and political culture.

Other essential works on southern culture and society include Bertram Wyatt-Brown's *Honor and Violence in the Old South* (1986), Elizabeth Fox-Genovese's *Within the Plantation Household: Black and White Women of the Old South* (1988), Catherine Clinton's *The Plantation Mistress: Woman's World in the Old South* (1982), Joan E. Cashin's *A Family Venture: Men and Women on the Southern Frontier* (1991), and Theodore Rosengarten's *Tombee: Portrait of a Cotton Planter* (1986).

John W. Blassingame's *The Slave Community: Plantation Life in the Antebellum South,* rev. and enlarged ed. (1979), Eugene D. Genovese's *Roll, Jordan, Roll: The World the Slaves Made* (1974), and Herbert G. Gutman's *The Black Family in Slavery and Freedom, 1750–1925* (1976) all stress the theme of a persisting and identifiable slave culture. On the question of slavery's profitability, see Robert William Fogel and Stanley L. Engerman's *Time on the Cross: The Economics of American Negro Slavery* (1974), and Edward E. Baptist's *The Half Has Never Been Told* (2014). Charles Joyner's *Down by the Riverside: A South Carolina Slave Community* (1984) offers a vivid reconstruction of one community.

Chapter 13

For background on Whig programs and ideas, see Michael F. Holt's *The Rise and Fall of the American Whig Party: Jacksonian Politics and the Onset of the Civil War* (1999). On John Tyler, see Edward P. Crapol's *John Tyler: The Accidental President* (2006). On the expansionist impulse westward, see Thomas R. Hietala's *Manifest Design: Anxious Aggrandizement in Late Jacksonian America* (1985), Walter Nugent's *Habits of Empire: A History of American Expansionism* (2008) and Richard White's *"It's Your Misfortune and None of My Own": A New History of the American West* (1991).

For the expansionism of the 1840s, see Steven E. Woodworth's *Manifest Destinies: America's Westward Expansion and the Road to the Civil War* (2010). The movement of settlers to the West is ably documented in John Mack Faragher's *Women and Men on the Overland Trail,* 2nd ed. (2001), and David Dary's *The Santa Fe Trail: Its History, Legends, and Lore* (2000).

Gene M. Brack's *Mexico Views Manifest Destiny, 1821–1846: An Essay on the Origins of the Mexican War* (1975) takes Mexico's viewpoint on U.S. designs on the West. For the American perspective on Texas, see Joel H. Silbey's *Storm over Texas: The Annexation Controversy and the Road to Civil War* (2005). On the siege of the Alamo, see William C. Davis's *Three Roads to the Alamo: The Lives and Fortunes of David Crockett, James Bowie, and William Barret Travis* (1998) and James Donovan's *The Blood of Heroes* (2012). An excellent biography related to the emergence of Texas is Gregg Cantrell's *Stephen F. Austin: Empresario of Texas* (1999).

On James K. Polk, see Robert W. Merry's *A Country of Vast Designs: James K. Polk, the Mexican War, and the Conquest of the American Continent* (2009). The best survey of the military conflict is John S. D. Eisenhower's *So Far from God: The U.S. War with Mexico, 1846–1848* (1989). The Mexican War as viewed from the perspective of the soldiers is ably described in Richard Bruce Winders's *Mr. Polk's Army: American Military Experience in the Mexican War* (1997). On the diplomatic aspects of Mexican-American relations, see David M. Pletcher's *The Diplomacy of Annexation: Texas, Oregon, and the Mexican War* (1973).

The best surveys of the forces and events leading to the Civil War include James M. McPherson's *Battle Cry of Freedom: The Civil War Era* (1988), Stephen B. Oates's *The Approaching Fury: Voices of the Storm, 1820–1861* (1997), and Bruce Levine's

Half Slave and Half Free: The Roots of Civil War (1992). The most recent narrative of the political debate leading to secession is Michael A. Morrison's *Slavery and the American West: The Eclipse of Manifest Destiny and the Coming of the Civil War* (1997).

Mark J. Stegmaier's *Texas, New Mexico, and the Compromise of 1850: Boundary Dispute and Sectional Crisis* (1996) probes that crucial dispute, while Michael F. Holt's *The Political Crisis of the 1850s* (1978) traces the demise of the Whigs. See also Fergus M. Bordewich's *America's Great Debate: Henry Clay, Stephen A. Douglas, and the Compromise That Preserved the Union* (2012). Eric Foner, in *Free Soil, Free Labor, Free Men: The Ideology of the Republican Party before the Civil War* (1970), shows how events and ideas combined in the formation of a new political party. The pivotal *Dred Scott* case is ably assessed in Earl M. Maltz's *Dred Scott and the Politics of Slavery* (2007).

On the role of John Brown in the sectional crisis, see Robert E. McGlone's *John Brown's War Against Slavery* (2009). A detailed study of the South's journey to secession is William W. Freehling's *The Road to Disunion*, vol. 1, *Secessionists at Bay, 1776–1854* (1990), and *The Road to Disunion*, vol. 2, *Secessionists Triumphant, 1854–1861* (2007). Robert E. Bonner traces the emergence of southern nationalism in *Mastering America: Southern Slaveholders and the Crisis of American Nationhood* (2009).

On the Buchanan presidency, see Jean H. Baker's *James Buchanan* (2004). Maury Klein's *Days of Defiance: Sumter, Secession, and the Coming of the Civil War* (1997) treats the Fort Sumter controversy. An excellent collection of interpretive essays is *Why the Civil War Came* (1996), edited by Gabor S. Boritt.

Chapter 14

On the start of the Civil War, see Adam Goodheart's *1861: The Civil War Awakening* (2011). The best one-volume overview of the Civil War period is James M. McPherson's *Battle Cry of Freedom: The Civil War Era* (1988). A more recent synthesis of the war and its effects is David Goldfield's *America Aflame: How the Civil War Created a Nation* (2011). A good introduction to the military events is Herman Hattaway's *Shades of Blue and Gray: An Introductory Military History of the Civil War* (1997). The outlook and experiences of the common soldier are explored in James M. McPherson's *For Cause and Comrades: Why Men Fought in the Civil War* (1997).

The northern war effort is ably assessed in Gary W. Gallagher's *The Union War* (2011). For emphasis on the South, see Gallagher's *The Confederate War* (1997). A sparkling account of the birth of the Rebel nation is William C. Davis's *"A Government of Our Own": The Making of the Confederacy* (1994). The same author provides a fine biography of the Confederate president in *Jefferson Davis: The Man and His Hour* (1991). On the leading Confederate commander, see Michael Korda's *Clouds of Glory: The Life and Legend of Robert E. Lee* (2014). On the key Union generals, see Lee Kennett's *Sherman: A Soldier's Life* (2001) and Josiah Bunting III's *Ulysses S. Grant* (2004).

The history of the North during the war is surveyed in Philip Shaw Paludan's *A People's Contest: The Union and Civil War, 1861–1865,* 2nd ed. (1996), and J. Matthew Gallman's *The North Fights the Civil War: The Home Front* (1994). See also Jennifer L. Weber's *Copperheads: The Rise and Fall of Lincoln's Opponents in the North* (2006). The central northern political figure, Abraham Lincoln, is the subject of many books. See James McPherson's *Abraham Lincoln* (2009) and Ronald C. White, Jr., *A. Lincoln: A Biography* (2009).

The experience of the African American soldier is surveyed in Joseph T. Glatthaar's *Forged in Battle: The Civil War Alliance of Black Soldiers and White Officers*

(1990) and Ira Berlin, Joseph P. Reidy, and Leslie S. Rowland's *Freedom's Soldiers: The Black Military Experience in the Civil War* (1998). For the African American woman's experience, see Jacqueline Jones's *Labor of Love, Labor of Sorrow: Black Women, Work and the Family, from Slavery to the Present* (1985). On Lincoln's evolving racial views, see Eric Foner's *The Fiery Trial: Abraham Lincoln and American Slavery* (2010). The war's impact on slavery is the focus of James Oakes's *Freedom National: The Destruction of Slavery in the United States, 1861-1865* (2013) and Bruce Levine's *The Fall of the House of Dixie* (2013). On the emancipation proclamation, see Louis P. Masur's *Lincoln's Hundred Days: The Emancipation Proclamation and the War for the Union* (2012).

Recent gender and ethnic studies include Nina Silber's *Gender and the Sectional Conflict* (2008), Drew Gilpin Faust's *Mothers of Invention: Women of the Slaveholding South in the American Civil War* (1996), George C. Rable's *Civil Wars: Women and the Crisis of Southern Nationalism* (1989), and William L. Burton's *Melting Pot Soldiers: The Union's Ethnic Regiments*, 2nd ed. (1998).

Chapter 15

The most comprehensive treatment of Reconstruction is Eric Foner's *Reconstruction: America's Unfinished Revolution, 1863–1877* (1988). On Andrew Johnson, see Hans L. Trefousse's *Andrew Johnson: A Biography* (1989) and David D. Stewart's *Impeached: The Trial of Andrew Johnson and the Fight for Lincoln's Legacy* (2009). An excellent brief biography of Grant is Josiah Bunting III's *Ulysses S. Grant* (2004).

Scholars have been sympathetic to the aims and motives of the Radical Republicans. See, for instance, Herman Belz's *Reconstructing the Union: Theory and Policy during the Civil War* (1969) and Richard Nelson Current's *Those Terrible Carpetbaggers: A Reinterpretation* (1988). The ideology of the Radicals is explored in Michael Les Benedict's *A Compromise of Principle: Congressional Republicans and Reconstruction, 1863–1869* (1974). On the black political leaders, see Phillip Dray's *Capitol Men: The Epic Story of Reconstruction through the Lives of the First Black Congressmen* (2008).

The intransigence of southern white attitudes is examined in Michael Perman's *Reunion without Compromise: The South and Reconstruction, 1865– 1868* (1973) and Dan T. Carter's *When the War Was Over: The Failure of Self-Reconstruction in the South, 1865–1867* (1985). Allen W. Trelease's *White Terror: The Ku Klux Klan Conspiracy and Southern Reconstruction* (1971) covers the various organizations that practiced vigilante tactics. On the massacre of African Americans, see Charles Lane's *The Day Freedom Died: The Colfax Massacre, the Supreme Court, and the Betrayal of Reconstruction* (2008).

The difficulties former slaves had in adjusting to the new labor system are documented in James L. Roark's *Masters without Slaves: Southern Planters in the Civil War and Reconstruction* (1977). Books on southern politics during Reconstruction include Michael Perman's *The Road to Redemption: Southern Politics, 1869–1879* (1984), Terry L. Seip's *The South Returns to Congress: Men, Economic Measures, and Intersectional Relationships, 1868–1879* (1983), and Mark W. Summers's *Railroads, Reconstruction, and the Gospel of Prosperity: Aid under the Radical Republicans, 1865–1877* (1984).

Numerous works study the freed blacks' experience in the South. Start with Leon F. Litwack's *Been in the Storm So Long: The Aftermath of Slavery* (1979). The Freedmen's Bureau is explored in William S. McFeely's *Yankee Stepfather: General O. O. Howard and the Freedmen* (1968). The situation of freed slave women is discussed in Jacqueline Jones's *Labor of Love, Labor of Sorrow: Black Women, Work and the Family, from Slavery to the Present* (1985).

On Roosevelt's war of words with isolationists, see Lynne Olsen's *Those Angry Days: Roosevelt, Lindbergh, and America's Fight over World War II, 1939-1942* (2013), and David Kaiser's *No End Save Victory: How FDR Led the Naiton into War* (2014). See also David Reynolds's *From Munich to Pearl Harbor: Roosevelt's America and the Origins of the Second World War* (2001). For the Japanese perspective, see Eri Hotta's *Japan 1941: Countdown to Infamy* (2014). On the surprise attack on Pearl Harbor, see Gordon W. Prange's *Pearl Harbor: The Verdict of History* (1986). Japan's perspective is described in Akira Iriye's *The Origins of the Second World War in Asia and the Pacific* (1987).

Chapter 24

For a sweeping survey of the Second World War, consult Anthony Roberts's *The Storm of War: A New History of the Second World War* (2011). The best detailed treatment of U.S. involvement is Rick Atkinson's multi-volume Pulitzer-prize winning series, *An Army at Dawn* (2007), *The Day of Battle* (2008), and *The Guns at Last Light* (2013). Roosevelt's wartime leadership is analyzed in Eric Larrabee's *Commander in Chief: Franklin Delano Roosevelt, His Lieutenants, and Their War* (1987).

Books on specific European campaigns include Anthony Beevor's *D-Day: The Battle for Normandy* (2010) and Charles B. MacDonald's *A Time for Trumpets: The Untold Story of the Battle of the Bulge* (1985). On the Allied commander, see Carlo D'Este's *Eisenhower: A Soldier's Life* (2002). Richard Overy assesses the controversial role of air power in *The Bombing War: Europe, 1939-1945* (2013).

For the war in the Far East, see John Costello's *The Pacific War, 1941–1945* (1981), Ronald H. Spector's *Eagle against the Sun: The American War with Japan* (1985), John W. Dower's award-winning *War without Mercy: Race and Power in the Pacific War* (1986), and Dan van der Vat's *The Pacific Campaign: The U.S.-Japanese Naval War, 1941–1945* (1991).

An excellent overview of the war's effects on the home front is Michael C. C. Adams's *The Best War Ever: America and World War II* (1994). On the transformation to the wartime economy, see Arthur Herman's *Freedom's Forge: How American Business Produced Victory in World War II* (2012) and Maury Klein's *A Call to Arms* (2013). Susan M. Hartmann's *The Home Front and Beyond: American Women in the 1940s* (1982) treats the new working environment for women. Kenneth D. Rose tells the story of problems on the home front in *Myth and the Greatest Generation: A Social History of Americans in World War II* (2008). Neil A. Wynn looks at the participation of blacks in *The Afro-American and the Second World War* (1976). The story of the oppression of Japanese Americans is told in Greg Robinson's *A Tragedy for Democracy: Japanese Confinement in North America* (2009). On the development of the atomic bomb, see Jim Baggott's *The First War of Physics: The Secret History of the Atomic Bomb* (2010). For the controversy over America's policies towards the Holocaust, see Richard Breitman and Alan J. Lichtman's *FDR and the Jews* (2013).

A detailed introduction to U.S. diplomacy during the conflict can be found in Gaddis Smith's *American Diplomacy during the Second World War, 1941–1945* (1965). To understand the role that Roosevelt played in policy making, consult Warren F. Kimball's *The Juggler: Franklin Roosevelt as Wartime Statesman* (1991). The most important wartime summit meeting is assessed in S. M. Plokhy's *Yalta: The Price of Peace* (2010). The issues and events that led to the deployment of atomic weapons are addressed in Martin J. Sherwin's *A World Destroyed: The Atomic Bomb and the Grand Alliance* (1975).

Chapter 25

The cold war remains a hotly debated topic. The traditional interpretation is best reflected in John Lewis Gaddis's *The Cold War: A New History (2005)*. Both superpowers, Gaddis argues, were responsible for causing the cold war, but the Soviet Union was more culpable. The revisionist perspective is represented by Gar Alperovitz's *Atomic Diplomacy: Hiroshima and Potsdam: The Use of the Atomic Bomb and the American Confrontation with Soviet Power*, 2nd ed. (1994). Also see H. W. Brands's *The Devil We Knew: Americans and the Cold War* (1993) and Melvyn P. Leffler's *For the Soul of Mankind: The United States, the Soviet Union, and the Cold War* (2007). On the architect of the containment strategy, see John L. Gaddis, *George F. Kennan: An American Life* (2011).

Frank Constigliola assesses Franklin Roosevelt's role in the start of the cold war in *Roosevelt's Lost Alliances: How Personal Politics Helped Start the Cold War* (2013). Arnold A. Offner indicts Truman for clumsy statesmanship in *Another Such Victory: President Truman and the Cold War, 1945–1953* (2002). For a positive assessment of Truman's leadership, see Alonzo L. Hamby's *Beyond the New Deal: Harry S. Truman and American Liberalism* (1973) and Robert Dallek's *The Lost Peace: Leadership in a Time of Horror and Hope, 1945-1953* (2010). The domestic policies of the Fair Deal are treated in William C. Berman's *The Politics of Civil Rights in the Truman Administration* (1970), Richard M. Dalfiume's *Desegregation of the U.S. Armed Forces: Fighting on Two Fronts, 1939–1953* (1969), and Maeva Marcus's *Truman and the Steel Seizure Case: The Limits of Presidential Power* (1977). The most comprehensive biography of Truman is David McCullough's *Truman* (1992).

For an introduction to the tensions in Asia, see Akira Iriye's *The Cold War in Asia: A Historical Introduction* (1974). For the Korean conflict, see Callum A. MacDonald's *Korea: The War before Vietnam* (1986) and Max Hasting's *The Korean War* (1987).

The anti-Communist crusade is surveyed in David Caute's *The Great Fear: The Anti-Communist Purge under Truman and Eisenhower* (1978). Arthur Herman's *Joseph McCarthy: Reexamining the Life and Legacy of America's Most Hated Senator* (2000) covers McCarthy himself. For a well-documented account of how the cold war was sustained by superpatriotism, intolerance, and suspicion, see Stephen J. Whitfield's *The Culture of the Cold War*, 2nd ed. (1996).

Chapter 26

Two excellent overviews of social and cultural trends in the postwar era are William H. Chafe's *The Unfinished Journey: America since World War II*, 6th ed. (2006), and William E. Leuchtenburg's *A Troubled Feast: America since 1945,* rev. ed. (1979). For insights into the cultural life of the 1950s, see Jeffrey Hart's *When the Going Was Good! American Life in the Fifties* (1982) and David Halberstam's *The Fifties* (1993).

The baby boom generation and its impact are vividly described in Paul C. Light's *Baby Boomers* (1988). The emergence of the television industry is discussed in Erik Barnouw's *Tube of Plenty: The Evolution of American Television,* 2nd rev. ed. (1990), and Ella Taylor's *Prime-Time Families: Television Culture in Postwar America* (1989).

On the process of suburban development, see Kenneth T. Jackson's *Crabgrass Frontier: The Suburbanization of the United States* (1985). Equally good is Tom Martinson's *American Dreamscape: The Pursuit of Happiness in Postwar Suburbia* (2000).

The middle-class ideal of family life in the 1950s is examined in Elaine Tyler May's *Homeward Bound: American Families in the Cold War Era,* rev. ed. (2008).

Thorough accounts of women's issues are found in Wini Breines's *Young, White, and Miserable: Growing Up Female in the Fifties* (1992). For an overview of the resurgence of religion in the 1950s, see George M. Marsden's *Religion and American Culture,* 2nd ed. (2000).

The origins and growth of rock and roll are surveyed in Carl Belz's *The Story of Rock,* 2nd ed. (1972). The colorful Beats are brought to life in Steven Watson's *The Birth of the Beat Generation: Visionaries, Rebels, and Hipsters, 1944–1960* (1995).

Scholarship on the Eisenhower years is extensive. A balanced treatment is Jean Edward Smith's *Eisenhower in War and Peace* (2012). For the manner in which Eisenhower conducted foreign policy, see Evan Thomas's *Ike's Bluff: President Eisenhower's Secret Battle to Save the World* (2012).

The best overview of American foreign policy since 1945 is Stephen E. Ambrose and Douglas G. Brinkley's *Rise to Globalism: American Foreign Policy since 1938* 9th ed. (2011). For the buildup of U.S. involvement in Indochina, consult Fredrik Logevall's *Embers of War: The Fall of an Empire and the Making of America's Vietnam* (2012). The Cold War strategy of the Eisenhower administration is the focus of Chris Tudda's *The Truth Is Our Weapon: The Rhetorical Diplomacy of Dwight D. Eisenhower and John Foster Dulles* (2006). To learn about the CIA's secret activities in Iran, see Ervand Abrahamian's *The Coup: 1953, the CIA, and the Roots of Modern U.S.-Iranian Relations* (2013).

The impact of the Supreme Court during the 1950s is the focus of Archibald Cox's *The Warren Court: Constitutional Decision as an Instrument of Reform* (1968). A masterly study of the important Warren Court decision on school desegregation is James T. Patterson's *Brown v. Board of Education: A Civil Rights Milestone and Its Troubled Legacy* (2001).

For the story of the early years of the civil rights movement, see Taylor Branch's *Parting the Waters: America in the King Years, 1954–1963* (1988) Robert Weisbrot's *Freedom Bound: A History of America's Civil Rights Movement* (1990), and David A. Nicholas's *A Matter of Justice: Eisenhower and the Beginning of the Civil Rights Revolution* (2007). On Rosa Parks, see Jeanne Theoharis's *The Rebellious Life of Mrs. Rosa Parks* (2013). On the testy relationship of Eisenhower and his vice president, Richard Nixon, see Jeffrey Frank's *Ike and Dick: Portrait of a Strange Political Marriage* (2013).

Chapter 27

A superb analysis of John Kennedy's life is Thomas C. Reeves's *A Question of Character: A Life of John F. Kennedy* (1991). The 1960 campaign is detailed in Gary A. Donaldson's *The First Modern Campaign: Kennedy, Nixon, and the Election of 1960* (2007). The best study of the Kennedy administration's domestic policies is Irving Bernstein's *Promises Kept: John F. Kennedy's New Frontier* (1991). See also Robert Dallek's *Camelot's Court: Inside the Kennedy White House* (2013), Thurston Clarke's *JFK's Last Hundred Days* (2013), and Ira Stoll's *JFK, Conservative* (2013). For details on the still swirling conspiracy theories about the assassination, see David W. Belin's *Final Disclosure: The Full Truth about the Assassination of President Kennedy* (1988).

On LBJ, see the magisterial multi-volume biography by Robert Caro's titled *The Years of Lyndon Johnson.* On the Johnson administration, see Vaughn Davis Bornet's *The Presidency of Lyndon B. Johnson* (1984).

Among the works that interpret liberal social policy during the 1960s, John E. Schwarz's *America's Hidden Success: A Reassessment of Twenty Years of Public Policy* (1983) offers a glowing endorsement of Democratic programs. For a contrasting perspective, see Charles Murray's *Losing Ground: American Social Policy, 1950–1980* (1994).

On foreign policy, see *Kennedy's Quest for Victory: American Foreign Policy, 1961–1963* (1989), edited by Thomas G. Paterson. To learn more about Kennedy's problems in Cuba, see Mark J. White's *Missiles in Cuba: Kennedy, Khrushchev, Castro and the 1962 Crisis* (1997). See also Aleksandr Fursenko and Timothy Naftali's *"One Hell of a Gamble": Khrushchev, Castro and Kennedy, 1958–1964* (1997).

American involvement in Vietnam has received voluminous treatment from all political perspectives. For an excellent overview, see Larry Berman's *Planning a Tragedy: The Americanization of the War in Vietnam* (1983) and *Lyndon Johnson's War: The Road to Stalemate in Vietnam* (1989), as well as Stanley Karnow's *Vietnam: A History,* 2nd rev. ed. (1997). An analysis of policy making concerning the Vietnam War is David M. Barrett's *Uncertain Warriors: Lyndon Johnson and His Vietnam Advisors* (1993). A fine account of the military involvement is Robert D. Schulzinger's *A Time for War: The United States and Vietnam, 1941–1975* (1997). On the legacy of the Vietnam War, see Arnold R. Isaacs's *Vietnam Shadows: The War, Its Ghosts, and Its Legacy* (1997).

Many scholars have dealt with various aspects of the civil rights movement and race relations in the 1960s. See especially Carl M. Brauer's *John F. Kennedy and the Second Reconstruction* (1977), David J. Garrow's *Bearing the Cross: Martin Luther King, Jr., and the Southern Christian Leadership Conference* (1986), and Adam Fairclough's *To Redeem the Soul of America: The Southern Christian Leadership Conference and Martin Luther King, Jr.* (1987). William H. Chafe's *Civilities and Civil Rights: Greensboro, North Carolina, and the Black Struggle for Freedom* (1980) details the original sit-ins. An award-winning study of racial and economic inequality in a representative American city is Thomas J. Sugrue's *The Origins of the Urban Crisis: Race and Inequality in Postwar Detroit* (1996).

Chapter 28

An engaging overview of the cultural trends of the 1960s is Maurice Isserman and Michael Kazin's *America Divided: The Civil War of the 1960s,* 3rd ed. (2007). The New Left is assessed in Irwin Unger's *The Movement: A History of the American New Left, 1959–1972* (1974). On the Students for a Democratic Society, see Kirkpatrick Sale's *SDS* (1973) and Allen J. Matusow's *The Unraveling of America: A History of Liberalism in the 1960s* (1984). Also useful is Todd Gitlin's *The Sixties: Years of Hope, Days of Rage,* rev. ed. (1993). For a focused study, see James T. Patterson's *The Eve of Destruction: How 1965 Transformed America* (2013).

For insights into the black power movement, see Peniel E. Joseph's *Stokely: A Life* (2014), and Joshua Bloom and Waldo E. Martin, Jr.'s *Black against Empire: The History and Politics of the Black Panther Party* (2013).

Two influential assessments of the counterculture by sympathetic commentators are Theodore Roszak's *The Making of a Counter-Culture: Reflections on the Technocratic Society and Its Youthful Opposition* (1969) and Charles A. Reich's *The Greening of America: How the Youth Revolution Is Trying to Make America Livable* (1970). A good scholarly analysis that takes the hippies seriously is Timothy Miller's *The Hippies and American Values* (1991).

The best study of the women's liberation movement is Ruth Rosen's *The World Split Open: How the Modern Women's Movement Changed America,* rev. ed. (2006). The organizing efforts of Cesar Chavez are detailed in Ronald B. Taylor's *Chavez and the Farm Workers* (1975). The struggles of Native Americans for recognition and power are sympathetically described in Stan Steiner's *The New Indians* (1968).

The best overview of the 1970s and 1980s is James T. Patterson's *Restless Giant: The United States from Watergate to Bush v. Gore* (2005). On Nixon, see Melvin Small's thorough analysis in *The Presidency of Richard Nixon* (1999). A good slim biography is Elizabeth Drew's *Richard M. Nixon* (2007). For an overview of the Watergate scandal, see Stanley I. Kutler's *The Wars of Watergate: The Last Crisis of Richard Nixon* (1990). For the way the Republicans handled foreign affairs, consult Tad Szulc's *The Illusion of Peace: Foreign Policy in the Nixon Years* (1978). The Nixon White House tapes make for fascinating reading. See *The Nixon Tapes* (2014), ed. by Douglas Brinkley and Luke Nichter. Rick Perlstein traces the effects of Nixon's career on the Republican party and the conservative movement in two compelling books: *Nixonland: The Rise of a President and the Fracturing of America* (2007) and *The Invisible Bridge: The Fall of Nixon and the Rise of Reagan* (2014).

The Communist takeover of Vietnam and the end of American involvement there are traced in Larry Berman's *No Peace, No Honor: Nixon, Kissinger, and Betrayal in Vietnam* (2001). William Shawcross's *Sideshow: Kissinger, Nixon and the Destruction of Cambodia*, rev. ed. (2002), deals with the broadening of the war, while Larry Berman's *Planning a Tragedy: The Americanization of the War in Vietnam* (1982) assesses the final impact of U.S. involvement. The most comprehensive treatment of the anti-war movement is Tom Wells's *The War Within: America's Battle over Vietnam* (1994).

A comprehensive treatment of the Ford administration is contained in John Robert Greene's *The Presidency of Gerald R. Ford* (1995). The best overview of the Carter administration is Burton I. Kaufman's *The Presidency of James Earl Carter, Jr.*, 2nd rev. ed. (2006). A work more sympathetic to the Carter administration is John Dumbrell's *The Carter Presidency: A Re-evaluation*, 2nd ed. (1995). Gaddis Smith's *Morality, Reason, and Power: American Diplomacy in the Carter Years* (1986) provides an overview. Background on how the Middle East came to dominate much of American policy is found in William B. Quandt's *Decade of Decisions: American Policy toward the Arab-Israeli Conflict, 1967–1976* (1977). For a biography of Carter, see Randall Balmer, *Redeemer: The Life of Jimmy Carter* (2014).

Chapter 29

The rise of modern political conservatism is well told in Patrick Allitt's *The Conservatives: Ideas and Personalities throughout American History* (2009) and Michael Schaller's *Right Turn: American Life in the Reagan-Bush Era, 1980-1992* (2007).

On Reagan, see John Patrick Diggins's *Ronald Reagan: Fate, Freedom, and the Making of History* (2007), Richard Reeves's *President Reagan: The Triumph of Imagination* (2005), and Sean Wilentz's *The Age of Reagan: A History, 1974–2008* (2008). The best political analysis is Robert M. Collins's *Transforming America: Politics and Culture during the Reagan Years* (2007). For insights into the 1980 election, see Andrew E. Busch's *Reagan's Victory: The Presidential Election of 1980 and the Rise of the Right* (2005). On Reaganomics, see David A. Stockman's *The Triumph of Politics: Why the Reagan Revolution Failed* (1986).

For Reagan's foreign policy in Central America, see James Chace's *Endless War: How We Got Involved in Central America—and What Can Be Done* (1984) and Walter LaFeber's *Inevitable Revolutions: The United States in Central America*, 2nd ed. (1993). On Reagan's second term, see Jane Mayer and Doyle McManus's *Landslide: The Unmaking of the President, 1984–1988* (1988). For a masterly work on the Iran-Contra affair, see Theodore Draper's *A Very Thin Line: The Iran Contra Affairs* (1991). Several collections of essays include varying assessments of the Reagan years. Among these are *The Reagan Revolution?* (1988), edited by B. B. Kymlicka and Jean

V. Matthews; *The Reagan Presidency: An Incomplete Revolution?* (1990), edited by Dilys M. Hill, Raymond A. Moore, and Phil Williams, and *Looking Back on the Reagan Presidency* (1990), edited by Larry Berman.

The 41st president is the focus of Timothy Naftali's *George H. W. Bush* (2007). On the 1988 campaign, see Sidney Blumenthal's *Pledging Allegiance: The Last Campaign of the Cold War* (1990). For a social history of the decade, see John Ehrman's *The Eighties: America in the Age of Reagan* (2005). On the Persian Gulf conflict, see Lester H. Brune's *America and the Iraqi Crisis, 1990–1992: Origins and Aftermath* (1993).

Chapter 30

Analysis of the Clinton years can be found in Joe Klein's *The Natural: The Misunderstood Presidency of Bill Clinton* (2002). Clinton's impeachment is assessed in Richard A. Posner's *An Affair of State: The Investigation, Impeachment, and Trial of President Clinton* (1999). The conflict between Clinton and Gingrich is explained in Elizabeth Drew's *The Struggle between Gingrich and the Clinton White House* (1996).

On changing demographic trends, see Sam Roberts's *Who We Are Now: The Changing Face of America in the Twenty-First Century* (2004). For a textured account of the exploding Latino culture, see Roberto Suro's *Strangers among Us: How Latino Immigration Is Transforming America* (1998). On social and cultural life in the 1990s, see Haynes Johnson's *The Best of Times: America in the Clinton Years* (2001). Economic and technological changes are assessed in Daniel T. Rogers's *Age of Fracture* (2011). The onset and growth of the AIDS epidemic are traced in *And the Band Played On: Politics, People, and the AIDS Epidemic,* 20th anniversary ed. (2007), by Randy Shilts.

On the religious right, see George M. Marsden's *Understanding Fundamentalism and Evangelicalism,* new ed. (2006) and Ralph E. Reed's *Politically Incorrect: The Emerging Faith Factor in American Politics* (1994).

On the invention of the computer and the Internet, see Paul E. Ceruzzi's *A History of Modern Computing,* 2nd ed. (2003), Janet Abbate's *Inventing the Internet* (1999), and Michael Lewis, *The New New Thing: A Silicon Valley Story* (1999). The booming economy of the 1990s is well analyzed in Joseph E. Stiglitz's *The Roaring Nineties: A New History of the World's Most Prosperous Decade* (2003).

For further treatment of the end of the cold war, see Michael R. Beschloss and Strobe Talbott's *At the Highest Levels: The Inside Story of the End of the Cold War* (1993) and Richard Crockatt's *The Fifty Years War: The United States and the Soviet Union in World Politics, 1941–1991* (1995).

On the transformation of American foreign policy, see James Mann's *Rise of the Vulcans: The History of Bush's War Cabinet* (2004), Claes G. Ryn's *America the Virtuous: The Crisis of Democracy and the Quest for Empire* (2003), and Stephen M. Walt's *Taming American Power: The Global Response to U.S. Primacy* (2005).

The disputed 2000 presidential election is the focus of Jeffrey Toobin's *Too Close to Call: The Thirty-Six-Day Battle to Decide the 2000 Election* (2001). On the Bush presidency, see *The Presidency of George W. Bush: A First Historical Assessment,* edited by Julian E. Zelizer (2010). See also Fred H. Israel and Jonathan Mann's *The Election of 2000 and the Administration of George W. Bush* (2003). Also see Dick Cheney's illuminating, if self-serving, account of his service as Bush's vice president in *In My Time: A Personal and Political Memoir* (2011).

On the attacks of September 11, 2001, and their aftermath, see *The Age of Terror: America and the World after September 11,* edited by Strobe Talbott and Nayan

Chanda (2001). For a devastating account of the Bush administration by a White House insider, see Scott McClellan's *What Happened: Inside the Bush White House and Washington's Culture of Deception* (2008). On the historic 2008 election, see Michael Nelson's *The Elections of 2008* (2009). The best biography of Obama is David Maraniss's *Barack Obama: The Story* (2012). A conservative critique is provided in Edward Klein's *The Amateur: Barack Obama in the White House* (2012).

The Great Recession is explained in Alan S. Blinder's *After the Music Stopped: The Financial Crisis, the Response, and the Work Ahead* (2013). The Tea Party movement is assessed in Theda Skocpol and Vanessa Williamson's *The Tea Party and the Remaking of Republican Conservatism* (2012) and Elizabeth Price Foley's *The Tea Party: Three Principles* (2012). The partisan gridlock in Congress is the focus of Thomas E. Mann and Norman J. Ornstein's *The Broken Branch: How Congress Is Failing America and How to Get it Back on Track* (2012). The tension between the conservative majority on the U.S. Supreme Court and the Obama administration is examined in Jeffrey Toobin's *The Oath: The Obama White Hosue and the Supreme Court* (2012). On the growing economic inequality in America, see Joseph Stiglitz's *The Price of Inequality: How Today's Divided Society Endangers Our Future* (2013).

Credits

Historical Society; **p. 627 (top):** Library of Congress; **p. 627 (bottom):** Corbis; **p. 628:** Library of Congress.

Chapter 18: p. 636: Bridgeman Art Library; **p. 641:** Library of Congress; **p. 643:** William Williams Papers, Manuscripts and Archives Division, The New York Public Library, Astor, Lenox and Tilden Foundations, Art Resource; **p. 645:** The Granger Collection; **p. 646:** Bettmann/CORBIS; **p. 648:** American Museum of Natural History; **p. 651:** Bridgeman Art Library; **p. 653:** Library of Congress; **p. 659:** Bettmann/Corbis; **p. 662:** Bettmann/Corbis; **p. 663:** Library of Congress; **p. 669:** Corbis; **p. 672 (top):** Corbis; **p. 672 (bottom):** Corbis.

Chapter 19: p. 676: Frederic Remington Art Museum; **p. 680:** The Granger Collection; **p. 681:** Corbis; **p. 683:** Wikimedia Commons; **p. 685 (top):** Corbis; **p. 685 (bottom):** Corbis; **p. 688:** The Granger Collection; **p. 691:** Corporal George J. Vennage c/o Ohio State University Rare Books and Manuscripts Library; **p. 694:** Bettmann/Corbis; **p. 699:** The Granger Collection; **p. 701:** Corbis; **p. 704:** The Granger Collection.

Chapter 20: p. 712: Getty Images; **p. 712:** Bettmann/Corbis; **p. 712:** The Granger Collection; **p. 712:** Art Resource; **p. 712:** Corbis; **pp. 714 & 715:** Getty Images; **p. 714:** From the Collections of The Henry Ford Museum; **p. 716:** The Granger Collection; **p. 721:** The Granger Collection; **p. 725:** Library of Congress; **p. 729:** Wikimedia Commons; **p. 731:** Corbis; **p. 732:** Library of Congress; **p. 733:** Library of Congress; **p. 735:** Library of Congress; **p. 737:** NYPL Digital Collection: **p. 739:** Art Resource; **p. 740:** The Granger Collection; **p. 743:** Donald C. & Elizabeth M. Dickinson Research Center, National Cowboy & Western Heritage Museum; **p. 744:** Library of Congress; **p. 750:** Corbis; **p. 751:** The Granger Collection.

Chapter 21: p. 758: Library of Congress; **p. 763:** Getty Images; **p. 765:** The Granger Collection; **p. 770:** Library of Congress; **p. 771:** Corbis; **p. 772:** Library of Congress; **p. 773:** Library of Congress; **p. 774:** Corbis; **p. 775:** Getty Images; **p. 777:** Wikimedia Commons; **p. 779:** The Granger Collection; **p. 786:** Corbis; **p. 787:** Corbis; **p. 790:** Corbis.

Chapter 22: p. 794: The Granger Collection; **p. 798:** The Granger Collection; **p. 799:** Bettmann/Corbis; **p. 800:** Wikimedia Commons; **p. 801:** From the Collections of The Henry Ford Museum; **p. 802:** Getty Images; **p. 804 (top):** Wikimedia Commons; **p. 804 (bottom):** Corbis; **p. 805:** Wikimedia Commons; **p. 806:** Art Resource; **p. 808 (top):** Library of Congress; **p. 808 (bottom):** Wikimedia Commons; **p. 809:** AP/Wide World Photos; **p. 810:** Ferdinand Schmutzer/Wikimedia; **p. 813:** Max Weber (American, born Russia, 1881-1961). Russian Ballet, 1916. Oil on canvas, 30 x 36 in. (76.2 x 91.4 cm). Brooklyn Museum, Bequest of Edith and Milton Lowenthal, 1992.11.29; **p. 817:** Corbis; **p. 820:** Alamy; **p. 821:** Corbis; **p. 829:** The Granger Collection; **p. 830:** Wikimedia Commons.

Chapter 23: p. 840: The Granger Collection; **p. 845:** Getty Images; **p. 847:** Bridgeman Art Library; **p. 849:** Corbis; **p. 850:** Library of congress; **p. 852 (left):** Corbis; **p. 852 (right):** Bettmann/Corbis; **p. 858:** Corbis; **p. 862 (top):** Getty Images; **p. 862 (bottom):** Getty Images; **p. 863:** Alamy; **p. 865:** Art Resource; **p. 866:** Bettmann/Corbis; **p. 867:** Bettmann/Corbis; **p. 870:** Art Resource; **p. 876:** Getty Images.

Chapter 24: p. 884: Corbis; **p. 887:** Getty Images; **p. 888:** Getty Images; **p. 890:** Alamy; **p. 892:** Library of Congress; **p. 895:** Alamy; **p. 896:** The Granger Collection; **p. 901:** Wikimedia Commons; **p. 902:** Wikimedia Commons; **p. 903:** Wikimedia Commons; **p. 906 (left):** The Granger Collection; **p. 906 (right):** The Granger Collection; **p. 907 (left):** The Granger Collection; **p. 907 (right):** AP/Wide World Photos; **p. 908:** Corbis; **p. 909:** Bettmann/Corbis; **p. 910:** Corbis; **p. 916:** Eisenhower Presidential Library; **p. 917:** Corbis; **p. 918:** Art Resource; **p. 920:** Art Resource; **p. 922:** Corbis; **p. 923:** National Archives; **p. 926:** Corbis; **p. 927:** Corbis.

Chapter 25: p. 938: Bettmann/Corbis; **p. 938:** Corbis; **p. 938:** Bettmann/Corbis; **p. 938:** Corbis; **p. 938:** Corbis; **pp. 940 & 941:** Bettmann/Corbis; **p. 940:** Corbis; **p. 941:** Corbis; **p. 944:** Corbis; **p. 946:** Corbis; **p. 951:** Corbis; **p. 953:** Corbis; **p. 958:** Bettmann/Corbis; **p. 959:** Corbis; **p. 962:** Getty Images; **p. 964 (top):** Corbis; **p. 964 (bottom):** Getty Images; **p. 966:** Corbis; **p. 971:** Getty Images; **p. 973:** Bridgeman Art Library.

Chapter 26: p. 980: Bridgeman Art Library; **p. 983:** Corbis; **p. 985:** Alamy; **p. 988:** Bridgeman Art Library; **p. 990:** Hulton Archives; **p. 992:** Getty Images; **p. 993 (left):** Corbis; **p. 993 (right):** Getty Images; **p. 995:** Getty Images; **p. 998:** Getty Images; **p. 999:** Getty Images; **p. 1004 (left):** Corbis; **p. 1004 (right):** Black Star/Stock Photo; **p. 1006:** Bettmann/Corbis; **p. 1010:** AP Photo; **p. 1011:** Getty Images; **p. 1017:** AP/Wide World Photos; **p. 1020:** AP/Wide World Photos.

Chapter 27: p. 1024: Bridgeman Art Library; **p. 1026:** The Granger Collection; **p. 1028:** Corbis; **p. 1029:** The Granger Collection; **p. 1030:** Bettmann/Corbis; **p. 1035 (left):** National Archives; **p. 1035 (right):** The Granger Collection; **p. 1037:** AP Photo; **p. 1041:** The Associated Press, **p. 1042:** National Archives; **p. 1043:** Corbis; **p. 1044:** Corbis; **p. 1046:** Corbis; **p. 1049:** Bettmann/Corbis; **p. 1052:** Corbis; **p. 1053:** Corbis; **p. 1056:** Jack Kightlinger, Lyndon Baines Johnson Library and Museum.

Chapter 28: p. 1066: Corbis; **p. 1070:** Corbis; **p. 1071:** AP/Wide World Photo; **p. 1072 (left):** Corbis; **p. 1072 (right):** Corbis; **p. 1073:** Corbis; **p. 1076:** © Globe Photos/ZUMAPRESS.com; **p. 1078 (left):** Corbis; **p. 1078 (right):** Corbis; **p. 1081:** Getty Images; **p. 1082:** Corbis; **p. 1090:** Getty Images; **p. 1092:** Bettmann/CORBIS; **p. 1095:** Corbis; **p. 1098:** Corbis; **p. 1101:** John Dominis/Getty Images; **p. 1107:** Corbis; **p. 1108:** Dirck Halstead/Time Life Pictures/Getty Images.

Chapter 29: p. 1114: Corbis; **p. 1117:** Corbis; **p. 1120:** Corbis; **p. 1121:** Corbis; **p. 1122:** Getty Images; **p. 1124:** Corbis; **p. 1128:** Corbis; **p. 1129:** Corbis; **p. 1134:** Corbis; **p. 1135:** Corbis; **p. 1139:** Corbis; **p. 1140:** Mark Thiesson © 1992 The NAMES Project; **p. 1141:** Corbis; **p. 1143:** Corbis; **p. 1145:** Getty Images.

Chapter 30: p. 1150: Corbis; **p. 1153:** AP/Wide World Photo; **p. 1156:** Getty Images; **p. 1160:** Corbis; **p. 1163:** Getty Images; **p. 1165:** Bettmann/Corbis; **p. 1166:** Bettmann/Corbis; **p. 1169:** Corbis; **p. 1171:** Mario Tama/Getty Images; **p. 1172:** AP Photo; **p. 1173:** Getty Images; **p. 1174:** AP Photo/Jae C. Hong; **p. 1180:** Jeff J Mitchell/Getty Images; **p. 1182:** AP Photo; **p. 1184:** Corbis; **p. 1188:** Wikimedia Commons; **p. 1147:** Chris Wilkins/Getty Images; **p. 1189:** AP Photo/Evgeniy Maloletka.

Index

Page numbers in *italics* refer to illustrations.